How to use this book

Welcome to the Guardian Media Directory 2007, the indispensable handbook for journalists, students and media professionals.

While this book is of course an excellent source of information, containing 13,000 contact phone numbers, listings and other vital mechanical information about the media, it also aims to be your one-stop guide to how the fast-moving and expanding media industry works.

Whether you are beginning your studies or career or plotting the sale of your independent production company while sizing-up a lovely villa in Tuscany, our aim is to give you an overview, analysis and advice on how each sector of the media is performing. We begin with an attempt to make sense of the glorious chaos with a **State of the media** overview (page 7). Here you'll find a guide to the top stories, an attempt to isolate the key trends and a summary of the media's financial performance (clue: largely awful).

The following chapters then summarise individual sectors. Each chapter includes an analysis of the sector plus a comment from a Guardian journalist or industry expert. Flick through this to find the contact details.

Dividing the media into industry sectors has become increasingly difficult and indeed arbitrary as convergence, that dreadful buzzword of the last five years, has become reality. Nevertheless, we have tried to set out sections of manageable sizes by defining companies by their core business. So if you're searching for a company, try first under its main business sector: News International, for example, despite its many investments in 2006 in the magazines and digital sectors, will be found under national newspapers.

News media is our blanket term for press, television, radio, digital media and global media. Within the press section you will find contact details for newspapers, national and regional, magazines as well as picture libraries and press agencies. **Creative media** comprises books, film and music and **Media services** includes the high-expense-account holders – advertising, PR and media law.

When I started buying the Guardian Media Guide (as it was then known), I was a student dreaming of a career in media and believed I needed to understand the fiendish world of ITV franchises and BBC funding. More specific advice for those of you with similar ambitions begins on page 359: training courses, recruitment agencies and the names of people to whom begging letters should be addressed.

And finally, at the back of this book, the **Contacts book**, a resource of information primarily for journalists. There's no need to expose your ignorance to colleagues by asking if anyone has a number for Downing Street. It'll be here.

I hope you find this book as useful as I have.

Janine Gibson

State of the media

Anticipated for almost as long as the second coming, the digital media era is finally upon us and that much misused word "convergence" has become meaningful. Newspapers are talking video journalism, broadcasters are talking downloads and web companies? Well, if you've got a blog, a site or, holy grail, a community, then your job is to look smug and talk hard cash.

From Murdoch's deal to buy MySpace to the selling of YouTube for more than a billion dollars after 18 months of trading, we are slap bang in the middle of the second dot.com boom. Don't even mention Google (the new Microsoft), whose founders, Sergey Brin and Larry Page, must be crossing off the days till it's time to become full-time philanthropists and cancel third-world debt.

However, the fortunes of the old media have looked somewhat less happy. Regional newspaper groups, still blinking from the novel glare of the spotlight, are being dragged into all sorts of alien arenas. Free newspapers (there are now three city-wide ones in London. At the time of writing. What with book lead times there may be eight or nine by the time you read this); local community websites; more cost-cutting, more mergers. Associated Newspapers, home of the Daily Mail, discovered it could barely give away its regional newspaper collection, Northcliffe. Trinity Mirror has embarked on another round of "what shall we do with this collection of nationals and regionals" and this time called it a formal review. The Daily Telegraph, meanwhile, under still relatively new owners the Barclay brothers, is on its third set of redundancies combined with a raft of new digital plans that must be leaving Colonel Bufton-Tuftons reeling all the way through the Cotswolds.

And broadcasters are faring no better. ITV, bless it, has had such a terrible time that it almost seems rude to intrude on what ought to be

Top 10 media events 2006
1 ITV: share price plummets, Greg Dyke launches failed takeover bid, chief executive resigns, Michael Grade poached from BBC
2 Sky launches broadband
3 Google buys YouTube
4 Newspapers go "web first" with news
5 Daily and Sunday Telegraph editors are both replaced
6 Capital Radio drops to no 3 in London
7 Telegraph group cuts 130 jobs
8 BBC plans to cut another 4,000 jobs
9 Both the London Evening Standard and News International launch free London papers to compete with Metro
10 Internet ad revenue reaches $5.8bn for the first half of the year

private grief. Charles Allen, the CEO with the strongest fingernails in media, has finally announced the ultimate manicure and departed in the summer. His replacement, and let no one say the ITV board rushed into a decision, has plenty to do. Michael Grade left the BBC in the lurch to become ITV's new executive chairman and hopes are high for his tenure which began this year. Five, after years of incremental growth from its newbie start-up position, has begun the inevitable decline so familiar to its terrestrial peers. Channel 4 has begun flirting with radio, Freeview and other media, while Sky has become a broadband provider. Such are the diverse ways that our leading media companies are attempting to continue to grow. And if you want to know what really frightens them, look at YouTube, bought by Google for a staggering $1.6bn.

The most quietly significant innovations in broadcasting this year have come from UK networks offering downloads of programmes over the internet for a small payment of around £2. The big US networks are already signed up to pay-per-play deals with iTunes. Some, such as NBC, offer catch-ups of recent episodes for free on their own websites.

In radio, GCap – the oddly bolted-together name resulting from the merger of GWR and Capital reflects the oddly bolted-together group – rivals only ITV for the financial disaster that has been 2006.

In fact there seems little to be cheerful about. And yet...

Whole-year trends	2005	2004
Total national newspaper circulation (per week)	83.1 million	86.3 million
Total regional newspaper circulation/distribution (weekly)	64.3 million	66.2 million
Total consumer magazine copies (sales per annum)	1438 million	1339 million
Total households with multichannel TV	18.1 million	15.6 million
Total radio reach	44.4 million	43.9 million
total number of DAB digital radios sold*	2.8 million	1.2 million
Total households and small businesses with internet access	16.3 million	15.2 million
total broadband connections	10.1 million	6.2 million
Total volume of books sold	306 million	295 million
Total measured ad spend	£19 billion	£18.4 billion

* Total to end of 2005   Sources: ABC, Newspaper Society, PPA, Rajar, Ofcom (Communication Market Report 2006), Books and the Consumer survey, Advertising Association

The trade magazine you don't get bored reading

The music. The business.

Music Week: a fresh angle on music

MediaGuardian 100

The MediaGuardian 100 is our annual guide to the most powerful people in the industry. A panel of experienced media watchers from the worlds of broadcast, journalism, marketing and the internet judged entrants using three criteria: cultural influence, economic clout and political power. The aim was to take a snapshot of the individuals who run or influenced the UK media in 2006.

It is cultural and economic powers that have dominated the debate. Candidates in this year's list are from all sectors of the media, including broadcasting, publishing, new media, advertising, and PR. With 29 new entries in this year's list, it makes interesting reading.

1. Mark Thompson

Photo: BBC

Job: BBC director general **Age:** 48
Industry: broadcasting, new media, publishing
Staff: 25,377 **Total group income:** £4bn **Salary:** £619,000
(including £10,000 expenses/benefits) **2005 ranking:** 1

Director general Mark Thompson has led the BBC from the aftershock of the Hutton report to the most important licence fee settlement in its history. In the process Thompson outlined his vision of a bold, expansionist BBC which puts new media at the core of its offerings, funded in part by the biggest round of job cuts the corporation has ever seen.

At the centre of Thompson's vision for the future of the corporation is the BBC iPlayer, an on-demand service offering immediate broadband access to programmes from the BBC Archive and the previous seven days' schedules. He dubbed it "martini media" – making programmes available "any time, any place, anywhere".

It was one of the key conclusions of Thompson's Creative Future, a review that aimed to define the BBC's on-air and online ambitions over the next five years.

Thompson is the most powerful person in the MediaGuardian 100 for the second year running. Last year he shared top billing with the BBC chairman, Michael Grade, now defected to ITV. But the feeling on the panel was that Thompson had come into his own in the past 12 months. The next year will reveal how Thompson and the corporation will fare without a chairman at such a critical point in its history.

The danger for Thompson is that the corporation could prove too successful for its own good. BBC Radio has a record lead over its commercial rivals of 12.8%. BBC Worldwide, the UK's third largest consumer magazine publisher, made record pre-tax profits of £89m. In a further commercialisation of the corporation's overseas activities, it will put advertising on its global website for the first time.

2. Steve Jobs

Job: co-founder and chief executive, Apple Computer
Age: 51 **Industry:** new media **Staff:** 14,800
Turnover: $17.31bn (year to April 1) **Salary:** $1
2005 ranking: 6

Apple's chief executive, Steve Jobs, transformed the music industry and in the process created a whole new demographic – the "iPod generation". With around 70% of the market, the one-billionth song was downloaded on iTunes this year (Coldplay's Speed of Sound, appropriately) prompting some observers to suggest that Apple was on the verge of becoming the most powerful retailer ever. Jobs is now gearing up to change the way we watch television with the launch of the video iPod, capable of showing films and TV programmes downloaded from the net.

Co-founded by Jobs in 1976, Apple celebrated its 30th birthday this year by winning its trademark battle with the Beatles over the use of its apple logo on iTunes. Apple reported its second-highest ever quarterly results in the second quarter of 2006, with a net profit of $410m on revenues of $4.36bn.

3. Rupert Murdoch

Job: chairman and chief executive, News Corporation
Age: 75 **Industry:** broadcasting, publishing, new media
Staff: 46,723 **Annual revenue:** $23.86bn
Salary: $23.6m (including $18.9m bonus) **2005 ranking:** 3

Murdoch is one of the biggest media moguls to react to the radical change brought about by the digital revolution. The year has seen him embark on a $2bn spending spree on new media properties including Intermix, the owner of the community website MySpace.com. Bought for $580m, it is now said to be worth more than $3bn.

Murdoch remains a bigger media player in the UK than he is in the US, with a 37% share in satellite broadcaster BSkyB and the News International stable of newspapers including the Sun, the Times, the News of the World and the Sunday Times.

In the US, Murdoch owns Fox, Fox News and Fox Filmed Entertainment, and newspapers including the New York Post. The global empire includes publishing house HarperCollins, Star TV in Asia, Foxtel in Australia and Sky Italia.

4. Sergey Brin and Larry Page

Job: co-founders and directors, Google
Age: Brin 32, Page 33 **Industry:** new media
Staff: 5,680 **Turnover:** $6.14bn **Salary:** $1
Worth: $7.3bn **2005 ranking:** 9

So ubiquitous has Google become that it is hard to imagine what we ever did without it. The ultimate convenience research tool, its founders, Brin and Page, are in the midst of transforming it from a search engine into a technology giant.

Locked in a race with Yahoo! and Microsoft to dominate the internet, Google's first-quarter earnings soared past the $2bn mark for the first time this year, making net profits of $592m (£330m). "Take over the world," says a 50-foot sign in Google's Silicon Valley headquarters. They appear to mean it.

Now branching out into telecoms with its internet telephone service, Google Talk, and online shopping with Froogle. Its products and services include Google Earth, Google Video and Google Mail (previously Gmail), with others are in the pipeline.

5. Andy Duncan

Job: chief executive, Channel 4 **Age:** 43
Industry: broadcasting **Staff:** 889 **Turnover:** £894.3m
Salary: £549,000 (including £133,000 bonus and benefits)
2005 ranking: 19

Quite a year for Andy Duncan, who joined Channel 4 two years ago with a fearsome reputation in marketing on the back of the successful launch of Freeview, but not much else. His multichannel strategy was a success story and resulted in unprecedented growth for Channel 4: it was the only terrestrial station to maintain its audience share; it launched a new channel, More4; took E4 and FilmFour free to air; it launched a broadband documentary channel, FourDocs; and became the first broadcaster to simulcast on the web around the clock.

As for ambitions — it wants to run its own national radio stations and will bid for the second national digital multiplex next year.

6. Charles Allen

Job: chief executive, ITV **Age:** 49 **Industry:** broadcasting
Staff: 5,952 **Turnover:** £2.2bn **Salary:** £1.85m (including bonus and benefits) **2005 ranking:** 4

Despite steeply falling ad revenue over the past two years and steadily declining audience share, Charles Allen lasted longer than anyone would have predicted as chief executive of ITV. The successful launch of four digital channels can only partially make up for the problems at ITV1, which accounts for two-thirds of the broadcaster's ad revenue. Allen faced two takeover bids fronted by his old foe Greg Dyke before his resignation in August.

7. Michael Grade

Job: BBC chairman **Age:** 63 **Industry:** broadcasting, new media, publishing **Staff:** 25,377 **Salary:** £110,000 (including £27,000 expenses/benefits) **2005 ranking:** 1

It has been quite a time of revolution for Michael Grade. Two years into his role as chairman at the BBC in the wake of its biggest crisis it was mission almost accomplished for Grade, with the BBC on the eve of the renewal of its royal charter, and a new licence fee settlement due at the beginning of next year.

He was due to head up the new BBC Trust, which he helped to create as a replacement for the board of governors. "What is happening with the trust is nothing short of a revolution in the way the BBC is governed," said Grade, "It will take time for the private sector to accept how radical this is."

But Grade surprised us all with his announcement to resign from the BBC to take up the post of executive chairman of ITV. The move could be brilliant for Grade (the hike in salary certainly is, up from £110,000 to around £850,000) to a position requiring strong creative leadership. But to succeed he will need to act swiftly to maintain shareholder confidence, generate momentum and a sense of direction.

8. Jana Bennett

Job: director of television, BBC **Age:** 49
Industry: broadcasting **Staff:** 300
Annual programming budget: £1.44bn (BBC's total spend on television) **Salary:** £353,000 (including £17,000 bonus and £15,000 benefits/expenses) **2005 ranking:** 36

Jana Bennett is the highest-placed woman in this year's MediaGuardian 100. She has been the BBC's director of television since 2002, with overall creative and leadership responsibility for the BBC's channels. A key lieutenant of BBC director general Mark Thompson, Bennett has been at the forefront of the BBC's Creative Future review and its drive to put content on to new media platforms such as broadband and mobile phones. Her influence has grown in the past year and is on the rise.

9. Bill Gates

Job: chairman and founder, Microsoft **Age:** 51
Industry: new media **Staff:** 61,000 **Turnover:** $39.79bn
Salary: $1m (including $400,000 bonus) **Worth:** £27bn
2005 ranking: new entry

The world's richest man: more than 90% of personal computers run on Gates's Microsoft Windows software. His ambition for global domination faces its greatest threat yet – Google. The outcome of the battle will determine how people use computers and find information in the future. Microsoft's other recent activities include investment in IPTV (television delivered over broadband internet) which will be installed in Freeview boxes this year.

Yet the Microsoft boss has become almost as famous for giving his money away as he has for running the world's computers. The Bill & Melinda Gates Foundation hands out grants of more than $1bn every year to fight diseases such as Aids, polio and malaria. Now one of the members of the Africa Progress Panel, set up to monitor the pledges on poverty made at the Gleneagles G8 summit in 2005, Gates will end his day-to-day involvement with Microsoft in two years' time to spend more time giving his money away. However, he will remain the company's non-executive chairman.

10. Paul Dacre

Job: editor-in-chief, Associated Newspapers **Age:** 57
Industry: publishing **Circulation:** Daily Mail 2,386,893 Jan–June 2006; Mail on Sunday 2,331,213; London Evening Standard 326,132 **Salary:** £997,000 (including £57,000 benefits) **2005 ranking:** 10

In his 15th year in charge of the Daily Mail, Paul Dacre remains the most powerful newspaper editor in Britain. His paper sets the news agenda like no other, and this year the team was boosted with the signing of the columnists Richard Littlejohn and Allison Pearson and the former editor of the Sunday Telegraph, Sarah Sands. As the editor-in-chief of Associated Newspapers, his empire extends from the Daily Mail to the Mail on Sunday, the London Evening Standard and Associated's successful commuter freesheet, Metro.

BBC

11. **Jenny Abramsky** director of BBC radio and music *broadcasting* (43)

12. **Rebekah Wade** editor, the Sun *publishing* (13)

13. **Andy Coulson** editor, News of the World *publishing* (15)

14. **Kevin Lygo** director of television, Channel 4 *broadcasting* (7)

15. **James Murdoch** chief executive, BSkyB *broadcasting* (11)

16. **Simon Shaps** director of television, ITV *broadcasting* (82)

17. **Helen Boaden** director of BBC news *broadcasting* (20)

18. **Tessa Jowell** culture secretary *politics* (5)

19. **Jonathan Ross** presenter, independent producer *broadcasting* NEW ENTRY

20. **Charles Dunstone** chief executive, Carphone Warehouse *telecommunications, new media* NEW ENTRY

21. **Ashley Highfield** BBC director of New Media and technology *broadcasting, new media* (23)

22. **Luke Johnson** chairman, Channel 4 *broadcasting* (26)

23. **Sir Martin Sorrell** group executive, WPP *advertising, marketing* (8)

24. **Viscount Rothermere** chairman, Daily Mail & General Trust *publishing* (24)

25. **Peter Fincham** controller, BBC *broadcasting* (12)

26. **Les Hinton** executive chairman, News International *publishing* (28)

27. **Tom Moloney** chief executive, Emap *broadcasting, publishing* (16)

28. **Russell T Davies** writer, executive producer *broadcasting* (14)

29. **Sir Richard Branson** founder, Virgin *broadcasting, telecommunications* NEW ENTRY

30. **Sir David and Sir Frederick Barclay** owners of the Telegraph Group, Press Holdings *publishing* (18)

31. **Dawn Airey** managing director, channels and services, Sky *broadcasting* (33)

32. **Sly Bailey** chief executive, Trinity Mirror *publishing* (32)

Graeme Robertson

33. **Ricky Gervais** writer, producer, actor, podcaster *broadcasting* NEW ENTRY

34. **Murdoch MacLennan** chief executive, Telegraph Group *publishing* (22)

35. **Alan Rusbridger** editor of the Guardian and executive editor of the Observer *publishing, new media* (51)

36. **Dame Marjorie Scardino** chief executive, Pearson *publishing, new media* (41)

37. **Lesley Douglas** controller, BBC Radio 2 and 6 Music *broadcasting* (65)

38. **Paul Abbott** writer *broadcasting* (25)

39. **Ivan Fallon** UK chief executive, Independent News & Media *publishing* (35)

40. **Ralph Bernard** chief executive, Gcap *broadcasting* (29)

41. **Robert Thomson** editor, the Times *publishing* (64)

42. **Chris Wright** chairman, Chrysalis *broadcasting* (37)

43. **Tony O'Reilly** chief executive, Independent News and Media *publishing* (48)

44. **Trevor East** director of sport, Setanta *broadcasting* NEW ENTRY

45. **John Witherow** editor, the Sunday Times *publishing* (47)

46. **Mark Damazer** controller, BBC Radio 4, BBC7 *broadcasting* (52)

47. **Richard Wallace** editor, Daily Mirror *publishing* (74)

48. **Nick Robinson** politcal editor, BBC *broadcasting* (94)

49. **Richard Desmond** chief executive, Northern & Shell, Express Newspapers *publishing* (27)

50 **Andy Parfitt** controller, BBC Radio 1, 1Xtra *broadcasting* (78)

51. **Paul O'Grady** TV presenter, producer *broadcasting* (76)

52. **John Bryant** editor-in-chief, Telegraph *publishing* (63)

53. **Simon Kelner** editor-in-chief, Independent, Independent on Sunday *publishing* (55)

54. **Nick Bogle** chief executive, Bartle Bogle Hegarty *advertising* NEW ENTRY

55. **Liz Forgan** chair, Scott Trust *publishing, new media* (58)

56. **Max Clifford** founder, Max Clifford Associates *public relations* (62)

57. **Jamie Oliver** TV Chef, independent producer *broadcasting* (30)

58. **Fru Hazlitt** chief executive, Virgin Radio *broadcasting* NEW ENTRY

59. **Paul Jackson** director of entertainment and comedy, ITV *broadcasting* NEW ENTRY

60. **Peter Bazalgette** chief creative officer, Endemol; chairman, Endemol Uk *broadcasting* NEW ENTRY

61. **Roly Keating** controller, BBC2 *broadcasting* (57)

62. **Roger Alton** editor, Observer *publishing* (77)

63. **Gerhard Zeiler** chief executive, RTL Group *broadcasting* (39)

64. **David Kershaw** chief executive, M&C Saatchi plc *advertising* NEW ENTRY

65. **Craig Newmark** customer service representative, founder, chairman, Craigslist *new media* (22)

66. **Jane Lighting** chief executive, Channel Five *broadcasting* (84)

67. **John Smith** chief executive, BBC Worldwide; chief operating officer, BBC *broadcasting, publishing, new media* NEW ENTRY

68. **Richard Scudamore** chief executive, Premier League *broadcasting* (72)

69. **David Bergg** director of programme strategy, ITV *broadcasting* (38)

70. **Ceri Thomas** editor, BBC Radio 4's Today programme *broadcasting* NEW ENTRY

71. **Dan Chambers** director of programmes, Channel Five *broadcasting* (44)

72. **Johnny Hornby** managing partner, Clemmow Hornby Inge *advertising* (81)

73. **David Mannion** editor-in-chief, ITV News *broadcasting* (66)

74. **Jane Featherstone** joint managing director, Kudos Productions *broadcasting* NEW ENTRY

75. **Nicholas Coleridge** managing director, Condé Nast *publishing* (63)

76. **Simon Cowell** TV presenter, producer *broadcasting* NEW ENTRY

77. **Ed Richards** chief operating officer, Ofcom *regulation* NEW ENTRY

78. **Julian Bellamy** controller, BBC3 *broadcasting* NEW ENTRY

79. **Lionel Barber** editor, Financial Times *publishing* NEW ENTRY

80. **Steve Morrison** chief executive, All3Media *broadcasting* NEW ENTRY

81. **Anthony McPartin and Declan Donnelly** presenters, producers *broadcasting* NEW ENTRY

82. **Sir Frank Lowe** founding partner, Red Brick *advertising* NEW ENTRY

83. **Richard Littlejohn** newspaper columnist *publishing* (34)

84. **Richard Woolfe** director of programming, Sky One, Sky Two and Sky Three *broadcasting* (85)

85. **Alison Sharman** ITV director of factual and daytime *broadcasting* (69)

86. **Matthew Freud** chairman, Freud Communications *public relations* (96)

87. **Patience Wheatcroft** editor, Sunday Telegraph *publishing* NEW ENTRY

88. **Jane Tranter** controller of drama commissioning, BBC *broadcasting* (79)

89. **Trevor Beattie** founder, Beattie, McGuinness, Bungay *advertising* (75)

90. **Duncan Edwards** managing director and chief executive officer, the National Magazine Company *publishing* (67)

91. **John Ryley** head of Sky News *broadcasting* NEW ENTRY

92. **Shaun Woodward** minister for creative industries and tourism *politics* NEW ENTRY

93. **Sir Christopher Meyer** chairman, Press Complaints Commission *regulation* (71)

94. **Carolyn McCall** chief executive designate, Guardian Media Group *publishing, broadcasting, new media* NEW ENTRY

95. **Peter Hill** editor, Daily Express *publishing* (86)

96. **Victoria Pile** writer, producer *broadcasting* NEW ENTRY

97. **Bob Shennan** controller, BBC Radio 5 Live, 5 Live Sports Extra, Asian Network *broadcasting* (92)

98. **Steven Lambert** chief creative officer, RDF Media *broadcasting* NEW ENTRY

99. **Ron Jones** executive chairman, Tinopolis *broadcasting* NEW ENTRY

100. **Greg Dyke** chairman, HIT Entertainment; wannabe chief executive, ITV *broadcasting* NEW ENTRY

● The panellists

Tess Alps

As chief executive of Thinkbox, the central marketing body for commercial TV, Alps is one of the most senior women executives in UK advertising. Prior to joining Thinkbox, she was chairman of the PHD Group media agency. Alps sits on the Committee of Advertising Practice general media panel for the Advertising Standards Authority. She is on the board of the MediaGuardian Edinburgh International TV Festival and a member of Bafta and the Royal Television Society.

Emily Bell

Bell has been editor-in-chief of Guardian Unlimited for six years, overseeing the rapid growth in the online operation of the newspaper, which has won accolades in the UK and abroad. Bell previously worked for the Observer as advertising correspondent, media business editor and finally business editor.

Janet Goldsmith

A leading proponent of multichannel television in the UK, Goldsmith appears as a regular commentator in newspapers and magazines. Over the past 12 years she has specialised in launching and restructuring a number of TV networks, both for start-up independent companies and multinational corporations and previously worked as managing director of Universal Studios Networks.

Lorraine Heggessey

Chief executive of Talkback Thames, one of the biggest production companies in the country, Heggessey is responsible for programmes as diverse as The X Factor, The Apprentice, Green Wing and Property Ladder. She joined Talkback Thames in 2005 after nearly five years in charge of BBC1, during which time the channel overtook ITV1 for the first time. Previously controller of Children's BBC and director of programmes at BBC Production, she also brought back Doctor Who.

Paul Robinson

Robinson is a media consultant to European and US broadcasters. He was senior vice-president at Walt Disney Television for seven years. Previously was chief executive of Talk Radio UK and spent seven years at the BBC. He joined Radio 1 as managing editor and was promoted to head of strategy for BBC Radios 1 to 5 Live.

Matt Wells

Wells started out as a reporter on the Edinburgh Evening News in 1995. He worked as a reporter, a news editor and London correspondent for the Scotsman before joining the Guardian in 1999. He was appointed media correspondent a year later and has edited the Guardian's media section since 2004. He is also editor and presenter of the Guardian's weekly media podcast, Media Talk.

News media

Press

Explainer: ABCs

What are ABCs?
ABCs are circulation figures published by the Audit Bureau of Circulation, an independent company that monitors and verifies sales of newspapers and magazines.

How often do ABCs come out?
National newspaper ABCs are published each month. Regional newspaper and magazine ABCs are published every six months, covering January–June and July–December each year.

What do the ABCs include?
The ABC publishes the number of copies of a publication sold at full price and sent to subscribers. They sometimes include "bulks" — copies distributed free to targeted places such as hotels and airlines – but now bulks must be reported by target audience, and the number of "actively purchased" copies is more often considered the headline figure. The figures in this book exclude bulks.

The Nationals

After 18 months of revolution, it could be said the British press has been running to stand still. If the treadmill in question is the overall and inexorable decline of the print industry, the little legs pounding away have been manoeuvring format changes, discounting, providing freesheets and giveaways, all in the name of reversing the circulation decline. Take a look at the ABC circulation figures (p 20) and it's evident very little has actually been gained in the past two years. In the quality press, those few papers that have not changed format (the Telegraph titles and the Sunday Times) have shown little sign of interest to do so.

Defenders of these moves would argue, that the slide would have been far worse if not for the makeover hullabaloo caused by the quality tabloids and midsize Berliner formats. But as the size of newspapers settles to these more convenient smaller shapes, where next for journalism and the publishing business? Go online, young man, and try not to look surprised – the press barons have cottoned on to this internet business and they're making up for lost time.

● The quality press

The Telegraph, nearly 170,000 readers adrift from its banker sale of 1 million of not so long ago, has experienced probably the worst identity crisis of the UK press. Its new owners, the Barclay brothers, have been through more editors than might be considered seemly at the stately titles and at the end of 2006 were set on dragging the titles into the future not via a new print size, but by focusing on the digital possibilities for their august organs. Success at first seemed far from certain – an early foray into video reports on the web was dubbed "Acorn Antiques" by Mediaguardian.co.uk's Media Monkey.

A former City journalist, Will Lewis, first elevated to the position of editorial managing director across both titles and then to editor of the daily, has gambled the shop on integrating the staff of papers and websites, launching video news on the web and shedding a further 130 staff (in addition to the 300 losses last year), all in the process of moving from Canary Wharf to new offices in Victoria. Outcry, perhaps inevitably, followed an announcement that several senior foreign correspondents would be made redundant as part of the cuts. The National Union of Journalists protested that the management had failed to abide by its own rules in carrying out consultations — perhaps most damagingly, it emerged that staff who were being considered for redundancy would not be allowed in to the new building until their future had been determined.

Internal strife continued with rumours that both the acting editor, John Bryant, and Patience Wheatcroft (lured away from her long-standing role as business editor of the Times to the Sunday) were unhappy with the encroachment of Lewis on to their turf. Wheatcroft was reported to have been consulting lawyers over the loss of some of her powers as editor; a report that she later denied, but it was symptomatic of the panic and uncertainty within the titles. Bryant, too, after an outburst in the paper's morning news conference, was said to have resigned his post. This rumour was also denied, but national newspapers being what they are, the stories of dissent kept coming. Bryant was in fact replaced as editor of the daily a few weeks later by Lewis but remains editor-in-chief of both titles at the time of writing.

Whether the most staid title in the market can survive such a huge shift in business and cultural focus will be preoccupying more media owners than just the Barclays in the near future. More than one press commentator has noted mournfully that should the Telegraph succeed in integrating, slimming down and multi-skilling its newsroom in one drastic move, the management will be hailed as visionaries and other titles will follow.

National daily circulations

	Editor	Jan–Jun 06	Jul–Dec 05	Jan–Jun 05	Year-on-year % change
Popular and midmarket titles					
Sun	Rebekah Wade	3,163,504	3,257,551	3,268,503	-3.21
Daily Mail	Paul Dacre	2,386,893	2,363,724	2,383,504	0.14
Daily Mirror	Richard Wallace	1,653,431	1,717,262	1,737,872	-4.86
Daily Express	Peter Hill	838,165	825,320	925,064	-9.39
Daily Star	Dawn Neesom	791,732	839,677	854,600	-7.36
Quality press					
Daily Telegraph	John Bryant	902,769	903,920	910,743	-0.88
Times	Robert Thomson	666,018	689,141	681,373	-2.25
Financial Times	Andrew Gowers	446,786	425,901	426,806	4.68
Guardian	Alan Rusbridger	381,790	382,291	368,294	3.66
Independent	Simon Kelner	254,827	259,178	261,043	-2.38

National Sunday circulations

	Editor	Jan–Jun 06	Jul–Dec 05	Jan–Jun 05	Year-on-year % change
Popular and midmarket titles					
News of the World	Andy Coulson	3,552,119	3,718,682	3,666,044	-3.11
Mail on Sunday	Peter Wright	2,331,213	2,292,809	2,339,022	-0.33
Sunday Mirror	Tina Weaver	1,463,809	1,506,268	1,540,574	-4.98
People	Mark Thomas	852,399	917,662	956,328	-10.87
Sunday Express	Martin Townsend	846,260	864,704	959,039	-11.76
Daily Star Sunday	Gareth Morgan	397,646	411,301	441,054	-9.84
Sunday Sport	Paul Carter	129,076	151,295	156,993	-17.78
Quality press					
Sunday Times	John Witherow	1,339,111	1,366,851	1,366,538	-2.01
Sunday Telegraph	Patience Wheatcroft	673,528	678,712	686,949	-1.95
The Observer	Roger Alton	487,307	438,483	445,119	9.48
Independent on Sunday	Tristan Davies	233,769	213,797	207,819	12.49

Source: ABC. All figures exclude bulks

Not quite so dramatically but equally significantly, the Times announced it would be publishing its UK and foreign news "web first", thereby ending the bizarre self-imposed embargo many newspapers have insisted on where you may not read news until tomorrow. Times TV and podcasts are also under feverish development as well as numerous very secret plans involving "community" on the Times website.

Indeed, community is the new, new thing in newspapers and the press industry en masse is taking it on board. In an attempt to wean advertisers away from the ABC figures as a measure of success (see explainer on ABCs, page 19), the industry has realised that it must mould its readers and users into some sort of identifiable shape. As a result, instead of selling ads with a pricing system based on copies sold, the newspaper industry has been able to shift to a rate card system based on eyeballs and repeat returns – terms more familiar in the broadcasting sector.

The good news for consumers is that the spectres of subscriptions and pay-per-view newspaper websites have all but receded. Of the mainstream papers, only the Independent will persist with this model in the short term and no one believes that's for any reason other than a reluctance to be online at all. The paper, which has enjoyed such a lively turnaround since initiating the conversion to tabloid, has seen its growth switch back to reverse, despite some equally lively stints with guest editors such as Bono and Georgio Armani. The Independent's editor, Simon Kelner, bravely continues to insist that throwing large sums at this new-fangled interweb is a mug's game. Instead, the Independent is to be published in India, it says, becoming the first British newspaper to be printed in the sub-continent and is expecting to distribute 5,000 copies there.

So, rest of the world beware, in one form or another the UK press is coming. Honed by years of cutthroat competition, it's largely leaner, more energetic and definitely more ruthless than you.

Guardian podcast... the way forward for the newspaper industry

Martin Argles

The Guardian began the year riding the success of its new format, picking up all the major awards for its editor, newspaper of the year and its website. As with the tabloid converters though, the huge year-on-year gains began to ebb as the paper announced it would be stepping up publishing in the US, just as the Times did.

This can be read not as a serious belief that selling copies in New York will transform the business, but as an attempt to generate traffic and awareness overseas. Rightly proud of having stuck by the internet in the lean years and been rewarded with the most-visited newspaper site in the world, the Guardian now finds itself in the unfamiliar territory of defending first-mover success as the others come pelting into the straight.

As a result we can expect more podcasts, shaky first steps into recruiting hacks with camcorders and more places to chat and debate on newspaper websites.

● Sundays

In 2006 the Observer adopted its stablemate the Guardian's Berliner format and enjoyed the fillip of immediate sales success. Its sales held up well through the year and its popular monthly magazines (Observer Food Monthly, Observer Sport Monthly, Observer Music Monthly and newcomer Observer Woman) enjoyed critical acclaim. Nicola Jeal, the editor of OFM and launch editor of Observer Woman, enjoyed the accolade of being nominated for both titles in the British Society of Magazine Editors awards. The Sunday Times continued to occupy most of the ground in the Sunday quality market with little change other than a stealth tabloidisation of its supplements, but it retains its broadsheet main section.

The Sunday Telegraph, by contrast, gained and lost an editor in the well-respected Sarah Sands, who moved from Saturday to Sunday within the group. Hampered by no format change, she none the less produced a revamped package with new supplements to the sound of deafening silence. She was replaced by Patience Wheatcroft, who began to unpick the changes midway through 2006.

The News of the World, under its editor, Andy Coulson, continued its spectacular feud with über-PR chief Max Clifford, baffling plenty of its readers with its continuing obsession with documenting every bump in the life of Kerry Katona (a Clifford client and somewhere, lost to history, at the heart of this incredibly long-running battle). Neither side shows any sign of backing down, leading us to wonder if perhaps the scoop-getting powers of the Mirror Group titles have been enhanced by the Clifford-Coulson hundred years' war. Coulson continues to be routinely described as the next editor of the Sun though the present incumbent, despite a night in the cells, shows no especial signs of departure.

The ticking time-bomb that may slow down Coulson's inexorable rise is the criminal investigation into tabloid reporting methods, just bubbling to the surface. The News of the World's royal editor, Clive Goodman, and two other men were arrested and charged after allegedly intercepting voicemail messages of the Prince of Wales' staff, leading to several uncannily accurate royal scoops. This practice is, according to numerous reports, not unheard of elsewhere in Fleet Street and threatens to bring down several houses of cards.

How much wall space do you have?

Trees of Britain

theguardian

We began 2006 wondering just how many free DVDs the UK newspaper consumer could feasibly consume. It became a commonly held belief that no one was actually watching the damn things, just picking them up because they were stupidly cheap. Entire conferences were convened, so it seemed, to discuss how to wean publishers off the expensive, long-term unhelpful, one-day hit of a free DVD buzz. Just as it seemed hopeless, a light dawned and the first wallchart of British fauna and flora appeared in the Guardian. (Note: the original authorship of wallcharts is as hotly contested as the Sudoku wars of 2004.) As sure as colliding stars form a black hole (I learn from my cosmology wallchart), the combination of DVD fatigue and possibly a new lust for learning in the British public provided a suitable sales boost. For a piece of paper with words and pictures on it — how refreshing (and cheap to produce) is that?

Two months later, there were wallcharts (apparently identical at that) in every paper. Missed mini-beasts? It'll be in the Mail tomorrow. Already got spiders? Don't worry, there's a whales chart in another paper. How long can the wallchart mania continue? Well, there's a question to which the answer must be, "How many fish are there in the sea?" (Marine life wallchart exclusively in Sunday's Telegraph).

● Daily tabloids

Kindly providing us media hacks with the most entertainment since Kelvin MacKenzie's headline writing, was the Sun's editor, Rebekah Wade, with the news one morning late in 2005 (broken, equally entertainingly, by Sky News) that she had spent the night in Wandsworth nick after a physical altercation with her husband, EastEnders hard man Grant Mitchell (the actor Ross Kemp). Though everyone tried very hard to maintain that domestic violence is no laughing matter, in the end, no one could bring themselves to great outrage and Wade managed to ride it out. Since this career high, though, the editor of the Sun has had a relatively quiet time, confining herself to spreading shock and awe through her pages, hiring the former editor MacKenzie to fill the capacious shoes of Richard Littlejohn, who finally joined the Mail after some nonsense litigation.

The Mail added Allison Pearson, late of many parishes, to its columnist line-up as a replacement for Lynda Lee-Potter, deciding against Amanda Platell, Liz Jones and various other pretenders to the crown, though those distinguished women are elsewhere in the paper. The biggest news at the Mail — overshadowed by far more life-threatening cuts elsewhere — has been the pruning of budgets on features, health and women. To its rivals, for whom the Mail's largesse has long been the subject of much speculation and envy, this was both comforting and disturbing news. If even Associated, a publisher that largely advocates selling papers by putting the money on the page, is cutting back, well, the sky really must be falling in.

In happier news, the success story of the year was the resurgent Daily Mirror. Not in circulation terms of course, but in the old-fashioned

A scoop year for the Daily Mirror

Major PCC decisions

● **February 2006** In September 2005, a Danish newspaper published a series of cartoons depicting the Prophet Muhammad, which caused widespread insult across the international Muslim community. In subsequent months, the decision by several newspapers in Europe and further afield to reprint the cartoons sparked demonstrations, flag burning, boycotts and death threats worldwide.

British Muslim leaders demanded that the PCC strengthen clause 12 of the code. In February 2006, the commission said it had received around 30 letters from the British public urging it to resist these demands. Clause 12 remained unchanged. However, the mainstream British press was unanimous in its decision not to publish the cartoons.

● **April 2006** In March 2006, Chat magazine ran a story about Sylvia Payne headlined, "Why I slept with my own son". Labour MP Laura Moffatt complained to the PCC objecting to the fact that Payne who had been convicted for having sex with her teenage son, had received money for the story.

The PCC ruled that Chat had breached clause 16 of the code, which says payment should not be made to convicted criminals for stories that "exploit a particular crime". Chat had paid an agency for the story, which in turn paid Payne and her son. The magazine accepted that, although the information had already been released to the public, no payment should have been made.

● **July 2006** A father complained to the commission that a photo had been published by Zoo magazine without consent in breach of clause 6 (children) of the code. The image depicted the complainant and his 10-year-old daughter apparently making Nazi salutes at an FA Cup semi-final.

However, a picture of a child taken and published without the consent of the parent will not in all cases breach the privacy code. The PCC considered that attending such a public event implied consent for the publication of photographs taken on the day. The complaint was not upheld.

● **August 2006** Following reports that the police were investigating a News of the World journalist for phone tapping, the PCC issued a statement calling interception of this kind "completely unacceptable".

The commission chairman pointed out that it could not comment for legal reasons but used the opportunity to reaffirm that journalists must abide by the press code of practice, in addition to the terms of the law.

scoop-getting business that used to be the daily press. First signs of life under its relatively new editor, Richard Wallace, came with the front-page pictures of Kate Moss apparently taking cocaine in a recording studio with her boyfriend, newspaper favourite Pete Doherty. While there were plenty of dissenters queuing up to dismiss this story as "supermodel takes coke, shock", there was no denying the Mirror owned one of those stories that runs for months. Indeed, the Moss/Doherty modern-day fable ran for most of 2006 in its many forms, to the great personal profit of almost everyone involved. A classic tabloid tale, then. Wallace performed a similar trick in the political arena with Prezza-gate (or "MP has extramarital fling, shock"); another exclusive that ran for months and was the beginning of a protracted end for the deputy prime minister. Through this invading of the classic Sunday newspaper turf – and casually taking out a Coronation Street star for crack addiction in passing – the Mirror proved that weekday tabs can still break stories and Wallace won editor of the year in the GQ awards in summer 2006 as well as the What the Papers Say crown in December. More will surely follow.

National newspaper ownership

Group name	Market share		Titles	Executive control
	Jan-Jun 06	Jan-Jun 05		
News International	34.4%	35.0%	Sun Times Sunday Times News of the World	Rupert Murdoch
Daily Mail and General Trust	20.5%	19.7%	Daily Mail Mail on Sunday	Viscount Rothermere
Trinity Mirror	15.1%	15.9%	Daily Mirror Sunday Mirror The People	Victor Blank
Northern and Shell	13.6%	14.4%	Daily Express Daily Star Sunday Express Daily Star Sunday	Richard Desmond
Telegraph Group	7.5%	7.2%	Daily Telegraph Sunday Telegraph	Barclay brothers
Guardian Media Group	3.4%	3.0%	Guardian Observer	Scott Trust
Pearson	3.3%	2.9%	Financial Times	Pearson board
Independent Newspapers	2.2%	1.9%	Independent Independent on Sunday	Anthony O'Reilly

Which newspaper will close next?

Stephen Brook

Years ago, when Rupert Murdoch predicted that the only daily newspapers to survive in the 21st century would be the Sun, the Times and the Daily Mail, Fleet Street scoffed. Of course, the great man had gone cheekily over the top, but it is fair at this point in British newspaper industry history to take his prediction to its logical endgame and bluntly ask, which newspaper will close next?

Fleet Street has been going through another wave of contraction and no titles are immune. Waves of redundancies at the Telegraph Media Group, Trinity Mirror and the Financial Times, belt tightening at the Times, even budget cuts at the Daily Mail. Newspapers are squashed between a sluggish British advertising market on one side and a rampant internet on the other. Add them together and it spells doom.

But which proud newspaper, or "legacy brand" – to use the scathing vernacular beloved of new media – will be first to vanish? By most accounts Sly Bailey, the chief executive of Trinity Mirror, is likeable enough, but I would rather go swimming with the sharks than stand between her and a potential efficiency saving. Thus the most uncomfortable newsroom to be in at the moment has to be that of the People.

While cutbacks hit many titles, they hit particularly hard at Trinity Mirror's People, where staff at the Sunday tabloid have been cut and cut again. Now star columnists, such as its TV reviewer, Garry Bushell, are off, because the paper apparently cannot afford them. It is hard to see how the great campaigning newspaper of years past, famed for its investigations in the 1970s, will survive. It is, as one Trinity Mirror executive says, "on the bones of its arse". Some weeks it rakes in not much more than £100,000 in advertising revenue. Add to that its sliding circulation – more than 100,000 sales have vanished, at last count. It is now selling an average of 790,000 and an amalgamation with its Trinity Mirror stablemate, the better-loved and more successful Sunday Mirror (circulation 1.4m), seems inevitable. Or the whole thing might just be put out of its misery.

Which brings us to Richard Desmond. In a historical footnote, the rambunctious owner of Northern & Shell apparently tried to buy the People in 2002. The offer price was in the region of £25m.

Trinity Mirror said no. It wanted £45m. Desmond went on to found the Daily Star Sunday at the end of that year, a further wound in what has turned into a fight for survival for the Sunday tabloid.

But Desmond has shown no mercy where his own titles are concerned. In what could become a sign of the future, he decided that the Press Association would be better – read cheaper – at producing the Daily Express City pages than staff journalists. He announced 35 redundancies and plans a similar amalgamation for the travel pages.

As advertising remains flat, Desmond and Bailey, in one respect, appear to be peas in a pod. Their tenures at the head of their companies has been about managing decline rather than going for growth. Bailey has a very unholy trinity she is attempting to satisfy: readers, advertisers and shareholders. It is an impossible task. Desmond makes his own demands on the profit levels of his titles. In Fleet Street's long game of survival they appear to be losers.

Where, if any, are the winners? With the state of mild panic afflicting the British newspaper industry deepening, no one can claim with any certainty that the future looks bright: circulation continues merrily on its downward curve, newspapers increase cover prices, cut costs, sack staff and grapple with digital integration. Newspaper websites are yet to overtake their print counterparts in terms of staffing or revenues, but many certainly have in terms of readers. More importantly, they are gaining critical mass. And newspapers are sober in the realisation that, even if websites exponentially increased their advertising and unique users, every print reader lost needs between 20 to 80 replacements on the web to maintain revenues.

Some companies decided to copy the great success across Europe of free newspapers. News International had the idea first with the London Paper, but its great rival, Associated Newspapers, got in first with London Lite. Both can't last as the market is too small. News International has quietly registered trademarks for the title in nearly a dozen major cities in England. Expect massive opposition from regional newspaper groups if any plans are put into operation. Such an event would send shockwaves through the industry, just as the closure of the People will. For while free newspapers and the internet show that the price of news has never been cheaper, those that run our newspapers know the weary truth that the costs have never been more crushingly expensive.

● Stephen Brook is press & publishing correspondent at Guardian Unlimited

The Regionals

It has been a tough time for the main regional newspaper groups: Trinity Mirror, Newsquest (owned by the US firm Gannett), the Daily Mail and General Trust (DMGT) and Johnston Press. After the consolidation boom of 2004 and a slowdown in 2005, 2006 proved to be a year of further circulation slides and advertising downturn, causing revenue warnings from Johnston and Trinity Mirror.

The tone was set when DMGT announced it would sell the country's third-largest regional group, Northcliffe, at the beginning of 2006, a move that stunned even the seasoned observer. DMGT, traditionally an investor in journalism, looked to be panicking at a time when the US-based website Craigslist, offering free classified advertising to users, put a face to the spectre haunting the industry. DMGT set itself ambitious targets for the group and did attract some bids (it said offers were around £1.2bn), but was forced to backtrack when the prices offered did not meet its expectations. It preferred, it said, to get more out of the papers itself. It's hard to say which announcement caused more surprise.

A month after calling off the sale, DMGT did sell Aberdeen Journals, publisher of the Aberdeen Press & Journal and Aberdeen Evening Express, to DC Thomson, publisher of, among other things, the Beano, in a deal worth £132m. It then merged the rest of the Northcliffe regional business with its national paper arm, Associated Newspapers. The move was designed, it said, to streamline management, save costs and combine its print and online operations to increase internet revenue.

The failure to sell the Northcliffe group may have caused a tipping point inside Trinity Mirror, where years of debate over whether its group would be worth more demerged (ie re-splitting the national and regional businesses coupled together in the post-Maxwell years) have finally resulted in a decision to put the group "under review". This is a traditional euphemism for "on the market", phrased only slightly more subtly than Northcliffe.

The abandoned sale of the Northcliffe group did unsettle the City which had a disastrous impact on the value of the sector as a whole, perhaps unfairly. For years these cash-generative, low-capital, high-

Top 10 regional publishers

	Number of papers	Weekly circulation (m)	% share
Trinity Mirror	234	13.8	21.5%
Newsquest Media Group	219	9.9	15.4%
Johnston Press	282	9.1	14.1%
Northcliffe Newspapers Group	111	7.5	11.7%
Associated Newspapers	11	6.7	10.4%
Archant	78	2.9	4.5%
Guardian Media Group	43	2.4	3.7%
The Midland News Association	19	2.0	3.1%
DC Thomson	6	2.0	3.1%
Iliffe News & Media	33	1.2	1.9%
Total top 10	**1036**	**57.5**	**89.4%**
Total all regional publishers	**1313**	**64.3**	

Data for 1 July 2006

Source: Newspaper Society

margin businesses remained City darlings while scepticism surrounded the future of the nationals. Chances are their time will come again.

In the meantime, the main groups have employed a number of new tactics to try and distract their advertisers from plunging sales. Despite the looming threats of online classified advertising and shrinking circulations, regional newspapers remain extremely profitable businesses; the city titles outside London and Manchester are proving resistant to freesheet mania and margins of 20-30% are not uncommon.

Industry-wide, the regionals are quietly rolling out hundreds of small, localised websites, attempting to link their existing paid-for classified advertising with a home for the kinds of free listings proving so successful in the US. These are, at present, little acorns.

Regional newspaper circulations

	Average net circulation			Frequency	Editor
	Jan–Jun 06	Jan–Jun 05	% change		
Top 20 paid-for regionals					
Sunday Mail, Scotland	532,545	562,543	-5.3%	Sunday	Allan Rennie
Sunday Post	451,530	481,767	-6.3%	Sunday	David Pollington
Daily Record, Scotland	443,464	469,232	-5.5%	morning	Bruce Waddell
Evening Standard, London	326,132	344,145	-5.2%	evening	Veronica Wadley
Express & Star, West Midlands	151,272	158,130	-4.3%	evening	Adrian Faber
Liverpool Echo	121,517	130,145	-6.6%	evening	Alastair Machray
Manchester Evening News	118,903	144,201	-17.5%	evening	Paul Horrocks
Belfast Telegraph	90,827	96,299	-5.7%	evening	Martin Lindsay
Evening Times, Glasgow	87,399	92,088	-5.1%	evening	Charles McGhee
Evening Chronicle, Newcastle	86,287	91,703	-5.9%	evening	Paul Robertson
Aberdeen Press & Journal	84,137	86,942	-3.2%	morning	Derek Tucker
Birmingham Mail	78,178	94,339	-17.1%	evening	Steve Dyson
Sunday Life, Belfast	77,817	84,082	-7.5%	Sunday	Jim Flanagan
Scotland on Sunday	77,230	82,756	-6.7%	Sunday	Tom Little
Dundee Courier & Advertiser	76,917	79,479	-3.2%	morning	Bill Hutcheon
Shropshire Star All Editions	76,568	80,394	-4.8%	evening	Sarah Jane Smith
Leicester Mercury	75,319	82,232	-8.4%	evening	Nick Carter
Herald, Glasgow	74,584	78,930	-5.5%	morning	Mark Douglas-Home
Sunday Sun, Newcastle	71,755	77,123	-7.0%	Sunday	Peter Montellier
The Sentinel, Stoke on Trent	70,567	74,892	-5.8%	daily	Mike Sassy
Eastern Daily Press, Norwich	66,515	68,599	-3.0%	morning	Peter Franzen
Nottingham Evening Post	65,364	71,080	-8.0%	evening	Graham Glen
Top 10 frees					
Metro, London	542,294*	480,698**	11.4%	morning	Kenny Campbell
Manchester Metro News	309,613	309,462	0.0%	weekly	Tim Oliver
Nottingham & Long Eaton Topper	212,750	212,236	0.2%	weekly	John Howarth
Nottingham Recorder	150,525	153,857	-2.2%	weekly	Graham Glen
Southampton Advertiser	143,103	148,895	-3.9%	weekly	Ian Murray
Herald & Post Edinburgh	134,537	142,963	-5.9%	weekly	Gail Milne
Wirral Globe	134,357	134,486	-0.1%	weekly	Leigh Marles
The Glaswegian	129,075	148,614	-13.1%	weekly	Garry Thomas
Coventry Observer	122,209	123,977	-1.4%	weekly	Mike Green
Derby Express	120,905	122,791	-1.5%	weekly	Andy Machin
Coventry Citizen	120,894	114,249	5.8%	weekly	Alan Kirby

Metro, London (now listed as ABC Bulk Distribution)   * 31 Jul-27 Aug 06   ** 1 Aug-28 Aug 05

● Free regional papers

The freesheet frenzy will prove to having an effect on the industry, though the full extent is still hard to read. It's important to remember that freesheets aren't actually a new phenomenon invented by Metro. Your local paid-for paper has probably had a free rival for the best part of 30 years. However, the current launch binge in major cities and the south-east involves big publishers and high stakes.

Associated moved first in London with the launch of London Lite — following Metro and Standard Lite into the giveaway market with a similar product. News International offered thelondonpaper, an all-new, internet-generation-friendly product ostensibly, but one whose launch seemed more vulnerable to mistakes and mockery (an infamous early error confused P Diddy and Pete Doherty in a small feature and ended up claiming the US star was a crack addict, to much hilarity from rival journalists who have plenty to gain from claiming such errors are due to too few, too inexperienced staff).

A few weeks after launch, both papers were claiming distribution of around the 400,000 mark (thelondonpaper said 360,000), with the Evening Standard's full-price sale down by anywhere between 10,000 and 40,000 copies, depending on whose figures you take. Thelondon-paper was generally better reviewed and a punchy Rupert Murdoch (is there any other kind?) declared that if the experiment proved successful he would roll out the model across the country posthaste.

In the other outpost of free-press wars, the Manchester Evening News (owned by the Guardian Media Group) free edition claimed to distribute 60,000 copies after launching in May 2006. Its paid-for editions seemed to lose around 10,000 copies, causing it to be overtaken by Trinity Mirror's Liverpool Echo. The MEN's editor, Paul Horrocks, told the Press Gazette that the reduction in paid-for copies would "continue to be replaced and supplemented by additional free copies".

"I don't see all our papers going free in the near future," said Horrocks, "but inevitably it is going in that direction."

How else to tackle the decline? Newsquest saw hope in turning night into day — or evening papers to morning titles in an attempt to increase readership. The York Evening Press, Oxford Mail and the Echo series in Essex were the first. Others including the Burton Mail, owned by Staffordshire Newspapers, followed.

Newsquest also converted its newsrooms into "multimedia centres" that will produce video clips for its websites and claimed 45,000 down-loads in the first month of the scheme. However, the production of videos prompted industrial action by journalists at the company's Southern Daily Echo in Southampton.

Johnston Press, meanwhile, after a quiet year, announced it would integrate around 60 of its larger newsrooms with online operations by the middle of 2007. Its CEO, Tim Bowdler, said younger readers were indeed using the websites. Little acorns...

Magazines

Leading new glossy... Grazia magazine

In the world of magazines it's entirely appropriate to begin with a neo-logistic coverline, then not really explain it in the rest of the piece. So here we go: Grazia is the new Heat.

It's about time someone was the new Heat because it's all old news with the old one (circulation is still growing, up 3.5% to 579,883; it is still outsold by Closer at 590,211, but since when did that matter?).

Sales figures aside, Grazia is where the buzz is. Launched in February 2005, a year later its circulation had risen 12.9% to 175,218 copies, not far off the 200,000 a month Elle sells or the 220,000 sold by Red. Grazia now sells more than 700,000 copies a month, making it by far the market-leading glossy in terms of volume. Is the women's market shifting from sedate monthlies to slightly scrappier weekly glossies? More style tips, more fashion, more gossip – in a way, the sheer volume of the 52 issues a year has tipped the scales.

Launches at the other end of the market have also distinguished them-selves. News International's home of gruesome real-life stories, Love It!, achieved a record debut circulation figure of 405,441. Few titles can hope for such heavy promotion and coupon offers in the Sun. Real People, the NatMags title that debuted in January, also celebrated reaching its target, with average sales of 318,105.

The effect of those two launches taking more than 700,000 sales per week has been catastrophic for the established titles. Take a Break lost 9.9% of its circulation in the year-on-year figures to June 2006 (still sells over 1m, though) and Woman's Own was down 13.3%, to 367,729. Its editor resigned a month after the ABC figures were published.

Men's monthlies are telling a similar tale: hit hard by the weeklies. The decline of the established titles is shocking: Maxim down 35.8% to 146,043 in the first half of 2006, Loaded down 21.9% and FHM down 24.9%, though it still leads the sector with 420,688 sales. Emap's Zoo and IPC's Nuts, fingered as the culprits responsible for this plummet, both seem to have reached a plateau, however – Zoo fell 12.5% to 228,024 and Nuts by just 0.7% to 304,785. This time the demon is, yes you guessed it, the web. Young men, too, are finding the internet irresistible.

Still, Nuts and Zoo have performed the marvellous trick of double-handedly reviving the old "top shelf" debate. In a flashback to the late 80s, concerned campaigners (reminiscent of Clare Short's attempt to ban Page 3) pointed out that these titles, plus a handful of others, market porn to children, notably teenage boys.

"As a nation, we have rightly become concerned about child safety and have put in place measures which keep our children away from harm," wrote Claire Curtis-Thomas, the Labour MP for Crosby, in the Guardian. "Control of the media has been inextricably linked with this campaign: the 9pm TV watershed was introduced; films are classified by age; DVDs carry specific warnings; the internet can be managed through parental controls and is monitored by police. These measures are designed to ensure that children are not exposed to unsuitable material which may harm their emotional or physical development. The time has come to extend these measures to the written word and to age-classify

Awards

British Press Awards, 2006

- *National newspaper of the year:*
  The Guardian

- *Front page of the year:*
  The Sun, "Harry the Nazi"

- *Scoop of the year:*
  Daily Mirror, "Cocaine Kate"

Regional Press Awards, July 2006

- *Regional newspaper of the year:*
  The Belfast Telegraph

- *Front page of the year:*
  The Belfast Telegraph, "Goodbye"

- *Scoop of the year:*
  Brighton, "The Argus"

PPA Awards, May 2006

- *Consumer magazine of the year:*
  Good Housekeeping (National Magazine Company)

- *Editor of the year, consumer:*
  Gill Hudson, Radio Times (BBC Magazines)

- *Consumer specialist magazine of the year:*
  Kerrang! (Emap Performance)

- *Consumer lifestyle magazine of the year:*
  Country Living (National Magazine Company)

- *Weekly business and professional magazine of the year:*
  Farmers Weekly (Reed Business Information)

- *Monthly business and professional magazine of the year:*
  Chemistry World (Royal Society of Chemistry)

- *Customer magazine of the year:*
  Waitrose Food Illustrated (John Brown)

Magazine top 10s

		Average circulation per issue		Year-on-year
		Jan–Jun 06	Jul–Dec 05	Jan–Jun 05	% change
Top 10 women's weeklies					
1	Take a Break	1,082,051	1,155,886	1,200,397	-9.9%
2	Closer	590,211	578,337	540,044	9.3%
3	Heat	579,883	575,267	560,438	3.5%
4	Chat	554,375	602,308	609,163	-9.0%
5	OK! Magazine	547,714	649,777	532,843	2.8%
6	Now	539,902	577,818	591,795	-8.8%
7	That's Life	490,220	550,036	569,631	-13.9%
8	New! *	458,751	426,161	373,039	23.0%
9	Pick Me Up	445,098	491,669	503,950	-11.7%
10	Woman	417,362	456,524	485,463	-14.0%
Top 10 women's lifestyle					
1	Glamour	586,056	585,984	609,626	-3.9%
2	Cosmopolitan	442,384	461,610	462,943	-4.4%
3	Good Housekeeping	441,151	468,579	475,838	-7.3%
4	Yours	400,312	421,438	440,070	-9.0%
5	Marie Claire	331,127	371,444	381,281	-13.2%
6	Woman & Home	325,223	335,922	327,554	-0.7%
7	Prima	321,617	331,715	326,231	-1.4%
8	Candis	301,114	312,547	319,914	-5.9%
9	Company	275,038	283,429	302,127	-9.0%
10	More! *	271,999	277,862	275,620	-1.3%
Top 10 men's lifestyle — including weeklies					
1	FHM	420,688	500,865	560,167	-24.9%
2	Nuts	304,785	306,802	304,751	0.0%
3	Men's Health	235,833	233,445	228,108	3.4%
4	Zoo	228,024	260,470	260,317	-12.4%
5	Loaded	185,268	232,001	237,083	-21.9%
6	Maxim	146,043	185,908	227,377	-35.8%
7	GQ	126,797	126,275	125,050	1.4%
8	Stuff	92,672	90,750	77,373	19.8%
9	Men's Fitness *	67,674	67,636	66,474	1.8%
10	Bizarre	65,959	71,776	76,328	-13.6%

* Not in last year's top 10

publications accordingly," added Curtis-Thomas, who presented an early-day motion on the subject.

It all amounted, naturally, to no more than a hill of beans. More tellingly, plenty of supermarkets have already moved Nuts and Zoo "upstairs" to the top shelf, in what is known as the Walmart effect. Wal-mart, the US mega-supermarket chain that practically invented the parental advisory sticker, responds not to legislation but market power and wields so much influence that it can determine the re-recording of a rap album with parentally friendly lyrics. The market will decide.

Back in the grim world of declining circulations, perhaps the most telling set of ABC circulation figures belong to the teen market. Feeling the effect of the networking sites MySpace and Bebo, many favoured brands slumped. Smash Hits closed and circulation figures for Bliss fell 22.7%, for Sugar by 29.8% and Mizz by 9.7%.

Magazine publishers have been among the least receptive to the inter-net, but towards the back end of 2006, that began to change. In two significant moves announced a day apart, NatMags – publisher of Cosmo, Good Housekeeping and Country Living among others – launched major websites for those titles. This followed the purchase of the seven-year-old women's site Handbag.com from the Barclay brothers for £22m.

"You could characterise us as watching rather than playing for the past five years," said the NatMags chief executive, Duncan Edwards. "We have now moved to take to the field."

● Business-to-business

Not so much taking to the field as heading for the hills, the trade publisher VNU announced it was prepared to sell its European magazine business. The Netherlands-based business-to-business publisher is one of the largest trade groups in the UK, with titles including Accountancy Age and a significant hold over the computer trade market. Though VNU seemed to have been one of the most successful translators of its business to the digital world, with online revenues hitting 25% (probably because of its natural affinity with the computer trade), it stated it wished to sell "because the group's activities are not well aligned with VNU's market-ing information and media measurement businesses". Generally one would read "not as profitable as", for "not well aligned with".

Top 50 consumer magazines

	Title	Average circulation/issue			Year-on-year
		Jan–Jun 06	Jul–Dec 05	Jan–Jun 05	% change
1	Sky the magazine	6,798,495	6,874,090	6,783,581	0.2%
2	AA Roadside	3,394,912	–	–	–
3	Asda Magazine	2,974,793	2,377,126	2,631,293	13.1%
4	Tesco Magazine	1,923,933	2,494,330	–	–
5	Prudential Magazine	1,708,257	1,909,855	–	–
6	The National Trust Magazine	1,665,483	1,655,088	1,573,615	5.8%
7	Boots Health & Beauty	1,591,393	1,689,490	1,724,587	-7.7%
8	**What's on TV**	1,509,519	1,502,977	1,673,790	-9.8%
9	U (Magazine for Unison members)	1,476,877	1,465,833	–	–
10	Sainsbury's Fresh Ideas	1,422,102	1,431,766	–	–
11	**TV Choice**	1,287,773	1,212,246	1,157,622	11.2%
12	Saga Magazine	1,105,140	1,230,639	1,245,006	-11.2%
13	The Somerfield Magazine	1,092,936	1,058,818	1,134,364	-3.7%
14	**Take a Break**	1,082,051	1,155,886	1,200,397	-9.9%
15	**Radio Times**	1,070,042	1,093,850	1,080,199	-0.9%
16	Asda Good For You! Magazine	959,440	976,100	–	–
17	Debenhams Desire	745,126	745,126	745,126	0.0%
18	**Reader's Digest**	737,345	735,138	776,902	-5.1%
19	Birds	621,198	623,857	624,118	-0.5%
20	**Closer**	590,211	578,337	540,044	9.3%
21	**Glamour**	586,056	585,984	609,626	-3.9%
22	**Heat**	579,883	575,267	560,438	3.5%
23	**Chat**	554,375	602,308	609,163	-9.0%
24	**OK! Magazine**	547,714	649,777	532,843	2.8%
25	Unlimited	542,250	386,400	338,000	60.4%
26	**Now**	539,902	577,818	591,795	-8.8%
27	Norwich Union Magazine	501,903	–	–	–
28	**That's Life**	490,220	550,036	569,631	-13.9%
29	**New!**	458,751	426,161	373,039	23.0%
30	**Pick Me Up**	445,098	491,669	503,950	-11.7%
31	**Cosmopolitan**	442,384	461,610	462,943	-4.4%
32	**Good Housekeeping**	441,151	468,579	475,838	-7.3%
33	Homebase Ideas	424,055	399,984	399,348	6.2%
34	**FHM**	420,688	500,865	560,167	-24.9%
35	**Woman**	417,362	456,524	485,463	-14.0%
36	Emma's Diary Pregnancy Guide	414,930	413,110	416,140	-0.3%
37	Legion	413,703	425,462	456,744	-9.4%
38	**Love It!**	405,441	–	–	–
39	**Hello!**	403,666	390,622	392,481	2.8%
40	**Yours**	400,312	421,438	–	–
41	Sky the magazine Ireland	397,478	364,768	348,136	14.2%
42	Your Family	392,475	–	–	–
43	**Woman's Weekly**	391,426	414,778	425,568	-8.0%
44	**TV Times**	372,712	407,878	418,192	-10.9%
45	Motoring & Leisure	371,552	371,940	365,010	1.8%
46	**Woman's Own**	367,729	409,616	424,292	-13.3%
47	The Vauxhall Magazine	365,882	372,754	394,846	-7.3%
48	**Best**	362,183	400,807	398,289	-9.1%
49	Sainsbury's: The Magazine	357,883	414,337	346,898	3.2%
50	**National Geographic Magazine**	355,956	356,438	350,253	1.6%

Newsstand titles in bold   Source: ABC. Top 50 excludes groups of titles

A mighty wind of change for magazines

David Hepworth

Arguably, the magazine launch that is probably being watched with most interest in some sectors of the industry is not on the newsstand. In fact it's not even on paper. It's a multimedia facsimile of a weekly lads' magazine called Monkey. It was launched a month ago and goes out free to anyone who signs up for a weekly mailout.

Monkey comes from Felix Dennis's company, which is instructive. This is the firm that has made a fortune out of selling young men's monthly magazines such as Maxim and (in the US) Stuff. The fact that Dennis's newest product is a weekly that's not on paper suggests that Felix probably hasn't changed his mind since 2000, when he went round telling everyone who would listen that there were Four Horsemen of the Apocalypse (new technology, environmentalism, illiteracy and distribution costs) riding into town to cut a scythe through the bland certainties of the previous 25 years.

At the other end of the spectrum are the people exuding sunny optimism in November after the British Society of Magazine Editors prizegiving, most of whom seemed to be saying "hold fast to your brand values, chase not short-term circulation gains, maintain editorial quality and you will outlast the storm". Cheerleader for this party is probably Condé Nast, whose December issue of GQ was so thick they ran out of folios.

I'm not sure I side with either party but at least Felix couldn't be accused of fooling himself. The notion that magazines are temporarily afflicted by a gadarene rush downmarket with an accompanying decline in editorial standards and will eventually awake is a delusion. It's a delusion that ignores the fact that, no matter what anybody's survey says, teenagers don't read in the numbers they used to. It's a delusion that ignores the evidence suggesting that a lot of the information people used to get from specialist magazines they now get from the web for free. It's a delusion that refuses to take note of the fact that a lot of the changes taking place are structural and permanent.

The teenage sector has already felt this mighty wind, which is why, earlier this year, Smash Hits closed in the UK and Teen People shut down in the US. (My colleague Andrew Harrison begs to point out here that Smash Hits is still a TV show but no longer a magazine while Top Of The Pops is still a magazine but no longer a TV show, which doesn't seem right.) If the government continues its stand against junk-food advertising in young people's media, life in the teen sector can only get harder.

Men's monthlies, whether specialist ones such as Max Power or general ones such as Maxim, are selling a fraction of what they once did and you can't attribute that entirely to the two weeklies, Nuts and Zoo. These two have been engaged in an energy-sapping, nipple-to-nipple, price-cutting contest that has seen their combined sales fall over the past year.

In the women's sector, the excitement has been mainly in the weeklies, though even here there are signs that growth is getting harder to come by, with Emap's launch First finding things tougher than anticipated and News International knocking out issues of Love It! at 30p (half its cover price). A few, such as Heat and Grazia, manage to stand aloof, but most are publishing on the back foot.

The newsstand is a war zone. The cumulative effect of all the gifting, price discounting and editorial saming is that the customer has no loyalty whatsoever. Duncan Edwards of National Magazines is not the only publisher of middle-market monthlies hoping for "a fundamental paradigm shift" away from its costly vicissitudes towards a subscription model. However, he also knows that giving massive discounts to subscribers who don't renew is even more wasteful than paying the retailers to ensure "display". What everybody's finding is that people are no less keen on their favourite magazines. It's simply that they don't so readily go and seek them out.

The Monkey experiment is an attempt to export the magazine approach to selling advertising, which is essentially all about environment, to the web, where it's all about massive numbers. The economics of the magazine industry are traditionally rooted in the idea that a Vogue reader is worth more than a Glamour reader who is worth more than a Closer reader. The web flattens out these distinctions, which may explain why cost per thousand in that medium is so under pressure.

The rumours for the new year are that we will see a male Grazia, that the Face is coming back as a website and that the News International bloke magazine is, as they say in Hollywood, "in turnaround". But then again, as they also say in Hollywood, nobody knows anything.

● David Hepworth is editorial director of Development Hell Ltd
    mail@davidhepworth.com

National press contacts

Daily Express
Express Newspapers, The Northern & Shell Building,
Number 10 Lower Thames Street, London EC3R 6EN
0871 434 1010
www.express.co.uk
firstname.surname@express.co.uk
Editor: Peter Hill
- *Deputy editor: Hugh Whittow; news: Greg Swift; political: Patrick O'Flynn*
- *Section editors – City: Stephen Kahn; comment: Laura Kibby; defence: John Ingham; features: Fergus Kelly; foreign: Gabriel Milland; health: Victoria Fletcher; money: Holly Thomas; showbiz: Mark Jagasia; sport: Bill Bradshaw; transport: John Ingham; TV: Charlotte Civil*
- *Production editor: Bob Smith; chief sub: Keith Ging*

Daily Mail
Associated Newspapers, Northcliffe House,
2 Derry Street, Kensington, London W8 5TT
020 7938 6000
www.dailymail.co.uk
firstname.surname@dailymail.co.uk
Editor: Paul Dacre
- *Deputy editor: Alistair Sinclair; news: Tony Gallagher; political: Ben Brogan*
- *Sections – city: Alex Brummer; diplomatic: Rebecca English; diary: Richard Kay; features: Leaf Kalfayan; money: Tony Hazell; showbiz: Nicole Lampert; sport: Tim Jotischky; transport: Ray Massey*
- *Correspondents – consumer affairs: Sean Poulter; education: Sarah Harris; health: Jenny Hope; industry: Becky Barrow; political: James Chapman, Graeme Wilson; social affairs: Steve Doughty*
- *Production editor: Harbans Baga; chief subs: Matthew Gocher (news); Robin Popham (features)*
- *Publicity: Charles Garside, 020 7938 6000*

Daily Mirror
MGN, One Canada Square, Canary Wharf, London E14 5AP
020 7293 3000
www.mirror.co.uk
firstname.surname@mirror.co.uk
Editor: Richard Wallace
- *Deputy editor: Conor Hanna; news: Anthony Harwood; political: Oonagh Blackman*
- *Sections – business: Clinton Manning; consumer: Ruki Sayid; fashion: Amber Morales; features: Carole Watson; foreign: Mark Ellis; health: Simone Cave; money: John Husband; sport: Dean Morse; TV: Nicola Methven*
- *Executive editor (production): Jon Moorhead; chief news sub: Pratima Sarwate; chief features sub: James Rettie; assistant editor (pictures): Ian Down; picture editor: Greg Bennett*
- *Publicity: Sarah Vaughan-Brown, 020 7293 3222*

Daily Sport
Sport Newspapers, 19 Great Ancoats Street,
Manchester M60 4BT
0161 236 4466
www.dailysport.net
firstname.surname@sportsnewspapers.co.uk
- *Publicity: Jane Field, 0161 238 8181*

Daily Star
Express Newspapers, The Northern & Shell Building,
Number 10 Lower Thames Street, London EC3R 6EN
0871 434 1010
www.dailystar.co.uk
firstname.surname@dailystar.co.uk
Editor: Dawn Neesom
- *Deputy editor: Jim Mansell; news: Kieron Saunders; political: Macer Hall; features: Samantha Taylor; sport: Howard Wheatcroft; Cashpoint: Michelle Carter*
- *Production editor: Bob Hadfield*

Daily Telegraph
Telegraph Group, 111 Buckingham Palace Road,
London SW1 0DT
020 7931 2000
www.telegraph.co.uk
firstname.surname@telegraph.co.uk
Acting editor: John Bryant
- *Deputy editor: Ian MacGregor; assistant editors: Corinna Honan, Andrew Pierce; managing director, editorial: William Lewis; editor at large: Jeff Randall; associate editor: Simon Heffer; news: Michael Smith; political: George Jones; home affairs: Philip Johnston; managing editor: John McGurk; night editor: David Lucas*
- *Sections – assistant editor (arts): Sarah Crompton; City: Damian Reece; executive foreign editor: Con Coughlin; fashion: Clare Coulson; features: Rachel Simhon; medical: Celia Hall; legal: Joshua Rozenberg; literary: Sam Leith; personal finance: Ian Cowie; science: Roger Highfield; sport: Keith Perry; TV: Neil Midgley; weekend: Jon Stock, education: Liz Lightfoot; consumer affairs: David Darbyshire*
- *Production editor: Steve Greaves*
- *Publicity: Danielle Howe, 020 7931 2000*

Financial Times
The Financial Times Group, 1 Southwark Bridge,
London SE1 9HL
020 7873 3000
www.ft.com
firstname.surname@ft.com
Editor: Lionel Barber
- *Deputy editor: Martin Dickson; news: Robert Shrimsley; political: James Blitz*
- *Sections – weekend: Michael Skapinker; Asia edition: John Ridding; FT magazine: Graham Watts; Europe: John Thornhill; comment: Brian Groom; public policy: Nick Timmins*
- *Production editor: Joe Russ*
- *Director of communications: Katy Hemmings; PR manager: Lucy Ellison*

The Guardian

Guardian News & Media, 119 Farringdon Road,
London EC1R 3ER
020 7278 2332
www.guardian.co.uk
firstname.surname@guardian.co.uk
Editor: Alan Rusbridger

- *Deputy editor: Paul Johnson; managing editor: Chris Elliott; home news: Nick Hopkins, David Taylor; home affairs: Alan Travis; political: Michael White, Patrick Wintour*
- Sections - *arts: Melissa Denes (Film & Music: Michael Hann); books: Claire Armitstead; City: Deborah Hargreaves, Julia Finch; Comment Is Free: Georgina Henry; diary: Jon Henley; economics: Larry Elliott; education: Claire Phipps; environment: John Vidal; Family: Becky Gardiner, Sally Weale; fashion: Jess Cartner-Morley; features: Katharine Viner; foreign: Harriet Sherwood; health: Sarah Boseley; media: Matt Wells; money: Patrick Collinson; northern: Martin Wainwright; obituaries: Phil Osborne; office hours: Vicky Frost; review: Lisa Allardice; rise: Ian Wylie; saturday: Ian Katz, Charlie English; social affairs: John Carvel; society: Patrick Butler; sport: Ben Clissitt; technology: Charles Arthur; travel: Andy Pietrasik; Weekend magazine: Merope Mills; women's page: Kira Cochrane; work: Ian Wylie*
- *Assistant editor (production): David Marsh; production editor, G2: Paul Howlett; production editor, weekend: Bill Mann*
- *Publicity: Sarah Jones: 020 7239 9818*

The Independent

Independent News and Media (UK), Independent House,
191 Marsh Wall, London E14 9RS
020 7005 2000
www.independent.co.uk
initial.surname@independent.co.uk
firstname.surname@ independent.co.uk
Editor-in-chief: Simon Kelner

- *Deputy editor: Ian Birrell; news: Danny Groom; political: Andrew Grice*
- Sections - *City: Jeremy Warner; diplomatic: Ann Penketh; education: Lucy Hodges; editor for education: Richard Garner; environment: Michael McCarthy; features: Adam Leigh; foreign: Leonard Doyle; health: Jeremy Laurance; labour: Barrie Clement; media: Ian Burrell; science: Steve Connor; sport: Matt Tench; transport: Barrie Clement*
- *Production editor: Carl Reader*
- *Marketing manager: David Greene, 020 7005 2000*

The Sun

News Group Newspapers, 1 Virginia Street,
London E98 1SN
020 7782 4000
www.thesun.co.uk
firstname.surname@the-sun.co.uk
Editor: Rebekah Wade

- *Deputy editor: Fergus Shanahan; executive editor: Chris Roycroft-Davis; managing editor: Graham Dudman; political: Trevor Kavanagh (deputy: George Pascoe-Watson, Whitehall: David Wooding); news: Christopher Pharo; chief reporter: John Kay*
- Sections - *bizarre: Victoria Newton; business: Ian King; crime: Mike Sullivan; defence: Tom Newton Dunn; features: Dominic Mohan; motoring: Ken Gibson; sport: Steve Waring; Sun woman: Sharon Hendry; TV: Sara Nathan*
- *Chief editorial production editor: Mike Fairbairn; chief sub, news: Jim Holgate*
- *Publicity: Lorna Carmichael, 020 7782 5000*

The Times

Times Newspapers, 1 Pennington Street, London E98 1TT
020 7782 5000
www.timesonline.co.uk
firstname.surname@thetimes.co.uk
Editor: Robert Thomson

- *Deputy editor: Ben Preston; home news: John Wellman, Oliver Wright; political: Philip Webster; social affairs: Rosemary Bennett; assistant politics: Peter Riddell; Washington correspondent: Tom Baldwin; Brussels correspondent: David Charter; Moscow correspondent: Tony Halpin; Whitehall: Jill Sherman; chief political correspondent: Anthony Browne*
- Sections - *business and City: James Harding; comment: Daniel Finkelstein; consumer and countryside: Valerie Elliott; defence: Michael Evans; diplomatic: Richard Beeston; education: Alex Frean; features: Michael Harvey; financial: Graham Searjeant; foreign: Bronwen Maddox; health: Nigel Hawkes; money: Antonia Senior; sport: Tim Hallissey*
- *Executive editors/chief subs: Chris McKane, Simon Pearson*
- *Communications director: Anoushka Healy, 020 7782 5000*

National Sunday newspapers

Daily Star Sunday

Express Newspapers, The Northern & Shell Building,
Number 10 Lower Thames Street, London EC3R 6EN
0871 434 1010
www.megastar.co.uk
firstname.surname@dailystar.co.uk
Editor: Gareth Morgan

- *Deputy editor: David Harbord; news: Michael Booker; political: Macer Hall*
- Sections - *features: Victoria Lissaman; sport: Ray Ansbro*
- *Chief sub: Mike Woods; picture editor: Tomassina Brittain*

The Independent on Sunday

Independent News and Media (UK), Independent House,
191 Marsh Wall, London E14 9RS
020 7005 2000
www.independent.co.uk
initial.surname@independent.co.uk
Editor: Tristan Davies

- *Deputy editor: Michael Williams; political: Andy McSmith (deputy: Francis Elliott)*
- Sections - *education: Richard Garner; environment: Geoffrey Lean; features: Nick Coleman; sport: Neil Morton; travel: Kate Simon; women's: Elizabeth Heathcote*
- *Production editor: Keith Howitt*
- *Marketing manager: Jonathan Grogan, 020 7005 2000*

The Mail on Sunday

Associated Newspapers, Northcliffe House,
2 Derry Street, Kensington, London W8 5TT
020 7938 6000
www.mailonsunday.co.uk
firstname.surname@mailonsunday.co.uk
Editor: Peter Wright

- *Deputy editor: Rod Gilchrist; news: Sebastian Hamilton; home affairs: Christopher Leake; political: Simon Walters*
- Sections - *education: Glen Owen; defence: Christopher Leake; environment: Jo Knowsley; features: Sian James; show business: Katie Nicholl; sport: Malcolm Vallerius*
- *Production editor: Tim Smith; executive production editors: Nic Petkovic, Derek Whitfield*
- *Managing editor: John Wellington, 020 7938 7015*

News of the World

News Group Newspapers, 1 Virginia Street,
London E98 1NW
020 7782 4000
www.thenewsoftheworld.co.uk
firstname.surname@notw.co.uk
Editor: Andy Coulson

- *Deputy editor: Neil Wallis; news: James Weatherup; assistant editor (news): Ian Edmondson; political: Ian Kirby; investigations: Mazher Mahmood; senior associate editor: Harry Scott*
- *Production editor: Richard Rushworth*
- *Publicity: Hayley Barlow, 020 7782 4529*

The Observer

Guardian News & Media, 3-7 Herbal Hill, London EC1R 5EJ
020 7278 2332
www.observer.guardian.co.uk
firstname.surname@observer.co.uk
Editor: Roger Alton

- *Deputy editors: John Mulholland, Paul Webster; managing editor: Jan Thompson; executive editor, news: Kamal Ahmed; political: Gaby Hinsliff*
- *Sections – arts: Sarah Donaldson; books: Robert McCrum; business: Ruth Sunderland; City: Richard Wachman; crime: Mark Townsend; economics: Heather Stewart; Escape: Joanne O'Connor; fashion: Jo Adams; foreign: Tracy McVeigh; health: Jo Revill; home affairs: Jamie Doward; media: Vanessa Thorpe; money and property: Jill Insley; Observer Magazine: Allan Jenkins; Observer Food Monthly: Nicola Jeal; Observer Woman: Nicola Jeal; Observer Music Monthly: Caspar Llewellyn Smith; Observer Sport Monthly: Jason Cowley; public affairs: Antony Barnett; Review: Jane Ferguson; science: Robin McKie; 7 days: Rob Yates; sport: Brian Oliver; TV: Mike Bradley*
- *Production editor: Bob Poulton; chief news sub: David Pearson; art director: Carolyn Roberts; picture editor: Greg Whitmore*
- *Publicity: Diane Heath, 020 7239 9936*

The People

MGN, One Canada Square, Canary Wharf, London E14 5AP
020 7293 3000
www.people.co.uk
firstname.surname@people.co.uk
Editor: Mark Thomas

- *Deputy editor and news: Ben Proctor; associate news editor: David Jeffs; political: Nigel Nelson*
- *Sections – features: Chris Bucktin; investigations: Roger Insall; showbiz: Debbie Manley; sport: Lee Horton*
- *Chief sub: Trisha Harbord; night editor: Matt Clarke; picture editor: Paula Derry*
- *Publicity: Sarah Vaughan-Brown, 020 7293 3222*

The Sunday Express

Express Newspapers, The Northern & Shell Building,
Number 10 Lower Thames Street, London EC3R 6EN
0871 434 1010
www.express.co.uk
firstname.surname@express.co.uk
Editor: Martin Townsend

- *Deputy editor: Richard Dismore; news: James Murray; political: Julia Hartley-Brewer*
- *Sections – arts: Rachel Jane; business: Lawrie Holmes; crime: Andrea Perry; defence & diplomatic: Kirsty Buchanan; environment: Stuart Winter; features: Giulia Rhodes; health: Hilary Douglas; royal: Keith Perry; sport: Scott Wilson; travel: Jane Memmler*
- *Night editor: Andy Hoban; assistant night editor (features): Stuart Kershaw; chief news sub: Keith Ging*

Sunday Mirror

MGN, One Canada Square, Canary Wharf, London E14 5AP
020 7293 3000
www.sundaymirror.co.uk
firstname.surname@sundaymirror.co.uk
Editor: Tina Weaver

- *Deputy editor: James Scott; associate editor: Mike Small; assistant editor (news): Nick Buckley; news: James Saville; political: Paul Gilfeather; chief reporter: Euan Stretch*
- *Sections – features: Nicky Dawson; investigations: Nick Owens; showbusiness: Ben Todd; sport: David Walker*
- *Chief subs: Brian Hancill (news and features); Phil Davies (sport); picture editor: Mike Sharp*
- *Publicity: Sarah Vaughan-Brown, 020 7293 3222*

Sunday Sport

Sport Newspapers, 19 Great Ancoats Street,
Manchester M60 4BT
0161 236 4466
www.sundaysport.com
Editor: Paul Carter

- *News editor: Jane Field; features: Mark Harris; sports: Mark Smith*

The Sunday Telegraph

Telegraph Group, 111 Buckingham Palace Road,
London SW1 0DT
020 7931 2000
www.telegraph.co.uk
firstname.surname@telegraph.co.uk
Editor: Patience Wheatcroft

- *Deputy editor: Richard Ellis; assistant editor: Iain Martin; news: Tim Woodward; political: Patrick Hennessy*
- *Sections – arts: Lucy Tuck; city: Dan Roberts; foreign: David Wastell; economics: Liam Halligan; Seven: Susanna Herbert; Stella: Anna Murphy; sport: Jon Ryan; night editor: Justin Williams; picture editor: Nigel Skelsey*
- *Publicity: Danielle Howe, 020 7931 2000*

The Sunday Times

Times Newspapers, 1 Pennington Street, London E98 1ST
020 7782 5000
www.sunday-times.co.uk
firstname.surname@sunday-times.co.uk
Editor: John Witherow

- *Deputy editor: Martin Ivens; managing editor: Richard Caseby; news: Charles Hymas; associate editor: Bob Tyrer; managing editor, news: Charles Hymas; political: David Cracknell (deputy: Isabel Oakeshott)*
- *Sections – arts: Richard Brooks; books: Caroline Gascoigne; business: John Waples; City: Grant Ringshaw; culture: Helen Hawkins; Ingear: Nick Rufford; Doors: David Johnson; economics: David Smith; financial editor: Paul Durman; Focus: Paul Nuki; foreign: Sean Ryan; home: Peter Conradi; home affairs: David Leppard; Insight: Jonathan Culvert; Ireland: Frank Fitzgibbon; medical: Sarah-Kate Templeton; money: Kathryn Cooper; News review: Eleanor Mills; science: Jonathan Leake; Scotland: Les Snowdon; sport: Alex Butler; Sunday Times Magazine: Robin Morgan; Style: Tiffanie Darke; travel: Christine Walker; TV: David Hutcheon*
- *Managing editor (production): Ian Coxon; chief subs: David Paton; Denise Boutall (arts and leisure); Arnis Biezais (business)*
- *Publicity: Sophie Bickford*

Regional press contacts

Main publishers

Archant
Prospect House, Rouen Road,
Norwich NR1 1RE
01603 772803
www.archant.co.uk
Chairman: Richard Jewson; CEO: John Fry; corporate communications manager: Keith Morris, 01603 772814

Archant Regional
01603 772824

Daily Mail & General Trust
Northcliffe House, 2 Derry Street,
London W8 5TT
020 7938 6000
www.dmgt.co.uk
Chairman: Viscount Rothermere; CEO: CJF Sinclair

Associated Newspapers
Northcliffe House, 2 Derry Street,
London W8 5TT
020 7938 6000
www.associatednewspapers.co.uk
MD: Kevin Beatty; editor-in-chief: Paul Dacre

Northcliffe Newspapers Group
31-32 John Street, London WC1N 2QB
020 7400 1100
www.thisisnorthcliffe.co.uk
MD: Michael Pelosi

DC Thomson
185 Fleet Street, London EC4A 2HS
020 7400 1030
www.dcthomson.co.uk

Guardian Media Group
75 Farringdon Road,
London EC1M 3JY
020 7278 2332
www.gmgplc.co.uk
Chairman: Paul Myners; CEO, regionals: Mark Dodson

Independent News and Media
Independent House,
2023 Bianconi Avenue, Citywest
Business Campus, Naas Road,
Dublin 24, Ireland
00 353 1 466 3200
www.inmplc.com
Chief executive: Anthony O'Reilly; CEO, Ireland: Vincent Crowley; CEO, UK: Ivan Fallon

Johnston Press
53 Manor Place, Edinburgh EH3 7EG
0131 225 3361
www.johnstonpress.co.uk
Non-executive chairman: Roger Parry; CEO: Tim Bowdler

**Midland News Association/
Express & Star**
51-53 Queen Street,
Wolverhampton WV1 1ES
01902 313131
www.mna-insite.co.uk

Newsquest Media
58 Church Street, Weybridge,
Surrey KT13 8DP
01932 821212
www.newsquest.co.uk
Chairman and chief executive: Paul Davidson

Scotsman Publications
Barclay House, 108 Holyrood Road,
Edinburgh EH8 8AS
0131 620 8620
www.scotsman.com
Publisher: Johnston Press; MD: Michael Johnston

Trinity Mirror
One Canada Square, Canary Wharf,
London E14 5AP
020 7293 3000
www.trinitymirror.com
Chairman: Sir Ian Gibson; CEO: Sly Bailey

Regional newspapers – England

● Major paid-for regionals

The Argus (Brighton)
Argus House, Crowhurst Road,
Hollingbury, Brighton BN1 8AR
01273 544544
www.theargus.co.uk
Daily. Owner: Newsquest. Editor: Michael Beard; news: Melanie Dowding; night news editor: David Wells; features: Jacqui Phillips; production: Chris Heath

Birmingham Evening Mail
PO Box 78, Weaman Street,
Birmingham, West Midlands B4 6AY
0121 236 3366
www.icbirmingham.co.uk
Daily. Owner: Trinity Mirror. Editor: Steve Dyson; news: Andy Richards; features: Alison Handley

Blackpool Gazette & Herald
Avroe House, Avroe Crescent,
Blackpool Business Park,
Blackpool FY4 2DP
01253 400888
www.blackpoolonline.co.uk
Daily. Owner: Johnston Press. Editor: David Halliwell; news: James Higgins; features: Paul McKenzie; chief sub: Linda Chatburn

Bolton Evening News
Newspaper House, Churchgate,
Bolton, Lancs BL1 1DE
01204 522345
www.thisisbolton.co.uk
Daily. Owner: Newsquest. Editor-in-chief: Steve Hughes; news: Cheryl Hague; features: Jill Galone; production: John Bird

Bristol Evening Post
Temple Way, Bristol BS99 7HD
0117 934 3000
www.thisisbristol.co.uk
Daily. Owner: Northcliffe Newspapers. Editor: Mike Norton; news: Kevan Blackadder; features: Bill Davis; chief sub: Helen Lawrence

Coventry Evening Telegraph
Corporation Street, Coventry CV1 1FP
024 7663 3633
www.iccoventry.co.uk
Daily. Owner: Trinity Mirror. Editor: Alan Kirby; news: John West; features: Steven Chilton; head of production: Barry Mathew

Daily Echo
Richmond Hill, Bournemouth BH2 6HH
01202 554601
www.thisisbournemouth.co.uk
Daily. Owner: Newsquest. Editor: Neal Butterworth; news: Andy Martin; features: Kevin Nash

Derby Evening Telegraph
Northcliffe House, Meadow Road,
Derby, Derbyshire DE1 2DW
01332 291111
www.thisisderbyshire.co.uk
*Daily. Owner: Northcliffe Newspapers.
Editor: Steve Hall; news: Nicola Hodgson;
features: Cheryl Hague; chief sub: Peter
Pheasant*

East Anglian Daily Times
Press House, 30 Lower Brook Street,
Ipswich IP4 1AN
01473 230023
www.eadt.co.uk
*Daily. Owner: Archant. Editor: Terry
Hunt; news: Aynsley Davidson; features:
Julian Ford*

Eastern Daily Press
Prospect House, Rouen Road,
Norwich NR1 1RE
01603 628311
www.edp24.co.uk
*Daily. Owner: Archant. Editor: Peter
Franzen*

Evening Chronicle (Newcastle)
Groat Market,
Newcastle upon Tyne NE1 1ED
0191 232 7500
www.icnewcastle.co.uk
*Daily. Owner: Trinity Mirror. Editor: Paul
Robertson; news: James Marley; features:
Jennifer Bradbury; chief sub: Beverley
Pearson*

Evening Gazette
Borough Road,
Middlesbrough TS1 3AZ
01642 245401
www.icteesside.co.uk
*Daily. Owner: Gazette Media Company
(Trinity Mirror). Editor: Darren
Thwaites; news: Jim Horsley; acting
features: Barbara Argument*

Evening Standard
Northcliffe House, 2 Derry Street,
London W8 5TT
020 7938 6000
www.thisislondon.co.uk
*Daily. Owner: Associated Newspapers.
Editor: Veronica Wadley; news: Ian
Walker; features: Simon Davies*

Express & Star
51–53 Queen Street, Wolverhampton,
West Midlands WV1 1ES
01902 313131
www.expressandstar.com
*Daily. Owner: Midland News Association.
Editor: Adrian Faber; news: Mark Drew;
features: Emma Farmer; chief sub: Tony
Reynolds*

Hull Daily Mail
Blundell's Corner, Beverley Road,
Hull HU3 1XS
01482 327111
www.thisishullandeastriding.co.uk
*Daily. Owner: Northcliffe Newspapers.
Editor: John Meehan; news: Jeremy
Deacon; deputy news editor: Paul Baxter;
features: Paul Johnson; chief sub: Daniel
Urben*

The Journal (Newcastle)
Groat Market,
Newcastle upon Tyne NE1 1ED
0191 201 6230
www.thejournal.co.uk
*Daily. Owner: Newcastle Chronicle &
Journal (Trinity Mirror). Editor: Brian
Aitken; night editor: Richard Kirkman;
news: Matt McKenzie; features: Jane Hall*

Lancashire Evening Post
Oliver's Place, Preston PR2 9ZA
01772 838103
www.prestontoday.net
*Daily. Owner: Johnston Press.
Editor: Simon Reynolds*

Lancashire Evening Telegraph
1 High Street, Blackburn,
Lancashire BB1 1HT
01254 298220
www.thisislancashire.co.uk
*Daily. Owner: Newsquest. Editor-in-chief:
Kevin Young; news: Andrew Turner;
features: John Anson*

Leicester Mercury
St George Street, Leicester LE1 9FQ
0116 251 2512
www.thisisleicestershire.co.uk
*Daily. Owner: Northcliffe Newspapers.
Editor: Nick Carter; news: Mark Charlton;
features: Alex Dawson*

Liverpool Daily Post & Echo
Old Hall Street, Liverpool L69 3EB
0151 227 2000
www.icliverpool.co.uk
*Daily. Owner: Trinity Mirror. Editor: Jane
Wolstenholme; news: Greg Fray*

Liverpool Echo
Old Hall Street, Liverpool L69 3EB
0151 227 2000
www.icliverpool.co.uk
*Daily. Owner: Trinity Mirror. Editor:
Alastair Machray; news: Alison Gow*

Manchester Evening News
164 Deansgate, Manchester M3 3RN
0161 832 7200
www.manchesteronline.co.uk
*Daily. Owner: Guardian Media Group.
Editor: Paul Horrocks; news: Ian Woods;
deputy features editor: Graham
McGilliard*

The News (Portsmouth)
Portsmouth Publishing & Printing,
The News Centre, London Road,
Hilsea, Portsmouth,
Hampshire PO2 9SX
023 9266 4488
www.portsmouth.co.uk
*Daily. Owner: Johnston Press. Editor:
Mike Gilson; news: Colin McNeill;
features: Graham Patfield*

Northern Echo
(Darlington & South West Durham)
Priestgate, Darlington,
County Durham DL1 1NF
01325 381313
www.thisisthenortheast.co.uk
*Daily. Owner: Newsquest. Editor: Peter
Barron; news: Nigel Burton; features:
Lindsay Jennings; chief sub: Dave Horsley*

Nottingham Evening Post
Castle Wharf House,
Nottingham NG1 7EU
0115 948 2000
www.thisisnottingham.co.uk
*Daily. Owner: Northcliffe Newspapers.
Editor: Graham Glen; news: Claire
Catlow; features: Jeremy Lewis*

Plymouth Evening Herald
17 Brest Road, Derriford Business
Park, Plymouth PL6 5AA
01752 765529
www.thisisplymouth.co.uk
*Daily. Owner: Northcliffe Newspapers.
Editor: Alan Qualtrough; news: James
Garnett; features: Su Carroll*

The Sentinel (Stoke-on-Trent)
Staffordshire Sentinel Newspapers,
Sentinel House, Etruria,
Stoke-on-Trent ST1 5SS
01782 602525
www.thisisthesentinel.co.uk
*Daily. Owner: Northcliffe Newspapers.
Editor: Mike Sassy; news: Richard
Bowyer; features: Charlotte Little-Jones;
chief sub: Chris Smith*

Shropshire Star
Shropshire Newspapers, Ketley,
Telford, Shropshire TF1 5HU
01952 242424
www.shropshirestar.com
*Daily. Owner: Midland News Association.
Editor: Sarah Jane Smith; news: John
Simcock; features: Carl Jones*

Southern Daily Echo
Newspaper House, Test Lane,
Redbridge, Southampton SO16 9JX
023 8042 4777
www.dailyecho.co.uk
*Daily. Owner: Newsquest. Editor: Ian
Murray; news: Gordon Sutter; chief sub:
Colin Jenkins*

The Star (Sheffield)
York Street, Sheffield,
South Yorkshire S1 1PU
0114 276 7676
www.sheffieldtoday.net
*Daily. Owner: Johnston Press. Editor:
Alan Powell; news: Bob Westerdale;
features: John Highfield; head of content:
Paul License*

Sunday Mercury
Weaman Street, Birmingham,
West Midlands B4 6AT
0121 236 3366
www.icbirmingham.co.uk
*Sunday. Owner: Trinity Mirror. Editor:
David Brookes; deputy: Paul Cole; news:
Tony Larner*

Sunday Sun (Newcastle)
Groat Market,
Newcastle upon Tyne NE1 1ED
0191 232 7500
www.icnewcastle.co.uk
*Sunday. Owner: Trinity Mirror. Editor:
Peter Montellier; news: Mike Kelly;
production: Colin Patterson; chief sub:
Lesley Oldfield*

Telegraph and Argus (Bradford)
Hall Ings, Bradford BD1 1JR
01274 729511
www.thisisbradford.co.uk
Daily. Owner: Newsquest. Editor: Perry Austin-Clarke; news: Martin Heminway; features: David Barnett; chief sub: Mel Jones

Western Daily Press (Bristol)
Temple Way, Bristol BS99 7HD
0117 934 3223
www.westpress.co.uk
Daily. Owner: Associated Press. Editor: Andrew Wright; backbench executive editor: Dave Edler; news: Cathy Ellis; features: Dave Webb; chief sub: Chris Brown

Western Morning News
17 Brest Road, Derriford Business Park, Plymouth PL6 5AA
01752 765500
www.thisisdevon.co.uk
Daily. Owner: Northcliffe Newspapers. Editor-in-chief: Alan Qualtrough; news: Mark Hughes, Steve Grant

York Evening Press
76–86 Walmgate, York YO1 9YN
01904 653051
www.yorkpress.co.uk
Daily. Owner: Newsquest. Editor: Kevin Booth; news: Scott Armstrong; features: Steven Lewis; chief sub: Simon Ritchie

Yorkshire Evening Post
PO Box 168, Wellington Street, Leeds LS1 1RF
0113 243 2701
www.leedstoday.net
Daily. Owner: Johnston Press. Editor: Neil Hodgkinson; news: Gillian Howorth; features: Anne Pickles; production: Howard Corry

Yorkshire Post
PO Box 168, Wellington Street, Leeds LS1 1RF
0113 243 2701
www.yorkshireposttoday.co.uk
Daily. Owner: Johnston Press. Editor: Peter Charlton; news: Hannah Start; features: Catherine Scott

Other local and regional papers – England

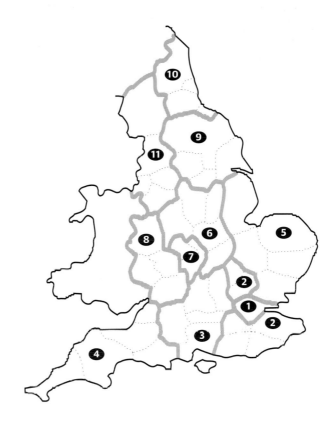

1 **London**   page 40

2 **South-east England**   page 43

3 **South England**   page 48

4 **South-west England**   page 52

5 **East England**   page 54

6 **Midlands**   page 59

7 **West Midlands**   page 62

8 **West England**   page 63

9 **North England**   page 65

10 **North-east England**   page 68

11 **North-west England**   page 69

REGIONAL contacts **Press**

● London

Barnes, Mortlake & Sheen Times
020 8940 6030
www.richmondandtwickenham
   times.co.uk
*Weekly (Fri). Owner: Newsquest.
Assistant editor: Scott Barr; news: Chris
Briddon*

Barnet & Potters Bar Times
020 8203 0411
www.barnettimes.co.uk
*Weekly (Thu). Owner: Newsquest.
Editor: John Killeen; news: Leigh Collins*

Barnet & Whetstone Press
020 8367 2345
*Weekly free (Thu). Owner: Trinity Mirror
Southern. Editor: Gary O'Keefe; news:
Tom Hutchinson*

Brent & Wembley Leader
020 8427 4404
*Weekly free (Fri). Owner: Trinity Mirror
Southern. Editor: Lindsey Coulson; news:
Claire Garner; features: Victoria Prewer*

Brentford, Chiswick & Isleworth
Times
020 8940 6030
www.richmondandtwickenham
   times.co.uk
*Weekly (Fri). Owner: Newsquest.
Assistant editor: Scott Barr; news: Chris
Briddon*

Bromley Times
020 8269 7000
www.archant.co.uk
*Weekly (Thu). Owner: Archant.
Editor: Melody Ryall; production: Sarah
Sharman*

Bromley News
01959 564766
www.bromley-today.co.uk
*Weekly (Thu). Owner: Tindle Newspapers.
Editor: Charlotte McDonnall*

Bromley News Shopper
01689 836211
www.newsshopper.co.uk
*Weekly (Weds). Owner: Newsquest.
Editor: Andrew Parkes; news: Matthew
Ramsden*

Camden Gazette
020 8340 6868
www.london24.net
*Weekly (Weds). Owner: Archant.
Editor: Tony Allcock; news: Rob Bleaney*

Camden New Journal
020 7419 9000
www.camdennewjournal.co.uk
*Weekly (Thu). Owner: New Journal
Enterprises. Editor: Eric Gordon; news:
Dan Carrier; features: Sunita Rappai;
production: Sarah Roberts*

Caterham & District Advertiser
020 8763 6666
www.croydonadvertiser.co.uk
*Weekly (Fri). Owner: Trinity Mirror
Southern. Editor: Ian Carter; news: Andy
Worden*

Chingford Guardian
020 8498 3400
www.chingfordguardian.co.uk
*Weekly (Thu). Owner: Newsquest.
Editor: Pat Stannard*

The Chiswick
020 8940 6030
www.richmondandtwickenham
   times.co.uk
*Weekly (Wed). Owner: Newsquest.
Editor: Scott Barr; news: Chris Briddon*

City AM
020 7015 1200
www.cityam.com
*Daily free. Owner: City AM Ltd. Editor:
David Parsley; news: Michael Glackin*

City of London & Dockland Times
020 7247 2524
Fortnightly (Mon). Editor: Mr D Delderfield

Croydon Advertiser
020 8763 6666
www.iccroydon.co.uk
*Weekly (Fri). Owner: Trinity Mirror
Southern. Editor: Ian Carter; news: Andy
Worden*

Croydon Borough Post
020 8977 2705
www.iccroydon.co.uk
*Weekly (Wed). Owner: Trinity Mirror
Southern. Editor: Ian Carter; news: Andy
Worden*

Croydon Guardian
020 8774 6565
www.croydonguardian.co.uk
*Weekly (Wed). Owner: Newsquest. Editor:
Helen Barnes; news: Danny Brierley*

Ealing & Acton Gazette
020 8579 3131
www.icealing.co.uk
*Weekly (Fri). Owner: Trinity Mirror
Southern. Editor: Sachin Nakrani; news:
Schuz Azan; features: Victoria Prewer*

Ealing Informer
020 8579 3131
www.icealing.co.uk
*Weekly (Wed). Owner: Trinity Mirror
Southern. Editor: Sachin Nakrani; news:
Schuz Azan; features: Victoria Prewer*

Ealing Leader
020 8579 3131
www.icealing.co.uk
*Weekly (Fri). Owner: Trinity Mirror
Southern. Editor: Sachin Nakrani; news:
Schuz Azan; features: Victoria Prewer;
chief sub: Joyce McKim*

Ealing Times
01494 755000
www.ealingtimes.co.uk
*Weekly (Thu). Owner: Newsquest.
Editor: Steve Cohen; news: James Young*

East End Life
020 7364 3059
*Weekly free (Sun). Owner: London Borough
of Tower Hamlets. Editor: Laraine Clay;
news: Helen Watson*

East London Advertiser
020 7791 7799
*Weekly (Thu). Owner: Archant. Editor:
Malcolm Starbrook; news: Mike Brooke*

East London Enquirer
01277 627300
www.theenquirer.co.uk
Weekly (Thu). Editor: Carol Driver

Edgware & Mill Hill Press
020 8367 2345
www.icnorthlondononline.co.uk
*Weekly free (Thu). Owner: Trinity Mirror
Southern. Editor: Gary O'Keefe; news:
Tom Hutchinson*

Edgware & Mill Hill Times
020 8203 0411
www.edgwaretimes.co.uk
*Weekly (Thu). Owner: Newsquest.
Editor: John Killeen; news: Colin O'Toole*

Eltham and Greenwich Times
020 8269 7000
www.archant.co.uk
*Weekly (Wed). Owner: Archant. Editor:
Melody Ryall; production: Sarah McLeod*

Enfield Advertiser
020 8367 2345
www.icnorthlondononline.co.uk
*Weekly (Wed). Owner: Trinity Mirror
Southern. Editor: Gary O'Keefe;
news: Tom Hutchinson*

Enfield Gazette
020 8367 2345
www.icnorthlondononline.co.uk
*Weekly (Thu). Owner: Trinity Mirror
Southern. Editor: Gary O'Keefe;
news: Tom Hutchinson*

Enfield Independent
020 8362 1431
www.enfieldindependent.co.uk
*Weekly (Wed). Owner: Newsquest.
Editor: Kate Russell*

Erith & Crayford Times
020 8269 7000
www.archant.co.uk
*Weekly (Wed). Owner: Archant. Editor:
Melody Ryall; production: Sarah McLeod*

Evening Standard
See page 38

Fulham Gazette
020 8579 3131
www.icealing.co.uk
*Weekly (Fri). Owner: Trinity Mirror
Southern. Editor: Sachin Nakrani*

Greenford & Northolt Gazette
020 8579 3131
www.icealing.co.uk
*Weekly (Fri). Owner: Trinity Mirror
Southern. Editor: Sachin Nakrani*

Greenwich Borough Mercury
020 8769 4444
www.icsouthlondon.co.uk
*Weekly (Wed). Owner: Trinity Mirror
Southern. Editor-in-chief: Hannah Walker*

Hackney Gazette
020 7791 7799
www.hackneygazette.co.uk
*Weekly (Thu). Owner: Archant.
Editor: Mick Ferris; news: Russ Lawrence*

Hammersmith & Fulham Chronicle
020 8572 1816
www.trinitymirrorsouthern.co.uk
*Weekly (Thu). Owner: Trinity Mirror
Southern. Content editor: Janice
Raycroft; features: Gerri Besgrove*

Hammersmith & Shepherd's Bush
Gazette
020 8579 3131
www.icealing.co.uk
*Weekly (Fri). Owner: Trinity Mirror
Southern. Editor: Sachin Nakrani*

Hampstead & Highgate Express
020 7433 0000
www.hamhigh.co.uk
Weekly (Fri). Owner: Archant. Editor:
Geoff Martin; news: Bridget Galton;
features: Melanie Smith

Harefield Gazette
01895 451000
www.icuxbridge.co.uk
Weekly (Wed). Owner: Trinity Mirror
Southern. Editor-in-chief: Adrian Seal;
content editor: David Tilley

Haringey Advertiser
020 8367 2345
www.icnorthlondononline.co.uk
Weekly (Wed). Owner: Trinity Mirror
Southern. Editor: Gary O'Keefe;
news: Tom Hutchinson

Harrow Leader
020 8427 4404
www.icharrow.co.uk
Weekly free (Fri). Owner: Trinity Mirror
Southern. Editor: Lindsay Coulson; news:
Claire Garner; features: Victoria Prewer;
production: Andre Erasmus

Harrow Observer
020 8427 4404
www.icharrow.co.uk
Weekly (Thu). Owner: Trinity Mirror
Southern. Editor: Lindsay Coulson; news:
Claire Garner; features: Victoria Prewer;
production: Andre Erasmus

Harrow Times
01923 216216
www.harrowtimes.co.uk
Weekly (Thu). Owner: Newsquest.
Editor: Charlie Harris

Hayes & Harlington Gazette
01895 451000
www.icuxbridge.co.uk
Weekly (Wed). Owner: Trinity Mirror
Southern. Editor-in-chief: Adrian Seal;
content editor: David Tilley

Hendon & Finchley Press
020 8367 2345
www.icnorthlondononline.co.uk
Weekly free (Thu). Owner: Trinity Mirror
Southern. Editor: Gary O'Keefe; news:
Tom Hutchinson

Hendon Times
020 8359 5959
www.hendontimes.co.uk
Weekly (Thu). Owner: Newsquest.
Editor: John Killeen; news: Colin O'Toole

Hillingdon & Uxbridge Times
01494 755000
www.hillingdontimes.co.uk
Weekly free (Thu). Owner: Newsquest.
Editor: Steve Cohen; news: James Young

Hornsey & Crouch End Journal
020 8340 6868
www.london24.net
Weekly (Thu). Owner: Archant. Editor:
Tony Allcock; news: Alison Campsie

Hounslow, Brentford & Chiswick
Informer
020 8572 1816
www.trinitymirrorsouthern.co.uk
Weekly free (Fri). Owner: Trinity Mirror
Southern. News editor: Sam Matthews

Hounslow Chronicle
020 8572 1816
www.trinitymirrorsouthern.co.uk
Weekly (Thu). Owner: Trinity Mirror
Southern. News editor: Sam Matthews;
features: Gerri Besgrove

Hounslow, Feltham & Hanworth
Times
020 8940 6030
www.hounslowguardian.co.uk
Weekly (Thu). Owner: Newsquest.
Editor: Scott Barr; news: Chris Briddon

Hounslow Guardian
020 8940 6030
www.hounslowguardian.co.uk
Weekly (Thu). Owner: Newsquest.
Editor: Scott Barr; news: Chris Briddon

Hounslow Informer
020 8572 1816
www.trinitymirrorsouthern.co.uk
Weekly free (Fri). Owner: Trinity Mirror
Southern. Features editor: Gerri
Besgrove; content editor: Janice Raycroft

Ilford Recorder
020 8478 4444
www.ilfordrecorder.co.uk
Weekly (Thu). Owner: Archant. Editor:
Chris Carter; production: Mike Cubitt

Islington Gazette
020 8340 6868
www.london24.net
Weekly (Thu). Owner: Archant.
Editor: Tony Allcock; news: Ollie Lane

Islington Tribune
020 7419 9000
www.camdennewjournal.co.uk
Weekly (Fri). Owner: New Journal
Enterprises. Editor: Eric Gordon; news:
Dan Carrier; features: Sunita Rappai;
production: Kelvin Morrison

Kensington & Chelsea Informer
020 8572 1816
www.trinitymirrorsouthern.co.uk
Weekly (Fri). Owner: Trinity Mirror
Southern. Content editor: Janice
Raycroft; features: Gerri Besgrove

Kilburn Times
020 8962 6868
www.wbtimes.co.uk
Weekly (Wed). Owner: Archant.
Editor: Tim Cole

Kingston & Surbiton Times
020 8940 6030
www.hounslowguardian.co.uk
Weekly (Fri). Owner: Newsquest
Editor: Scott Barr; news: Chris Briddon

Kingston Guardian
020 8940 6030
www.kingstonguardian.co.uk
Weekly (Thu). Owner: Newsquest.
Editor: Sean Duggan

Kingston Informer
020 8572 1816
www.trinitymirrorsouthern.co.uk
Weekly (Fri). Owner: Trinity Mirror
Southern. Content editor: Janice
Raycroft; features: Gerri Besgrove

Lewisham & Greenwich Mercury
020 8769 4444
www.icsouthlondon.co.uk
Weekly free. Owner: Trinity Mirror
Southern. Editor-in-chief: Hannah
Walker; news: Christina Salzano

Lewisham Borough Mercury
020 8769 4444
www.icsouthlondon.co.uk
Weekly (Wed). Owner: Trinity Mirror
Southern. Editor-in-chief: Hannah
Walker; chief reporter: Keely Sherbird

Lewisham News Shopper
020 8646 5772
www.newsshopper.co.uk
Weekly (Thu). Owner: Newsquest.
Editor: Andrew Parkes; news: Matthew
Ramsden; chief sub: Tim Miles

Leyton & Leytonstone Guardian
020 8498 3400
www.leytonguardian.co.uk
Weekly (Thu). Owner: Newsquest.
Editor: Pat Stannard

London Lite
020 7938 7516
www.thisislondon.co.uk
Daily free. Owner: Associated
Newspapers. Editor: Ted Young

The London Paper
020 7782 4848
www.thelondonpaper.com
Daily free. Owner: News International.
Editor: Stefano Hatfield

Marylebone & Paddington Informer
020 8572 1816
www.trinitymirrorsouthern.co.uk
Weekly (Fri). Owner: Trinity Mirror
Southern. Content editor: Janice
Raycroft; features: Gerri Besgrove

Marylebone & Paddington Mercury
020 8572 1816
www.trinitymirrorsouthern.co.uk
Weekly (Fri). Owner: Trinity Mirror
Southern. Content editor: Janice
Raycroft; features: Gerri Besgrove

Mayfair Times
020 7259 1050
www.pubbiz.com
Monthly free (1st Mon). Editor-in-chief:
Eric Brown; editor: Thelma Day

Metro London
020 7651 5200
www.metro.co.uk
Daily. Owner: Associated Newspapers.
Editor: Kenny Campbell; news: Sarah
Getty; features: Kieran Meeke

Mitcham, Morden & Wimbledon
Post
020 8769 4444
www.icsouthlondon.co.uk
Weekly free (Fri). Owner: Trinity Mirror
Southern. Editor-in-chief: Hannah
Walker; news: Christina Salzano

Muswell Hill & Crouch End Times
020 8359 5959
www.london24.net
Weekly (Thu). Owner: Newsquest.
Editor: John Killeen; news: Colin O'Toole

Muswell Hill Journal
020 8340 6868
www.london24.net
Weekly (Thu). Owner: Archant. Editor:
Tony Allcock; news: Alison Campsie

New Addington Advertiser
020 8763 6666
www.icsurrey.co.uk
Weekly (Fri). Owner: Trinity Mirror
Southern. Editor: Ian Carter; news: Andy
Worden

Newham Recorder
020 8472 1421
www.recorderonline.co.uk
Weekly (Wed). Owner: Archant. Editor:
Colin Grainger; deputy editor: John Finn;
news: Pat Coughtrey

Pinner Observer
020 8427 4404
www.icharrow.co.uk
Weekly (Thu). Owner: Trinity Mirror
Southern. Editor: Lindsay Coulson; news:
Claire Garner; features: Victoria Prewer;
production: Andre Erasmus

The Press (north London)
020 8364 4040
Weekly free (Thu). Owner: Trinity Mirror
Southern. Editor: Gary O'Keefe; news:
Tom Hutchinson

Richmond & Twickenham Informer
020 8572 1816
www.trinitymirrorsouthern.co.uk
Weekly (Fri). Owner: Trinity Mirror
Southern. Content editor: Janice
Raycroft; features: Gerri Besgrove

Richmond & Twickenham Times
020 8940 6030
www.richmondandtwickenham
    times.co.uk
Weekly (Fri). Owner: Newsquest. Editor:
Paul Mortimer; news: James Adlam

Richmond Borough Guardian
020 8940 6030
www.kingstonguardian.co.uk
Weekly (Thu). Owner: Newsquest.
Editor: Scott Barr; news: Chris Briddon

Ruislip & Northwood Gazette
01895 451000
www.icuxbridge.co.uk
Weekly (Wed). Owner: Trinity Mirror
Southern. Editor-in-chief: Adrian Seal;
content editor: David Tilley

St John's Wood & Maida Vale
Express (Wood & Vale)
020 7433 0000
www.islingtonexpress.co.uk
Weekly (Fri). Owner: Archant. Editor:
Geoff Martin; news: Jeni Conniveer;
features: Bridget Galton: chief sub:
Melanie Smith

South Bucks Star
01494 755000
www.southbucksstar.co.uk
Weekly free (Thu). Owner: Newsquest.
Editor: Steve Cohen; news: Victoria Birch;
features: Lindy Bilgorri

South London Press
020 8769 4444
www.icsouthlondon.co.uk
Twice-weekly (Tue, Fri). Owner: Trinity
Mirror Southern. Editor-in-chief:
Hannah Walker; news: Christina Salzano

Southall Gazette
020 8579 3131
www.icealing.co.uk
Weekly (Fri). Owner: Trinity Mirror
Southern. Editor: Sachin Nakrani

Southwark Weekender
020 7231 5258
Fortnightly free (Fri). Editor: Chris Mullany
and Kevin Quinn

Stanmore Observer
020 8427 4404
www.icharrow.co.uk
Weekly (Thu). Owner: Trinity Mirror
Southern. Editor: Lindsay Coulson; news:
Claire Garner; features: Victoria Prewer;
production: Andre Erasmus

Stratford & Newham Express
020 7791 7799
Weekly (Wed). Owner: Archant. Editor:
Pat O'Connor; reporter: Charlotte Smith

Stratford Guardian
020 8498 3431
www.stratfordguardian.co.uk
Weekly (Thu). Owner: Archant. Editor:
Chris Carter; production: Mike Cubitt

Streatham Guardian
020 8646 6336
www.streathamguardian.co.uk
Weekly (Thu). Owner: Newsquest. Editor:
Dave Tilley; features: June Sampson

Streatham, Clapham &
West Norwood Post
020 8769 4444
www.icsouthlondon.co.uk
Weekly free (Thu). Owner: Trinity Mirror
Southern. Editor-in-chief: Hannah
Walker; news: Christina Salzano

Teddington & Hampton Times
020 8940 6030
Weekly (Fri). Owner: Newsquest.
Editor: Scott Barr; news: Chris Briddon

Tottenham & Wood Green Journal
020 8340 6868
www.london24.net
Weekly (Thu). Owner: Archant. Editor:
Tony Allcock; news: Alison Campsie

Tottenham Independent
020 8362 1432
www.tottenhamindependent.co.uk
Weekly (Fri). Owner: Newsquest.
Editor: Kate Russell

Tower Hamlets Recorder
020 8472 1421
www.recorderonline.co.uk
Weekly (Thu). Owner: Archant. Editor:
Colin Grainger; deputy editor: John Finn;
news: Pat Coughtrey

Uxbridge & Hillingdon Leader
01895 451000
www.icuxbridge.co.uk
Weekly free (Thu). Owner: Trinity Mirror
Southern. Editor-in-chief: Adrian Seal;
content editor: David Tilley

Uxbridge & W Drayton Gazette
01895 451000
www.icuxbridge.co.uk
Weekly (Tue). Owner: Trinity Mirror
Southern. Editor-in-chief: Adrian Seal;
content editor: David Tilley

Walthamstow Guardian
020 8498 3400
www.walthamstowguardian.co.uk
Weekly (Thu). Owner: Newsquest.
Editor: Pat Stannard

Wandsworth Guardian
020 8646 6336
www.wandsworthguardian.co.uk
Weekly (Thu). Owner: Newsquest.
News editor: Alison Hepworth; features:
June Sampson

Wembley & Kingsbury Times
020 8962 6868
www.wbtimes.co.uk
Weekly (Wed). Owner: Archant.
Editor: Tim Cole

Wembley Leader
020 8427 4404
www.icharrow.co.uk
Weekly (Thu). Owner: Trinity Mirror
Southern. Editor: Lindsay Coulson; news:
Claire Garner; features: Victoria Prewer;
production: Andre Erasmus

Wembley Observer
020 8427 4404
www.icharrow.co.uk
Weekly (Thu). Owner: Trinity Mirror
Southern. Editor: Lindsay Coulson; news:
Claire Garner; features: Victoria Prewer;
production: Andre Erasmus

West End Extra
020 7419 9000
www.camdennewjournal.co.uk
Weekly (Fri). Owner: New Journal
Enterprises. Editor: Eric Gordon; news:
Joel Taylor; features: Sunita Rappai;
production: Kelvin Morrison

Westender
020 7607 6060
Monthly free (last week in month).
Editor: Eileen Martin; news: Bina
Gowrea; features: Eileen Duff;
production: Jason Kent

Westminster & Pimlico News
020 8572 1816
www.trinitymirrorsouthern.co.uk
Weekly (Fri). Owner: Trinity Mirror
Southern. Content editor: Janice
Raycroft; features: Gerri Besgrove

Westminster Independent
020 8961 3345
www.londonlocals.co.uk
Monthly (last Fri). Editor: Jan Mappin;
news: Jaz Walia

The Wharf
020 7510 6306
www.icthewharf.co.uk
Weekly free (Thu). Owner: Trinity Mirror
Southern. Editor: Tom Derbyshire;
deputy editor: Lucy Walters

Willesden & Brent Times
020 8962 6868
www.wbtimes.co.uk
Weekly (Wed). Owner: Archant.
Editor: Tim Cole

Willesden Observer
020 8427 4404
www.icharrow.co.uk
Weekly (Thu). Owner: Trinity Mirror
Southern. Editor: Lindsay Coulson; news:
Claire Garner; features: Victoria Prewer;
production: Andre Erasmus

Wimbledon Guardian
020 8646 6336
www.wimbledonguardian.co.uk
Weekly (Thu). Owner: Newsquest. Editor:
Dave Tilley; features: June Sampson

Wimbledon News
020 8646 6336
www.wimbledonnews.co.uk
Weekly (Wed). Owner: Newsquest. Editor:
Dave Tilley; features: June Sampson

● South-east England

Bedfordshire, East Sussex, Hertfordshire, Kent, Surrey, West Sussex

Addlestone and Byfleet Review
01483 508700
www.surreyad.co.uk
Weekly (Wed). Owner: Guardian Media Group. Group editorial director: Marnie Wilson

Adscene (Ashford & Tenterden)
01227 767321
www.trinitymirrorsouthern.co.uk
Weekly free (Fri). Owner: Trinity Mirror Southern. Publishing director: Lesley Finlay; features: Julia Rogers; chief sub: Catherine Langston

Adscene (Canterbury)
01227 767321
www.trinitymirrorsouthern.co.uk
Weekly free (Thu). Owner: Trinity Mirror Southern. Editor: John Nurden; features: Julia Rogers; chief sub: Paul Taylor; production: Mark Silva

Adscene (Folkestone & Dover)
01227 767321
www.trinitymirrorsouthern.co.uk
Weekly free (Wed). Owner: Trinity Mirror Southern. Editor: Simon Finlay

Adscene (Maidstone)
01622 690339
www.ickent.co.uk
Weekly free (Thu). Owner: Trinity Mirror Southern. Editor: Diane Nicholls

Adscene (Medway)
01227 767321
www.trinitymirrorsouthern.co.uk
Weekly free (Thu). Owner: Trinity Mirror Southern. Editor: Diane Nicholls

Adscene (Sittingbourne & Sheppey)
01227 767321
www.trinitymirrorsouthern.co.uk
Weekly free (Thu). Owner: Trinity Mirror Southern. Editor: Christine Rayner

Adscene (Thanet)
01227 767321
www.trinitymirrorsouthern.co.uk
Weekly free (Wed). Owner: Trinity Mirror Southern. Editor: Rebecca Smith; news: Jenny De Freitas

Aldershot News
01483 508700
www.aldershot.co.uk
Weekly (Tue). Owner: Guardian Media Group. Group editorial director: Marnie Wilson

The Argus (Brighton)
See page 37

Ashford KM Extra
01233 623232
www.kentonline.co.uk
Weekly (Tue). Owner: Kent Messenger Group. Editor: Leo Whitlock; news: Simon Alford; chief sub: Claire Stevens; production: Gary Barker

Barnet & Potters Bar Times
020 8359 5959
www.barnettimes.co.uk
Weekly (Thu). Owner: Newsquest. Group editor: John Kileen; chief reporter: Leigh Collins

Bedford Times & Citizen
01234 405060
www.bedfordtoday.co.uk
Weekly (Fri). Owner: Johnston Press. Editor: Chris Hall; deputy editor: Olga Norford; news: Mark Lewis

Bedfordshire on Sunday
01234 300888
www.seriousaboutnews.com
Weekly (Sun). Owner: LSN Media. Editor: Steve Lowe; news: Liz O'Reilly; production: Julia Course

Bexhill AdNews
01424 730555
www.bexhilltoday.co.uk
Weekly free (Wed). Owner: Johnston Press. Deputy editor: John Dowling; news: Daniel Collins

Bexhill-on-Sea Observer
01424 730555
www.bexhilltoday.co.uk
Weekly (Fri). Owner: Johnston Press. Deputy editor: John Dowling; news: Daniel Collins

Bexley Express
020 8269 7000
www.bexleyexpress.co.uk
Weekly free (Wed). Owner: Archant. Editor: Melody Ryall; production: Mick Taylor

Bexley Dartford & Gravesham News Shopper
01689 885701
www.newsshopper.co.uk
Weekly (Wed). Editor: Andrew Parkes

Bexley Mercury
020 8769 4444
www.icsouthlondon.co.uk
Weekly free (Wed/Thu). Owner: Trinity Mirror Southern. Editor: Hannah Walker

Bexleyheath & Welling Times
020 8269 7000
Weekly (Wed). Owner: Archant. Editor: Melody Ryall; production: Mick Taylor

Biggin Hill News
01959 564766
www.biggin-hill-today.co.uk
Weekly (Thu). Owner: Tindle Newspapers. Editor: Charlotte McDonald

Biggleswade & Sandy Comet
01438 866000
www.thecomet.net
Weekly (Thu). Owner: Archant. Editor: Darren Isted; news: John Adams

Biggleswade Advertiser
01462 441020
www.hitchinadvertiser.co.uk
Weekly (Wed). Owner: Observer Standard Newspapers. General manager: Ricky Allan

Biggleswade Chronicle
01767 222333
www.biggleswadetoday.co.uk
Weekly (Fri). Owner: Johnston Press. Editor: Jim Stewart

Bishops Stortford Citizen
01992 572285
www.eppingforestguardian.co.uk
Weekly (Thu). Owner: Newsquest. Editor: David Jackman

Bishops Stortford Herald
01279 624331
www.herald24.co.uk
Weekly (Thu). Owner: Archant. Editor: Barry Hunt; reporter: Laura Fineberg

Bognor Regis Guardian
01243 534133
www.chichester.co.uk
Weekly free (Wed). Owner: Johnston Press. Editor: Alicia Denny

Bognor Regis Observer
01243 828777
www.chichester.co.uk
Weekly (Thu). Owner: Johnston Press. Chief sub: David Philip; features: Kevin Smith

Borehamwood & Elstree Times
020 8359 5959
www.borehamwoodtimes.co.uk
Weekly (Fri). Owner: Newsquest. Group editor: John Kileen; chief reporter: Leigh Collins

Brighton & Hove Leader
01273 544544
www.thisisbrightonandhove.co.uk
Weekly (Fri). Owner: Newsquest. Editor: Chris Chandler; news: Mike Dunford

Bromley Times
020 8269 7000
www.bromleytimes.co.uk
Weekly (Thu). Owner: Archant. Editor: Melody Ryall; production: Mick Taylor

Camberley Courier
01252 339760
www.camberley.co.uk
Weekly free (Wed). Owner: Guardian Media Group. Editor: Elaine Cole; news: Adam Clark

Camberley News & Mail
01252 339760
www.camberley.co.uk
Weekly (Fri). Owner: Guardian Media Group. Editor: Elaine Cole; news: Adam Clark

Canterbury KM Extra
01227 768181
www.kentonline.co.uk
Weekly (Tue). Owner: Kent Messenger Group. Editor: Bob Bounds; news: Trisha Jamieson; production: Gary Barker

Cheshunt & Waltham Mercury
01992 414141
www.herts-essex-news.co.uk
Weekly (Fri). Owner: Herts & Essex Newspapers. Editor: Ian Rogerson; news: Pat Roberts

Chichester & Selsey Journal
01243 534133
www.chichester.co.uk
Weekly free (Wed). Owner: Johnston Press. Editor: Alicia Denny

Chichester Observer
01243 539389
www.chiobserver.co.uk
Weekly (Thu). Owner: Johnston Press. Chief sub: David Phillip; features: Sue Gilson

Cranleigh Times
01483 508700
Weekly free (Wed). Owner: Guardian Media Group. Group editorial director: Marnie Wilson

Crawley News
01737 732000
www.icsurrey.co.uk
Weekly (Wed). Owner: Trinity Mirror Southern. Editor-in-chief: Ian Carter; content editor: Harriet Shelley

Crawley Observer
01293 562929
www.crawleyobserver.co.uk
Weekly (Wed). Owner: Johnston Press. Editor: Lesley Hickson; news: Andrew Newman; chief sub: Mark Dunford

Crowborough Courier
01892 681000
www.thisiskentandeastsussex.co.uk
Weekly (Fri). Owner: Northcliffe Newspapers. Editor: Roger Watkins; news: Faith Lee; Today editor: Melanie Yey; editorial production: Lindsay Jones

Croydon Advertiser
020 8763 6666
www.iccroydon.co.uk
Weekly (Fri). Owner: Trinity Mirror Southern. Editor-in-chief: Ian Carter; content editor: Andy Worden

Croydon Guardian
020 8774 6590
www.croydonguardian.co.uk
Weekly (Wed). Owner: Newsquest. Editor: Danny Brierly; news: Helen Barnes

Croydon Post
01737 732000
www.iccroydon.co.uk
Weekly (Thu). Owner: Trinity Mirror Southern. Editor-in-chief: Ian Carter; content editor: Andy Worden

Dartford & Swanley Extra Informer
01322 220791
www.kentonline.co.uk
Weekly (Thu). Owner: Kent Messenger Group. Editor: Sandra Hembury; news: Louise Edwards

Dartford Express
020 8269 7000
www.dartfordexpress.co.uk
Weekly free (Wed). Owner: Archant. Editor: Melody Ryall; production: Mick Taylor

Dartford Messenger
01322 220791
www.kentonline.co.uk
Weekly (Thu). Owner: Kent Messenger Group. Editor: Sandra Hembury; news: Louise Edwards

Dartford Times
020 8269 7000
www.dartfordtimes.co.uk
Weekly (Thu). Owner: Archant. Editor: Melody Ryall; production: Mick Taylor

Dover Express
01227 767321
www.trinitymirrorsouthern.co.uk
Weekly (Thu). Owner: Trinity Mirror Southern. Editor: Simon Finlay

Dover Mercury
01304 240380
Weekly (Thu). Owner: Kent Messenger Group. Editor: Graham Smith

Downs Mail
01622 630330
www.downsmail.co.uk
Monthly (variable). Editor: Dennis Fowle

Dunstable Gazette
01582 526000
www.lutontoday.co.uk
Weekly (Wed). Owner: Johnston Press. Editor: Geoff Cox

East Grinstead Courier
01892 681000
www.thisiskentandeastsussex.co.uk
Weekly (Thu). Owner: Northcliffe Newspapers. Editor: Roger Watkins; news: Faith Lee; Today editor: Melanie Yey; editorial production: Lindsay Jones

East Grinstead Observer
01737 732000
www.icsurrey.co.uk
Weekly (Wed). Owner: Trinity Mirror Southern. Editor-in-chief: Ian Carter

East Kent Gazette
01227 767321
www.trinitymirrorsouthern.co.uk
Weekly (Thu). Owner: Trinity Mirror Southern. Editor: Christine Rayner

East Kent Mercury
01304 238970
www.eastkentmercury.co.uk
Weekly (Thu). Owner: Kent Messenger Group. Editor: Graham Smith

Eastbourne & District Advertiser
01323 722091
www.eastbournetoday.co.uk
Weekly free (Thu). Owner: Johnston Press. Editor: Peter Austin; commercial editor: Andrew Bennett; sports editor: Ken McEwan

Eastbourne Gazette
01323 722091
www.eastbournetoday.co.uk
Weekly (Wed). Owner: Johnston Press. Editor: Peter Austin; commercial editor: Andrew Bennett; sports editor: Ken McEwan

Eastbourne Herald
01323 722091
www.eastbournetoday.co.uk
Weekly (Fri). Owner: Johnston Press. Editor: Peter Austin; commercial editor: Andrew Bennett; sports editor: Ken McEwan

Edenbridge Chronicle
01959 564766
www.edenbridge-today.co.uk
Weekly (Thu). Owner: Tindle Newspapers. Editor: Signid Sherrell

Edenbridge County Border News
01959 564766
www.edenbridge-today.co.uk
Weekly (Thu). Owner: Tindle Newspapers. Editor: Kevin Black

Edenbridge Courier
01892 681000
www.thisiskentandeastsussex.co.uk
Weekly (Fri). Owner: Northcliffe Newspapers. Editor: Roger Watkins; news: Faith Lee; Today editor: Melanie Yey; editorial production: Lindsay Jones

Edgware & Mill Hill Times
020 8359 5959
www.edgwaretimes.co.uk
Weekly (Wed). Owner: Newsquest. Group editor: John Kileen; chief reporter: Leigh Collins

Elmbridge Guardian
020 8646 6336
www.elmbridgeguardian.co.uk
Weekly (Thu). Owner: Newsquest. Editor: Sean Duggan

Epsom, Ewell & Banstead Post
020 8763 6666
www.iccroydon.co.uk
Weekly (Fri). Owner: Trinity Mirror Southern. Editor: Ian Carter; news: Patsy Payne

Epsom Guardian
020 8646 6336
www.epsomguardian.co.uk
Weekly (Thu). Owner: Newsquest. Editor: Sean Duggan

Esher News & Mail
01483 508700
www.esher.co.uk
Weekly (Fri). Owner: Guardian Media Group. Group editorial director: Marnie Wilson

Farnham Herald
01252 725224
www.farnham-herald-today.co.uk
Weekly (Fri). Owner: Tindle Newspapers. Editor: Sandy Baker; chief reporter: Corina Larby

Farnham Post
01420 88949
Fortnightly free (Mon). Owner: Guardian Media Group. General manager: Alan Wooler

Faversham KM Extra
01227 534545
www.kentonline.co.uk
Weekly (Tue). Owner: Kent Messenger Group. Editor: Bob Bounds; news: Trisha Jamieson; production: Gary Barker

Faversham News
01795 532345
www.kentonline.co.uk
Weekly (Thu). Owner: Kent Messenger Group. Editor: Bob Bounds; news: Trisha Jamieson; production: Gary Barker

Faversham Times
01795 536555
www.trinitymirrorsouthern.co.uk
Weekly (Thu). Owner: Trinity Mirror Southern. Editor: Christine Rayner; features: Julia Rogers

Folkestone & Hythe Extra
01303 850676
Weekly (Wed). Owner: Kent Messenger Group. Editor: Leo Whitlock; production: Gary Barker

Folkestone Express
01233 623232
www.kentonline.co.uk
Weekly (Wed). Owner: Kent Messenger Group. Editor: Leo Whitlock; news: Simon Alford; chief sub: Claire Stevens

Folkestone Herald
01303 850999
www.trinitymirrorsouthern.co.uk
Weekly (Thu). Owner: Trinity Mirror Southern. Editor: Simon Finlay

Friday-Ad
0870 162 9999
www.friday-ad.co.uk
Weekly (Fri). Editor: David Sommerville

Gatwick Skyport
020 8538 2236
www.trinitymirrorsouthern.co.uk
Weekly free (Fri). Owner: Trinity Mirror Southern. Editor: Suzy Shanley

Godalming Times
01483 508700
Weekly free (Wed). Owner: Guardian Media Group. Group editorial director: Marnie Wilson; news: Debby Thompson

Gravesend Express
020 8269 7000
www.gravesendexpress.co.uk
Weekly free (Wed). Owner: Archant. Editor: Melody Ryall; production: Mick Taylor

Gravesend KM Extra
01474 333381
www.kentonline.co.uk
Weekly (Fri). Owner: Kent Messenger Group. Editor: Denise Eaton

Gravesend Messenger
01474 333381
www.kent-online.co.uk
Weekly (Thu). Owner: Kent Messenger Group. Editor: Sandra Hembury; news: Denise Eaton

Gravesend Reporter
020 8269 7000
www.gravesendreporter.co.uk
Weekly (Thu). Owner: Archant. Editor: Melody Ryall; production: Mick Taylor

Guildford Times
01483 508700
www.surreyad.co.uk
Weekly free (Wed). Owner: Guardian Media Group. Group editorial director: Marnie Wilson; news: Debby Thompson

Hailsham Gazette
01323 722091
www.eastbournetoday.co.uk
Weekly (Wed). Owner: Johnston Press. Editor: Peter Austin; commercial editor: Andrew Bennett; sports editor: Ken McEwan

Harpenden Observer
01727 834411
www.stalbansobserver.co.uk
Weekly (Wed). Owner: Newsquest. Editor: Claire Bourke

Haslemere Times & Mail
01252 716444
www.haslemere-herald-today.co.uk
Weekly free (Tue). Owner: Tindle Newspapers. Editor: Sandy Baker; subeditor: Tony Short

Hastings & St Leonards Observer
01424 854242
www.hastingstoday.co.uk
Weekly (Fri). Owner: Johnston Press. Group editor: Peter Lindsey; chief reporter: Chris Pollard

Hastings AdNews
01424 854242
www.hastingstoday.co.uk
Weekly (Fri). Owner: Johnston Press. Group editor: Peter Lindsey; chief reporter: Chris Pollard

Hemel Hempstead Gazette
01442 262311
www.hemeltoday.co.uk
Weekly (Wed). Owner: Johnston Press. Editor: David Feldstein; sports editor: Graham Caygill

Hendon & Finchley Times
020 8359 5959
www.hendontimes.co.uk
Weekly (Thu). Owner: Newsquest. Group editor: John Kileen; chief reporter: Leigh Collins

Herne Bay Gazette
01227 475901
www.kentonline.co.uk
Weekly (Thu). Owner: Kent Messenger Group. Editor: Bob Bounds; news: Trisha Jamieson; production: Gary Barker

Herne Bay KM Extra
01227 768181
www.kentonline.co.uk
Weekly (Tue). Owner: Kent Messenger Group. Editor: Bob Bounds; news: Trisha Jamieson; production: Gary Barker

Herne Bay Times
01227 771515
Weekly (Thu). Owner: Trinity Mirror Southern. Editor: John Nurden; features: Julia Rogers; chief sub: Paul Taylor

Hertford Times
01707 327551
www.whtimes.co.uk
Weekly (Wed). Owner: Archant. Editor: Terry Mitchinson; news: Chris Lennon

Hertfordshire Mercury
01992 526625
www.hertsessexnews.co.uk
Weekly (Fri). Owner: Herts & Essex Newspapers. Editor: Paul Winspear

Hertfordshire on Sunday
01992 526625
www.hertsessexnews.co.uk
Weekly (Sun). Owner: Herts & Essex Newspapers. Editor: Bridget McAlpine

Hertfordshire Star
01992 526625
www.hertsessexnews.co.uk
Weekly (Wed). Owner: Herts & Essex Newspapers. Editor: Chris Bristow

Herts & Essex Observer
01279 866355
www.hertsessexnews.co.uk
Weekly (Thu). Owner: Archant. Editor: Val Drown; news: Sandra Perry

Herts Advertiser
01727 865165
www.hertsad.co.uk
Weekly (Thu). Owner: Archant. Editor: Noel Cantillon

Hitchin Advertiser
01462 441020
www.hitchinadvertiser.co.uk
Weekly (Wed). Owner: Observer Standard Newspapers. General manager: Ricky Allan

Hitchin Comet
01438 866200
www.thecomet.net
Weekly (Thu). Owner: Archant. Editor: Darren Isted; news: John Adams

Hoddesdon & Broxbourne Mercury
01992 414141
www.hertsessexnews.co.uk
Weekly (Fri). Owner: Herts & Essex Newspapers. Editor: Ian Rogerson; news: Pat Roberts

Horsham Advertiser
01403 751200
www.horshamtoday.co.uk
Weekly (Fri). Owner: Johnston Press. Editor: Gary Shipton; chief sub: Steve Payne

Hythe Herald
01227 767321
www.trinitymirrorsouthern.co.uk
Weekly (Thu). Owner: Trinity Mirror Southern. Editor: Simon Finlay

Isle of Thanet Gazette
01227 767321
www.trinitymirrorsouthern.co.uk
Weekly (Thu). Owner: Trinity Mirror Southern. Editor: Rebecca Smith; news: Jenny De Freitas

Kent & Sussex Courier
01892 681000
www.thisiskentandeastsussex.co.uk
Weekly (Fri). Owner: Northcliffe Newspapers. Editor: Roger Watkins; features: Melanie Whittaker; production: Richard Page

Kent Messenger
01622 695666
www.kentonline.co.uk
Weekly (Fri). Owner: Kent Messenger Group. Editor: Bob Dimond; community editor: Cathy Tyce

Kent on Sunday
01303 817000
www.kentnews.co.uk
Weekly (Sun). Owner: KOS Media (Publishing). Editor: Ian Patel; news: Bernard Ginns; chief sub: Dave Hobday; production: Jason Pyne

Kentish Express
01233 623232
www.kentonline.co.uk
Weekly (Thu). Owner: Kent Messenger Group. Editor: Leo Whitlock; news: Simon Alford; chief sub: Claire Stevens; production: Gary Barker

Kentish Gazette
01227 768181
www.kentonline.co.uk
Weekly (Thu). Owner: Kent Messenger Group. Editor: Bob Bounds; news: Trisha Jamieson; production: Gary Barker

Kingston Guardian
020 8646 6336
www.kingstonguardian.co.uk
Weekly (Thu). Owner: Newsquest. Editor: Sean Duggan

Lea Valley Star
01992 526625
www.hertsessexnews.co.uk
Weekly (Wed). Owner: Herts & Essex Newspapers. Editor: Chris Bristow

Leatherhead Advertiser
01737 732000
www.icsurreyonline.co.uk
Weekly (Thu). Owner: Trinity Mirror Southern. Editor-in-chief: Ian Carter; content editor: Katherine Newton

Leatherhead Guardian
020 8646 6336
www.leatherheadguardian.co.uk
Weekly (Thu). Owner: Newsquest.
Editor: Sean Duggan

Leighton Buzzard & Linslade Citizen
01908 651200
www.miltonkeynestoday.co.uk
Weekly free (Thu). Owner: Johnston
Press. Editor: Alan Legg

Leighton Buzzard Observer
01525 858400
www.miltonkeynestoday.co.uk
Weekly (Tue). Owner: Johnston Press.
Editor: Nick Wormley; news: Mike King

Leighton Buzzard On Sunday
01908 809000
www.seriousaboutnews.com
Sunday. Owner: LSN Media. Editor:
Gaynor Selby; news: Martin Bughair

Letchworth & Baldock Comet
01438 866000
www.thecomet.net
Weekly (Thu). Owner: Archant. Editor:
Darren Isted; news: John Adams

Limited Edition (Hertfordshire)
01923 216220
Monthly (1st Tue). Owner: Newsquest.
Editor: Deborah Aspinall

Littlehampton Gazette
01903 230051
www.littlehamptontoday.co.uk
Weekly (Thu). Owner: Johnston Press.
Editor: Roger Green

Luton & Dunstable on Sunday
01582 707707
www.seriousaboutnews.com
Weekly (Sun). Owner: LSN Media. Editor:
Gaynor Selby; news: Martin Bughair

Luton Herald & Post
01582 700600
www.lutontoday.co.uk
Weekly (Thu). Owner: Johnston Press.
Editor: John Francis

Luton News
01582 526000
www.lutontoday.co.uk
Weekly (Wed). Owner: Johnston Press.
Assistant editor: Geoff Cox

Maidstone KM Extra
01622 695666
www.kentonline.co.uk
Weekly free (Fri). Owner: Kent Messenger
Group. Editor: Bob Dimond; community
editor: Cathy Tyce

Medway Messenger
(Rochester, Chatham, Gravesend)
01634 227800
www.kentonline.co.uk
Weekly (Mon, Fri). Owner: Kent
Messenger Group. Editor: Bob Dimond;
news: Sarah Clarke; features: Lynn Cox;
chief sub: Alan Roots

Medway News
01227 767321
www.trinitymirrorsouthern.co.uk
Weekly (Thu). Owner: Trinity Mirror
Southern. Editor: Diane Nicholls

Medway Standard
01227 767321
www.trinitymirrorsouthern.co.uk
Weekly (Fri). Owner: Trinity Mirror
Southern. Editor: Diane Nicholls

The Messenger (Haslemere)
01428 653999
www.messenger-online.co.uk
Weekly free (Wed). Editor: Guy Butchers;
news: Sheila Checkley

Mid Sussex Citizen
01444 452201
www.midsussextoday.co.uk
Weekly free (Wed). Owner: Johnston
Press. Editor: Grahame Campbell

Mid Sussex Leader
01273 544544
www.thisismidsussex.co.uk

Mid Sussex Times
01444 452201
www.midsussextoday.co.uk
Weekly (Thu). Owner: Johnston Press.
Editor: Grahame Campbell

Midhurst & Petworth Observer
01730 813557
www.midhurstandpetworth.co.uk
Weekly (Thu). Owner: Johnston Press.
Chief sub: David Philip; news: Jane Hunt

News & Mail
01483 508900
www.surreyad.co.uk
Weekly (Wed). Owner: Guardian Media
Group. Group editorial director: Marnie
Wilson

News in Focus
01732 228000
www.thisiskent.co.uk
Weekly (Tue). Owner: Northcliffe
Newspapers. Editor: Ian Reid

News Shopper Guide
01689 885701
www.newsshopper.co.uk
Weekly (Thu). Owner: Newsquest.
Editor: Andrew Parkes; news: Matthew
Ramsden; chief sub: Tim Miles

Orpington & Petts Wood Times
020 8269 7000
Weekly (Thu). Owner: Archant. Editor:
Melody Ryall; production: Mick Taylor

Paddock Wood Courier
01892 681000
www.thisiskentandeastsussex.co.uk
Weekly (Fri). Owner: Northcliffe
Newspapers. Editor: Roger Watkins;
features: Melanie Whittaker; production:
Richard Page

Redhill, Reigate & Horley Life
01403 223180
www.redhillandreigatelife.co.uk
Weekly (Wed). Owner: Newsquest.
Editor: Chris Chandler

Reigate Post
020 8770 7171
www.icsurrey.co.uk
Weekly (Thu). Owner: Trinity Mirror
Southern. Editor: Ian Carter; content
editor: James Osbourne

Reigate, Redhill & Horley Post
01737 732000
www.icsurrey.co.uk
Weekly (Wed). Owner: Trinity Mirror
Southern. Editor-in-chief: Ian Carter;
content editor: James Osbourne

Romney Marsh Herald
01227 767321
www.trinitymirrorsouthern.co.uk
Weekly (Wed). Owner: Trinity Mirror
Southern. Editor: Diane Nicholls

Royston & Buntingford Mercury
01992 526600
www.hertsessexnews.co.uk
Weekly (Fri). Owner: Herts & Essex
Newspapers. Editor: Paul Winspear;
news: Paul Brackley; features: Bridget
McAlpine

Royston Crow
01763 245241
www.royston-crow.co.uk
Weekly (Thu). Owner: Archant.
Editor: Les Baker

Rye & Battle Observer
01424 854242
www.ryeandbattletoday.co.uk
Weekly (Fri). Owner: Johnston Press.
Associate editor: Russell Claughton;
news: Andy Hemsley

St Albans & Harpenden Review
01727 834411
www.stalbansobserver.co.uk
Weekly free (Wed). Owner: Newsquest.
Editor: Claire Bourke

St Albans Observer
01727 834411
www.stalbansobserver.co.uk
Weekly (Thu). Owner: Newsquest.
Editor: Claire Bourke

Seaford Gazette
01323 722091
www.eastbournetoday.co.uk
Weekly (Wed). Owner: Johnston Press.
Editor: Peter Austin; commercial editor:
Andrew Bennett; sports editor:
Ken McEwan

Sevenoaks Chronicle
01732 228000
www.thisiskentandeastsussex.co.uk
Weekly (Thu). Owner: Northcliffe
Newspapers. Editor: Ian Reid

Sheerness Times Guardian
01795 580300
Weekly (Thu). Owner: Kent Messenger
Group. Editor: Duncan Marsh; news:
Gemma Constable

Sheppey Gazette
01227 767321
www.trinitymirrorsouthern.co.uk
Weekly (Thu). Owner: Trinity Mirror
Southern. Editor: Christine Rayner

Shoreham Herald
01903 230051
www.shorehamtoday.co.uk
Weekly (Thu). Owner: Johnston Press.
Editor: Michelle Neville

Sittingbourne KM Extra
01795 580300
www.kentonline.co.uk
Weekly (Wed). Owner: Kent Messenger
Group. Editor: Duncan Marsh; news:
Gemma Constable

South Coast Leader
01273 544544
www.thisisbrightonandhove.co.uk
Weekly (Fri). Owner: Newsquest. Editor:
Chris Chandler; news: Mike Dunford

Staines & Ashford News
01932 561111
www.trinitymirrorsouthern.co.uk
Weekly free (Wed). Owner: Trinity Mirror Southern. Editor: Mike Hawkins; publishing director: Liz Dixon

Staines & Egham News
01932 561111
www.trinitymirrorsouthern.co.uk
Weekly free (Wed). Owner: Trinity Mirror Southern. Editor: Mike Hawkins; publishing director: Liz Dixon

Staines Guardian
020 8940 6030
www.stainesguardian.co.uk
Weekly (Thu). Owner: Newsquest. Editor: Paul Mortimer; news: James Adlam

Staines Informer
01932 561111
www.trinitymirrorsouthern.co.uk
Weekly (Thu). Owner: Trinity Mirror Southern. Editor: Mike Hawkins; publishing director: Liz Dixon

Staines Leader
01932 561111
www.trinitymirrorsouthern.co.uk
Weekly (Thu). Owner: Trinity Mirror Southern. Editor: Mike Hawkins

Star Classified (Bishops Stortford)
01279 866355
www.hertsessexnews.co.uk
Weekly (Thu). Owner: Archant. Editor: Val Brown; news: Sandra Perry

Stevenage Advertiser
01462 441020
www.hitchinadvertiser.co.uk
Weekly (Wed). Owner: Observer Standard Newspapers. General manager: Ricky Allan

Stevenage Comet
01438 866000
www.thecomet.net
Weekly (Thu). Owner: Archant. Editor: Darren Isted; news: John Adams

Stevenage Herald
01438 866000
www.thecomet.net
Weekly free (Wed). Owner: Archant. Editor: Darren Isted; news: John Adams

Surrey & Hants News
01252 716444
www.farnham-herald-today.co.uk
Weekly free (Tue). Owner: Tindle Newspapers. Editor: Sandy Baker; sub: Tony Short

Surrey Advertiser
01483 508700
www.surreyad.co.uk
Weekly (Fri). Owner: Guardian Media Group. Group editorial director: Marnie Wilson

Surrey Comet
020 8646 6336
www.surreycomet.co.uk
Weekly (Wed). Owner: Newsquest. Editor: Sean Duggan

Surrey Hants Star
01252 316311
www.shstar.co.uk
Weekly free (Thu). Owner: Guardian Media Group. Editor: Joanne Jones

Surrey Herald
01932 561111
www.trinitymirrorsouthern.co.uk
Weekly (Wed). Owner: Trinity Mirror Southern. Editor: Mike Hawkins

Surrey Mirror
020 8770 7171
www.icsurrey.co.uk
Weekly (Wed). Owner: Trinity Mirror Southern. Editor: Ian Carter; news: James Osbourne; features: Christine Malthouse; chief sub: Sherif El Alfay

Sussex Express
01273 480601
www.lewestoday.co.uk
Weekly (Fri). Owner: Johnston Press. Editor: Paul Watson; deputy editor: Michael McKenzy

Sutton Advertiser
020 8763 6666
www.iccroydon.co.uk
Weekly (Fri). Owner: Trinity Mirror Southern. Editor: Ian Carter

Sutton Borough Post
020 8763 6666
www.iccroydon.co.uk
Weekly (Wed). Owner: Trinity Mirror Southern. Editor: Ian Carter

Sutton Guardian
020 8646 6336
www.suttonguardian.co.uk
Weekly (Thu). Owner: Newsquest. Editor: Sean Duggan

Swanley Messenger
01322 220791
www.kent-online.co.uk
Weekly (Thu). Owner: Kent Messenger Group. Editor: Sandra Hembury; news: Louise Edwards

Swanley Times
020 8269 7000
Weekly (Thu). Owner: Archant. Editor: Melody Ryall; production: Mick Taylor

Tandridge Chronicle
01959 564766
www.tandridge-today.co.uk
Weekly (Thu). Owner: Tindle Newspapers. Editor: Signid Sherrell

Tandridge County Border News
01959 564766
www.tandridge-today.co.uk
Weekly (Thu). Owner: Tindle Newspapers. Editor: Kevin Black

Tenterden Express
01233 623232
www.kentonline.co.uk
Weekly (Tue). Owner: Kent Messenger Group. Editor: Leo Whitlock; news: Simon Alford; chief sub: Claire Stevens

Tenterden KM Extra
01233 623232
www.kentonline.co.uk
Weekly (Tue). Owner: Kent Messenger Group. Editor: Leo Whitlock; news: Simon Alford; chief sub: Claire Stevens

Thanet KM Extra
01622 717880
www.kentonline.co.uk
Weekly (Wed). Owner: Kent Messenger Group. Editor: Bob Bounds

Thanet Times
01227 767321
www.trinitymirrorsouthern.co.uk
Weekly (Tues). Owner: Trinity Mirror Southern. Editor: Rebecca Smith; news: Jenny De Freitas

Tonbridge Courier
01892 681000
www.thisiskentandeastsussex.co.uk
Weekly (Fri). Owner: Northcliffe Newspapers. Editor: Roger Watkins; features: Melanie Whittaker; production: Richard Page

Tunbridge Wells Courier
01892 681000
www.thisiskentandeastsussex.co.uk
Weekly (Fri). Owner: Northcliffe Newspapers. Editor: Roger Watkins; features: Melanie Whittaker; production: Richard Page

Tunbridge Wells Extra
01892 525111
www.kentonline.co.uk
Weekly (Fri). Owner: Kent Messenger Group. Editor: Bob Dimond; news: Linda Mitchell

Virginia Water Villager
01753 523355
Fortnightly (Thu). Owner: Clyde & Forth Press. Editor: Sally Stevens

Walton & Weybridge Informer
01932 561111
www.trinitymirrorsouthern.co.uk
Weekly free (Thu). Owner: Trinity Mirror Southern. Editor: Mike Hawkins

Watford Free Observer
01923 216216
www.watfordobserver.co.uk
Weekly (Thu). Owner: Newsquest. Editor: Peter Wilson-Leary; news: Frazer Ansell

Watford Review
01923 216212
www.stalbansobserver.co.uk
Weekly free (Wed). Owner: Newsquest. Editor: Peter Wilson-Leary

Weald Courier
01892 681000
www.thisiskentandeastsussex.co.uk
Weekly (Fri). Owner: Northcliffe Newspapers. Editor: Roger Watkins; features: Melanie Whittaker; production: Richard Page

Wealden Advertiser
01580 753322
www.wealdenad.co.uk
Weekly free (Fri). Editor: Graham Thorn

Weekend Herald (Crawley, Horsham, Horley)
01293 562929
www.crawleyobserver.co.uk
Weekly free (Fri). Owner: Johnston Press. Editor: Lesley Hixon; chief sub: Mark Dunford

Welwyn & Hatfield Review
01727 834411
www.stalbansobserver.co.uk
Weekly (Thu). Owner: Newsquest. Editor: Claire Bourke

Welwyn & Hatfield Times
01707 327551
www.whtimes.co.uk
Weekly (Wed). Owner: Archant. Editor: Terry Mitchinson; news: Chris Lennon

Westerham County Border News
01959 564766
www.westerham-today.co.uk
*Weekly (Thu). Owner: Tindle
Newspapers. Editor: Kevin Black*

West Sussex County Times
01403 751200
www.horshamonline.co.uk
*Weekly (Fri). Owner: Johnston Press.
Editor: Gary Shipton; deputy editor:
Tim Hopewell-Ash*

West Sussex Gazette
01903 230051
www.worthingtoday.co.uk
*Weekly (Wed). Owner: Johnston Press.
Editor: Jeannie Knight; chief sub: Phil
Reynolds*

Weybridge Villager
01753 523355
*Fortnightly (Thu). Owner: Clyde & Forth
Press. Editor: Sally Stevens*

Whitstable Gazette
01227 372233
www.kentonline.co.uk
*Weekly (Thu). Owner: Kent Messenger
Group. Editor: Bob Bounds; news: Trisha
Jamieson; production: Gary Barker*

Whitstable KM Extra
01227 768181
www.kentonline.co.uk
*Weekly (Tue). Owner: Kent Messenger
Group. Editor: Bob Bounds; news: Trisha
Jamieson; production: Gary Barker*

Whitstable Times
01227 771515
*Weekly (Thu). Owner: Trinity Mirror
Southern. Editor: John Nurden; features:
Julia Rogers; chief sub: Paul Taylor;
production: Mark Silva*

Woking Informer
01932 561111
www.trinitymirrorsouthern.co.uk
*Weekly free (Thu). Owner: Trinity Mirror
Southern. Editor: Liz Dixon; news: Irlene
Watchmore*

Woking News & Mail
01483 755755
www.woking.co.uk
*Weekly (Thu). Owner: Guardian Media
Group. Editor: Penny Bray; news: Simon
Ashall*

Woking Review
01483 755755
www.woking.co.uk
*Weekly (Wed). Owner: Guardian Media
Group. Editor: Penny Bray; news: Simon
Ashall*

Worthing Advertiser
01903 230051
www.worthingtoday.co.uk
*Weekly (Wed). Owner: Johnston Press.
Editor: Tony Mayes*

Worthing Guardian
01903 230051
www.worthingtoday.co.uk
*Weekly (Fri). Owner: Johnston Press.
Editor: Nikki Jeffrey*

Worthing Herald
01903 230051
www.worthingtoday.co.uk
*Weekly (Thu). Owner: Johnston Press.
Editor: John Buss; news: Nicola McClaren*

● South England

**Berkshire, Buckinghamshire, Hampshire,
Oxfordshire, Wiltshire**

Abingdon Herald
01865 425262
www.thisisoxfordshire.co.uk
*Weekly (Thu). Owner: Newsquest.
Editor: Derek Holmes*

The Advertiser (Newbury)
01635 524111
www.newburynews.co.uk
*Weekly (Tue). Owner: Blacket Turner.
Editor: Brien Beharrell; news: Martin
Robertshaw*

Aldershot Courier
01252 339760
www.aldershot.co.uk
*Weekly free (Wed). Owner: Guardian
Media Group. Editor: Elaine Cole;
news: Adam Clark*

Aldershot Mail
01252 339760
www.aldershot.co.uk
*Weekly (Tue). Owner: Guardian Media
Group. Editor: Elaine Cole; news:
Adam Clark*

Aldershot News
01252 339760
www.aldershot.co.uk
*Weekly (Fri). Owner: Guardian Media
Group. Editor: Elaine Cole; news:
Adam Clark*

Alresford Gazette
01420 84446
*Weekly (Wed). Owner: Tindle
Newspapers. Editor: Christine
McDerment; news: Paul Ferguson*

Alton Times & Mail
01252 716444
www.alton-herald-today.co.uk
*Weekly free (Tue). Owner: Tindle
Newspapers. Editor: Tony Short*

Amersham & Chesham Free Press
01494 755081
www.bucksfreepress.co.uk
*Weekly (Fri). Owner: Newsquest.
Editor: Steve Cohen; news: Victoria Birch;
features: Lindi Bilgorri*

Amersham Examiner
01753 888333
www.buckinghamtoday.co.uk
*Weekly (Thu). Owner: Trinity Mirror
Southern. Editor: Julie Voyce; news:
Ben Steele*

Andover Advertiser
01264 323456
www.andoveradvertiser.co.uk
*Weekly (Fri). Owner: Newsquest. Editor:
Joe Scicluna; deputy editor: Judy Belbin;
features: Simon Reeve; chief sub: Judith
Hughes*

Andover Advertiser Midweek
01264 323456
www.andoveradvertiser.co.uk
*Weekly (Wed). Owner: Newsquest. Editor:
Joe Scicluna; deputy editor: Judy Belbin;
features: Simon Reeve; chief sub: Judith
Hughes*

Ascot News
01344 456611
www.icberkshire.co.uk
*Weekly (Thu). Owner: Trinity Mirror
Southern. Editor: Joe Wise; chief reporter:
Richard Crowe*

Ash & Farnham Mail
01252 339760
www.aldershot.co.uk
*Weekly (Tue). Owner: Guardian Media
Group. Editor: Elaine Cole; news: Adam
Clark*

Banbury Cake
01295 256111
www.thisisoxfordshire.co.uk
*Weekly (Thu). Owner: Newsquest.
Editor: Derek Holmes; news and features:
Jason Collie*

Banbury Review
01295 227777
www.banburyguardian.co.uk
*Weekly free (Fri). Owner: Johnston Press.
Editor: Bridget Dakin; news: Cally
Reynolds*

Banbury Guardian
01295 227777
www.banburyguardian.co.uk
*Weekly (Thu). Owner: Johnston Press.
Editor: Bridget Dakin; news: Cally
Reynolds*

**Basingstoke & Northampton
Gazette**
01256 461131
www.thisishampshire.net
*Weekly (Mon). Owner: Newsquest. Editor:
Mark Jones; news: Hugh Cadman; chief
sub: Jonathan Lee; production manager:
Alan Cranham*

Basingstoke Extra
01256 461131
www.thisishampshire.net
*Weekly free (Wed). Owner: Newsquest.
Editor: Mark Jones; news: Hugh Cadman;
chief sub: Jonathan Lee; production
manager: Alan Cranham*

Basingstoke Independent
01962 859 559
www.hantsmedia.co.uk
*Weekly (Fri). Owner: Hampshire Media.
Editor: Pete Harvey*

Basingstoke Observer
01256 694121
*Weekly (Thu). Owner: Tri Media
Publishing. Editor: Steve Davies; head of
production: Tony Allsop*

Beaconsfield Advertiser
01753 888333
www.buckinghamtoday.co.uk
*Weekly (Thu). Owner: Trinity Mirror
Southern. Editor: Julie Voyce; news: Ben
Steele*

Berkhamsted & Tring Gazette
01442 262311
www.hemelonline.co.uk
*Weekly (Wed). Owner: Johnston Press.
Editor: David Feldstein; news: Ann
Traynor; sports editor: Graham Caygill*

Bicester Advertiser
01865 425262
www.thisisoxfordshire.co.uk
*Weekly (Fri). Owner: Newsquest.
Editor: Derek Holmes*

Bicester Review
01280 813434
www.buckinghamtoday.co.uk
Weekly (Fri). Owner: Buckingham
Advertiser Group. Editor: Rob Gibbard;
deputy editor: Clare Wale

Bordon Post
01730 264811
www.petersfield.co.uk
Weekly (Wed). Owner: Johnston Press.
Editor: Graeme Moir; chief reporter:
Will Parsons

Bordon Times & Mail
01252 716444
Weekly free (Tue). Owner: Tindle
Newspapers. Editor: Tony Short;
features: Angie Williamson

Brackley & Towcester Advertiser
01280 813434
www.buckinghamtoday.co.uk
Weekly (Fri). Owner: Buckingham
Advertiser Group. Editor: Rob Gibbard;
deputy editor: Clare Wale

Bracknell & Ascot Times
0118 936 6180
www.getbracknell.co.uk
Weekly (Thu). Owner: Guardian Media
Group. Editor: Adam D Smith; deputy
editor: David Allan; sports editor: Steve
Skerry

Bracknell Midweek News
01344 456611
www.icberkshire.co.uk
Weekly (Thu). Owner: Trinity Mirror
Southern. Editor: Joe Wise; chief reporter:
Richard Crowe

Bracknell News
01344 456611
www.icberkshire.co.uk
Weekly (Thu). Owner: Trinity Mirror
Southern. Editor: Joe Wise; chief reporter:
Richard Crowe

Bracknell Standard
0118 936 6180
www.getbracknell.co.uk
Weekly (Thu). Owner: Guardian Media
Group. Editor: Adam D Smith; deputy
editor: David Allan; sports editor: Steve
Skerry

Buckingham & Winslow Advertiser
01280 813434
www.buckinghamtoday.co.uk
Weekly (Fri). Owner: Buckingham
Advertiser Group. Editor: Rob Gibbard;
deputy editor: Clare Wale

Buckinghamshire Advertiser
01753 888333
Weekly (Thu). Owner: Trinity Mirror
Southern. Editor: Julie Voyce; news:
Ben Steele

Buckinghamshire Echo
0116 253 8194
Weekly journal (Tue). Owner: Journal
Publishing Company. Editor: Elaine Ellis

Buckinghamshire Examiner
01753 888333
www.buckinghamtoday.co.uk
Weekly (Thu). Owner: Trinity Mirror
Southern. Editor: Julie Voyce; news:
Ben Steele

Bucks Free Press
01494 755000
www.bucksfreepress.co.uk
Weekly (Fri). Owner: Newsquest.
Editor: Steve Cohen; news: Victoria Birch

Bucks Free Press Midweek
01494 755081
www.bucksfreepress.co.uk
Weekly (Tue). Owner: Newsquest.
Editor: Steve Cohen; news: Victoria Birch;
features: Lindi Bilgorri

Bucks Herald
01296 318300
www.bucksherald.co.uk
Weekly (Wed). Owner: Johnston Press.
Editor: David Summers; news: Sarah
Young; features: Janet Gleghorne

Chippenham, Corsham Advertiser
01225 760945
Weekly (Thu). Owner: Northcliffe
Newspapers. Editor: Sam Holiday;
news: Paul Wiltshire; features: George
McCready; production: Marion Wild

Crowthorne & Sandhurst Times
0118 936 6180
www.getbracknell.co.uk
Weekly (Wed). Owner: Guardian Media
Group. Editor: Adam D Smith; news:
David Allan; sport: Steve Skerry

Crowthorne, Sandhurst, Owlsmoor Newsweek
01344 456611
www.icberkshire.co.uk
Weekly (Thu). Owner: Trinity Mirror
Southern. Editor: Joe Wise; chief reporter:
Richard Crowe

Devizes, Melksham & Vale of Pewsey News
01793 528144
www.thisisswindon.co.uk
Weekly free (Wed). Owner: Newsquest.
Editor: Mark Waldron; news: Tom Morton

Didcot Herald
01865 425262
www.thisisoxfordshire.co.uk
Weekly (Thu). Owner: Newsquest.
Editor: Derek Holmes

Eastleigh News Extra
01962 841772
www.thisishampshire.net
Weekly free (Thu). Owner: Newsquest.
Editor: Mary Payne; news: Kit Neilson

Eton Observer
01753 523355
www.thisisslough.com
Weekly (Fri). Owner: Clyde & Forth Press.
Editor: Sally Stevens; assistant editor:
Mike Sim

Evening Advertiser (Swindon)
01793 528144
www.thisisswindon.co.uk
Daily. Owner: Newsquest. Editor:
Mark Waldron; news: Cath Turnbull

Fareham & Gosport Journal
023 9266 4488
www.portsmouth.co.uk
Weekly free (Thu). Owner: Johnston
Press. Editor: Mike Gilson; news: Colin
McNeill; features: Graham Patsfield

Fareham & Gosport News
See The News, page 38

Farnborough News & Mail
01252 339760
www.farnborough.co.uk
Weekly (Tue). Owner: Guardian Media
Group. Editor: Elaine Cole

Fleet News & Mail
01252 339760
www.fleet-online.co.uk
Weekly (Tue). Owner: Guardian Media
Group. Editor: Elaine Cole

Frome Times and White Horse News
01225 704761
www.fromenews.co.uk
Fortnightly free (Thu). Owner: Wiltshire
Publications. Editor: Ian Drew

Hamble Valley Journal
023 9266 4488
www.portsmouth.co.uk
Weekly free (Thu). Owner: Johnston
Press. Editor: Mike Gilson; news: Colin
McNeill; features: Graham Patsfield

Hampshire Chronicle
01962 841772
www.thisishampshire.net
Weekly (Fri). Owner: Newsquest.
Editor: Keith Redbourn; deputy editor:
Kit Neilson

Hants & Dorset Avon Advertiser
01722 426500
www.salisburyjournal.co.uk
Weekly (Wed). Owner: Newsquest.
Editor: Bill Browne; news: David Vallis;
features: Lesley Bates

Hart Courier
01252 339760
www.surreyad.co.uk
Weekly (Fri). Owner: Guardian Media
Group. Editor: Elaine Cole

Havant & Waterlooville Journal
023 9266 4488
www.portsmouth.co.uk
Weekly free (Thu). Owner: Johnston
Press. Editor: Mike Gilson; news: Colin
McNeill; features: Graham Patsfield

Havant & Waterlooville News
See The News, page 38

Hemel Hempstead Herald & Express
01442 262311
www.hemeltoday.co.uk
Weekly (Thu). Owner: Johnston Press.
Editor: David Feldstein; news: Ann
Traynor; sports editor: Graham Caygill

Henley Standard
01491 419444
www.henley-on-line.co.uk
Weekly (Thurs). Editor: George Tuckfield;
news: Richard Reid

Isle of Wight County Press
01983 521333
www.iwcp.co.uk
Weekly (Fri). Editor: Brian Dennis;
news: Phil Wolsey

Liphook Times & Mail
01252 716444
Weekly free (Tue). Owner: Tindle
Newspapers. Editor: Tony Short

Lymington Times
01425 613384
Weekly (Fri). Editor: Charles Curry

Maidenhead Advertiser
01628 680680
www.maidenhead-advertiser.co.uk
*Weekly (Thurs). Editor: Martin Trepte;
news: Glenn Mitchell*

Maidenhead Express
01753 825111
www.icberkshire.co.uk
*Weekly (Fri). Owner: Trinity Mirror
Southern. Editor: Paul Thomas;
news: Francis Batt*

Marlow Free Press
01494 755081
www.bucksfreepress.co.uk
*Weekly (Fri). Owner: Newsquest.
Editor: Steve Cohen; news: Victoria Birch;
features: Lindi Bilgorri*

Melksham Independent News
01225 704761
www.melkshamnews.com
*Fortnightly free (Thu). Owner: Wiltshire
Publications. Editor: Ian Drew*

Meon Valley News
023 9263 2767
www.meonvalleynews.org.uk
*Monthly (Mon). Owner: Tindle
Newspapers. Editor: Christine Miller;
assistant editor: Angela Ennis*

Mid Hampshire Observer
01962 859559
www.hantsmedia.co.uk
*Weekly (Wed). Owner: Hampshire Media.
Editor: Pete Harvey*

Milton Keynes Citizen
01908 371133
www.miltonkeynes.co.uk
*Weekly free (Thu). Owner: Johnston Press.
Editor: Jan Henderson; news: Steve Larner*

Milton Keynes Journal
0116 251 1113
*Weekly (Tue). Owner: Journal Publishing
Company. Editor: Emily Davison*

Milton Keynes News
01908 809000
www.mk-news.co.uk
*Weekly (Wed). Owner: LSN Media.
Editor: David Gale*

Monday Gazette
01256 461131
www.thisishampshire.net
*Weekly (Mon). Owner: Newsquest. Editor:
Mark Jones; news: Hugh Cadman; chief
sub: Jonathan Lee; production manager:
Alan Cranham*

New Forest Post
01590 613888
www.thisishampshire.net
*Weekly (Thu). Owner: Newsquest.
Editor: Ian Murray*

New Milton Advertiser
01425 613384
Weekly (Fri). Editor: Charles Curry

Newbury & Thatcham Chronicle
01635 32812
www.icberkshire.co.uk
*Weekly free (Wed). Owner: Trinity Mirror
Southern. Editor: Morris O'Brien*

Newbury Weekly News
01635 524111
www.newburynews.co.uk
*Weekly (Thu). Owner: Blacket Turner.
Editor: Brien Beharrell; news: Martin
Robertshaw*

The News (Portsmouth)
See page 38

Oxford Courier
01235 553444
www.oxfordshirecourier.co.uk
*Weekly (Thu). Owner: Courier
Newspapers. Editor: Lawrence Web,
01235 547806; production: Tony Allsopp*

Oxford Journal
01235 553444
www.oxfordjournal.co.uk
*Weekly (Fri). Owner: Courier
Newspapers. Editor: Lawrence Web,
01235 547806; production: Tony Allsopp*

Oxford Mail
01865 425262
www.thisisoxfordshire.co.uk
*Daily. Owner: Newsquest. Editor: Simon
O'Neill*

Oxford Star
01865 425262
www.thisisoxfordshire.co.uk
*Weekly (Thu). Owner: Newsquest.
Editor: Simon O'Neill*

Oxford Times
01865 425262
www.thisisoxfordshire.co.uk
*Weekly (Fri). Owner: Newsquest. Editor:
Derek Holmes; news: Jason Collie; chief
sub: Marc Evans*

Oxfordshire Weekly
01865 425262
www.thisisoxfordshire.co.uk
*Weekly (Wed). Owner: Newsquest.
Editor: Derek Holmes*

Petersfield Mail
01252 716444
*Weekly free (Tue). Owner: Tindle
Newspapers. Editor: Tony Short*

Petersfield Post
01730 264811
www.petersfield.co.uk
*Weekly (Wed). Owner: Johnston Press.
Editor: Graeme Moir; chief reporter:
Will Parsons*

Portsmouth & Southsea Journal
023 9266 4488
www.portsmouth.co.uk
*Weekly free (Thu). Owner: Johnston
Press. Editor: Mike Gilson; news: Colin
McNeill; features: Graham Patsfield*

Property Chronicle (Berkshire)
0118 950 3030
www.icberkshire.co.uk
*Weekly (Wed, Thu). Owner: Trinity
Mirror Southern. Editor: Simon Jones;
news: Maurice O'Brien; features: Alec
Kingham; production: Phil Atkinson*

Reading Post
0118 918 3000
www.getreading.co.uk
*Weekly (Thu). Owner: Guardian Media
Group. Editor: Andy Murrill; Deputy
editor: Hiliary Scott; chief sub: Alan
Blayney*

Reading Chronicle
0118 950 3030
www.icberkshire.co.uk
*Weekly (Thu). Owner: Trinity Mirror
Southern. Editor: Simon Jones; news:
Maurice O'Brien; features: Alec Kingham;
production: Phil Atkinson*

Reading Evening Post
0118 918 3000
www.getreading.co.uk
*Daily (Mon-Fri). Owner: Guardian Media
Group. Editor: Andy Murrill; news: Lucy
Allan; features: Jenny Laurence; chief
sub: Alan Blayney*

Romsey Advertiser
023 8042 4777
www.thisishampshire.net
 /hampshire/romsey
*Weekly (Fri). Owner: Newsquest. Editor:
Ian Murray; news: Gordon Sutter; chief
sub: Colin Jenkins*

Salisbury Avon Advertiser
01722 426500
www.thisiswiltshire.co.uk
*Weekly (Wed). Owner: Newsquest. Editor:
Bill Browne; news: David Vallis; features:
Lesley Bates; chief sub: Jane Warner*

Salisbury Journal
01722 426500
www.thisissalisbury.co.uk
*Weekly (Thu). Owner: Newsquest. Editor:
Bill Browne; news: David Vallis; features:
Lesley Bates; chief sub: Jane Warner*

Sandhurst & Crowthorne Mail
01252 339760
www.aldershot.co.uk
*Weekly (Tue). Owner: Guardian Media
Group. Editor: Elaine Cole*

Sandhurst & Crowthorne News
01252 339760
www.aldershot.co.uk
*Weekly (Fri). Owner: Guardian Media
Group. Editor: Elaine Cole*

Slough Express
01753 825111
www.icberkshire.co.uk
*Weekly (Fri). Owner: Trinity Mirror
Southern. Editor: Paul Thomas; news:
Francis Batt*

Slough Observer
01753 523355
www.thisisslough.com
*Weekly (Wed). Owner: Clyde & Forth
Press. Editor: Sally Stevens; assistant
editor: Mike Sim*

Southern Daily Echo
See page 38

**South Bucks, Wycombe & Chiltern
Star and Midweek**
01494 755000
www.hillingdontimes.co.uk
*Weekly (Tue, Thu). Owner: Newsquest.
Editor: Steve Cohen; news: Sharon
Walters*

Southampton Advertiser
023 8042 4777
*Weekly (Thu). Owner: Newsquest. Editor:
Ian Murray; news: Gordon Sutter; chief
sub: Colin Jenkins*

South Oxfordshire Courier
01235 553444
www.southoxfordcourier.co.uk
*Weekly (Thu). Owner: Courier
Newspapers. Editor: Lawrence Web,
01235 547806; production: Tony Allsopp*

Surrey & Hampshire Guardian
01788 543077
www.surreyandhampshireguardian
.co.uk
*Daily. Owner: Journal Publishing
Company. Editor: Jag Basra; news:
Keith Brailford; features: Andrew Woods*

Swindon Star
01793 528144
www.thisisswindon.co.uk
*Weekly free (Thu). Owner: Newsquest.
Editor: Mark Waldron; news: Tom Morton*

Tadley Gazette
01256 461131
www.thisishampshire.net
*Weekly free (Weds). Owner: Newsquest.
Editor: Mark Jones; news: Hugh Cadman;
chief sub: Jonathan Lee; production
manager: Alan Cranham*

Thame Gazette
01296 318300
www.aylesburytoday.co.uk
*Weekly (Fri). Owner: Johnston Press.
Editor: David Summers; news: Sarah
Young; features: Janet Gleghorne*

Thatcham News
01635 524111
www.newburynews.co.uk
*Weekly (Thu). Owner: Blacket Turner.
Editor: Brien Beharrell; news: Martin
Robertshaw*

**Trowbridge, Melksham,
Bradford-on-Avon Advertiser**
01225 760945
www.thisiswiltshire.co.uk
*Weekly (Thu). Owner: Northcliffe
Newspapers. Editor: Sam Holiday;
news: Paul Wiltshire; features: George
McCready; production: Marion Wild*

Twyford Times
0118 936 6180
www.getbracknell.co.uk
*Weekly (Wed). Owner: Guardian Media
Group. Editor: Adam D Smith; deputy
editor: David Allan; sports editor:
Steve Skerry*

Wallingford Herald
01865 425262
www.thisisoxfordshire.co.uk
*Weekly (Thu). Owner: Newsquest.
Editor: Derek Holmes*

Wantage Herald
01865 425262
www.thisisoxfordshire.co.uk
*Weekly (Thu). Owner: Newsquest.
Editor: Derek Holmes*

Warminster & Westbury Standard
01373 462379
www.thisissomerset.co.uk
*Weekly (Thu). Owner: Northcliffe
Newspapers. Editor: Sam Holiday*

Warminster Journal
01985 213030
*Weekly (Fri). Editors: RC Shorto and
DJ Watkins*

West & North Wilts Star
01225 777292
www.thisiswiltshire.co.uk
*Weekly free (Fri). Owner: Newsquest.
Editor: Andy Sambidge; news: Craig Evry;
features: Amy Watkins*

Westbury, Warminster Advertiser
01225 760945
www.wiltshirepublications.com
*Weekly (Thu). Owner: Northcliffe
Newspapers. Editor: Sam Holliday;
news: Paul Wiltshire; features: George
McCready; production: Marion Wild*

Wilts & Gloucestershire Standard
01285 642642
www.thisiscirencester.com
*Weekly (Thu). Owner: Newsquest.
Editor: Skip Walker; news: Simon Davis*

Wiltshire Gazette and Herald
01793 528144
www.thisisswindon.co.uk
*Weekly (Thu). Owner: Newsquest.
Editor: Gary Lawrence*

Wiltshire Guardian
024 7622 0742
*Weekly free (Thu). Owner: Journal
Publishing Company. Editor: Jag Basra;
features: Kelly Turrall*

Wiltshire Times
01225 777292
www.thisiswiltshire.co.uk
*Weekly (Fri). Owner: Newsquest.
Editor: Andy Sambidge; news: Craig Evry;
features: Sarah Seamarks*

Winchester News Extra
01962 841772
www.thisishampshire.net
*Weekly free (Thu). Owner: Newsquest.
Editor: Keith Redbourn; news: Brian
Mustoe*

Winchester Shopper
023 8042 4777
www.dailyecho.co.uk
*Weekly (Sun). Owner: Newsquest. Editor:
Ian Murray; news: Gordon Sutter; chief
sub: Colin Jenkins*

**Windsor, Ascot & Maidenhead
Observer**
01753 523355
www.thisiswindsor.com
*Weekly (Fri). Owner: Clyde & Forth Press.
Editor: Sally Stevens; assistant editor:
Mike Sim*

Windsor Express
01753 825111
www.icberkshire.co.uk
*Weekly free (Fri). Owner: Trinity Mirror
Southern. Editor: Paul Thomas; news:
Francis Batt*

Witney & West Oxfordshire Gazette
01865 425262
www.thisisoxfordshire.co.uk
*Weekly (Wed). Owner: Newsquest.
Editor: Derek Holmes*

Wodley Times
0118 936 6180
www.getbracknell.co.uk
*Weekly (Wed). Owner: Guardian Media
Group. Editor: Adam D Smith; deputy
editor: David Allan; sports editor: Steve
Skerry*

Woking Midweek
01344 456611
www.icberkshire.co.uk
*Weekly (Wed). Owner: Trinity Mirror
Southern. Editor: Joe Wise; chief
reporter: Richard Crowe*

Wokingham News
01344 456611
www.icberkshire.co.uk
*Weekly (Wed). Owner: Trinity Mirror
Southern. Editor: Joe Wise; chief
reporter: Richard Crowe*

Wokingham Standard
0118 936 6180
www.getbracknell.co.uk
*Weekly (Thu). Owner: Guardian Media
Group. Editor: Adam D Smith, deputy
editor: David Allan; sports editor: Steve
Skerry*

Wokingham Times
0118 936 6180
www.getbracknell.co.uk
*Weekly (Thu). Owner: Guardian Media
Group. Editor: Adam D Smith; deputy
editor: David Allan; sports editor: Steve
Skerry*

Woodley & Earley Chronicle
0118 963 3030
www.icberkshire.co.uk
*Weekly (Thu). Owner: Trinity Mirror
Southern. Editor: Simon Jones; news:
Maurice O'Brien; features: Alec Kingham;
production: Phil Atkinson*

Yateley Mail
01252 339760
www.aldershot.co.uk
*Weekly (Tue). Owner: Guardian Media
Group. Editor: Elaine Cole*

Yateley News
01252 339760
www.aldershot.co.uk
*Weekly (Fri). Owner: Guardian Media
Group. Editor: Elaine Cole*

● South-west England

Cornwall, Devon, Dorset,
Somerset & Avon

Bath Chronicle
01225 322322
www.thisisbath.co.uk
*Daily. Owner: Northcliffe Newspapers.
Editor: Sam Holliday; news: Paul
Wiltshire; features: Georgette McCready;
chief sub: Graham Holburn*

Bath Times
01225 322322
www.thisisbath.co.uk
*Weekly (Tues). Owner: Northcliffe
Newspapers. Editor: Sam Holliday;
news: Paul Wiltshire*

Bournemouth Advertiser
01202 554601
www.thisisbournemouth.co.uk
*Weekly free (Thu). Owner: Newsquest.
Editor: Neal Butterworth; news: Andy
Martin; features: Kevin Nash*

Bridgwater Mercury
01823 365151
www.thisisthewestcountry.co.uk
*Weekly (Tue). Owner: Newsquest.
Editor-in-chief: Ken Bird; deputy group
editor: Bob Drayton*

Bridgwater Star
01823 365151
www.thisisthewestcountry.co.uk
*Weekly (Thu). Owner: Newsquest.
Editor-in-chief: Ken Bird; deputy group
editor: Bob Drayton*

Bridgwater Times
01275 335100
www.thisissomerset.co.uk
*Weekly (Thu). Owner: Northcliffe
Newspapers. Editor: Carol Deacon*

Bridport & Lyme Regis News
01308 425884
www.bridportnews.co.uk
*Weekly (Fri). Owner: Newsquest.
Editor: Holly Robinson*

Bristol Evening Post
See page 37

Brixham News
01803 864212
*Weekly free (Wed). Owner: Tindle
Newspapers. Editor: Gina Coles*

Bude & Stratton Post
01566 772424
*Weekly (Thu). Owner: Tindle
Newspapers. Editor: Geoff Seccombe;
news: Keith Whitford*

Burnham & Highbridge Mercury
01823 365151
www.thisisthewestcountry.co.uk
*Weekly (Tue). Owner: Newsquest.
Editor-in-chief: Ken Bird; deputy group
editor: Bob Drayton*

Burnham & Highbridge Times
01275 335100
www.thisissomerset.co.uk
*Weekly (Thu). Owner: Northcliffe
Newspapers. Editor: Carol Deacon;
news: Juliette Auty*

Burnham & Highbridge Weekly News
01823 365151
www.thisisthewestcountry.co.uk
*Weekly (Thu). Owner: Newsquest.
Editor-in-chief: Ken Bird; deputy group
editor: Bob Drayton*

Camborne and Redruth Packet
01326 213333
www.thisisthewestcountry.co.uk
*Weekly free (Wed). Owner: Newsquest.
Editor: Terry Lambert; news: Stephen
Ivall; chief sub: David Robinson*

Camelford & Delabole Journal Gazette
01566 772424
*Weekly (Fri). Owner: Tindle Newspapers.
Editor: Geoff Seccombe; news: Keith
Whitford*

Camelford & Delabole Post
01566 772424
*Weekly (Thu). Owner: Tindle Newspapers.
Editor: Geoff Seccombe; news: Keith
Whitford*

Central Somerset Gazette
01749 832300
www.thisissomerset.co.uk
*Weekly (Thurs). Owner: Northcliffe
Newspapers. Editor: Philip Welch*

Chard & Ilminster News
01823 365151
www.thisisthewestcountry.co.uk
*Weekly (Wed). Owner: Newsquest.
Editor-in-chief: Ken Bird; deputy group
editor: Bob Drayton*

Chard & Ilminster News (Somerset)
01460 67474
www.thisisthewestcountry.co.uk
*Weekly (Wed). Owner: Newsquest. Editor:
Ken Bird; chief reporter: Alex Cameron*

Chard Advertiser
01297 357504
www.chard-today.co.uk
*Weekly free (Weds). Owner: Tindle
Newspapers. Editor: Tony Woodman*

Cheddar Valley Gazette
01749 832300
www.thisissomerset.co.uk
*Weekly (Thu). Owner: Northcliffe
Newspapers. Editor: Philip Welch*

Chew Valley Gazette
01275 332266
www.chewvalleygazette.co.uk
*Monthly (last Fri). Owner: Northcliffe
Newspapers. Editor: Rowland Janes;
features: Anne Collier*

Clevedon Mercury
01275 335142
www.thisissomerset.co.uk
*Weekly (Thu). Owner: Northcliffe
Newspapers. Editor: Carol Deacon;
chief sub: Kevin Lee*

Cornish & Devon Post
01566 772424
*Weekly (Thu). Owner: Tindle
Newspapers. Editor: Geoff Seccombe;
news: Keith Whitford*

Cornish Guardian
01208 78133
www.thisiscornwall.co.uk
*Weekly (Thu). Owner: Northcliffe
Newspapers. Editor: Andy Cooper; news:
Ian Sheppard; chief sub: Anna Witney*

The Cornishman
01736 362247
www.thisiscornwall.co.uk
*Weekly (Thu). Owner: Northcliffe
Newspapers. Editor: Jeremy Ridge;
features: Joyce Channon*

Cornish Times
01579 342174
www.cornwall-today.co.uk
*Weekly (Fri). Owner: Tindle Newspapers.
Editor: John Noble*

Crewkerne Advertiser
01297 631120
www.crewkerne-today.co.uk
*Weekly free (Fri). Owner: Tindle
Newspapers. Editor: Tony Woodman*

Culm, Crediton & Tiverton Gazette
01884 252725
*Weekly (Tue). Owner: Northcliffe
Newspapers. Editor: Richard Best*

Daily Echo
See page 37

Dartmouth Chronicle
01548 856353
www.dartmouth-today.co.uk
*Weekly (Fri). Owner: Tindle Newspapers.
Editor: Gina Coles; chief sub: Lucy
Baker-Kind*

Dawlish Gazette
01626 355566
www.dawlish-today.co.uk
*Weekly (Fri). Owner: Tindle Newspapers.
Editor: Ruth Davey; news: John Belment;
chief sub: Steven Taylor*

Dawlish Post
01626 355566
www.dawlish-today.co.uk
*Weekly (Fri). Owner: Tindle Newspapers.
Editor: Ruth Davey; news: John Belment;
chief sub: Steven Taylor*

Dorchester Advertiser
01305 830930
www.thisisdorset.net
*Weekly (Thu). Owner: Newsquest. Editor:
David Murdock; news: Paul Thomas;
features: Dirmaid Macdonagh; chief sub:
Nick Horton*

Dorset Echo
01305 830930
www.thisisdorset.net
*Weekly (Thu). Owner: Newsquest. Editor:
David Murdock; news: Paul Thomas;
features: Dirmaid Macdonagh*

Exeter Express and Echo
01392 442211
www.thisisexeter.co.uk
*Daily. Owner: Northcliffe Newspapers.
Acting editor: Mark Astley; news: Sue
Kemp; features: Lynne Turner; production:
Jerry Charge*

Exeter Leader
01392 442211
www.thisisexeter.co.uk
*Weekly free (Wed). Owner: Northcliffe
Newspapers. Editor: Mark Astley; news:
Sue Kemp; features: Lynne Turner*

Exmouth Herald
01392 888444
www.exmouthherald.co.uk
*Weekly free (Fri). Owner: Archant.
Chief sub: Phil Griffin*

Falmouth Packet
01326 213333
www.thisisthewestcountry.co.uk
Weekly (Wed). Owner: Newsquest. Editor: Terry Lambert; news: Stephen Ivall

Frome & Somerset Standard
01225 322322
www.thisissomerset.co.uk
Weekly (Thu). Owner: Northcliffe Newspapers. Assistant Editor: Stephanie Feldwicke; News Editor: Chloe Boyce

Frome Times
01225 704761
www.frometimes.co.uk
Fortnightly free (Thu). Editor: Ian Drew; news: Jessica Fox-Taylor

Hayle Times
01736 795813
www.stivesnews.co.uk
Weekly (Fri). Editor: Toni Carver; news: Paul Pocock; features: Tricia Carver

Helston Gazette
01326 213333
www.thisisthewestcountry.co.uk
Weekly (Wed). Owner: Newsquest. Editor: Terry Lambert; news: Stephen Ivall

Holsworthy Post
01566 778220
Weekly (Thu). Owner: Tindle Newspapers. Editor: Keith Whitford

Honiton Advertiser
01297 35750
www.honiton-today.co.uk
Weekly (Wed). Owner: Tindle Newspapers. General manager: Keith Hawkins; editorial manager: Tony Woodman

Ivybridge, South Brent & South Hams Gazette
01548 853101
www.ivybridge-today.co.uk
Weekly (Fri). Owner: Tindle Newspapers. Editor: Gina Coles; chief sub: Steve Harvey

Journal (Exmouth)
01392 888444
www.devon24.co.uk
Weekly (Thu). Owner: Archant. Editor: Phil Griffin

Kingsbridge & Salcombe Gazette
01548 853101
Weekly (Fri). Owner: Tindle Newspapers. Editor: Gina Coles; chief sub: Steve Harvey

Launceston Journal Gazette
01566 772424
Weekly (Fri). Owner: Tindle Newspapers. Editor: Geoff Seccombe; news: Keith Whitford

Liskeard Gazette & Journal
01579 342174
Weekly (Thu). Owner: Tindle Newspapers. Editor: Mary Richards

Mid Cornwall Advertiser
01726 66755
www.cornwalladvertisers.co.uk
Monthly (middle of month). Owner: Tindle Newspapers. Editor: Fiona Jolley

Mid Devon Advertiser
01626 355566
www.newton-abbot-today.co.uk
Weekly (Fri). Owner: Tindle Newspapers. Editor: Ruth Davey; news: John Belment; chief sub: Steven Taylor

Mid Devon Star
01823 365151
www.thisisthewestcountry.co.uk
Weekly (Fri). Owner: Newsquest. Editor-in-chief: Ken Bird; deputy group editor: Bob Drayton

Midweek Herald
01392 888444
www.devon24.co.uk
Weekly (Wed). Owner: Archant. Editor: Peter Le Riche

Newquay Voice
01637 878298
www.newquayvoice.co.uk
Weekly (Wed). Editor: Matt Bond

North Cornwall Advertiser
01208 815096
www.northcornwall-today.co.uk
Monthly free (1st Wed). Owner: Tindle Newspapers. Editor: Tony Gregan

North Devon Gazette & Advertiser
01271 344303
www.northdevongazette.co.uk
Weekly (Wed). Owner: Archant. Editor: David Tanner

North Devon Journal
01271 343064
www.thisisnorthdevon.co.uk
Weekly (Thu). Owner: Northcliffe Newspapers. Managing editor: Andy Cooper; deputy editor: Richard Best; features: Sue Robinson

North Somerset Times
01934 422622
www.thewestonmercury.co.uk
Weekly (Wed). Owner: Archant. Editor: Heather Pickstock; news: Andy Ridgeway

Okehampton Times
01822 613666
www.okehampton-today.co.uk
Weekly (Thu). Owner: Tindle Newspapers. Editor: Colin Brent

Ottery Advertiser
01297 35750
Weekly (Wed). Owner: Tindle Newspapers. General manager: Keith Hawkins; editorial manager: Tony Woodman

Penwith Pirate
01326 213333
www.thisisthewestcountry.co.uk
Weekly free (Wed). Owner: Newsquest. Editor: Terry Lambert; news: Stephen Ivall; chief sub: David Robinson

Plymouth Evening Herald
See page 38

Plymouth Extra
01752 765500
www.thisisplymouth.co.uk
Weekly free (Thu). Owner: Northcliffe Newspapers. Editor: Paul Atkins

Plympton Plymstock & Ivybridge News
01548 853101
Weekly (Fri). Owner: Tindle Newspapers. Editor: Gina Coles

Poole Advertiser
01202 675413
Weekly free (Thu). Owner: Newsquest. Editor: Neal Butterworth; news: Andy Martin; features: Kevin Nash

Post Advertiser
01305 830900
Monthly free (Mon). Owner: Newsquest. Editor: Bob Conway

Princetown Times
01822 613666
www.thisisthewestcountry.co.uk
Weekly (Thu). Owner: Tindle Newspapers. Editor: Colin Brent

St Ives Times & Echo
01736 795813
www.stivesnews.co.uk
Weekly (Fri). Editor: Toni Carver; news: Paul Pocock; features: Tricia Carver

Shepton Mallet Journal
01749 832300
www.thisissomerset.co.uk
Weekly (Thu). Owner: Northcliffe Newspapers. Editor: Philip Welch

Sidmouth Herald
01392 888444
www.archantdevon.co.uk
Weekly (Fri). Owner: Archant. Editor: Emma Silverthorne

Somerset County Gazette
01823 365151
www.thisisthewestcountry.co.uk
Weekly (Thu). Owner: Newsquest. Editor-in-chief: Ken Bird; deputy group editor: Bob Drayton

Somerset Guardian
01225 322322
www.thisissomerset.co.uk
Weekly (Thu). Owner: Northcliffe Newspapers. Editor: Joanne Roughton; features: Aliya Frostick

South Devon & Plymouth Times
01584 856353
www.thisisthewestcountry.co.uk
Weekly (Thu). Owner: Tindle Newspapers. Editor: Gina Coles

Swanage and Wareham District Advertiser
01929 427428
www.thisisdorset.net
Weekly free (Thu). Owner: Newsquest. Editor: Neal Butterworth; news: Eric Randolph

Taunton Star
01823 365151
www.tauntonstar.co.uk
Weekly (Wed). Owner: Newsquest. Editor: Neal Butterworth; deputy group editor: Bob Drayton

Taunton Times
01823 250500
www.thisissomerset.co.uk
Weekly free (Thu). Owner: Northcliffe Newspapers. Editor: Martin Heale

Tavistock Times Gazette
01822 613666
www.tavistock-today.co.uk
Weekly (Thu). Owner: Tindle
Newspapers. Editor: Colin Brent

Teignmouth News
01626 355566
www.teignmouth-today.co.uk
Weekly (Fri). Owner: Tindle Newspapers.
Editor: Ruth Davey; news: John Belment;
chief sub: Steven Taylor

Teignmouth Post & Gazette
01626 355566
www.teignmouth-today.co.uk
Weekly (Fri). Owner: Tindle Newspapers.
Editor: Ruth Davey; news: John Belment;
chief sub: Steven Taylor

Torbay Weekender
01803 676000
www.thisissouthdevon.co.uk
Weekly (Thu). Owner: Northcliffe
Newspapers. Editor: Brendan Hanrahan;
news: Jim Parker; features: Tracy
Gwynne; chief sub: Nigel Lines

Torquay Herald Express
01803 676000
www.thisissouthdevon.co.uk
Weekly (Thu). Owner: Northcliffe
Newspapers. Editor: Brendan Hanrahan;
news: Jim Parker; features: Tracy
Gwynne; chief sub: Nigel Lines

Totnes News
01548 853101
Weekly (Fri). Owner: Tindle Newspapers.
Editor: Gina Coles

Totnes Times Gazette
01584 856353
www.thisisthewestcountry.co.uk
Weekly (Wed). Owner: Tindle
Newspapers. Editor: Gina Coles

Trader News (West Somerset)
01984 632731
Weekly free (Wed). Owner: Northcliffe
Newspapers. Editor: Gareth Purcell

Truro Packet
01326 213333
www.thisisthewestcountry.co.uk
Weekly (Wed). Owner: Newsquest. Editor:
Terry Lambert; news: Stephen Ivall; chief
sub: David Robinson

Wellington Weekly News
01823 250500
www.thisissomerset.co.uk
Weekly (Wed). Owner: Northcliffe
Newspapers. Editor: Debbie Rundle;
news: Steve Weatherill

Wells Journal
01749 832300
www.thisissomerset.co.uk
Weekly (Thu). Owner: Northcliffe
Newspapers. Editor: Philip Welch

The West Briton
01872 271451
www.thisiscornwall.co.uk
Weekly (Thu). Owner: Northcliffe
Newspapers. Editor: Jeremy Ridge

West Somerset Free Press
01984 632731
www.west-somerset-today.co.uk
Weekly (Fri). Owner: Northcliffe
Newspapers. Editor: Gareth Purcell

Western Daily Press (Bristol)
See page 39

Western Gazette
01935 700500
www.westgaz.co.uk
Weekly (Thu). Owner: Northcliffe
Newspapers. Editor: Martin Heal; news:
Zena O'Rourke; features: Carla Gale

Western Morning News (Plymouth)
See page 39

Weston & Worle News
01275 335140
www.thisissomerset.co.uk
Weekly (Thu). Owner: Northcliffe
Newspapers. Editor: Carol Deacon; news:
Juliette Auty; chief sub: Kevin Lee

Weston Mercury
01934 422622
www.thewestonmercury.co.uk
Weekly (Fri). Owner: Archant. Editor:
Judy Kisiel; news: Andy Ridgeway

Weston-super-Mare Admag
01934 422622
www.thewestonmercury.co.uk
Weekly (Wed). Owner: Archant. Editor:
Judy Kisiel; news: Andy Ridgeway

Weymouth & Portland Advertiser
01305 830930
www.thisisdorset.net
Weekly (Thu). Owner: Newsquest. Editor:
David Murdock; news: Paul Thomas;
features: Dirmaid Macdonagh

Yeovil Express
01823 365151
www.thisisthewestcountry.co.uk
Weekly (Thu). Owner: Newsquest. Editor-
in-chief: Ken Bird; deputy group editor:
Bob Drayton

Yeovil Times
01935 700500
Weekly free (Wed). Owner: Northcliffe
Newspapers. Editor: Martin Heal; news:
Zena O'Rourke; features: Carla Gale

● East England

Cambridgeshire, Essex, Lincolnshire,
Norfolk, Suffolk

Alford Standard
01754 897120
www.skegnesstoday.co.uk
Weekly (Wed). Owner: Johnston Press.
Editor: John Coupe

Axholme Herald
01427 874417
Weekly (Wed). Owner: Northcliffe
Newspapers. Editor: Ron Shipley

Barking & Dagenham Post
0845 070 0161
www.bdpost.co.uk
Weekly (Wed). Owner: Archant. Editor:
Barry Kirk; news: Wayne Tuckfield

Barking & Dagenham Recorder
020 8478 4444
www.bdrecorder.co.uk
Weekly (Thu). Owner: Archant.
Editor: Chris Carter

Barking & Dagenham Weekender
0845 070 0161
Weekly (Fri). Owner: Archant. Editor:
Barry Kirk; news: Wayne Tuckfield;
chief sub: Graham Whitmore

Barking & Dagenham Yellow
Advertiser
01268 503400
www.trinitymirrorsouthern.co.uk
Weekly (Thu). Owner: Trinity Mirror
Southern

Basildon & Wickford Recorder
01268 522792
www.thisisessex.co.uk
Daily. Owner: Newsquest. Editor: Martin
McNeill; news: Chris Hatton; chief sub:
Neal Reeve

Basildon Yellow Advertiser
01268 503400
www.icessex.co.uk
Weekly (Thu). Owner: Trinity Mirror
Southern. Features: Liz Wade

Beccles & Bungay Journal
01603 628311
www.edp24.co.uk
Weekly (Fri). Owner: Archant.
Editor: Terry Redhead

Billericay & Wickford Gazette
01277 219222
www.thisisessex.co.uk
Weekly (Wed). Owner: Northcliffe
Newspapers. Editor: Mat Holder;
news: Sheelagh Bree

Boston Citizen
01205 311433
www.bostontoday.co.uk
Weekly (Fri). Owner: Johnston Press.
Editor: Julia Ogden; news: Pam Browne;
chief sub: Warren Moody

Boston Standard
01205 311433
www.bostontoday.co.uk
Weekly (Wed). Owner: Johnston Press.
Editor: Julia Ogden; news: Pam Browne;
chief sub: Warren Moody

Boston Target
01522 820000
www.thisislincolnshire.co.uk
*Weekly (Wed). Owner: Northcliffe
Newspapers. Editor: Glyn Belsher*

Braintree & Witham Times
01376 343344
www.thisisessex.co.uk
*Weekly (Thu). Owner: Newsquest.
Editor: Ainsley Davidson*

Braintree Chronicle
01245 600700
www.thisisessex.co.uk
*Weekly (Wed/Thu). Owner: Northcliffe
Newspapers. Editor: Stuart Rawlins;
news: Matt Adams; features: Darryl
Webber*

**Brentwood, Billericay &
Havering Recorder**
01708 771500
www.romfordrecorder.co.uk
*Weekly (Fri). Owner: Archant. Editor:
Mark Sweetingham; news: Eden Black*

Brentwood Gazette
01277 219222
www.thisisessex.co.uk
*Weekly (Wed). Owner: Northcliffe
Newspapers. Editor: Mat Holder;
news: Sheelagh Bree*

Brentwood Weekly News
01268 522792
www.thisisessex.co.uk
*Weekly (Thu). Owner: Newsquest. Editor:
Martin McNeill; news: Chris Hatton;
chief sub: Neal Reeve*

Brentwood Yellow Advertiser
01268 503400
www.trinitymirrorsouthern.co.uk
*Weekly (Thu). Owner: Trinity Mirror
Southern. Features: Liz Wade*

Bury Free Press
01284 768911
www.buryfreepress.co.uk
*Weekly (Fri). Owner: Johnston Press.
Editor: Barry Peters; news: Lesley
Anslow; features: Sue Green*

Bury St Edmunds Citizen
01284 768911
*Weekly (Fri). Owner: Johnston Press.
Editor: Barry Peters; news: Lesley
Anslow; features: Sue Green*

Bury St Edmunds Mercury
01284 702588
www.edp24.co.uk
*Weekly (Fri). Owner: Archant.Editor:
Paul Couch; news: Will Grahame-Clarke*

Cambridge Crier
01223 434434
www.cambridge-news.co.uk
*Weekly (Fri). Owner: Cambridge
Newspapers. Editor: Nigel Brookes;
features: James Fuller*

Cambridge Evening News
01223 434434
www.cambridge-news.co.uk
*Daily. Owner: Cambridge Newspapers.
Editor: Murray Morse; news: John Deex;
features: Paul Kirkley*

Cambridge Weekly News
01223 434434
www.cambridge-news.co.uk
*Weekly (Wed). Owner: Cambridge
Newspapers. Editor: Nigel Brookes*

Cambridgeshire Times
01354 652621
*Weekly. Owner: Archant. Editor: Brian
Asplin; news: John Elworthy; features:
Maggie Gibson*

Castle Point Yellow Advertiser
01268 503400
www.trinitymirrorsouthern.co.uk
*Weekly (Thu). Owner: Trinity Mirror
Southern*

Castlepoint & Rayleigh Standard
01268 522792
www.thisisessex.co.uk
*Weekly (Wed). Owner: Newsquest. Editor:
Martin McNeill; news: Chris Hatton; chief
sub: Neal Reeve*

Chatteris Times
01354 652621
www.cambs-times.co.uk
*Weekly (Thu). Owner: Archant. Editor:
Brian Asplin; news: John Elworthy;
features: Maggie Gibson*

Chelmsford Chronicle
01245 600700
www.thisisessex.co.uk
*Weekly (Wed, Thu). Owner: Northcliffe
Newspapers. Editor: Stuart Rawlins; news:
Matt Adams; features: Darryl Webber*

Chelmsford Weekly News
01245 493444
www.thisisessex.co.uk
*Weekly (Thu). Owner: Newsquest. Editor:
Chris Richards; news: Denise Rigby*

Chelmsford Yellow Advertiser
01268 503400
www.trinitymirrorsouthern.co.uk
*Weekly (Thu). Owner: Trinity Mirror
Southern*

Clacton & Frinton Gazette
01255 221221
www.thisisessex.co.uk
*Weekly (Thu). Owner: Newsquest.
Chief sub: Nigel Brown*

Colchester Evening Gazette
01206 506000
www.nqe.info
*Daily. Owner: Newsquest. Editor-in-chief:
Irene Kettle; news: Sally Teatheredge;
features: Iris Clapp, chief sub: Will
Bramhill*

Dereham & Fakenham Times
01603 628311
www.edp24.co.uk
*Weekly (Thu). Owner: Archant.
Editor: Terry Redhead*

Diss Express
01379 642264
www.dissexpress.co.uk
*Weekly (Fri). Owner: Johnston Press.
Editor: Stephen Penny*

Diss Mercury
01603 628311
www.edp24.co.uk
*Weekly (Fri). Owner: Archant.
Editor: Terry Redhead*

Dunmow & Stansted Chronicle
01245 600700
www.thisisessex.co.uk
*Weekly (Wed/Thu). Owner: Northcliffe
Newspapers. Editor: Stuart Rawlins;
news: Matt Adams; features: Darryl
Webber*

Dunmow Broadcast and Recorder
01371 874537
www.dunmow-broadcast.co.uk
*Weekly free (Thu). Owner: Archant.
Editor: Barry Hunt; reporter: Jenny
Oliveira*

Dunmow Observer
01279 866355
www.herts-essex-news.co.uk
*Weekly (Thu). Owner: Herts & Essex
Newspapers. Editor: Val Brown; news:
Sandra Perry*

East Anglian Daily Times
See page 38

East Herts Herald
01279 624331
www.herald24.co.uk
*Weekly (Thu). Owner: Archant. Editor:
Barry Hunt; news: Tracey Hubbard*

Eastern Daily Press
See page 38

Ely Standard
01353 667831
www.ely-standard.co.uk
*Weekly free (Thu). Owner: Archant.
Editor: Debbie Davies; news: Leslie Innes*

**Epping & Waltham Yellow
Advertiser**
01268 503400
www.trinitymirrorsouthern.co.uk
*Weekly free (Fri). Owner: Trinity Mirror
Southern*

Epping Guardian
01992 572285
www.eppingguardian.co.uk
*Weekly (Thu). Owner: Newsquest.
Editor: David Jackman*

Epping Independent
020 8498 3400
www.newsquest.co.uk
*Weekly (Fri). Owner: Newsquest.
Editor: David Jackman*

Epworth Bells & Crowle Advertiser
01427 872202
www.epworthtoday.co.uk
*Weekly (Thu). Owner: Johnston Press.
Editor: Janet Harrison*

Essex Chronicle
01245 600700
www.thisisessex.co.uk
*Weekly (Wed/Thu). Owner: Northcliffe
Newspapers. Editor: Stuart Rawlins;
news: Matt Adams; features: Darryl
Webber*

Essex County Standard
01206 506000
www.nqe.info
*Weekly (Fri). Owner: Newsquest.
Editor: Irene Kettle; features: Iris Clapp;
chief sub: Will Bramhill*

Essex Enquirer
01277 627300
www.theenquirer.co.uk
Weekly (Thu). Editor: Carol Driver

Evening Echo (Essex)
01268 522792
www.thisisessex.co.uk
Daily. Owner: Newsquest. Editor: Martin McNeill; news: Chris Hatton; chief sub: Neal Reeve

Evening News (Norwich)
01603 628311
www.eveningnews24.co.uk
Daily. Owner: Archant. Editor: David Bourn

Evening Star (Ipswich)
01473 324788
www.eveningstar.co.uk
Daily. Owner: Archant. Editor: Nigel Pickover; news: Martin Davey; features: Tracy Sparling

Fenland Citizen
01945 586100
www.fenlandtoday.co.uk
Weekly (Wed). Owner: Johnston Press. Editor: Keith Drayton

Gainsborough Standard
01427 615323
www.gainsboroughtoday.co.uk
Weekly (Thu). Owner: Johnston Press. Editor: Janet Harrison

Gainsborough Target
01522 820000
www.thisislincolnshire.co.uk
Weekly (Fri). Owner: Northcliffe Newspapers. Editor: Jon Grubb

Goole Courier
01405 782400
www.gooletoday.co.uk
Weekly (Thu). Owner: Johnston Press. Editor: Janet Harrison; news: Stephanie Bateman

Goole Times/Selby Post
01405 720110
www.gooletimes.co.uk
Weekly (Thu). Owner: Northcliffe Newspapers. Editor: Peter Butler

Grantham Citizen
01476 562291
www.granthamtoday.co.uk
Weekly (Tue). Owner: Johnston Press. Editor: Tim Robinson; news: John Pinchbeck

Grantham Journal
01476 562291
www.granthamtoday.co.uk
Weekly (Tue). Owner: Johnston Press. Editor: Tim Robinson; news: John Pinchbeck

Great Yarmouth & Gorleston Advertiser
01493 601206
www.advertiser-online.co.uk
Weekly (Thu). Owner: Archant. Editor: Anne Edwards

Great Yarmouth Mercury
01603 628311
www.edp24.co.uk
Weekly (Tue). Owner: Archant. Editor: Terry Redhead

Grimsby Evening Telegraph
01472 360360
www.thisisgrimsby.co.uk
Daily. Owner: Northcliffe Newspapers. Editor: Michelle Lalor; news: Lucy Wood; features: Barrie Farnsworth

Grimsby Target
01472 360360
www.thisisgrimsby.co.uk
Daily. Owner: Northcliffe Newspapers. Editor: Michelle Lalor; news: Lucy Wood; features: Barrie Farnsworth

Halstead Gazette
01376 343344
www.thisisessex.co.uk
Weekly (Fri). Owner: Newsquest. Editor: Ainsley Davidson

Harlow Herald
01279 624331
www.herald24.co.uk
Weekly (Thu). Owner: Archant. Editor: Barry Hunt; news: Tracey Hubbard

Harlow Star
01279 838111
www.herts-essex-news.co.uk
Weekly (Thu). Owner: Herts & Essex Newspapers. Editor: Barry Hunt; news: Mark Fletcher

Harold Gazette
01277 219222
www.thisisessex.co.uk
Weekly (Wed). Owner: Northcliffe Newspapers. Editor: Roger Watkins; news: Sheelagh Bree; features: Josie Stephenson

Harold Recorder
01708 771500
www.recorderonline.co.uk
Weekly (Fri). Owner: Archant. Editor: Mark Sweetingham; news: Eden Black

Haverhill Echo
01440 703456
www.haverhilltoday.co.uk
Weekly (Thu). Owner: Johnston Press. News editor: David Hart

Haverhill Weekly News
01223 434434
www.cambridge-news.co.uk
Weekly (Thu). Owner: Cambridge Newspapers. Editor: Nigel Brookes

Havering Herald
0845 070 0161
Weekly free (Fri). Owner: Archant. Editor: Richard Thompson

Havering Yellow Advertiser
01268 503400
www.trinitymirrorsouthern.co.uk
Weekly (Wed). Owner: Trinity Mirror Southern

Horncastle News
01507 353200
www.horncastletoday.co.uk
Weekly (Wed). Owner: Johnston Press. Managing editor: Tim Robinson

Huntingdon Town Crier
01480 402100
www.cambridge-news.co.uk
Weekly (Thu). Owner: Johnston Press. Editor: Richard Yetman

Huntingdon Weekly News
01223 434434
www.cambridge-news.co.uk
Weekly (Wed). Owner: Newsquest. Editor: Murray Morse; news: John Deex

Hunts Post
01480 411481
www.huntspost.co.uk
Weekly (Wed). Owner: Archant. Editor: Andy Veale; deputy editor: Angela Singer

Ilford & Redbridge Post
0845 070 0161
Weekly free (Wed). Owner: Archant. Editor: Wayne Tuckfield; chief sub: Graham Whitmore

Ipswich Advertiser
01473 324700
www.ipswichadvertiser.co.uk
Weekly (Thu). Owner: Archant. Editor: Paul Couch

Island Times (Canvey Island)
01702 477666
Monthly (Tue). Owner: Archant. Editor: Michael Guy

Leigh Times
01702 477666
Fortnightly (Tue). Owner: Archant. Editor: Michael Guy

Lincoln Target
01522 820000
www.thisislincolnshire.co.uk
Weekly (Wed). Owner: Northcliffe Newspapers. Editor: Jon Grubb

Lincolnshire Echo
01522 820000
www.thisislincolnshire.co.uk
Daily. Owner: Northcliffe Newspapers. Editor: Jon Grubb

Lincolnshire Free Press
01775 725021
www.spaldingtoday.co.uk
Weekly (Tue). Owner: Johnston Press. Editor: Nick Woodhead; news: David Crossley; features: Julie Williams; chief sub: Tracey Vale

The Local (Bourne)
01778 425876
Weekly (Fri). Owner: Johnston Press. Editor: Lisa Bruen

Loughton, Chigwell & Buckhurst Hill Guardian
01992 572285
www.eppingguardian.co.uk
Weekly (Thu). Owner: Newsquest. Editor: David Jackman

Louth Citizen
01507 353200
www.louthtoday.co.uk
Weekly (Fri). Owner: Johnston Press. Managing editor: Tim Robinson; editor: Charles Ladbrooke

Louth Leader
01507 353200
www.louthtoday.co.uk
Weekly (Wed). Owner: Johnston Press. Managing editor: Tim Robinson; editor: Charles Ladbrooke

Lowestoft Journal
01603 628311
www.edp24.co.uk
Weekly (Fri). Owner: Archant. Editor: Terry Redhead

Lynn News
01553 761188
www.lynnnews.co.uk
*Weekly (Tue, Fri). Owner: Johnston Press.
Editor: Malcolm Powell; news: Donna
Semmens*

Maldon & Burnham Chronicle
01245 600700
www.thisisessex.co.uk
*Weekly (Wed/Thu). Owner: Northcliffe
Newspapers. Editor: Stuart Rawlins;
news: Matt Adams; features: Darryl
Webber*

Maldon & Burnham Standard
01621 852233
*Weekly (Thu). Owner: Newsquest.
Editor: Neil Thomas*

Market Rasen Mail
01507 353200
www.marketrasentoday.co.uk
*Weekly (Wed). Owner: Johnston Press.
Managing editor: Tim Robinson;
editor: Jason Hipsley*

Newmarket Journal
01638 564104
www.newmarketjournal.co.uk
*Weekly (Thu). Owner: Johnston Press.
Assistant editor: Alison Hayes*

Newmarket Weekly News
01223 434434
www.cambridge-news.co.uk
*Weekly (Thu). Owner: Cambridge
Newspapers. Editor: Nigel Brookes*

Norfolk Citizen
01553 761188
*Weekly (Fri). Owner: Johnston Press.
Editor: Chris Hornby*

Norfolk North Advertiser
01603 772487
www.advertiser24.co.uk
*Weekly (Fri). Owner:Archant.
Editor: Terry Redhead*

North Essex Advertiser
01473 324700
www.advertiser-online.co.uk
*Weekly (Fri). Owner: Archant. Editor:
Paul Couch; news: Nicola Durrant*

**North Norfolk & Broadland Town
& Country News**
01692 582287
*Monthly (Fri nearest 1st).
Editor: Lawrence Watts*

North Norfolk News
01603 628311
www.edp24.co.uk
*Weekly (Thu). Owner: Archant.
Editor: Terry Redhead*

Norwich Advertiser
01603 772487
www.advertiser24.co.uk
*Weekly (Fri). Owner:Archant.
Editor: Terry Redhead*

Ongar & North Weald Gazette
01277 219222
www.thisisessex.co.uk
*Weekly (Wed). Owner: Northcliffe
Newspapers. Editor: Roger Watkins; news:
Sheelagh Bree; features: Josie Stephenson*

Ongar Guardian
01992 572285
www.eppingguardian.co.uk
*Weekly (Thu). Owner: Newsquest.
Editor: David Jackman*

Peterborough Citizen
01733 555111
www.peterboroughnow.co.uk
*Weekly (Wed). Owner: Johnston Press.
Editor: Rebecca Stephens; news: Rebecca
Goding; features: Rachel Gordon;
production: Brad Barnes*

Peterborough Evening Telegraph
01733 555111
www.peterboroughnow.co.uk
*Daily. Owner: Johnston Press Editor:
Rebecca Stephens; news: Rebecca Goding;
features: Rachel Gordon; production:
Brad Barnes*

Peterborough Herald & Post
01733 318600
www.peterborough.net
   /heraldandpost
*Weekly (Thu). Owner: Midlands Weekly
Media (Trinity Mirror). Editor: Steve
Rose; features: Amanda Franklin*

Ramsey Post
01480 411481
*Weekly (Thu). Owner: Archant.
Editor: Paul Richardson; deputy editor:
Angela Singer*

Rayleigh Times
01702 477666
*Monthly. Owner: Archant.
Editor: Michael Guy*

Redbridge Yellow Advertiser
01268 503400
www.trinitymirrorsouthern.co.uk
*Weekly (Thu). Owner: Trinity Mirror
Southern*

**Redbridge, Waltham Forest &
West Essex Guardian**
020 8498 3400
www.newsquest.co.uk
*Weekly (Thu). Owner: Newsquest.
Editor: Pat Stannard*

Romford & Havering Post
0845 070 0161
www.haveringpost.co.uk
*Weekly free (Wed). Owner: Archant.
Editorial director: Richard Thompson;
editor: Amanda Patterson*

Romford Recorder
01708 771500
www.recorderonline.co.uk
*Weekly (Fri). Owner: Archant. Editor:
Mark Sweetingham; news: Eden Black*

Royston Weekly News
01223 434434
www.cambridge-news.co.uk
*Weekly (Thu). Owner: Cambridge
Newspapers. Editor: Nigel Brookes*

Rutland & Stamford Mercury
01780 762255
www.stamfordtoday.co.uk
*Weekly (Fri). Owner: Johnston Press.
Editor: Eileen Green; news: Suzanne Moon*

Saffron Walden Observer
01279 866355
www.herts-essex-news.co.uk
*Weekly (Thu). Owner: Herts & Essex
Newspapers. Editor: Val Brown; news:
Sandra Perry*

Saffron Walden Weekly News
01223 434434
www.cambridge-news.co.uk
*Weekly (Thu). Owner: Cambridge
Newspapers. Editor: Nigel Brookes*

**Saffron Walden, Stansted &
Sawston Reporter**
01799 525100
www.thisisessex.co.uk
*Weekly (Thu). Owner: Archant.
Editor: Barry Hunt*

St Ives Town Crier
01480 402100
www.stivestoday.co.uk
*Weekly (Thu). Owner: Johnston Press.
Editor: Richard Yetman*

St Ives Weekly News
01223 434434
www.cambridge-news.co.uk
*Weekly (Thu). Owner: Cambridge
Newspapers. Editor: Murray Morse*

St Neots Town Crier
01480 402100
www.stneotstoday.co.uk
*Weekly (Thu). Owner: Johnston Press.
Editor: Richard Yetman*

St Neots Weekly News
01223 434434
www.cambridge-news.co.uk
*Weekly (Wed). Owner: Newsquest.
Editor: Murray Morse*

Scunthorpe Target
01724 273273
www.thisisscunthorpe.co.uk
*Weekly (Thu). Owner: Northcliffe
Newspapers. Editor: Jane Manning;
chief sub: John Curtis*

Scunthorpe Telegraph
01724 273273
www.thisisscunthorpe.co.uk
*Daily. Owner: Northcliffe Newspapers.
Editor: Jane Manning; chief sub:
John Curtis*

Skegness Citizen
01507 353200
*Weekly (Fri). Owner: Johnston Press.
Managing editor: Tim Robinson;
editor: John Cowpe*

Skegness Standard
01507 353200
www.skegnesstoday.co.uk
*Weekly (Wed). Owner: Johnston Press.
Managing editor: Tim Robinson;
editor: John Cowpe*

Skegness Target
01205 315000
*Weekly (Wed). Owner: Northcliffe
Newspapers. Editor: Glyn Belsher*

Sleaford Citizen
01529 413646
*Weekly (Fri). Owner: Johnston Press.
Editor: John Lavery; news: Andy Hubbert*

Sleaford Standard
01529 413646
Weekly (Wed). Owner: Johnston Press.
Editor: John Lavery; news: Andy Hubbert

Sleaford Target
01522 820000
www.thisislincolnshire.co.uk
Weekly (Wed). Owner: Northcliffe
Newspapers. Editor: Glyn Belsher

South Woodham & Maldon Weekly News
01621 852233
www.thisisessex.co.uk
Weekly (Thu). Owner: Newsquest.
Editor: Neil Thomas

Southend Standard
01268 522792
www.thisisessex.co.uk
Weekly (Thu). Owner: Newsquest. Editor:
Martin McNeill; news: Chris Hatton;
chief sub: Neal Reeve

Southend Times
01702 477666
Weekly (Tue). Owner: Archant.
Editor: Michael Guy

Southend Yellow Advertiser
01268 503400
www.trinitymirrorsouthern.co.uk
Weekly free (Thu). Owner: Trinity Mirror
Southern

Spalding Guardian
01775 725021
www.spaldingtoday.co.uk
Weekly (Thu). Owner: Johnston Press.
Editor: Nick Woodhead; news: David
Crossley; features: Julie Williams;
chief sub: Tracey Vale

Spalding Herald
01775 713723
www.spaldingherald.co.uk
Monthly free (1st of month).
Editor: Natalie Ward

Spilsby Standard
01754 897120
www.skegnesstoday.co.uk
Weekly (Wed). Owner: Johnston Press.
Editor: John Cowpe

Spilsby Target
01205 315000
Weekly (Wed). Owner: Northcliffe
Newspapers. Editor: Glyn Belsher

Stamford Citizen
01780 762255
www.stamfordmercury.co.uk
Weekly free (Tue). Owner: Johnston Press.
Editor: Eileen Green; news: Suzanne Moon

Stamford Herald & Post
01733 318600
Weekly (Thu). Owner: Midlands Weekly
Media (Trinity Mirror). Editor: Steve
Rose; features: Amanda Franklin

Stansted Observer
01279 866355
www.herts-essex-news.co.uk
Weekly (Thu). Owner: Herts & Essex
Newspapers. Editor: Val Brown;
news: Sandra Perry

Sudbury Mercury
01284 702588
www.edp24.co.uk
Weekly (Fri). Owner: Archant. Editor:
Paul Couch; reporter: Will Wright

Suffolk Advertiser
01473 324700
www.advertiser24.co.uk
Weekly (Fri). Owner: Archant. Editor:
Paul Couch; news: Nicola Durrant

Suffolk Free Press
01787 375271
www.sudburytoday.co.uk
Weekly free (Thu). Owner: Johnston
Press. Editor: Mark Crossley; news:
Nick Wells

Swaffham Mercury
01603 628311
www.edp24.co.uk
Monthly. Owner: Archant. Editor: Terry
Redhead

Swaffham News
01553 761188
Weekly (Fri). Owner: Johnston Press.
Editor: Malcolm Powell; news: Donna
Semmens

Tendring Weekly News
01206 506000
www.thisisessex.co.uk
Weekly free (Wed). Owner: Newsquest.
Editor-in-chief: Irene Kettle; news:
Sally Teatheredge

Thetford & Brandon Times
01603 628311
www.edp24.co.uk
Weekly (Wed). Owner: Archant.
Editor: Terry Redhead

Thetford Citizen
01284 768911
www.burystedmundstoday.co.uk
Weekly. Owner: Johnston Press.
Editor: Barry Peters; news: Lesley
Anslow; features: Sue Green

Thurrock Gazette
01375 411502
www.thisisessex.co.uk
Weekly free (Fri). Owner: Newsquest.
Editor: Neil Speight

Thurrock, Lakeside & Grays Post
0845 070 0161
Weekly (Thu). Owner: Archant. Editor:
Barry Kirk; news: Wayne Tuckfield;
chief sub: Graham Whitmore

Thurrock Recorder
01708 771500
www.romfordrecorder.co.uk
Weekly (Fri). Owner: Archant. Editor:
Mark Sweetingham; news: Eden Black

Thurrock Yellow Advertiser
01268 503400
www.trinitymirrorsouthern.co.uk
Weekly free (Thu). Owner: Trinity Mirror
Southern

Walden Local
01799 516161
www.thisisessex.co.uk
Weekly (Wed). Editor: John Brooker

Waltham Forest Guardian
020 8498 3400
www.newsquest.co.uk
Weekly (Thu). Owner: Newsquest.
Editor: Pat Stannard

Waltham Forest Independent
020 8498 3400
www.newsquest.co.uk
Weekly (Fri). Owner: Newsquest.
Editor: Pat Stannard

Watton & Swaffham Times
01603 628311
www.edp24.co.uk
Weekly (Fri). Owner: Archant.
Editor: Terry Redhead

Waveney Advertiser
01493 601206
www.advertiser-online.co.uk
Weekly (Fri). Owner: Archant.
Managing editor: Anne Edwards

Whittlesey Times
01354 652621
www.cambs-times.co.uk
Weekly (Fri). Owner: Archant. Editor:
Brian Asplin; news: John Elworthy;
features: Maggie Gibson

Wisbech Standard
01354 652621
www.wisbech-standard.co.uk
Weekly (Thu). Owner: Archant. Editor:
Brian Asplin; news: John Elworthy;
features: Maggie Gibson

Witham Chronicle
01245 600700
www.thisisessex.co.uk
Weekly (Wed/Thu). Owner: Northcliffe
Newspapers. Editor: Stuart Rawlins;
news: Matt Adams; features: Darryl
Webber

Woodham Chronicle
01245 600700
www.thisisessex.co.uk
Weekly (Wed/Thu). Owner: Northcliffe
Newspapers. Editor: Stuart Rawlins;
news: Matt Adams; features: Darryl
Webber

Wymondham & Attleborough Mercury
01603 628311
www.edp24.co.uk
Weekly (Fri). Owner: Archant.
Editor: Terry Redhead

● Midlands

Derbyshire, Leicestershire,
Northamptonshire, Nottinghamshire,
Staffordshire

The Advertiser (Staffordshire)
01782 602525
www.thisisthesentinel.co.uk
*Weekly free (Thu). Owner: Northcliffe
Newspapers. Editor: Mike Sassi; news:
Robert Cotterill; features: Charlotte
Little-Jones*

Alfreton & Ripley Echo
01773 834731
www.derbyshiretoday.com
*Weekly (Fri). Owner: Johnston Press.
Editor: David Hopkinson*

Alfreton Chad
01623 456789
www.johnstonpress.co.uk
/yorkshire.asp
*Weekly (Fri). Owner: Johnston Press.
Editor: Jeremy Plews; news: Joy
Thompson; chief sub: Karen Robinson*

Ashbourne News Telegraph
01283 512345
www.ashbournenewstelegraph.co.uk
*Weekly (Wed). Owner: Staffordshire
Newspapers. Editor: Paul Hazeldine;
news: Steve Doohan; features: Bill
Pritchard; production: Diane Finn*

Ashby & Coalville Mail
0116 251 2512
www.thisisleicestershire.co.uk
*Weekly (Tue). Owner: Northcliffe
Newspapers. Editor: Nick Carter; news:
Mark Charlton; features: Alex Dawson*

Ashby Times
01530 813101
*Weekly (Fri). Owner: Trident Midland
Newspapers. News editor: Robin Flingsby*

Ashfield Chad
01623 456789
www.ashfieldtoday.co.uk
*Weekly (Wed). Owner: Johnston Press.
Editor: Jeremy Plews; news: Joy
Thompson; chief sub: Karen Robinson*

Atherstone Herald
01827 848535
*Weekly (Thu). Owner: Northcliffe
Newspapers. Editor: Sam Holliday*

Belper Express
01332 291111
*Weekly free (Tue). Owner: Northcliffe
Newspapers. Editor: Andy Machin*

Belper News
01629 762120
www.matlocktoday.co.uk
*Weekly (Wed). Owner: Johnston Press.
Editor: Amanda Hatfield; news: Helen
Taylor*

Biddulph Advertiser
01260 281012
www.thisisthesentinel.co.uk
*Weekly (Thu). Owner: Northcliffe
Newspapers. Editor: Paul Dutton*

Biddulph Chronicle
01260 273737
www.chronicleseries.com
Weekly (Fri). Editor: Jeremy Condliffe

Birstall Post
0116 267 4213
www.birstallpost.co.uk
*Monthly free (1st of month). Owner: The
Birstall Post Society. Editor: Jerry Jackson*

Bolsover & District Advertiser
01246 202291
www.chesterfieldtoday.co.uk
*Fortnightly free (Wed). Owner: Johnston
Press. Editor: Mike Wilson; assistant
editor: Phil Bramley; news: Tracy
Mitchell; assistant news editor: Sean Boyle*

Brackley Post
01604 614600
www.midlandweeklymedia.co.uk
*Weekly (Fri). Owner: Midlands Weekly
Media (Trinity Mirror). Editor: Richard
Howarth; production: Julie Fisher*

Burntwood Mercury
01827 848535
*Weekly (Thu). Owner: Northcliffe
Newspapers. Editor: Sam Holliday*

Burton & South Derbyshire Advertiser
01283 512345
www.uttoxeteradvertiser.co.uk
*Weekly (Wed). Owner: Staffordshire
Newspapers. Editor: Paul Hazeldine;
news: Steve Doohan; features: Bill
Pritchard; production: Diane Finn*

Burton Mail
01283 512345
www.burtonmail.co.uk
*Daily. Owner: Staffordshire Newspapers.
Editor: Paul Hazeldine; news: Steve
Doohan; features: Bill Pritchard;
production: Diane Finn*

Burton Trader
01283 512200
*Weekly (Wed). Owner: Midlands Weekly
Media (Trinity Mirror). Editor: Pam
Thomas; news: Paul Henshall; chief sub:
Alan Payne*

Buxton Advertiser
01298 767070
www.buxtontoday.co.uk
*Weekly (Thu). Owner: Johnston Press.
Editor: John Phillips; chief reporter:
Emma Downes; subeditor: Alan Charnley*

Buxton Times
01298 767070
www.buxtontoday.co.uk
*Weekly free (Fri). Owner: Johnston Press.
Editor: John Phillips; chief reporter:
Emma Downes; subeditor: Alan Charnley*

Cannock & Rugeley Chronicle
01543 506311
www.expressandstar.com/chronicle
*Weekly (Fri). Owner: Midland News
Association. Editor: Mark Ship*

Cannock & Rugeley Mercury
01827 848535
*Weekly (Thu). Owner: Northcliffe
Newspapers. Editor: Linda Young*

Cannock Chase & Burntwood Post
01543 501700
*Weekly (Thu). Owner: Midlands Weekly
Media (Trinity Mirror). Editor: Mike
Lockley*

Cheadle & Tean Times
01538 753162
Weekly (Wed). Editor: Nigel Titterton

Cheadle Post & Times
01538 750011
www.staffordshiresentinel.co.uk
*Weekly (Wed). Owner: Northcliffe
Newspapers. Editor: Doug Pickford*

Chesterfield Advertiser
01246 202291
www.chesterfieldtoday.co.uk
*Weekly free (Fri). Owner: Johnston Press.
Editor: Mike Wilson; assistant editor: Phil
Bramley; news: Tracy Mitchell; assistant
news editor: Sean Boyle*

Chesterfield Express
01246 504500
*Weekly free (Wed). Owner: Johnston
Press. Editor: Mike Wilson; assistant
editor: Phil Bramley; news: Tracy
Mitchell; assistant news editor: Sean Boyle*

Chronicle and Echo (Northampton)
01604 467000
www.northantsnews.com
*Daily. Owner: Johnston Press. Editor:
Mark Edwards; news: Richard
Edmondson; production: Graham Tebbutt*

Coalville & Ashby Echo
01509 635807
*Weekly (Tue). Owner: Midlands Weekly
Media (Trinity Mirror). Editor: Pete
Warrington*

Coalville Times
01530 813101
*Weekly (Fri). Owner: Trident Midland
Newspapers. Editor: Nick Hudson*

Coleshill Herald
01827 848535
www.tamworthherald.co.uk
*Weekly (Thu). Owner: Northcliffe
Newspapers. Editor: Sam Holliday*

Corby Citizen
01536 506100
www.northantsnews.com
*Weekly (Thu). Owner: Johnston Press.
Acting deputy editor: Mark Edwards;
acting news editor: Kristy Ward; features:
Joni Ager; chief sub: Kathryn Dunn*

Corby Herald & Post
01604 614600
www.midlandweeklymedia.co.uk
*Weekly (Thu). Owner: Midlands Weekly
Media (Trinity Mirror). Editor: Richard
Howarth; production: Julie Fisher*

Daventry Express
01327 703383
www.daventrytoday.co.uk
*Weekly (Thu). Owner: Johnston Press.
Editor: Jason Gibbons; news: Chris
Livington*

Derby Evening Telegraph
See page 38

Derby Express
01332 291111
*Weekly free (Tue). Owner: Northcliffe
Newspapers. Editor: Andy Machin*

Derby Trader
01332 253999
*Weekly (Thu). Owner: Midlands Weekly
Media (Trinity Mirror). Editor: Patrick
O'Connor; features: Steve Eyley; chief
sub: Richard Taylor*

Derbyshire Times
01246 504500
www.derbyshiretimes.co.uk
*Weekly (Thu). Owner: Johnston Press.
Editor: Mike Wilson; assistant editor: Phil
Bramley; news: Tracy Mitchell; assistant
news editor: Sean Boyle*

Dronfield Advertiser
01246 202291
www.chesterfieldtoday.co.uk
*Weekly free (Wed). Owner: Johnston
Press. Editor: Mike Wilson; assistant
editor: Phil Bramley; news: Tracy
Mitchell; assistant news editor: Sean Boyle*

Dukeries Advertiser
01636 681234
*Weekly (Fri). Editor: Harry Whitehouse;
news: Lucy Millard; chief sub: Chris Prine*

Eastwood & Kimberley Advertiser
01773 537850
www.eastwoodtoday.co.uk
*Weekly (Fri). Owner: Johnston Press.
Editor: John Shawcroft*

Eckington Leader
01246 437310
*Weekly (Fri). Owner: Johnston Press.
Editor: Mike Wilson; assistant editor: Phil
Bramley; news: Tracy Mitchell; assistant
news editor: Sean Boyle*

The Evening Telegraph (Northants)
01536 506100
www.northantsnews.com
*Daily. Owner: Johnston Press. Acting
deputy editor: Mark Edwards; acting
news editor: Kristy Ward; features: Joni
Ager; chief sub: Kathryn Dunn*

Glossop Chronicle
0161 304 7691
www.tamesidereporter.com
*Weekly (Thu). Owner: Ashton Weekly
Newspapers. Editor: Nigel Skinner*

Harborough Mail
01858 462626
www.harboroughtoday.co.uk
*Weekly (Thu). Owner: Johnston Press.
Editor: Brian Dodds; news: Maria
Thompson*

High Peak Courier
01298 22118
www.buxtontoday.co.uk
*Weekly free (Fri). Owner: Johnston Press.
Editor: John Phillips; chief reporter:
Emma Downes; subeditor: Alan Charnley*

Hinckley Herald & Journal
01455 891981
www.hinckley-times.co.uk
*Weekly (Wed). Owner: Coventry
Newspapers (Trinity Mirror).
Editor: Andrew Punchon*

Hinckley Times
01455 891981
www.hinckley-times.co.uk
*Weekly (Thu). Owner: Coventry
Newspapers (Trinity Mirror).
Editor: Andrew Punchon*

Hucknall & Bulwell Dispatch
01623 456789
www.hucknalltoday.co.uk
*Weekly (Fri). Owner: Johnston Press.
Editor: Richard Silverwood*

Ilkeston & Ripley Trader
01332 253999
*Weekly (Fri). Owner: Midlands Weekly
Media (Trinity Mirror). Editor: Patrick
O'Connor; features: Steve Eyley; chief
sub: Richard Taylor*

Ilkeston Advertiser
0115 944 6160
www.ilkestontoday.co.uk
*Weekly (Thu). Owner: Johnston Press.
Editor: David Horne*

Ilkeston Express
01332 291111
*Weekly free (Tue). Owner: Northcliffe
Newspapers. Editor: Pete Noble*

Ilkeston Shopper
0115 944 6160
www.ilkestontoday.co.uk
*Weekly free (Tue). Owner: Johnston Press.
Editor: David Horne*

Kenilworth Citizen
024 7663 3633
*Weekly free (Thu). Owner: Coventry
Newspapers (Trinity Mirror). Editor:
Jonathan Sever*

Kettering Citizen
01536 506100
www.northantsnews.com
*Weekly (Thu). Owner: Johnston Press.
Editor: Jeremy Clifford; news editor:
Kirsty Ward; features: Joni Ager;
chief sub: Kathryn Dunn*

Kettering Evening Telegraph
01536 506100
www.northantsnews.com
*Weekly (Thu). Owner: Johnston Press.
Editor: Jeremy Clifford; news editor:
Kirsty Ward; features: Joni Ager;
chief sub: Kathryn Dunn*

Kettering Herald & Post
01604 614600
www.midlandweeklymedia.co.uk
*Weekly (Thu). Owner: Midlands Weekly
Media (Trinity Mirror). Editor: Richard
Howarth; production: Julie Fisher*

Leek Post & Times
01538 399599
www.leekpostandtimes.co.uk
*Weekly (Wed). Owner: Northcliffe
Newspapers. Editor: Doug Pickford;
news: Jane Griffiths*

Leicester Mail
0116 251 2512
www.thisisleicestershire.co.uk
*Weekly free (Tue). Owner: Northcliffe
Newspapers. Editor: Nick Carter; news:
Mark Charlton; features: Alex Dawson*

Leicester Mercury
See page 38

Leicestershire Times Today
0115 982 7338
www.leicestertimestoday.com
*Weekly (Fri). Owner: Journal Publishing
Company. Editor: Matthew Palmer*

**Lichfield & Burntwood Edition
Express and Star**
01902 313131
www.expressandstar.com
*Daily. Owner: Midland News Association.
Editor: Adrian Faber*

Lichfield Mercury
01827 848535
www.lichfieldmercury.co.uk
*Weekly (Thu). Owner: Northcliffe
Newspapers. Editor: Sam Holliday*

Lichfield Post
01543 258523
www.iclichfield.co.uk
*Weekly (Thu). Owner: Midlands Weekly
Media (Trinity Mirror). Editor: Pam
Thomas*

Long Eaton Advertiser
0115 946 2837
*Weekly (Wed). Owner: Midlands Weekly
Media (Trinity Mirror). Editor: David
Godsall*

Long Eaton Recorder
0115 948 2000
www.thisisnottingham.co.uk
*Weekly free (Thu). Owner: Northcliffe
Newspapers. Editor: Graham Glen; news:
Claire Catlow; features: Jeremy Lewis*

Long Eaton Trader
0115 946 9909
*Weekly (Thu). Owner: Midlands Weekly
Media (Trinity Mirror). Editor: Patrick
O'Connor; features: Steve Eyley*

Loughborough Echo
01509 232632
*Weekly (Thu). Owner: Midlands Weekly
Media (Trinity Mirror). Editor: Andy
Rush; news: Rachel Harrison*

Loughborough Mail
0116 251 2512
www.thisisleicestershire.co.uk
*Weekly (Tue). Owner: Northcliffe
Newspapers. Editor: Nick Carter; news:
Mark Charlton; features: Alex Dawson*

Lutterworth Mail
01858 462626
www.harboroughtoday.co.uk
*Weekly (Thu). Owner: Johnston Press.
Editor: Brian Dodds; news: Maria
Thompson*

Mansfield & Ashfield Observer
01623 456789
*Weekly free (Thu). Owner: Johnston
Press. Editor: Tony Spittles*

Mansfield & Ashfield Recorder
01623 420000
*Weekly free (Wed). Owner: Northcliffe
Newspapers. Editor: Graham Glen*

Mansfield Chad
01623 456789
www.mansfieldtoday.co.uk
*Weekly (Wed). Owner: Johnston Press.
Editor: Jeremy Plews; news: Joy
Thompson; chief sub: Karen Robinson*

Market Harborough Herald & Post
01604 614600
www.midlandweeklymedia.co.uk
*Weekly (Thu, Fri). Owner: Midlands
Weekly Media (Trinity Mirror). Editor:
Richard Howarth; production: Julie
Fisher*

Matlock Mercury
01629 762120
www.matlocktoday.co.uk
*Weekly (Thu). Owner: Johnston Press.
Editor: Amanda Hatfield; news: Helen
Taylor*

Melton Citizen
01664 410041
www.meltontoday.co.uk
Weekly free (Tue). Owner: Johnston Press.
Editor: Michael Cooke

Melton Times
01664 410041
www.meltontoday.co.uk
Weekly (Thu). Owner: Johnston Press.
Editor: Michael Cooke

Mid Staffs Edition Express and Star
01543 506311
www.expressandstar.com
Daily. Owner: Midland News Association.
Editor: Adrian Faber; news: Mark Drew

Moorlands Advertiser
01782 602 525
www.thisisthesentinel.co.uk
Weekly (Wed). Owner: Post & Times.
Editor: Mike Sassi

Mountsorrel Post
0116 267 4213
4pa. Owner: The Birstall Post Society.
Editor: Jerry Jackson

Newark Advertiser
01636 681234
www.newarkadvertiser.co.uk
Weekly (Fri). Editor: Harry Whitehouse;
news: Lucy Millard

Newcastle Advertiser
01782 619830
www.staffordshiresentinel.co.uk
Daily. Owner: Northcliffe Newspapers.
Editor: Sean Dooley; news: Robert
Cotterill; features: Charlotte Little-Jones

North West Leics &
South Derbyshire Leader
01530 813101
Weekly (Wed). Owner: Trident Midland
Newspapers. Editor: Robin Slingsby

Northampton Herald & Post
01604 614600
www.midlandweeklymedia.co.uk
Weekly (Thu). Owner: Midlands Weekly
Media (Trinity Mirror). Editor: Richard
Howarth; production: Julie Fisher

Northampton Mercury
01604 467000
www.northantsnews.com
Weekly (Thu). Owner: Johnston Press.
Editor: Steve Scholes; news: Richard
Edmondson; production: Graham Tebbutt

Northants on Sunday
01604 467000
www.northantsnews.com
Sunday. Owner: Johnston Press. Editor:
Steve Scoles; news: Richard Edmondson;
features: Angela Pownall; production
manager: Graham Billing

Nottingham & Trent Valley Journal
0115 982 7337
Weekly (Fri). Owner: Journal Publishing
Company. Editor: Matthew Palmer

Nottingham & Long Eaton Topper
0115 969 6000
www.toppernewspapers.co.uk
Weekly free (Wed). Owner: Topper
Newspapers. Editor: John Howarth

Nottingham Evening Post
See page 38

Nottingham Recorder
0115 948 2000
www.thisisnottingham.co.uk
Weekly free (Wed). Owner: Northcliffe
Newspapers. Editor: Graham Glen; news:
Claire Catlow; features: Jeremy Lewis

Oadby & Wigston Mail
0116 251 2512
www.thisisleicestershire.co.uk
Weekly (Tue). Owner: Northcliffe
Newspapers. Editor: Nick Carter; news:
Mark Charlton; features: Alex Dawson

Peak Advertiser
01629 812159
Fortnightly free (Thu). Editor: Steve Wild

Peak Times
01629 582432
www.matlocktoday.co.uk
Weekly free (Fri). Owner: Johnston Press.
Editor: Amanda Hatfield; news: Helen
Taylor

Potteries Advertiser
01782 602525
www.thisisthesentinel.co.uk
Weekly free (Thu). Owner: Northcliffe
Newspapers. Editor: Sean Dooley; news:
Robert Cotterill; features: Charlotte
Little-Jones

Retford & Bawtry Guardian
01909 500500
www.retfordtoday.co.uk
Weekly (Thu). Owner: Johnston Press.
Editor: George Robinson; news: Jackie
Laver

Retford, Gainsborough & Worksop
Times
01777 702275
Weekly (Thu). Owner: Northcliffe
Newspapers. Editor: Nick Purkiss

Retford Trader
01909 500500
www.retfordtoday.co.uk
Weekly free (Fri). Owner: Johnston
Press. Editor: George Robinson; news:
Jackie Laver

Ripley & Heanor News
01629 582432
www.matlocktoday.co.uk
Weekly (Thu). Owner: Johnston Press.
Editor: Amanda Hatfield; news: Helen
Taylor

Rugeley Mercury
01543 414414
www.thisisstaffordshire.co.uk
Weekly (Thu). Owner: Northcliffe
Newspapers. Editor: Tim Hewitt;
news: Andy Kerr

Rugeley Post
01543 258523
Weekly (Thu). Owner: Midlands Weekly
Media (Trinity Mirror). Editor: Pam
Thomas

Rutland Times
01572 757722
www.rutlandtoday.co.uk
Weekly (Thu). Owner: Johnston Press.
Editor: Andy Plaice

The Sentinel (Stoke-on-Trent)
See page 38

Sentinel Sunday
See The Sentinel, page 38

Shepshed Echo
01509 232632
Weekly (Thu). Owner: Midlands Weekly
Media (Trinity Mirror). Editor: Andy
Rush; news: Rachel Harrison

Sherwood/Rainworth Chad
01623 456789
Weekly (Wed). Owner: Johnston Press.
Editor: Jeremy Plews; news: Joy Thompson

Shirebrook & Bolsover Chad
01623 456789
Weekly (Wed). Owner: Johnston Press.
Editor: Jeremy Plews; news: Joy Thompson

South Notts Advertiser
01636 681234
Weekly (Fri). Editor: Harry Whitehouse;
news: Lucy Millard

Stafford & Stone Chronicle
01785 247290
www.expressandstar.com/chronicle
Daily. Owner: Midland News Association.
Editor: Klooran Wills

Stafford Post
01543 501700
www.icstafford.co.uk
Weekly (Thu). Owner: Midlands Weekly
Media (Trinity Mirror). Editor: Mike
Lockley

Staffordshire Newsletter
01785 257700
www.staffordshirenewsletter.co.uk
Weekly (Thu). Owner: Staffordshire
Newspapers. Editor: Klooran Wills

Stapleford & Sandiacre News
0115 946 2837
Weekly (Wed). Owner: Midlands Weekly
Media (Trinity Mirror). Editor: David
Godsall

Stratford & Banbury Why
0845 600 9742
Weekly free (Fri). Owner: Northcliffe
Newspapers. Ad Director: Hazel Pilling

Swadlincote Times
01530 813101
Weekly (Fri). Owner: Trident Midland
Newspapers. News editor: Nick Hudson

Tamworth Herald
01827 848535
www.tamworthherald.co.uk
Weekly (Thu). Owner: Northcliffe
Newspapers. Editor: Sam Holiday

Tamworth Times
01827 308000
Weekly (Thu). Owner: Midlands Weekly
Media (Trinity Mirror). Editor: Pam
Thomas

Towcester Post
01604 614600
www.midlandweeklymedia.co.uk
Weekly (Fri). Owner: Midlands Weekly
Media (Trinity Mirror). Editor: Richard
Howarth; production: Julie Fisher

Trader Pictorial
01636 681234
www.newarkadvertiser.co.uk/trader
Weekly (Wed). Editor: Harry Whitehouse;
news: Lucy Millard

Uttoxeter Advertiser
01889 562050
www.uttoxeteradvertiser.co.uk
Weekly (Tue). Owner: Staffordshire
Newspapers. Editor: Alan Harris

Uttoxeter Post & Times
01889 568999
Weekly (Thu). Owner: Northcliffe
Newspapers. Editor: Doug Pickford;
news: Jane Griffiths

Warsop Chad
01623 456789
Weekly (Wed). Owner: Johnston Press.
Editor: Jeremy Plews; news: Joy
Thompson; chief sub: Karen Robinson

Wellingborough & East Northants
Evening Telegraph
01536 506100
www.northantsnews.com
Daily. Owner: Johnston Press. Acting
deputy editor: Mark Edwards; acting
news editor: Kristy Ward; features: Joni
Ager; chief sub: Kathryn Dunn

Wellingborough & Rushden Citizen
01536 506100
www.northantsnews.com
Weekly (Thu). Owner: Johnston Press.
Acting deputy editor: Mark Edwards;
acting news editor: Kristy Ward; features:
Joni Ager; chief sub: Kathryn Dunn

Wellingborough & Rushden
Herald & Post
01604 614600
www.midlandweeklymedia.co.uk
Weekly (Thu). Owner: Midlands Weekly
Media (Trinity Mirror). Editor: Richard
Howarth; production: Julie Fisher

Worksop Guardian
01909 500500
www.worksoptoday.co.uk
Weekly (Fri). Owner: Johnston Press.
Editor: George Robinson; news: Jackie
Laver

Worksop Trader
01909 500500
Weekly free (Wed). Owner: Johnston
Press. Editor: George Robinson; news:
Jackie Laver

Your Leek Paper
01538 371807
www.yourleekpaper.co.uk
Weekly (Wed). Independent. Editor: Gary
Shenton

● West Midlands

West Midlands, Warwickshire

Ad News (Willenhall, Wednesbury
& Darlaston)
01543 501700
Weekly (Wed). Owner: Midlands Weekly
Media (Trinity Mirror). Editor: Mike
Lockley

Bedworth Echo
01455 891965
www.iccoventry.co.uk
Weekly (Fri). Owner: Coventry
Newspapers (Trinity Mirror). Editor:
Andrew Punchon; news: Emma Ray;
features: Emma Ray

Birmingham Evening Mail
See page 37

Birmingham Independent
0121 446 1345
www.birminghamindependent.co.uk
Weekly (Fri). Owner: Birmingham
Independent. Editor: Paul Blair

Birmingham News
0121 234 5048
www.icbirmingham.co.uk
Weekly (Thu). Owner: Birmingham Post
& Mail (Trinity Mirror). Editor: Russ
Crawford; news: Victoria Thomas

Birmingham Post
0121 236 3366
www.icbirmingham.co.uk
Daily. Owner: Birmingham Post & Mail
(Trinity Mirror). Editor: Marc Reeves;
news: Mohammed Ilyas; features: Sarah
Probert

Black Country Bugle
01384 567678
www.blackcountrybugle.co.uk
Weekly (Thu). Owner: Staffordshire
Newspapers. Editor: Robert Taylor

Coventry Citizen
024 7663 3633
www.iccoventry.co.uk
Weekly (Thu). Owner: Coventry
Newspapers (Trinity Mirror). Editor:
Alan Kirby; news: John West; features:
Steven Chilton

Coventry Evening Telegraph
See page 37

Coventry Observer
024 7649 5900
www.coventryobserver.co.uk
Weekly free (Thu). Owner: Observer
Standard Newspapers. Editor: Mike Green

Daventry Express
01327 703383
www.daventryonline.co.uk
Weekly (Thu). Owner: Johnston Press.
Editor: Jason Gibbons

Dudley Chronicle
01384 353211
www.expressandstar.com
Weekly (Fri). Owner: Midland News
Association. Editor: John Nash; features:
Dave Pearce; chief sub: Jane Reynolds

Dudley Edition Express & Star
01384 355355
www.expressandstar.com
Daily. Owner: Midland News Association.
Editor: Adrian Faber; news: Mark Drew;
features: Dylan Evans; chief sub: Tony
Reynolds

Dudley News
01384 358050
www.dudleynews.co.uk
Weekly (Fri). Owner: Newsquest.
Editor: Jeff Gepheott

Express & Star
See page 38

Express & Star (Stourbridge)
01384 399914
www.expressandstar.com
Daily. Owner: Midland News Association.
Editor: Adrian Faber

Express & Star (Walsall)
01922 444444
www.expressandstar.com
Daily. Owner: Midland News Association.
Editor: Adrian Faber

Great Barr & Erdington Chronicle
0121 553 7171
www.expressandstar.com
Weekly free (Thu). Owner: Midland News
Association. Editor: John Nash

Great Barr Observer
01827 848535
www.tamworthherald.co.uk
Weekly (Fri). Owner: Northcliffe
Newspapers. Editor: Mark Eustace

Halesowen Chronicle
01384 353211
Weekly (Fri). Owner: Midland News
Association. Editor: John Nash; features:
Dave Pearce; chief sub: Jane Reynolds

Halesowen News
01384 358050
www.halesowennews.co.uk
Weekly (Fri). Owner: Newsquest.
Editor: Jeff Gepheott

Heartland Evening News
024 7635 3534
www.hen-news.com
Daily. Editor: Tony Parrott; news: Kevin
Cooke; features: John Jevons; production:
Bob Clemens

Kenilworth Times
024 7650 0375
Weekly (Wed). Owner: Trinity Mirror.
Editor: Darren Parkin

Kenilworth Weekly News
01926 457777
www.kenilworthonline.co.uk
Weekly (Fri). Owner: Johnston Press.
Editor: Gemma Lynn

Leamington Spa Courier
01926 457777
www.leamingtononline.co.uk
Weekly (Fri). Owner: Johnston Press.
Editor: Martin Lawson

Leamington Spa Observer
01926 451900
www.leamington-now.com
Weekly free (Thu). Owner: Observer
Standard Newspapers. Editor: Ian Hughes

Leamington Spa Review
01926 457777
www.leamingtonspatoday.co.uk
Weekly (Thu). Owner: Johnston Press.
Editor: Martin Lawson

Metro (Birmingham)
020 7938 6000
www.metrobirmingham.co.uk
Daily. Owner: Associated Newspapers.
Editor: Kenny Campbell; news: Sarah
Getty; features: Kieran Meeke

Nuneaton Weekly Tribune
024 7663 3633
www.iccoverntry.co.uk
*Weekly (Thu). Owner: Coventry
Newspapers (Trinity Mirror). Editor:
Alan Kirby; news: John West; features:
Steven Chilton*

Royal Leamington Spa Times
024 7650 0375
*Weekly (Wed). Owner: Trinity Mirror.
Editor: Darren Parkin*

Rugby Advertiser
01788 535363
www.rugbyadvertiser.co.uk
*Weekly (Thu). Owner: Johnston Press.
Editor: Peter Hengenheister*

Rugby Observer
01788 535147
www.therugbyobserver.co.uk
*Weekly free (Thu). Owner: Observer
Standard Newspapers. Editor: Chris Smith*

Rugby Review
01788 535363
www.rugbyreviewtoday.co.uk
*Weekly (Thu). Owner: Johnston Press.
Editor: Peter Hengenheister*

Rugby Times
01604 614 643
*Weekly (Tues). Owner: Trinity Mirror.
Editor: Duncan Gibbons*

Sandwell Chronicle
0121 553 7171
www.expressandstar.com
*Weekly free (Thu). Owner: Midland News
Association. Editor: John Nash*

Solihull News
0121 711 5723
www.midlandweeklymedia.co.uk
*Weekly (Fri). Owner: Midlands Weekly
Media (Trinity Mirror). Editor: Ross
Crawford*

Solihull Observer *
0121 683 0707
www.solihull.observertoday.co.uk
*Weekly (Thurs). Owner: Observer
Standard Newspapers. Editor: Charlotte
Burch*

Solihull Times
0121 711 5723
www.midlandweeklymedia.co.uk
*Weekly (Wed). Owner: Midlands Weekly.
Media (Trinity Mirror) Editor: Ross
Crawford*

Stourbridge Chronicle
01384 399914
www.expressandstar.com
*Weekly (Fri). Owner: Midland News
Association. Editor: John Nash; features:
Dave Pearce; chief sub: Jane Reynolds*

Stourbridge News
01384 358050
www.thisisstourbridge.co.uk
*Weekly (Thu). Owner: Newsquest.
Editor: Jeff Gepheott*

Stratford-upon-Avon Herald
01789 266261
www.stratford-herald.co.uk
*Weekly (Thu). Owner: Stratford Herald.
Editor: Chris Towner; news: Dale Levack*

Stratford-upon-Avon Midweek
01789 266261
www.stratford-herald.co.uk
*Weekly (Tue). Owner: Stratford Herald.
Editor: Chris Towner; news: Dale Levack*

Stratford-upon-Avon Observer
01789 415717
www.stratfordstandard.co.uk
*Weekly free (Thu). Owner: Observer
Standard Newspapers. Editor: Clare
Fitzsimmons*

Sunday Mercury (Birmingham)
0121 236 3366
www.icbirmingham.co.uk
*Weekly (Sun). Owner: Birmingham Post
& Mail (Trinity Mirror). Editor: David
Brookes; news: Tony Larner; features:
Paul Cole*

Sutton Coldfield News
0121 355 7070
www.icsuttoncoldfield.co.uk
*Weekly (Fri). Owner: Midlands Weekly
Media (Trinity Mirror). Editor: Pam
Thomas*

Sutton Coldfield Observer
01827 848535
www.tamworthherald.co.uk
*Weekly (Fri). Owner: Northcliffe
Newspapers. Editor: Gary Phelps*

Walsall Advertiser
01827 848535
www.tamworthherald.co.uk
*Weekly (Thu). Owner: Northcliffe
Newspapers. Editor: Natalie Missenden*

Walsall Chronicle
01922 444444
www.expressandstar.com
*Weekly (Thu). Owner: Midland News
Association. Editor: John Nash*

Walsall Observer
01922 636666
www.thisiswalsall.co.uk
*Weekly (Fri). Owner: Midlands Weekly
Media (Trinity Mirror). Editor: Mike
Lockley*

Warwick Times
0247 6500 375
*Weekly (Wed). Owner: Trinity Mirror.
Editor: Darren Parkin*

Why Coventry, Nuneaton & Hinckley
0845 600 9742
*Weekly free (Fri). Owner: Northcliffe
Newspapers. Editor: Hazel Pilling*

Why Solihull & District
0845 600 9742
*Weekly free (Fri). Owner: Northcliffe
Newspapers. Editor: Hazel Pilling*

Why Warwick & Leamington
0845 600 9742
*Weekly free (Fri). Owner: Northcliffe
Newspapers. Editor: Hazel Pilling*

Wolverhampton Ad News
01543 501700
*Weekly (Wed). Owner: Midlands Weekly
Media (Trinity Mirror). Editor: Mike
Lockley*

Wolverhampton Chronicle
01902 313131
www.expressandstar.com
*Weekly free (Thu). Owner: Midland News
Association. Editor: John Nash; news:
Mark Drew; features: Dave Pearce; chief
sub: Tony Reynolds*

● West England

Gloucestershire, Herefordshire,
Shropshire, Worcestershire

Alcester Chronicle
01527 453500
www.thisisworcestershire.co.uk
*Weekly (Wed). Owner: Newsquest. Editor:
Paul Walker; news: Emily Bridgwater*

Berrow's Worcester Journal
01905 748200
www.berrowsjournal.co.uk
*Weekly. Owner: Newsquest. Editor:
Stewart Gilbert; news: Stephanie Preece;
chief sub: Jim Collins*

Bridgnorth Journal
01746 761411
www.bridgnorthjournal.co.uk
*Weekly (Fri). Owner: Midland News
Association. Editor: John Griffiths*

Bromsgrove Advertiser
01527 837000
www.thisisworcestershire.co.uk
*Weekly (Wed). Owner: Newsquest.
Editor: Alan Wallcroft; chief reporter:
Peter Lammas*

Bromsgrove Messenger
01527 837000
www.thisisworcestershire.co.uk
*Weekly (Wed). Owner: Newsquest.
Editor: Alan Wallcroft; chief reporter:
Peter Lammas*

Bromsgrove Standard
01527 574111
www.bromsgrovestandard.co.uk
*Weekly free (Fri). Owner: Observer
Standard Newspapers. Editor: Tristan
Harris*

Cheltenham Independent
01453 762412
www.thisisstroud.com
*Weekly (Wed). Owner: Newsquest.
Editor: Sue Smith; news: Tamash Lal*

Cheltenham News
01242 271900
www.thisisgloucestershire.co.uk
*Weekly free (Thu). Owner: Northcliffe
Newspapers. Editor: Anita Syvret*

Cheltenham/Tewkesbury News
01452 420632
www.thisisgloucestershire.co.uk
*Weekly free (Thu). Owner: Northcliffe
Newspapers. Editor: Chris Hill*

Chipping Sodbury/Yate Gazette
01453 544000
www.thisisthesouthcotswolds.co.uk
*Weekly (Fri). Owner: Newsquest.
Editor: Kathryn Turnbull*

Cotswold Journal
01608 651456
www.thisistewkesbury.com
*Weekly (Thu). Owner: Newsquest. Editor:
John Murphy; news: Tony Donnelly*

County Independent
01453 762412
www.thisisstroud.com
*Weekly (Wed). Owner: Newsquest.
Editor: Sue Smith; news: Tamash Lal*

Droitwich Spa Advertiser
01527 837000
www.thisisdroitwichspa.co.uk
Weekly (Wed). Owner: Newsquest.
Editor: Alan Wallcroft; deputy editor:
Alex Wellings

Droitwich Standard
01527 574111
www.droitwich.standardtoday.co.uk

Evesham Journal
01608 651456
www.thisisworcestershire.co.uk
Weekly (Thu). Owner: Newsquest. Editor:
John Murphy; news: Tony Donnelly

Express and Star (Kidderminster)
01902 313131
www.expressandstar.com
Daily. Owner: Midland News Association.
Editor: Adrian Faber

Forest of Dean and Wye Valley
Review
01594 841113
www.forest-and-wye-today.co.uk
Weekly free (Wed). Owner: Tindle
Newspapers. Editor: John Powell

The Forester
01594 820600
www.thisisgloucestershire.co.uk
Weekly (Thu). Owner: Northcliffe
Newspapers. Editor: Viv Hargreaves

Gloucester Citizen
01242 271900
www.thisisgloucestershire.co.uk
Daily. Owner: Northcliffe Newspapers.
Editor: Ian Mean

Gloucester Independent
01453 762412
www.thisisstroud.com
Weekly (Wed). Owner: Newsquest.
Editor: Sue Smith; news: Tamash Lal

Gloucester News
01242 271900
www.thisisgloucestershire.co.uk
Weekly free (Thu). Owner: Northcliffe
Newspapers. Editor: Chris Hill

Gloucestershire County Gazette
01453 544000
www.thisisthesouthcotswolds.co.uk
Weekly (Fri). Owner: Newsquest.
Editor: Skip Walker; news: Carole Taylor

Gloucestershire Echo
01242 271900
www.thisisgloucestershire.co.uk
Daily. Owner: Northcliffe Newspapers.
Editor: Anita Syvret; news: Sam
Shepherd; features: Tanya Gledhill;
chief sub: Peter Gavan

Hereford Admag
01432 376120
Weekly (Wed). Owner: Northcliffe
Newspapers. Features editor: Richard
Green

Hereford Journal
01432 355353
www.herefordjournal.co.uk
Weekly free (Wed). Owner: Midland News
Association. Editor: Mike Robinson;
news: Colin Osborne

Hereford Times
01432 274413
www.thisisherefordshire.co.uk
Weekly (Thu). Owner: Newsquest. Editor:
Liz Griffin; news: Nigel Heins

Jobs Today
(Cheltenham & Gloucester)
01453 544000
www.thisisthesouthcotswolds.co.uk
Weekly (Fri). Owner: Newsquest.
Editor: Kathryn Turnbull

Kidderminster Chronicle
01562 829500
www.thisisworcestershire.co.uk
/worcestershire/kidderminster
Weekly (Wed). Owner: Newsquest.
Editor: Clive Joyce; chief reporter:
Peter McMillan

Kidderminster Shuttle and Times
and Stourport News
01562 633333
www.thisisworcestershire.co.uk
/worcestershire/kidderminster
Weekly (Thu). Owner: Newsquest. Editor:
Clive Joyce; chief reporter: Peter
McMillan

Ledbury Reporter
01684 892200
www.thisisworcestershire.co.uk
Weekly (Fri). Owner: Newsquest.
Editor: Nick Howells; news: Jo Lafferty

Leominster Journal
01432 355353
www.leominsterjournal.com
Weekly free (Wed). Owner: Midland News
Association. Editor: Mike Robinson;
news: Colin Osborne

Ludlow Advertiser
01584 873796
www.thisisludlow.co.uk
Weekly (Thu). Owner: Newsquest. News
editor: Jean Kingdon; general reporter:
Michael Baws

Ludlow Journal
01743 248248
www.ludlowjournal.co.uk
Weekly free (Fri). Owner: Midland News
Association. Editor: Mike Robinson;
chief reporter: Vince Buston

Malvern Gazette
01684 892200
www.thisisworcestershire.co.uk
Weekly (Fri). Owner: Newsquest.
Editor: Nick Howells

Market Drayton Advertiser
01630 698113
www.marketdraytonadvertiser.co.uk
Weekly (Fri). Owner: Midland News
Association. Editor: Samantha Taylor;
deputy editor: Gary Scattergood

Newport Advertiser
01952 811500
www.newportadvertiser.co.uk
Weekly (Fri). Owner: Midland News
Association. Editor: Samantha Taylor;
deputy editor: Gary Scattergood

North Shropshire Chronicle
01743 248248
www.northshropshirechronicle.com
Weekly (Thu). Owner: Midland News
Association. Editor: John Butterworth

Oswestry & Border Counties
Advertiser
01691 655321
www.bordercountiesadvertiser.co.uk
Weekly (Wed). Owner: North Wales
Newspapers. Editor: Sue Perry

Redditch Advertiser
01527 453500
www.thisisworcestershire.co.uk
/worcestershire/redditch
Weekly (Wed). Owner: Newsquest. Editor:
Paul Walker; news: Emily Bridgwater

Redditch Standard
01527 588688
www.redditchstandard.co.uk
Weekly free (Fri). Owner: Observer
Standard Newspapers. Editor: Andrew
Powell

Ross Gazette
01989 562007
www.ross-today.co.uk
Weekly (Thu). Owner: Tindle
Newspapers. Editor: Chris Robertson;
chief reporter: Jo Scriven

Ross-on-Wye Journal
01432 355353
www.rossonwyejournal.com
Weekly free (Wed). Owner: Midland News
Association. Editor: Mike Robinson;
news: Colin Osborne

Shrewsbury Admag
01743 241414
www.northshropshirechronicle.com
Weekly (Thu). Owner: Northcliffe
Newspapers. General manager: Jan
Edwards

Shrewsbury Chronicle
01743 248248
www.shrewsburychronicle.co.uk
Weekly (Thu). Owner: Midland News
Association. Editor: John Butterworth

Shropshire Star
See page 38

South Shropshire Journal
01584 876311
www.southshropshirejournal.co.uk
Weekly (Fri). Owner: Midland News
Association. Editor: Mike Robinson;
news: Vince Buston

Stourport News
01562 633330
Weekly free (Thu). Owner: Newsquest.
Editor: Clive Joyce; deputy editor:
Alison Grange; news: Peter McMillan

Stratford Observer
01789 415717
www.stratfordobserver.co.uk
Weekly (Thu). Owner: Observer Standard
Newspapers. Editor: Clare Fitzsimmons

Stroud News & Journal
01453 762142
www.thisisstroud.com
Weekly (Wed). Owner: Newsquest.
Editor: Sue Smith; news: Tamash Lal

Telford Journal
01743 248248
www.telfordjournal.co.uk
Weekly free (Thu). Owner: Midland News
Association. Editor: David Sharpe

Tenbury Wells Advertiser
01584 873796
www.thisistenbury-wells.co.uk
Weekly (Thu). Owner: Newsquest.
Editor: Liz Griffin

Thornbury Gazette
01453 544000
www.thisisthesouthcotswolds.co.uk
Weekly (Fri). Owner: Newsquest.
Editor: Kathryn Turnbull

Why Evesham
0845 600 9742
Weekly free (Fri). Owner: Northcliffe
Newspapers. Editor: Tushy Sanghera

Why Redditch & District
0845 600 9742
Weekly free (Fri). Owner: Northcliffe
Newspapers. Editor: Tushy Sanghera

**Why Worcester, Malvern
& Kidderminster**
0845 600 9742
Weekly free (Fri). Owner: Northcliffe
Newspapers. Editor: Tushy Sanghera

Wilts & Gloucestershire Standard
01285 642642
www.thisiscirencester.com
Weekly (Thu). Owner: Newsquest.
Editor: Skip Walker; news: Simon Davies

Worcester Evening News
01905 748200
www.thisisworcestershire.co.uk
Weekly. Owner: Newsquest. Editor:
Stewart Gilbert; news: Stephanie Preece;
chief sub: Jim Collins

Worcester Standard
01905 726200
www.worcesterstandard.co.uk
Weekly free (Thu). Owner: Observer
Standard Newspapers. Editor: James
Illes; news: David Dunham

● North England

East, North, South & West Yorkshire

Aire Valley Target
01274 729511
Weekly (Thu). Owner: Newsquest.
Editor: Perry Austin-Clarke; news:
Martin Heminway; features: David
Barnett; chief sub: Mel Jones

Axholme Herald
01472 874417
Weekly (Fri). Owner: Northcliffe
Newspapers. Editor: Ron Shipley

Barnsley Chronicle
01226 734734
www.barnsley-chronicle.co.uk
Weekly (Fri). Editor: Robert Cockroft;
news: Stephanie Daley; features: Maureen
Middleton; chief sub: John Threlkeld

Barnsley Independent
01226 734734
www.barnsley-chronicle.co.uk
Weekly (Tue). Editor: Robert Cockroft;
news: Stephanie Daley; features: Maureen
Middleton; chief sub: John Threlkeld

Batley News
01924 468282
www.dewsburytoday.co.uk
Weekly (Thu). Owner: Johnston Press.
Editor: Richard Firth; news: Vicky Dacre

Beverley Advertiser
01482 327111
Weekly (Thu). Owner: Northcliffe
Newspapers. Editor: Alex Leys

Beverley Guardian
01377 241122
www.beverleytoday.co.uk
Weekly free (Fri). Owner: Johnston Press.
Editor: Dennis Sissons; news: Steve Petch;
chief sub: Gill Pick

Birstall News
01924 468282
www.dewsburytoday.co.uk
Weekly (Thu). Owner: Johnston Press.
Editor: Richard Firth

Bradford Target
01274 729511
Weekly (Thu). Owner: Newsquest.
Editor: Perry Austin-Clarke; news:
Martin Heminway; features: David
Barnett; chief sub: Mel Jones

Bridlington Free Press
01262 606606
www.bridlingtontoday.co.uk
Weekly (Thu). Owner: Johnston Press.
Editor: Nick Procter; news: Simon
Haldenby; features: John Edwards

Bridlington Gazette & Herald
01262 606606
www.bridlingtontoday.co.uk
Weekly free (Tue). Owner: Johnston
Press. Editor: Nick Procter; news: Simon
Haldenby; features: John Edwards

Brighouse Echo
01422 260200
www.brighousetoday.co.uk
Weekly (Fri). Owner: Johnston Press.
Editor: Stephen Firth

Calderdale News
01422 260200
www.halifaxtoday.co.uk
Weekly free (Wed). Owner: Johnston
Press. Editor: John Furbisher; production:
Gordon Samson

Colne Valley Chronicle
01484 437747
www.ichuddersfield.co.uk
Weekly (Fri). Owner: Trinity Mirror
Huddersfield. Editor: Chris Burgess

Craven Herald & Pioneer
01756 794117
www.cravenherald.co.uk
Weekly (Fri). Owner: Newsquest.
Editor: Ian Lockwood; deputy editor:
Lindsey Moore

Dearne Advertiser
01709 303050
www.doncastertoday.co.uk
Weekly (Fri). Owner: Johnston Press.
Editor-in-chief: Graham Huston

Dearne Valley Weekender
01709 571111
www.rotherhamadvertiser.com
Weekly (Fri). Owner: Garnet Dickinson
Publishing. Editor: Doug Melloy

Dewsbury Reporter
01924 468282
www.dewsburytoday.co.uk
Weekly (Thu). Owner: Johnston Press.
Editor: Richard Firth; news: Vicky Dacre

Dinnington & Maltby Guardian
01909 550500
www.dinningtontoday.co.uk
Weekly (Fri). Owner: Johnston Press.
Editor: George Robinson; news: Jackie
Laver

Dinnington & Maltby Trader News
01909 550500
Weekly (Thu). Owner: Johnston Press.
Editor: George Robinson; news: Jackie
Laver

Doncaster Advertiser
01302 347213
Weekly (Fri). Owner: Johnston Press.
Editor: Martin Edmunds; news: John
Hepperstall

Doncaster Free Press
01302 347264
www.doncastertoday.co.uk
Weekly (Thu). Owner: Johnston Press.
Editor: Graham Huston; news: Kath
Finlay; features: Darren Burke;
production: David Crossland

Doncaster Star
01302 347264
www.doncastertoday.co.uk
Daily. Owner: Johnston Press.
Reporter: David Kessen

Driffield Post
01377 241122
www.driffieldtoday.co.uk
Weekly (Fri). Owner: Johnston Press.
Editor: Dennis Sissons; news: Steve Petch;
chief sub: Gill Pick

Driffield Times
01377 241122
www.driffieldtoday.co.uk
Weekly (Wed). Owner: Johnston Press.
Editor: Dennis Sissons; news: Steve Petch;
chief sub: Gill Pick

Easingwold Advertiser & Weekly News
01347 821329
www.ghsmith.com/advertiser
Weekly (Thu). Editor: Margery Smith

East Hull Advertiser
01482 327111
Weekly (Wed). Owner: Northcliffe Newspapers. Editor: Alex Leys

East Riding Advertiser
01482 327111
Weekly (Thu). Owner: Northcliffe Newspapers. Editor: Alex Leys

East Riding News
01482 887700
www.eastridinggov.co.uk
Monthly (1st week). Editor: Sarah Mainprize

Elmsall & South Elmsall Express
01977 640107
www.wakefieldexpress.co.uk
Weekly (Thu). Owner: Johnston Press. Editor: Delia Kitson

Epworth Bells & Crowle Advertiser
01427 615323
Weekly (Thu). Owner: Johnston Press. Editor: Eddir Mardell; deputy editor: Andy Staples

Filey & Hunmanby Mercury
01723 363636
www.scarboroughtoday.co.uk
Daily. Owner: Johnston Press. Editor: Ed Asquith; news: Steve Hartley; chief sub: Steve Banbridge

Gainsborough News
01427 872202
Weekly free (Fri). Owner: Johnston Press. Editor: Janet Harrison; deputy editor: Andy Staples

Gainsborough Standard
01427 615323
Weekly (Thu). Owner: Johnston Press. Editor: Janet Harrison; deputy editor: Andy Staples

Halifax Evening Courier
01422 260200
www.halifaxtoday.co.uk
Daily. Owner: Johnston Press. Editor: John Furbisher

Harrogate Advertiser
01423 564321
www.harrogatetoday.co.uk
Weekly (Fri). Owner: Johnston Press. Editor: Jean Macquarrie; assistant editor: Sophie Bradley; chief sub: Sarah Kelly

Harrogate Herald
01423 564321
www.harrogatetoday.co.uk
Weekly (Fri). Owner: Johnston Press. Editor: Jean Macquarrie; assistant editor: Sophie Bradley; chief sub: Sarah Kelly

Hebden Bridge Times
01422 260200
www.halifaxtoday.co.uk
Weekly (Fri). Owner: Johnston Press. Editor: Sheila Tordoff

Heckmondwike Herald
01924 468282
www.dewsburytoday.co.uk
Weekly (Fri). Owner: Johnston Press. Editor: Richard Firth

Holderness & Hornsea Gazette
01964 612777
www.holderness-online.com
Weekly (Thu). Publisher: Brian Adcock; news: Chris Leek

Holderness Advertiser
01482 327111
Weekly (Wed). Owner: Northcliffe Newspapers. Editor: Alex Leys

Holme Valley Express
01484 430000
www.ichuddersfield.co.uk
Weekly (Tue). Owner: Trinity Mirror Huddersfield. Editor: Chris Burgess

Huddersfield Daily Examiner
01484 430000
www.ichuddersfield.co.uk
Daily. Owner: Trinity Mirror Huddersfield. Editor: Roy Wright; news: Neil Atkinson; features: Andrew Flynn

Huddersfield District Chronicle
01484 437747
www.ichuddersfield.co.uk
Weekly (Fri). Owner: Trinity Mirror Huddersfield. Editor: Chris Burgess

Hull Daily Mail
See page 38

Ilkley Gazette
01943 607022
www.ilkleygazette.co.uk
Weekly (Thu). Owner: Newsquest. Editor: Mel Vasey; chief reporter: Paul Langan

The Journal (Hull)
01482 327111
Monthly (24th). Owner: Northcliffe Newspapers. Editor: Roy Woodcock

Keighley & Craven Target
01274 729511
Weekly (Tue). Owner: Newsquest. Editor: Perry Austin-Clarke; news: Martin Heminway; features: David Barnett; chief sub: Mel Jones

Keighley News
01535 606611
www.keighleynews.co.uk
Weekly (Thu). Owner: Newsquest. Editor: Malcolm Hoddy; news: Alistair Shand; chief sub: Ralph Badham

Knaresborough Post
01423 564321
www.knaresboroughtoday.co.uk
Weekly (Fri). Owner: Johnston Press. Editor: Jean Macquarrie; assistant editor: Sophie Bradley; chief sub: Sarah Kelly

Leeds Weekly News
0113 243 2701
Weekly (Thu). Owner: Johnston Press. Editor: Sheila Holmes

Look Local (Sheffield)
0114 283 1100
www.looklocal.org.uk
Weekly (Wed). Editor: James Evans; head of production: Adrian von Werzbach

Malton & Pickering Mercury
01723 363636
www.maltontoday.co.uk
Daily. Owner: Johnston Press. Editor: Ed Asquith; news: Steve Hartley; chief sub: Steve Banbridge

Metro Yorkshire
020 7651 5200
www.metro.co.uk
Daily. Owner: Associated Newspapers. Editor: Kenny Campbell; news: Sarah Getty; features: Kieran Meeke

Mirfield Reporter
01924 468282
www.dewsburytoday.co.uk
Weekly (Fri). Owner: Johnston Press. Editor: Richard Firth

Morley Advertiser
0113 252 4020
www.morleytoday.co.uk
Weekly (Wed). Owner: Johnston Press. Editor: Robert Evans; news: Sarah Hall

Morley Observer
01924 468282
www.dewsburytoday.co.uk
Weekly (Fri). Owner: Johnston Press. Editor: Richard Firth

North Yorkshire Advertiser
01325 381313
www.theadvertiserseries.co.uk
Weekly free (Tue). Owner: Newsquest. Editor: Peter Barron; production editor: Sally Taylor

North Yorkshire Herald & Post
01642 245401
www.ncjmediainfo.co.uk
Weekly (Thu). Owner: Gazette Media Company (Trinity Mirror). Editor: Sue Giles

North Yorkshire News
01765 601248
www.northallertontoday.co.uk
Weekly free (Wed). Owner: Johnston Press. Editor: Steve Barton; news: Stephen Pass

Northallerton, Thirsk & Bedale Times
01765 601248
www.northallertontoday.co.uk
Weekly (Fri). Owner: Johnston Press. Editor: Steve Barton; news: Stephen Pass

Ossett Observer
01924 375111
www.wakefieldtoday.co.uk
Weekly free (Fri). Owner: Johnston Press. Editor: Mark Bradley; news: Lisa Rookes

Pateley Bridge & Nidderdale Herald
01423 564321
www.nidderdaletoday.co.uk
Weekly (Fri). Owner: Johnston Press. Editor: Jean Macquarrie; assistant editor: Sophie Bradley; chief sub: Sarah Kelly

Pocklington Post
01759 301003
www.pocklingtontoday.co.uk
Weekly (Thu). Owner: Johnston Press. Chief reporter: Nick Frame

Pontefract & Castleford Express
01977 737200
www.wakefieldexpress.co.uk
Weekly (Thu). Owner: Johnston Press. Editor: David Ward; news: Julie Hawksworth

Pontefract & Castleford Extra
01977 737200
www.wakefieldexpress.co.uk
Weekly free (Fri). Owner: Johnston Press.
Editor: David Ward; news: Julie
Hawksworth

Pudsey Times
01943 466750
Weekly (Thu). Owner: Johnston Press.
Editor: Kate Evans

Ripon Gazette & Boroughbridge Herald
01423 564321
www.ripontoday.co.uk
Weekly (Fri). Owner: Johnston Press.
Editor: Jean Macquarrie; assistant editor:
Sophie Bradley; chief sub: Sarah Kelly

Rotherham & South Yorkshire Advertiser
01709 768000
www.rotherhamadvertiser.com
Weekly (Fri). Owner: Garnet Dickinson
Publishing. Editor: Doug Melloy; news:
Ann Charlton

Rotherham Record
01709 768000
www.rotherhamadvertiser.com
Weekly (Wed). Owner: Garnet Dickinson
Publishing. Editor: Doug Melloy; news:
Ann Charlton

Scarborough Evening News
01723 363636
www.scarboroughcveningnews.co.uk
Daily. Owner: Johnston Press. Editor: Ed
Asquith; news: Steve Hartley; chief sub:
Steve Banbridge

Scarborough Trader
01723 352269
www.tradertoday.co.uk
Weekly free (Thu). Owner: Johnston Press.
Editor: Ed Asquith

Selby Chronicle
01757 702198
www.selbytoday.co.uk
Weekly free (Fri). Owner: Johnston Press.
Editor: Chris Page; news: Richard Parker

Selby Post
01405 720110
www.selbypost.co.uk
Weekly (Thu). Owner: Northcliffe
Newspapers. Editor: Peter Butler

Selby Star
01904 653051
www.yorkpress.co.uk
Weekly free (Wed). Owner: Newsquest.
Editor: Lynne Martin

Selby Times
01757 702802
www.selbytoday.co.uk
Weekly (Thu). Owner: Johnston Press.
Editor: Chris Page; news: Richard Parker

Sheffield & South Yorkshire Times Today
0115 956 8858
Weekly free (Wed). Owner: GPC General
Publishing Company. Editor: Matthew
Palmer

Sheffield Journal
0114 276 7676
www.sheffieldtoday.net
Weekly free (Thu). Owner: Johnston
Press. Editor: Alan Powell; news: Charles
Smith; features: John Highfield; head of
content: Paul License

Sheffield Mercury
0114 276 3633
Weekly (Wed). Editor: David Hayes

Sheffield Telegraph
0114 276 7676
www.sheffieldtoday.net
Weekly (Fri). Owner: Johnston Press.
Editor: David Todd; news: Peter Kay;
head of content: Paul License

Sheffield Weekly Gazette
0114 276 7676
www.sheffieldtoday.net
Weekly (Thu). Owner: Johnston Press.
Editor: Alan Powell; news: Bob
Westerdale; features: John Highfield;
head of content: Paul License

South Yorkshire Times
01709 303050
www.dearnetoday.co.uk
Weekly (Thu). Owner: Johnston Press.
Editor: Linda Waslidge

Spenborough Guardian
01924 468282
www.dewsburytoday.co.uk
Weekly (Fri). Owner: Johnston Press.
Editor: Richard Firth

The Star (Sheffield)
See page 38

Telegraph and Argus (Bradford)
See page 39

Todmorden News & Advertiser
01422 260200
www.halifaxtoday.co.uk
Weekly (Fri). Owner: Johnston Press.
Editor: Sheila Tordoff

The Town Crier (Bradford)
01274 729511
Weekly (Thu). Owner: Newsquest.
Editor: Perry Austin-Clarke; news:
Martin Heminway; features: David
Barnett; chief sub: Mel Jones

Wakefield Express
01924 375111
www.wakefieldexpress.co.uk
Weekly free (Fri). Owner: Johnston Press.
Editor: Mark Bradley; news: Lisa Rookes

Wakefield, Rothwell & Alton Extra
01924 375111
www.wakefieldexpress.co.uk
Weekly free (Thu). Owner: Johnston Press.
Editor: Mark Bradley; news: Lisa Rookes

Weekly Advertiser
01924 468282
www.dewsburytoday.co.uk
Weekly free (Fri). Owner: Johnston Press.
Editor: Richard Firth

West Hull Advertiser
01482 327111
Weekly (Wed). Owner: Northcliffe
Newspapers. Editor: Alex Leys

Wetherby News
01423 564321
www.harrogatetoday.co.uk
Weekly (Fri). Owner: Johnston Press.
Editor: Jean Macquarrie; assistant editor:
Sophie Bradley; chief sub: Sarah Kelly

Wharfe Valley Times
01943 466750
Weekly (Thu). Owner: Johnston Press.
Editor: Kate Evans

Wharfedale & Airedale Observer
01943 465555
www.wharfedaleobserver.co.uk
Weekly (Thu). Owner: Newsquest. Editor:
Mel Vasey; chief reporter: Paul Langhan

Whitby Gazette
01947 602836
www.whitbytoday.co.uk
Twice-weekly (Tue, Fri). Owner: Johnston
Press. Editor: Damien Holmes

York Evening Press
See page 39

York Star
01904 653051
www.yorkstar.co.uk
Weekly free (Wed). Owner: Newsquest.
Editor: Lynne Martin

Yorkshire Evening Post
See page 39

Yorkshire Express
0115 956 8858
Weekly free (Wed). Owner: GPC General
Publishing Company. Editor: Matthew
Palmer

Yorkshire Gazette & Herald
01904 653051
www.thisisryedale.co.uk
Weekly (Wed). Owner: Newsquest.
Editor: Chris Buxton

Yorkshire Post
See page 39

● North-east England

Cleveland, Durham, Northumberland, Tyne & Wear

Berwick Advertiser
01289 306677
www.berwicktoday.co.uk
Weekly (Thu). Owner: Johnston Press. Editor: Janet Workershaw; news: Ian Smith; features: Thomas Baldwin; chief sub: Keith Hamblin

Berwick Gazette
01289 306677
www.tweedalepress.co.uk
Weekly (Thu). Owner: Johnston Press. Editor: Janet Workershaw; news: Ian Smith; features: Thomas Baldwin; chief sub: Keith Hamblin

Chester-le-Street Advertiser
01325 381313
www.thisisthenortheast.co.uk
Weekly free (Thu). Owner: Newsquest. Editor: Peter Barron; news: Nigel Burton; features: Lindsey Jennings; chief sub: Ken Farrier

Citylife (Newcastle)
0191 211 5093
www.newcastle.gov.uk/citylife
Monthly (last week of month). Editor: Jane Byrne

Consett & Stanley Advertiser
01325 381313
www.thisisthenortheast.co.uk
Weekly free (Thu). Owner: Newsquest. Editor: Peter Barron; news: Nigel Burton; features: Lindsey Jennings; chief sub: Ken Farrier

Darlington & Stockton Times
01325 381313
www.thisisthenortheast.co.uk
Weekly (Fri). Owner: Newsquest. Editor: Malcolm Warne; news: Mike Bridgen; chief sub: Andy Brown

Darlington, Aycliffe & Sedgefield Advertiser
01325 381313
www.thisisthenortheast.co.uk
Weekly free (Wed). Owner: Newsquest. Editor: Peter Barron; news: Nigel Burton; features: Lindsey Jennings; chief sub: Ken Farrier

Darlington Herald & Post
01325 262000
www.icteesside.co.uk
Weekly (Thu). Owner: Johnston Press. Editor: Sue Giles

Durham Advertiser
01325 381313
www.thisisthenortheast.co.uk
Weekly free (Thu). Owner: Newsquest. Editor: Peter Barron; news: Nigel Burton; features: Lindsey Jennings; chief sub: Ken Farrier

East Cleveland Advertiser
01325 381313
www.theclarion.co.uk
Weekly free (Fri). Owner: Newsquest. Editor: Peter Barron; news: Nigel Burton; features: Lindsey Jennings; chief sub: Ken Farrier

East Cleveland Herald & Post
01642 234227
www.icteesside.co.uk
Weekly (Wed). Owner: Gazette Media Company (Trinity Mirror). Editor: Sue Giles

Evening Chronicle (Newcastle)
See page 38

Evening Gazette
See page 38

Gateshead Herald and Post
0191 201 6405
www.icnewcastle.co.uk
Weekly (Wed). Owner: Newcastle Chronicle & Journal (Trinity Mirror). Editor: Catherine Welford; news: Zoe Burn

Hartlepool Mail
01429 239333
www.hartlepoolmail.co.uk
Daily. Owner: Johnston Press. Editor: Joy Yates; deputy editor: Brian Nuttley

Hartlepool Star
01429 239333
www.hartlepoolmail.co.uk
Weekly free (Thu). Owner: Johnston Press. Editor: Joy Yates; deputy editor: Brian Nuttley

Hexham Courant
01434 602351
www.hexham-courant.co.uk
Weekly (Fri). Owner: Cumbrian News Group. Editor: Collin Tapping; news: Brian Tilley

Houghton Star
0191 501 5800
Weekly free (Thu). Owner: Johnston Press. Editor: Betty Long

The Journal (Newcastle)
See page 38

Metro North East
0191 477 7445
www.metro.co.uk
Daily. Owner: Newcastle Chronicle & Journal (Trinity Mirror). Editor: Deane Hodgson

Middlesbrough Herald & Post
01642 234227
www.icteesside.co.uk
Weekly (Wed). Owner: Gazette Media Company (Trinity Mirror). Editor: Sue Giles

Morpeth Herald
01670 510522
www.morpethtoday.co.uk
Weekly (Thu). Owner: Johnston Press. Editor: Terry Hackett

Newcastle Herald & Post
0191 201 6405
www.icnewcastle.co.uk
Weekly (Wed). Owner: Newcastle Chronicle & Journal (Trinity Mirror). Editor: Catherine Welford; news: Zoe Burn

Newcastle Times
01332 205900
www.regional-media.co.uk
Weekly (Thu). Owner: Journal Publishing Company. Editor: Charlie Davenport; news: Simon Howorth; features: Katie Doherty; production: Fiona Smith

News Post Leader (Whitley Bay)
0191 251 8484
www.blyth-wansbecktoday.co.uk
Weekly. Owner: Johnston Press. Editor: Ross Weeks

Northeast Guardian
01452 300 037
www.cmcnewspapers.co.uk
Weekly (Thurs). Owner: Gazette. Editor: Elaine Morgan

North Tyneside Herald & Post
0191 201 6405
www.icnewcastle.co.uk
Weekly (Wed). Owner: Newcastle Chronicle & Journal (Trinity Mirror). Editor: Catherine Welford; news: Zoe Burn

Northern Echo
See page 38

Northumberland Gazette
01665 602234
www.northumberlandtoday.co.uk
Weekly (Thu). Owner: Johnston Press. Editor: Paul Larkin

Northumberland Herald and Post
0191 201 6405
Weekly (Wed). Owner: Newcastle Chronicle & Journal (Trinity Mirror). Editor: Catherine Welford; news: Zoe Burn

Peterlee Star
0191 501 5800
Weekly free (Thu). Owner: Johnston Press. Editor: Betty Long

Seaham Star
0191 501 5800
Weekly free (Thu). Owner: Johnston Press. Editor: Betty Long

South Durham Herald & Post
01642 234227
www.icteesside.co.uk
Weekly (Fri). Owner: Gazette Media Company (Trinity Mirror). Editor: Sue Giles

South Shields Gazette
0191 455 4661
www.southtynesidetoday.co.uk
Daily. Owner: Johnston Press. Editor: John Syzmanski

South Tyne Star
0191 455 4661
Weekly free (Thu). Owner: Johnston Press. Editor: John Syzmanski

South Tyneside Herald & Post
0191 201 6405
www.icnewcastle.co.uk
Weekly (Wed). Owner: Newcastle Chronicle & Journal (Trinity Mirror). Editor: Catherine Welford; news: Zoe Burn

Stockton & Billingham Herald & Post
01642 234227
www.icteesside.co.uk
Weekly (Wed). Owner: Gazette Media Company (Trinity Mirror). Editor: Sue Giles

Sunday Sun (Newcastle)
See page 38

Sunderland Echo
0191 501 5800
www.sunderland-today.co.uk
Daily. Owner: Johnston Press. Editor: Rob Lawson; news: Gavin Foster; features: Paul Taylor; production: Jerry Kenny

Sunderland Star
0191 501 5800
Weekly free (Thu). Owner: Johnston Press. Editor: Betty Long

Teesside Focus
01332 365811
www.regional-media.co.uk
Weekly free (Mon). Owner: Journal Publishing Company. General Manager: Martin Scott

Teesside Herald & Post
01642 234227
www.icteesside.co.uk
Weekly (Wed). Owner: Gazette Media Company (Trinity Mirror). Editor: Sue Giles

Wallsend News Guardian
0191 251 8484
www.northtynesidetoday.co.uk
Weekly free (Thu). Owner: Johnston Press. Editor: Ross Weeks

Washington Star
0191 501 5800
Weekly free (Thu). Owner: Johnston Press. Editor: Betty Long

Wear Valley Mercury
01388 768 758
www.wearvalleymercury.co.uk
Weekly (Fri). Owner: Teesdale Mercury. Editor: Adrian Braddy

Whitley Bay News Guardian
0191 251 8566
www.northtynesidetoday.co.uk
Weekly free (Thu). Owner: Johnston Press. Editor: Ross Weeks

● North-west England

Cheshire, Cumbria, Lancashire, Manchester, Merseyside

Accrington Observer
01254 871444
www.accringtonobserver.co.uk
Weekly (Fri). Owner: Guardian Media Group. Editor: Mervyn Kay; news: Stephanie Turner

Advertising Times
01200 422324
Weekly (Fri). Owner: Trinity Mirror Cheshire. Editor: Vivien Meath; news: Duncan Smith

Anfield and Walton Star
0151 472 2701
www.icliverpool.co.uk
Weekly (Thu). Owner: Trinity Mirror Merseyside. Editor: Jane Daly; news editor: Ed Casson

Ashton-under-Lyne Reporter
0161 303 1910
Weekly (Thu). Editor: Nigel Skinner

Asian News
01706 354321
www.theasiannews.co.uk
Monthly (4th Fri). Owner: Guardian Media Group. Editor: Steve Hammond

Barnoldswick & Earby Times
01282 612561
www.eastlancashireonline.co.uk
Weekly (Fri). Owner: Johnston Press. Editor: Roy Prenton; news: Peter Dewhurst

Barrow Advertiser
01229 840150
www.cumbria-online.co.uk
Weekly free (Thu). Owner: Cumbrian News Group. Editor: Steve Brauner; news: Jon Townend; features: Pete Leach; chief sub: Ann McVea

Bentham Guardian
01524 32525
Weekly (Fri). Owner: Johnston Press. Editor: Sue Riley; news: Louise Bryning; features: Paul Collins; chief sub: Bryan Carter

Birkenhead News
0151 647 7111
www.icwirral.co.uk
Weekly (Wed). Owner: Trinity Mirror Merseyside. Editor: Colin Walker

Blackburn Citizen
01254 678678
www.thisislancashire.co.uk
Weekly (Thu). Owner: Newsquest. Editor-in-chief: Kevin Young; news: Andrew Turner; features: John Anson

Blackpool & Fylde Citizen
01772 824631
www.thisislancashire.co.uk
Weekly (Thu). Owner: Newsquest. Editor: Jill Ellis; news: Steve Dunthorne

Blackpool Gazette & Herald
See page 37

Blackpool Reporter
01253 361842
www.blackpoolonline.co.uk
Daily. Owner: Johnston Press. Assistant Editor: Alison Bott

Bolton Evening News
See page 37

Bolton Journal
01204 522345
www.thisisbolton.co.uk
Weekly (Thu). Owner: Newsquest. Editor-in-chief: Steve Hughes; editor: Derrick Grewcock; news: James Higgins; features: Andrew Mosley; production: John Bird

Bootle Times
0151 932 1000
www.icliverpool.co.uk
Weekly (Thu). Owner: Trinity Mirror Merseyside. Editor: Peter Harvey; news: Lloyd Jones

Bromborough & Bebington News
0151 647 7111
Weekly (Wed). Owner: Trinity Mirror Merseyside. Editor: Colin Walker

Burnley Citizen
01254 678678
www.thisislancashire.co.uk
Weekly (Thu). Owner: Newsquest. Editor-in-chief: Kevin Young; news: Andrew Turner; features: John Anson

Burnley Express
01282 426161
www.burnleytoday.co.uk
Weekly (Tue, Fri). Owner: Johnston Press. Editor: Chris Daggett; news: Margaret Parsons; features: Barry Bradshaw; production: Paul Watson

Bury Journal
0161 764 9421
www.thisisbury.co.uk
Weekly (Wed). Owner: Newsquest. Editor: Ian Savage; news: Steve Orrell; chief sub: John Ellavy

Bury Times
0161 764 9421
www.thisisbury.co.uk
Weekly (Wed). Owner: Newsquest. Editor: Ian Savage; news: Steve Orrell; chief sub: John Ellavy

Buy Sell Cheshire
0151 330 4991
www.cheshirenews.co.uk
Weekly (Thu). Owner: Trinity Mirror Cheshire. Editor: Ali McRae

Carnforth Guardian
01524 32525
Weekly (Fri). Owner: Johnston Press. Editor: Sue Riley; news: Louise Bryning; features: Paul Collins; chief sub: Bryan Carter

Chester & District Standard
01244 304500
www.chesterstandard.co.uk
Weekly (Thu). Owner: North Wales Newspapers. Editor: Jonathan White

Chester Chronicle
01244 340151
www.cheshirenews.co.uk
Weekly (Fri). Owner: Trinity Mirror Cheshire. Editor-in-Chief: Eric Langton

Chester Mail
01244 340151
www.cheshirenews.co.uk
Weekly (Fri). Owner: Trinity Mirror Cheshire. Editor-in-Chief: Eric Langton

Chorley Citizen
01257 269313
www.thisislancashire.co.uk
/lancashire/chorley
Weekly (Wed). Owner: Johnston Press. Editor-in-chief: Kevin Young

Chorley Guardian
01257 264911
www.chorleytoday.co.uk
*Weekly (Wed). Owner: Johnston Press.
Editor: Chris Maguire; news: Vanessa
Taylor; chief sub: Mal Morris*

Chronicle Weekend (Oldham)
0161 633 2121
www.oldham-chronicle.co.uk
*Daily. Editor: Jim Williams; news: Mike
Attenborough; chief sub: Steve Sutcliffe*

Clitheroe Advertiser & Times
01200 422324
www.clitheroe.co.uk
*Weekly (Thu). Owner: Johnston Press.
Editor: Vivien Meath; news: Duncan Smith*

Colne Times
01282 612561
www.eastlancashireonline.co.uk
*Weekly (Fri). Owner: Johnston Press.
Editor: Roy Prenton; news: Peter Dewhurst*

Community News (Macclesfield)
01625 503322
*Weekly (Thu). Owner: Northcliffe
Newspapers. Editor: Carla Slynn*

Congleton Advertiser
01782 602525
*Weekly free (Thu). Owner: Northcliffe
Newspapers. Editor: Micheal Saffy;
news: Robert Cotterill; features: Charlotte
Little-Jones*

Congleton Chronicle
01260 273737
www.chronicleseries.com
Weekly (Fri). Editor: Jeremy Condliffe

Congleton Guardian
01260 280686
www.thisischeshire.co.uk
*Weekly (Fri). Owner: Newsquest.
Editor: Carla Slynn; news: Ian Ross*

Crewe & Nantwich Guardian
01925 434000
www.thisischeshire.co.uk
*Weekly (Thu). Owner: Newsquest.
Editor: Nicola Priest*

Crewe Chronicle
01270 256631
www.cheshirenews.co.uk
*Weekly (Wed). Owner: Trinity Mirror
Cheshire. Editor: Dave Fox; news:
Jan Roberts*

Crewe Mail
01270 256631
www.cheshirenews.co.uk
*Weekly (Fri). Owner: Trinity Mirror
Cheshire. Editor: Dave Fox; news:
Jan Roberts*

Crosby Herald
0151 932 1000
www.icseftonandwestlancs.co.uk
*Weekly (Thu). Owner: Trinity Mirror
Merseyside. Editor: Peter Harvey;
news: Lloyd Jones*

**Cumberland and Westmorland
Herald**
01768 862313
www.cwherald.com
*Weekly (Sat). Editor: Colin Maughan;
news: Liz Stannard; features: Helen
Phillips*

Cumberland News
01228 612600
www.cumberland-news.co.uk
*Weekly (Fri). Owner: Cumbrian News
Group. Editor: Keith Sutton; news:
Sue Crawford; features: Mary Ingham;
production: Andy Nixon*

Deeside Chronicle
01244 340151
www.cheshirenews.co.uk
*Weekly (Fri). Owner: Trinity Mirror
Cheshire. Editor-in-Chief: Eric Langton*

East Cumbrian Gazette
01228 612600
www.cumbria-online.co.uk
*Weekly free (Thu). Owner: Cumbrian
News Group. Editor: Keith Sutton; news:
Sue Crawford; features: Mary Ingham;
production: Andy Nixon*

Ellesmere Port Pioneer
0151 355 5181
www.cheshirenews.co.uk
*Weekly (Wed). Owner: Trinity Mirror
Cheshire. Editor: Phil Robinson*

Ellesmere Port Standard
01244 304500
www.ellesmereportstandard.co.uk
*Weekly (Thu). Owner: North Wales
Newspapers. Editor: Jonathan White*

Evening Leader (Chester)
01352 707707
*Daily. Editor: Barry Jones; features:
Joanne Shone; chief sub: Joanne Shone;
production: Karen Perry*

**Fleetwood Weekly News
and Chronicle**
01253 772950
www.fleetwoodtoday.co.uk
*Weekly (Wed). Owner: Johnston Press.
Editor: Gary Miller; news: Karen Evans;
chief sub: Linda Chatburn*

Flint & Holywell Chronicle
01244 821911
www.cheshirenews.co.uk
*Weekly (Fri). Owner: Trinity Mirror
Cheshire. Editor: Kevin Hughes;
news: James Shepherd*

Formby Champion
01704 392392
www.championline.net
*Weekly (Wed). Owner: Champion Media
Group. Editor: Martin Hovden*

Formby Times
01704 872237
www.icformby.co.uk
*Weekly (Thu). Owner: Trinity Mirror
Merseyside. Editor: Hazel Shaw*

Frodsham & Helsby Chronicle
01244 340151
www.cheshirenews.co.uk
*Weekly (Fri). Owner: Trinity Mirror
Cheshire. Editor-in-Chief: Eric Langton*

Garstang Courier
01995 602494
www.garstangtoday.co.uk
*Weekly (Fri). Owner: Johnston Press.
Editor: Richard Machin; news: Tony
Coppin*

Garstang Guardian
01524 32525
www.prestontoday.net
*Weekly (Fri). Owner: Johnston Press.
Editor: Sue Riley; news: Louise Bryning;
features: Paul Collins; chief sub: Bryan
Carter*

Heswall News
0151 647 7111
*Weekly (Wed). Owner: Trinity Mirror
Merseyside. Editor: Colin Walker*

Heywood Advertiser
01706 360626
www.heywoodadvertiser.co.uk
*Weekly (Wed). Owner: Guardian Media
Group. Editor: Paul Harrison*

Hoylake & West Kirby News
0151 647 7111
*Weekly (Wed). Owner: Trinity Mirror
Merseyside. Editor: Colin Walker*

Huyton & Roby Star
0151 236 2000
*Weekly (Thu). Owner: Trinity Mirror
Merseyside. News editor: Jane Daly*

Keswick Reminder
01768 772140
www.keswickreminder.co.uk
Weekly (Fri). Editor: Jane Grave

Kirkby Extra
07831 090566
Monthly (1st Wed). Editor: Chris O'Shea

Kirkham Express
01253 724236
*Weekly (Thu). Owner: Johnston Press.
Editor: Gary Miller; news: Chris Dixon*

Knowsley Challenge
0151 236 2426
www.knowsleychallenge.co.uk
*Monthly (15th). Owner: Trinity Mirror
Merseyside. Editor: Alan Birkett*

Knutsford Guardian
01925 434000
www.thisischeshire.co.uk
*Weekly (Wed). Owner: Newsquest.
Editor: Nicola Priest*

Lakeland Echo
01524 833111
www.lakelandtoday.co.uk
*Weekly (Fri). Owner: Johnston Press.
Editor: David Waddington*

Lancashire Evening Post
See page 38

Lancashire Evening Telegraph
See page 38

Lancaster & Morecambe Citizen
01524 382121
www.thelancasterandmorecambe
citizen.co.uk
*Weekly (Wed). Owner: Newsquest Media
Group. Editor: Phil Fleming*

Lancaster Guardian
01524 32525
www.lancastertoday.co.uk
*Weekly (Fri). Owner: Johnston Press.
Editor: Sue Riley; news: Louise Bryning;
features: Paul Collins; chief sub: Bryan
Carter*

Leigh Journal
01942 672241
www.thisislancashire.co.uk
*Weekly (Thu). Owner: Newsquest.
Editor: Mike Hulme*

Leigh Reporter
01942 603334
www.leightoday.co.uk
Weekly free (Thu). Owner: Johnston Press. Editor: Wendy Moss

Leyland Guardian
01257 264911
www.leylandtoday.co.uk
Weekly (Wed). Owner: Johnston Press. Editor: Tracy Bruce; news: Vanessa Taylor; chief sub: Mal Morris

Liverpool Daily Post & Echo
See page 38

Longridge News
01772 783265
www.thisislancashire.co.uk
Weekly (Thu). Owner: Johnston Press. Editor: Richard Machin

Lytham St Annes & Fylde Express
01253 724236
Weekly (Thu). Owner: Johnston Press. Editor: Gary Miller; news: Chris Dixon

Macclesfield Express
01625 424445
www.macclesfield-express.co.uk
Weekly (Wed). Owner: Guardian Media Group. Editor: Mike Quilley; news: Pat Hills

Macclesfield Times
01625 424445
www.manchesteronline.co.uk /newspapers/macctimes.html
Weekly (Thu). Owner: Guardian Media Group. Editor: Mike Quilley; news: Pat Hills

Maghull & Aintree Star
0151 236 2000
www.icseftonandwestlancs.co.uk /icmaghull
Weekly (Thu). Owner: Trinity Mirror Merseyside. News editor: Jane Daly

Maghull Champion
01704 392392
www.championline.net
Weekly (Wed). Owner: Champion Media Group. Editor: Martin Hovden

Manchester Evening News
See page 38

Manchester Metro News
0161 834 9677
www.metronews.co.uk
Daily free. Editor: Tim Oliver

Marketplace (Wirral)
0151 906 3000
Weekly (Thu). Owner: Newsquest. Editor: Leigh Marles

Metro North West
0161 836 5152
www.metro.co.uk
Daily free. Owner: Associated Newspapers. Editor: Kenny Campbell

Middleton & North Manchester Guardian
0161 643 3615
www.middletonguardian.co.uk
Weekly (Thu). Owner: Guardian Media Group. Editor: Gerry Sammon

Middlewich Chronicle
01244 340151
www.cheshirenews.co.uk
Weekly (Fri). Owner: Trinity Mirror Cheshire. Editor-in-Chief: Eric Langton

Middlewich Guardian
01925 434000
www.thisischeshire.co.uk
Weekly (Wed). Owner: Newsquest. Editor: Nicola Priest

Midweek Advertiser
01695 572501
Weekly (Thu). Owner: Trinity Mirror Merseyside. Editor: Rob Hopkins; news: Clifford Birchall

Mold & Buckley Chronicle
01244 340151
www.cheshirenews.co.uk
Weekly (Fri). Owner: Trinity Mirror Cheshire. Editor-in-Chief: Eric Langton

Morecambe Guardian
01524 32525
Weekly (Fri). Owner: Johnston Press. Editor: Sue Riley; news: Louise Bryning; features: Paul Collins; chief sub: Bryan Carter

Morecambe Visitor
01524 833111
www.morecambetoday.co.uk
Weekly (Wed). Owner: Johnston Press. Editor: Glen Cooper; news: Ingrid Kent

Nantwich Chronicle
01244 340151
www.cheshirenews.co.uk
Weekly (Fri). Owner: Trinity Mirror Cheshire. Editor-in-Chief: Eric Langton

Nelson Leader
01282 612561
www.burnleytoday.co.uk
Weekly (Fri). Owner: Johnston Press. Editor: Roy Prenton; news: Peter Dewhurst

Neston News
0151 647 7111
Weekly (Wed). Owner: Trinity Mirror Merseyside. Editor: Colin Walker

News & Star (Carlisle)
01228 612600
www.news-and-star.co.uk
Daily (Mon-Thu). Owner: Cumbrian News Group. Editor: Keith Sutton; news: Sue Crawford; features: Mary Ingham; production: Andy Nixon

Newton & Golborne Guardian
01925 434000
www.thisischeshire.co.uk
Weekly (Thu). Owner: Newsquest. Editor: Nicola Priest

Northwest Evening Mail (Barrow)
01229 821835
www.nwemail.co.uk
Daily. Owner: Cumbrian News Group. Editor: Steve Brauner; news: Jon Townend; features: Pete Leach; chief sub: Ann McVea

Northwich & District Guardian
01925 434000
www.thisischeshire.co.uk
Weekly (Wed). Owner: Newsquest. Editor: Nicola Priest

Northwich Chronicle
01244 340151
www.cheshirenews.co.uk
Weekly (Fri). Owner: Trinity Mirror Cheshire. Editor-in-Chief: Eric Langton

Northwich Herald & Post
01244 340151
www.cheshirenews.co.uk
Weekly (Fri). Owner: Trinity Mirror Cheshire. Editor-in-Chief: Eric Langton

Northwich Mail
01606 42272
Weekly (Thu). Owner: Trinity Mirror Cheshire. Editor: Paul Brown

Oldham Evening Chronicle
0161 633 2121
www.oldham-chronicle.co.uk
Daily. Editor: Jim Williams; news: Mike Attenborough; chief sub: Steve Sutcliffe

Ormskirk Advertiser
01695 572501
Weekly (Thu). Owner: Trinity Mirror Merseyside. Editor: Rob Hopkins; news: Clifford Birchall

Ormskirk Champion
01704 392392
www.championline.net
Weekly (Wed). Owner: Champion Media Group. Editor: Martin Hovden

Padiham Express
01282 426161
www.burnleytoday.co.uk
Weekly (Tue, Fri). Owner: Johnston Press. Editor: Chris Daggett; news: Margaret Parsons

Pendle & Burnley Reporter
01282 612561
Weekly free (Fri). Owner: Johnston Press. Editor: Roy Prenton; news: Peter Dewhurst

Pendle Express
01282 612561
www.burnleytoday.co.uk
Weekly (Tue, Fri). Owner: Johnston Press. Editor: Roy Prenton; news: Peter Dewhurst

Poynton Times
01625 424445
www.manchesteronline.co.uk
Weekly (Wed). Owner: Guardian Media Group. Editor: Mike Quilley; news: Pat Hills

Preston & Leyland Reporter
01772 838103
Weekly free (Thu). Owner: Johnston Press. Editor: Simon Reynolds

Preston & Leyland Citizen
01772 824631
www.thisislancashire.co.uk
Weekly (Thu). Owner: Newsquest. Editor: Gill Ellis; news: Jane Willis

Prestwich & Whitefield Guide
0161 764 9421
www.thisisbury.co.uk
Weekly (Wed). Owner: Newsquest. Editor: Ian Savage; news: Steve Orrell; chief sub: John Ellavy

Prestwich Advertiser
0161 789 5015
www.prestwichadvertiser.co.uk
Weekly (Fri). Owner: Guardian Media Group. Editor: Vince Hale

Radcliffe Times
0161 764 9421
www.thisisbury.co.uk
Weekly (Wed). Owner: Newsquest. Editor: Ian Savage; news: Steve Orrell; chief sub: John Ellavy

Rochdale Express
01706 354321
www.manchesteronline.co.uk/news
papers/rochdaleexpress.html
*Weekly free (Fri). Owner: Guardian
Media Group. Editor: Claire Mooney*

Rochdale Observer
01706 354321
www.rochdaleobserver.co.uk
*Weekly (Wed, Sat). Owner: Guardian
Media Group. Editor: Claire Mooney*

Rossendale Free Press
01706 213311
www.therossendalefreepress.co.uk
*Weekly (Thu). Owner: Guardian Media
Group. Editor: Stuart Robertson*

Runcorn and Widnes Herald & Post
0151 424 5921
*Weekly (Fri). Owner: Trinity Mirror
Cheshire. Editor: Ian Douglas; news:
Simon Drury*

Runcorn Weekly News
0151 424 5921
www.cheshireonline.icnetwork.co.uk
*Weekly (Thu). Owner: Trinity Mirror
Cheshire. Editor: Ian Douglas; news:
Simon Drury*

Runcorn World
0845 603 7854
www.runcornworld.co.uk
*Weekly (Wed). Owner: Newsquest.
Editor: Nicola Priest; assistant editor:
Stephen Hallmark*

St Helens Star
01925 434000
www.thisisst-helens.co.uk
*Weekly (Thu). Owner: Newsquest.
Editor: Nicola Priest*

**St Helens, Prescot & Knowsley
Reporter**
01744 22285
www.sthelenstoday.net
*Weekly (Wed). Owner: Johnston Press.
Editor: Andy Moffatt*

Sale & Altrincham Messenger
0161 908 3360
www.messengernewspapers.co.uk
*Weekly (Thu). Owner: Newsquest.
Editor: Lynn Hughes*

Salford Advertiser
0161 789 5015
www.salfordadvertiser.co.uk
*Weekly (Fri). Owner: Guardian Media
Group. Editor: Vince Hale*

Skelmersdale Advertiser
01695 572501
www.icseftonandwestlancs.co.uk
*Weekly (Thu). Owner: Trinity Mirror
Merseyside. Editor: Rob Hopkins;
news: Clifford Birchall*

Skelmersdale Champion
01704 392392
www.championline.net
*Weekly (Wed). Owner: Champion Media
Group. Editor: Martin Hovden*

South Cheshire Advertiser
01782 602525
*Weekly free (Thu). Owner: Northcliffe
Newspapers. Editor: Michael Saffy;
news: Robert Cotterill; features:
Charlotte Little-Jones*

South Cheshire Guardian
01925 434000
www.thisischeshire.co.uk
*Weekly (Wed). Owner: Newsquest.
Editor: Nicola Priest*

South Cheshire Mail
01270 256631
www.cheshirenews.co.uk
*Weekly (Wed). Owner: Trinity Mirror
Cheshire. Editor: Dave Fox; news:
Jan Roberts*

South Lakes Citizen
01539 720555
www.thisisthelakedistrict.co.uk
*Weekly free (Wed). Owner: Newsquest.
Editor: Mike Glover; news: Mike Addison;
chief sub: Richard Belk*

South Liverpool Merseymart
0151 734 4000
*Weekly (Thu). Owner: Trinity Mirror
Merseyside. News editor: Kevin Mathews*

South Manchester Reporter
0161 446 2213
www.southmanchesterreporter.co.uk
*Weekly (Thu). Owner: Guardian Media
Group. Editor: Laurence Matheson; news:
Gareth Tidman*

South Wirral News
0151 355 5181
*Weekly free. Owner: Trinity Mirror
Cheshire. Editor: Phil Robinson*

Southport Champion
01704 392392
www.championline.net
*Weekly (Wed). Owner: Champion Media
Group. Editor: Martin Hovden*

Stockport Citizen
0161 491 5700
*Fortnightly (Thu). Independent.
Editor: Mike Shields*

Stockport Express
0161 480 4491
www.stockportexpress.co.uk
*Weekly (Wed). Owner: Guardian Media
Group. Editor: Mandy Leigh; news:
Duncan Ponter; features: Lisa Woodhouse*

Stockport Times East
0161 475 4834
www.stockportexpress.co.uk
*Weekly (Thu). Owner: Guardian Media
Group. Editor: Mandy Leigh; news:
Duncan Ponter; features: Lisa Woodhouse*

Stockport Times West
0161 475 4834
www.stockportexpress.co.uk
*Weekly (Thu). Owner: Guardian Media
Group. Editor: Mandy Leigh; news:
Duncan Ponter; features: Lisa Woodhouse*

Stretford & Urmston Messenger
0161 908 3360
www.messengernewspapers.co.uk
*Weekly (Thu). Owner: Newsquest.
Editor: Lynn Hughes*

Tameside Advertiser
0161 339 7611
www.tamesideadvertiser.co.uk
*Weekly free (Thu). Owner: Guardian
Media Group. Editor: David Porter*

Tameside Reporter
0161 304 7691
www.tamesidereporter.com
*Weekly (Thu). Owner: Ashton Weekly
Newspapers. Editor: Nigel Skinner*

**Thornton, Cleveleys & Poulton
Citizen**
01772 824631
www.thisislancashire.co.uk
*Weekly (Thu). Owner: Newsquest.
Editor: Jill Ellis; news: Steve Dunthorne*

Village Visiter (Lancashire)
01695 572501
*Weekly (Thu). Owner: Trinity Mirror
Merseyside. Editor: Rob Hopkins;
news: Clifford Birchall*

Wallasey News
0151 647 7111
*Weekly (Wed). Owner: Trinity Mirror
Merseyside. Editor: Colin Walker*

Warrington Guardian
01925 434000
www.thisischeshire.co.uk
*Weekly (Thu). Owner: Newsquest. Editor:
Nicola Priest; news: Gareth Dunning*

Warrington Guardian Midweek
01925 434000
www.thisischeshire.co.uk
*Weekly free (Tue). Owner: Newsquest.
Editor: Nicola Priest*

Warrington Mercury
01925 434000
www.thisischeshire.co.uk
*Weekly free (Fri). Owner: Newsquest.
Editor: Nicola Priest*

West Cumberland Times and Star
01900 607600
www.times-and-star.co.uk
*Weekly (Fri). Owner: Cumbrian News
Group. Editor: Stephen Johnson; deputy
editor: Ian Brogden*

West Cumbrian Gazette
01228 612600
www.cumbria-online.co.uk
*Weekly free (Thu). Owner: Cumbrian
News Group. Editor: Keith Sutton; news:
Sue Crawford; features: Mary Ingham;
production: Andy Nixon*

West Derby & Tuebrook Star
0151 236 2000
*Weekly (Thu). Owner: Trinity Mirror
Merseyside. Editor: Jane Daly; news
editor: Ed Casson*

Westmorland Gazette
01539 720555
www.thisisthelakedistrict.co.uk
*Weekly (Fri). Owner: Newsquest.
Editor: Mike Glover; news: Mike Addison;
chief sub: Richard Belk*

Westmorland Messenger
01539 720555
www.thisisthelakedistrict.co.uk
*Weekly (Wed). Owner: Newsquest.
Editor: Mike Glover; news: Mike Addison;
chief sub: Richard Belk*

Whitchurch Herald
01948 662332
*Weekly (Thu). Owner: Trinity Mirror
Cheshire. Editor: Andrew Bowan*

Whitehaven News
01946 595100
www.whitehaven-news.co.uk
*Weekly (Thu). Owner: Cumbrian News
Group. Editor: Colin Edgar; deputy
editor: Alan Cleaver; news: David Siddall*

Widnes Weekly News
0151 424 5921
www.iccheshire.co.uk
Weekly (Thu). Owner: Trinity Mirror
Cheshire. Editor: Ian Douglas;
news: Simon Drury

Widnes World
0151 907 8525
www.widnesworld.co.uk
Weekly (Wed). Owner: Newsquest.
Editor: Nicola Priest; assistant editor:
Stephen Hallmark

Wigan Courier
01257 400026
www.wigancourier.co.uk
Monthly (last Fri). Independent.
Editor: John Callon

Wigan Evening Post
01772 838103
www.wigantoday.net
Daily. Owner: Johnston Press.
Editor: Simon Reynolds; head of content:
Blaise Tapp

Wigan Observer
01772 838103
www.wigantoday.net
Daily. Owner: Johnston Press.
Editor: Simon Reynolds; head of content:
Blaise Tapp

Wigan Reporter
01772 838103
www.wigantoday.net
Weekly free (Thu). Owner: Johnston
Press. Editor: Simon Reynolds; head
of content: Blaise Tapp

Wilmslow Citizen
0161 491 5700
Fortnightly (Thu). Independent.
Editor: Mike Shields

Wilmslow Express
01625 529333
www.thewilmslowexpress.co.uk
Weekly (Wed). Owner: Guardian Media
Group. Editor: Jackie Doran; news:
Betty Anderson

Winsford Chronicle
01244 340151
www.cheshirenews.co.uk
Weekly (Fri). Owner: Trinity Mirror
Cheshire. Editor-in-Chief: Eric Langton

Winsford Guardian
01925 434000
www.thisischeshire.co.uk
Weekly (Wed). Owner: Newsquest.
Editor: Nicola Priest

Wirral Chronicle
01244 340151
www.cheshirenews.co.uk
Weekly (Fri). Owner: Trinity Mirror
Cheshire. Editor-in-Chief: Eric Langton

Wirral Globe
0151 906 3000
www.thisiswirral.co.uk
Weekly (Wed). Owner: Newsquest.
Editor: Leigh Marles

Wirral Target
0151 906 3000
www.thisiswirral.co.uk
Fortnightly free (Wed). Owner:
Newsquest. Editor: Leigh Marles

Wythenshawe World
0161 998 4786
Fortnightly free (Fri). Editor: John Oatway

Isle of Man

Isle of Man Courier
01624 695695
www.iomonline.co.im
Weekly (Thu). Owner: Johnston Press.
Editor: John Sherrocks; news: Jo Overty;
chief sub: Dave Corbett

Isle of Man Examiner
01624 695695
www.iomonline.co.im
Weekly (Tue). Owner: Johnston Press.
Editor: John Sherrocks; news: Jo Overty;
chief sub: Dave Corbett

The Manx Independent
01624 695695
www.iomonline.co.im
Weekly (Fri). Owner: Johnston Press.
Editor: John Sherrocks; news: Jo Overty;
chief sub: Dave Corbett

Regional newspapers – Wales

● Major regionals

Wales on Sunday
Thomson House, Havelock Street,
Cardiff CF10 1XR
029 2058 3583
www.icwales.co.uk
Weekly (Sun). Owner: Western Mail
& Echo (Trinity Mirror). Editor:
Tim Gordon; news: Laura Kemp

Western Mail
Thomson House, Havelock Street,
Cardiff CF10 1XR
029 2058 3583
www.icwales.co.uk
Daily. Owner: Western Mail & Echo
(Trinity Mirror). Editor: Alan Edmunds;
news: Paul Carey

South Wales Echo
Thomson House, Havelock Street,
Cardiff CF10 1XR
029 2058 3583
www.icwales.co.uk
Daily. Owner: Western Mail & Echo
(Trinity Mirror). Editor: Richard
Williams; news: Cathy Owen

South Wales Evening Post
PO Box 14, Adelaide Street,
Swansea SA1 1QT
01792 510000
www.swep.co.uk
Daily. Owner: Northcliffe Newspapers.
Editor: Spencer Feeney; news: Peter Slee;
features: Catherine Ings; chief sub: Lynne
Fernquest

● North Wales

Abergele Visitor
01492 584321
www.icnorthwales.co.uk
Weekly (Thu). Owner: Trinity Mirror
North Wales. Editor: Alan Davies;
news: Steve Stratford

Bangor Chronicle
01248 387400
www.northwaleschronicle.co.uk
Weekly (Thu). Owner: North Wales
Newspapers. Editor: Emlyn Roberts;
news: Claire Hart; features: Tony Coates

Bangor/Anglesey Mail
01286 671111
www.icnorthwales.co.uk
Weekly (Wed). Owner: Trinity Mirror
North Wales. Editor: Jeff Eames; news:
Linda Roberts; production: Mark Jones

Buy Sell (Flintshire Edition)
01978 290400
Weekly (Wed). Owner: Trinity Mirror
Cheshire. No editorial

Caernarfon & Denbigh Herald
01286 671111
www.icnorthwales.co.uk
Weekly (Thu). Owner: Trinity Mirror
North Wales. Editor: Jeff Eames; news:
Linda Roberts; production: Mark Jones

Y Cymro
01970 615000
www.y-cymro.co.uk
Weekly (Mon). Owner: Tindle Newspapers.
Editor: Beverley Davies

Daily Post
01492 574455
www.icnorthwales.co.uk
Daily. Owner: Trinity Mirror North Wales.
Editor: Rob Irvine

Denbighshire Free Press
01745 813535
www.denbighshirefreepress.co.uk
Weekly (Thu). Owner: North Wales
Newspapers. Editor: Alistair Syme

Flintshire Chronicle
01244 821911
www.icnorthwales.co.uk
Weekly (Fri). Owner: North Wales
Newspapers. Editor: Kevin Hughes;
news: James Shepherd

Flintshire Leader
01244 304500
www.chesterstandard.co.uk
Weekly (Thu). Owner: North Wales
Newspapers. Editor: Barrie Jones

Flintshire Leader & Standard
01352 707707
www.flintshirestandard.co.uk
Weekly (Thu). Editor: Barrie Jones;
features: Joanne Shone; chief sub:
Joanne Shone; production: Karen Perry

Gwynedd Chronicle
01248 387400
www.chroniclenow.co.uk
Weekly (Thu). Owner: North Wales
Newspapers. Editor: Emlyn Roberts;
news: Claire Hart; features: Tony Coates

Yr Herald
01286 671111
www.icnorthwales.co.uk
Weekly (Sat). Owner: Trinity Mirror
North Wales. Editor: Jeff Eames; news:
Linda Roberts; production: Mark Jones

Holyhead & Anglesey Mail
01286 671111
www.icnorthwales.co.uk
Weekly (Wed). Owner: Trinity Mirror
North Wales. Editor: Jeff Eames; news:
Linda Roberts; production: Mark Jones

North Wales Chronicle
01248 387400
www.chroniclenow.co.uk
Weekly (Thu). Owner: North Wales
Newspapers. Editor: Emlyn Roberts;
news: Claire Hart; features: Tony Coates

North Wales Pioneer
01492 531188
www.northwalespioneer.co.uk
Weekly (Thu). Owner: North Wales
Newspapers. Editor: Steve Rogers

North Wales Weekly News
01492 584321
www.icnorthwales.co.uk
Weekly (Thu). Owner: Trinity Mirror
North Wales. Editor: Alan Davies;
news: Steve Stratford

Rhyl & Prestatyn Visitor
01745 334144
www.icnorthwales.co.uk
Weekly free (Wed). Owner: Trinity Mirror
North Wales. Editor: Alan Davies;
news: Dave Jones

Rhyl, Prestatyn & Abergele Journal
01745 357500
www.rhyljournal.co.uk
Weekly (Thu). Owner: North Wales
Newspapers. Editor: Steve Rogers; deputy
editor: Terry Canty

Vale Advertiser
01492 584321
icnorthwales.icnetwork.co.uk
/news/valeadvertiser
Weekly (Fri). Owner: Trinity Mirror
North Wales. Editor: Alan Davies;
news: Steve Stratford

Wrexham Evening Leader
01978 355151
www.eveningleader.co.uk
Daily. Owner: North Wales Newspapers.
Editor: Barrie Jones

Wrexham Leader
01978 355151
www.bigleader.co.uk
Weekly free (Fri). Owner: North Wales
Newspapers. Editor: Barrie Jones

Wrexham Mail
01978 351515
www.icnorthwales.co.uk
Weekly (Thu). Owner: Trinity Mirror
Cheshire. Editor: Kevin Hughes; news:
James Shepherd

Ynys Mon Chronicle
01248 387400
www.chroniclenow.co.uk
Weekly (Thu). Owner: North Wales
Newspapers. Editor: Emlyn Roberts;
news: Claire Hart; features: Tony Coates

● **South Wales**

Abergavenny Chronicle
01873 852187
www.abergavenny.co.uk
Weekly (Thu). Owner: Tindle
Newspapers. Editor: Liz Davies

Abergavenny Free Press
01873 857497
www.thisismonmouthshire.co.uk
Weekly (Wed). Owner: Newsquest.
Editor: Andy Downie

Barry & District News
01446 704981
www.thisisbarry.co.uk
Weekly (Thu). Owner: North Wales
Newspapers. Editor: Shira Valek

Barry Gem
01446 774484
www.barry-today.co.uk
Weekly (Thu). Owner: Tindle
Newspapers. Editor: Caroline Patuto

Brecon & Radnor Express
01874 610111
www.brecon-radnor.co.uk
Weekly (Wed). Owner: Tindle
Newspapers. Editor: Clare Graham

Bridgend & District Recorder
01446 774484
Weekly (Tue). Owner: Tindle Newspapers.
Editor: Caroline Patuto

Cambrian News
01970 615000
www.aberystwyth-today.co.uk
Weekly (Wed). Owner: Tindle
Newspapers. Editor: Beverly Davies;
news: Simon Middlehurst

Campaign Blackwood
01633 777212
www.thisisgwent.co.uk
Weekly (Fri). Owner: North Wales
Newspapers. Editor: Andy Downie;
chief sub: Gina Robertson

Campaign Caerphilly
01633 777212
www.thisisgwent.co.uk
Weekly (Fri). Owner: North Wales
Newspapers. Editor: Andy Downie;
chief sub: Gina Robertson

Campaign North Gwent
01633 777212
www.thisisgwent.co.uk
Weekly (Fri). Owner: North Wales
Newspapers. Editor: Andy Downie;
chief sub: Gina Robertson

Campaign Pontypridd
01633 777212
www.thisisgwent.co.uk
Weekly (Fri). Owner: North Wales
Newspapers. Editor: Andy Downie;
chief sub: Gina Robertson

Cardiff Advertiser & Property Times
029 2030 3900
www.thecardiffandsouthwales
advertiser.co.uk
Weekly (Fri). Independent.
Editor: David Hynes

Cardigan & Tivyside Advertiser
01239 614343
www.thisistivyside.net
Weekly (Wed). Owner: Newsquest.
Editor: Areurin Evans; news: Sue Lewis

Carmarthen Herald
01267 227222
www.thisissouthwales.co.uk
Weekly free (Fri). Owner: Northcliffe
Newspapers. Editor: Robert Lloyd;
news: Rachael Misstear

Carmarthen Journal
01267 227222
www.thisissouthwales.co.uk
Weekly (Wed). Owner: Northcliffe
Newspapers. Editor: David Hardy;
news: Diane Williams

Chepstow Free Press
01291 621882
www.thisismonmouthshire.co.uk
Weekly (Wed). Owner: Newsquest.
Editor: Andy Downie; news: Alex Cinus

County Echo (Newport)
01348 874445
www.newport-today.co.uk
Weekly (Fri). Owner: Tindle Newspapers.
Editor: Bev Davies

County Times & Gazette (Brecon)
01938 553354
www.countytimes.co.uk
Weekly (Thu). Owner: North Wales
Newspapers. Editor: Martin Wright

Courier (Neath)
01792 510000
Weekly (Tue). Owner: Northcliffe Newspapers. Editor: Paul Turner

Cowbridge Gem
01446 774484
www.cowbridge-today.co.uk
Weekly (Thu). Owner: Tindle Newspapers. Editor: Caroline Patuto

Cynon Valley Leader
01685 873136
www.icwales.co.uk
Weekly (Wed). Owner: Western Mail & Echo (Trinity Mirror). Editor: Gary Marsh

Glamorgan Gazette
01656 304924
www.icwales.co.uk
Weekly (Thu). Owner: Western Mail & Echo (Trinity Mirror). Editor: Deborah Rees

Gwent Gazette
01495 304589
www.icwales.co.uk
Weekly (Tue). Owner: Western Mail & Echo (Trinity Mirror). Editor: Sarah Harris

Heart of Wales Chronicle
01874 610111
Weekly (Mon). Owner: Tindle Newspapers. Editor: Clare Graham

Llanelli Star
01554 745300
www.thisissouthwales.co.uk
Weekly (Wed, Thu). Owner: Northcliffe Newspapers. Editor: Rob Lloyd; assistant editor: Susanne Oakley

Llantwit Major Gem
01446 774484
www.llantwit-major-today.co.uk
Weekly (Thu). Owner: Tindle Newspapers. Editor: Caroline Patuto

Metro Cardiff
01179 343 728
www.metro.co.uk
Daily. Owner: Associated newspapers. Editor: Clare Ogden

Merthyr Express
01685 856500
Weekly (Fri). Owner: Western Mail & Echo (Trinity Mirror). Editor: Gordon Caldicott

Mid Wales Journal
01743 283312
www.midwalesjournal.co.uk
Weekly (Fri). Owner: Midland News Association. Editor: Mike Robinson; deputy Editor: Mary Queally

Milford & West Wales Mercury
01646 698971
www.thisismilfordhaven.co.uk
Weekly (Thu). Owner: Newsquest. Editor: Fiona Phillips News editor: Richard Harris

Monmouth Free Press
01600 713631
www.thisismonmouthshire.co.uk
Weekly (Wed). Owner: Newsquest. Editor: Andy Downie; news: Andy Sherwill

Monmouthshire Beacon
01600 712142
www.monmouth-today.co.uk
Weekly (Thu). Owner: Tindle Newspapers. Editor: Robert Williams

Narbeth & Whitland Observer
01834 843262
Weekly (Fri). Owner: Tindle Newspapers. Editor: Neil Dickinson

Neath & Port Talbot Guardian
01639 778885
Weekly (Thu). Owner: Western Mail & Echo (Trinity Mirror). Editor: Rhodri Evans

Neath & Port Talbot Tribune
01792 510000
Monthly (2nd Fri). Owner: Northcliffe Newspapers. Editor: Paul Turner

Penarth Times
029 2070 7234
www.thisispenarth.co.uk
Weekly (Thu). Owner: North Wales Newspapers. News editor: Shira Valek

Pontypool Free Press
01495 751133
www.thisismonmouthshire.co.uk
Weekly (Wed). Owner: Newsquest. Editor: Andy Downie; news: Adrian Osmond

Pontypridd Observer
01443 665161
www.icwales.com
Weekly (Wed). Owner: Western Mail & Echo (Trinity Mirror). Editor: Wayne Nowaczyk

Rhondda Leader
01443 665151
Weekly (Thu). Owner: Western Mail & Echo (Trinity Mirror). Editor: Kayrin Davies; news: Dave Edwards

South Wales Argus
01633 810000
www.thisisgwent.co.uk
Daily. Owner: Newsquest. Editor: Gerry Keighley; chief sub: Caroline Woolard

South Wales Guardian
01269 592781
www.thisisammanford.co.uk
Weekly (Wed). Owner: Newsquest. Editor: Elizabeth Cartwright; news: Emma Evans; features: Richard Sharpe

Swansea Herald
01792 514630
Weekly (Thu). Owner: Northcliffe Newspapers. Editor: Spencer Feeney

Tenby Observer
01834 843262
www.tenby-today.co.uk
Weekly (Fri). Owner: Tindle Newspapers. Editor: Neil Dickinson

Tenby Times
01834 843262
Monthly free (1st Wed). Owner: Tindle Newspapers. Editor: Neil Dickinson

Weekly Argus
01633 810000
www.thisisgwent.co.uk
Weekly (Thu). Owner: Newsquest. Editor: Gerry Keighley; chief sub: Caroline Woolard

Western Telegraph
01437 763133
www.thisispembrokeshire.net
Weekly (Wed). Owner: Newsquest. Editor: Fiona Philips

● Main regionals

Aberdeen Press and Journal
Aberdeen Journals, Lang Stracht, Mastrick, Aberdeen AB15 6DF
01224 690222
www.thisisnorthscotland.co.uk
Daily. Owner: Northcliffe Newspapers. Editor: Derek Tucker; news: Andrew Hebdon; features: Richard Neville; chief sub: Jim Urquart

Courier and Advertiser
80 Kingsway East, Dundee DD4 8SL
01382 223131
www.thecourier.co.uk
Daily. Owner: DC Thomson. Editor: Bill Hutcheon; news: Arliss Rhind; features: Catriona Macinnes; production: Brian Clarkson

Daily Record
One Central Quay, Glasgow G3 8DA
0141 309 3000
www.dailyrecord.co.uk
Daily. Owner: Mirror Group. Editor: Bruce Waddell; news: Tom Hamilton; features: Melanie Harvey

Edinburgh Evening News
Barclay House, 108 Holyrood Road, Edinburgh EH8 8AS
0131 620 8620
www.edinburghnews.com
Daily. Owner: Scotsman Publications. Editor: John McLellan; news: Euan McGrory; features: Gina Davidson; chief sub: Howard Dorman; production: Mark Eadie

Glasgow Evening Times
200 Renfield Street, Glasgow G2 3QB
0141 302 7000
www.eveningtimes.co.uk
Daily. Owner: Newsquest. Editor: Charles McGhee; news: Hugh Boag; features: Garry Scott; chief sub: Andy Clark

Glasgow Herald
200 Renfield Street, Glasgow G2 3QB
0141 302 7000
www.theherald.co.uk
Daily. Owner: Newsquest. Editor: Mark Douglas-Home; news: Magnus Llewellin; features: Mark Smith; chief sub: Chris Macrae

Scotland On Sunday
Barclay House, 108 Holyrood Road, Edinburgh EH8 8AS
0131 620 8620
www.scotlandonsunday.com
Sunday. Owner: Scotsman Publications. Editor: Tom Little; news: Peter Laing; features: Claire Hay; chief sub: Martin Allen; production: Chris Dry

The Scotsman
Barclay House, 108 Holyrood Road,
Edinburgh EH8 8AS
0131 620 8620
www.scotsman.com
*Daily. Owner: Scotsman Publications.
Editor: Ian Stewart; news: James Hall;
assistant features editor: Gaby Soutar;
production editors: John Ellingham and
Alistair Norman (subs), Alastair Clark
(opinion)*

Scottish Daily Mirror
1 Central Quay, Glasgow G3 8DA
0141 221 2121
www.mirror.co.uk
*Daily. Owner: Trinity Mirror.
News: Maggie Barrie*

Sunday Herald
200 Renfield Street, Glasgow G2 3QB
0141 302 7800
www.sundayherald.com
*Sunday. Owner: Newsquest. Editor:
Richard Walker; news: Charlene Sweeney;
features: Susan Flockhart; production:
Roxanne Sorooshian*

Sunday Mail
One Central Quay, Glasgow G3 8DA
0141 309 3000
www.sundaymail.co.uk
*Sunday. Owner: Mirror Group. Editor:
Allan Rennie; news: Brendan McGinty*

Sunday Post
DC Thomson & Co, 2 Albert Square,
Dundee DD1 9QJ
01382 223131
www.thesundaypost.co.uk
*Sunday. Owner: DC Thomson. Editor:
David Pollington; deputy editor; Alastair
Bennett; news: Tom McKay; features:
Bruce Allan*

● Other newspapers

Aberdeen & District Independent
01224 618300
www.aberdeen-indy.co.uk
*Weekly (Thu). Independent. Editor:
Derek Piper; news: Donna Morrison*

Aberdeen Citizen
01224 690222
*Weekly (Wed). Owner: Northcliffe
Newspapers. Editor: Damien Bates;
deputy: Richard Prest; news: Louise
Redvers; chief sub: James Donaldson*

Aberdeen Evening Express
01224 690222
www.eveningexpress.co.uk
*Daily. Owner: Northcliffe Newspapers.
Editor: Damien Bates; deputy: Richard
Prest; news: Louise Redvers; chief sub:
James Donaldson*

The Advertiser (Midlothian)
0131 561 6600
*Weekly (Wed). Owner: Johnston Press.
Editor: Roy Scott; news: Alex Hogg*

Airdrie & Coatbridge Advertiser
01236 748648
www.icscotland.co.uk
*Weekly (Wed). Owner: Scottish &
Universal Newspapers (Trinity Mirror).
Editor: John Murdoch*

Alloa & Hillfoots Advertiser
01259 214416
*Weekly (Thu). Owner: Dunfermline Press
Group. Editor: Kevin McRoberts; news:
Faye Thomson*

Annandale Herald
01461 202078
*Weekly (Thu). Owner: Dumfriesshire
Newspapers. Editor: Bryan Armstrong;
news: Alan Hall*

Annandale Observer
01461 202078
*Weekly (Fri). Owner: Dumfriesshire
Newspapers. Editor: Bryan Armstrong;
news: Alan Hall*

Arbroath Herald
01241 872274
*Weekly (Fri). Owner: Johnston Press.
Editor: Craig Nisbet; news: Brian Forsythe*

Ardrossan & Saltcoats Herald
01294 464321
www.ardrossanherald.com
*Weekly (Fri). Owner: Scottish & Universal
Newspapers (Trinity Mirror). Editor: Alex
Clarke; news: Craig Nisbet*

Argyllshire Advertiser
01631 563058
www.argyllshireadvertiser.co.uk
*Weekly (Fri). Owner: Oban Times. Editor:
Stewart Mackenzie; news: Joanne Simms*

Arran Banner
01631 568000
www.obantimes.co.uk
*Weekly (Sat). Owner: Oban Times.
Editor: Stewart Mackenzie*

Ayr Advertiser
01292 267631
*Weekly (Wed). Owner: Ayrshire Weekly
Press. Editor: Alex Clarke; news: Caroline
Paterson*

Ayrshire Extra
01292 611666
*Weekly (Thu). Owner: Archant.
Editor: John Matthews*

Ayrshire Post
01292 261111
www.icscotland.co.uk
*Weekly (Wed). Owner: Scottish &
Universal Newspapers (Trinity Mirror).
Editor: Alan Woodison; deputy editor:
Cheryl McEvoy; features: Yonnie McInnes*

Ayrshire Weekly Press
01294 464321
*Weekly (Fri). Owner: Scottish & Universal
Newspapers (Trinity Mirror). Editor:
Alex Clarke; news: Craig Nisbet*

Ayrshire World
01294 272233
www.icscotland.co.uk
*Weekly free (Wed). Owner: Scottish &
Universal Newspapers (Trinity Mirror).
Editor: Alan Woodison; news: Lex Brown*

Banffshire Herald
01542 886262
www.bannfshireherald.com
*Weekly (Fri). Owner: J&M Publishing.
Editor: Lorna Campbell*

Barrhead News
0141 887 7055
*Weekly (Wed). Owner: Clyde & Forth
Press. Editor: James Walsh*

Bearsden, Milngavie & Glasgow Extra
0141 427 7878
www.icscotland.co.uk
*Weekly (Thu). Owner: Archant. Editor:
Allan Hodge; news: Colin Macdonald;
chief sub: Jim Cameron*

Bellshill Speaker
01698 264611
*Weekly (Thu). Owner: Johnston Press.
Editor: Archie Fleming*

Berwick Gazette
01289 306677
www.berwicktoday.co.uk
*Weekly (Thu). Owner: Johnston Press.
Editor: Sandy Brydon*

Berwickshire News
01289 306677
www.berwickshiretoday.co.uk
*Weekly (Thu). Owner: Johnston Press.
Editor: Sandy Brydon*

Blairgowrie Advertiser
01250 872854
www.icscotland.co.uk
*Weekly (Thu). Owner: Scottish &
Universal Newspapers (Trinity Mirror).
Editor: Alison Lowson*

Border Telegraph
01896 758395
www.bordertelegraph.com
*Weekly (Tue). Owner: Dunfermline Press.
Editor: Atholl Innes*

Brechin Advertiser
01356 622767
www.brechinadvertiser.com
*Weekly (Thu). Owner: Angus County
Press. Editor: Alan Ducat; news: Phillip
Murray; features: Jenny Hill*

Buchan Observer
01779 472017
www.buchanie.co.uk
*Weekly (Tue). Owner: Archant.
Editor: Ken Duncan*

The Buteman
01700 502503
www.icscotland.co.uk
*Weekly (Fri). Owner: Angus County Press.
Editor: Craig Borland*

Caithness Courier
01955 602424
www.caithness-courier.co.uk
*Weekly (Wed). Owner: North of Scotland
Newspapers. Editor: Alan Henry; news:
Karen Macdonald*

Campbell Times Courier
01631 563058
*Weekly (Sat). Owner: Oban Times. Editor:
Stewart Mackenzie; news: Joanne Simms*

Campbeltown Courier & Argyllshire Advertiser
01586 554646
www.campbeltowncourier.co.uk
*Weekly (Fri). Owner: Oban Times.
Senior Reporter: Aileen McLennon*

Carrick Gazette
01671 402503
*Weekly (Thu). Owner: Angus County
Press. Editor: Stephen Norris*

Central Fife Times & Advertiser
01383 728201
*Weekly (Wed). Owner: Dunfermline Press
Group. Editor: Jim Stark; chief sub: Susan
Dryburgh*

Clydebank Post
0141 952 0565
Weekly (Thu). Owner: Clyde & Forth Press.
Editor: James Walsh

Clyde Weekly News
01294 273421
www.icScotland.co.uk
Weekly (Wed). Owner: Scottish &
Universal Newspapers (Trinity Mirror).
Editor: Alex Clarke

Craigmillar Chronicle
0131 661 0791
www.craignet.org.uk/chronicle
Monthly free (1st of month).
Editor: Sally Fraser

Cumbernauld News & Advertiser
01236 725578
www.falkirktoday.co.uk
Weekly free (Fri). Owner: Johnston Press.
Editor: Alistair Blyth; chief sub: Neil Smith

Cumbernauld News &
Kilsyth Chronicle
01236 725578
www.falkirktoday.co.uk
Weekly (Wed). Owner: Johnston Press.
Editor: Alistair Blyth; chief sub: Neil Smith

Cumnock Chronicle
01290 421633
Weekly (Wed). Owner: Ayrshire Weekly
Press. Editor: Douglas Skelton

Deeside Piper
01330 824955
www.deesidepiper.com
Weekly (Fri). Owner: Angus County Press.
Editor: Phil Allan

Donside Piper & Herald
01330 824955
www.donsidepiper.com
Weekly (Fri). Owner: Angus County Press.
Editor: Phil Allan

Dumbarton & Vale Of Leven
Reporter
01436 673434
Weekly (Tue). Owner: Clyde & Forth Press.
Editor: Alan Green; news: Steve MacIlroy

Dumfries & Galloway Standard
01387 240342
www.icscotland.co.uk
Weekly (Wed). Owner: Scottish &
Universal Newspapers (Trinity Mirror).
Editor: Elizabeth Martin; news: Ian Pollock

Dumfries and Galloway Today
01387 240342
www.icscotland.co.uk
Weekly (Wed). Owner: Scottish &
Universal Newspapers (Trinity Mirror).
Editor: Elizabeth Martin; news: Ian Pollock

Dumfries Courier
01461 202078
Weekly free (Fri). Owner: Dumfriesshire
Newspapers. Editor: Bryan Armstrong;
news: Alan Hall

Dunfermline Press &
West of Fife Advertiser
01383 728201
www.snpa.org.uk
Weekly (Thu). Owner: Dunfermline Press
Group. Editor: Tom Davidson; news:
Simon Harris

Dunoon Observer &
Argyllshire Standard
01369 703218
www.dunoon-observer.co.uk
Weekly (Fri). Owner: E&R Ingles.
Editor: Bill Jardin

East Fife Mail
01592 261451
www.fifenow.co.uk
Weekly free (Wed). Owner: Johnston
Press. Editor: Ian Muirhead

East Kilbride Mail
01355 270510
www.eastkilbridemail.com
Weekly (Wed). Owner: Forth
Independent. Editor: Ross McKay

East Kilbride News
01355 265000
www.iclanarkshire.co.uk
Weekly (Wed). Owner: Scottish &
Universal Newspapers (Trinity Mirror).
Editor: Gordon Bury; news: Lynda Nichol

East Kilbride World
01698 283200
Weekly free (Fri). Owner: Scottish &
Universal Newspapers (Trinity Mirror).
Editor: Joseph Kelly

East Lothian Courier
01620 822451
www.eastlothiancourier.com
Weekly (Thu). Owner: Dunfermline Press
Group. Editor: Elaine Reid

East Lothian Herald
01289 306677
www.berwickshire-news.co.uk
Weekly (Thu). Owner: Johnston Press.
Editor: Sandy Brydon

East Lothian News
0131 561 6600
www.eastlothiantoday.co.uk
Weekly (Thu). Owner: Johnston Press.
Editor: Roy Scott; news: Alex Hogg

East Lothian Times
0131 561 6600
Weekly free (Fri). Owner: Johnston Press.
Editor: Roy Scott; news: Alex Hogg

Ellon Advertiser
01888 563589
Weekly (Fri). Owner: W Peters & Son.
Editor: Joyce Summers

Ellon Times & East Gordon
Advertiser
01779 472017
Weekly (Thu). Owner: Archant.
Acting editor: Ken Duncan

Eskdale and Liddesdale Advertiser
01387 380012
Weekly (Thu). Owner: Cumbrian News
Group. Editor: Keith Sutton; news:
Rachael Norris

Evening Telegraph (Dundee)
01382 223131
Daily. Owner: DC Thomson. Editor:
Gordon Wishart; news: Elaine Harrison;
features: Phillip Smith

The Extra (Ayrshire)
01292 611666
www.theextra24.co.uk
Weekly (Thu). Owner: Archant.
Editor: John Matthews

Falkirk Herald
01324 624959
www.falkirktoday.co.uk
Weekly (Thu). Owner: Johnston Press.
Editor: Colin Hume; assistant editor:
Duncan McCallum

Falkirk, Grangemouth & Linlithgow
Advertiser
01324 638314
Weekly (Wed). Owner: Johnston Press.
Editor: Colin Hume; assistant editor:
Duncan McCallum

Fife & Kinross Extra
01383 728201
Weekly free (Fri). Owner: Dunfermline
Press Group. Editor: Andrew Cowie

Fife Free Press
01592 261451
www.fifenow.co.uk
Weekly free (Thu). Owner: Johnston Press.
Editor: Allen Crow

Fife Herald
01592 261451
www.fifenow.co.uk
Weekly free (Fri). Owner: Johnston Press.
Editor: Graham Scott

Fife Leader
01592 261451
www.fifenow.co.uk
Weekly free (Tue). Owner: Johnston Press.
Editor: Jack Snedden

Forfar Dispatch
01307 464899
www.forfardispatch.com
Weekly (Tue). Owner: Angus County
Press. Editor: Alan Ducat

Forres Gazette
01309 672615
www.forres-gazette.co.uk
Weekly (Wed). Scottish Provincial Press.
Editor: Ken Smith

Fraserburgh Herald
01779 472017
Weekly (Fri). Owner: Archant.
Editor: Alex Shand

Galloway Gazette
01671 402503
www.gallowaygazette.com
Weekly (Thu). Owner: Angus County
Press. Editor: Peter Jeal

Galloway News
01556 504141
www.icscotland.co.uk
Weekly (Thu). Owner: Scottish &
Universal Newspapers (Trinity Mirror).
Editor: Elizabeth Martin; chief sub.
Chris McIntyre

The Gazette (Paisley)
0141 887 7055
Weekly (Wed). Owner: Clyde & Forth
Press. Editor: James Walsh

Glasgow East News
0141 573 5060
Weekly (Fri). Owner: Johnston Press.
Editor: Jim Holland; chief sub: Allan Muir

Glasgow South & Eastwood Extra
0141 427 7878
www.icscotland.co.uk
Weekly (Thu). Owner: Archant. Editor:
Allan Hodge; news: Colin Macdonald;
chief sub: Jim Cameron

Glasgow West Extra
0141 427 7878
www.icscotland.co.uk
Weekly (Thu). Owner: Archant. Editor: Allan Hodge; news: Colin Macdonald; chief sub: Jim Cameron

The Glaswegian
0141 309 3132
Weekly free. Owner: Scottish Daily Record & Sunday Mail (Trinity Mirror). Editor: Garry Thomas

Glenrothes Gazette
01592 261451
www.fifenow.co.uk
Weekly free (Wed). Owner: Johnston Press. Editor: Brian Stormont

Gorgie Dalry Gazette
0131 337 2457
Monthly (Fri). Independent. Editor: Brian Montgomery

Greenock Telegraph
01475 726511
www.greenocktelegraph.co.uk
Weekly (Wed). Owner: Clyde & Forth Press. Editor: Tom McConingley

Hamilton Advertiser
01698 283200
www.icScotland.co.uk
Weekly (Thu). Owner: Scottish & Universal Newspapers (Trinity Mirror). Editor: Joseph Kelly

Hamilton Extra People
01698 261321
Weekly (Fri). Owner: Archant. Editor: Martin Clark

Hawick News
01750 21581
www.hawicktoday.co.uk
Weekly (Fri). Owner: Johnston Press. Editor: Michael Mee

Helensburgh Advertiser
01436 673434
Weekly (Thu). Owner: Clyde & Forth Press. Editor: Alan Green; news: Steve Macllroy

Herald & Post Edinburgh
0131 620 8620
Weekly free (Thu). Owner: Scotsman Publications. Editor: Gail Milne

Highland News
01463 732222
www.highland-news.co.uk
Weekly (Thu). Owner: Scottish Provincial Press. Editor: Helen Macrae

Huntly Express
01466 793622
Weekly (Fri). Owner: J&M Publishing. Editor: Pat Scott

Ileach (Islay & Jura)
01496 810355
www.ileach.co.uk
Fortnightly (Sat). Independent. Editor: Carl Reavey

Inverclyde Extra
01475 726511
Weekly free (Wed). Owner: Clyde & Forth Press. Editor: Tom McConigley

Inverness & Nairnshire Herald
01463 732222
Weekly (Thu). Owner: Scottish Provincial Press. Editor: Helen Macrae

Inverness Courier
01463 233059
www.inverness-courier.co.uk
Twice-weekly (Tue, Fri). Owner: Scottish Provincial Press. Contact: Robert Taylor

Inverurie Advertiser
01888 563589
Weekly (Fri). Owner: W Peters & Son. Editor: Joyce Summers

Inverurie Herald
01467 625150
www.inverurieherald.com
Weekly (Thu). Owner: Angus County Press. Editor: David Duncan

Irvine & North Ayrshire Extra
01292 611666
www.theextra24.co.uk
Weekly (Thu). Owner: Archant. Editor: John Matthews

Irvine Herald
01294 222288
www.icscotland.co.uk
Weekly (Wed). Owner: Scottish & Universal Newspapers (Trinity Mirror). Editor: Alan Woodison; news: Lex Brown; chief sub: Murray Stevenson

Irvine Times
01294 273421
Weekly (Wed). Owner: Scottish & Universal Newspapers (Trinity Mirror). Editor: Alex Clarke

John O'Groat Journal
01955 602424
www.johnogroat-journal.co.uk
Weekly (Fri). Owner: North of Scotland Newspapers. Editor: Alan Henry; news: Karen Macdonald

Kilmarnock & District Extra
01292 611666
www.theextra24.co.uk
Weekly (Thu). Owner: Archant. Editor: John Matthews

Kilmarnock Standard
01563 525115
www.icscotland.co.uk
Weekly (Wed). Owner: Scottish & Universal Newspapers (Trinity Mirror). Editor: Alan Woodison; news: Lex Brown

Kincardineshire Observer
01561 377283
Weekly (Fri). Owner: Angus County Press. Editor: Charles Wallace

Kirkintilloch Herald
0141 775 0040
www.kirkintillochtoday.co.uk
Weekly (Wed). Owner: Johnston Press. Editor: Jim Holland; chief sub: Allan Muir

Kirriemuir Herald
01307 464899
www.kirriemuirherald.com
Weekly (Wed). Owner: Angus County Press. Editor: Alan Ducat

Lanark Gazette
01555 663937
Weekly (Thu). Owner: Johnston Press. Editor: Aileen McCulloch

Lanarkshire Extra
01698 261321
www.icscotland.co.uk
Weekly (Thu). Owner: Archant. Editor: Martin Clark

Lanarkshire World
01698 283200
www.icscotland.co.uk
Weekly (Wed). Owner: Scottish & Universal Newspapers (Trinity Mirror). Editor: Joseph Kelly

Largs & Millport Weekly News
01475 689009
Weekly (Wed). Owner: Clyde & Forth Press. Editor: Andrew Cochrane

Lennox Herald
01389 742299
www.icscotland.co.uk
Weekly (Wed). Owner: Scottish & Universal Newspapers (Trinity Mirror). Editor: Alan Woodison

Linlithgowshire Journal & Gazette
01506 844592
www.icscotland.co.uk
Weekly (Fri). Owner: Johnston Press. Editor: Jack Shennan; features: Julie Currie

Lochaber News
01463 732222
www.lochaber-news.co.uk
Weekly (Thu). Owner: Scottish Provincial Press. Editor: Helen Macrae

Lothian Times East
0131 561 6600
Weekly free (Fri). Owner: Johnston Press. Editor: Roy Scott; news: Alex Hogg

Mearns Leader
01569 762139
www.mearnsleader.com
Weekly (Fri). Owner: Angus County Press. Editor: John McIntosh

Metro Scotland
020 7651 5200
www.metroscot.co.uk
Daily. Owner: Associated Newspapers. Editor: Kenny Campbell

Midlothian Times
0131 561 6600
Weekly free (Fri). Owner: Johnston Press. Editor: Roy Scott; news: Alex Hogg

Midlothian Advertiser
0131 561 6600
Weekly (Wed). Owner: Johnston Press. Editor: Roy Scott; news: Alex Hogg

Milngavie & Bearsden Herald
0141 956 3533
Weekly (Fri). Owner: Johnston Press. Editor: Allan McIntyre; news: Rena O'Neill

Moffat News
01461 202078
Weekly (Thu). Owner: Dumfriesshire Newspapers. Editor: Bryan Armstrong; news: Alan Hall

Montrose Review
01674 672605
www.montrosereview.net
Weekly (Thu). Owner: Angus County Press. Editor: Douglas Hill

Motherwell Extra
01698 261321
Weekly (Fri). Owner: Archant. Editor: Martin Clark

Motherwell Times
01698 264611
Weekly (Thu). Owner: Johnston Press. Editor: Archie Fleming

Musselburgh News
0131 561 6600
Weekly (Thu). Owner: Johnston Press.
Editor: Roy Scott; news: Alex Hogg

North Ayrshire World
01294 272233
www.icScotland.co.uk
Weekly (Wed). Owner: Scottish &
Universal Newspapers (Trinity Mirror).
Editor: Alan Woodison; news: Lex Brown

North East Gazette
01224 618300
www.aberdeen-indy.co.uk
Weekly (Fri). Editor: Derek Piper;
news: Donna Morrison

North Edinburgh News
0131 467 3972
www.northedinburghnews.co.uk
Monthly free (2nd Wed). Editor: Mary
Burnside

North Star
01463 732222
www.highland-news.co.uk
Weekly (Thu). Owner: Scottish Provincial
Press. Editor: Helen Macrae

North West Highlands Bratach
01641 561214
www.bratach.co.uk
Monthly (1st Thu). Editor: Donald McCloud

Northern Scot
01343 548777
www.northern-scot.co.uk
Weekly (Fri). Owner: Scottish Provincial
Press. Editor: Pauline Taylor

Northern Times
01408 633993
www.northern-times.co.uk
Weekly (Thu). Owner: Scottish Provincial
Press. Editor: Duncan Ross

Oban Times
01631 563058
www.obantimes.co.uk
Weekly (Thu). Owner: Oban Times. Editor:
Stewart Mackenzie; news: Joanne Simms

The Orcadian
01856 879000
www.orcadian.co.uk
Weekly (Thu). Editor: Stuart Laundy

Paisley & District People
0141 887 7055
Weekly free (Fri). Owner: Clyde & Forth
Press. Editor: James Walsh

Paisley & Renfrewshire Extra
0141 427 7878
www.icscotland.co.uk
Weekly (Thu). Owner: Archant. Editor:
Allan Hodge; news: Colin Macdonald;
chief sub: Jim Cameron

Paisley Daily Express
0141 887 7911
www.icscotland.co.uk
Daily. Owner: Scottish & Universal
Newspapers (Trinity Mirror). News:
Anne Dalrymple

Peebles Times
0131 561 6600
Weekly free (Fri). Owner: Johnston Press.
Editor: Roy Scott; news: Alex Hogg

Peeblesshire News
01896 758395
www.peeblesshirenews.com
Weekly (Fri). Owner: Dunfermline Press.
Editor: Atholl Innes

Perth Shopper
01738 626211
Weekly (Fri). Owner: Scottish & Universal
Newspapers (Trinity Mirror). Editor:
Alison Lowson

Perthshire Advertiser
01738 626211
www.icperthshire.co.uk
Weekly (Tue, Fri). Owner: Scottish &
Universal Newspapers (Trinity Mirror).
Editor: Alison Lowson

Ross-shire Herald
01463 732222
Weekly (Thu). Owner: Scottish Provincial
Press. Editor: Helen Macrae

Ross-shire Journal
01349 863436
www.rsjournal.co.uk
Weekly (Fri). Owner: Scottish Provincial
Press. Editor: Hector McKenzie; features:
Shirley Hastings

Rutherglen Reformer
0141 647 2271
www.icscotland.co.uk
Weekly (Thu). Owner: Scottish &
Universal Newspapers (Trinity Mirror).
Editor: Joe Kelly

St Andrews Citizen
01592 261451
www.fifenow.co.uk
Weekly free (Fri). Owner: Johnston Press.
Editor: Mike Rankin

Selkirk Advertiser
01750 21581
www.selkirktoday.co.uk
Weekly (Fri). Owner: Johnston Press.
Editor: Susan Windram

Shetland Life
01595 693622
www.shetlandtoday.co.uk
Monthly (1st Fri). Editor: Andrew Morrison

Shetland News
01806 577332
www.shetland-news.co.uk
Daily, online. Editor: Hans Marter

Shetland Times
01595 693622
www.shetlandtoday.co.uk
Weekly. Editor: Jonathan Lee

Southern Reporter
01750 21581
www.borderstoday.co.uk
Weekly (Fri). Owner: Johnston Press.
Editor: Susan Windram

Stirling News
01259 214416
Weekly free (Thu). Owner: Dunfermline
Press Group. Editor: Kevin McRoberts

Stirling Observer
01786 451110
www.icstirlingshire.co.uk
Twice-weekly free (Wed, Fri). Owner:
Scottish & Universal Newspapers (Trinity
Mirror). Editor: Alan Rennie; deputy
editor: Donald Morton

Stirling/Alloa & Hillfoots Shopper
01786 451110
Weekly free (Fri). Owner: Scottish &
Universal Newspapers (Trinity Mirror).
Editor: Alan Rennie; deputy editor:
Donald Morton

**Stornoway Gazette & West Coast
Advertiser**
01851 702687
www.stornowaygazette.co.uk
Weekly (Thu). Editor: Melinda Gillen

**Stranraer & Wigtownshire
Free Press**
01776 702551
www.stranraer.org/freepress
Weekly (Wed). Editor: John Neil

Strathearn Herald
01738 626211
www.icperthshire.co.uk
Weekly (Fri). Owner: Scottish & Universal
Newspapers (Trinity Mirror).
Editor: Alison Lowson

Strathkelvin Advertiser
0141 775 0040
Weekly (Sat). Owner: Johnston Press.
Editor: Jim Holland; chief sub: Allan Muir

Strathspey Herald
01479 872102
www.sbherald.co.uk
Weekly (Wed). Owner: Scottish Provincial
Press. Editor: Gavin Musgrove

Turriff Advertiser
01888 563589
Weekly (Fri). Owner: W Peters & Son.
Editor: Joyce Summers

Wee County News
01259 724724
www.wee-county-news.co.uk
Weekly (Thu). Editor: Joan McCann;
chief sub: Ronnie Paterson; production:
Bryan Watson

West Highland Free Press
01471 822464
www.whfp.co.uk
Weekly (Thu). Editor: Ian McCormack

West Lothian Courier
01506 633544
www.icscotland.co.uk
Weekly (Thu). Owner: Scottish &
Universal Newspapers (Trinity Mirror).
Acting editor: John Murdoch

West Lothian Herald & Post
0131 620 8620
Weekly free (Thu). Owner: Scotsman
Publications. Editor: Gail Milne

Wishaw Press
01698 373111
www.icscotland.co.uk
Weekly (Wed). Owner: Scottish &
Universal Newspapers (Trinity Mirror).
Editor: John Murdoch

Wishaw World
01698 283200
www.icscotland.co.uk
Weekly (Fri). Owner: Scottish & Universal
Newspapers (Trinity Mirror). Editor:
Joseph Kelly

News media

Regional papers - Northern Ireland

● Main regionals

Belfast Telegraph
124–144 Royal Avenue,
Belfast BT1 1EB
028 9026 4000
www.belfasttelegraph.co.uk
Daily. Owner: Independent News & Media. Editor: Martin Lindsay; news: Paul Connolly; features: Gail Walker

Sunday Life
124–144 Royal Avenue,
Belfast BT1 1EB
028 9026 4000
www.sundaylife.co.uk
Sunday. Owner: Independent News & Media. Editor: Jim Flanagan; news: Martin Hill; features: Audrey Watson

Daily Ireland
028 9061 2345
www.dailyireland.com
Daily. Owner: Andersonstown News Group. Editor: Maria McCourt; deputy editor: Colin O'Carroll

The Daily Mirror (NI)
028 9056 8000
www.mirror.co.uk
Daily. Owner: Mirror Group. Editor: Jerry Miller; news: Morris Fitzmaurice; features: Jilly Beattie

Irish News
028 9032 2226
www.irishnews.com
Daily. Owner: Morton Group. Editor: Noel Doran; news: Steven O'Reilly; features: Joanna Braniff

News Letter
028 9068 0000
www.belfasttoday.net
Daily. Owner: Century Newspapers. Editor: Darwin Templeton; news: Rick Clarke; features: Jeff Hill

The People (NI)
028 9056 8000
www.people.co.uk
Sunday. Owner: Mirror Group. Editor: Stephen McQuire; news: Liz Trainor

Sunday Mirror
028 9056 8000
www.sundaymirror.co.uk
Sunday. Owner: Mirror Group. Editor: Christian McCashin; assistant editor: Donna Carton

● Other newspapers

Andersonstown News
028 9061 9000
www.irelandclick.com
Twice-weekly (Mon, Thu). Owner: Andersonstown News Group. Editor: Robin Livingstone

Antrim Guardian
028 9446 2624
www.ulster-ni.co.uk
Weekly (Wed). Owner: Alpha Group. Editor: Liam Hesfron

Antrim Times
028 9442 8572
www.antrimtoday.co.uk
Weekly (Wed). Owner: Johnston Press. Editor: Gareth Fullerton

Armagh Observer
028 8772 2557
Weekly (Wed). Independent. Editor: Desmond Mallon; news: Desmond Mallon Junior

Armagh-Down Observer
028 8772 2557
Weekly (Thu). Independent. Editor: Desmond Mallon; news: Desmond Mallon Junior

Ballycastle Chronicle
028 7034 3344
www.ulsternet-ni.co.uk/chronicle/pages/ballycastle.htm
Weekly (Wed). Owner: Northern News Group. Editor: John Fillis

Ballyclare Advertiser
028 9336 3651
www.ulsternet-ni.co.uk
Weekly (Wed). Owner: Alpha Group. Editor: Raymond Hughes

Ballymena Chronicle
028 8772 2557
Weekly (Wed). Independent. Editor: Desmond Mallon; news: Desmond Mallon Junior

Ballymena Guardian
028 2564 1221
www.ulsternet-ni.co.uk
Weekly (Wed). Owner: Alpha Group. Editor: Maurice O'Neil; assistant editor: Shaun O'Neil

Ballymena Times
028 2565 3300
www.ballymenatoday.co.uk
Weekly (Tue). Owner: Morton News Group. Editor: Desmond Blackadder; advertising: Stephanie Manson

Ballymoney & Coleraine Chronicle
028 7034 3344
www.ulsternet-ni.co.uk/chronicle/pages/ballymoney.htm
Weekly (Wed). Owner: Northern News Group. Editor: John Fillis

Ballymoney Times
028 2766 6216
www.ballymoneytoday.co.uk
Weekly (Wed). Owner: Morton News Group. Editor: Lyle McMullen; news: Clare Smith; features: Rachael Stamford

Banbridge Chronicle
028 4066 2322
Weekly (Wed). Independent. Editor: Bryan Hooks

Banbridge Leader
028 4066 2745
www.banbridgetoday.co.uk
Weekly (Wed). Independent. Editor: Damien Wilson

Bangor Spectator
028 9127 0270
Weekly (Thu). Owner: DE Alexander & Sons. Editor: Paul Flowers

Belfast News
028 9068 0000
www.icnorthernireland.co.uk
Weekly (Thu). Owner: Century Newspaper. Editor: Julie McClay; news: Rick Clarke; features: Jeff Hill

Carrick Gazette
028 9336 3651
www.ulster-ni.co.uk
Weekly (Wed). Owner: Alpha Group. Editor: David Hull

Carrick Times
028 3839 3939
www.carricktoday.co.uk
Weekly (Thu). Owner: Morton News Group. Editor: David Armstrong; assistant editor: Lyle McMullen

Carrickfergus Advertiser
028 8772 2274
www.carricktoday.co.uk
Weekly (Wed). Owner: Alpha Group. Editor: David Hull

City News
028 7127 2200
www.derrytoday.com
Weekly (Wed). Owner: Local Press. Editor: Martin Mcganley; deputy editor: Bernie Mullen

Coleraine Times
028 7035 5260
www.colerainetoday.co.uk
Weekly (Wed). Owner: Morton News Group. Editor: David Rankin

County Down Spectator
028 9127 0270
Weekly (Thu). Owner: Spectator Newspapers. Editor: Paul Flowers

Craigavon Echo
028 3839 3939
www.craigavontoday.co.uk
Weekly free (Wed). Owner: Morton News Group. Editor: David Armstrong; assistant editor: Hugh Vance

Derry Journal
028 7127 2200
www.derrytoday.com
Twice-weekly (Tues, Fri). Owner: Local Press. Editor: Martin Mcganley; deputy editor: Bernie Mullen

Derry Journal (Sunday)
028 7127 2200
www.derrytoday.com
Weekly (Sun). Owner: Local Press. Editor: Martin Mcganley; deputy editor: Bernie Mullen

Derry News
028 7129 6600
Twice-weekly (Mon, Thu). Independent.
Editor: Joanne McCool; news: Mark
Mullen; head of production: Ann Breslin

Derry on Monday
028 7127 2200
www.derrytoday.com
Weekly (Mon). Owner: Local Press.
Editor: Martin Mcganley; deputy editor:
Bernie Mullen

Down Democrat
028 4461 4400
www.downdemocrat.com
Weekly (Tue). Owner: TCH Group.
Editor: Terry McLaughlin; sales editor:
Tina McGuire

Down Recorder
028 4461 3711
www.thedownrecorder.co.uk
Weekly (Wed). Independent. Editor:
Paul Symington

Dromore Leader
028 3839 3939
www.dromoretoday.co.uk
Weekly (Wed). Owner: Morton News
Group. Editor: Marc Bian

Dungannon News & Tyrone Courier
028 8772 2271
www.ulsternet-ni.co.uk/courier
/cpages/cmain.htm
Weekly (Wed). Owner: Alpha Group.
Editor: Ian Grear

Dungannon Observer
028 8772 2557
Weekly (Fri). Independent. Editor:
Desmond Mallon; news: Desmond
Mallon Jr

East Antrim Advertiser
028 2827 2303
Monthly. Owner: Morton News Group.
Editor: Hugh Vance

East Antrim Guardian
028 2564 1221
www.macunlimited.net
Weekly (Wed). Owner: Northern Alpha
Group. Editor: Maurice O'Neil; assistant
editor: Shaun O'Neil

Farming Life
028 9068 0000
www.farminglife.com
Twice-weekly (Wed, Sat). Owner: Century
Newspapers. Editor: Darwin Templeton;
news: Rick Clarke; features: Jeff Hill

Fermanagh Herald
028 6632 2066
www.fermanaghherald.com
Weekly (Wed). Owner: North West of
Ireland Printing Co. Editor: Pauline Leary

Fermanagh News
028 8772 2557
Weekly (Fri). Independent. Editor:
Desmond Mallon; news: Desmond Mallon
Junior

Foyle News
028 7127 2200
www.derryjournal.com
Weekly (Weds). Owner: Local Press.
Editor: Martin Mcganley; deputy editor:
Bernie Mullen

Impartial Reporter
028 6632 4422
www.impartialreporter.com
Weekly (Thu). Independent.
Editor: Denzil McDaniel

The Journal (Derry)
028 7127 2200
www.derryjournal.com
Weekly (Thu). Owner: Local Press

Lakeland Extra
028 6632 4422
www.impartialreporter.com
Monthly free (3rd Mon). Independent.
Editor: Denzil McDaniel; news: Sarah
Sanderson; features editor Lily Dane;
head of production: Tony Quinn

Larne Gazette
028 9336 3651
www.ulster-ni.co.uk
Weekly (Wed). Owner: Alpha Group.
Editor: David Hull

Larne Times
028 3839 3939
www.larnetoday.co.uk
Weekly (Thu). Owner: Morton News
Group. Editor: Hugh Vance

The Leader (Banbridge/Dromore)
028 2827 2303
Weekly (Wed). Owner: Morton News
Group. Editor: Damien Wilson

The Leader (Coleraine)
028 7034 3344
www.ulsternet-ni.co.uk/leader
/pages/leader.htm
Weekly (Mon). Owner: Northern News
Group. Editor: John Fillis

Limavady Chronicle
028 7034 3344
www.ulsternet-ni.co.uk/chronicle
/pages/limavady.htm
Weekly (Wed). Owner: Northern News
Group. Editor: John Fillis

Lisburn Echo
028 3839 3939
www.lisburntoday.co.uk
Weekly free (Wed). Owner: Morton News
Group. Editor: Hugh Vance

Londonderry Sentinel
028 7134 8889
www.londonderrytoday.co.uk
Weekly (Wed). Owner: Morton News
Group. Editor: Robin Young; assistant
editor: Donna Deeney

Lurgan & Portadown Examiner
028 8772 2557
Weekly (Wed). Independent. Editor:
Desmond Mallon; news: Desmond Mallon
Junior

Lurgan Mail
028 3832 7777
www.lurgantoday.co.uk
Weekly (Thu). Owner: Morton News
Group. Editor: Clint Aitken; assistant
editor: John Bingham; news: Richard
Burton; head of production: Lesley Wiley

**Magherafelt & Limavady
Constitution**
028 7034 3344
www.ulsternet-ni.co.uk/ncon
/pages/limavady.htm
Weekly (Wed). Owner: Northern News
Group. Editor: John Fillis

Mid-Ulster Echo
028 8676 2288
www.midulstertoday.co.uk
Weekly free (Wed). Owner: Morton News
Group. Editor: Mark Bain; assistant
editor: Alan Rogers

Mid-Ulster Mail
028 8676 2288
www.midulstertoday.co.uk
Weekly (Thu). Owner: Morton News
Group. Assistant editor: Alan Rogers

Mid-Ulster Observer
028 8772 2557
Weekly (Wed). Independent. Editor:
Desmond Mallon; news: Desmond
Mallon Jr

**Mourne Observer & County Down
News**
028 4372 2666
www.mourneobserver.com
Weekly (Wed). Independent.
Editor: Terrance Bowman

Newry Advertiser
028 8772 2557
Monthly free. Independent. Editor:
Desmond Mallon; news: Desmond
Mallon Jr

Newry Democrat
028 3025 1250
www.newrydemocrat.com
Weekly (Tue). Owner: Thomas Crosby
Holdings. Editor: Jacky Mckeown;
features: Patrick Ryan; head of
production: Stephen Burns

Newtownabbey Times
028 3839 3939
www.newtownabbeytoday.co.uk
Weekly (Thu). Owner: Morton News
Group. Editor: Hugh Vance

Newtownards Chronicle
028 9127 0270
Weekly (Thu). Owner: Spectator
Newspapers. Editor: Paul Flowers

Newtownards Spectator
028 9127 0270
Weekly (Thu). Owner: Spectator
Newspapers. Editor: Paul Flowers

North Belfast News
028 9058 4444
www.irelandclick.com
Weekly (Fri). Owner: Andersonstown
News Group. Editor: Andrea McKernon;
features: Aine McEntee

North West Echo
028 3839 3939
Weekly free (Wed). Owner: Morton News
Group. Editor: David Armstrong;
assistant editor: John Fillis

Northern Constitution
028 7034 3344
www.ulsternet-ni.co.uk/ncon
/pages/coleraine.htm
Weekly (Wed). Owner: Northern News
Group. Editor: John Fillis

The Outlook (Portadown)
028 4063 0202
www.ulsternet-ni.co.uk
Weekly (Wed). Owner: Alpha Group.
Editor: Ruth Rogers

Portadown Times
028 3833 6111
www.portadowntimes.com
Weekly (Fri). Owner: Morton News
Group. Editor: David Armstrong

Roe Valley Sentinel
028 3839 3939
www.roevalleytoday.co.uk
Weekly (Wed). Owner: Morton News
Group. Editor: David Armstrong;
assistant editor: John Fillis

South Belfast News
028 9061 9000
www.irelandclick.com
Weekly (Fri). Owner: Andersonstown
News Group. Editor: Maria McCourt

Strabane Chronicle
028 8224 3444
www.strabanechronicle.com
Weekly (Thu). Owner: North West
of Ireland Printing Co. Editor: Darach
Mcdonald

Strabane Weekly News
028 8224 2721
www.ulsternet-ni.co.uk
Weekly (Thu). Owner: Alpha Group.
Editor: Wesley Atchison; features:
Geraldine Wilson

Tyrone Constitution
028 8224 2721
www.ulsternet-ni.co.uk
Weekly (Thu). Owner: Alpha Group.
Editor: Wesley Atchison; features:
Geraldine Wilson

Tyrone Herald
028 8224 3444
www.tyroneherald.com
Weekly (Mon). Owner: The North West
of Ireland Printing & Publishing Co.
Editor: Morris Kennedy

Tyrone Times
028 8775 2801
www.tyronetoday.co.uk
Weekly (Fri). Owner: Morton News
Group. Editor: Peter Bayne

Ulster Gazette & Armagh Standard
028 3752 2639
www.ulsternet-ni.co.uk
Weekly (Thu). Owner: Alpha Group.
Editor: Richard Stewart

Ulster Herald
028 8224 3444
www.ulsterherald.com
Weekly (Thu). Owner: North West
of Ireland Printing Co. Editor: Darach
McDonald

Ulster Star
028 9267 9111
www.ulsterstar.com
Weekly (Fri). Owner: Morton News
Group. Editor: David Fletcher; news:
Mary McGee

Magazine contacts

Main magazine & contract magazine publishers

Archant
Prospect House, Rouen Road,
Norwich NR1 1RE
01603 772803
www.archant.co.uk
Chief executive: John Fry; MD, Archant Life: Johnny Hustler, 01603 664212; general manager, Archant Dialogue customer publishing: Chris Rainer, 01603 772532

Archant Specialist
The Mill, Bearwalden Business Park,
Royston Road, Wendens Ambo,
Essex CB11 4GB
01799 544200
MD: Farine Clarke
Press: Keith Morris, 01603 772814

Brooklands Group
Westgate, 120-128 Station Road,
Redhill, Surrey RH1 1ET
01737 786800
mail@brooklandsgroup.com
www.brooklandsgroup.com
Chief executive: Darren Styles, account director: Matthew Jenns
Press: 020 8875 2853

BBC Worldwide
Woodlands, 80 Wood Lane,
London W12 0TT
020 8433 2000
www.bbcworldwide.com
MD: Peter Phippen

Cedar
Pegasus House, 37-43 Sackville Street, London W1S 3EH
020 7534 2400
info@cedarcom.co.uk
www.cedarcom.co.uk
MD: Clare Broadbent; editorial director: Mark Jones

Centaur
50 Poland Street, London W1F 7AX
020 7970 4000
firstname.secondname@centaur.co.uk
www.centaur.co.uk
Publishing directors: Robin Coates, Roger Beckett, Howard Sharman, Tim Potter, Nigel Roby, Annie Swift

CMP Information
Ludgate House, 245 Blackfriars Road, London SE1 9UY
020 7921 5000
www.cmpinformation.com
Part of United Business Media. Chief executive: Gary Hughes

Condé Nast
Vogue House, Hanover Square,
London W1S 1JU
020 7499 9080
www.condenast.co.uk
MD: Nicholas Coleridge

DC Thomson
185 Fleet Street, London EC4A 2HS
020 7400 1030
shout@dcthomson.co.uk
www.dcthomson.co.uk

Dennis
30 Cleveland Street, London W1T 4JD
020 7907 6000
firstname_secondname@dennis.co.uk
www.dennis.co.uk
Chief executive: James Tye; MD, consumer: Bruce Sandell

Emap
Wentworth House, Wentworth Street, Peterborough PE1 1DS
020 7278 1452
www.emap.com
Group chief executive: Tom Maloney

Emap Communications
Scriptor Court, 155 Farringdon Road,
London EC1R 3AD
020 7841 6600
Chief executive: Derek Carter

Emap Consumer Media
Endeavour House, 189 Shaftesbury Avenue, London WC2H 8JG
020 7437 9011
Chief executive: Paul Keenan; MD: Dharmash Mistry

Emap Performance
Mappin House, 4 Winsley Street,
London W1W 8HF
020 7436 1515

Future
Beauford Court, 30 Monmouth Street, Bath BA1 2BW
01225 442244
firstname.secondname@futurenet.com
www.futurenet.com
Chief executive: Stevie Spring; MD: Robert Price

London office
2 Balcombe Street, London NW1 6NW
020 7042 4000
Press: 01225 732235/822517

H Bauer
Academic House, 24-28 Oval Road,
London NW1 7DT
020 7241 8000
www.bauer.co.uk
MD: David Goodchild

Hachette Filipacchi
64 North Row, London W1K 7LL
020 7150 7000
www.hf-uk.com
Chairman: Kevin Hand; general manager women's group: Julie Harris

Haymarket
174 Hammersmith Road,
London W6 7JP
020 8267 5000
hpg@haymarketgroup.com
www.haymarketgroup.com
Group MD: Simon Daukes; joint MDs, Haymarket magazines: Kevin Costello, Simon Daukes; chairman and MD, Haymarket business publications: Martin Durham

Haymarket Customer Publishing
Broom Road, Teddington,
Middlesex TW11 9BE
020 8267 5411
haycustpub@haynet.com
www.haycustpub.com
MD: Patrick Fuller

IPC Media
King's Reach Tower, Stamford Street,
London SE1 9LS
0870 444 5000
www.ipcmedia.com
Owned by Time Warner. CEO: Sylvia Auton; editorial director: Mike Soutar

John Brown Citrus
The New Boathouse, 136-142
Bramley Road, London W10 6SR
020 7565 3000
www.jbcp.co.uk
MD: Dean Fitzpatrick, 020 7565 3202; editorial director: Paul Colbert

National Magazine Company
National Magazine House,
72 Broadwick St, London W1F 9EP
020 7439 5000
www.natmags.co.uk
MD: Jessica Burley

Publicis Blueprint
Whitfield House, 83-89 Whitfield Street, London W1A 4XA
020 7462 7777
www.publicis-blueprint.com
MD: Jason Frost

Rare Publishing
102 Sydney Street, London SW3 6NJ
020 7368 9000
Bristol office 0117 929 7680
www.rarecontent.co.uk
Part of Chime Communications. MD: Julian Downing; publishing and commercial director: Sarah Kermode; editorial director: Maureen Rice; editor-in-chief: Matthew Cowen

Redwood
7 St Martin's Place,
London WC2N 4HA
020 7747 0700
info@redwoodgroup.net
www.redwoodgroup.net
MD: Keith Grainger

Reed Business Information
Quadrant House, The Quadrant,
Sutton SM2 5AS
020 8652 3500
www.reedbusiness.co.uk
Part of Reed Elsevier. Chief executive:
Keith Jones

River Group
Victory House, Leicester Square,
London WC2H 7QH
020 7306 0304
info@river.co.uk
www.therivergroup.co.uk
Joint MD and sales and marketing
director: Nicola Murphy; joint MD and
editorial director: Jane Wynn

Seven
20 Upper Ground, London SE1 9PD
020 7775 7775
info@7publishing.co.uk
www.7publishing.com
Chairman: Michael Potter

VNU Business
VNU House, 32–34 Broadwick Street,
London W1A 2HG
020 7316 9000
firstname_secondname@vnu.co.uk
www.vnunet.com
MD: Brin Bucknor

Consumer magazines

● Adult

Erotic Review
020 7907 6000
www.theeroticreview.co.uk
Monthly. Owner: Dennis.
Editor: Rowan Pelling

Escort
020 7292 8000
Monthly. Owner: Paul Raymond.
Editor: James Hundleby

Fiesta
01376 534549
www.fiesta.co.uk
13pa. Owner: Galaxy. Editor: Ross Gilfillan

For Women
020 7308 5363
9pa. Owner: Fantasy Publications.
Editor: Liz Beresford

Knave
01376 534549
www.knave.co.uk
13pa. Owner: Galaxy. Editor: Ross Gilfillan

Mayfair
020 7292 8000
Monthly. Owner: Paul Raymond.
Editor: David Rider

Men Only
020 7292 8000
Monthly. Owner: Paul Raymond.
Editor: Pierre Perrone

Skin Two
020 7498 5533
www.skintwo.co.uk
4pa. Owner: Tim Woodward.
Editor: Tony Mitchell

Viz
020 7907 6000
www.viz.co.uk
Monthly. Owner: Dennis

● Arts, music, film & TV

247
01752 294130
www.twenty4-seven.co.uk
Monthly. Owner: Afterdark Media.
Editor: Lucy Griffiths

All About Soap
020 7150 7000
www.allaboutsoap.co.uk
Fortnightly. Owner: Hachette Filipacchi
UK. Editor: Jonathan Hughes

Amateur Photographer
020 7261 5100
www.amateurphotographer.co.uk
Weekly. Owner: IPC Media.
Editor: Garry Coward-Williams

AN Magazine
0191 241 8000
www.a-n.co.uk
Monthly. Owner: F22The Artists
Information Company.
Editor: Gillian Nicol

The Art Book
01865 776868
www.blackwellpublishing.com
4pa. Owner: Blackwell Publishing.
Editor: Sue Ward, Marion Arnold

The Art Newspaper
020 7735 3331
www.theartnewspaper.com
Monthly. Independent.
Editor: Cristina Ruiz

Art Quarterly
020 7225 4818
www.artfund.org
4pa. Owner: National Art Collection
Fund. Editor: Caroline Bugler

Art Review
020 7246 3350
www.art-review.com
Monthly. Owner: ArtReview.
Editor: Daniel Kunitz

The Artist
01580 763315
www.theartistmagazine.co.uk
Monthly. Owner: The Artists' Publishing
Company. Editor: Sally Bulgin

Artists & Illustrators
020 7700 8500
www.aimag.co.uk
Monthly. Owner: Quarto Magazines.
Editor: John Swinfield

Arts East
01223 434434
www.cambridgenewspapers.co.uk
Monthly. Owner: Cambridge Newspapers.
Editor: Louise Cummings

BBC Music Magazine
0117 927 9009
www.bbcmagazines.com/music
Monthly. Owner: Origin Publishing.
Editor: Oliver Condy

The Big Cheese
020 7607 0303
www.bigcheesemagazine.com
Monthly. Independent.
Editor: Eugene Butcher

Billboard
020 7420 6000
www.billboard.com
Weekly. Owner: VNU. Group Editorial
Director: Scott McKenzie

Blues & Soul
020 7402 6897
www.bluesandsoul.com
Fortnightly. Owner: Blues & Soul.
Editor: Bob Killbourn

The Brighton Source
01273 561617
www.brightonsource.co.uk
Monthly. Owner: Newsquest.
Editor: Richard Gilpin

Buzz Magazine
029 2025 6883
www.buzzmag.co.uk
Monthly. Editor: Emma Clark

Cineworld
01225 737300
www.cineworld.co.uk
Bi-monthly. Owner: Concept.
Editor: Sally Thomson

Classic FM – The Magazine
020 8267 5000
www.haymarketpublishing.co.uk
Monthly. Owner: Haymarket.
Editor-in-chief: John Evans

Classic Rock
020 7317 2654
www.classicrockmagazine.com
13pa. Owner: Future. Editor: Scott Rowley

Classical Music
020 7333 1742
www.rhinegold.co.uk
Fortnightly. Owner: Rhinegold.
Editor: Keith Clarke

Country Music People
020 8854 7217
www.countrymusicpeople.com
Monthly. Owner: Music Farm.
Editor: Craig Baguley

Country Music Round-up
01472 821707
www.cmru.co.uk
Monthly. Owner: CMRU.
Editor: John Emptage

The Crack
0191 230 3038
www.thecrackmagazine.com
Monthly. Editor: Robert Meddes

Cult Times
020 8875 1520
www.visimag.com
Monthly. Owner: Visual Imagination.
Editor: Paul Spragg

Dance Europe
020 8985 7767
www.danceeurope.net
Monthly. Editor: Emma Manning

Dance Gazette
020 7326 8000
www.rad.org.uk
3pa. Owner: Royal Academy of Dance.
Editor: David Jays

DJ
020 7042 4000
www.djmag.com
Fortnightly. Owner: Future.
Editor: Lesley Wright

DMC Update
020 7262 6777
www.dmcworld.com/update
Weekly. Owner: DMC.
Publisher: Tony Prince

DVD Monthly
01392 434477
www.predatorpublishing.co.uk
Monthly. Owner: Predator.
Editor: Tim Isaac

DVD Review
020 7331 1000
www.dvdreview.net
13pa. Owner: Future. Editor: Paul Morgan

Early Music Today
020 7333 1744
www.rhinegold.co.uk
6pa. Owner: Rhinegold.
Editor: Lucien Jenkins

Empire
020 7182 8093
www.empireonline.co.uk
Monthly. Owner: Emap.
Editor: Colin Kennedy

Entertainer
01302 347225
www.doncastertoday.co.uk
Weekly. Owner: Johnston Press.
Editor: Martin Edmonds

EP Magazine
0845 644 5513
www.vigilante.co.uk
10pa. Owner: Vigilante Publications.
Editor: Jon Ewing

Film Review
020 8875 1520
www.visimag.com
Monthly. Owner: Visual Imagination.
Editor: Nikki Baughan

The Fly
020 7691 4555
www.the-fly.co.uk
Monthly. Owner: Channelfly Enterprises.
Editor: Will Kinsman

Freetime
01252 621513
www.freetimemag.co.uk
4pa. Owner: VRA. Editor: Vic Robbie

fRoots
020 8340 9651
www.frootsmag.com
Monthly. Owner: Southern Rag.
Editor: Ian Anderson

Future Music
01225 442244
www.futuremusic.co.uk
13pa. Owner: Future. Editor: Andy Jones

Gramophone
020 8267 5136
www.gramophone.co.uk
Monthly. Owner: Haymarket.
Editor: James Jolly

Granta
020 7704 9776
www.granta.com
4pa. Owner: Granta. Editor: Ian Jack

Guitar
020 8726 8303
www.ipcmedia.com
Monthly. Owner: IPC Media.
Editor: Marcus Leadley

Guitar Buyer
01353 665577
Monthly. Owner: MB Media.
Editor: Mick Taylor

Guitar Techniques
01225 442244
www.futurenet.com/guitartechniques
13pa. Owner: Future.
Editor: Neville Marten

Guitarist
01225 442244
www.futurenet.com/guitarist
13pa. Owner: Future.
Editor: Michael Leonard

Hip Hop Connection
01223 210536
www.hiphop.co.uk
Monthly. Owner: Infamous Ink.
Editor: Andy Cowan

Hollywood Reporter
020 7420 6004
www.hollywoodreporter.com
Weekly. Owner: VNU.
Editor: Cynthia Littleton

Home Cinema Choice
020 7331 1000
www.homecinemachoice.com
Monthly. Owner: Future.
Editor: Steve May

Impact
01484 435011
www.martialartsltd.co.uk/impact/
Monthly. Owner: MAI Publications.
Editor: John Mosby

Inside Soap
020 7150 7000
www.insidesoap.co.uk
Weekly. Owner: Hachette Filipacchi UK.
Editor: Steven Murphy

It's Hot
020 8433 3910
www.bbcmagazines.com/hot
13pa. Owner: BBC Worldwide. Acting
editor: Shelley Moulden

Jazz at Ronnie Scott's
020 7485 9803
www.ronniescotts.co.uk
Bi-monthly. Editor: Jim Godbolt

Jazz Guide
01908 312392
Monthly. Editor: Bernie Tyrrell

Jazz UK
029 2066 5161
www.jazzservices.org.uk
Bi-monthly. Owner: Jazz Services.
Editor: John Fordham

Kerrang!
020 7182 8000
www.kerrang.com
Weekly. Owner: Emap.
Editor: Paul Brannigan

Knowledge
020 8533 9300
www.knowledgemag.co.uk
10pa. Owner: Vision Publishing.
Editor: Colin Steven

Leisure Painter
01580 763315
www.leisurepainter.co.uk
Monthly. Owner: The Artists' Publishing
Company. Editor: Ingrid Lyon

The List
0131 550 3050
www.list.co.uk
Fortnightly; extra festival issues in
August. Editor: Nick Barley

London Review of Books
020 7209 1101
www.lrb.co.uk
Fortnightly. Owner: LRB.
Editor: Mary-Kay Wilmers

London Theatre Guide
020 7557 6700
www.officiallondontheatre.co.uk
Fortnightly. Owner: The Society of
London Theatre. Editor: Philippa Smart

M8
0141 840 5980
www.m8magazine.com
Monthly. Editor: Kevin McFarlane

Magpie
0870 071 1611
www.magpiedirect.com
Bi-monthly. Editor: Mark Rye

Metal Hammer
020 7317 2691
www.metalhammer.co.uk
13pa. Owner: Future.
Editor: Jamie Hibbard

Mixmag
020 7817 8805
www.mixmag.net
Monthly. Owner: Emap.
Features editor: Andrew Harrison

Mojo
020 7436 1515
www.mojo4music.com
Monthly. Owner: Emap.
Editor: Phil Alexander

Movie Mag International
020 8567 3662
www.movie-mag.net
Monthly. Editor: Bharathi Pradhan

Music Tech
01225 489984
www.musictechmag.co.uk
Monthly. Owner: Anthem Publishing.
Editor: Neil Worley

Music-Zine
01279 865070
www.music-zine.com
Bi-monthly. Editor: Simon Baker

National Gallery Season Guide
020 7747 2836
www.nationalgallery.org.uk
3pa. Owner: National Gallery.
Editor: Andrea Easey

NME
020 7261 5564
www.nme.com
Weekly. Owner: IPC Media.
Editor: Conor McNicholas

Official Elvis Presley Fan Club
Magazine
0116 253 7271
www.elvisweb.co.uk
Bi-monthly. Editor: Todd Slaughter

Opera
020 8563 8893
www.opera.co.uk
Monthly. Editor: John Allison

Opera Now
020 7333 1740
www.rhinegold.co.uk
6pa. Owner: Rhinegold.
Editor: Ash Khandekar

Piano
020 7333 1724
www.rhinegold.co.uk
6pa. Owner: Rhinegold.
Editor: Jeremy Siepmann

The Potteries Post
01782 575569
Monthly. Owner: Potteries Publications.
Editor: Terry Winter

Q
020 7182 8000
www.q4music.com
Monthly. Owner: Emap. Editor: Paul Rees

RA Magazine
020 7300 5820
www.ramagazine.org.uk
4pa. Owner: Royal Academy of Arts.
Editor: Sarah Greenberg

Radio Times
0870 608 4455
www.radiotimes.com
Weekly. Owner: BBC Worldwide.
Editor: Gill Hudson

Record Buyer
01522 511265
Monthly. Owner: Aceville.
Editor: Paul Rigby

Rhythm
01225 442244
www.futurenet.com/rhythm
13pa. Owner: Future. Editor: Louise King

Rock Sound
020 7877 8770
www.rock-sound.net
Monthly. Editor: Darren Taylor

Rolling Stone
00 1 212 484 1616
www.rollingstone.com
26pa. Owner: Rolling Stone Magazine.
Editor: Jann S Wenner

Screen International
020 7505 8096
www.screendaily.com
Weekly. Owner: Emap.
Editor: Michael Gubbins

SFX
01225 442244
www.sfx.co.uk
13pa. Owner: Future. Editor: Dave Bradley

Shivers
020 8875 1520
www.visimag.com
Monthly. Owner: Visual Imagination.
Editor: David Miller

Sight & Sound
020 7957 8963
www.bfi.org.uk/sightandsound
Monthly. Owner: British Film Institute.
Editor: Nick James

Soaplife
020 7261 7568
www.ipcmedia.com
Fortnightly. Owner: IPC Media.
Editor: Hellen Gardner

Songlines
020 7371 2777
www.songlines.co.uk
Bi-monthly. Editor: Simon Broughton

Sound on Sound
01954 789888
www.soundonsound.com
Monthly. Owner: SOS Publications Group.
Editor: Paul White

The Stage
020 7403 1818
www.thestage.co.uk
Weekly. Editor: Brian Attwood

Starburst
020 8875 1520
www.visimag.com
Monthly. Owner: Visual Imagination.
Editor: Stephen Payne

Stardust International
020 7224 2600
www.stardustindia.com
Monthly. Owner: Magna.
Editor: Ashwin Varde

The Strad
020 7618 3095
www.thestrad.com
Monthly. Owner: Newsquest.
Editor: Naomi Sadler

Straight No Chaser
020 8533 9999
www.straightnochaser.co.uk
Bi-monthly. Editor: Paul Bradshaw

Theatregoer
020 7439 2777
www.theatregoer.net
Monthly. Owner: Whatsonstage.
Editor: Terri Paddock

This is London Magazine
020 7434 1281
www.thisislondontickets.co.uk
Weekly. Publisher: Julie Jones

Time Out
020 7813 3000
www.timeout.com
Weekly. Owner: Time Out Group.
Editor: Gordon Thomson

Time Out Student Guide
020 7813 3000
www.timeout.com
Annually. Owner: Time Out Group.
Editor: Tom Lomont

Times Literary Supplement
020 7782 3000
www.the-tls.co.uk
Weekly. Owner: TSL Education.
Editor: Peter Stothard

Top of the Pops Magazine
020 8433 3910
www.bbcmagazines.com/totp
Monthly. Owner: BBC Worldwide.
Editor: Peter Hart

Total DVD
020 7331 1000
www.totaldvd.net
12pa. Owner: SMD Publishing.
Editor: Chris Jenkins

Total Film
020 7042 4000
www.totalfilm.co.uk
13pa. Owner: Future.
Deputy Editor: Matt Mueller

Total Guitar
01225 442244
www.totalguitar.co.uk
13pa. Owner: Future.
Editor: Stephen Lawson

Total TV Guide
020 7241 8000
www.bauer.co.uk
Weekly. Owner: H Bauer. Editor: Jon Peake

TV & Satellite Week
020 7261 7534
www.tvandsatelliteweek.com
Weekly. Owner: IPC Media.
Editor: Jonathan Bowman

TV Choice
020 7241 8000
www.bauer.co.uk
Weekly. Owner: H Bauer.
Editor: Jon Peake

TV easy
020 7261 5000
www.ipcmedia.com
Weekly. Owner: IPC Media.
Editor: Richard Clark

TV Hits!
01206 851 117
www.tvhits.co.uk
Monthly. Owner: Hachette Filipacchi UK.
Assistant Editor: Charlotte Acock

TV Quick
020 7241 8000
www.bauer.co.uk
Weekly. Owner: H Bauer.
Editor: Jon Peake

TV Times
020 7261 7816
www.ipcmedia.com
Weekly. Owner: IPC Media.
Editor: Ian Abbott

TV Zone
020 8875 1520
www.visimag.com
Monthly. Owner: Visual Imagination.
Editor: Jan Vincent-Rudzki

Ultimate DVD
020 8875 1520
www.visimag.com
Monthly. Owner: Visual Imagination.
Editor: David Richardson

Uncut
020 7261 6992
www.uncut.co.uk
Monthly. Owner: IPC Media.
Editor: Allan Jones

V&A Magazine
020 7942 2505
www.vam.ac.uk
3pa. Owner: Culture Shock.
Editor: Charlotte Mullins

Variety
020 7611 4580
www.variety.com
Daily and weekly. Owner: Reed Business
Information. Editor: Alex Romanelli

What's on in London
020 7278 4393
www.whatsoninlondon.co.uk
Weekly. Editor: Michael Darvell

What's on TV
020 7261 7535
www.ipcmedia.com
Weekly. Owner: IPC Media.
Editor: Colin Tough

Where London
020 7611 7885
Monthly. Owner: Where Publications.
Editor: Mary Anne Evans

The Wire
020 7422 5014
www.thewire.co.uk
Monthly. Editor: Chris Bohn

Word
020 7520 8625
www.wordmagazine.co.uk
Monthly. Owner: Development Hell.
Editor: Mark Ellen

Writers' News
0113 200 2929
www.writersnews.co.uk
Monthly. Owner: Warners.
Editor: Derek Hudson

X-pose
020 8875 1520
www.visimag.com
Monthly. Owner: Visual Imagination.
Editor: Anthony Brown

● Children and teenage

2000 AD
01865 200603
www.2000adonline.com
Weekly. Owner: DC Thomson.
Editor: Matt Smith

Action Man
01892 500100
www.paninicomics.co.uk
18pa. Owner: Panini UK.
Editor: Simon Frith

Animal Action
0870 010 1181
www.rspca.org.uk
Bi-monthly. Owner: RSPCA.
Editor: Sarah Evans

Animals and You
01382 223131
www.dcthomson.co.uk
Monthly. Owner: DC Thomson.
Editor: Margaret Monaghan

Aquila Children's Magazine
01323 431313
www.aquila.co.uk
Monthly. Owner: New Leaf Publishing.
Editor: Jackie Berry

Art Attack
01892 500100
www.paninicomics.co.uk
18pa. Owner: Panini UK.
Editor: Karen Brown

Balamory Magazine
020 8433 2356
www.bbcmagazines.com
13pa. Owner: BBC Worldwide.
Editor: Siobhan Keeler

Barbie
020 7380 6452
www.egmontmagazines.co.uk
Fortnightly. Owner: Egmont Magazines.
Editor: Claire Noonan

BBC Toybox
020 8433 2356
www.bbcmagazines.com/toybox/
13pa. Owner: BBC Worldwide. Editors:
Nora Kerezovic, Paddy Kempshall

Beano
01382 223131
www.beanotown.com
Weekly. Owner: DC Thomson.
Editor: Euan Kerr

Bliss
020 7437 9011
www.blissmag.co.uk
Monthly. Owner: Emap.
Editor: Lisa Smosarski

Breakout
01235 553444
www.couriergroup.com
6pa. Owner: Courier Newspaper Group.
Editor: Lawrence Webb

CosmoGirl!
020 7439 5000
www.cosmogirl.co.uk
Monthly. Owner: National Magazine
Company. Editor: Celia Duncan

Daisy
020 7380 6474
www.egmontmagazines.co.uk
Monthly. Owner: Egmont.
Editor: Joanna Tubbs

Dandy
01382 223131
www.dandy.com
Weekly. Owner: DC Thomson.
Editor: Morris Heggie

Disney & Me
020 7380 6449
www.egmontmagazines.co.uk
Fortnightly. Owner: Egmont Magazines.
Editor: Jeanette Ryall

Disney Princess
020 7380 6449
www.egmontmagazines.co.uk
Fortnightly. Owner: Egmont Magazines.
Editor: Jeanette Ryall

Dora the Explorer
020 7565 3000
Monthly. Owner: G E Magazines.
Editor: Harriet Murphy

Elle Girl
020 7150 7000
www.hf-uk.com
Monthly. Owner: Hachette Filipacchi UK.
Editor: Claire Irvin

Fimbles Magazine
020 8433 2000
www.bbcmagazines.com
13pa. Owner: BBC Worldwide.
Editor: Nora Kerezovic

Girl
01392 664141
Monthly. Owner: LCD Publishing.
Editor: Joanne Trump

Girl Talk
020 8433 3825
www.bbcmagazines.com/girltalk
Fortnightly. Owner: BBC Worldwide.
Editor: Samantha McEvoy

Go Girl
020 7380 6471
www.egmontmagazines.co.uk
Fortnightly. Owner: Egmont Magazines.
Editor: Sarah Delmege

Guiding
020 7592 1821
www.girlguiding.org.uk
Monthly. Owner: GirlGuiding UK.
Editor: Wendy Kewley

Hot Wheels
020 7380 6467
www.egmontmagazines.co.uk
Monthly. Owner: Egmont Magazines.
Editor: Matt Crossick

Mizz
01892 500105
www.paninionline.com
Fortnighty. Owner: Panini UK

Pony
01428 601020
www.ponymag.com
Monthly. Owner: DJ Murphy Publishers.
Editor: Janet Rising

Postman Pat
01892 500 100
www.paninicomics.co.uk
3 weekly. Owner: Panini.
Editor: Karen Brown

Power Rangers
020 7380 6449
www.egmontmagazines.co.uk
Monthly. Owner: Egmont Magazines.
Editor: Jeanette Ryall

Rugrats
0161 624 0414
13pa. Owner: Toontastic Publishing.
Editor: Emma Boff

Scouting Magazine
020 8433 7219
www.scouts.org.uk/magazine/
Bi-monthly. Owner: Redactive Publishing.
Editor: Matt Oakes

Shout Magazine
01382 223131
www.dcthomson.co.uk
Fortnightly. Owner: DC Thomson.
Editor: Ria Welch

Simpsons Comic
020 7620 0200
www.titanmagazines.com
Monthly. Owner: Titan Publishing.
Editor: Paul Terry

Spectacular Spider-Man
01892 500100
www.paninicomics.co.uk
17pa. Owner: Panini UK.
Editor: Tom O'Malley

Sugar
020 7150 7087
www.sugarmagazine.co.uk
Monthly. Owner: Hachette Filipacchi UK.
Editor: Annabel Brog

Thomas & Friends
020 7380 6454
www.egmontmagazines.co.uk
Fortnightly. Owner: Egmont Magazines.
Editor: Audrey Wong

Toxic
020 7380 6465
www.egmontmagazines.co.uk
Fortnightly. Owner: Egmont Magazines.
Editor: Matt Yeo

Tweenies Magazine
020 8433 2356
www.bbcmagazines.com
Fortnightly. Owner: BBC Worldwide

Wallace & Gromit
020 7803 1209
www.titanmagazines.com
Monthly. Owner: Titan Magazines.
Editor: Steve White

Winnie the Pooh
020 7380 6449
www.egmontmagazines.co.uk
Monthly. Owner: Egmont Magazines.
Editor: Jeanette Ryall

Witch
020 8433 3825
www.bbcmagazines.com
/content/magazines/witch
Monthly. Owner: BBC. Editor: Bea Appleby

Wolverine & Deadpool
01892 500100
www.paninicomics.co.uk
13pa. Owner: Panini UK. Editor: Scott Gray

Young Scot
0131 313 2488
www.youngscot.org
Monthly. Editor: Fiona McIntyre

● Computing & gadgets

.net
01225 442244
www.netmag.co.uk
13pa. Owner: Future. Editor: Lisa Jones

3D World
01225 442244
www.3dworldmag.co.uk
13pa. Owner: Future. Editor: Jim Thacker

Computer Arts
01225 442244
www.computerarts.co.uk
13pa. Owner: Future. Editor: Gillian Carson

Computer Arts Projects
01225 442244
www.computerarts.co.uk
13pa. Owner: Future. Editor: Rob Carney

Computer Buyer
020 7907 6000
www.computerbuyer.co.uk
Monthly. Owner: Dennis.
Editor: James Nixon

Computer Shopper
020 7907 6000
www.computershopper.co.uk
Monthly. Owner: Dennis.
Editor: Paul Sanders

ComputerActive
020 7316 9000
www.computeractive.co.uk
Fortnightly. Owner: VNU.
Editor: Dylan Armbrust

Computing Which?
020 7770 7564
www.computingwhich.co.uk
Bi-monthly. Owner: Which?
Editor: Jessica Ross

Digital Camera Buyer
01202 586200
www.imagine-publishing.co.uk
6pa. Owner: Imagine Publishing.
Editor: Chris Lean

Digital Home
01225 442244
www.digitalhomemag.co.uk
13pa. Owner: Future. Editor: Dean Evans

Digital Photo
01733 264666
www.emap.com
Monthly. Owner: Emap. Editor: Jon Adams

Digital Video
www.digitalvideomag.co.uk
13pa. Owner: Future. Editor: Robert Hull

Edge
01225 442244
www.edge-online.co.uk
13pa. Owner: Future. Editor: Tony Mott

Games Domain
0121 326 0900
www.gamesdomain.com
Website, updated daily. Owner: Yahoo!

Games TM
01202 586257
www.gamestm.co.uk
13pa. Owner: Imagine Publishing.
Editor: Paul Morgan

GamesMaster
01225 442244
www.futurenet.com/gamesmaster
13pa. Owner: Future. Editor: Robin Alway

Hi-Fi Choice
020 7042 4000
www.hifichoice.co.uk
13pa. Owner: Future. Editor: Tim Bowern

Hi-Fi News
020 8726 8000
www.hifinews.com
Monthly. Owner: IPC Media.
Editor: Steve Fairclough

Hi-Fi World
01275 371386
www.hi-fiworld.co.uk
Monthly. Editor: David Price

Home Cinema Choice
020 7042 4000
www.homecinemachoice.co.uk
Monthly. Owner: Future. Editor: Steve May

iCreate
01202 586205
www.icreatemagazine.com
9pa. Owner:Imagine Publishing.
Editor: Ben Harvell

Internet and Broadband Advisor
01225 442244
www.netadvisor.co.uk
13pa. Owner: Future.
Editor: Alex Summersby

Internet World
020 8232 1600
www.internetworld.co.uk
Monthly. Owner: Penton Media Europe.
Editor: Mark Dye

Jetix
01225 442244
www.jetix.co.uk
13pa. Owner: Future. Editor: Cavan Scott

Linux Format
01225 442244
www.linuxformat.co.uk
13pa. Owner: Future. Editor: Nick Veitch

Login Magazine
01702 589169
Monthly. Owner: Enterbrain.
Editor: Rick Haynes

MacFormat
01225 442244
www.macformat.co.uk
13pa. Owner: Future.
Editor: Graham Barlow

MacUser
020 7907 6000
www.macuser.co.uk
Fortnightly. Owner: Dennis.
Editor: Nick Rawlinson

Macworld
020 7071 3621
www.macworld.co.uk
13pa. Owner: IDG London.
Editor: Mark Hattersley

Micro Mart
020 7907 6000
www.micromart.co.uk
Weekly. Owner: Dennis.
Editor: Simon Brew

Official PlayStation 2 Magazine
01225 442244
www.playstation.co.uk
13pa. Owner: Future.
Editor: Stephen Pierce

Official Xbox Magazine
020 7042 4000
www.officialxboxmagazine.co.uk
13pa. Owner: Future. Editor: Steve Brown

PC Advisor
020 7071 3615
www.pcadvisor.co.uk
Monthly. Owner: IDG London.
Editor: Matthew Bath

PC Answers
01225 442244
www.pcanswers.co.uk
13pa. Owner: Future.
Editor: Simon Pickstock

PC Format
01225 442244
www.pcformat.co.uk
13pa. Owner: Future. Editor: Adam Oxford

PC Gamer
01225 442244
www.pcgamer.co.uk
13pa. Owner: Future. Editor: Mark Donald

PC Plus
01225 442244
www.pcplus.co.uk
13pa. Owner: Future. Editor: Ian Robson

PC Pro
020 7907 6000
www.pcpro.co.uk
Monthly. Owner: Dennis. Editor: James Morris

PC Utilities
0871 223 1112
www.pc-utilities.co.uk
13pa. Owner: Magnesium Media International. Editor: Gavin Burrell

PC Zone
020 7042 4000
www.pczone.co.uk
13pa. Owner: Future. Editor: Jamie Sefton

PDA Essentials
01202 586254
www.pda-essentials.co.uk
13pa. Owner: Imagine.
Deputy editor: Andy Betts

Personal Computer World
01858 438881
www.pcw.co.uk
Monthly. Owner: VNU. Editor: Rob Jones

Play
01202 586216
www.play-mag.co.uk
13pa. Owner: Imagine. Editor: Nick Jones

PSM2
01225 442244
www.futurenet.com/psm2
13pa. Owner: Future. Editor: Daniel Griffith

PSW
020 7042 4000
www.myfavouritemagazines.co.uk
13pa. Owner: Future. Editor: Lee Nutter

Stuff
020 8267 5036
www.stuffmagazine.co.uk
Monthly. Owner: Haymarket.
Editor: Oliver Irish

T3
020 7042 4000
www.t3.co.uk
13pa. Owner: Future. Editor: James Beechinor-Collins

Total Mobile
020 7331 1000
www.camuser.co.uk
13pa. Owner: Future. Editor: Phil Lattimore

Web Designer
01202 299900
www.webdesignermag.co.uk
13pa. Owner:Imagine. Editor: Mark Billen

Web User
020 7261 7294
www.webuser.co.uk
Fortnightly. Owner: IPC Media.
Editor: Andrew Craig

What Digital Camcorder
020 7331 1000
www.whatcamcorder.net
13pa. Owner: Future. Editor: Ali Upham

What Hi-Fi? Sound and Vision
020 8267 5000
www.whathifi.com
Monthly, plus awards issue.
Owner: Haymarket

What Home Cinema
020 7331 1000
www.homecinemachoice.com/whathomecinema/magazine
Monthly. Owner: Future.
Editor: Adrian Justins

What Satellite and Digital TV
020 7331 1000
www.wotsat.com
Monthly. Owner: Future. Editor: Alex Lane

What Video and Widescreen TV
020 7331 1000
www.whatvideomag.com
Monthly. Owner: Future.
Editor: Danny Phillips

Windows XP Made Easy
01202 586253
www.windowsmadeeasy.co.uk
13pa. Owner: Imagine.
Editor: Stuart Tarrant

Windows XP: The Official Magazine
01225 442244
www.windowsxpmagazine.co.uk
13pa. Owner: Future.
Editor: Richard Keith

● Current affairs

AFF Families Journal
01980 615525
www.aff.org.uk
4pa. Owner: Army Families Federation.
Editor: Sue Bonney

The American
01747 830520
www.the-american.co.uk
Monthly. Owner: Blue Edge Publishing.
Editor: Michael Burland

Big Issue
020 7526 3388
www.bigissue.com
Weekly. Editor: A. John Bird

Big Issue in Scotland
0141 418 7000
www.bigissuescotland.com
Weekly. Editor: Claire Harris

Big Issue in the North
0161 834 6300
www.bigissueinthenorth.com
Weekly. Editor: Ato Erzan

Challenge Newsline
0845 166 8463
www.challengenewsline.com
Monthly. Owner: Verité.
Editor: Debbie Bunn

Connect Magazine
020 7865 8100
www.greenpeace.org.uk
4pa. Owner: Greenpeace.
Editor: Stokeley Webster

Diplo
020 7833 9766
www.diplo-magazine.co.uk
Monthy. Owner: Editor: Charles Baker

EarthMatters
020 7490 1555
www.foe.co.uk
3pa. Owner: Friends of the Earth.
Editors: Adam Bradbury, Nicola Baird

Ecologist
020 7351 3578
www.theecologist.org
10pa. Editor: Zac Goldsmith

Economist
020 7830 7000
www.economist.com
Weekly. Owner: The Economist Newspaper. Editor: John Micklethwait

Glasgow Magazine
0141 287 0907
www.glasgow.gov.uk
Bi-monthly. Owner: Glasgow City Council.
Editor: John Keil

Green Futures
020 7324 3660
www.greenfutures.org.uk
Bi-monthly. Owner: Forum for the Future.
Editor: Martin Wright

The House Magazine
020 7091 7530
www.epolitix.com
Weekly. Owner: Dods Parliamentary Communications.
Editor: Sir Patrick Cormack

Impact International
020 7263 1417
www.impact-magazine.com
Monthly. Owner: News and Media.
Editor: Ahmad Irfan

Index on Censorship
020 7278 2313
www.indexonline.org
4pa. Owner: Taylor & Francis.
Editor: Judith Bidal-Hall

The Liberty Newsletter
020 7403 3888
www.liberty-human-rights.org.uk
4pa. Owner: Liberty, The National Council for Civil Liberties.
Editor: Zoe Gillard

New African
020 7713 7711
www.africasia.com
Monthly. Owner: IC Publications.
Editor: Baffour Ankomah

New Internationalist
01865 811400
www.newint.org
Monthly.
Editorial contact: David Ransom

New Statesman
020 7730 3444
www.newstatesman.com
Weekly. Editor: John Kampfner

News Africa
020 7713 8135
www.newsafrica.net
Monthly. Editor: Moffat Ekoriko

Newsweek
020 7851 9799
www.newsweek.com
Weekly. Editor: Fareed Zakaria

Outrage - magazine of Animal Aid
01732 364546
www.animalaid.co.uk
4pa. Editor: Mark Gold

Parliamentary Brief
020 7381 1611
www.thepolitician.org
Monthly. Editor: Roderick Crawford

Party Politics
020 7324 8500
www.sagepub.co.uk
6pa. Owner: Sage Publications.
Editor: David M Farrell

Private Eye
020 7437 4017
www.private-eye.co.uk
Fortnightly. Owner: Pressdram.
Editor: Ian Hislop

Prospect
020 7255 1281
www.prospect-magazine.co.uk
Monthly. Owner: Prospect Publishing.
Editor: David Goodhart

Red Pepper
020 7281 7024
www.redpepper.org.uk
*Monthly. Owner: Socialist Newspaper
(Publications). Editor: Hilary Wainwright*

Report
020 7930 6441
www.askatl.org.uk
*10pa. Owner: Association of Teachers and
Lecturers. Editor: Heather Pinnell*

SchNEWS
01273 685913
www.schnews.org.uk
Weekly. Editor: Jo Makepeace

Socialism Today
020 8988 8773
www.socialismtoday.org
Monthly. Editor: Lynn Walsh

The Socialist
020 8988 8777
www.socialistparty.org.uk
*Weekly. Owner: Eastway Offset.
Editor: Ken Smith*

Socialist Review
020 7819 1176
www.socialistreview.org.uk
*11pa. Owner: Socialist Workers Party
(Britain). Editor: Yuri Prasad*

Socialist Worker
020 7819 1180
www.socialistworker.co.uk
*Weekly. Owner: Newsfax.
Editor: Chris Bambery*

Spectator
020 7405 1706
www.spectator.co.uk
Weekly. Editor: Matthew d'Ancona

The Sticks Magazine
01462 486810
www.the-sticks.com
*Monthly. Owner: The Plain English
Publishing Company. Editor: John Boston*

Time
020 7499 4080
www.time.com
*Weekly. Owner: Time.
Editor: Michael Elliot*

Tribune
020 7433 6410
www.tribuneweb.co.uk
Weekly. Editor: Chris McLaughlin

Unite
01582 663880
www.pensioneronline.com
*8pa. Owner: National Federation of Royal
Mail and BT Pensioners. Editor: Lee Wilson*

The Week
020 7907 6180
www.theweek.co.uk
*Weekly. Owner: Dennis.
Editor: Jeremy O'Grady*

The World Today
020 7957 5712
www.theworldtoday.org
*Monthly. Owner: The Royal Institute
of International Affairs.
Editor: Graham Walker*

WWF News
01483 426444
www.wwf.org.uk
Quarterly. Owner: WWF. Editor: Guy Jowett

● Food & drink

BBC Good Food
020 8433 3342
www.bbcmagazines.com/goodfood
*Monthly. Owner: BBC Worldwide.
Editor: Gillian Carter*

Big Cook Little Cook
020 8433 2356
www.bbcmagazines.com/content
/magazines/bigcooklittlecook
*Monthly. Owner: BBC Worldwide.
Editor: Sarah O'Neill*

Decanter
020 7261 5000
www.decanter.com
*Monthly. Owner: IPC Media.
Editor: Amy Wislocki*

Delicious
020 7775 7757
www.deliciousmagazine.co.uk
*Monthly. Owner: Seven Publishing.
Editor: Mitzie Wilson*

Easy Cook
020 8433 2000
www.bbcmagazines.com
*Bi-monthly. Owner: BBC Worldwide.
Editor: Sara Buenfeld*

Food & Travel
020 7501 0511
www.foodandtravel.com
*Monthly. Owner: Green Pea Publishing.
Editor: Laura Tennant*

Food Chain
01603 274130
www.foodchain-magazine.com
*Bi-monthly. Owner: Schofield Publishing.
Editor: Libbie Hammond*

Foodie Magazine
01527 61122
www.thefoodie.co.uk/magazine.php
*Monthly. Owner: CW Corporate
Communications. Editor: Alison Davison*

Italian Wines & Spirits
020 8458 4860
www.iwines.it
*Website updated monthly.
Editor: Pino Khail*

M&S Magazine
020 7747 0700
www.redwoodgroup.net
*4pa. Owner: Redwood.
Editor: Diane Kenwood*

Olive
020 8433 1828
www.olivemagazine.co.uk
*Monthly. Owner: BBC Worldwide.
Editor: Christine Hayes*

Sainsbury's Magazine
020 7633 0266
www.sainsburysmagazine.co.uk
*Monthly. Owner: New Crane Publishing.
Editor: Sue Robinson*

Somerfield Magazine
0117 989 7808
www.somerfield.co.uk
*13pa. Owner: Rare Publishing.
Editor: Hannah Smith*

The Vegetarian
0161 925 2000
www.vegsoc.org
*4pa. Owner: The Vegetarian Society of the
United Kingdom. Editor: Jane Bowler*

Waitrose Food Illustrated
020 7565 3000
www.jbcp.co.uk
*Monthly. Owner: John Brown Publishing
Group. Editor: William Sitwell*

What's Brewing
01727 798454
www.camra.org.uk
*Monthly. Owner: Camra.
Editor: Ted Bruning*

Whisky Magazine
01603 633808
www.whiskymag.com
*8pa. Owner: Paragraph Publishing.
Editor: Dominic Roskrow*

Wine
01293 846550
www.wineint.com
*Monthly. Owner: Quest Magazines
& Events. Editor: Catharine Lowe*

● Gay and lesbian

» *See page 119*

● General interest

American in Britain
020 8661 0186
www.americaninbritain.co.uk/
*4pa. Owner: The American Hour.
Editor: Helen Elliott*

Another Magazine
020 7336 0766
www.anothermag.com
*2pa. Owner: Dazed Group.
Editor: Jefferson Hack*

Asian Image
01254 298263
www.asianimage.co.uk
*Monthly. Owner: Newsquest.
Editor: Shuiab Khan*

Astronomy Now
01903 266165
www.astronomynow.com
*Monthly. Owner: Pole Star Publications.
Editor: Stuart Clark*

BBC History Magazine
0117 927 9009
www.bbchistorymagazine.com
*Monthly. Owner: Origin Publishing.
Editor: Greg Neale*

Brighton & Hove Life
01903 604226
www.archantlife.co.uk
*Monthly. Owner: Archant.
Editorial contact: Viv Craske*

Cambridge Agenda
01223 309224
www.thecambridgeagenda.co.uk
*Monthly. Owner: Life Publishing.
Editor: Nick Jordan*

Cheshire Life
01772 722022
www.archantlife.co.uk
Monthly. Owner: Archant.
Editor: Patrick O'Neill

Choice
01733 555123
www.choicemag.co.uk
Monthly. Editor: Norman Wright

Contemporary
020 7740 1704
www.contemporary-magazine.com
Monthly. Owner: Art 21.
Editor: Michele Rebecchi

Cornwall Life
01803 860910
www.archantlife.co.uk
Monthly. Owner: Archant.
Publisher: Anita Newcombe

Cotswold Life
01242 216050
www.archantlife.co.uk
Monthly. Owner: Archant.
Publisher: Peter Waters

Dazed & Confused
020 7336 0766
www.confused.co.uk
Monthly. Owner: Dazed Group.
Editor: Rod Stanley

Der Spiegel
020 8605 3893
www.spiegel.de
Weekly. Editor: Stefan Aust

Devon Life
01803 860928
www.archantlife.co.uk
Monthly. Owner: Archant.
Editor: Jan Barwick

Dorset
01305 211840
www.archantlife.co.uk
Monthly. Owner: Archant.
Editor: Bridget Swann

DV8
01202 388388
www.dv8online.co.uk
Monthly. Editor: Helen Mayson

EDP Norfolk Magazine
01603 772469
www.edp24.co.uk
Monthly. Owner: Archant.
Editor: Carolyn Bowden

Epicurean Life
020 7376 5959
www.epicureanlife.co.uk
4pa. Editor: Azzy Asghar

Essex Life & Countryside
01799 544273
www.archant.co.uk
Monthly. Owner: Archant.
Editor: Robyn Bechelet

Expression
01392 263052
www.exeter.ac.uk/alumni
2pa. Owner: University of Exeter Alumni
Network. Editor: Karen Lippoldt

Focus
0117 933 8040
www.focusmag.co.uk
Monthly. Owner: Origin Publishing.
Editor: Paul Parsons

Folio
0117 942 8491
www.foliomag.com
Monthly. Owner: Venue Publishing.
Editor: Ali Stevens

Forward
0118 983 8243
www.guidedogs.org.uk
4pa. Editor: Sarah Hall

Freemasonry Today
01359 240820
www.freemasonrytoday.co.uk
4pa. Editor: Michael Baigent

Fresh Direction
020 7449 0900
www.freshdirection.co.uk
3pa. Owner: Antonville.
Editor: Paul Russell

The Green
020 7792 2626
www.archantlife.co.uk
Monthly. Owner: Archant.
Editor: Maxine Briggs

The Guide Magazine
020 8297 0809
www.archantlife.co.uk
Monthly. Owner: Archant.
Editor: Lee Cheshire

H&E Naturist
01405 760298
www.henaturist.co.uk
Monthly. Owner: New Freedom
Publications. Editor: Sara Backhouse

Hampshire Life
01242 216053
www.archantlife.co.uk
Monthly. Owner: Archant.
Editor: Mike Lowe

Hertfordshire Life
01799 544273
www.archantlife.co.uk
Monthly. Owner: Archant.
Editor: Robyn Bechelet

The Hill
020 7792 2626
www.archantlife.co.uk
Monthly. Owner: Archant.
Editor: Pendle Harte

History Today
020 7534 8000
www.historytoday.com
Monthly. Owner: History Today.
Editor: Peter Furtado

Hot Press
00 353 1 241 1500
www.hotpress.com
Fortnightly. Owner: Osnovina.
Editor: Niall Stokes

Hotline (Virgin Trains)
020 7306 0304
www.therivergroup.co.uk
Quarterly. Owner: River Publishing.
Editor: Rod Stanley

i-D
020 7490 9710
www.i-dmagazine.co.uk
Monthly. Editor: Ben Reardon

Illustrated London News
020 7805 5555
www.ilng.co.uk
Bi-annual. Owner: Illustrated London
News. Editor: Alison Booth

The Insight
01273 724300
www.theinsight.co.uk
Monthly. Owner: The Insight.
Publisher: Mike Holland

Kent Life
01622 762818
www.archantlife.co.uk
Monthly. Owner: Archant.
Editor: Sarah Sturt

Kindred Spirit
01803 866686
www.kindredspirit.co.uk
6pa. Editor: Richard Beaumont

Lancashire Life
01772 722022
www.archantlife.co.uk
Monthly. Owner: Archant.
Editor: Roger Borrell

Let's Talk! Norfolk
01603 772413
www.edp24.co.uk
Monthly. Owner: Archant.
Editor: Cathy Brown

Let's Talk! Suffolk
01473 324795
www.archant.co.uk
Monthly. Owner: Archant.
Editor: Anne Gould

The Lifeboat
01202 662254
www.rnli.org.uk
4pa. Owner: RNLI. Editor: Liz Cook

Limited Edition
01689 885661
www.newsshopper.co.uk
/limitededition
Monthly. Owner: Newsquest.
Editor: Andrew Parkes

Living South
020 7223 0022
www.archant.co.uk
Monthly. Owner: Archant.
Editor: Shannon Denny

Magnet – The Village
Communicator
01825 732796
www.magnetpublications.com
Monthly. Editor: Mary Hillyar

Majesty
020 7436 4006
www.majestymagazine.com
Monthly. Owner: Rex Publications.
Editor-in-chief: Ingrid Seward

Mayfair and St James's Life
020 7344 9121
www.mayfairlife.co.uk
Monthly. Editor: Stephen Goringe

MQ – Masonic Quarterly
020 7793 4140
www.mqmagazine.co.uk
Quarterly. Owner: Grand Lodge
Publications. Editor: John Jackson

New Humanist
020 7436 1151
www.newhumanist.org.uk
Bi-monthly. Owner: Rationalist Press Association. Editor: Frank Jordans

Nexus
01342 322854
www.nexusmagazine.com
Bi-monthly. Editor: Duncan Roads

Norfolk Roots
01603 772184
www.norfolkroots24.co.uk
Bi Monthly. Owner: Archant. Editor: Robin Vyrnwy-Pierce

North Magazine
020 7359 5500
www.archantlife.co.uk
Monthly. Owner: Archant. Editor: Mark Kebble

NW
020 7792 2626
www.archantlife.co.uk
Monthly. Owner: Archant. Editor: Danielle Monroe

Occasions
020 7650 2000
www.occasions-mag.com
4pa. Owner: Ethnic Media Group. Editor: Sheri Mill

The Oldie
020 7436 8801
www.theoldie.co.uk
Monthly. Owner: Oldie Publications. Editor: Richard Ingrams

Oxfordshire Life
01242 216050
www.archantlife.co.uk
Monthly. Owner: Archant. Publisher: Paul Bates

Password
020 7261 9878
Bi-monthly. Editor: Alistair Gordon

Platform
0115 848 1510
www.trentstudents.org
Fortnightly. Owner: Nottingham Trent Students Union. Editor: Loay El Hady

Psychologies
0870 129 8800
www.psychologies.co.uk
Monthly. Owner: Hachette Fillipacchi. Editor: Maureen Rice

Quicksilver Magazine
020 7747 9390
www.pspcom.com
Bi-monthly. Owner: PSP Communications. Editor: Garth Gibbs

Reader's Digest
020 7715 8000
www.readersdigest.co.uk
Monthly. Owner: Reader's Digest. Editor: Katherine Walker

Reform
020 7916 8630
www.urc.org.uk
11pa. Owner: United Reformed Church. Editor: Brenda Guest

The Resident
020 7384 9124
www.metropolispublishing.co.uk
Monthly. Owner: Metropolis Publishing. Editor: Amanda Constance

Royal Berkshire Life
01242 216050
www.archantlife.co.uk
Monthly. Owner: Archant. Publisher: Paul Bates

Royalty
020 8201 9978
www.royalty-magazine.com
Monthly. Owner: Sena Julia Publicatus. Editor: M Houston

Salvationist
020 7367 4890
www.salvationarmy.org.uk
/salvationist
Weekly. Owner: Salvation Army. Editor: Dean Pallant

Scots Magazine
01382 223131
www.scotsmagazine.com
Monthly. Owner: DC Thomson. Editor: John Methven

Sixer
0114 250 6300
www.northernlifestyle.com
Monthly. Owner: Regional Magazine Company. Editor: Chris Wilson

Somerset Life
01803 860910
www.archantlife.co.uk
Monthly. Owner: Archant. Editor: Nicki Lukehurst

The Spark
0117 914 3434
www.thespark.co.uk
4pa. Editor: John Dawson

Surrey Life
01737 247188
www.archantlife.co.uk
Monthly. Owner: Archant. Editor: Elizabeth Hammond

Sussex Life
01903 604200
www.archantlife.co.uk
Monthly. Owner: Archant. Editor: Jonathan Keeble

SW
020 7223 0022
www.archantlife.co.uk
Monthly. Owner: Archant. Editor: Sarah Hodgson

Tank
020 7434 0110
www.tankmagazine.com
Quarterly. Owner: Tank Publications. Editor: Masoud Golsorkhi

Toni & Guy
020 7462 7777
www.publicis-blueprint.co.uk
4pa. Owner: Publicis Blueprint. Editor: Scarlett Brady

Town & Country News
01692 582287
Monthly. Owner: Leisure Publishing. Editor: Laurence Watts

Trafford Magazine
020 7387 9888
www.babersmith.co.uk
2pa. Owner: Baber Smith. Editor: Heather Wood

The Village
020 7792 2626
www.archantlife.co.uk
Monthly. Owner: Archant. Editor: Pendle Harte

The Visitor
01963 351256
Monthly. Editor: Helen Dunion

Wavelength
01872 247456
www.wavelengthmag.co.uk
Monthly. Owner: Cornwall & Devon Media. Editor: Tim Nunn

Weekly News
01382 223131
www.dcthomson.co.uk
Weekly. Owner: DC Thomson. Editor: Dave Burness

Which?
020 7770 7373
www.which.co.uk
Monthly. Owner: Which? Editor: Neil Fowler

Yorkshire Life
01772 722022
www.archantlife.co.uk
Monthly. Owner: Archant. Editor: Esther Leach

You Can! Magazine
01242 544905
3pa. Owner: Independent News & Media (UK). Editor: Anthony McClaran

Your Family Tree
01225 442244
www.yourfamilytreemag.co.uk
Monthly. Owner: Future. Editor: Garrick Webster

Yours
01733 264666
www.emap.com
Monthly. Owner: Emap. Editor: Valerie McConnell

● Home and garden

25 Beautiful Homes
020 7261 5015
www.ipcmedia.com
Monthly. Owner: IPC Media. Editor: John Smigielski

25 Beautiful Kitchens
020 7261 5015
www.ipcmedia.com
10pa. Owner: IPC Media. Editor: Ysanne Brooks

Amateur Gardening
01202 440840
www.ipcmedia.com
Weekly. Owner: IPC Media. Editor: Tim Rumball

BBC Gardeners' World
020 8433 3959
www.gardenersworld.com
Monthly. Owner: BBC Worldwide. Editor: Adam Pasco

BBC Good Homes
0870 444 2607
www.bbcmagazines.com/goodhomes
Monthly. Owner: BBC Worldwide.
Editor: Lisa Allen

BBC Homes & Antiques
0117 927 9009
www.bbcmagazines.com
   /homesandantiques
Monthly. Owner: BBC Magazines Bristol.
Editor: Gail Dixon

Country Homes & Interiors
020 7261 6434
www.ipcmedia.com
Monthly. Owner: IPC Media.
Editor: Rhoda Parry

Country Living
020 7439 5000
www.countryliving.co.uk
Monthly. Owner: National Magazine
Company. Editor: Susy Smith

Horsemart
0870 122 2710
www.country-mkt.co.uk
Monthly. Editor: David Somerville

Easy Living
0870 837 8507
www.easylivingmagazine.co.uk
Monthly. Owner: Condé Nast.
Editor: Abigail Chisman

Elle Decoration
020 7150 7000
www.hf-uk.com
Monthly. Owner: Hachette Filipacchi UK.
Editor: Michelle Ogunadehin

The English Garden
020 7751 4800
www.theenglishgarden.co.uk
Monthly. Owner: Archant.
Editor: Janine Wookey

The English Home
020 7751 4800
www.theenglishhome.co.uk
Monthly. Owner: Archant.
Editor: Charlotte Coward-Williams

The Essential Kitchen, Bathroom & Bedroom Magazine
01206 851117
www.essentialpublishing.co.uk
Monthly. Owner: Essential Publishing.
Acting editor: Natalie Kelly

Fabric
020 7747 0700
www.redwoodgroup.net
Monthly. Owner: Redwood.
Editor: Steven Short

The Garden
01733 775775
www.rhs.org.uk
Monthly. Owner: RHS Publications.
Editor: Ian Hodgson

Garden Answers
01733 264666
www.emap.com
Monthly. Owner: Emap. Editor: Neil Pope

Garden News
01733 264666
www.emap.com
Weekly. Owner: Emap

Gardening Which?
020 7770 7564
www.which.co.uk/gardeningwhich
10pa. Owner: Which? Editor: Julia Bolton

Gardens Illustrated
0870 444 2611
www.bbcmagazines.com
   /gardensillustrated
10pa. Owner: BBC Worldwide.
Editor: Juliet Roberts

Gardens Monthly
01689 899297
www.gardening.co.uk
11pa. Owner: Encanta. Editor: Liz Dobbs

Good Housekeeping
020 7439 5000
www.goodhousekeeping.co.uk
Monthly. Owner: National Magazine
Company. Editor: Lindsay Nicholson

Home & Country
020 7731 5777
www.womens-institute.co.uk
Monthly. Owner: Women's Institute.
Editor: Joanna Gray

Home Furnishing News (HFN)
020 7240 0420
www.hfnmag.com
Weekly. Owner: Fairchild.
Editor: Warren Shoulberg

Home Life Magazine
028 3832 4006
Monthly. Editor: M Kinsella

Home View
01277 366134
www.homeviewproperty
   magazine.com
Bi-monthly. Editor: Garry Clarke

Homebase Ideas
020 7462 7777
www.publicis-blueprint.co.uk
Quarterly. Owner: Publicis Blueprint.
Editor: Ward Hellewell

Homebuilding & Renovating
01527 834400
www.moveorimprove.co.uk
Monthly. Owner: Centaur.
Editor: Jason Orme

Homes & Gardens
020 7261 5678
www.homesandgardens.com
Monthly. Owner: IPC Media.
Editor: Deborah Barker

Homes & Interiors Scotland
0141 221 5559
www.homesandinteriorsscotland.com
Bi-monthly. Owner: International
Magazines. Editor: Kate Hamilton

Homes Overseas
020 7002 8300
www.homesoverseas.co.uk
Monthly. Owner: Blendon
Communications. Editor: Mike Hayes

Homes Review
01206 506249
Monthly. Owner: MS Publications

HomeStyle
01206 851117
www.essentialpublishing.co.uk
Monthly. Owner: Essential Publishing.
Editor: Sarah Gallaher

House & Garden
020 7499 9080
www.houseandgarden.co.uk
Monthly. Owner: Condé Nast.
Editor: Susan Crewe

House & Home Ideas
01823 288 344
www.houseandhomeideas.co.uk
Monthly. Owner: Giraffe Media.
Editor: Rachel Southwood

House Beautiful
020 7439 5000
www.housebeautiful.co.uk
Monthly. Owner: National Magazine
Company. Editor: Julia Goodwin

Ideal Home
020 7261 6474
www.ipcmedia.com
Monthly. Owner: IPC Media.
Editor: Susan Rose

International Homes
01245 358877
www.international-homes.com
Monthly. Editor: Jill Keene

Ireland's Homes Interiors & Living
028 9147 3979
www.irelandshomesinteriors
   andliving.com
Monthly. Editor: Samantha Blair

KBB – Kitchens, Bedrooms & Bathrooms Magazine
020 8515 2000
www.dmgworldmedia.com
Monthly. Owner: DMG World Media.
Editor: Jackie Daly

Key
020 7494 3155
www.real-london.com
2pa. Owner: Real London Ltd.
Editor: Clare Weatherall

Livingetc
020 7261 6603
www.ipcmedia.com
Monthly. Owner: IPC Media.
Editor: Suzanne Imre

Location, Location, Location
01737 786800
www.brooklandsgroup.com
Monthly. Owner: Brooklands Media.
Editor: Nigel Lewis

Period House
01206 851117
www.essentialpublishing.co.uk
Monthly. Owner: Essential Publishing.
Editor: Charlotte Barber

Period Ideas
01206 505976
www.periodideas.com
Monthly. Owner: Aceville Publications.
Editor: Jeannine McAndrew

Period Living & Traditional Homes
020 7970 4000
www.periodliving.co.uk
Monthly. Owner: Centaur.
Editor: Liz Walker

Real Homes Magazine
020 7150 7000
www.hhc.co.uk
Monthly. Owner: Hachette Filipacchi.
Editor: Lisa McFarlane

Renovations
020 7384 1985
4pa. Editor: Liz Cowley

Scottish Home & Country
0131 225 1724
www.swri.org.uk
Monthly. Owner: Scottish Women's Rural Institutes. Editor: Liz Ferguson

Traditional Homes & Interiors
01795 599191
www.cplmedia.co.uk
11pa. Owner: CPL Media. Editor: Vicki Watson

Wallpaper*
020 7322 1177
www.wallpaper.com
Monthly. Owner: IPC Media. Editor: Jeremy Langmead

World of Interiors
020 7499 9080
www.worldofinteriors.co.uk
Monthly. Owner: Condé Nast. Editor: Rupert Thomas

Your Home
01206 851117
www.essentialpublishing.co.uk
Monthly. Owner: Essential Publishing. Editor: Hayley Chilver

Your New Home
01732 878800
www.yournewhome.co.uk
4pa. Owner: New Concept Group. Editor: Karen Keeman

● Leisure

Absolute Horse
01473 731220
www.ahmagazine.com
Monthly. Owner: PCD Media. Editor: Diana Goldstone

Aeroplane
020 7261 5849
www.aeroplanemonthly.com
Monthly. Owner: IPC Media. Editor: Michael Oakey

Air Enthusiast
01780 755131
www.airenthusiast.com
Bi-monthly. Owner: Key Publishing. Editor: Ken Ellis

Air Transport World
01628 477775
www.atwonline.com
Monthly. Owner: Penton Media. Editor: Perry Flint

Aircraft Illustrated
01932 266600
www.aircraftillustrated.com
Monthly. Owner: Ian Allan Publishing. Editor: Alan Burney

Airliner World
01780 755131
www.airlinerworld.com
Monthly. Owner: Key Publishing. Editor: Tony Dixon

Animal Life
0870 010 1181
www.rspca.org.uk
Quarterly. Owner: RSPCA. Editor: Amanda Bailey

Antique Collecting
01394 389950
www.antique-acc.com
10pa. Owner: Antique Collectors Club. Editor: Susan Wilson

Antique Dealer & Collectors Guide
020 8691 4820
www.antiquecollectorsguide.co.uk
Bi-monthly. Owner: Status Court. Editor: Philip Bartlam

Antiques and Collectibles
01225 786835
www.antiques-collectables.co.uk
13pa. Owner: Merricks Media. Editor: Rachel Harrison

At Home in Cardiff Bay
029 2045 0532
www.athomeincardiffbay.com
Bi-monthly. Owner: City Publications. Editor: Alison Tucker

Aviation News
01424 720477
www.aviation-news.co.uk
Monthly. Owner: HPC Publishing. Editor: Barry Wheeler

Aviation Week & Space Technology
020 7434 3126
www.aviationnow.com
Weekly. Owner: McGraw-Hill. Editor-in-chief: Anthony Velocci; London bureau chief: Douglas Barrie

Award Journal
01753 727470
www.theaward.org
3pa. Editor: Dave Wood

BBC Wildlife Magazine
0117 927 9009
www.bbcwildlifemagazine.com
Monthly. Publisher: Bristol Magazines Ltd. Editor: Sophie Stafford

Bird Life
01767 680551
www.rspb.org.uk
Bi-monthly. Owner: RSPB. Editor: Derek Niemann

Birds
01767 680551
www.rspb.org.uk
4pa. Owner: RSPB. Editor: Rob Hume

Birdwatch
020 8881 0550
www.birdwatch.co.uk
Monthly. Owner: Solo Publishing. Editor: Dominic Mitchell

Bird Watching
01733 264666
www.emap.com
Monthly. Owner: Emap. Editor: Kevin Wilmott

BMFA News
0116 244 0028
www.bmfa.org/news
Bi-monthly. Editor: Eric Clark

Boat International
020 8547 2662
www.boatinternational.com
Monthly. Owner: Edisea. Editor: Amanda McCracken

Boats & Yachts for Sale
01243 533394
www.boatshop24.co.uk
Monthly. Owner: Marine Trader Media.

Book & Magazine Collector
0870 732 8080
13pa. Publisher: Diamond. Editor: Jonathan Scott

Bridge Magazine
020 7388 2404
www.bridgemagazine.co.uk
Monthly. Editor: Mark Horton

British Birds
01424 815132
www.britishbirds.co.uk
Monthly. Editor: Roger Riddington

British Horse
0870 120 2244
www.bhs.org.uk
Bi-monthly. Owner: The British Horse Society. Editor: David Prince

British Naturism
01604 620361
www.british-naturism.org.uk
4pa. Editor: Tracey Major

Budgerigar World
01678 520262
Monthly. Owner: County Press. Editor: G Evans

Buy a Boat (for under £20,000)
01243 533394
www.boatshop24.co.uk
Monthly. Owner: Marine Trader Media

Cage & Aviary Birds
020 7261 6201
www.ipcmedia.com
Weekly. Owner: IPC Media. Editor: Donald Taylor

Camping & Caravanning
024 7647 5270
www.campingandcaravanningclub.co.uk
Monthly. Owner: The Camping & Caravanning Club. Editor: Nick Harding

Camping Magazine
01778 391000
www.campingmagazine.co.uk
10pa. Owner: Warners. Editor: Mike Cowton

Canal & Riverboat
01603 708930
www.canalsandrivers.co.uk
Monthly. Owner: Morgan Publications. Editor: Chris Cattrall

Canal Boat
0118 977 1677
www.canalboatmag.co.uk
Monthly. Owner: Archant. Editor: Kevin Blick

Caravan Club Magazine
01342 336804
www.caravanclub.co.uk
Monthly. Owner: The Caravan Club. Editor: Gary Martin

Caravan Magazine
020 8726 8249
www.ipcmedia.com
Monthly. Owner: IPC Media. Editor: Steve Rowe

Cat World
01903 884988
www.catworld.co.uk
Monthly. Owner: Ashdown. Editor: Jess White

Chess
020 7388 2404
www.chess.co.uk
Monthly. Editor: Jimmy Adams

Church Music Quarterly
01722 424848
www.rscm.com
4pa. Owner: Royal School of Church Music. Editor: Esther Jones

Classic Boat
020 8726 8130
www.ipcmedia.com
Monthly. Owner: IPC Media. Editor: Dan Houston

Coast
020 7439 5000
www.coastmagazine.co.uk
Monthly. Publisher: National Magazine Company. Editor: Susy Smith

Coin News
01404 46972
www.tokenpublishing.com
Monthly. Owner: Token Publishing. Editor: John Mussell

Coin Yearbook
01404 46972
www.tokenpublishing.com
Yearly. Owner: Token Publishing. Editor: John Mussell

Collect it!
01778 391000
www.collectit.info
Monthly. Owner: Warner Publishing Group. Editor: Jean Hodge

Collections
020 7870 9000
www.bostonhannah.co.uk
3pa. Owner: Boston Hannah International. Editor: Charles Ford

Collector
020 8740 7020
www.artefact.co.uk
Bi-monthly. Owner: Barrington Publications. Editor: Paul Hooper

Collectors Gazette
01778 391000
www.collectorsgazette.com
Monthly. Owner: Warners. Editor: Denise Burrows

Companions Magazine
01952 290999
www.pdsa.org.uk
4pa. Owner: PDSA. Editor: Clare Evans

Continental Modeller
01297 20580
www.peco-uk.com
Monthly. Owner: Peco Publications & Publicity. Editor: Andrew Burnham

Country Illustrated
020 7291 8609
www.countryclubuk.com
Monthly. Owner: St Martin's Magazines. Editor: Julie Spencer

Country Life
020 7261 6400
www.countrylife.co.uk
Weekly. Owner: IPC Media. Editor: Mark Hedges

Country Smallholding
01392 888481
www.countrysmallholding.com
Monthly. Owner: Archant. Editor: Diane Cowgill

Country Walking
01733 264666
www.emap.com
Monthly. Owner: Emap. Editor: Jonathan Manning

The Countryman
01756 701381
www.countrymanmagazine.co.uk
Monthly. Owner: Country Publications. Editor: Paul Jackson

The Countryman's Weekly
01822 855281
www.countrymansweekly.com
Weekly. Owner: Diamond. Editor: David Venner

Countryside La Vie
0116 212 2555
www.countryside-lavie.com
Bi-monthly. Editor: Sue Brindley

Crafts
020 7806 2538
www.craftscouncil.org.uk
Bi-monthly. Owner: Crafts Council. Editor: Caroline Roux

Crafts Beautiful
01206 505989
www.crafts-beautiful.com
Monthly. Owner: Aceville Publications. Editor: Sarah Crosland

Crafty Carper
0114 258 0812
www.anglingpublications.co.uk
Monthly. Owner: Angling Publications. Editorial director: Martin Ford

Cross Stitch Collection
01225 442244
www.crossstitchcollection.co.uk
13pa. Owner: Future. Editor: Catherine Hood

Cross Stitcher
01225 442244
www.cross-stitchermagazine.co.uk
13pa. Owner: Future. Editor: Catherine Hood

Cumbria
01756 701033
www.dalesman.co.uk
Monthly. Owner: Country Publications. Editor: Terry Fletcher

Dalesman
01756 701033
www.dalesman.co.uk
Monthly. Owner: Country Publications. Editor: Terry Fletcher

Dartmoor Magazine
01822 614899
www.dartmoormagazine.co.uk
4pa. Owner: Quay Publications. Editor: Elisabeth Stanbrook

Dog World
01233 621877
www.dogworld.co.uk
Weekly. Editor: Stuart Baillie

Dogs Today
01276 858880
www.dogstodaymagazine.co.uk
Monthly. Editor: Beverley Cuddy

Doll Magazine
01903 884988
www.dollmagazine.com
Bi-Monthly. Owner: Ashdown.co.uk. Editor: Sue Brewer

Dolls House World
01903 884988
www.dollshouseworld.com
Monthly. Owner: Ashdown.co.uk. Editor: Laura Quiggan

Engineering in Miniature
01926 614101
www.engineeringinminiature.co.uk
Monthly. Owner: Tee Publishing. Editor: CL Deith

EOS Magazine
01869 331741
www.eos-magazine.com
4pa. Owner: Robert Scott Associates. Editor: Angela August

ESP Magazine
01733 253477
www.espmag.co.uk
Monthly. Editor: Sharon McAllister

Evergreen
01242 537900
www.thisengland.co.uk
4pa. Owner: This England. Editor: Stephen Garnet

Everyday Practical Electronics
01202 873872
www.epemag.co.uk
Monthly. Owner: Wimborne Publishing. Editor: Mike Kenward

Families East
020 8694 8694
www.familiesonline.co.uk
Bi-monthly. Owner: Families Magazines. Editor: Mewe Mechese

Families Edinburgh
0131 624 0049
www.familiesonline.co.uk
Bi-monthly. Owner: Families Magazines. Editor: Louise Armour

Families Liverpool
0151 601 8270
www.familiesonline.co.uk
Bi-monthly. Owner: Families Magazines. Editor: Jennifer-Paige Deenihan

Families North
020 7794 5690
www.familiesonline.co.uk
Bi-monthly. Owner: Families Magazines. Editor: Cathy Youd

Families Together
01903 821082
www.cfnetwork.co.uk
3pa. Owner: Christian Publishing and Outreach. Editor: Russ Bravo

Families Upon Thames
01932 254584
www.familiesonline.co.uk
Bi-monthly. Owner: Families Magazines. Editor: Francis Loates

The Flower Arranger
020 8748 2673
www.theflowerarrangermagazine.co.uk
4pa. Owner: The National Association of Flower Arrangement Societies (NAFAS). Editor: Judith Blacklock

Flyer
01225 481440
www.flyer.co.uk
13pa. Owner: Seager Publishing.
Editor: Philip Whiteman

FlyPast
01780 755131
www.flypast.com
13pa. Owner: Key Publishing.
Editor: Ken Ellis

Fortean Times
020 7907 6000
www.forteantimes.com
13pa. Owner: Dennis. Editor: David Sutton

Galleries
020 8740 7020
www.galleries.co.uk
Monthly. Owner: Barrington
Publications. Editor: Andrew Aitken

Gibbons Stamp Monthly
01425 472363
www.gibbonsstampmonthly.com
Monthly. Owner: Stanley Gibbons
Publications. Editor: Hugh Jefferies

Good Woodworking
01225 442244
www.futurenet.com
13pa. Owner: Future. Editor: Nick Gibbs

The Great Outdoors
0141 302 7700
www.newsquest.co.uk
Monthly. Owner: Newsquest.
Editor: Cameron McNaish

Gulliver's World
01228 404350
www.lilliputlane.co.uk
4pa. Owner: Enesco.
Editor: Lynne Thompson

Hali
020 7970 4000
www.hali.co.uk
6pa. Owner: Centaur.
Editor: Daniel Shaffer

Heritage Magazine
020 7751 4800
www.heritagemagazine.co.uk
Bi-monthly. Owner: Archant.
Editor: Penelope Rance

Hoofprint
01565 872107
Monthly. Owner: Penn House Publishing.
Editor: Barry Hook

Horoscope
01202 873872
www.horoscope.co.uk
Monthly. Owner: Wimborne Publishing.
Editor: Mike Kenward

Horse
020 7261 5867
www.ipcmedia.com
Monthly. Owner: IPC Media.
Editor: Amanda Williams

Horse & Hound
020 7261 6453
www.horseandhound.co.uk
Weekly. Owner: IPC Media.
Editor: Lucy Higginson

Horse & Rider
01428 601020
www.horseandridermagazine.co.uk
Monthly. Owner: DJ Murphy Publishers.
Editor: Alison Bridge

International Boat Industry
020 8726 8134
www.ibinews.com
Monthly. Owner: IPC Media.
Editor: Ed Slack

K9 Magazine
0870 011 4115
www.k9magazine.com
Quarterly. Owner: K9 Media Solutions.
Editor: Ryan O'Meara

Kew
020 8332 5906
www.rbgkew.org.uk
4pa. Editor: Sue Seddon

Koi Carp
01202 735090
www.koi-carp.com
Monthly. Owner: Freestyle Publications.
Editor: Christina Evatt

Lakeland Walker
01778 391000
www.warnersgroup.co.uk
Bi-monthly. Owner: Warners Group.
Editor: Michael Cowton

Legion – Royal British Legion
020 7880 7666
www.britishlegion.org.uk
Bi-monthly. Owner: Redactive Publishing.
Editor: Claire Townley-Jones

Leisure Painter
01580 763315
www.leisurepainter.co.uk
Monthly. Owner: The Artists' Publishing
Company. Editor: Ingrid Lyon

Leisure Scene
01494 888433
www.cssc.co.uk
3pa. Owner: CSSC Sports & Leisure.
Editor: Ian Cooper

Lifewatch Magazine
020 7449 6363
www.zsl.org
3pa. Owner: Zoological Society of
London. Editor: Debbie Curtis

Marine Modelling International
01684 588500
www.marinemodelmagazine.com
Monthly. Owner: Traplet Publications.
Editor: Chris Jackson

Microlight Flying (The British Microlight Aircraft Assocation official magazine)
01524 841010
www.pagefast.co.uk
6pa. Owner: Pagefast.
Editor: David Bremner

Military Illustrated Past & Present
0870 870 2345
www.publishingnews.co.uk
Monthly. Owner: Publishing News.
Editor: Tim Newark

Military in Scale
01684 588500
www.militaryinscale.com
Monthly. Owner: Traplet Publications.
Editor: Spencer Pollard

Military Modelling
01525 370389
www.militarymodelling.com
15pa. Owner:Encanta. Editor: Ken Jones

Miniature Wargames
01202 297344
www.miniwargames.com
Monthly. Owner: Pireme Publishing.
Editor: Iain Dickie

Model & Collectors Mart
0121 233 8712
www.modelmart.co.uk
Monthly. Owner: Trinity Publications.
Editor: Dean Shepherd

Model Boats
01525 382847
13pa. Owner: Encanta.
Editor: John Cundell

Model Collector
020 8726 8238
www.modelcollector.co.uk
Monthly. Owner: IPC Media.
Editor: Lindsey Amrani

Model Engineer
01689 899255
26pa. Owner: Encanta.
Editor: David Carpenter

Model Engineers' Workshop
01738 583832
11pa. Owner: Encanta.
Editor: David Fenner

Model Helicopter World
01684 588500
www.modelheliworld.com
Monthly. Owner: Traplet Publications.
Editor: Jon Tanner

Motor Boat & Yachting
020 7261 7257
www.ybw.com
Monthly. Owner: IPC Media.
Editor: Hugo Andreae

Motor Boats Monthly
020 7261 5308
www.motorboatsmonthly.com
Monthly. Owner: IPC Media. Editor:
Simon Collis

Motor Caravan Magazine
020 8726 8248
www.motorcaravanmagazine.co.uk
Monthly. Owner: IPC Media.
Editor: Helen Avery

Motor Caravanner
01480 496130
www.motorcaravanners.org.uk
Monthly. Owner: The Motor
Caravanners' Club. Editor: Kate Jones

Motorcaravan & Camping Mart
01778 391000
www.caravanmart.co.uk
11pa. Owner: Warners Group.
Editor: Peter Sharpe

Motorhome Monthly
020 8302 6150
www.stoneleisure.com
Monthly. Owner: Stone Leisure.
Editor: Robert Griffiths

Natural World
020 8962 3020
www.thinkpublishing.co.uk
3pa. Owner: Think Publishing.
Editor: Rupert Paul

New Stitches
01227 750215
www.newstitches.com
*Monthly. Owner: Creative Crafts
Publishing. Editor: Mary Hickmott*

Our Dogs
0870 731 6500
www.ourdogs.co.uk
*Weekly. Owner: Our Dogs Publishing.
Editor: Anne Williams*

Paddles
01202 735090
www.freestyle-group.com
*Monthly. Owner: Freestyle Publications.
Editor: Richard Parkin*

PaperCraft Inspirations
01225 442244
www.futurenet.com/papercraft
13pa. Owner: Future. Editor: Jenny Dixon

Park Home & Holiday Caravan
020 8726 8253
www.ipcmedia.com
*Monthly. Owner: IPC Media.
Editor: Emma Bartlett*

Patchwork & Quilting
01684 588500
www.pandqmagazine.com
*Monthly. Owner: Traplet Publications.
Editor: Di Huck*

Paws
020 7627 9293
www.dogshome.org
*4pa. Owner: Battersea Dogs Home.
Editor: Helen Tennant*

The People's Friend
01382 223131
www.dcthomson.co.uk
*Weekly. Owner: DC Thomson.
Editor: Margaret McCoi*

Pet Patter
020 7415 7100
www.mediamark.co.uk
*Quarterly. Owner: Mediamark
Publishing. Editor: Pip Jones*

Pilot
01799 544200
www.pilotweb.aero
*Monthly. Owner: Archant.
Editor: Nick Bloom*

Popular Patchwork
01727 866664
*13pa. Owner: Encanta.
Editor: Davina Thomas*

Practical Boat Owner
01202 440820
www.pbo.co.uk
*Monthly. Owner: IPC Media.
Editor: Sarah Norbury*

Practical Caravan
020 8267 5000
www.practicalcaravan.com
*Monthly. Owner: Haymarket.
Editor: Carl Rodgerson*

Practical Fishkeeping
01733 282764
www.emap.com
*Monthly. Owner: Emap.
Editor: Karen Youngs*

Practical Wireless
0870 224 7810
www.pwpublishing.co.uk
*Monthly. Owner: PW Publishing.
Editor: Rob Mannion*

Practical Woodworking
01689 899256
www.getwoodworking.com
*13pa. Owner: Encanta.
Editor: Mark Ramuz*

Prediction
020 8726 8257
www.predictionmagazine.co.uk
*Monthly. Owner: IPC Media.
Editor: Marion Williamson*

Quick & Crafty
01206 505980
www.crafts-beautiful.com
*Monthly. Owner: Aceville Publications.
Editor: Lynn Martin*

Quick & Easy Cross Stitch
01225 442244
www.futurenet.com
/quickandeasycrossstitch
13pa. Owner: Future. Editor: Ruth Spolton

RA Magazine
020 7300 5820
www.ramagazine.org.uk
*4pa. Owner: Royal Academy of Arts.
Editor: Sarah Greenberg*

Racecar Engineering
020 8726 8362
www.racecar-engineering.com
*Monthly. Owner: IPC Media.
Editor: Charles Armstrong-Wilson*

RadCom
0870 904 7373
www.rsgb.org
*Monthly. Owner: Radio Society of Great
Britain. Editor: Alex Kearns*

Radio Control Jet International
01684 588500
www.rcjetinternational.com
*Bi-monthly. Owner: Traplet Publications.
Editor: John Wright*

Radio Control Model Flyer
01525 222573
www.modelflyermagazine.com
*Monthly. Owner: ADII Publishing.
Editor: Ken Shepherd*

Radio Control Model World
01684 588500
www.rcmodelworld.com
*Monthly. Owner: Traplet Publications.
Editor: Tony Van Geffen*

Radio Race Car International
01684 588500
www.radioracecar.com
*Monthly. Owner: Traplet Publications.
Editor: Des Chand*

Rail Express
01780 470086
www.railexpress.co.uk
*Monthly. Owner: Foursight Publications.
Editor: Philip Sutton*

Railway Modeller
01297 20580
www.peco-uk.com
*Monthly. Owner: Peco Publications
& Publicity. Editor: John Brewer*

Raw Vision
01923 856644
www.rawvision.com
4pa. Editor: John Maizels

RCM & E
01689 899258
*13pa. Owner: Encanta.
Editor: Graham Ashby*

RIB International
01884 266100
www.ribmagazine.com
*Bi-monthly.
Editor: Hugo Montgomery-Swan*

RYA Magazine
023 8060 4100
www.rya.org.uk
*Quarterly. Owner: Royal Yachting
Association. Editor: Deborah Cornick*

Sailing Today
01489 580836
www.sailingtoday.co.uk
Monthly. Editor: John Goode

Scale Aviation Modeller
0870 733 3373
www.sampublications.com
*Monthly. Owner: Sam Publications.
Editor: Neil Robinson*

ScrapBook Inspirations
01225 442244
www.myfavouritemagazines.co.uk
*13pa. Owner: Future.
Editor: Joanne Mullen*

Sew Bridal
01243 379009
www.sewbridal.co.uk
*Annually. Owner: McCall Butterick &
Vogue. Editor: Julie Watkins*

Sewing World
01684 588500
www.sewingworldmagazine.com
*Monthly. Owner: Traplet Publications.
Editor: Wendy Gardiner*

Sew Today
01243 379009
www.sewdirect.com
*10pa. Owner: McCall Butterick & Vogue.
Editor: Julie Watkins*

Ships Monthly
01283 542741
www.ipcmedia.com
*Monthly. Owner: IPC Media. Editor: Iain
Wakefield*

Radio User Magazine
0870 224 7810
www.pwpublishing.co.uk
*Monthly. Owner: PW Publishing.
Editor: Elaine Richards*

Simply Knitting
01225 442244
www.futurenet.com
/simplyknittingmagazine
*13pa. Owner: Future. Editor: Debora
Bradley*

Stamp Magazine
020 8726 8243
www.stampmagazine.co.uk
*Monthly. Owner: IPC Media.
Editor: Guy Thomas*

Steam Days
01202 304849
www.steamdaysmag.co.uk
Monthly. Owner: Redgauntlet
Publications Ltd. Editor: Douglas Kennedy

Steam Railway
01733 264666
www.emap.com
Monthly. Owner: Emap.
Editor: Tony Streeter

Styleyes Magazine
020 7747 0700
www.redwoodgroup.net
2pa. Owner: Redwood.
Editor: Laurence Weinberger

Surrey Nature
01483 795440
www.surreywildlifetrust.org
3pa. Owner: Surrey Wildlife Trust.
Editor: Chris Parker

The Teddy Bear Club International
01903 884988
www.teddybeartimes.com
Monthly. Owner: Ashdown.
Editor: Kirste McCool

Time Out Shopping Guide
020 7813 3000
www.timeout.com
Annual. Owner: Time Out Group.
Editor: Jan Fuscoe

Toy Soldier & Model Figure
01903 884988
www.toy-soldier.com
Monthly. Owner: Ashdown.co.uk.
Editor: Stuart Hessney

Treasure Hunting
01376 521900
www.greenlightpublishing.co.uk
Monthly. Owner: Greenlight Publishing.
Editor: Greg Payne

Trends
020 8342 5777
www.independentregionals.com
4pa. Owner: Archant. Editor: Tony Allcock

Truck Model World
01684 588500
Monthly. Owner: Traplet Publications.
Editor: Peter White

Used Bike Guide
01507 529300
www.usedbikeguide.com
Monthly. Owner: Mortons Media Group.
Editor: Chris Pearson

Wag
020 7837 0006
www.dogstrust.org.uk
3pa. Owner: Dogs Trust.
Editor: Deana Selby

Walk
020 7339 8500
www.ramblers.org.uk
Quarterly. Owner: The Ramblers
Association/Think Publishing.
Editor: Christopher Ord

Waterways
01283 790447
www.waterways.org.uk
Quarterly. Owner: Inland Waterways
Association. Editor: Harry Arnold

Waterways World
01283 742951
Monthly. Editor: Richard Hayhurst

Which Caravan
01778 391000
www.whichcaravan.co.uk
Monthly. Owner: Warners Group.
Editor: Mark Sutcliffe

Wild Times
01767 680551
www.rspb.org.uk
Quarterly. Owner: RSPB.
Editor: Derek Niemann

Wildfowl & Wetlands
01453 891187
www.wwt.org.uk
4pa. Owner: Wildfowl & Wetlands Trust.
Editor: Mike Daw

Woodcarving
01273 477374
www.thegmcgroup.com
Bi-monthly. Owner: Guild of Master
Craftsmen

Woodturning
01273 477374
www.thegmcgroup.com
13pa. Owner: Guild of Master Craftsmen.
Editor: Colin Simpson

The Woodworker
01689 899256
www.getwoodworking.com
14pa. Owner: Encanta.
Editor: Mark Ramuz

Workbox
01579 340100
www.ebony.co.uk/workbox
Bi-monthly. Owner: Ebony Media.
Editor: Victor Briggs

The World of Yachts & Boats (pan-Arab)
020 7328 3334
www.worldofyachts.com
Bi-monthly. Owner: The World of Yachts
& Boats. Editor: Nabil Farhat

The Yellow Book
01483 211535
www.ngs.org.uk
Yearly. Owner: National Garden Scheme.
Editor: Julia Grant

You & Your Vet
020 7636 6541
www.bva-awf.org.uk
4pa. Owner: British Veterinary
Association. Editor: Martin Alder

Your Cat
01780 766199
www.yourcat.co.uk
Monthly. Owner: Bourne Publishing
Group. Editor: Sue Parslow

Your Dog
01780 766199
www.yourdog.co.uk
Monthly. Owner: Bourne Publishing
Group. Editor: Sarah Wright

Your Horse
01733 264666
www.emap.com
Monthly. Owner: Emap.
Editor: Nicola Dela-Croix

● **Men's interest**

Arena
020 7437 9011
www.emap.com
Monthly. Owner: Emap.
Editor: Anthony Noguera

Arena Homme Plus
020 7437 9011
www.emap.com
2pa. Owner: Emap. Editor: Joanne Furness

Bizarre
020 7907 6000
www.bizarremag.com
Monthly. Owner: Dennis.
Editor: Alex Godfrey

Boys Toys
01202 735090
www.boystoys.co.uk
Monthly. Owner: Freestyle Publications.
Editor: Duncan Madden

Details
020 7240 0420
www.men.style.com/details
10pa. Owner: Fairchild.
Editor: Daniel Peres

DNR
020 7240 0420
www.dnrnews.com
Weekly. Owner: Fairchild.
Editor: Jon Birmingham

Esquire
020 7439 5000
www.esquire.co.uk
Monthly. Owner: National Magazine
Company. Editor: Simon Tiffin

FHM
020 7436 1515
www.fhm.com
Monthly. Owner: Emap. Editor: Ross Brown

GQ
020 7499 9080
www.gq.com
Monthly. Owner: Condé Nast.
Editor: Dylan Jones

Loaded
020 7261 5562
www.loaded.co.uk
Monthly. Owner: IPC Media.
Editor: Martin Daubney

Maxim
020 7907 6000
www.maxim-magazine.co.uk
Monthly. Owner: Dennis.
Editor: Derek Harbinson

Men's Fitness
020 7907 6000
www.mensfitnessmagazine.co.uk
Monthly. Owner: Dennis.
Editor: Peter Muir

Men's Health
020 7439 5000
www.menshealth.co.uk
11pa. Owner: National Magazine
Company. Editor: Morgan Rees

Muscle & Fitness
01423 504516
www.muscle-fitness.co.uk
Monthly. Owner: Weider Publishing.
Editor: Geoff Evans

Musclemag International
0845 345 0916
www.emusclemag.com
Monthly. Owner: Tropicana Health &
Fitness. Editor: Gary Hill; Sophie Adey

Nuts
020 7261 5660
www.nuts.co.uk
Weekly. Owner: IPC Media.
Editor: Phil Hilton

Zoo Weekly
020 7182 8000
www.zooweekly.co.uk
Weekly. Owner: Emap.
Editor: Anthony Noguera

● Money and property

Bloomberg Money
020 7484 9771
www.investegate.co.uk
Monthly. Owner: Incisive Media.
Editor: Sarah Godfrey

The Business
020 7961 0000
www.thebusinessonline.com
Weekly. Owner: Press Holdings. Publisher
and editor-in-chief: Andrew Neil; editor:
Ian Watson

Business Week
020 7176 6060
www.businessweek.com
Weekly. Owner: McGraw-Hill.
Bureau chief: Stanley Reed

Country Landowner and Rural
Business
01392 447766
www.cla.org.uk
Monthly. Owner: Country Land and
Business Association. Publisher: Archant.
Editor: Tom Quinn

Euroslot
01622 687031
www.datateam.co.uk
Monthly. Owner: Dateam Publishing.
Editor: Alan Campbell

Forbes
020 7534 3900
www.forbes.com
Fortnightly. Owner: Forbes.
Editor: William Baldwin

Fortune
020 7322 1074
www.fortune.com
Fortnightly. European editor, Fortune
Europe: Nelson Schwartz

Investors Chronicle
020 7775 6292
www.investorschronicle.co.uk
Weekly. Owner: Financial Times
Business. Editor: Matthew Vincent

ISA Direct
020 7409 1111
www.allenbridge.co.uk
2pa. Owner: Allenbridge.
Editor: Anthony Yadgaroff

London Property News
01933 271611
www.londonpropertynews.co.uk
Monthly. Editor: Alistair Moxey

The MBA Career Guide
020 7284 7200
www.topmba.com/careers
2pa. Editor: Nunzio Quacquarelli

Money Observer
020 7713 4188
www.moneyobserver.com
Monthly. Owner: Guardian Media Group.
Editor: Andrew Pitts

Moneywise
020 7382 4300
www.moneywise.co.uk
Monthly. Editor: Rachel Williams

The Mortgage Edge
020 7430 5129
www.mortgageedge.co.uk
Monthly. Editor: Christina Jordan

Mortgage Finance Gazette
020 7827 5457
www.mfgonline.co.uk
Monthly. Owner: Charterhouse
Communications. Editor: John Murray

Mortgage Introducer
020 7827 5429
www.mortgageintroducer.com
Weekly. Owner: Charterhouse
Communications. Editor: Scott Philipson

Negotiator
01252 843566
www.negotiator-magazine.co.uk
Fortnightly.
Owner: Inside Communications.
Editor: Rosalind Renshaw

Optima
020 8420 4488
www.optimamagazine.co.uk
Fortnightly. Editor: Jill Glenn

Personal Finance Confidential
020 7633 3600
www.agoralifestyles.com
Monthly. Owner: Agora Lifestyles.
Managing editor: Dave Fedash

Personal Finance Magazine
020 7827 5454
www.pfmagazine.co.uk
Monthly. Owner: Charterhouse
Communications. Editor: Martin Fagan

Post Magazine
020 7484 9700
www.postmagazine.co.uk
Weekly. Owner: Incisive Media.
Editor: Jonathan Swift

Property Ladder
01737 786 800
www.brooklandsgroup.com
      /magazines/property-ladder
      /index.html
Monthly. Owner: Brooklands.
Editor: Helen Bazuaye

The Property Magazine
01480 494944
www.property-platform.com
Monthly. Owner: Guild of Professional
Estate Agents. Editor: Malcolm Lindley

Scotland's New Home Buyer
0131 556 9702
4pa. Owner: Pinpoint Scotland.
Editor: Anna Baird

What Investment
020 7827 5454
www.what-investment-mag.co.uk
Monthly. Owner: Charterhouse
Communications. Editor: Kieron Root

What Investment Trust
020 7827 5454
www.charterhouse-
communications.co.uk
3pa. Owner: Charterhouse
Communications. Editor: Kieron Root

What ISA
020 7827 5454
www.charterhouse-
      communications.co.uk
3pa. Owner: Charterhouse
Communications. Editor: Amanda Jarvis

What Mortgage
020 7827 5454
www.what-mortgage-mag.co.uk
Monthly. Owner: Charterhouse
Communications. Editor: Nia Williams

Your Money: Savings & Investments
020 7484 9700
www.yourmoney.com
Quarterly. Owner: Incisive Media.
Editor: Mike Collins

Your Mortgage
020 7484 9700
www.yourmortgage.co.uk
Monthly. Owner: Incisive Media.
Editor: Paula John

Your New Home
01732 878800
www.yournewhome.co.uk
6pa. Owner: New Concept.
Editor: Karen Keeman

● Motoring

4x4 Magazine
020 8726 8374
www.4x4i.com
Monthly. Owner: IPC Media.
Editor: John Carroll

100% Biker
01244 663400
www.100-biker.co.uk
Monthly. Owner: Jazz Publishing.
Editor: Nick Samson

911 & Porsche World Magazine
01737 814311
www.chpltd.com
Monthly. Owner: CH Publications.
Editor: Steve Bennett

Advanced Driving
01483 230300
www.iam.org.uk
3pa. Owner: Institute of Advanced
Motorists. Editor: Ian Webb

American Motorcycle Dealer
01892 511516
www.dealer-world.com
Monthly. Owner: Dealer World.
Editor: Robin Bradley

Audi Driver
01525 750500
www.autometrix.co.uk
Monthly. Owner: AutoMetrix
Publications. Editor: Paul Harris

The Audi Magazine
01590 683222
2pa. Owner: Clive Richardson Communications.
Editor: Clive Richardson

Autocar
020 8267 5000
www.autocarmagazine.co.uk
Weekly. Owner: Haymarket.
Editor: Steve Copley

Auto Express
020 7907 6000
www.autoexpress.co.uk
Weekly. Owner: Dennis.
Editor: David Johns

Auto Italia
01707 273999
www.auto-italia.co.uk
13pa. Owner: TRMG. Editor: Philip Ward

AutoTrader
020 8544 7000
www.autotrader.co.uk
Weekly. Owner: Trader Media Group

The Automobile
01483 268818
Monthly. Owner: Enthusiast Publishing.
Editor: Michael Bowler

Back Street Heroes
020 7772 8300
www.insidecom.co.uk
Monthly. Owner: Inside Communications.
Editor: Stu Garland

Banzai
01732 748000
www.banzaimagazine.com
Monthly. Owner: Unity Media.
Editor: Joe Clifford

BBC Top Gear
020 8433 2313
www.topgear.com
Monthly. Owner: BBC Worldwide.
Editor: Michael Harvey

Bike
01733 468000
www.emap.com
12pa. Owner: Emap. Editor: John Westlake

BMW Car
01732 748000
www.bmwcarmagazine.com
Monthly. Owner: Unity Media.
Editor: Bob Harper

BMW Magazine
020 7534 2400
www.cedarcom.co.uk
Quarterly. Owner: Cedar.
Editor: Andrew Gillingwater

Car
01733 468000
www.car-magazine.co.uk
12pa. Owner: Emap. Editor: Jason Barlow

Car Mechanics
01959 541444
www.carmechanicsmag.co.uk
Monthly. Owner: Kelsey Publishing.
Editor: Peter Simpson

CarSport Magazine
028 9078 3200
www.carsportmag.net
Monthly. Owner: Greer Publications.
Editor: Pat Burns

Classic & Sports Car
020 8267 5000
www.classicandsportscar.com
Monthly. Owner: Haymarket.
Editor: James Elliott

Classic American
0161 877 9977
www.classic-american.com
Monthly. Owner: Guardian Media Group.
Editor: Ben Klemenzson

Classic Bike
01733 468000
www.emap.com
12pa. Owner: Emap. Editor: Hugo Wilson

The Classic Bike Guide
01507 529404
www.classicbikeguide.com
Monthly. Owner: Mortons Media Group.
Editor: Tim Britton

Classic Car
01733 468000
www.emap.com
12pa. Owner: Emap. Editor: Phil Bell

Classic Car Mart
0121 233 8712
www.classic-car-mart.co.uk
Monthly. Owner: Trinity Publications.
Editor: Frank Westworth

Classic Car Weekly
01733 347559
www.classic-car-weekly.co.uk
Weekly. Owner: Kelsey Publishing.
Editor: Richard Gunn

Classic Ford
01225 442244
www.classicfordmag.co.uk
Monthly. Owner: Future.
Editor: Steve Phillips

Classic Military Vehicle
01959 541444
www.kelsey.co.uk
Monthly. Owner: Kelsey Publishing.
Editor: Pat Ware

Classic Motor Monthly
01204 657212
www.classicmotor.co.uk
Monthly. Editor: John Hodson

Classic Motorcycle
01507 529300
www.classicmotorcycle.co.uk
Monthly. Owner: Mortons Media Group.
Editor: James Robinson

Classic Racer
01507 529300
www.classicracer.com
Bi-monthly. Owner: Mortons Media Group. Editor: Nigel Clark

Classics
01225 442244
www.futurenet.com
13pa. Owner: Future.
Editor: Gary Stretton

Custom Car
01959 541444
www.kelsey.co.uk
Monthly. Owner: Kelsey Publishing.
Editor: Dave Biggadyke

Dirt Bike Rider
01524 834077
www.dirtbikerider.com
Monthly. Editor: Sean Lawless

Enjoying MG
01954 231125
www.mgcars.org.uk
Monthly. Owner: Polestar Colchester.
Editor: Richard Ladds

Evo
020 7907 6000
www.evo.co.uk
Monthly. Owner: Dennis.
Editor: Harrison Metcalfe

Fast Bikes
01225 442244
www.fastbikesmag.com
www.futurenet.com
13pa. Owner: Future.
Editor: Richard Newland

Fast Car
01689 887200
www.fastcar.co.uk
www.futurenet.com
13pa. Owner: Future. Editor: Gez Jones

Fast Ford
01225 442244
www.fastfordmag.co.uk
Monthly. Owner: Future.
Editor: Simon Woolley

Good Motoring
01342 825676
www.motoringassist.com
Quarterly. Owner: Gem Motoring Assist.
Editor: James Luckhurst

Intersection
020 7608 1166
www.intersectionmagazine.com
Quarterly. Owner: Intersection Media.
Editor: Dan Ross

Jaguar Driver
01582 419332
www.jaguardriver.co.uk
Monthly. Owner: Jaguar Drivers Club.
Editor: Steve Fermore

Jaguar World Monthly
01959 541444
www.jaguar-world.com
Monthly. Owner: Kelsey Publishing.
Editor: Matt Skelton

J-Tuner
01225 442244
www.jtunermagazine.co.uk
Monthly. Owner: Future.
Editor: Steve Chalmers

Land Rover Enthusiast
01379 890056
www.landroverenthusiast.com
Monthly. Editor: James Taylor

Land Rover Owner International
01733 468000
www.lro.com
13pa. Owner: Emap. Editor: John Pearson

Land Rover World
020 8726 8000
www.landroverworld.co.uk
Monthly. Owner: IPC Media.
Editor: John Carroll

Lexus Magazine
020 7837 8337
www.mccann.com
4pa. Owner: Story Worldwide.
Editor: Lucy Callington

LRM – Land Rover Monthly
01359 240066
www.lrm.co.uk
Monthly. Editor: Richard Howell-Thomas

MaxPower
01733 468000
www.maxpower.co.uk
13pa. Owner: Emap.
Editor: Simon Penson

Mazda Magazine
020 7833 7410
www.northstarpublishing.com
4pa. Owner: Northstar Publishing.
Editor: Mark Walton

Mercedes
01789 490530
3pa. Owner: Impact Press & PR.
Editor: Eric Lafone

Mercedes Enthusiast
020 8639 4400
www.mercedesenthusiast.co.uk
Monthly. Owner: Sundial Magazines.
Editor: Dan Trent

MG Enthusiast Magazine
01924 499261
www.mg-enthusiast.com
6pa. Editor: Martyn Wise

Mini Magazine
01225 442244
www.minimag.co.uk
Monthly. Owner: Future.
Editor: Helen Webster

MiniWorld
020 8726 8354
www.ipcmedia.com
Monthly. Owner: IPC Media.
Editor: Monty Watkins

Motor Cycle News (MCN)
01733 468000
www.motorcyclenews.com
Weekly. Owner: Emap.
Editor: Marc Potter

Motor Sport
020 8267 5000
www.haymarketpublishing.co.uk
Monthly. Owner: Haymarket.
Editor: Paul Fearnley

Motorcycle Mechanics
01507 529442
www.classicmechanics.com
Monthly. Owner: Mortons Media Group.
Editor: Rod Gibson

Motorcycle Racer
01353 665577
www.motorcycleracer.com
Monthly. Owner: MB Media.
Editor: Larry Carter

Motorcycle Rider
01652 680060
www.bmf.co.uk
4pa. Owner: RBP. Editor: Andy Dukes

Motorcycle Sport & Leisure
01507 529300
www.mslmagazine.co.uk
Monthly. Owner: Mortons Media Group.
Editor: Phil Turner

Motoring & Leisure
01273 744757
www.csma.uk.com
10pa. Owner: CSMA.
Editor: David Arnold

Performance Bikes
01733 468000
www.emap.com
Monthly. Owner: Emap.
Editor: Tim Thompson

Performance VW
01732 748000
www.performancevwmag.com
Monthly. Owner: Unity Media.
Editor: Elliot Roberts

Peugeot Rapport
0117 925 1696
www.specialistuk.com
3pa. Owner: Specialist.
Editor: Karen Ellison

Porsche Post
01608 652911
www.porscheclubgb.com
Monthly. Editor: Stephen Mummery

Post Office Motoring
0191 418 3970
www.emap.com
4pa. Owner: The Post Office Auto Club.
Editor: Alan Fairbairn

Practical Classics
01733 468000
www.emap.com
13pa. Owner: Emap. Editor: Matt Wright

Redline
01225 442244
www.redlinemag.co.uk
13pa. Owner: Future. Editor: Dan Lewis

The Renault Magazine
01737 786800
www.brooklandsgroup.com
4pa. Owner: Brooklands Publishing.
Editor: Ann Wallace

Retro Cars
01225 442244
www.retrocarsmag.co.uk
Monthly. Owner: Future.
Editor: Paul Wager

Ride
01733 468000
www.emap.com
13pa. Owner: Emap. Editor: Steve Rose

Saab Magazine
01603 664242
www.archant.co.uk
2pa. Owner: Archant. Editor: Zoe Francis

Safety Fast!
01235 555552
www.mgcc.co.uk
Monthly. Editor: Andy Knott

Scootering
01507 529300
www.scootering.com
Monthly. Owner: Mortons Media Group.
Editor: Andy Gillard

Street Fighters
020 7772 8300
www.insidecom.co.uk
Monthly. Owner: Inside Communications.
Editor: Stu Garland

SuperBike Magazine
020 8726 8445
www.superbike.co.uk
Monthly. Owner: IPC Media.
Editor: Kenny Pryde

Tag Magazine
01507 529408
www.twistngo.com
Bi-Monthly. Owner: Mortons Media
Group. Editor: Mau Spencer

Torque
01455 891515
www.triumph.co.uk
Quarterly. Owner: Riders Association
of Triumph. Editor: Simon Carter

Total BMW
01225 442244
www.totalbmag.co.uk
Monthly. Owner: Future.
Editor: Matt Robinson

Total Vauxhall
01225 442244
www.totalvauxhall.co.uk
Monthly. Owner: Future.
Editor: Barton Brisland

TWO – Two Wheels Only
020 8267 5000
www.haymarketpublishing.co.uk
Monthly. Owner: Haymarket.
Assistant editor: Tim Dickson

Used Bike Guide
01507 529300
www.usedbikeguide.com
Monthly. Owner: Mortons Media Group.
Editor: Chris Pearson

VM – Vauxhall
01582 426909
www.vmonline.co.uk
3pa. Owner: Brooklands Publishing.
Editor: Michelle Howard

Volks World
020 8726 8347
www.volksworld.com
Monthly. Owner: IPC Media.
Editor: Ivan McCutcheon

Volkswagen Driver
01525 750500
www.autometrix.co.uk
Monthly. Owner: AutoMetrix
Publications. Editor: Neil Birkitt

The Volvo Magazine
020 7747 0700
www.redwoodgroup.net
3pa. Owner: Redwood.
Editor: Zac Assemakis

VW Magazine
01778 391000
www.vwmonline.co.uk
Monthly. Owner: Warners Group.
Editors: Richard Copping, Ken Cservenka

What Car?
020 8267 5000
www.whatcar.co.uk
Monthly. Owner: Haymarket.
Editor: David Motton

Which Kit?
01737 222030
www.which-kit.com
Monthly. Editor: Peter Filby

● Photography

Digital Camera Buyer
01202 299900
www.digicambuyer.co.uk
13pa. Owner: Imagine. Editor: Chris Lean

Digital Camera Magazine
01225 442244
www.dcmag.co.uk
13pa. Owner: Future.
Editor: Marcus Hawkins

Digital Camera Shopper
01225 442244
www.dcmag.co.uk
13pa. Owner: Future. Editor: Mark Sparrow

Digital Photographer
01202 299900
www.dphotographer.co.uk
13pa. Owner: Imagine.
Dep editor: Kirsty Eaglesham

Photography Monthly
0845 650 1065
www.photographymonthly.co.uk
Monthly. Owner: Archant.
Acting editor: Will Cheung

What Camera
020 7681 1010
www.ipcmedia.com
4pa. Owner: IPC Media. Editor: Joel Lacey

What Digital Camera
020 7261 5323
www.what-digital-camera.com
Monthly. Owner: IPC Media.
Editor: Nigel Atherton

Which Digital Camera?
01799 544240
www.archant.co.uk
Monthly. Owner: Archant.
Technical editor: Darren Harbar

● Puzzles

100 Crosswords
01737 378700
www.puzzler.co.uk
13pa. Owner: Puzzler Media.
Editor: Debbie Hardy

Code Words
01737 378700
www.puzzler.co.uk
13pa. Owner: Puzzler Media.
Editor: Charles Sloan

Fundoku
0870 787 9234
www.puzzler.co.uk
Monthly. Owner: Puzzler Media.
Editor: Ariane Blok

Kakuro
0870 428 1295
www.puzzler.co.uk
Monthly. Owner: Puzzler Media.
Editor: Ariane Blok

Kriss Kross
01737 378700
www.puzzler.co.uk
13pa. Owner: Puzzler Media.
Editor: Jo MacLeod

Logic Problems
01737 378700
www.puzzler.co.uk
13pa. Owner: Puzzler Media.
Editor: Steve Bull

Pocket Puzzler Crosswords
01737 378700
www.puzzler.co.uk
13pa. Owner: Puzzler Media.
Editor: Maggie Ayres

Puzzle Compendium
01737 378700
www.puzzler.co.uk
10pa. Owner: Puzzler Media.
Editor: Birgitta Bingham

Puzzle Corner Special
01737 378700
www.puzzler.co.uk
10pa. Owner: Puzzler Media.
Editor: Debbie Hardy

Puzzle Selection
020 7241 8000
www.bauer.co.uk
Monthly. Owner: H Bauer.
Editor: Sonia Garner

Puzzler
01737 378700
www.puzzler.co.uk
13pa. Owner: Puzzler Media.
Editor: Catherine Filby

Puzzler Quiz Kids
01737 378700
www.puzzler.co.uk
7pa. Owner: Puzzler Media.
Editor: Jackie Guthrie

Sudoku
01737 378700
www.puzzler.co.uk
8pa. Owner: Puzzler Media.
Contact: Tim Preston

Sudoku Puzzles
0870 787 9306
www.puzzler.co.uk
Monthly. Owner: Puzzler Media.
Editor: Ariane Blok

Take a Break
020 7241 8000
www.bauer.co.uk
Weekly. Owner: H Bauer.
Editor: John Dale

Take a Crossword
020 7241 8000
www.bauer.co.uk
13pa. Owner: H Bauer.
Editor: David Moore

Take a Puzzle
020 7241 8000
www.bauer.co.uk
13pa. Owner: H Bauer.
Editor: Michael Jones

● Sport

Ace
020 7381 7000
Monthly. Owner: Tennis GB.
Editor: Nigel Billen

Air Gun World
0118 977 1677
www.airgunshooting.org
Monthly. Owner: Archant.
Editor: Adam Smith

Air Gunner
0118 977 1677
www.archant.co.uk
Monthly. Owner: Archant.
Editor: Nigel Allen

Airgun World
0118 977 1677
www.archant.co.uk
Monthly. Owner: Archant.
Editor: Adam Smith

Angler's Mail
020 7261 5829
www.ipcmedia.com
Weekly. Owner: IPC Media.
Editor: Tim Knight

Angling Times
01733 237111
www.anglingtimes.co.uk
Weekly. Owner: Emap.
Editor: Richard Lee

Angling Times Advanced
01733 465510
www.atadvanced.co.uk
Monthly. Owner: Emap. Editor: Steve Cole

The Arsenal Magazine
020 7704 4138
www.arsenal.com
Monthly. Owner: Arsenal Football Club.
Editor: Andy Exley

Athletics Weekly
01733 898440
www.athletics-weekly.com
Weekly. Owner: Descartes Publishing.
Editor: Jason Henderson

Autosport
020 8267 5000
www.autosport.com
Weekly. Owner: Haymarket.
Editor: Biranit Goren

Badminton Magazine
01908 268400
www.badmintonengland.co.uk
Quarterly. Owner: Badminton England.
Contact: Gerry Cronin

Boxing Monthly
020 8986 4141
www.boxing-monthly.co.uk
Monthly. Owner: Topwave.
Editor: Glyn Leach

Boxing News
020 7618 3069
www.boxingnewsonline.net
Weekly. Owner: Newsquest.
Editor: Claude Abrams

British Homing World
01938 552360
www.pigeonracing.com
Weekly. Editor: Steven Richards

British Waterski & Wakeboard
01932 570885
www.britishwaterski.org.uk
5pa. Owner: British Water Ski.
Editor: Gavin Kelly

Bunkered
0141 950 2216
www.bunkered.co.uk
8pa. Owner: Pro Sports Promotions.
Editor: Martin Dempster

Calcio Italia
01225 489984
www.calcioitalia.co.uk
Monthly. Owner: Anthem Publishing.
Editor: John Taylor

Canoe Focus
01480 465081
www.canoefocus.co.uk
Bi-monthly. Owner: 2B Graphic Design.
Editor: Peter Tranter

Carpworld
0114 258 0812
www.anglingpublications.co.uk
Monthly. Owner: Angling Publications.
Publishing editor: Tim Paisley

Carve Surfing Magazine
01637 878074
www.orcasurf.co.uk
8pa. Owner: Orca Publications.
Editor: Chris Power

Celtic View
0141 551 4218
www.celticfc.net
Weekly. Owner: Cre8. Editor: Paul Cuddihy

Clay Shooting
01264 889533
www.clay-shooting.com
Monthly. Owner: Brunton Business
Publications. Editor: Richard Rawlingson

Climb
01298 72801
www.planetfear.com
Monthly. Owner: Greenshires Group.
Editor: Neil Pearson

Climber
01778 391000
www.climber.co.uk
Monthly. Owner: Warners.
Editor: Bernard Newman

Combat
0121 344 3737
www.martialartsinprint.com
Monthly. Owner: Martial Arts
Publications. Editor: Paul Clifton

Combat & Survival
01484 435011
www.combatandsurvival.com
Monthly. Owner: MAI Publications.
Editor: Bob Morrison

Country Walking
01733 264666
www.emap.com
Monthly. Owner: Emap.
Editor: Jonathan Manning

Cricket World Magazine
01476 561944
www.cricketworld.com
Quarterly. Editor: Alistair Symondson

Cycle
0870 873 0060
www.ctc.org.uk
Bi-monthly. Owner: Cyclists' Touring
Club. Editor: Dan Joyce

Cycle Sport
020 8726 8000
www.cyclesport.co.uk
Monthly. Owner: IPC Media.
Editor: Robert Garbutt

Cycling Plus
01225 442244
www.cyclingplus.co.uk
13pa. Owner: Future.
Editor: Tony Farrelly

Cycling Weekly
020 8726 8000
www.cyclingweekly.co.uk
Weekly. Owner: IPC Media.
Editor: Robert Garbutt

Daily Mail Ski & Snowboard Magazine
020 8515 2000
www.metroskishow.co.uk
6pa Sep-Mar. Owner: DMG World Media.
Editor: Henry Druce

Darts World
020 8650 6580
www.dartsworld.com
Monthly. Owner: World Magazines.
Editor: Tony Wood

Direct Hit
020 7953 7473
www.surreycricket.com
5pa. Owner: Trinorth.
Editor: Matt Thacker

Dirt MTB Magazine
01305 251263
www.dirtmag.co.uk
Bi-monthly. Owner: 4130 Publications.
Editor: Mike Rose

Distance Running
0141 810 9000
www.inpositionmedia.co.uk
4pa. Owner: In Position Media.
Editor: Hugh Jones

DIVE Magazine
020 8940 0555
www.divemagazine.co.uk
Monthly. Editor: Simon Rogerson

Diver
020 8943 4288
www.divernet.com
Monthly. Owner: The Diver Group.
Editor: Steve Weinman

Document Skateboard
01305 251263
www.documentskateboard.com
9pa. Owner: 4130 Publications.
Editor: Percy Dean

Document Snowboard
01733 293250
www.fall-line.co.uk
Monthly Oct-Mar. Owner: Fall-Line
Media. Editor: Ian Sansom

Dog Training Weekly
01348 875011
www.dogtrainingweekly.com
Weekly. Owner: Canine Press.
Editor: Angela Barrah

England Rugby
01707 273999
www.rfu.com
Quarterly. Owner: TRMG.
Editor: Howard Johnson

Equi-Ads
01738 567700
www.equiads.net
Monthly. Editor: Mary Moore

Evening Times Wee Red Book
0141 302 6606
Yearly. Owner: Newsquest.
Editor: Frasier Gibson

Eventing
020 7261 5388
www.ipcmedia.com
Monthly. Owner: IPC Media.
Editor: Julie Harding

The Evertonian
0151 285 8412
Monthly. Owner: Trinity Mirror.
Editor: Ken Rogers

F1 Racing
020 8267 5000
www.haymarketpublishing.co.uk
Monthly. Owner: Haymarket.
Editor: Matt Bishop

The Fairway Golfing News
01633 666700
www.fairway.org.uk
Monthly. Editor: John Doherty

Fall-Line Skiing
01733 293250
www.fall-line.co.uk
Monthly Oct-Feb. Owner: Fall-Line
Media. Editor: Ian Sansom

The Field
020 7261 5198
www.thefield.co.uk
Monthly. Owner: IPC Media.
Editor: Jonathan Young

Fighters
0121 344 3737
www.martialartsinprint.com
Monthly. Owner: Martial Arts
Publications. Editor: Malcolm Martin

First Down
020 7005 2000
www.independent.co.uk
Weekly. Owner: Independent News
& Media (UK). Editor: Tony Prince

Fitness First
020 8544 2900
www.fitnessfirst.com
Quarterly. Owner: Weybridge Press.
Editor: Iain Mackie

FitPro
0870 513 3434
www.fitpro.com
Bi-monthly. Owner: Fitness Professionals.
Editor: Gemma Carr

Flex
01423 504516
www.flex-europe.com
Monthly. Owner: Weider Publishing.
Editor: Geoff Evans

Football Insider
020 7963 7888
www.sportservicesgroup.com
Bi-annual; also daily email. Owner: PA
Sport Services Group. Editor: Jay Stuart

Football Italia
01494 564564
www.channel4.co.uk/sport
/football_italia
Monthly. Owner: Anthem Publishing.
Editor: John Taylor

FourFourTwo
020 8267 5000
www.haymarketpublishing.co.uk
Monthly. Owner: Haymarket.
Deputy editor: Mat Snow

Gamefisher
020 7283 5838
www.salmon-trout.org
2pa. Owner: Salmon & Trout Association.
Editor: Carmel Jorgensen

Going for Golf
01268 554100
www.goingforgolf.com
Quarterly. Editor: Neil Webber

**The Golf Guide: Where to Play/
Where to Stay**
0141 887 0428
www.holidayguides.com
Yearly. Owner: FHG Guides.
Editor: Anne Cuthbertson

Golf International
020 7828 3003
www.golfinternationalmag.co.uk
10pa. Editor: Richard Simmons

Golf Monthly
020 7261 7237
www.golf-monthly.co.uk
Monthly. Owner: IPC Media.
Editor: Jane Carter

Golf News
020 7269 8900
www.golfnews.co.uk
Monthly. Owner: Golf News.
Editor: Nick Bayly

Golf World
01733 288011
www.emap.com
Monthly. Owner: Emap.
Editor: Paul Hamblin

Good Ski Guide
020 7332 2000
www.goodskiguide.com
*4pa in winter. Owner: Profile Sports
Media. Editor: John Hill*

Greenside
01753 646815
www.foremostonline.com
3pa. Owner: Foremost Golf.
Editor: Jenni O'Connor

The Gymnast
0116 247 8766
www.british-gymnastics.org
Bi-monthly. Editor: Trevor Low

Improve Your Coarse Fishing
01733 237111
www.emap.com
Monthly. Owner: Emap.
Editor: Kevin Green

In The Know
0870 333 2062
www.itkonline.com
Monthly. Editor: Darren Croft

International Rugby News
020 7005 2000
www.independent.co.uk
*Monthly. Owner: Independent News
& Media (UK). Editor: Russell Stander*

Ireland's Equestrian Magazine
028 3833 4272
www.irelandsequestrian.co.uk
*Bi-monthly. Owner: Mainstream
Publishing. Editor: Dianne Ray*

Karting
01689 897123
www.kartingmagazine.com
Monthly. Owner: Lodgemark Press.
Editor: Mark Burgess

The Kop
0151 285 8412
Monthly. Owner: Trinity Mirror.
Editor: Paul Dove

Lady Golfer
01274 851323
Monthly. Owner: Sports Publications.
Editor: Mickey Walker

LFC
0151 285 8412
Weekly. Owner: Trinity Mirror.
Editor: Steve Hanrahan

Liverpool Monthly
01392 664141
Monthly. Owner: LCD Publishing.
Editor: Joanne Trump

London Cyclist
020 7234 9310
www.lcc.org.uk
*Bi-monthly. Owner: London Cycling
Campaign. Editors: Lynette Eyb,
Rebecca Lack*

Martial Arts Illustrated
01484 435011
www.martialarts.co.uk
Monthly. Owner: MAI Publications.
Editor: Bob Sykes

Match
01733 237111
www.matchmag.co.uk
Weekly. Owner: Emap. Editor: Ian Forster

Match Fishing Magazine
01327 311999
www.total-fishing.com
Monthly. Owner: DHP.
Editor: Dave Harrell

Moto
01305 251263
www.motomagazine.co.uk
Bi-monthly. Owner: 4130 Publications.
Assistant Editor: Geoff Perrett

Motor Sport
020 8267 5000
www.haymarketpublishing.co.uk
Monthly. Owner: Haymarket.
Editor: Richard Robinson

Motorsport News
020 8267 5385
www.haymarketpublishing.co.uk
Weekly. Owner: Haymarket.
Editor: Jim Holder

Motorsports Now!
01753 765000
www.msauk.org
*Quarterly. Owner: The Really Motoring
Group (TRMG). Editor: Pete Wadsworth*

Mountain Bike Rider
020 8726 8000
www.mountainbikerider.co.uk
Monthly. Owner: IPC Media.
Editor: John Kitchiner

Mountain Biking UK
01225 442244
www.mbuk.com
13pa. Owner: Future. Editor: Tim Manley

Muscle & Fitness
01423 504516
www.muscle-fitness-europe.com
Monthly. Owner: Weider Publishing.
Editor: Geoff Evans

Musclemag International
0845 345 0916
www.emusclemag.com
*Monthly. Owner: Tropicana Health &
Fitness. Editor: Gary Hill*

National Club Golfer
01274 851323
www.nationalclubgolfer.com
Monthly. Owner: Sports Publications.
Editor: Chris Bertram

The Non-League Paper
020 8971 4333
www.thenlp.net
*Twice weekly (Aug-May), weekly
(May-Aug). Owner: Greenways Media.*
Editor: David Emery

The Official Tour de France Guide
020 7042 4761
www.procycling.com
Yearly. Owner: Future.
Editor: Peter Cossins

The Outdoor Adventure Guide
01733 293250
www.fall-line.co.uk
Bi-monthly. Owner: Fall-Line Media.
Editor: Martina Hanlon

PQ International
020 7924 2550
www.pqinternational.co.uk
4pa. Owner: Euromedia Services.
Editor: Roger Chatterton-Newman

Procycling
020 7042 4000
www.procycling.com
Monthly. Owner: Future.
Editor: Jeremy Whittle

Pull!
01780 766199
www.countrypursuits.co.uk
10pa. Owner: Bourne Publishing Group.
Editor: Mike Barnes

Raceform Update
020 7293 3000
www.racingpost.co.uk
Weekly. Owner: Trinity Mirror.
Editor: Bernie Ford

Racing Calendar
0870 871 2000
www.britishcycling.org.uk
*Quarterly. Owner: British Cycling
Federation. Editor: Phil Ingham*

Racing Pigeon Weekly
01689 600006
www.racingpigeon.co.uk
Weekly. Editor: Steve Dunn

Racing Post
020 7293 3000
www.racingpost.co.uk
Daily. Owner: Racing Post.
Editor: Chris Smith

Ride BMX
01305 251263
www.ridebmxmag.co.uk
9pa. Owner: 4130 Publications.
Editor: Mark Noble

Rugby League World
01484 401895
www.totalrl.com
Monthly. Owner: League Publications.
Editor: Tim Butcher

Rugby Leaguer & League Express
01484 401895
www.totalrl.com
Weekly. Owner: League Publications.
Editor: Martyn Sadler

Rugby Times
01484 401895
www.rugbytimes.com
Weekly. Owner: League Publications.
Editor: Jon Newcombe

Rugby World
020 7261 6810
www.rugbyworld.com
Monthly. Owner: IPC Media.
Editor: Paul Morgan

Runner's World
020 7439 5000
www.runnersworld.co.uk
Monthly. Owner: National Magazine
Company. Editor: Steven Seaton

Running Fitness
01733 347559
www.running-fitness.co.uk
Monthly. Owner: Kelsey Publishing.
Editor: Paul Larkins

Scuba World
01202 735090
www.freestyle-group.com
Monthly. Owner: Freestyle Publications.
Acting editor: Mark Nuttall

Sea Angler
01733 237111
www.emap.com
Monthly. Owner: Emap. Editor: Mel Russ

Seahorse
01590 671899
www.seahorsemagazine.com
Monthly. Owner: Fairmead
Communications. Editor: Andrew Hurst

Shoot Monthly
020 7261 6287
www.shootmonthly.co.uk
Monthly. Owner: IPC Media.
Editor: Colin Mitchell

The Shooting Gazette
01780 485 351
www.ipcmedia.com
Monthly. Owner: IPC Media.
Editor: Will Hetherington

Shooting Sports
01206 525697
www.shooting-sports.net
Monthly. Owner: Aceville Publications.
Editor: Peter Moore

Shooting Times
020 7261 6180
www.shootingtimes.co.uk
Weekly. Owner: IPC Media.
Editor: Robert Gray

Sidewalk Skateboarding Magazine
01235 536229
www.sidewalkmag.com
Monthly. Owner: Permanent Publishing
UK. Editor: Ben Powell

Snooker Scene
0121 585 9188
www.snookersceneshop.co.uk
Monthly. Owner: Evertons News Agency.
Editor: Clive Everton

Speedway Star
020 8335 1100
www.speedwaystar.net
Weekly. Owner: Pinegen.
Editor: Richard Clark

Sport Cities and Venues
020 7963 7888
www.sportservicesgroup.com
Bi-annual; also weekly email.
Owner: Sport Services Group.
Editor: Caroline Reid

Sport Diver
01799 544200
www.sportdiver.co.uk
Monthly. Owner: Archant.
Editor: Mark Evans

Sport Insider
020 7963 7888
www.sportservicesgroup.com
Bi-annual; weekly email, Sport Insider.
Owner: PA Sport Services Group.
Editor: Jay Stewart.

Sporting Gun
08704 445000
www.ipcmedia.com
Monthly. Owner: IPC Media.
Editor: Robin Scott

Sporting Shooter
020 7751 4800
www.sportingshooter.co.uk
Monthly. Owner: Archant.
Editor: James Marchington

Sportsbetting Update
020 7963 7888
www.sportservicesgroup.com
Weekly email. Owner: PA Sport Services
Group. Editor: Andrew Gellatly

Sportsmedia
020 7963 7888
www.sportservicesgroup.com
Bi-annual; also daily email. Owner: PA
Sport Services Group. Editor: Jay Stuart

The Squash Player
01753 775511
www.squashplayer.co.uk
10pa. Owner: McKenzie Publishing.
Editor: Ian McKenzie

Summit
0870 010 4878
www.thebmc.co.uk
Quarterly. Owner: Warners Group.
Editor: Alex Messenger

Surf News
01637 878074
www.britsurf.co.uk
4pa. Owner: Orca Publications.
Editor: Chris Power

The Surfer's Path
01235 536229
www.surferspath.com
Bi-monthly. Owner: Permanent
Publishing UK. Editor: Alex Dick-Read

Swimming
01509 632230
www.britishswimming.org
Monthly. Owner: Amateur Swimming
Association. Editor: Peter Hassall

Swimming Pool News
0870 442 0935
www.swimmingpoolnews.co.uk
Bi-monthly. Owner: Archant.
Editor: Christina Connor

Taekwondo & Korean Martial Arts Magazine
0121 344 3737
www.martialartsinprint.com
Monthly. Owner: Martial Arts
Publications. Editor: Malcolm Martin

Thoroughbred Owner and Breeder
020 7408 0903
www.racehorseowners.net
Monthly. Owner: Racehorse Owners
Association. Editor: Richard Griffiths

Today's Golfer
01733 237111
www.emap.com
Monthly. Owner: Emap.
Editor: Paul Hamblin

Today's Pilot
01780 755131
www.todayspilot.co.uk
Monthly. Owner: Key Publishing.
Editor: Dave Unwin

Total Carp
01327 311999
www.total-fishing.com
Monthly. Owner: DHP.
Editor: Mark Coulson

Traditional Karate
0121 344 3737
www.martialartsinprint.com
Monthly. Owner: Martial Arts
Publications. Editor: Malcolm Martin

Trail
01733 264666
www.trailroutes.com
Monthly. Owner: Emap.
Editor: Guy Procter

Trials & Motorcross News
01524 834030
www.tmxnews.co.uk
Weekly. Owner: Johnston Press.
Editor: John Dickinson

Trout & Salmon
01733 237111
www.emap.com
Monthly. Owner: Emap.
Editor: Andrew Flitcroft

Ultra-Fit
01736 350204
www.ultra-fitmagazine.com
8pa. Editor: Charles Mays

Unity
01993 811181
8pa. Owner: Arcwind.
Editor: Steve Glidewell

Warren Miller's Tour Magazine
020 7240 4071
www.warrenmiller.co.uk
Yearly. Editor: Guy Chambers

What Mountain Bike
01225 442244
www.whatmtb.co.uk
13pa. Owner: Future. Editor: Jane Bentley

When Saturday Comes
020 7729 1110
www.wsc.co.uk
Monthly. Editor: Andy Lyons

105

White Lines Snowboarding Magazine
01235 536229
www.whitelines.com
6pa (Oct-Mar). Owner: Permanent Publishing UK. Editor: Matt Barr

Windsurf Magazine
01993 811181
www.windsurf.co.uk
10pa. Owner: Arcwind.
Editor: Mark Kasprowicz

Women & Golf
020 7261 7237
www.ipcmedia.com
Monthly. Owner: IPC Media.
Editor: Jane Carter

World Soccer
020 7261 5714
www.worldsoccer.com
Monthly. Owner: IPC Media.
Editor: Gavin Hamilton

Yachting Monthly
020 7261 6040
www.yachtingmonthly.com
Monthly. Owner: IPC Media.
Editor: Paul Gelder

Yachting World
020 7261 6800
www.ybw.com
Monthly. Owner: IPC Media.
Editor: Andrew Bray

Yachts & Yachting
01702 582245
www.yachtsandyachting.com
Fortnightly. Editor: Gael Pawson

● Travel

A Place in the Sun
01737 786820
www.aplaceinthesunmag.co.uk
Monthly. Owner: Brooklands Media.
Editor: Matt Havercroft

Activity Wales
01437 766888
www.activitywales.com
Yearly. Editor: Matthew Evans

Adventure Travel
01789 450000
www.atmagazine.co.uk
Bi-monthly. Editor: Alun Davies

Arab Traveller
01621 842745
Bi-monthly. Owner: Fanar Publishing WLL. Editor: Jeremy Wright

BA Impressions
020 7613 8777
www.impressions-ba.com
Quarterly. Owner: Ink Publishing.
Editor: Edward Chamberlain

Best of Britain
020 7611 7891
www.morriseurope.com
Yearly. Owner: Morris Visitor Publications. Editor: Chris Johnson

Bradmans Business Travel Guides
020 7613 8777
www.bradmans.com
Yearly. Owner: Ink Publishing.
Editor: Richard Bence

Canada News
01323 726040
www.emigrate2006.co.uk
Monthly. Owner: Outbound Publishing.
Editor: Paul Beasley

City to Cities
01322 311600
www.swanpublishing.co.uk
6pa. Owner: Swan Publishing.
Editor: David Tickner

CN Traveller (Condé Nast Traveller)
020 7499 9080
www.cntraveller.com
Monthly. Owner: Condé Nast.
Editor: Sarah Miller

Destination New Zealand
01323 726040
www.emigrate2006.co.uk
Monthly. Owner: Outbound Publishing.
Editor: Paul Beasley

Easyjet Magazine
020 7613 8777
www.easyjetinflight.com
Monthly. Owner: Ink Publishing.
Editor: Piers Townley

Edinburgh Shopping & Tourist Guide
01506 508001
2pa. Owner: Capital Group.
Editor: Roger Sadler

Education Travel Magazine
020 7440 4025
www.hothousemedia.com
Bi-monthly. Owner: Hothouse Media.
Editor: Amy Baker

Emigrate America
01323 726040
www.emigrate2006.co.uk
Bi-monthly. Owner: Outbound Publishing. Editor: Paul Beasley

Emigrate Australia
01323 726040
www.emigrate2006.co.uk
Monthly. Owner: Outbound Publishing.
Editor: Paul Beasley

Enjoy Dorset & Hampshire Magazine
01202 737678
www.enjoydorset.co.uk
Yearly. Owner: Eastwick Publishing.
Editor: Zoe Wilson

Ensign
01202 414200
Yearly. Editor: Karen Portnall

Essentially America
020 7243 6954
www.phoenixip.com
Quarterly. Owner: Phoenix International Publishing. Editor: Mary Moore Mason

Flybe. Uncovered
020 8649 7233
www.bmipublications.com
Bi-monthly. Owner: BMI Publications.
Editor: Alan Orbell

Food & Travel
020 7501 0511
www.foodandtravel.com
Monthly. Owner: Green Pea Publishing.
Editor: Janine Furness

France
01242 216050
www.francemag.com
Monthly. Owner: Archant.
Editor: Nick Wall

French Property News
020 8543 3113
www.french-property-news.com
Monthly. Owner: Archant.
Editor: Karen Tait

Gap Year
0870 241 6704
www.gapyear.com
Website. Editor: Tom Griffiths

Geographical
020 8332 2713
www.geographical.co.uk
Monthly. Owner: Circle Publishing.
Editor: Geordie Torr

Greece
01225 786835
www.merricksmedia.co.uk
Bi-monthly. Owner: Merricks Media.
Editor: Diana Cambridge

High Life
020 7534 2400
www.cedarcom.co.uk
Monthly. Owner: Cedar.
Editor: Kerry Smith

Holiday Which?
020 7770 7564
www.which.co.uk
4pa. Owner: Which? Editor: Lorna Cowan

Holiday, The RCI Magazine
01536 310101
www.rci.com
3pa. Owner: RCI Europe.
Editor: Simon McGrath

Homes Overseas
020 7002 8300
www.homesoverseas.co.uk
Monthly. Owner: Blendon Communications. Editor: Mike Hayes

In Britain
020 7751 4800
www.archant.co.uk
Bi-monthly. Owner: Archant.
Editor: Andrea Spain

In London
020 7611 7891
www.morriseurope.com
Bi-monthly. Owner: Morris Visitor Publications. Editor: Chris Johnson

Italia
01225 489984
www.italia-magazine.com
Monthly. Owner: Anthem Publishing.
Editor: Paul Pettengale

Italy
01305 266360
www.italymag.co.uk
Monthly. Owner: Poundbury Publishing.
Editor: Melissa Ormaston

Kuoni World Magazine
01306 744555
www.kuoni.co.uk
4pa. Owner: Kuoni Travel.
Editor: Naomi Wilkinson

Livewire
020 7805 5555
www.ilng.co.uk
Bi-monthly. Owner: The Illustrated London News Group.
Editor: Claire Roberts

Living France
01242 216050
www.livingfrance.com
Monthly. Owner: Archant.
Editor: Nick Wall

The London Guide
020 7611 7891
www.morriseurope.com
Monthly. Owner: Morris Visitor Publications. Editor: Chris Johnson

London Hotel Magazine
020 7373 7282
www.goodlifemedia.co.uk
Bi-monthly. Owner: Goodlife Media.
Editor: ER Spence

London Planner
020 7751 4915
www.archant.co.uk
Monthly. Owner: Archant.
Editor: Rachael Bull

Med Life
020 7841 0340
www.touchline.com
Quarterly. Owner: Touchline Publishing.
Editor: Glyn Wilmshurst

My Travel Recline & Life Magazines
020 7613 8777
www.mytravelmag.com
Quarterly. Owner: Ink Publishing.
Editor: Michael Keating

National Geographic
00 1 813 979 6845
www.nationalgeographic.com
Monthly. Editor: Bill Allen

Orient-Express Magazine
020 7805 5555
4pa. Owner: The Illustrated London News Group. Editor: Alison Booth

Overseas
020 7408 0214 x205
www.rosl.org.uk
4pa. Owner: The Royal Over-Seas League.
Editor: Vicky Baker

Pride of Britain
020 7389 0870
www.prideofbritainhotels.com
2pa. Owner: Freeway Media.
Editor: Sophie MacKenzie

The Railway Magazine
020 7261 5821
www.ipcmedia.com
Monthly. Owner: IPC Media.
Editor: Nick Pigott

Redhot Magazine
020 7613 8777
www.ontoeurope.com
Quarterly. Owner: Ink Publishing.
Editor: Bethen Rider

South Africa News
01323 726040
www.southafricanews.co.uk
Bi-monthly. Owner: Outbound Publishing. Editor: Paul Beasley

Spain
0131 226 7766
www.spainmagazine.co.uk
Monthly. Owner: The Media Company.
Editor: Sue Hitchen

Spanish Homes
01225 442244
www.buyingabroad.net
Monthly. Owner: Future.
Editor: Mike Shakespeare

Sunday Times Travel
020 7413 9302
www.sundaytimestravel.co.uk
Monthly. Owner: River Publishing.
Editor: Ed Grenby

TNT Magazine
020 7373 3377
www.tntmagazine.com
Weekly (Mon). Owner: TNT.
Editor: Lyn Eyb

Travel & Leisure
020 8554 4456
www.tlmags.com
4pa. Owner: Travel & Leisure Magazines.
Editor: Helen Hodge

Travel Australia
01424 223111
www.consylpublishing.co.uk
2pa. Owner: Consyl Publishing.
Editor: Shirley Gilbertson

Travel GBI
020 7729 4337
Monthly. Editor: Richard Cawthorne

Traveller
020 7589 3315
www.traveller.org.uk
Quarterly. Owner: WEXAS.
Editor: Amy Sohanpaul

Travelmag
01672 810202
www.travelmag.co.uk
Online magazine. Editor: Jack Barker

Wanderlust
01753 620426
www.wanderlust.co.uk
Bi-monthly. Editor: Lyn Hughes

Welcome to London
020 8297 4444
www.welcometolondon.com
Bi-monthly. Owner: Pareto.
Editor: Melanie Armstrong

Where London
020 7611 7891
www.morriseurope.com
Monthly. Owner: Morris Visitor Publications. Editor: Mary Anne Evans

● Women and health

Accent Magazine
0191 284 9994
Monthly. Editor: Kevin Wright

Al-Jamila
020 7831 8181
www.hhsaudi.com
Weekly. Owner: Saudi Research & Publishing. Editor: Sanaa Elhadethee

Allergy Magazine
0207 747 9392
www.allergymagazine.com
Bi-monthly. Owner: Ink Publishing.
Editor: Faye Rowe

Asian Woman
0870 755 5501
www.asianwomanmag.com
Bi-monthly. Owner: Asian Interactive Media. Editor: Brianne Ragel

Asthma
020 7786 5000
www.asthma.org.uk
4pa. Owner: Asthma UK.
Editor: Laura Smith

A–Z of Calories
01984 623014
Bi-monthly. Owner: Octavo Publications.
Editor: Gertrude Sharrock

Balance
020 7424 1010
www.diabetes.org.uk
Bi-monthly. Owner: Diabetes UK.
Editor: Martin Cullen

Be Slim
01984 623014
4pa. Owner: Octavo Publications.
Editor: Gertrude Sharrock

Beautiful Brides
0117 934 3742
www.thisisbristol.co.uk
/beautifulbrides
4pa. Owner: BUP Niche Publications.
Editor: Harry Mottram

Bella
020 7241 8000
www.bauer.co.uk
Weekly. Owner: H Bauer.
Editor: Jayne Marsden

Best
020 7439 5000
www.natmags.co.uk
Weekly. Owner: National Magazine Company. Editor: Louise Court

Black Beauty & Hair
020 7720 2108
www.blackbeautyandhair.com
Bi-monthly. Owner: Hawker Consumer Publications. Editor: Irene Shelley

Blackhair
01376 534549
Bi-monthly. Owner: Haversham Publications. Editor: Jane MacArthur

Bliss for Brides
01376 534549
www.blissforbrides.co.uk
Bi-monthly. Owner: For the Bride Publishing. Editor: Angela Cole

Brides
020 7499 9080
www.bridesmagazine.co.uk
Bi-monthly. Owner: Condé Nast.
Editor: Debra Joseph

Caduceus Journal
01926 451897
www.caduceus.info
4pa. Editor: Sarida Brown

Candis
0870 745 3002
www.candis.co.uk
Monthly. Owner: New Hall Publications.
Editor: Jenny Campbell

Chat
020 7261 6570
www.ipcmedia.com
Weekly. Owner: IPC Media.
Editor: Gilly Sinclair

Closer
020 7437 9011
www.emap.com
Weekly. Owner: Emap.
Editor: Jane Johnson

Company
020 7439 5000
www.company.co.uk
Monthly. Owner: National Magazine
Company. Editor: Victoria White

Cosmopolitan
020 7439 5000
www.cosmopolitan.co.uk
Monthly. Owner: National Magazine
Company. Editor: Sam Baker

Cosmopolitan Hair & Beauty
020 7439 5000
www.cosmohairandbeauty.co.uk
Monthly. Owner: National Magazine
Company. Editor: Melanie Goose

Elle
020 7150 7000
www.hf-uk.com
Monthly. Owner: Hachette Filipacchi UK.
Editor: Lorraine Candy

Emma's Diary Pregnancy Guide
media@emmasdiary.co.uk
www.emmasdiary.co.uk
Weekly. Owner: Lifecycle Marketing

Essentials
020 7261 5553
www.ipcmedia.com
Monthly. Owner: IPC Media.
Editor: Julie Barton-Breck

Eve
020 8267 8223
www.evemagazine.co.uk
Monthly. Owner: Haymarket.
Editor: Sara Cremer

Family Circle
020 7261 6193
www.ipcmedia.com
Monthly. Owner: IPC Media.
Editor: Karen Livermore

Family Magazine
01200 453000
www.family-mag.co.uk
Bi-monthly. Owner: RVPL.
Editor: Jeremy Nicholls

First
020 7437 9011
www.emap.com
Weekly. Owner: Emap.
Editor: Julian Linley

For the Bride
01376 534549
www.forthebride.co.uk
Bi-monthly. Owner: For the Bride
Publishing. Editor: Angela Cole

Full House
020 7406 1582
www.fullhousemagazine.co.uk
Weekly. Owner: Hubert Burda Media UK.
Editor: Samm Taylor

Glamour
020 7499 9080
www.glamourmagazine.co.uk
Monthly. Owner: Condé Nast.
Editor: Jo Elvin

Grazia
020 7437 9011
www.graziamagazine.co.uk
Weekly. Owner: Emap. Editor-in-chief:
Fiona McIntosh; editor: Jane Bruton

Hair
020 7261 6974
www.ipcmedia.com
Bi-monthly. Owner: IPC Media.
Editor: Zoe Richards

Hair & Beauty
020 7436 9766
Bi-monthly. Owner: Style Media.
Editor: Laura Curtis

Hair Now
020 7436 9766
Bi-monthly. Owner: Style Media.
Editor: Tim Frisby

Hairflair
01376 534549
9pa. Owner: Hairflair Magazines.
Editor: Ruth Page

Hairstyles Only
01376 534549
9pa. Owner: Hairflair Magazines.
Editor: Ruth Page

Happy
0871 434 1010
www.happymagazine.co.uk
Monthly. Owner: Northern and Shell.
Editor: Eilidh Macaskill

Harpers & Queen
020 7439 5000
www.harpersandqueen.co.uk
Monthly. Owner: National Magazine
Company. Editor: Lucy Yeomans

Health & Fitness
020 7331 1000
www.hfonline.co.uk
Monthly. Owner: Future.
Editor: Mary Comber

The Health Store Magazine
0115 9555 255
www.thehealthstore.co.uk
Bi-monthly. Editor: Jane Garton

Healthy
020 7306 0304
www.therivergroup.co.uk
Bi-monthly. Owner: River Publishing.
Editor: Heather Beresford

Healthy Times
020 7819 1111
www.squareonegroup.co.uk
Quarterly. Owner: Square One Group.
Editor: Michelle Simmons

Heat
020 7437 9011
www.emap.com
Weekly. Owner: Emap. Editor: Mark Frith

Hello!
020 7667 8901
www.hellomagazine.com
Weekly; website updated daily.
Editor: Ronnie Whelan

Hia
020 7539 2270
Monthly. Owner: Al Madina Printing &
Publishing Company. Editor: Mai Badr

InStyle
020 7261 4747
www.ipcmedia.com
Monthly. Owner: IPC Media.
Editor: Louise Chunn

In the Know
020 7424 7113
www.intheknowmagazine.co.uk
Weekly. Owner: H. Bauer.
Editor: Keith Kendrick

Jane
020 7240 0420
www.janemag.com
Monthly. Owner: Fairchild.
Editor: Brendon Holley

Junior
020 7761 8900
www.juniormagazine.co.uk
Monthly. Owner: Future.
Editor: Catherine O'Dolan

Junior Pregnancy & Baby
020 7761 8900
www.juniormagazine.co.uk
Monthly. Owner: Future.
Editor: Debora Stottor

Ladies First
029 2039 6600
www.hilspublications.com
4pa. Owner: Hils Publications.
Editor: Hilary Ferda

The Lady
020 7379 4717
www.lady.co.uk
Weekly. Editor: Arline Usden

Marie Claire
020 7261 5177
www.ipcmedia.com
Monthly. Owner: IPC Media.
Editor: Marie O'Riordan

More!
020 7859 8606
www.moremagazine.co.uk
Fortnightly. Owner: Emap.
Editor: Alison Hall

Mother & Baby
020 7874 0200
www.emap.com
Monthly. Owner: Emap.
Editor: Eleanor Dalrymple

MS Matters
020 8438 0700
www.mssociety.org.uk
Bi-monthly. Owner: Multiple Sclerosis
Society. Editor: Debbie Reeves

My Weekly
01382 223131
www.dcthomson.co.uk
Weekly. Owner: DC Thomson.
Editor: Sally Hampton

New Woman
020 7437 9011
www.newwoman.co.uk
Monthly. Owner: Emap.
Editor: Helen Johnston

New!
0871 434 1010
Weekly. Owner: Northern and Shell.
Editor. Kirsty Mouatt

Now
020 7261 6274
www.nowmagazine.com
Weekly. Owner: IPC Media.
Editor: Jane Ennis

Number Ten
020 7439 9100
www.numberten.co.uk
Bi-annual. Owner: Arberry Pink.
Editor: Laura Sheed

OK!
0871 434 1010
www.ok-magazine.com
Weekly. Owner: Northern and Shell.
Editor: Lisa Palta

Parent News UK
020 8337 6337
www.parents-news.co.uk
Monthly. Editor: Penny McCarthy

Parent Talk
020 7450 9073
www.parentalk.co.uk
Website updated weekly.
Editor: Hannah Jenkins

People
020 7322 1134
www.people.com
Weekly. Owner: Time Life.
Editor: Simon Perry

Pick Me Up
020 7261 5588
www.pick-me-up.co.uk
Weekly. Owner: IPC Media.
Editor: June Smith Sheppard

Practical Parenting
020 7261 5058
www.ipcmedia.com
Monthly. Owner: IPC Media.
Editor: Susie Boon

Pregnancy and Birth
020 7347 1885
www.emap.com
Monthly. Owner: Emap.
Acting Editor: Katie Holland

Pregnancy Magazine
020 7331 1000
Monthly. Owner: Future.
Editor: Claire Roberts

Pride Magazine
020 7228 3110
www.pridemagazine.com
Monthly. Owner: Pride Media.
Editor: Sherry Dixon

Prima
020 7439 5000
www.primamagazine.co.uk
Monthly. Owner: National Magazine
Company. Editor: Maire Fahey

Prima Baby
020 7439 5000
www.primababy.co.uk
Monthly. Owner: National Magazine
Company. Editor: Julia Goodwin

Real
01206 851117
www.essentialpublishing.co.uk
Fortnightly. Owner: Essential Publishing.
Editor: Sally Merroway

Real Health & Fitness
020 7306 0304
www.therivergroup.co.uk
Bi-monthly. Owner: River Publishing.
Editor: Andy Darling

Red
020 7150 7000
www.redmagazine.co.uk
Monthly. Owner: Hachette Filipacchi UK.
Editor: Trish Halpin

Reveal
020 7439 5000
www.natmags.co.uk
Weekly. Owner: National Magazine
Company. Editor: Michael Butcher

Rosemary Conley Diet & Fitness Magazine
01509 620444
www.rosemary-conley.co.uk
9pa. Owner: Quorn House Publishing.
Editor: Allison Barlow

She
020 7439 5000
www.she.co.uk
Monthly. Owner: National Magazine
Company. Editor: Sian Rees

Slimmer, Healthier, Fitter
01206 505972
www.slimmerrecipes.co.uk
10pa. Owner: Aceville Publications.
Editor: Rachel Callen

Slimming World
01773 546360
www.slimming-world.com
7pa. Editor: Christine Michael

Star
0871 434 1010
Weekly. Owner: Northern and Shell.
Editor: Busola Odulate

Take a Break
020 7241 8000
www.bauer.co.uk
Weekly. Owner: H Bauer.
Editor: John Dale

Tatler
020 7499 9080
www.tatler.co.uk
Monthly. Owner: Condé Nast.
Editor: Geordie Greig

That's Life!
020 7241 8000
www.bauer.co.uk
Weekly. Owner: H Bauer.
Editor: Jo Checkley

Tiara
029 2039 6600
www.hilspublications.com
3pa. Owner: Hils Publications.
Editor: Hilary Ferda

Top Santé Health & Beauty
020 7437 9011
www.emap.com
Monthly. Owner: Emap.
Editor: Lauren Libbert

Twins, Triplets & More Magazine
0870 770 3305
www.tamba.org.uk
4pa. Owner: The Twins and Multiple
Births Association. Editor: Jane Williams

Ulster Bride
028 9066 3311
www.ulstertatler.com
Bi-monthly. Owner: Ulster Talter
Publications. Editor: Christopher Sherry

Ulster Tatler
028 9066 3311
www.ulstertatler.com
Monthly. Owner: Ulster Talter
Publications. Editor: Richard Sherry

Ultra-Fit
01736 350204
www.ultra-fitmagazine.com
8pa. Editor: Charles Mays

Vanity Fair
020 7499 9080
www.vanityfair.co.uk
Monthly. Owner: Condé Nast.
Editor: Henry Porter

Vogue
020 7499 9080
www.vogue.com
Monthly. Owner: Condé Nast.
Editor: Alexandra Shulman

W
020 7240 0420
www.style.com/w
Monthly. Owner: Fairchild.
Editor: Patrick McCarthy

Wave
01273 818160
www.wavemagazine.co.uk
Monthly. Owner: The Latest.
Editor: Matt Chittock

Wedding
020 7261 7471
www.weddingandhome.co.uk
Monthly. Owner: IPC Media.
Editor: Katherine Westwood

Wedding Day
020 7761 8980
www.beachpublishing.co.uk
Bi-monthly. Owner: Beach Publications.
Editor: Alice Kodell

Wedding Journal
028 9045 7457
www.weddingjournalonline.com
Quarterly. Owner: Penton Group.
Editor: Tara Craig

WeightWatchers
020 8882 2555
8pa. Owner: Castlebar Publishing.
Editor: Barbara Raine-Allen

WM
029 2022 3333
www.icwales.co.uk
Quarterly. Owner: Trinity Mirror.
Editor: Sarah Drew Jones

Woman
020 7261 7023
www.ipcmedia.com
Weekly. Owner: IPC Media.
Editor: Jackie Hatton

Woman & Home
020 7261 5176
www.womanandhome.com
Monthly. Owner: IPC Media.
Editor: Sue James

Woman Alive
01903 821082
www.womanalive.co.uk
*Monthly. Owner: Christian Publishing
and Outreach. Editor: Jackie Stead*

Woman's Own
020 7261 5500
www.ipcmedia.com
*Weekly. Owner: IPC Media.
Editor: Elsa McAlonan*

Woman's Weekly
020 7261 6131
www.ipcmedia.com
*Weekly. Owner: IPC Media.
Editor: Gilly Sinclair*

Women's Wear Daily (WWD)
020 7240 0420
www.wwd.com
*Daily. Owner: Fairchild.
Editor: Patrick Mcarthy*

Yoga and Health
020 7480 5456
www.yogaandhealthmag.co.uk
*Monthly. Owner: Yoga Today.
Editor: Jane Sill*

You & Your Wedding
020 7439 5000
www.youandyourwedding.co.uk
*6pa. Owner: National Magazine
Company. Editor: Colette Harris*

You are What You Eat
01737 786 871
www.brooklandsgroup.com
/magazines/you-are-what-you-eat
*Monthly. Owner: Brooklands.
Editor: Francis Cottam*

Zest
020 7439 5000
www.zest.co.uk
*Monthly. Owner: National Magazine
Company. Editor: Alison Pylkkanen*

Major customer magazines

Asda Magazine
020 7462 7777
www.publicis-blueprint.co.uk
*Monthly. Publisher: Publicis Blueprint.
Editor: Helen Williams*

BMW Magazine
020 7534 2400
www.cedarcom.co.uk
*Quarterly. Publisher: Cedar.
Editor: Andrew Gillingwater*

Boots Health and Beauty
020 7747 0700
www.redwoodgroup.net
*6pa. Publisher: Redwood.
Editor: Elise Wells*

Caravan Club Magazine
01342 336804
www.caravanclub.co.uk
*Monthly. Publisher: The Caravan Club.
Editor: Gary Martin*

Carlos – Virgin Atlantic Upper Class
020 7565 3000
www.jbcp.co.uk
*Monthly. Publisher: John Brown
Publishing Group. Editor: Andy Raughton*

Debenhams Desire
020 7462 7777
www.publicis-blueprint.co.uk
*5pa. Publisher: Publicis Blueprint.
Editor: Amanda Morgan*

Harrods
020 7499 9080
*2pa. Owner: Condé Nast.
Editor: Nicola Loftus*

Harvey Nichols Magazine
020 7747 0700
www.redwoodgroup.net
4pa. Owner: Redwood. Editor: Deborah Bee

Heritage Today
020 7565 3000
www.english-heritage-books.org.uk
*Quarterly. Publisher: John Brown
Publishing Group. Editor: Francine
Lawrence*

High Life
020 7534 2400
www.cedarcom.co.uk
*Monthly. Publisher: Cedar.
Editor: Kerry Smith*

Homebase Ideas
020 7462 7777
www.publicis-blueprint.co.uk
*Quarterly. Publisher: Publicis Blueprint.
Editor: Ward Hellewell*

Honda Dream
020 7306 0304
www.therivergroup.co.uk
*Quarterly. Publisher: River Publishing.
Editor: Chris Hatherill*

Hotline (Virgin Trains)
020 7306 0304
www.therivergroup.co.uk
*Quarterly. Publisher: River Publishing.
Editor: Rod Stanley*

M&S Magazine
020 7747 0700
www.redwoodgroup.net
*4pa. Publisher: Redwood.
Editor: Diane Kenwood*

Motoring & Leisure
01273 744757
www.csma.uk.com
*10pa. Publisher: CSMA.
Editor: David Arnold*

National Trust Magazine
01793 817400
www.nationaltrust.org.uk
*3pa. Publisher: National Trust.
Editor: Sue Herdman*

O Magazine
020 7565 3000
www.jbcp.co.uk
*Monthly. Publisher: John Brown
Publishing Group. Editor: Sarah Notton*

The Renault Magazine – Vanguard
020 7462 7777
www.publicis-blueprint.co.uk
*Quarterly. Publisher: Publicis Blueprint.
Editor: Neil Anderson*

Saga Magazine
01303 771523
www.saga.co.uk
*Monthly. Publisher: Saga Group.
Editor: Emma Soames*

Sainsbury's Magazine
020 7633 0266
www.sainsburysmagazine.co.uk
*Monthly. Publisher: New Crane
Publishing. Editor: Sue Robinson*

Sky The Magazine
020 7565 3000
www.jbcp.co.uk
*Monthly. Publisher: John Brown
Publishing Group. Editor: Simon Geller*

Somerfield Magazine
0117 989 7808
www.somerfield.co.uk
*13pa. Publisher: Rare Publishing.
Editor: Hannah Smith*

Spirit of Superdrug
020 7306 0304
www.therivergroup.co.uk
*Monthly. Publisher: River Publishing.
Editor: Natalie Gibbons*

Triangle
020 8267 5000
www.haymarketpublishing.co.uk
*2pa. Publisher: Haymarket.
Editor: Emma Murfer*

Unlimited
0117 927 9009
www.originpublishing.co.uk
*10pa. Publisher: Origin Publishing.
Editor: Pat Reid*

VM – Vauxhall
01582 426909
http://vauxhall.co.uk/vmmagazine/
*3pa. Publisher: Brooklands Publishing.
Editor: Michelle Howard*

Waitrose Food Illustrated
020 7565 3000
www.jbcp.co.uk
*Monthly. Publisher: John Brown
Publishing Group. Editor: William Sitwell*

Business and trade press

● Business

Accountancy
020 8247 1387
www.accountancymagazine.com
Monthly. Owner: CCH. Editor: Chris Quick

Accountancy Age
020 7316 9000
www.accountancyage.com
Weekly. Owner: VNU.
Editor: Damian Wild

Accounting & Business
020 7059 5966
www.accaglobal.com
10pa. Owner: Certified Accountants
(Publications). Editor: John Prosser

Accounting Technician
020 7837 8600
www.accountingtechnician.co.uk
Monthly. Owner: Association of
Accounting Agencies.
Editor: Fritha Sutherland

Assessment
020 7801 2884
www.pcs.org.uk/revenue
Monthly. Owner: Public & Commercial
Services Union. Editor: Colin Edwards &
Alistair McClane

Bradmans Business Travel Guides
020 7613 8777
www.bradmans.com
Yearly. Owner: Ink Publishing.
Editor: Richard Bence

Brand Strategy
020 7970 4000
www.mad.co.uk
Monthly. Owner: Centaur.
Editor: Robert Mortimer

Business Informer
0191 518 4281
Bi-monthly. Owner: Deneholme
Publishing. Editor: Alan Roxborough

Business Traveller
020 7845 6510
www.businesstraveller.com
10pa. Owner: Panacea Publishing
International. Editor: Tom Otley

CFO Europe
020 7830 1090
www.cfoeurope.com
11pa. Owner: The Economist Newspaper.
Editor: Janet Kersnar

CorpComms Magazine
020 7251 7500
www.thecrossbordergroup.com
Monthly. Owner: Cross Border Ltd.
Editor: Helen Dunne

Corporate Citizenship Briefing
020 7940 5610
www.ccbriefing.co.uk
Bi-monthly. Founding editor: Mike Tuffrey

Creative Review
020 7970 4000
www.mad.co.uk
Monthly. Owner: Centaur.
Editor: Patrick Burgoyne

Design Week
020 7970 4000
www.mad.co.uk
Weekly. Owner: Centaur.
Editor: Lynda Relph-Knight

Director
020 7766 8950
www.iod.com
Monthly. Owner: Director Publications.
Editor: Joanna Higgins

Employee Benefits
020 7970 4000
www.employeebenefits.co.uk
Monthly. Owner: Centaur.
Editor: Amanda Wilkinson

Euromoney
020 7779 8888
www.euromoneyplc.com
Monthly. Owner: Euromoney
Institutional Investor. Editor: Peter Lee

Finance Week
020 7970 4000
www.financeweek.co.uk
Weekly. Owner: Centaur.
Editor: Dearbail Jordan

Financial Advisor
00 1 732 450 8866
www.financialadvisormagazine.com
Weekly. Owner: Charter Financial
Publishing Network. Senior editor:
Raymond Fazzi

Financial Management
020 7368 7177
www.cimaglobal.com
Monthly. Owner: Caspian.
Editor: Ruth Prickett

Financial News
020 7426 3333
www.efinancialnews.com
Weekly. Editor: William Wright

Financial World
020 7493 0173
www.financialworld.co.uk
Monthly. Owner: Caspian.
Editor: Denise Smith

First Voice of Business
01223 477411
www.campublishers.com
Bi-monthly. Owner: Cambridge
Publishers. Editor: Mike Sewell

Fund Strategy
020 7970 4000
www.fundstrategy.co.uk
Weekly. Owner: Centaur.
Editor: Daniel Ben-Ami

Growing Business
020 8334 1661
www.gbmag.co.uk
Monthly. Owner: Crimson Publishing.
Deputy editor: Matt Thomas

Human Resources
020 8267 4641
www.humanresourcesmagazine.com
11pa. Owner: Haymarket.
Editor: Trevor Merriden

Industrial Focus
020 7014 0300
www.industrialfocus.co.uk
Bi-monthly. Owner: Tower Publishing.
Editor: Mike Wearing

Institutional Investor –
International Edition
020 7779 8888
www.iilondon.co.uk
Monthly. Owner: Euromoney Institutional
Investor. Editor: Michael Carol

In-Store
020 7970 4000
www.mad.co.uk
Monthly. Owner: Centaur.
Editor: Matthew Valentine

Insurance Age
020 7484 9776
www.insuranceage.com
Monthly. Owner: Incisive Media.
Editor: Michelle Worvell

Investor Relations
020 7251 7500
www.thecrossbordergroup.com
Monthly. Owner: Cross Border Ltd.
Executive editor: Neil Stewart

The Journal
020 7534 2400
www.cedarcom.co.uk
Bi-monthly. Owner: Cedar.
Editor: John Guy

Landscape and Amenity Product
Update
01952 200809
www.landscapespecification.com
6pa. Owner: Tanner Stiles Publishing.
Editor: Katie Wilcox

Logistics Manager
020 7970 4000
www.logisticsmanager.co.uk
Monthly. Owner: Centaur.
Editor: Mannery Davis

Management Today
020 8267 5000
www.mtmagazine.co.uk
Monthly. Owner: Haymarket.
Editor: Emma de Bita

Marketing Week
020 7970 4000
www.mad.co.uk
Weekly. Owner: Centaur.
Editor: Stuart Smith

Money Marketing
020 7970 4000
www.centaur.co.uk
Weekly. Owner: Centaur.
Editor: John Lappin

Mortgage Strategy
020 7970 4000
www.mortgagestrategy.co.uk
Weekly. Owner: Centaur.
Editor: Robyn Hall

New Business
020 7407 9800
www.newbusiness.co.uk
Quarterly. Owner: IBMG.
Editor: Nick Martindale

New Media Age
020 7970 4000
www.nma.co.uk/
Weekly. Owner: Centaur.
Editor: Michael Nutley

OS Magazine
0141 567 6000
www.peeblesmedia.com
Bi-monthly. Owner: Peebles Media Group.
Editor: Mike Travers

Overseas Trade
020 7368 9600
www.overseas-trade.co.uk
Monthly. Owner: Rare Publishing.
Editor: Janet Tibble

Pensions & Investments
020 7457 1430
www.pionline.com
Fortnightly. Owner: Crain
Communications. Editor: Nancy Webman

Pensions Age
020 7426 0424
www.pensions-age.com
Monthly. Owner: Pensions Age Magazine.
Editor: Francesca Fabrizi

People Management
020 7880 6200
www.peoplemanagement.co.uk
Fortnightly. Owner: Redactive Publishing.
Editor: Steve Crabb

Personnel Today
020 8652 3941
www.personneltoday.com
Weekly. Owner: Reed Business
Information. Editor: Karen Dempsey

Professional Manager
020 7421 2705
www.managers.org.uk
Bi-monthly. Owner: Chartered
Management Institute. Editor: Sue Mann

Public Private Finance
020 7970 4000
www.publicprivatefinance.co.uk
Monthly. Owner: Centaur.
Editor: Michael Kapoor

Real Business
020 7368 7177
www.realbusiness.co.uk
Monthly. Owner: Caspian.
Editor: Adam Leyland

Recruiter Magazine
020 7970 4000
www.recruitermagazine.co.uk
Fortnightly. Owner: Redactive Publishing.
Editor: Dee Dee Doke

StartUps.co.uk
020 8334 1721
www.startups.co.uk
Website, updated hourly.
Online editor: Oliver Milman

Supply Management
020 7880 6200
www.supplymanagement.co.uk
Fortnightly. Owner: Redactive Publishing.
Editor: Geraint John

What's New In Industry
020 7970 4000
www.centaur.co.uk
Monthly. Owner: Centaur.
Editor: David Keighley

● Construction
and engineering

ABC&D
01527 834400
www.abc-d.co.uk
Monthly. Owner: Centaur.
Editor: Claire Mackle

Architecture Today
020 7837 0143
www.architecturetoday.co.uk
10pa. Editor: Chris Foges

Builder & Engineer
0161 236 2782
www.builderandengineer.co.uk
Monthly. Owner: Excel Publishing.
Editor: Richard Stirling

Building
020 7560 4149
www.building.co.uk
Weekly. Owner: CMP Information.
Editor: Denise Chevin

Building Design
020 7921 5000
www.bdonline.co.uk
Weekly. Owner: CMP Information.
Editor: Amanda Baillieu

Building Products
0870 049 4424
www.buildingproducts.co.uk
Monthly. Owner: Quantum Business
Media. Editor: James Stagg

Construction Manager
020 7560 4153
www.construction-manager.co.uk
10pa. Owner: The Builder Group.
Editor: Kristina Smith

Construction News
020 7505 6868
www.cnplus.co.uk
Weekly. Owner: Emap.
Editor: Aaron Morby

Construction Products
020 7505 6868
www.cnplus.co.uk
Monthly. Owner: Emap.
Editor: Julian Birch

Contract Journal
020 8652 4761
www.contractjournal.com
Weekly. Owner: Reed Business
Information. Editor: Emma Penny

Electronics
01622 699162
www.connectingindustry.com
11pa. Editor: Joanne Bennett

Electronics Weekly
020 8652 3650
www.electronicsweekly.com
Weekly. Owner: Reed Business
Information. Editor: Richard Wilson

Engineering and Technology
01438 313311
www.iee.org/Publish/Journals
Monthly. Owner: The Institution of
Electrical Engineers. Editor: Dickon Ross

The Engineer
020 7970 4000
www.e4engineering.com
Fortnightly. Owner: Centaur.
Editor: Andrew Lee

Gas Installer
0870 401 2529
www.shoreline-media.com
Monthly. Owner: Corgi.
Editor: Nicole Perry

Global Pipeline Monthly
01494 675139
www.pipemag.com
Monthly. Owner: Scientific Surveys.
Editor: John Tiratsoo

Metal Working Production
020 7970 4000
www.mwp.co.uk
Monthly. Owner: Centaur.
Editor: Mike Excell

New Civil Engineer
020 7505 6600
www.nceplus.co.uk
Weekly. Owner: Emap.
Editor: Antony Oliver

Offshore
01992 656 657
www.offshore-mag.com
Monthly. Owner: Penwell Corporation.
Editor: Eldon Ball

PIR Construction
0870 749 0220
www.pirnet.co.uk
6pa. Owner: The Bellmont Agency.
Editor: Steve Lucas

Process Engineering
020 7970 4000
www.processengineering.co.uk
Monthly. Owner: Centaur.
Editor: Mike Spear

Professional Electrician & Installer
01923 237799
www.hamerville.co.uk
11pa. Owner: Hamerville Magazines.
Editor: Richard Pagett

Professional Engineering
020 7973 1299
www.profeng.com
Fortnightly. Owner: Professional
Engineering Publishing.
Editor: John Pullin

Professional Heating & Plumbing Installer
01923 237799
www.hamerville.co.uk
11pa. Owner: Hamerville Magazines.
Editor: Stuart Hamilton

Public Sector Building
01527 834400
www.centaur.co.uk
6pa. Owner: Centaur.
Publisher: Angela Smith

RIBA Journal
020 7921 8560
www.ribajournal.com
Monthly. Owner: The Builder Group.
Editor: Eleanor Young

What's New In Building
020 7560 4245
www.wnibonline.com/
Monthly. Owner: CMP information.
Editor: Mark Pennington

● Defence

Airforces Monthly
01780 755131
www.airforcesmonthly.com
Monthly. Owner: Key Publishing.
Editor: Alan Warnes

Jane's Defence Weekly
020 8700 3700
www.janes.com
Weekly. Owner: Jane's.
Editor: Robert Hewson

Navy News
023 9229 4228
www.navynews.co.uk
Monthly. Editor: Sarah Fletcher

Soldier
01252 347356
www.soldiermagazine.co.uk
Monthly. Editor: John Elliott

● Education

Child Education
0845 850 4411
www.scholastic.co.uk
Monthly. Owner: Scholastic.
Deputy editor: Michael Ward

Education Today
020 7947 9536
www.collegeofteachers.ac.uk
Quarterly. Owner: College of Teachers.
Editorial assistant: Morag Hughes

Education Travel Magazine
020 7440 4025
www.hothousemedia.com
Bi-monthly. Owner: Hothouse Media.
Editor: Amy Baker

English Teaching Professional
01243 576600
www.keywayspublishing.com
Bi-monthly. Owner: Keyways.
Editor: Helena Gomm

FE Now
020 7005 2741
www.aoc.co.uk
4pa. Owner: The Association of Colleges.
Editor: Kate Hilpern

Gair Rhydd
029 2078 1400
www.cardiffstudents.com
Weekly. Owner: Cardiff Union Services.
Editor: Perry Lewis

Governors' News
0121 643 5787
www.nagm.org.uk
5pa. Owner: National Association of School Governors. Editor: Sally Thorne

Higher Education Review
020 8341 1366
www.highereducationreview.com
3pa. Editor: John Pratt

ICT for Education
020 8334 1600
www.ictforeducation.co.uk
Monthly. Owner: Crimson Publishing.
Editor: Ian Delaney

LSE Magazine
020 7955 7582
www.lse.ac.uk
2pa. Owner: London School of Economics.
Editor: Judith Higgin

The Magic Key
020 8433 2883
www.bbcmagazines.com
Monthly. Owner: BBC Worldwide.
Editor: Stephanie Cooper

Nursery Education
01926 887799
www.scholastic.co.uk
Monthly. Owner: Scholastic.
Editor: Sarah Sodhi

Nursery World
020 7782 3000
www.nurseryworld.co.uk
Weekly. Owner: TSL Education.
Editor: Liz Roberts

Open Learner
01223 400362
www.nec.ac.uk
Website. Editor: Sarah Lawrence

Oxford Today
01865 280545
www.oxfordtoday.ox.ac.uk
3pa. Owner: University of Oxford.
Editor: Georgina Ferry

Report
020 7930 6441
www.askatl.org.uk
10pa. Owner: Association of Teachers and Lecturers. Editor: Victoria Poskit

Right Start
020 7878 2338
www.rightstartmagazine.co.uk
Bi-monthly. Owner: McMillan-Scott.
Editor: Lynette Lowthian

Scottish Educational Journal
0131 225 6244
www.eis.org.uk
5pa. Owner: Educational Institute of Scotland. Editor: Simon MacAulay

Sesame
01908 653011
www.open.ac.uk/sesame
4pa. Owner: Open University.
Editor: Tracy Archbold

Special Schools Guide
020 7970 4000
www.centaur.co.uk
Annual. Owner: Centaur.
Publisher: Derek Rogers

Student Direct
0161 275 2943
www.student-direct.co.uk
Weekly during term.
Editor: Alexa Gainsbury

The Teacher
020 7380 4708
www.teachers.org.uk
8pa. Owner: National Union of Teachers.
Editor: Elyssa Campbell-Barr

Teaching Today
0121 457 6140
www.teachersunion.org.uk
5pa. Owner: NASUWT. Editor: Joe Devo

Times Educational Supplement
020 7782 3000
www.tes.co.uk
Weekly. Owner: TSL Education.
Editor: Judith Judd

Times Higher Education Supplement
020 7782 3000
www.thes.co.uk
Weekly. Owner: TSL Education.
Editor: John O'Leary

UC
020 7837 3636
www.ucu.org.uk
5pa. Owner: UCU. Editors: Brenda Kirsch

● Farming

British Dairying
01438 716220
Monthly. Owner: WB Publishing.
Editor: Mike Green

Crop Production Magazine
01743 861122
www.cpm.gb.net
Monthly Feb-Oct. Editor: Angus McKirdy

Crops
020 8652 4923
www.reedbusiness.co.uk
Fortnightly. Owner: Reed Business Information. Editor: Charles Abel

Dairy Farmer
01732 377273
16pa. Owner: CMP Information.
Editor: Peter Hollinshead

Farmers Guardian
01772 799411
www.farmersguardian.com
Weekly. Owner: CMP Information.
Editor: Liz Falkingham

Farmers Weekly
020 8652 4940
www.fwi.co.uk
Weekly. Owner: Reed Business Information. Editor: Michael Targett

Feed International
00 31 30 659 2236
www.wattnet.com
Monthly. Owner: Watt Publishing.
Editor: Clayton Gill

Living Earth
0117 914 2434
www.soilassociation.org
3pa. Editor: Elisabeth Winkler

NFU Horticulture
020 7331 7359
www.nfuonline.com
3pa. Owner: NFU
Editor: Martin Stanhope

Poultry International
00 31 30 659 2234
www.wattnet.com
Monthly. Owner: Watt Publishing.
Editor: Jackie Linden

Scottish Farmer
0141 302 7700
www.newsquest.co.uk
Weekly. Owner: Newsquest.
Editor: Alistair Fletcher

Tractor & Machinery
01959 541444
www.kelsey.co.uk
Monthly. Owner: Kelsey Publishing.
Editor: Peter Love

● Health and social care

Arthritis News
020 7380 6521
www.arthritiscare.org.uk
*Bi-monthly. Owner: Arthritis Care.
Editor: Rosie Loft*

BMJ
020 7387 4499
www.bmj.com
*Weekly. Owner: BMJ Publishing Group.
Editor: Fiona Godlee*

Community Care
020 8652 4886
www.communitycare.co.uk
*Weekly. Owner: Reed Business
Information. Editor: Mark Ivory*

Doctor
020 8652 8740
www.doctorupdate.net
*Weekly. Owner: Reed Business
Information. Editor: Charles Creswell*

Druglink
020 7922 8605
www.drugscope.co.uk
*Bi-monthly. Owner: DrugScope.
Editor: Harry Shapiro*

GP
020 8267 4846
www.gponline.com
*Weekly. Owner: Haymarket.
Editor: Bronagh Miskelly*

Health Service Journal
020 7874 0200
www.hsj.co.uk
*Weekly. Owner: Emap.
Editor: Nick Edwards*

Hospital Doctor
020 8652 8745
www.hospital-doctor.net
*Weekly. Owner: Reed Business
Information. Editor: Mike Broad*

Journal of Family Healthcare
01243 576600
www.keywayspublishing.com
*Bi-monthly. Owner: Keyways Publishing.
Editor: Pat Scowan*

The Lancet
020 7424 4910
www.lancet.com
*Weekly. Owner: Elsevier.
Editor: Richard Horton*

Medeconomics
020 8267 5000
www.gponline.com
*Monthly. Owner: Haymarket.
Editor: Jacki Buist*

MIMS
020 8267 5000
www.gponline.com
*Monthly. Owner: Haymarket.
Editor: Colin Duncan*

Nursing Standard
020 8423 1066
www.nursing-standard.co.uk
*Weekly. Owner: RCN Publishing.
Editor: Ken Edwards*

Nursing Times
020 7874 0502
www.nursingtimes.net
*Weekly. Owner: Emap.
Editor: Rachel Downey*

The Pharmaceutical Journal
020 7572 2414
www.pjonline.com
*Weekly. Owner: Royal Pharmaceutical
Society of Great Britain.
Editor: Olivia Timbs*

The Practitioner
020 7921 8113
www.practitioner-i.co.uk
*Monthly. Owner: CMP Information.
Editor: Gavin Atkin*

The Psychologist
0116 252 9573
www.bps.org.uk/publications
/thepsychologist
*Monthly. Owner: The British
Psychological Society.
Editor: Dr Jon Sutton*

Pulse
020 7921 8106
www.pulse-i.co.uk
*49pa. Owner: CMP Information.
Editor: Joe Haynes*

RCN Bulletin
020 8423 1066
www.nursing-standard.co.uk
*Weekly. Owner: RCN Publishing.
Editor: Ken Edwards*

Update
020 8652 8760
www.doctorupdate.net
*Monthly. Owner: Reed Business
Information. Editor: Anna Sayburn*

》 See also disability page 119

● Housing

Housing Association Magazine
0121 682 8881
www.wavcoms.co.uk
*Bi-monthly. Owner: Waverley
Communications. Editor: Bruce Meecham*

Inside Housing
020 7772 8300
www.insidehousing.co.uk
*Weekly. Owner: Inside Communications.
Editor: Karen Day*

Regeneration & Renewal
020 8267 4381
www.regenerationmagazine.com
*Weekly. Owner: Haymarket.
Editor: Richard Garlick*

Roof
020 7505 2161
www.roofmag.org.uk
*Bi-monthly. Owner: Shelter.
Editor: Emma Hawkey*

● Law

The In-House Lawyer
020 7396 5672
10pa. Editor: Eduardo Reyes

The Lawyer
020 7970 4000
www.centaur.co.uk
*Weekly. Owner: Centaur.
Editor: Catrin Griffiths*

Law Society Gazette
020 7841 5546
www.lawgazette.co.uk
*Weekly. Owner: The Law Society.
Editor: Jonathan Ames*

Legal Business
020 7396 9308
www.legalbusiness.co.uk
10pa. Editor: Tom Freeman

Legal Week
020 7566 5600
www.legalweek.com
*Weekly. Owner: Legal Week Global Media.
Editor: Caroline Pearce*

Media Lawyer
01229 716622
www.medialawyer.press.net
*Bi-monthly. Owner: Press Association.
Editor: Mike Dodd*

● Media

● Police

Constabulary Magazine
0870 350 1892
*Monthly. Owner: National Press Publishers.
Editor-in-chief: Christopher Locke*

Police Magazine
020 8335 1000
www.polfed.org
*Monthly. Owner: Police Federation of
England & Wales. Editor: Metin Enver*

Police Review
020 8276 4729
www.policereview.com
*Weekly. Owner: Jane's.
Editor: Catriona Marchant*

Policing Today
01243 576600
www.keywayspublishing.com
*Quarterly. Owner: Keyways Publishing.
Editor: Peter Shipley*

● Property

Estates Gazette
020 7911 1805
www.reedbusiness.co.uk
*Weekly. Owner: Reed Business
Information. Editor: Peter Bill*

Facilities Management Journal
020 8771 3614
www.fmarena.com
*Monthly. Owner: Market Place
Publishing. Editor: Becca Wilson*

Facilities Management UK
0161 683 8032
www.worldsfair.co.uk
Bi-monthly. Owner: World's Fair.
Editor: Mike Appleton

● Retail and catering

Asian Trader
020 7928 1234
www.gg2.net
Fortnightly. Owner: Garavi Gujarat
Publications. Editor: R Solanki

Caterer and Hotelkeeper
020 8652 4210
www.reedbusinessinformation.co.uk
Weekly. Owner: Reed Business
Information. Editor: Mark Lewis

Caterer and Licensee News
01202 552333
www.catererlicensee.co.uk
Monthly. Owner: RBC Publishing.
Editor: Peter Adams

Catering Update
020 8652 8307
www.reedbusiness.co.uk
Monthly. Owner: Reed Business
Information. Editor: Kathy Bowry

Chain Leader UK
020 8652 3370
www.reedbusiness.co.uk
Monthly. Owner: Reed Business
Information. Editor: Helen Adkins

Class
01293 610442
www.william-reed.co.uk
Monthly. Owner: William Reed
Publishing. Editor: Paul Wootton

Convenience Store
01293 610218
www.william-reed.co.uk
Fortnightly. Owner: William Reed
Publishing. Editor: David Rees

DNR
020 7240 0420
www.dnrnews.com
Weekly, Owner: Fairchild.
Editor: John Birmingham

Drapers
020 7812 3700
www.drapersonline.com
Weekly. Owner: Emap.
Editor: Josephine Collins

Eat Out
01471 571436
www.dewberryredpoint.co.uk
Monthly. Owner: Dewberry Redpoint.
Editor: David Foad

Food Manufacture
01293 610231
www.foodmanufacture.co.uk
Monthly. Owner: William Reed
Publishing. Editor: Rick Pendrous

Footwear News (FN)
020 7240 0420
www.footwearnews.com
Weekly. Owner: Fairchild.
Editor: Neil Weilheimer

Forecourt Trader
01293 610219
www.william-reed.co.uk
Monthly. Owner: William Reed
Publishing. Editor: Merril Boulton

The Franchise Magazine
01603 620301
www.franchise-group.com
8pa. Owner: Franchise Development
Services. Editor: Stuart Anderson

The Grocer
01293 610259
www.grocertoday.co.uk
Weekly. Owner: William Reed Publishing.
Editor: Sheila Sheridan

Hospitality
0161 236 2782
www.excelpublishing.co.uk
Monthly. Owner: Excel Publishing.
Editor: Elizabeth Donavan

Independent Retail News
01322 611240
www.irn-talkingshop.co.uk
Fortnightly. Owner: Nexus Holdings.
Editor: Charles Morrissey

Leisure Report
01293 846 559
www.martin-info.com
Monthly. Owner: William Reed
Publishing. Acting editor: Duncan Rowe

On Trade Scotland
0141 222 5389
www.william-reed.co.uk
Fortnightly. Owner: William Reed
Publishing. Editor: Michelle Robertson

MBR
01293 610268
www.william-reed.co.uk
Monthly. Owner: William Reed
Publishing. Editor: James Parker

Morning Advertiser
01293 610480
www.william-reed.co.uk
Weekly. Owner: William Reed Publishing.
Editor: Andrew Pring

Off Licence News
01293 610226
www.william-reed.co.uk
Fortnightly. Owner: William Reed
Publishing. Editor: Graham Holter

Party Times
01926 886588
www.partytimes.biz
Bi-monthly. Owner: Plaza Publishing.
Editor: Andrew Maiden

PubChef
01293 610487
www.william-reed.co.uk
Monthly. Owner: William Reed
Publishing. Editor: Jo Bruce

The Publican
020 7955 3736
www.thepublican.com
42pa. Owner: United Advertising
Publications. Editor: Caroline Nodder

Sales Promotion
01799 544200
www.salespromo.co.uk
Monthly. Owner: Greenhill Publishing.
Publisher: Matt Sullivan

Shopping Centre
01293 610294
www.william-reed.co.uk
Monthly. Owner: William Reed
Publishing. Editor: Graham Parker

Supermarket News
020 7240 0420
www.supermarketnews.com
Weekly. Owner: Fairchild.
Editor-in-chief: David Merrefield

Toy News
01992 535646
www.toynewsmag.com
Monthly. Owner: Intent Media.
Editor: Ronnie Dungan

The Trader
0870 049 4363
www.thetrader.co.uk
Monthly. Owner: United Advertising.
Publications

Women's Wear Daily (WWD)
020 7240 0420
www.wwd.com
Daily. Owner: Fairchild.
Editor: Ed Nardoza

WWDBeautyBiz
020 7240 0420
www.wwd.com
9pa. Owner: Fairchild. Editor: Jenny Fine

● Science

Clinical Laboratory International
01442 877777
www.cli-online.com
8pa. Owner: Reed Business Information.
Editor: Frances Bushrod

Nature
020 7833 4000
www.nature.com
Weekly. Owner: Nature Publishing Group.
Editor: Phil Campbell

New Scientist
020 7611 1201
www.newscientist.com
Weekly. Owner: Reed Business
Information. Editor: Jeremy Webb

Science
01223 326500
www.sciencemag.org
Weekly. Owner: American Association
for the Advancement of Science.
Editor: Andrew Sugden

● Technology

British Photographic Industry News
01799 544200
www.archant.co.uk
Monthly. Owner: Archant.
Editor: Ian Farrell

Computer Business Review
020 7675 7910
www.cbronline.com
Monthly. Owner: Business Review.
Editor: Jason Stamper

Computer Weekly
020 8652 8450
www.computerweekly.com
Weekly. Owner: Reed Business
Information. Editor: Hooman Bassirian

Computing
020 7316 9000
www.computing.co.uk
Weekly. Owner: VNU. Editor: Toby Wolpe

Develop
01992 535646
www.developmag.com
Monthly. Owner: Intent Media.
Editor: Michael French

Developer Network Journal
0117 930 0255
www.dnjonline.com
Website. Owner: Matt Publishing.
Editor: Matt Nicholson

Information Age
020 7612 9300
www.infoconomy.com
Monthly. Owner: Infoconomy.
Editor: Kenny MacIver

IT Week
020 7316 9000
www.itweek.co.uk
Weekly. Owner: VNU. Editor: Lem Bingley

ITNOW
01793 417474
www.bcs.org
Bi-monthly. Owner: British Computer
Society. Editor: Brian Runciman

Mobile Entertainment
01992 535646
www.mobile-ent.biz
Monthly and website. Owner: Intent
Media. Editor: Stuart O'Brien

PC Retail
01992 535646
www.pcretailmag.com
Monthly. Owner: Intent Media.
Editor: Scott Bicheno

Professional Photographer
01799 544200
www.professionalphotographer.co.uk
Monthly. Owner: Archant.
Editor: Ian Farrell

Scientific Computing World
01223 477411
www.europascience.com
Bi-monthly. Owner: Europa Science.
Editor: Tom Wilkie

● Transport

Aerospace International
020 7670 4300
www.aerosociety.com
Monthly. Owner: The Royal Aeronautical
Society. Editor: Richard Gardner

Air International
01780 755131
www.airinternational.com
Monthly. Owner: Key Publishing.
Editor: Malcolm English

Automotive Engineer
020 7304 6809
www.pepublishing.com
Monthly. Owner: Professional
Engineering Publishing.
Editor: John Pullin

Autowired
01565 872107
www.autowired.co.uk
Daily. Owner: Eurotax Glass.
Editor: Barry Hook

Commercial Motor
020 8652 3612
www.reedbusinessinformation.co.uk
Weekly. Owner: Reed Business
Information. Editor: Andy Salter

Flight International
020 8652 4395
www.flightinternational.com
Weekly. Owner: Reed Business
Information. Editor: Murdo Morrison

Helicopter International
01934 822524
www.helidata.rotor.com
Bi-monthly. Owner: Avia Press
Associates. Editor: Elfan ap Rees

Motor Trader
01322 611301
www.motortrader.co.uk
Weekly. Owner: Nexus Holdings.
Editor: Curtis Hutchinson

Motor Transport
020 8652 3285
www.reedbusinessinformation.co.uk
Weekly. Owner: Reed Business
Information. Editor: Andrew Brown

Professional Motor Mechanic
01923 237799
www.hamerville.co.uk
11pa. Owner: Hamerville Magazines.
Editor: Richard Bowler

Rail
01733 264666
www.emap.com
Fortnightly. Owner: Emap.
Editor: Nick Randle

Railnews
020 7278 6100
www.railnews.co.uk
Monthly. Owner: Clarity Publishing.
Editor: Paul Whiting

Truck & Driver
020 8652 3303
www.reedbusinessinformation.co.uk
Weekly. Owner: Reed Business
Information. Editor: Dave Young

Trucking
01225 442244
www.truckingmag.co.uk
Monthly. Owner: Future.
Deputy editor: Steve Hayes

● Travel

Travel Trade Gazette
020 7921 8029
www.ttglive.com
Weekly. Owner: CMP Information.
Editor: John Welsh

Travel Weekly
020 8652 8227
www.travelweekly.co.uk
Weekly. Owner: Reed Business
Information. Editor: Richard Siddle

Minority press

● Cultural and ethnic minorities

Ad-Diplomasi News Report
Focus Press (UK)
020 7286 1372
subscribe@ad-diplomasi.com
www.ad-diplomasi.com
Monthly. Arabic and English. Political
affairs covering the Middle East.
Editor: Raymond Atallah

Al-Ahram
Al-Ahram
weeklymail@ahram.org.eg
http://weekly.ahram.org.eg
Weekly. English, serving Arab world.
Editor-in-chief: Assem El-Kersh

Al-Arab
Al Arab Publishing House
020 7021 0966
editor@alarab.co.uk
www.alarabonline.org
Daily and online. Arabic.
Editor: Elhouni Mohammed

Anandabazar Patrika
subscription@abpmail.com
www.anandabazar.com
Daily. Bengali. Editor: Shrabani Basu

Anglo-Hellenic Review
Anglo-Hellenic League
020 7267 3877
paul.watkins@virgin.net
www.hellenicbookservice.com
/ahr.htm
2pa. Cultural affairs covering Greece and
Britain. Editor: Paul Watkins

Ashraq Al Awsat
Saudi Research and Marketing UK
020 7831 8181
editorial@asharqalawsat.com
www.aawsat.com
Daily. Arabic. Editor: Tariq Al Homayed

Asian Entertainment Guide
020 7723 6797
Weekly. Editor: N Gosai

Asian Leader Midlands
Urban Media
0871 872 9893
zakia@asianleader.com
Fortnightly. English, free.
Editor: Zakia Yousaf

Asian News
Guardian Media Group
01706 357086
asiannews@gmwn.co.uk
www.theasiannews.co.uk
Monthly. Editor: Steve Hammond;
chief reporter: Shelina Begum

Asian Post
Hussain Media
020 8558 9127
leali@theasianpost.co.uk
Weekly. English. Editor: Murtaza Ali Shah

Asian Times
Ethnic Media Group
020 7650 2000
news@asiantimes.co.uk
www.asiantimesonline.co.uk
Weekly. English. Editor: Burhan Ahmad

Asians in Media
020 8893 5646
sunny.hundal@asiansinmedia.org
www.asiansinmedia.org
Weekly. Guide to the British Asian media industry. Editor: Sunny Hundal

Awaaz
Awaaz Multi Media
01924 510512
info@awaaz.com
www.awaaznews.com
Monthly. English, Urdu and Gujarati. Head of Comms: Shakir Daji

Barficulture.com
020 8561 6855
www.barficulture.com
Website. Young British Asians. Editor: Sunny Hundal

Blacknet
0870 746 5000
junior@blacknet.co.uk
www.blacknet.co.uk
Community website for black people in Britain. Editor: Junior Wilson

Black Information Link
020 7582 1990
blink1990@blink.org.uk
www.blink.org.uk
Website. Editor: Lester Holloway

Canada Post
020 8840 9765
info@canadapost.co.uk
www.canadapost.co.uk
Monthly. Managing editor: Paula Adamick

Caribbean Times
Ethnic Media Group
020 7650 2000
caribbeantimes@ethnicmedia.co.uk
www.caribbeantimes.co.uk
Weekly. Editor: Ron Shillingford

Chinatown
CTM Publishing
0161 245 3252
enquiries@
    chinatownthemagazine.com
www.chinatownthemagazine.com
Bi-monthly. English for Chinese. Publisher: William Ong; editor: Davidine Sim

Chup magazine
020 8983 6567
info@chupmagazine.com
www.chupmagazine.com
Bi-monthly. English for British Bengalis. Editor: Jasmine

Clickwalla.com
MeMedia
020 7693 8416
amit@memediagroup.com
www.clickwalla.com
Website. Editor: Amit Daryamani

Daily AUSAF
020 8521 8555
ausaflondon@aol.com
www.dailyausaf.com
Daily. Urdu. Chief editor: Mehtab Khan

Daily Jang London
Jang Publications
020 7403 5833
editor@janglondon.co.uk
www.jang.com.pk
Daily. English and Urdu. Editor: Zahoor Niazi

Des Pardes
020 8571 1127
despadesuk@btconnect.com
Weekly. Punjabi for Indian expatriates. Editor: GS Virk

Dziennik Polski
The Polish Daily (Publishers)
020 8740 1991
editor@dziennikpolski.co.uk
www.polishdailynews.com
Daily. Polish. Editor: Taroslaw Kozminski

Eastern Eye
Ethnic Media Group
020 7650 2000
editor@easterneyeuk.co.uk
www.easterneyeonline.co.uk
Weekly. For Indian, Pakistani, Sri Lankan and Bangladeshi communities in Britain. Editor: Hamnt Verma

Echo Me
Multi Ethnic (Aberdeen)
01224 645268/645200
info@multiethnic.co.uk
www.multiethnic.co.uk
Bi-monthly. All ethnic groups

Eikoku News Digest
News Digest International
020 7616 1100
info@newsdigest.co.uk
www.newsdigest.co.uk
Weekly. Japanese. Editor: Mikiko Toshima

Euro Bangla
Newsfax
020 7377 0311
info@eurobangla.co.uk
www.eurobangla.co.uk
Weekly. Bangla and English. Managing Director: Masaddik Ahmed

Garavi Gujarat
Asian Media & Marketing Group
020 7928 1234
garavi@gujarat.co.uk
www.gg2.net
Weekly. English and Gujarati. Editor: Ramniklal Solanki

The Gleaner
020 7737 7377
www.jamaica-gleaner.com
Weekly. Deputy editor: Vic Moutne

Gujarat Samachar/ Asian Voice
Asian Business Publications
020 7749 4080
support@abplgroup.com
www.gujarat-samachar.com
Weekly. Editor: C Patel

Hia
HH Saudi Research & Marketing UK
020 7831 8181
hia@hhsaudi.com
Monthly. Arab women. Editor: Mai Badr

Hurriyet
020 7734 1211
www.hurriyetim.com
Daily. Turkish. Editor: Aysegul Richardson

Impact International
020 7263 1417
editor@impact-magazine.com
Monthly. Muslim current affairs. Editor: Ahmed Irfan

India Monitor
shiv@journalist.com
www.indiamonitor.com
Website

India Times
Times Internet
servicedesk@timesgroup.com
http://timesofindia.indiatimes.com
Daily and website. Managing director & chief executive officer: Dinesh Wadhawan

Irish Post
020 8741 0649
irishpost@irishpost.co.uk
www.irishpost.co.uk
Weekly. Editor: John Miles

Irish World
Newsfax
020 8453 7800
sales@theirishworld.com
www.theirishworld.com
Weekly. Acting editor: Frank Murphy

Janomot
Publication 1969
020 7377 6032
janomot@btconnect.com
www.janomotnews.com
Weekly. Bengali. Editor: Nabab Uddin

Jewish Chronicle
020 7415 1500
webmaster@thejc.com
www.thejc.com
Weekly and website. Editor: David Rowan

Jewish Telegraph
0141 621 4422
mail@jewishtelegraph.com
www.jewishtelegraph.com
Weekly. Editor: Paul Harris

KAL
020 7439 9100
www.kalmagazine.com
Bi-annual. Careers and recruitment for ethnic minority students. Editor: Laura Sheed

La Voce degli Italiani
020 7735 5164
www.lavoce.com
Bi-Monthly. Italians in Europe. Editor: Padre Giandomenico Ziliotto

London Turkish Gazette
020 8889 5025
news@londragazete.com
www.londragazete.com
Weekly. Turkish and English. Publisher: Yilmaz Ozyigit; editor: Artun Goksan

London Welsh Magazine
London Welsh Association
020 7837 3722
ddaniel@streamline-cm.co.uk
www.londonwelsh.org
Quarterly. Editor: David Daniel

Maghreb Review
020 7388 1840
maghrab@maghrabreview.com
www.maghrabreview.com
Quarterly. English and French.
North Africa, sub-Saharan Africa,
Middle East and Islam. Islamic studies:
history, geopolitics, environment.
Editor: Mohammed Ban-madani

MIL Matchmaker Magazine
Matchmaker International
020 8868 1879
info@perfect-partner.com
www.perfect-partner.com
3pa. Asians seeking partners.
Editor: Mr Bharat Raithatha

Mauritian Abroad
Sankris Publishing
01795 539499
eveer77807@aol.com
Quarterly. English and French.
Editor: Krish Veeramah

Mauritius News
020 7498 3066
editor@mauritiusnews.co.uk
www.mauritiusnews.co.uk
Monthly. Editor: Peter Chellen

Milap Weekly
020 7385 8966
Weekly. Urdu-speaking community.
Editor: Ramesh Soni

Muslim News
Visitcrest
020 8863 8586
editor@muslimnews.co.uk
www.muslimnews.co.uk
Monthly. Editor: Ahmed Versi

Muslim Weekly
020 7377 1919
info@themuslimweekly.com
www.themuslimweekly.com
Weekly. Editor: Ahmed Malik

Navin Weekly
020 7385 8966
Weekly. Hindi. Editor: Ramesh Kumar

New Nation
Ethnic Media Group
020 7650 2000
general@ethnicmedia.co.uk
www.newnation.co.uk
Weekly. Black African-Caribbean news.
Editorial director: Michael Eboda

New World
020 77002673
dhirennewworld@blueyonder.co.uk
Fortnightly. Editor and publisher:
Dhiren Basu

New Zealand News UK
Southern Link Media
020 7463 2100
editor@southernlink.co.uk
www.nznewsuk.co.uk
Weekly. Editor: Ellie van Baren

The News
Jang Publications
020 7403 5833
thenewsse1@yahoo.com
www.jang.com.pk
Daily. English and Urdu.
Editor: Shahid Sadullah

Noticias Latin America
020 7686 1633
informacion@noticias.co.uk
www.noticias.co.uk
Monthly. Spanish. Editor: Alberto Rojas

Notun Din Bengali Newsweekly
Din Publishers
020 7247 6280
news@notundin.plus.com
Weekly. Bengali.
Editor: Mohib Chowdhury

Occasions Magazine
Ethnic Media Group
020 7650 2000
sheri@occasions.co.uk
www.occasions.co.uk
Quarterly. Asians worldwide.
Editor: Sheri Mill

Opportunity
020 7005 2250
Quarterly. 16–25, all ethnic minority
backgrounds. Magazine manager:
Brian Keith

Pakistan Post
Hussain Media
020 8558 9127
editor@thepakistanpost.net
www.thepakistanpost.net
Weekly. Urdu and English. Editor in Urdu:
Faizan Arif; editor in English: Murtaza
Ali Shah

Parikiaki
info@parikia.com
www.parikia.com/greek/parikiaki.html
Weekly. Cypriots in UK

Pride Magazine
020 72283110
info@pridemagazine.com
www.pridemagazine.com
Monthly. Black African, black Caribbean,
mixed race. Publisher: Carl Cushnie;
editor: Sherry Dixon

Punjabi Guardian
0121 5543995
punjabiguardian@hotmail.com
Fortnightly. Punjabi and English.
Editor: Indarjit Singh

Punjab Mail International
020 8522 0901
Monthly. Punjabi and English.
Editor: Gurdip Singh Sandhu

Punjab Times International
PTI Derby Media
01332 372851
panjabtimes@aol.com
Weekly. Punjabi and English. Punjabi
community in UK. Editor: Ms Purewal

Red Hot Curry
01707 269 666
www.redhotcurry.com
Website. South Asian, British Asian, and
East African Asian. Editor: Lopa Patel

Sayidaty
Saudi Research and Marketing UK
020 7831 8181
sayidaty@hhsaudi.com
www.sayidaty.net
Weekly. Arab issues.
Editor: Hani Nakshbandi

Sikh Courier International
The World Sikh Foundation
020 8864 9228
2pa. Sikhs. Editor: SS Kapoor

Sikh Messenger
020 8540 4148
sikhmessenger@aol.com
Quarterly. Editor: Indarjit Singh

Sikh Times
Archline Midland
0121 523 0115
info@thesikh-times.co.uk
www.thesikh-times.co.uk
Weekly. English, Punjabi.
Editor: Jas Pal Singh

SomethingJewish.co.uk
07976 220273
editor@somethingjewish.co.uk
www.somethingjewish.co.uk
Website. UK Jewish. Editor: Leslie Bunder

Spectrum
020 7439 9100
laura@arberrypink.co.uk
www.spectrummagazine.co.uk
Bi-annual. Careers and recruitment
for ethnic minority students.
Editor: Laura Sheed

Surma
020 7377 9787
info@surmanewsgroup.co.uk
www.surmanewsgroup.co.uk
Weekly. Bangla. Publisher: Sarz Ahmed;
editor: Mohammed Emadadul Choudhury

TNT Magazine
Trader Media Group
020 7373 3377
enquiries@tntmag.co.uk
www.tntmagazine.com
Weekly. International travellers.
Editor: Lyn Eyb

Travellers' Times
c/o The Rural Media Company
01432 344039
travellerstimes@ruralmedia.co.uk
www.travellerstimes.org.uk
Quarterly. Gypsies and Travellers.
Editor: Bill Laws

Ukrainian Thought
Association of Ukrainians in GB
020 7229 8392
administrator@augb.co.uk
www.augb.co.uk/ukrainian
_thought.htm
Weekly. Ukrainian.
Administrator: Mrs Anna Mikulin

Ultra Journey
Japan Journals
020 7255 3838
info@japanjournals.com
www.japanjournals.com
Monthly. Japanese. Editor: Ko Tejima

The Voice
020 7737 7377
www.voice-online.co.uk
Weekly. For black community in Britain.
Deputy editor: Vic Moutne

Weekly Journey
Japan Journals
020 7255 3838
lina@japanjournals.com
www.japanjournals.com
Weekly. Japanese in Britain.
Editor: K Tejima

● Disability

Big Print
0800 124007
bigprint@rnib.org.uk
www.big-print.co.uk
Weekly. Large print news.
Editor: Trevor Buckley

Breathing Space
The British Lung Foundation
020 7688 5555
enquiries@blf-uk.org
www.lunguk.org/
Quarterly. Lung disease.
Editor: Humphrey Couchman

Communication
The National Autistic Society
020 7833 2299
publications@nas.org.uk
www.nas.org.uk
3pa. Autism. Editor: Miranda Kemp

Devon Link
Devon County Council
   and Torbay Council
01392 382332
joanne.white@devon.gov.uk
www.devon.gov.uk/devonlink
Quarterly. People with physical and sensory disabilities, and carers.
Editor: Sarah Wilson

Disability Now
Scope
020 7619 7323
editor@disabilitynow.org.uk
www.disabilitynow.org.uk
Monthly. Acting editor: Sarah Hobson

Disabled and Supportive Carer
Euromedia Associates
01254 390066
editorial@euromedia-al.com
6pa. Editor: Richard Cheeseborough

DISH Update
DISH
01727 813815
info@dish.uk.net
www.dish.uk.net
Quarterly. Disability info for people in Hertfordshire. Editor: Jane Fookes

Epilepsy Today
Epilepsy Action
0113 2108800
smitchell@epilepsy.org.uk
www.epilepsy.org.uk
Quarterly. Editor: Sue Mitchell

FreeHand
Abucon
020 7834 1066
info@abucon.co.uk
www.abucon.co.uk
4pa. Elderly disabled in their own homes.
Editor: Liza Jones

Jigsaw
DISH
01727 813815
info@dish.uk.net
www.dish.uk.net
Quarterly. Disability info for young people. Editor: Jane Fookes

MS Matters
MS Society
020 8438 0700
info@mssociety.org.uk
www.mssociety.org.uk
6pa. Editor: Debbie Reeves

New Beacon
Royal National Institute of the Blind
020 7878 2307
beacon@rnib.org.uk
www.rnib.org.uk
11pa. For those with sight problems.
Editor: Ann Lee

New Pathways
The MS Resource Centre
01206 505444
info@msrc.co.uk
www.msrc.co.uk
6pa. MS issues. Editor: Judy Graham

Ouch!
020 8752 5444
ouch@bbc.co.uk
www.bbc.co.uk/ouch
Website. Editor: Damon Rose

One in Seven Magazine
The Royal National Institute for
   Deaf People
020 7296 8000
oneinseven@rnid.org.uk
www.rnid.org.uk
6pa. For the deaf. Editor: Dawn Diamond

The Parkinson Magazine
Parkinson's Disease Society of the UK
020 7931 8080
lhurst@parkinsons.org.uk
www.parkinsons.org.uk
Quarterly. Information manager:
Aislneg Kearney

Positive Nation
The UK Coalition of People Living
   with HIV and Aids (UKC)
020 7564 2121
editor@positivenation.co.uk
www.positivenation.co.uk
11pa. Issues for people with HIV Aids.
Editor: Amanda Elliott; news editor:
Martin Flynn

Soundaround
Soundaround Associations
020 8741 3332
nigel@soundaround.org
www.soundaround.org
Monthly. Visually impaired, worldwide.
Executive editor: Nigel Vee

Stroke News
The Stroke Association
020 7566 0300
www.stroke.org.uk
Quarterly. Editor: Maggie Warburton

Talk
The National Deaf Children's Society
020 7490 8656
ndcs@ndcs.org.uk
www.ndcs.org.uk
6pa. For deaf children. Editor: Jane Fookes

Talking Sense
Sense, National Deafblind and
Rubella Association
020 7272 7774
enquiries@sense.org.uk
www.sense.org.uk
3pa. Deafblind. Editor: Colin Anderson

Typetalk Update
Paver Downes Associates
0151 293 0505
smith@paverdownes.co.uk
www.typetalk.org
6pa. Down's syndrome.
Editor: Rachel Smith

Viewpoint
Mencap
020 7696 5599
viewpoint@mencap.org.uk
www.mencap.org.uk/viewpoint
6pa. Learning disabilities.
Editor: Faiza Fareed

Vitalise
(formerly Winged Fellowship Trust)
020 7017 3420
admin@vitalise.org.uk
www.vitalise.org.uk
2pa. Disabled people and their carers.
Editor: Alison Wadley

● Gay and lesbian

3sixty
City Pride Publications
01273 570570
info@3sixtymag.co.uk
www.3sixtymag.co.uk
Monthly. Editor: David Harvey

Attitude
Northern & Shell
020 7308 5090
adam.mattera@attitudemag.co.uk
www.attitude.co.uk
Monthly. Editor: Adam Mattera

AXM
Millivres-Prowler
020 7424 7400
m.miles@axm-mag.com
www.axm-mag.com
Monthly. Editor: Matthew Miles

Bent
All Points North Publications
020 7837 2660
editor@bent.com
www.bent.com
11-12pa. Editor: Jenny Parkin

Boyz
020 7025 6120
gage@boyz.co.uk
www.boyz.co.uk
Weekly. Editor: Simon Gage

Diva
Millivres-Prowler
020 7424 7400
edit@divamag.co.uk
www.divamag.co.uk
Monthly. Editor: Jane Czyzselska

G3
G3 Magazine
020 7272 0093
info@g3magazine.co.uk
www.g3magazine.co.uk
Monthly. Editor: Sarah Garrett

Gay Times
Millivres-Prowler
020 7424 7400
joseph@gaytimes.co.uk
www.gaytimes.co.uk
Monthly. Editor: Joseph Galliano

Gay.com UK
020 7440 0660
stewart.who@planetoutinc.co.uk
www.uk.gay.com
Editor: Christine Townsend

Midlands Zone
What's On Magazine Group
01743 281777
info@zonemag.com
www.zonemag.com
Monthly. Editor: Martin Monahan

Outnorthwest
0161 235 8035
editor@outnorthwest.com
www.lgf.org.uk
*Monthly free, published by the Lesbian
and Gay Foundation. Editor: Grahame
Robertson*

Pink Paper
Millivres-Prowler
020 7424 7400
tris@pinkpaper.com
www.pinkpaper.com
Weekly. Editor: Tris Reid-Smith

Refresh
Wild Publishing
01322 225392
david@wildpublishing.com
www.refreshmag.co.uk
Monthly. Editor: David Tickner

Stonewall Newsletter
Stonewall
020 7881 9440
info@stonewall.org.uk
www.stonewall.org.uk
Quarterly. Editor: Jodie West

UKBlackOut.com
www.ukblackout.com
Website. For black lesbians and gays

● **Religion**

All The World
The Salvation Army
020 7332 0101
kevin_sims@salvationarmy.org
www.salvationarmy.org
Quarterly. Editor: Kevin Sims

Baptist Times
Baptist Times
01235 517670
editor@baptisttimes.co.uk
www.baptisttimes.co.uk
*Weekly. Church leaders.
Editor: Mark Woods*

Catholic Herald
020 7588 3101
editorial@catholicherald.co.uk
www.catholicherald.co.uk
Weekly. Acting Editor: Luke Coppen

Catholic Times
Gabriel Communications
0161 236 8856
kevin.flaherty@totalcatholic.com
www.totalcatholic.com
Weekly. Editor: Kevin Flaherty

Christianity and Renewal
Premier Media Group (PMG)
020 7316 1450
ccp@premier.org.uk
www.christianitymagazine.com
Monthly. Editor: John Buckeridge

Daily Bread
Scripture Union Publishing
01908 856000
nigelh@scriptureunion.org.uk
www.dailybread.org.uk
*Quarterly. Adult Bible readers.
Editor: Tricia Williams*

Home and Family
The Mothers' Union
020 7222 5533
homeandfamily@
   themothersunion.org
www.themothersunion.org
Quarterly. Editor: Jill Worth

Jewish Chronicle
020 7415 1500
editorial@thejc.com
www.thejc.com
Weekly and website. Editor: David Rowan

Jewish Telegraph
0141 621 4422
mail@jewishtelegraph.com
www.jewishtelegraph.com
Weekly. Editor: Paul Harris

Jewish.net
07976 220273
admin@jewish.net
www.jewish.net
Website

The Life
Scripture Union Publishing
01908 856000
media@scriptureunion.org.uk
Quarterly

Life and Work
Board of Communications
0131 225 5722
magazine@lifeandwork.org
www.lifeandwork.org
*Monthly. Church of Scotland.
Editor: Lynne McNeil*

The Muslim News
Visitcrest
020 8863 8586
editor@muslimnews.co.uk
www.muslimnews.co.uk
Monthly. Editor: A Versi

New Day
The Leprosy Mission
01733 370505
karendup@tlmew.org.uk
www.leprosy.org.uk
2pa. Editor: Karen Duplessis

Presbyterian Herald
Presbyterian Church in Ireland
028 9032 2284
herald@presbyterianireland.org
www.presbyterianrianireland.org
Monthly. Editor: Rev Arthur Clarke

Scottish Catholic Observer
0141 221 4956
info@scottishcatholicobserver.com
www.scottishcatholicobserver.com
Weekly. Editor: Harry Conroy

Sikh Courier International
World Sikh Foundation
020 8864 9228
bablibharara@hotmail.com
www.sikhfoundation.org
2pa. Editor: Sukhbir Singh

SomethingJewish.co.uk
07976 220273
editor@somethingjewish.co.uk
www.somethingjewish.co.uk
UK Jewish website. Editor: Leslie Bunder

Ummah.com
info@ummah.com
www.ummah.org.uk
Website. English. Islam

The Universe
Gabriel Communications
0161 236 8856
newsdesk@the-universe.net
www.totalcatholic.com
*Weekly. Roman Catholics and Ireland.
Editor: Joe Kelly*

War Cry
Salvation Army
020 7367 4900
warcry@salvationarmy.org.uk
www.salvationarmy.org.uk/warcry
*Weekly. Christian current affairs.
Editor: Major Nigel Bovey*

Journalism trade press

Best Sellers
020 7689 3357
sarah.longbottom@newtrade.co.uk
www.newtrade.co.uk
*2pa. Owner: Newtrade Publishing.
Consumer magazine data and ABC
results. Editor: Sarah Longbottom*

British Journalism Review
020 7324 8500
editor@bjr.org.uk
www.bjr.org.uk
*Quarterly. Owner: SAGE Publications.
Managing editor: Brian Bass; Editor:
Bill Hagerty*

CPU Quarterly
020 7583 7733
cpu@cpu.org.uk
www.cpu.org.uk
*Quarterly. Owner: Commonwealth
Press Union. In-house newspaper
of the Association of Commonwealth
Newspapers. Executive director: Lindsay
Ross; editorial contact: Rosie Vlasto;
press officer: Harry Wilson*

The Journal
020 7252 1187
memberservices@ioj.co.uk
www.ioj.co.uk
*Owner: The Chartered Institute of
Journalists. Quarterly. Editor: Andy Smith*

journalism.co.uk
Mousetrap Media
01273 384293
info@journalism.co.uk
www.journalism.co.uk
*Website. Editor/publisher: John Thompson;
news: Oliver Luft*

The Journalist
020 7278 7916
timg@nuj.org.uk
www.nuj.org.uk
10pa. Owner: National Union of
Journalists. Free to union members.
Editor: Tim Gopsill

Magazine Retailer
020 7689 3357
sarah.longbottom@newtrade.co.uk
www.newtrade.co.uk
2pa. Owner: Newtrade Publishing.
Information on magazine sales in all
sectors. Editor: Sarah Longbottom

Magazine World
020 7404 4169
info@fipp.com
www.fipp.com
Quarterly. Owner: FIPP. International
consumer and B2B publishing trends.
Editor: Christina Esposito

News from NewstrAid
01371 874198
oldben@newstraid.org.uk
www.newstraid.org.uk
Annual. Owner: Newstraid Benevolent
Society. Charity for the newspaper
industry. Editorial contact: Tansey Bolsom

Press Gazette
020 7936 6402
ianr@pressgazette.co.uk
www.pressgazette.co.uk
Weekly. Independent. Editor: Ian Reeves;
features editor: Julie Tomlyn

Ulrich's Periodical Directory
01342 310450
sales@bowker.co.uk
www.ulrichsweb.com
Annual; updated quarterly on CD,
monthly on website. Owner: Bowker.
Editor: Laurie Kaplan

Useful associations

Association of American
Correspondents in London
c/o Time Life International,
Brettenham House, Lancaster Place,
London WC2E 7TL
020 7499 4080
monique_jessen@peoplemag.com

Association of British Science
Writers
Wellcome Wolfson Building,
165 Queen's Gate, London SW7 5HE
0870 770 3361
absw@absw.org.uk
www.absw.org.uk

Association of Freelance Writers
Sevendale House, 7 Dale Street,
Manchester M1 1JB
0161 228 2362
fmn@writersbureau.com
www.writersbureau.com
/resources.htm

Audit Bureau of Circulations (ABC)
Saxon House, 211 High Street,
Berkhamsted, Hertfordshire HP4 1AD
01442 870800
marketing@abc.org.uk
www.abc.org.uk

Authors' Club
40 Dover Street, London W1S 4NP
020 7499 8581
circles@author.co.uk
www.author.co.uk

British Copyright Council
29–33 Berners Street,
London W1T 3AB
01986 788122
secretary@britishcopyright.org
www.britishcopyright.org

British Guild of Beer Writers
68B Elmwood Road,
London SE24 9NR
07973 465081
peterhaydon@onetel.net.uk
www.beerguild.com

British Guild of Travel Writers
51B Askew Crescent,
London W12 9DN
020 8749 1128
charlotte.c@virtualnecessities.com
www.bgtw.org

British Newspaper Library
The British Library,
Newspaper Library, Colindale Avenue,
London NW9 5HE
020 7412 7353
newspaper@bl.uk
www.bl.uk/catalogues
/newspapers.html

British Society of Magazine Editors
137 Hale Lane, Edgware,
Middlesex HA8 9QP
020 8906 4664
admin@bsme.com
www.bsme.com

Broadcasting Press Guild
Tiverton, The Ridge, Woking,
Surrey GU22 7EQ
01483 764895
torin.douglas@bbc.co.uk

Bureau of Freelance
Photographers
Focus House, 497 Green Lanes,
London N13 4RP
020 8882 3315
info@thebfp.com
www.thebfp.com

Campaign for Freedom of
Information
Suite 102, 16 Baldwins Gardens,
London EC1N 7RJ
020 7831 7477
admin@cfoi.demon.co.uk
www.cfoi.org.uk

Campaign for Press and
Broadcasting Freedom
2nd Floor, Vi and Garner Smith
House, 23 Orford Road,
Walthamstow, London E17 9NL
020 8521 5932
freepress@cpbf.org.uk
www.cpbf.org.uk

Chartered Institute of Journalists
2 Dock Offices, Surrey Quays Road,
London SE16 2XU
020 7252 1187
memberservices@ioj.co.uk
www.ioj.co.uk

Foreign Press Association in London
11 Carlton House Terrace,
London SW1Y 5AJ
020 7930 0445
reception@foreign-press.org.uk
www.foreign-press.org.uk

Garden Writers' Guild
c/o Institute of Horticulture,
14/15 Belgrave Square,
London SW1X 8PS
020 7245 6943
gwg@horticulture.org.uk
www.gardenwriters.co.uk

Guild of Agricultural Journalists
Charmwood, 47 Court Meadow,
Rotherfield, East Sussex TN6 3LQ
01892 853187
don.gomery@farmingline.com
www.gaj.org.uk

Guild of Food Writers
020 7610 1180
guild@gfw.co.uk
www.gfw.co.uk

Guild of Motoring Writers
39 Beswick Avenue,
Bournemouth BH10 4EY
01202 518808
chris@whizzco.freeserve.co.uk
www.guildofmotoringwriters.co.uk

International Newspaper
Marketing Association
10300 North Central Expressway,
Suite 467, Texas 75231 USA
00 1 214 373 9111
www.inma.org

MediaWise Trust
University of the West of England,
Canon Kitson, Oldbury Court Road,
Bristol BS16 2JP
0117 939 9333
info@mediawise.org.uk
www.mediawise.org.uk
Media ethics charity

Medical Writers' Group
The Society of Authors,
84 Drayton Gardens,
London SW10 9SB
020 7373 6642
info@societyofauthors.org
www.societyofauthors.org

National Union of Journalists
Acorn House, 308-312 Gray's Inn
Road, London WC1X 8DP
020 7278 7916
info@nuj.org.uk
www.nuj.org.uk

Newspaper Marketing Agency
Empire House, 175 Piccadilly,
London W1J 9EN
020 7887 6112
enquiries@nmauk.co.uk
www.nmauk.co.uk

Newspaper Society
Bloomsbury House, 74–77 Great
Russell Street, London WC1B 3DA
020 7636 7014
ns@newspapersoc.org.uk
www.newspapersoc.org.uk

Outdoor Writers' Guild
PO Box 520, Bamber Bridge,
Preston, Lancashire PR5 8LF
01772 321243
secretary@owg.org.uk
www.owg.org.uk

**Periodical Publishers Association
(PPA)**
Queens House, 28 Kingsway,
London WC2B 6JR
020 7404 4166
info1@ppa.co.uk
www.ppa.co.uk

Picture Research Association
c/o 1 Willow Court, off Willow Street,
London EC2A 4QB
chair@picture-research.org.uk
www.picture-research.org.uk

Press Complaints Commission
Halton House, 20/23 Holborn,
London EC1N 2JD
020 7831 0022
complaints@pcc.org.uk
www.pcc.org.uk

**Scottish Newspaper Publishers
Association**
48 Palmerston Place,
Edinburgh EH12 5DE
0131 220 4353
info@snpa.org.uk
www.snpa.org.uk

**Scottish Print Employers
Federation and Scottish Daily
Newspaper Society**
48 Palmerston Place,
Edinburgh EH12 5DE
0131 220 4353
info@spef.org.uk
www.spef.org.uk

Society of Editors
University Centre, Granta Place,
Mill Lane, Cambridge CB2 1RU
01223 304080
info@societyofeditors.org
www.societyofeditors.org

**Society of Women Writers and
Journalists**
swwriters@aol.com
www.swwj.co.uk

**Sports Journalists' Association
of Great Britain**
c/o Start2Finish Event Management,
Unit 92, Capital Business Centre,
22 Carlton Road, Surrey CR2 0BS
020 8916 2234
petta.naylor@sportengland.org
www.sportsjournalists.co.uk

Picture library contacts

British Association of Picture Libraries and Agencies
18 Vine Hill, London EC1R 5DZ
020 7713 1780
enquiries@bapla.org.uk
www.bapla.org

Picture Research Association
c/o 1 Willow Court, Off Willow Street, London EC2A 4QB
020 7739 8544
chair@picture-research.org.uk
www.picture-research.org.uk
Fine arts collection for museums throughout the world

4Corners Images*
12 Larden Road, London W3 7ST
020 8811 1010
info@4cornersimages.com
www.4cornersimages.com

A1PIX*
40 Bowling Green Lane, Finsbury Business Centre, London EC1R ONE
020 7415 7045
london@a1pix.com
www.a1pix.com
Travel, business, lifestyle, children, nature, animals and illustrations. Hi-res download facility, personal search service

AA World Travel Library*
13th Floor, Fanum House,
Basing View, Basingstoke RG21 4EA
01256 491588
travel.images@theaa.com

ACESTOCK.COM*
Satellite House, 2 Salisbury Road,
Wimbledon, London SW19 4FZ
020 8944 9944
library@acestock.com
www.acestock.com

Action Images*
Image House, Station Road,
London N17 9LR
020 8885 3000
info@actionimages.com
www.actionimages.com

Action Library*
Bretton Court, Bretton,
Peterborough PE3 8DZ
0870 062 8287
nicholas.schaffer@emap.com
www.actionlibrary.com

Action Plus Sports Images*
54/58 Tanner Street, London SE1 3PH
020 7403 1558
osha@actionplus.co.uk
www.actionplus.co.uk

Adam (Amnesty Digital Asset Management)*
Audio Visual Resources,
Amnesty International, International Secretariat, 1 Easton Street,
London WC1X ODW
020 7413 5893
audiovis@amnesty.org

Adams Picture Library*
Unit 1 Canalot Production Studios,
222 Kensal Road, London W10 5BN
020 8964 8007
mail@adamspicturelibrary.com
www.adamspicturelibrary.com

Advertising Archives*
45 Lyndale Avenue, London NW2 2QB
020 7435 6540
library@advertisingarchives.co.uk
www.advertisingarchives.co.uk
British and American press ads, magazine illustration

Aerofilms Photo Library*
32-34 Station Close, Potters Bar,
Hertfordshire, EN6 1TL
01707 648390
library@aerofilms.com
www.simmonsaerofilms.com

africanpictures.net*
Leighton Street No. 17,
Pietermaritzburg, KwaZulu-Natal,
South Africa 3201
00 27 33 345 9445
pictures@africanpictures.net
www.africanpictures.net

Agripicture Images*
1 Bowdens Lane, Shillingford,
Tiverton, Devon EX16 9DG
01398 331598
info@agripicture.com
www.agripicture.com

akg-images*
5 Melbray Mews, 158 Hurlingham Road, London SW6 3NS
020 7610 6103
enquiries@akg-images.co.uk
www.akg-images.co.uk

Alamy Images*
Central 127 Milton Park, Abingdon,
Oxfordshire OX14 4SA
01235 844600
sales@alamy.com
www.alamy.com

Alinari Archives*
Largo Fratelli Alinari 15,
50123 Firenze, Italy 50123
00 39 055 239 5239
fototeca@alinari.it
www.alinariarchives.it

All Action Digital*
Pavilion House, 16 Castle Boulevard,
Nottingham NG7 1FL
0115 844 7447
info@empics.com
www.empics.com

AllStar & Sportsphoto*
20 Clifton Street,
Scarborough YO12 7SR
01723 367264
library@allstarpl.com
www.allstarpl.com
Worldwide sports, politics, travel

Alpine Club Photo Library*
55 Charlotte Road, London EC2A 3QF
020 7033 0203
photos@alpine-club.org.uk
www.alpine-club.org.uk

Alvey & Towers
The Springboard Centre, Mantle Lane,
Coalville, Leicestershire LE67 3DW
01530 450011
office@alveyandtowers.com
www.alveyandtowers.com
Transport

Ancient Art & Architecture Collection Library*
Suite 1, 410-420 Rayners Lane,
Pinner, Middlesex HA5 5DY
020 8429 3131
library@aaacollection.co.uk
www.aaacollection.com

Andes Press Agency*
26 Padbury Court, London E2 7EH
020 7613 5417
apa@andespressagency.com
www.andespressagency.com
Travel and social documentary worldwide, Latin America, UK, Middle East

Andreas von Einsiedel Archive*
72-80 Leather Lane,
London EC1N 7TR
020 7242 7674
federica@einsiedel.com
www.einsiedel.com

Andrew N Gagg's Photo Flora*
Town House Two, Fordbank Court,
Henwick Road, Worcester WR2 5PF
01905 748515
andrew.n.gagg@ntlworld.com
homepage.ntlworld.com/a.n.gagg
  /photo/photoflora.html

Angelo Hornak Library*
17 Alwyne Villas, London N1 2HG
020 7354 1790
angelohornak@mac.com
www.angelohornak.co.uk

Animal Photography*
4 Marylebone Mews, New Cavendish Street, London W1G 8PY
020 7935 0503
stephen@animal-photography.co.uk
www.animal-photography.co.uk

Ann & Bury Peerless Picture Library*
22 Kings Avenue, Minnis Bay,
Birchington On Sea, Kent CT7 9QL
01843 841428
ann@peerlessmail.com;
picturelibrary@peerlessmail.com
www.peerlessimages.com

Anthony Blake Photo Library*
20 Blades Court, Deodar Road,
Putney, London SW15 2NU
020 8877 1123
info@abpl.co.uk
www.abpl.co.uk

Antiquarian Images*
PO Box 20, Chislehurst, Kent BR7 5SZ
020 8467 6297
enquiries@antiquarianimages.co.uk
www.antiquarianimages.com

Aquarius Library*
PO Box 5, Hastings,
East Sussex TN34 1HR
01424 721196
aquarius.lib@clara.net
www.aquariuscollection.com

Arcaid Picture Library*
Parc House, 25–37 Cowleaze Road,
Kingston upon Thames,
Surrey KT2 6DZ
020 8546 4352
arcaid@arcaid.co.uk
www.arcaid.co.uk

Arcangel Images
46 Chestnut Avenue, Buckhurst Hill,
Essex IG9 6EW
020 8559 1545
sales@arcangel-images.com
www.arcangel-images.com

arcblue.com*
93 Gainsborough Road,
Richmond TW9 2ET
020 8940 2227
info@arcblue.com
www.arcblue.com

Architectural Association Photo Library*
36 Bedford Square, London WC1B 3ES
020 7887 4066
valerie@aaschool.ac.uk
www.aaschool.ac.uk/photolib

Ardea*
35 Brodrick Road, London SW17 7DX
020 8672 2067
ardea@ardea.com
www.ardea.com
Wildlife, pets, environment

ArenaPAL*
Lambert House, 55 Southwark
Street, London SE1 1RU
020 7403 8542
searches@arenapal.com
www.arenapal.com

Arkreligion.com*
57 Burdon Lane, Cheam,
Surrey SM2 7BY
020 8642 3593
images@artdirectors.co.uk
www.arkreligion.com
www.artdirectors.co.uk

Aroomwithviews*
Bluff House, Stoulgrove Lane,
Woodcroft, Chepstow NP16 7QE
01594 529111
aroomwithviews@
    molyneuxassociates.com
www.aroomwithviews.com

Art Archive, The*
2 The Quadrant, 135 Salusbury Road,
London NW6 6RJ
020 7624 3500
info@picture-desk.com
www.picture-desk.com

Art Directors and Trip Photo Library*
57 Burdon Lane, Cheam,
Surrey SM2 7BY
020 8642 3593
images@artdirectors.co.uk
www.artdirectors.co.uk
Worldwide countries and religion

artimagedirect.com*
29 High Street, Stalham,
Norwich NR12 9AH
01692 580205
enquiries@artimagedirect.com
www.artimagedirect.com

ARWP*
Studio 444, 80 High Street,
Winchester SO23 9AT
01264 731238
sales@andyrouse.co.uk
www.andyrouse.co.uk

Aspect Picture Library*
40 Rostrevor Road, London SW6 5AD
020 7736 1998
aspect.Ldn@btinternet.com
www.aspect-picture-library.co.uk

Associated Press Images*
Associated Press House, 12 Norwich
Street, London EC4A 1BP
020 7427 4333
london_photolibrary@ap.org
www.apimages.com

Atmosphere Picture Library*
Willis Vean, Mullion, Helston,
Cornwall TR12 7DF
01326 240180
pix@atmosphere.co.uk
www.atmosphere.co.uk

Auto Express Picture Library*
Dennis Publishing, 30 Cleveland
Street, London W1T 4JD
020 7907 6132
pictures@dennis.co.uk
www.autoexpressimages.co.uk

Aviation Picture Library*
30 Wyndham Road, West Ealing,
London W13 9TE
07860 670073; 020 8566 7712
avpix@aol.com
www.aviationpictures.com
Aviation, aerial, architecture and travel

Aviation-Images.com*
42 Queens Road, Wimbledon,
London SW19 8LR
020 8944 5225
pictures@aviation-images.com
www.aviation-images.com
Aviation and aerial photography

Axel Poignant Archive*
115 Bedford Court Mansions,
Bedford Avenue, London WC1B 3AG
020 7636 2555
rpoignant@aol.com
Anthropology, ethnography

Axiom Photographic Agency*
The Saga Building, 326 Kensal Road,
London W10 5BZ
020 8964 9970
jen@axiomphoto.co.uk;
jennifer.dove@axiomphoto.co.uk
www.axiomphoto.co.uk

BAA Aviation Photo Library*
Green Dragon Vaults, Parliament
Square, Hertford SG14 1PT
01992 501134
sales@in-press.co.uk
www.baa.com/photolibrary

BananaStock
The Stables, West Barn, Brightwell,
Baldwin, Oxfordshire OX49 5NP
01491 613800
team@bananastock.com
www.bananastock.com

Barnardos'*
Tanners Lane, Bakingside, Ilford,
Essex IG6 1QG
020 8498 7345
stephen.pover@barnardos.org.uk
www.barnardos.org.uk

BBC Photo Library*
B116 BBC Television Centre,
Wood Lane, London W12 7RJ
020 8225 7193
Research-Central@bbc.co.uk
www.bbcresearchcentral.com

BDI Images*
56 Five Ash Down, Uckfield,
East Sussex TN22 3AL
01825 733095/732006
info@bdi-images.com
www.bdi-images.com

Beachfeature.com*
41 Trebarwith Crescent, Newquay,
Cornwall TR7 1DX
01637 870430
info@beachfeature.com
www.beachfeature.com

Beken of Cowes*
16 Birmingham Road, Cowes,
Isle of Wight PO31 7BH
01983 297311
beken@beken.co.uk
www.beken.co.uk

The Best of Morocco
38 Market Place, Chippenham,
Wiltshire SN15 3HT
01380 828533
steve@realmorocco.com
www.realmorocco.com

BFI Stills, Posters and Designs*
21 Stephen Street, London W1T 1LN
020 7957 4797
stills.films@bfi.org.uk
www.bfi.org.uk

* Member of BAPLA, the British Association of Picture Libraries and Agencies

Big Pictures*
50-54 Clerkenwell Road,
London EC1M 5PS
020 7250 3555
alan.williams@bigpictures.co.uk
www.bigpicturesphoto.com

Birmingham Central Library*
Chamberlain Square,
Birmingham B3 3HQ
0121 303 4439
pete.james@birmingham.gov.uk
www.birmingham.gov.uk

**Birmingham Museums & Art
Gallery Picture Library***
Chamberlain Square,
Birmingham B3 3DH
0121 303 3155
picture_library@birmingham.gov.uk
www.bmag.org.uk

Birmingham Picture Library*
14 St. Bernard's Road, Olton,
Solihull B92 7BB
0121 765 4114
office@bplphoto.co.uk
www.bplphoto.co.uk

Bluegreen Pictures*
11 Bath Road, Cowes,
Isle of Wight PO31 7QN
01983 282233
info@bluegreenpictures.com
www.bluegreenpictures.com

BM Totterdell Photography*
Constable Cottage, Burlings Lane,
Knockholt, Sevenoaks TN14 7PE
01959 532001
btrial@btopenworld.com

Bridgeman Art Library*
17-19 Garway Road, London W2 4PH
020 7727 4065
admin@bridgeman.co.uk
www.bridgeman.co.uk

Britain on View*
Thames Tower, Black's Road,
Hammersmith, London W6 9EL
020 8563 3120
bovsales@visitbritain.org
www.britainonview.com

British Antarctic Survey*
High Cross, Madingley Road,
Cambridge CB3 0ET
01223 221412
pictures@bas.ac.uk
www.antarctic.ac.uk
www.photo.antarctic.ac.uk

**British Geological Survey –
National Archive of Geological
Photographs (NAGP)***
Murchison House, West Mains Road,
Edinburgh EH9 3LA
0131 650 0335
nagp@bgs.ac.uk
www.bgs.ac.uk

British Library Imaging Services*
96 Euston Road, London NW1 2DB
020 7412 7614
imagesonline@bl.uk
www.bl.uk/imagesonline
Images, maps, historical and engravings

**British Motor Industry
Heritage Trust***
Heritage Motor Centre, Banbury
Road, Gaydon, Warwick CV35 0BJ
01926 645 073
photo@bmiht.com
www.heritage-motor-centre.co.uk

**British Museum Photography
and Imaging***
The British Museum Company,
38 Russell Square, London WC1B 3QQ
020 7079 0944
customerservices@bmimages.com
www.bmimages.com

**Bryan and Cherry Alexander
Photography***
Higher Cottage, Manston,
Sturminster Newton, Dorset DT10 1EZ
01258 473006
alexander@arcticphoto.co.uk
www.arcticphoto.com
Arctic and Antarctic specialists

Bubbles Photolibrary*
3 Rose Lane, Ipswich IP1 1XE
01473 288605
info@bubblesphotolibrary.co.uk
www.bubblesphotolibrary.co.uk

Built Vision*
49 Lucknow Drive,
Nottingham NG3 5EU
0115 962 1112
office@builtvision.co.uk
www.builtvision.co.uk

Burall Floraprint*
Oldfield Lane, Wisbech,
Cambridgeshire PE13 2TH
0870 728 7222
zbrown@burall.com

Buzz Pictures*
14 Shanklin Road, London N8 8TJ
020 8374 2596
office@buzzpictures.co.uk
www.buzzpictures.co.uk

Cadenza Archive*
81 Clifton Road, Wokingham,
Berkshire RG41 1NJ
01189 791404
peter@cadenza-archive.co.uk
www.cadenza-archive.co.uk

Camera Press*
21 Queen Elizabeth Street,
London SE1 2PD
020 7378 1300
sales@camerapress.com
www.camerapress.com
Worldwide photographic library

Capital Pictures*
85 Randolph Avenue, London W9 1DL
020 7286 2212
sales@capitalpictures.com
www.capitalpictures.com

CartoonStock*
Unit 2, Lansdown Mews, Bath BA1 5DY
01225 789600
admin@cartoonstock.com
www.cartoonstock.com

Celebrity Pictures*
98 De Beauvoir Road, London N1 4EN
020 7275 2700
steve@celebritypictures.co.uk
www.celebritypictures.co.uk

Cephas Picture Library*
A1 Kingsway Business Park, Oldfield
Road, Hampton, Middlesex TW12 2HD
020 8979 8647
pictures@cephas.com
www.cephas.com
*Wine and vineyards, whisky and brandy,
food and drink*

Chatsworth Photo Library*
Chatsworth, Bakewell,
Derbyshire DE45 1PP
01246 565300
photolibrary@chatsworth.org
www.chatsworth.org

Chris Bonington Picture Library*
Badger Hill, Hesket Newmarket,
Wigton, Cumbria CA7 8LA
01697 478286
frances@bonington.com
www.bonington.com

**Chris Howes/Wild Places
Photography**
PO Box 100, Abergavenny NP7 9WY
01873 737707
photos@wildplaces.co.uk
*Travel, topography and natural history,
plus action sports and caving*

Christian Aid Photo Section*
PO Box 100, London SE1 7RT
020 7523 2235
jcabon@christian-aid.org

Christian Him's Jazz Index*
26 Fosse Way, London W13 0BZ
020 8998 1232
christianhim@jazzindex.co.uk
www.jazzindex.co.uk

Christie's Images*
1 Langley Lane, Vauxhall,
London SW8 1TJ
020 7582 1282
imageslondon@christies.com
www.christiesimages.com
Fine and decorative art

**Christopher Hill
Photographic Library***
17 Clarence Street, Belfast BT2 8DY
028 9024 5038
sales@scenicireland.com
www.scenicireland.com

CIRCA Photo Library*
Joanne Robinson, 39 Beech Grove,
Sale, Cheshire M33 6RT
0161 9692 483
joanner@arcworld.org

Collections*
13 Woodberry Crescent,
London N10 1PJ
020 8883 0083
collections@btinternet.com
www.collectionspicturelibrary.co.uk
*Britain and Ireland: people and
traditional culture*

Construction Photography*
3 Morocco Street, London SE1 3HB
020 7403 8866
Lucy@constructionphotography.com
www.constructionphotography.com

Corbis*
111 Salusbury Road, London NW6 6RG
0800 731 9995
info@corbis.com
www.corbis.com

Cornish Picture Library*
Trelawney Lodge, Keveral Lane,
Seaton, Cornwall PL11 3JJ
01503 250673
info@imageclick.co.uk
www.imageclick.co.uk

Cornwall, Norways in
Parc Webban, Gulval Churchtown,
Penzance, Cornwall TR18 3BB
01736 365056
graeme@norways.co.uk
www.norways.co.uk

Country Life Picture Library*
King's Reach Tower, Stamford Street,
London SE1 9LS
020 7261 6337
camilla_costello@ipcmedia.com
www.clpicturelibrary.co.uk
*Architecture, country pursuits, gardens,
crafts, black and white pictures*

**Countryside Agency Photographic
Library***
John Dower House, Crescent Place,
Cheltenham, Gloucestershire GL50 3RA
01242 521381

**Courtauld Institute of Art
Image Libraries***
Somerset House, Strand,
London WC2R 0RN
020 7848 2879
galleryimages@courtauld.ac.uk
www.courtauld.ac.uk and
www.artandarchitecture.org.uk

Crafts Council Picture Library*
44a Pentonville Road, Islington,
London N1 9BY
020 7806 2503
photostore@craftscouncil.org.uk
www.craftscouncil.org.uk/photostore

Crash Picture Agency*
No1 Innovation Centre,
Silverstone Circuit, Silverstone,
Northamptonshire NN12 8GX
0870 350 5044
photos@crash.net
www.crashpa.net

Create Online*
The Mansion, Bletchley Park,
Milton Keynes MK3 6EB
0845 658 2470
enquiries@createonline.net
www.createonline.net

Creative Image Library*
Brook Cottage, Hale Oak Road,
Weald, Sevenoaks TN14 6NQ
01892 723388
sales@creativeimagelibrary.com
www.creativeimagelibrary.com

The Culture Archive*
193 Ditchling Road, Brighton BN1 6JB
01273 552929
culture@pavilion.co.uk
www.fulltable.com/index.htm

Cumbria Photo
Ashleigh, Holly Road, Windermere,
Cumbria LA23 2AQ
0845 658 2470
bbarden@gocumbria.org
www.cumbriaphoto.co.uk

**Dance Picture Library and Circus
Images***
4 Ongar Place, Addlestone,
Surrey KT15 1JF
07956 319362
linda-rich@dancepicturelibrary.com
www.dancepicturelibrary.com

David Hoffman Photo Library*
c/o Bapla office, 18 Vine Hill,
London EC1R 5DZ
020 8981 5041
lib@hoffmanphotos.com
www.hoffmanphotos.com
*Social issues, built from journalistic work
since the 1970s*

David King Collection*
90 St Pauls Road, London N1 2QP
020 7226 0149
postmaster@davidkingcollection.com
www.davidkingcollection.com
*Soviet Union and other images of the
Communist movements*

David Noble Photography*
Longleigh, 28 Coolinge Lane,
Folkestone, Kent CT20 3QT
01303 254263
djn@noblepics.co.uk
www.noblepics.co.uk

David Tipling Photo Library*
9 Eccles Road, Holt,
Norfolk NR25 6HJ
07973 181375
dt@windrushphotos.demon.co.uk
www.davidtipling.com

David Williams Picture Library*
50 Burlington Avenue,
Glasgow G12 0LH
0141 339 7823
david@scotland-guide.co.uk

**Dee Conway Ballet & Dance
Picture Library***
110 Sussex Way, London N7 6RR
020 7272 7845
www.ddance.co.uk

The Defence Picture Library
14 Mary Seacole Road, The Millfields,
Plymouth, Devon PL1 3JY
01752 312061
pix@defencepictures.com
www.defencepictures.com

Diomedia*
4, 34–35 Grand Parade,
London N4 1AQ
020 7193 1389
info@diomedia.com
www.diomedia.com

DIY Photolibrary
The Covert, Pickhurst Rise,
West Wickham, Kent BR4 0AA
020 8777 5025
info@diyphotolibrary.com
www.diyphotolibrary.com

DK Images*
80 Strand, London WC2 0RL
020 7010 4500
enquiries@dkimages.com
www.dkimages.com

DN – Images*
Cambridge Lodge, Gate Lane,
Freshwater Bay,
Isle of Wight PO40 9QD
01983 759918
info@dn-images.com
www.dn-images.com

Dominic Photography*
4b Moore Park Road, London SW6 2JT
020 7381 0007
office@catherineashmore.co.uk

dopeshots.com*
27 Orchard Park, Holmer Green,
Buckinghamshire HP15 6QX
01494 717 118
info@dopeshots.com
www.dopeshots.com

Double Red Photographic*
The Old School, Thorn Lane, Goxhill,
Barrow upon Humber DN19 7JE
01469 531416
s.ward@doublered.co.uk
pix@doublered.co.uk
www.doublered.co.uk
Motorsport photography

E&E Picture Library*
Beggars Roost, Woolpack Hill,
Brabourne Lees, Ashford,
Kent TN25 6RR
01303 812608
isobel@
   picture-library.freeserve.co.uk
www.heritage-images.com
World religion, heritage and architecture

Ecoscene*
Empire Farm, Throop Road,
Templecombe BA8 0HR
01963 371700
pictures@ecoscene.com
www.ecoscene.com

Edifice*
Cutterne Mill, Southwood,
Evercreech, Somerset BA4 6LY
01749 831400
info@edificephoto.com
www.edificephoto.com
*Buildings, architecture and exteriors
of all kinds*

Education Photos*
April Cottage, Warners Lane, Albury
Heath, Guildford GU5 9DE
01483 203846
johnwalmsley@educationphotos.co.uk
www.educationphotos.co.uk
Education, work, homes, signs

* Member of BAPLA, the British Association of Picture Libraries and Agencies

Elizabeth Whiting & Associates*
70 Mornington Street,
London NW1 7QE
020 7388 2828
ewa@elizabethwhiting.com
www.elizabethwhiting.com

EMPICS*
Pavilion House, 16 Castle Boulevard,
Nottingham NG7 1FL
0115 844 7447
info@empics.com
www.empics.com

EMRIC Images*
64 Union Street, Barnet,
London EN5 4HZ
020 8364 9506
emric-images@virgin.net
www.emric-images.com

English Heritage Photo Library*
NMRC, Kemble Drive,
Swindon SN2 2GZ
01793 414903
photo.library@
   english-heritage.org.uk
www.english-heritage.org.uk

**English Heritage, National
Monuments Record***
English Heritage, Kemble Drive,
Swindon SN2 2GZ
01793 414600
nmrinfo@english-heritage.org.uk
www.english-heritage.org.uk

**Environmental Investigation
Agency***
62–63 Upper Street, London N1 0NY
020 7354 7968
tomthistlethwaite@
   eia-international.org
www.eia-international.org

ePicscotland.com*
Unit 5 Hathaway Business Centre,
21/29 Hathaway Street,
Glasgow G20 8TD
0141 945 0000
info@epicscotland.com
www.epicscotland.com

**Eric Hepworth Golf Course
Picture Library***
72 Apley Road, Hyde Park,
Doncaster DN1 2AY
01302 322674
eric@hepworthgolfphotography.com
www.hepworthgolfphotography.com

Esler Crawford Photography
37a Lisburn Road, Belfast BT9 7AA
028 9032 6999
esler.crawford@btclick.com
www.eslercrawford.com

Eureka*
2 Astley Avenue, London NW2 WAD
020 8452 1006
chris@bobelsdale.com
www.alamy.com/stock-photography
   /0F959F0F-006F-4714-983B-6B
6DE5B5DF0E/Eureka.htm

Everynight Images*
Top Floor Studio, 127 Strathleven
Road, Brixton, London SW2 5JS
020 7738 7297
info@everynight.co.uk
www.everynight.co.uk

EWA Stock
70 Mornington Street,
London NW1 7QE
020 7388 2828
info@ewastock.com
www.ewastock.com

Exile Images*
1 Mill Row, Weston Hill Road,
Brighton BN1 3SU
01273 208741
pics@exileimages.co.uk
www.exileimages.co.uk
*Refugees, protest, asylum seekers, conflict.
Middle East, Balkans, south-east Asia*

Eye Ubiquitous/Hutchison*
65 Brighton Road, Shoreham-by-sea,
West Sussex BN43 6RE
01273 440113
library@eyeubiquitous.com
www.eyeubiquitous.com

eyevine*
3 Mills Film Studios, Three Mill Lane,
London E3 3DU
020 8709 8709
info@eyevine.com
www.eyevine.com

Fairfaxphotos.com
201 Sussex Street,
Sydney 2000, Australia
00 61 2 9282 2429
fairfaxphotos@fairfax.com.au
www.fairfaxphotos.com

Famous*
13 Harwood Road, London SW6 4QP
020 7731 9333
info@famous.uk.com
www.famous.uk.com

ffotograff
10 Kyveilog Street, Cardiff CF11 9JA
029 2023 6879
ffotograff@easynet.co.uk
www.ffotograff.com
*Travel, exploration, arts, architecture,
culture, Wales, Middle East, Far East*

FilmMagic*
Suite 501, 77 Oxford Street,
London W1D 2ES
020 7399 1823
billy.robertson@filmmagic.com
www.filmmagic.com

Financial Times Pictures
1 Southwark Bridge, London SE1 9HL
020 7873 3000
photosynd@ft.com
www.ft.com

Fine Art Photographic Library*
2a Milner Street, London SW3 2PU
020 7589 3127
info@fineartphotolibrary.com
www.fineartphotolibrary.com

Firepix International
68 Arkles Lane, Anfield,
Liverpool L4 2SP
0151 260 0111
info@firepix.com
www.firepix.com

The Flight Collection*
Quadrant House, The Quadrant,
Sutton SM2 5AS
020 8652 8888
qpl@rbi.co.uk
www.theflightcollection.com

Flowerphotos*
71 Leonard Street, London EC2A 4QU
020 7684 5668
sales@flowerphotos.com
www.flowerphotos.com

FLPA – Images of Nature*
Pages Green House, Wetheringsett,
Stowmarket IP14 5QA
01728 860789
pictures@flpa-images.co.uk
www.flpa-images.co.uk

Fogden Wildlife Photographs*
16 Locheport, North Uist,
Western Isles HS6 5EU
01876 580245
susan.fogden@virgin.net
www.fogdenphotos.com

Food Features*
Stream House, West Flexford Lane,
Wanborough, Guildford GU3 2JW
01483 810840
frontdesk@foodpix.co.uk
www.foodpix.co.uk

foodanddrinkphotos*
Studio 4, Sun Studios,
30 Warple Way, London W3 0RX
020 8740 6610
info@foodanddrinkphotos.com
www.foodanddrinkphotos.com

**Forest Commission Life
Picture Library**
231 Corstorphie Road,
Edinburgh EH12 7AT
0131 314 6411
neil.campbell@forestry.gsi.gov.uk
www.forestry.gov.uk

Fortean Picture Library
Henblas, Mwrog Street,
Ruthin LL15 1LG
01824 707278
janet.bord@forteanpix.demon.co.uk
www.forteanpix.demon.co.uk

Fotografique
43a Gunter Grove, Chelsea,
London SW10 0UN
020 7376 5843
duncan@fotografique.com
www.fotografique.com

fotoLibra*
22 Mount View Road, London N4 4HX
020 8348 1234
professionals@fotolibra.com
www.fotolibra.com

Fotomas Index UK
12 Pickhurst Rise,
West Wickham BR4 0AL
020 8776 2772

Framed Picture Library*
18 Vine Hill, London EC1R 5DZ
020 7713 1780

Francis Frith Collection, The*
Frith's Barn, Teffont,
Salisbury SP3 5QP
01722 716376
sales@francisfrith.co.uk
www.francisfrith.co.uk

Frank Lane Picture Agency
Pages Green House, Pages Green,
Wetheringsett, Suffolk IP14 5QA
01728 860789
pictures@flpa-images.co.uk
www.flpa-images.co.uk
*Natural history, environment, pets,
weather*

FremantleMedia Stills Library, The*
Unit 5, Teddington Business Park,
Station Road, Teddington,
Middlesex TW11 9BQ
020 8977 2134
stills.library@fremantlemedia.com
www.fremantlemediastills.com

Galaxy Picture Library*
34 Fennels Way, Flackwell Heath,
High Wycombe HP10 9BY
01628 521338
robin@galaxypix.com
www.galaxypix.com
Astronomy and the sky

GAP Photos Ltd
95 Holloway Road, Heybridge,
Maldon, Essex CM9 4SW
01621 858379
info@gapphotos.com
www.gapphotos.com

**Garden and Wildlife Matters
Photo Library***
Marlham, Watermill Lane, Henley's
Down, Battle, East Sussex TN33 9BN
01424 830566
gardens@gmpix.com
www.gardenmatters.uk.com

The Garden Collection*
6 Dorset Road, Harrow,
Middlesex HA1 4JG
020 8863 8298
info@garden-collection.com
www.garden-collection.com

Garden Exposures Photo Library*
316 Kew Road, Kew Gardens,
Richmond, Surrey TW9 3DU
020 8287 0600
pictures@gardenexposures.co.uk
www.gardenexposures.com

Garden Photo Library*
239a Hook Road, Chessington,
Surrey KT9 1EQ
020 8397 3761
derek@gardenphotolibrary.com
www.gardenphotolibrary.com

Garden Picture Library*
Unit 12, Ransome's Dock,
35 Parkgate Road, London SW11 4NP
020 7228 4332
sales@gardenpicture.com
www.gardenpicture.com
Gardening

Garden World Images*
Grange Studio, Woodham Road,
Battlesbridge, Wickford,
Essex SS11 7QU
01245 325725
info@gardenworldimages.com
www.gardenworldimages.com

Geo Aerial Photography*
4 Christian Fields, London SW16 3JZ
0115 981 9418
geo.aerial@geo-group.co.uk
www.geo-group.co.uk

Geoff Wilkinson Image Library*
The Old Stables,
rear of 84 Nightingale Lane,
Wanstead, London E11 2EZ
020 8530 4612
mjw@gwimlib.com
www.gwimlib.com

GeoScience Features Picture Library*
6 Orchard Drive, Wye, Kent TN25 5AU
01233 812707
gsf@geoscience.demon.co.uk
www.geoscience.demon.co.uk

Geoslides Photography*
4 Christian Fields, London SW16 3JZ
0115 981 9418
geoslides@geo-group.co.uk
www.geo-group.co.uk
Landscape and human interest

Getty Images*
101 Bayham Street, London NW1 0AG
0800 376 7977
sales@gettyimages.co.uk
www.gettyimages.co.uk
Live feed photo agency

Glasgow Museums Photo Library*
The Burrell Collection, Pollok
Country Park, 2060 Pollokshaws
Road, Glasgow G43 1AT
0141 287 2595
photolibrary@cls.glasgow.gov.uk
www.glasgowmuseums.com

Golf Picture Library*
7 Bourne Road, Berkhamstead,
Hartfordshire HP4 3JU
01442 863434
requests@golfpicturelibrary.com
www.golfpicturelibrary.com

Great Stock Photo Library*
PO Box 87622, Houghton,
Johannesburg, South Africa 2041
00 27 11 880 7826
enquiries@greatstock.co.za
www.greatstock.co.za

Greenpeace Images*
Canonbury Villas, London N1 2PN
020 7865 8294
pix@uk.greenpeace.org
www.greenpeace.org.uk

Greenpeace International Images*
Photo Library, Otto Heldringstraat 5,
Amsterdam 1066 AZ
00 31 20 718 2116
julieanne.wilce@int.greenpeace.org
www.greenpeace.org

Guzelian*
5 Victoria Road, Saltaire, Bradford,
Yorkshire BD18 3LA
01274 532300
pictures@guzelian.co.uk
www.guzelian.co.uk

Hali Archive*
Hali Publications Ltd, St Giles House,
50 Poland Street, London W1F 7AX
020 7970 4600
hali@centaur.co.uk
www.hali.com

Harpur Garden Library*
44 Roxwell Road, Chelmsford,
Essex CM1 2NB
01245 257527
info@harpurgardenlibrary.com
www.harpurgardenlibrary.co.uk

Heather Angel/Natural Visions*
6 Vicarage Hill, Farnham,
Surrey GU9 8HG
01252 716700
hangel@naturalvisions.co.uk
www.naturalvisions.co.uk
*Online images of worldwide wildlife
and plants*

Heritage Image Partnership*
18–20 St John Street, Islington,
London EC1M 4NX
020 7251 5091
info@heritage-images.com
www.heritage-images.com

Heseltine Archive*
Mill Studios, Frogmarsh Mills,
South Woodchester,
Gloucestershire GL5 5ET
01453 873792
john@heseltine.co.uk
www.heseltine.co.uk

Historic Royal Palaces*
Apartment 25, Hampton Court
Palace, East Molesey, Surrey KT8 9AU
020 8781 9775
annie.heron@hrp.org.uk
www.hrp.org.uk

**Historic Scotland
Photographic Library***
Historic Scotland, Longmore House,
Salisbury Place, Edinburgh EH9 1SH
0131 668 8647
hs.images@scotland.gsi.gov.uk
www.historic-scotland.gov.uk

**History of Advertising Trust
Archive (HAT)***
HAT House, 12 Raveningham Centre,
Raveningham, Norwich NR14 6NU
01508 548623
enquiries@hatads.org.uk
www.hatads.org.uk

Historystore
29 Churton Street, London SW1V 2LY
020 7976 6040
claire@historystore.ltd.uk
www.historystore.ltd.uk

* Member of BAPLA, the British Association of Picture Libraries and Agencies

Hobbs Golf Collection*
5 Winston Way, New Ridley,
Stocksfield, Northumberland NE43 7RF
01661 842933
info@hobbsgolfcollection.com
www.hobbsgolfcollection.com

Holt Studios
Pages Green House, Wetheringsett,
Stowmarket IP14 5QA
01728 860789
jean@flpa-images.co.uk
www.holt-studios.co.uk
*World agriculture and horticulture,
wildlife, pests and diseases*

Houghton's Horses*
Radlet Cottage, Spaxton,
Bridgwater, Somerset TA5 1DE
01278 671362
kit@enterprise.net
www.houghtonshorses.com

Hungry Eye Images*
Ground Floor, 25 Phipp Street,
London EC2A 4NP
020 7033 0022
info@hungryeye.co.uk
www.hungryeyeimages.com

Hutchison Picture Library
65 Brighton Road, Shoreham on sea,
West Sussex BN43 6RE
01273 440113
library@hutchisonpictures.co.uk
www.hutchisonpictures.co.uk
Worldwide contemporary images

ICCE Photolibrary*
Burcott House, Wing,
Leighton Buzzard LU7 0JU
01296 688245
jacolyn@iccephotolibrary.co.uk
www.iccephotolibrary.co.uk

Idarta Travel Images*
522 The Greenhouse, Custard
Factory, Birmingham B9 4AA
sales@idartatravelimages.com
www.idartatravelimages.com

Idols Licensing and Publicity*
593-599 Fulham Road,
London SW6 5UA
020 7385 5121
info@idols.co.uk
www.idols.co.uk

**Illustrated London News
Picture Library***
20 Upper Ground, London SE1 9PF
020 7805 5585
research@ilnpictures.co.uk
www.ilnpictures.co.uk

Image Option*
73 Jarrow Road, Chadwell Heath,
Essex RM6 5RL
01708 732336
info@imageoption.co.uk
www.imageoption.co.uk

Image Quest Marine*
The Moos, Poffley End, Witney,
Oxfordshire OX29 9UW
01993 704050
info@imagequestmarine.com
www.imagequestmarine.com

Image Solutions*
P.O Box 62429, UAE
00 971 4 340 4092
info@gulfimages.com
www.gulfimages.com

Image Source*
41 Great Pulteney Street,
London W1F 9NZ
020 7851 5700
info@imagesource.com
www.imagesource.com

image100
4th Floor, 79 New Cavendish Street,
London W1W 6XB
020 7612 1550
info@image100.com
www.image100.com

Images of Africa Photobank*
11 The Windings, Lichfield,
Staffordshire WS13 7EX
01543 262898
info@imagesofafrica.co.uk
www.imagesofafrica.co.uk
130,000 images of 20 African countries

Images of Empire*
British Empire & Commonwealth
Museum, Temple Meads,
Bristol BS1 6QH
0117 929 3851
jo.hopkins@empiremuseum.co.uk

Imagestate
Ramillies House, 1-2 Ramillies Street,
London W1F 7LN
020 7734 7344
sales@imagestate.co.uk
www.imagestate.com

Impact Photos*
18-20 St John Street,
London EC1M 4NX
020 7251 5091
library@impactphotos.com
www.impactphotos.com

Imperial Images.com*
Porta Leacach House, Kildonan,
Isle of Arran KA27 8SD
01770 820644
inquiries@imperialimages.com
www.imperialimages.com

Imperial War Museum*
Photograph Archive, All Saints Annexe,
Austral Street, London SE11 4SL
020 7416 5333
photos@iwm.org.uk
www.iwm.org.uk

Infoterra
Atlas House, 41 Wembley Road,
Leicester LE3 1UT
0116 273 2314
info@infoterra-global.com
www.infoterra-global.com

Inmagine Limited*
Suite 319, Waterloo Business Centre,
117 Waterloo Road, London SE1 8UL
0808 222 8888
info.uk@inmagine.com
www.inmagine.com

Inpho Sports Photography*
15A Lower Baggot Street, Dublin 2
00 353 1 7088 084
norman@inpho.ie
www.inpho.ie

Institution of Mechanical Engineers*
1 Birdcage Walk, London SW1H 9JJ
020 7304 6836
m_claxton@imeche.org.uk
www.imeche.org.uk

Interior Archive*
1 Ruston Mews, London W11 1RB
020 7221 9922
karen@
    interior-archive.netkonect.co.uk
www.interiorarchive.com

International Photobank
Unit D1, Roman Hill Business Park,
Broadmayne, Dorset BT2 8LY
01305 854145
peter@internationalphotobank.co.uk
www.internationalphotobank.co.uk
400,000 travel images

Irish Image Collection*
Ballydowane East, Bunmahon,
Kilmacthomas, Co Waterford
00 353 51 292020
george@theirishimagecollection.ie
www.theirishimagecollection.ie

Irish Picture Library*
69b Heather Road, Sandyford
Industrial Estate, Dublin 18
00 353 1 2950 799
info@fatherbrowne.com
www.fatherbrowne.com/ipl

islide*
51 Church Hill, Ironbridge,
Shropshire TF8 7QB
05600 439229
ross@islide.co.uk
www.islide.co.uk

Jacqui Hurst
66 Richford Street, London W6 7HP
020 8743 2315
jacquih@dircon.co.uk
www.jacquihurstphotography.co.uk
*Designers and applied artists, regional
food producers and markets*

**Jaguar Daimler
Photographic Library***
B/1/002, Browns Lane, Allesley,
Coventry CV5 9DR
024 7620 2743
kram4@jaguar.com
www.jdht.com

James Davis Worldwide
65 Brighton Road, Shoreham on sea,
West Sussex BN43 6RE
01273 452252
library@eyeubiquitous.com
www.eyeubiquitous.com
Travel collection

Janine Wiedel Photo Library*
8 South Croxted Road,
London SE21 8BB
020 8761 1502
wiedelphoto@compuserve.com
www.wiedel-photo-library.com

---

* Member of BAPLA, the British Association of Picture Libraries and Agencies

Jellypics Limited*
25 Kellerton Road, London SE13 5RB
020 8852 0352
info@jellypics.com
www.jellypics.com

Jessica Strang*
504 Brody House, Strype Street,
London E1 7LQ
020 7247 8982
jessica@jessicastrang.plus.com
Architecture, interiors and gardens

JGA
7 Holborn View, Woodhouse,
Leeds LS6 2RD
0113 295 0446
sales@canalstock.co.uk
www.canalstock.co.uk

Jim Henderson Photography*
Crooktree, Kincardine O'Neil,
Aboyne, Aberdeenshire AB34 4JD
01339 882149
JHende7868@aol.com
www.jimhendersonphotography.com
*Aberdeenshire, aurora borealis, ancient
Egypt*

**John Birdsall Social Issues
Photo Library***
89 Zulu Road, New Basford,
Nottingham NG7 7DR
0115 978 2645
photos@johnbirdsall.co.uk
www.johnbirdsall.co.uk

**John Cleare/Mountain Camera
Picture Library***
Hill Cottage, Fonthill Gifford,
Salisbury SP3 6QW
01747 820320
cleare@btinternet.com
www.mountaincamera.com
*Landscapes of the UK and worldwide
- mountains and trekking*

John Heseltine Archive
Mill Studio, Frogmarsh Mills, South
Woodchester, Gloucester GL5 5ET
01453 873792
john@heseltine.co.uk
www.heseltine.co.uk
*Landscapes, architecture, food and
travel: Italy and UK*

John Warburton-Lee Photography*
The Grange, Walcot, Sleaford,
Lincolnshire NG34 0ST
01529 497223
info@johnwarburtonlee.com
www.johnwarburtonlee.com

Jon Arnold Images*
7 Rydes Avenue, Guildford GU2 9SR
01483 451245
info@jonarnoldimages.com
www.jonarnold.com

Jupiterimages*
5 Finch Drive, Springwood Industrial
Estate, Braintree, Essex CM7 2SF
0800 056 7533
sales@jupiterimages.co.uk
www.jupiterimages.co.uk

Just-London.com*
Unit K, Suite 3, Kemp Road,
Chadwell Heath, Essex RM8 1SL
020 8598 9317
info@just-london.com
www.just-london.com

Katz
109 Clifton Street, London EC2A 4LD
020 7749 6012
info@katzpictures.com
www.katzpictures.com

The Kennel Club*
1-5 Clarges Street, London WIJ 8AB
020 7749 6000
picturelibrary@
  the-kennel-club.org.uk
www.the-kennel-club.org.uk

Kevin Allen Photography*
The Malthouse, Low Road, Tasburgh,
Norfolk NR15 1AR
01508 470030
kevin_allen@mac.com
www.kevinallenphotography.co.uk

Kobal Collection*
2 The Quadrant, 135 Salusbury Road,
London NW6 6RJ
020 7518 1035
info@picture-desk.com
www.picture-desk.com

Kos Picture Source*
7 Spice Court, Ivory Square,
Plantation Wharf, London SW11 3UE
020 7801 0044
images@kospictures.com
www.kospictures.com
Water-based images

LAT Photographic*
Somerset House, Somerset Road,
Teddington, Middlesex TW11 9BE
020 8251 3000
zoe.mayho@haynet.com
www.latphoto.co.uk

Latent Light*
P.O Box 1426, Mangotsfield,
Bristol BS16 9ZJ
0870 043 5536
enquiries@latentlight.com
www.latentlight.com

**Lebrecht Music and Arts
Photo Library***
58b Carlton Hill, London NW8 0ES
020 7625 5341
pictures@lebrecht.co.uk
www.lebrecht.co.uk

Lee Miller Archives*
Farley Farmhouse, Muddles Green,
Chiddingly, East Sussex BN8 6HW
01825 872691
archives@leemiller.co.uk
www.leemiller.co.uk

Lephoto.com*
Studio 71, Chesterfield Avenue,
Gedling, Nottingham NG4 4GE
07788 101144
contact@lephoto.com
www.lephoto.com

Leonard Smith Collection*
Greenacre, Brantham Hill, Brantham,
Manningtree, Essex CO11 1TB
01206 393321
library@leonardsmith.co.uk
www.leonardsmith.co.uk

Lesley & Roy Adkins*
10 Acre Wood, Whitestone,
Exeter EX4 2HW
01392 811357
mail@adkinsarchaeology.com
www.adkinsarchaeology.com
Archaeology and heritage

Lickerish*
36 Eastcastle Street,
London W1W 8DP
020 7323 1999
robert@lickerish.biz
www.lickerish.biz

**Lindley Library, Royal Horticultural
Society***
80 Vincent Square, London SW1P 2PE
020 7821 3051
picturelibrary@rhs.org.uk
www.rhs.org.uk

Link Picture Library*
41A The Downs, London SW20 8HG
020 8944 6933
library@linkpicturelibrary.com
www.linkphotographers.com

London Aerial Photo Library*
Studio D1, Fairoaks Airport,
Chobham, Surrey GU24 8HU
01276 855997
info@londonaerial.co.uk
www.londonaerial.co.uk
*Aerial imagery (oblique and vertical)
covering most of the UK*

Londonstills.com*
5 Keswick Road, Putney,
London SW15 2HL
020 8874 4905
info@londonstills.com
www.londonstills.com

Lonely Planet Images*
72-82 Rosebery Avenue,
Clerkenwell, London EC1R 4RW
020 7841 9062
lpi@lonelyplanet.co.uk
www.lonelyplanetimages.com

Loop Images*
The Studio, 61 Park Road, Woking,
Surrey GU22 7BZ
01483 830120
paul@loopimages.com
www.loopimages.com

Loupe Images*
20-21 Jockey's Fields,
London WC1R 4BW
020 7025 2249
info@loupeimages.com
www.loupeimages.com

**MacQuitty International
Photographic Collection***
7 Elm Lodge, River Gardens,
Stevenage Road, London SW6 6NZ
020 7385 5606
miranda.macquitty@btinternet.com

* Member of BAPLA, the British Association of Picture Libraries and Agencies

Magnum Photos*
Ground Floor, 63 Gee Street,
London EC1V 3RS
020 7490 1771
magnum@magnumphotos.co.uk
www.magnumphotos.com

**Manchester Art Gallery
Picture Library***
Mosley Street, Manchester M2 3JL
0161 235 8863
t.walker@manchester.gov.uk
www.manchestergalleries.org

**Mander and Mitchenson Theatre
Collection***
Jerwood Library of the Performing
Arts, Trinity College of Music,
King Charles Court, Old Royal Naval
College, London SE10 9JF
020 8305 4426
rmangan@tcm.ac.uk
www.mander-and-mitchenson.co.uk

Marianne Majerus Photography*
1 Mason's Place, off Moreland Street,
London EC1V 8DU
020 7253 5551
mm@mariannemajerus.com
www.mariannemajerus.com

Marsden Archive, The*
The Presbytery, Hainton, Market
Rasen, Lincolnshire LN8 6LR
01507 313646
info@marsdenarchive.com
www.marsdenarchive.com

Marx Memorial Library Pictures*
37a Clerkenwell Green,
London EC1R 0DU
020 7253 1485
marx.library@britishlibrary.net
www.marxlibrary.net

Mary Evans Picture Library*
59 Tranquil Vale, Blackheath,
London SE3 0BS
020 8318 0034
pictures@maryevans.com
www.maryevans.com
Historical images

Masterfile UK Limited*
90 Long Acre, London WC2E 9RZ
0870 351 7928
sales.london@masterfile.com
www.masterfile.com

Massive Pixels
07956 505186
info@massivepixels.com
www.massivepixels.com

mattonimages.co.uk*
2 Western Avenue Business Park,
Mansfield Road, London W3 0BZ
020 8753 7000
info@mattonimages.co.uk
www.mattonimages.co.uk

M-Dash
11 Sandringham Drive, Bramcote,
Nottingham NG9 3EA
0115 925 8802
info@m-dash.com
www.m-dash.com

Mediablitz Images (UK) Ltd*
11 Beaumont Road, Canford Cliffs,
Poole, Dorset BH13 7JJ
01202 701584
enquiries@mediablitzimages.com
www.mediablitzimages.com

Mediscan*
2nd Floor, Patman House,
23–27 Electric Parade, George Lane,
London E18 2LS
020 8530 7589
info@mediscan.co.uk
www.mediscan.co.uk

Merseyside Photo Library*
Suite 6 , Egerton House, Tower
Road, Birkenhead, Wirral CH41 1FN
0151 666 2289
ron@rja-mpl.com
www.merseysidephotolibrary.com

Michael Cole Camerawork*
The Coach House, 27 The Avenue,
Beckenham, Kent BR3 5DP
020 8658 6120
mikecole@dircon.co.uk
www.tennisphotos.com

Mike Watson Images*
52 Lime Street, London EC3M 7NL
020 7469 6946
Sarah.McNab@mikewatsonimages.com
www.mikewatsonimages.co.uk

**The Military Picture Library
International***
PO BOX 3350, Shepton Mallet,
Somerset BA4 4WX
01749 850560
info@mpli.co.uk
www.militarypicturelibrary.com

**Millbrook House Picture Library
(Railphotos)***
Unit 1, Oldbury Business Centre,
Pound Road, Oldbury,
West Midlands B68 8NA
0121 544 2970

Millennium Images*
48 Belsize Square, London NW3 4HN
020 7794 9194
mail@milim.com
www.milim.com

Mirrorpix*
21 Bruton Street, Mayfair,
London W1J 6QD
020 7293 3700
desk@mirrorpix.com
www.mirrorpix.com

Monitor Picture Library*
The Forge, Roydon, Harlow,
Essex CM19 5HH
01279 792700
sales@monitorpicturelibrary.com
www.monitorpicturelibrary.com
UK and international personalities

Mooney Photo*
25 Armitage Bridge Mills, Armitage
Bridge, Huddersfield HD4 7NR
01484 663698
keely@mooney-photo.co.uk
www.mooney-photo.co.uk

Mother & Baby Picture Library*
Emap Esprit, Greater London House,
Hampstead Road, London NW1 7EJ
020 7347 1867
mother.baby.pl@emap.com
www.motherandbaby
picturelibrary.com

Motoring Picture Library*
National Motor Museum, Beaulieu,
Brockenhurst, Hampshire SO42 7ZN
01590 614656
motoring.pictures@beaulieu.co.uk
www.motoringpicturelibrary.com

Moviestore Collection*
2nd Floor, Chartwell House, 61–65
Paulet Road, London SE5 9HW
020 7733 9990
sales@moviestorecollection.com
www.moviestorecollection.com

Museum of Antiquities*
The University, Newcastle NE1 7RU
0191 222 7846
l.allason-jones@ncl.ac.uk
www.museums.ncl.ac.uk

Museum of English Rural Life*
The University of Reading,
Redlands Road, Reading RG1 5EX
0118 378 8660
merl@reading.ac.uk
www.merl.org.uk

**Museum of London
Picture Library***
London Wall, London EC2Y 5HN
020 7814 5604/12
picturelib@museumoflondon.org.uk
www.museumoflondon.org.uk

nagelestock.com*
Parkgate, West Approach Drive,
Cheltenham GL52 3AD
01242 242952
look@nagelestock.com
www.nagelestock.com

Narratives (Interiors Food Travel)*
11 Gibraltar Walk, London E2 7LH
020 7366 6658
pictures@narratives.co.uk
www.narratives.co.uk

**National Archives Image Library
(Public Record Office)***
Ruskin Avenue, Kew,
Richmond TW9 4DU
020 8392 5225
image-library@
nationalarchives.gov.uk
www.nationalarchives.gov.uk
British and colonial history

National Army Museum*
Royal Hospital Road, Chelsea,
London SW3 4HT
020 7730 0717
photo@national-army-museum.ac.uk
www.national-army-museum.ac.uk

National Galleries of Scotland*
Picture Library, The Dean Gallery,
73 Belford Road, Edinburgh EH4 3DS
0131 624 6258
picture.library@nationalgalleries.org
www.nationalgalleries.org

---

* Member of BAPLA, the British Association of Picture Libraries and Agencies

National Gallery of Ireland Picture Library*
Merrion Square West, Dublin 2
00 353 1 6633 526/7
mmcfeely@ngi.ie
www.nationalgallery.ie

National Gallery Picture Library*
St Vincent House, 30 Orange Street,
London WC2H 7HH
020 7747 5994
picture.library@nationalgallery.co.uk
www.nationalgallery.co.uk/library

National Maritime Museum*
Picture Library, National Maritime
Museum, Greenwich,
London SE10 9NF
020 8312 6645
picturelibrary@nmm.ac.uk
www.nmm.ac.uk/picturelibrary

National Museums Liverpool*
127 Dale Street, Liverpool L2 2JH
0151 478 4657
photography@
liverpoolmuseums.org.uk
www.liverpoolmuseums.org.uk

National Museums of Scotland Picture Library*
Chambers Street, Edinburgh EH1 1JF
0131 247 4236
h.osmani@nms.ac.uk
www.nms.ac.uk

National Portrait Gallery Picture Library*
St Martin's Place, London WC2H 0HE
020 7312 2475
picturelibrary@npg.org.uk
www.npg.org.uk/picturelibrary
Portraits

The National Trust for Scotland*
28 Charlotte Square,
Edinburgh EH2 4ET
0131 243 9315
irobertson@nts.org.uk
www.nts.org.uk

National Trust Photo Library*
Heelis, Kemble Drive,
Swindon SN2 2NA
020 7447 6788
photo.library@nationaltrust.org.uk
www.nationaltrust.org.uk/photolibrary

Natural History Museum Picture Library*
Cromwell Road, South Kensington,
London SW7 5BD
020 7942 5401
nhmpl@nhm.ac.uk
www.nhm.ac.uk/piclib

Natural Science Photos*
PO Box 397, Welwyn Garden City,
Hertfordshire AL8 6LG
01707 690561
natasha@naturalsciencephotos.com
www.naturalsciencephotos.com

Nature Photographers
West Wit, New Road Little London,
Tadley, Hampshire RG26 5EU
01256 850661
paul@naturephotographers.co.uk
www.naturephotographers.co.uk
Worldwide natural history

Nature Picture Library*
BBC Broadcasting House,
Whiteladies Road, Bristol BS8 2LR
0117 974 6720
info@naturepl.com
www.naturepl.com
Wildlife

Neil Williams Classical Collection
22 Avon Hockley, Tamworth,
Staffordshire B77 5QA
01827 286086
neil@classicalcollection.co.uk
Classical music

Neill Bruce's Automobile Photo Library*
Grange Cottage, Harts Lane,
Burghclere, Newbury RG20 9JN
01635 278342
neillb@brucephoto.co.uk
www.brucephoto.co.uk

Network Photographers
127 Milton Park, Abingdon,
Oxfordshire OX14 4SA
01235 844600
sales@alamy.com
www.alamy.com

News Team International*
35 Gas Street, Birmingham B1 2JT
0121 246 5120
syndication@newsteam.co.uk
www.newsteam.co.uk

NewsCast*
The Coach House, 4 Cannon Hill,
London N14 7HG
020 8886 5895
contact@newscast.co.uk;
photo@newscast.co.uk
www.newscast.co.uk

NewsCom*
700 12th Street NW, Suite 1000,
Washington DC 20005, USA
001 202 383 6070
support@newscom.com
www.newscom.com

Newspix*
2 Holt Street, Level 2, Sydney
NSW 2010, Australia
0612 9288 2829
newspix@newsltd.com.au
www.newspix.com.au

Newsquest (Herald & Times)*
200 Renfield Street,
Glasgow G2 3QB
0141 302 7364
rights@glasgow.newsquest.co.uk
www.thepicturedesk.co.uk

NHPA Ltd/Photoshot Holdings
29–31 Saffron Hill, London EC1N 8SW
020 7421 6003
nhpa@nhpa.co.uk
www.nhpa.co.uk
Natural history

NI Syndication*
1 Virginia Street, London E98 1SY
020 7711 7888
enquiries@nisyndication.com
www.nisyndication.com

Novosti Photo Library*
3 Rosary Gardens, London SW7 4NW
020 7370 1873
photos@novosti.co.uk
http://en.rian.ru

Nunn Syndication*
PO Box 56303, London SE1 2TD
020 7357 9000
production@nunn-syndication.com
www.nunn-syndication.com

Oceans-Image Pictures*
2nd Floor, 83–84 George Street,
Richmond TW9 1HE
020 8332 8422
matthew@oceans-image.com
www.oceans-image.com

Offside Sports Photography*
271–273 City Road, London EC1V 1LA
020 7253 3344
mail@welloffside.com
www.welloffside.com

OnAsia*
30 Cecil Street, Prudential Tower,
Level 15, Singapore 049712
00 66 2655 4680
info@onasia.com
www.onasia.com

Organics Image Library*
The Studios, 27 Hogarth Road,
Brighton & Hove BN3 5RH
01273 701557
info@organicsimagelibrary.com
www.organicsimagelibrary.com

The Original Double Red Photographic*
The Old School, Thorn Lane, Goxhill,
North Lincolnshire DN19 7JE
01469 531416
doublered@atlas.co.uk
www.doublered.co.uk

Oxford Picture Library*
15 Curtis Yard, North Hinksey Lane,
Oxford OX2 0LX
01865 723404
opl@cap-ox.com
www.cap-ox.com

Oxford Scientific (OSF)*
Ground Floor, Network House,
Station Yard, Thame,
Oxfordshire OX9 3UH
01844 262370
enquiries@osf.co.uk
www.osf.co.uk

Panos Pictures*
1 Honduras Street, London EC1Y 0TH
020 7253 1424
pics@panos.co.uk
www.panos.co.uk
Documentary library specialising in developing world

Papilio*
155 Station Road, Herne Bay,
Kent CT6 5QA
01227 360996
library@papiliophotos.com
www.papiliophotos.com
Natural history subjects worldwide

* Member of BAPLA, the British Association of Picture Libraries and Agencies

Patrick Eagar Photography*
1 Queensberry Place, Richmond,
Surrey TW9 1NW
020 8940 9269
patrick@patrickeagar.com
www.patrickeagar.com

PBPA – Paul Beard Photo Agency
PBPA House, 33 Sanctuary Close,
St John's, Worcester WR2 5PY
0845 644 7975
Paul@pbpa.co.uk
www.pbpa.co.uk

Peter Dazeley Photography
The Studios, 5 Heathman's Road,
Parsons Green, London SW6 4TJ
020 7736 3171
studio@peterdazeley.com

Peter Sanders Photography
24 Meades Lane, Chesham,
Buckinghamshire HP5 1ND
01494 773674
photos@petersanders.com
www.petersanders.com

PGI-Images*
64 Union Street, High Barnet EN5 4HZ
020 8364 9506
emric-images@virgin.net

Phil Sheldon Golf Picture Library*
Southcroft, 40 Manor Road,
Barnet EN5 2JQ
020 8440 1986
info@philsheldongolfpics.co.uk;
Gill@philsheldongolfpics.co.uk
www.philsheldongolfpics.co.uk
More than 500,000 images of golf

Photega*
Telford Way, Waterwells Business
Park, Quedgeley, Gloucester GL2 2AB
01452 541220
images@photega.com
www.photega.com

Photofusion Picture Library*
17a Electric Lane, Brixton,
London SW9 8LA
020 7733 3500
library@photofusion.org
www.photofusionpictures.org
*Contemporary social and environmental
issues*

Photogold
40 Dunvegan Place, Polmont,
Falkirk FK2 0NX
01324 720038
sales@photogold.co.uk
www.castlepictures.com
Scotland

Photolibrary Wales*
2 Bro-Nant, Church Road, Pentyrch,
Cardiff CF15 9QG
029 2089 0311
info@photolibrarywales.com
www.photolibrarywales.com

photolibrary.com*
4th Floor, 83-84 Long Acre,
Covent Garden, London WC2E 9NG
020 7836 5591
uksales@photolibrary.com
www.photolibrary.com

**Photomax Specialist Aquarium
Picture Library***
118-122 Magdalen Road,
Oxford OX4 1RQ
01865 372981
info@photomax.org.uk
www.photomax.org.uk

Photos 12*
20, Rue Lalande, Paris 75014
00 33 1 5680 1440
meurin@photo12.com
www.photo12.com

Photos Horticultural*
PO Box 105, Ipswich IP1 4PR
01473 257329
library@photos-horticultural.com
www.photos-horticultural.com

Photoshot*
29-31 Saffron Hill, London EC1N 8SW
020 7421 6000
charles@uppa.co.uk
www.photoshot.com

Photostage*
8 Drakes Mews, Crownhill Industry,
Milton Keynes MK8 0ER
01908 262324
info@photostage.co.uk
www.photostage.co.uk

Pictoreal*
The Westall Centre, Hoberrow Green,
Redditch, Worcestershire B96 6JY
01386 793555
peter.smith@pictoreal.com
www.pictoreal.com

Picture Business*
PO Box 6275, Wareham BH20 9AG
020 7731 6076
picturebusiness@easynet.co.uk
www.picturebusiness.co.uk

The Picture Library*
16 Crescent Road, London N22 7RS
020 8365 8389
joanne@thepicturelibraryltd.net
www.alandavidson.net

PictureBank Photo Library*
Parman House, 30-36 Fife Road,
Kingston Upon Thames KT1 1SY
020 8547 2344
info@picturebank.co.uk
www.picturebank.co.uk

Pictures Colour Library*
10 James Whatman Court, Turkey Mill,
Ashford Road, Maidstone ME14 5SS
01622 609809
enquiries@picturescolourlibrary.co.uk
www.picturescolourlibrary.co.uk

Pictures of Britain*
Alma House, 73 Rodney Road,
Cheltenham GL50 1HT
01242 537923
info@picturesofbritain.co.uk
www.picturesofbritain.co.uk

picturesofmanchester.com
13 Alan Road, Withington,
Manchester M20 4NQ
0161 448 2034
info@picturesofmanchester.com
www.picturesofmanchester.com

Poker Images*
1 Barb Mews, London W6 7PA
020 7605 8018
sales@pokerimages.com
www.pokerimages.com

Popstar Ltd
Central Warehouse, North London
Freight Terminal, York Way,
London N1 0UZ
020 7833 1066
www.popstarpictures.co.uk
Glamour and celebrity pictures

PPL Photo Agency*
Booker's Yard, The Street,
Walberton, near Arundel,
Sussex BN18 0PF
01243 555561
ppl@mistral.co.uk
www.pplmedia.com
*Watersports, sub-aqua, business, travel,
Sussex scenes and historical images*

Practical Pictures*
Hermes House, 88-89 Blackfriars
Road, London SE18HA
020 7775 4407
piclibrary@anness.com
www.practicalpictures.com

Premaphotos Wildlife*
Amberstone, 1 Kirland Road,
Bodmin, Cornwall PL30 5JQ
01208 78258
enquiries@premaphotos.com
www.premaphotos.com
Natural history worldwide

Print Fair Ltd*
Glaisdale Drive East,
Nottingham NG8 4JJ
0115 929 3419
davidhyams@print-fair.com
www.print-fair.com

Professional Sport UK *
18-19 Shaftesbury Quay,
Hertford SG14 1SF
01992 505000
pictures@prosport.co.uk
www.professionalsport.com

Proper Gander Imaging*
94 Leonard Street, London EC2A 4RH
020 7729 6789
info@proper-gander.co.uk
www.proper-gander.com

Pulse Picture Library*
CMP Information Ltd, Ludgate
House, 245 Blackfriars Road,
London SE1 9UY
020 7921 8099
mcollard@cmpinformation.com
www.cmpimages.com

Punch Cartoon Library*
87-135 Brompton Road,
Knightsbridge, London SW1X 7XL
020 7225 6710
punch.library@harrods.com
www.punch.co.uk

PunchStock*
Sherwood House, Forest Road,
Kew, Surrey TW9 3BY
0800 073 0760
service@punchstock.co.uk
www.punchstock.co.uk

---

* Member of BAPLA, the British Association of Picture Libraries and Agencies

PYMCA*
St John's Building, 2nd Floor, 43
Clerkenwell Road, London EC1M 5RS
020 7251 8338
info@pymca.com
www.pymca.com

QA Photos*
Webster House, Jesmond Street,
Folkestone, Kent CT19 5QW
01303 894141
pix@qaphotos.com
www.qaphotos.com

Rail Images*
5 Sandhurst Crescent, Leigh-on-Sea,
Essex SS9 4AL
01702 525059
info@railimages.co.uk
www.railimages.co.uk

Railways – Milepost 92 ½*
Milepost 92 ½, Newton Harcourt,
Leicestershire LE8 9FH
0116 259 2068
contacts@milepost92-half.co.uk
www.railphotolibrary.com

Raleigh International
Raleigh House, 27 Parsons Green
Lane, London SW6 4HZ
020 7371 8585
www.raleighinternational.org

**Raymond Mander & Joe Mitchenson
Theatre Collection**
Jerwood Library of Performing Arts,
Trinity College of Music, King
Charles Court, Old Royal Naval
College, London SE10 9JF
020 8305 4426
rmangan@tcm.ac.uk
www.mander-and-mitchenson.co.uk

Red Cover*
Unit 7, Aura House, 53 Oldridge Road,
London SW12 8PP
020 8772 1110
info@redcover.com
www.redcover.com

Redferns Music Picture Library*
7 Bramley Road, London W10 6SZ
020 7792 9914
info@redferns.com
www.redferns.com

Repfoto London*
74 Creffield Road, Acton,
London W3 9PS
020 8992 2936
repfoto@btinternet.com
www.repfoto.com

Report Digital*
4 Clarence Road,
Stratford upon Avon CU37 9DL
01789 262151
info@reportdigital.co.uk
www.reportdigital.co.uk
*Work issues and occupations, leisure,
economy, health, education, politics,
social issues, protest, trades union,
environmental issues and culture*

reportphotos.com*
c/o 19 Quernmore Road,
London N4 4QT
07973 219201
library@reportphotos.com
www.reportphotos.com

Retna Pictures*
Pinewood Studios, Pinewood Road,
Iver Heath, Buckinghamshire SLO ONH
01753 785450
info@retna.com
www.retna.co.uk
Celebrity music and lifestyle

Retrograph Archive Collection
10 Hanover Street, Brighton,
East Sussex BN2 9SB
01273 687554
retropix1@aol.com
www.retrograph.com
*Vintage consumer advertising, art,
decorative art*

Reuters*
The Reuters Building, South
Colonnade, Canary Wharf,
London E14 5EP
020 7542 4899
kim.lee@reuters.com
www.reuters.com/pictures

Rex Features*
18 Vine Hill, London EC1R 5DZ
020 7278 7294
info@rexfeatures.com
www.rexfeatures.com

Rex Interstock*
18 Vine Hill, London EC1R 5DZ
020 7278 6989
interstock@rexfeatures.com
www.rexinterstock.com

Robbie Jack Photography*
45 Church Road, Hanwell,
London W7 3BD
020 8567 9616
robbie@robbiejack.com
www.robbiejack.com
Performing arts

Robert Estall Photo Agency*
12–14 Swan Street, Boxford,
Sudbury, Suffolk CO10 5NZ
01787 210111
robertestall@mac.com
www.africanceremonies.com

Robert Forsythe Picture Library
16 Lime Grove, Prudhoe,
Northumberland NE42 6PR
01661 834511
robert@forsythe.demon.co.uk
www.forsythe.demon.co.uk
*Original ephemera and transparencies of
industrial and transport heritage*

Robert Harding World Imagery*
58–59 Great Marlborough Street,
London W1F 7JY
020 7478 4000
info@robertharding.com
www.robertharding.com

Ronald Grant Archive*
The Masters House, The Old Lambeth
Workhouse, 2 Dugard Way,
off Renfrew Road, London SE11 4TH
020 7840 2200
pixdesk@rgapix.com
www.ronaldgrantarchive.com

Round the World Images*
Wrotham Business Park, Barnet,
Hertfordshire EN5 4SZ
020 8275 1040
martin.smith@worldonfilm.com
www.worldonfilm.com

Royal Air Force Museum*
Grahame Park Way, Hendon,
London NW9 5LL
020 8205 2266
photographic@rafmuseum.org
www.rafmuseum.org

Royal Armouries Image Library*
Royal Armouries, Armouries Drive,
Leeds LS10 1LT
0113 220 1891
image.library@armouries.org.uk
www.armouries.org.uk

Royal Collection Enterprises*
Picture Library, St James's Palace,
London SW1A 1JR
020 7839 1377
picturelibrary@royalcollection.org.uk
www.royalcollection.org.uk
Royal family

**Royal Geographical Society
Picture Library***
1 Kensington Gore, London SW7 2AR
020 7591 3060
pictures@rgs.org
www.rgs.org/picturelibrary

RSPB Images*
PO Box 7515, Heath Road, Ramsden
Heath, Billericay, Essex CM11 1HR
01268 711471
rspb@thatsgood.biz
www.rspb-images.com

RSPCA Photolibrary*
Wilberforce Way, Southwater,
Horsham, West Sussex RH13 9RS
0870 754 0150
pictures@rspcaphotolibrary.com
www.rspcaphotolibrary.com

Russia and Eastern Images*
Sonning, Cheapside Lane, Denham,
Uxbridge, Middlesex UB9 5AE
01895 833508
easteuropix@btinternet.com
www.easteuropix.com

S&O Mathews Photography
Little Pit Place, Brighstone,
Isle of Wight PO30 4DZ
01983 741098
oliver@mathews-photography.com
www.mathews-photography.com
Gardens, plants and landscapes

Sally and Richard Greenhill*
357 Liverpool Road, London N1 1NL
020 7607 8549
sr.greenhill@virgin.net
www.srgreenhill.co.uk

* Member of BAPLA, the British Association of Picture Libraries and Agencies

Scala, London*
1 Willow Court, off Willow Street,
London EC2A 4QB
020 7782 0044
info@scala-art.demon.co.uk
www.scalarchives.it
Art and culture

Science & Society Picture Library*
Science Museum, Exhibition Road,
London SW7 2DD
020 7942 4400
piclib@nmsi.ac.uk
www.scienceandsociety.co.uk
*Science Museum, National Railway
Museum; photography, film and television*

Science Photo Library*
327–329 Harrow Road,
London W9 3RB
020 7432 1100
info@sciencephoto.com
www.sciencephoto.com

Scope Features & Scope Beauty*
26–29 St Cross Street, Hatton
Garden, London EC1N 8UH
020 7405 2997
images@scopefeatures.com
www.scopefeatures.com

**Scott Polar Research Institute
Picture Library***
University of Cambridge, Lensfield
Road, Cambridge CB2 1ER
01223 336547
picture.library@spri.cam.ac.uk
www.spri.cam.ac.uk/lib/pictures

Scottish Viewpoint*
64 Polwarth Gardens,
Edinburgh EH11 1LL
0131 622 7174
info@scottishviewpoint.com
www.scottishviewpoint.com

**Shell Photographic Services
and Library***
Shell International Limited,
Shell Centre, London SE1 7NA
020 7934 4820
photographicservices@shell.com

SIN*
89a North View Road, Crouch End,
London N8 7LR
020 8348 8061
sales@sin-photo.co.uk
www.sin-photo.co.uk

Skishoot-Offshoot
Hall Place, Upper Woodcott,
Whitchurch, Hampshire RG28 7PY
01635 255527
info@skishoot.co.uk
www.skishoot.co.uk
Winter sports

Skyscan Photolibrary*
Oak House, Toddington,
Cheltenham GL54 5BY
01242 621357
info@skyscan.co.uk
www.skyscan.co.uk
Aviation and aerial sports

**Snookerimages
(Eric Whitehead Photography)**
Larch House, 10 Brow Close, Bowness
on Windermere, Cumbria LA23 2HA
015394 48894
snooker@snookerimages.co.uk
www.snookerimages.co.uk

SNS Group*
15 Fitzroy Place, Glasgow G3 7RW
0141 221 3602
info@snspix.com
www.snspix.com

SOA Photo Agency*
Lovells Farm, Dark Lane,
Stoke St Gregory, Taunton TA3 6EU
020 7870 6437
info@pictureocean.net
www.pictureocean.net
*Humour, sports, travel, modern
European*

**Société Jersiaise Photographic
Archive***
7 Pier Road, St Helier, Jersey JE2 4XW
01534 633 398
photoarchive@societe-jersiaise.org
www.societe-jersiaise.org

Sonia Halliday Photographs*
22 Bates Lane, Weston Turville,
Buckinghamshire HP22 5SL
01296 612266
info@soniahalliday.com
www.soniahalliday.com

Sotheby's Picture Library*
Level 2 Olympia, Hammersmith
Road, London W14 8UX
020 7293 5383
piclib@sothebys.com
www.sothebys.com

South American Pictures*
48 Station Road, Woodbridge,
Suffolk IP12 4AT
01394 383963
morrison@southamericanpictures.com
www.southamericanpictures.com

Splash News UK Limited*
1 Sekforde Street, London EC1R 0BE
020 7107 2666
dellis@splashnews.com
www.splashnews.com

SplashdownDirect.com*
1 Glen Cottages, Sandy Lane,
Abbots Leigh, Bristol BS8 3SE
01275 375520
tom@splashdowndirect.com
www.splashdowndirect.com

Stay Still*
29–31 Saffron Hill, London EC1N 8SW
020 7922 1313
staystill@staystill.com
www.staystill.com

Steve Bloom Images*
Middlefield House, Olantigh Road,
Wye, Ashford, Kent TN25 5EP
01233 813777
kathy@stevebloom.com
www.stevebloom.com

Still Moving Picture Company
1c Castlehill, Doune,
Edinburgh FK16 6BU
01786 842790
info@stillmovingpictures.com
www.stilldigital.co.uk
Scotland and sport

**Still Pictures – The Whole Earth
Photo Library***
199 Shooters Hill Road, Blackheath,
London SE3 8UL
020 8858 8307
info@stillpictures.com
www.stillpictures.com
*Environment, nature, social and
developing world issues*

Stock Scotland*
The Croft Studio, Croft Roy, Crammond
Brae, Tain, Ross-shire IV19 1JG
01862 892298
info@stockscotland.com
www.stockscotland.com

Stockfile*
5 High Street, Sunningdale SL5 0LX
01344 844428
info@stockfile.co.uk
www.stockfile.co.uk
Mountain biking and cycling

StockShot*
2b St Vincent Street,
Edinburgh EH3 6SH
0131 557 6688
info@stockshot.co.uk
www.stockshot.co.uk

**Sue Anderson Island Focus
Scotland***
Pony Park, Letterwalton,
Benderloch, Oban, Argyll PA37 1SA
01631 720078
info@islandfocus.co.uk
www.islandfocus.co.uk

Sue Cunningham Photographic
56 Chatham Road,
Kingston Upon Thames KT1 3AA
020 8541 3024
info@scphotographic.com
www.scphotographic.com

Superstock*
1st Floor Grayton House, 498–502
Fulham Road, London SW6 5NH
020 7386 4380
info@superstock.co.uk
www.superstock.co.uk

Surfpix*
1 High Street, St Davids,
Pembrokeshire SA62 6SA
01437 721188
info@surfpix.co.uk
www.surfpix.co.uk

Sutton Motorsport Images*
The Chapel, 61 Watling Street,
Towcester, Northants NN12 6AG
01327 352188
customerservices@
  sutton-images.com
www.sutton-images.com

---

* Member of BAPLA, the British Association of Picture Libraries and Agencies

Swift Imagery
The Old Farm House, Hexworthy,
Yelverton, Devon PL20 6SD
01364 631405
info@theswiftgroup.co.uk
www.theswiftgroup.co.uk

Sylvia Cordaiy Photo Library*
45 Rotherstone, Devizes,
Wiltshire SN10 2DD
01380 728327
info@sylvia-cordaiy.com
www.sylvia-cordaiy.com
170 countries, from obscure to stock images

Tate Images*
The Lodge, Millbank,
London SW1P 4RG
020 7887 8890
picture.library@tate.org.uk
www.tate.org.uk

Tessa Traeger*
7 Rossetti Studios, 72 Flood Street,
London SW3 5TF
020 7352 3641
info@tessatraeger.com
www.tessatraeger.com

Theimagefile.com*
3000 Hillswood Drive, PO Box 241,
Chertsey, Surrey KT16 0YZ
0870 224 2454
sales@theimagefile.com
www.theimagefile.com

Thoroughbred Photography *
The Hornbeams, 2 The Street,
Worlington, Suffolk IP28 8RU
01638 713 944
mail@thoroughbredphoto.com
www.thoroughbredphoto.com

Tibet Images*
3rd Floor, 5 Torrens Street,
London EC1V 1NQ
020 7278 2377
info@tibetimages.co.uk
www.tibetimages.co.uk

Tim Graham*
020 7435 7693
mail@timgraham.co.uk
www.royalphotographs.com

TimeArts Picture Library*
29–31 Distons Lane, Chipping Norton,
Oxfordshire OX7 5NY
01608 643334
info@3sco.co.uk
www.3sco.co.uk

TIPS Images *
3000 Hillswood Drive, PO Box 241,
Chertsey, Surrey KT16 0YZ
ossie@tipsimages.com
www.tipsimages.com

Tom Hanley*
41 Harefield, Hinchley Wood, Esher,
Surrey KT10 9TG
020 8972 9165
tomhanley31@hotmail.com

TopFoto*
PO Box 33, Edenbridge,
Kent TN8 5PF
01732 863939
requests@topfoto.co.uk
www.TopFoto.co.uk

Travel Ink Photo Library*
The Old Coach House,
14 High Street, Goring on Thames,
Reading RG8 9AR
01491 873011
info@travel-ink.co.uk
www.travel-ink.co.uk

The Travel Library*
Unit 7, The Kiln Workshops,
Pilcot Road, Crookham Village,
Fleet GU51 5RY
01252 627233
info@travel-library.co.uk
www.travel-library.co.uk

travel-shots.com*
3b Uplands Close, London SW14 7AS
020 8878 2226
sales@travel-shots.com
www.travel-shots.com

Trevillion Images*
1 Bellman's Court, 2 Reform Street,
Beith KA15 2AE
0845 223 5451
info@trevillion.com
www.codyimages.com

TRH Pictures*
Bradley's Close, 74–77 White Lion
Street, London N1 9PF
020 7520 7647
trh@trhpictures.co.uk
www.trhpictures.co.uk

TROPIX Photo Library*
44 Woodbines Avenue, Kingston
upon Thames, Surrey KT1 2AY
020 8546 0823
veronica@tropix.co.uk
www.tropix.co.uk

True North Photo Library
Louper Weir, Ghyll Head,
Windermere, Cumbria LA23 3LN
07941 630420
hurlmere@btinternet.com
*Picture collection of landscapes and life
of the North*

UKstockimages*
St Cross, Havant, Hampshire PO9 2QR
023 9247 8643
grant@ukstockimages.com
www.ukstockimages.com

Ulster Museum Picture Library*
Botanic Gardens, Belfast BT9 5AB
028 9038 3113
patricia.maclean@magni.org.uk
www.ulstermuseum.org.uk
*Art, archaeology, ethnography, natural
history, Irish history*

**Universal Pictorial Press and
Agency/Photoshot***
29–31 Saffron Hill, London EC1N 8SW
020 7421 6000
ctaylor@uppa.co.uk
www.uppa.co.uk

Untitled*
Radar Studio, Coldblow Lane,
Thurnham, Maidstone ME14 3LR
01622 737722
info@untitled.co.uk
www.untitled.co.uk

urbanlip.com*
Ivy Cottage, Lampard Lane, Churt,
Surrey GU10 2HJ
01428 717548
team@urbanlip.com
www.urbanlip.com

V&A Images*
Victoria and Albert Museum,
Cromwell Road, South Kensington,
London SW7 2RL
020 7942 2489
vanda.images@vam.ac.uk
www.vandaimages.com

**Vaughan Williams
Memorial Library**
Cecil Sharpe House, Regents Park
Road, London NW1 7AY
020 7485 2206
info@efdss.org
www.efdss.org
Traditional music and culture

Venturepix *
29 London Road, Sawbridgeworth,
Hertfordshire CM21 9EH
07970 262505
images@venturepix.com
www.venturepix.com

View Pictures*
14 The Dove Centre,
109 Bartholomew Road,
London NW5 2BJ
020 7284 2928
info@viewpictures.co.uk
www.viewpictures.co.uk

VinMag*
84–90 Digby Road, London E9 6HX
020 8533 7588
piclib@vinmag.com
www.vinmagarchive.com
*Twentieth-century history: books,
newspapers, posters, adverts, photos,
film, ephemera*

Vision Vault
123–125 Curtain Road, Shoreditch,
London EC2A 3BX
020 7739 4488
visionvault@taylorjames.com
www.taylorjames.com/visionvault

VK Guy *
Browhead Cottage, Troutbeck,
Windermere, Cumbria LA23 1PG
01539 433519
mike@vkguy.co.uk
www.vkguy.co.uk

Volunteering England Image Bank*
Regent's Wharf, 8 All Saints Street,
London N1 9RL
0845 305 6979
marketing@volunteeringengland.org
www.volunteering.org.uk/imagebank

WalesPics (Cambrian Images)*
The Arches, West Street, Rhayader,
Powys LD6 5AB
01597 810915
sales@cambrian-images.co.uk
www.cambrian-images.co.uk

* Member of BAPLA, the British Association of Picture Libraries and Agencies

Waterways Photo Library*
39 Manor Court Road, Hanwell,
London W7 3EJ
020 8840 1659
watphot39@aol.com
www.waterwaysphotolibrary.com
Inland waterways

**Wellcome Trust Medical
Photographic Library***
210 Euston Road, London NW1 2BE
020 7611 8348
medphoto@wellcome.ac.uk
www.medphoto.wellcome.ac.uk

Werner Forman Archive *
36 Camden Square,
London NW1 9XA
020 7267 1034
wfa@btinternet.com
www.werner-forman-archive.com

Wilderness Photographic Library*
4 Kings Court, Kirkby Lonsdale,
Cumbria LA6 2BP
01524 272149
wildernessphoto@btinternet.com
www.wildernessphoto.co.uk

**Window on the World
Picture Library***
The Garden Studio, 2 Jeffreys Walk,
Jeffreys Road, London SW4 6QF
020 7928 3448
usill@winworld.co.uk
www.winworld.co.uk

WireImage*
77 Oxford Street, London W1D 2ES
020 7659 2815
jc@wireimage.com
www.wireimage.com

Woodfall Wild Images*
17 Bull Lane, Denbigh LL16 3SN
01745 815903
wwimages@woodfall.com
www.woodfall.com

Woodland Trust*
Autumn Park, Dysart Road,
Grantham, Lincolnshire NG31 6LL
01476 581111
woodlandpictures@
   woodland-trust.org.uk
www.woodlandpictures.com

**World Entertainment News
Network Ltd***
35 Kings Exchange, Tileyard Road,
London N7 9AH
020 7607 2757
lloyd@wenn.com
www.wenn.com

World Pictures*
3rd Floor, 43–44 Berners Street,
London W1T 3ND
020 7580 1845
worldpictures@btinternet.com
www.worldpictures.co.uk
Travel

World Religions Photo Library*
53a Crimsworth Road,
London SW8 4RJ
020 7720 6951
co@worldreligions.co.uk
www.worldreligions.co.uk

Writer Pictures*
33/5 Mertoun Place,
Edinburgh EH11 1JX
020 8241 0039
info@writerpictures.com
www.writerpictures.com

WWF-UK Photo-Library*
Panda House, Weyside Park,
Godalming, Surrey GU7 1XR
01483 412336
phototemp@wwf-uk.org
www.wwf-uk.org

www.cumbriaphoto.co.uk
Windermere Road, Staveley, Kendal,
Cumbria LA8 9PL
01539 822222
bbarden@gocumbria.org
www.cumbriaphoto.co.uk

Xposure Photo Agency Limited
32-38 Scrutton Street,
London EC2A 4SS
020 7377 2770
david@xposurephotos.com
www.xposurephotos.com

**York Archaeological Trust
Picture Library**
Cromwell House, 13 Ogleforth,
York YO1 7FG
01904 663000
enquiries@yorkarchaeology.co.uk
www.yorkarchaeology.co.uk
Archaeology in York area

Zoological Society of London*
Regents Park, London NW1 4RY
020 7449 6274
leonie.lambert@zsl.org
www.zsl.org

**National Association
of Press Agencies**
41 Lansdowne Crescent,
Leamington Spa,
Warwickshire CV32 4PR
01926 424181
secretariat@napa.org.uk
www.napa.org.uk

7 Day Press
132 West Nile Street, Glasgow G1 2RQ
0141 572 0060
daypress@aol.com
www.7daypress.co.uk
Scottish sport

24/7 Media (Photography)
200 St Andrews Road, Bordesley
Village, Birmingham,
West Midlands B9 4JG
0121 753 1329
0121 753 1329
Jamie Jones: 07976400043
*Photographer covering news, sports,
features, PR and commercial*

Advance Media Information
Princess Court, 1 Horace Road,
Kingston-upon-Thames,
Surrey KT1 2SL
020 8547 0077
sales@amiplan.com
www.amiplan.com
*Future news, entertainment, lifestyle
and business events*

AFX News
Finsbury Tower, 103–105 Bunnhill
Row, London EC1Y 8TN
020 7422 4870
john.manley@afxnews.com
www.afxnews.com
International financial news

Agence France-Presse, UK
78 Fleet Street, London EC4Y 1NB
020 7353 7461
london.bureau@afp.com
www.afp.com
Major agency

Agencia EFE
299 Oxford Street, 6th Floor,
London W1C 2DZ
020 7493 7313
www.efe.com
Spanish news agency

Airtime Television News
PO Box 258, Maidenhead SL6 9YR
01628 482763
info@airtimetv.co.uk
www.airtimetv.co.uk
Heathrow airport

Allscot News Agency
PO Box 6, Haddington EH41 3NQ
01620 822578
101324.2142@compuserve.com
Scottish news

Anglia Press Agency
17A Whiting Street, Bury St Edmunds,
Suffolk IP33 1NR
01284 702421
news@angliapressagency.co.uk
East Anglia, words and pictures

ANSA News Agency
Essex House, 12–13 Essex Street,
London WC2R 3AA
020 7240 5514
ansalondra@yahoo.com
www.ansa.it
News worldwide

Apex News and Picture Agency
Priests Court, Main Road, Exminster,
Exeter EX6 8AP
01392 824024
info@apexnewspix.com
www.apexnewspix.com
Based in south-west. All news and features

APTN
The Interchange, Oval Road,
Camden Lock, London NW1 7DZ
020 7482 7400
aptninfo@ap.org
www.aptn.com
International newsgathering

Associated Press News Agency
12 Norwich Street, London EC4A 1BP
020 7353 1515
www.ap.org
Worldwide all news

Associated Sports Photography
21 Green Walk, Leicester LE3 6SE
0116 232 0310
asp@sports-photos.co.uk
www.sporting-heroes.net
Worldwide sports, travel

Australian Associated Press
Associated Press Building,
12 Norwich Street, London EC4A 1QJ
020 7353 0153
news.london@aap.com.au
www.aap.com.au
European news to Australia

Bellis News Agency
14B Kenelm Road, Rhos on Sea,
Colwyn Bay, North Wales LL28 4ED
01492 549503
bellisd@aol.com;
glynbellis@dsl.pipex.com
North Wales

Big Picture Press Agency
50–54 Clerkenwell Road,
London EC1M 5PS
020 7250 3555
picturedesk@bigpictures.co.uk
www.bigpicturesphoto.co.uk
Celebrities

Bloomberg LP
City Gate House, 39–45 Finsbury
Square, London EC2A 1PQ
020 7330 7500
newsdesk@bloomberg.net
www.bloomberg.com
Worldwide financial

**Bournemouth News &
Picture Service**
Unit 1, 1st Floor, 40–44 Holdenhurst
Road, Bournemouth BH8 8AD
01202 558833
news@bnps.co.uk
www.bnps.co.uk
News and features

Calyx Multimedia
41 Churchward Avenue,
Swindon SN2 1NJ
01793 520131
richard@calyxpix.com
www.calyxpix.com
Stills, news and freelance cameraman

Capital Press Agency
14 Canongate Venture, New Street,
Edinburgh EH8 8BH
0131 652 3999
capitalnews@hemedia.co.uk,
capitalpix@hemedia.co.uk
www.hemedia.co.uk
Edinburgh, Lothians and borders

Capital Pictures
85 Randolph Avenue, London W9 1DL
020 7286 2212
sales@capitalpictures.com
www.capitalpictures.com
International celebrities

**Cassidy & Leigh Southern
News Service**
Exchange House, Hindhead Road,
Hindhead GU26 6AA
01428 607330
denis@cassidyandleigh.com
News and pictures

Caters News Agency
Queens Gate, Suite 40,
121 Suffolk Street Queensway,
Birmingham B1 1LX
0121 616 1100
news@catersnews.com
features@catersnews.com
*West Midlands news, featuring pictures
and sport*

Cavendish Press and CPMedia
3rd Floor, Albert House, 17 Bloom
Street, Manchester M1 3HZ
0161 237 1066
newsdesk@cavendish-press.co.uk
www.cavendish-press.co.uk
www.cpmedia.co.uk
News and pictures

Celtic News
Box 101, Powys NP8 1WZ
01874 731 185
features@celticnews.co.uk
www.sellmystory.co.uk
*UK-wide features for nationals
and magazines*

Central News Network
Suite 7, 350 Main Street, Canelon,
Falkirk FK1 4EG
01324 630505
jimdavisofcnn@aol.com
Central Scotland news features

Central Press Features
5th Floor, BEP Building, Temple Way,
Bristol BS99 7HD
0117 934 3605
sam.bush@pa.press.net
http://pa-entertainment.co.uk
Worldwide editorial syndication

Centre Press Agency
2 Clairmont Gardens, Glasgow G3 7LW
0141 332 8888
centrenews@hemedia.co.uk,
centrepix@hemedia.co.uk
www.hemedia.co.uk
Central and southern Scotland

Chapman & Page
Dengate House, Amber Hill,
Boston PE20 3RL
01205 290477
chapmanpage@internett.demon.co.uk
Syndicated features agency

Chester News Service
Linen Hall House, Stanley Street,
Chester CH1 2LR
01244 304500
news@chesterstandard.co.uk
www.chesterstandardnow.co.uk
North Wales area

Chester Press Bureaux
Riverside House, Brymau 3 Trading
Estate, River Lane Saltney,
Chester CH4 8RQ
01244 678575
ron@chesterpb.freeserve.co.uk
*North-west area press agency and
contract publishing*

Computer Wire
Charles House, 108-110 Finchley Road,
London NW3 5JJ
020 7675 7000
kevin.white@computerwire.co.uk
www.computerwire.com
Worldwide IT index links

Copyline Scotland
70 Tomnahurich Street,
Inverness IV3 5DT
01463 231415
copylinescotland@aol.com
Scottish Highlands

Cotswold & Swindon News Service
256 Marlborough Road,
Swindon SN3 1NR
01793 485461
cotswin@stares.co.uk
www.stares.co.uk
Swindon area

Coventry News Service
4 Edison Building, Electric Wharf,
Sandy Lane, Coventry CV1 4JA
024 7663 3777
adent@advent-
communications.co.uk
www.advent-communications.co.uk
Coventry area

DBSP
112 Cornwall Street South,
Glasgow G41 1AA
0141 427 5344
stewart.mcdougall@btclick.com
Worldwide sport

Dobson Agency
20 Seafield Avenue, Osgodby,
Scarborough YO11 3QG
01723 585141; 07802 530583
pix@dobsonagency.co.uk
www.dobsonagency.co.uk
*Covering Yorkshire, Cleveland,
Humberside and rest of UK*

Double Red Photographic
The Old School, Thorn Lane, Goxhill,
Barrow upon Humber DN19 7JE
01469 531416
s.ward@doublered.co.uk;
pix@doublered.co.uk
www.doublered.co.uk
Motorsport photography

Dow Jones Newswires
10 Fleet Place, Limeburner Lane,
London EC4M 7QN
020 7842 9900
djequitiesnews.london@
  dowjones.com
www.djnewswires.com
International financial news

DPA (German Press Agency)
30 Old Queen Street, St James's
Park, London SW1H 9HP
020 7233 2888
london@dpa.com
www.dpa.com
Global media services

Dragon News & Picture Agency
21 Walter Road, Swansea SA1 5NQ
01792 464800
mail@dragon-pictures.com
www.dragon-pictures.com
All news and PR

Emirates News Agency
The Studio, 143 Lavender Hill,
London SW11 5QJ
020 7228 1060
mia@mia.gb.com
www.mia.gb.com
News from Arab peninsula

Empics Sports Photo Agency
Pavilion House, 16 Castle Boulevard,
Nottingham NG7 1FL
0115 844 7447
info@empics.com
www.empics.com
Sports worldwide, celebrities

Entertainment News
Dragon Court, 27-29 Mackin Street,
London WC2B 5LX
020 7190 7795
info@entnews.co.uk
www.entnews.co.uk
Diary for entertainment news

Essex News Service
2 The Street, Great Tay,
Colchester CO6 1AE
01206 211413
perfect@teynews.fsnet.co.uk
Essex area news and features

Evertons News Agency
1st Floor Offices, Hayley Green
Court, 130 Hagley Road, Halesowen,
West Midlands B63 1DY
0121 585 9188
clive.everton@talk21.com
Snooker and golf. Magazine journalist

Feature Story News
The Interchange, Oval Road,
London NW1 7DZ
020 7485 0303
drewc@featurestory.com
www.featurestory.com and
www.featurestorynews.com
*Domestic and international radio and
TV news*

Ferrari Press Agency
7 Summerhill Road, Dartford,
Kent DA1 2LP
01322 628444
news@ferraripress.com
www.ferraripress.com
*Kent, south London, south Essex,
East Sussex, Calais and Boulogne etc*

Foresightnews
Dragon Court, 27-29 Mackin Street,
London WC2B 5LX
020 7190 7788
info@foresightnews.co.uk
www.foresightnews.co.uk
Forward planning media news diary

Frank Ryan News Service
Cargenriggs, Islesteps, Dumfries
DG2 8ES
01387 253700
smeddum@btinternet.com
*South-west Scotland, general news
and features*

Freemans Press Agency
3 Youlston Close, Shirwell,
Barnstable EX31 4JW
01271 850255
freemans.pa@virgin.net
www.bipp.com
All news, north Devon

Future Events News Service
FENS House, 8-10 Wiseton Road,
London SW17 7EE
020 8672 3191
editorial@fensintl.com
www.fens.com
*Diary news service, UK and international
Entertainment and business*

Getty Images
101 Bayham Street, London NW1 1OG
0800 376 7981
sales@gettyimages.co.uk
www.gettyimages.com
Images of news

Gloucestershire News Service
Maverdine Chambers, 26 Westgate
Street, Gloucester GL1 2NG
01452 522270
john.hawkins@glosnews.com
www.glosnews.com
Gloucester general news

Gosnay's Sports Agency
Park House, 356 Broadway,
Horsforth, Leeds LS18 4RE
0113 258 5864
gosnays@aol.com
Sports news

Government News Network
London
Hercules House, Hercules Road,
London SE1 7DU
020 7217 3091
london@gnn.gsi.gov.uk
www.gnn.gov.uk
Government press office

West Midlands
5 St Phillips Place, Birmingham B3 2PW
0121 352 5500
birmingham@gnn.gsi.gov.uk
www.gnn.gov.uk

East Midlands
Belgrave Centre, Stanley Place,
Talbot Street, Nottingham NG1 5GG
0115 971 2780
nottingham@gnn.gov.uk
www.gnn.gov.uk

North-west
25th Floor, Sunley Tower,
Piccadilly Plaza, Manchester M1 4BT
0161 952 4500
manchester@gnn.gsi.gov.uk
www.gnn.gov.uk
All north-west, Carlisle to Stoke

North-east
Citygate, Gallowgate,
Newcastle upon Tyne NE1 4WH
0191 202 3600
newcastle@gnn.gov.uk
www.gnn.gov.uk

Yorkshire & Humber
1st Floor, City House,
New Station Street, Leeds LS1 4JG
0113 283 6599
leeds@gnn.gsi.gov.uk
www.gnn.gov.uk

Harrison Photography
37/39 Great Northern Street,
Belfast BT9 7FJ
028 9066 3100
mail@harrisonphotography.co.uk
www.harrisonphotography.co.uk
*All Northern Ireland. Business, PR,
photography*

Hayters Teamwork
Image House, Station Road,
London N17 9LR
020 8808 3300
sport@haytersteamwork.com
www.haytersteamwork.com
Home and international sports

IPS Photo Agency
21 Delisle Road, London SE28 0JD
020 8855 1008
info@ips-net.co.uk
*Agents in Japan, Italy, Germany, Spain,
France, Scandinavia*

Independent Radio News (IRN)
ITN Radio, 200 Gray's Inn Road,
London WC1X 8XZ
020 7430 4814
irn@itn.co.uk
www.irn.co.uk
National and international news

Independent Sports Network
London Television Centre,
Upper Ground, London SE1 9LT
020 7827 7700
jane.tatnall@isntv.co.uk
www.isntv.co.uk
UK sport transmissions

Islamic Republic News Agency (IRNA)
3rd Floor, Imperial Life House,
390–400 High Road, Wembley,
Middlesex HA9 6AS
020 8903 5531
irna@irna.ir
www.irna.ir
Islamic Republic news agency

Information Telegraph Agency of Russia (ITAR-TASS)
Suite 12–20, 2nd Floor, Morley
House, 314–320 Regent Street,
London W1B 3BD
020 7580 5543
iborisenko@yahoo.co.uk
www.itar-tass.com
Russian business news agency

Jarrold's Press Agency
68 High Street, Ipswich IP1 3QJ
01473 219193
jarroldspress@cix.compulink.co.uk
*Suffolk, north Essex, south Norfolk,
East Anglia and football coverage*

Jenkins Group
Berkeley House, 186 High Street,
Rochester ME1 1EY
01634 830888
nickandmarion@hotmail.com
PR worldwide

Jewish Chronicle News Agency
25 Furnival Street, London EC4A 1JT
020 7415 1500
marketing@thejc.com
www.thejc.com
Worldwide news

JIJI Press
4th Floor, International Press Centre,
76 Shoe Lane, London EC4A 3JB
020 7936 2847
edit@jiji.co.uk
www.jiji.co.jp
London economic news

John Connor Press Associates
57a High Street, Lewes BN7 1XE
01273 486851
news@jcpa.co.uk
News and features in Sussex

John Fairfax (UK)
1 Bath Street, London EC1V 9LB
020 7688 2777
linda@fairfaxbn.com
www.f2.com
Worldwide news

John Wardle Agency
Trafalgar House, 5 High Lane,
Manchester M21 9DJ
0161 861 8015
iwhittell@aol.com
Sports agency nationwide

Kuwait News Agency (KUNA)
6th Floor, New Premier House,
150 Southampton Row,
London WC1B 5AL
020 7278 5445
kuwait@btclick.com
www.kuwait-info.com
News around the world

Lakeland Press Agency
16 Stonecroft, Ambleside,
Lancashire LA22 0AU
01539 431749
craigwilson23@yahoo.co.uk
*Cumbria/Lake District. All news and
features*

Lappas of Exeter
7 Waylands Road, Tiverton,
Devon EX16 6UT
01884 254555
lappas@freeuk.com
www.richardlappas.com
Devon, Cornwall, Somerset, Dorset

M&Y News Agency
65 Osborne Road, Southsea,
Portsmouth PO5 3LS
023 9282 0311
mynews@dircon.co.uk
www.mynewsagency.co.uk
*News, sports and pictures. Hampshire,
Sussex, Dorset*

M2 Communications
PO Box 505, Coventry CV1 1ZQ
020 7047 0200
webmaster@M2.com
www.m2.com
Global news

Maghreb Arabe Press
35 Westminster Bridge Road,
London SE1 7JB
020 7401 8147; 07832147146
aouifia@aol.com; mapldn@aol.com
www.map.ma/eng
*News in North Africa, Middle East and
Mediterranean*

Market News International
Ocean House, 10–12 Little Trinity Lane,
London EC4V 2AR
020 7634 1655
ukeditorial@marketnews.com
www.marketnews.com
*International economics, politics and
financial markets*

Marshall's Sports Service
2 Newfield Drive,
Kingswinford DY6 8HY
01384 274877
marshall@bham-sport.demon.co.uk
West Midlands sports

Masons News Service
Unit 2, Clare Hall, Parsons Green,
St Ives, Cambridgeshire PE27 4WY
01480 302302
newsdesk@masons-news.co.uk
www.campix.co.uk
General news from East Anglia

Media Features
36 Holcroft Court, Carburton Street,
London W1W 5DJ
020 7436 3678
leozanelli@aol.com
Worldwide press syndication

Mercury Press Agency
Unit 218, Century Buildings,
Tower Street, Liverpool L3 4BJ
0151 709 6707
reporters@mercurypress.co.uk
www.mercurypress.co.uk
*Merseyside, Lancashire, Cheshire, parts
of North Wales*

National News Agency
4–5 Academy Buildings,
Fanshaw Street, London N1 6LQ
020 7684 3000
pix@nationalnews.co.uk
www.nationalpictures.co.uk
General news. London and south-east

News of Australia
1 Virginia Street, London E98 1NL
020 7702 1355
amy.westmore@newsint.co.uk;
sarah.parker@newsint.co.uk
www.news.com.au
Australian news

News Team International
35 Gas Street, Birmingham B1 2JT
0121 246 5511
picture.desk@newsteam.co.uk
www.newsteam.co.uk
Midlands, London news

Newsflash Scotland
3 Grosvenor Street, Edinburgh,
Scotland EH12 5ED
0131 226 5858
news@nflashed.co.uk
www.newsflashscotland.com
Scotland

North News and Pictures
The Newgate Centre, 69 Grainger
Street, Newcastle upon Tyne NE1 5JE
0191 233 0223
northscotnews@hemedia.co.uk;
northscotpix@hemedia.co.uk
www.hemedia.co.uk
North-east England, Cumbria and borders

North West News Service
10 Broseley Avenue,
Manchester M20 6JX
07980 006606
northwestnews@ntlworld.com
www.nw-news.co.uk

Northscot Press Agency
18 Adelphi, Aberdeen AB11 5BL
01224 212141
northnews@hemedia.co.uk;
northpix@hemedia.co.uk
www.hemedia.co.uk
Grampian and Highlands

Nunn Syndication
PO Box 56303, London SE1 2TD
020 7357 9000
production@nunn-syndication.com
www.nunn-syndication.com
London press agency

Press Association (PA)
292 Vauxhall Bridge Road,
London SW1V 1AE
020 7963 7000
information@pa.press.net
www.pa.press.net
*National news agency of UK and Ireland;
provider of real-time news and sports
information and images*

PA News Birmingham
312–313 The Custard Factory, Gibb
Street, Digbeth, Birmingham B9 4AA
0121 224 7686
pa_birmingham@hotmail.com
www.pa.press.net

PA News Liverpool
PO Box 48, Old Hall Street,
Liverpool L69 3EB
0151 472 2548
paliverpool@pa.press.net
www.pa.press.net

PA News Scotland
1 Central Quay, Glasgow G3 8DA
0870 830 6725
news@scottishpressassociation.co.uk
www.thepagroup.com

Press Gang News
137 Endlesham Road, Balham,
London SW12 8JN
0208 673 4229 Fax: 0208 673 3205
mail@pressgangnews.co.uk
www.pressgangnews.co.uk

Pacemaker Press International
787 Lisburn Road, Belfast BT9 7GX
028 9066 3191
david@pacemakerpressintl.com
www.pacemakerpressintl.com
Northern Ireland, Republic of Ireland

Page One Photography
11 West Avenue, West Bridgeford,
Nottingham, NG2 7NL
0115 981 8880
pictures@pageonephotography.com
www.pageonephotography.com
*Central and East Midlands. Corporate
and editorial photography*

Parliamentary & EU News Service
19 Douglas Street, Westminster,
London SW1P 4PA
020 7233 8283
info@parliamentary-monitoring.co.uk
www.parliamentary-monitoring.co.uk
Parliamentary news service

The Picture Library
16 Crescent Road, London N22 7RS
020 8365 8389
joanne@thepicturelibraryltd.net
www.alandavidson.net

Press Agency (Gatwick)
1a Sunview Avenue,
Peacehaven BN10 8PJ
01273 583103
petershirley2@hotmail.com
*Gatwick and south coast, mostly national
press*

Press Team Scotland
22 St John's Street, Coatbridge,
Lanarkshire ML5 3EJ
01236 440077
news@pressteam.co.uk
Lanarkshire, Glasgow and west Scotland

Press Trust of India
PTI Building, 4 Parliament Street,
New Delhi 110 001
00 91 11 031 61872
trans@pti.com
www.ptinews.com
Worldwide news and photos

Profile Group (UK)
Dragon Court, 27–29 Macklin Street,
London WC2B 5LX
020 7190 7777
info@profilegroup.co.uk
www.profilegroup.co.uk
Future events info and business leads

Racenews
85 Blackstock Road, London N4 2JW
020 7704 0326
racenews@compuserve.com
www.racenews.co.uk
Worldwide horse racing

Raymonds Press Agency
3rd Floor Abbots Hill Chambers,
Gower Street, Derby DE1 1SD
01332 340404
news@raymondspress.com
Sports, news and photography

Reuters
The Reuters Building, South
Colonnade, Canary Wharf E14 5EP
020 7250 1122
robert.woodward@reuters.com
www.reuters.com
Worldwide news and features

Rex Features
18 Vine Hill, London EC1R 5DZ
020 7278 7294
rex@rexfeatures.com
www.rexfeatures.com
International and US picture agency

Richard Harris News
Woody Glen, How Mill,
Branton CA8 9JY
01228 670381
richardwjharris@aol.com
News in north Cumbria

Ross Parry Agency
40 Back Town Street, Farsley,
Leeds LS28 5LD
0113 236 1842
newsdesk@rossparry.co.uk
www.rossparry.co.uk
Yorkshire, news features and photos

**Russian Information Agency –
Novosti (RIA-Novosti)**
3 Rosary Gardens, London SW7 4NW
020 7370 3002
ria@novosti.co.uk
www.rian.ru
Russia

Scottish News Agency
Avian House, 4 Lindsay Court,
Dundee Technology Park,
Dundee DD2 1SW
01382 427035
g.ogilvy@scottishnews.com
*East and central Scotland, Perthshire,
Fife, Edinburgh, Lothians and Borders*

Scottish News & Sport
15 Fitzroy Place, Glasgow G3 7RW
0141 221 3602
info@snspix.com
www.snspix.com
Scotland sport

Shetland News Agency
The Knowes, Lunning, Vidlin,
Shetland
01806 577332
hans@shetland-news.co.uk
www.shetland-news.co.uk

Smith Davis Press
Queens Chambers, 8 Westport Road,
Burslem, Stoke on Trent ST6 4AW
01782 829850
smith-davis@smith-davis.co.uk
www.smith-davis.co.uk
*Photography, graphic design, freelance
journalists and contract publishing*

Snowmedia Consultancy
Unit G4, Broadway Studio, 28 Tooting
High Street, London SW17 0RG
020 8672 9800
info@snowmedia.net
www.snowmedia.net
*Nationwide lifestyle profiles on health
and sport*

Solent News and Photo Agency
23 Mitchell Point, Ensign Way,
Hamble, Southampton SO31 4RF
023 8045 8800
news@solentnews.biz
www.solentnews.biz
*Hampshire, Wiltshire, Isle of Wight news
features for all media*

Somerset News Service
3 Lewis Road, Taunton,
Somerset TA2 6DU
01823 331856
somersetnews@boltblue.com
Contact: Richard Briers

Somerset Photo News
12 Jellalabad Court, The Mount,
Taunton, Somerset TA1 3RZ
01823 282053, 07860 207333
somersetphotonews@boltblue.com
Somerset

South Beds News Agency
Bramingham Park Business Centre,
Enterprise Way, Bramingham Park,
Luton, Bedfordshire LU3 4BU
01582 572222
southbedsnews@btconnect.com
*Hertfordshire, Bedfordshire,
Buckinghamshire, Northamptonshire*

South West News & Picture Service
Media Centre, Emma-Chris Way,
Abbeywood Park, Bristol BS34 7JU
0117 906 6500
news@swns.com
www.swns.com
*South-west general news, features
and photos*

Space Press News and Pictures
Bridge House, Blackden Lane,
Goostrey, Cheshire CW4 8PZ
01477 533403
scoop2001@aol.com
*Knutsford, Macclesfield, Crewe, Nantwich,
Wilmslow, Alderley Edge, Northwich,
Cheshire, Shropshire and North-west*

Specialist News Services
27 Newton Street, London WC2B 5EL
020 7831 3267
desk@snsnews.co.uk
*National. Consumer, media, city, travel
and motor industry, advertising and
marketing, new products, science and
nature*

Speed Media One
3 Kings Court, Horsham RH13 5UR
01403 259661
info@speedmediaone.co.uk;
greg@speedmediaone.co.uk
www.speedmediaone.co.uk
*General news and features. Sport, sport
development, education, local
government, environment, overseas
property, investments*

Sport & General Press Agency
63 Gee Street, London EC1V 3RS
020 7253 7705
info@alphapress.com
www.alphapress.com

Sportsphoto
20 Clifton Street,
Scarborough YO12 7SR
01723 367264
stewart@sportsphoto.co.uk
www.allstarpl.com
*All sport and entertainment, national
and international*

Tim Wood Agency
Press Room, Central Criminal Courts,
London EC4M 7EH
020 7248 3277
*Court cover at Old Bailey, Southwark and
Knightsbridge crown courts*

Tony Scase News Service
Little Congham House,
Congham, Kings Lynn PE32 1DR
01485 600650
news@scase.co.uk
www.scase.co.uk
East Anglia news

TV News
Feature Story News, The Interchange,
Oval Road, London NW1 7DZ
020 7485 0303
newsdesk3@featurestory.com
www.fsntv.com
*TV news for north America, south-east
Asia, southern Africa*

UK Press
Unit 27, The Limehouse Cut,
46 Morris Road, London E14 6NQ
020 7515 3878
info@ukpress.com
www.ukpress.com
UK and European photography

Unique Entertainment News
50 Lisson Street, London NW1 5DF
020 7453 1650
philip.chryssikos@
   entertainmentnews.co.uk
www.entertainmentnews.co.uk
Purely entertainment news

Universal Pictorial Press & Agency
29-31 Saffron Hill, London EC1N 8SW
020 7421 6000
contacts@uppa.co.uk;
maurice@uppa.co.uk
www.photoshot.com
*Press and worldwide commercial
photography, celebrities, sport, politicians*

Wales News & Picture Service
Market Chambers, 5-7 St Mary's
Street, Cardiff CF10 1AT
029 2066 6366
news@walesnews.com
www.walesnews.com
Wales. General news and features

**Warwickshire News & Picture
Agency**
41 Lansdowne Crescent,
Leamington Spa CV32 4PR
01926 424181
barrie@tracynews.co.uk
*Midlands. General news, features
and pictures*

Wessex Features and Photos Agency
Neates Yard, 108 High Street,
Hungerford RG17 0NB
01488 686810
news@britishnews.co.uk
www.britishnews.co.uk
Women's news, nationwide

West Coast News
Renaissance House, Parracombe,
Barnstaple, Devon EX31 4QH
01598 763296
westcoast.news@dial.pipex.com
Devon, Cornwall, west Somerset

White's Press Agency
46 London Road, Heeley,
Sheffield S2 4HP
0114 255 3975
news@whites-press-sheffield.co.uk
Men's sport, south Yorkshire

Wireimage UK
77 Oxford Street, London W1D 2ES
020 7659 2815
jc@wireimage.com
www.wireimage.com
*Worldwide coverage of entertainment
news and sport*

World Entertainment News Network
35 Kings Exchange, Tileyard Road,
London N7 9AH
020 7607 2757
info@wenn.com
yasmin@wenn.com
www.wenn.com
Worldwide entertainment and photos

Xinhua News Agency of China
8 Swiss Terrace, Belsize Road,
Swiss Cottage, London NW6 4RR
020 7586 8437
xinhua@easynet.co.uk
www.xinhuanet.com
News of China

ITV

Graeme Robertson

New force at ITV... Michael Grade

How can you spend five months not finding a chief executive, then suddenly produce a surprise right from under everyone's noses? The end of the year turnaround in ITV's story produced by the snatching of Michael Grade from the BBC was in fact the only good news out of the broadcaster all year.

Consider the situation prior to the great Grade robbery: ratings are predictably down; ad revenue has, naturally, been better; the 2006 World Cup didn't do the bottom-line inflating rescue job that the company required. The programme schedule looks tired and over-reliant on former glories. The chairman was, according to reports, racing the chief executive out of the building. The share price has been languishing under 100p for the majority of the year. Perhaps the worst of all is that its rival, BSkyB has just spent £1bn buying 18% of the company's stock. Just because it can.

By autumn 2006, if you weren't part of a secret bid team with a plan to buy out ITV and install your own people to turn it round, well, you weren't really anyone in television. Or banking. Or catering, probably.

Charles Allen, the chief executive of Granada who merged the ITV companies, finally stopped fighting halfway through 2006. Announcing his departure, he set about writing his legacy with a MacTaggart Lecture at the MediaGuardian Edinburgh International Television Festival. Proving the old adage that if you stick around long enough you'll become a national treasure, Allen was hailed as a master negotiator who won vital concessions from regulators and government alike.

As the new executive chairman Michael Grade will probably get 18 months to rescue ITV. In real terms this means about six months before cost cutting is demanded. Good luck there.

Through all of this, the core channel's performance continued to tank. A poor start to the year, disappointing ad takes from the World Cup and diminishing returns from its banker hit programme, The X-Factor, all added up to tough times. Arguably, the lowlight was a very weak season of Love Island (later axed), no longer even pretending to feature celebrities, which managed to make the umpteenth season of Big Brother look fresh and innovative.

The return of two ITV stalwarts, Cracker and Prime Suspect, didn't so much consolidate its reputation as a quality programmer as remind everyone how good it used to be. Like many businesses, broadcasting is cyclical, and ITV seems determined to explore just how low that curve can go before it turns the corner.

Media agencies will always try and paint the worst possible picture of ITV in order to negotiate better ad deals for next year, but there was no denying the back end of 2006 looked bad. In 2000, ITV1 had an audience of 44% of all commercial viewing by the key group 16- to 34-year-olds. In 2006, that figure was forecasted to have fallen to 22%. The same agencies were predicting revenue to fall by £215m — or 14% — in 2006, compared with 2005.

If ITV can keep its total of younger viewers higher than anyone else, then it continues to win, thanks to that broadcasting double jeopardy whereby you can still charge a premium for reaching more people than anyone else. Even if the big number is smaller than it used to be.

However, as the ratings gap between the main channels continues to shrink, agencies began to describe a "tipping point" where they might be spreading their spend between Channel 4 and other digital channels.

One senior media planner was quoted as saying "For the first time, it is possible to not have [ITV] on the schedule [for advertisers' campaigns]. ITV isn't doing anything to rebuff that at the moment and the argument is gathering momentum."

Cheerier times at the multichannel outposts of ITV2, ITV3 and ITV4, however. ITV2 beat Channel 4 in peaktime in September, where repeats of Saturday Night Takeaway and The X-Factor pulled a 5% share against Channel 4's 4.6% in the same period. (It had taken Five out a couple of weeks earlier.) ITV2 even pulled in one of the anticipated US imports of the year with HBO's Entourage. Its ratings were lacklustre, but the prestige and coverage were both disproportionately high.

The ITV family of digital channels became the second biggest player in multichannel TV in the first half of 2006, overtaking the UKTV portfolio, to attract a 4.03% total share of viewing. Still some way behind Sky's 8.75%, but Sky is falling fast.

● Regional franchises

With all the fuss made about "one ITV network" it's easy to forget that in the Channel Islands, Northern Island and parts of Scotland the franchises are independently controlled. SMG, which owns the Scottish and Grampian ITV franchises, did its best to remind us it's still here by

Audience share in all homes 2006

Terrestrial channels	Aug	July	Jun	May	April	March	Feb	Jan	Total % share 2005
BBC1	22.2	23.8	24.9	23.0	22.3	22.6	22.3	22.2	23.3
BBC2	8.3	8.5	7.9	8.7	9.3	9.3	9.8	9.3	9.4
ITV (inc GMTV)	17.2	16.8	20.5	19.5	19.5	21.0	20.2	20.5	21.5
C4	9.8	11.3	11.0	10.5	9.6	9.4	9.9	11.0	9.7
Five	5.7	6.1	5.4	5.8	5.8	6.0	6.0	5.8	6.4
Other viewing	37.0	33.5	30.3	32.6	33.3	31.8	31.8	31.3	29.6
Audience share of viewing in multichannel homes									
All Sky Movies	2.1	2.4	1.8	2.5	2.7	2.4	2.2	2.2	
Sky Sports	3.4	2.3	1.8	3.2	3.5	3.4	3.0	3.3	
Total Sky	9.0	7.8	6.9	8.8	9.1	8.8	8.8	9.2	
All other channels	3.6	3.5	3.4	3.4	3.6	3.6	3.8	3.8	
Total non terrestrial channels	**46.3**	**42.5**	**38.4**	**41.7**	**42.7**	**41.2**	**42.2**	**41.5**	
Total terrestrial	**53.6**	**57.5**	**61.6**	**58.3**	**57.3**	**58.8**	**57.8**	**58.5**	

Source: BARB

indulging in a spectacular boardroom row at the end of 2006. The entire board threatened to resign over who should run the company as one of its biggest shareholders, Fidelity, tried to oust the chairman, Chris Masters.

The year struck a low for SMG, which also owns Virgin Radio and the Pearl & Dean cinema advertising business, with profits warnings, the loss of its chief executive, and a couple of takeover attempts (including one by Ulster TV). Fidelity, of course, is widely credited with having ousted Michael Green from Carlton.

BBC

The perennial question of how much the nation is prepared to pay for the BBC was debated furiously again in 2006. Resting on this momentous decision apparently were not only the programming plans of the corporation, the digital future of the entire nation and the preserving of Terry Wogan for another generation, but, brilliantly, also the entire economy of the north-west (way to raise the stakes, BBC!).

Mark Thompson, the BBC's director-general was playing tough: all the familiar weapons of negotiation were wheeled out through 2006. Further lay-offs of staff helping to prove the BBC is pared to the bone and not awash with cash? Check. An extensive restructure to show the corporation is busily engaging with the new world order? Check. A prestigious costume drama for the early autumn Sunday evenings as a reminder that there are some programmes only the BBC can do? Jane Eyre, check.

By pledging to move certain BBC services to Manchester (where quite a lot of them used to be, incidentally) only *if* the licence-fee settlement was high enough to cover the costs of the move, Thompson figured he'd played the winning move. Matters became slightly bad-tempered when the chancellor, Gordon Brown, let it be known (via the now traditional route of speculative news stories in Sunday papers) he was not minded to give any extra money to the BBC. An overtaxed nation could live without another episode of EastEnders if it meant better food in hospitals, seemed to be the gist of the argument.

HE HATES CHANGE, SO HE RECORDS HIS OWN REPEATS.

BBC

Thompson reacted with unexpected force, in a speech that – if he gets his way on the proposed annual rise of 1.8% above inflation in the licence fee – will be carefully studied by future director-generals. Cleverly focusing the blame on Rupert Murdoch, who may well be a global media visionary but has never been hugely popular among either voters or licence-fee payers, Thompson accused Sky of trying to sabotage digital switchover by impoverishing the BBC. He then suggested that perhaps Murdoch's much-discussed and boasted-of influence in Nos 10 and 11 was behind the current havering. Was it enough?

It is an unusually subtle and political battle this time round. When John Birt last saddled up for licence-fee war, the fight was for the hearts and minds of Sun readers, who were being urged to refuse to pay their licence fee in protest. But research by the government and Ofcom suggests that the public is not only prepared to pay for the BBC, but accepts that an increase is inevitable. Whether the shift in public opinion is due to the weakness of some of the BBC's rivals, its (overdue) focus on family viewing or the growing take-up of digital services so that those who previously didn't understand where all the money was going can now see BBC3, BBC4 and CBeebies, or a combination of all those factors, the corporation has won the hard part of the battle.

Less convincing was the formation of the BBC Trust, a new group of the great and the good, to govern the executive branch but entirely different to the BBC governors in many, many ways, all of which are far too complicated to explain here. Leaving the BBC for ITV, Michael Grade explained that being chairman of the BBC Trust was going to be a bit less interesting than being chairman of the BBC board of governors.

As if to prove that not all innovation is necessarily great, at least one BBC foray into new services proved a convincing failure. "Tardisodes", heavily publicised one-minute episodes of Doctor Who designed for mobile phones, attracted just 3,000 downloads an episode. While PC downloads of the teasers reached 2.6 million users, the mobile service seemed to stutter over the charges involved (between £1.50 and £2 to phone operators rather than the BBC). As with so many things in the new world order, it seems that the market is out there, but it simply isn't prepared to pay.

● BBC programming

Though Robin Hood, pitched as the new Doctor Who for family audiences, failed to match the latter's critical and popular success, BBC1 has enjoyed a steady success in its programming while avoiding public outcry over religion, arts, cheap reality shows and even current affairs in primetime. The closest it has come to a scandal during the year came with a much-trailed and over-hyped Panorama investigation into "football bungs", which promised to bring down the careers of several key Premiership figures. It did not.

Disaster struck the hit comedy The Thick of It, lauded by critics as the brightest and sharpest new comedy to emerge from the corporation for some time. In the middle of a year in which its writer, Armando Iannucci, and talented cast including Chris Langham and Peter Capaldi won a stream of awards, Langham was arrested and charged with several offences relating to child porn and indecent assault. It was hastily announced that the planned Christmas special would go ahead without him and he stepped down from all ongoing BBC projects.

The new Sunday prestige costume drama, Jane Eyre, performed solidly and will doubtless scoop plenty of Baftas, while a heavily cross-promoted prequel, The Wide Sargasso Sea, also did well for BBC4.

The BBC proves its worth with costume drama Jane Eyre

Mike Hogan / BBC

Gutsy strategist... Channel 4 chief
Andy Duncan

Martin Godwin

Channel 4

The greatest threat to Channel 4 seems to be the possibility, raised almost constantly, that its senior executive team will decamp en masse to rescue ITV. As all the relevant figures deny any interest in selling their souls to big money at every opportunity, this move can surely be only moments away. As things stand though, the channel continues reliably, though its large year-on-year gains in audience are now behind it.

The chief executive, Andy Duncan, has followed a strategy not unknown to the former BBC executive, who helped launch the digital terrestrial service Freeview. Adapting the BBC's "be free, everywhere" plan, Duncan took the pay channels E4 and then FilmFour on to the Freeview platform as well as launch the niche service More 4 there. He explained his moves with the declaration that the economics of multichannel television had changed and there was far more to be gained in advertising revenue than in subscription. (To be fair to ITV, they had already proved this to be the case with the success of ITVs 2 and 3.)

Channel 4's digital channels increased its share of multichannel viewing from 1.42% in the first half of 2005 to 2.87% in the six months to the end of June 2006. Its digital channel E4, which became available on Freeview in May 2005, increased from 1.1% to 1.75% year on year, and is challenging ITV2 and Sky One for the mantle of most-watched digital network. Even newcomer More4 attracted a 0.57% share in the first half of 2006.

With a portfolio of free-to-air channels, Duncan turned his attention to new ground and Channel 4 announced it would bid for a digital multiplex and attempt to add radio to its output, possibly with a commercial partner. Welcomed by advertisers, many of whom believe Channel 4 could provide serious competition to BBC Radio 4, this plan was not necessarily hugely popular with the big radio groups.

In programming, Channel 4 recaptured its daytime stronghold with one of the most annoying, addictive and (I'm sorry to say it) iconic new hit shows: Deal Or No Deal. Resurrecting the career of its host, Noel Edmonds, and based on the seemingly innocuous premise that in one of 22 boxes lies the chance to win £250,000 if the contestant can find it, this Endemol format did a "Millionaire" and laid waste to all around it in daytime. A US version performed similarly well in primetime.

In fact, daytime dominated Channel 4's headlines. The new Countdown host, Des Lynam, had barely ridden out his natural disadvantage of not being the late lamented Richard Whiteley when he caused a huge stink by asking for the show to be moved from Leeds to nearer his southeast home. The ensuing row prompted Lynam to resign and the now annual hunt for a new Countdown host to begin again.

Meanwhile, Paul O'Grady, who defected from ITV to Channel 4 a year ago in a very entertaining coup, recovered from a heart attack to return to his 5pm slot and take on Sharon Osbourne in the daytime talkshow wars. The head-to-head caused both sides to lose audience, but O'Grady was pronounced the victor as Osbourne, undoubtedly suffering from X-Factor overexposure, admitted that the early editions of her programme were "not the best". Indeed.

How could primetime compete with such wrangling? Not all that well, was the answer. Some of Channel 4's hardy perennial makeover shows were not looking so hardy in 2006. Big Brother performed well against Love Island but failed to shrug off speculation as to whether enough is enough. A new star, Charlotte Church, took on the Friday night post-pub crowd to great personal acclaim but the show left much to be desired. Green Wing, a great hope when it launched, bowed out after a less successful second series and returning drama continued to be a problem area, though one-offs such as Longford still do the credibility business if not the ratings.

Five

It has been a mixed time for the fifth channel recently. In some areas, things started to look up. After years of meandering in strategy confusion, hampered by its complicated shareholding structure, unable to invest properly in its core service, let alone look ambitiously at the rest of the broadcast landscape, 2006 saw the channel able to take some tiny steps forward.

Having finally achieved single ownership under the German group RTL, Five set about diversifying to offset the beginning of audience decline. And not a moment too soon.

Five's audience share fell to 6% in the first half of 2006 (from 6.7% the previous year). RTL said profits rose 21% to a record £333m and pointed to the "outperformance" of Five in previous years, which made the decline in share "a little less painful". Still, this is the second year that performance has fallen for Five and suggestions that it is directly linked to the success of Freeview imply that it may be permanent.

And so, two new channels launched under the Five umbrella in October 2006: Five Life and Five US. The latter raised a few eyebrows with a deliberately controversial ad campaign, first declaring "nothing good ever came out of America" before swiftly revealing that (surprise!) lots of good things have come out of America, namely CSI, Grey's Anatomy, House and other such shows that Five broadcasts. The other newbie, Five Life, will mix its successful children's strand, Milkshake, with lifestyle programming aimed at women.

There are some signs of life in the main channel's schedule, as the director of programmes, Dan Chambers, invested in the thirtysomething comedy-drama genre, which can prove so attractive to advertisers. Perfect Day, Tiger Aspect's ensemble piece, has become a trilogy and Mike Bullen's (of Cold Feet) Tripping Over found its home on Five rather than ITV. Of course, this being the perverse world of television, almost as soon as his new efforts began to hit the screens, Chambers was fired to make way for Lisa Opie, an executive from the multichannel world. Opie's task will be to spend 2006 trying to resurrect the channel's audience share, presumably with little or no original programming. Either that or she'll be smiling nicely at the people from Sky when they come to take over the channel.

Another innovation saw video on demand on Five's website. The first to offer unbroadcast episodes for sale, Five launched with CSI, both new and old, for sale at £2.49 and £1.49 an episode respectively. Purchasers are in effect buying a licence that allows them to watch the episodes an unlimited number of times for 14 days. Eventually, Five hopes to offer the entire back catalogue of all three series of CSI. Though how this will be distinguished from its primetime schedule is unclear...

Multichannel

Digital take-up hit 70% of UK households in 2006, which seems like a lot until you realise that switchover has already begun in some areas and there are just five years to go until complete switchover. Research suggesting that a good number of Freeview boxes are on second television sets rather than in fully converted digital homes, shows how far there is left to go in luring the refusniks voluntarily into the future.

NTL, having finally merged with Telewest as well as a slightly bizarre merger with Virgin mobile in order to get a bit of Virgin branding, began a long-overdue marketing campaign for cable as a concept. Tagged "if you can you should", it suggested that the attraction of getting your phone, broadband and television from one company was pure simplicity. Indeed. If only cable had been able to get its collective act together ten years ago...

As Channel 4 switched its premium digital channels to free, it became clear that the model for multichannel success has switched from subscription- to advertiser-funded. ITVs digital channels ITV2, ITV3 and ITV4 are currently propping up falling revenue from the main channel and even Five got in on the act with two new channels.

The number of viewers increased incrementally, with some notable exceptions proving that digital no longer necessarily means niche. When the BBC decided to air the Doctor Who spin-off Torchwood as a BBC3 premiere, its opening episode garnered 2.4 million viewers. In itself that is the largest ever audience for a UK programme (ie not sport) broadcast on multichannel television. Given that multichannel ratings are generally dominated by live football matches and episode of The Simpsons, Torchwood might even be seen as a landmark moment for homegrown television.

More significantly, perhaps, 2.4 million is the kind of audience for a primetime show that neither BBC2, Channel 4 nor Five would be unhappy with. The "flattening out" of channels, certainly audiences in Freeview households, is upon us.

Of course, the real question is whether quality drama such as Torchwood, is economically viable for broadcast on multichannel television unless you are the BBC. So far, the most successful shows on multichannel (in terms of cost-per-rating) have been the kind of live post-match analysis that follows big reality shows. The many Big Brother talk shows, Xtra Factor and the Strictly Come Dancing endless streaming, come with their own built-in audience recognition and "turn over now" prompting from the main channel.

The BBC can afford to spend millions on a Torchwood and use it to boost BBC3, because it will air on BBC2 in the same week (where it also performed creditably). It may be too optimistic, though, to hope that a rash of similarly ambitious projects will suddenly appear throughout the multichannel schedules. Not yet, anyway.

Milestone for digital channels... millions watch Torchwood drama on BBC3

Steven Brown / BBC

149

● Sky

Undoubtedly the single biggest thing Sky did last year was spend nearly £1bn one Friday afternoon to become the largest shareholder in ITV. Though many have attempted to post-rationalise this move into a strategic purpose, it was essentially done because Murdoch can. They bought the stake to stop NTL (or anyone else) buying ITV without a Murdoch say-so. Having done that, while saying (with an insincere smile) "we're here to help ITV", it turns out they actually did help ITV. The Murdochs (and let's be honest, this is their plan, not BSkyB's) bought the ITV board enough time to install a new man — which in turn has probably bought them enough time to have a stab at making a go of it. Was that Sky's intention? Probably not. Funny how things turn out.

In programming terms, Sky has been relatively quiet, though earth-shattering news from its news division suggests all might not be well. Nick Pollard, the long-serving, respectable face of satellite broadcasting, resigned from his post as the head of Sky News in 2006 following a much-derided relaunch of the channel. Pollard, an incredibly well-respected figure in a largely backbiting industry, denied he was leaving because of the relaunch. Certainly there have been a number of cuts at the channel with which he might not have agreed; Sky News has always been a loss leader for BSkyB, but its value as an example of quality satellite broadcasting and importance as a rival to the terrestrial providers was never in dispute. Recently, though, the BBC's News 24 has closed the ratings gap, an effect probably caused by uptake of the Freeview service, and Sky News has been under pressure to maintain its status as the leading 24-hour news channel. Some comfort came when it won a pitch, ahead of the BBC, to provide news services into train stations.

Richard Woolfe, the award-winning head of LivingTV, joined Sky One with the aim to make sense of that woebegotten channel and has focused on stunt programming involving minor celebrities to some effect. A world-exclusive interview with Kylie Minogue, however, failed to reach the dizzy ratings heights of its notorious Rebecca Loos predecessor.

BSkyB has preferred, it seems, to focus on its business as a platform provider. The first half of the year was taken up with pushing High Definition — the new broadcasting technology by which every pore on a presenter's face (or, in a more marketable phrase, every blade of grass on a football pitch) is visible to the home viewer. Having decided to push HD for the World Cup, Sky hit every marketing button and plenty of stories suggested it had sold out of HD boxes.

Digital and multichannel TV

	Main operators	Connected homes		Year-on-year rise	Audience share at 30 June 06
		31-Mar-06	31-Mar-05		
Analogue terrestrial					28.0%
Satellite	Sky	7.7m	7.35m	5%	30.7%
	Free-to-view	645,000	445,000	31%	2.8%
Digital terrestrial	Freeview	6.4m	5.06m	21%	25.3%
Cable	ntl:Telewest	3.3m	3.29m	0%	13.1%
of which digital		2.8m	2.54m	9%	
ADSL		50,400	20,000	60%	0.2%
Total digital		**17.6m**	**15.42m**	**12%**	**70.2%**
Total multichannel		**18.1m**	**16.16m**	**11%**	**72.0%**

Source: Ofcom, BSkyB

Whether the public has taken to HD or not is unclear. Some reports suggested the first-generation HD boxes weren't up to the hype; perhaps more tellingly, retailers reported a glut of HD-ready big-screen TVs after the World Cup had ended and many resorted to heavy discounting of plasmas, LCDs and the like in what must have seemed like a very early January sale.

However, with the BBC expanding its HD test broadcasts and Sky launching two new HD movie channels, the broadcasters are gambling that the public won't notice that they've already been sold digital on the promise of higher-quality pictures and will fork out again for the next new thing.

The incumbents of Isleworth, Sky's home outside London, spent the second half of the year focusing on broadband. Beginning with some heavily over-subscribed free offers to its existing subscribers, Sky came crashing into the free broadband market with typical enthusiasm. Again, supply seemed unable to keep up with demand at first, though Sky insists it will be upping capacity in the near future. As part of these offers, the satellite broadcaster is flirting with several "fringe" innovations, such as enabling programming your Sky+ box via a mobile or downloading movies from the Sky website. It has yet to settle on the next Sky+ though – that is, the technology that will drive a new wave of those reluctant subscribers to Sky rather than to Freeview.

Independent production companies

The independent sector has changed almost unrecognisably from the early days of Channel 4 and the start-up of boutique studios in Soho selling a limited number of beautifully-crafted programmes a year. The "let a thousand flowers bloom" of the early indie sector saw at one point more than 900 trading companies supplying just four channels. Now with nearer 900 channels, the casual observer could be forgiven for thinking there are just four independent producers. Consolidation has been good for the founders of these companies and City money has flowed in, whether it be through floating on AIM (the alternative investment market), mergers between themselves, or selling out to a European utilities company (in the case of Endemol/Telefonica).

The diversity factor provided by the independent sector has, however, been stifled as broadcasters prefer to work with known and trusted providers. Pact, the producers' association, which has lobbied effectively for better rights agreements, including that of allowing producers to retain their programmes after a broadcaster has bought a licence to air it, is now turning its attention to quantity.

Yes, the talk is back to quotas. Not for the total share of independent production, but for the number of producers used. As ever, television pretends to be a free market, but the regulation involved in the masquerade grows ever more complex.

Top shows of 2005

	Title	Viewers (m)	% Share	Broadcaster/producer
1	Coronation Street	14.35	57.39	ITV1
2	EastEnders	14.34	57.85	BBC1
3	I'm a Celebrity... Get me out of Here!	12.30	49.73	ITV1
4	The Vicar of Dibley	11.57	42.70	BBC1/Tiger Aspect
5	Emmerdale	11.18	48.80	ITV1
6	Comic Relief: Red Nose Night Live 05	10.93	45.09	BBC1
7	Doctor Who	10.81	44.84	BBC1
8	Strictly Come Dancing	10.80	41.95	BBC1
9	A Touch of Frost	10.28	40.24	ITV1
10	Little Britain	10.17	40.68	BBC1
11	Uefa Champions League Live	10.11	44.78	ITV1
12	Ahead of the Class	10.06	40.21	ITV1
13	The X Factor	10.04	48.65	ITV1/Thames Syco
14	Diamond Geezer	9.94	43.83	ITV1
15	The Royal Variety Show	9.80	37.50	ITV1
16	Midsomer Murders	9.70	41.72	ITV1/Bentley
17	Heartbeat	9.58	38.31	ITV1
18	Ten O'Clock News	9.56	43.55	BBC1
19	Doc Martin	9.26	37.62	ITV1/Buffalo Pictures
20	Casualty	9.24	36.43	BBC1
21	Dalziel and Pascoe	9.22	35.31	BBC1
22	The Royal	9.13	35.04	ITV1
23	Life Begins	9.09	38.11	ITV1
24	Creature Comforts	9.01	35.51	ITV1/Aardman
25	Ant & Dec's Gameshow Marathon	9.00	42.52	ITV1
26	Trial and Retribution	8.99	36.69	ITV1/La Plante
27	Casualty at Holby City	8.90	35.86	BBC1
28	The Green Green Grass	8.88	39.81	BBC1
29	Like Father Like Son	8.85	35.45	ITV1/Ecosse
30	Ant and Dec's Saturday Night Takeaway	8.84	40.30	ITV1
31	Match of the Day Live	8.75	46.24	BBC1
32	Waking the Dead	8.58	35.20	BBC1
33	The Bill	8.55	33.76	ITV1/Thames
34	Who wants to be a Millionaire?	8.45	37.85	ITV1/Celador
35	Walk Away and I Stumble	8.38	36.17	ITV1
36	New Tricks	8.25	34.96	BBC1/Wall To Wall
37	Grand National Grandstand	8.21	51.23	BBC1
38	Comic Relief Does Fame Academy	8.18	35.66	BBC1
39	The British Soap Awards	8.14	37.67	ITV1
40	The Stepfather	8.13	32.57	ITV1
41	Holby City	8.09	31.92	BBC1
42	Supervolcano	8.07	31.89	BBC1
43	Agatha Christie's Marple	8.04	30.72	ITV1
44	Silent Witness	8.02	35.65	BBC1
45	Heartless	8.00	33.81	ITV1/Ecosse
46	The Eurovision Song Contest 2005	7.97	38.52	BBC1
47	Wire in the Blood	7.94	33.53	ITV1
48	Ocean's Eleven	7.93	32.95	ITV1
48	The Two Ronnies Christmas Sketchbook	7.93	38.31	BBC1
48	The National Lottery: Jet Set	7.93	34.70	BBC1

	Title	Viewers (m)	% Share	Broadcaster/producer
51	Distant Shores	7.91	31.30	ITV1
52	Judge John Deed	7.84	31.70	BBC1
53	Live8	7.82	41.79	BBC1
54	The Commander	7.79	31.71	ITV1
55	The Two Ronnies Sketchbook	7.69	33.63	BBC1
56	Big Brother	7.65	37.72	C4/Endemol
57	William and Mary	7.61	31.97	ITV1
58	Red Nose 05 Goes Live	7.53	33.13	BBC1
59	The National Television Awards	7.52	32.52	ITV1
60	Fat Friends	7.50	31.20	ITV1/Rollem
61	Emmerdale Greatest Love Triangles	7.49	32.59	ITV1
61	Egypt	7.49	30.03	BBC1
63	An Audience with Joe Pasquale	7.48	32.43	ITV1
64	The Queen's Castle	7.46	28.47	BBC1/RDF
65	Footprints in the Snow	7.36	33.86	ITV1/Oxford Films
65	The Royal Wedding: Charles and Camilla	7.36	53.36	BBC1
67	Where the Heart Is	7.32	30.99	ITV1
67	Bleak House	7.32	30.82	BBC1
67	Bend It Like Beckham	7.32	27.32	BBC1
70	Antiques Roadshow	7.31	32.35	BBC1
71	Falling	7.27	32.78	ITV1
72	Eurovision – Making Your Mind Up	7.22	31.59	BBC1
73	Malice Aforethought	7.17	30.48	ITV1
74	Cold Blood	7.09	30.87	ITV1
75	Messiah 4	7.07	30.62	BBC1
76	Vincent	7.02	28.99	ITV1
76	Rome	7.02	28.05	BBC2
78	Taggart	6.99	29.28	ITV1/SMG
79	Class of '76	6.92	29.34	ITV1/Zenith
80	Bridget Jones's Diary	6.90	32.11	BBC1
81	The Inspector Lynley Mysteries	6.88	28.58	BBC1
82	The National Lottery – Wright Around...	6.87	29.36	BBC1
83	Footballers' Wives	6.85	29.75	ITV1/Shed
84	Spooks	6.84	29.82	BBC1/Kudos
85	Queen Mania	6.80	30.26	ITV1
86	Harry Potter/ Philosopher's Stone	6.77	38.30	BBC1
87	Marian, Again	6.76	30.17	ITV1 Company
88	Rugby Union	6.75	32.70	BBC1
88	Lost	6.75	32.17	C4
90	Monarch of the Glen	6.73	28.17	BBC1/Ecosse
91	Sea of Souls	6.72	28.35	BBC1
92	The National Lottery – In It to Win It	6.70	36.21	BBC1
93	Shrek	6.69	47.47	BBC1
94	Ronnie Barker – A Life in Comedy	6.67	34.48	BBC1
95	Strictly Dance Fever Results	6.66	30.60	BBC1
95	Watchdog	6.66	29.53	BBC1
95	Airline	6.66	35.16	ITV1
98	Six O'Clock News	6.65	36.33	BBC1
99	The National Lottery Come and Have a Go	6.64	33.78	BBC1
100	Indiana Jones and the Last Crusade	6.63	28.81	BBC1

Source: Broadcast Jan 06 issue

ITV finally makes the Grade

Steve Hewlett

Many of the most interesting stories about television in 2006 have had little directly to do with what appears on screen.

Michael Grade's abrupt departure from the BBC was one of a number of "coming home" moments. When Grade announced to cheering ITV staffers that he felt he had "arrived home", some seasoned media watchers experienced a sense of deja vu: he had said more or less the same when he arrived at the BBC in the wake of the hurried post-Hutton departures of Greg Dyke and Gavin Davies. Peter Salmon – the newly appointed chief creative officer of BBC Vision – said he'd "arrived home" from a couple of tortured years in the independent sector. Funnily enough, he more or less swapped jobs with the former BBC director of factual and learning, John Willis, who said he was thrilled to be returning to his real home – programme making – as chief executive of Mentorn, the independent production company that Salmon had just left. Charles Allen, the chief executive of ITV, and Dan Chambers, the programme director at Five, really did return to their homes. Literally.

For commercial television in the UK, 2006 will go down as a dysfunctional year. Relative optimism at the start of the year quickly gave way to foreboding as some audiences and revenues began to decline. Revenues dipped by some 6.5% year on year. ITV1 took the biggest hit, with revenues declining some 15%.

The impact of the contract rights renewal system – felt fully for the first time in 2006 – didn't just cripple ITV but is widely regarded to be a key factor in dragging the whole market down. As the architect of the system – offered up by ITV to secure the Carlton/Granada merger – Charles Allen was vulnerable but when the World Cup failed to deliver any of the predicted financial benefits, he was almost certain to be shown the red card in the second half. And on August 9, he was.

With shareholders looking on in vain for signs of improvement in ITV's fortunes, the corporate vultures began to circle. An attempt to buy ITV earlier in the year by a venture capital consortium headed by the former ITV executive and BBC director general Greg Dyke was successfully resisted by the ITV board on the promise of future improvement. But that didn't come and following Allen's departure and the prolonged failure of the board to find a replacement NTL moved in for the kill. RTL (owners of Five) were also reported to be concocting a bid. City expectation was that ITV, bereft of a chief executive, would most likely be bought and quite possibly broken up. Respite was only brought by a sharp move by Sky, which bought 18% of ITV's stock at a price far higher than NTL could reasonably afford to pay, and the sudden and unexpected coup by the ITV board of pinching Michael Grade from the BBC.

Industry estimates for advertising revenues in 2007 are again relatively optimistic at flat to up a little. If that turns out to be right, the short-term difficulties of ITV could ease (provided it gets the programmes right).

And what about dear old Auntie? It was all going so well. Awards for programming excellence poured in and the BBC's main channels held up better than most in audience terms (BBC2 peak-time share actually went up). Friends and enemies alike looked on with awe at the BBC's prowess in the new media field. The Grade-Thompson dream team had delivered a new 10-year charter, persuaded the government of their vision of a "Big BBC" funded by a compulsory licence fee at the centre of the nation's cultural life in the digital age and seen off the threat of external regulation. All that remained was the small matter of the level of the licence fee itself.

The BBC's request for RPI (inflation) plus 2.3% looked audacious and was regarded, predictably, as merely an opening bid. But much of the process was conducted – much to the BBC's credit and for the first time ever – in public. However, the rot began with the publication of a report by the accountancy firm PKF hired by the Department for Culture, Media and Sport to check out the BBC bid. Too many of the BBC's figures either didn't add up or were based on questionable assumptions, and thus began a lengthy series of detailed negotiations with government. The biggest risk of a low settlement is not that the BBC won't manage – because it will – but that the period of intense introspection that goes with it will disable, albeit temporarily, Britain's foremost and most forward-looking cultural institution.

● Steve Hewlett is media columnist at the Guardian

Television contacts

BBC

BBC
020 8743 8000
info@bbc.co.uk
www.bbc.co.uk
*Acting chair of governors: Chitra Bharucha;
vice-chairman: Anthony Salz; governors:
Deborah Bull, Dame Ruth Deech, Dermot
Gleeson, Professor Merfyn Jones, Professor
Fabian Monds, Angela Sarkis, Ranjit
Sondhi, Richard Tait; director-general:
Mark Thompson*
Press: 020 8576 1865
   press.office@bbc.co.uk
   www.bbc.co.uk/pressoffice

Addresses

Television Centre
Wood Lane, London W12 7RJ

BBC White City
201 Wood Lane, London W12 7TS

Broadcasting House
Portland Place, London W1A 1AA

● BBC TV

Television Centre
020 8743 8000
www.bbc.co.uk/television
*Director of television: Jana Bennett;
controller, programme acquisition:
George McGhee*
Press: 020 8576 9900
   publicity.frontdesk@bbc.co.uk

● Nations and regions

Director of nations and regions:
Pat Loughrey

BBC Northern Ireland
Broadcasting House, Ormeau
Avenue, Belfast BT2 8HQ
028 9033 8000
www.bbc.co.uk/northernireland
Controller: Anna Carragher

BBC Scotland
Broadcasting House, Queen
Margaret Drive, Glasgow G12 8DG
0141 339 8844
www.bbc.co.uk/scotland
Controller: Ken MacQuarrie

BBC Wales
Broadcasting House, Llandaff,
Cardiff CF5 2YQ
029 2032 2000
www.bbc.co.uk/wales
Controller: Menna Richards

BBC ENGLISH REGIONS

Controller: Andy Griffee

BBC London
35c Marylebone High Street,
London W1U 4QA
020 7224 2424
yourlondon@bbc.co.uk
www.bbc.co.uk/london
*Head of regional and local programmes:
Michael MacFarlane*

BBC East
The Forum, Millennium Plain,
Norwich NR2 1BH
01603 619 331
look.east@bbc.co.uk
www.bbc.co.uk/england/lookeast
*Head of regional and local programmes:
Tim Bishop*

BBC East Midlands
London Road, Nottingham NG2 4UU
0115 955 0500
emt@bbc.co.uk
www.bbc.co.uk/england
   /eastmidlandstoday
*Head of regional and local programmes:
Alison Ford*

BBC North
2 St Peter's Square, Leeds LS9 8AH
0113 244 1188
look.north@bbc.co.uk
www.bbc.co.uk/england
   /looknorthyorkslincs
*Head of regional and local programmes:
Helen Thomas*

BBC North East and Cumbria
Broadcasting Centre, Barrack Road,
Newcastle upon Tyne NE99 2NE
0191 232 1313
newcastlenews@bbc.co.uk
www.bbc.co.uk/england
   /looknorthnecumbria
*Head of regional and local programmes:
Wendy Pilmer*

BBC North West
New Broadcasting House,
Oxford Road, Manchester M60 1SJ
0161 200 2020
nwt@bbc.co.uk
www.bbc.co.uk/manchester
*Head of regional and local programmes:
Tamsin O'Brien*

BBC South
Broadcasting House, Havelock Road,
Southampton SO14 7PU
023 8022 6201
south.today@bbc.co.uk
www.bbc.co.uk/england/southtoday
*Head of regional and local programmes:
Eve Turner*

BBC South East
The Great Hall, Mount Pleasant
Road, Tunbridge Wells TN1 1QQ
01892 670000
southeasttoday@bbc.co.uk
www.bbc.co.uk/england
   /southeasttoday
*Head of regional and local programmes:
Laura Ellis*

BBC South West
Broadcasting House, Seymour Road,
Mannamead, Plymouth PL3 5BD
01752 229201
spotlight@bbc.co.uk
www.bbc.co.uk/england/devon
*Head of regional and local programmes:
John Lilley*

BBC West
Broadcasting House,
Whiteladies Road, Bristol BS8 2LR
0117 973 2211
pointswest@bbc.co.uk
www.bbc.co.uk/england/pointswest
*Head of regional and local programmes:
Andrew Wilson*

BBC West Midlands
The Mailbox, Birmingham B1 1XL
0121 567 6767
midlands.today@bbc.co.uk
www.bbc.co.uk/birmingham
*Head of regional and local programmes:
David Holdsworth*

● Channels

BBC One
Television Centre
020 8743 8000
www.bbc.co.uk/bbcone
Controller: Peter Fincham

BBC Two
Television Centre
020 8743 8000
www.bbc.co.uk/bbctwo
*Controller: Roly Keating; controller of
daytime, Jay Hunt*

BBC Three
Television Centre
020 8743 8000
www.bbc.co.uk/bbcthree
Controller: Julian Bellamy

BBC Four
Television Centre
0870 010 0222
www.bbc.co.uk/bbcfour
Controller: Janice Hadlow

CBBC
Television Centre
020 8743 8000
www.bbc.co.uk/cbbc
Controller: Richard Deverell

CBeebies
Television Centre
020 8743 8000
www.bbc.co.uk/cbeebies
Controller: Richard Deverell

BBC America
PO Box 6266, Florence,
KY 41022-6266, USA
00 1 859 342 4070
www.bbcamerica.com
Programme executive: Alison Fredericks

BBC Canada
121 Bloor Street East, Suite 200,
Toronto, Ontario, Canada M4W 3M5
00 416 967 3249
feedback@bbccanada.com
www.bbccanada.com

BBC Food
PO Box 5054, London W12 0ZY
020 8433 2221
www.bbcfood.com
Editor: David Weiland

BBC News 24
Television Centre
020 8743 8000
bbcnews24@bbc.co.uk
www.bbc.co.uk/bbcnews24
Editoral director: Mark Popescu

BBC Parliament
4 Millbank, London SW1P 3JA
020 7973 6216
parliament@bbc.co.uk
www.bbc.co.uk/bbcparliament

BBC Prime
PO Box 5054, London W12 0ZY
020 8433 2221
bbcprime@bbc.co.uk
www.bbcprime.com
Editor: David Weiland

BBC World
PO Box 5054, London W12 0ZY
020 8433 2221
bbcworld@bbc.co.uk
www.bbcworld.com
Editorial director: Sian Kevill

BBC Japan
PO Box 5054, London W12 0ZY
www.bbcjapan.tv

● Interactive TV

BBCi
Television Centre
020 8743 8000
www.bbc.co.uk/digital/tv
*Controller: Rahul Chakkara; head,
interactive TV programming: Emma
Somerville*

● Ceefax

Television Centre
020 8743 8000

Genres

● BBC News

Television Centre
020 8743 8000
www.bbc.co.uk/news
*Director of BBC News: Helen Boaden;
deputy: Mark Damazer; head of
newsgathering: Adrian Van Klaveren*

- Editors – *business: Jeff Randall;
diplomatic: Brian Hanrahan; home:
Mark Easton; Middle East: Jeremy
Bowen; political: Nick Robinson; world
affairs: John Simpson*

- UK correspondents – *defence: Paul
Adams; diplomatic: Jonathan Marcus;
education: Mike Baker; health: Karen
Allen; home affairs: Margaret Gilmore;
political: Laura Trevelyan; royal:
Nicholas Witchell, Peter Hunt; rural
affairs: Tom Heap; security: Frank
Gardner; social affairs: Daniel Sandford*

- Special correspondents – *Fergal Keane,
Gavin Hewitt; TV news: Ben Brown;
BBC News 24: Philippa Thomas*

- World correspondents – *world affairs:
Peter Biles. Europe: Tim Franks, Chris
Morris, Stephen Sackur; Paris: Allan
Little, Caroline Wyatt; Berlin: Ray
Furlong; Rome: David Willey; Greece:
Richard Galpin; Moscow: Damian
Grammaticas; south Europe: Brian
Barron; central Europe: Nick Thorpe.
Middle East: Orla Guerin, James
Reynolds, Paul Wood; Turkey: Jonny
Dymond. Americas - Washington: Nick
Bryant, Matt Frei, Jon Leyne, Clive
Myrie, Ian Pannell, Justin Webb;
California: David Willis; Mexico and
central America: Claire Marshall; South
America: Elliott Gotkine. Other - Africa:
Hilary Andersson; east Africa: Andrew
Harding; south Asia: Adam Mynott;
south-east Asia: Kylie Morris; central
Asia: Monica Whitlock. World media:
Sebastian Usher. Also Dominic Hughes,
Jill McGivering, Matthew Price*

Political programmes unit
BBC Westminster, 4 Millbank,
London SW1P 3JA
020 7973 6000
*Head of political programmes: Sue
Inglish; political editor: Nick Robinson*

TV News
Room 1502, Television Centre
020 8624 9141
*Head of television news: Peter Horrocks;
deputy: Rachel Attwell*

PROGRAMMES

Breakfast
Room 1605, News Centre,
Television Centre
020 8624 9700
breakfasttv@bbc.co.uk
*Editor: Richard Porter; presenters:
Dermot Murnaghan, Natasha Kaplinsky*

Newsnight
Television Centre
020 8624 9800
*Editor: Peter Barron; presenters: Jeremy
Paxman, Kirsty Wark, Gavin Esler*

Panorama
Room 1118, BBC White City
020 8752 7152
panorama@bbc.co.uk
*Editor: Mike Robinson; deputy editors:
Andrew Bell and Sam Collyns*

Politics Show
4 Millbank, London SW1P 3JQ
020 7973 6199
politicsshow@bbc.co.uk
Presenter: John Sopel

Question Time
Mentorn, 43 Whitfield Street,
London W1T 4HA
020 7258 6800
Presenter: David Dimbleby

Six O'Clock News
Television Centre
020 8624 9996
*Presenters: George Alagiah, Sophie
Raworth*

Ten O'Clock News
Television Centre
020 8624 9999
*Editor: Kevin Bakhurst; presenters:
Huw Edwards, Fiona Bruce*

● Factual and learning

Director of factual and learning
John Willis
020 8752 6501

Controller, factual TV
Glenwyn Benson
020 8743 8000

Arts
2nd Floor, BBC White City
020 8752 4092
claire.lewis.02@bbc.co.uk
*Executive producer: Claire Lewis;
commissioner, arts and culture:
Franny Moyle*

Arts (Wales)
Room 4001, BBC Wales
029 2032 2943
Acting head of arts, Wales: Gail Evans

Classical music
Room EG09, Television Centre
020 8895 6541
*Head of TV, classical music and
performance: Peter Maniura*

Current affairs
Room 1172, BBC White City
020 8752 7005
Head of current affairs: George Entwistle

Documentaries and
contemporary factual
Room 3559, BBC White City
020 8743 8000
genfact.proposals@bbc.co.uk
Head of documentaries: Keith Scholey

Education
Room 3416, BBC White City
020 8752 5241
Executive editor: Karen Johnson

Education (Northern Ireland)
Education Unit, First Floor,
BBC Northern Ireland
028 9033 8445
Editor, learning, NI: Kieran Hegarty

Education (Scotland)
Room 230, BBC Scotland
0141 338 1507
Editor, education, Scotland: Moira Scott

Education (Wales)
Room E3106, BBC Wales
029 2032 2834
*Head of education and learning,
Wales: Dr Eleri Wyn Lewis*

Factual (Northern Ireland)
2nd Floor, BBC Northern Ireland
028 9033 8553
*Editor, factual TV: Paul McGuigan; head
of factual network production, NI: Fiona
Campbell, 020 8752 6074*

Factual (Scotland)
Room 3178, BBC Scotland
0141 338 3646
andrea.miller.01@bbc.co.uk
*Head of factual programmes, Scotland:
Andrea Miller*

Factual (Wales)
Room 4020, BBC Wales
029 2032 2976
*Head of factual programmes,
Wales: Adrian Davies*

Lifeskills TV
Room 2308, BBC White City
020 8752 4574
Head of Lifeskills TV: Seetha Kumar

Music (Wales)
Room E4113, BBC Wales
029 2032 2111
davidm.jackson@bbc.co.uk
Head of music, Wales: David Jackson

Specialist factual, current affairs and arts
Room 2156, BBC White City
020 8743 8000
specfact.proposals@bbc.co.uk
*Head of independent commissioning:
Adam Kemp; commissioner, specialist
factual: Emma Swain; senior
commissioning executives: Krishan
Arora, Lucy Hetherington; executive
editor: Jacquie Hughes*

PROGRAMMES

Arena
Room 2168, BBC White City
020 8752 5172
Series editor: Anthony Wall

Everyman
Room 5048, BBC Manchester,
Broadcasting House, Oxford Road,
Manchester M60 1SJ
0161 244 3321
ruth.pitt@bbc.co.uk
Creative director: Ruth Pitt

Horizon
Room 4523, BBC White City
020 8752 6134
horizon@bbc.co.uk
Editor: Andrew Cohen

Imagine
Arts Department, 2nd Floor,
BBC White City
020 8752 4092
ian.macmillan@bbc.co.uk
Series producer: Ian Macmillan

Money programme
Room 4116, BBC White City
020 8752 7400
Executive editor: Clive Edwards

One Life
Room 5503, BBC White City
020 8752 6608
todd.austin@bbc.co.uk
Commissioning editor: Todd Austin

Panorama
Room 1118, BBC White City
020 8752 7152
Editor: Mike Robinson

Storyville
Room 201, 1 Mortimer Street,
London W1T 3JA
020 7765 5211
storyville@bbc.co.uk
Commissioning editor: Nick Fraser

This World
Room 1362, BBC White City
020 8752 7500
thisworld@bbc.co.uk
Editor: Karen O'Connor

Timewatch
Room 3150, BBC White City
020 8752 7079
Editor: John Farren

● Drama and entertainment

*Director of drama, entertainment
and CBBC* Alan Yentob

Comedy
Room 4045, Television Centre
020 8743 8000
*Head of comedy commissioning:
Lucy London*

Comedy and entertainment (Scotland)
Room 3167, BBC Scotland
0141 338 2370
*Head of comedy and entertainment,
Scotland: Alan Tyler*

Daytime
Room 3560, BBC White City
020 8752 6225
*Senior commissioning executive, daytime:
Lindsay Bradbury*

Daytime entertainment
Room 6070, Television Centre
020 8576 9960
*Commissioning executive, daytime
entertainment: Gilly Hall*

Drama
Room 2145, Television Centre,
56 Wood Lane, London W12 7RJ
020 8576 1861

Drama (Northern Ireland)
BBC Northern Ireland
020 8576 1664
Head of drama, NI: Patrick Spence

Drama (Scotland)
Room 2170, BBC Scotland
0141 338 2517
*Head of television drama, Scotland:
Anne Mensah*

Drama (Wales)
Room E2106, BBC Wales
029 2032 2935
Head of drama, Wales: Julie Gardner

Entertainment
Room 6070, Television Centre
020 8225 6992
*Controller, entertainment,
commissioning: Jane Lush*

Entertainment (Northern Ireland)
Room 229, BBC Northern Ireland
028 9033 8375
mike.edgar@bbc.co.uk
*Head of entertainment, events and sport,
NI: Mike Edgar*

● Children

CBBC
Room E1012, Television Centre
020 8576 1280
*Director: Anne Gilchrist; controller:
Richard Deverell*

Acquisitions
Room E185, Television Centre
020 8576 8245
*Head of acquisitions and co-productions:
Jesse Cleverly*

CBBC Creates
Room E1200, Television Centre
020 8576 1040
*Development executive, CBBC Creates:
Michael Carrington*

CBBC Scotland
Room 2104, BBC Scotland
0141 338 2012
Head of Scotland: Donalda MacKinnon

Drama
Room E817, Television Centre
020 8576 8245
Head of drama: Jon East

Entertainment
Room E701, Television Centre
020 8225 9269
Head of entertainment: Anne Gilchrist

News and factual
Room E111, Television Centre
020 8576 3118
Head of news and factual: Tim Levell

Pre-school
Room N105, Neptune House,
BBC Elstree, Clarendon Road,
Borehamwood, Herts WD6 1JF
020 8228 7072
Head of pre-school: Clare Elstow

● Sport

Director of sport Roger Mosey

Live sport and highlights
Room 5060, Television Centre
020 8225 8400
andrew.thompson.01@bbc.co.uk
Head of new media, sports news and development: Andrew Thompson

● Films

BBC Films
Grafton House, 379 Euston Road,
London NW1 3AU
020 7765 0251
Head of BBC Films: David Thompson; executive producer: Anne Pivcevic

>> *See page 295*

● Radio

>> *See page 200*

● New media

BBC New Media
Broadcast Centre, Media Village,
201 Wood Lane, London W12 7TP
020 8008 1300
www.bbc.co.uk
Director of new media and technology: Ashley Highfield; controller, internet: Tony Ageh; controller, emerging platforms: Angel Gambino

>> *See page 237*

● Business services

BBC Costumes and Wigs
Victoria Road, London W3 6UL
020 8576 1761
costume@bbc.co.uk
wigs@bbc.co.uk
www.bbcresources.com

BBC International Unit
020 8576 1963
international.unit@bbc.co.uk
www.bbc.co.uk/international
Supplies TV facilities to overseas broadcasters transmitting from UK. Manager: Peter James

BBC Monitoring
Marketing Unit, Caversham Park,
Reading RG4 8TZ
0118 948 6289
csu@mon.bbc.co.uk
www.bbcmonitoringonline.com
www.monitor.bbc.co.uk
Monitors world media

BBC Outside Broadcasts
Kendal Avenue, London W3 0RP
020 8993 9333
ob@bbc.co.uk
www.bbcresources.com

BBC Post-Production
Television Centre
020 8225 7702
postproduction@bbc.co.uk
www.bbcresources.com
Bristol
Broadcasting House,
White Ladies Road, Bristol BS8 2LR
0117 974 6666
Birmingham
The Mailbox, Birmingham B1 1XL
0121 567 6767

BBC R&D
BBC Kingswood Warren,
Tadworth, Surrey KT20 6NP
01737 839500
info@rd.bbc.co.uk
www.bbc.co.uk/rd
Head of research: Ian Childs

BBC Research Central
Broadcasting House
research-central@bbc.co.uk
www.bbcresearchcentral.com
Information, footage, pronunciation, radio and photo research services. Senior researchers: Helen Turner, Huw Martin, Guy Watkins, Angie Francis, Kyla Thorogood, Richard Jeffery, Jacqueline Faulkner, Michael Paige

BBC Studios
Television Centre
020 8576 7666
tvstudio.sales@bbc.co.uk
www.bbcresources.com

BBC Training and Development
35 Marylebone High Street,
London W1U 4PX
0870 122 0216
training@bbc.co.uk
www.bbctraining.co.uk
Training for programme-making, broadcasting and new media
Press: 01993 823011
   louise@energypr.co.uk
   (Louise Findlay-Wilson)
Elstree
Clarendon Road, Borehamwood,
Herts WD6 1JF
Wood Norton Training Centre
Evesham, Worcestershire WR11 4YB

BBC Worldwide
Woodlands, 80 Wood Lane,
London W12 0TT
020 8433 2000
www.bbcworldwide.com
Commercial arm: businesses include distribution, TV channels, magazines, books, videos, spoken word, music, DVDs, licensed products, CD-ROMs, English language teaching, videos for education and training, interactive telephony, co-production, library footage. Chief executive: John Smith

Advisory bodies

Broadcasting Council for Scotland
The Secretary, Broadcasting House,
Queen Margaret Drive,
Glasgow G12 8DG
0141 339 8844

Broadcasting Council for Wales
The Secretary, Broadcasting House,
Llandaff, Cardiff CF5 2YQ
029 2032 2000

Broadcasting Council for Northern Ireland
Head of Public Affairs and Secretary,
Broadcasting House, Ormeau
Avenue, Belfast BT2 8HQ
028 9033 8000

Central Religious Advisory Committee
The Secretary, Broadcasting House,
London W1A 1AA
020 7580 4468

English National Forum
Head of Press and Public Affairs,
English Regions, BBC Birmingham,
The Mailbox, Birmingham B1 1XL
0121 567 6767

Governors' World Service Consultative Group
BBC World Service, Bush House,
Strand, London WC2B 4PH
020 8743 8000

● ITV Network (ITV1)

200 Grays Inn Road,
London WC1X 8HF
020 7843 8000
www.itv.com/itv1
www.itvregions.com
*Controllers run commissioning and
scheduling across ITV1 national network -
including non-ITV plc regions. Network
controllers - acquisitions: Jay Kondola,
020 7843 8120; arts, current affairs and
religion: Dominic Crossley-Holland;
factual and daytime: Alison Sharman,
020 7843 8132; comedy: Paul Jackson,
020 7843 8093; drama: Nick Elliot, 020
7843 8202 (head of continuing series:
Corinne Hollingworth); entertainment:
Paul Jackson, 020 7843 8105; sport:
Mark Sharman*

● ITV plc

London Television Centre,
Upper Ground, London SE1 9LT
020 7843 8000
*Controls 11 of the 15 ITV1 franchises,
ITV2, ITV3, ITV News Channel, and
Granada production company. Chief
executive: Michael Grade; chairman: Sir
Peter Burt; director of regional affairs:
Susan Woodward; controller of regional
affairs: Jane Luca. Communications
director: Brigitte Trafford*
Press: 020 7620 1620

ITV Broadcast
020 7843 8000
Runs ITV plc's 11 regional ITV1
franchises; runs ITV2 and ITV3
Director of Television: Simon Shaps

ITV1 FRANCHISES

ITV Anglia
Anglia House, Norwich NR1 3JG
01603 615151
firstname.lastname@itv.com
www.angliatv.com
*MD: Neil Thompson; controller of
programmes and regional news: Neil
Thompson; head of regional affairs:
Jim Woodrow*

News at Anglia
0870 240 6003
news@angliatv.com

Cambridge regional office
26 Newmarket Road,
Cambridge CB5 8DT
01223 467076

Chelmsford regional office
64–68 New London Road,
Chelmsford CM2 0YU
01245 357676

Ipswich regional office
Hubbard House, Ipswich IP1 2QA
01473 226157

Luton regional office
16 Park Street, Luton LU1 2DP
01582 729666

Northampton regional office
77b Abington Street,
Northampton NN1 2BH
01604 624343

Peterborough regional office
6 Bretton Green,
Peterborough PE3 8DY
01733 269440

ITV Border
The Television Centre, Durranhill,
Carlisle CA1 3NT
01228 525101
www.border-tv.com
*MD: Paddy Merrall; head of news: Ian
Proniewicz; head of features: Jane
Bolesworth*
Press and regional affairs manager:
Louise Maving

ITV Central
Gas Street, Birmingham B1 2JT
0121 643 9898
firstname.lastname@itv.com
www2.itv.com/central
*MD: Ian Squires; controller of news and
operations: Mike Blair; head of regional
programming: Duncan Rycroft; editor,
Central News West: Dan Barton*
Press officer: Christopher Strange

Central News East
Terry Lloyd House, 1 Regan Way,
Chetwynd Business Park,
Nottingham NG9 6RZ
0115 986 3322
News editor: Mike Blair

Central News South
9 Windrush Court,
Abingdon Business Park, Abingdon,
Oxford OX14 1SA
01235 554123
News editor: Steve Lambdon

ITV Granada
Quay Street, Manchester M60 9EA
0161 832 7211
firstname.lastname@itv.com
www.granadatv.com
*MD: Susan Woodward; controller of
programmes: Duncan Ryecroft; controller
of regional affairs: Jane Luca; news
editor: Richard Frediani*

Liverpool office
The Liver Building, Liverpool L3 1HU
0151 473 8600

Lancaster office
White Cross, Lancaster LA1 4XQ
01524 60688

ITV London
London Television Centre,
Upper Grounds, London SE1 9LT
020 7620 1620
firstname.lastname@itv.com
www2.itv.com/london
*MD: Christy Swords; controller of
regional programming: Emma Barker;
head of regional affairs: Helen Andrews*

London News Network
200 Grays Inn Road,
London WC1X 8HF
020 7430 4000
firstname.lastname@itvlondon.com
www.itvlondon.co.uk
*Planning editor: Arti Lukha; head of
news: Stuart Thomas; news editors:
Brendan McGowan, Robin Campbell*

ITV Meridian
Forum One, Parkway,
Solent Business Park, Whiteley,
Hampshire PO15 7PA
01489 442000
news@meridiantv.com
www.meridiantv.co.uk

Maidstone news office
Maidstone Studios, Vinters Park,
Maidstone, Kent ME14 5NZ
01489 442000

Newbury news office
Strawberry Hill House, Strawberry
Hill, Newbury, Berkshire RG14 1NG
01635 552266

ITV Tyne Tees
Television House, The Watermark,
Gateshead NE11 9SZ
0191 4048700
news@tynetees.tv
firstname.lastname@itv.com
www.tynetees.tv
*MD and controller of programmes:
Graeme Thompson; head of regional
affairs: Norma Hope; head of news:
Graham Marples*

*Tees Valley & North Yorkshire
news office*
Belasis Hall Technology Park,
Billingham, Teesside TS23 4EG
01642 566999
newstoday@tynetees.tv
Senior editor: Bill Campbell

ITV Wales
The Television Centre,
Culverhouse Cross, Cardiff CF5 6XJ
029 2059 0590
info@itvwales.com
news@itvwales.com
firstname.lastname@itvwales.com
www.itvwales.com
*MD: Roger Lewis; controller of
programmes: Elis Owen; head of regional
affairs: Mansel Jones; head of news: John
G Williams*
Press contact: Mansel Jones

Carmarthen news office
Coopers Chambers, Lammas Street,
Carmarthen
01267 236806
West Wales correspondent: Giles Smith

Colwyn Bay news office
Celtic Business Centre, Plas Eiriasm
Heritage Gate, Abergele Road,
Colwyn Bay LL29 8BW
01492 513888
colwyn@itvwales.com
*North Wales correspondents: Carole
Green, Ian Lang*

contacts **TV**

159

Newtown news office
St David's House, Newtown SY16 1RB
01686 623381
Mid-Wales correspondent: Rob Shelley

Wrexham news office
Crown Buildings, 31 Chester Street,
Wrexham LL13 8BG
01978 261462
North Wales correspondent: Paul Mewies

ITV West
Television Centre, Bath Road,
Bristol BS4 3HG
0117 972 2722
reception@itv.com
firstname.lastname@itv.com
www.itv1west.com
*MD: Mark Haskell; controller of
programmes: Jane McCloskey; head of
features and current affairs: James Garrett;
head of regional affairs: Richard Lister*
Press: 0117 972 2214

Newsdesk
0117 972 2151/2
itvwestnews@itv.com
Head of news: Liz Hannam

ITV Westcountry
Langage Science Park, Western
Wood Way, Plymouth PL7 5BQ
01752 333333
firstname.lastname@itv.com
www.westcountry.co.uk
*MD: Mark Haskell; director of
programmes: Jane McCloskey; controller,
business affairs: Peter Gregory; director of
production technology: Mark Chaplin;
regional affairs: Rebecca Payne*

Main newsdesk
01752 333329
news@westcountry.co.uk
Controller of news: Phil Carrodus

Barnstaple news office
1 Summerland Terrace,
Barnstaple EX32 8JL
01271 324244

Exeter news office
St Luke's Campus, Magdalene Road,
Exeter EX4 4WT
01392 499400

Penzance news office
Parade Chambers, 10 Parade Street,
Penzance TR18 4BU
01736 331483

Taunton news office
Foundry Cottage, Riverside Place,
St James Street, Taunton TA1 1JH
01823 322335

Truro news office
Courtleigh House, Lemon Street,
Truro TR1 2PN
01872 262244

Weymouth news office
8 King Street, Weymouth DT4 7BP
01305 760860

ITV Yorkshire
The Television Centre, Kirkstall
Road, Leeds, West Yorkshire LS3 1JS
0113 243 8283
firstname.lastname@itv.com
www.yorkshiretv.com
*MD: David Croft, 0113 222 7184;
controller of regional programmes: Clare
Morrow, 0113 222 8724; head of regional
affairs: Mark Covell, 0113 222 7091*
Press: 0113 222 7129

Grimsby office
Immage Studios, Margaret Street,
Immingham, Grimsby DN40 1LE
01469 510661
Head of news: Will Venters

Hull office
23 The Prospect Centre,
Hull HU2 8PM
01482 324488

Lincoln office
88 Bailgate, Lincoln LN1 3AR
01522 530738

Sheffield office
23 Charter Square, Sheffield S1 4HS
0114 272 7772

York office
York St John's College,
Lord Mayors Walk, York YO31 7EX
01904 610066

● Channels

ITV2
020 7843 8000
www.itv.com/itv2
*Editor: Zai Bennett, 020 7843 8332;
controller of commissioned programmes:
Daniella Neumann, 020 7843 8101*

ITV3
020 7843 8000
www.itv.com/itv3
*Editor: Steve Arnell, 020 7843 8337;
controller of commissioned programmes:
Daniella Neumann, 020 7843 8101*

● ITV News Group
020 7396 6000
*Includes ITV1's national and
international news output, and regional
news for ITV plc franchises (see above);
plus ITV plc's 40% stake in ITN. Chief
executive: Clive Jones*

ITV News
ITN, 200 Grays Inn Road,
London WC1X 8XZ
020 7833 3000
www.itv.com/news
*ITN is 40% owned by ITV plc. Editor-in-
chief: David Mannion; editor: Deborah
Turness; deputy editor: Jonathan Munro;
managing editor: Robin Elias*
• Key presenters: *Mary Nightingale;
  Katie Derham; Mark Austin; Nicholas
  Owen; Alastair Stewart; Nina Hossain,
  Joyce Ohaja, Steve Scott*
• Editors - *business: Lauren Taylor;
  consumer affairs: Chris Choi;
  international: Bill Neely; political: Tom*

*Bradby; science: Lawrence McGinty;
Senior Correspondent: James Mates; UK
correspondents - news: Juliet Bremner,
Neil Connery, Paul Davies, Tim Ewart,
Philip Reay-Smith; Harry Smith;
political: Angus Walker, Libby Wiener;
north of England: Tim Rogers; Wales
and west of England: Helen Callaghan;
medical: Sue Saville; crime: Adrian
Britton; media and arts: Nina Nannar;
royalty: Romilly Weeks; social affairs:
Helen Wright; sport: Geraint Vincent*
• World correspondents - *international:
  Andrea Catherwood, Penny Marshall;
  Europe: Robert Moore; Washington:
  John Irvine; Middle East: Julian
  Manyon; Africa: Martin Geissler;
  China: John Ray*
Press: 020 7430 4825
    saskia.wirth@itn.co.uk
Press releases to:
    itvplanning@itn.co.uk

ITV News Channel
ITN, 200 Grays Inn Road,
London WC1X 8XZ
020 7833 3000
Editor: John Ray

Regional news offices
*Part of ITV News Group; listed under ITV
franchises, above*

● Other ITV plc divisions

Granada
020 7620 1620
*Production arm. Chief executive:
Simon Shaps*
Press: 020 7843 8218/9

ITV Consumer
020 7396 6051
*Builds direct consumer revenues. Chief
executive officer: Jeff Henry*

ITV Sales
020 7396 6000
*MD: Graham Duff; director of ITV sales:
Gary Digby; director of sales operations:
Jill Kerslake; director of knowledge
management: Andy Bagnall; director
of customer relationship management:
Justin Sampson*

● Other ITV1 franchise-holders

Scottish Media Group
Acting chief executive: Donald Emslie

Grampian TV
Television Centre, Craigshaw
Business Park, West Tullos,
Aberdeen AB12 3QH
01224 848848
firstname.lastname@smg.plc.uk
www.grampiantv.co.uk
*MD and controller of regional
programmes: Derrick Thomson; head of
news: Henry Eagles*
Press: Lyndsay Scatterty
  01224 848820
lyndsay.scatterty@grampiantv.co.uk

Scottish TV
200 Renfield Street, Glasgow G2 3PR
0141 300 3000
firstname.lastname@smg.plc.uk
www.scottishtv.co.uk
*MD and controller of regional
programmes: Bobby Hain; head of news:
Paul Mckinney. Newsdesk: 0141 300 3360*
Press: Kirsten Elsby
  0141 300 3670
  kirstin.elsby@smg.plc.uk

INDEPENDENT FRANCHISES

Channel Television
Television Centre, La Pouquelaye,
St Helier, Jersey JE1 3ZD
01534 816816
broadcast@channeltv.co.uk
www.channeltv.co.uk
*MD: Michael Lucas; director of
programmes: Karen Rankine
(karen.rankine@channeltv.co.uk);
director of special projects: Gordon de Ste
Croix (gordon@channeltv.co.uk); director
of resources and transmission: Kevin
Banner. Newsroom: 01534 816688*

Guernsey office
Television House, Bulwer Avenue,
St Sampson, Guernsey GY2 4LA
01481 241888
broadcast.gsy@channeltv.co.uk

London office
Enterprise House, 1–2 Hatfields,
London SE1 9PG
020 7633 9902

UTV
Ormeau Road, Belfast BT7 1EB
028 9032 8122
info@utvplc.com
www.u.tv
*Group chief executive: John McCann;
director of television: Alan Bremner*
Press: 028 9026 2187

Channel 4

124 Horseferry Road,
London SW1P 2TX
020 7396 4444
www.channel4.co.uk
*Chief executive: Andy Duncan, 020 7306
8700; commercial director: Andy Barnes,
020 7306 8200; director of television:
Kevin Lygo, 020 7306 3775*
Press: Matt Baker, 020 7306 8666

● Commissioning

*Managing editor: Janey Walker,
020 7306 8623 (assistant: Anuja
Manoharan, 020 7306 8282); disability
advisor: Alison Walsh, 020 7306 8125*

Comedy
*Head of comedy and comedy films:
Caroline Leddy, 020 7306 8718*

Daytime and features
*Commissioning editor, daytime:
Adam MacDonald, 020 7306 8033;
editor, daytime and features:
Mark Downie, 020 7306 5150*

Documentaries
*Head: Danny Cohen, 020 7306 6912;
commissioning editors:
Meredith Chambers, 020 7306 5571;
Simon Dickson, 020 7306 3799;
Dominique Walker, 020 7306 3763*

E4
*Head: Danny Cohen, 020 7306 6436;
commissioning editor:
Angela Jain, 020 7306 8515; head of
scheduling: David Booth, 020 7306 6582*

Education
*Head: Janey Walker; commissioning
editor: Deborah Ward*

Entertainment
*Head: Andrew Newman,
020 7306 6382*

Factual entertainment
*Head: Danny Cohen , 020 7306 6436;
editors: Nav Raman, 020 7306 8746,
and Andrew Mackenzie, 020 7306 3680*

Features
*Head: Sue Murphy, 020 7306 8279;
commissioning editors:
Andrew Jackson, 020 7306 8476,
Philippa Ransford, 020 7306 8424,
and Liam Humphreys, 020 7306 6932*

Film and drama
*Head: Tessa Ross, 020 7306 6455; senior
commissioning editor: Francis Hopkinson,
020 7306 6970; editor (series): Camilla
Campbell, 020 7306 3783; deputy
commissioning editor (events): Hannah
Weaver, 020 7306 5536; assistant
editor: Liz Pilling, 020 7306 8621;
head of development: Katherine Butler;
head of Filmfour Lab: Peter Carlton*

History, science, religion and arts
*Head: Hamish Mykura, 020 7306 1036;
commissioning editors:
Aaqil Ahmed, 020 7306 8065, and Jan
Younghusband, 020 7306 5153. Editor:
Louise Bolch, 020 7306 8039*

Nations and regions
Director: Stuart Cosgrove, 0141 568 7105

News and current affairs
*Head: Dorothy Byrne, 020 7306 8568;
commissioning editor (investigations):
Kevin Sutcliffe, 020 7306 1068*

Programming planning and strategy
*Head: Jules Oldroyd, 020 7306 8229;
editor: Neil McCallum, 020 7306 8588;
assistant editor: Cath Lovesey,
020 7306 5622*

Sport
*Deputy commissioning editor:
Deborah Poulton, 020 7306 8501*

Programme acquisition
Jeff Ford, 020 7306 8747

● Broadcasting

*Controller: Rosemary Newell, 020 7306
8620; head of schedules: Jules Oldroyd,
020 7306 8229; deputy scheduler: John
Williams, 020 7306 8257; planner: Lynne
Jarrett, 020 7306 8231; senior planner:
Lucy Rogers, 020 7306 8401
Sales and marketing – agency sales:
Matt Shreeve, 020 7306 8240;
airtime management: Merlin Inkley,
020 7306 8254; marketing director:
Polly Cochrane, 020 7306 6446; research
and insight: Claire Grimmond,
020 7306 8779; sponsorship: David
Charlesworth, 020 7306 8043; strategic
sales: Mike Parker 020 7306 8242; strategy:
Jonathan Thompson, 020 7306 8799*

● Business services

124 Facilities
Tony Chamberlain, 020 7306 8110

Channel Four International
Graeme Mason, 020 7306 3796

Consumer products
Mike Morris, 020 7306 5364

Digital channels
Dan Brooke, 020 7306 6497
E4
Danny Cohen, 020 7306 6436
FilmFour
Tom Sykes, 020 7306 6442

New media
Andy Taylor, 020 7306 3651

● Channel 4 News

ITN
200 Grays Inn Road,
London WC1X 8XZ
020 7833 3000
www.channel4.com/news
*Editor: Jim Gray; deputy editor: Martin
Fewell; managing editor: Gay Flashman.
Newsdesk: 020 7430 4601*
• Presenters – *anchor: Jon Snow; noon
anchor: Krishnan Guru-Murthy; senior
reporter: Sue Turton; presenter: Samira
Ahmed*

- Senior editors – *home: Yvette Edwards; foreign: Deborah Rayner. International editor: Lindsey Hilsum*
- Commissioning editor, independent productions: *Fiona Campbell*
- Chief correspondent: *Alex Thomson. Other correspondents – Asia: Kylie Morris; arts: Nicholas Glass; economics: Liam Halligan; foreign affairs: Jonathan Miller; home affairs: Simon Israel; Midlands: Carl Dinnen; political: Gary Gibbon; science: Tom Clarke; science/defence: Julian Rush; social affairs: Victoria Macdonald; correspondent: Sarah Smith*
Press: 020 7430 4220
   fiona.railton@itn.co.uk

Five

2 Long Acre, London WC2E 9LY
020 7550 5555
firstname.lastname@five.tv
www.five.tv
Director of programmes: Dan Chambers, 020 7550 5673 (PA: Sarah Jackson, 020 7550 5522); controller of broadcast services: David Burge, 020 7691 6260; history: Alex Sutherland

- Controllers – *arts, daytime and religion: Kim Peat, 020 7421 7107; children's programmes: Nick Wilson; factual entertainment: Steve Gowans (deputy commissioning editor: Ian Dunkley, 020 7550 5659); features and entertainment: Ben Frow, 020 7421 7118; news: Chris Shaw, 020 7421 7122 (deputy: Ian Russell, 020 7550 5529); science: Justine Kershaw, 020 7421 7112; sport: Robert Charles, 020 7421 7185; special events and pop features: Sham Sandhu, 020 7421 7184*
- Drama editor: *Abigail Webber*
- Press: *020 7550 5533; head of press and corporate affairs: Paul Leather, 020 7550 5541; deputy: Tracey O'Connor, 020 7550 5553; marketing and publicity executive: Louise Bowers, 020 7550 5662*
- Heads of publicity – *acquisitions and drama: Tamara Bishopp, 020 7550 5539; factual and features: Louise Plank, 020 7550 5659*
- Publicists – *arts, history and daytime: Allison Broodie, 020 7550 5587; entertainment: Nick Dear, 020 7550 5634; factual and features: Stephanie Faber, 020 7550 5589; science and pop features: Elin Rees, 020 7550 5538*

● five news

Unit 1, Sky News, Grant Way, Isleworth, Middlesex TW7 5QD
020 7800 2705
www.five.tv/news
Editor: Mark Calvert; deputy editor: Josie MacRae; head of newsgathering: James Burtles

- Presenters: *Kirsty Young, Kate Sanderson, Lara Lewington*
- Political editor: *Andy Bell*
- Chief correspondent: *Stuart Ramsay*
- Correspondents – *northern: Peter Lane; sport: Alex Thomas*
- Reporters and correspondents: *Cathy Jones, Catherine Jacob, Lindley Gooden, Jason Farrel*
Press: 020 7800 4289.
Senior publicist: Stella Tooth

● Other departments

Acquisitions
*Director: Jay Kandona, 020 7421 7166
Controller: Vanessa Brookman, 020 7421 7166*

Interactive
Producer: Steven Bonner, 020 7550 5663

Scheduling and planning
Director: Susanna Dinnage, 020 7550 5588

RTÉ (Ireland)

Radio Telefís Éireann
Donnybrook, Dublin 4, Ireland
00 353 1 208 3111
info@rte.ie
www.rte.ie
*Irish national broadcaster.
Managing director of television: Noel Curran; managing director of news: Ed Mulhall; director of communications: Bride Rosney*
Press: 00 353 1 208 3434
   press@rte.ie

- Press contacts (*firstname.lastname@rte.ie*) *– acquisitions and drama: Sharon Brady; entertainment: Dympna Clerkin; factual: Dervla Keating; Fair City (soap): Tara O'Brian; music, sport and young people: Richie Ryan; news and current affairs: Carolyn Fisher*

KEY GOVERNMENT CONTACTS FOR DIGITAL TV

Department for Culture, Media and Sport
2–4 Cockspur Street,
London SW1Y 5DH
020 7211 6000
firstname.surname@
culture.gsi.gov.uk
www.culture.gov.uk
Culture secretary: Tessa Jowell
Press: 020 7211 6267
mark.devane@culture.gsi.gov.uk
SwitchCo press office: 020 7737 7008

DTI
1 Victoria Street, London SW1H 0ET
020 7215 5000
dti.enquiries@dti.gsi.gov.uk
www.dti.gov.uk/industries
/broadcasting
Head of broadcasting policy and director of digital television project: Jane Humphreys; deputy project manager, digital television: David Fuhr; head of broadcasting technology: Ian Dixon
Press: 020 7215 6403
nic.fearon-low@dti.gsi.gov.uk

● BSkyB

British Sky Broadcasting
Grant Way, Isleworth TW7 5QD
0870 240 3000
www.sky.com
Chief executive: James Murdoch; chief operating officer: Richard Freudenstein; chief marketing officer: Jon Florsheim; MD, Sky Sports: Vic Wakeling; director of corporate communications: Julian Eccles; director of publicity: Adrian Lee; head of programme publicity: Richard Turner; Sky One: Chris Aylott; Sky Movies: Phil Evans; Sky Sports: Chris Haynes; consumer PR: Gabby Bennett
Press: 0870 240 3000

SKY CHANNELS
Grant Way, Isleworth TW7 5QD
0870 240 3000

Sky Bet
www.skybet.com
Marketing director: Simon Miller; consumer PR manager: Heidi Bruckland
Press: 020 7705 3275

Sky Box Office
www.skymovies.com
Head of pay-per-view: Karen Saunders; publicity manager: Phil Evans
Press: 020 7800 4252
skymoviespublicity@bskyb.com

Sky Cinema 1 & 2
www.skymovies.com
Director of film channels and acquisitions: Sophie Turner-Laing; publicity manager: Phil Evans
Press: 020 7800 4252
skymoviespublicity@bskyb.com

Sky Customer Channel
Consumer PR manager: Heidi Bruckland
Press: 020 7705 3275

Sky Movies 1–9
www.skymovies.com
Director of film channels and acquisitions: Sophie Turner-Laing; publicity manager: Phil Evans
Press: 020 7800 4252
skymoviespublicity@bskyb.com

Sky News
Newsdesk: news.plan@bskyb.com
www.skynews.co.uk
Head of Sky News: Nick Pollard
• Key presenters - *Afternoon: Kay Burley, Mark Longhurst; Live at Five: Anna Botting, Jeremy Thompson*
• Correspondents - *business: Michael Wilson; crime: Martin Brunt; entertainment: Neil Sean, Matt Smith; foreign: Richard Bestic, Rachel Amatt, Emma Hurd, Laurence Lee, Tim Marshall, David Chater, Dominic Waghorn, Andrew Wilson, Ian Woods; health: Nicola Hill, Thomas Moore; political: Adam Boulton, Jon Craig, Jenny Percival, Peter Spencer, Glen O'Glaza; royal: Geoff Meade; other: David Bowden, Michelle Clifford, Lisa Holland, Peter Sharp*
Press: 020 7800 4289
Senior publicist: Stella Tooth; head of programme publicity: Richard Turner

Sky One
www.skyone.co.uk
Controller: James Baker. Acting publicity manager: Chris Aylott; head of programme publicity: Richard Turner; publicists for programmes - 24: Tom Mackey; Battlestar Galactica, Law & Order, Enterprise: Chris Aylott; Cold Case, Malcolm in the Middle: Gayle Hemmings and Melanie Adorian; Nip/Tuck, The Simpsons: Lee Robson
Press: 020 7805 7276

Sky Mix
www.skyone.co.uk
Controller: James Baker
Press: 020 7805 7276
Acting publicity manager: Chris Aylott; head of programme publicity: Richard Turner

Sky Sports 1, 2 & 3
www.skysports.com
MD: Vic Wakeling
Press: 020 7800 4254
Head of press and publicity: Chris Haynes

Sky Sports Extra
www.skysports.com
MD: Vic Wakeling
Press: 020 7800 4254
Head of press and publicity: Chris Haynes

Sky Sports News
www.skysports.com
MD: Vic Wakeling
Press: 020 7800 4254
Head of press and publicity: Chris Haynes

Sky Travel
www.skytravel.co.uk
General manager: Barbara Gibbon
Press: richard.turner@bskyb.com

Sky Travel Extra
www.skytravel.co.uk
General manager: Barbara Gibbon
Press: richard.turner@bskyb.com

Sky Travel Shop
www.skytravel.co.uk
General manager: Barbara Gibbon
Press: richard.turner@bskyb.com

Sky Travel +1
www.skytravel.co.uk
General manager: Barbara Gibbon
Press: richard.turner@bskyb.com

Sky Vegas Live
www.skyvegaslive.com
Executive producer: Peter Ward
Press: 020 7705 3416
Consumer PR executive: Tara Hicks

DEPARTMENTS

Sky Active
www.sky.com/skyactive
MD, Sky Interactive: Ian Shepherd

Sky Business
www.sky.com/business
Sales to non-domestic clients. Commercial marketing director: Iain Holden

Sky Ventures
www.sky.com/ventures
Joint venture channels and services. Director of Sky Ventures: Matthew Imi

● Cable

NTL
NTL House, Bartley Wood Business Park, Bartley Way, Hook, Hampshire RG27 9UP
01256 752000
www.ntl.com
CEO: Steve Burch
Press: 01256 752663
Head of corporate PR: Justine Smith; head of consumer PR: Rachel Turner

Cablecom Investments
The Coach House, Bill Hill Park, Wokingham, Berks RG40 5QT
0845 230 0028
customer@cablecom.co.uk
www.cablecom.co.uk
MD: Charles Tompkins

Telewest Global
Export House, Cawsey Way, Woking, Surrey GU21 6QX
01483 750900
www.telewest.co.uk
Acting chief executive: Barry Elson
Press: 020 7299 5888
Head of media relations: Kirstine Cox

WightCable
56 Love Lane, Cowes,
Isle of Wight PO31 7EU
01983 242424
enquiries@wightcable.com
www.wightcable.com
CEO: Duncan Kerr

WightCable North
3 Chalmers Place, Riverside Business
Park, Irvine, North Ayrshire KA11 5DH
01294 230000
enquiries@wightcablenorth.com
www.wightcablenorth.com
MD: Sandra Ayres
Press: 01294 231145
 pr@wightcablenorth.com
 Contact: Gillian Gordon

Video Networks
205 Holland Park Avenue,
London W11 4XB
020 7348 4000
info@videonetworks.com
www.videonetworks.com
Chairman and CEO: Roger Lynch
Press: 020 7348 4110
Head of PR: Nick Southall

● Digital terrestrial

Freeview
Broadcast Centre, (BC3 D5),
201 Wood Lane, London W12 7TP
020 8743 8000
www.freeview.co.uk
*Free-to-view digital terrestrial service,
owned by Crown Castle, BBC and BSkyB.
General manager: Lib Charlesworth*
Press: 020 7229 4400
*Consumer: Lucy Mayo;
corporate: Hannah Bailey – both
firstname.lastname@nelsonbostock.com*

Arqiva
Crawley Court, Winchester,
Hampshire SO21 2QA
01962 823434
firstname.surname@arqiva.com
www.arqiva.com
*Formerly NTL Broadcast. CEO: Tom
Bennie; MD, media solutions: Steve
Holebrook*
Press: 01962 822582
Communications manager: Bruce Randall

Crown Castle UK
Warwick Technology Park,
Gallows Hill, Heathcote Lane,
Warwick CV34 6TN
01926 416000
MarketingUK@crowncastle.co.uk
www.crowncastle.co.uk
*Digital terrestrial transmitter operator;
part-owner of Freeview. MD: Peter Abery*
Press: 01926 416870
Communications manager: Stephen Arnold

Top-Up TV
PO Box 208, Twickenham TW1 2YF
0870 054 5354
enquiries@topuptv.com
www.topuptv.com
*Offers top-up pay channels for Freeview
viewers. Chairman: David Chance*

● TV Channels

ABC1
Chiswick Park, Building 12,
566 Chiswick High Road,
London W4 5AN
020 8636 2000
VP programming: James Neal
Press: rachel.babington@disney.com

Adventure One
Grant Way, Isleworth TW7 5QD
0870 240 3000
www.nationalgeographic.co.uk
Contact: Emma Moloney

African and Caribbean TV
28F Lawrence Road, London N15 4EG
020 8809 7700
actv4@yahoo.com
www.actv.org.uk
Programme controller: Dawn Grant

Animal Planet
Discovery House, Chiswick Park
Building 2, 566 Chiswick High Road,
London W4 5YB
020 8811 3000
www.discoverychannel.co.uk
Acting channel director: Mark Wilde
Press: delyth_hughes@
 discovery-europe.com

Artsworld
Great West House (15th floor),
Great West Road, Brentford,
Middlesex TW8 9DF
020 7805 2404
www.artsworld.com
Scheduling manager: Kate Potter
Press: alyssa.bonic@artsworld.com

AsiaNet
Asianet Complex, Puliyarakonam PO,
Trivandrum 695 573 India
00 91 471 237 8407
www.asianetglobal.com

ATN Bangla
WASA Bhaban, 1st Floor,
98 Kazi Nazrul Islam Avenue,
Kawran Bazar, Dhaka 1215,
Bangladesh
00 880 811 1207/08/09/10
info@atnbangla.tv
www.atnbangla.tv

attheraces
11–13 Charlotte Street,
London W1T 1RH
020 7566 8911
studio@attheraces.co.uk
www.attheraces.co.uk
MD: Matthew Imi

Authentic TV
www.authentictv.tv

Avago
PO Box 42514, London E1W 2WA
0845 006 0235
www.avago.tv
Head of gaming: Damian Cope

B4
37 Harwood Road, London SW6 4QP
020 7371 5999
sarah@chartshow.tv
Head of channels: Chris Boardman

B4U
Transputec House, 19 Heather Park
Drive, Wembley HA0 1SS
020 8795 7171
www.b4utv.com
Programme controller: Anita Roy
Press: Kevin Rego

B4U Music
Transputec House, 19 Heather Park
Drive, Wembley HA0 1SS
020 8795 7171
www.b4utv.com
Programme controller: Anita Roy
Press: Kevin Rego

Bad Movies
179–181 The Vale, London W3 7RW
020 8600 9700
www.sit-up.tv
MD: Chris Manson

BBC America
PO Box 6266, Florence,
KY 41022-6266 USA
00 1 859 342 4070
www.bbcamerica.com
Programme executive: Alison Fredericks

BBC Canada
121 Bloor Street East, Suite 200,
Toronto, Ontario, Canada M4W 3M5
00 416 967 3249
feedback@bbccanada.com
www.bbccanada.com

BBC Food
PO Box 5054, London W12 0ZY
020 8433 2221
www.bbcfood.com
Editor: David Weiland

BBC Four
Television Centre
0870 010 0222
www.bbc.co.uk/bbcfour
Controller: Janice Hadlow

BBC Japan
PO Box 5054, London W12 0ZY
www.bbcjapan.tv

BBC News 24
Television Centre
020 8743 8000
bbcnews24@bbc.co.uk
www.bbc.co.uk/bbcnews24
Editorial director: Mark Popescu

BBC One
Television Centre
020 8743 8000
www.bbc.co.uk/bbcone
Controller: Peter Fincham

BBC Parliament
4 Millbank, London SW1P 3JA
020 7973 6216
parliament@bbc.co.uk
www.bbc.co.uk/bbcparliament

BBC Prime
PO Box 5054, London W12 0ZY
020 8433 2221
bbcprime@bbc.co.uk
www.bbcprime.com
Editor: David Weiland

BBC Three
Television Centre
020 8743 8000
www.bbc.co.uk/bbcthree
Controller: Stuart Murphy

BBC Two
Television Centre
020 8743 8000
www.bbc.co.uk/bbctwo
Controller: Roly Keating; controller of daytime: Jay Hunt

BBC World
PO Box 5054, London W12 0ZY
020 8433 2221
bbcworld@bbc.co.uk
www.bbcworld.com
Editorial director: Sian Kevill

BBCi (interactive TV)
Television Centre
020 8743 8000
www.bbc.co.uk/digital/tv
Controller: Rahul Chakkara; head, interactive TV programming: Emma Somerville

BEN
25 Ashley Road, London N17 9LJ
020 8808 8800
info@bentelevision.com
www.bentelevision.com
Head of programming: Ife Akim

Best Direct
Sentinel House, Poundwell,
Modbury PL21 0ZZ
0871 555 5252
www.bestdirect.tv
Account manager: Mary Hastings

Bid TV
Sit-Up House, 179-181 The Vale,
London W3 7RW
0870 165 1647
www.hid.tv

Big Game TV
PO Box 5372, London W1A 8WN
020 7432 7300
www.biggame.tv

Biography Channel
Grant Way, Isleworth TW7 5QD
020 7371 5399
www.thebiographychannel.co.uk
Channel director: Richard Melman
Press: 020 7941 5199
biographychannelpress@bskyb.com

Bloomberg
City Gate House, 39-45 Finsbury
Square, London EC2A 1PQ
020 7330 7797
newsalert@bloomberg.net
www.bloomberg.com/tv
Executive editor, broadcast: Ken Cohn

Boomerang
Turner House, 16 Great Marlborough
Street, London W1F 7HS
020 7693 1000
www.cartoonnetwork.co.uk
Channel manager: Dan Balaam
Press: alastair.edwards@turner.com
www.europe.turnerinfo.com

The Box
Mappin House, 4 Winsley Street,
London W1W 8HF
020 7182 8000
www.emap.com
Programme director: Dave Young; director of music: Simon Sadler
Press: maureen.corish@emap.com

Bravo
160 Great Portland Street,
London W1W 5QA
020 7299 5000
www.bravo.co.uk
Programme controller: Jonathan Webb
Press: jakki_lewis@flextech.co.uk

British Eurosport
Feltham Media Centre,
Sussex House, 2 Plane Tree Crescent,
Felthambrook Industrial Estate,
Middlesex TW13 7HF
020 7468 7777
www.eurosport.co.uk
Programming director: Dave Kerr
Press: mhorler@eurosport.com,
020 8818 1400

British Eurosport 2
Feltham Media Centre,
Sussex House, 2 Plane Tree Crescent,
Felthambrook Industrial Estate,
Middlesex TW13 7HF
020 7468 7777
www.eurosport.com
Programming director: Dave Kerr
Press: mhorler@eurosport.com
020 8818 1400

Channel 4
124 Horseferry Road,
London SW1P 2TX
020 7396 4444
www.channel4.com
Chief executive: Andy Duncan, 020 7306 8700; commercial director: Andy Barnes, 020 7306 8200; director of television: Kevin Lygo, 020 7306 3775

Cartoon Network
Turner House, 16 Great Marlborough
Street, London W1F 7HS
020 7693 1000
www.cartoonnetwork.co.uk
Channel manager: Don Gardiner
Press: alastair.edwards@turner.com
www.europe.turnerinfo.com

CBBC
Television Centre
020 8743 8000
www.bbc.co.uk/cbbc
Controller: Alison Sharman; chief operating officer: Richard Deverell

CBeebies
Television Centre
020 8743 8000
www.bbc.co.uk/cbeebies
Controller: Alison Sharman

CCTV9
cctv-9-mail1@cctv-9.com
www.cctv9.tv

CFC TV
The Christian Family Channel,
2 Silver Rd, Shepherds Bush,
London W12 7SG
www.cfctv.com

Challenge
160 Great Portland Street,
London W1W 5QA
020 7299 5000
www.challenge.co.uk
Programme controller: Jonathan Webb
Press: jakki_lewis@flextech.co.uk

Channel U
Video Interactive Television,
Studio4, 3 Lever Street,
London EC1V 3QU
020 7054 9010
info@vitv.co.uk
www.u-music.tv

Chart Show TV
37 Harwood Road, London SW6 4QP
020 7371 5999
info@chartshow.tv
www.chartshow.tv
Music coordinator: Sarah Gaughan

Chelsea TV
Stamford Bridge, Fulham Road,
London SW6 1HS
020 7915 1980
chelseatv@chelseafc.com
www.chelseafc.com
MD: Chris Tate

Chinese Channel
Teddington Studios, Broom Road,
Teddington TW11 9NT
020 8614 8364
newseditor@chinese-channel.co.uk
www.chinese-channel.co.uk
Head of programming: Desmond Ng

Classic FM TV
7 Swallow Place, London W1B 2AG
020 7343 9000
classicfmtv@classicfm.com
www.classicfm.com/tv
Station manager: Darren Henley

Classics TV
The Media Centre, 131-151 Great
Titchfield Street, London W1W 5BB
020 7663 3651
www.classicstv.co.uk
Contact: Petra Oblak

CNBC Europe
10 Fleet Place, London EC4M 7QS
020 7653 9300
www.cnbceurope.com
Executive producers: Harry Fuller, John Casey
Press:
cblenkinsop@cnbceurope.com

CNN
Turner House, 16 Great Marlborough
Street, London W1F 7HS
020 7693 1000
www.cnn.com
International managing editor for EMEA: Nick Wrenn
Press: 020 7693 0942
chris.dwyer@turner.com

Community Channel
3-7 Euston Centre, Regent's Place,
London NW1 3JG
020 7874 7626
info@communitychannel.org
www.communitychannel.org
Channel controller: Nick Ware

Create and Craft
Ideal Home House,
Newark Road, Peterborough,
Cambridgeshire PE1 5WG
08700 777002
customerservices@
idealshoppingdirect.co.uk
www.createandcraft.tv
CEO: Andrew Fryatt

Dating Channel
130 City Road, London EC1V 2NW
020 7748 1500
info@thedatingchannel.com
www.thedatingchannel.com
Mobile technical manager: Paul Doyle

Digital Broadcasting Company
Radio House, 19 Clifftown Road,
Southend-on-Sea SS0 1AB
01702 337321
www.digitalbroadcastingcompany
.co.uk

Discovery Channel
Discovery House, Chiswick Park
Building 2, 566 Chiswick High Road,
London W4 5YB
020 8811 3000
www.discoverychannel.co.uk
*Channel director, senior vice-president:
Jill Offman*
Press: lynn_li@
discovery-europe.com

Discovery Civilisation
Discovery House, Chiswick Park
Building 2, 566 Chiswick High Road,
London W4 5YB
020 8811 3000
www.discoverychannel.co.uk
*Channel director, senior vice-president:
Jill Offman*
Press: kate_buddle@
discovery-europe.com

Discovery Home & Health
Discovery House, Chiswick Park
Building 2, 566 Chiswick High Road,
London W4 5YB
020 8811 3000
www.discoverychannel.co.uk
Channel director: Clare Laycock
Press: libby_rowley@
discovery-europe.com

Discovery Kids
Discovery House, Chiswick Park
Building 2, 566 Chiswick High Road,
London W4 5YB
020 8811 3000
www.discoverychannel.co.uk
Channel director: Clare Laycock
Press: libby_rowley@
discovery-europe.com

Discovery Real Time
Discovery House, Chiswick Park
Building 2, 566 Chiswick High Road,
London W4 5YB
020 8811 3000
www.realtimetv.co.uk
*Channel director, vice-president: Paul
Welling*
Press: claire_phillips@
discovery-europe.com

Discovery Science
Discovery House, Chiswick Park
Building 2, 566 Chiswick High Road,
London W4 5YB
020 8811 3000
www.discoverychannel.co.uk
*Channel director, senior vice-president:
Jill Offman*
Press: kate_buddle@
discovery-europe.com

Discovery Travel and Living
Discovery House, Chiswick Park
Building 2, 566 Chiswick High Road,
London W4 5YB
020 8811 3000
www.travelandliving.co.uk
*Channel director, vice-president: Paul
Welling*
Press: claire_phillips@
discovery-europe.com

Discovery Wings
Discovery House, Chiswick Park
Building 2, 566 Chiswick High Road,
London W4 5YB
020 8811 3000
www.discoverychannel.co.uk
*Channel director, senior vice-president:
Jill Offman*
Press: kate_buddle@
discovery-europe.com

Disney Channel
Chiswick Park, Building 12,
566 Chiswick High Road,
London W4 5AN
020 8636 2000
www.disneychannel.co.uk
VP programming: James Neal
Press: rachel.babington@
disney.com

DM Digital
Lower Ground Floor,
33/35 Turner Street,
Manchester M4 1DW
0161 795 4844
zahidh76@yahoo.com
Contact: Zahidh Hussain

DW-TV
Voltastr. 6, D-13355 Berlin, Germany
00 49 30 4646 0
www.dw-world.de/dw
Head DW-TV: Christoph Lanz

E!
www.eonline.com

E4
124 Horseferry Road,
London SW1P 2TX
020 7396 4444
www.channel4.com/e4
Head: Danny Cohen

eeZee TV
Regis Road, Kentish Town,
London NW5 3EG
0870 1287 288
www.eezeetv.co.uk
Press: 020 7691 3822
press@eezeetv.com

Escape
681 Falmouth Road, Mashpee,
MA 02649 USA
00 1 508 477 9385
info@escapetv.tv
www.escapetv.tv

Euro News
60, Chemin des Mouilles, BP 131,
F-69131 Lyon-Ecully, France
00 33 4 7218 0000
www.euronews.net
Press: 00 33 4 72 18 80 56

Exchange & Mart TV
Link House, 25 West Street, Poole,
Dorset BH15 1LL
01202 445000
tim.brown@unitedadvertising.co.uk
www.exchangeandmart.co.uk/tv
*Business development manager:
Tim Brown*

Express Shopping Channel
Griffin House, 40 Lever Street,
Manchester M60 6ES
020 7308 5283
expressyourself@expressshopping.tv
www.expressshopping.tv
Channel controller: David Holmans

Extreme Sports Channel
The Media Centre, 19 Bolsover
Street, London W1W 5NA
020 7886 0770
www.extreme.com
Head of acquisitions: Alex Barnes
Press: stuart@extreme
sportschannel.com

Fantasy Channel
Suite 14, Burlington House,
St Saviours Road, St Helier,
Jersey JE2 4LA
01534 703700
pfarell@nasnet.je
Programme controller: Peter Farell

Fashion TV
Production Paris,
49 rue Jules Guesde,
92300 Levallois Perret France
00 33 1 4505 4545
info@ftv.com
www.ftv.com
London office: jessica@ftv.com

FilmFour
124 Horseferry Road,
London SW1P 2TX
020 7396 4444
www.channel4.com/film/ffchannel
Head: Tom Sykes, 020 7306 6442

five
22 Long Acre, London WC2E 9LY
020 7550 5555
firstname.lastname@five.tv
www.five.tv
Director of programmes: Dan Chambers,
020 7550 5673 (PA Sarah Jackson,
020 7550 5522); controller of broadcast
services: David Burge, 020 7691 6260
Press: 020 7550 5533

Fizz
Video Interactive Television,
Studio4, 3 Lever Street,
London EC1V 3QU
020 7054 9010
info@vitv.co.uk
Contact: Darren Platt

Flaunt
Grant Way, Isleworth TW7 5QD
0870 240 3000
www.flaunt.tv

Fox News
1211 Avenue of the Americas,
New York NY 10036
00 1 888 369 4762
foxaroundtheworld@foxnews.com
www.foxnews.com
Senior vice-president, corporate
communications: Brian Lewis, 001 212
301 3331, brian.lewis@foxnews.com;
vice-president, media relations: Irena
Briganti, 001 212 301 3608,
irena.briganti@foxnews.com

FTN
160 Great Portland Street,
London W1W 5QA
020 7299 5000
www.flextech.co.uk
Programme controller: Claudia
Rosencrantz
Press: judy_wells@flextech.co.uk
jessica_alder@flextech.co.uk

FX and Fox Movie Channel
10000 Santa Monica Blvd,
Los Angeles, CA 90067 USA
00 1 310 286 3800
www.fxnetworks.com
Vice-president, public relations: John
Solberg, 00 1 310 789 4689; manager,
public relations: Roslyn Bibby, 00 1 310
789 4640

Game Network
Via Bisceglie 71\73,
20152 Milano, Italy
www.game-network.net

Gay Date TV
Suite 407, Copper Gate House,
16 Brune Street, London, E1 7NJ
020 7748 1500
info@gaydatetv.co.uk
www.gaydatetv.co.uk
Mobile technical manager: Mark Adams

Gems TV
Eagle Road Studios, Eagle Road,
Redditch B98 9HF

GEO TV
geouk@geo.tv
www.geo.tv

Get Lucky TV
www.getlucky.tv

God TV
Angel House, Borough Road,
Sunderland, Tyne and Wear SR1 1HW
0191 568 0800
info@god.tv
www.god.tv
UK regional director: Johnny Woodrow

The Golf Channel UK
1 Kingsgate, Bradford Business Park,
Canal Road, Bradford, West
Yorkshire BD1 4SJ
www.thegolfchanneluk.com
Press: press@golftvinfo.co.uk

Hallmark
234a Kings Road, London SW3 5UA
020 7368 9100
info@hallmarkchannel.co.uk
www.hallmarkchannel.co.uk
Director of acquisitions: Rosy Hill-Davies
Press: janemuirhead@
hallmarkchannel.com

History Channel
Grant Way, Isleworth TW7 5QD
020 7705 3000
www.thehistorychannel.co.uk
Channel director: Richard Melman
Press: 020 7941 5199
historychannelpress@bskyb.com

Hits Channel
Mappin House, 4 Winsley Street,
London W1W 8HF
020 7182 8000
www.emapadvertising.com
Programme director: Dave Young;
director of music: Simon Sadler
Press: Vicky Timmons

Hollywood.com Television (HTV)
2255 Glades Road, Suite 219A,
Boca Raton, FL 33431 USA
00 1 561 998 8000
www.hollywood.com
Chairman and CEO: Mitchell Rubenstein

The Horror Channel
info@horrorchannel.com
www.thehorrorchannel.tv

Ideal Vitality
Ideal Home House,
Newark Road, Peterborough,
Cambridgeshire PE1 5WG
08700 777002
customerservices@
idealshoppingdirect.co.uk
www.idealvitality.tv
CEO: Andrew Fryatt

Ideal World
Ideal Home House,
Newark Road, Peterborough,
Cambridgeshire PE1 5WG
08700 777002
customerservices@
idealshoppingdirect.co.uk
www.idealworld.tv
CEO: Andrew Fryatt

INI
Charlotte, North Carolina USA
00 1 704 525 9800
info@ini.tv
www.ini.tv

Islam Channel
14 Bonhill Street, London EC2A 4BX
020 7374 4516
www.islamchannel.tv
Press: pr@islamchannel.tv

ITV News
200 Grays Inn Road,
London WC1X 8XZ
020 7833 3000
www.itv.com/news
Editor: Ben Rayner

ITV1
200 Grays Inn Road,
London WC1X 8HF
020 7843 8000
www.itv.com/itv1
ITV Network contacts: see page 159

ITV2
200 Grays Inn Road,
London WC1X 8HF
020 7843 8000
www.itv.com/itv2
Channel editor: Zai Bennett; controller
of commissioned programmes: Matthew
Littleford

ITV3
200 Grays Inn Road,
London WC1X 8HF
020 7843 8000
www.itv.com/itv3
Channel editor: Steve Arnell; controller
of commissioned programmes: Matthew
Littleford

Jetix
3 Queen Caroline Street,
Hammersmith, London W6 9PE
020 7554 9000
www.jetix.co.uk

Kerrang TV
Mappin House, 4 Winsley Street,
London W1W 8HF
020 7182 8000
www.emapadvertising.com
Programme director: Dave Young;
director of music: Simon Sadler
Press: maureen.corish@emap.com

Kiss TV
Mappin House, 4 Winsley Street,
London W1W 8HF
020 7182 8000
www.emapadvertising.com
Programme director: Dave Young;
director of music: Simon Sadler
Press: maureen.corish@emap.com

Living
160 Great Portland Street,
London W1W 5QA
020 7299 5000
www.livingtv.co.uk
Programme controller: Claudia
Rosencrantz
Press: judy_wells@flextech.co.uk
jessica_alder@flextech.co.uk

Look4Love TV
Unit 20, Intec 2, Basingstoke,
Hampshire RG24 8NE
0871 550 0055
enquiries@look4love.tv
www.look4love.tv

Magic TV
Mappin House, 4 Winsley Street,
London W1W 8HF
020 7182 8000
www.emapadvertising.com
*Programme director: Dave Young;
director of music: Simon Sadler*
Press: maureen.corish@emap.com

Majestic TV
CC.Comercial La Colonia Edificio II,
Locales 25-27, San Pedro de
Alcantara, 29670 Malaga
00 34 952 799 518
www.majestictv.co.uk

Matinee Movies
179-181 The Vale, London W3 7RW
020 8600 9700
www.sit-up.tv
MD: Chris Manson

MATV National
Combine House, 7 Woodboy Street,
Leicester LE1 3NJ
0116 2532288
info@matv.co.uk
www.matv.co.uk
MD: Vinod Popat

Men and Motors
200 Grays Inn Road,
London WC1X 8HF
020 7843 8000
info@menandmotors.co.uk
www.menandmotors.co.uk
Commissioning editor: Joe Talbot
Press: 020 7843 8392

Motors TV
855, avenue Roger Salengro,
92370 Chaville, France
00 33 1 4115 9852
www.motorstv.com
Press: service.presse@
          motorstv.com

MTA – Muslim TV
16 Gressenhall Road,
London SW18 5QL
020 8870 0922
info@mta.tv
www.mta.tv

MTV, MTV2, Base, Dance, Hits
MTV, Hawley Crescent,
London NW1 8TT
020 7284 7777
www.mtv.co.uk
*Head of development (for programme
commissions): Chris Sice*
Press: curlewis.samantha@
          mtvne.com

Music Choice Europe
The Old Truman Brewery,
91 Brick Lane, London E1 6QL
020 3107 0300
contactus@musicchoice.co.uk
www.musicchoice.co.uk

Musicians Channel
PO BOX 5784,
Southend on Sea SS1 9BYN
01702 350530
info@musicianschannel.tv
www.musicianschannel.tv

MUTV
4th Floor, 274 Deansgate,
Manchester M3 4JB
0161 834 1111
mutv@mutv.com
www.manutd.com/mutv

Nation 217
6&7 Princes Court, Wapping Lane,
London E1W 2DA
020 7942 7942
william.van.rest@nation217.tv
www.nation217.tv

National Geographic Channel
Grant Way, Isleworth TW7 5QD
020 7705 3000
natgeoweb@bskyb.com
www.nationalgeographic.co.uk
General manager: Simon Bohrsmann

Nick Jr
Nickelodeon, 15-18 Rathbone Place,
London W1T 1HU
020 7462 1000
abigail.hutton@nickelodeon.co.uk
www.nickjr.co.uk
Director of channels: Howard Litton

Nick Toons TV
Nickelodeon, 15-18 Rathbone Place,
London W1T 1HU
020 7462 1000
abigail.hutton@nickelodeon.co.uk
www.nick.co.uk/toons
Director of channels: Howard Litton

Nickelodeon
Nickelodeon, 15-18 Rathbone Place,
London W1T 1HU
020 7462 1000
abigail.hutton@nickelodeon.co.uk
www.nick.co.uk
Director of channels: Howard Litton

OBE
Crown House, North Circular Road,
London NW10 7PN
0870 240 4474
info@obetv.co.uk
www.obetv.co.uk

Open Access
6 Hoxton Square, London N1 6NU
0870 744 2041
info@openaccess.tv
www.openaccess.tv

Paramount Comedy
UK House, 4th Floor, 180 Oxford
Street, London W1D 1DS
020 7478 5300
www.paramountcomedy.co.uk
Director of programming: Heather Jones
Press: zoe.diver@
          paramountcomedy.com

**PCNE Phoenix Chinese News
& Entertainment**
The Chiswick Centre, 414 Chiswick
High Road, London W4 5TF
020 8987 4320/1
info@phoenixcnetv.com
www.phoenixcne.com
MD: Wen Guang

Performance
4 Farleigh Court, Long Ashton,
Bristol BS48 1UL
0870 850 8102
info@performancetv.co.uk
www.performance-channel.com
*CEO: Steve Timmins; channel manager:
Matthew Clements*

Poker Channel
020 8600 2698
info@thepokerchannel.co.uk
www.thepokerchannel.co.uk
*CEO: Crispin Nieboer; head of
programming: James Hopkins; director
of television: Chiara Cipriani*
Press: sophie.moore@
          thepokerchannel.co.uk

POP
37 Harwood Road, London SW6 4QP
020 7384 2243
francesca@chartshow.tv
www.popclub.tv
Head of channels: Keith MacMillan

Price Drop TV
Sit-Up House, 179-181 The Vale,
London W3 7RW
0870 165 1647
www.price-drop.tv

Q TV
Mappin House, 4 Winsley Street,
London W1W 8HF
020 7182 8000
www.emapadvertising.com
*Programme director: Dave Young;
director of music: Simon Sadler*
Press: maureen.corish@emap.com

QVC
Marco Polo House,
346 Queenstown Road,
Chelsea Bridge, London SW8 4NQ
020 7705 5600
www.qvcuk.com
Planning manager: Susan Hellyar
Press: 020 7886 8440

Real Estate TV
1-6 Falconberg Court,
London W1D 3AB
020 7440 1090
info@realestatetv.tv
www.realestatetv.tv
Head of channel: Mark Dodds

Reality TV
105-109 Salusbury Road,
London NW6 6RG
020 7328 8808
www.realitytv.co.uk
Press: jane.wynward@
          zonevision.com

Record TV
tvrecord@recordnetwork.net
www.rederecord.com.br

Revelation TV
117a Cleveland Street,
London W1T 6PX
020 7631 4446
howard@revelationtv.com
lesley@revelationtv.com
www.revelationtv.com
Head of programming: Howard Conder

RTÉ 1 + 2
Donnybrook, Dublin 4, Ireland
00 353 1 208 3111
info@rte.ie
www.rte.ie/tv
*Commissioning editor, Irish language,
multiculture and education programmes:
Máiread Ní Nuadháin*

S4C
Parc Ty Glas, Llanishen,
Cardiff CF14 5DU
Cardiff: 029 20747444
Caernarfon: 01286 674622
www.s4c.co.uk

Sci-Fi
5-7 Mandeville Place,
London W1U 3AX
020 7535 3500
www.scifi.com
*Head of programming and acquisitions:
Monica Iglesias*

Screenshop
179-181 The Vale, London W3 7RW
020 8600 9700
www.sit-up.tv
MD: Chris Manson

Scuzz
Grant Way, Isleworth TW7 5QD
0870 240 3000
www.scuzz.tv

Setanta Sport UK
4th Floor, Waterloo Place,
London SW1Y 4BE
0870 050 6980
setantauk@setanta.com
www.setanta.com
MD, Setanta UK & Ireland: Roger Hall

Shop on TV
020 8453 1120
enquiries@shopon.tv
www.shopon.tv

Shop Vector
64-66 Coleman Street,
London EC2R 5BX
020 8104 0493
customerservice@simplymedia.tv
fran.hales@simplymedia.tv
www.vectordirect.tv
Media manager: Fran Hales

Simply Ideas
64-66 Coleman Street,
London EC2R 5BX
020 8104 0493
customerservice@simplymedia.tv
fran.hales@simplymedia.tv
www.simplyshoppingtv.co.uk
Media manager: Fran Hales

Simply Shopping
64-66 Coleman Street,
London EC2R 5BX
020 8104 0493
customerservice@simplymedia.tv
fran.hales@simplymedia.tv
www.simplyshoppingtv.co.uk
Media manager: Fran Hales

Sky Bet
Grant Way, Isleworth TW7 5QD
0870 240 3000
www.skybet.com
Marketing director: Simon Miller
Press: 020 7705 3275.
Consumer PR manager: Heidi Bruckland

Sky Box Office
Grant Way, Isleworth TW7 5QD
0870 240 3000
www.skymovies.com
Head of PPV: Karen Saunders
Press: 020 7800 4252
skymoviespublicity@bskyb.com
Publicity manager: Phil Evans

Sky Cinema 1 & 2
Grant Way, Isleworth TW7 5QD
0870 240 3000
www.skymovies.com
*Director of film channels and
acquisitions: Sophie Turner-Laing*
Press: 020 7800 4252
skymoviespublicity@bskyb.com
Publicity manager: Phil Evans

Sky Customer Channel
Grant Way, Isleworth TW7 5QD
0870 240 3000
Press: 020 7705 3275.
Consumer PR manager: Heidi Bruckland

Sky Mix
Grant Way, Isleworth TW7 5QD
0870 240 3000
www.skyone.co.uk
Controller: James Baker
Press: 020 7805 7276.
*Acting publicity manager: Chris Aylott;
head of programme publicity: Richard
Turner*

Sky Movies 1-9
Grant Way, Isleworth TW7 5QD
0870 240 3000
www.skymovies.com
*Director of film channels and
acquisitions: Sophie Turner-Laing*
Press: 020 7800 4252
skymoviespublicity@bskyb.com
Publicity manager: Phil Evans

Sky News
Grant Way, Isleworth TW7 5QD
0870 240 3000
Newsdesk: news.plan@bskyb.com
www.skynews.co.uk
*Head of Sky News: John Riley. Presenters
and correspondents: see page 163*
Press: 020 7800 4289
*Senior publicist: Stella Tooth; head of
programme publicity: Richard Turner*

Sky One
Grant Way, Isleworth TW7 5QD
0870 240 3000
www.skyone.co.uk
Controller: Richard Woolfe
Press: 020 7805 7276.
*Acting publicity manager: Chris Aylott;
head of programme publicity: Richard
Turner. Publicists for programmes -
24: Tom Mackey; Battlestar Galactica,
Law & Order, Enterprise: Chris Aylott;
Cold Case, Malcolm in the Middle:
Gayle Hemmings and Melanie Adorian;
Nip/Tuck, The Simpsons: Lee Robson*

Sky Sports 1, 2 & 3
Grant Way, Isleworth TW7 5QD
0870 240 3000
www.skysports.com
MD: Vic Wakeling
Press: 020 7800 4254
Head of press and publicity: Chris Haynes

Sky Sports Extra
Grant Way, Isleworth TW7 5QD
0870 240 3000
www.skysports.com
MD: Vic Wakeling
Press: 020 7800 4254
Head of press and publicity: Chris Haynes

Sky Sports News
Grant Way, Isleworth TW7 5QD
0870 240 3000
www.skysports.com
MD: Vic Wakeling
Press: 020 7800 4254
Head of press and publicity: Chris Haynes

Sky Travel
Grant Way, Isleworth TW7 5QD
0870 240 3000
www.skytravel.co.uk
General manager: Barbara Gibbon
Press: richard.turner@bskyb.com

Sky Travel +1
Grant Way, Isleworth TW7 5QD
0870 240 3000
www.skytravel.co.uk
General manager: Barbara Gibbon
Press: richard.turner@bskyb.com

Sky Travel Extra
Grant Way, Isleworth TW7 5QD
0870 240 3000
www.skytravel.co.uk
General manager: Barbara Gibbon
Press: richard.turner@bskyb.com

Sky Travel Shop
Grant Way, Isleworth TW7 5QD
0870 240 3000
www.skytravel.co.uk
General manager: Barbara Gibbon
Press: richard.turner@bskyb.com

Sky Vegas Live
Grant Way, Isleworth TW7 5QD
0870 240 3000
www.skyvegaslive.com
*Executive producer: Peter Ward.
Consumer PR executive: Tara Hicks*
Press: 020 7705 3416

Sky Welcome
Grant Way, Isleworth TW7 5QD
0870 240 3000
Consumer PR executive: Tara Hicks
Press: 020 7705 3416

Smash Hits Channel
Mappin House, 4 Winsley Street,
London W1W 8HF
020 7182 8000
www.emapadvertising.com
*Programme director: Dave Young;
director of music: Simon Sadler*
Press: maureen.corish@emap.com

Snatch It
Factory Outlet TV,
Eagle Road Studios, Eagle Road,
Redditch B98 9HF
0845 3 670670
customercare@gemstv.com
www.gemstv.com
MD: Steve Bennett

Sony Entertainment TV Asia
34 Foubert's Place, London W1V 2BH
020 7534 7575
www.setasia.tv
*Vice president for international business:
Neeraj Arora*
Press: ash_jaswal@spe.sony.com

Sound TV
21 East Links, Tollgate,
Chandlers Ford, Southampton,
Hampshire SO53 3TG
023 8065 2777
info@soundtv.co.uk
www.soundtv.co.uk
*MD: Richard Digance; head of
programmes for children: Morag Thorpe;
public relations associate: Steve Blacknell*

Soundtrack Channel
1335 Fourth Street, Santa Monica,
California 90401 USA
00 1 310 899 1315
contactstc@stcchannel.com
www.stcchannel.com

Star TV/ News/ Plus
Great West House (15th floor),
Great West Road, Brentford,
Middlesex TW8 9DF
020 7805 2326
www.uk.startv.com
*Senior marketing executive: Gurpreet
Braich*
Press: gurpreet.braich@bskyb.com

SUBtv
140 Buckingham Palace Road,
London SW1W 9SA
020 7881 2540
info@sub.tv
www.subtvnetwork.com
Creative director: Jon Kingdon

Superstore TV
64-66 Coleman Street,
London EC2R 5BX
020 8104 0493
customerservice@simplymedia.tv
fran.hales@simplymedia.tv
www.superstore.tv
Media manager: Fran Hales

TBN Europe
PO Box 240, Hatfield,
Hertfordshire AL9 6BH
info@tbneurope.org
www.tbneurope.org

TCM
Turner House, 16 Great Marlborough
Street, London W1V 1AF
020 7693 1000
tcminfo@turner.com
www.tcm.com

Teachers' TV
16-18 Berners Street,
London W1T 3LN
020 7182 7430
info@teachers.tv
www.teachers.tv
Chief executive: Nigel Dacre

Teletext Holidays
Building 10, Chiswick Park,
566 Chiswick High Road,
London W4 5TS
0870 731 3000
www.teletextholidays.co.uk

TG4
Baile na hAbhann, Co. na Gaillimhe,
Ireland
00 353 91 505050
eolas@tg4.ie
www.tg4.ie
*Director of television: Alan Esslemont;
programmes department: Mícheál Ó
Meallaigh*

Thane Direct
248-250 Tottenham Court Road,
London W1T 7RA
020 7580 6110
info@thanedirect.tv
www.thanedirect.co.uk
MD: Thomas Parrot

Thane Stop and Shop
248-250 Tottenham Court Road,
London W1T 7RA
020 7580 6110
info@thanedirect.tv
www.thanedirect.co.uk
MD: Thomas Parrot

Thomas Cook TV
8 Park Place, Lawn Lane, Vauxhall,
London SW8 1UD
020 7820 4470
www.thomascooktv.com

Tiny Pop
37 Harwood Road, London SW6 4QP
020 7371 5999 / 7384 2243
francesca@chartshow.tv
Head of channels: Keith MacMillan

TMF
MTV, Hawley Crescent,
London NW1 8TT
020 7284 7777
www.vh1.co.uk
*Acting general manager (for programme
commissions): Steve Shannon*
Press: hershon.mandy@mtvne.com

Toonami
Turner House, 16 Great Marlborough
Street, London W1V 1AF
020 7693 1000
www.toonami.co.uk

Travel Channel
64 Newman Street, London W1T 3EF
020 7636 5401
www.travelchannel.co.uk
Head of programming: Annabelle Parmes
Press: petra@travelchannel.co.uk

Trouble
160 Great Portland Street,
London W1W 5QA
020 7299 5000
www.trouble.co.uk
Programme controller: Jonathan Webb
Press: jakki_lewis@flextech.co.uk

True Movies
020 7371 5999

Turner Classic Movies
Turner House, 16 Great Marlborough
Street, London W1F 7HS
020 7693 1000
www.tcmonline.co.uk
Channel manager: Alan Musa
Press: ann.rosen@turner.com
www.europe.turnerinfo.com

TV Warehouse
Chalfont Grove,
Narcot Lane, Chalfont St Peter,
Buckinghamshire SL9 8TW
0800 013 1464
www.tvwarehouseonline.co.uk
MD: John Bramm

TV-Shop
P.O Box 64, Hadleigh IP7 6WF
08700 191019
tvshop-support@portica.co.uk
www.tvshop.com
MD: Ruth Oliver

UCB TV
PO Box 255, Stoke-on-Trent ST4 8YY
0845 604 0401
www.ucb.co.uk
TV broadcasting manager: John Green

UKTV Bright Ideas
160 Great Portland Street,
London W1W 5QA
020 7299 6200
www.uktv.co.uk
Channel editor: Gareth Williams
Press: Penny Groom

UKTV Documentary
160 Great Portland Street,
London W1W 5QA
020 7299 6200
www.uktv.co.uk
Channel editor: James Newton
Press: rebecca.hook@uktv.co.uk

UKTV Drama
160 Great Portland Street,
London W1W 5QA
020 7299 6200
www.uktv.co.uk
Channel editor: Richard Kingston
Press: Zoe Clapp

UKTV Food
160 Great Portland Street,
London W1W 5QA
020 7299 6200
www.uktvfood.co.uk
Channel editor: Paul Morton
Press: Penny Groom

UKTV G2
160 Great Portland Street,
London W1W 5QA
020 7299 6200
www.uktv.co.uk
Channel editor: Steve North
Press: Zoe Clapp

UKTV Gold
160 Great Portland Street,
London W1W 5QA
020 7299 6200
www.uktv.co.uk
Channel editor: James Newton
Press: Zoe Clapp

UKTV History
160 Great Portland Street,
London W1W 5QA
020 7299 6200
www.uktv.co.uk
Channel editor: Adrian Wills
Press: Chris Masters

UKTV People
160 Great Portland Street,
London W1W 5QA
020 7299 6200
www.uktv.co.uk
Channel editor: Steve North
Press: Chris Masters

UKTV Style
160 Great Portland Street,
London W1W 5QA
020 7299 6200
www.uktvstyle.co.uk
Channel editor: Catherine Cattion
Press: Penny Groom

The Vault
37 Harwood Road, London SW6 4QP
020 7384 2243
sarah@chartshow.tv

Vectone 4U, Bangla, Bolly, Tamil, Urdu and World
Vectone Media, 54 Marsh Wall,
Canary Wharf, London E14 9TP
020 7517 4322
a.sharma@vectone.com
CEO: Amitabh Sharma

VH1
MTV, Hawley Crescent,
London NW1 8TT
020 7284 7777
www.vh1.co.uk
Acting general manager (for programme commissions): Steve Shannon
Press: hershon.mandy@mtvne.com

VH1 Classic
MTV, Hawley Crescent,
London NW1 8TT
020 7284 7777
www.vh1.co.uk
Acting general manager (for programme commissions): Steve Shannon
Press: hershon.mandy@mtvne.com

VH2
MTV, Hawley Crescent,
London NW1 8TT
020 7284 7777
www.vh1.co.uk
Acting general manager (for programme commissions): Steve Shannon
Press: hershon.mandy@mtvne.com

Wine Network
88 Kearny Street, Suite 2100,
San Francisco CA 94108 USA
00 1 415 772 3639
info@winetv.tv
www.winetv.tv
CEO: Patrick Brunet; COO: Lorie Kim

Wrestling Channel
114 St Martins Lane,
London WC2N 4BE
020 7599 8959
info@thewrestlingchannel.tv
www.thewrestlingchannel.tv

YES661
Harper Road,
Sharston Industrial Estate,
Sharston, Manchester M22 4RG
0161 947 2580
www.yes661.com
MD: David Ades

YooPlay
Northumberland House,
155-157 Great Portland Street,
London W1W 6QP
020 7462 08/0
oiyoo@yooplay.com
www.yoomedia.com/yooplay

Zee TV
Unit 7, Belvue Business Centre,
Belvue Road, Northolt UB5 5QQ
020 8839 4000
www.zeetv.co.uk
Programmes manager: Pranab Kapadia
Press: media@zeenetwork.com

Data services

Ceefax
BBC Television Centre, Wood Lane,
London W12 7RJ
020 8743 8000

Teletext
Building 10, Chiswick Park,
566 Chiswick High Road,
London W4 5TS
0870 731 3000
editor@teletext.co.uk
www.teletext.co.uk
Has a licence to use spare capacity within the Channel 3 (ITV) signal. Head of television: Mishma Patel

Other broadcasters

Abacus TV
01603 812800
sales@abacustv.co.uk
www.abacustv.co.uk
Producer: Jane Scarfe

BFBS Forces Radio and TV
01494 878290
sarah.dornford-may@ssvc.com
www.ssvc.com
Controller of television: Helen Williams

BTV - Bloomsbury Television (University College London)
020 7387 3827
btv@ucl.ac.uk
http://welcome.to/btv

BVTV
01582 581753
info@bvtv.co.uk
www.bvtv.co.uk

Capital TV (Wales)
029 2048 8500
enquiries@capital.tv
www.capital.tv
MD: David Morris Jones

Channel M
0161 475 4855
info@channelM.co.uk
www.channelm.co.uk
Operations manager: Susan Steenson

EBS New Media
01462 895999
ben@newmediagroup.co.uk
www.newvisiongroup.co.uk
MD: Ben Tagg

Glasgow University Student Television (GUST)
0141 341 6216
gust@src.gla.ac.uk
www.src.gla.ac.uk/gust
Station controller: Chris Hall

Leeds University Union TV (ls:tv)
0113 380 1423
stationmanager@lstv.co.uk
www.lstv.co.uk

Loughborough Students Union TV (LSUTV)
01509 635045
manager@lsutv.co.uk
www.lsutv.co.uk
Head of media: Anna Bowden

Middlesex Broadcasting Corporation (MATV Channel 6)
0116 253 2288
info@matv.co.uk
www.matv.co.uk
MD: Vinod Popat

Nerve TV
01202 595777
jhawkins@bournemouth.ac.uk
www.nervemedia.net
Media services manager: Jason Hawkins

Nexus UTV
01603 592270
nexusutv@gmail.com
www.uea.ac.uk/~sunexus

**North West Television Services
(Channel 9 – Coleraine, Limavady,
Londonderry/Derry)**
028 7131 4400
info@c9tv.tv
www.c9tv.tv
Director: Gary Porter

Northern Visions
028 9024 5495
info@northernvisions.org
www.northernvisions.org

SIX TV – The Oxford Channel
01865 314700
admin@oxfordchannel.com
www.oxfordchannel.com

Solent TV (Isle of Wight)
01983 522344
info@solent.tv
www.solent.tv

**STOIC Student Television of
Imperial College**
020 7594 8100
info@stoictv.com
www.union.ic.ac.uk/media/stoic
Contact: John Anderson

XTV
01392 263598
xtv@ex.ac.uk
www.xtv.org.uk

YCTV – Youth Culture Television
020 8964 4646
stuartr@yctv.org
www.yctv.org

**York University St John Student
Television (YSTV)**
01904 624624
marketing@yorksj.ac.uk
www.yorksj.ac.uk

Independent production companies

● Key companies

ALL3MEDIA
87–91 Newman Street,
London W1T 3EY
020 7907 0177
information@allthreemedia.co.uk
www.allthreemedia.com
*MD: Louise Pedersen; head of press and
marketing: Rachel Glaister; senior sales
and marketing executive: Peter Grant*

Assembly TV
Riverside Studios, Crisp Road,
London W6 9RL
020 8237 1075
judithmurrell@riversidestudios.co.uk
www.allthreemedia.com
Chief executive: William Burdett-Coutts
• *Black Books; Jo Brand's Hot Potatoes;
In Exile*

Bentley Productions
Pinewood Studios, Pinewood Road,
Iver, Bucks SL0 0NH
01753 656594
www.allthreemedia.com
MD: Brian True-May
• *Midsomer Murders; Ultimate Force*

Cactus TV
373 Kennington Road,
London SE11 4PS
020 7091 4900
touch.us@cactustv.co.uk
www.cactustv.co.uk
MDs: Simon Ross, Amanda Ross
• *Richard & Judy*

Lion Television
Lion House, 26 Paddenswick Road,
London W6 0UB
020 8846 2000
Scotland: 0141 331 0450
New York: 00 1 212 206 8633
LA: 00 1 310 566 6285
mail@liontv.co.uk
www.liontv.co.uk
*MDs: Richard Bradley, Nick Catliff,
Shahana Meer, Jeremy Mills*
• *Bad Behaviour; Days That Shook the
World; Britain's Finest; Castles; Royal
Deaths and Diseases; Passport to the Sun*

North One TV
Mayward House, 46–52 Pentonville
Road, London N1 9HF
020 7502 6000
annelise.unitt@northonetv.com
www.allthreemedia.com
*MD: Neil Duncanson; chief executive:
John Wohlgemuth*
• *Formula One; World Rally; The Top Ten
series; Speed Sunday; Fifth Gear; The
Gadget Show; The Victoria Cross*

At It Productions
68 Salusbury Road, Queens Park,
London NW6 6NU
020 8964 2122
enquiries@atitproductions.com
www.atitproductions.com
MDs: Martin Cunning, Chris Fouracre
• *T4; LA Pool Party; Sun Sea and Silicone;
Perfect Getaway; Chancers; Popworld,
25 Years of Smash Hits; Bride and
Grooming; Born Without a Face*

Celador Productions
39 Long Acre, London WC2 9LG
020 7845 6999
tvhits@celador.co.uk
www.celador.co.uk
*MDs: Paul Smith, Danielle Lux; head of
entertainment: Colman Hutchinson; head
of production: Heather Hampson;
development executives, comedy: Vanessa
Haynes, Humphrey Barclay*
• *You Are What You Eat; It's Been A Bad
Week; Who Wants To Be a Millionaire?;
Winning Lines; Britain's Brainiest; 24
Carrott Gold*

Diverse
Gorleston Street, London W14 8XS
020 7603 4567
reception@diverse.tv
www.diverse.tv
*MD: Paul Sowerbutts; creative director:
Roy Ackerman; head of post production:
Paul Bates; head of production: Janet
Smyth; executive producer: Adam Barker*
• *Musicality: The Winners' Story; Let 'Em
All In; Guyana: The Politics of Paradise;
If We Could Stop the Violence; The Real
Dad's Army*

Endemol UK
Shepherds Building Centre,
Clarecroft Way, Shepherds Bush,
London W14 0EE
0870 333 1700
info@endemoluk.com
www.endemoluk.com
*Chairman: Peter Bazalgette; chief
creative officer: Tim Hincks; director of
production: Clare Pickering*
• *Big Brother; Fame Academy; Orange
British Academy Film Awards; Ground
Force; Changing Rooms; Restoration;
The Salon 2; The Games; Restoration;
8 Out of 10 Cats; Soccer Aid; Ready
Steady Cook*

Hat Trick Productions
10 Livonia Street, London W1F 8AF
020 7434 2451
info@hattrick.com
www.hattrick.com
*MD: Jimmy Mulville; head of
entertainment: Leon Wilde*
• *Have I Got News For You; Bodies;
Bromwell High; Room 101; The Kumars
at No 42; Father Ted; Jeffrey Archer -
The Truth; Underworld; Drop The Dead
Donkey*

HIT Entertainment
Maple House, 5th Floor,
149–150 Tottenham Court Road,
London W1T 7NF
020 7554 2500
www.hitentertainment.com
*MD: Charles Burvick; head of production:
Jocelyn Stephenson*
• *Barney and Friends; Art Attack;
Angelina Ballerina; Pingu; Toddworld;
Fireman Sam; Bob the Builder;
Rubbadubbers; Sooty; Thomas the
Tank Engine*

IWC Media
St George's Studio,
93–97 St George's Road,
Glasgow G3 6JA
0141 353 3222
London: 020 7317 2230
info@iwcmedia.co.uk
www.iwcmedia.co.uk
*MD: Sue Oriel; creative directors: Alan
Clements, Zad Rogers; head of production:
Jonathan Warne; director of drama:
Eileen Quinn*
• *Ultimate Cars; 18th Street; Other Side;
Location, Location, Location; The
Planman; Changemakers; Hunt for Jill
Dando's Killer; Survival of the Richest;
Relocation Relocation; Root of all Evil*

Princess Productions
Whiteley's Centre, 151 Queensway,
London W2 4SB
020 7985 1985
reception@princess.tv.com
www.princess.tv.com
*MD: Sebastian Scott; head of production:
Sarah Buckenham*
• *Ruby Does the Business; Back to Reality;
Bump 'n' Grind; Rise; The Wright Stuff;
The Friday Night Project; Secrets of the
CIA; Doctor Doctor*

Prospect Pictures
Wandsworth Plain, London SW18 1ET
020 7636 1234
Capital studios,
London: 020 8877 1234
Wales 029 2055 1177
rhys@prospect-uk.com
www.prospect-uk.com
MD: Liam Hamilton
• *Saturday Kitchen; Great Food Live;
Under One Roof; Ready Steady Cook;
Nigella*

Ragdoll (UK)
Timothy's Bridge Road,
Stratford Upon Avon CV37 9NQ
01789 404100
USA: 00 1 212 966 4477
info@ragdoll.co.uk
www.ragdoll.co.uk
Director of production: Sue James
• *Open a Door; Rosie and Jim; Tots TV;
Brum; Teletubbies; Teletubbies
Everywhere; Boohbah*

RDF Media
The Gloucester Building,
Kensington Village, Avonmore Road,
London W14 8RF
020 7013 4000
contactus@rdfmedia.com
www.rdfmedia.com
*Chief executive: David Frank; chief
creative officer: Stephen Lambert; chief
operating officer: Joely Fether*
• *Faking It 4; Wife Swap; Celebrity Wife
Swap; Scrapheap Challenge 5; Century
of the Self; Holiday Showdown;
Ian Wright's Supersize Kids; Britain's
Top Dog*

September Films
Glen House, 22 Glenthorne Road,
London W6 0NG
020 8563 9393
USA: 00 1 323 960 8085
september@septemberfilms.com
www.septemberfilms.com
*Chief executive: Sammy Nourmand;
director of production: Elaine Day;
head of drama and film development:
Nadine Mellor*
• *Holiday Homes Nightmares; Clubbing
on the Frontline; The Bottom Line; New
Tycoons; Secrets and Lies; Instant
Wedding; Making It; Beauty & The
Geek; Celebrity Bodies; Haunted Homes*

Shine
140 Kensington Church Street,
Notting Hill, London W8 4BN
020 7985 7000
info@shinelimited.com
www.shinelimited.com
MD: Elizabeth Murdoch
• *Dispatches; Fit to Eat; Take That;
Masterchef Goes Large; Charles &
Camilla: Madly In Love; 100 Greatest
Series*

Talkback Thames Productions
20–21 Newman Street,
London W1T 1PG
020 7861 8000
reception@talkbackthames.tv
www.talkbackthames.tv
*Chief executive: Lorraine Heggessey;
executive editor: Daisy Goodwin*
• *Family Affairs; Bo' Selecta!; I'm Alan
Partridge; Jamie's Kitchen; Perfect
Strangers; The Apprentice; Grand
Designs; Green Wing; Nathan Barley;
How Clean Is Your House?; House
Doctor; The Bill*

Tiger Aspect Productions
7 Soho Street, London W1D 3DQ
020 7434 6700
general@tigeraspect.co.uk
www.tigeraspect.co.uk
*MD: Andrew Zein; executive producer,
entertainment: Drew Pearce; head of
factual: Paul Sommers; head of comedy:
Sophie Clarke-Jervoise. Comedy, drama,
entertainment, factual and animation.*
• *Teachers; Murphy's Law; Streetmate;
Gimme Gimme Gimme; Vicar of Dibley;
Lenny Henry Show; Murphy's Law;
Vital Signs; 3 Minute Wonder*

Tinopolis
Tinopolis Centre, Park Street,
Llanelli, Carmarthenshire SA15 3YE
01554 880880
Mentorn London: 020 7258 6800
Oxford Mentorn: 01865 318 450
Glasgow Mentorn: 0141 204 6600
info@tinopolis.com
www.tinopolis.com
Executive chairman: Ron Jones
• *Robot Wars; Britain's Worst …;
Botham's Ashes; Gillette World Sport;
Hitler's Legacy; Club Culture; Question
Time; The Real Monty; Take My
Mother-in-Law; Hamburg Cell; Traffic
Cops; Car Wars*

TWI (Trans World International)
Pier House, Strand on the Green,
London W4 3NN
020 8233 5000
kmullins@imgworld.com
www.imgworld.com
Head of production: Graham Fry
• *Japan's War (in colour series);
Wimbledon; The Olympics; Premier
League; PGA European Tour; Colour
of War*

Twofour Productions
3 Bush Park, Estover,
Plymouth PL6 7RG
01752 727400
enq@twofour.co.uk
www.twofour.co.uk
*CEO: Charles Wace; managing director of
communications: Charles Mills; managing
director of broadcast: Melanie Leach*
• *G Girls; Gardens Through Time; Dead
Famous; The City Gardener; Ideal Home
Show; Extreme: Celebrity Surgery;
Extreme: Celebrity Skint; Little Dom's
Big Adventure*

Wall To Wall
8–9 Spring Place, Kentish Town,
London NW5 3ER
020 7485 7424
mail@walltowall.co.uk
www.walltowall.co.uk
*CEO: Alex Graham; Head of production:
Helena Ely*
• *Life Beyond the Box: Norman Stanley
Fletcher; New Tricks; The Regency
House Party; Texas Ranch House; The
Battle That Made Britain; The History
of Photography; Who Do You Think You
Are?*

Zenith Entertainment
43–45 Dorset Street,
London W1U 7NA
020 7224 2440
general@zenith-
entertainment.co.uk
www.zenith-entertainment.co.uk
MD of production: Alan Fairholm
• *Byker Grove; 2000 Acres of Sky;
Headliners; Garden Rivals; Room Rivals;
Brian's Boyfriends; Murder Most Foul;
SMTV; CDUK*

Zig Zag Productions
13–14 Great Sutton St, Clerkenwell,
London EC1V 0BX
020 7017 8755
production@zigzag.uk.com
www.zigzagproductions.tv
*MD: Danny Fenton; head of factual
entertainment: Jes Wilkins; production
executive: Sophie Ardern; head of
development: Ben Paul*
• *Fashion is Football Challenge; Inside the
Mind of Frank Bruno; Three Lions; DIY
Births; Celebrity Gladiators; X-Rated:
The Ads They Couldn't Show; That's So
Last Week; Essex Boys; World's Most
Deadliest Gangs*

● Other production companies

1A Productions
01360 620855
office@1AProductions.co.uk
MD; Norman Stone
• Tales From the Madhouse; Man Dancin';
CS Lewis: Beyond Narnia; Ain't
Misbehavin'; The Journey; Breathless

3BM Television
020 8740 4780
3bmtv@3bmtv.co.uk
www.3bmtv.co.uk
Chairman and creative director: Simon
Berthon
• War Lords; Children of Abraham; Zero
Hour: Ten Days to D-Day; The British
Working Class; Tsunami: Where Was
God?

12 Yard Productions
020 7432 2929
contact@12yard.com
www.12yard.com
MD: David Young
• Weakest Link; In It To Win It; Without
Prejudice?; Double Cross; EggHeads;
Here Comes The Sun; Three's A Crowd

The 400 Company
020 8746 1400
info@the400.co.uk
www.the400.co.uk
MD: Mark Sloper
• The Real TT Heroes; Full Throttle
Famous; Property Ladder; To Buy Or
Not To Buy; Conflicts; The Games;
Extreme Makeover

Aardman Animations
0117 984 8485
mail@aardman.co.uk
www.aardman.com
MD: Sonia Davis
• Walkers' Mr Potato Head commercial;
Robinson's Boogie commercial;
Chicken Run

Absolutely Productions
020 7644 5575
info@absolutely-uk.com
www.absolutely.biz
MD: Pete Baikie
• Barry Welsh; Stressed Eric; Trigger
Happy TV; Baggage

Acacia Productions
020 8341 9392
projects@acaciaproductions.co.uk
www.acaciaproductions.co.uk
MD: J Edward Milner
• Documentary and news, environment,
current affairs and human rights

Accomplice Television
00 353 1 660 3235
office@accomplice-tv.com
www.accomplice-tv.com
MD: David Collins
• Pure Mule; Bachelors Walk Series 1, 2 & 3

Addictive Television
020 7700 0333
mail@addictive.com
www.addictive.com
Head of production: Nik Clarke; Graham
Daniels
• Spaced Out; Transambient; Night Shift;
The Web Review; Mixmasters (ITV1);
Visual Stings (Magnetic Channel);
Optronica

Aimimage Production Company
020 7482 4340
atif@aimimage.com
www.aimimage.com
MD: Ahmad Zadeh
• Terra Circa; Balls to Basra; The Family
Portrait

Angel Eye
0845 230 0062
office@angeleye.co.uk
www.angeleye.co.uk
MD: Richard Osborne
• Holy Offensive; Beginners Luck; Estate
Agents; Lady Macbeth; The Last Chances

Antelope
01243 370806
mick.csaky@antelope.co.uk
www.antelope.co.uk
Chief executive and creative director:
Mike Csaky
• Docs: Mozart in Turkey; Rebel Music:
The Bob Marley Story; Geiko Girl; Africa
Live; Epic Journey; 13-part series about
Kyoto

APT Films
020 7284 1695
admin@aptfilms.com
www.aptfilms.com
MD: Jonny Persey
• Wondrous Oblivion (feature); Solomon
and Gaenor (Oscar nomination, best
foreign film); The Chosen Ones; Solo
One; When I Lived in Modern Times;
Deep Water

Atlantic Productions
020 7371 3200
info@atlanticproductions.tv
www.atlanticproductions.tv
MD: Anthony Geffen
• Spartans; The Queen of Sheba; Nefertiti
Resurrected; Mystery of the Tibetan
Mummy; The Real Jules Verne;
Tutankhamen: a murder mystery;
Saladin; Seven Wonders of Ancient
Rome; Who Killed Cleopatra?; Richard
the Lionheart; The American Dream; The
Greeks; Nefertiti; The Promised Land

Attaboy TV
020 7740 3000
info@attaboytv.com
www.attaboytv.com
MD: Michael Wood
• The High Road; End of the Line; A
Question of Colin; Life at the Sport; Vets
in Hong Kong

Avalon
020 7598 7280
enquiries@avalonuk.com
www.avalonuk.com
MD: John Thoday
• Harry Hill's TV Burp; The Frank
Skinner Show; Jerry Springer – The
Opera; Kelsey Grammer presents The
Sketch Show (Fox Network USA)

Betty TV
020 7290 0660
tammy@bettytv.co.uk
www.bettytv.co.uk
MD: Liz Warner
• Spendaholics; Rude Britannia

Big Bear Films
020 7229 5982
office@bigbearfilms.co.uk
www.bigbearfilms.co.uk
Directors: John Stroud, Marcus Mortimer
• My Hero; Strange; Hairy Bikers
Cookbook

Big Heart Media
020 7608 0352
info@bigheartmedia.com
www.bigheartmedia.com
MD: Colin Izod
• GridClub/music studio; Spin 'n Groove;
Street Corner Symphony; Rewind; Cape
Farewell; Teachers' TV

Big Umbrella Media
0121 506 9620
production@bigumbrellamedia.co.uk
www.bigumbrellamedia.co.uk
MD: Martin Head
• Living with the New Cross Fire; Sir
Frank Whittle: The Man who Shrank the
World

Big Wave Productions
01243 532531
info@bigwavetv.com
www.bigwavetv.com
MD: Sarah Cunliffe
• Bug Attack; Death on the Amazon;
Secret Weapons; Revenge of the
Crocodiles; HK; Death: The Inside Story;
Alien Worlds

Blackwatch Productions
0141 222 2640
info@blackwatchtv.com
www.blackwatchtv.com
MD: Nicola Black
• Boys with Breasts; Snorting Coke with
the BBC; Designer Vagina

Blakeway Productions
020 8743 2040
admin@blakeway.co.uk
www.blakeway.co.uk
MD: Denys Blakeway
• Empire: how Britain made the modern
world; Strike: When Britain Went to
War; American Colossus; Prince William;
Winston's War; The Major Years

Blast! Films
020 7267 4260
blast@blastfilms.co.uk
www.blastfilms.co.uk
MD: Edmund Coulthard
• *Principles of Lust; The Death of Klinghoffer; Tales from Pleasure Beach; Days in the Life*

Blue Egg Television/ Blue Egg Studios
0870 765 0007
info@blueegg.tv
www.blueegg.tv
MD: Jill Scott
• *James Bond: Die Another Day; San Antonio; Orange commercial*

Box TV
020 7297 8040
info@box-tv.co.uk
www.box-tv.co.uk
MD: Justin Thomson-Glover
• *Sunday; Trust; Boudica; Gunpowder, Treason and Plot; Sweeney Todd*

Brechin Productions
020 8876 2046
clivedoig@blueyonder.co.uk
www.brechin.com
MD: Clive Doig
• *Jigsaw; See it, Saw it; Turnabout; Eureka*

Brian Waddell Productions
028 9042 7646
strand@bwpltv.co.uk
www.bwpltv.co.uk
MD: Brian Waddell
• *Futureweapons; When Sports Stars See Red; Ireland's Richest; Getaways; How Long Will You Live?; Belfast Zoo; The Formal; Wanted Farmers; House Traders*

Brighter Pictures
020 8222 4100
info@brighter.co.uk
www.brighter.co.uk
MD: Gavin Hay
• *Take the Mike; Bombay Blush; Diet Another Day; You Can't Fire Me I'm Famous; Larger Than Life; A Girls Guide to 21st Century Sex; Chantelle's Dream Dates*

Brighter Pictures Scotland
0141 572 0861
scotland@brighter.co.uk
www.brighter.co.uk
MD: Gavin Hay
• *Get a New Life (BBC2); Tabloid Tales (BBC1); Nick Nairn and the Dinner Ladies (BBC Scotland)*

Brighton TV
01273 224280
info@brighton.tv
www.brighton.tv
MD: David Pounds
• *Tales of the Living Dead; Big Boutique; Secrets of the Bog People; Sleepwalkers Who Kill*

Broadway
0115 955 6909
info@intermedianotts.co.uk
www.broadway.org.uk
MD: Ceris Morris
• *One For The Road; Slot Art; Shifting Units; The Entertainer; First Cut*

Brook Lapping Productions
020 7428 3100
info@brooklapping.com
www.brooklapping.com
MD: Brian Lapping
• *I Met Osama Bin Laden; The Fall of Milosevic; Avenging Terror; Before the Booker; I Met Adolf Eichmann; The Death of Yugoslavia; Israel and the Arabs; Live Aid Remembered (2 parts); Surviving Katrina; Europe's 9/11; Stanley Goes to Europe*

Cactus TV
020 7091 4900
touch.us@cactustv.co.uk
www.cactustv.co.uk
MDs: Amanda Ross, Simon Ross
• *The Spirit of Diana, The Debate; Songs of Bond; Cliff Richard, The Hits I Missed; Richard & Judy; British Soap Awards*

Caledonia, Sterne And Wyld
0141 564 9100
info@caledonia-tv.com
www.caledonia-tv.com
MD: Seona Robertson
• *Sun Worshippers; King Jamie and the Angel; The Real Tartan Army II*

Carnival (Films and Theatre)
020 8968 0968
info@carnival-films.co.uk
www.carnival-films.co.uk
MD: Brian Eastman
• *Shadowlands; Firelight; Bugs; As If; Poirot; Rosemary and Thyme; Hotel Babylon*

Century Films
020 7378 6106
info@centuryfilmsltd.com
www.centuryfilmsltd.com
MDs: Brian Hill, Katie Bailiff
• *Drinking for England; Feltham Sings; Shot; Men at Fifty; David Beckham: A Footballer's Story; Tightwads; Songbirds; Bully 4 U*

Chameleon TV
0113 205 0010
www.chameleontv.com
MD: Allen Jewhurst
• *Edge of the City; Love 2 shop; Faith and Music Series; Britain's First Suicide Bombers*

Channel X
020 7566 8160
info@channelx.co.uk
www.channelx.co.uk
MD: Alan Marke
• *Reeves & Mortimer; Date That; Popetown; Catterick*

Cicada Films
020 7266 4646
cicada@cicadafilms.com
www.cicadafilms.com
MD: Frances Berrigan
• *Ancient inventions; NYPD Animal Squad; Fat Fiancees; The Abyss; Beyond Pompeii; Bikini; Tiger Traffic; A Year Without Summer*

Clearcut Communications
0161 427 3052
info@clearcut.freeserve.co.uk
MD: Robin Anderson
• *Sex and the Village; On the Edge (Granada); Sense of Place (BBC1); Shanghai'd (BBC2); Proof Positive (pilot for Discovery America)*

Clerkenwell Films
020 7608 2726
andy@clerkenwellfilms.com
MD: Murray Ferguson
• *Quite Ugly One Morning; Dr Jekyll and Mr Hyde (Universal TV); Inspector Rebus; Afterlife Series 1 & 2; Losing It*

Collingwood O'Hare Entertainment
020 8993 3666
info@crownstreet.co.uk
www.collingwoodohare.com
MD: Christopher O'Hare
• *Animal Stories; Eddy and the Bear; The King's Beard; Yoko! Jakamoko! Toto!*

The Comedy Unit
0141 305 6666
comedyunit@comedyunit.co.uk
www.comedyunit.co.uk
MDs: Colin Gilbert, April Chamberlain
• *Still Game; The Karen Dunbar Show; Offside; Yo! Diary!; Taxi for Cowan Spanish Special; New Year specials: Chewin' The Fat; Only An Excuse?*

Company Pictures
020 7380 3900
enquiries@companypictures.co.uk
www.companypictures.co.uk
MDs: Charlie Pattinson, George Faber
• *Life and Death of Peter Sellers; Shameless; Forty; White Teeth; Anna Karenina; Wild at Heart*

Cosgrove Hall Films
0161 882 2500
animation@chf.co.uk
www.chf.co.uk
MD: Anthony Utley
• *Andy Pandy; Bill & Ben; Postman Pat; Enjie Benji; Dangermouse; Rupert the Bear*

CTVC
020 7940 8480
ctvc@ctvc.co.uk
www.ctvc.co.uk
CEO: Nick Stuart
• *Imber, Britain's Lost Village; Tonight; Shariah TV; Victim 001; Bethlehem Year Zero; John Meets Paul; A Mediterranean Journey; Understanding Islam; The M25 Rapist; Codex*

Dai4Films
01570 471368
info@dai4films.com
www.dai4films.com
MD: Neil Davies
• *The Montserrat Volcano; Islands in the Sun; Working Machines; Double or Nothing; Raw Spice; Dirty Streets*

Dan Films
020 7916 4771
enquiries@danfilms.com
www.danfilms.com
Director: Julie Baines
• *Creep; Sons of the Wind; The Republic of Love; Severance*

Darlow Smithson Productions
020 7482 7027
mail@darlowsmithson.com
www.darlowsmithson.com
MD: John Smithson
• *Touching the Void; We Built this City; Dragons - A Fantasy Made Real; Living the Quake; E=MC²*

Darrall Macqueen
020 7407 2322
info@darrallmacqueen.com
www.darrallmacqueen.com
MDs: Maddy Darrall, Billy Macqueen
• *The Crust; Play the Game; Smile series 1, 2, 3; U Get Me series 1, 2, 3; Animal Spies; Feel the Fear; Smile*

Dazed Film and TV
020 7549 6840
info.film&tv@dazegroup.com
www.dazedfilmtv.com
MD: Laura Hastings-Smith
• *Perfect; Stop for a Minute; Untold Beauty; The Lives of the Saints; Hero2Hero*

DLT Entertainment UK
020 7631 1184
jbartlett@dltentertainment.co.uk
www.dltentertainment.com
MD: John Bartlett
• *As Time Goes By; Love on a Branch Line; My Family; Meet My Folks*

DNA Films
020 7292 8700
info@dnafilms.com
www.dnafilms.com
MD: Andrew MacDonald
• *28 Days Later*

Eagle and Eagle
020 8995 1884
producer@eagletv.co.uk
www.eagletv.co.uk
Producer: Robert Eagle
• *The Nuclear Boy Scout; Robo Sapiens; Big Questions*

Eagle Films
01372 844484
enquiries@eaglefilms.co.uk
www.eaglefilms.co.uk
Producer: Katrina Moss
• *Bitter Honey; The Sins of the Father; It Started with a Kiss; The Road to Somewhere; Shaking Dreamland*

Ecosse Films
020 7371 0290
webmail@ecossefilms.com
www.ecossefilms.com
MD: Douglas Rae
• *Amnesia; Like Father Like Son; Monarch of the Glen; The Ambassador; Mrs Brown; Charlotte Gray; Heartless; Under the Greenwood Tree; Wilderness; Becoming Jane*

Educational Broadcasting Services Trust
020 7613 5082
enquiries@ebst.co.uk
www.ebst.co.uk
Chief executive: Dr Jim Stevenson
• *Looking at Learning; Maths for Engineers; Maths tutor (Series)*

Electric Sky
01273 224240
info@electricsky.com
www.electricsky.com
MD: David Pounds
• *Who Killed Diana; Clash of Worlds; 37 Uses of a Dead Sheep; Fireballs of Tutankhamun; Sashan Avenue with Jodie Kidd*

The Elstree Production Company
01932 572680
enquiries@elsprod.com
www.elsprod.com
Producer: Greg Smith
• *Agnes Brown; George Orwell's Animal Farm; David Copperfield*

FACE Television
01256 350022
paula@facetv.co.uk
www.facetv.co.uk
MD: Paul Friend
• *Wildlife SOS series 1, 2; Lifeboat Rescue; Wildlife Photographer*

Faction Films
020 7690 4446
faction@factionfilms.co.uk
www.factionfilms.co.uk
MDs: David Fox, Sylvia Stevens, Peter Day
• *Aphrodite's Drop; Murder in the Family; Love for Sale; Resistencia; Cinematic Orchestra; Sonic Revolution; Point Annihilation*

The Farnham Film Company
01252 710313
info@farnfilm.com
www.farnfilm.com
MD: Ian Lewis
• *Dance with the Devil; Intergalactic Kevin; Mona the Vampire; The Druid's Tune*

Festival Film and TV
020 8297 9999
info@festivalfilm.com
www.festivalfilm.com
MD: Ray Marshall
• *Feature films: Man Dancin'; The Colour; Grievous Angel*

Film and Music Entertainment
020 7434 6655
info@fame.uk.com
www.fame.uk.com
MD: Mike Downey
• *Guy X; Deathwatch; The Enemy*

Films of Record
020 7286 0333
zoek@filmsofrecord.com
www.filmsofrecord.com
MD: Jane Bevan
• *Malaria; The Protectors; Remember the Secret Policeman's Ball; Rail Cops*

Flame Television
020 7713 6868
contact@flametv.co.uk
www.theflamegroup.co.uk
Chairman: Roger Bolton; MD and head of production: Clare Featherstone
• *Don't Get Done, Get Dom; Tarrence Way; Churchill's Girl; Celebrity Swap*

Flashback Television
020 7490 8996
Bristol: 0117 973 8755
mailbox@flashbacktv.co.uk
bristol@flashbacktv.co.uk
www.flashbacktv.co.uk
MD: Taylor Downing
• *D-Day: The Lost Evidence; Regency Feast; The Badness of King George IV; Nigella Bites; Speed Machines; Battlestations*

Flick features
020 7385 7338
info@flickfeatures.com
www.flickfeatures.co.uk
Director: John Deery
• *Hell4Leather; Conspiracy of Silence; Pictures of Anna (in development)*

Flying Elephant Films
020 7871 0686
info@flyingelephant.co.uk
www.flyingelephant.co.uk
MD: Preeyf Nair
• *A Story That Begins at the End; A Different Life; You Know What I'm Saying; A Different Life (1,2 and 3)*

Focus Productions
0117 904 6292
Stratford-upon-Avon:
   01789 298948
martinweitz@focusproductions.co.uk
maddern@focusproductions.co.uk
www.focusproductions.co.uk
MD: Martin Weitz
• *Pharaoh's Holy Treasure; This Sceptred Isle; The Jewish Journey. Winner, Sony Gold Award. Projects 2003: Witness on Saint-making; The Godfather of the Blues; The Real Rainman; Brainman; Painting the Mind; The Musical Genius*

Footstep Productions
020 7836 9990
info@footstep-productions.com
www.footstepproductions.com
MD: Collette Thomson
• *Worktalk; Voces Espanolas*

Free@Last TV
020 7242 4333
barry@freeatlasttv.co.uk
www.freeatlasttv.co.uk
Executive producer: Barry Ryan
• *Revisiting Brideshead; The Wonderful World of Roald Dahl; Super Sleuths; 20 Reasons to Love Star Trek; A Portrait of George Galloway; The Story of Punk*

Fresh One Productions
020 7359 1000
www.freemantlemedia.com
MD: Andrew Conran
• *Jamie's School Dinners; Oliver's Twist; Jamie's Kitchen*

Fulcrum TV
020 7939 3160
info@fulcrumtv.com
www.fulcrumtv.com
MDs: Christopher Hird, Richard Belfield
• *The Twelfth; Don't Worry; Can You Live Without?... (Series 1 & 2); Egypt Week Live*

Genesis Media Group
029 2066 6007
alan@genesis-media.co.uk
www.genesis-media.co.uk
Producer and programme director: Alan Torjussen
• *Peter Warlock; Ceiri and his Music; Love Talk; Leila Megane*

Ginger Television
020 7882 1000
production@ginger.tv
www.ginger.tv
MD: Elisabeth Partyka
• *Jack Osbourne - Adrenaline Junkie; Crucify Me; Whatever*

Glasshead
020 8740 0024
media@glasshead.co.uk
www.glasshead.co.uk
MD: Lambros Atteshlis
• *Blue Dragon; Watch Magic Grandad; Real Science*

Grand Slamm Children's Films
020 7388 0789
info@gscfilms.com
www.gscfilms.com
MD: Ginger Gibbons
• *Percy the Park Keeper; Angelina Ballerina; Kipper; Dot Wot; The Hairdresser's Dog, The Magic Bed; Sheeep*

Green Bay Media
029 2064 2370
john-geriant@green-bay.tv
www.green-bay.tv
MD: Phil George, John Geriant
• *An Archbishop Like This; A Bloody Good Friday; Do Not Go Gentle; The World's Most Dangerous Roads; The Physics Of Rock Guitar; Going for Growth*

Green Inc Productions
028 9057 3000
tv@greeninc.tv
www.greeninc.tv
MD: Stephen Stewart
• *The Afternoon Show; Patrick Kielty Almost Live; Red Bull DJ Academy; Anderson In; Brendan Courtney Show*

Green Umbrella
0117 906 4336
postmaster@umbrella.co.uk
www.umbrella.co.uk
MD: Nigel Ashcroft
• *Journey to Centre of the Earth; Escape from Berlin; Galileo's Daughter; John and Abigail Adams: American Experience; Elephant Exodus; Bridging the Atlantic*

Greenlit Productions
020 7287 3545
info@greenlit.co.uk
www.greenlit.co.uk
MD: Jill Green
• *Foyle's War; The Swap; Menace; Trust*

Greenpoint Films
020 7240 7066
info@greenpointfilms.com
www.greenpointfilms.co.uk
MDs: Patrick Cassavetti, Ann Scott, Simon Relph
• *Only Human; Hideous Kinky; The Land Girls; The Only Boy For Me*

Grosvenor Park Productions
020 7493 8030
chris.chrisafis@grosvenorpark.com
www.grosvenorpark.com
MD: Daniel Taylor
• *Reign of Fire; Being Julia; Colour Me Kubrick; Count of Monte Cristo; Spider*

Gruber Films
0870 366 9313
office@gruberfilms.com
www.gruberfilms.com
MD: Richard Holmes
• *Shooting Fish; Waking Ned; The Abduction Club*

Hand Pict Productions
0131 346 1111
ask@handpict.com
www.handpict.com
Director: George Cathro
• *Adoption Stories; East Coast Boy, West Coast Man; Numero Una*

Hanrahan Media
01789 450182
info@hanrahanmedia.com
www.hanrahanmedia.tv
MD: Will Hanrahan
• *Your Stars; Renovation Creation; Star Lives; World's Biggest Ghost Hunt, Most Haunted Live; Men's Healthy Cash Crop Circles; Verdict; Going to Work Naked; Conversion*

Hasan Shah Films
020 7722 2419
hsfilms@blueyonder.co.uk
MD: Hasan Shah
• *Short: Art Of The Critic. Feature in development 2003: A Little Scary*

Hewland International
020 8215 3345
jcook@hewland.co.uk
www.harchester.net
MD: Jane Hewland
• *Dream Team; Stranger than Fiction; Dial a Date; Dream Team Retro; Mile High; Can't Buy Me Love*

Hopscotch Films
0141 221 2828
info@hopscotchfilms.co.uk
www.hopscotchfilms.co.uk
MDs: Charlotte Wontner, Clara Glynn, John Archer
• *Writing Scotland; Detox or Die; Last Train to Beechwood; Scots: The Language of the People; Cinema Iran; On the Road with Kiarostami; The Big Scots Road Trip*

Hot Shot Films
028 9031 3332
info@hotshotfilms.com
www.hotshotfilms.com
MDs: Brendan J. Byrne, Jimmy McAleuvey
• *The Secret Life of Words; Living History; Blind Vision; Street Detectives; So You Thought You Knew the Plantation; Heroes; Sons of Ulster; The Visitors*

Hotbed Media
0121 248 3900
mail@hotbedmedia.co.uk
www.hotbedmedia.co.uk
MD: Johannah Dyer
• *Under the Hammer; Songs of Praise; Real Brassed Off; 100 Worst Britons; Everything Must Go; 100 Worst Pop Records; Star Portraits with Rolf Harris; Build, Buy or Restore*

Hourglass Productions
020 8540 8786
productions@hourglass.co.uk
www.hourglass.co.uk
MD: Martin Chilcott
• *Energy for Nature; DNA and Rocket Science, Living Donation*

HRTV
020 7494 3011
mail@hrtv-online.com
www.hrtv-online.com
MD: Jerry Hibbert
• *Tractor Tom; Stressed Eric series II*

Hyphen Films
020 7734 0632
nmk@hyphenfilms.com
www.hyphenfilms.com
MD: N.M. Kabir
• *Spotlights and Saris; Bollywood Dancing; Bollywood Women - Intros; Bismillah of Benaras; Bollywood Celebrites; Bollywood 2006*

I2I Productions
01698 794100
enquiries@ i2itv.com
www.i2itv.com
Director: Gordon Ross
• *Crimewatch; Panorama; Holiday Programme*

Icon Films
0117 970 6882
info@iconfilms.co.uk
www.iconfilms.co.uk
MD: Laura Marshall
• *Belgrano; King Cobra; Einstein's Brain*

Illumina Digital
020 8600 9300
info@illumina.co.uk
www.illumina.co.uk
MD: Andrew Chitty
- DFES; National Theatre; Culture; Net Cymru

Illuminations Films
020 7288 8400
mail@illumin.co.uk
www.illumin.co.uk
MD: Linda Zuck
- The Piano Tuner of Earthquakes; London Orbital; Little Otik; TV Heaven; The A-Z of TV; 1001 Nights of TV

Images Of War
020 7430 4480
derek@dircon.co.uk
www.warfootage.com
MD: Derek Blades
- Mass for Peace; Invasion; D-Day; Footage for Hitler's Britain; 300 hours of war-related material

Imago Productions
01603 727600
mail@imagoproductions.tv
www.imagoproductions.tv
MD: Vivica Parsons
- Grudge Match; Perfect Man; The Coach; Sporty Facts; Bryan's Olde and Bitter; Coastal Kitchen; Coastal Inspirations; My Horror Home; Secrets Beneath Our Feet

Independent Image
01883 654867
info@indimage.com
www.indimage.com
MD: David Wickham
- Chefs in the City; Cannabis from the Chemist; Interpol's Most Wanted; David Dimbleby's India; Quest for the Lost Civilisation

Infonation
020 7370 1082
mail@infonation.org.uk
www.infonation.org.uk
MD: Ron Blythe
- Under One Umbrella; Protected Meal Times; Challenge UK

International Media Productions (IMP)
020 8690 9674
improductions@tiscali.co.uk
www.improductions.co.uk
Producer, director: Paul Moody
- Arriva; Tiny Lives; A Beacon for Culture

ITN factual
020 7430 4511
itn.factual@itn.co.uk
www.itn.co.uk
Head of ITN Factual: Philip Armstrong
- Reign of Terror; Europe's Richest; Madam Cyn's Home Movies; Travels with Diana; The First Head Transplant

IWC Media
0141 353 3222
info@iwcmedia.co.uk
www.warkclements.com
MD: Sue Oriel
- Relocation, Relocation, Relocation; Location, Location, Location; Jeopardy; The First World War (C4); No Sex Please We're Teenagers; Survival of the Richest

Jay Media
01270 884453
media@jaymedia.co.uk
www.jaymedia.co.uk
MD: Nigel Jay
- Skill City; Manchester Evening News; Preston City Council; Mersey Family Business Awards; UK Trade & Investment; Manchester City Council; Scope

The Jim Henson Company
020 7428 4000
fanmail@henson.com
www.henson.com
MD: Brian Henson
- Muppet series; Aliens in the Family; Bear in the Big Blue House; Sesame Street

Juniperblue
0117 3305938
richard@juniperblue.com
www.juniperblue.com
MD: Richard Moore
- Tate – Henry Moore Recumbent Figure; Marine Conservation Society; Good Beach Guide; Wild Battlefields Wolf and Polar Bear; Allied Domecq- Courvoisier XO

Keo Films
020 7490 3580
keo@keofilms.com
www.keofilms.com
MD: Andrew Palmer
- River Cottage Diner; Surviving Extremes; The Great Race; Save Lullingstone Castle

Kudos
020 7812 3270
info@kudosfilmandtv.com
www.kudosfilmandtv.com
MDs: Stephen Garrett, Jane Featherstone
- Spooks; Life on Mars; Hustle II; Pleasureland

Landmark Films
01865 297220
info@landmarkfilms.com
www.landmarkfilms.com
MD: Nick O'Dwyer
- Extraordinary People; Beauty School; Real Life Swap; Angry Britain; Limo Fever

Landseer Productions
020 7485 7333
mail@landseerfilms.com
www.landseerfilms.com
MD and producer: Derek Bailey

Leopard Films
0870 420 4232
mail@leopardfilms.com
www.leopardfilms.com
MD: James Burstall
- Car Booty; Cash in the Attic; Money Spinners; Elvis Mob; Stately Suppers; Found

Liberty Bell Productions
0191 222 1200
info@libertybell.tv
www.libertybell.tv
MD: Stuart Prebble; head of features: Judith Holder
- Grumpy Old Men; Victoria Wood's Big Fat Documentary; Stella's Story; For the Benefit of Mr Parris; Heroes for Six Minutes; After They Were Famous – Grease; Stars Reunited

Libra Television
0161 236 5599
hq@libratelevision.com
www.libratelevision.com
MDs: Madeline Wiltshire, Louise Lynch
- Gross; Citizen Power; How to be a Bully; Copycat Kids; History Busters; Road Safety; Sorted 2; Curriculum Bites RE

Little Bird
00 353 1 613 1710
info@littlebird.ie
www.littlebird.ie
Co Chairmen: James Mitchell, Jonathan Cavendish
- Bridget Jones 2 – The Edge of Reason; Trauma; Churchill the Hollywood Years; In My Father's Den; Whisky Echo

Loose Moose
020 7287 3821
info@loosemoose.net
www.loosemoose.net
MD: Glenn Holberton
- Peperami; Chips Ahoy!; Brisk Iced Tea; Alone Amongst Friends; League of Gentlemen; Thunder Pig

Lupus Films
020 7419 0997
info@lupusfilms.net
www.lupusfilms.net
MDs: Camilla Deakin, Ruth Fielding
- Little Wolf's Book of Badness; Wilde Stories; Little Wolf's Adventure Academy; Mia, Cool Hunter

Macmillan Media
0870 350 2150
info@macmillanmedia.co.uk
www.macmillanmedia.co.uk
MD: Michael Macmillan
- Corporate video

Malachite
01790 763538
info@malachite.co.uk
www.malachite.co.uk
MD: Charles Mapleston
- Fiore; Children of the Mafia; Dressing up for the Carnival – a Portrait of Carol Shields

Maverick Television
0121 771 1812 London: 020 7383 2727
mail@mavericktv.co.uk
www.mavericktv.co.uk
Chairman: Johnnie Turpie
- Ten Years Younger; Celebrity Disfigurement; How to Look Good Naked

Maya Vision International
020 7796 4842
john@mayavisionint.com
www.mayavisionint.com
Producer and director: Rebecca Dobbs
• *Hitler's Search for the Holy Grail;*
  Conquistadors; In Search of Shakespeare;
  Two Moons; In Search of Myths and
  Heroes

Mentorn
020 7258 6800
mentorn@mentorn.co.uk
www.mentorn.co.uk
MD: Steve Anderson
• *Robot Wars; Question Time; 30 minutes;*
  Body Shock; Big Ideas that Change the
  World

Mint Productions
028 9024 0555
Belfast 028 9024 0555
Dublin 00 353 1 491 3333
info@mint.ie
www.mint.ie
MD: Steve Carson
• *Abu Hamza; Two Day Coup; De Lorean;*
  Workers Strike; Crash; Emmet; All the
  Queen's Men; Who Kidnapped Shergar?

Monkey
020 7749 3110
info@monkeykingdom.com
www.monkeykingdom.com
MD: Dom Loehnis
• *What Sadie Did Next; Swag;*
  He's Starsky I'm Hutch

Multi Media Arts
0161 374 5566
info@mmarts.com
www.mmarts.com
MD: Michael Spencer
• *Powerhouse; The Blizzard of Odd;*
  Reality Bites

Mute Marmalade
020 7449 2552
info@mutemarmalade.com
www.mutemarmalade.com
MD: Jonathan Bentata
• *Black Soles; The Runner; Making*
  Mistakes

Nexus Productions
020 7749 7500
info@nexusproductions.com
www.nexusproductions.com
MD: Chris O'Reilly
• *Honda; Vodafone; Thunderbirds; iToy;*
  Coca Cola; Franz Ferdinand

Objective Productions
020 7202 2300
info@objectiveproductions.com
www.objectiveproductions.net
MDs: Andrew O'Connor, Michael Vine
• *Derren Brown: Trick of the Mind;*
  Peep Show; Dirty Tricks; Balls of Steel;
  Greatest TV Moments

October Films
020 7284 6868
info@octoberfilms.co.uk
www.octoberfilms.co.uk
MD: Tom Roberts
• *The Beslan Siege; The Fight for Ground*
  Zero; The Insurgency; True Horror with
  Anthony Head

Open Mind Productions
020 7437 0624
enquiries@openmind.co.uk
www.openmind.co.uk
MD: Roland Tongue
• *Paz; The Shiny Show; The Number Crew*

Optomen
020 7967 1234
otv@optomen.com
www.optomen.com
MD: Mike Bibby
• *Ramsay's Kitchen Nightmares series 2*

Outline Productions
020 7428 1560
mail@outlineproductions.co.uk
www.outlineproductions.co.uk
MDs: Helen Veale, Laura Mansfield
• *House of Tiny Tearaways; Mongrel*
  Nation; Homefront; Violent Nation;
  Conspiracies On Trial

ORTV
020 8614 7200
reception@ortv.co.uk
www.ortv.co.uk
MD: Christopher Mitchell
• *John McCarthy - Out of the Shadows;*
  Heart of the Lioness; Saddam's Iraq

Oxford Film And Television
020 7483 3637
email@oftv.co.uk
www.oftv.co.uk
Creative director: Nicholas Kent
• *Lionheart - The Crusade; Second*
  Generation (C4); Superfly, Terry Jones'
  Medieval Tales, National Trust (BBC);
  The Spectator Affair; Vic Reeves: Rogues
  Gallery; Building Britain; 2003 Visions
  Of Space

Paladin Invision
020 7371 2123
clive@pitv.com
www.pitv.com
MDs: William Cran, Clive Syddall
• *Commanding Heights; Do You Speak*
  American; Dark Star; All Or Nothing At
  All: The Life of Frank Sinatra

Pepper's Ghost Productions
020 8546 4900
enquiries@peppersghost.com
www.peppersghost.com
MD: Paul Michael
• *Tiny Planets, Policecat Fuzz; Bus Stop;*
  Kingfisher Tailor

Pesky
020 7703 2080
hodge@pesky.com
www.pesky.com
Partners: David Hodgson, Clare
Underwood
• *Stress Maniacs; Amazing Adrenalini*
  Brothers; MissyMiss; Invisible INK;
  CyberPest

Pilot Film and TV Productions
020 8960 2771
info@pilot.co.uk
www.pilotguides.com
Director: Ian Cross
• *Globe Trekker; Pilot Guides; Planet*
  Food; Ian Wright Live

Pioneer Productions
020 8748 0888
pioneer@pioneertv.com
www.pioneertv.com
MD: Stuart Carter
• *Naked Science; Danger Man;*
  Tycoon Toys

Planet 24 Productions
020 7486 6268
alice@planet24.co.uk
www.planet24.com
MD: Ed Forsdick
• *Mechanick; How to Pull... ;*
  Big Breakfast

Planet Wild
0161 233 3090
office@planetwild.co.uk
www.planetwild.co.uk
MD: Paula Trafford
• *Cilla in Black and White; George Best's*
  Story; Pushy Parents

Presentable
029 2057 5729
all@presentable.co.uk
www.presentable.co.uk
MD: Megan Stuart
• *Poker Nations Cup, Late Night Poker,*
  Wales: The Making of a People, Family
  Detectives.

Prism Entertainment
020 8969 1212
info@prism-e.com
www.prismentertainment.co.uk
MDs: Mike Crosby, Amelia Johnson
• *The Stables; FAQ series 3; Beat the*
  Cyborgs; PXG; Star Munchies;
  Invention SOS

The Producers
020 7636 4226
jenny@theproducersfilms.co.uk
www.theproducersfilms.co.uk
MDs: Jenny Edwards, Jeanna Polley
• *Belonging; Seeing Red; The Politician's*
  Wife

Quickfire Media
0117 946 6838
info@quickfiremedia.com
www.quickfiremedia.com
MD: Mark Fielder
• *The Bobby Moore Story-The Secret*
  Life of a Superhero; In the Footsteps of
  Churchill; Dispatches: Barrack Room
  Bullies; Natural World; Wolves of the
  Barren Lands

Raw Charm
029 2064 1511
enquiries@rawcharm.tv
www.rawcharm.tv
MD: Kate Jones-Davies
• *War Stories; Grave Detectives; Simon*
  Weston's War Heroes; The Weston Front

Real Life Media Productions
0113 237 1005
info@reallife.co.uk
www.reallife.co.uk
MD: Ali Rashid
• *Mum, I'm a Muslim; Baby Baby;*
  Britain's Most Dangerous Prisoner

Red Green and Blue Company
020 8746 0616
max@rgbco.com
www.rgbco.com
Directors: Max Whitby, Cathy Collis
• *DNA Interactive*

Red Kite Animations
0131 554 0060
info@redkite-animation.com
www.redkite-animation.com
MD: Ken Anderson
• *The Secret World of Benjamin Bear; The Loch Ness Kelpie; Wilf the Witch's Dog; The Imp; BBC Radio Scotland*

Red Production Company
0161 827 2530
info@redlimited.co.uk
www.redproductioncompany.com
MD: Andrew Critchley
• *Conviction; Jane Hall; Mine All Mine*

Reef Television
020 7836 8595
mail@reeftv.com
www.reef.tv
MD: Richard Farmbrough
• *Sun, Sea & Bargain Spotting; Put Your Money Where Your House Is; Foreign Exchange; Uncharted Territory; The People's Museum; My Favourite Garden*

Renting Eyeballs Entertainment
020 7437 4188
malcolm.rasala@rentingeyeballs.com
www.rentingeyeballs.com
MD: Mark Maco
• *Commercials, promos, brand television, motion pictures*

Resource Base
023 8023 6806
post@resource-base.co.uk
www.resource-base.co.uk
MD: Karen Gilchrist, Hilary Durman
• *VEE-TV; Without You; World of Difference; Lion Mountain; Who Cares?*

Ricochet Films
020 7251 6966
mail@ricochet.co.uk
www.ricochet.co.uk
MD: Nick Powell
• *Supernanny; Living in the Sun; Flying Heavy Metal; How Not to Decorate; Risking It All; Mirror, Signal, Manoeuvre*

Ronin Entertainment
020 7734 3884
mail@ronintv.com
www.ronintv.com
MDs: Richard Hearsey, Robin Greene
• *The Impressionable Jon Culshaw; Fort Boyard; It's a Knockout*

RS Productions
0191 224 4301
info@rsproductions.co.uk
www.rsproductions.co.uk
MD: Mark Lavender
• *Frozen; Elephants and Angels; Laughter When We're Dead; Thereby Hangs a Tale*

Sally Head Productions
020 8607 8730
admin@shpl.demon.co.uk
MD: Sally Head
• *Forefathers; Plastic Man; Tipping The Velvet; The Cry; Mayor of Casterbridge; The Return; Fingersmith; A Good Murder*

Samson Films
00 353 1 667 0533
info@samsonfilms.com
www.samsonfilms.com
MD: David Collins
• *Co-producer: Blind Flight; Honeymooners; Abduction Club; Most Fertile Man in Ireland. Feature development: Mir Friends; Immortal; Havoc*

Scream Films
020 8995 8255
info@screamfilms.com
www.screamfilms.com
MD: Susie Dark
• *Famous and Frightened; Dale Winton's Wedding; Terror Alert*

Screenhouse Productions
0113 266 8881
info@screenhouse.co.uk
www.screenhouse.co.uk
Chief executive: Barbara Govan
• *Star Date; Science Shack; Snapshot*

Seventh Art Productions
01273 777678
info@seventh-art.com
www.seventh-art.com
MD: Phil Grabsky
• *Tim Marlow on ... Edward Hopper; Easter in Art; Pelé - World Cup Hero; Great Artists II; The Boy Who Plays on the Buddhas of Bamiyan; In Search of Mozart*

Shed Productions
020 8215 3387
shed@shedproductions.com
www.shedproductions.com
MD: Eileen Gallagher
• *Footballers Wives; Bad Girls; Waterloo Road*

SMG Productions
0141 300 3000
website@smgproductions.tv
www.smgproductions.tv
MD: Elizabeth Partyka
• *Taggart; Club Reps: The Workers; Good Bye Mr Chips; Medics of the Glen; Squeak!; How 2*

Slinky Pictures
020 7247 6444
info@slinkypics.com
www.slinkypics.com
MD: Maria Manton
• *Who I Am and What I Want; Look For Me; Stalk; The Census Taker*

Smith And Watson Productions
01803 863033
info@smithandwatson.com
www.smithandwatson.com
MD: Nick Smith
• *Building a Dream; Bill Wyman's Blues; A Story of Peter Rabbit and Beatrix Potter; Joss Stone in Uganda*

Smoking Dogs Films
020 7249 6644
info@smokingdogsfilms.com
www.smokingdogsfilms.com
MD: David Lawson
• *Urban Soul - Making of Modern R&B; The Wonderful World of Louis Armstrong; Goldie - When Satin Returns*

So Television
020 7960 2000
info@sotelevision.co.uk
www.sotelevision.co.uk
Director: Jon Magnusson
• *Comedy Lab; v Graham Norton; Bigger Picture*

Specific Films
020 7580 7476
info@specificfilms.com
MD: Michael Hamlyn
• *Last Seduction II; Paws; Mr Reliable; Priscilla, Queen of the Desert; The Proposition*

Spire Films
01865 371979
mail@spirefilms.co.uk
www.spirefilms.co.uk
MD: David Willcock
• *Delia Smith; Romans*

Stampede
01582 727330
dave@stampede.co.uk
www.stampede.co.uk
MD: Mike Chamberlain
• *Putting the Fun in Fundamental; Lin and Ralph - A Love Story; Fierce People; Before The Flood*

Sunset + Vine
020 7478 7300
reception@sunsetvine.co.uk
www.sunsetvine.co.uk
MD: John Leach
• *Channel 4 Cricket; Gillette World Sport; Rad; European Poker Tour; Football on Five; John Barnes Football Night*

Sunstone Films
sunstonefilms@aol.com
www.sunstonefilms.co.uk
• *Before Columbus; Lords of the Maya; Warhorse; Gladiators: The Brutal Truth; It Ain't Necessarily So*

Talent Television
020 7421 7800
entertainment@talenttv.com
www.talenttv.com
Creative director: John Kaye Cooper
• *Best of Friends; Casino, Casino; Test The Nation; The Man With Eighty Wives*

Telemagination
020 7434 1551
mail@tmation.co.uk
www.telemagination.co.uk
Head of studio: Beth Parker
• *Pongwiffy; Little Ghosts; Something Else; Metalheads; Cramp Twins; Heidi*

Television Junction
0121 248 4466
info@televisionjunction.co.uk
www.televisionjunction.co.uk
MDs: Paul Davies, Yvonne Davies
• *Double Act; Seeing Science; Think About It; The Way We Were*

Wish Films
020 8324 2308
info@wishfilms.com
www.wishfilms.com
MD: Helen Cadwallader
• *Jim Jam and Sunny*

Ten Alps TV
020 7089 3686
info@tenalps.com
www.tenalps.com
MD: Sam Cash
• *Peaches Geldof: Inside the Mind of a Teenager; Jeremy Vine Meets... series 2; Geldof on Fathers; Geldof on Divorce; 50 Greatest Goals; Top Dog*

Tern Television
01224 211123
Glasgow: 0141 243 5658
info@terntv.com
www.terntv.com
MDs: David Strachan, Gwyneth Hardy
• *Chancers; Fraserburgh; 2003 Reloaded; Mapman; Beachgrove Garden; The Greenmount Garden*

Testimony Films
0117 925 8589
mail@testimonyfilms.com
MD: Steve Humphries
• *Lovechild; Sex in a Cold Climate; Britain's Boy Soldiers; Some Liked It Hot*

Tigress Productions
020 7434 4411
Bristol: 0117 933 5600
general@tigressproductions.co.uk
general@tigressbristol.co.uk
www.tigressproductions.co.uk
MD: Jeremy Bradshaw
• *Snakemaster; The Jeff Corwin Experience; Dolphin Murders; The Science of Combat*

Torpedo
01443 231989
info@torpedoltd.co.uk
www.torpedoltd.co.uk
Chairman: Mark Jones
• *Fishlock's Sea Stories II; Jigsaw III; V.E.T.S*

Touch Productions
01225 484666
enquiries@touchproductions.co.uk
www.touchproductions.co.uk
MD: Malcolm Brinkworth
• *Mind Shock: Transplanting Minds; Separating Twins; Angela's Dying Wish; British Made; Paris In The Sun; Brit School; The Four-Year-Old Boy Who Ran 40 Miles*

TransAtlantic Films
020 8735 0505
Hereford: 01497 831800
mail@transatlanticfilms.com
www.transatlanticfilms.com
MD: Corisande Albert
• *Amazing Animal Adaptors; Extreme Body Parts; Science of Love*

Turn On Television
0161 247 7700
mail@turnontv.co.uk
www.turnontv.co.uk
MD: Angela Smith
• *Unlikely Lovers; Baby's Birthday; Inside Criminal Minds*

TV6
020 7610 0266
mail@tv6.co.uk
www.tv6.co.uk
MD: Richard Reisz
• *Horizon: Percy Pilcher's Flying Machines; Horizon: King Solomon's Tablet of Stone; Landscape Mysteries; Into the Great Pyramid; Tutankhamun's Fireball*

Unique Communications Group
020 7605 1200
ucg@uniquegroup.co.uk
info@uniquecomms.com
www.uniquecomms.com
MD: Noel Edmonds
• *British Comedy Awards 2003; Stars Behind Bars; Harley Street; I'm the Answer; Survivors; Make Me Rich*

Vera Productions
020 7436 6116
cree@vera.co.uk
MD: Geoff Atkinson
• *Bremner Bird and Fortune*

Vivum Intelligent Media
020 7729 2749
livewire@vivum.net
www.vivum.net
MD: Nick Rosen
• *2003 World Trade Centre series; high-brow factual content*

Wag TV
020 7688 1711
post@wagtv.com
www.wagtv.com
MD: Martin Durkin
• *Divine Designs; Dave Courtney's Underworld; The Great Scientist; Kings of Construction; Industrial Revelations; Face of Britain; How Do They Do It?*

Wild Dream Films
01432 840732
mail@wild-dream.com
www.wild-dream.com
MD: Stuart Clarke
• *Map Makers; Ancient Discoveries series 1/2*

Wild Rover Productions
028 9050 0980
enquiries@wild-rover.com
www.wild-rover.com
MD: Philip Morrow
• *Just For Laughs; A Day In The Westlife of Shane; Would You Pass the Eleven Plus?; Get Smarter in a Week*

Wilton Films
020 7749 7282
info@wiltonfilms.com
cvs@wiltonfilms.com
www.wiltonfilms.com
MD: Paul Mitchell
• *Hotspots; Chechnya; The Alternative Rock 'n' Roll Years; Lords of the Spin; Future for Lebanon; How to Make a Revolution; How Putin Came to Power*

Windfall Films
020 7251 7676
enquiries@windfallfilms.com
www.windfallfilms.com
MD: David Dugan
• *D-Day: The Ultimate Conflict; The Great Escape Revealed; Men of Iron*

World Of Wonder
020 7428 3444
wow@worldofwonder.co.uk
www.worldofwonder.net
Chief executive: Fenton Bailey
• *Matt's Old Masters; Housebusters; The Art Show – Spoils of War*

World Wide Pictures
020 7434 1121
info@worldwidegroup.ltd.uk
www.worldwidegroup.ltd.uk
MDs: Richard King, Ray Townsend, Chris Courtenay-Taylor
• *Bad Girls; videos for the Office of the Deputy Prime Minister*

World's End Productions
020 7386 4900
info@worldsendproductions.com
www.worldsendproductions.com
MDs: Jim Philips, Jerry Drew
• *Shoot Me; Going Down to South Park; Dead Casual; Live at Johnny's; Fighting Talk. Co-production with Celador: Johnny & Denise*

Zeal Television
020 8780 4600
sheila.humphreys@zealtv.net
www.zealtv.net
Chief executive: Peter Christiansen
• *Building the Dream; Britain's Hardest; Resistance; Demolition; Super Human; Sushi TV*

Zeppotron
0870 333 1700
contact@zeppotron.com
www.zeppotron.com
Creative directors: Neil Webster, Ben Caudell, Charlie Brooker
• *People's Book of Records; Playing Tricks; The Cowboy Trap; Space Cadets*

TV and film studios

124 Facilities
124 Horseferry Road,
London SW1P 2TX
020 7306 8040
www.124.co.uk
*Part of the Channel 4 group. General
manager: Tony Chamberlain; studio
managers: Tony Kibbles, Tim Moulson*

3 Mills Studios
Three Mill Lane, London E3 3DU
020 7363 3336
info@3mills.com
www.3mills.com
*MD: Daniel Dark; studio manager: Jason
Taylor*

3sixty Media
Quay Street, Manchester M60 9EA
0161 827 2020
enquiry@3sixtymedia.com
www.3sixtymedia.com
Head of studios: Paul Bennett

400 Company
B3 The Workshops,
2A Askew Crescent, Shepherds Bush,
London W12 9DP
020 8746 1400
info@the400.co.uk
www.the400.co.uk
Studio manager: Christian Riov

Arqiva
Crawley Court, Crawley,
Winchester SO21 2QA
01962 823434
info@arqiva.com
www.arqiva.com
*MD: Peter Douglas. Formerly NTL
Broadcast*

Ascent Media
1 Stephen Street, London W1T 1AL
020 7691 6000
www.ascentmedia.co.uk
Studio manager: Tony Shepherd

APTN
The Interchange, Oval Road,
Camden Lock, London NW1 7DZ
020 7482 7580
aptnbookings@ap.org
www.aptn.com
Studio manager: James Lewis

Ardmore Studios
Herbert Road, Bray,
Co Wicklow, Ireland
00 353 1 286 2971
film@ardmore.ie
www.ardmore.ie
MD: Kevin Moriarty

BBC Elstree Centre
Clarendon Road, Borehamwood,
Herts WD6 1JF
020 8228 7102
www.bbc.co.uk
Senior facility manager: Sue Spree

BBC TV Centre Studios
Wood Lane, Shepherds Bush,
London W12 7RJ
020 8743 8000
bbcresources@bbc.co.uk
www.bbcresources.co.uk
Principal facilities manager: Keith Clark

Bray Studios
Down Place, Water Oakley, Windsor,
Berks SL4 5UG
01628 622111
General manager: Nathan Hendricks

Broadley Productions
Broadley House, 48 Broadley
Terrace, London NW1 6LG
020 7258 0324
markfrench@broadley.tv
www.broadley.tv
MD and studio manager: Mark French

Canalot Production Studios
222 Kensal Road, London W10 5BN
020 8960 8580
eliza.davis@workspacegroup.co.uk
www.workspacegroup.co.uk
Studio manager: Eliza Davis

Capital Studios
13 Wandsworth Plain,
London SW18 1ET
020 8877 1234
bobbi.johnstone@capitalstudios.com
www.capitalstudios.co.uk
Studio manager: Bobbi Johnstone

Central Studios
Location House, 5 Dove Lane,
Bristol BS2 9HP
0117 955 4777
info@centralstudios.co.uk
www.centralstudios.co.uk
Studio manager: Dave Garbe

Centre Stage
28-30 Osnaburgh Street,
London NW1 3ND
07775 948700
mail@centrestagestudios.co.uk
www.centrestagestudios.co.uk
*MD: Saul Barrington; studio manager:
Toby Gair*

**CTS and Lansdowne Recording
Studios**
Lansdowne House, Lansdowne Road,
London W11 3LP
020 7727 0041
info@cts-lansdowne.co.uk
www.cts-lansdowne.co.uk
Studio manager: Chris Dibble

Desisti Lighting (UK)
15 Old Market Street, Thetford,
Norfolk IP24 2EQ
01842 752909
info@desisti.co.uk
www.desisti.co.uk
Director: John Reay-Young

Ealing Studios
Ealing Green, London W5 5EP
020 8567 6655
info@ealingstudios.com
www.ealingstudios.com
Studio manager: Jeremy Pelzer

East Side Studios
40A River Road, Barking,
Essex IG11 0DW
020 8507 7572
info@eastsidestudios.com
www.eastsidestudios.com
Studio manager: Susan Noy

Elstree Film and Television Studios
Shenley Road, Borehamwood,
Herts WD6 1JG
020 8953 1600
info@elstreefilmtv.com
www.elstreefilmtv.com
Directors: Julie Wicks, Neville Reid

Enfys
Unit 31 Portanmoor Road,
East Moors, Cardiff,
South Glamorgan CF2 5HB, Wales
029 2049 9988
mail@enfys.tv
www.enfys.tv
Studio manager: Sarah-Jane Salmon

Fountain TV Studios
128 Wembley Park Drive,
Wembley, Middlesex HA9 8HQ
020 8900 5800
everyone@ftv.co.uk
www.ftv.co.uk
Studio manager: Tony Edwards

Greenford Studios
5-11 Taunton Road,
Metropolitan Centre, Greenford,
Middlesex UB6 8UQ
020 8575 7300
studios@panavision.co.uk
www.panavision.co.uk
Studio manager: Kate Tufano

Handstand Productions
13 Hope Street, Liverpool L1 9BH
0151 708 7441
info@handstand-uk.com
www.handstand-uk.com
*Director producers: Han Duijvendak,
Nick Stanley*

Holborn Studios
49/50 Eagle Wharf Road,
London N1 7ED
020 7490 4099
studiomanager@
    holborn-studios.co.uk
www.holborn-studios.co.uk
Studio manager: Billy McCartney

The Hospital
24 Endell Street, Covent Garden,
London WC2H 9HQ
020 7170 9112
studio@thehospital.co.uk
www.thehospital.co.uk
Studio manager: Anne Marie Phelan

IAC
Moorside Road, Winchester,
Hampshire S23 7US
01962 873000
info@iacl.co.uk
www.iacl.co.uk
Studio manager: Ian Rich

ICA Theatre
The Mall, London SW1Y 5AH
020 7930 0493
info@ica.org.uk
www.ica.org.uk
Technical director: Lee Curran

Island Studios
9-11 Alliance Road, Acton,
London W3 0RA
020 8956 5600
info@islandstudios.net
www.islandstudios.net
MD and studio manager: Steve Guidici

London Studios
London Television Centre,
Upper Ground Floor, London SE1 9LT
020 7737 8888
sales@londonstudios.co.uk
www.londonstudios.co.uk
MD: Debbie Hills; head of sales: Kathy Schulz

Maidstone Studios
New Cut Road, Vinters Park,
Maidstone, Kent ME14 5NZ
01622 691111
info@maidstonestudios.com
www.maidstonestudios.com
MD: Geoff Miles; liaison manager: Denise Buckland

Metro Imaging
76 Clerkenwell Road,
London EC1M 5TN
020 7865 0000
info@metroimaging.co.uk
www.metroimaging.co.uk
Studio manager: Steve Jackson

Millbank Studios
4 Millbank, London SW1P 3JA
020 7233 2020
production@millbank-studios.co.uk
www.millbank-studios.co.uk
Production manager: Caroline Bloomfield

Millennium Studios
5 Elstree Way, Borehamwood,
Herts WD6 1SF
020 8236 1400
info@millenniumstudios.co.uk
www.millenniumstudios.co.uk
MD: Ronan Willson; studio manager: Toni Cullip

Molinare Studios
34 Fouberts Place, London W1F 7PX
020 7478 7000
bookings@molinare.co.uk
www.molinare.co.uk
Studio manager: Mick Harley

Park Royal Studios
1 Barretts Green Road,
London NW10 7AE
020 8965 9778
info@parkroyalstudios.com
www.parkroyalstudios.com
Studio manager: Francois van de Langkruis

Phaebus Communications
The Brewery Tower,
The Deva Centre, Trinity Way,
Manchester M3 7BF
0161 605 9999
solutions@phaebus.co.uk
www.phaebus.co.uk
Studio manager: Steve Bettridge

Pinewood Studios
Pinewood Road, Iver Heath,
Bucks SL0 0NH
01753 651700
firstname.lastname@
   pinewoodgroup.com
www.pinewoodgroup.com
Studio manager: Peter Hicks

Production House NI/ Stage Services North
Unit 5, Prince Regent Retail Park,
Prince Regent Road, Belfast BT5 6QP
028 9079 8999
info@productionhouse.net
Studio manager: Neil Lewis

Pyramid TV
36 Cardiff Road, Llandaff, Cardiff,
Wales CF5 2DR
029 2057 6888
keith@pyramidtv.co.uk
www.pyramidtv.co.uk
Studio manager: Martin Dodwell

RC Film & TV Set Construction
Unit C11 Dundonald Enterprise Park,
Carrowreagh Road, Dundonald
BT16 1QT, Northern Ireland
028 9055 7557
MD: Russell Fulton

Riverside Studios
Crisp Road, Hammersmith,
London W6 9RL
020 8237 1000
alexcotterill@riversidestudios.co.uk
www.riversidestudios.co.uk
Centre manager: Alex Cotterill

Sands Film Studios
Grices Wharf, 119 Rotherhithe Street,
London SE16 4NF
020 7231 2209
OStockman@sandsfilms.co.uk
www.sandsfilms.co.uk
MD: Olivier Stockman

Shepperton Studios
Studios Road, Shepperton,
Middlesex TW17 0QD
01932 562611
firstname.lastname@
   pinewoodgroup.com
www.pinewoodgroup.com
Studio manager: David Godfrey

Studio
Cabul Road, London SW11 2PR
020 7228 5228
thestudio@filmed.com
www.the-studio.co.uk
Studio manager: Gemma Masters

Sumners
Suite 401, Barclay House,
35 Whitworth Street West,
Manchester M1 5NG
0161 228 0330
andy@sumners.co.uk
www.sumners.co.uk
General manager and chief engineer: Brian Hardman

Technicolor Network Services
Chiswick Park, Building 12,
566 Chiswick High Road,
London W4 5AN
020 8100 1000
lucia.davella@thomson.net
www.technicolor.com
Facilities manager: Marco Bellini

Teddington Studios
Broom Road, Teddington,
Middlesex TW11 9NT
020 8977 3252
sales@teddington.tv
www.teddington.co.uk
Studio manager: Ray Gearing

The Worx
10 Heathmans Road, Fulham,
London SW6 4TJ
020 7371 9777
enquiries@theworx.co.uk
www.theworx.co.uk
MDs: Jackie Mallory, Jonathan Mallory

Twickenham Studios
The Barons, St Margarets,
Twickenham, Middlesex TW1 2AW
020 8607 8888
caroline@
   twickenhamfilmstudios.com
www.twickenhamstudios.com
Studio manager: Caroline Tipple

VFX Company
Dukes Island Studios, Dukes Road,
London W3 0SL
020 8956 5674
info@thevfxco.co.uk
www.thevfxco.co.uk
Operations manager: Digna Nigoumi

Waterfall Studios
2 Silver Road, Wood Lane,
London W12 7SG
020 8746 2000
enquiries@waterfall-studios.com
www.waterfall-studios.com
Studio manager: Samantha Leese

Post-production

3sixty Media
Quay Street, Manchester M60 9EA
0161 839 0360
enquiry@3sixtymedia.com
www.3sixtymedia.com
Independent. Effects and virtual reality.
Post-production manager: John Mariner
- *Island at War; Tonight with Trevor*
  MacDonald; Blue Murder; Vincent;
  Coronation Street

3 Wise Men
Ingestre Court, Ingestre Place,
London W1F 0JL
020 7343 6623
daz@3wisemen.tv
www.3wisemen.tv
Independent. Offline editing. MD: Darren
Jonusas
- *Seven Industrial Wonders; Battlefield*
  Britain; Horizon; Journeys into the Ring
  of Fire; Truth About Food

4x4
First Floor, 21 Ormeau Avenue,
Belfast BT2 8HD
028 9027 1950
4@4x4post.com
www.4x4post.com
Independent. Effects; graphics;
commercials; audio. Directors: Katy
Jackson; Paula Campbell; Alan Perry;
Jonathan Featherstone
- *Disability commercials; BTNI*
  commercial; Just for a Laugh

422 Manchester
4th Floor, South Central,
11 Peter Street, Manchester M2 5QR
0161 839 6080
production@422.tv
www.422manchester.com
Animation, graphics, commercials,
special effects and audio. Production
director: Richard Wallwork
- *Vimto; Pingu; Mastermind; A Question*
  of Sport

422 South
St John's Court, Whiteladies Road,
Bristol BS8 2QY
0117 946 7222
debbiet@422.com
www.422south.com
Factual television and animation, digital
effects, commercials production.
Production director: Andy Davies-Coward
- *The British Isles – A Natural History;*
  Journey of Life; Royal British Legion

Ascent Media Camden
13 Hawley Crescent,
London NW1 8NP
020 7284 7900
www.ascent-media.co.uk
Nine other sites. Film processing
laboratory; video; tape; DVD
- *Poirot; Auf Weidersehen Pet; Hustle*

Anvil
Denham Media Park,
North Orbital Road, Denham,
Uxbridge, Middlesex UB9 5HL
020 8799 0555
mike.anscombe@thomson.net
www.anvilpost.com
Audio. Part of Technicolor (Thomson
Group). Studio manager: Mike Anscombe
- *The Brief; Ultimate Force; Midsomer*
  Murders; Like Father, Like Son; Doc
  Martin; Auf Wiedersehen Pet; Heartless

Arena P3
74 Newman Street, London W1T 3EL
020 7436 4360
edit@arenap3.tv
www.arenap3.tv
Part of 2D video facilities. Effects; audio;
documentaries; comedy. MD: Juliet
Gonsales
- *Bo' Selecta!; Trouble at Top;*
  Scambusters; Brassed-Off Britain

Arion Communications
Global House, Denham Media Park,
North Orbital Road, Denham,
Uxbridge Middlesex UB9 5HL
01895 834484
sales@arion.co.uk
www.arion.co.uk
Independent. Telecine; DVD duplication;
editing. MD: Neil Mockler
- *Hitchhiker's Guide to the Galaxy; Basic*
  Instinct 2; Sahara

Barcud Derwen
Cibyn, Caernarfon,
Gwynedd LL55 2BD
01286 684300
Cardiff 029 2061 1515
info@barcudderwen.com
www.barcudderwen.com
Drama, graphics. MD: Tudor Roberts
- *Celebrity Poker; Tracy Beaker series;*
  Mountains and Man

Blue
58 Old Compton Street,
London W1D 4UF
020 7437 2626
info@bluepp.co.uk
www.bluepp.co.uk
VTR Group. Special effects; graphics;
commercial; audio. MD: Simon Briggs
- *Equator; My New Home; Britain's*
  Biggest Spenders; Hellman's
  commercial

Capital FX
3rd Floor, 20 Dering Street,
London W1S 1AJ
020 7493 9998
ian.buckton@capital-fx.co.uk
www.capital-fx.co.uk
Independent. Special effects; graphics;
taped film transfer. MD: Ian Buckton
- *Harry Potter; Troy; Lord of the Rings*

Cine Wessex
Westway House,
19 St Thomas Street, Winchester,
Hampshire SO23 9HJ
01962 865454
info@cinewessex.co.uk
www.cinewessex.co.uk
Independent. Editing; camera kit and
crew hire; 2D and 3D graphics; VHS, CD
and DVD. Facilities director: Joe Conman
- *City Gardener; Mappin Murder; Room*
  for Improvement

Clear
37 Dean St, London W1D 4PT
020 7734 5557
reception@clearpost.co.uk
www.clearpost.co.uk
Sister company Finally Cut. Visual
effects, commercials and films. Head of
production: Pierre Fletcher
- *28 Days Later; BBC Talking Head*
  preview; Millions

Clear Cut Hires
Pinewood Studios, Pinewood Road,
Iver Heath, Bucks SL0 0NH
0845 257 0500
fazal@clearcuthires.com
www.clearcuthires.com
Sister company Clear Cut Pictures.
Dry hire post-production equipment.
MD: Fazal Shah
- *Celeb Deck; Glastonbury festival; Liquid*
  News; United 93; After Thomas; Miss
  Potter

Clear Cut Pictures
1 Springvale Terrace,
London W14 0AE
020 7605 1700
info@clearcutpictures.com
www.clearcutpictures.com
Sister company Clear Cut Hires. Graphics
and digital rostrum; video and sound.
MD: Jo Beighton
- *Crimewatch; Horizon; Money*
  Programme

Component
5 Berners Mews, London W1T 3AJ
020 7631 4477
mike@component.co.uk
www.component.co.uk
Independent. Pure graphics. Director:
Mike Kenny
- *Hell's Kitchen; Destination D-Day;*
  Without Prejudice; SAS Jungle; Clive
  Anderson Now; Crimewatch; Wogan
  Now and Then; Ron Manager

Computamatch
117 Wardour Street, London W1F 0NU
020 7287 1316
edl@computamatch.com
www.ascent-media.co.uk
Part of Ascent Group. Film negative
cutting service. MD: Marilyn Sommer
- *5 Children and It; Guinness; Levi's*

Computer Film Services
66b Unit, York Road, Weybridge,
Surrey KT13 9DY
01932 850034
enquiries@computerfilm.com
www.computerfilm.com
*Independent. Digital disc recorders and
post-production systems. Director: Peter
Holland*

Concrete
34-35 Dean Street, London W1D 4PR
020 7439 9080
bookings@concretepost.co.uk
www.concretepost.co.uk
*Part of Arena Digital. Audio; graphics;
sound; editing; telecine. MD: Dave
Thompson*
• *Brassed off Britain; Blag; Celebrity
Penthouse; Car Booty; Monty Don
Project (BBC)*

Crow TV
Shepherds Building East,
Richmond Way, London W14 0DQ
020 7471 7970
jocelyn@crowtv.com
www.crowtv.com
*Independent. Graphics; editing for
television; pogle colour grade; online/
offline editing; audio. MD: Jocelyn
Buckley*
• *Vincent, The Full Story; South Bank
Show; The Challenge; Mediterranean
Tales*

Cut and Run
Cinema House, 93 Wardour Street,
London W1F 0UD
020 7432 9696
editors.uk@cutandrun.co.uk
www.cutandrun.co.uk
*Independent. Offline editing. MD: Simon
Gosling*
• *Commercials: Castrol; Rimmel; Diet
Coke; UPS; Lynx*

DB Dubbing
4 St Pauls Road, Clifton, Bristol,
Avon BS8 1LT
0117 904 8210
miles@dbdubbing.tv
Independent. Audio. MD: Miles Harris
• *Secret Nature; Built for the Kill; Eden
Project*

De Lane Lea
75 Dean Street, London W1D 3PU
020 7432 3800
info@delanelea.com
www.delanelea.com
*Part of Ascent group. Sound for post-
production TV and film. Chief operating
officer: Hugh Penalt-Jones*
• *Cold Mountain; Harry Potter, the
Prisoner of Azkaban; Two Brothers;
Bond: Casino Royale; Children of Man;
United 93*

DGP
Portland House, 12-13 Greek Street,
London W1D 4DL
020 7734 4501
mail@dgpsoho.co.uk
www.dgpsoho.co.uk
*Independent. Editing; graphics; DVD;
authoring. MD: Julian Day*
• *Murder City; Yahoo; Friends; The Last
Samurai; Lord of the Rings: Return of
the King; Six Feet Under*

DVA Associates
7/8 Campbell Court, Bramley,
Tadley, Hampshire RG26 5EG
01256 882032
info@dva.co.uk
www.dva.co.uk
*Independent. Graphics; audio; DVD;
commercials. MD: Barrie Gibson*
• *SAS Survival Secrets; Life of David
Kelly; Goalrush for Meridian*

Evolutions Television
5 Berners Street, London W1T 3LF
020 7580 3333
bookings@evolutionstelevision.com
www.evolutionstelevision.com
*Independent. Graphics; documentaries;
commercials; audio. MD: Simon Kanjee*
• *Top of the Pops titles; Jump London;
Other People's Houses; Top Gear; MTV
The Lick; MTV Pimp My Ride*

The Farm
13 Soho Square, London W1D 3QF
020 7437 6677
info@farmgroup.tv
www.farmgroup.tv
*Partner with Home, The Shed and Uncle.
Online/offline editing, audio dubbing;
high definition edit and grading. MDs:
Nicky Sargent, Vikki Dunn*
• *Dunkirk; Friday night with Jonathan
Ross; One Life; X-Factor*

Films at 59
59 Cotham Hill, Bristol, Avon BS6 6JR
0117 906 4300
info@filmsat59.com
www.filmsat59.com
*Independent. Audio; high definition;
equipment hire; online/offline dubbing.
MD: Gina Lee Fucci*
• *Teachers; Big Cat Diary; Building the
Dream*

Final Cut
55-57 Great Marlborough Street,
London W1F 7JX
020 7556 6300
zoe.henderson@finalcut-uk.com
www.finalcut-edit.com
Offline editing. Producer: Zoe Henderson
• *Commercials: Sony PlayStation;
Mountain; Mercedes "movement"; Nike*

Finishing Post
10, Gilt Way, Giltbrook, Nottingham,
Notts NG16 2GN
0115 945 8800
info@finishing-post.co.uk
www.finishing-post.co.uk
*Independent. Graphics; editing; DVD
authoring. MD: Mark Harwood*
• *Commercials: Jaguar; Peugeot;
Heart of the Country; Carlton Country*

Framestore CFC
9 Noel Street, London W1F 8GH
020 7208 2600
info@framestore-cfc.com
www.framestore-cfc.com
*Independent. Effects; computer generated
commercials; films. Chief executive:
William Sergeant*
• *Thunderbirds; Walking with Sea
Monsters*

Frontier Post
67 Wells Street, London W1T 3PZ
020 7291 9191
info@frontierpost.co.uk
www.frontierpost.co.uk
*Independent. Graphics; audio; online/
offline grading. MD: Neil Hatton*
• *Property Dreams; Howard Goodall's
20th Century Greats; Pagans of the
Roman Empire*

Fusion Broadcast
56 Ballynahinch Road, Dromara,
Dromore, County Down BT25 2AL
028 9753 1004
sales@fusionbroadcast.co.uk
www.fusionbroadcast.co.uk
*Independent. Crew supplying. MD: John
Morriffey*
• *BBC Northern Ireland; BBC Network*

Frontline Television
35 Bedfordbury, Covent Garden,
London WC2 4DU
020 7836 0411
public@frontline-tv.co.uk
www.frontline-tv.co.uk
*Independent. Editing; graphic design;
audio; Avid online/offline; duplication.
MD: Bill Cullen*
• *Bum Fights; VTV programme for the
Deaf; The Curse of Reality TV; Spooks
interactive; Little Britain interactive;
Industrial Revelations*

Future Post Production
25 Noel Street, London W1F 8GX
020 7434 6655
info@futurefilmgroup.com
www.futurefilmgroup.com
*Part of Future Films Group. Sound; two
dolby mix studios. MDs: Tim Levy,
Stephen Margolis*
• *King Arthur; Exorcist, The Beginning;
Harry Potter 3*

Glassworks
33-34 Great Pulteney Street,
London W1F 9NP
020 7434 1182
nina@glassworks.co.uk
www.glassworks.co.uk
*Independent. Special effects; animation;
all online. MD: Hector Macleod*
• *Dream Keeper; Bjork's All is Full of
Love; Sprite commercials*

Goldcrest Post-Production
1 Lexington Street, 36-44 Brewer
Street, London W1F 9LX
020 7437 7972
mail@goldcrestpost.co.uk
www.goldcrestpost.co.uk
*Independent. Sound and telecine.
MD: Peter Joly*
• *Cold Mountain; Lord of the Rings,
Two Towers; Girl with a Pearl Earring*

Golden Square
11 Golden Square, London W1F 9JB
020 7300 3555
info@goldensq.com
www.goldensq.com
*Independent. Commercials; special
effects. MD: Phil Gillies*
• *Campari; Tomb Raiders; Volkswagen*

Hackenbacker Audio Post Production
10 Bateman Street, London W1D 4AQ
020 7734 1324
reception@hackenbacker.com
www.hackenbacker.com
*Independent. Audio; sound effects; films;
trailers. MDs: Julian Slater, Nigel Heath*
• *Shaun of the Dead; Girl with a Pearl
Earring; Spooks*

The Hive
37 Dean Street, London W12 4PT
020 7565 1000
contact@hiveuk.com
www.hiveuk.com
*Part of VTR Group. Telecine; online
editing; special effects; 3D and 2D
graphics; animation. MD: Simon Huhtala*
• *Direct Line sponsorship; BBC Bitesize;
Hell's Kitchen promotion*

Home Post Productions
12-13 Richmond Buildings, Soho,
London W1D 3HG
020 7292 0200
info@homepost.co.uk
www.farmgroup.tv
*Independent. Graphics; audio; effects;
commercials. MD: Paul Napier*
• *Dunkirk; Friday Night with Jonathan
Ross; One Life*

Lime
4th Floor, Epatra House, 58-60
Berners Street, London W1T 3NQ
020 7637 3210
james@limepost.co.uk
www.limepost.co.uk
*Part of M2 Group. 3D animation; 2D
effects; storyboarding; direction; studio
shooting; graphics. Producer: Michelle
Marsden*
• *Troy; Q Channel Broadcasting;
Waking the Dead; Silent Witness;
Airwick Sponsorship Campaign; MTV;
Discovery Channel*

Lip Sync Post
123 Wardour Street, London W1F 0UU
020 7534 9123
info@lipsyncpost.co.uk
www.lipsync.co.uk
*Independent. Sound; graphics; editing;
5.1 dolby ex mixing. MD: Norman Merry*
• *Silent Witness; Touch the Void;
Trolleywood; Severage; Highland of 5;
Creep*

Liquid TV
1-2 Portland Mews, London W1F 8JE
020 7437 2623
info@liquid.co.uk
www.liquid.co.uk
*Independent. Title branding; special
effects. MD: Asra Alikhan*
• *Restoration; Film 2004; Horizon; Troy*

Lola
14-16 Great Portland Street,
London W1W 8BL
020 7907 7878
info@lola-post.com
www.lola-post.com
*Independent. Visualeffects; commercials;
films and TV. MDs: Grahame Andrew,
Rob Harvey*
• *Troy; 5 Children and It; Ancient
Egyptians*

M2 Television
Ingestre Court, Ingestre Place,
London W1F 0JL
020 7343 6543
info@m2tv.com
www.m2tv.com
Edit; visual; audio. MD: Tom Jones
• *Revenge; Human Mind; Bodysnatchers*

The Machine Room
54-58 Wardour Street,
London W1D 4JQ
020 7734 3433
info@themachineroom.co.uk
www.themachineroom.co.uk
*Part of VTR Group. Online editing;
telecine suites; DVD; teramix machine;
archive restoration department. Facilities
manager: Luci Weir; online services
director: Vanessa Arden-Wood*
• *Love, Actually; Bad Girls; Footballers
Wives*

Maidstone
New Cut Road, Vintners Park,
Maidstone Kent
01622 684428
www.maidstonestudios.com
*Independent. Edit. General Manager
Kenton Oxley*
• *Reeves and Mortimer*

Mediahouse
Hogarth Business Park,
3 Burlington Lane, London W4 2TH
020 8233 5400
info@mediahouse.tv
www.mediahouse.tv
*IMG Media Group. Video; graphics;
DVD; transmission studio. Head of
post-production: Karen Mullins*
• *Bremner, Bird and Fortune; Planet's
Funniest Animals*

Men-from-Mars
Unit 6, Walpole Court, Ealing Green,
London W5 5ED
020 8280 9000
info@men-from-mars.com
www.men-from-mars.com
*Part of Barcud Derwen. Visual effects
for film and TV. Creative director: Philip
Attfield; production director: Simon
Frame*
• *Gladiatress; Chasing Liberty; Jekyll and
Hyde; Hamburg Cell; Sons of the Wind;
De-Lovely; Trial and Retribution: Blue
Eiderdown*

Metro Broadcast
5-7 Great Chapel Street,
London W1F 8FF
020 7434 7700
Metro Suffolk Street: 020 7202 2000
Metro Ecosse Edinburgh:
0131 554 9421
Metro Ecosse Glasgow:
0141 419 1660
info@metrobroadcast.com
www.metrobroadcast.com
*Editing inc HD; crewing and equipment
rental; audio and video restoration;
DVD production; webcasting;
duplications and standards conversion.
Directors: Mark Cox, Paul Beale*
• *EPKs for Mr Bean; Rugby World Cup
promo; NHK various programmes, shot
and edited in HD*

The Mill
40-41 Great Marlborough Street,
London W1F 7JQ
020 7287 4041
info@mill.co.uk
www.mill.co.uk
*Independent. Commercials; 3d
animation; edition. MD: Pat Joseph*
• *Commercials: Mercedes; Honda; O2*

MGB Facilities
Capital House, Sheepscar Court,
Meanwood Road, Leeds, West
Yorkshire LS7 2BB
0113 243 6868
contact@mgbtv.co.uk
www.mgbtv.co.uk
*Independent. Graphics; commercials;
DVD; animation. MD: Mike Gaunt*
• *Hasbro commercial; Brazilian Football;
DFS Furniture*

Molinare
34 Fouberts Place, London W1F 7PX
020 7478 7000
bookings@molinare.co.uk
www.molinare.co.uk
*Independent. Graphics; DVD; audio. MD:
Mark Foligno*
• *Faking It; Make Me Honest; Poirot*

Moving Picture Company
127 Wardour Street, London W1F 0NL
020 7434 3100
mpc@moving-picture.com
www.moving-picture.com
*Independent. Commercials; effects;
animation; editing. MD: David Jeffers*
• *Troy; Dunkirk; Guinness moth
commercial*

Nats
10 Soho Square, London W1D 3NT
020 7287 9900
bookings@nats.tv
www.nats.tv
*Independent. Editing; audio; telecine;
effects; graphics. MD: Simon Kanjee*
• *Seven Wonders of the Industrial World;
Grand Designs; The National Trust;
Property Ladder; Picture of Britain;
Around the World in 80 Treasures; The
South Bank Show; A Place in France;
Jamie's Kitchen*

Oasis Television
6-7 Great Pulteney Street,
London W1F 9NA
020 7434 4133
sales@oasistv.co.uk
www.oasistv.co.uk
Independent. Audio; editing; graphics;
duplication. MD: Gareth Mullaney
• *State of Play; The Young Visitors;*
  May 33rd

One
71 Dean Street, London W1D 3SF
020 7439 2730
matt.adams@onepost.tv
www.onepost.tv
Part of Ascent Group. Commercials;
telecine; animation. DI Producers: Matt
Adams; Jo'Ann Darby
• *Jaguar; American Express; Aerosmith*

Outpost Facilities
Pinewood Studios, Pinewood Road,
Iver, Buckinghamshire SL0 0NH
01753 630770
charlie@outpostfacilities.co.uk
www.outpostfacilities.co.uk
Independent. Commercials; films;
broadcast; TV. MD: Nigel Gourley
• *My Family; Everything I Know About*
  Men; Teletubbies Everywhere; Scrapheap
  Challenge; Wild Thing I Love You

Pepper
3 Slingsby Place, London WC2E 9AB
020 7836 1188
mailuf@pepperpost.tv
www.pepperpost.tv
Independent. Effects; graphics; dramas.
MDs: Patrick Holzen; Shane Warden
• *Dirty War; Midsomer Murders; White*
  Noise; Spooks; The Sally Lockheart
  Mysteries; Cracker; Prime Evil

Phaebus Communications Group
The Brewery Tower, The Deva centre
Trinity Way, Manchester M3 7BF
0161 605 9999
info@phaebus.co.uk
www.phaebus.co.uk
Two branches. DVD; authoring;
TV production. MD: Steve Bettridge
• *BBC channel idents; Andy Pandy;*
  Thomas Cook conference events

Pink House
33 West Park Clifton, Bristol,
Avon BS8 2LX
0117 923 7087
anita.nandwami@pinkhousepp.com
www.filmsat59.com
Part of Films at 59. Broadcast; audio;
pictures; effects; commercials. Contact:
Anita Nandwani
• *Building the Dream; Big Cook Little*
  Cook; Animal Camera

Red Vision
Cambos House, 3 Canal Street,
Manchester M1 3HE
0161 907 3764
London 020 7419 2010
Bristol 0117 946 6633
info@redvision.co.uk
www.redvision.co.uk
Computer graphics for film and TV.
MD: David Mousley
• *Touching the Void; D-Day: Men and*
  Machines

Resolution
341 Old Street, London EC1V 9LL
020 7749 9300
London 020 7437 1336
info@resolution.tv
www.resolution.tv
Broadcast; commercials; offline/online;
audio; graphics. MD: Mike Saunders
• *Big Brother; Top Gear; Fame Academy*

Rushes
66 Old Compton Street,
London W1D 4UH
020 7437 8676
info@rushes.co.uk
www.rushes.co.uk
Part of Ascent media. Effects; telecine for
commercial video. MD: Joyce Capper
• *Commercials: Hewlett Packard;*
  Offspring; Ford Mondeo (Tom and Jerry)

Savalas
Film City Glasgow, 11 Merryland St,
Glasgow G51 2QG
linda@savalas.co.uk
www.savalas.co.uk
Independent. Music production; audio;
sound design. MDs: Giles Lamb; Michael
MacKinnon; Karl Henderson
• *Magdalene Sisters; Relocation,*
  Relocation, Relocation; Sea of Souls;
  Russian Revolution; Asylum; American
  Cousins

2nd Sense Broadcast
Millennium Studios, Elstree Way
Borehamwood, Herts WD6 1SF
020 8236 1133
info@2ndsense.co.uk
www.2ndsense.co.uk
Independent. Audio. MD: Wendy Hewitt
• *Top of the Pops 2; Chuckle Vision; East*
  Enders Revealed

Skaramoosh
9-15 Neal Street, London WC2H 9PW
020 7379 9966
reception@skaramoosh.co.uk
www.skaramoosh.com
Independent. Audio; Video. MD: Wendy
Hewitt
• *Strictly Come Dancing; Football*
  Factory; Naked Science

Soho Images
8-14 Meard Street, London W1F 0EQ
020 7437 0831
info@sohoimages.com
www.sohoimages.com
Independent. Effects; graphic design;
animation. MD: Daniel Slight
• *Murder in Mind; Bloody Sunday;*
  Mrs Brown

Sound Monsters
70 Grafton Way, London W1T 5DT
020 7387 3230
info@soundmonsters.com
www.soundmonsters.com
Independent. Audio; sound; transfer;
animation. MD: Cliff Jones
• *Death in Gaza; State of Texas; Real*
  Great Escapes

St Anne's Post
20 St Anne's Court,
London W1F 0BH
020 7155 1500
info@saintannespost.co.uk
www.saintannespost.co.uk
Part of Ascent Group. Audio; editing;
telecine. MD: Keith Williams
• *Brothers Grimm; Alfie; Night Detective*

Stream
61 Charlotte Street, London W1T 4PF
020 7208 1567
info@streamdm.co.uk
www.streamdm.co.uk
Part of Ascent Group. DVD; design
compression; authoring facility. MD: Paul
Kind
• *The Office; Where We're Calling From;*
  My Big Fat Greek Wedding

Strongroom
120-124 Curtain Road,
London EC2A 3SQ
020 7426 5100
nina@strongroom.com
www.strongroom.tv
Part of Strongroom Studios. Audio post
production for DVD, television and film.
Post-production manager: Sally Drury
• *New World War; Holiday Exchange;*
  Pepsi ident; Shaun of the Dead; The
  Stone Roses; Little Britain

Suite
28 Newman Street, London W1T 1PR
020 7636 4488
shelley@suitetv.co.uk
www.suitetv.co.uk
Independent. Editing for TV. MD: Shelley
Fox
• *The Office; Swiss Toni; The Lenny Henry*
  Show; Extras 2; Virgin Diaries (MTV);
  Rob Brydon's Annually Retentive;
  Randomist; Catherine Tate

Sumners
Suite 401, Berkeley House,
35 Whitworth Street West,
Manchester M1 5NG
0161 228 0330
janet@sumners.co.uk
www.sumners.co.uk
Independent. Online/offline; graphics;
very reality studio. MDs: Janet Sumner,
Andrew Sumner
• *Best Sitcoms; Songs of Praise;*
  Bank of Mum and Dad

Television Set
22 Newman Street, London W1T 1PH
020 7637 3322
terry.bettles@tvsetgroup.co.uk
www.thetelevisionset.co.uk
2 branches. Restoration of old archives for
reuse; audio; grading; telecine. MD: Terry
Bettles
• *D-Day plus 60; Poirot remastering;*
  Let it Be

Television Services International
10 Grape Street, London WC2H 8TG
020 7379 3435
enquiries@tsi.co.uk
www.tsi.co.uk
Independent. Longform and shortform in light entertainment and documentaries. MD: Simon Peach
• *Ali G; My New Best Friend; Who Rules the Roost?*

Top Banana
The Studio, Broome, Stourbridge,
West Midlands DY9 0HA
01562 700404
info@top-b.com
www.top-b.com
Independent. Animation; DVD; duplication; effects; graphics. MDs: Nick Terry; Richard Bridge
• *Sindy; Jellies; Butt Ugly Martians*

Todd-ao creative services
13 Hawley Crescent,
London NW1 8NP
020 7284 7900
schedule@todd-ao.co.uk
www.todd-ao.co.uk
Part of Ascent Group. Telecine grading; negative film processing; video dailies; offline/online editing. MD: Samantha Webb
• *Monarch of the Glen; Canterbury Tales; Taggart*

Videosonics
68a Delancey Street,
London NW1 7RY
020 7209 0209
info@videosonics.com
www.videosonics.com
Independent. Audio. MD: Denis Weinreich
• *Young Adam; Bright Young Things; Sexy Beast; Alien Vs Predator; Glastonbury; White Noise*

VTR
64 Dean Street, London W1D 4QQ
020 7437 0026
reception@vtr.co.uk
www.vtr.co.uk
Independent. Effects; commercials; telecine. MD: Anshul Doshi
• *Christina Aguilera; McDonalds; Persil; Philadelphia; Rimmel; Dairylea*

Wild Tracks Audio Studio
2nd Floor, 55 Greek Street,
London W1D 3DT
020 7734 6331
bookings@wildtracks.co.uk
www.wildtracks.co.uk
Independent. Audio. MD: Graham Pickford
• *Canon; Bob the Builder; Pingu*

Yellow Moon
30 Shaw Road, Holywood,
County Down BT18 9HX
028 9042 1826
general@yellowmoon.net
www.yellowmoon.net
Independent. Editing. MD: Greg Darby
• *Citizen Alec; Christine's Children; Sven-Goran Eriksson*

Film and music libraries

BBC Birmingham, Information & Archives
The Mailbox, Birmingham B1 1RF
0121 567 6767
www.bbc.co.uk
Music, news requests, productions

BFI National Film and TV Archives
Kingshill Way, Berkhamsted,
Herts HP4 3TP
01442 876301
darren.long@bfi.org.uk
www.bfi.org.uk
Large collection from 1895 to the present day

East Anglian Film Archive
The Archive Centre, Martineau Lane,
Norwich NR1 2DQ
01603 592 664
eafa@uea.ac.uk
www.uea.ac.uk/eafa
Moving images relating to the region of East Anglia

Film and Video Archive, Imperial War Museum
All Saints Annexe, Austral Street,
London SE11 4SL
020 7416 5290/1
film@iwm.org.uk
www.iwm.org.uk/collections/film.htm
Images of conflict - 1914 to the present day

Film Institute of Ireland/ Irish Film Archive
6 Eustace Street, Temple Bar,
Dublin 2
00 353 1 679 5744
info@irishfilm.ie
www.irishfilm.ie
Films worldwide. Every Irish film ever made

GMTV Library Sales
London TV Centre, Upper Ground,
London SE1 9TT
020 7827 7363/6
librarysales@gm.tv
www.gm.tv

Huntley Film Archive
22 Islington Green, London N1 8DU
020 7226 9260
films@huntleyarchives.com
www.huntleyarchives.com
Rare and vintage documentary film from 1895

Images Of War
31a Regents Park Road,
London NW1 7TL
020 7267 9198
derek@warfootage.com
www.warfootage.com
Images of war archive. 1900 to first Gulf war

ITN Archive
200 Grays Inn Road,
London WC1X 8XZ
020 7833 3000
sales@itnarchive.com
www.itnarchive.com
More than 500,000 hours of news and feature material

ITV Central
Gas Street, Birmingham B1 2JT
0121 643 9898
www.itv.com

JW Media Music
10–11 Great Turnstile,
London WC1V 7JU
020 7681 8900
info@jwmediamusic.co.uk
www.jwmediamusic.com
Music production and publishing

Media Archive for Central England
1 Salisbury Road, University of Leicester, Leicester LE1 7RQ
0115 846 6448
mace@nottingham.ac.uk
www.nottingham.ac.uk/film/mace
East and West Midlands

National Screen and Sound Archive of Wales
Aberystwyth, Ceredigion SY23 3BU
01970 632828
agssc@llgc.org.uk
http://screenandsound.llgc.org.uk
Wales

North West Film Archive
Minshull House,
47–49 Chorlton Street,
Manchester M1 3EU
0161 247 3097
n.w.filmarchive@mmu.ac.uk
www.nwfa.mmu.ac.uk
The north-west, 1897 to present day

Northern Region Film and Television Archive
School of Arts & Media,
University of Teesside,
Middlesbrough TS1 3BA
01642 384022
leo@nrfta.org.uk
l.enticknap@tees.ac.uk
www.nrfta.org.uk
Public sector moving image archive serving County Durham, Cumbria, Northumberland, Tees Valley and Tyne & Wear

Pathé Pictures
14–17 Market Place, London W1W 8AR
020 7323 5151
www.pathe.co.uk
Worldwide images

Royal Television Society, Library & Archive
info@rts.org.uk
www.rts.org.uk
Archive TV pictures, award ceremonies and monthly dinners

Scottish Screen Archive
39–41 Montrose Avenue,
Hillington Park, Glasgow G52 4LA
0845 366 4600
archive@scottishscreen.com
www.scottishscreen.com/archivelive
Scotland since the 1890s

South East Film & Video Archive
University of Brighton, Grand Parade, Brighton BN2 0JY
01273 643 213
screenarchive@brighton.ac.uk
www.brighton.ac.uk/screenarchive
The south-east: Kent, Surrey, East and West Sussex, Brighton & Hove and Medway

South West Film and Television Archive
Melville Building, Royal William Yard, Stonehouse, Plymouth PL1 3RP
01752 202 650
info@tswfta.co.uk
www.tswfta.co.uk
The south-west from 1890 to the present day

Wessex Film and Sound Archive
Hampshire Record Office, Sussex Street, Winchester SO23 8TH
01962 847742
david.lee@hants.gov.uk
www.hants.gov.uk /record-office /film/index.html
Central southern England. Film records 1897 to the present day, sound records 1890 to the present day.

Wiener Library
4 Devonshire Street, London W1W 5BH
020 7636 7247
info@wienerlibrary.co.uk
www.wienerlibrary.co.uk
Modern Jewish history

Yorkshire Film Archive
York Lord St John College, Mayors Walk, York YO31 7EX
01904 716 550
info@yorkshirefilmarchive.com
www.yorkshirefilmarchive.com
Moving images of the Yorkshire region

TV & film training and support

BBC Training and development: Broadcast Training
0870 122 0216
training@bbc.co.uk
www.bbctraining.com
All strands of broadcast training

Birds Eye View
020 7288 7444
rosiestrang@birds-eye-view.co.uk
www.birds-eye-view.co.uk
Emerging female film-makers

Film Education
020 7851 9450
postbox@filmeducation.org
www.filmeducation.org

First Film Foundation
info@firstfilm.co.uk
www.firstfilm.co.uk
Training for new film writers, producers and directors

FT2 – Film and Television Freelance Training
020 7407 0344
info@ft2.org.uk
www.ft2.org.uk
Training for new broadcast freelancers

New Producers Alliance (NPA)
020 7613 0440
queries@npa.org.uk
www.npa.org.uk
Training and support for film-makers

Shooting People
contact@shootingpeople.org
http://shootingpeople.org
Online network for filmmakers to exchange information and ideas

Skillset: The Sector Skills Council for the Audio Visual Industries
020 7520 5757
info@skillset.org
www.skillset.org
Owned by broadcast industry; accredits courses, publishes handbooks and runs Skillsformedia service (www.skillsformedia.com)

Women in Film and TV
020 7240 48/5
emily@wftv.org.uk
www.wftv.org.uk
Membership association open to women with at least one year's professional experience in the television, film and/or digital media industries

» See also page 396

Trade press

Advance Production News
020 8305 6905
www.crimsonuk.com
Monthly. Listings for production companies. Owner: Crimson Communications. Editor: Alan Williams

Broadband TV News
01223 464359
jclover@broadbandtvnews.com
www.broadbandtvnews.com
Free weekly emails and subscription newsletters. Editor, international edition: Julian Clover

Broadcast
020 7505 8000
broadcastnews@emap.com
www.broadcastnow.co.uk
Weekly. TV and radio industry. Owner: Emap Media. Editor: Conor Dignam; news: Chris Curtis; features editor and deputy: Emily Booth; chief sub: Angus Walker

Cable & Satellite Europe
020 7017 5533
www.telecoms.com
10pa. Owner: Informa Media and Telecoms. Editor: Stuart Thomson

Cable & Satellite International
020 7426 0101
neil.howman@cable-satellite.com
www.cable-satellite.com
6pa. Owner: Perspective Publishing. Editor: Karen Gonn

Channel 21 International magazine
020 7729 7460
press@c21media.net
www.c21media.net
10pa. Owner: C21 Media. Editor-in-chief: David Jenkinson; editor: Ed Waller

Commonwealth Broadcaster
020 7583 5550
cba@cba.org.uk
www.cba.org.uk
Quarterly of the Commonwealth Broadcasting Association. Editor: Elizabeth Smith

Contacts – The Spotlight Casting Directories
020 7437 7631
info@spotlight.com
www.spotlight.com
Annual. Contacts for stage, film, TV and radio. Editor: Kate Poynton

Crewfinder
028 9079 7902
mail@adleader.co.uk
www.crewfinderwales.co.uk
Annual. Wales's film, TV and video directory. Owner: Adleader Publications. Proprietor: Stan Mairs

Digital Spy
nwilkes@digitalspy.co.uk
www.digitalspy.co.uk
Web. Digital TV. Editor: Neil Wilkes

FilmBang
0141 334 2456
info@filmbang.com
www.filmbang.com
Annual. Scotland's film and video directory. Editor: Marianne Mellin

IBE
01895 421111
editor@ibeweb.com
www.ibeweb.com
12pa. International broadcast engineering. Owner: BPL Business Media. Editor: Neil Nixon

Kemps Film, TV, Video Handbook (UK edition)
01342 335861
kemps@reedinfo.co.uk
www.kftv.com
Annual. Guide to international production. Owner: Reed Business Information. Editorial contact: Pat Huson

The Knowledge
020 8977 7711
orders@hollis-publishing.com
www.hollis-publishing.com
Annual. Production directory. Owner: Hollis Publishing. Editorial contact: Louise Baynes

Line Up
01905 381725
editor@lineup.biz
www.lineup.biz
6pa. Journal of the Institute of Broadcast Sound. Owner: Line Up Publications. Editor: Hugh Robjohns

Multichannel News
00 1 646 746 6590
www.multichannel.com
*Weekly. Owner: Reed Business
Information. Editor: Kent Gibbons; news:
Mike Reynolds; copy chief: Michael
Demenchuk*

Pact
020 7067 4367
enquiries@pact.co.uk
www.pact.co.uk
*Annual. Directory of independent
producers*

Pro Sound News Europe
020 7921 8319
david.robinson@cmpi.biz
www.prosoundnewseurope.com
*12pa. Audio industry. Owner: CMP
Information. Editor: David Robinson;
managing editor: Camilla Edwards*

The Production Guide
020 7505 8000
theproductionguide@Emap.com
www.productionguideonline.com
*Annual. Information on production.
Owner: Emap Media. Editor: Mei Mei
Rogers*

Satellite Finance
020 7251 2967
ross.bateson@satellitefinance.com
www.satellitefinance.com
*11pa. Finance journal for executives.
Owner: Thompson Stanley Publishers.
Editor: Ross Bateson*

Stage Screen and Radio
020 7346 0900
janice@stagescreenandradio.org.uk
www.bectu.org.uk
*10pa. Magazine of broadcasting union
Bectu. Editor: Janice Turner*

Televisual
020 7970 4000
tim.dams@centaur.co.uk
www.mad.co.uk
*Monthly. Trade magazine for TV. Owner:
Centaur Holdings. Editor: Tim Dams;
news editor: Jonathan Creamer*

TV International
020 7017 5533
media.enquiries@informa.com
www.telecoms.com
*Daily. International TV listings. Owner:
Informa Media and Telecoms. Editor:
Stewart Clarke*

**TBI (Television Business
International)**
020 7017 5533
media.enquiries@informa.com
www.telecoms.com
*Annual. Directory of businesses. Owner:
Informa Media and Telecoms. Editor:
Kevin Scott*

TV Technology and Production
01480 461555
www.imaspub.com
*6pa. Broadcasting and production
technology. Owner: IMAS Publishing UK.
Editor: Mark Hallinger*

TVB Europe
00 353 1 882 4444
tvbeurope@scope.ie
www.tvbeurope.com
*Monthly. Broadcasting innovation and
technology. Owner: CMP Information.
Editor-in-chief: Fergal Ringrose*

VLV Bulletin
01474 352835
info@vlv.org.uk
www.vlv.org.uk
*Quarterly magazine of Voice of the
Listener and Viewer. Advocates citizen
and consumer interests in broadcasting.
Editor: Jocelyn Hay*

Zerb
01795 535468
cfox@urbanfox.com
www.gtc.org.uk
*2pa. For camera operators. Owner: The
Deeson Group. Editor: Christina Fox*

》 Consumer film and TV magazines
see page 84

Events

Bafta Awards
195 Piccadilly, London W1J 9LN
020 7734 0022
www.bafta.org
Film, TV and interactive industries

**MediaGuardian Edinburgh
International Television Festival**
117 Farringdon Road,
London EC1R 3BX
020 7278 9515
www.mgeitf.co.uk

TV & film associations

**Association of Motion Picture
Sound**
28 Knox Street, London W1H 1FS
020 7723 6727
admin@amps.net
www.amps.net
Film and TV sound technicians

**Bafta (British Academy of Film and
Television Arts)**
195 Piccadilly, London W1J 9LN
020 7734 0022
www.bafta.org
Awards, training and education

**Barb (Broadcasters' Audience
Research Board)**
020 7529 5531
enquiries@barb.co.uk
www.barb.co.uk
Industry-owned audience data
Press: 020 7591 9610

**Bectu (Broadcasting,
Entertainment, Cinematograph
and Theatre Union)**
373-377 Clapham Road,
London SW9 9BT
020 7346 0900
info@bectu.org.uk
www.bectu.org.uk
*Union for broadcasting, entertainment
and theatre*

BKSTS – The Moving Image Society
Pinewood Studios, Iver Heath,
Bucks SL0 0NH
01753 656656
Info@bksts.com
www.bksts.com
*Film foundation, TV and digital tech,
foundation sound for film and video,
broadcasting engineering*

British Board of Film Classification
3 Soho Square, London W1D 3HD
020 7440 1570
contact_the_bbfc@bbfc.co.uk
www.bbfc.co.uk

British Film Institute
21 Stephen Street, London W1T 1LN
020 7255 1444
publishing@bfi.org.uk
www.bfi.org.uk
Education, exhibitions and resources

**British Universities Film & Video
Council**
77 Wells Street, London W1T 3QJ
020 7393 1500
ask@bufvc.ac.uk
www.bufvc.ac.uk
*To promote the use of media within higher
education*

British Video Association
167 Great Portland Street,
London W1W 5PE
020 7436 0041
general@bva.org.uk
www.bva.org.uk
*Represents the interests of publishers and
rights owners of pre-recorded home
entertainment on video*

Broadcasting Press Guild
Tiverton, The Ridge, Woking,
Surrey GU22 7EQ
01483 764895
torin.douglas@bbc.co.uk
*Promotes professional interests of
journalists who write or broadcast about
the media*

**Cinema and Television Benevolent
Fund**
22 Golden Square, London W1F 9AD
020 7437 6567
info@ctbf.co.uk
www.ctbf.co.uk
Trade charity

Drama Association of Wales
The Old Library Building, Singleton
Road, Splott, Cardiff CF24 2ET
029 2045 2200
aled.daw@virgin.net
www.amdram.co.uk

**DigiTAG (Digital Terrestrial
Television Action Group)**
17a Ancienne Route, CH-1218 Grand
Saconnex, Geneva, Switzerland
00 41 22 717 2735
projectoffice@digitag.org
www.digitag.org
Not-for-profit international association

Digital Television Group
7 Old Lodge Place, St Margarets,
Twickenham TW1 1RQ
020 8891 1830
www.dtg.org.uk
International industry-led consortium.
Director general: Marcus Coleman

Digital Video Broadcasting Project (DVB)
Project Office, 17a Ancienne Route,
CH-1218 Grand Saconnex, Geneva,
Switzerland
00 41 22 717 2714
dvb@dvb.org
www.dvb.org
Not-for-profit international association

Directors' Guild of Great Britain
4 Windmill Street, London W1T 2HZ
020 7580 9131
guild@dggb.org
www.dggb.org

Documentary Film-makers Group
225a Brecknock Road,
London N19 5AA
020 7428 0882
info@dfglondon.com
www.dfglondon.com

Equity
Guild House, Upper St Martins Lane,
London WC2H 9EG
020 7379 6000
info@equity.org.uk
www.equity.org.uk
Actors' union

Federation of Entertainment Unions
1 Highfield, Twyford, Nr Winchester,
Hampshire SO21 1QR
01962 713134
harris.s@btconnect.com

Film Archive Forum
c/o British Universities Film & Video
Council, 77 Wells Street,
London W1T 3QJ
020 7393 1508
luke@bufvc.ac.uk
www.bufvc.ac.uk/faf

Film Distributors' Association
www.launchingfilms.com
Trade body representing theatrical film distributors in the UK

Focal International
Pentax House, South Hill Avenue,
South Harrow HA2 0DU
020 8423 5853
info@focalint.org
www.focalint.org
Trade association for libraries and researchers

Guild of British Camera Technicians
c/o Panavision (UK), Metropolitan
Centre, Bristol Road, Greenford,
Middlesex UB6 8GD
020 8813 1999
admin@gbct.org
www.gbct.org

Guild of Television Cameramen
01822 614405
chairman@gtc.org.uk
www.gtc.org.uk

Guild of Vision Mixers
www.guildofvisionmixers.org.uk

Institute of Broadcast Sound
PO Box 932, Guildford GU4 7WW
01483 575450
info@ibs.org.uk
www.ibs.org.uk

International Federation of Film Archives (FIAF)
1 Rue Defacqz, B-1000 Brussels,
Belgium
00 322 538 3065
info@fiafnet.org
www.fiafnet.org

International Visual Communication Association (IVCA)
19 Pepper Street, Glengall Bridge,
London E14 9RP
020 7512 0571
info@ivca.org
www.ivca.org
Promotes corporate visual communication

MCPS and PRS Alliance
29-33 Berners Street,
London W1T 3AB
020 7580 5544
www.mcps-prs-alliance.co.uk
Collects and distributes music royalties

NaSTA (National Student Television Association)
nasta@warwicktv.co.uk
www.nasta.org.uk
Student-run TV stations

National Film Theatre
Belvedere Road, South Bank,
Waterloo, London SE1 8XT
020 7928 3535
nft@bfi.org.uk
www.bfi.org.uk

Office of Communications (Ofcom)
Riverside House, 2A Southwark
Bridge Road, London SE1 9HA
020 7981 3000
www.ofcom.org.uk
Press: 020 7981 3033,
mediaoffice@ofcom.org.uk

Pact (Producers Alliance for Cinema and Television)
Procter House, 1 Procter Street,
London WC1V 6DW
020 7067 4367
enquiries@pact.co.uk
www.pact.co.uk
Trade association for independent production companies

The Picture Research Association
c/o 1 Willow Court, off Willow
Street, London EC2A 4QB
chair@picture-research.org.uk
www.picture-research.org.uk

Production Guild
N&P Complex,
Pinewood Studios, Iver Heath,
Buckinghamshire SL0 0NH
01753 651767
patrick@productionguild.com
www.productionguild.com

Production Managers Association
Ealing Studios, Ealing Green, Ealing,
London W5 5EP
020 8758 8699
pma@pma.org.uk
www.pma.org.uk

Professional Lighting and Sound Association - Plasa
38 St Leonards Road,
Eastbourne BN21 3UT
01323 410335
www.plasa.org

Royal Television Society
5th Floor, Kildare House,
3 Dorset Rise, London EC4Y 8EN
020 7822 2810
info@rts.org.uk
www.rts.org.uk
Membership and events organisation

The Satellite & Cable Broadcasters Group
29 Harley Street, London W1G 9QR
07968 125959
info@scbg.org.uk
www.scbg.org.uk
The trade association for satellite and cable programme providers

Sgrin, Media Agency for Wales
33-35 West Bute St, Cardiff Bay,
Cardiff CF10 5LH
029 2033 3300
sgrin@sgrin.co.uk
www.sgrin.co.uk
Film agency for Wales

Voice of the Listener and Viewer (VLV)
101 King's Drive, Gravesend,
Kent DA12 5BQ
01474 352835
info@vlv.org.uk
www.vlv.org.uk
Independent, non-profit society working to ensure independence, quality and diversity in broadcasting

UK Film Council
10 Little Portland Street,
London W1W 7JG
020 7861 7861
info@ukfilmcouncil.org.uk
www.ukfilmcouncil.org.uk
Promotes UK as a production centre

UK Post
47 Beak Street, London W1F 9SE
020 7734 0000
info@ukpost.org.uk
www.ukpost.org.uk
Trade body charged with representing the post-production and special effects sector at home and internationally

Writernet
Cabin V, Clarendon Buildings,
25 Horsell Road, Highbury,
London N5 1XL
020 7609 7474
info@writernet.org.uk
www.writernet.org.uk
Information and guidance for playwrights and performance writers

Poor GCap. The company's problems have proved to be more of a challenge than it ever expected. Having been stitched together from two of the biggest commercial radio companies, GWR and Capital, in a multi-million pound merger with the aim to create synergies, savings and other useful efficiencies, GCap Media has entirely failed to live up to its potential. Instead, a previously successful flagship service (in this case Capital) has been transformed into a limping shadow of its former self.

The news is not relentlessly bad: GCap remains the country's largest commercial radio operator and some of its stations are performing well. Classic FM and the digital station Planet Rock posted good Rajar figures in 2006 and contributed to the rise of commercial radio overall.

Yet Capital, disproportionately influential because of its lucrative London advertising base, continues to plummet disastrously, having lost its coveted status as "London's number one" status to Magic. The station lost almost one-fifth of its audience in 2006; hitting an all-time low in London for the second successive quarter with 5% of listening.

Worse, its confidence has been shaken severely. The management has looked uncertain since the loss of Chris Tarrant in 2004 and a schedule makeover has proved unconvincing. The Johnny Vaughan breakfast show – though Capital insists its demographic breakdown is better than Tarrant's with younger men tuning in – is less successful in volume terms.

When Tarrant left, the breakfast show audience was 1.37 million. It is now 782,000. (Jamie Theakston, on Capital's rival Heart FM, attracts 768,000 listeners). As a consolation both Vaughan and Theakston can claim victory in the breakfast show wars, because while Vaughan has 14,000 more listeners in overall reach, Theakston has a greater share of the audience. (This puzzle is due to the fact that radio ratings are fiendishly complex. Reach is the total number of listeners who stay with you for 15 minutes or more during a week. Share is the average share of listeners and factors in those who listen for longer.) Tarrant, incidentally, has announced he will return to radio with a new show, though he hasn't signed with a network at the time of writing.

Breakfast show warrior Jamie Theakston at Heart FM

Adding to Capital's woes is the pledge it made to cap adverts to two per break. This brave move seems to have backfired as revenues have taken an inevitable hit, with little impact on audiences. Revenues for the group fell 9% to the six months ending September 2006. The share price rallied a little, however, when it sold some regional stations to the Guardian Media Group (the parent company that publishes this guide).

Yet, the situation looks to be improving for Capital. A new programme director, Scott Muller, has arrived. The station will start marketing again. And, even more excitingly, it emerged at the end of 2006 that Birmingham

City's Karen Brady ("the first woman of football") is in the running to take over as managing director of the station.

Though she might not seem the obvious choice, Brady is on the board of Channel 4 and chairman of Emap's rock radio station Kerrang! If nothing else, the floating of Brady's name has given many journalists hours of fun conjuring footballing metaphors for Capital's plight.

● Digital radio

Thanks to the introduction of a wide range of DAB digital radio sets on the market from the impossibly modern to the sturdily retro, digital radio is beginning to achieve some impact in the UK. Penetration is estimated to be 13.9% by the end of 2006, and should reach 50% by 2010 according to the Digital Radio Development Bureau. It is still a far from startling statistic but nonetheless would represent a fourfold growth over four years. Its popularity has been attributed in part to the increasing availability of cheaper digital radios. Already the first mobile phone able to receive DAB stations, the Virgin Mobile Lobster 700, has been launched, while MP3 players featuring DAB receivers are already on the market.

National digital radio stations

	Digital One	Sky Digital	NTL Digital	Telewest Broadband	Freeview	Online
On BBC network						
1Xtra*	●	●	●	●	●	●
6 Music*	●	●	●	●	●	●
Asian Network*	●	●	●	●	●	●
BBC 7*	●	●	●	●	●	●
BBC Radio 1	●	●	●	●	●	●
BBC Radio 2	●	●	●	●	●	●
BBC Radio 3	●	●	●		●	●
BBC Radio 4	●				●	●
BBC Radio 5 Live	●	●	●	●	●	●
BBC World Service	●	●	●	●	●	●
Five Live Sports Extra*	●	●	●	●	●	●

* Exclusive to digital radio

	Digital One	Sky Digital	NTL Digital	Telewest Broadband	Freeview	Online
Capital Life	●					●
ClassicFM*	●	●	●	●		●
Core	●	●	●	●		●
Oneword Radio	●	●			●	●
Planet Rock	●	●	●	●		●
talkSPORT*	●	●	●	●	●	●
Virgin Radio*	●	●	●	●	●	●

	Digital One	Sky Digital	NTL Digital	Telewest Broadband	Freeview	Online
Local/regional stations available nationally on digital terrestrial television						
3C Contiuous Cool Country					●	●
Heat Radio		●			●	●
The Hits		●	●		●	●
Kerrang!*		●	●		●	●
Kiss 100*		●	●		●	●
Magic 105.4*		●	●		●	●
Premier Christian Radio*		●	●		●	●
Smash! Hits		●	●		●	●

* Also available on analogue

But it is still a minority sport, which makes the kerfuffle over the next set of digital multiplex licences all the less explicable.

The race to become the UK's second national digital radio multiplex operator is well underway, with all the usual suspects bidding as well as a newcomer to radio – Channel 4, with its promises of real competition for the BBC speech services. A multiplex is essentially a chunk of available broadcasting spectrum allowing the launch of a number of new stations, in this case up to 10. The more bandwidth you use for a service, the better the quality. Of course, it's the opposite if you try to squeeze an extra service into the spectrum – as the BBC did with Five Live, and caused a row over the drop in quality of sound on Radio 3. Channel 4's chief executive Andy Duncan has already invested considerable time and resource in digital radio as a future-proofing strategy for Channel 4 – a bold and innovative move. Having gone about it so publicly, he almost cannot afford not to win at least a share of the multiplex and is believed to have been talking to most of the more established radio groups about the possibility of a partnership or joint bid for the multiplex. No details of any such deal have so far been forthcoming.

However Duncan and his radio team, largely mined from the pre-merger Capital group, have been making some pre-bid moves in the medium. They have promised a rival to BBC Radio 4's flagship The Today programme based on the well-respected Channel 4 News should they be successful in their bid. And banking on the fact that opinion formers (especially politicians one assumes) would relish competition for John Humphrys et al.

If that all sounds a bit staid for the future, Channel 4 has also recently launched a revival of the TV programme The Tube over the internet at Channel4radio.com. Featuring bleeding edge bands of the sort that the over-30s could never hope to have heard of, the youth-friendly service will, Channel 4 hopes, be music to the ears of the regulators who dish out licences. Certainly, having developed some products for radio makes Channel 4 look less of a dilettante when up against established radio players.

GCap had initially resisted the launch of a new multiplex and threatened legal action against Ofcom for even mentioning the possibility of another one. GCap, of course, is the majority owner (63%) of the original national commercial radio multiplex, Digital One. It felt the launch of a new series of services would damage its own assets and threaten its already perilous status.

However, Ofcom has declared that the new multiplex must feature complementary rather than competitive stations and GCap has called off the lawyers for the time being.

So the auditioning period begins and applicants will spend the first three months of 2007 honing their bids (expect plenty of carefully-crafted public service commitments and big names on advisory panels). The following three months will be spent waiting for a decision, expected early summer that year. The services themselves will not be able to launch until 2008, by which time they will have changed unrecognisably from the promised offerings if past experience is anything to go by. Yes, it's the fast-moving, cutting-edge world of digital radio here, kids.

In addition to the national multiplex, Ofcom is also offering 12 local multiplex licences, aimed at rural areas that currently have little or no access to digital radio. These multiplexes will allow for up to 74 existing

National listening figures, second quarter 2006

Top 20 national stations	Reach (m)	Reach (%)	Share (%)
BBC Radio 2	13.3	27	15.7
BBC Radio 1	10.4	21	10.3
BBC Radio 4	9.2	18	10.7
BBC Radio FIVE LIVE (inc Sports Extra)	6.1	12	4.7
Classic FM	5.8	12	4.2
Heart*	3.1	6	2.4
Magic*	3.1	6	2.3
Galaxy*	2.5	5	1.7
Kiss*	2.4	5	1.2
Virgin Radio*	2.3	5	1.5
talkSPORT (Talk Radio)	2.2	4	1.7
BBC Radio 3	1.8	4	1.1
Century*	1.7	3	1.1
Real Radio*	1.6	3	1.6
Smooth*	1.5	3	1.2
BBC World Service	1.3	3	0.7
Kerrang!*	1.2	2	0.6
Capital Gold*	1.2	2	0.7
The Hits	1.1	2	0.4
XFM*	1.1	2	0.8
ALL BBC	**32.9**	**66**	**54.7**
All BBC network radio	28.7	58	44.0
BBC local/regional	10.0	20	10.7
ALL COMMERCIAL	**30.7**	**62**	**42.9**
All local commercial	24.8	50	32.2
All national commercial	13.3	27	10.7

* Total networks   Source: Rajar

Top 20 local/regional stations by reach, second quarter 2006

		Reach (m)	Reach (%)	Share (%)
Magic 105.4	London	1,867	18	6.5
Heart 106.2 FM	London	1,664	16	6.1
Capital Radio	London	1,641	16	5.0
Kiss 100 FM	London	1,499	14	4.4
BBC Radio Scotland		927	22	7.4
Galaxy*	Yorkshire	900	21	8.0
100.7 Heart FM*	Birmingham	820	24	10.1
105.4 Century FM	Manchester	751	15	5.5
Real Radio*	Scotland	723	27	15.5
Smooth FM	North West	670	12	6.5
Clyde 1 FM*	Glasgow	595	33	16.6
Capital Gold	London	590	6	1.3
XFM 104.9	London	548	5	2.3
Smooth FM	London	537	5	2.1
Key 103*	Manchester	524	23	9.0
96.4 BRMB*	Birmingham	519	26	8.0
BBC Radio Ulster		510	37	27.5
Radio City 96.7*	Liverpool	506	28	13.6
Choice FM	London	493	5	1.9
Galaxy*	North East	478	22	8.6
All local commercial radio		**24,749**	**51**	**32.8**
BBC local radio		**7,641**	**19**	**10.3**

* figures taken from Jan–Jun   Source: RAJAR/Ipsos-RSL, second quarter 2006

Awards

local FM and analogue services and all BBC local and regional stations to switch to digital.

Digital radio is absolutely key to the future success of commercial radio, because of the link between new services and younger (more desirable) listeners. The top 20 digital radio stations by weekly reach read like the "young people" shelf of a newsagents – The Hits, Smash Hits Radio (both Emap), BBC7 (comedy), BBC Asian Network, Planet Rock, BBC6 Music, 1Xtra, Q and Heat (again both Emap). Like the internet five years ago, there's no real money in it yet, but the operators sense there's gold in them thar hills if they just hang around long enough.

● Commercial v BBC

Despite its relatively low penetration, digital radio is slowly changing the listening landscape, to the benefit of commercial radio which is making small gains against the BBC. The BBC's lead in audience share has narrowed to just under 11% (overall 54.3%), with Radio 1 the only one of its five main national stations to increase its audience year on year in the third quarter of 2006.

BBC's Five Live, suffering in a quarter that included a televised World Cup in the right time zone for primetime, dropped 5% of its audience and was the biggest loser of share for the BBC. Though its commercial rival TalkSport actually gained 8.4% year on year.

Commercial radio's overall share of listening, at 43.6% is up both on quarter and on year.

● Regional networks

If the largest concern in the regional radio industry is supposed to be the homogenisation of local radio, listeners appear unconcerned.

The diverse and specialised BBC local radio network is in fact struggling, having lost around 1 in 10 of its listeners during 2006, while the national regional services in Scotland and Ulster fared little better. Only Wales has shown a slight increase in listeners.

The corporation's losses have made for a cheery picture in regional commercial radio, where the story is one of success. Emap, with its brands of Magic, Kerrang!, the Big City network and digital stations The Hits and Smash Hits is performing well, attracting roughly a quarter of all listening to commercial radio.

Chrysalis, which has been thwarted somewhat in its acquisitions strategy having failed to acquire GMG's radio stations, is enjoying success regardless with its Galaxy and LBC networks.

GMG Radio (again, owned by the company which publishes this directory) has improved reach across its Real Radio and Smooth FM stations. Having rejected the Chrysalis bid and purchased two Century stations for £60m from GCap, GMG seems – following a strategic review of all its assets – to have decided to remain firmly in radio for the time being.

GMG Radio has reported record reach across its Real Radio and Smooth FM stations, attracting a total of 3.1 million listeners a week. Real Radio Scotland recorded its biggest ever audience of 736,000. Even GCap has, as a group, added 3.3m listener hours and 93,000 extra listeners.

There is, however, a caveat. Of course. The miseries of the advertising market are not confined to national media, nor is radio exempt. The new digital stations do not yet have the penetration to attract any serious advertising, so the analogue stations must divide up the shrinking pot of

Radio

197

advertisers' money between the existing services and the new ones. Nor can they turn off the old services yet until the new ones have a greater penetration. A tipping point is urgently needed.

The squeeze is compounded by the revelation that young people are losing their appetite for radio as with other old media. Listening among 15-24 year olds has dropped over the last five years by more than 14m hours a week.

As MediaGuardian's radio columnist Paul Robinson noted, "The challenge for the industry, if it is to remain relevant to today's youth, is to embrace new delivery platforms that take radio way beyond the tranny on the kitchen windowsill."

Digital multiplex licence-holders

Holder	Owners	Multiplexes number	location
NATIONAL			
BBC	Public	1	80% of the country
Digital One	GCap Media and Arqiva	1	85% of the country
Total national		2	
LOCAL AND REGIONAL *			
CE Digital Ltd	GCap Media, Emap Digital Radio	3	London, Birmingham, Manchester
Digital Radio Group London	GCap Media, Carphone Warehouse, UTV, SMG	1	London
Emap Digital Radio	Emap Radio	7	Humberside, Leeds, Liverpool, South Yorkshire, Teeside, Tyne & Wear
MXR	Chrysalis Radio, GCap Media, Guardian Media Group, UBC and Ford	5	The North-East, North-West, West Midlands, Yorkshire, South Wales & Severn Estuary
Now Digital	GCap Media	12	Bristol & Bath, Coventry, Wolverhampton, Southend & Chelmsford, Bournemouth, Exeter & Torbay, Peterborough, Norwich, Swindon & Wiltshire, Cambridge, Reading
Now Digital East Midlands	GCap Media, Chrysalis, Sabras Radio	2	Leicester, Nottingham
Now Digital Southern (formerly Capital Digital)	GCap Media	4	Cardiff and Newport, South Hampshire, Sussex Coast, Kent
Score Digital	Emap Radio	5	Northern Ireland, Dundee/Perth, Edinburgh, Glasgow, Inverness
South West Digital Radio Limited	GCap Media, UKRD	1	Plymouth & Cornwall
Switchdigital	UTV Radio	3	London and Aberdeen (local), central Scotland (regional)
UTV-Emap Digital Ltd	UTV Radio, Emap Digital Radio	3	Swansea, Stoke onTrent, Bradford and Huddersfield
Total local and regional		46	

* Local licences unless stated

Radio reshuffles its talent

Paul N Robinson

Despite ratings and mergers dominating the headlines in recent times, both the BBC and commercial radio managed to churn out programmes that had the average listener tuning in for nearly a whole day every week. Presenters came and went: Sue Lawley departed and Chris Evans re-arrived, this time at Radio 2. Radio 4's Woman's Hour proved its sustainability despite an anachronistic title by celebrating its 60th birthday, and also celebrating 60 years was the Third Programme, now Radio 3.

The first big talent move of the year was in January when Christian O'Connell arrived at Virgin Radio to take over the breakfast show from Pete and Jeff, in a mission to push up ratings. O'Connell sounded comfortable on the national station from week one, helped perhaps by the format, which was a direct lift from his former XFM slot. Nevertheless Who's Calling Christian did the business with over 150 celebrities calling, although giving Tony Blair the prize (albeit for charity) seemed like "brown nosing" in the extreme.

Breakfast show presenters often host the drivetime slot before being given the premier morning show. The former Capital FM DJ Neil Fox, now on Magic in London, made a decent job of helping the station in its three-way fight with Heart and Capital Radio, but the drivetime hire that made headlines was controller Leslie Douglas's appointment of Chris Evans to the slot formerly occupied by Johnnie Walker on BBC Radio 2. The press claimed there were vast numbers of complaints (there was merely a small trickle) and commercial radio moaned that the BBC had paid a handsome price for Evans' services (probably true).

When Sue Lawley announced she was leaving Radio 4's Desert Island Discs, there was speculation on a grand scale about her successor. To put the change of anchor into perspective, she was only the third presenter of the programme (the first two being Roy Plomley, the creator, followed by Michael Parkinson) after decades on air. The choice of Kirsty Young, whose radio experience includes Radio Scotland and national commercial station Talk Radio (before Kelvin arrived), was inspired. In case you need to know for Trivial Pursuit, her first castaway was Quentin Blake.

The summer at Radio 1 saw a revamp of the evening schedule, the signing of specialist talent Eddie Halliwell and trophy wins with Colin Murray being given a new weekday evening show. The former Radio 1 DJ Simon Bates, whose weepy feature Our Tune can still be heard on radio, took the Special award at the Commercial Radio Arqiva awards and the Sony Radio Academy awards continued to go from strength to strength with a new record number of entries. The commercial sector was relieved to take a best-ever number of Sony gongs this year, including 12 golds. And finally on talent and future award-winners, the digital station BBC6 Music's loss was Radio 2's gain, with the start in November of Russell Brand's Saturday night show. He compared the national station to Hogwarts, but suggestions that magic is the reason for the station's stellar audience figures are wide of the mark.

Commercial radio made strides developing network programming, with every local station in England participating in February's The Big Quit, a campaign to motivate smokers to give up, followed in October by the launch of an R&B chart called the Fresh 40, broadcast on stations such as Galaxy and Kiss.

Channel 4 declared its intention to get into radio and made a promising start online, with shows ranging from Jon Snow's Morning Report to offbeat reporter Sid Kipper's Country Code, Richard and Judy's Book Club and a revival of the iconic TV music show, The Tube.

BBC Radio 3 demonstrated its credentials as the UK's patron of live classical music, with Listen Up, a festival featuring more than 30 British orchestras and 20 living composers, including Judith Weir and Michael Omer. The festival coincided with the network's 60th birthday.

The year ended with GCap Media launching a new national digital jazz music station and Ofcom consulting on the future of the medium and commercial radio in particular.

● Paul Robinson is the chief executive at PR Media Consulting Ltd

Radio

Radio contacts

News media

BBC radio

Broadcasting House,
Portland Place,
London W1A 1AA
020 7580 4468

Director of audio and music:
Jenny Abramsky, 020 7765 4561

Head of radio news:
Stephen Mitchell

Head of radio current affairs:
Gwyneth Williams

Controller, radio production:
Graham Ellis, 020 7765 4809

Controller, interactive radio and music:
Simon Nelson, 020 7765 2545

Press

Head of press and publicity, BBC radio:
Sue Lynas, 020 7765 4990

Nations and regions:
Tim Brassell, 020 8008 1239

Digital radio:
Jamie Austin, 020 7765 0426

Regional press offices
London: 020 7765 4990
Birmingham: 0121 567 6274
Bristol: 0117 974 2130
Manchester: 0161 244 4888
Leeds: 0113 224 7152
Newcastle: 0191 244 1296

» *See also separate press contacts*

● Radio stations

BBC Radio 1/1xtra
Yalding House,
152-156 Great Portland Street,
London W1N 6AJ
www.bbc.co.uk/radio1
www.bbc.co.uk/1xtra
Controller: Andy Parfitt; head of mainstream programmes: Ben Cooper, 020 7765 2236; head of specialist live music: Ian Parkinson, 020 7765 0365; breakfast show: Chris Moyles (Radio 1), Rampage (1xtra)
Press: Alison Hunter, 020 7765 1030

BBC Radio 2
Western House,
99 Great Portland Street,
London W1A 1AA
www.bbc.co.uk/radio2
Controller: Lesley Douglas, 020 7765 3493; managing editor: Antony Bellekom, 020 7765 4612; editor, mainstream programmes: Phil Hughes, 020 7765 4159; editor, specialist programmes: Dave Barber, 0121 432 9854; breakfast show: Terry Wogan
Press: Hester Nevill, 020 7765 5712

BBC Radio 3
Broadcasting House, Portland Place,
London W1A 1AA
www.bbc.co.uk/radio3
Controller: Roger Wright, 020 7765 2523; head of speech programmes: Abigail Appleton, 020 7765 3277; head of music programming: John Evans, 020 7765 0481; controller, Proms, live events and TV classical music: Nicholas Kenyon, 020 7765 4928
Press: Clare Fisher, 020 7765 5887

BBC Radio 4
Broadcasting House, Portland Place,
London W1A 1AA
www.bbc.co.uk/radio4
Controller: Mark Damazer, 020 7765 3836; network manager: Denis Nowlan, 020 7765 4615; head of radio drama: Alison Hindell, 020 7557 1006; editor, entertainment: Caroline Raphael, 020 7765 1870; editor, drama: Jeremy Howe 020 7765 4505; editor, general factual: Jane Ellison (features) 020 7765 0631; editor, specialist factual: Andrew Caspari, 020 7765 2660
Press: Sian Davis, 020 7765 2629

BBC Radio Five Live & Five Live Sports Extra
Television Centre, Wood Lane,
London W12 7RJ
www.bbc.co.uk/fivelive
Controller: Bob Shennan, 020 8624 8956; head of radio sport: Gordon Turnbull, 020 8225 6206; head of news, Radio Five Live: Mat Morris, 020 8624 8946; commissioning editor: Moz Dee, 020 8624 8948
Press: Andy Bate, 020 8576 1694

BBC 6 Music
Western House,
99 Great Portland Street,
London W1A 1AA
020 7765 3493
www.bbc.co.uk/6music
Controller: Lesley Douglas, 020 7765 3493; head of programmes: Ric Blaxill; breakfast show: Phill Jupitus; see also Radio 2 contacts

BBC Asian Network
Epic House, Charles Street,
Leicester LE1 3SH
0116 251 6688
www.bbc.co.uk/asiannetwork
Controller: Bob Shennan; breakfast: Sonia Deol
Press: Andy Bate, 020 8225 1694

BBC World Service
Bush House, Strand,
London WC2B 4PH
020 7557 2941
www.bbc.co.uk/worldservice
Director: Mark Byford

Today programme
Room G630, Stage 6, Television Centre, Wood Lane, London W12 7RJ
www.bbc.co.uk/radio4/today
Editor: Ceri Thompson; presenters: John Humphrys, James Naughtie, Ed Stourton, Sarah Montague; comms manager: Karen Rosine, 020 8576 8367
Press: 020 8576 8928

● Nations and regions

BBC Radio Scotland
Queen Margaret Drive,
Glasgow G12 8DG
0141 339 8844
scottishplanning@bbc.co.uk
www.bbc.co.uk/scotland
92-95 FM; 810 AM. Controller: Ken MacQuarrie

BBC Radio Nan Gaidheal
52 Church Street, Stornoway,
Isle of Lewis HS1 2LS
01851 705000
feedback@bbc.co.uk
www.bbc.co.uk/scotlandalba/radio
103-105 FM. Editor: Marion MacKinnon; news editor: Norman Campbell

BBC Radio Wales/Cymru
Broadcasting House, Llandaff,
Cardiff CF5 2YQ
0870 010 0110
radiowales@bbc.co.uk
www.bbc.co.uk/radiowales
93-104 FM. Managing editor: Sali Collins; head of news: Geoff Williams; breakfast show: Richard Evans/Felicity Evans/Rhun Ap Iorwerth/Jo Kiernan/Sarah Dickens

BBC Radio Ulster
Broadcasting House, Belfast BT2 8HQ
028 9033 8000
radioulster@bbc.co.uk
www.bbc.co.uk/radioulster
92-95.4 FM. Head of radio: Susan Lovell; head of music: Declan McGovern; head of news: Kathleen Carragher

BBC Radio Foyle
Northland Road, Derry,
Londonderry BT48 7GD
028 7137 8600
radiofoyle@bbc.co.uk
www.bbc.co.uk/radiofoyle
93.1 FM; 792 AM. Head of radio: Paul McCauley

● BBC local radio

BBC Radio Berkshire
PO Box 1044, Reading RG4 8FH
0118 946 4200
berkshireonline@bbc.co.uk
www.bbc.co.uk/berkshire
94.6 FM; 95.4 FM; 104.1 FM; 104.4 FM. Editor: Lizz Loxam; breakfast show: Andrew Peach

BBC Radio Bristol and Somerset Sound
PO Box 194, Bristol BS99 7QT
01179 741111
radio.bristol@bbc.co.uk
www.bbc.co.uk/radiobristol and
www.bbc.co.uk/bristol
95.5, 94.9 FM; 1548, 1566 AM. Managing editor, Bristol: Tim Pemberton; assistant editors: Dawn Trevett (Bristol), Simon Clifford (Somerset Sound); breakfast show: Nigel Dando/ Rachael Burden

BBC Radio Cambridgeshire
PO Box 96, 104 Hills Road,
Cambridge CB2 1LD
01223 259696
cambs@bbc.co.uk
www.bbc.co.uk/cambridgeshire
96 FM; 95.7 FM. News editor: Alison Daws; managing editor: Jason Horton; breakfast show: Steve Richardson

BBC Radio Cleveland
PO Box 95FM, Newport Road,
Middlesbrough TS1 5DG
01642 225211
bbcradiocleveland@bbc.co.uk
www.bbc.co.uk/tees
95 FM. Managing editor: David Clayton; news editor: Peter Harris; breakfast show: Matthew Davies

BBC Radio Cornwall
Phoenix Wharf, Truro,
Cornwall TR1 1UA
01872 275421
radio.cornwall@bbc.co.uk
www.bbc.co.uk/cornwall
103.9 FM; 95.2 FM. Managing editor: Pauline Causey; news editor: Ed Goodrich; breakfast show: Pam Spriggs and James Churchfield

BBC Radio Cumbria
Annetwell Street, Carlisle CA3 8BB
01228 592444
cumbria@bbc.co.uk
www.bbc.co.uk/radiocumbria
95.6 FM; 96.1 FM; 104.1 FM. Managing editor: Nigel Dyson; news editor: Tom Stight; breakfast show: Richard Corrie and Richard Nankivell

BBC Radio Derby
PO Box 104.5, Derby DE1 3HL
01332 361111
radio.derby@bbc.co.uk
www.bbc.co.uk/radioderby
1116 AM; 104.5 AM; 95.3 FM; 96FM. Managing editor: Simon Cornes; news editor: John Atkin; breakfast show: Andy Whitaker

BBC Radio Devon
PO Box 1034, Plymouth PL3 5BD
01752 260323
devon.online@bbc.co.uk
www.bbc.co.uk/devon
103.4 FM. Managing editor: Robert Wallis; news editor: Emma Clements; breakfast show: Michael Chequer

BBC Essex
198 New London Road, Chelmsford,
Essex CM2 9XB
01245 616000
essex@bbc.co.uk
www.bbc.co.uk/essex
103.5 FM; 95.3 FM; 765 AM; 1530 AM; 729 AM. Managing editor: Margaret Hyde; news editor: Alison Hodgkins-Brown; breakfast show: Etholle George and John Hayes

BBC Radio Gloucestershire
London Road, Gloucester GL1 1SW
01452 308585
radio.gloucestershire@bbc.co.uk
www.bbc.co.uk/gloucestershire
104.7 FM; 1413 AM. Managing editor: Mark Hurrell; news editor: Graham Day; breakfast show: Mark Cummings

BBC Radio Guernsey
Bulwer Avenue, St Sampsons,
Guernsey GY2 4LA
01481 200600
radio.guernsey@bbc.co.uk
www.bbc.co.uk/guernsey
93.2 FM; 1116 AM. Managing editor: David Martin; news editors: Simon Alexander and Kay Longlay; breakfast show: Adrian Gidney

BBC Hereford and Worcester
Hylton Road, Worcester WR2 5WW
01905 748485
bbchw@bbc.co.uk
www.bbc.co.uk/worcester or
www.bbc.co.uk/hereford
104 FM; 104.6 FM; 94.7 FM. Managing editor: James Coghill; news editor: Jo Baldwin; breakfast show: Howard Bentham

BBC Radio Humberside
Queens Court, Queens Gardens,
Hull HU1 3RP
01482 323232
radio.humberside@bbc.co.uk
www.bbc.co.uk/humber
95.9 FM; 1485 AM. Managing editor: Simon Pattern; news editor: Kate Slade; breakfast show: Andy Comfort

BBC Radio Jersey
18 Parade Road, St Helier,
Jersey JE2 3PL
01534 837228
jersey@bbc.co.uk
www.bbc.co.uk/jersey
88.8 FM. Managing editor: Denzil Dudley; news editor: Sarah Scriven; breakfast show: Joe Pignatiello

BBC Radio Kent
The Great Hall,
Mount Pleasant Road,
Tunbridge Wells, Kent TN1 1QQ
01892 670000
radio.kent@bbc.co.uk
www.bbc.co.uk/kent
96.7 FM; 97.6 FM; 104.2 FM. Managing editor: Paul Leuper; news editors: Sally Dunk and Simon Longprice; breakfast show: Steve Ladner

BBC Radio Lancashire and BBC Open Centre
26 Darwen Street, Blackburn,
Lancs BB2 2EA
01254 262411
radio.lancashire@bbc.co.uk
www.bbc.co.uk/lancashire
95.5 FM. Managing editor: John Clayton; news editor: Chris Rider; breakfast show: Alison Butterworth

BBC Radio Leeds
Broadcasting Centre,
2 St Peters Square, Leeds LS9 8AH
0113 244 2131
radio.leeds@bbc.co.uk
www.bbc.co.uk/leeds
92.4 FM. Managing editor: Phil Roberts; news editor: Andy Evans; breakfast show: Andrew Edwards and Georgie Spanswick

BBC Radio Leicester
9 St Nicholas Place, Leicester LE1 5LB
0116 251 6688
leicester@bbc.co.uk
www.bbc.co.uk/leicester
104.9 FM. Managing editor: Kate Squire; breakfast show: Ben Jackson

BBC Radio Lincolnshire
PO Box 219, Newport,
Lincoln LN1 3XY
01522 511411
radio.lincolnshire@bbc.co.uk
www.bbc.co.uk/lincolnshire
94.9 FM; 1368 FM; 104 FM. Managing editor: Charlie Partridge; news editor: Andy Farrant; breakfast show: Rod Whiting

BBC London 94.9
35 Marylebone High Street,
London W1U 4QA
020 7224 2424
yourlondon@bbc.co.uk
www.bbc.co.uk/london
*94.9 FM. Managing editor: David Robey;
breakfast show: Danny Baker*

BBC Radio Manchester
PO Box 951, Oxford Road,
Manchester M60 1SD
0161 200 2000
manchester.online@bbc.co.uk
www.bbc.co.uk/manchester
*95.1 FM; 104.6 FM. Managing editor:
John Ryan; news editor: Mark Elliott;
breakfast show: Terry Christian*

BBC Radio Merseyside and
BBC Open Centre
PO Box 95.8, 31 College Lane,
Liverpool L69 1ZJ
0151 708 5500
radio.merseyside@bbc.co.uk
www.bbc.co.uk/liverpool
*95.8 FM. Managing editor: Mike Ord;
news editor: Andy Ball; breakfast show:
Simon O'Brian and Lucinda Moore*

BBC Radio Newcastle
Broadcasting Centre, Barrack Road,
Newcastle upon Tyne NE99 1RN
0191 232 4141
radio.newcastle@bbc.co.uk
www.bbc.co.uk/england
   /radionewcastle
*95.4 FM. Managing editor: Graham Moss;
news editor: Doug Morris; breakfast
show: Mike Parr*

BBC Radio Norfolk
The Forum, Millennium Plain,
Norwich NR2 1BH
01603 617411
radionorfolk@bbc.co.uk
www.bbc.co.uk/norfolk
*104.4 FM; 95.1 FM; 855 AM; 873 AM.
Managing editor: David Clayton; news
editor: Sarah Kings; breakfast show:
Stephen Bumfrey*

BBC Radio Northampton
Broadcasting House, Abington
Street, Northampton NN1 2BH
01604 239100
northampton@bbc.co.uk
www.bbc.co.uk/northamptonshire
*104.2, 103.6 FM. Managing editor: Laura
Moss; news editor: Laura Cook; breakfast
show: Anna Murby*

BBC Radio Nottingham
London Road, Nottingham NG2 4UU
0115 955 0500
radio.nottingham@bbc.co.uk
www.bbc.co.uk/nottingham
*103.8 FM. Managing editor: Mike
Bettison; news editor: Mike Yound;
breakfast show: Karl Cooper*

BBC Radio Oxford
269 Banbury Road, Oxford OX2 7DW
01865 311444
oxford@bbc.co.uk
www.bbc.co.uk/radiooxford
*95.2 FM. Managing editor: Steve
Taschini; news editor: Mike Day*

BBC Radio Sheffield and
BBC Open Centre
54 Shoreham Street, Sheffield S1 4RS
0114 273 1177
radio.sheffield@bbc.co.uk
www.bbc.co.uk/england
   /radiosheffield
*88.6 FM. Managing editor: Gary Keown;
news editor: Mike Woodcock; breakfast
show: Antonia Brickell*

BBC Radio Shropshire
2-4 Boscobel Drive,
Shrewsbury SY1 3TT
01743 248484
radio.shropshire@bbc.co.uk
www.bbc.co.uk/shropshire
*96 FM; 95.7 FM. Managing editor: Tim
Beach; news editor: Sharon Simcock;
breakfast show: Eric Smith*

BBC Radio Solent
Broadcasting House, Havelock Road,
Southampton SO14 7PW
02380 631311
radio.solent@bbc.co.uk
www.bbc.co.uk/radiosolent
*96.1 FM. Managing editor: Mia Costello;
breakfast show: Julian Clegg*

BBC Southern Counties Radio
Broadcasting Centre,
Guildford GU2 7AP
01483 306306
southern.counties@bbc.co.uk
www.bbc.co.uk/southerncounties
*104-104.8 FM; 95-95.3 FM. Managing
editor: Mike Hapgood; news editor: Mark
Carter; breakfast show: Sarah Gorrell, Ed
Douglas, John Radford*

BBC Radio Stoke and
BBC Open Centre
Cheapside, Hanley,
Stoke on Trent ST1 1JJ
01782 208080
radio.stoke@bbc.co.uk
www.bbc.co.uk/stoke
*94.6 FM. Managing editor: Sue Owen;
breakfast show: Janine Machin*

BBC Radio Suffolk
Broadcasting House,
St Matthew's Street, Ipswich,
Suffolk IP1 3EP
01473 250000
radiosuffolk@bbc.co.uk
www.bbc.co.uk/suffolk
*105.5 FM; 104.5 FM; 103 FM. Managing
editor: Gerald Main; news editor: Lis
Henderson; breakfast show: Mark
Murphy*

BBC Radio Swindon
PO Box 1234, Swindon SN1 3RW
01793 513626
radio.swindon@bbc.co.uk
www.bbc.co.uk/wiltshire
*103.6 FM. Managing editor: Tony
Worgan; news editor: Kirsty Ward and
Jillian Moody; breakfast show: Mark
O'Donnell*

BBC Three Counties Radio
PO Box 3CR, Luton,
Bedfordshire LU1 5XL
01582 637400
3cr@bbc.co.uk
www.bbc.co.uk/threecounties
*95.5 FM; 104.5 FM; 103 FM. Managing
editor: Angus Moorat; breakfast show:
Roberto Perrone*

BBC Radio Wiltshire
PO Box 1234, Bedfordshire LU1 5XL
01793 513626
radio.wiltshire@bbc.co.uk
www.bbc.co.uk/wiltshire
*103.6 FM. Managing editor: Tony
Worgan; news editor: Kirsty Ward and
Jillian Moody; breakfast show: Mark
O'Donnell*

BBC WM (Birmingham)
The Mailbox, Birmingham B1 1RF
0121 567 6000
birmingham@bbc.co.uk
www.bbc.co.uk/birmingham or
www.bbc.co.uk/blackcountry
*95.6 FM. Managing editor: Keith Beech;
news editor: Raj Ford; breakfast show:
Adrian Goldberg*

BBC WM (Coventry)
1 Holt Court, Greyfriars Road,
Coventry CV1 2WR
024 7655 1000
coventry@bbc.co.uk
warwickshire@bbc.co.uk
www.bbc.co.uk/coventry
*103.7 FM; 94.8 FM; 104 FM. Managing
editor: David Clargo; breakfast show:
Annie Othen*

BBC North Yorkshire – Radio York
20 Bootham Row, York YO30 7BR
01904 641351
northyorkshire.news@bbc.co.uk
www.bbc.co.uk/northyorkshire
*1260 AM; 666 AM; 104.3 FM; 103.7 FM;
95.5 FM. Managing editor: Matt Youdale;
news editor: Anna Evans; breakfast show:
Allan Watkiss, Anna Wallace*

● Resources

BBC Radio Resources
Brock House, 19 Langham Street,
London W1A 1AA
020 7765 3208
radio.resources@bbc.co.uk
www.bbcradioresources.com
*Senior operations manager: Martin
Hollister; controller operations and
technology: Miles Hosking;
communications and marketing
manager: Holly Senior*

Event Services
Room 112 Brock House,
19 Langham Street, London W1A 1AA
020 7765 5100
rr-events-team@bbc.co.uk
www.bbcradioresources.com
*Events manager: Mark Diamond; events
assistant: Joanne Wye, 020 7765 2375*

Outside Broadcasts
Room 112 Brock House,
19 Langham Street, London W1A 1AA
020 7765 4888
duncan.smith@bbc.co.uk
www.bbcradioresources.com
*Operations manager: Will Garrett; radio
outside broadcasts manager: Duncan
Smith*

● Studios

Birmingham Studios
The Mailbox, Birmingham B1 1RF
0121 567 6767
www.bbc.co.uk/birmingham
*Operations co-ordinator: Liz Treacher;
facilities manager: Caroline Smith*

Bristol Broadcasting House
Whiteladies Road, Bristol BS8 2LR
0117 973 2211
www.bbc.co.uk/bristol
*Radio operations planner: Maria
Clutterbuck; sound manager: Iain Hunter*

Broadcasting House Studios
Brock House, 19 Langham Street,
London W1A 1AA
020 8743 8000
www.bbc.co.uk
*Marketing executive in music
management: Amanda Bates; senior
operations manager: Martin Hollister*

Maida Vale Studios
1-129 Delaware Road, London W9 2LG
020 7765 2091
www.bbc.co.uk
Facilities manager: John Hakrow

Manchester Studios
New Broadcasting House, PO Box 27,
Oxford Road, Manchester M60 1SJ
0161 244 4607
www.bbc.co.uk
*Operations co-ordinator: Alison Turner;
operations manager: Richard Savage*

Commercial radio

Commercial Radio Companies Association
77 Shaftesbury Avenue,
London W1D 5DU
020 7306 2603
info@crca.co.uk
www.crca.co.uk
*Chief executive: Paul Brown; research
and communications manager: Alison
Winter*

● Main commercial radio groups

CN Group
Dalston Road, Carlisle,
Cumbria CA2 5UA
01228 612600
news@cumbrian-newspapers.co.uk
www.cumbria-online.co.uk
*Chief executive: Robin Burgess; managing
director: Christopher Bisco; deputy
managing director: Terry Hall*

Chrysalis Radio Group
The Chrysalis Building,
13 Bramley Road, London W10 6SP
020 7221 2213
info@chrysalis.com
www.chrysalis.com
*Chief executives: Richard Huntingford
(whole group), Phil Riley (radio)*

Classic Gold Digital
Network Centre, Chiltern Road,
Dunstable LU6 1HQ
01582 676200
www.classicgolddigital.com
*Managing director: John Baish;
programme controller: Stewart Davies*

Emap Performance Network
Mappin House, 4 Winsley Street,
London W1W 8HF
020 7436 1515
www.emap.com
*Group managing director: Dee Ford;
advertising director: Dave King;
programme director: Phil Roberts*

GCap Media
30 Leicester Square,
London WC2H 7LA
020 7766 6000
www.gcapmedia.com
*Chief executive: Ralph Bernard;
director of communications: Jane Wilson*

Lincs FM
Witham Park, Waterside South,
Lincoln LN5 7JN
01522 549900
enquiries@lincsfm.co.uk
www.lincsfm.co.uk
*Chief executive: Michael Betton; director
of operations and press: Keith Briggs*

SMG
200 Renfield Street, Glasgow G2 3PR
0141 300 3300
www.smg.plc.uk
Acting chief executive: Donald Emslie

Tindle Radio Holdings
Ground Floor, Radio House, Orion
Court, Great Blakenham IP6 0LW
01473 836100
info@tindleradio.com
www.tindleradio.com
*Chief executive: Kevin Stewart; deputy
chief executive: David Lovell; group
programme controller: Mark Franklin*

UKRD Group
Carn Brea Studios, Wilson Way,
Redruth, Cornwall TR15 3RQ
01209 310435
enquiries@ukrd.co.uk
www.ukrd.com
*Chairman: Trevor Smallwood; chief
executive: William Rogers; group
programme director: Phil Angell*

The Wireless Group
18 Hatfields, London SE1 8DJ
020 7959 7900
www.thewirelessgroup.net
Chief executive: Scott Taunton

● National commercial digital radio

Digital One
30 Leicester Square,
London WC2H 7LA
020 7288 4600
info@digitalone.co.uk
www.ukdigitalradio.com
*Joint venture backed by GWR and NTL.
Chief executive: Quentin Howard*

Freeview
DTV Services Ltd, PO Box 7630,
Mansfield MG18 4YL
020 7792 7412
www.freeview.co.uk
*Five shareholders: BBC, Crown Castle
International, BSkyB, ITV and Channel 4*
Press: 07813 783181

● Stations on AM, DAB* and Freeview

3c – continuous cool country
Scottish Radio Holdings,
Clydebank Business Park, Clydebank,
Glasgow G81 2RF
0141 565 2307
3c@3cdigital.com
www.3cdigital.com
*Country music. DAB; Freeview; internet.
Station manager, programme controller
and breakfast show: Pat Geary*

The Arrow
Chrysalis Group, 1 The Square,
111 Broad Street, Birmingham,
West Midlands B15 1AS
0121 695 0000
paul.fairburn@chrysalis.com
www.thearrow.co.uk
*Rock. DAB; Freeview. Managing director:
Paul Fairburn; programme director: Alan
Caruther*

** only those stations with widespread
urban coverage*

Capital Disney
GCap Media, 30 Leicester Square,
London WC2H 7LA
020 7766 6000
will.chambers@
   capitalradiogroup.com
www.capitaldisney.co.uk
*Current pop aimed at eight- to 14-year-olds.
DAB. Head of sponsorship and
promotions: Laurette Holmes;
programme controller: Will Chambers*

Choice FM
GCap Media, 30 Leicester Square,
London WC2H 7LA
020 7766 6810
info@choicefm.com
www.choicefm.com
*Hip-hop and R&B. DAB; 107.1FM.
Managing director: Graham Bryce;
programme controller: Ivor Etienne
Studio: 08702 027000*

Classic FM
GCap Media, 7 Swallow Place,
London W1B 2AG
020 7343 9000
enquiries@classicfm.co.uk
www.classicfm.com
*Classical music. DAB; 99.9–102 FM.
Station manager: Darren Henley;
managing editor: Giles Pearman
Studio: 08700 702969*

Core
GCap Media, 30 Leicester Square,
London WC2H 7LA
020 7766 6000
fresh@corefreshhits.com
www.corefreshhits.com
*Pop, dance and R&B. DAB; Sky; cable;
internet. Programme contoller: Bern
Leckie; digital content manager: Nick
Piggott*

Gaydar Radio
Q Soft Consulting, 6th Floor,
2 Holly Road, Twickenham TW1 4EG
020 8744 1287
contact@gaydarradio.com
www.gaydarradio.com
*Pop, dance, diva-led house. DAB;
Sky; internet. Managing director:
Henry Badenhorst; programme director:
Jamie Crick*

Heart 106.2
Chrysalis Group, The Chrysalis
Building, 13 Bramley Road,
London W10 6SP
020 7468 1062
firstname.lastname@heart1062.co.uk
www.heart1062.co.uk
*70s, 80s and 90s. 106.2 FM. Programme
controller: Mark Browning; head of news:
Jonathan Richards; breakfast show:
Jamie Theakston and Harriet Scott*

Heat
Emap Performance Network,
Mappin House, 4 Winsley Street,
London W1W 8HF
020 7436 1515
www.heatradio.co.uk
*Adult contemporary. DAB; Freeview.
Development director: Shaun Gregory;
programme controller: Andy Roberts*

The Hits
Emap Performance Network,
Castle Quay, Castlefield,
Manchester M15 4PR
0161 288 5000
studio@thehitsradio.com
www.thehitsradio.com
*Contemporary music. DAB in Greater
London; Freeview; Sky. Station manager:
Phil Mackenzie; programme controller:
Anthony Gay*

Smooth FM
Guardian Media Group,
26–27 Castlereagh Street,
London W1H 5DL
020 7706 4100
studio@jazzfm.com
www.jazzfm.com
*Soul, jazz and R&B. DAB in central
Scotland, Greater London, south Wales
and Severn estuary; Freeview; 102.2FM in
West Midlands. Managing director: Roy
Bennett; programme director: Mark
Walker. Studio: 08444 158181*

Kerrang!
Emap Performance Network,
Kerrang! House, 20 Lionel Street,
Birmingham B3 1AQ
08450 531052
brendan.moffett@emap.com
http://digital.kerrangradio.co.uk
*Rock. Freeview; Sky; cable. Programme
director: Andrew Jefferies; managing
director: Adrian Serle. Studio: 08453
451022*

Kiss
Emap Performance Network,
Mappin House, 4 Winsley Street,
London W1W 8HF
020 7436 1515
feedback@kissonline.co.uk
www.kiss100.com
*Rhythmic. DAB; Freeview; Sky; 100 FM
in Greater London. Managing director:
Mark Story; programme director:
Simon Long. Studio: 020 7617 9100.
Studio: 08456 880908*

Capital Life
Capital Radio Group, 30 Leicester
Square, London WC2H 7LA
020 7766 6000
studio@listentolife.com
www.ukcapitallife.com
*Pop. DAB. Programme manager: Kevin
Palmer*

Magic
Emap Performance Network,
Mappin House, 4 Winsley Street,
London W1W 8HF
020 7975 8100
studio@magicradio.com
www.magic1054.co.uk
*Soft melodic. Freeview; Sky; cable.
Managing director: Andria Vidler;
programme director: Richard Park*

Mojo
Emap Performance Network,
Mappin House, 4 Winsley Street,
London W1W 8HF
020 7436 1515
studio@mojo4music.com
www.mojo4music.com
*Classic rock and soul. Freeview.
Chairman: Dee Ford; Programme director:
Andy Roberts. Studio: 020 7436 1054*

Oneword Radio
50 Lisson Street, London NW1 5DF
020 7453 1600
info@oneword.co.uk
www.oneword.co.uk
*Contemporary music. DAB; Freeview;
Sky; internet. Managing director: Simon
Blackmore*

Planet Rock
30 Leicester Square,
London WC2H 7LA
020 7766 6000
joinus@planetrock.com
www.planetrock.com
*Classic radio. DAB. Station director: Mark
Lee; Executive producer: Trevor White*

Premier Christian Radio
Premier Media Group,
22 Chapter Street, London SW1P 4NP
020 7316 1300
enquiries@premier.org.uk
www.premier.org.uk
*Contemporary Christian music. Freeview;
Sky; cable; 1305, 1332, 1413 AM. Managing
director: Peter Kerridge; programme
controller: Charmaine Noble-Mclean*

Q Radio
Emap Performance Network,
Mappin House, 4 Winsley Street,
London W1W 8HF
020 7436 1515
brendan.moffett@emap.com
www.q4music.com
*Contemporary music. Freeview; Sky;
cable. Programme director: Shaun Gregory*

Smash! Hits
Emap Performance Network,
Mappin House, 4 Winsley Street,
London W1W 8HF
020 7436 1515
brendan.moffett@emap.com
www.smashhits.net
*Chart hits. Freeview; Sky; cable.
Programme director: Anthony Gay*

TalkSport
The Wireless Group,
18 Hatfields, London SE1 8DJ
020 7959 7800
www.talksport.net
*Talk, sport and current affairs. Digital
One; 1107, 1053, 1089 AM. Managing
director: Michael Franklyn; programme
director: Bill Ridley. Studio: 08704
202020*

Virgin Radio
SMG, No 1 Golden Square,
London W1F 9DJ
020 7434 1215
reception@virginradio.co.uk
studio@virginradio.co.uk
www.virginradio.co.uk
*Rock. Digital One; Sky; 1197, 1215, 1233,
1242, 1260 AM. Head of production:
Mark Bingham; programme director:
Paul Jackson*

XFM
GCap Media, 30 Leicester Square,
London WC2H 7LA
020 7054 8000
www.xfm.co.uk
*Alternative music. DAB; Sky; cable;
internet; 104.9 FM. Managing director:
Nick Davidson; programme controller:
Andy Ashton. Studio: 08712 221049;
08707 301215*

Yarr Radio
Sunrise Radio, Sunrise Radio House,
Merrick Road, Southall,
Middlesex UB2 4AU
020 843 5313 CHK
info@yaarradio.com
www.yarrradio.com
*Asian music. DAB; Sky; internet. Station
manager: Ajmer Grewel; chief executive:
Avtar Lit. Studio: 020 8574 6262*

● News services

ITN Radio
200 Grays Inn Road,
London WC1X 8XZ
020 7430 4090
radio@itn.co.uk
www.itn.co.uk
*Managing director: John Perkins; editor:
Jon Godel. Newsdesk: 020 7430 4814*

Independent Radio News (IRN)
200 Grays Inn Road,
London WC1X 8XZ
020 7430 4090
irn@itn.co.uk
news@irn.co.uk
www.irn.co.uk
*Managing director: John Perkins; editor:
Jon Godel. Newsdesk: 020 7430 4814*

● Commercial local radio: England

LONDON

95.8 Capital FM
30 Leicester Square,
London WC2H 7LA
020 7766 6000
info@capitalradio.com
www.capitalfm.com
*Pop. Greater London. 95.8 FM. Owner:
GCap Media. Managing director: Carl
Lyons; news editor: Matthew Schofield;
breakfast show: Johnny Vaughan*

107.3 Time FM
2-6 Basildon Road, Abbey Road,
London SE2 OEW
020 8311 3112
www.timefm.com
*All-time favourites. South-east London.
106.8, 107.3 FM. Owner: London Media
Group. Station managing director: Mike
Huston; news editor: Alex Hornall;
breakfast show: Jonathan Miles*

Capital Gold (1548)
30 Leicester Square,
London WC2H 7LA
020 7054 8000
info@capitalradio.com
www.capitalgold.com
*Hits of the 60s, 70s and 80s. Greater
London. 1548 AM. Owner: GCap Media.
Programme director: Andy Turner; head
of news: Justin King; breakfast show:
David Jensen*

Choice 107.1 FM
30 Leicester Square,
London WC2H 7LA
020 7378 3969
info@choicefm.com
www.choicefm.com
*R&B. North London. 107.1 FM. Owner:
GCap Media. Managing director: Ivor
Etienne; news editor: Pam Joseph;
breakfast show: George Kay*

Club Asia
Asia House, 227-247 Gascoigne
Road, Barking, Essex IG11 7LN
020 8594 6662
info@clubasiaonline.com
www.clubasiaonline.com
*Young Asian hit music. Greater London.
972 AM. Independent. Managing director:
Ash Kavia; creative director: John Ogden;
breakfast show: Jas "The Man" and the
Breakfast Clan*

Easy Radio
Radio House, Merrick Road,
Southall, Middlesex UB2 4AU
020 8843 5341
info@easy1035.com
www.easy1035.com
*Easy listening. Greater London. 1035 AM.
Owner: Easy Radio. Programme controller:
Paul Owens; breakfast show: Ron Brown*

Heart 106.2
The Chrysalis Building,
Bramley Road, London W10 6SP
020 7468 1062
www.heart1062.co.uk
*Adult contemporary. Greater London.
106.2 FM. Owner: Chrysalis Radio.
Programme controller: Mark Browning;
head of news: Jonathan Richards;
breakfast show: Jamie Theakston and
Harriet Scott*

Kiss 100
Mappin House, 4 Winsley Street,
London W1W 8HF
020 7975 8100
firstname.lastname@kiss100.com
www.kiss100.com
*Rhythmic. Greater London. 100 FM.
Managing director: Mark Story;
programme director: Simon Long;
breakfast show: James Merritt*

LBC 97.3 FM
The Chrysalis Building,
Bramley Road, London W10 6SP
020 7314 7300
firstname.lastname@lbc.co.uk
www.lbc.co.uk
*Talk radio. Greater London. 97.3 FM.
Owner: Chrysalis. Managing director:
David Lloyd; programme controller: Scott
Solder; head of news: Jonathan Richards;
breakfast show: Nick Ferrari*

LBC News 1152 AM
The Chrysalis Building,
Bramley Road, London W10 6SP
020 7314 7300
newsroom@lbc.co.uk
www.lbc.co.uk
*News. Greater London. 1152 AM. Owner:
Chrysalis. Editorial director: Jonathan
Richards*

London Greek Radio
437 High Road, London N12 OAP
020 8349 6950
sales@lgr.co.uk
www.lgr.co.uk
*Greek music. North London. 103.3 FM.
Independent. Programme controller and
head of news: G Gregoriou; breakfast
show: Soula Viola Ri*

London Turkish Radio LTR
185B High Road, Wood Green,
London N22 6BA
020 8881 0600
info@londontv.org
www.londonturkishradio.org
*Turkish and English music. North
London. 1584 AM. Independent.
Programme controller: Umit Dandul;
managing director: Erkan Pastirmacioglu;
breakfast show: Fatos Sarman*

Magic 105.4 FM
Mappin House, 4 Winsley Street,
London W1W 8HF
020 7955 1054
firstname.lastname@emap.com
www.magic1054.co.uk
*Soft melodic. Freeview; Sky; cable.
Managing director: Andria Vidler;
programme director: Richard Park;
breakfast show: Gary Vincent*

Premier Christian Radio
22 Chapter Street, London SW1P 4NP
020 7316 1300
premier@premier.org.uk
www.premier.org.uk
Contemporary Christian music. Freeview;
Sky; cable; 1305, 1332, 1413 AM. Managing
director: Peter Kerridge; programme
controller: Charmaine Noble-Mclean;

Smooth FM 102.2
26–27 Castlereagh Street,
London W1H 5DL
020 7706 4100
jazzinfo@jazzfm.com
www.jazzfm.com
Soul, jazz and R&B. DAB in central
Scotland, Greater London, south Wales
and Severn estuary; Freeview; 102.2 FM
in West Midlands. Managing director:
Roy Bennett; programme director: Mark
Walker; breakfast show: David Prever

Spectrum Radio
4 Ingate Place, Battersea,
London SW8 3NS
020 7627 4433
name@spectrumradio.net
www.spectrumradio.net
Multi-ethnic. Greater London. 558 AM.
Independent. General manager: Paul
Hogan; managing director: Toby Aldrich

Sunrise Radio
Sunrise House, Merrick Road,
Southall, Middlesex UB2 4AU
020 8574 6666
Reception@sunriseradio.com
www.sunriseradio.com
Asian music. Greater London. 1458 AM.
Independent. Chief executive: Avtar Lit;
MD: Tony Lit; news editor: David
Landau; breakfast show: Tony Patti

Virgin 105.8
1 Golden Square, London W1F 9DJ
020 7434 1215
reception@virginradio.co.uk
www.virginradio.co.uk
Rock. Greater London. 105.8 FM. Owner:
SMG. Programme director: Paul Jackson;
head of news: Andrew Bailey; breakfast
show: Christian O'Connell

Xfm
30 Leicester Square,
London WC2H 7LA
020 7054 8000
info@xfm.co.uk
www.xfm.co.uk
Alternative music. Greater London.
104.9 FM. Owner: GCap Media. Managing
director: Nick Davidson; programme
controller: Andy Ashton; news centre:
Chris Smith

SOUTH-EAST

2-Ten FM
PO Box 2020, Calcot, Reading,
Berkshire RG31 7FG
0118 945 4400
tim.parker@creation.com
www.musicradio.com
All types of music. Reading, Basingstoke,
Newbury and Andover. 103.4 FM;
97 FM; 102.9 FM. Owner: GCap Media.
Programme controller: Tim Parker; head
of news: Susie Southgate; breakfast show:
Foxy and Tom

96.4 The Eagle
Dolphin House, North Street,
Guildford GU1 4AA
01483 300964
onair@964eagle.co.uk
www.964eagle.co.uk
Adult contemporary. Guildford. 96.4 FM,
1566AM. Owner: UKRD Group. Managing
director: Valeria Handley; programme
director: Peter Gordon; head of news: Lucy
Skitmore; breakfast show: Peter Gordon

103.2 Power FM
Radio House,
Whittle Avenue, Segensworth,
West Fareham PO15 5SH
01489 589911
info@powerfm.co.uk
www.powerfm.com
20 years to up-to-date pop. South
Hampshire. 103.2 FM. Owner: GCap
Media. Programme director: John
O'Hara; head of news: Alison Law;
breakfast show: Dan Morrissey

107.4 The Quay
Flagship Studios PO Box 1074,
Portsmouth PO2 8YG
023 9236 4141
mail@quayradio.com
www.quayradio.com
Pop. Portsmouth. 107.4 FM. Owner:
Radio Investments. Programme controller
and breakfast show: Sam Matterface

107.5 Sovereign Radio
14 St Mary's Walk, Hailsham,
East Sussex BN27 1AF
01323 442700
info@1075sovereignradio.co.uk
www.1075sovereignradio.co.uk
Music. Eastbourne. 107.5 FM. Owner:
Radio Investments. Brand manager: Nigel
Ansell; commercial manager: Karen
Dyball; breakfast show: Ian Dore

107.6 Kestrel FM
Paddington House, Festival Place,
Basingstoke RG21 7LJ
01256 694000
studio@kestrelfm.com
www.kestrelfm.com
70s, 80s, 90s and today. Basingstoke.
107.6 FM. Owner: Milestone Group.
Managing director: Paul Allen;
programme manager: Pat Simmons; head
of news: Emily Lang-Stewart; breakfast
show: Pat Sissons

107.8 Arrow FM
Priory Meadow Centre, Hastings,
East Sussex TN34 1PJ
01424 461177
info@arrowfm.co.uk
www.arrowfm.co.uk
Adult contemporary. Hastings. 107.8 FM.
Owner: Radio Investments. Programme
controller: Mike Buxton; head of news:
Vicky Jones; breakfast show: Andy Knight

107.8 Radio Jackie
The Old Post Office 110–112,
Tolworth Broadway, Surbiton,
Surrey KT6 7JD
020 8288 1300
info@radiojackie.com
www.radiojackie.com
Adult contemporary. Kingston-upon-
Thames. 107.8 FM. Independent.
Managing director: Peter Stremes;
programme controller: Dave Owen; head
of news: Rod Bradbury; breakfast show:
Neil Long

Bright 106.4
The Market Place Shopping Centre,
Burgess Hill, West Sussex RH15 9NP
01444 248127
reception@bright1064.com
www.bright1064.com
70s, 80s, 90s and latest. Burgess Hill and
Haywards Heath. 106.4 FM. Independent.
Managing director: Allan Moulds; sales
director: Mak Norman; programme
director: Mark Chapple; head of news:
Alan Lewis; breakfast show: Andrew
Dancey

Capital Gold (1170 and 1557)
Radio House, Whittle Avenue,
Segensworth West, Farnham,
Hampshire PO15 5SH
01489 589911
info@capitalgold.com
www.capitalgold.com
Hits of the 60s, 70s and 80s. South
Hampshire. 1557 AM; 1170 AM. Owner:
GCap Media. Programme director: Andy
Turner; head of news: Alison Law;
breakfast show: David Jensen

Capital Gold (1242 and 603)
Radio House, John Wilson Business
Park, Whitstable, Kent CT5 3QX
01227 772004
info@capitalgold.co.uk
www.capitalgold.com
Hits of the 60s, 70s and 80s. Maidstone,
Medway and East Kent. 603 AM; 1242 AM.
Owner: GCap Media. Programme director:
Andy Turner; head of news: Clare Martin;
breakfast show: David Jensen

Capital Gold (1323 and 945)
Radio House, PO Box 2000,
Brighton BN41 2SS
020 7766 6000
info@capitalgold.co.uk
www.capitalgold.com
Hits of the 60s, 70s and 80s. Maidstone,
Medway and East Kent. 603 AM; 1242 AM.
Owner: GCap Media. Programme director:
Andy Turner; head of news: Clare Martin;
breakfast show: David Jensen

Classic Gold 1431 and 1485

The Chase, Calcot, Reading RG31 7RB
0118 945 4400
enquiries@classicgolddigital.com
www.classicgolddigital.com
*80s, 90s and modern. Reading,
Basingstoke and Andover. 1431 AM;
1485 AM. Owner: Classic Gold Digital.
Network head of programmes: Bill
Overton and Paul Baker; head of news:
Suzie Southgate*

Classic Gold (1521)

The Stanley Centre, Kelvin Way,
Crawley, West Sussex RH10 9SE
01293 519161
studio@musicradio.com
www.musicradio.co.uk
*60s and 70s. Reigate and Crawley. 1521 AM.
Owner: Classic Gold Digital. Sales team
leader: Amanda Masters; network head
of programmes: Bill Overton and Paul
Baker; head of news: Gareth Davies;
breakfast show: Tony Blackburn*

County Sound Radio 1566 AM

Dolphin House North Street,
Guildford GU1 4AA
01483 300964
onair@countysound.co.uk
www.ukrd.com
*Adult contemporary. Guildford. 1566 AM.
Owner: UKRD Group. Managing director:
Valerie Handley; programme director:
Peter Gordon; head of news: Lucy
Skitmore; breakfast show: Dave Johns*

CTR 105.6 FM

6-8 Mill Street, Maidstone ME15 6XH
01622 662500
enq@ctrfm.com
www.ctrfm.com
*Adult contemporary. Maidstone. 105.6 FM.
Independent. Managing director: John
Maxfield; head of news: Helen Fisher;
breakfast show: Ant Payne*

Delta FM

Tindle House, High Street, Bordon,
Hants GU35 0AY
01420 473473
studio@deltaradio.co.uk
www.deltaradio.co.uk
*Yesterday and today. Alton, Hampshire.
101.6 FM; 102 FM; 97.1 FM; 101.8 FM.
Owner: UKRD Group and Tindle
Newspapers. Managing director: David
Way; sales manager: Andy Wise; head of
news: James Sloane; breakfast show:
David Way*

FM 103 Horizon

14 Vincent Avenue Crownhill,
Milton Keynes MK8 0AB
01908 269111
reception@horizon.musicradio.com
www.musicradio.com
*80s, 90s and today. Milton Keynes.
103.3 FM. Owner: GCap Media.
Programme controller: Trevor Marshall;
breakfast show: Gareth James*

Invicta FM

Radio House, John Wilson Business
Park, Whitstable, Kent CT5 3QX
01227 772004
info@invictaradio.co.uk
www.invictafm.com
*Pop. Maidstone, Medway and East Kent.
95.9 FM; 102.8 FM; 96.1 FM; 97 FM;
103.1 FM. Owner: GCap Media. Programme
controller: Max Hailey; head of news:
Nicola Everitt; breakfast show: The
Morning Zoo*

Isle of Wight Radio

Dodnor Park, Newport,
Isle of Wight PO30 5XE
01983 822557
admin@iwradio.co.uk
www.iwradio.co.uk
*Adult contemporary and pop. Isle of
Wight. 102 FM; 107 FM. Owner: Radio
Investments. Programme director:
Tom Stroud; head of news: Lucy Morgan;
breakfast show: Andy Shier*

Juice 107.2

170 North Street, Brighton BN1 1EA
01273 386107
info@juicebrighton.com
www.juicebrighton.com
*Commercial dance. Brighton. 107.2 FM.
Owner: Brighton & Hove Ltd. Managing
director: Matthew Bashford; programme
controller: Sam Wulker; head of news:
Graham Levitt; breakfast show: Terry
Garoghan*

Kick FM

The Studios, 42 Bone Lane,
Newbury, Berkshire RG14 5SD
01635 841600
mail@kickfm.com
www.kickfm.com
*Adult contemporary. Newbury. 105.6 FM;
107.4 FM. Owner: Milestone Group.
Managing director: Sur Reynolds; head of
news: Sally Beadle; programme controller:
James O'Neill; breakfast show: Chris Rose
and Charlotte Butt*

Kmfm for Canterbury

9 St George's Place, Canterbury,
Kent CT1 1UU
01227 475950
reception@kmfm.co.uk
www.kmfm.co.uk
*Adult contemporary. Canterbury. 106 FM.
Owner: KM Radio. Group programme
controller: Spencer Cork; head of news:
Anthony Masters; breakfast show:
Russ Lowe*

Kmfm for Folkestone and Dover

93-95 Sandgate Road,
Folkestone, Kent CT20 2BQ
01303 220303
Scork@kmfm.co.uk
www.kmfm.co.uk
*60s, 70s, 80s and 90s. Dover and
Folkestone. 106.8 FM; 96.4 FM. Owner:
KM Radio. Group programme controller:
Spencer Cork; head of sales: Suzanne
Fitzsimons; breakfast show: Spencer Cork*

Kmfm for Medway

Medway House, Ginsbury Close,
Sir Thomas Longley Road,
Strood ME2 4DU
pcarter@kmfm.co.uk
www.kmfm.co.uk
*Adult contemporary. Medway Towns.
100.4 FM; 107.9 FM. Owner: KM Radio.
Group programme controller: Steve
Fountain; breakfast show: Richard Walters*

Kmfm for Thanet

181-183 Northdown Road,
Cliftonville, Kent CT9 2PA
01843 220222
initialsurname@kmgroup.co.uk
www.kmfm.co.uk
*Classic hits from 70s and current. Thanet.
107.2 FM. Owner: KM Radio. Group
programme controller: Steve Fountain;
head of news: Julia Walsh; breakfast
show: Johnny Lewis*

Kmfm for West Kent

1 East Street, Tonbridge,
Kent TN9 1AR
01732 369200
tunbridgestudio@kmfm.co.uk
www.kmfm.co.uk
*Adult contemporary. Tunbridge Wells
and Sevenoaks. 96.2 FM; 101.6 FM.
Owner: KM Radio. Group programme
controller: Steve Fountain; head of news:
Julia Walsh; breakfast show: James Dean*

Mercury FM

The Stanley Centre, Kelvin Way,
Crawley, West Sussex RH10 9SE
01293 519161
studio@musicradio.com
www.musicradio.com
*60s and 70s. Reigate and Crawley.
97.5 FM; 102.7 FM. Owner: GCap Media.
Programme controller: Dan Jennings;
head of news: Gareth Davies; breakfast
show: Dan Jennings*

Mix 96

Friars Square Studios, 11 Bourbon
Street, Aylesbury HP20 2PZ
01296 399396
info@mix96.co.uk
www.mix96.co.uk
*70 to present day. Aylesbury. 96.2 FM.
Owner: Radio Investments. Station
manager: Rachael Faulkner; programme
controller: James O'Neil; head of news:
Penny Harper; breakfast show: Ian
Sandford*

Mix 107 FM

PO Box 1107, High Wycombe,
Buckinghamshire HP13 6EE
01494 446611
sales@mix107.co.uk
www.mix107.co.uk
*Adult contemporary. High Wycombe.
107.4 FM. Owner: Radio Investments.
Programme director: Andy Muir; head
of news: Hilary Cogan; breakfast show:
Big Fun Breakfast with Rory and Steve*

Ocean FM
Radio House,
Whittle Avenue, Segensworth,
West Fareham PO15 5SH
01489 589911
info@oceanfm.co.uk
www.oceanfm.com
*70s, 80s and 90s. South Hampshire.
96.7 FM; 97.5 FM. Owner: GCap Media.
Programme controller: Stuart Ellis; head
of news: Alison Law; breakfast show:
Richard Williams*

Reading 107 FM
Radio House, Madejski Stadium,
Reading, Berkshire RG2 0FN
0118 986 2555
firstname@reading107fm.com
www.reading107fm.com
*Beatles to Bangles. Reading. 107 FM.
Independent. Managing director: Ian
Smith; programme controller: Robert
Kenny; acting marketing director: Andy
Carter; breakfast show: Simon Ross*

Southern FM
Radio House, PO Box 2000,
Brighton BN41 2SS
01273 430111
news@southernfm.co.uk
www.southernfm.com
*Pop. Brighton, Eastbourne and Hastings.
103.5 FM; 96.9 FM; 102.4 FM; 102 FM.
Owner: GCap Media. Sales director:
Lorraine Wynn; programme controller:
Tony Aldridge; news editor: Laurence
King; breakfast show: Danny & Nicky
in the Morning*

Spirit FM
9-10 Dukes Court, Bognor Road,
Chichester PO19 8FX
01243 773600
info@spiritfm.net
www.spiritfm.net
*Easy listening. Chichester, Bognor Regis,
Littlehampton. 102.3 FM; 96.6 FM, 106.6
FM. Independent. Managing director:
Ann Dyson; programme controller: Ed
Bretton; head of news: Caroline Kingsmill;
breakfast show: Paul Williams*

Splash FM
Guildbourne Centre, Worthing,
West Sussex BN11 1LZ
01903 233005
mail@splashfm.com
www.splashfm.com
*60s, 70s, 80s, 90s and today. Worthing.
107.7 FM. Independent. Managing
director: Roy Stannard; programme
controller: Simon Osborne; news editor:
Kerry Worman; breakfast show: Dave Hunt*

Star 106.6
The Observatory Shopping Centre,
Slough SL1 1LH
01753 551066
onair@star1066.co.uk
www.star1066.co.uk
*Adult contemporary. Slough, Maidenhead,
Windsor. 106.6 FM. Owner: UKRD Group.
Programme controller: Mark Watson;
head of news: Angie Walker; breakfast
show: Mark and Sarah*

Time 107.5
Lambourne House, 7 Western Road,
Romford, Essex RM1 3LD
01708 731643
info@timefm.com
www.timefm.com
*Soul. Romford, Barking and Dagenham.
107.5 FM. Owner: Sunrise Radio.
Managing director: Neil Romain;
programme director: Mark Dover;
breakfast show: Mike Porter*

Wave 105 FM
5 Manor Court, Barnes Wallis Road,
Segensworth East, Fareham,
Hampshire PO15 5TH
01489 481057
martin.ball@wave105.com
www.wave105.com
*70s, 80s and 90s hits. Solent. 105.2 FM;
105.8 FM. Owner: ScottishRadio Holdings.
Managing director: Martin Ball;
programme controller: Dave Shearer;
head of news: Jason Beck; breakfast
show: Steve Power*

Win 107.2
PO Box 107,
The Brooks Shopping Centre,
Winchester, Hampshire SO23 8FT
01962 841071
jo@winfm.co.uk
www.winfm.co.uk
*Adult contemporary. Winchester. 107.2 FM.
Owner: Radio Investments. Station
manager: Ceri Hurford-Jones; head of
news:Dina Burgess; breakfast show: Ben
Shoveller*

SOUTH-WEST

2CR FM
5-7 Southcote Road,
Bournemouth, Dorset BH1 3LR
01202 234900
newsbournemouth@creation.com
www.musicradio.com
*80 and 90s and chart music.
Bournemouth and Hampshire. 102.3 FM.
Owner: GCap Media. Programme
controller: Graham Mack; sales director:
Jane Suttie; breakfast show: Chris Wright*

97 FM Plymouth Sound
Earl's Acre, Plymouth PL3 4HX
01752 275600
mail@plymouthsound.musicradio.com
www.musicradio.com
*80s, 90s and today. Plymouth. 97 FM;
96.6 FM. Owner: GCap Media. Programme
controller: Dave Harbour; head of news:
Darryl Jenner; breakfast show: Morning
Crew*

97.4 Vale FM
Longmead Studios, Shaftesbury,
Dorset SP7 8QQ
01747 855711
studio@valefm.co.uk
www.valefm.co.uk
*Adult contemporary. Shaftesbury. 97.4 FM;
96.6 FM. Owner: Radio Investments.
Programme controller: Stewart Smith;
head of news: Kevin Gover; breakfast
show: Cameron Smith*

104.7 Island FM
12 Westerbrook, St Sampsons,
Guernsey GY2 4QQ
01481 242000
firstname@islandfm.guernsey.net
www.islandfm.guernsey.net
*Chart music. Rock show in evenings.
Guernsey. 104.7 FM; 93.7 FM. Owner:
Tindle Radio. Programme controller:
Gary Burgess; head of news: Katie Collins;
breakfast show: James Bentley*

107.5 3TR FM
Riverside Studios, Boreham Mill,
Bishopstow, Warminster BA12 9HQ
01985 211111
admin@3trfm.com
www.3trfm.com
*Classics. Warminster. 107.5 FM. Owner:
Radio Investments. Managing director:
John Baker; sales manager: Will
Brougham; head of news: Tessa Bickers;
breakfast show: Jono & Tess*

Bath FM
Station House, Ashley Avenue,
Lower Weston, Bath BA1 3DS
01225 471571
news@bath.fm
www.bath.fm
*Adult contemporary. Bath. 107.9 FM.
Independent. Managing director: Jo
Woods; programme controller and head
of news: Steve Collins; breakfast show:
Karl & Poonam*

BCRfm
Royal Clarence House,
York Buildings High Street,
Bridgwater TA6 3AT
01278 727701
studio@bcrfm.co.uk
www.bcrfm.co.uk
*Music from last four decades. Bridgwater.
107.4 FM. Independent. Chairman: Paul
Andrews; programme controller and
breakfast show: David Englefield*

Channel 103 FM
6 Tunnell Street, St Helier,
Jersey JE2 4LU
01534 888103
firstname@channel103.com
www.channel103.com
*Broad mix of pop and rock. Jersey.
103.7 FM. Owner: Tindle Radio.
Managing director: Linda Burnham;
programme controller: Gary Burgess;
head of news: Christina Ghidona;
breakfast show: Peter Mac*

Classic Gold 666/954
Hawthorn House,
Exeter Business Park, Exeter EX1 3QS
01392 444444
*Classic Hits. Exeter, Torbay. 954 AM;
Owner: Classic Gold Digital. Head of
programmes: Paul Baker; head of news:
Michelle Horsley; breakfast show: Tony
Blackburn*

Classic Gold 774

Bridge Studios, Eastgate Centre, Gloucester GL1 1SS
01452 572400
www.classicgolddigital.com
Various sounds. Gloucester, Cheltenham. 774 AM. Owner: Classic Gold Digital. Head of programmes: Paul Baker; head of news: Vicky Breakwell; breakfast show: Tony Blackburn

Classic Gold 828

5 Southcote Road, Bournemouth, Dorset BH1 3LR
01202 234900
newsbournemouth@creation.com
www.classicgolddigital.com
Popular music. Bournemouth. 828 AM. Owner: Classic Gold Digital. Head of programmes: Paul Baker; breakfast show: Tony Blackburn

Classic Gold 936/1161 AM

1st Floor, Chiseldon House Stonehill Green Westlea, Swindon, Wiltshire SN5 7HB
01793 663000
reception@musicradio.com
www.musicradio.com
Popular music. Swindon. 936 AM; 1161 AM. Owner: Classic Gold Digital. Managing director: John Baish; head of programming: Bill Overton; breakfast show: Tony Blackburn

Classic Gold 1152 AM

Earl's Acre, Plymouth PL3 4HX
01752 275600
www.classicgolddigital.com
70s, 80s and 90s. Plymouth. 1152 AM. Owner: Classic Gold Digital. Head of programmes: Paul Baker; head of news: Daryl Jenner; breakfast show: Tony Blackburn

Classic Gold 1260

One Passage Street, Bristol BS99 7SN
0117 984 3200
admin@classicgolddigital.com
www.classicgolddigital.com
Chart Music. Bristol and Bath. 1260 AM. Owner: Classic Gold Digital. Head of programmes: Paul Baker; head of news: Cormac Macmahon; breakfast show: Tony Blackburn

Fire 107.6FM

Quadrant Studios, Old Christchurch Road, Bournemouth BH1 2AD
01202 318100
firstname@fire1076.com
www.fire1076.com
Rhythmic and contemporary. Bournemouth and Poole. 107.6 FM. Owner: Radio Investments. Station manager: Sarah Val; head of news: Justin Gladdis; breakfast show: Northern and Gemma

FOX FM

Brush House, Pony Road, Oxford OX4 2XR
01865 871000
reception@foxfm.co.uk
www.foxfm.co.uk
Adult contemporary. Oxford and Banbury. 102.6 FM; 97.4 FM. Owner: Capital Radio. Programme controller: Chris Baughen; head of news: Huw James; breakfast show: Debbie & Adam

Gemini FM

Hawthorn House, Exeter Business Park, Exeter EX1 3QS
01392 444444
gemini@geminifm.musicradio.com
www.musicradio.com
Top 40. Exeter, Torbay. 97 FM; 103 FM; 96.4 FM. Owner: GWR Group. Content Director: Dirk Anthony; head of news: Michelle Horsley; breakfast show: Matt & Charlie

GWR FM and Classic Gold Digital

PO Box 2000, One Passage Street, Bristol BS99 7SN
0117 984 3200
reception@musicradio.com
www.musicradio.com
70s, 80s and 90s and today. Swindon and west Wiltshire. 102.2 FM; 96.5 FM; 97.2 FM. Owner: GCap Media. Programme controller: Paul Andrew; head of news: Vicky Breakwell; breakfast show: Join Paulina and Russ

GWR FM (Bath)

PO Box 2000, One Passage Street, Bristol BS99 7SN
0117 984 3200
reception@gwrfm.musicradio.com
www.musicradio.com
Chart music. Bristol and Bath. 103 FM. Owner: GCap Media. Content director: Dirk Anthony; programme controller: Paul Andrew; head of news: Vickie Brakewell; breakfast show: Join Paulina and Russ

GWR FM (Bristol)

PO Box 2000, One Passage Street, Bristol BS99 7SN
0117 984 3200
reception@gwrfm.musicradio.com
www.musicradio.com
Chart music. Bristol and Bath. 103 FM; 96.3 FM. Owner: GCap Media. Managing director: Dirk Anthony; programme controller: Paul Andrew; head of news: Vickie Brakewell; breakfast show: Tony and Michaela

Ivel FM

The Studios, Middle Street, Yeovil, Somerset BA20 1DJ
reception: 01935 848488
studio: 08712 777105
all@ivelfm.co.uk
www.ivelfm.com
60s, 70s, 80s to present day. Yeovil. 105.6 FM, 106.6 FM. Owner: Local Radio Company. Programme controller: Steve Carpenter; heads of news: Fiona Biggs and Fiona Honan; breakfast show: Steve Carpenter

Lantern FM

2b Lauder Lane, Roundswell Business Park, Barnstaple EX31 3TA
01271 342342
paul.hopper@gcapmedia.com
www.musicradio.com
Late 90s to present day. Barnstaple. 97.3 FM; 96.2 FM. Owner: GCap Media. Sales director: Jim Trevelyan; programme controller: Paul Hopper; head of news: Tim Pryor; breakfast show: Hopps and Chapple

Orchard FM

Haygrove House, Taunton, Somerset TA3 7BT
01823 338448
orchardfm@musicradio.com
www.musicradio.com
Top 40. Yeovil and Taunton. 102.6 FM; 97.1 FM; 96.5 FM. Owner: GCap Media. Programme controller: Jon White; journalists: Nicola Maxey and Darren Bevan; breakfast show: Ian and Laura

Passion 107.9

270 Woodstock Road, Oxford OX2 7NW
01865 315980
info@passion1079.com
www.passion1079.com
Dance and pop. Oxford. 107.9 FM. Owner: Absolute Radio. Programme controller and station manager: Ian Walker; breakfast show: Darren Lee

Pirate FM

Carn Brea Studios, Wilson Way, Redruth, Cornwall TR15 3XX
01209 314400
enquiries@piratefm.co.uk
www.piratefm.co.uk
Various pop. Cornwall and west Devon. 102.2 FM; 102.8 FM. Owner: UKRD Group. Managing director: Beverley Warne; programme director: Bob McCreadie; head of news: Tristan Hunkin; breakfast show: Bob McCreadie

Quay West Radio

The Harbour Studios, The Esplanade, Watchet, Somerset TA23 0AJ
01984 634900
studio@quaywest.fm.net
Adult contemporary. West Somerset. 102.4 FM. Independent. Programme director: David Mortimer; head of news: Spencer Bishop; breakfast show: David Mortimer

Severn Sound

Bridge Studios, Eastgate Centre, Gloucester GL1 1SS
01452 572400
www.musicradio.com
Various sounds. Gloucester and Cheltenham. 103 FM; 102.4 FM. Owner: GCap Media. Programme controller: Marcus Langreiter; sales manager: Lorraine Milkins; breakfast show: Gav and Vicky

South Hams Radio
Unit 1G, South Hams Business Park,
Churchstow, Kingsbridge,
Devon TQ7 3QH
01548 854595
reception@southhamsradio.com
www.southhamsradio.com
*Adult contemporary. South Hams.
101.9 FM; 100.8 FM; 100.5 FM; 101.2 FM.
Owner: GCap Media. Station manager:
David Fitzgerald; head of news: Steph
Wright; breakfast show: Graham Russell*

Spire FM
City Hall Studios, Malthouse Lane,
Salisbury, Wiltshire SP2 7QQ
01722 416644
info@spirefm.co.uk
www.spirefm.co.uk
*Chart hits. Salisbury. 102 FM. Owner:
Local Radio Company. Managing director:
Ceri Hurford-Jones; programme
controller: Stuart McGinley; breakfast
show: Chris Ewington*

Star 107
Unit 3 Brunel Mall, London Road,
Stroud, Gloucester GL5 2BP
01453 767369
studio@star1079.co.uk
www.star1079.co.uk
*70s, 80s and 90s and greatest hits. Stroud.
107.3 FM; 107.9 FM. Owner: UKRD Group.
Head of sales: Junie Lewis; programme
manager: Brody Swain; head of news:
Simon Hancock; breakfast show: Star
breakfast*

Star 107.2
Bristol Evening Post Building,
Temple Way, Bristol BS99 7HD
0117 910 6600
www.starbristol.co.uk
*Adult contemporary and soul. Bristol.
107.2 FM. Owner: UKRD Group. Station
manager: Sue Brooks; head of news:
Stephanie Mousey; breakfast show: JP*

Star 107.5
Cheltenham Film Studios, 1st Floor,
West Suite Arle Court, Hatherley
Lane, Cheltenham GL51 6PN
01242 699555
studio@star1075.co.uk
www.star1075.co.uk
*70s, 80s and 90s and greatest hits. Stroud.
107.3 FM; 107.9 FM. Owner: UKRD Group.
Head of sales: Junie Lewis; programme
manager: Brody Swain; head of news:
Simon Hancock; breakfast show: Brody
Swain*

Star 107.7 FM
11 Beaconsfield Road,
Weston Super Mare BS23 1YE
01934 624455
name@star1077.co.uk
www.star1077.co.uk
*70s, 80s and 90s popular music. Weston
Super Mare. 107.7 FM. Owner: UKRD
Group. Programme controller: Ian
Downs; head of news: Laura Harrison;
breakfast show: Ian Downs*

Vibe 101
26 Baldwin Street, Bristol BS1 1SE
0117 901 0101
info@vibe101.co.uk
www.vibe101.co.uk
*Dance and R&B. South Wales and Severn
estuary. 97.2 FM; 101 FM. Owner: Scottish
Radio Holdings. Managing director:
Beverley Cleall-Harding; programme
controller: Trevor James; head of news:
Lucy Perrett; breakfast show: Darren Daley*

Wessex FM
Radio House, Trinity Street,
Dorchester DT1 1DJ
01305 250333
admin@wessexfm.com
www.wessexfm.com
*Hits of 60s, 70s, 80s. Weymouth and
Dorchester. 97.2 FM; 96 FM. Owner: Local
Radio Company. Station manager: Steve
Bulley; head of news: Maria Greenwood;
breakfast show: Jason Herbert*

EAST ENGLAND

96.9 Chiltern FM
5, Abbey Court, Fraser Road,
Priory Business Park, Bedford,
Bedfordshire MK44 3WH
01234 272400
firstname.surname@musicradio.com
www.musicradio.com
*80s, 90s to today. Bedford. 96.9 FM.
Owner: GCap Media. Sales manager:
Sharon Rush; programme controller:
Stuart Davies; head of news: Mark
Grinnell; breakfast show: Andy Gelder*

97.6 Chiltern FM
Chiltern Road, Dunstable,
Bedfordshire LU6 1HQ
01582 676200
firstname.surname@musicradio.co.uk
www.musicradio.com
*Easy listening. Hertfordshire,
Bedfordshire, Buckinghamshire.
97.6 FM. Owner: GCap Media. Programme
controller: Stuart Davies; head of news:
Mark Grinnell; breakfast show: Gareth
Wesley and Karen Carpenter*

102.7 Hereward FM
PO Box 225 Queensgate Centre,
Peterborough PE1 1XJ
01733 460460
firstname.surname@gcapmedia.com
www.musicradio.com
*Adult contemporary. Greater
Peterborough. 102.7 FM. Owner: GCap
Media. Programme controller: Tom
Haynes; head of news: Sarah Spence;
breakfast show: Matt and Sarah*

103.4 The Beach
PO Box 103.4, Lowestoft,
Suffolk NR32 2TL
0845 345 1035
103.4@thebeach.co.uk
www.thebeach.co.uk
*Chart past and present. Great Yarmouth
and Lowestoft. 103.4 FM. Owner: Tindle
Radio. Managing director: David Blake;
news editor: John Boltitude; breakfast
show: Paul Carter*

Broadland 102
St George's Plain, 47–49 Colgate,
Norwich NR3 1DB
01603 630621
firstname.surname@gcapmedia.com
www.musicradio.com
*80s, 90s and today. Norfolk and north
Suffolk. 102.4 FM. Owner: GCap Media.
Programme controller: Steve Martin;
head of news: Harry Mitchell; breakfast
show: Rob and Chrissie*

Classic Gold 792/828
Chiltern Road, Dunstable,
Beds LU6 1HQ
01582 676200
firstname.surname@
    classicgolddigital.com
www.classicgolddigital.com
*60s to modern. Luton, Bedford. 792 AM;
828 AM. Owner: Opus Group/Classic Gold
Digital. Programme controller: John
Baish; head of news: Mark Grinnell;
breakfast show: Tony Blackburn and
Laura Pittson*

Classic Gold 1332 AM
PO Box 225, Queensgate Centre,
Peterborough PE1 1XJ
01733 460460
firstname.surname@
    classicgolddigital.com
www.classicgolddigital.com
*Classic hits. Peterborough. 1332 AM.
Owner: Opus Group/Classic Gold Digital.
Programme controller: Mickey Gavin;
head of news: Sarah Spence; breakfast
show: Tony Blackburn*

Classic Gold Amber
St George's Plain,
47–49 Colgate, Norwich NR3 1DB
01603 630621
firstname.surname@
    classicgolddigital.com
www.classicgolddigital.com
*80s, 90s and today. Norwich. 1152 AM.
Owner: GCap Media/Classic Gold Digital.
Programme controller: Paul Baker; sales
centre manager: Rod Walker; breakfast
show: Tony Blackburn*

Classic Gold Amber 1152
Alpha Business Park, 6–12 White
House Road, Ipswich IP1 5LT
01473 461000
firstname.surname@
    classicgolddigital.com
www.classicgolddigital.com
*70s and 80s. Ipswich and Bury St
Edmunds. 1251 AM; 1170 AM. Owner:
Classic Gold Digital. Programme
controller: Steve Springett; breakfast
show: Tony Blackburn*

Classic Gold Breeze
Radio House, 31 Glebe Road,
Stanford, Essex CN1 1QG
01245 524500
firstname.surname@
    classicgolddigital.com
www.classicgolddigital.com
*Classic 60s, 70s, 80s. Southend and
Chelmsford. 1359 AM; 1431 AM. Owner:
Opus Group/Classic Gold Digital.
Programme controller: Paul Baker;
breakfast show: Tony Blackburn*

Dream 100 FM
Northgate House, St Peter's Street,
Colchester, Essex CO1 1HT
01206 764466
info@dream100.com
www.dream100.com
70s to today. North Essex and south
Suffolk. 100.2 FM. Owner: Tindle Radio.
Managing director: Jamie Brodie;
programme controller: David Rees; head
of news: Scott Wilson; breakfast show:
Chris Sturgess

Dream 107.7
Cater House, High Street,
Chelmsford CM1 1AL
01245 259400
firstname.surname@dream107.com
www.dream107.com
Adult contemporary. Chelmsford. 107.7
FM. Owner: Tindle Radio. Managing
director: Ian Wootton; programme
controller and head of news: Nick Hull;
breakfast show: Tracy Young

Essex FM
Radio House, 31 Glebe Road,
Stanford, Essex CN1 1QG
01245 524500
firstname.surname@gcapmedia.com
www.musicradio.com
Adult contemporary. Chelmsford. 107.7
FM. Owner: Tindle Radio. Managing
director: Ian Wootton; programme
controller and head of news: Brian
O'Neill; breakfast show: Tracy Young

Fen Radio 107.5 FM
5 Church Mews, Wisbech,
Cambridgeshire PE13 1HL
01945 467107
studio@fenradio.co.uk
www.fenradio.co.uk
70s to today. Fenland. 107.1 FM; 107.5 FM.
Owner: UKRD Group. Station manager
and programme director: Mark Pryke;
programme manager: Richard Grant;
sales director: Anthony Johnson;
breakfast show: Joe Rudd

Hertbeat FM
The Pump House, Knebworth Park,
Hertford, Hertfordshire SG3 6HQ
01438 810900
info@hertbeat.com
www.hertbeat.com
80s/90s, specialist programmes weekend.
Hertfordshire. 106.9 FM; 106.7 FM.
Independent. Station manager: Brett
Harley; programme controller: Steve
Folland; news editor: Ruth Gibbon;
breakfast show: Steve Folland

KL.FM 96.7
18 Blackfriars Street, Kings Lynn,
Norfolk PE30 1NN
01553 772777
admin@klfm967.co.uk
www.klfm967.co.uk
Best of past 30 years. Kings Lynn and
west Norfolk. 96.7 FM. Owner: UKRD
Group. Managing director: William
Rogers; Station manager: Mark Pryke;
programme controller: Simon Rowe; head
of news: Gary Phillips; breakfast show:
Simon Roe and Amanda Eade

Lite FM
2nd Floor, 5 Church Street,
Peterborough PE1 1XB
01733 898106
info@lite1068.com
www.lite1068.com
Adult contemporary. Peterborough.
106.8 FM. Owner: Forward Media Group.
Managing director: David Myatt

North Norfolk Radio
The Studio, Breck Farm, Stody,
Norfolk NR24 2ER
01263 860808
info@northnorfolkradio.com
www.northnorfolkradio.com
Adult contemporary. North Norfolk.
103.2 FM; 96.2 FM. Owner: Tindle Radio.
Programme controller: Tom Koy; head
of news: John Bultitude

Q103 FM
Enterprise House, The Vision Park,
Chivers Way, Histon,
Cambridgeshire CB4 9WW
01223 235255
firstname.surname@gcapmedia.com
www.musicradio.com
Mix of today. Cambridge and Newmarket.
103 FM. Owner: GCap Media. Area
programme controller: James Keen; sales
director: Sharon Rush; head of news:
Sarah Spence; breakfast show: Charlie
and Helen

SGR Colchester
Abbey Gate Two, 9 Whitewell Road,
Colchester CO2 7DE
01206 575859
sgrcolchester@musicradio.com
www.musicradio.com
80s, 90s and today. Colchester. 96.1 FM.
Owner: GCap Media. Programme
controller: Jonathon Hemmings; sales
director: Sue Rudland; head of news:
Emma Carrick; senior presenter: Paul
Morris; breakfast show: Louise and
Graham

SGR FM
Alpha Business Park, 6-12 White
House Road, Ipswich Suffolk IP1 5LT
01473 461000
firstname.surname@gcapmedia.com
www.sgrfm.co.uk
80s, 90s and current hits. Suffolk.
96.4 FM; 97.1 FM. Owner: GCap Media.
Programme controller: Paul Morris;
head of news: Peter Cook

Star 107.9
Radio House, Sturton Street,
Cambridge CB1 2QF
01223 722300
admin@star107.co.uk
www.star1079.co.uk
Mainstream adult contemporary.
Cambridge. 107.1 FM, 107.9 FM. Owner:
UKRD Group. Programme controller:
James Keen; head of news: Lynda Hardy;
breakfast show: Andy Gall

Ten 17
Latton Bush Centre, Southern Way,
Harlow, Essex CM18 7BB
01279 431017
firstname.surname@musicradio.com
www.musicradio.com
Pop. East Herts, west Essex. 101.7 FM.
Owner: GCap Media. Programme director:
Freddie Scherer; news editor: Jack Taylor;
breakfast show: Neil Grayson

Vibe FM
Reflection House,
The Anderson Centre, Olding Road,
Bury St Edmunds IP33 3TA
01284 715300
general@vibefm.co.uk
www.vibefm.co.uk
Dance and R&B. East of England.
105-108 FM. Owner: Emap. Managing
director and programme controller: Gary
Robinson; news editors: Dawn Ferguson
and Neil Didsbury; breakfast show:
Stuart Grant

Watford's Mercury 96.6
Unit 5, The Metro Centre,
Dwight Road, Watford WD18 9UP
01923 205470
firstname.surname@
    hertsmercury.co.uk
www.hertsmercury.co.uk
Popular music. St Albans and Watford.
96.6 FM. Independant. Programme
controller: Tank Montana; head of news:
Eric Johnson; breakfast show: Tom and Kez

EAST MIDLANDS

96 Trent FM
29-31 Castle Gate,
Nottingham NG1 7AP
0115 873 1500
firstname.surname@musicradio.com
www.musicradio.com
All types of music. Nottinghamshire. 96
FM. Owner: GCap Media. Programme
controller: Luis Clark; head of news: Lewis
Scrimshaw; breakfast show: Jo and Twiggy

102.8 RAM FM
35-36 Irongate, Derby DE1 3GA
01332 205599
ramfm@musicradio.com
www.ramfm.co.uk
All current pop music. Derby. 102.8 FM.
Owner: GCap Media. Programme
controller: James Daniels; head of news:
Lewis Scrimshaw; breakfast show: Deano
and Pete

107 Oak FM
7 Waldron Court,
Prince William Road, Loughborough,
Leicestershire LE11 5GD
01509 211711
studio@oak107.co.uk
www.oak107.co.uk
60s to today. Charnwood and north-west
Leicestershire. 107 FM. Owner: CN Group.
Station manager: Gregg Parker;
programme manager: Don Douglas;
breakfast show: Gavin Sandways

Centre FM

5-6 Aldergate, Tamworth,
Staffordshire B79 7DJ
01827 318000
studio@cnradio.co.uk
www.touchtbl.co.uk
80s, 90s and today. South-east Staffordshire. 101.6 FM; 102.4 FM. Owner: CN Group. Managing director: Greg Parker; programme manager: Dave James; head of news: Mike Thomas; breakfast show: Dave James

Classic Gold 1557

Northamptonshire,
19-21 St Edmunds Road,
Northampton NN1 5DT
01604 795600
firstname.surname@
classicgolddigital.com
www.classicgolddigital.com
Classic music. Northampton. 1557 AM. Owner: Classic Gold Digital. Programme controller: Chris Rick; head of news: Sarah Spence; breakfast show: Tony Blackburn

Classic Hits

PO Box 262, Worcester WR6 5ZE
01432 360246
officemanager@classichits.co.uk
www.classichits.co.uk
Last four or five decades of hits. Hereford and Worcester. 954 AM; 1530 AM. Owner: Murfin Media International. Managing director: Muff Murfin; head of news: Andrew Currie; breakfast show: Paul Smith

Classic Gold GEM

29-31 Castle Gate,
Nottingham NG1 7AP
0115 873 1500
firstname.surname@
classicgolddigital.com
www.classicgolddigital.com
Classic chart hits. Nottingham, Derby. 999 AM; 945 AM. Owner: Classic Gold Digital. Managing director: John Daish; programme controller: Luis Clark; head of news: Lewis Scrimshaw; breakfast show: Tony Blackburn

Connect FM

Unit 1, Centre 2000, Kettering,
Northamptonshire NN16 8PU
01536 412413
info@connectfm.com
www.connectfm.com
70s, 80s and 90s and today. Kettering, Corby. 107.4 FM; 97.2 FM. Owner: Forward Media Group. Group managing director: David Myatt; Station manager: Martin Parr; programme manager: Danny Gibson; head of news: John Reading; breakfast show: Ian Sharpe

Dearne FM

PO Box 458, Barnsley S71 1XP
01226 321733
enquiries@dearnefm.co.uk
www.dearnefm.co.uk
60s, 70s, 80s and 90s and current hits. Barnsley. 97.1 FM; 102 FM. Owner: Lincs FM Group. Programme controller: Matt Jones; head of news: James Marriott; breakfast show: James Brandon

Fosseway Radio

PO Box 107, Hinckley,
Leicestershire LE10 1WR
01455 614151
studios@fossewayradio.co.uk
www.fossewayradio.co.uk
70s, 80s and 90s and hits of today. Hinckley, Nuneaton. 107.9 FM. Owner: Lincs FM. Chief executive: Michael Betton; programme manager: Ian Ison; head of news: James Wall; breakfast show: Julien Saunders

Heart 106 FM

City Link, Nottingham NG2 4NG
0115 910 6100
news@heart106.com
www.heart106.com
80s, 90s and contemporary. East Midlands. 106 FM. Owner: Chrysalis; Managing Director: Chris Jones; breakfast show: Sam and Amy

Leicester Sound

6 Dominus Way, Meridian Business
Park, Leicester LE19 1RP
0116 256 1300
www.musicradio.com
90s and today. Leicester. 105.4 FM. Owner: GCap Media. Programme controller: Simon Ritchie; head of sales: Bina Chauhan; head of news: Hayley Brewer; breakfast show: Rae and Kev

Lincs FM

Witham Park, Waterside South,
Lincoln LN5 7JN
01522 549900
enquiries@lincsfm.co.uk
www.lincsfm.co.uk
Pop. Lincoln. 102.2 FM; 97.6 FM; 96.7 FM. Owner: Lincs FM. Chief executive: Michael Betton; programme manager: Katie Trinder; news editor: Shaun Dunderdale; breakfast show: John Marshall

Mansfield 103.2

The Media Suite,
4 Brunts Business Centre,
Samuel Brunts Way, Mansfield,
Nottinghamshire NG18 2AH
01623 646666
info@mansfield103.co.uk
www.mansfield103.co.uk
70s, 80s and 90s and present day. Mansfield and District. 103.2 FM. Independent. Managing director: Tony Delahunty; programme director: Katie Trinder; head of news: Ian Watkins; breakfast show: Katie Trinder

Northants 96

19-21 St Edmunds Road,
Northampton NN1 5DY
01604 795600
firstname.surname@gcapmedia.com
www.northants96.co.uk
Pop. Northampton. 96.6 FM. Owner: GCap Media. Programme controller: Chris Rick; head of news: Hayley Brewer; breakfast show: Jagger and Woody

Peak 107 FM

Radio House, Foxwood Road,
Chesterfield S41 9RF
01246 269107
info@peak107.com
www.peakfm.net
50/50 music mix. Chesterfield, north Derbyshire, south Sheffield and Peak District. 102 FM; 107.4 FM. Owner: UTV. Group programme controller: Chris Buckley; head of news: Naz Premiji; breakfast show: Sean Goldsmith and Beck Measures

Rutland Radio

40 Melton Road, Oakham,
Rutland LE15 6AY
01572 757868
enquiries@rutlandradio.co.uk
www.rutlandradio.co.uk
Last 40 years' hits. Rutland and Stamford. 97.4 FM; 107.2 FM. Owner: Lincs FM. Station manager: Julie Baker; senior journalist: breakfast show: Rob Persani

Sabras Radio

Sabras Sound, Radio House,
63 Melton Road, Leicester LE4 6PN
0116 261 0666
neal@sabrasradio.com
www.sabrasradio.com
Asian music. Leicester. 1260 AM. Independent. Managing director and programme controller: Don Kotak; breakfast show: Alpa

Saga 106.6 FM

Saga Radio House, Alder Court,
Riverside Business Park,
Nottingham NG2 1RX
0115 986 1066
reception@saga1066fm.co.uk
www.saga1066fm.co.uk
Easy listening from past six decades. East Midlands. 106.6 FM. Owner: Saga Group. Managing director: Phil Dixon; programme director: Paul Robey; head of news: Lisa Teanby; breakfast show: John Peters

Signal 1

Stoke Road, Stoke on Trent ST4 2SR
01782 441300
info@signalradio.com
www.signal1.co.uk
Pop music. Stoke on Trent. 96.4 FM; 102.6 FM; 96.9 FM. Owner: The Wireless Group. Group programme director: John Dash; managing director: Chris Hurst; head of news: Paul Sheldon; breakfast show: Andy Golding and Louise Stone

Signal Two

Stoke Road, Stoke on Trent ST4 2SR
01782 441300
info@signalradio.com
www.signal2.co.uk
Pop music. Stoke on Trent. 1170 AM. Owner: The Wireless Group. ILR group programme: John Dash; managing director: Chris Hurst; head of news: Paul Sheldon; breakfast show: Johnny Owen

Trax FM
PO Box 444, Worksop,
Nottinghamshire S80 1HR
01909 500611
enquiries@traxfm.co.uk
www.traxfm.co.uk
*Adult contemporary. Bassetlaw.
107.9 FM. Owner: Lincs FM. Programme
controller: Nick Hancock; head of
news: Tina Masters; breakfast show:
Nick Hancock*

WEST MIDLANDS

96.4 FM BRMB
Nine Brindleyplace, 4 Ooozells
Square, Birmingham B1 2DJ
0121 245 5000
info@brmb.co.uk
www.brmb.co.uk
*Chart music. Birmingham. 96.4 FM.
Owner: GCap Media. Commercial
controller: Jane Davis; programme
controller: Adam Bridge; breakfast show:
The Big Brum Breakfast*

100.7 Heart FM
1 The Square, 111 Broad Street,
Birmingham B15 1AS
0121 695 0000
news@heartfm.co.uk
www.heartfm.co.uk
*Easy listening. West Midlands. 100.7 FM.
Owner: Chrysalis Radio. Managing
director: Paul Fairburn; programme
director: Alan Carruthers; head of news:
Chris Kowalik; breakfast show: Ed James*

107.1 Rugby FM
Dunsmore Business Centre,
Spring Street, Rugby CV21 3HH
01788 541100
studio@rugbyfm.co.uk
www.rugbyfm.co.uk
*60s, 70s, 80s and 90s and to date. Rugby.
107.1 FM. Owner: Milestone Radio Group.
Sales director: Nathalie Toner; head
of news: Laura Skelsie; breakfast show:
Matt Hollick*

107.4 Telford FM
Shropshire Star, Waterloo Road,
Ketley, Telford TF1 5HU
01952 280011
staff@telfordfm.co.uk
www.telfordfm.co.uk
*Easy listening. Telford. 107.4 FM
Independent. Programme director:
Pete Wagstaff; breakfast show: Paul
Shuttleworth*

107.7 The Wolf
10th Floor, Mander House,
Wolverhampton WV1 3NB
01902 571070
firstname@thewolf.co.uk
www.thewolf.co.uk
*50/50 mix of yesterday and today.
Wolverhampton. 107.7 FM. Owner:
Wireless Group. Group programme
director: John Evington; breakfast show:
Dickie Dodd*

Beacon FM
267 Tettenhall Road,
Wolverhampton WV6 0DE
01902 461300
firstname.surname@creation.com
www.musicradio.com
*Popular mix. Wolverhampton.
97.2 FM; 103.1 FM. Owner: GCap Media.
Programme director: Chris Pegg; head
of news: Adam Edward; breakfast show:
Mark Jeeves and Jo Jesmond*

The Bear 102
The Guard House Studios,
Banbury Road,
Stratford-upon-Avon CV37 7HX
01789 262636
info@thebear.co.uk
www.thebear.co.uk
*Classic and current hits. Stratford-upon-
Avon. 102 FM. Owner: CN Group. Station
director: Chris Arnold; programme
controller: Steve Hyden; head of news:
Daniel Bruce; breakfast show: Steve Hyden*

Capital Gold (1152)
30 Leicester Square,
London WC2H 7LA
020 7766 6000
info@capitalgold.co.uk
www.capitalgold.com
*Hits of the 60s, 70s and 80s.
Birmingham. 1152 AM. Owner: GCap
Media. Programme director: Andy
Turner; head of news: Justin King;
breakfast show: Tom Ross*

Classic Gold 1359
Hertford Place, Coventry CV1 3TT
02476 868200
firstname.surname@
classicgolddigital.com
www.classicgolddigital.com
*70s, 80s and 90s. Coventry. 1359 AM.
Owner: Classic Gold Digital. Programme
controller: Russ Williams; breakfast
show: Tony Blackburn*

Classic Gold WABC
267 Tettenhall Road,
Wolverhampton WV6 0DE
01902 461300
firstname.surname@
classicgolddigital.com
www.classicgolddigital.com
*Classic 80s, 90s onward.
Wolverhampton. 990 AM; 1017 AM.
Owner: Classic Gold Digital. Programme
controller: Chris Pegg; head of news:
Adam Edward; breakfast show: Tony
Blackburn*

Galaxy 102.2
1 The Square, 111 Broad Street,
Birmingham B15 1AS
0121 695 0000
galaxy1022@galaxy1022.co.uk
www.galaxy1022.co.uk
*Easy listening. Birmingham. 102.2 FM.
Owner: Chrysalis Radio. Managing
director: Paul Fairburn; programme
director: Neil Greenslade; head of news:
Chris Kowalik; breakfast show: Dave Clark*

Kix 96
Watch Close Spon Street,
Coventry CV1 3LN
024 7652 5656
firstname.lastname@cnradio.co.uk
www.intouchfm.co.uk
*Pop and Dance. Coventry. 96.2 FM.
Owner: CN Group. Sales director: Mark
Wright; programme manager: Don
Douglas; head of news: Daniel Bruce;
breakfast show: Stefan Latouche*

Mercia FM
Hertford Place, Coventry CV1 3TT
024 7686 8200
merciafm@musicradio.com
www.musicradio.com
*80s, 90s and modern. Coventry.
102.9 FM; 97 FM. Owner: GCap Media.
Programme controller: Russ Williams;
head of news: Tony Attwater; breakfast
show: Ru, and James*

Radio XL 1296 AM
KMS House Bradford Street,
Birmingham B12 0JD
0121 753 5353
arun@radioxl.net
www.radioxl.net
*Indian and Asian mixes. Birmingham.
1296 AM. Independent. Managing
director: Arun Bajaj; programme director:
Sukjoinder Ghataore; breakfast show: Tej*

Saga 105.7 FM
3rd Floor, Crown House,
Beaufort Court, 123 Hagley Road,
Edgbaston B16 8LD
0121 452 1057
onair@saga1057fm.co.uk
www.saga1057fm.co.uk
*40s onwards. West Midlands. 105.7 FM.
Owner: Saga Group. Managing director:
Phil Dickson; programme director: Paul
Robey; news editor: Colin Palmer;
breakfast show: Mike Wyer*

Wyvern FM
5-6 Barbourne Terrace,
Worcester WR1 3JZ
01905 612212
wyvern.news1@gcapmedia.com
www.musicradio.com
*Pop music. Hereford and Worcester.
102.8 FM; 97.6 FM; 96.7 FM. Owner:
GCap Media. Programme controller:
Rick Symmons, head of news: Jonathan
Dunbar; breakfast show: Lee Stone*

NORTH-EAST

Alpha 103.2
Radio House, 11 Woodland Road,
Darlington Co., Durham DL3 7BJ
01325 255552
studio@alphafm.co.uk
www.alphafm.co.uk
*Classic hits from last 30 years.
Darlington. 103.2 FM. Owner: Radio
Investments. Station manager: Angela
Bridgen; programme manager: Emma
Hignet; head of news: Kirsty Watt;
breakfast show: Tim West*

Century FM
Church Street, Gateshead NE8 2YY
0191 477 6666
info@centuryfm.co.uk
www.100centuryfm.com
80s, 90s and today. North-east England.
96.2 FM; 96.4 FM; 100.7 FM; 101.8 FM.
Owner: GCap Media. Programme
controller: Paul Drogan; head of news: Rick
Martin; breakfast show: Daryl and Mick

Galaxy 105–106
Kingfisher Way, Silverlink Business
Park, Tyne and Wear NE28 9NX
0191 206 8000
matt.mcclure@galaxy1056.co.uk
www.galaxy1056.co.uk
Dance and R&B. North-east England.
105.3 FM; 105.6 FM; 105.8 FM; 106.4 FM.
Owner: Chrysalis Radio. Programme
director: Matt McClure; Journalist:
Mandy Simpson; breakfast show: Kate Fox

Magic 1152
55 Degrees North, Pilgrim Street.
Newcastle upon Tyne NE1 6BS
0191 230 6100
paul.chantler@metroandmagic.com
www.magic1152.co.uk
Classic 60s and 70s. Tyne and Wear.
1152 AM. Owner: Emap Performance
Network. Managing director: Sally
Aitchaison; programme director: Paul
Chantler; breakfast show: Nick Wright

Magic 1170
Radio House, Yales Crescent,
Thornaby, Stockton-on-Tees TS17 6AA
01642 888222
colin.paterson@tfmradio.com
www.tfmradio.co.uk
Adult contemporary. Teesside. 1170 AM.
Owner: Emap Performance Network.
Managing director: Catherine Ellington;
programme director: Colin Paterson;
head of news: Myles Ashby; breakfast
show: Peter Grant

Metro Radio
Longrigg, Swalwell,
Newcastle upon Tyne NE99 1BB
0191 420 0971
paul.chantler@metroandmagic.com
www.magic1152.co.uk
Adult contemporary and chart. Tyne
and Wear. 97.1 FM. Owner: Emap
Performance Network. Managing director:
Sally Aitchison; programme director: Paul
Chantler; breakfast show: Tony Horn

Sun FM
PO Box 1034, Sunderland SR5 2YL
0191 548 1034
progs@sun-fm.com
www.sun-fm.com
Adult contemporary. Sunderland. 103.4
FM. Owner: Local Radio Company. Brand
controller: Simon Grundy; head of news:
Mark Selling; breakfast show: Ashley
Whitfield

TFM
Radio House, Yales Crescent,
Thornaby, Stockton-on-Tees TS17 6AA
01642 888222
colin.paterson@tfmradio.com
www.tfmradio.co.uk
Adult contemporary. Teesside. 96.6 FM.
Owner: Emap Performance Network.
Managing director: Catherine Ellington;
programme director: Colin Paterson;
head of news: Myles Ashley; breakfast
show: Tom Davies and Cara

YORKSHIRE AND HUMBERSIDE

96.3 Radio Aire
51 Burley Road, Leeds LS3 1LR
0113 283 5500
firstname.lastname@radioaire.com
www.radioaire.co.uk
Adult contemporary. Leeds. 96.3 FM.
Owner: Emap Performance Network.
Managing director: Alexis Thompson;
programme director: Stuart Baldwin;
head of news: Richard Pervis; breakfast
show: Cameron and Jamie

96.9 Viking FM
The Boat House, Commercial Road,
Hull HU1 2SG
01482 325141
reception@vikingfm.co.uk
www.vikingfm.co.uk
Variety. Hull. 96.9 FM. Owner: Local
Radio Company. Programme director:
Craig Beck; head of news: Jo Taylor;
breakfast show: Sam and Mark

97.2 Stray FM
The Hamlet, Hornbeam Park Avenue,
Harrogate HG2 8RE
01423 522972
mail@strayfm.com
www.strayfm.com
60s and 70s. Harrogate. 97.2 FM. Owner:
Local Radio Company. Managing director:
Sarah Barry; programme director: Mark
Brooks; head of news: Patrick Dunlop;
breakfast show: Mark Brooks

Classic Gold 1278/1530 AM
Pennine House, Forster Square,
Bradford, West Yorkshire BD1 5NE
01274 203040
general@pulse.co.uk
www.pulse.co.uk
Oldies. Bradford, Halifax and
Huddersfield. 1278 AM; 1530 AM.
Owner: The Wireless Group. ILR group
programme director: John Evington;
managing director: Tony Wilkinson; head
of news: Richard Murie; breakfast show:
Tony Blackburn and Laura Pittson

Compass FM
26a Wellowgate, Grimsby DN32 ORA
01472 346666
enquiries@compassfm.co.uk
www.compassfm.co.uk
Easy listening. Grimsby. 96.4 FM. Owner:
Lincs FM. Station Manager: Richard
Lyon; head of news: Shaun Dunderdale;
breakfast show: Richard Lyon

Fresh Radio
Firth Mill, Firth Street, Skipton,
North Yorkshire BD23 2PT
01756 799991
info@freshradio.co.uk
www.freshradio.co.uk
Adult contemporary. Yorkshire Dales with
Skipton. 1431 AM; 1413 AM; 936 AM.
Independent. Managing director: Dave
Parker; head of news: James Wilson;
breakfast show: Nick Bewes

Galaxy 105
Joseph's Well, Hannover Walk,
off Park Lane, Leeds LS3 1AB
0113 213 0105
mail@galaxy105.co.uk
www.galaxy105.co.uk
Dance and R&B. Yorkshire. 105.8 FM;
105.6 FM; 105.1 FM; 105.6 FM; DAB; Sky;
cable. Owner: Chrysalis Radio. Managing
director: Martin Healy; head of news and
programme director: Mike Cass; breakfast
show: Hirsty, Danny and JoJo

Hallam FM
Radio House 900 Herries Road,
Sheffield S6 1RH
0114 209 1000
Programmes@hallamfm.co.uk
www.hallamfm.co.uk
All types of music. South Yorkshire.
102.9 FM; 103.4 FM; 97.4 FM. Owner:
Emap Performance Network. Managing
director: Iain Clasper; head of news and
programming: Gary Stein; breakfast
show: Big John Breakfast Show

Home 107.9
The Old Stableblock, Lockwood
Park, Huddersfield HD1 3UR
01484 321107
info@home1079.com
www.home1079.com
Pop from past three decades.
Huddersfield. 107.9 FM. Owner: Radio
Investments. Programme controller: John
Harding; sales director: Susie Sweeny;
head of news: Steven Naylor; breakfast
show: Chris Bell

Magic 828
51 Burley Road, Leeds LS3 1LR
0113 283 5500
firstname.lastname@radioaire.com
www.radioaire.co.uk
Adult contemporary. Leeds. 828 AM.
Owner: Emap Performance Network.
Managing director: Alexis Thompson;
programme director: Stuart Baldwin;
head of news: Richard Pervis; breakfast
show: Paul Carrington

Magic 1161 AM
The Boat House, Commercial Road,
Hull HU1 2SG
01482 325141
reception@magic1161.co.uk
www.magic1161.co.uk
60s to present day. Humberside (east
Yorkshire and north Lincolnshire). 1161
AM. Owner: Emap Performance Network.
Managing director: Mike Bauden;
programme director: Darrell Woodman;
head of news: Kirsty Moore; breakfast
show: Steve Jordan

Magic AM
Radio House, 900 Herries Road,
Sheffield S6 1RH
0114 209 1000
Programmes@magicam.co.uk
www.magicam.co.uk
*Popular music. South Yorkshire.
990 AM; 1305 AM; 1545 AM. Owner:
Emap Performance Network. Managing
director: Iain Clasper; head of news and
programming: Gary Stein; breakfast
show: Howie*

Minster FM
PO Box 123, Dunnington,
York YO19 5ZX
01904 488888
general@minsterfm.com
www.minsterfm.com
*Past few decades. York. 104.7 FM;
102.3 FM. Owner: Radio Investments.
Commercial station manager: Sarah
Barry; programme controller: Ed Bretton;
head of news: Tristan Hunkin; breakfast
show: Ed Bretton*

The Pulse
Pennine House, Forster Square,
Bradford, West Yorkshire BD1 5NE
01274 203040
general@pulse.co.uk
www.pulse.co.uk
*Oldies. Bradford, Huddersfield and
Halifax. 102.5 FM; 97.5 FM. Owner: The
Wireless Group. ILR group programme
director: John Evington; managing
director: Esther Morton; head of news:
Richard Murie; breakfast show: Jackie
and Steve*

Real Radio (Yorkshire)
Sterling Court, Capitol Park,
Leeds WF3 1EL
0113 238 1114
info@realradiofm.com
www.realradiofm.com
*90s and popular. South and West
Yorkshire. 107.6 FM; 106.2 FM; 107.7 FM.
Owner: Guardian Media Group Radio.
Managing director: Shaun Bowron;
programme director: Terry Underhill;
head of news: James Rea; breakfast show:
Guy Harris*

Ridings FM
PO Box 333, Wakefield WF2 7YQ
01924 367177
enquiries@ridingsfm.co.uk
www.ridingsfm.co.uk
*Popular music. Wakefield. 106.8 FM.
Owner: Lincs FM. Station manager: Keith
Briggs; head of news: Andy Smith;
breakfast show: Kev Wilson*

Sunrise FM
Sunrise House, 30 Chapel Street,
Little Germany, Bradford BD1 5DN
01274 735043
usha@sunriseradio.fm
www.sunriseradio.fm
*Asian music. Bradford. 103.2 FM.
Independent. Managing director and
programme controller: Usha Parmar;
head of news: Gail Papworth; breakfast
show: Gail and Sadia*

Trax FM
PO Box 44, Doncaster DN4 5GW
01302 341166
events@traxfm.co.uk
www.traxfm.co.uk
*All sorts. Doncaster. 107.1 FM. Owner:
Lincs FM. Programme controller: Rob
Wagstaff; sales manager: Peggy Watson;
head of news: Tina Master; breakfast
show: Mick Hancock*

Yorkshire Coast Radio
PO Box 962, Scarborough,
North Yorkshire YO11 3ZP
01723 581700
studio@yorkshirecoastradio.com
www.yorkshirecoastradio.com
*Chart hits. Bridlington, Scarborough,
Whitby. 96.2 FM; 103.1 FM. Owner: Radio
Investments. Station manager and
programme controller: Chris Sigsworth;
head of news: Al Ross; breakfast show:
Ben Fry*

Yorkshire Coast Radio
The Old Harbour Master's Office,
Harbour Road, Bridlington,
East Yorkshire YO15 2NR
01262 404400
enquiries@yorkshirecoastradio.com
www.yorkshirecoastradio.com
*Adult contemporary. Bridlington.
102.4 FM. Owner: Radio Investments.
Commercial and brand manager:
Chris Sigsworth; sales director: Peter
Bilsborough; breakfast show: Greg Dukeson*

NORTH-WEST

2BR
Imex Lomeshaye Business Village,
Nelson, Lancashire BB9 7DR
01282 690000
info@2br.co.uk
www.2br.co.uk
*70s to current. Burnley. 99.8 FM.
Owner: Local Radio Company. Managing
director: Mark Matthews; breakfast show:
Brooksy n Diane*

96.2 The Revolution
PO Box 962, Oldham OL1 3JF
0161 621 6500
info@therevolution.uk.com
www.revolutiononline.co.uk
*Classic and chart hits. Oldham. 96.2 FM.
Owners: UKRD; Hirst Kidd & Rennie.
Station manager: Jackie Sulkowski;
programme controller and head of news:
Chris Gregg; breakfast show: John
Warburton*

97.4 Rock FM
PO Box 974, Preston PR1 1YE
01772 477700
firstname.lastname@rockfm.co.uk
www.rockfm.co.uk
*Adult contemporary. Preston and
Blackpool. 97.4 FM. Owner: Emap
Performance Network. Programme
director: Brian Paige; head of news: Clare
Hannah; breakfast show: Dave Miller*

100.4 Smooth FM
8 Exchange Quay, Manchester M5 3EJ
0161 877 1004
jazzinfo@jazzfm.com
www.jazzfm.com
*Smooth and R&B. North-west England.
100.4 FM. Owner: Guardian Media Group
Radio. Managing director: Roy Bennett;
programming director: Steve Collins;
head of music: Derek Webster; breakfast
show: Chris Best*

102.4 Wish FM
Orrell Lodge, Orrell Road, Orrell,
Wigan WN5 8HJ
01942 761024
studio@wish_fm.com
www.wishfm.net
*80s, 90s, up to date. Wigan. 102.4 FM.
Owner: The Wireless Group. Programme
manager: Jo Heuston; head of news: Stuart
Arrowsmith; breakfast show: Ben and Jo*

106.7 FM The Rocket
The Studios, Cables Retail Park,
Prescot, Merseyside, L34 5SW
Reception: 0151 290 1501
Studio: 0845 051 1067
www.kcr1067.com
*60s to modern. Knowsley. 106.7 FM.
Owner: Local Radio Company. Managing
director: Ray Ferguson; programme
controller: Brian Cullen; head of news:
Sophia Livert; breakfast show: John
Cooper*

106.9 Silk FM
Radio House, Bridge Street,
Macclesfield, Cheshire SK11 6DJ
01625 268000
mail@silkfm.com
www.silkfm.com
*Adult contemporary. Macclesfield.
106.9 FM. Owner: Radio Investments.
Programme manager: Andy Bailey; head
of news: Helen Croydon; breakfast show:
Andy Bailey*

107.2 Wire FM
Warrington Business Park,
Long Lane, Warrington WA2 8TX
01925 445545
info@wirefm.com
www.wirefm.com
*Adult contemporary. Warrington.
107.2 FM. Owner: The Wireless Group.
Station director: Mathew Allitt; head of
news: Mark Bell; breakfast show: Dominic
Walker*

Asian Sound Radio
Globe House, Southall Street,
Manchester M3 1LG
0161 288 1000
info@asiansoundradio.co.uk
www.asiansoundradio.com
*Asian hip-hop. East Lancashire. 963 AM;
1377 AM. Independent. Managing
director and programme director: Shujat
Ali; head of news: Mazar Hussain*

The Bay
PO Box 969, St Georges Quay,
Lancaster LA1 3LD
01524 848747
information@thebay.fm
www.thebay.fm
*Adult contemporary. Morecambe Bay,
South Lakes, Cumbria. 102.3 FM; 96.9
FM; 103.2 FM. Station director: Jason
Gill; programme controller: Dave Collins;
head of news: Peter Storry; breakfast
show: Phil Holmes*

Century 105 FM
Laser House, Waterfront Quay,
Salford Quays, Manchester M50 3XW
0161 662 4700
info1054@centuryfm.co.uk
www.1054centuryfm.com
*Pop. North-west England. 105.4 FM.
Owner: GCap Media. Managing director:
Nick Davidson; Brand programme
director: Giles Squire; head of news: Matt
Bowen; breakfast show: Darren Proctor*

Classic Gold Marcher 1260 AM
The Studios, Mold Road,
Wrexham LL11 4AF
01978 752202
firstname.surname@
     classicgolddigital.com
www.classicgolddigital.com
*Classical music. Wrexham and Chester.
1260 AM. Owner: Classic Gold Digital.
Programme controller: Paul Baker; head
of news: Elina Cavanagh; breakfast show:
Tony Blackburn*

Dee 106.3
2 Chantry Court, Chester CH1 4QN
01244 391000
info@dee1063.com
www.dee1063.com
*Adult contemporary. Chester. 106.3 FM.
Independent. Station manager: Steve
Howarth; Head of news: Mairead O Kane;
breakfast show: Gavin and Irene*

Dune FM
The Power Station, Victoria Way,
Southport PR8 1RR
01704 502500
studio@dunefm.co.uk
www.dunefm.co.uk
*Adult contemporary. Southport.
107.9 FM. Owner: Local Radio Company.
Programme controller: John Storey;
head of news: Charlotte Maher; breakfast
show: John Storey*

Galaxy 102
5th Floor, The Triangle,
Hanging Ditch, Manchester M4 3TR
0161 279 0300
mail@galaxy102.co.uk
www.galaxy102.co.uk
*Dance and R&B. Manchester. 102 FM.
Owner: Chrysalis Radio. Managing
director: Martyn Healey; programme
director: Mike Cass; breakfast show: Wes*

Imagine FM
Regent House, Heaton Lane,
Stockport SK4 1BX
0161 609 1400
info@imaginefm.com
www.imaginefm.co.uk
*Hits 70s to 90s and today. Stockport.
104.9 FM. Owner: The Wireless Group.
Head of news and programme controller:
Ashley Burne; breakfast show: Paul Willett*

Juice 107.6
27 Fleet Street, Liverpool L1 4AR
0151 707 3107
mail@juiceliverpool.com
www.juice.fm
*R&B. Liverpool. 107.6 FM. Owner:
Absolute Radio. Managing director: Chris
Hurst; programme director: Grainne
Landowski; head of news: Catherine
Davies; breakfast show: Louis Hurst*

Key 103
Castle Quay, Castlefield,
Manchester M15 4PR
0161 288 5000
first.name@key103.co.uk
www.key103.com
*Mainstream. Manchester. 103 FM.
Owner: Emap Performance Network.
Managing director: Liz Larner;
programme director: Anthony Gay; head
of news: John Pickford; breakfast show:
Mike Toolan*

Lakeland Radio
Lakeland Food Park, Plumgarths,
Crook Road, Kendal, Cumbria LA8 8QJ
01539 737380
info@lakelandradio.co.uk
www.lakelandradio.co.uk
*60s to modern. Kendal and Windermere.
100.8 FM; 100.1 FM. Independent.
Managing director: Peter Fletcher; head
of music: Colin Yare; breakfast show:
Sarah Newman*

Magic 999
St Pauls Square, Preston PR1 1YE
01772 477700
name.surname@magic999.co.uk
www.magic999.co.uk
*Adult contemporary. Preston and
Blackpool. 999 AM. Owner: Emap
Performance Network. Programme
director: Brian Paige; head of news: Clare
Hannah; breakfast show: Rob Charles*

Magic 1152
Castle Quay, Castlefield,
Manchester M15 4PR
0161 288 5000
firstname.lastname@magicradio.com
www.manchestersmagic.co.uk
*80s, 90s. Manchester. 1152 AM. Owner:
Emap Performance Network. Managing
director: Liz Larner; programme director:
Anthony Gay; head of news: John Pickford;
breakfast show: Macdonald snd Maguire*

Magic 1548
St Johns Beacon, 1 Houghton Street,
Liverpool L1 1RL
0151 472 6800
firstname@magic1548.com
www.radiocity.co.uk
*Adult contemporary. Liverpool. 1548 AM.
Owner: Emap Performance Network.
Managing director: Sean Marlev;
programme director: Richard Maddock;
head of news: Steve Hothersell; breakfast
show: Phil Easton*

Marcher Sound
The Studios, Mold Road, Gwersyllt,
Nr Wrexham LL11 4AF
01978 752202
firstname.surname@gcapmedia.com
www.mymfm.co.uk
*Pop music. Wrexham and Chester. 103.4
FM. Owner: GCap Media. Managing
director: Sarah Smithard; programme
controller: Lisa Marrey; head of news:
Alina Cavanagh; breakfast show: Jamie
and Bec*

Radio City 96.7
St Johns Beacon, 1 Houghton Street,
Liverpool L1 1RL
0151 472 6800
firstname.surname@
     radiocity967.com
www.radiocity.co.uk
*Pop. Liverpool. 96.7 FM. Owner: Emap
Performance Network. Managing
director: Iain McKenna; programme
director: Richard Maddock; head of news:
Steve Hothersell; breakfast show: Kev Seed*

Tower FM
The Mill, Brownlow Way,
Bolton BL1 2RA
01204 387000
info@towerfm.co.uk
www.towerfm.co.uk
*Traditional music. Bolton and Bury.
107.4 FM. Owner: Wire Group. Sales
director: Victoria Cullen; programme
director: Kevin McLean; head of news:
Sophie Hubberstey; breakfast show: Vicks
and Martin*

Wave FM
965 Mowbray Drive, Blackpool,
Lancashire FY3 7JR
01253 304965
wave@thewavefm.co.uk
www.wave965.com
*Chart and retro. Blackpool. 96.5 FM.
Owner: The Wireless Group. Group
managing director: Scott Taunton;
programme manager: Helen Bowden;
Station director: Mel Booth; breakfast
show: Roy and Janine*

Wirral's Buzz FM
Pacific Road Arts Centre, Pacific
Road, Birkenhead CH41 1LJ
0151 650 1700
sarah.smithard@musicradio.com
www.musicradio.com
*Chart 80s and 90s. Wirral. 97.1 FM.
Owner: GWR Group. Programme
controller: Lisa Marrey; head of news:
Alina Cavanagh; breakfast show: Becky
and Jeff*

● Commercial local radio: Wales

96.4 FM The Wave
PO Box 964, Swansea SA4 3AB
01792 511964
info@thewave.co.uk
www.thewave.co.uk
Chart hits. Swansea. 96.4 FM. Owner: The Wireless Group. ILR Programme director: Steve Barnes; station manager: Carrie Mosley; head of news: Emma Thomas; breakfast show: Badger and Emma

Bridge FM
PO Box 1063, Bridgend CF35 6WF
0845 890 4000
firstname.surname@bridge.fm
www.bridge.fm
Adult contemporary. Bridgend. 106.3 FM. Owner: Tindle Radio. Managing director: Mark Franklyn; programme controller: Lee Thomas; head of news: Kayley Thomas; breakfast show: Gareth Davies

Champion FM
Llys y Dderwen Parc Menai, Bangor LL57 4BN
01248 673400
sarah.smithard@musicradio.com
www.musicradio.com
Modern music. Caenafon. 103 FM. Owner: GCap Media. Managing director: Sarah Smithard; Area programme controller: Steve Simms; head of news: David Grundy; breakfast show: Kevin Bach

Coast FM
PO Box 963, Bangor LL57 4ZR
01248 673400
firstname.surname@musicradio.com
www.coastfm.co.uk
Modern music. North Wales coast. 96.3 FM. Owner: GCap Media. Managing director: Sarah Smithard; programme controller: Steve Simms; head of news: David Grundy; breakfast show: Craig Pilling

Radio Ceredigion
Yr Hen Ysgol Gymraeg, Aberystwyth, Ceredigion SY23 1LF
01970 627999
admin@ceredigionfmf9.co.uk
www.ceredigionradio.com
Adult contemporary Welsh. Ceredigion. 97.4 FM; 103.3 FM; 96.6 FM. Independent. Programme controller: Mark Simon; head of news: Rhoori Darey; breakfast show: Thomo

Radio Maldwyn
The Studios, The Park, Newtown, Powys SY16 2NZ
01686 623555
radio.maldwyn@ukonline.co.uk
www.magic756.net
Adult contemporary. Montgomeryshire. 756 AM. Owner: Murfin Media International. Managing director, operations director and programme controller: Austin Powell; head of news: Andrew Curry; breakfast show: Mark Edwards

Radio Pembrokeshire
Unit 14 The Old School Estate, Station Road, Narberth, Pembrokeshire SA67 7DU
01834 869384
enquiries@radiopembrokeshire.com
www.radiopembrokeshire.com
Adult contemporary rock. Pembrokeshire, West Carmarthenshire. 102.5 FM. Independent. Managing director and programme controller: Keri Jones; head of news: Tim John; breakfast show: Keri Jones

Real Radio (South Wales)
Unit 1, Ty-Nant Court, Ty-Nant Road Morganstown, Cardiff CF15 8LW
029 2031 5100
info@realradiofm.com
www.realradiofm.com
70s to modern. South Wales regional. 105.9 FM; 106 FM; 105.2 FM; 105.4 FM. Owner: Guardian Media Group Radio. Programme director: Sarah Graham; head of news: Gareth Setter; breakfast show: Ian Brannan

Red Dragon FM & Capital Gold
Atlantic Wharf, Cardiff Bay CF10 4DJ
029 2066 2066
firstname.lastname@
   reddragonfm.co.uk
www.reddragonfm.co.uk
Chart music. Cardiff and Newport. 103.2 FM; 97.4 FM. Owner: GCap Media. Programme controller: Gavin Marshall; head of news: Angharad Thomas; breakfast show: Clare Lloyd

Sunshine 855
Unit 11, Burway Trading Estate, Bromfield Road, Ludlow, Shropshire SY8 1EN
01584 873795
sunshine855@ukonline.co.uk
www.sunshine855.com
Adult contemporary. Ludlow. 855 AM. Owner: Murfin Media International. Operations director and programme controller: Ginny Murfin; head of news: Andrew Currie; breakfast show: Nick Jones

Swansea Sound
Victoria Road, Gowerton, Swansea SA4 3AB
01792 511170
info@swanseasound.co.uk
www.swanseasound.co.uk
Chart hits. Swansea. 1170 AM. Owner: The Wireless Group. Station manager: Carrie Mosley; head of news: Emma Thomas; head of music: Andy Miles; breakfast show: Kevin Johns

Valleys Radio
Festival Park Victoria, Beech Grove, Ebbw Vale NP23 8XW
01495 301116
admin@valleysradio.co.uk
www.valleysradio.co.uk
Adult contemporary. Heads of south Wales valleys. 1116 AM; 999 AM. Owner: The Wireless Group. Managing director: Chris Hurst; head of news: Emma Thomas; breakfast show: Tony Peters

● Commercial local radio: Scotland

96.3 QFM
65 Sussex Street, Glasgow G41 1DX
0141 429 9430
sales@q-fm.com
www.q96.net
All types. Paisley. 96.3 FM. Owner: The Wireless Group. Managing director: Scott Taunton; head of news: Angela Carr; breakfast show: Joe and Lynne

Argyll FM
27-29 Longrow, Campbeltown, Argyll PA28 6ER
01586 551800
argyllradio@hotmail.com
www.argyllfm.co.uk
Adult contemporary. Kintyre, Islay and Jura. 107.7 FM; 107.1 FM; 106.5 FM. Independent. Managing director: Colin Middleton; programme controller: Kenny Johnson; head of news: Ian Henderson; breakfast show: Bill Young

Beat 106
Four Winds Pavilion, Pacific Quay, Glasgow G51 1EB
0141 566 6106
info@beat106.com
www.beat106.com
Dance. Central Scotland. 106.1 FM; 105.7 FM. Owner: GCap Media. Programme controller: Claire Pattenden; news editor: Vicky Lee; breakfast show: Paul Harper and Frazier Thompson

Central FM
201 High Street, Falkirk FK1 1DU
01324 611164
mail@centralfm.co.uk
www.centralfm.co.uk
Hits and memories. Stirling and Falkirk. 103.1 FM. Owner: Radio Investments. Programme controller: Tom Bell; head of news: Tadek Kopszywa; breakfast show: Tom Bell

CFM
PO Box 964, Carlisle CA1 3NG
01228 818964
reception@cfmradio.com
www.cfmradio.com
Best mix of music. Carlisle. 96.4 FM; 102.5 FM. Owner: Scottish Radio Holdings. Managing director: Cathy Kirk; programme controller: David Bain; head of news: Bill McDonald; breakfast show: Robbie Dee

Clan FM
Radio House, Rowantree Avenue, Newhouse Ind. Estate, Newhouses, Lanarkshire ML1 5RX
01698 733107
reception@clanfm.com
www.clanfm.com
Adult contemporary. North Lanarkshire. 107.9 FM; 107.5 FM. Owner: Kingdom Group. Station manager: Janis Melville; programme controller: Darren Stenhouse; breakfast show: David Ross; head of news: Andrew Thompson

Clyde 1 FM
Clydebank Business Park,
Glasgow G81 2RX
0141 565 2200
info@clyde1.com
www.clyde1.com
*Pop. Glasgow. 97 FM; 103.3 FM; 102.5 FM.
Owner: Scottish Radio Holdings.
Managing director: Paul Cooney;
programme controller: Ross Macfadyen;
head of news: Russell Walker; breakfast
show: Gavin Pearson*

Clyde 2
Clydebank Business Park,
Glasgow G81 2RX
0141 565 2200
info@clyde2.com
www.clyde2.com
*Hits from last few decades. Glasgow.
1152 AM. Owner: Scottish Radio Holdings.
Managing director: Paul Cooney;
programme controller: Ross Macfadyen;
head of news: Russell Walker; breakfast
show: John McCauley*

Forth One
Forth House, Forth Street,
Edinburgh EH1 3LE
0131 556 9255
info@forthone.com
www.forthone.com
*Adult contemporary. Edinburgh. 97.6 FM;
102.2 FM; 97.3 FM. Owner: Scottish Radio
Holdings. Managing director: Camille
Craig; programme director: Luke
McCullough; head of news: Paul
Robertson; breakfast show: Grant Scott*

Forth Two
Forth House, Forth Street,
Edinburgh EH1 3LE
0131 556 9255
info@forth2.com
www.forth2.com
*60s, 70s, 80s, 90s and today. Edinburgh.
1548 AM. Owner: Scottish Radio
Holdings. Managing director: Camille
Craig; programme director: Luke
McCullough; head of news: Paul
Robertson; breakfast show: Darren Adam*

Heartland FM
Atholl Curling Rink, Lower Oakfield
Pitlochry, Perthshire PH16 5HQ
01796 474040
mailbox@heartlandfm.co.uk
www.heartlandfm.co.uk
*Classic hits. Pitlochry and Aberfeldy.
97.5 FM; 102.7 FM. Independent.
Programme controller: Peter Ramsden;
head of news: Margaret Stevenson;
breakfast show: Bruce P*

Isles FM
PO Box 333, Stornoway,
Isle of Lewis HS1 2PU
01851 703333
studio@isles.fm
www.isles.fm
*Adult contemporary. Western Isles.
103 FM. Independent. Director of
operations: David Morrison; head of
news: Iain MacIver*

Kingdom FM
Haig House, Haig Business Park
Markinch, Fife KY7 6AQ
01592 753753
info@kingdomfm.co.uk
www.kingdomfm.co.uk
*Across-the-board mix. Fife. 95.2 FM;
105.4 FM; 96.6 FM; 106.3 FM; 96.1 FM.
Independent. Managing director: Kevin
Brady; programme director: Darren
Stenhouse; head of news: Chris Hodge;
breakfast show: Mike Pelosi*

Lochbroom FM
Radio House, Mill Street, Ullapool,
Ross-shire IV26 2UN
01854 613131
radio@lochbroomfm.co.uk
www.lochbroomfm.co.uk
*Adult contemporary. Ullapool. 96.8 FM;
102.2 FM. Independent. Chairman: Iain
Boyd; programme controller and
breakfast show: Maddain Mhath*

Moray Firth Radio (MFR)
Scorguie Place, Inverness IV3 8UJ
01463 224433
mfr@mfr.co.uk
www.mfr.co.uk
*Contemporary and chart. Inverness.
96.6 FM; 96.7 FM; 97.4 FM; 102.5 FM;
102.8 FM. Owner: Scottish Radio
Holdings. Managing director: Gary
Robinson; head of news: Susan Rose;
breakfast show: Tich McCooey*

NECR
The Shed, School Road, Kintore,
Aberdeenshire AB51 0UX
01467 632878
necrradio102.1fmsales@supanet.com
www.necrfm.co.uk
*Recent hits and classic gold and specialist
country, Irish and Scottish. Inverurie.
102.1 FM; 102.6 FM; 97.1 FM; 103.2 FM;
101.9 FM; 106.4FM. Independent.
Managing director: Colin Strong;
programme controller: John Dean;
head of news: John Dean; breakfast show:
John Dean*

Nevis Radio
Ben Nevis Estate, Claggan,
Fort William PH33 6PR
01397 700007
studio@nevisradio.co.uk
www.nevisradio.co.uk
*Daily chart music. Evening specialist.
Fort William and parts of Lochaber.
96.6 FM; 102.4 FM; 97 FM; 102.3 FM.
Independent. Head of news, station
manager and programme controller:
Willie Cameron; breakfast show:
David Ogg*

Northsound One
Abbotswell Road, West Tullos,
Aberdeen AB12 3AJ
01224 337000
northsound@srh.co.uk
www.northsound1.co.uk
*Modern music. Aberdeen and north-east
Scotland. 96.9 FM; 97.6 FM; 103 FM.
Owner: Scottish Radio Holdings.
Managing director: Ken Massie;
programme controller: Chris Thomson;
head of news: Neil Metcalf; breakfast
show: Greigsy*

Northsound Two
Abbotswell Road, West Tullos,
Aberdeen AB12 3AJ
01224 337000
northsound@srh.co.uk
www.northsound2.co.uk
*Modern music. Aberdeen and north-east
Scotland. 1035 AM. Owner: Scottish Radio
Holdings. Managing director: Ken Massie;
programme controller: Chris Thomson;
head of news: Neil Metcalf; breakfast
show: John McCruvie*

Oban FM
132 George Street, Oban,
Argyll PA34 5NT
01631 570057
obanfmradio@btconnect.com
www.obanfm.tk
*Gaelic to modern pop. Oban. 103.3 FM.
Independent. Station manager: Ian
Mackay; programme director: Tina
Robertson; head of news: Coll McDougall*

Radio Borders
Tweedside Park, Galashiels TD1 3TD
01896 759444
programming@radioborders.com
www.radioborders.com
*Hits and memories. Borders. 96.8 FM;
103.1 FM; 103.4 FM; 97.5 FM. Owner:
Scottish Radio Holdings. Programme
controller: Stuart McCulloch; head of
news: Claire Reilly; breakfast show:
Keith Clarkson*

Real Radio (Scotland)
PO Box 101, Parkway Court, Glasgow
Business Park, Glasgow G69 6GA
0141 781 1011
contact.name@realradiofm.com
www.realradiofm.com
*Wide variety. Central Scotland.
100.3 FM; 101.1 FM. Owner: Guardian
Media Group Radio. Managing director:
Billy Anderson; programme director: Jay
Crawford; head of news: Heather Kane;
breakfast show: Robin Galloway*

River FM
Stadium House, Alderstone Road,
Livingstone, West Lothian EH54 7DN
01506 410411
office@river-fm.com
www.river-fm.com
*Adult contemporary and charts. West
Lothian. 107.7 FM; 103.4 FM. Owner:
Kingdon Radio Group. Programme
controller: Donny Hughes; sales director:
Wahida Wilson; breakfast show: James
Russell*

RNA FM
Radio North Angus, Arbroath
Infirmary, Rosemount Road,
Arbroath, Angus DD11 2AT
01241 879660
info@radionorthangus.co.uk
www.radionorthangus.co.uk
*Classic/Scottish and pop. Arbroath,
Carnoustie. 96.6 FM. Independent.
Managing director and head of news:
Malcolm Finlayson*

SIBC

Market Street, Lerwick,
Shetland ZE1 0JN
01595 695299
info@sibc.co.uk
www.sibc.co.uk
*Rock and pop. Shetland. 96.2 FM;
102.2 FM. Independent. Managing
director and programme controller: Inga
Walterson; head of news: Ian Anderson*

South West Sound

Unit 40, The Loreburne Centre,
High Street, Dumfries DG1 2BD
01387 250999
firstname.lastname@
   southwestsound.co.uk
www.southwestsound.co.uk
*Chart music. Dumfries and Galloway.
96.5 FM; 97 FM; 103 FM. Owner: Scottish
Radio Holdings. Managing director:
Sheena Borthwick; programme director:
Alan Toomey; head of news: Jo Leavesley;
breakfast show: Tommy Jardine*

Tay AM

6 North Isla Street, Dundee DD3 7JQ
01382 200800
tayam@radiotay.co.uk
www.radiotay.co.uk
*Various music. Dundee and Perth. 1584
AM; 1161 AM. Owner: Scottish Radio
Holdings. Managing director and
programme director: Ally Ballingall; head
of news: Amanda Mezzullo; breakfast
show: Grant Reed*

Tay FM

6 North Isla Street, Dundee DD3 7JQ
01382 200800
tayam@radiotay.co.uk
www.radiotay.co.uk
*Various music. Dundee and Perth.
102.8 FM; 96.4 FM. Owner: Scottish
Radio Holdings. Managing director and
programme director: Ally Ballingall; head
of news: Amanda Mezzullo; breakfast
show: Stuart Webster*

Two Lochs Radio

Gairloch, Rossshire IV21 2BQ
0870 741 4657
info@2lr.co.uk
www.2lr.co.uk
*Broad mix and Scottish Gaelic. Gairloch
and Loch Ewe. 106.6 FM. Independent.
Programme director: Colin Pickering;
chairman and station manager: Alex Gray*

Wave 102

8 South Tay Street, Dundee DD1 1PA
01382 900102
studio@wave102.co.uk
www.wave102.co.uk
*80s, 90s and today. Dundee. 102 FM.
Owner: The Wireless Group. Managing
director: Chris Hurst; programme
controller: Peter McInulty; head of news:
Mandy Carter; breakfast show: Peter Mac*

Waves Radio Peterhead

7 Blackhouse Circle,
Peterhead AB42 1BW
01779 491012
waves@radiophd.freeserve.co.uk
www.wavesfm.com
*Current and classic. Peterhead. 101.2 FM.
Independent. Managing director and
chairman: Norman Spence; head of news:
Glenn Moir; program controller: Kenny
King; breakfast show: Kenny King*

West FM

Radio House, 54a Holmston Road,
Ayr KA7 3BE
01292 283662
info@westfm.co.uk
www.westfm.co.uk
*Wide variety including music. Ayr.
97.5FM; 96.7 FM. Owner: Scottish Radio
Holdings. Managing director: Sheena
Borthwick; programme director: Alan
Toomey; head of news: Ian Wilson;
breakfast show: Alan Shaw*

West Sound AM

Radio House, 54a Holmston Road,
Ayr KA7 3BE
01292 283662
info@westsound.co.uk
www.westsound.co.uk
*Wide variety of music. Ayr. 1035 AM.
Owner: Scottish Radio Holdings.
Managing director: Sheena Borthwick;
programme director: Alan Toomey; head
of news: Ian Wilson; breakfast show:
Kenny Campbell*

Your Radio

Pioneer Park Studios, Unit 1-3,
80 Castlegreen Street,
Dumbarton G82 1JB
01389 734422
info@yourradio.com
www.yourradiocom
*Popular music. Dumbarton. 103 FM;
106.9 FM. Independent. Station
manager: Susan Dignon; programme
controller: Dave Ross; head of news: Gary
Pews; breakfast show: Derek McIntyre*

● Commercial local radio: Northern Ireland

Cool FM

PO Box 974, Belfast BT1 1RT
028 9181 7181
music@coolfm.co.uk
www.coolfm.co.uk
*Pop. Northern Ireland. 97.4 FM.
Owner: Scottish Radio Holdings.
Managing director: David Sloan MBE;
head of news: Harry Castles; breakfast
show: Pete Snodden*

Downtown Radio

Newtownards, Co Down,
Northern Ireland BT23 4ES
028 9181 5555
Programmes@downtown.co.uk
www.downtown.co.uk
*Adult contemporary. Northern Ireland.
97.1 FM; 103.1 FM; 103.4 FM; 102.4 FM;
1026 AM; 96.6 FM; 102.3 FM; 96.4 FM.
Owner: Scottish Radio Holdings.
Programme controller: David Sloan MBE;
head of news: Harry Castles; breakfast
show: Paul Thomas*

Mid FM

2c Park Avenue, Burn Road,
Cookstown BT80 8AH
028 8675 8696
firstnamelastname@
   midfm106fm.co.uk
www.mid106fm.co.uk
*80s, 90s mix. Mid-Ulster. 106 FM. Owner:
CN Group. Station director: Neil McLeod
Berriskell; news manager: Donagh
Mckeown; breakfast show: Francie Quinn*

Q101

42A Market Street, Omagh,
Co. Tyrone BT78 1EH
028 8224 5777
Manager@q101west.fm
www.q101west.fm
*Chart and pop. Omagh and Enniskillen.
101.2 FM. Owner: Q Radio Network.
Programme controller: Frank
McLaughlin; head of news: Eve Blair;
breakfast show: Stuart Gordon*

Q102

The Riverview Suite,
87 Rossdowney Road, Waterside,
Londonderry BT47 5SU
028 7134 4449
Manager@q102.fm
www.q102.fm
*70s to today. Londonderry. 102.9 FM.
Owner: Q Radio Network. Managing
director and programme controller:
Frank McLaughlin; head of news: Jimmy
Cadden; breakfast show: Adrian Johnson*

Q97.2 Causeway Coast Radio

24 Cloyfin Road, Coleraine,
Co Londonderry BT52 2NU
028 7035 9100
Manager@q972.fm
www.q972.fm
*Adult contemporary. Coleraine. 97.2 FM.
Owner: Q Radio Network. Programme
controller: Frank McLaughlin; head of
news: Roger Donnelly; breakfast show:
Barrie Owler*

Minor stations *

Adventist World Radio
01344 401401
www.awr.org
Community and religious programmes. Satellite. Programme director: Ray Allen

Amrit Bani
020 8606 9292
info@amritbaniradio.com
www.amritbani.com
Religious Asian broadcasting. Digital. Operational director: Surjit Singh Dusanjh

Apna Radio
www.apnaradio.com
Punjabi, Hindi and Pakistani music. Internet

Asian Gold
020 8571 7200
info@sukhsagarradio.com
www.sukhsagarradio.com
Ethnic Asian. Digital. Chief executive director: Zorawar Gakhal

Bloomberg Radio
020 7330 7575
ecoleman4@bloomberg.net
www.bloomberg.co.uk
Financial news. 1130 AM. Radio editor: Eric Coleman

Calvary Chapel Radio
020 8466 5365
07779 507032
ccradio@btconnect.com
www.calvarychapelradio.co.uk
Christian radio. Sky. Managing director: Brian Brodersen; programme controller: Alison Johnstone-White

Club Asia
020 8594 6662
info@clubasiaonline.com
www.clubasiaonline.com
Young British Asians. 963 AM, 972 AM. Programme controller: Sumerad Ahmed

Easy Radio
0845 612 8040
info@easy1035.com
www.easy1035.com
DAB. Programme controller: Paul Owens

ETBC London
www.etbclondon.com
Tamil language

Family Radio
00 1 800 543 1495
www.familyradio.com
Christian gospel. Internet

FCUK FM
020 8749 7272
ian@deliciousdigital.com
www.fcuk.com
Music only. Internet. Managing director: O Raphael; director: Ian Taylor

HCJB World Radio
01274 721810
info@hcjb.org.uk
www.hcjb.org
Religious. International shortwave

Holiday FM
www.holidayfmradio.co.uk
Gran Canaria, Lanzarote, Tenerife, Costa del Sol, Ibiza, Costa Blanca

Kool AM
020 8373 1075
pfmnews@email.com
www.koolam.co.uk
Harlow. 1134 AM. Programme controller: Joe Bone

Laser Radio
01342 327842
laser@ukmail.com
www.laserradio.net
Baltic sea area and Scandinavia. 9290 AM. Managing director: Andrew Yeates

Music Choice
020 3107 0300
www.musicchoice.co.uk
Non-stop music compilation channels. Sky; internet. CEO: Margo Daly

NPR Worldwide (National Public Radio)
00 1 202 513 2000
www.npr.org/worldwide
Vice president, communications: Andi Sporkin

Panjab Radio
020 8848 8877
info@panjabradio.co.uk
www.panjabradio.co.uk
DAB and internet

Radio Caroline
020 8340 3831
info@radiocaroline.co.uk
www.radiocaroline.co.uk
Album rock music. Sky and internet. Programme controller and station manager: Peter Moore

Radio France Internationale (RFI)
00 33 1 5640 1212
www.rfi.fr
France's "World Service". Internet

Radio Telefis Eireann
00 353 1 208 3111
info@rte.ie
www.rte.ie
Ireland's public service broadcaster. Managing director: Adrian Moynes

Real Radio
029 2031 5100
ricky.durkin@realradiofm.com
www.realradiofm.com
60s to present day. 105-106 FM. Managing director: Andy Carter; programme director: Ricky Durkin

Spectrum Digital 1
020 7627 4433
enquiries@spectrumradio.net
www.spectrumradio.net
Multi-ethnic. 558 AM. General manager: Paul Hogan

The Storm
020 7911 7300
mail@stormradio.co.uk
www.stormradio.co.uk
Modern rock. Digital. Station manager: Bern Leckie

Sunrise Radio
020 8574 6666
reception@sunriseradio.com
www.sunriseradio.com
Asian. 1458 AM. Managing director: Tony Lit; programme controller: Tony Patti

talkGospel.com
020 7316 1300
enquiries@talkgospel.com
www.talkgospel.com
African and Caribbean churches. Sky and internet

TBC Radio
07817 063682
info@tbcuk.com
www.tbcuk.com
Political analysis, news, Asian music. Satellite. Managing director: V Ramarag

TotalRock
info@totalrock.com
www.totalrock.com
Rock and metal. Sky and internet. Editorial contact: Malcolm Dome

Trans World Radio UK
0161 923 0270
web@twr.org.uk
www.twr.org.uk
Christian music. Sky and internet; 1467 AM Saturday and Sunday 11.15pm; short-wave 9.87 MHz and 11.865 MHz each morning. Chief executive: Russell Farnworth

Voice of America
00 1 202 203 4000
publicaffairs@voa.gov
www.voanews.com
News, information, educational and cultural programming. Satellite

WorldSpace UK
020 7494 8200
ukservice@worldspace.com
www.worldspace.com
Music, news. Satellite. Senior vice-president: Safia Safwat

* Stations available in UK only on cable, satellite or internet, or on a small number of local DAB licences

Community radio

7 Waves
0151 691 1595
pauline.murphy@merseymail.com
www.7waves.co.uk
Leasowe, Wirral. Project coordinator: Pauline Murphy

209 Radio
01223 488418
getinvolved@209radio.co.uk
www.209radio.co.uk
Cambridge. Project manager: Karl Hartland

ACE Consortium
0115 970 6882
info@ace-consortium.net
Nottingham. Secretary: Kelbert Henriques

Aldershot Garrison FM
01748 830050
hq@garrisonradio.com
www.army.mod.uk/garrisonradio
Programme director: John McCray

Alive in the Spirit of Plymouth FM
01752 242262
chris@cornerstonevision.com
Programme manager: Christopher Girdler

ALL FM
0161 248 6888
alex@allfm.org
www.allfm.org
Manchester. Station manager: Alex Green

Angel Radio Havant
023 9248 1988
angelradio@37.com
Contact: Tony Smith

Angel Radio Isle of Wight
01983 246810
angelradioiw@hotmail.com
Contact: Chris Gutteridge

Asian Star
07841 918434
sbba1@yahoo.co.uk
Slough. Administration manager: Shba Siddique

BCB
01274 771677
info@bcbradio.co.uk
www.bcb.yorks.com
Bradford. Director: Mary Dowson; broadcast manager: Jonathan Pinfield

Betar Bangla
020 7729 4333
betarbangla@btconnect.com
London. Chief executive and director: Golam Mohammed Chowdhury

Bexley Community Media Association
01322 447767
info@bcma.biz
www.bcma.biz
Chief executive: Andrew Sayers

Branch FM
01924 454750
studio@branchfm.co.uk
Dewsbury. Contact: Stephen Hodgson

Bristol Community FM
07870 467245
phil@bcfm.org.uk
www.bcfm.org.uk
Project manager: Phil Gibbons

BRFM
01795 876045
office@brfm.net
www.brfm.net
Isles of Sheppey. Station manager: Danny Lawrence

Burst FM (Bristol University)
0117 954 5777
info@burstradio.org.uk
www.burstradio.org.uk
Station manager: Martin MacLachlan

Cambridge University Radio
01223 501004.
sm@cur1350.co.uk
www.cur1350.co.uk
Station manager: Michael Brooks

Canalside Community Radio FM
01625 576689
nick@ccr-fm.co.uk
www.ccr-fm.co.uk
Bollington, Macclesfield. Programme controller and coordinator: Nick Wright

Carillon Radio
01509 564433
carillonradio@aol.com
Loughborough. Station manager: Jon Sketchley

Castledown Radio
01264 791929
studio@castledownradio.info
www.castledownradio.info
Ludgershall, Wiltshire. Project manager: Baz Reilly

Catterick Garrison FM
01748 830050
hq@garrisonradio.com
www.army.mod.uk/garrisonradio/
Programme director: John McCray

Chelmsford Calling
01245 355274
jim.salmon@blueyonder.co.uk
www.chelmsfordcalling.com
Managing director: James Salmon

Cheshire FM
01606 737844
info@cheshirefm.com
www.cheshirefm.com
Northwich. Managing Director: David Duffy

Chesterfield Broadcasting Network
01246 851150
info@trustfm.co.uk
Station director: Ivan Spenceley

Colchester Garrison Radio
01206 782589
colchester@garrisonradio.com
www.garrisonradio.com
Managing director: Mark Page

Crescent Radio
01706 340786
faheem@myself.com
www.crescentradio.net
Rochdale. Contact: Faheem Chishti

Cross Rhythms City Radio
08700 118008
jonathan.bellamy@
crossrhythms.co.uk
www.crossrhythms.co.uk
Stoke on Trent (Hanley). General manager: Jon Bellamy

Cross Rhythms Teesside
07787 531759
Joel.hauxwell@gmail.com
www.crossrhythmsteesside.co.uk
Stockton on Tees. General manager: Joel Hauxwell

Demo FM
020 8655 7209
gracembailey@yahoo.co.uk
London. Record producer: Charles Bailey

Desi Radio
020 8574 9591
info@desiradio.org.uk
www.desiradio.org.uk
West London. Manager: Amarjit Khera

Diverse FM
01582 400906
diversefm@hotmail.com
www.diversefm.com
Luton. Coordinator: Ashuk Ahmed

Drystone Radio
01535 635392
drystoneradio@fsmail.net
www.drystoneradio.co.uk
Yorkshire Dales. Contact: David Adams

Express FM
023 9282 2112
studio@expressfm.com
www.expressfm.com
South Hampshire. Managing director: Cheryl Buggy

Focus FM Radio
0117 944 4497
info@focusradio.com
www.focusradio.com
Bristol. Director: Theo Stephenson

Forest FM
01202 820003
vwradio@aol.com
www.forestfm.co.uk or
www.forestfm.com
Verwood Dorset. Managing director: Steve Saville

Forest of Dean Community Radio
01594 820722
contactus@fodradio.org
www.fodradio.org
Cinderford, Glos. Director: Martin Harrison

Future Radio
01603 250505
info@nr5project.co.uk
www.futurefmradio.co.uk
Norwich. Radio manager: Tom Buckham

Generation Radio Clapham Park
020 8623 9419
studio@generationradio.co.uk
www.generationradio.co.uk
London. Programme director: Andy Sayers

Gloucester FM
01452 546400
admin@gloucesterfm.com
www.gloucesterfm.com
Chairman: Derrick Francis

Harborough FM
01858 464666
barry.badger@harboroughfm.co.uk
www.hfm.freeservers.com
Market Harborough. Station manager:
Barry Badger

Hayes Community Radio
020 8573 7992
office@hayesfm.org
www.hayesfm.org
Operations manager: Surish Sharma

Hope FM
01202 780396
jblaircrawford@aol.com
www.hopefm.com
Bournemouth. Executive director:
Blair Crawford

Indian Muslim Welfare Society
01924 500555
info@imws.org.uk
Batley. Centre manager: Mr Muza Kazi

Ipswich Community Radio
01473 418022
info@icrfm.co.uk
www.icrfm.co.uk
Contact: Nick Greenland

Life FM
020 8963 0935
bryan@lifefm.org.uk
www.lifefm.org.uk
London. Project director: Bryan Anderson

Link FM
01708 378378
dave.butler@haveringbep.co.uk
www.linkfm.net
Romford. Managing director: Dave Butler

Lionheart Radio
01665 602244
studio@lionheartradio.co.uk
www.lionheartradio.co.uk
Alnwick, Northumberland. Contact:
George Millar

Lune Valley Radio
01524 271294
paul@lakelandtoday.com
Kirby Lonsdale. Contact: Paul Broadbent

New Style Radio 98.7 FM
0121 456 3826
newstyle@acmccentre.co.uk
www.newstyleradio.co.uk
Birmingham. Chairman: Martin Blissett

NuSound Radio
07909 998927
tari.sian@nusoundradio.com
www.nusoundradio.com
Ilford. Project director: Tari Sian

Pendle Community Radio
01282 723 455
info@mwfuk.org
www.mwfuk.org
Manager: Sagheer Akhtar

Phoenix FM (Essex)
01277 234555
studio@phoenixfm.com
www.phoenixfm.com
Brentwood and Billericay.
Station manager: Paul Golder

Phoenix FM (Halifax)
01422 365923
sales@phoenixfm.co.uk
www.phoenixfm.co.uk
Contact: Anna Lombardi

Publicmedia UK
01322 223493
vb@publicmedia.co.uk
www.publicmedia.co.uk
Wigan. Enterprise director:
Vince Braithwaite

Pure Radio
0161 474 5961
info@pureradio.org.uk
www.pureradio.org.uk
Stockport. Radio project officer:
Dave Stearn

Raaj Radio
0116 2756212
infor@raajradio.co.uk
www.raajradio.co.uk
Leicester. Chief executive: Dr CPS Johal

Radio Barnsley
01226 216319
richodr@blueyonder.co.uk
www.ymcaradiobarnsley.co.uk
Barnsley. Training manager: Dave
Richardson

Radio CD (Radio Cultural Diversity)
01865 766032
jwoodman@doctors.org.uk
www.radiocd.org
Oxford. Programme director: Dr Woodman

Radio Faza 91.1 FM
0115 844 0052
radiofaza@hotmail.com
www.radiofaza.org.uk
Nottingham. Marketing manager: Javed
Mirza

Radio Faza FM/Karimia Institute
0115 841 5807
bmccnottingham@hotmail.com
www.karimia.com
Nottingham. Director: Dr Musharaf
Hussain

Radio Hartlepool
01429 275222
jason@radiohartlepool.co.uk
www.radiohartlepool.co.uk
Managing director: Jason Anderson

Radio Reverb
01273 323040
info@earshot.org.uk
www.radioreverb.com
Brighton. Contact: Karen Cass

Radio Scilly
01720 423304
radioscilly@aol.com
www.radioscilly.co.uk
Studio manager: Peter Hobson

Radio Teesdale
01833 696750
alastair@teesdaleenterprise.co.uk
Contact: Alastair Dinwiddie

Radio Ummah
020 8548 4647
www.radioummah.com
Internet. Chief Operating Officer: Saleem
Ahmed

Radio Verulam
07711 286488
studio@radioverulam.com
www.radioverulam.com
St Albans and Hemel Hempstead. Station
manager: Phil Richards

Redbridge FM
07814 450586

Resonance FM
020 7836 3664
info@resonancefm.com
www.resonancefm.com
London. Station managers:
Richard Thomas and Chris Weaver

Seaside Radio
01964 611427
lyz@seasideradio.org
Withernsea, E Yorks. Project manager:
Lyz Turner

Shalom FM
shalomfm@hotmail.com
www.shalomfm.com
London. Director: Richard Brian Ford

Sheffield Live
0114 2814082
sangita@thedrum.org.uk
Sheffield. Project leader: Sangita Basudev

Siren FM
01522 886270
brudd@lincoln.ac.uk
Lincoln. Contact: Bryan Rudd

Skyline Community Radio
01489 799008
webmaster@
    skylinecommunityradio.co.uk
www.skylinecommunityradio.co.uk
Southampton. Managing director: David
Algate

Sound Radio
info@soundradio.info
www.soundradio.org.uk
East London. Contact: Lol Gellor

Stourbridge Radio Group
01902 696425
info@stourbridgeradio.com
www.stourbridgeradio.com
Chairman and chief executive: Dr Paul
Collins

Sussex Surrey Radio
01737 644259
info@susyradio.com
www.susyradio.com
Redhill and Reigate. Contact: Colin Pearse

Takeover Radio
0116 2999600
sharon@takeoverradio.com
www.takeoverradio.com
Leicester. Contact: Sharon Komrska

Tameside Community Radio
07867 532 850
studio@tcrfm.com
www.tcrfm.com
Contact: Simon Walker

Tidworth Bulford Garrison FM
01748 830050
hq@garrisonradio.com
www.army.mod.uk/garrisonradio
Programme director: John McCray

Tyneside Community Broadcast
0191 278 2957
admin@cbit.org.uk
www.cbit.org.uk
Newcastle. Manager: Elaine Parker

Unity Radio 24
023 8023 3239
kelly@unity101.org
www.unity24.org
*Southampton. Project manager: Ram
Kalyan ("Kelly")*

Voice of Africa Radio
020 8471 9111
info@voiceofafricaradio.com
www.voiceofafricaradio.com
London. Project manager: Space Clottey

Walsall FM
01922 637666
pw004t5791@blueyonder.co.uk
Contact: Pam Weaver

Wayland Community Radio
07769 833868
wayland.radio@tesco.net
*Watton, Norfolk. Project manager: David
Hatherly*

**West Hull Community Radio
(WHCR FM)**
07711 117042
contact@whcrfm.com
www.whcrfm.com
Contact: John Harding

Wetherby Community Radio Group
01937 589088
bobpreedy@yahoo.co.uk
Contact: RE Preedy

Wharfedale FM
01943 463502
nigelfrancis@btinternet.com
Otley, Leeds. Chairman: Nigel Francis

Wirral Christian Media
0151 643 1696
office@flamefmwirral.org.uk
www.flamefmwirral.org.uk
Manager: Norman Polden

**Wolverhampton Community
Radio Training**
01902 572260
whitehousep@wolvcoll.ac.uk
www.wcrfm.com
Chairman: Peter Whitehouse

Wythenshawe FM
0161 237 5454
phil@radioregen.org
www.radioregen.org
Director: Phil Korbel

Youth Community Media
0845 226 1246
chris@youthcommunitymedia.org.uk
www.youthcommunitymedia.org.uk
Worcester. Station Manager: Chris Fox

● Wales

Afan FM
07791 375999
craig@afanfm.co.uk
www.afanfm.co.uk
*Port Talbot. Station manager: Craig
Williams*

Beats FM
029 2064 0500
john.lenney@immtech.co.uk
www.immtech.co.uk
Cardiff. Director: John Lenny

BRFM
01495 312567
studio@brfm.co.uk
www.brfm.co.uk
*Blaenau Gwent. Station manager: Chris
Lewis*

Calon FM
01978 293373
mail@nadira.co.uk
www.newi.ac.uk
*Wrexham. Head of communications,
technology and environment: Nadira
Tudor (07765 276880)*

GTFM
01443 406111
news@gtfm.co.uk
www.gtfm.co.uk
*Pontypridd. Station manager: Andrew
Jones*

Toradio
01495 791599
tormedia@softhome.net
www.tormedia.info/toradio.htm
Torfaen. Contact: Alan Fossey

● Scotland

Awaz FM
0141 420 6666
info@awazfm.co.uk
www.awazfm.co.uk
Glasgow. Contact: Javed Sattar

Black Diamond FM
0131 271 3711
admin@midlothianradio.org.uk
www.midlothianradio.org.uk
Edinburgh. Chairman: John Ritchie

Celtic Music
0141 812 7570
info@celticmusicradio.org.uk
www.celticmusicradio.org.uk
Glasgow. Contact: Robert McWilliam

East End Broadcast
0141 550 3954
Glasgow. Project manager: William Faulds

Edinburgh Garrison FM
01748 830050
hq@garrisonradio.com
www.army.mod.uk/garrisonradio/
Programme director: John McCray

Leith FM
0131 553 5304
info@leithmediaworks.com
www.leithmediaworks.co.uk
Edinburgh. Contact: Sandy Campbell

Ness Community Radio
01463 731740
colin.macphail@virgin.net
Inverness. Admin director: Colin MacPhail

Radio Asia Scotland
0141 570 5731
Radioasiascotland@hotmail.com
*Glasgow. Contact: Mohammed Nasar
Moughal*

Revival Radio
01236 823810
info@revivalradio.org.uk
www.revivalradio.org.uk
Cumbernauld. Chairman: Ian Dunlop

RNIB Scotland VIP ON AIR
0141 3345530
ross.macfayien@viponair.com
www.viponair.com
*Glasgow. Station manager: Ross
Macfayien*

Station House Media Unit
01224 487174
info@shmu.org.uk
www.shmu.org.uk
Aberdeen. Co-ordinator: Murray Dawson

Sunny Govan
0141 440 0600
sunnygovanradio@hotmail.com
www.sunnygovan.org
Glasgow. Contact: Heather McMillan

Superstation Orkney
01856 831835
info@thesuperstation.co.uk
www.thesuperstation.co.uk
Contact: Dave Miller

● Northern Ireland

BFBS – Lisburn
01494 878702
marc.tyley@bfbs.com
www.bfbs.com
Deputy controller: Marc Tyley

Down FM
028 4461 5815
ian.mccormick@edifhe.ac.uk
www.edifhe.ac.uk
*Downpatrick. Head of information and
design: Ian McCormick*

Féile FM
028 90 242002
emma@feilebelfast.com
www.feilebelfast.com
Belfast. Station manager: Emma Mullen

Raidió Fáilte
028 9020 8040
mary@aislingghear.tv
*Belfast. Contact: Máire Uí
Mhaoilchiaráin*

Hospital, student and sporting event radio

1287 AM Insanity
01784 414268
studio@su.rhul.ac.uk
www.insanityradio.com
Egham. Student radio. 1287 AM.
Station manager: Chris Jackson-Jones

1503 AM Radio Diamonds
01933 652000
press.office@rd-fc.co.uk
Matchday service for Rushden and
Diamonds FC. 1503 AM. Contact: Simon
Hitchcox

B-1000
01895 203094
www.brunel.ac.uk
Uxbridge. Brunel University. 999 AM

Bailrigg FM
01524 593902
station.manager@bailriggfm.co.uk
www.bailriggfm.co.uk
Lancaster University. 87.7 FM.
Station manager: Sara Bury

Basildon Hospital Radio
01268 282828
studios@bhr1287.net
www.bhr1287.net
1287 AM. Chairman: Alan Newman

Bedrock AM
01708 738700
www.musicinhospital.org.uk
Romford. Oldchurch Hospital. 846 AM

BFBS
01494 878701
adminofficer@bfbs.com
www.bfbs.com
Chalfont St Peter. Forces radio. Northern
Ireland only. 1287 AM. Radio controller:
Charles Foster

Big Blue
020 7386 1677
gary@bigbluedigital.co.uk
Chelsea. Matchday service. 96.3 FM.
Contact: Gary Taphouse

Blast 1386
0118 967 5068
blast1386@reading-college.ac.uk
www.blast1386.com
Reading. Student radio. 1386 AM;
internet. Station manager: Bob Goertz

Bridge FM
01382 496333
info@bridgefm.org.uk
www.bridgefm.org.uk
Dundee. Hospital, Tayside. 87.7 FM.
Presenter: Barry Hampton; station
manager: Bob McNally

C4 Radio
01227 782510
c4radio@cant.ac.uk
Canterbury. Christchurch College.
999 AM. Station manager: Lucy Drury

Canterbury Hospital Radio
01227 864161
www.chradio.org.uk
Canterbury. 945 AM. Studio manager:
Martin Pauley

Canterbury Student Radio
01227 824703
www.csrfm.com
University of Kent. 1350 AM. Liz Nicholson

Cardiff Stadium Radio
01264 369369
paul.forsyth@sounddec.com
www.sounddeck.com
Cardiff. Rugby referee match
commentary. Sales director: Paul Forsyth

Carillon Radio
01509 564433
carillonradio@aol.com
Loughborough. Loughborough Hospital,
Coalville Hospital. 1386 AM

Carlett Radio
0151 551 7777
enquiries@wmc.ac.uk
Wirral Metropolitan College. 1287 AM

Chichester Hospital Radio
01243 788122 x3000
studio@chr1431.org.uk
www.chr1431.org.uk
St Richard's Hospital. 1431 AM.
Presenter: Mark Hughes

City Hospital Radio
01442 262222
general@hemelradio.com
www.hemelradio.com
Hemel Hempstead. St Albans City Hospital.
1350 AM; 1287AM. Chairman: Neil O'Hara

Crush
01707 285005
uhsu.comms@herts.ac.uk
http://uhsu.herts.ac.uk/media/crush/
Hatfield. University of Hertfordshire.
1278 AM. Station manager: Domhnall
Cosgrave

CUR
01223 569509
studio@cur1350.co.uk
www.cur1350.co.uk
Cambridge. Churchill College, University
of Cambridge. 1350 AM. Station manager:
Michael Brooks

D:One
01332 590500
http://done.udsu.co.uk/
Derby. University of Derby. 1278 AM.
Station manager: Richard Green

Dorton Radio Station
01732 592500
karen.campbell@rlsb.org.uk
www.rlsb.org.uk
Sevenoaks. Dorton College. 1350 AM.
Station manager: Karen Campbell

Frequency
01772 894895
www.yourunion.co.uk
Preston. University of Central
Lancashire. 1350 AM. Station manager:
Emma Syer

GU2
01483 681350
studio@gu2.co.uk
www.gu2.co.uk
Guildford. Student. 1350 AM. Head of
Creative: Tom Knight

Hospital Radio Basingstoke
01256 313521
mail@hrbasingstoke.co.uk
www.hrbasingstoke.co.uk
945 AM. Programme controller: Neil Ogden

Hospital Radio Crawley
01293 534859
1287 AM

Hospital Radio Plymouth
01752 763441
www.hospitalradioplymouth.org.uk
87.7 FM. Station Manager: Bob Smith

Hospital Radio Pulse
01527 512048
studio@hospitalradiopulse.com
www.hospitalradiopulse.com
Redditch. 1350 AM. Programme
controller: Ian Barstow

Hospital Radio Reading
0118 950 7420
requests@hospitalradioreading.co.uk
www.hospitalradioreading.org.uk
Royal Berkshire and Battle Hospitals. 945
AM. Programme controller: Stephen Ham

Hospital Radio Rossendale
01706 233334
945 AM. Contact: David S Foster

Hospital Radio Yare
01493 842613
jean@birchwell.co.uk
www.radioyare.com
Great Yarmouth. James Paget, Northgate,
Lowestoft hospitals. 1350 AM. Chairman:
Jean Thorpe; programme controller: Phil
Marshall

IC Radio
020 7594 8100
info@icradio.com
www.icradio.com
South Kensington. Imperial College halls
of residence. 999 AM. Station manager:
Mike Jones

Insanity
01784 414268
studio@su.rhul.ac.uk
www.insanityradio.com
Egham. Royal Holloway, University of
London. 1287 AM

Jam 1575
01482 466999
email@jam1575.com
www.jam1575.com
Hull. Hull University. 1575 AM. Station
manager: Oliver Tripp

Junction 11
0118 986 5159
studio@1287am.com
www.1287am.com
Reading. Reading University. 1287 AM.
Station manager: Dave Wiley

Kendal Radio
01539 795420
Info@kendalhospitalradio.com
www.kendalhospitalradio.org.uk
Hospital radio. Chairman: John Fulstow

Kingstown Radio
01482 327711
onair@kingstownradio.com
www.kingstownradio.co.uk
Hull. Hull hospital radio. 1350 AM.
Station manager: Nick Palmer

Kool AM
020 8373 1075
pfmnews@email.com
www.koolam.co.uk
Edmonton. 1134 AM. Programme
controller: Joe Bone

Livewire
01603 592512
manager@livewire1350.com
www.livewire1350.com
Norwich. UEA students. 1350 AM.
Station manager: Alan Milford

Loughborough Campus Radio
01509 635050
studio@lcr1350.co.uk
www.lcr1350.co.uk
Loughborough. Student radio. 1350 AM.
Head of media: Lucy Pritchard; station
manager: Oliver Folkerd

Mid-Downs Hospital Radio
01444 441350
studio@ndr.org.uk
Haywards Heath. Hospital radio.
1350 AM. Station manager: Alan French

Nerve Radio
01202 595765
Jhawkins@bournemouth.ac.uk
www.nervemedia.net
Bournemouth. Bournemouth University.
87.7 FM. Web manager: Jason Hawkins

Nevill Hall Sound
01873 858633
info@nevillhallsound
www.nevillhallsound.com
Abergavenny. Nevill Hall Hospital.
1287 AM. Station manager: Steve Powell

Newbold Radio
01344 454607 x324
www.newbold.ac.uk
Binfield. Newbold College. 1350 AM

Oakwell 1575 AM
enquiries@oakwell1575am.co.uk
www.oakwell1575am.co.uk
Barnsley. Matchday service for Barnsley
FC. 1575 AM. Station manager: Dave
Parker

Palace Radio 1278 AM
020 8653 5796
info@palaceradio.net
www.palaceradio.net
London. Matchday service for Crystal
Palace FC. 1278 AM. Station Manager:
Jerry Clark

Portsmouth Hospital Broadcasting
023 9262 6299
www.qaradio.co.uk
Queen Alexandra Hospital and St Mary's
Hospital. 945 AM. Station manager:
Barrie Swann

Radio Air3
01786 467179
stationManager@airthrey.co.uk
http://susaonline.org.uk
Sterling. Student, music, politics. 1350 AM.
Station manager: Matt Ludlow

Radio Branwen
01766 781911
radiobranwen@yahoo.co.uk
Harlech. Student, music. 87.7 FM.
Station manager: Trevor Andrews

Radio Brockley
020 8954 6591
studio@radiobrockley.org
www.radiobrockley.org
London. Stanmore's Royal National.
Orthopaedic Hospital. 999 AM

Radio Bronglais
01970 635363
office@radiobronglais.co.uk
www.radiobronglais.co.uk
Aberystwyth. Bronglais General Hospital.
87.8 FM. Station manager: Martin Oakes

Radio Cavell
0161 620 3033
info@radiocavell1350.org.uk
www.radiocavell1350.org.uk
Royal Oldham Hospital. 1350 AM.
Broadcasting manager: Phil Edmunds

Radio Chelsea and Westminster
0702 880 1234
www.chelwest.nhs.uk
Hospital radio. Chairman: Anthony
Davis; station manager: James Healy

Radio Glangwili
01267 227504
Carmarthen. West Wales General
Hospital. 87.7 FM

Radio Gosh
020 8203 2226
peter@radiogosh.co.uk
www.radiogosh.co.uk
London. Great Ormond Street Hospital.
999 AM. Chairman: Peter Losch

Radio Heatherwood
01344 625818
www.radioheatherwood.org.uk
Ascot. Heatherwood Hospital. 999 AM.
Station manager: Dave Smith

Radio Hotspot
01473 326200
www.royalhospitalschool.org
Ipswich. The Royal Hospital School.
1287 AM. Manager: Don Topley

Radio Lonsdale
01229 877877
studio@radiolonsdale.co.uk
www.radiolonsdale.co.uk
Hospital. 87.7 FM. Station manager:
Julian Ackred

Radio Nightingale
01709 304244
Admin@radionightingale.org.uk
www.radionightingale.org.uk
Rotherham District General Hospital.
1350 AM

Radio North Angus
01382 424095
info@radionorthangus.co.uk
www.radionorthangus.co.uk
Arbroath Infirmary and Brechin
Infirmary. 96.6 FM, 87.7 FM. Managing
director: Malcolm Finlayson

Radio North Tees
01642 624337
info@radionorthtees.com
www.radionorthtees.com
Stockton on Tees. Hospital radio.
Station manager: Elliot Kennedy

Radio Northwick Park
020 8869 3959
info@radionorthwickpark.org
www.radionorthwickpark.org
North-west London. Hospital radio.
Programme controller: Matt Blank

Radio Reading
0118 322 6560
www.hospitalradioreading.org.uk
Aberdeen. Royal Aberdeen Children's
Hospital. 945 AM

Radio Redhill
01737 768511
studio@radioredhill.co.uk
www.radioredhill.co.uk
East Surrey Hospital. 1287 AM.
Station manager: Nigel Gray

Radio Rovers
01254 261413
touchline@radiorovers.com
www.gjmedia.co.uk/rrovers
Blackburn. Blackburn Rovers matchday
service. 1404 AM. Station manager:
Alan Yardley

Radio Tyneside
0191 273 6970
info@radiotyneside.co.uk
www.radiotyneside.co.uk
Newcastle General Hospital. 1575 AM

Radio Warwick
024 7657 3077
studio@radio.warwick.ac.uk
www.radio.warwick.ac.uk
Warwick. Student radio. 1251 AM.
Station manager: James Buckland

Radio West Suffolk
01284 713403
peteowen1350@hotmail.com
www.radiowestsuffolk.co.uk
Bury St Edmunds. West Suffolk Hospital.
1350 AM. Vice chairman: P Owen

Radio Wexham
01753 570033
Wexham Park Hospital. 945 AM

Radio Ysbyty Glan Clwyd
01745 584229
Conway. Glan Clwyd District General
Hospital. 1287 AM. Manager: Morag Jelly

Ram Air
01274 233269
studio@ramair.co.uk
www.ramair.co.uk
Bradford. University of Bradford.
1350 AM. Station manager: Ben Nunney

Range Radio
0161 861 9727
studio@rangeradio.co.uk
www.rangeradio.co.uk
Manchester. Student radio. 1350 AM.
Station manager: Roy Appleby

Red
01206 863211
red@essex.ac.uk
www.essexstudent.com/media
/redradio
Colchester. Student radio. 1404 AM.
Station manager: Shruti Budhia

RK1 FM
01691 773671
singletonr@moretonhall.com
www.moretonhall.org/radio
_report.html
Oswestry. Moreton Hall Educational
Trust. 87.7 AM. Head of science: Richard
Singleton

Rookwood Sound Hospital Radio
029 2031 3796
chief@rookwoodsound.co.uk
www.rookwoodsound.co.uk
Llandaff. Rookwood Hospital. 945 AM.
Programme controller: Matthew Morrissey

The Saint 107.8 FM
023 8033 0300
studio@saintsfc.co.uk
www.saintsfc.co.uk
Adult contemporary, Southampton FC.
Southampton. 107.8 FM. Independent.
Programme controller: Stewart Dennis;
station director: Tim Manns; breakfast
show: Stewart Dennis

Sports! Link-fm
01225 835553
info@sportslinkfm.com
www.sportslinkfm.com
Live sports commentary. 87.7 to 105 FM.
Managing director: Peter Downey

SNCR
0115 914 6467
Nottingham. South Nottingham College.
1278 AM

Solar AM
01744 623454
solar1287am@hotmail.com
www.sthelens.ac.uk/college
/facilities/solar.asp
St Helens. St Helens College. 1287 AM.
Station manager: Terry Broughton

Southside Hospital Broadcasting
01642 854742
info@southsideradio.com
www.southsideradio.com
James Cook University Hospital. Contact:
Alex Lewczuk

Stoke Mandeville Hospital Radio
01296 331575
info@smhr.co.uk
www.smhr.co.uk
1575 AM

Storm FM
01248 383235
admin@stormfm.com
www.stormfm.com
Bangor. University of Wales Bangor.
87.7 FM. Manager: Spencer George

Storm Radio
01206 500700
storm@colchsfc.ac.uk
www.colchsfc.ac.uk
Colchester. Student radio. 999 AM.
Station manager: Shirley Hart

Subcity Radio
0141 341 6222
manager@subcity.org
www.subcity.org
Glasgow. Student radio. 1350 AM.
Station manager: Sean Murphy

Surge
023 8059 1287
office@surgeradio.co.uk,
studio@surgeradio.co.uk
www.surgeradio.co.uk
University of Southampton. 1287 AM.
Station manager: Alex Duffy; programme
controller: Richard Bennett; head of
music: James Hickson

Trust AM
01909 502909
studio@trustam.com
www.trustam.com
Doncaster. Doncaster and Bassetlaw
Foundation Trust group of hospitals.
1278 AM. Programme controllers:
Steve Roberts and Andy Morton

Tunbridge Wells Hospital Radio
01892 528528
info@hrtw.org.uk
www.hrtw.org.uk
Kent and Sussex, Pembury and Tonbridge
Cottage hospitals. 1350 AM. Programme
controller: Chris Manser

UCA
01292 886358
Marcus.Bowman@paisley.ac.uk
www.ucaradio.paisley.ac.uk
Ayr. University campus, Ayr. 87.7 FM;
DAB. Station manager: Marcus Bowman

University Radio Falmer
01273 678999
exec@urfonline.com
www.urfonline.com
Falmer. University of Sussex and Brighton
University Falmer Campus. 1431 AM.
Station manager: Daniel Parslow

University Radio York
01904 433840
ury@ury.york.ac.uk
http://ury.york.ac.uk
York. Student radio. 1350 AM.
Programme controller: Matt Wareham

URB
01225 386611
studio@bath.ac.uk
www.1449urb.com
Bath. Student radio. 1449 AM.
Station manager: Mark Farrington

URF
01273 678999
exec@urfonline.com
www.urfonline.com
Brighton. Student radio. 1431 AM.
Station manager: Jonathan Pascoe

URN
0115 846 8722
manager@urn1350.net
www.urn1350.net
Nottingham. University of Nottingham.
1350 AM. Station manager: Paul Hughes;
head of music: Philippa Treverton-Jones

Viva AM
01925 722298
head@penketh.warrington.sch.uk
www.penkethhigh.com/vivaradio.htm
Warrington. Penketh High School. 1386
AM. Programme controller: Jonathan Kay

VRN
07940 591479
www.classicvrn.org.uk
Kirkaldy. Victoria Hospital, Kirkaldy.
1287 AM. Programme controller: Sandy
Izatt

WCR AM
01902 572260
training@wcr1350.co.uk
www.wcr1350.co.uk
Wolverhampton. College radio. 1350 AM.
Manager: Nicola Stewart

Withybush FM
01437 773564
studio@withybushfm.co.uk
www.withybushfm.co.uk
Withybush Hospital. 87.7 FM.
Station manager: Hilary Raymond

Xpression
01392 263568
stationManager@Xpressionfm.com
www.Xpressionfm.com
Exeter. Student radio. 87.7 FM.
Station manager: Chloe Aust

Xtreme
01792 295989
studio@xtremeradio.info
www.xtremeradio.info
Swansea. Student radio. 1431 AM.
Station Manager: Richard Lewis

Radio associations

Association for International Broadcasting
PO Box 141, Cranbrook TN17 9AJ
020 7993 2557
info@aib.org.uk
www.aib.org.uk
Trade organisation

Broadcasting Press Guild
Tiverton, The Ridge, Woking,
Surrey GU22 7EQ
01483 764895
torin.douglas@bbc.co.uk
Promotes interests of journalists who write or broadcast about the media

Commercial Radio Companies Association
The Radiocentre, 77 Shaftesbury Avenue, London W1D 5DU
020 7306 2603
info@radiocentre.org
www.radiocentre.org

Creators' Rights Alliance
British Music House, 26 Berners Street, London W1T 3LR
020 7436 7296
info@creatorsrights.org
www.creatorsrights.org.uk
Campaigns to protect creators' rights; operates in all media areas

Digital Radio Development Bureau (DRDB)
The Radiocentre, 77 Shaftesbury Avenue, London W1D 5DU
020 7306 2630
info@drdb.org
www.drdb.org
Trade body; funded and supported by BBC and commercial radio multiplex operators

Musicians Union
60–62 Clapham Road,
London SW9 0JJ
020 7840 5534
london@musiciansunion.org.uk
www.musiciansunion.org.uk

Office of Communications (Ofcom)
Riverside House, 2A Southwark Bridge Road, London SE1 9HA
020 7981 3000
mediaoffice@ofcom.org.uk
www.ofcom.org.uk
Broadcasting super-regulator

Performing Rights Society
29–33 Berners Street,
London W1T 3AB
020 7580 5544
mediaquery@mcps-prs-alliance.co.uk
www.prs.co.uk
Collects and distributes royalties
Press: 020 7306 4803

Rad10
rad10@rad10.com
www.rad10.com
Free training resource for radio volunteers looking at going professional; offers advice for community radio groups

Radio Joint Audience Research (Rajar)
Paramount House,
162–170 Wardour St,
London W1F 8ZX
020 7292 9040
info@rajar.co.uk
www.rajar.co.uk
Audience measurement system. Wholly owned by the Commercial Radio Companies Association and the BBC

The Radio Academy
5 Market Place, London W1W 8AE
020 7255 2010
info@radioacademy.org
www.radioacademy.org
Professional body for radio; aims to promote excellence and a greater understanding of the medium

Voice of the Listener and Viewer (VLV)
101 King's Drive, Gravesend,
Kent DA12 5BQ
01474 352835
info@vlv.org.uk
www.vlv.org.uk
Independent, non-profit society working to ensure independence, quality and diversity in broadcasting

Women's Radio Group
27 Bath Road, London W4 1LJ
Fax: 020 8995 5442
wrg@zelo.demon.co.uk
www.womeninradio.org.uk
Training and networking charity

World Radio Network
PO Box 1212, London SW8 2ZF
020 7896 9000
email@wrn.org
www.wrn.org
Home to series of global radio networks; hosts transmission services for world's leading broadcasters

Radio trade press

Advance Production News
Crimson Communications,
211a Station House,
Greenwich Commercial Centre,
49 Greenwich High Road,
London SE10 8JL
020 8305 6905
www.crimsonuk.com
Monthly. Listings for production companies. Editor: Alan Williams

Audio Media
IMAS Publishing UK, Atlantica House, 11 Station Road, St Ives, Cambs PE27 5BH
01480 461555
p.mac@audiomedia.com
j.miller@audiomedia.com
www.audiomedia.com
Monthly. Professional audio. Editor: Paul Mac; news: Jonathan Miller; editorial manager: Sarah Johnston

Broadcast
Emap Media, 33–39 Bowling Green Lane, London EC1R 0DA
020 7505 8000
admin@broadcastnow.co.uk
www.broadcastnow.co.uk
Weekly. TV and radio industry. Editor: Conor Dignam; news: Chris Curtis; features and deputy editor: Emily Booth; chief sub: Angus Walker

Commonwealth Broadcaster
Commonwealth Broadcasting Association, 17 Fleet Street, London EC4Y 1AA
020 7583 5550
cba@cba.org.uk
www.cba.org.uk
Quarterly. Editor: Elizabeth Smith

Contacts – The Spotlight Casting Directories
The Spotlight, 7 Leicester Place, London WC2H 7RJ
020 7437 7631
info@spotlight.com
www.spotlight.com
Annual. Contacts for stage, film, TV and radio. Editor: Kate Poynton

Line Up
Line Up Publications, The Hawthornes, 4 Conference Grove, Crowle WR7 4SF
01905 381725
editor@lineup.biz
www.lineup.biz
Bi-monthly. Journal of the Institute of Broadcast Sound. Editor: Hugh Robjohns

Pro Sound News Europe
CMP Information, Ludgate House, 245 Blackfriars Road, London SE1 9UR
020 7921 8319
david.robinson@cmpi.biz
www.prosoundnewseurope.com
12pa. Audio industry. Owner: CMP Information. Editor: David Robinson; managing editor: Camilla Edwards

QSheet

10 Northburgh Street,
London EC1V 0AT
020 7253 8888
www.qsheet.com
*Monthly. Support material for presenters
and producers. Editor: John Reynolds;
features and interviews: Nik Harta; art
direction and design: Dominic Philcox*

Radcom

Radio Society of Great Britain,
Lambda House, Cranbourne Road,
Potters Bar EN6 3JE
0870 904 7373
radcom@rsgb.org.uk
www.rsgb.org
Monthly. Radio enthusiasts

Radio Magazine

Crown House, 25 High Street,
Rothwell, Northants NN14 6AD
01536 418558
name@theradiomagazine.co.uk
www.theradiomagazine.co.uk
*Weekly. Radio news for industry. Editor:
Paul Boon; features and assistant editor:
Collette Hillier; advertising and technical
manager: Tom Hooper*

Stage Screen and Radio

Bectu, 373–377 Clapham Road,
London SW9 9BT
020 7346 0900
jturner@bectu.org.uk
www.bectu.org.uk
*10pa. Broadcasting union. Editor: Janice
Turner*

VLV Bulletin

Voice of the Listener and Viewer,
101 Kings Drive,
Gravesend DA12 5BQ
01474 352835
info@vlv.org.uk
www.vlv.org.uk
*Quarterly. Advocates citizen and
consumer interests in broadcasting.
Editor: Jocelyn Hay*

Digital media

The sector formerly known as new media is this year rechristened digital media. This will not, I fear, be the last renaming of this sector, but at least the change recognises that the technology is no longer new. As the phrase "bubble 2.0" begins to gain traction — suggesting that the rash of big buyouts and multi-billion dollar deals are overvaluing the potential of the internet all over again, the very least we can do is suggest the sector has a history.

With longevity comes respectability and with respectability comes responsibility. Internet cowboys who consider themselves beyond the law now simply have too much money to be ignored.

There's also the issue of copyright, copyright, copyright. As soon as big corporate owners start getting involved, there are assets that are worth suing over — as the new site owners of MySpace.com and YouTube.com have found out. If you are (as YouTube was) two guys in a room above a pizza shop trying out a cool new idea, chances are that a company such as Viacom, for example, will ignore your blatant infringement of its copyright because you're not worth bothering with. But almost as the ink was drying on the deal between Google and YouTube, the new owners were forced to step up the removal of copyrighted material from the site. Whole episodes of The Daily Show (previously one of the staples of the site's content) disappeared overnight, though the show's owner, Comedy Central, decided to be magnanimous over "clips".

News Corporation's newly acquired MySpace was next in line to clean up, announcing it would license technology allowing it to stop users illegally posting copyrighted material — largely music and music videos. This decision followed public criticism and presumably private threats

YouTube website celebrates acquisition by Google

David Sillitoe

from movie studios and music labels. The chairman of Universal Music, Doug Morris, used an investor conference to decry both MySpace and YouTube as "copyright infringers" who "owe us tens of millions of dollars". Later Universal decided if you can't beat 'em, form a partnership which it did with YouTube – though it has launched lawsuits against smaller sites such as Bolt and Grouper.

The technology MySpace will rely on has been used by iTunes for a while. Gracenote, which provides song titles and "sleeve notes" on downloaded tracks, will be able to identify copyrighted material uploaded to the site and block anything being used without consent.

And why did MySpace cave in with so little resistance? It plans to begin selling music, initially with songs from unsigned bands, but aiming to offer signed acts. And you can't do that if you're at war with the record companies. Of course, the wild west mentality of the world wide web suggests that as soon as MySpace and YouTube "go legal", the hep cats will move on somewhere else, leaving News Corporation and Google with expensive empty prairies.

These companies can surely just keep buying the next big thing. The numbers speak for themselves: UK internet advertising is worth almost half of TV advertising – just under £1bn in the first six months of 2006, up 40.3%, year on year and predicted to top £2bn by the end of the year. It overtook press advertising spend for 2006, doubles the size of outdoor spend (posters and billboards), is twice the amount spent on magazines and three times the size of radio advertising.

Where's all the money coming from? Pretty much everywhere: recruitment, finance, entertainment, media and automotive. This extraordinary rate of growth is attributed partly to the rapid take-up of broadband in the UK – 10m households are now broadband-enabled. And with better web access comes more hours spent online – an average of 23 hours a week, according to a YouGov survey of internet users.

Most interestingly, where is all the money going? In a one-word answer, Google. Of that predicted £2bn in 2006, Google is estimated to have taken £900m. Nearly half of all UK advertising. This big round number was put very effectively into context by Channel 4's chief

ROCKET SCIENCE MADE SIMPLE

RELEVANT, TARGETED AND EFFICIENT DIGITAL MARKETING SOLUTIONS FOR ADVERTISERS AND PUBLISHERS

- Behavioural targeting, advanced analytics, Rich Media and integrated ad-serving

- More than 1,000 websites serving over 30 billion impressions every month

- Rated number one search engine marketing services and technology provider*

*Rated N°1 in the 2006 Jupiter Research Constellation Report

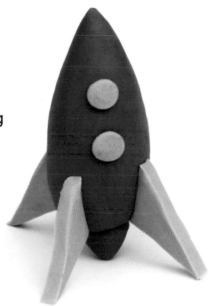

THE SCIENCE OF DIGITAL MARKETING

Online ad spend		
Year	Spend £m	Market share %
2005	1272	7.2
2004	784	4.5
2003	448	2.7
2002	192	1.2
2001	164	1.0
2000	153	0.9
1999	51	0.3
1998	20	0.1

Source: Advertising Association

executive, Andy Duncan, who pointed out that this "structural change" in the ad industry meant that Google would make more money than his 24-year-old broadcast station (at roughly £800m).

As with the copyright rows, this diversion of a huge slice of total advertising spend has hit the critical mass where big companies are starting to take serious notice. With that kind of attention comes the inevitable question of regulation. In television, for example, ITV's dominance of the ad market requires regulation. It is inevitable that Google's rivals (and that now means everyone in media) will soon begin lobbying for some sort of equivalent.

Google has not maintained a low profile in sucking up the cash either. Last year, it scrapped the 15% gross discount it traditionally offered agencies and replaced it with a new net pricing system. Its big problem now is how to retain its market position without tipping over into Microsoft territory and attracting measures to curb its dominance.

It would be naive to think that Google hasn't already spotted this potential thorn. Less than two months before the mid-term congressional elections, it registered a political action committee with the US federal election commission – a first step towards making corporate donations to support candidates seeking elected office.

In the UK, Google's chairman and chief executive, Eric Schmidt, has kept his political options open, forging links with both the government and the opposition. Google Europe has been hiring from the political arena, too, bringing both a former union activist and the partner of a prominent Tory advisor into its communications unit.

So far, Google has claimed its NetPAC exists solely to promote a free market on the internet. (Let's not forget, its founding principle is "don't be evil".) But as Warren Cowan, head of the London-based internet search marketing consultancy Greenlight was quoted in the Guardian:

"As Google moves far beyond search to become a global media owner, it is throwing its tendrils out into non-search related areas. If its business had been based more in the 'real' world rather than online, then the regulators would have eyed it up long ago."

It might not be unrelated to this point to note that Eric Schmidt has called a moratorium on new developments by the firm, saying it needed to focus on providing better versions of its existing projects. That said, it has bought out a firm that builds "wiki" style communities and launched a new search facility, Google Co-Op, which will allow users and businesses to build customised search engines to be placed on their own sites. Google Co-op will be free, but Google will display ads alongside all the results.

Of course, when you get too big in the new world, you attract not just government intervention but also annoying hackers. Apple is cursing the renowned hacker Jon Lech Johansen, a California-based Norwegian who claims to have found a way of bypassing the copy protection on the iPod. His discovery means that you can play tracks not bought from either the Apple store or taken from a CD on your iPod. Johansen's breakthrough could potentially unlock the popular music player – which has sold nearly 68m units around the world since it was launched five years ago – and make it compatible with tracks sold by other online retailers.

Johansen has form: when he was 15, he cracked the copy protection software used to encrypt DVDs. Though the film industry spent years trying to prosecute him, he was acquitted and his code is available all over the internet.

I
SPY
SEARCH
MARKETING

I Spy is passionate about search engine marketing and the results it will deliver for your business.

We specialise in search engine marketing and offer a focussed, customised and integrated solution for your search marketing success for both Paid Search Campaign Management and Natural Search Engine Optimisation.

Call: Chris Whitelaw

Tel: 020 7096 1797

Email: information@ispysearch.com

● Content

The big movers in internet content, MySpace and YouTube, have been bought out. Next, if only judging by its phenomenal public profile is Second Life, the virtual world in which its million inhabitants play games, dress up as more glamorous versions of themselves, flirt and shop. The simulated land has hosted concerts by established artists and is home to various "virtual stores" started by big name brands. Two rules set down by its founders are key to its success: first, that all its users own the copyright to anything they build or create within Second Life. Second, the money that is used for trading "in-world" has an exchange with US dollars. It is, therefore, possible to spend one's working life there as well as recreational hours, and make an income. Virtual real-estate agents (it's a status symbol to own property within Second Life and trading is fast approaching, if not central London levels, then certainly a smart bit of Manchester), shop owners and casino proprietors have all gone on record testifying to the possibility of living online.

Blogs and podcasts have become so ubiquitous that, to borrow a TV term, the moment when they jump the shark cannot be far away. The arrival of political parties into the blogosphere can only hasten the "so over" moment. The Tories' much-derided Webcameron — a video diary of, yes, the Conservative Party leader David Cameron mostly doing the washing up — upset everyone by being unutterably naff. The Labour Party retaliated with labourspace.com, a "grassroots" site where supporters are encouraged to write about issues they care about.

The internet TV station 18 Doughty Street launched with some fanfare as the home of UK neocons. It is, let's face it, only a matter of time, before a more attractive version of your local MP starts campaigning in Second Life. That'll kill it stone dead.

The industry to have fallen most quickly in love with the internet must surely be the press. Entirely unsurprisingly if you refer back to the figures at the beginning of this chapter detailing the movement of advertising money. Rupert Murdoch's turnaround with regards to the internet has finally started to sweep through to his mainstream media. The Sun newspaper has launched its own social networking site — My Sun. Based loosely on MySpace (both are owned by parent company News Corporation), My Sun allows users to post pictures, profiles, reviews, comment and chat and blogs on the Sun's website. The Times Online has redesigned its site to promote consumer activity, scheduled to relaunch

Webcasting mania... Nick Razzell takes part

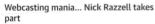
Webcameron down with the kids

Nicholas Razzell

Top 10 web audiences			
Name	Unique audience 2006 (m)	Unique audience 2005 (m)	Growth in unique audience
1 Google	19.5	17.3	13%
2 MSN/Windows Live	16.8	–	–
3 Microsoft	14.7	–	–
4 Yahoo!	12.9	13.5	-5%
5 BBC	12.8	10.9	17%
6 eBay	11.8	11.6	2%
7 Amazon	6.9	7.1	-2%
8 Apple	6.3	5.4	15%
9 Lycos Europe	6.2	3.7	67%
10 AOL	6.0	6.5	-8%

* Coding change to Microsoft and MSN parameters means trended data comparison unavailable

Source: Nielsen//NetRatings

before the end of 2006. The Times newspaper has been concentrating on communities, podcasts and Times Online TV, announcing that it would screen clips from Sky News.

Associated Newspapers, owners of the Daily Mail, was the slowest mover to the internet and resisted putting even its daily paper's content up until very recently. However, the revamped site became one of the year's fastest growers. The Telegraph, as discussed in the press section, has effectively integrated its paper and web teams overnight – a gamble that has yet to play out but which will be hugely influential whether it comes off or not.

The Guardian Unlimited has been the biggest UK newspaper on the web for some years – largely because its trust status meant its management could argue for investment on the web while its shareholder-owned rivals were cutting back. Now, however, the Guardian faces challenges from all quarters. It has reacted by launching two new super-blogs, Comment Is Free and Arts and Entertainment. It too is flirting with video and podcasts. Late in 2006 it announced that creators of the highly-successful TV programme The Office, Ricky Gervais and Stephen Merchant, would be bringing their world-record-holding podcast back to the Guardian site.

Awards

Webby Awards, May 2006

- *Best copy/writing* — NewYorker.com   www.newyorker.com
- *Blog – Business* — 5 Blogs Before Lunch   http://daveibsen.typepad.com/5_blogs_before_lunch
- *Blog – Culture/Personal* — we make money not art   http://we-make-money-not-art.com
- *Blog – Political* — The Huffington Post   www.huffingtonpost.com
- *Community* — BBC Cumbria website/Digital Lives   www.bbc.co.uk/cumbria/digital_lives
- *Film* — 2006 Sundance Film Festival   http://festival.sundance.org/2006
- *Guides/Ratings/Reviews* — UCS HybridCenter   www.hybridcenter.org
- *Magazine* — National Geographic Magazine Online   http://ngm.com
- *Music* — Fabchannel.com – Concerts Online   www.fabchannel.com
- *News* — BBC News   http://news.bbc.co.uk
- *Newspaper* — Guardian Unlimited   www.guardian.co.uk
- *Politics* — OpenSecrets   www.opensecrets.org
- *Radio* — NPR.org   www.npr.org
- *Telecommunications* — Orange 'Talking Point'   http://talkingpoint.orange.co.uk
- *TV* — Creating the Scene   www.hbo.com/carnivale/behind/creating_the_scene/index.html

Bafta Games Awards, October 2006

- *Best game* — Tom Clancy's Ghost Recon Advanced Warfighter
- *Action and Adventure* — Shadow of the Colossus
- *Strategy* — Rise And Fall: Civilizations at War
- *Simulation* — The Movies
- *Multiplayer* — Dungeons & Dragons Online: Stormreach
- *Sports* — Fight Night Round 3
- *Technical Achievement* — Tom Clancy's Ghost Recon Advanced Warfighter
- *Artistic Achievement* — Shadow of the Colossus

Digital comes of age

Bobbie Johnson

The past year has seen a rapid resurrection of the dotcom boom, with entrepreneurs and investors piling into new ventures around the world. They can sniff something revolutionary in the air — a chance, once again, to turn ideas into business opportunities.

It's all a stark contrast to the situation five years ago, when it was tumbleweed — not bright ideas — that blew through Britain's silicon alleys. The bursting of the dotcom bubble, which had been dangerously expanded by incredible hubris and buccaneer attempts at profiteering, brought an entire industry to its knees even more swiftly than it had built it up.

But half a decade later, and with a little more wisdom, a renewed sense of optimism and innovation has emerged. At the centre lies the increasing cross-pollination of different media and different audiences.

With it have come spine-tingling reminders of the late 1990s, such as the re-emergence of the dotcom whizzkid and tales of nerds in garages turning into millionaires overnight. But for all the triumphal whoops, many insiders — and the money people who back them — are quick to say that they have learned their lessons.

Other fragments of the past remain, too. The BBC continues to dominate the UK's new media scene. And thanks to a new digital-age strategy dreamt up by its director general, Mark Thompson, and his hi-tech coterie, Auntie is now working on the kind of cross-media commissioning that once seemed the preserve of funky young independents. The result of his so-called "Creative Future" strategy seems to have been the increase in the influence of technology inside the corporation, and more power to the elbow of new media guru Ashley Highfield. Executives must now commission programming and content across all media platforms, and are brought together under three banners; journalism, audio & music and vision. Highfield is responsible for the pan-organisational division Future Media and Technology, tasked with taking the BBC further into the 21st century.

And the popular concept of community-generated information and user content is also flexing its muscles — with plans afoot to create an online BBC that connects to people directly, as well as letting them connect with each other.

Such futuristic public service concepts — and existing ones such as Backstage, which promises to open up many of Auntie's online services to talented hackers and programmers — are not only trying to catch the zeitgeist but are also vital in maintaining the BBC's status as a publicly-funded organisation well into the future... even if the departure of Michael Grade threw an unexpected spanner into the works. Thompson's talk of "convergence" and "platforms" might sound more like a consultant's game of buzzword bingo than the inheritor of Reith's vision, but — if nothing else — it indicates the increasing influence that the internet age is exerting on old media organisations.

Even though the Beeb, with its deep pockets, casts a long shadow, it also offers illumination. Many of the brightest talents in our digital media industry have been forged, at least in part, in its labyrinthine corridors and offices — though many have chosen to escape. And while giants such as Google, Microsoft and Yahoo continue to expand their operations in the UK, the sheer dominance of a very British organisation actually helps illustrate some of the advantages we have over our transatlantic cousins.

Unlike the United States — where Silicon Valley, Madison Avenue and the bright lights of Hollywood exist in their own separate worlds, interacting only when business needs to be done — the UK's digital media world benefits from tightness. The heart of our thriving internet industry pulses to the beat of the nearby advertising agencies. And the talent that it produces (or the audiences it serves) are no more than a few hours' drive away, rather than divided by a cross-continental schlep.

Central to future growth is the rise of video on the web. What once was difficult to watch (characterised by jerky, slow-loading films) is now fast-becoming a mainstay of the online media industry. The rapid deployment of broadband internet has breathed life into a troublesome outlet, until the tipping point was reached when YouTube commanded $1.65bn of Google's money despite being barely 18 months old. Rumours of other buyouts swirl around the industry with the power of a hurricane, and the unstoppable growth of user-generated product threatens to turn the old models of television on their head.

While user-generated content has been the buzzphrase du jour for some time, getting the content for free doesn't mean much if you can't work out what to do with it. Where such ventures prove financially successful it is through bringing traditional media — stories, sounds and films — to the internet and coupling them with advertising.

How will analogue media convert to the digital age? Radio stations have already jumped on the podcasting bandwagon, but it remains to be seen whether TV broadcasters will be brave or foolhardy enough to do the same.

● Bobbie Johnson is technology correspondent at the Guardian

Digital media contacts

In this section we provide details of some of the key companies involved in the digital sector, online publishers, digital media agencies and associations. However, to avoid repetition in the book many companies are not listed here, but can be found listed under their core businesses.

Main search engines/ portals

AltaVista
New London House, 172 Drury Lane, London WC2B 5QR
angela.bloor@overture.com
www.altavista.co.uk
Press: 020 7071 3510

Ask
53 Parker Street, London WC2B 5PT
020 7400 2222
infogeneral@ask.com
www.ask.com
Press: 020 7400 2222

Excite UK
Viale G Baccelli, 70,
00153 – Roma, Italy
00 39 06 570231
bberger@staff.excite.lt
www.excite.co.uk
Press: 00 39 06 5702 3208

Google UK
European HQ:
Gordon House, Barrow Street, Dublin 04, Ireland
UK sales office:
Belgrave House, 76 Buckingham Palace Road, London SW1W 9TQ
020 7031 3000
UK@google.com
www.google.co.uk
Press: 020 7031 3130

Kelkoo UK
125 Shaftesbury Avenue,
London WC2H 8AD
sales@kelkoo.co.uk
www.kelkoo.co.uk
Shopping search engine owned by Yahoo!
Press: press@kelkoo.co.uk

Lycos UK
8th Floor, 1 Stephen Street,
London W1T 1AL
020 7462 9200
www.lycos.co.uk
Press: ukpressoffice@lycos-europe.com

MSN
Microsoft House, 10 Great Pulteney Street, London W1R 3DG
0870 601 0100
www.msn.co.uk
Press: 0870 2077 377
ukprteam@microsoft.com

Yahoo! UK
125 Shaftesbury Avenue,
London WC2H 8AD
020 7131 1000
www.yahoo.co.uk

Main software publishers

Activision UK
3 Roundwood Avenue, Stockley Park, Uxbridge UB11 1AF
020 3060 1000
www.activision.com
Games

Adobe
3 Roundwood Avenue, Stockley Park, Uxbridge, Middlesex UB1 1AY
020 8606 4000
www.adobe.co.uk
Design and publishing software

Apple Computer UK
2 Furzeground Way, Stockley Park East, Uxbridge, Middlesex UB11 1BB
020 8218 1000
uk.marketing@euro.apple.com
www.apple.com/uk
Computer hardware/software
Press: appleuk.pr@euro.apple.com
apple@bitepr.com

Atari UK
Landmark House, Hammersmith Bridge Road, London W6 9EJ
020 8222 9700
www.atari.co.uk
Games

Codemasters
Stoneythorpe, Southam, Warwickshire CV47 2DL
01926 814132
www.codemasters.co.uk
Games
Press: press@codemasters.co.uk

Eidos Interactive
Wimbledon Bridge House,
1 Hartfield Road,
Wimbledon SW19 3RU
020 8636 3000
plc@eidos.co.uk
www.eidos.co.uk
Games

Electronic Arts
2000 Hillswood Drive, Chertsey, Surrey KT16 0EU
http://uk.ea.com
Independent developer and publisher of interactive entertainment software
Press: 01932 450000

Focus Multimedia
The Studios, Lea Hall Enterprise Park, Wheelhouse Road, Rugeley, Staffordshire WS15 1LH
01889 570156
info@focusmm.co.uk
www.focusmm.co.uk
CD-roms

IBM Lotus
PO Box 41, North Harbour, Portsmouth, Hampshire PO6 3AU
023 9256 1000
www.lotus.co.uk, www.ibm.com
Office software

Linux
59 East River St, #2, Ogdensburg, NY13669 USA
00 1 315 393 1202
www.linux.org.uk
Free operating system
Press: pr@linux.org

Microsoft UK
Microsoft Campus, Thames Valley Park, Reading, Berkshire RG6 1WG
0870 601 0100
www.microsoft.com/uk
Software house
Press: 0870 207 7377
ukprteam@microsoft.com

McAfee UK
227 Bath Road, Slough, Berkshire SL1 5PP
01753 217500
www.mcafee.com
Anti-virus

RealNetworks
1st Floor, 233 High Holborn, London WC1B 7DN
020 7618 4000
www.real.co.uk
Audio and video
Press: real@axicom.com

Symantec UK
Hines Meadow, St Cloud Way, Maidenhead, Berkshire SL6 8XB
01628 592 222
www.symantec.co.uk
Information security provider
Press: 01628 592365

Main ISPs

AOL UK
80 Hammersmith Road,
London W14 8UD
020 7348 8000
www.aol.co.uk
Press: ukmediaoffice@aol.com

British Telecom
BT Centre, 81 Newgate Street, London EC1A 7AJ
020 7356 5000
www.bt.com
Press: 020 7356 5000

Claranet UK
21 Southampton Row,
London WC1B 5HA
020 7685 8310
info@clara.net
www.clara.net
Press: 020 7685 8019

Demon
322 Regents Park Road, Finchley,
London N3 2QQ
0800 027 5848
netsales@demon.net
www.demon.net

Easynet
1 Brick Lane, London E1 6PU
020 7900 4444
business@uk.Easynet.net
www.easynet.net
Press: 0870 770 4767

Entanet
Stafford Park 6, Telford,
Shropshire TF3 3AT
0870 770 9588
www.enta.net
Press: 0870 770 4996

Nildram
1 Triangle Business Park,
Stoke Mandeville,
Buckinghamshire HP22 5BD
0800 197 1490
info@nildram.net
www.nildram.net

NTL UK
NTL House, Bartley Wood Business
Park, Hook, Hampshire RG27 9UP
01256 752000
www.ntl.com
Press: 020 7466 5000

One.Tel
3rd Floor, Building 1, Chiswick Park
High Road, London W4 5BY
020 7181 9991
www.onetel.co.uk

Orange UK
Verulam Point, Station Way,
St Albans AL1 5HE
0870 373 5605
www.orange.co.uk
Press: 0870 373 5517

Pipex
Pipex House, 4 Falcon Gate, Shire Park,
Welwyn Garden City AL7 1TW
0845 077 2537
www.pipex.co.uk

PlusNet Technologies
Technology Building, Terry Street,
Sheffield S9 2BU
0845 140 0200
www.Plus.net

Surfanytime
12 Beckford Business Centre,
Beckford Street, Hamilton ML3 OBT
0870 141 7113
www.surfanytime.co.uk

Telewest
Export House, Cawsey Road,
Woking, Surrey GU21 6QX
01483 750900
www.telewest.co.uk
Press: 020 7299 5888

Tiscali UK
20 Broadwick Street,
London W1F 8HT
020 7087 2000
www.tiscali.co.uk

Virgin.net
The Communications Building,
48 Leicester Square,
London WC2H 7LT
www.virgin.net
Press: 020 7907 7803

Vispa Internet
The Courtyard, 160a Moss Lane,
Altrincham, Cheshire WA15 8AU
0870 1624 888
info@vispa.net
www.vispa.co.uk

Yahoo! UK
125 Shaftesbury Avenue,
London WC2H 8AD
020 7808 4000
agency@uk.yahoo-inc.com
www.yahoo.co.uk

Main telecoms companies

British Telecom
BT Centre, 81 Newgate Street,
PO Box 163, London EC1A 7AJ
020 7356 5000
www.bt.com
Press: 020 7356 5000

Cable and Wireless
Lakeside House, Cain Road,
Bracknell, Berkshire RG12 1XL
01908 845000
www.cw.com

Colt Communications
Beaufort House, 15 St Botolph Street,
London EC3A 7QN
020 7863 5000
info@colt.net
www.colt.net

Coms
Coms.com Ltd, 77 Queen Victoria
Street, London EC4V 4AY
020 7618 9000
info@coms.com
www.coms.com
Press: techteam@midnight.co.uk

Hutchinson 3G UK
3 Media Centre, 27b Floral Street,
Covent Garden, London WC2E 9DP
0870 733 0333
www.three.co.uk
Press: 01628 765000

Kingston Communications
37 Carr Lane,
Kingston upon Hull HU1 3RE
01482 602000
www.kcom.com
Press: 01482 602711

NTL UK
NTL House, Bartley Wood Business
Park, Hook, Hampshire RG27 9UP
01256 752000
www.ntl.com
Press: 020 7466 5000

O2
Wellington Street, Slough SL1 1YP
0113 272 2000
www.o2.com
Press: 01753 628402

Orange
The Point, 37 North Wharf Road,
London W2 1AG
0870 373 1500
www.orange.co.uk
Press: 020 7984 2000

Talk Talk
1 Portal Way, London W3 6RS
0870 4441820
pressoffice@cpw.co.uk
www.talktalk.co.uk

Telewest
Export House, Cawsey Road,
Woking, Surrey TU21 6QX
01483 750900
www.telewest.co.uk
Press: 020 7299 5888

Thus
1/2 Berkley Square,
99 Berkley Street, Glasgow G3 7HR
0141 567 1234
www.thus.net

T-Mobile (UK)
Hatfield Business Park, Hatfield,
Hertfordshire AL10 9BW
01707 315000
www.t-mobile.co.uk
Press: 07017 150150

Verizon Business
Reading International Business Park,
Basingstoke Road, Reading,
Berkshire RG2 6DA
0118 905 5000
pressoffice_uk@lists.mci.com
www.verizonbusiness.com
Press: ukpressoffice@
                verizonbusiness.com

Virgin Mobile
5th Floor, Communication Building,
48 Leicester Square,
London WC2H 7LT
020 7484 4300
www.virginmobile.com

Vodafone
Vodafone House, The Connection,
Newbury, Berkshire RG14 2FN
0700 050 0100
www.vodafone.co.uk
Press: 0845 444 4466/01635 664444

UK news online

BBC News.co.uk
TV Centre, Wood Lane,
London W12 7RJ
020 8743 8000
www.bbc.co.uk

Belfast Telegraph
Independent News and Media
(Northern Ireland), Internet
Department, 124–144 Royal Avenue,
Belfast BT1 1EB
028 9026 4000
www.belfasttelegraph.co.uk

FT.com
One Southwark Bridge, London SE1 9HL
020 7873 3000
joanna.manning-cooper@ft.com
www.ft.com
Press: 020 787 34447

Guardian Unlimited
119 Farringdon Road, London EC1R 3ER
020 7278 2332
editor@guardianunlimited.co.uk
www.guardian.co.uk
Press: 020 7239 9818

The Independent
Independent House, 191 Marsh Wall,
London E14 9RS
020 7005 2000
www.independent.co.uk

ITV News
200 Grays Inn Road, London WC1X 8HF
editor@itn.co.uk
www.itv.com/news

Online Mirror
MGN, 1 Canada Square, Canary Wharf,
London E14 5AP
020 7293 3000
mirrornews@mgn.co.uk
www.mirror.co.uk
Press: 020 7293 3222

Orange
Marshall Mill, Marshall Street,
Leeds LS11 9YJ
0113 367 4600
simon.glover@orange.co.uk
www.ananova.com

Reuters
30 The Reuters Building,
South Colonnade, Canary Wharf,
London E14 5EP
020 7250 1122
www.reuters.co.uk
Press: 020 7542 7457

The Scotsman
Barclay House, 108 Holyrood Road,
Edinburgh EH8 8AS
0131 620 8620
enquiries@scotsman.com
www.scotsman.com
Press: 0131 620 8507

Sky News
Grant Way, Isleworth TW7 5QD
0870 240 3000
www.sky.com/skynews

The Sun Online
Level 6, 1 Virginia Street,
London E98 1SN
020 7782 4000
corporate.info@the-sun.co.uk
www.thesun.co.uk

Telegraph Online
111 Buckingham Palace Road,
London SW1W 0DT
020 7538 3235
corporateaffairs@telegraph.co.uk
www.telegraph.co.uk

The Times
1 Pennington Street, Wapping,
London E98 1TA
020 7782 5000
online.editor@thetimes.co.uk
www.timesonline.co.uk

Online publishers

CTO Media
St Augustines House,
Werrington Street, London
07974 581357
online@camden.tv
www.camden.tv
*Londons first web-based community
television station*

Handbag.com
151 Oxford Street, London W1D 2JG
editor@handbag.com
www.handbag.com
Women's consumer site

Motley Fool UK
2nd Floor, Lasenby House,
32 Kingly Street, London W1B 5QQ
020 7025 5500
ukwebfool@fool.co.uk
www.fool.co.uk
Personal finance

MyVillage
105 Ladbroke Grove, London W11 1PG
020 7792 0624
info@myvillage.co.uk
www.myvillage.co.uk
Leisure guide

Petite Personal Shopper
PO Box 218, Aberystwyth SY23 3XS
07779 084573
yasmin@petitepersonalshopper.com
www.petitepersonalshopper.com
*Fashion magazine website aimed at the
petite market*

Popbitch
hello@popbitch.com
www.popbitch.com
Celeb gossip email and forum

Rapnews.co.uk
editorial@rapnews.co.uk
www.rapnews.co.uk
*The leading online resource for hiphop
culture and rap music*

Salon.com
101 Spear Street, Suite 203,
San Francisco, CA 94105, USA
00 1 415 645 9200
www.salon.com
US online magazine

Slate
251 West 57th Street, 19th Floor,
New York, NY 10019-1894, USA
00 1 212 445 5330
www.slate.com
US online magazine
Press: press@slate.com

Upmystreet.com
10th Floor, Portland House,
Stag Place, London SW1E 5BH
020 7802 2992
content@upmystreet.com
www.upmystreet.com
Local information
Press: pr@upmystreet.com

Wikipedia
200 2nd Avenue South 358,
St Petersburg, Florida 33701, USA
00 1 727 231 0101
Press@wikimedia.org
www.wikipedia.org
User-edited encyclopaedia
Press: 00 1 727 231 0101

YourKindaTV.com
8-10 Neal's Yard, Covent Garden,
London WC2H 9DP
020 7096 0802
contact@yourkindatv.com
www.yourkindatv.com
*Online news and views which combines
user submitted content with professionally
produced content.*
Press: 020 7612 1155

New media agencies

3T Productions
0161 492 1400
queries@3t.co.uk
www.3t.co.uk

Abacus e-media
London: 020 7549 2500
Portsmouth: 023 9289 3600
info@abacusemedia.com
www.abacusemedia.com

Agency.com
020 7964 8200
info.london@agency.com
www.agency.com

Agency Republic
020 7942 0000
chat@agencyrepublic.com
www.agencyrepublic.com/home.asp

AKQA
020 7780 4786
info@akqa.com
www.akqa.com

Amaze
0870 2401700
generalenquiries@amaze.com
www.amaze.com

Aspect Group
020 7504 6900
contactus@lbicon.co.uk
www.lbicon.co.uk

Babel Media
01273 764100
info@babelmedia.com
www.babelmedia.com

Big Picture Advertising
020 7240 6582
simon@bigpictureadvertising.co.uk
www.bigpictureadvertising.co.uk

Bostock and Pollitt
020 7379 6709
info@bostockandpollitt.com
www.bostockandpollitt.com

Carlson Digital
020 8875 0875
www.carlsonmarketing.co.uk

Cimex Media Ltd
020 7324 7780
contact@cimex.com
www.cimex.com
*Consultancy through to digital design,
technical and content services*

CMW Interactive
020 7224 4050
d-smith@cmw-uk.com
www.cmwinteractive.com

Complete
020 7383 5300
general@complete.co.uk
www.complete.co.uk

Conchango
01784 222222
www.conchango.com

Craik Jones Digital
020 7734 1650
digital@craikjones.co.uk
www.digital.craikjones.co.uk

cScape
020 7689 8800
m.daniels@cscape.com
www.cscape.com

Custom Communication
07949 830256
info@customcommunication.co.uk
www.customcommunication.co.uk
Online contract publishing/social media strategies

Dare Digital
020 7612 3600
us@daredigital.com
www.daredigital.com

DC Interact
London: 020 7689 1200
Edinburgh: 0131 556 1172
hello@dcinteract.com
www.dcinteract.com

Deal Group Media
020 7691 1880
www.dgm-uk.com

Detica
01483 442000
info@detica.com
www.detica.com

Digit
020 7377 4000
info@digitlondon.com
www.digitlondon.com

Digital TMW
020 7349 4000
info@tmw.co.uk
www.tmw.co.uk

Digiterre
020 7381 7910
info@digiterre.com
www.digiterre.com

DNA
020 7907 4545
info@dna.co.uk
www.dna.co.uk

Draft London
020 7589 0800
john.minnec@draftlondon.com
www.draftlondon.com

DVA
01256 882032
info@dva.co.uk
www.dva.co.uk

E3 Media
0117 9021333
info@e3media.co.uk
www.e3media.co.uk

EHS Brann
020 7017 1000
www.ehs.co.uk

Euro RSCG Interaction UK
020 7240 4111
info-interaction@eurorscg.com
www.eurorscginteraction.co.uk

Framfab
020 7446 7500
info.uk@framfab.com
www.framfab.co.uk

Freestyle New Media Group
01926 652832
info@fsnm.co.uk
www.fsnm.co.uk

Global Beach
020 7384 1188
info@globalbeach.com
www.globalbeach.com

Glue London
020 7739 2345
www.gluelondon.com

Good Technology
020 7299 7000
almira.mohamed@
  goodtechnology.com
www.goodtechnology.com

Greenlight
020 7253 7000
rfi@greenlight.co.uk
www.greenlight.co.uk
Search Engine Marketing company

GT Network
01476 514687
info@gtns.co.uk
www.gtns.net

Gurus
023 80231219
info@gurumedia.net
www.gurumedia.net

Haygarth Direct
020 8971 3300
stephen.m@haygarth.co.uk
www.haygarth.co.uk

The Hub Communications
020 3008 6260
www.thehub.co.uk

Interesource New Media
020 7613 8200
www.interesource.com

Ioko365
01904 438 000
info@ioko.com
www.ioko.com

IR Group
020 7436 3140
mark.hill@the-group.net
www.the-group.net

IS Solutions
01932 893333
www.issolutions.co.uk

iTouch
020 7613 6000
info@itouch.co.uk
www.itouch.co.uk

itraffic
020 7964 8500
www.itraffic.com

Lateral
020 7613 4449
www.lateral.net

Latitude Group Ltd
01925 413 513
office@searchlatitude.com
www.searchlatitude.com

Lawton eMarketing
023 8082 8522
steve.sponder@lawton.co.uk
www.lawtonemarketing.com

LB Icon (UK)
020 7504 6900
contactus@lbicon.co.uk
www.lbicon.co.uk

Lightmaker Group
01892 615015
sales@lightmaker.com
www.lightmaker.com

Lightmaker Manchester
0161 834 9889
matt.farrar@lightmaker.com
www.lightmaker.com

louter productions
0121 443 2835/07916152215
fabrice.millet@louterproductions.com
www.louterproductions.com
Audio visual solutions for the charitable/art sector

Madgex
01273 775100
info@madgex.com
www.madgex.com
Works with B2B publishers to develop their online titles, drive web traffic and increase revenue

McCann-i
01625 822 200
info@mccann-i.com
www.mccann-i.com

M-Corp
01425 477766
enquiries@m-corp.com
www.m-corp.com

MediaVest IP
020 7190 8000
ecombe@uk.starcomww.com
www.mediavest.co.uk

MitchellConnerSearson Group
020 7420 7991
london@choosemcs.co.uk
www.mitchellconnersearson.com

Modem Media
020 7874 9400
info@modemmedia.com
www.modemmedia.com

Netstore
0870 300 6400
www.netstore.co.uk

Ogilvy Interactive
020 7345 3000
www.ogilvy.com

Poulters
0113 383 4200
enquiries@poulters.com
www.poulters.com

Profero
020 7387 2000
contact@profero.com
www.profero.com

Proximity London
020 7298 1000
info@proximitylondon.com
www.proximitylondon.com

Rathergood
07796 487538
joel@rathergood.com
www.rathergood.com
Animations, songs, commercials

Reading Room
020 7025 1800
info@readingroom.com
www.readingroom.com

Realise
020 7743 7150
www.realise.com

Recreate Solutions
020 8233 2916
contactus@recreatesolutions.com
www.recreatesolutions.com

Redbee Media
020 8008 0080
www.redbeemedia.com

Redskin
020 7636 8262
info@redskin7.com
www.bravemarketing.com

Rufus Leonard
020 7404 4490
enquiries@rufusleonard.com
www.rufusleonard.com

Sapient
020 7786 4500
eu_sales@sapient.com
www.sapient.co.uk

Sift Group
0117 915 9600
service@sift.co.uk
www.sift.co.uk

Souk Digital
020 7420 7880
mail@soukdigital.com
www.soukdigital.co.uk

Syzygy UK
020 7460 4080
london@syzygy.net
www.syzygy.net

Tangozebra
020 7535 9850
info@tangozebra.com
www.tangozebra.com

TBG
020 7428 6650
info@tbglondon.com
www.tbglondon.com
Full service digital marketing agency that provides creative, strategy, media planning and technology services

TBWA\GGT
020 7440 1100
info@tequila-uk.com
www.tequila-uk.com

Them
020 8392 6868
talktous@themlondon.com
www.themlondon.com

Tribal DDB
020 7258 4500
www.tribalddb.com

TVF Medical Communications
020 7837 3000
lynette.coetzee@tvf.co.uk
www.tvfcommunications.com

twentysix London
020 7535 9800
info@twentysixlondon.com
www.twentysixlondon.com

Urbandevcorp
07906 292373
info@urbandevcorp.com
www.urbandevcorp.com

Victoria Real
020 8222 4591
www.victoriareal.com

Web Technology Group
020 7339 8600
info@webtechnologygroup.co.uk
www.webtechnologygroup.co.uk

Wheel
London: 020 7348 1000
Glasgow: 0141 225 6560
www.wheel.co.uk

Wireless Information Network
01494 750500
businessdevelopment@winplc.com
www.winplc.com

Write Image
020 7959 5400
info@write-image.co.uk
www.write-image.com

XM London
020 7724 7228
xminfo@ccgxm.com
www.xmlondon.co.uk

Digital media planning and buying

All Response Media
020 7017 1450
www.allresponsemedia.com
www.digit-all.co.uk

Carat Interactive
020 7430 6320
reception@carat.com
www.carat.com

Cheeze
01473 236892
info@cheeze.com
www.cheeze.com

i-level
020 7340 2700
www.i-level.com

Isobar UK
020 7405 1050
info@isobarcommunications.com
www.isobarcommunications.com

MediaCom North
0161 839 6600
johnmarshall@mediacomnorth.com
www.mediacomnorth.com

MediaVest
020 7190 8000
ecombe@uk.starcomww.com
www.mediavest.co.uk

Outrider
001 314 209 1005
contact.us@outrider.com
www.outrider.com

PHDiQ
020 7446 0555
callen@phd.co.uk
www.phd.co.uk

Profero
020 7387 2000
contact@profero.com
www.profero.co.uk

Quantum
020 7287 8768
info@quantum-media.co.uk
www.quantum-media.co.uk

Starcom Digital
020 7190 8000
ecombe@uk.starcomww.com
www.starcomww.co.uk

TBG
020 7428 6650
info@tbglondon.com
www.tbglondon.com
Full service digital marketing agency that provides creative, strategy, media planning and technology services

Tribal DDB
020 7258 4500
www.tribalddb.com

Unique Digital Marketing
020 7354 6566
mark@unique-digital.co.uk
www.unique-digital.co.uk

Zed
01923 815 913
design@zed.co.uk
www.zed.co.uk

New media trade press

3G Mobile
Informa Telecoms & Media
020 7017 5537
telecoms.enquiries@informa.com
www.informatm.com
Fortnightly. Editor: Gavin Patterson; news and features: Nick Lane; chief sub: Charles Gordon

Computer Weekly
Reed Business Information
020 8652 3500
editorial@computerweekly.com
www.computerweekly.com
Weekly. Editor: Hooman Bassirian; news and features: Mike Simons; production: Stuart Nissen

Computing
VNU Business Publications
020 7316 9000
catrina_attard@vnu.co.uk
www.computing.vnu.co.uk
Weekly. Editor: Toby Wolpe; news, features and production: Catrina Attard

EI magazine
Ark Publishing
020 8785 2700
publishing@ark-group.com
www.eimagazine.com
Monthly. Editor: Graeme Burton; features and production: Emma Palfreyman

Informa Telecoms & Media
Informa Telecoms & Media
020 7017 4852
Kathryn.Bushnell@informa.com
www.arcgroup.com
Strategic research reports

IT Europa
IT BPL
01895 454458
contact@ITEuropa.com
www.iteuropa.com
20pa. Editor: Andrew Seymour

IT Week
VNU Business Publications
020 7316 9000
itweek_letters@vnu.co.uk
www.itweek.co.uk
*Weekly. Editor: Toby Wolpe; news,
features and production: Catrina Attard*

Journalism.co.uk
Mousetrap Media, 68 Middle Street,
Brighton BN1 1AL
01273 384293
info@journalism.co.uk
www.journalism.co.uk
*Website editor/publisher: John Thompson;
news reporter: Oliver Luft; sales/marketing
manager: Kiera Schacht; production
manager: Clare Fisher*

NetImperative
020 8535 7565
editorial@netimperative.com
www.netimperative.com
*Email and online news service, daily and
weekly newsletters. Editor: Mike Butcher*

New Media Age
Centaur Media
020 7970 4000
www.nma.co.uk
*Weekly. Editor: Michael Nutely; features:
Justin Pearson; production: George Stewart*

Online Journalism Review
Annenberg School of Journalism
001 213 740 3914
rniles@usc.edu
www.ojr.org
*Online. Publisher: Geoffrey Cowan;
editor: Robert Niles*

The Online Reporter
Rider Research
01280 820560
info@newsriderresearch.com
www.riderresearch.com
Weekly. Editor: Charles Hall

The Register
020 7462 7744
news@theregister.co.uk
www.theregister.co.uk
*Website. Editor-in-chief: Drew Cullen;
editor: Joe Fay*

Revolution
Haymarket Business Publications
020 8267 4947
revolution.ads@haynet.com
www.revolutionmagazine.com
*Monthly. Editor: Philip Smith; news:
Emma Rigby; features: Philip Buxton;
art editor: David Grant; production:
Vic Johnstone*

VNUnet.com
VNU Publications
020 7316 9000
newseditor@vnunet.com
www.vnunet.com
*Online. Editor: Robert Jaques; chief sub:
Francis Abberley*

Wired
001 415 276 8400
www.wired.com
*Monthly. Managing editor: Marty Cortinas;
senior reporter: Kim Zetter; content
editor: Leander Kahney; copy chief: Tony
Long; production manager: Jeremy Barna*

World Telemedia
0870 7327 327
info@worldtelemedia.co.uk
www.worldtelemedia.co.uk
/wtmag.htm
*Quarterly. Publisher: Toby Padgham;
editor: Paul Skeldon*

ZDNet UK and Silicon.com
CNet Networks
020 7903 6800
www.cnet.com
*Online. Editors: Matt Loney, Tony Hallett;
news: Graham Weirdon*

Internet associations

Association of Freelance Internet Designers
a.carson@uku.co.uk
www.afid.net

Association of Online Publishers (AOP)
Queens House, 28 Kingsway,
London WC2B 6JR
020 7400 7510
alex.white@ukaop.org.uk

British Interactive Media Association
Briarlea House, Southend Road,
South Green, Billericay CM11 2PR
01277 658107
info@bima.co.uk
www.bima.co.uk

British Internet Publishers Alliance (BIPA)
49 Park Town, Oxford OX2 6SL
01865 310732
angela.mills@wade.uk.net
www.bipa.co.uk

British Web Design and Marketing Association
PO Box 3227, London NW9 9LX
020 8204 2474
info@bwdma.co.uk
www.bwdma.co.uk

Entertainment and Leisure Software Publishers Association
167 Wardour Street, London W1F 8WL
020 7534 0580
info@elspa.com
www.elspa.com
Trade association for games industry

HTML Writers Guild/International Webmasters Association
(IWA-HWG), 119 E Union Street,
Suite F, Pasadena, CA 91103 USA
help@iwanet.org
www.hwg.org
Training body for web designers

Internet Advertising Bureau
Adam House, 7-10 Adam Street,
Strand, London WC2N 6AA
Press: 020 7886 8282
info@iabuk.net
www.iabuk.net

Internet Corporation for Assigned Names and Numbers (ICANN)
4676 Admiralty Way, Suite 330,
Marina del Rey, CA 90292-6601, USA
00 1 310 823 9358
icann@icann.org
www.icann.org

Internet Service Providers Association
23 Palace Street, London SW1E 5HW
0870 050 0710
pressoffice@ispa.org.uk
www.ispa.org.uk

Internet Watch Foundation
East View, 5 Coles Lane, Oakington,
Cambridge CB4 5BA
01223 237 700
media@iwf.org.uk
www.iwf.org.uk
*Operates hotline for public to report
inadvertent exposure to illegal internet
content*

London Internet Exchange (Linx)
2nd Floor, Geneva House, 3 Park
Road, Peterborough PE1 2UX
Press: 01733 207700
info@linx.net
www.linx.net

Global media

Ahead of the game... Rupert Murdoch

Any discussion of global media from a UK perspective must begin with one question: "What's Rupert Murdoch up to?" It's a measure of how far the media industry has come in the past five years that there are even supplementary questions at all, to be honest.

But to deal with that first question, Murdoch has been pleasingly distracted by the UK at the back end of 2006. The buying of an 18% stake in ITV in November for nigh on £1bn was a substantial blocking move to protect BSkyB's position in the UK. Arguably it might also prove to help expand BSkyB by providing leverage to buy, say Channel Five, from RTL should the German group wish to make a move on ITV. As a standalone defensive deal, though, it had few rivals. Murdoch himself should know how this kind of stake-taking works – he's been in a similar situation with all its problems for years with John Malone's Liberty Media gradually buying up shares in News Corporation.

Murdoch's Fox network has had a mixed year – American Idol continues to dominate all and has the highest ad revenue of any show on US network television while the medical drama House continues to sweep all before it, with even higher ratings in its third season. The rest of the schedule is less distinguished. In general, though, US network television continues to enjoy its revival. CBS, through its phenomenally successful CSI franchise enjoys a consistently strong share; ABC's Desperate Housewives and Lost, though having shed some of their shine, continue to rate well. NBC, in an extraordinary four-year slump, is still struggling.

The president of NBC, Jeff Zucker, caused some consternation when, having made a substantial number of CNBC staff redundant in early autumn, he announced that the network would no longer be developing drama or scripted comedy for the 8pm to 9pm hour. That, he said, would have to be the preserve of cheaper reality and game show television, as the alternatives were economically unsustainable.

Whether this is actually a prescient analysis of the future of mass market television, or merely a reflection of NBC's troubles, is arguable. The network had actually built up to a strong 2006/2007 season. Its pre-season season looked great – one of the first networks on either side of the Atlantic to release shows, trails and teasers to YouTube. The first also to offer full reruns of its new shows on its website for free. It did an innovative deal with the US DVD-rental service Netflix to offer its pilot shows to subscribers. In short, the broadcaster looked to be in touch with the new world and actually a few steps ahead of its rivals.

Sadly, the shows, with the exception of its new hit, Heroes, have not been up to the pre-publicity. It is CBS's boss, Les Moonves, who is now at the forefront of deal-making, this time with iTunes and YouTube. And people actually want to see his programmes on different platforms.

Moonves' boss, the irascible head of Viacom, Sumner Redstone, rivals only Rupert Murdoch in the "very old media moguls who just keep on trucking" stakes. Redstone, fresh from very publicly ditching Tom Cruise from his expensive deal with Paramount Studios, fired the popular and apparently successful Tom Freston, who co-founded MTV and was president and CEO of Viacom. Months later, the reason why Freston had to go is still unclear, though plenty of US media speculation has pointed the finger at the failure of Viacom to move on, say, MySpace.

Which brings us back to Murdoch. His joy at seeing his US tabloid newspaper, the New York Post, overtake the Daily News in circulation was tempered slightly by the embarrassing debacle over his Harper Collins/Fox TV joint venture, If I Did It. This is a book and spin-off TV programme detailing in OJ Simpson's own words how he might have killed his ex-wife and her friend, if he had. The multimillion-dollar deal outraged even some of the most outrageous of Murdoch's Fox News commentators. If Bill O'Reilly is shocked and dismayed by your corporate behaviour then you may be in some trouble.

Murdoch pulped the book and cancelled the show with hours to spare, an act of rare contrition but necessary under the circumstances.

● The newspaper sector in the US

Elsewhere in the US, signs of life began to emerge in the newspaper sector. This is due largely to the English trend catching on here where very wealthy people decide it might be nice to own a paper – you know, as a hobby. The erstwhile music mogul and film studio partner David Geffen was rumoured to have made a cash offer for the LA Times. As the owners of the Tribune Company, of which the Times is a subsidiary, decided to put the whole shebang on the market, the field became rather crowded with such billionaires as Ron Burkle (friend of Bill Clinton) and Eli Broad, pitching in, but also Gannett, the huge newspaper conglomerate.

Murdoch showed some tentative interest in Newsday (also part of the Tribune group) and others wandered round kicking the metaphorical tyres of the Chicago Cubs baseball team. If you didn't know that the Tribune Company owned the Chicago Cubs, then you don't remember the last big media trend, for owning sports clubs, about five years ago. No? Well don't worry, because they're all being sold now. And we're back to megalomaniac newspaper proprietors.

Cashing in on the unexpected rash of potential Citizen Kanes, other newspapers began to look like selling. Titles such as the Boston Globe, Wall Street Journal and oh, something like the Hartford Courant, were being linked with bids by the end of the year. Knight Ridder, a mighty US newspaper company that rivalled Gannett, was broken up. In some circles, it was whispered (and indeed reported) that the New York Times might have to restructure its ownership.

The Observer's Edward Helmore wrote from New York of this spate of would-be newspaper barons: "There is a strong argument to suggest that the kind of overhaul the US newspaper business now needs is better suited to private ownership. While worrying about relentless shareholder, financial, and advertiser pressures, media organisations have shown themselves to be vulnerable to strong-arming from government to follow the official line. Under private ownership, the theory goes, they could be less easily intimidated."

The UK's own David Montgomery (late of the Mirror Group) has been romping round Europe buying newspapers and clearly believes there's life in the old media yet. Monty, as he is affectionately known by the many UK journalists he made redundant over the years, first made his move on the German publishing group Berliner Verlag, then swooped for Hamburg's second-biggest newspaper, Hamburger Morgenpost, and finally paying £647m, through his investment vehicle, Mecom, for the Norwegian group Orkla Media. As Montgomery continues to quietly build a European newspaper force, the UK analysts wonder out loud if he is eyeing the Mirror titles, his old stomping ground, for purchase next.

● AOL Time Warner

If nothing else could prove a cautionary tale to oversized, publicly owned newspaper groups, surely the ballad of AOL Time Warner would give pause to some. In a move guaranteeing some tearful shareholders closure, if nothing else, Steve Case finally apologised for merging AOL with Time Warner in early 2000. The co-founder of AOL told US broadcaster Charlie Rose he was "sorry [he] did it". About time, really, for a deal universally regarded as one of the worst corporate mergers in history and one which wiped $200bn of shareholder value from the company. It won't stop another similarly horrendous "web 2.0" merger occurring this time around, of course.

● Non-stop news

Meanwhile, there's been an extraordinary boom in international news channels. From al-Jazeera's international channel, now known as al-Jazeera English, born a mere six months late, to the final gestation of France 24, Jacques Chirac's French version of CNN, anyone who's anyone has their own 24-hour news channel these days. The rationale for all these services is the same: there's a need to get a different take on the world's news out there, because those Americans are having it all their own way. Next will be BBC Arabic, a BBC version of al-Jazeera, due in 2007. BBC Arabic will, as with the World Service, be part-funded by the Foreign Office and is undoubtedly an attempt to do the reverse (that is, take "British" news to the Middle East).

● Growth in India and China

For all that the likes of Rupert Murdoch and advertising giant Sir Martin Sorrell enjoy waxing lyrical about China, India is where all the action is. Newspapers, television and new media and tech businesses are opening where, apparently, the old media are reborn.

The International Herald Tribune, Metro International and Financial Times are all moving to India, either through launches or investments. The Daily Mail is understood to be looking at opportunities in the country and the Independent's parent company has already spent £19m on a stake in the Hindi newspaper group Jagran Prakashan. The Indy will launch in India in English, "very soon".

Why? There are currently 204 million newspaper readers in India – an increase of 12.6 million on 2005. It's just maths, really. Plus there's a window. Internet penetration in India is still low, despite its growing tech industry. Where China has around 120 million internet users, India has between 15 and 30 million, depending on which estimates you go by. From a population of 1 billion, that leaves quite a lot of eyeballs still open to persuasion to print.

Speaking of China, let's return one more time to the adventures of Rupert Murdoch. The 75-year-old mogul paid a visit to China at the end of 2006 and let it be known that MySpace China was next on the launch list. Those 120 million Chinese web users are still less than 10% of its 1.3 billion population, leaving some room for growth. It is the largest internet market in the world, after the US.

While MySpace China faces all sorts of potential problems (the state censorship issues that bugged Google's China launch are inevitable and the government is said to be considering banning short films on the internet without permission), Murdoch's wife is set to take a board position on the launch. So, in essence, don't bet against it.

Next stop, total world domination.

Forging new relationships

Matt Wells

When Rupert Murdoch gobbled up MySpace for $580m in 2005, it seemed like an astonishingly large amount of money to pay for a website that amounted to little more than spotty teenagers sharing pictures of each other getting drunk and having sex. Now, with some analysts valuing the site at upwards of $4bn and the social networking phenomenon sweeping the globe, it seems remarkably good value.

Murdoch, ever the expert at spotting a bandwagon just before its brakes were being released, realised that survival in the digital age means engaging with the people who consume his content (formerly known as readers). Online conversations are breaking out all over the world; if you don't give people space to talk about what you produce, they'll do it somewhere else.

And so now you can't move on a news publisher's website without stumbling over an array of blogs, talkboards, podcasts and vodcasts. For media professionals around the world, this revolution has forged new relationships with consumers. As Murdoch noted in a speech on his 75th birthday: "Power is moving away from the old elite in our industry – the editors, the chief executives and, let's face it, the proprietors ... A new generation of media consumers has risen, demanding content delivered when they want it, how they want it, and very much as they want it."

Those who have failed to embrace this shift in the balance of power are in the biggest trouble. The New York Times has admitted that the US newspaper market is "in freefall". Of the top 25 newspapers in the United States, only three posted circulation rises in the six months to September 2006. The Los Angeles Times was down 8%, the New York Times down 3.5%, and the Washington Post fell by 3.3%. Two of the biggest newspaper groups in the US, Knight Ridder and Tribune, have been broken up or sold. Audiences for the main news shows on the three main broadcast networks continue to decline.

Meanwhile, the audience for US newspaper websites is soaring – up almost a third in 2005. Unfortunately, advertising revenue is not following the audience and traditional media groups are struggling to bridge the gap. As MediaGuardian's US-based columnist Jeff Jarvis noted: "Newspapers must set a date soon where they plan past paper and then figure out how to get there – fast."

In Europe, the media landscape is changing almost as rapidly. The free paper phenomenon has swept the continent, with London the latest capital to find its streets strewn with newsprint. The freebie culture is eating its way into the foundation pillars of the mainstream media, from television (under threat from YouTube and BitTorrent), through newspapers (hit by online and giveaways) to radio (undermined by filesharing and podcasts).

Around the world, all is not doom and gloom. The media industries in India are exploding. As a result of a change in the law in 2002 that for the first time allowed foreign investment in India's media, western media organisations in trouble in their home markets are looking to this area of potentially enormous growth. According to the Indian Readership Survey, the country has 204 million newspaper readers; this in a nation of 1 billion people. No surprise, then, that the Financial Times should invest $3m for a stake in Business Standard, India's second-largest business title. Or that Dow Jones should hook up with the publishers of the Times of India, the biggest-selling English-language title in India, or that Independent News and Media should invest €25.5m in return for a 21% stake in Jagran Prakashan, publisher of India's largest read daily newspaper. Combined, the television, radio, publishing, film, music and advertising industries are already worth an estimated 353bn rupees ($4bn). According to PricewaterhouseCoopers' Global Entertainment and Media Outlook 2006-2010, this will grow by 24% over the next five years.

The same PWC report predicts that China will become the largest media and entertainment market in Asia in three years, overtaking Japan. The growth is being driven largely by the rise in broadband access – predicted to grow by 30% a year. This extraordinary growth in Asian markets has meant global advertising revenue is increasing, despite poor performances in Europe and the US.

But there are still vast obstacles for foreign media owners to overcome: in 2005, Murdoch said in relation to his Chinese media ambitions that he had hit a "brick wall". In 2006, however, he revealed he had sent his wife, Wendi Deng, to China with senior News Corporation executives to try and find a way of taking MySpace to the country. And Google's controversial foray into the country marked a turning point in its image from upstart outsider to global corporate player. Every international media organisation wants to get into China – and is busy figuring out how to do it.

● Matt Wells is media editor at the Guardian

Global media contacts

Global media groups

Bertelsmann
Carl-Bertelsmann-Strasse 270,
33311 Gütersloh, Germany
00 49 5241 800
andreas.grafemeyer@bertelsmann.de
www.bertelsmann.com
Press: 00 49 5241 802 466
oliver.herrgesell@bertelsmann.com

Clear Channel
200 East Basse Road, San Antonio,
TX 78209, USA
00 1 210 822 2828
www.clearchannel.com
Press: lisacdollinger@
clearchannel.com

ComCast
1500 Market Street, Philadelphia,
PA 19102, USA
00 1 866 281 2100
www.comcast.com

Gannett
7950 Jones Branch Drive,
McLean VA 22107, USA
00 1 703 854 6000
www.gannett.com
Press: tjconnel@gannett.com

NewsQuest Media Group
58 Church Street, Weybridge,
Surrey KT13 8DP
01932 821212
enquiries@newsquestmedia.co.uk
www.newsquestmedia.co.uk

General Electric/NBC
3135 Easton Turnpike,
Fairfield CT 06828, USA
00 1 203 373 2211
www.ge.com/en
Press: gary.sheffer@ge.com

NewsCorp
1211 Avenue of Americas, 8th Floor,
New York, NY 10036, USA
00 1 212 852 7017
www.newscorp.com
Press: abutcher@newscorp.com

Sony
550 Madison Avenue, New York,
NY 10022, USA
00 1 212 833 8000
www.sony.com; www.sony.co.uk
Press: press@eu.sony.com

Time Warner
1 Time Warner Centre, 58th and 8th
Avenue, New York, NY 10019, USA
00 1 212 484 8000
www.timewarner.com

Viacom
1515 Broadway, New York,
NY 10036, USA
00 1 212 258 6000
www.viacom.com
Press: press@viacom.com

Vivendi Universal
42 avenue de Friedland,
75380 Paris Cedex 08, France
00 33 1 7171 1000
New York: 00 1 212 572 7000
www.vivendi.com
Press: 00 33 1 7171 1180

Walt Disney
500 South Buena Vista Street,
Burbank, CA 91521-9722, USA
00 1 818 560 1000
www.disney.go.com
Press: kim.kerscher@dig.com

Global news outlets

● Ireland

Connacht Tribune
15 Market Street, Galway, Ireland
00 353 91 536222
www.connacht-tribune.ie
*Weekly. Editor: John Cunningham;
features: Brendon Carol; head of
production: Declan Maguire*

Cork Evening Echo
Academy Street, Cork, Ireland
00 353 21 480 2142
www.eveningecho.ie
*Daily. Editor: Maurice Gubbins; news:
Emma Connolly; features: John Dolan*

Daily Ireland
See page 80

Evening Herald
27–32 Talbot Street, Dublin 1, Ireland
00 353 1 705 5333
www.independent.ie
*Daily. Editor: Gerry Oregan; news: Philip
Maloy; features: Dave Lawlor*

Ireland on Sunday
3rd Floor, Embassy House,
Herbert Park Lane, Ballsbridge,
Dublin 4, Ireland
00 353 1 637 5800
*Sunday. Editor: Philip Maloy; news:
Paul Drury; features: Aileen Doherty;
head of production: Ciaran O'Tuama*

Irish Daily Star
62a Terenure Road North,
Terenure, Dublin 6W, Ireland
00 353 1 490 1228
www.thestar.ie
*Daily. Editor: Gerard Colon; news:
Michael O'Cain; features: Danny Smyth*

Irish Examiner
Academy Street, Cork, Ireland
00 353 21 427 2722
www.examiner.ie
*Daily. Editor: Tim Vaughan; news: John
O'Mahoney; features: Fionnuala Quinlan*

Irish Independent
27–32 Talbot Street, Dublin 1, Ireland
00 353 1 705 5333
www.independent.ie
*Daily. Editor: Vincent Doyle; news: Philip
Dunne; features: Peter Carvosso*

Irish Times
10–16 D'Olier Street, Dublin 2,
Ireland
00 353 1 675 8000
www.ireland.com
*Daily. Editor: Geraldine Kennedy; news:
John Maher; features: Shelia Wayman*

Kerryman
Clash, Tralee, County Kerry, Ireland
00 353 66 714 5500
www.kerryman.ie
*Weekly. Editor: Declan Malone; news:
Diedre Walsh; features: Marisa Reidy*

Leinster Leader
18/19 South Main Street, Naas,
County Kildare, Ireland
00 353 45 897302
www.leinsterleader.ie
*Weekly. Editor: Michael Sheenan;
features: Sylvia Pownall*

Limerick Leader
54 O'Connell Street, Limerick,
Ireland
00 353 61 214503/6
www.limerickleader.ie
*Weekly. Editor: Brendon Halligan;
news: Eugene Phelan*

Limerick Post
Town Hall Centre, Rutland Street,
Limerick, Ireland
00 353 61 413322
www.limerickpost.ie
*Weekly. Editor: Billy Ryan;
news: Clare Doyle; features: Rose Rush*

RTÉ
New Library Building, Donnybrook,
Dublin 4, Ireland
00 353 1 208 3111
info@rte.ie
www.rte.ie
*Irish national broadcaster.
Acquisitions and drama: Sharon Brady;
entertainment: Dympna Clerkin;
factual: Dervla Keating; Fair City (soap):
Tara O'Brian; music, sport and young
people: Richie Ryan; news and current
affairs: Carolyn Fisher - all
firstname.lastname@rte.ie*
Press: 00 353 1 208 3434.

Sunday Business Post
80 Harcourt Street, Dublin 2, Ireland
00 353 1 602 6000
www.thepost.ie
*Sunday. Editor: Cliff Taylor; news: Gavin
Daley; features: Fiona Neff; head of
production: Tom McHale*

Sunday Independent
27–32 Talbot Street, Dublin 1, Ireland
00 353 1 705 5333
www.independent.ie
Sunday. Editor: Angus Faning; news:
Willy Kealy; features: Anne Harris

Sunday Tribune
15 Lower Baggot Street, Dublin 2,
Ireland
00 353 1 631 4300
www.tribune.ie
Sunday. Editor: Noirin Hegarty; deputy
editor: Diarmuid Doyle; news: Olivia
Doyle; features: Lise Hand; head of
production: Paul Howe

Sunday World
27–32 Talbot Street, Dublin 1, Ireland
00 353 1 884 9000
www.sundayworld.com
Sunday. Editor: Colm McGinty; news:
John Donlon; features: Eamon Dillon;
head of production: John Noonan

TG4
Baile na hAbhann, Co na Gaillimhe,
Ireland
00 353 91 505050
www.tg4.ie
Irish-language broadcaster. Director of
television: Alan Esslemont

● Other Europe

Corriere della Sera
28 via Solferino, Milano 20121, Italy
00 39 026 339
www.corriere.it
Italian daily. Editor: Paulo Mieli

Cyprus Mail
24 Vassiliou Voulgaroctonou Street,
PO Box 21144, 1502 Nicosia, Cyprus
00 357 22 818 585
editor@cyprus-mail.com
www.cyprus-mail.com
English-language daily. Editor: Kosta
Pavlowitch

Deutsche Welle
Public Broadcasting Service,
Kurt-Schumacher-Str. 3, 53113 Bonn,
Germany
00 49 228 429 0
www.dw-world.de
German broadcaster. European focus.
Editor: Erik Bettermann

Diario de Noticias
Altzutzate 8, Polígono Industrial
Areta, HUARTE-PAMPLONA,
Portugal
00 351 948 33 25 33
dnot@dn.pt
www.noticiasdenavarra.com
Portuguese daily. Editor: Pablo Munoz

EuroNews
BP 161, 60 Chemin de Mouilles,
69131 Lyon Ecully, France
00 33 4 7218 8000
info@euronews.net
www.euronews.net
Pan-European TV news

Le Figaro
37 rue du Louvre,
75002 Paris, France
00 33 1 4221 6200
www.lefigaro.fr
Rightwing quality daily

Frankfurter Allgemeine Zeitung
Hellerhofstraße 2-4, 60327
Frankfurt am Main, Germany
00 49 1805 810 811
KaiN.Pritzsche @pri
www.faz.net
Right-leaning daily. Editor: Kai N.
Pritzsche

Gazeta Wyborcza
Szewska, 5, 31009 Krakow, Poland
00 48 12 629 5000
www.gazeta.pl
Poland's most popular daily

International Herald Tribune
6 bis, rue des Graviers,
92521 Neuilly Cedex, France
00 33 1 4143 9322
iht@iht.com
www.iht.com
Editor: Alison Smale

Kathimerini
D Falireos & E Makariou St 2,
185–47 N Faliron, Piraeus, Greece
00 30 210 480 8000
editor@ekathimerini.com
www.ekathimerini.com
English-language daily. Editor: Nikos
Konstandaras

Libération
11, rue Béranger,
75154 Paris Cedex 03, France
00 33 1 42 76 17 89
www.libe.com
Left-leaning quality daily.
Editor: Antoine de Grudemar

Le Monde
80 Boulevard Auguste Blanqui,
75013 Paris, France
00 33 1 5728 2000
mediateur@lemonde.fr
www.lemonde.fr
France's bestselling quality daily.
Editor: Gerrard Courtoes

Moscow Times
Ulitsa Vyborgskaya 16, Bldg 4,
125212 Moscow, Russia
00 7 095 937 3399
editors@themoscowtimes.com
www.moscowtimes.ru
Respected English-language daily.
Editor: Lynn Berry

El Mundo
Calle Pradillo, 42, 28002 Madrid,
Spain
00 34 91 586 48 00
www.elmundo.es
Progressive Spanish daily. Editor: Pedro
Ramirez

El País
Miguel Yuste 40, 28037 Madrid,
Spain
00 34 91 337 8200
redaccion@prisacom.com
www.elpais.es
Spain's biggest daily paper.
Editor: Jesus Ceberio

Prague Post
Stepanska 20, Prague 1, 110 00,
Czech Republic
00 420 2 9633 4400
info@praguepost.com
www.praguepost.com
The Czech Republic's best English-
language daily. Editor: Will Tizard

Radio France Internationale
116, avenue du President Kennedy,
Paris 75016, France
00 33 1 5640 1212
www.rfi.fr
France's "World Service"

Radio Netherlands
Box 222, 1200 JG Hilversum,
The Netherlands
00 31 35 672 4211
letters@rnw.nl
www.rnw.nl
Holland's best English-language news
service

La Repubblica
Piazza Indipendenza, 11/b,
Rome 00185, Italy
00 39 06 49821
larepubblica@repubblica.it
www.repubblica.it
Liberal Rome based daily. In Italian.
Editor: Azio Maruo

Der Standard
Schenkenstrasse 4/6,
A-1010 Wien, Austria
00 43 1 53 170
chefredaktion@derStandard.at
www.derstandard.at
(In German.) Liberal daily. Editor: Oscar
Bronnir

Süddeutsche Zeitung
Sendlinger Strasse 8, 80331
Munchen, Germany
00 49 89 21830
redaktion@sueddeutsche.de
www.sueddeutsche.de
(In German.) Major Munich based paper.
Broadly liberal. Editor: Hans Werner Kilz

De Telegraaf
30 Basisweg, 1043 Amsterdam,
The Netherlands
00 31 20 585 9111
redactie-i@telegraaf.nl
www.telegraaf.nl
(In Dutch.) Holland's largest national
daily. Editor: E Bos

● Middle East

Al-Ahram
Galaa St., Cairo, Egypt
00 20 2578 6441
weeklyeditor@ahram.org.eg
http://weekly.ahram.org.eg
Editor: Galal Nassar; web editor: Amira Howeidy

Al-Jazeera
PO Box 22300, Doha, Qatar
00 974 438 2777
info@aljazeera.net.qa
www.aljazeera.net
Arabic-language satellite channel, based in Qatar

Aljazeera Publishing
London, UK
http://english.aljazeera.net

Daily Star
Marine Tower 6th floor, Rue de La Ste Famille, Gemaizeh, Achrafieh, Beirut, Lebanon
00 961 1 587277
www.dailystar.com.lb
Lebanese daily. Publisher: Mr Hanna Anbar

Ha'aretz
21 Schocken St, PO Box 233, Tel Aviv 61001, Israel
00 972 3 512 1212/1204
contact@haaretz.co.il
www.haaretzdaily.com/
English edition of Israel's moderate national daily, published in Tel Aviv. Editor: David Landam

Jerusalem Post
Jerusalem Post Building, PO Box 81, Jerusalem 91000, Israel
00 972 2531 5666
eedition@jpostmail.com
www.jpost.com
Conservative English-language daily. Editor: David Horovitz

Jordan Times
Jordan Press Foundation, PO Box 6710, Queen Rania Al Abdullah Street, Amman, Jordan
00 962 6 560 0800
jotimes@jpf.com.jo
www.jordantimes.com
Jordan's only English-language daily. Editor: Jennifer Hamarneh

Middle East Times
8 Nikis Avenue, Office 201, 2nd Floor, Nicosia 1086, Cyprus
00 357 22 45 47 57
editor@middleastimes.net
www.metimes.com
Quality English-language weekly, based in Egypt. Editor: Claude Salhani

● US and Canada

CBS Television Network
51 W 52nd St, NY 10019, USA
00 1 212 975 4321
www.cbs.com
News network

CNN
100 International Blvd, Atlanta, GA 30303, USA
00 1 404 827 1500
www.cnn.com
News network

International Herald Tribune
6 bis, rue des Graviers, 92521 Neuilly Cedex, France
00 33 1 4143 9322
iht@iht.com
www.iht.com
International daily, owned by the New York Times. Editor: Alison Smale

LA Times
202 W 1st St, Los Angeles, CA 90012, USA
00 1 213 237 5000
www.latimes.com
Biggest west-coast daily. Editor: John Carroll

NBC
30 Rockefeller Plaza, New York, NY 10112, USA
00 1 212 664 4444
www.nbc.com
News network

New York Times
229 West 43rd Street, New York, New York 10036, USA
00 1 212 556 1234
editorial@nytimes.com
www.nytimes.com
National paper of record. Editor: Bill Keller

Wall St Journal
200 Liberty Street, New York, NY 10281, USA
00 1 212 416 2000
wsj.ltrs@wsj.com
www.wsj.com
Conservative financial daily. Editor: Paul E Steiger

Wall St Journal Europe
87 Boulevard Brand Whitlock, 1200 Brussels, Belgium
00 32 2 741 1211
www.europesubs.wsj.com
Global business news for Europe. Editor: Frederick Kempe

Washington Post
1150 15th Street NW, Washington, DC 20071, USA
00 1 202 334 6000
www.washingtonpost.com
The New York Times' main rival. Editor: Leonard Downie

● Canada

Toronto Globe and Mail
444 Front Street West, Toronto, Ontario M5V 2S9, Canada
00 1 416 585 5000
newsroom@GlobeAndMail.ca
www.theglobeandmail.com
Quality daily, Canada. Editor: Angus Frame

● Africa

Daily Mail and Guardian
PO Box 91667, Auckland Park, Johannesburg 2006, South Africa
00 27 11 250 7300
editoronline@mg.co.za
www.mg.co.za
South African daily. Editor: Ferial Haffejee

Daily Nation
Nation Centre, Kimathi Street, Nairobi, Kenya
00 254 20 320 88 000
www.nationmedia.com
Kenya's biggest daily paper. Editor: Joseph Odindo

Daily News
PO Box 47549, Greyville, 4023 Zimbabwe, South Africa
00 27 31 308 2911
pather@nn.independent.co.za
www.dailynews.co.za
Daily independent paper. Editor: Dennis Pather

The East African
Kenya
00 254 20 540 633
comments@nationaudio.com
www.nationaudio.com/News/EastAfrican/current

East African Standard
Likoni Road, PO Box 30080, Nairobi, Kenya
00 254 20 322 2111
editorial@eastandard.net
www.eastandard.net
Editor: Chaacha Mwita

Le Matin
1 Rud Birchir Attar, Algiers, Algeria
00 213 216 706 85
(In French.) Moderate, secular paper

Monitor, Uganda
Plot 29–35, 8th Street, Industrial Area (PO Box 12141), Kampala, Uganda
00 256 41 232 367
info@monitor.co.ug
www.monitor.co.ug
Major independent daily. Editor: Peter Mwesige

SABC
Private Bag X1, Auckland Park, 2006, South Africa
00 27 11 714 5150
feedback@sabcnews.com
www.sabcnews.com
South African broadcaster

Sunday Times (South Africa)
2nd floor, Johnnic Publishing House,
4 Biermann Avenue, Rosebank,
2196, South Africa
00 27 11 280 3000
suntimes@sundaytimes.co.za
www.suntimes.co.za

● Asia

Asahi Shimbun
104–8011, Tokyo, Chuo Ku, Tsukiji 5,
Chome 3-2, Japan
00 81 3545 0131
www.asahi.com
Japanese daily

Dawn
Haroon House,
Dr Ziauddin Ahmed Road,
Karachi 74200, Pakistan
00 92 21 111 444 777
webmaster@dawn.com
www.dawn.com
English-language daily. Editor: Tahir Mirza

Hindustan Times
Hindustan Times House,
18–20, Kasturba Gandhi Marg,
New Delhi-110001, INDIA
00 91 11 23361234
salil@hindustantimes.com
www.hindustantimes.com
Editor: Shailesh Shekhar

Jakarta Post
Jl. Palmerah Selatan 15,
Jakarta 10270, Indonesia
00 62 21 5300476
editorial@thejakartapost.com
www.thejakartapost.com
Editor: Endy M Bayuni

JoongAng Ilbo
7, Sunhwa-dong, Jung-gu,
Seoul 100-759, Korea
00 82 2 751 9215
iht@joongang.co.kr
http://joongangdaily.joins.com
Korean daily. Editor: Charles D Sherman

South China Morning Post
16F Somerset House, Taikoo Place,
979 King's Road, Quarry Bay,
Hong Kong
00 852 2565 2222
peter.dedi@scmp.com
www.scmp.com
English-language daily. Editor: Peter Dedi

Star News Asia
8th Floor, One Harbourfront,
18 Tak Fung Street, Hunghom,
Kowloon, Hong Kong
00 852 2621 8888
http://startv.com

Straits Times
1000 Toa Payoh North,
News Centre, Singapore 31944
00 65 6319 5397
STI@sph.com.sg
http://straitstimes.asia1.com.sg
Singapore's most widely circulated English-language paper: close ties to the government. Editor: Cheong Yip Seng

Taipei Times
14F, NO. 399, Ruiguang Rd., Neihu
District, Taipei City 11492, Taiwan
00 886 2 2656 1000
inquiries@taipeitimes.com
www.taipeitimes.com

● Latin America and Caribbean

O Estado de Sao Paulo
Av Celestino Bourroul, 68,
1 andar Bairro do Limão,
São Paulo, Brazil
00 55 11 3856 2122
atende@estado.com.br
www.estado.estadao.com.br
Editor: Sandro Vaia

El Mercurio
Santiago, Chile
00 56 2330 1111
www.elmercurio.cl
Daily. Editor: Juan Pablo Illanes

La Nacion
Bouchard 551, 1106, Buenos Aires,
Argentina
00 54 11 4319 1600
cescribano@lanacion.com.ar
www.lanacion.com.ar
Editor: Bartolome Mitre

El Tiempo
Terra Networks Colombia, Diagonal
97 No. 17-60 Oficina 402, Bogotá,
Colombia
00 57 160 29898
http://eltiempo.terra.com.co
Editor: Roberto Pombo

El Universal
Burcarlini 8, Colony Centre,
Mexico City, Mexico
00 52 55 5709 1313/6917
enrique.cardenas@
    eluniversal.com.mx
www.el-universal.com.mx
Editor: Enrique Cárdenas

● Caribbean

Jamaica Gleaner
7 North Street, PO Box 40, Kingston,
Jamaica
00 1 876 922 3400
feedback@jamaica-gleaner.com
www.jamaica-gleaner.com
Editor: Garfield Grandison

● Pacific

ABS-CBN (Philippines)
Manila, Phillipines
00 63 2 924 4101
newsfeedback@abs-cbn.com
www.abs-cbnnews.com
News network

The Age, Melbourne
250 Spencer Street, Melbourne
3000, Australia
00 61 3 9600 4211
inquiries@theage.com.au
www.theage.com.au
Editor: Andrew Jaspan

New Zealand Herald
PO Box 32, Auckland, New Zealand
00 64 9 379 5050
www.nzherald.co.nz
Editor: Tim Murphy

Sydney Morning Herald
201 Sussex St, GPO Box 506, Sydney
NSW 2001, Australia
00 61 2 9282 2833
newsdesk@smh.com.au
www.smh.com.au
Quality daily. Editor: Robert Whitehead

Global journalism bodies

**Association of European
Journalists, British section**
40 Bruce Road, London E3 3HL
020 8981 4691
aejuk@btopenworld.com
www.aej-uk.org

**AMARC (World Association of
Community Broadcasters)**
705 Bourget Street, Suite 100,
Montreal, Quebec, H4C 2M6, Canada
00 1 514 982 0351
amarc@amarc.org
www.amarc.org

Article XIX
6-8 Amwell Street, London EC1R 1UQ
020 7278 9292
info@article19.org
www.article19.org
Combats censorship

Committee to Protect Journalists
330 7th Avenue 11th Floor, New York
NY 10001, USA
00 1 212 465 1004
info@cpj.org
www.cpj.org
Independent, non-profit body defending right of journalists to report without fear of reprisal

**Foreign Press Association in
London**
11 Carlton House Terrace,
London SW1Y 5AJ
020 7930 0445
reception@foreign-press.org.uk
www.foreign-press.org.uk

**Institute for War and Peace
Reporting**
48 Grays Inn Road,
London WC1X 8LT
020 7831 1030
yigal@iwpr.net
www.iwpr.net
Training in conflict areas

International Centre for Journalists
1616 H Street NW, Third Floor,
Washington DC 20006, USA
00 1 202 737 3700
www.icfj.org

**International Consortium
of Investigative Journalists**
910 17th Street, NW, 7th Floor,
Washington, DC 20006, USA
00 1 202 466 1300
www.icij.org

International Federation of Journalists
IPC-Residence Palace, Bloc C,
Rue de la Loi 155,
B-1040 Brussels, Belgium
00 32 2 235 2200
ifj@ifj.org
www.ifj.org

International Federation of the Periodical Press
Queens House,
55-56 Lincoln's Inn Fields,
London WC2A 3LJ
020 7404 4169
info@fipp.com
www.fipp.com
Works for benefit of magazine publishers worldwide

International Freedom of Expression
555 Richmond St W, PO Box 407,
Toronto, Ontario, Canada M5V 3B1
00 1 416 515 9622
ifex@ifex.org
www.ifex.org

International News Safety Institute
Residence Palace, Block C,
International Press Centre,
155 Rue de la Loi,
1040 Brussels, Belgium
00 32 2 235 2201
info@newssafety.com
www.newssafety.com
Safety network for journalists in conflict zones

International Press Institute
Spiegelgasse 2, A-1010 Vienna,
Austria
00 43 1 512 90 11
ipi@freemedia.at
www.freemedia.at
Network of editors, executives and senior journalists

International Women's Media Foundation
1625 K Street NW, Suite 1275,
Washington, DC 20006, USA
00 1 202 496 1992
info@iwmf.org
www.iwmf.org
Role of women in news media

InterNews
1640 Rhode Island Avenue NW,
7th Floor, Washington DC 20036,
USA
00 1 202 833 5740
info@ internews.org
www.internews.org
News around the world

InterWorld Radio
Panos Institute, 9 White Lion Street,
London N1 9PD
020 7239 7633
anna.egan@panos.org.uk
www.interworldradio.org
Global network for radio stations and journalism

Overseas Press and Media Association
OPMA Secretariat, 15 Magrath
Avenue, Cambridge CB4 3AH
01223 512631
membership@opma.co.uk
www.opma.co.uk

Panos London
9 White Lion Street, London N1 9PD
020 7278 1111
info@panos.org.uk
www.panos.org.uk
Journalism in developing countries

Reporters Sans Frontières
5 Rue Geoffroy-Marie,
75009 Paris, France
00 33 1 4483 8484
rsf@rsf.org
www.rsf.org
Reporters without borders - freedom of the press

World Association of Newspapers
7 Rue Geoffroy St. Hilaire,
75005 Paris, France
00 33 1 4742 8500
www.wan-press.org
Senior newsroom editors' forum

World Press Freedom Committee
11690-C Sunrise Valley Drive,
Reston, VA 20191, USA
00 1 703 715 9811
freepress@wpfc.org
www.wpfc.org

World Press Photo
Jacob Obrechtstraat 26, 1071 KM
Amsterdam, The Netherlands
00 31 20 676 6096
office@worldpressphoto.nl
www.worldpressphoto.nl

Global media trade press

The Fourth Estate
00 61 416 178 908
michael@walsh.net
www.fourth-estate.com
Website and weekly newsletter. Editor: Mike Walsh. Digital techology and media

MediaChannel
575 8th Avenue, #2200, New York,
NY 10018, USA
00 1 212 246 0202
editor@mediachannel.org
www.mediachannel.org
Website. Executive director: Timothy Karr; executive editor: Danny Schechter

Middle East Media Guide
PO Box 72280, Dubai, UAE
00 971 50 553 0209
editor@middleeastmediaguide.com
www.middleeastmediaguide.com
Annual. Editor: Ben Smalley

Online Journalism Review
3502 Watt Way, Los Angeles, CA
90089, USA
00 1 213 740 0948
rniles@usc.edu
www.ojr.org
Website. Editor: Larry Pryor

PR Week
Haymarket Professional
Publications, 174 Hammersmith
Road, London W6 7JP
020 8267 4429
prweek@haynet.com
www.prweek.com
Weekly. Editor-in-chief: Kate Nicholas; news editor: Ravi Chandiramani

World Press Freedom Review
IPI Headquarters, Spiegelgasse 2,
A-1010 Vienna, Austria
00 43 1 512 90 11
ipi@freemedia.at
www.freemedia.at/wpfr/world_m.htm
Website. Director: Johann P Fritz

Global media bodies

Association for International Broadcasting
PO Box 990, London SE3 9XL
020 8297 3993
info@aib.org.uk
www.aib.org.uk
Market intelligence, representation, contacts and other services

Association for Progressive Communications
PO Box 29755, Melville 2109,
South Africa
00 27 11 726 1692
webeditor@apc.org
www.apc.org
Internet and ICTs for social justice and development

APC secretariat
Presidio Building 1012, Torney
Avenue, PO Box 29904, San
Francisco, CA 94129, USA

Committee of Concerned Journalists (CCJ)
Project for Excellence in Journalism,
1850 K St, NW Suite 850,
Washington, DC 20006, USA
001 202 293 7394
mail@journalism.org
www.journalism.org
Initiative by journalists to clarify and raise the standards of American journalism

European Audio-Visual Observatory
76, allee de la Robertsau, 67000
Strasbourg, France
00 33 388 144400
obs@obs.coe.int
www.obs.coe.int
European media observatory. Operates within framework of Council of Europe

European Broadcasting Union
17A, Ancienne Route, CH-1218
Grand-Saconnex, Switzerland
00 41 22 717 2111
ebu@ebu.ch
www.ebu.ch/en/index.php
Professional association of national broadcasters

International Advertising Association

521 Fifth Avenue, Suite 1807,
New York, NY 10175, USA
00 1 212 557 1133
iaa@iaaglobal.org
www.iaaglobal.org
Advocates consumer and advertiser free choice

International Center for Journalists (ICFJ)

1616 H Street, NW, Third Floor,
Washington, DC 20006, USA
00 1 202 737 3700
editor@icfj.org
www.icfj.org
Aims to help journalists and raise standards, esp in places with little tradition of a free press

International Classified Media Association (ICMA)

ICMA Head Office,
Koggestraat 9H, 1012 TA
Amsterdam, The Netherlands
00 31 20 638 2336
info@icmaonline.org
www.icmaonline.org
Represents major publishers

International Communications Forum

24 Greencoat Place,
London SW1P 1RD
020 7798 6010
icforum@yahoo.co.uk
www.icforum.org
Goodwill network

International Institute of Communications

Regent House, 24-25 Nutford Place,
London W1H 5YN
020 7323 9622
enquiries@iicom.org
www.iicom.org
Industry, government and academic forum

International Newspaper Marketing Association

10300 North Central Expressway,
Suite 467, Dallas, Texas 75231, USA
00 1 214 373 9111
www.inma.org

International Press Institute (IPI)

Spiegelgasse 2, A-1010 Vienna,
Austria
00 43 1 512 90 11
ipi@freemedia.at
www.freemedia.at
Global network of editors, media executives and leading journalists. Supports press freedom, free flow of information, and improved journalism standards

International Public Relations Association

1, Dunley Hill Court, Ranmore
Common, Dorking, Surrey RH5 6SX
01483 280 130
iprasec@btconnect.com
www.ipra.org
Network of PR pioneers

International Publishers Association

Ave de Miremont 3, 1206 Geneva,
Switzerland
00 41 22 346 3018
secretariat@ipa-uie.org
www.ipa-uie.org
NGO with consultative status to UN

International Telecommunication Union

Place des Nations,
CH-1211 Geneva 20, Switzerland
00 41 22 730 51 11
itumail@itu.int
www.itu.int
UN body for coordination of global telecom services

International Webcasting Association

4206 F Technology Court, Chantilly,
VA 20151, USA
info@webcasters.org
www.webcasters.org

World Associations of Newspapers (WAN)

7 Rue Geoffroy St. Hilaire,
75005 Paris, France
00 33 1 4742 8500
contact_us@wan.asso.fr
www.wan-press.org
Defends press freedom and economic independence of newspapers

World Federation of Advertisers

120, Avenue Louise, 1050 Brussels,
Belgium
00 32 2 502 57 40
www.wfanet.org

World Summit on the Information Society

Executive Secretariat,
Place des Nations,
1211 Geneva 20, Switzerland
00 41 22 730 60 48
wsis@itu.int
www.itu.int/wsis

Creative media

Books

Challenges are flowing thick and fast for Britain's publishers. The once genteel book trade, aloof from the travails of the media, entertainment or retail industries, is now being buffeted on all sides.

This new reality can be traced to the collapse of the Net Book Agreement in 1995, when the old certainties upheld by price-fixing evaporated. Paradoxes are all-pervasive. The mass market is expanding at breathtaking pace, but many publishers are specialising in ever-smaller niches. Wannabe authors either get spectacular six-figure book deals almost overnight, or are ignored by literary agents in perpetuity. Books are setting the media agenda as never before, yet literary reviews have lost their impact. Publishing has become a game of scale where only the largest survive, but independent houses such as Profile and Faber thrive.

In 2007 these gaps will grow wider still, as all sides of the book industry finally confront the digital era. Whether or not the year brings an "iPod moment", when an e-reading device finally takes off, publishers will sort out their online strategies. Developing digital marketing and online content is crucial, through audio downloads, serialisations, poems for mobile phones, reference databases, and full-blooded websites. This should be the year that print-on-demand technology finally comes of age, enabling publishers to produce titles for tiny audiences.

As information becomes commoditised, the opportunities for high-value print publishing grow. From first editions to signed copies, books are gaining value as treasured objects and even status symbols. Expect to see publishers produce more lavish hardbacks and collectable limited editions in 2007.

● Book sales

The UK book market continues to grow steadily, if unspectacularly. In 2005, book sales were up 3.7% to £1.65bn according to Nielsen BookScan, which monitors actual till purchases from the vast majority of UK retailers. The number of copies shifted was up 5.9% to 216.7 million books. The disparity in the two figures reflects increased discounting, an inexorable feature of the bookselling landscape (see below). As I write this, sales for the first 11 months of 2006 are in turn up 2.7% compared with 2005. These figures fit a long-term pattern: over the past decade, high-street book sales in the UK have grown at an average of around 4% – more in a Harry Potter year, less without the boy wizard.

Da Vinci Code fever may have been quelled by the critically panned Tom Hanks film, yet Dan Brown's novel stayed top of the end-of-year charts in 2006, quietly racking up sales of another million copies. Booksellers badly need Brown to finish his follow-up novel, a conspiracy tale set in the secretive world of the Masons, tentatively titled The

Solomon Key. They'd also like JK Rowling to round off her Harry Potter series with a bang.

Behind Brown in the 2006 paperback league was Kate Mosse, who co-founded the Orange Prize for Fiction before turning author. Mosse's Labyrinth took Brown's "quest thriller" formula to medieval France; when it was picked by Richard & Judy for their book club, sales rocketed. Other Richard & Judy success stories were Victoria Hislop's The Island and Richard Benson's memoir The Farm. Against all the odds, the daytime TV duo has become the stamp (or sticker) of publishing quality, trusted by millions. Can they sustain their influence in 2007?

Book categories showing strongest growth are misery memoirs (despite publishers plumbing the depths with shameless titles such as Please, Daddy, No!), quirky fact books (the New Scientist's surprise Christmas 2005 bestseller Does Anything Eat Wasps? was followed up with another hit, Why Don't Penguins' Feet Freeze?), retro magazine annuals (from Smash Hits to The Best of Jackie), and celebrity autobiographies (see page 261).

● The new force of retail

The fastest-changing face of the book market is retail, which used to be known as plain old bookselling. No one could have missed the media storm when the UK's largest dedicated book chain, Waterstone's, plotted a takeover of its smaller rival Ottakar's, a group of smaller stores mainly in market towns. Years of frustrations from publishers, authors and agents boiled over, and they successfully lobbied the Office of Fair Trading to have the deal referred to the Competition Commission. After a 17-week investigation, the commission's finest lawyers dismissed the concerns, finding that the UK book market was in "robust health" and that the merger would not restrict consumer choice. Waterstone's ended up taking Ottakar's for £63m, a cool £33m less than it originally offered. But chastened by the force of the opposition, it promised to blend the best of both businesses, and recruited some of Ottakar's finest staff talent to run the combined 340 shops.

One driving force behind the deal was the external competition faced by all high-street booksellers. The most ubiquitous new force is Amazon, which continues to steamroll ahead with its combination of aggressive discounts, targeted marketing and strong customer service. Waterstone's launched its own website in autumn 2006, and other new players such

Top 10 paperbacks 2005

Ranking / Title	Author	Volume sold	RRP
1 The Da Vinci Code	Dan Brown	2,223,328	£6.99
2 Angels and Demons	Dan Brown	1,464,729	£6.99
3 Deception Point	Dan Brown	960,411	£6.99
4 Digital Fortress	Dan Brown	858,239	£6.99
5 The Time Traveler's Wife	Audrey Niffenegger	652,015	£7.99
6 The Other Side of the Story	Marian Keyes	488,058	£7.99
7 The Broker	John Grisham	480,406	£6.99
8 Nights of Rain and Stars	Maeve Binchy	455,313	£6.99
9 The Rule of Four	Ian Caldwell & Dust Thomason	451,747	£6.99
10 Small Island	Andrea Levy	427,501	£7.99

Source: Nielsen Bookscan

Ali Smith's book 'The Accidental' sold more copies at Tesco than at any other store

as LoveReading and Play.com are emerging, but they have their work cut out to combat Amazon.

Then there's the supermarkets, taking an ever larger slice of the best-sellers and forcing high-street chains into an un-winnable discount battle. It's not just the latest Jamie Oliver that Tesco can shift: it is expanding deep into book-lover territory, for example selling more copies of Ali Smith's challenging Orange prize-shortlisted The Accidental than any other retailer.

This retail frenzy leaves independent booksellers exposed. While many still have loyal local customers, others are being forced to close their doors at an alarming rate. Publishers such as Faber, Profile and Penguin have responded by offering them special deals: but is it too little, too late?

● Industry moves

Publishers have not been immune to takeover fever. The biggest trade publishing deal of 2006 saw Time Warner Books, the transatlantic giant, sold to French media group Hachette Livre. The deal catapulted Hachette ahead of Random House Group to the overall UK number one publisher, controlling a suite of imprints including Orion, Weidenfeld & Nicolson, Gollancz, Little Brown, Orbit, John Murray, Hodder & Stoughton, Head-line, Sceptre, Mitchell Beazley, Cassell, Watts, and Orchard. In other industries such a merger would be followed by mass redundancies and office closures, but the Hachette approach is the opposite: to wield conglomerate clout when dealing with printers and suppliers, but also to nurture distinct literary identities. Random House fought back with a canny deal with the BBC, buying a majority stake in its tie-in publishing arm BBC Books.

In the more profitable arena of academic publishing, America's John Wiley & Sons snapped up Blackwell Publishing, which grew out of the separate Blackwell's university bookshop chain. Wiley, also a family com-pany, paid a record £572m for Blackwell, and the deal makes it the second-largest scholarly publisher in the world behind Reed Elsevier. Both companies needed more scale to cope with changing library buying patterns and investment in digital programmes.

● Digital impact

The book industry has a digital divide: while educational, academic and professional publishing groups have spent millions on developing online content, their sister companies in general books are still only starting to make digital moves. This is partly because of several false dawns such as the CD-rom revolution. There's also no equivalent to the iPod for books. Yet nobody doubts that within five years there will be a viable consumer device for downloads. So Random House, Macmillan and HarperCollins are among those who have started to digitise their backlists and build "digital warehouses". They are also using online marketing, creating dedicated websites for authors and new launches, and exploiting social networking sites such as MySpace.

● Classics: the new battleground

As the digital dawn draws nearer, it is ironic that the books of past centuries are still subject to fierce competition. The "classics war" started with the BBC's Big Read in 2003, when The Lord of the Rings narrowly pipped Pride and Prejudice to be named the nation's best-loved book. Publishers realised that out-of-copyright work could sell in huge quantities, and without the need for high advances or royalty payments. So companies large and small flooded the market, with everything from throwaway £1 editions to lavish collector's hardbacks.

In early 2006 the aggressively commercial publisher Headline "rebranded" Jane Austen as a modern women's romance author. The standard period painting covers on her six novels were replaced by swirly, flowery designs and sold in supermarkets and petrol stations. Headline then tried a similar trick on Sherlock Holmes, repackaging Sir Arthur Conan Doyle's novels as crime thrillers. Nor has the giant of classics publishing, Penguin, sat still. It launched a new series of "Red Classics", giving old favourites a new twist at lower prices. It also used the 60th anniversary of its famous black-spined classics list as an excuse for a major marketing campaign and the release of limited edition "Designer Classics" with handmade covers by the likes of Sir Paul Smith and Manolo Blahnik. In August 2007 Random House will jump into the classics arena, launching a new Vintage Classics list in an effort to erode Penguin's dominance and protect its own authors from being swallowed up when their work slips out of copyright.

Awards

British Book Awards 2006
www.britishbookawards.com

- *Book of the year:* Harry Potter and the Half Blood Prince, by JK Rowling (Bloomsbury)
- *Best read of the year:* Labyrinth, by Kate Mosse (Orion)
- *Author of the year:* Alan Bennett
- *Newcomer award:* Marina Lewycka for A short history of tractors in the Ukraine (Penguin)

British book trade awards 2006

- *Publisher of the year:* Faber
- *Imprint and editor of the year:* Corgi/Black Swan, Bill Scott-Kerr
- *Small publisher of the year:* Profile/Snowbooks

Orange prize 2006
www.orangeprize.co.uk

- On Beauty, by Zadie Smith (Penguin)

Orange prize for new writers 2006
www.orangeprize.co.uk

- Disobedience, by Naomi Alderman (Penguin Viking)

Man Booker prize 2006
www.themanbookerprize.com

- The Inheritance of Loss, by Kiran Desai (Hamish Hamilton)

Guardian first book award 2005
http://books.guardian.co.uk/fba2005

- Stewart: A Life Backwards, by Alexander Masters (Fourth Estate)

Guardian children's fiction prize 2005
http://books.guardian.co.uk/childrensfictionprize2005

- The New Policeman, by Kate Thompson (Bodley Head Children's Books)

Whitbread awards 2006

- *Book of the year:* Matisse: The Master, by Hilary Spurling (Hamish Hamilton)
- *First novel:* The Harmony Silk Factory, Tash Aw (Fourth Estate)
- *Biography:* Matisse: The Master, by Hilary Spurling (Hamish Hamilton)
- *Poetry:* Logue's Homer Cold Calls: War Music Continued: Vol 1, by Christopher Logue (Faber)
- *Children's:* The New Policeman, by Kate Thompson (Bodley Head Children's Books)

Celebrity publishing: stars in their eyes

Joel Rickett

The celebrity autobiography is nothing new. From Casanova to Anthea Turner, those in the public eye have always wanted to set the record straight through the pages of a book. What is remarkable is that in this age of Heat magazine, MTV and MySpace, the humble printed page has retained its lustre.

When Sharon Osbourne's memoir was released in autumn 2005, few expected it to top the charts. After all, who could want or need to know more about the wife of Ozzie Osbourne, whose family life had already been subject to a long-running reality TV series, and who was venting her opinions every week on ITV's The X Factor? The answer was at least a million of us. Extreme, her rollercoaster story of living "50 lives in 50 years", went on to become the biggest-selling hardback autobiography since records began.

In retrospect the signs were there for all to see. Katie Price, the glamour model known as Jordan, initially struggled to get a book deal. Yet when John Blake, the former Daily Mirror editor turned publisher, signed her up, he had an instant sensation on his hands. The book trade, partly through the new force of the supermarkets, was reaching a new type of customer: young women. Celebrities provided a ready-made brand to get on to shelves, and maybe even trigger a reading habit.

So in the first few months of 2006, publishers scrambled to sign up their own version of Jordan or Osbourne. Chequebooks were brandished with abandon. The biggest deals of £1m-plus were for the actor Rupert Everett, the former Take That star Gary Barlow, the Iraq war veteran Johnson Beharry, Terry Wogan, and the Bolton comedian Peter Kay. Nary a week passed without another six-figure memoir deal, from the sublime (Bill Bryson) to the ridiculous (Celebrity Big Brother winner Chantelle). A beleaguered band of ghostwriters were dispatched to produce the books in a few weeks on the basis of some snatched interviews. At least 50 celebrity life stories were lined up for the autumn season, elbowing each other off the bookshelves.

The first casualties were the England footballers. In the run-up to the 2006 World Cup, patriotic fervour provoked publishers to snap up books by the likes of Rio Ferdinand, Ashley Cole and Frank Lampard; topping them all was HarperCollins' £5m, 12-year deal with Wayne Rooney. Yet after a lacklustre performance in Germany, nobody wanted to read the details of their pampered lives, and most only sold a few thousand copies. The exception is Stephen Gerrard, who chronicled his European Cup and FA Cup triumphs for the benefit of his fervent Liverpool FC fanbase.

The national press quickly lambasted David Blunkett (whose diaries sold less than 5,000 copies before Christmas) and Big Brother star Pete Bennett (who told the Guardian that he hadn't read a word of his own book). Yet there have also been unmatched successes for those celebs who inspire real affection and have a genuine story to tell. Peter Kay was selling an astonishing 65,000 copies a week in November. Others with a reason for festive cheer were Gordon Ramsay, Terry Wogan, Kerry Katona, Chris Moyles, Victoria Beckham, and Jeremy Clarkson.

Some publishers will have gaping holes in their balance sheets in early 2007; others will have made the advances back through newspaper serialisation deals. But if you're a publishing conglomerate you can afford to write off a few wasted £1m advances; the scarier prospect is having nothing to push to the front of the supermarket displays. The death of the celebrity memoir has been greatly exaggerated.

● Joel Rickett is deputy editor of The Bookseller

Book contents

Book publishers

A&C Black
(see Bloomsbury Publishing)

AA Publishing
The Automobile Association,
14th Floor, Fanum House,
Basingstoke, Hampshire RG21 4EA
01256 491519
ian.harvey@theaa.com
www.theaa.co.uk
Maps, atlases and guidebooks

Abacus
(see Time Warner Books)

ABC-Clio
26 Beaumont Street,
Oxford OX1 2NP
01865 517222
salesuk@abc-clio.com
www.abc-clio.com
Academic and general reference

Absolute Press
Scarborough House,
29 James Street West, Bath BA1 2BT
01225 316013
info@absolutepress.co.uk
www.absolutepress.co.uk
Non-fiction

Abson Books London
5 Sidney Square, London E1 2EY
020 7790 4737
absonbooks@aol.com
www.absonbooks.co.uk
Language glossaries

Acair
7 James Street, Stornoway,
Isle of Lewis HS1 2QN
01851 703020
info@acairbooks.com
www.acairbooks.com
Scottish history and culture, Gaelic

Acumen Publishing
15A Lewins Yard,
East Street, Chesham,
Buckinghamshire HP5 1HQ
01494 794398
steven.gerrard@
    acumenpublishing.co.uk
www.acumenpublishing.co.uk
Philosophy, history and politics

Addison-Wesley
(see Pearson Education)

African Books Collective
Unit 13, Kings Meadow,
Ferry Hinksey Road,
Oxford OX2 0DP
01865 726686
abc@africanbookscollective.com
www.africanbookscollective.com
*Publishing and distribution of African
books*

Age Concern England
1268 London Road,
London SW16 4ER
020 8765 7200
media@ace.org.uk
www.ageconcern.org.uk

Aidan Ellis Publishing
Whinfield, Herbert Road, Salcombe,
South Devon TQ8 8HN
01548 842755
mail@aidanellispublishing.co.uk
www.aepub.demon.co.uk
General publishing and non-fiction

Albatross Publishing
The Dairy Studios,
Runfold St George, Farnham,
Surrey GU10 1PL
01252 781994
sbutler@albatrosspublishing.com
www.albatrosspublishing.com
Reference and non-fiction

Allen & Unwin
(see Orion Publishing Group)

Allen Lane
(see Penguin Books)

Allison & Busby
Suite 111, Bon Marche Centre,
241 Ferndale Road, London SW9 8BJ
020 7580 1080
susie@allisonandbusby.com
www.allisonandbusby.com
Crime; literary fiction and non-fiction

Allyn & Bacon
(see Pearson Education)

Amber Lane Press
Cheorl House, Church Street,
Charlbury, Oxfordshire OX7 3PR
01608 810024
info@amberlanepress.co.uk
www.amberlanepress.co.uk
Plays and theatre

Andersen Press
20 Vauxhall Bridge Road,
London SW1V 2SA
020 7840 8701
andersenpress@randomhouse.co.uk
www.andersenpress.co.uk
Children's books and fiction

Anness Publishing
Hermes House,
88–89 Blackfriars Road,
London SE1 8HA
020 7401 2077
sbaldwin@anness.com
www.annesspublishing.com
General non-fiction

Anova Books
151 Freston Road, London W10 6TH
020 7314 1400
eproffit@anovabooks.com
www.anovabooks.com
• **Batsford** - *Specialist and technical
illustrated non-fiction: embroidery, lace,
chess, bridge, practical art, film and
furniture*

• **Collins & Brown** - *Illustrated non-
fiction: photography, crafts
and practical arts; national magazine
branded books; health, mind, body
and spirit (formerly Vega)*
• **Conway Maritime** - *Maritime history,
ship modelling and naval*
• **Pavilion** - *High-end coffee table books:
celebrity, lifestyle, interiors, cookery,
garden, art and photography*
• **Robson** - *Sports, humour and biography,
especially celebrity; some fiction*

Anthem Press
(see Wimbledon Publishing Press)

Antique Collectors' Club
Sandy Lane, Old Martlesham,
Woodbridge, Suffolk IP12 4SD
01394 389950
sales@antique-acc.com
www.antiquecollectorsclub.com

Anvil Press Poetry
Neptune House, 70 Royal Hill,
London SE10 8RF
020 8469 3033
anvil@anvilpresspoetry.com
www.anvilpresspoetry.com
Poetry

APA Publications
58 Borough High Street,
London SE1 1XF
020 7403 0284
berlitz@apaguide.co.uk
www.berlitzpublishing.co.uk
*Owned by Langenscheidt Publishing
Group. Travel and languages.
Imprint: Berlitz Publishing*

Appletree Press
The Old Potato Station,
14 Howard Street South,
Belfast BT7 1AP
028 9024 3074
reception@appletree.ie
www.appletree.ie
*Cookery and Celtic interest, bespoke
publications*

Arc Publications
Nanholme Mill, Shaw Wood Road,
Todmorden, Lancashire OL14 6DA
01706 812338
info@arcpublications.co.uk
www.arcpublications.co.uk
Contemporary poetry

Arcadia Books
15-16 Nassau Street,
London W1W 7AB
020 7436 9898
info@arcadiabooks.co.uk
www.arcadiabooks.co.uk
*Literary fiction, crime, biography,
gender studies and travel*

Architectural Association Publications
36 Bedford Square,
London WC1B 3ES
020 7887 4021
publications@aaschool.ac.uk
www.aaschool.info/publications
Publishing arm of Architectural Association School of Architecture

Arcturus Publishing
26/27 Bickels Yard,
151–153 Bermondsey Street,
London SE1 3HA
020 7407 9400
info@arcturuspublishing.com
www.arcturuspublishing.com
Non-fiction

Arrow
(see Random House Group)

Ashgrove Publishing
27 John Street, London WC1N 2BX
020 7831 5013
gmo73@dial.pipex.com
www.ashgrovepublishing.com
Owned by Hollydata Publishers. Mind, body and spirit

Ashley Drake Publishing
PO Box 733, Cardiff CF14 2YX
029 2056 0343
post@ashleydrake.com
www.ashleydrake.com
Imprints: Welsh Academic Press (academic titles in English); St David's Press (general trade); Y Ddraig Fach (children's books in Welsh); Gwasg Addysgol Cymru (educational in Welsh)

Ashmolean Museum Publications
(see Oxford University)

Atlantic Books
Ormond House,
26–27 Boswell Street,
London WC1N 3JZ
020 7269 1610
enquiries@groveatlantic.co.uk
www.groveatlantic.co.uk
Literary fiction, non-fiction and reference

Atom
(see Time Warner Books)

Aurum Press
25 Bedford Avenue,
London WC1B 3AT
020 7637 3225
editorial@aurumpress.co.uk
www.aurumpress.co.uk
Non-fiction

Australian Consolidated Press UK
Moulton Park Business Centre,
Red House Road, Moulton Park,
Northampton NN3 6AQ
01604 497531
books@acpuk.com
www.acpuk.com
Home interest

Authentic Media
9 Holdom Avenue, Bletchley,
Milton Keynes MK1 1QR
01908 364200
info@authenticmedia.co.uk
www.authenticmedia.co.uk
Imprints: Authentic (Christian life); Paternoster (academic and theological titles and theses); Authentic Music

Autumn Publishing
Appledram Barns,
Birdham Road, near Chichester,
West Sussex PO20 7EQ
01243 531660
autumn@autumnpublishing.co.uk
www.autumnpublishing.co.uk
Early learning. Imprint: Dyeway Books

Award Publications
The Old Riding School,
Welbeck Estate, Worksop,
Nottinghamshire S80 3LR
01909 478170
info@awardpublications.co.uk
www.awardpublications.co.uk
Children's fiction and reference. Imprint: Horus Editions

Axis Publishing
8C Accommodation Road,
London NW11 8ED
020 8731 8080
admin@axispublishing.co.uk
www.axispublishing.co.uk
Illustrated full colour books

Bantam/Bantam Press
(see Random House Group)

Barefoot Books
124 Walcot Street, Bath BA1 5BG
01225 322400
info@barefootbooks.co.uk
www.barefootbooks.com
Highly illustrated children's picture books

Barny Books
The Cottage,
Hough on the Hill, near Grantham,
Lincolnshire NG32 2BB
01400 250246
Children's books, adult fiction and non-fiction

Barrington Stoke
18 Walker Street, Edinburgh EH3 7LP
0131 225 4113
info@barringtonstoke.co.uk
www.barringtonstoke.co.uk
Remedial children's reading

Batsford
(see Anova Books)

BBC Bookshop
PO Box 308, Sittingbourne,
Kent ME9 8LW
0870 241 5490
bbcshop@bbc.co.uk
www.bbcshop.com

Benjamin Cummings
(see Pearson Education)

Berg Publishers
1st Floor Angel Court,
81 St Clements Street,
Oxford OX4 1AW
01865 245104
enquiry@bergpublishers.com
www.bergpublishers.com
Various academic. Imprint: Oswald Wolff Books

Berghahn Books
3 Newtec Place, Magdalen Road,
Oxford OX4 1RE
01865 250011
salesuk@berghahnbooks.com
www.berghahnbooks.com
Academic books and journals

BFI Publishing
British Film Institute,
21 Stephen Street, London W1T 1LN
020 7255 1444
publishing@bfi.org.uk
www.bfi.org.uk/books
Part of the British Film Institute

BFP Books
Focus House, 497 Green Lanes,
London N13 4BP
020 8882 3315
info@thebfp.com
www.thebfp.com
Publishing arm of the Bureau of Freelance Photographers

BIOS Scientific Publishers
(see I&F Informa)

Birlinn
West Newington House,
10 Newington Road,
Edinburgh EH9 1QS
0131 668 4371
info@birlinn.co.uk
www.birlinn.co.uk
History, folklore, Scottish interest and fiction

Black & White Publishing
99 Giles Street, Edinburgh EH6 6BZ
0131 625 4500
mail@blackandwhitepublishing.com
www.blackandwhitepublishing.com
General fiction and non-fiction

Black Spring Press
Curtain House,
134–146 Curtain Road,
London EC2A 3AR
020 7613 3066
general@blackspringpress.co.uk
www.blackspringpress.co.uk
Fiction and non-fiction

Black Swan
(see Random House Group)

Blackstaff Press
4c Heron Wharf,
Sydenham Business Park,
Belfast BT3 9LE
028 9045 5006
info@blackstaffpress.com
www.blackstaffpress.com
Fiction, non-fiction and poetry

Blackwell Publishing
9600 Garsington Road,
Oxford OX4 2DQ
01865 776868
www.blackwellpublishing.com
Journals and textbooks

Bloodaxe Books
Highgreen, Tarset,
Northumberland NE48 1RP
01434 240500
publicity@bloodaxebooks.com
www.bloodaxebooks.com
Poetry

Bloomsbury Publishing
38 Soho Square, London W1D 3HB
020 7494 2111
publicity@bloomsbury.com
www.bloomsbury.com
*Adult and children's fiction and
non-fiction (including Harry Potter)*

A&C Black (Publishers)
Alderman House, 37 Soho Square,
London W1D 3QZ
020 7758 0200
enquiries@acblack.com
www.acblack.com
*Reference and non-fiction; Writers' and
Artists' Yearbook*

BMJ Books
(incorporated into Blackwell
Publishing)

The Bodley Head
(see Random House Group)

Book Guild
Temple House, 25 High Street,
Lewes, East Sussex BN7 2LU
01273 472534
info@bookguild.co.uk
www.bookguild.co.uk
Fiction and non-fiction

**Boulevard Books & The Babel
Guides**
71 Lytton Road, Oxford OX4 3NY
01865 712931
info@babelguides.com
www.babelguides.com
Contemporary world fiction and guides

Bowker (UK)
1st Floor, Medway House,
Canteloupe Road, East Grinstead,
West Sussex RH19 3BJ
01342 310450
sales@bowker.co.uk
www.bowker.co.uk
*Part of the Cambridge Information Group
(CIG). Reference and biography*

Boydell & Brewer
PO Box 9, Woodbridge,
Suffolk IP12 3DF
01394 610600
trading@boydell.co.uk
www.boydell.co.uk
Non-fiction, principally medieval studies

Boxtree
(see Macmillan Publishers)

Bradt Travel Guides
23 High Street, Chalfont St Peter,
Buckinghamshire SL9 9QE
01753 893444
info@bradtguides.com
www.bradtguides.com
Travel guides

Breedon Books Publishing Co
Breedon House, 3 Parker Centre,
Mansfield Road, Derby DE21 4SZ
01332 384235
sales@breedonpublishing.co.uk
www.breedonbooks.co.uk
Local history and heritage, sport

British Academy
10 Carlton House Terrace,
London SW1Y 5AH
020 7969 5200
secretary@britac.ac.uk
www.britac.ac.uk

British Library
96 Euston Road, London NW1 2DB
020 7412 7469
blpublications@bl.uk
www.bl.uk

British Museum Press
38 Russell Square,
London WC1B 3QQ
020 7323 1234
sales@britishmuseum.co.uk
www.britishmuseum.co.uk

Brooklands Books
PO Box 146, Cobham,
Surrey KT11 1LG
01932 865051
sales@brooklands-books.com
www.brooklands-books.com
Motoring titles and technical catalogues

Brown Watson
The Old Mill, 76 Fleckney Road,
Kibworth Beauchamp,
Leicestershire LE8 0HG
0116 279 6333
books@brownwatson.co.uk
www.brownwatson.co.uk
General children's interest

Brown, Son & Ferguson
4–10 Darnley Street,
Glasgow G41 2SD
0141 429 1234
info@skipper.co.uk
www.skipper.co.uk
Nautical textbooks and Scottish plays

Browntrout Publishers
Redland Office Centre,
157 Redland Road, Redland,
Bristol BS6 6YE
0117 973 9191
sales@browntroutuk.com
www.browntrout.com
Fine art and photography calendars

Brunner-Routledge
(see T&F Informa)

Bryntirion Press
Bryntirion, Bridgend,
Mid-Glamorgan CF31 4DX
01656 655886
office@emw.org.uk
www.emw.org.uk
*Owned by the Evangelical Movement
of Wales. Christian books in English
and Welsh*

Business Education Publishers
The Teleport, Doxford International,
Sunderland, Tyne & Wear SR3 3XD
0191 525 2410
info@bepl.com
www.bepl.com

Butterworth
(see Reed Elsevier)

Cadogan Guides
2nd Floor, 233 High Holborn,
London WC1V 7DN
020 7611 4660
info@cadoganguides.co.uk
www.cadoganguides.com
*Owned by US firm, Morris Publications.
Travel guides*

Calder Publications
51 The Cut, London SE1 8LF
020 7633 0599
info@calderpublications.com
www.calderpublications.com
*Formerly John Calder (Publishers).
Biography, drama, music, poetry
and translations*

Cambridge University Press
The Edinburgh Building,
Shaftesbury Road,
Cambridge CB2 2RU
01223 312393
information@cambridge.org
www.cambridge.org

Camden Press
43 Camden Passage, London N1 8EA
020 7226 4673
Social issues. Imprint: Mindfield

Campbell Books
(see Macmillan Publishers)

Canongate Books
14 High Street, Edinburgh EH1 1TE
0131 557 5111
info@canongate.co.uk
www.canongate.net
Literary fiction and non-fiction, music

Capall Bann Publishing
Auton Farm, Milverton,
Somerset TA4 1NE
01823 401528
enquiries@capallbann.co.uk
www.capallbann.co.uk
British traditional works and folklore

Capstone Publishing
(see John Wiley & Sons)

Carcanet Press
4th Floor, Alliance House,
30 Cross Street, Manchester M2 7AQ
0161 834 8730
info@carcanet.co.uk
www.carcanet.co.uk
*Poetry, academic works, literary
biography, fiction in translation*

Cardiff Academic Press
St Fagans Road, Fairwater,
Cardiff CF5 3AE
029 2056 0333
cap@drakeed.com
www.drakeed.com/cap

Carfax
(see T&F Informa)

Carlton Publishing Group
20 Mortimer Street,
London W1T 3JW
020 7612 0400
enquiries@carltonbooks.co.uk
www.carltonbooks.co.uk
*Illustrated entertainment and leisure
titles. Imprints: Carlton Books, Granada
Media, Manchester United Books,
Andre Deutsche and Prion Books*

Carroll & Brown Publishers
20 Lonsdale Road, London NW6 6RD
020 7372 0900
mail@carrollandbrown.co.uk
www.carrollandbrown.co.uk
Lifestyle

Cassell Reference/Cassell Military
(see Orion Publishing Group)

Catholic Truth Society (CTS)
40–46 Harleyford Road,
London SE11 5AY
020 7640 0042
editorial@cts-online.org.uk
www.cts-online.org.uk
*Roman Catholic books, including
Vatican documents*

Cavendish Publishing
The Glass House, Wharton Street,
London WC1X 9PX
020 7278 8000
info@cavendishpublishing.com
www.cavendishpublishing.com
Academic and practitioner law books

CBA (Publishing Department)
St Marys House, 66 Bootham,
York YO30 7BZ
01904 671417
info@britarch.ac.uk
www.britarch.ac.uk
*Publishing arm of the Council for British
Archaeology. Archaeology, practical
handbooks*

CBD Research
Chancery House, 15 Wickham Road,
Beckenham, Kent BR3 5JS
020 8650 7745
cbd@cbdresearch.com
www.cbdresearch.com
Directories

Century
(see Random House Group)

Chambers Harrap Publishers
7 Hopetoun Crescent,
Edinburgh EH7 4AY
0131 556 5929
admin@chambersharrap.com
www.chambersharrap.com
Dictionaries and reference

Channel 4 Books
(see Random House Group)

Chapman Publishing
4 Broughton Place,
Edinburgh EH1 3RX
0131 557 2207
chapman-pub@blueyonder.co.uk
www.chapman-pub.co.uk
*Scottish writers including poetry, drama,
short stories*

**Chartered Institute of Personnel
and Development**
151 The Broadway, London SW19 1JQ
020 8263 3387
publish@cipd.co.uk (books) and
editorial@peoplemanagement.co.uk
www.cipd.co.uk
Part of CIPD Enterprises (magazine)

Chatto & Windus
(see Random House Group)

Chicken House Publishing
2 Palmer Street, Frome,
Somerset BA11 1DS
01373 454 488
chickenhouse@doublecluck.com
www.doublecluck.com
Children's fiction

Child's Play (International)
Ashworth Road, Bridgemead,
Swindon, Wiltshire SN5 7YD
01793 616286
allday@childs-play.com
www.childs-play.com

Chris Andrews Publications
15 Curtis Yard, North Hinksey Lane,
Oxford OX2 0LX
01865 723404
chris.andrews1@btclick.com
www.cap-ox.co.uk
*Owns the Oxford Picture Library. Coffee
table books, calendars and diaries*

Christian Focus Publications
Geanies House, Fearn, Tain,
Ross-shire IV20 1TW
01862 871011
info@christianfocus.com
www.christianfocus.com
Christian books for adults and children

Chrysalis Books
(incorporated into Anova Books)

Cicerone Press
2 Police Square, Milnthorpe,
Cumbria LA7 7PY
01539 562069
info@cicerone.co.uk
www.cicerone.co.uk
Guidebooks for outdoor enthusiasts

Cisco Press
(see Pearson Education)

Co & Bear Productions (UK)
565 Fulham Road, London SW6 1ES
020 7385 0888
bvincenzini@cobear.co.uk
www.scriptumeditions.co.uk
*High quality illustrated books.
Imprint: Scriptum Editions*

Colin Smythe
PO Box 6, Gerrards Cross,
Buckinghamshire SL9 8XA
01753 886000
sales@colinsmythe.co.uk
www.colinsmythe.co.uk
Anglo-Irish literature and criticism

Collins
(see HarperCollins Publishers)

Collins & Brown
(see Anova Books)

Colourpoint Books
Colourpoint House,
Jubilee Business Park,
21 Jubilee Road, Newtownards,
Co Down BT23 4YH
028 9182 0505
info@colourpoint.co.uk
www.colourpoint.co.uk
School textbooks, transport, Irish interest

Compass Maps
The Coach House, Beech Court,
Winford BS40 8DW
01275 474737
info@popoutmaps.com
www.mapgroup.net
Pocket maps and guides

Compendium Publishing
1st Floor, 43 Frith Street,
London W1V 5TE
020 7287 4570
info@compendiumpublishing.com
Historical

Constable & Robinson
3, The Lanchesters,
162 Fulham Palace Road,
London W6 9ER
020 8741 3663
enquiries@constablerobinson.com
www.constablerobinson.com
*Fiction and non-fiction: lifestyle,
reference, children's, current affairs
and politics*

**Continuum International
Publishing Group**
(see Thompson Learning)

Conway Maritime
(see Anova Books)

Corgi
(see Random House Group)

Country Publications
The Watermill, Broughton Hall,
Skipton, North Yorkshire BD23 3AG
01756 701381
editorial@dalesman.co.uk
www.dalesman.co.uk
*Magazines and regional books
(Countryman, Cumbria, Dalesman and
the Yorkshire nostalgia magazine Down
Your Way)*

Countryside Books
Highfield House, 2 Highfield Avenue,
Newbury, Berkshire RG14 5DS
01635 43816
info@countrysidebooks.co.uk
www.countrysidebooks.co.uk
Local interest and walking books

CRC
(see T&F Informa)

265

Creative media

Crecy Publishing
Unit 1a, Ringway Trading Estate,
Shadowmoss Road,
Manchester M22 5LH
0161 499 0024
enquiries@crecy.co.uk
www.crecy.co.uk
Aviation and naval military history

Cressrelles Publishing Co
10 Station Road Industrial Estate,
Colwall, Malvern,
Worcestershire WR13 6RN
01684 540154
simonsmith@
    cressrelles4drama.fsbusiness.co.uk
*Plays and theatre texts. Imprints: Actinic
Press*

Crowood Press
The Stable Block, Crowood Lane,
Ramsbury, Marlborough,
Wiltshire SN8 2HR
01672 520320
enquiries@crowood.com
www.crowood.com
*Aviation, military history, country,
sports, hobby and leisure pursuits*

Curzon Press
(see T&F Informa)

CW Daniel Company
(see Random House Group)

Darton, Longman & Todd
1 Spencer Court,
140-142 Wandsworth High Street,
London SW18 4JJ
020 8875 0155
mail@darton-longman-todd.co.uk
www.darton-longman-todd.co.uk
Spirituality, theology and Christianity

David & Charles Publishers
Brunel House, Forde Close,
Newton Abbot, Devon TQ12 4PU
01626 323200
postmaster@davidandcharles.co.uk
www.davidandcharles.co.uk
*Subsidiary of F&W, USA. Illustrated
non-fiction*

David Fickling Books
(see Random House Group)

David Fulton (Publishers)
(see Granada Learning Group)

Debrett's
18-20 Hill Rise, Richmond,
Surrey TW10 6AU
020 8939 2250
people@debretts.co.uk
www.debretts.co.uk
Specialist reference works

Dedalus
Langford Lodge, St Judith's Lane,
Sawtry, Cambridgeshire PE28 5XE
01487 832382
info@dedalusbooks.com
www.dedalusbooks.com
*English contemporary fiction and
European fiction in translation, concept
books such as The Decadent Handbook
and The Dedalus Book of Absinthe*

Dewi Lewis Publishing
8 Broomfield Road, Heaton Moor,
Stockport SK4 4ND
0161 442 9450
mail@dewilewispublishing.com
www.dewilewispublishing.com
Fiction, photography and visual arts

Dorling Kindersley
(see Penguin Books)

**Doubleday/Doubleday Picture
Books**
(see Random House Group)

Drake Educational Associates
St Fagans Road, Fairwater,
Cardiff CF5 3AE
029 2056 0333
info@drakeav.com
www.drakeav.com
Audio-visual, educational

Dref Wen
28 Church Road, Whitchurch,
Cardiff CF14 2EA
029 2061 7860
sales@drefwen.com
Welsh language

Duncan Baird Publishers
Castle House, 75-76 Wells Street,
London W1T 3QH
020 7323 2229
enquiries@dbairdpub.co.uk
www.dbponline.co.uk
General non-fiction

Duncan Petersen Publishing
C7, Old Imperial Laundry,
Warriner Gardens, London SW11 4XW
020 7371 2356
charmingsmall.hotels@zen.co.uk
www.charmingsmallhotels.co.uk
Non-fiction

Ebury Press
(see Random House Group)

Eden
(see Random House Group)

Edinburgh University Press
22 George Square, Edinburgh EH8 9LF
0131 650 4218
Timothy.Wright@eup.ed.ac.uk
www.eup.ed.ac.uk

Edward Elgar Publishing
Glensanda House,
Montpellier Parade, Cheltenham,
Gloucestershire GL50 1UA
01242 226934
info@e-elgar.co.uk
www.e-elgar.com
Economics, business and environment

Egmont Books
239 Kensington High Street,
London W8 6SA
020 7761 3500
info@euk.egmont.com
www.egmont.com
*Children's entertainment. Imprints:
Heinemann Young Books, Methuen
Children's Books, Hamlyn Children's
Books, Mammoth, Dean*

Eland Publishing
Third Floor, 61 Exmouth Market,
Clerkenwell, London EC1R 4QL
020 7833 0762
info@travelbooks.co.uk
www.travelbooks.co.uk
*Classic travel literature, Spirit of Place
novels, poetry and history of the Islamic
world*

Elliot Right Way Books
Kingswood Buildings,
Brighton Road, Lower Kingswood,
Tadworth, Surrey KT20 6TD
01737 832202
info@right-way.co.uk
www.right-way.co.uk
Practical non-fiction paperbacks

Elliott & Thompson
27 John Street, London WC1N 2BX
020 7831 5013
gmo73@dial.pipex.com
www.elliottthompson.com
History, biography, literary and fiction

Elm Consulting
Seaton House,
Kings Ripton, Huntingdon,
Cambridgeshire PE28 2NJ
01487 773254
sritchie@elm-training.co.uk
www.elm-training.co.uk
Educational aids

Elsevier
(see Reed Elsevier)

Emissary Publishing
PO Box 33, Bicester,
Oxfordshire OX26 4ZZ
01869 323447
www.manuscriptresearch.co.uk
Humorous paperbacks

Emma Treehouse
2nd Floor, The Old Brewhouse,
Lower Charlton Trading Estate,
Shepton Mallet, Somerset BA4 5QE
01749 330529
treehouse-books@btconnect.com
www.emmatreehouse.com
Children's pre-school

Encyclopaedia Britannica (UK)
2nd Floor, Unity Wharf, Mill Street,
London SE1 2BH
020 7500 7800
enquiries@britannica.co.uk
www.britannica.co.uk

English Heritage (Publishing)
Kemble Drive, Swindon SN2 2GZ
01793 414619
customers@english-heritage.org.uk
www.english-heritage.org.uk
General and specialist history

Enitharmon Press
26B Caversham Road,
London NW5 2DU
020 7482 5967
books@enitharmon.co.uk
www.enitharmon.co.uk
*Poetry, literary criticism, fiction, art and
photography, memoirs and translations*

Euromonitor
60-61 Britton Street,
London EC1M 5UX
020 7251 8024
info@euromonitor.com
www.euromonitor.com
*Business reference, market analysis and
information directories*

Europa Publications
(see T&F Informa)

Evans Publishing Group
(see Thomson Learning)

Everyman
(see Orion Publishing Group)

Everyman's Library
Northburgh House,
10 Northburgh Street,
London EC1V 0AT
020 7566 6350
books@everyman.uk.com
*Imprint of Alfred A Knopf (subsidiary of
Random House, USA). Literature, poetry,
children's and travel*

Exley Publications
16 Chalk Hill, Watford,
Hertfordshire WD19 4BG
01923 248328
enquiries@exleypublications.co.uk
www.helenexleygiftbooks.com
*Giftbooks, quotation anthologies and
humour*

Expert Books
(see Random House Group)

FA Thorpe (Publishing)
(see Ulverscroft Group)

Faber & Faber
3 Queen Square, London WC1N 3AU
020 7465 0045
info@faber.co.uk
www.faber.co.uk
Fiction, non-fiction and poetry

Facet Publishing
7 Ridgmount Street,
London WC1E 7AE
020 7255 0590/0505 (text phone)
info@facetpublishing.co.uk
www.facetpublishing.co.uk
*Publishing arm of CILIP (Chartered
Institute of Library and Information
Professionals). Library and information
science*

Findhorn Press
305a The Park, Findhorn, Forres,
Morayshire IV36 3TE
01309 690582
info@findhornpress.com
www.findhornpress.com
*New Age, personal development and
alternative health*

First & Best in Education
Unit K, Earlstrees Court,
Earlstrees Road, Corby,
Northamptonshire NN17 4HH
01536 399005
info@firstandbest.co.uk
www.firstandbest.co.uk
*Educational books for schools.
Imprints: School Improvement Reports*

Fitzwarren Publishing
2 Orchard Drive,
Aston Clinton, Aylesbury,
Buckinghamshire HP22 5HR
01296 632627
pen2paper@btopenworld.com
Legal handbooks for the layman

Floris Books
15 Harrison Gardens,
Edinburgh EH11 1SH
0131 337 2372
floris@florisbooks.co.uk
www.florisbooks.co.uk
*Scientific, religion, holistic health,
children's, bio dynamics and organics*

Fodor's
(see Random House Group)

Folens Publishers
20 Apex Business Centre,
Boscombe Road, Dunstable LU5 4RL
0870 609 1237
folens@folens.com
www.folens.com
Educational books. Imprint: Belair

Footprint Handbooks
6 Riverside Court,
Lower Bristol Road, Bath BA2 3DZ
01225 469141
ariddle@footprintbooks.com
www.footprintbooks.com
*Travel. Activity guides to hundreds
of cities and countries*

For Dummies
(see John Wiley & Sons)

Fountain Press
Newpro UK , Old Sawmills Road,
Faringdon, Oxfordshire SN7 7DS
01367 242411
sales@newprouk.co.uk
Photography and natural history

Fourth Estate
(see HarperCollins Publishers)

Frances Lincoln Publishers
4 Torriano Mews, Torriano Avenue,
London NW5 2RZ
020 7284 4009
reception@frances-lincoln.com
www.franceslincoln.com
Highly illustrated non-fiction

Frank Cass
(see T&F Informa)

Free Association Books
PO Box 37664, London NW7 2XU
020 8906 0396
info@fabooks.com
www.fabooks.com
*Psychoanalysis and psychotherapy,
social science, psychology*

Frommer's
(see John Wiley & Sons)

FT Prentice Hall
(see Pearson Education)

Gaia Books
2-4 Heron Quays, London E14 4JP
020 7531 8439
info@gaiabooks.com
www.gaiabooks.co.uk
*Illustrated natural health, mind body
spirit, natural living and environmental
issues*

Garland Science
(see T&F Informa)

Garnet Publishing
8 Southern Court, South Street,
Reading, Berkshire RG1 4QS
0118 959 7847
enquiries@garnetpublishing.co.uk
www.garnetpublishing.co.uk
*Imprints: Garnet (Middle East); Ithaca
Press (business books)*

Geddes & Grosset
David Dale House,
New Lanark ML11 9DJ
01555 665000
info@geddesandgrosset.co.uk
www.geddesandgrosset.co.uk
*Children's and reference books.
Imprint: Beanobooks (children's)*

**Geological Society Publishing
House**
Unit 7, Brassmill Enterprise Centre,
Brassmill Lane, Bath BA1 3JN
01225 445046
sales@geolsoc.org.uk
www.geolsoc.org.uk/bookshop
*Publishing arm of the Geological Society.
Undergraduate and postgraduate texts in
the earth sciences*

George Mann Books
PO Box 22, Maidstone,
Kent ME14 1AH
01622 759591
Original non-fiction and selected reprints

Gibson Square Books
47, Lonsdale Square, London N1 1EW
020 7096 1100
publicity@gibsonsquare.com
www.gibsonsquare.com/
*Biography and personal experience.
Imprints: Gibson Square, New Editions*

Giles de la Mare Publishers
PO Box 25351, London NW5 1ZT
020 7485 2533
gilesdelamare@dial.pipex.com
www.gilesdelamare.co.uk
*Art and architecture, biography, history,
music*

Gollancz
(see Orion Publishing Group)

GMP (Gay Men's Press)
Unit M, Spectrum House,
32/34 Gordon House Road,
London NW5 1LP
020 7424 7400
www.millivres.co.uk
*Part of the Millivres Prowler Group.
Literary gay fiction. Imprint: Zipper
Books (gay male erotic fiction)*

Gomer Press
Llandysul, Ceredigion SA44 4JL
01559 362371
gwasg@gomer.co.uk
www.gomer.co.uk
Adult fiction and non-fiction.
Imprint: Pont Books

Good Web Guide
65 Bromfelde Road,
London SW4 6PP
020 7720 8919
marketing@thegoodwebguide.co.uk
www.thegoodwebguide.co.uk

Granada Learning Group
Television Centre, Quay Street,
Manchester M60 9EA
0161 827 2927
info@granada-learning.co.uk
www.granada-learning.co.uk

David Fulton Publishers
The Chiswick Centre,
414 Chiswick High Road,
London W4 5TF
020 8996 3610
mail@fultonpublishers.co.uk
www.fultonpublishers.co.uk
Books for Initial Teacher Training courses,
continuing professional development and
for special educational needs teachers

Leckie and Leckie
3rd Floor, 4 Queen Street,
Edinburgh EH2 1JF
01334 475656
enquiries@leckieandleckie.co.uk
www.leckieandleckie.co.uk
Study guides for students preparing for
the Scottish Standard Grade and Higher
exams

Letts Educational
The Chiswick Centre
0845 602 1937
mail@lettsed.co.uk
www.letts-successzone.com
Examination study and revision guides

nferNelson
The Chiswick Centre
020 8996 8444
information@nfernelson.co.uk
www.nfer-nelson.co.uk
Tests, assessments and assessment services

SEMERC
Television Centre
0161 827 2927
www.semerc.com
ICT special needs

Granta Books
2-3 Hanover Yard, Noel Road,
London N1 8BE
020 7704 9776
ltaylor@granta.com
www.granta.com
Literary fiction and general non-fiction

Green Books
Foxhole, Dartington, Totnes,
Devon TQ9 6EB
01803 863260
edit@greenbooks.co.uk
www.greenbooks.co.uk
Green issues

Greenhill Books/Lionel Leventhal
Park House, 1 Russell Gardens,
London NW11 9NN
020 8458 6314
info@greenhillbooks.com
www.greenhillbooks.com
Aviation, military, Napoleonic.
Imprint: Chatham Publishing (naval)

Gresham Books
46 Victoria Road, Summertown,
Oxford OX2 7QD
01865 513582
info@gresham-books.co.uk
www.gresham-books.co.uk
Hymn and service books

Griffith Institute
(see Oxford University)

Grub Street Publishing
4 Rainham Close, London SW11 6SS
020 7924 3966/7738 1008
post@grubstreet.co.uk
www.grubstreet.co.uk
Lifestyle and military

**Guild of Master Craftsman
Publications**
166 High Street, Lewes,
East Sussex BN7 1XU
01273 477374
pubs@thegmcgroup.com
www.gmcbooks.com
Craft and woodworking

Guinness World Records
338 Euston Road, London NW1 3BD
020 7891 4567
press@guinnessworldrecords.com
www.guinnessworldrecords.com

Gullane
(see Pinwheel)

Gwasg Carreg Gwalch
12 Iard yr Orsaf, Llanrwst,
Conwy LL26 0EH
01492 642031
books@carreg-gwalch.co.uk
www.carreg-gwalch.co.uk
Welsh fiction and non-fiction; books on
Wales

Halban Publishers
22 Golden Square, London W1F 9JW
020 7437 9300
books@halbanpublishers.com
www.halbanpublishers.com
Fiction, memoirs, history, biography
and books of Jewish interest

Halsgrove
Halsgrove House, Lower Moor Way,
Tiverton Business Park, Tiverton,
Devon EX16 6SS
01884 243242
sales@halsgrove.com
www.halsgrove.com
South-west regional books, cookery,
biography and art

Hambledon and London
102 Gloucester Avenue,
London NW1 8HX
020 7586 0817
office@hambledon.co.uk
www.hambledon.co.uk
History and biography

Hamish Hamilton
(see Penguin Books)

Harcourt Education
(see Reed Elsevier)

Harlequin Mills & Boon
Eton House, 18-24 Paradise Road,
Richmond, Surrey TW9 1SR
020 8288 2800
www.millsandboon.co.uk
Subsidiary of Harlequin, Canada.
Popular fiction

Harley Books
Martins, Great Horkesley,
Colchester, Essex CO6 4AH
01206 271216
harley@harleybooks.co.uk
www.harleybooks.com
Natural history

HarperCollins Publishers
77-85 Fulham Palace Road,
London W6 8JB
020 8741 7070
webcontact@harpercollins.co.uk
www.harpercollins.co.uk
• Collins - www.collins.co.uk
Reference books, cartography,
education, dictionaries
• General books -
www.harpercollinschildrensbooks.co.uk
HarperCollins Childrens Books. Picture
books, fiction and properties (Dr Seuss,
Paddington Bear, Noddy etc.)
• HarperEntertainment - *Imprints:*
Entertainment (media-related); Collins
Willow (sports); Tolkien and Estates
(works by JRR Tolkien, Agatha Christie,
CS Lewis); HarperCollins Audio
• HarperFiction -
www.voyager-books.co.uk
www.collins-crime.co.uk
www.readinggroups.co.uk
Imprints: HarperCollins Fiction (crime
and popular fiction); Voyager (sci-fi and
fantasy)
• HarperPress - *Imprints: HarperCollins*
Non-Fiction (history, current affairs,
travel and biography); Fourth Estate
(innovative fiction and non fiction);
HarperPerennial (literary paperbacks)
• Thorsons - www.thorsons.co.uk
Health, mind, body and spirit, personal
development books. Imprint: Thorsons
and Element (colour illustrated)

Harvard University Press/MIT Press
Fitzroy House, 11 Chenies Street,
London WC1E 7EY
020 7306 0603
info@HUP-MITpress.co.uk
http://mitpress.mit.edu
European office of US company

Harvill Secker
(see Random House Group)

Haynes Publishing
Sparkford, Near Yeovil,
Somerset BA22 7JJ
01963 440635
www.haynes.co.uk
Owns Sutton Publishing. Car and
motorcycle service and repair manuals

Heinemann
(see Reed Elsevier)

Helicon Publishing
RM, New Mill House,
183 Milton Park, Abingdon,
Oxfordshire OX14 4SE
0870 920 0200
helicon@rm.com
www.helicon.co.uk
CD-Roms and online reference and cartography

Helm Information
Crowham Manor, Main Road,
Westfield, Hastings,
East Sussex TN35 4SR
01424 882422
amandahelm@
   helm-information.co.uk
www.helm-information.co.uk
Academic

Helter Skelter Publishing
South Bank House, Black Prince
Road, London SE1 7SJ
020 7463 2204
info@helterskelterpublishing.com
www.helterskelterbooks.com
*Obscure music. Co-imprint with
SAF Publishing: Firefly Publishing
(mainstream rock and pop)*

Hesperus Press
4 Rickett Street, London SW6 1RU
020 7610 3331
info@hesperuspress.com
www.hesperuspress.com
Classic fiction in paperback

Hobsons Publishing
Challenger House, 42 Adler Street,
London E1 1EE
020 7958 5000
info@hobsons.co.uk
www.hobsons.com/uk
*Part of the Daily Mail & General Trust.
Course and career guides*

Hodder Headline Group
338 Euston Road, London NW1 3BH
020 7873 6000
www.hodderheadline.co.uk and
www.madaboutbooks.com
Owned by Hatchett & Every

Hodder Headline Ireland
8 Castlecourt Centre, Castleknock,
Dublin 15
00 353 1 824 6288
*Adult fiction and non-fiction.
Imprint: HHI Lir (fiction)*

Hodder Headline Scotland
2A Christie Street, Paisley PA1 1NB
0141 848 1609
bob.mcdevitt@hodder.co.uk

General
• Hodder & Stoughton - *Imprints:
Sceptre (literary); NEL (crime);
Coronet (commercial fiction); Mobius
(mind, body & spirit); Flame (fiction)*
• Headline - *Imprints: Review (literary);
Headline (commercial fiction and non-
fiction)*
• John Murray - *Fiction, history, travel,
literature and memoir*

Education
• Hodder Arnold - *Imprints: teach
yourself (home reference); Hodder +
Stoughton (reference including FA
Guides and Michelle Thomas)*
• Hodder Murray - *Curriculum materials*
• Hodder Gibson - 0141 848 1609
hoddergibson@hodder.co.uk
*Textbooks and revision support for the
Scottish market*

Religious
• Hodder Religious - *Imprints: Hodder &
Stoughton (gift and inspirational); HY
[help yourself] (home reference); HCB
(Hodder Christian Books); NIV [New
International Version] (bible translation)*

Children's
• Hodder Children's Books - *Fiction for
children and young adults*
• Hodder Wayland -
   www.hodderwayland.co.uk
Non-fiction educational books

Honeyglen Publishing
56 Durrels House, Warwick Gardens,
London W14 8QB
020 7602 2876
History and fiction

Honno Welsh Women's Press
c/o Canolfan Merched Y Wawr,
Vulcan Street, Aberystwyth,
Ceredigion SY23 1JH
01970 623150
post@honno.co.uk
www.honno.co.uk
*Reprints of classics, children's, fiction,
poetry, short stories and Welsh women
writers*

House of Lochar
Isle of Colonsay, Argyll PA61 7YR
01951 200232
lochar@colonsay.org.uk
www.houseoflochar.com
*Mostly Scottish titles. Imprint: Colonsay
Books*

How To Books
Spring Hill House, Spring Hill Road,
Begbroke, Oxford OX5 1RX
01865 375794
info@howtobooks.co.uk
www.howtobooks.co.uk
Reference and self-help books

Hurst Publishers
41 Great Russell Street,
London WC1B 3PL
020 7255 2201
hurst@atlas.co.uk
www.hurstpub.co.uk
*Current affairs, politics, contemporary
history*

Hutchinson
(see Random House Group)

Ian Allan Publishing
Riverdene Business Park,
Molesey Road, Hersham,
Surrey KT12 4RG
01932 266600
info@ianallanpublishing.co.uk
www.ianallan.com
*Maritime, road, rail, aviation, militaria
and military history. Imprints: Midland
Publishing, OPC Railway, Classic
Publications, Lewis Masonic*

Ian Henry Publications
20 Park Drive, Romford,
Essex RM1 4LH
01708 749119
info@ian-henry.com
www.ian-henry.com
History and Sherlock Holmes

IB Tauris
(see Thomson Learning)

Icon Books
The Old Dairy, Brook Road, Thriplow,
Cambridge SG8 7RG
01763 208008
info@iconbooks.co.uk
www.iconbooks.co.uk
*History, children's fiction and non-fiction,
adult non-fiction*

IMP Fiction
PO Box 69, Church Stretton,
Shropshire SU6 6WZ
0169 472 0049
info@impbooks.com
www.impbooks.com
Original fiction

Independent Music Press
PO Box 69, Church Stretton,
Shropshire SU6 6WZ
0169 472 0049
info@impbooks.com
www.impbooks.com
Music biography and youth culture

Interpet
Interpet House, Vincent Lane,
Dorking, Surrey RH4 3YX
01306 873840
publishing@interpet.co.uk
Pet, aquatic and water gardening books

Inter-Varsity Press
Norton Street, Nottingham NG7 3HR
0115 978 1054
ivp@ivpbooks.com
www.ivpbooks.com
*Christian belief and lifestyle.
Imprints: IVP, Apollos, Crossway*

Isis Publishing
(see Ulverscroft Group)

Ithaca Press
(see Garnet Publishing)

**James Clarke & Co Lutterworth
Press**
PO Box 60, Cambridge CB1 2NT
01223 350865
publishing@jamesclarke.co.uk
www.jamesclarke.co.uk
*Parent company of The Lutterworth Press.
Theological, directory and reference*

James Currey Publishers
73 Botley Road, Oxford OX2 0BS
01865 244111
editorial@jamescurrey.co.uk
www.jamescurrey.co.uk
Academic books on Africa and third world

Jane's Information Group
163 Brighton Road, Coulsdon,
Surrey CR5 2YH
020 8700 3700
info@janes.com
www.janes.com
Defence, aerospace and transport

Janus Publishing Company
105–107 Gloucester Place,
London W1U 6BY
020 7580 7664
publisher@januspublishing.co.uk
www.januspublishing.co.uk
Fiction and non-fiction. Imprint:
Empiricus Books

Jarrold Publishing
Whitefriars, Norwich,
Norfolk NR3 1JR
01603 763300
publishing@jarrold.com
www.jarrold-publishing.co.uk
Heritage and leisure, walking guides.
Imprints: Pitkin, Unichrome

Jessica Kingsley Publishers
116 Pentonville Road,
London N1 9JB
020 7833 2307
post@jkp.com
www.jkp.com
Social and behavioural sciences

John Blake Publishing
3 Bramber Court, 2 Bramber Road,
London W14 9PB
020 7381 0666
words@blake.co.uk
www.blake.co.uk
General non-fiction, esp true crime,
popular culture, general biography.
Includes Richard Cohen, Smith Gryphon
and Blake Publishing. Imprints: Metro
Books (health, fitness, cookery and
lifestyle)

John Hunt Publishing
The Bothy, Deershot Lodge,
Park Lane, Ropley,
Hampshire SO24 0BE
01962 773768
office1@o-books.net
www.johnhunt-publishing.com
www.o-books.net
World religions. Imprint: O Books (mind,
body and spirit)

John Murray
(see Hodder Headline Group)

John Wiley & Sons
The Atrium, Southern Gate,
Chichester PO19 8SQ
01243 779777
cs-books@wiley.co.uk
www.wileyeurope.com
Scientific, technical and medical;
professional and trade; textbooks and
educational materials.
• **Capstone Publishing** – *Business and*
personal development
www.capstoneideas.com

• **Fernhurst Books** – *Sailing and*
watersports
• **For Dummies** – *Reference series*
• **Frommer's** – *Travel guides*
• **Jossey-Bass** – *Management, education*
and religion
• **The Unofficial Guide** – *Travel, computing*
• **Visual/Redhat Press/Wrox** – *Computing*
• **Wiley** – *Scientific, technical and*
medical; professional and trade;
textbooks and educational materials
• **Wiley Interscience** – *Scientific, technical*
and medical; print and online reference
materials
• **Wiley-Academy** – *Architecture*
• **Wiley-Liss** – *Life and medical*
• **Wiley-VCH** – *Scientific, technical and*
medical

Jonathan Cape
(see Random House Group)

Kahn & Averill
9 Harrington Road, London SW7 3ES
020 8743 3278
kahn@averill23.freeserve.co.uk
Books on music

Kenilworth Press
Wykey House, Wykey, Shrewsbury,
Shropshire SY4 1JA
01939 261616
editorial@kenilworthpress.co.uk
www.kenilworthpress.co.uk
Equestrian

Kenneth Mason Publications
The Book Barn, Westbourne,
Emsworth, Hampshire PO10 8RS
01243 377977
info@researchdisclosure.com
www.researchdisclosure.com
Lifestyle, nutrition and nautical.
Imprint: Research Disclosure

Kevin Mayhew Publishers
Buxhall, Stowmarket,
Suffolk IP14 3BW
01449 737978
info@kevinmayhewltd.com
www.kevinmayhew.com
Christian music resources

Kingfisher Publications
New Penderel House,
283–288 High Holborn,
London WC1V 7HZ
020 7903 9999
sales@kingfisherpub.com
www.kingfisherpub.com
Children's fiction and non-fiction

Kogan Page
120 Pentonville Road,
London N1 9JN
020 7278 0433
kpinfo@kogan-page.co.uk
www.kogan-page.co.uk
Business and management

Kyle Cathie
122 Arlington Road,
London NW1 7HP
020 7692 7215
general.enquiries@kyle-cathie.com
www.KyleCathie.com
Lifestyle

Ladybird
(see Penguin Books)

Landmark Publishing
Ashbourne Hall, Cokayne Avenue,
Ashbourne, Derbyshire DE6 1EJ
01335 347349
landmark@clara.net
www.landmarkpublishing.co.uk
Travel guides, and industrial and local
history

Laurence King Publishing
71 Great Russell Street,
London WC1B 3BP
020 7430 8850
enquiries@laurenceking.co.uk
www.laurenceking.co.uk
Illustrated arts

Lawrence & Wishart
99A Wallis Road, London E9 5LN
020 8533 2506
lw@lwbooks.co.uk
www.lwbooks.co.uk
Current and world affairs

Leckie and Leckie
(see Granada Learning Group)

Lennard Associates
Windmill Cottage, Mackerye End,
Harpenden, Hertfordshire AL5 5DR
01582 715866
stephenson@lennardqap.co.uk
Sporting yearbooks. Imprints and
divisions include: Lennard Publishing,
Queen Anne Press

Letts Educational
(see Granada Learning Group)

LexisNexis
(see Reed Elsevier)

Lion Hudson
Mayfield House, 256 Banbury Road,
Oxford OX2 7DH
01865 302750
enquiries@lionhudson.com
www.lionhudson.com
Formed through merger of Lion Publishing
and Angus Hudson. Christian books.
Imprints: Lion, Lion Children's, Candle,
Monarch

Little, Brown
(see Time Warner Books)

Little Tiger Press
Magi Publications,
1 The Coda Centre,
189 Munster Road, London SW6 6AW
020 7385 6333
info@littletiger.co.uk
www.littletigerpress.com
Children's picture and novelty books.
Imprints: Little Tiger, Caterpillar Books

Liverpool University Press
4 Cambridge Street,
Liverpool L69 7ZU
0151 794 2233
sbell@liv.ac.uk
www.liverpool-unipress.co.uk

Lonely Planet Publications
72–82 Rosebery Avenue,
Clerkenwell, London EC1R 4RW
020 7841 9000
go@lonelyplanet.co.uk
www.lonelyplanet.com
Travel guides

Longman
(see Pearson Education)

Lutterworth Press
(see James Clarke & Co Lutterworth Press)

Macmillan Publishers
4 Crinan Street, London N1 9XW
020 7843 3600
www.macmillan.com

Nature Publishing Group
4 Crinan Street, London N1 9XW
020 7843 4000
www.nature.com
Scientific journals and reference publishing

Macmillan Education
Macmillan Oxford,
4 Between Towns Road,
Oxford OX4 3PP
01865 405700
www.macmillaneducation.com
ELT learning materials for international markets

Palgrave Macmillan
Brunel Road, Houndmills,
Basingstoke, Hampshire RG21 6XS
01256 329242
bookenquiries@palgrave.com
www.palgrave.com
Academic, scholarly and reference publishing in the social sciences and humanities

Pan Macmillan
20 New Wharf Road, London N1 9RR
020 7014 6000
www.panmacmillan.com
Fiction and non-fiction for adults and children. Imprints: Macmillan, Pan, Picador, Young Picador, Boxtree, Sidgwick and Jackson, Papermac, Macmillan Children's Books, Campbell Books, Priddy Books. US imprints: Picador USA; St Martin's Press; Farrar, Straus and Giroux Inc.; Henry Holt; Tor. Australian imprints: Pan Macmillan Australia, Pancake. South African imprints: Pan Macmillan South Africa, Picador Africa. Irish imprints: Gill and Macmillan

Magna Large Print Books
(see Ulverscroft Group)

Mainstream Publishing Co (Edinburgh)
7 Albany Street, Edinburgh EH1 3UG
0131 557 2959
enquiries@
    mainstreampublishing.com
www.mainstreampublishing.com
General non-fiction and popular paperbacks

Management Books 2000
Forge House, Limes Road,
Kemble, Cirencester,
Gloucestershire GL7 6AD
01285 771441
info@mb2000.com
www.mb2000.com
Working books for working managers

Manchester University Press
Oxford Road, Manchester M13 9NR
0161 275 2310
mucp@manchester.ac.uk
www.manchesteruniversitypress
.co.uk

Manson Publishing
73 Corringham Road,
London NW11 7DL
020 8905 5150
www.mansonpublishing.com
Scientific, technical, medical and veterinary

Marion Boyars Publishers
24 Lacy Road, London SW15 1NL
020 8788 9522
catheryn@marionboyars.com
www.marionboyars.co.uk
Formerly Calder and Boyars. Literary fiction, fiction in translation, social affairs, film, music, drama

Marshall Cavendish
119 Wardour Street,
London W1F 0UW
020 7565 6000
www.marshallcavendish.co.uk
Adults' and children's and educational

Marston House
Marston House, Marston Magna,
Yeovil, Somerset BA22 8DH
01935 851331
alphaimage@
    marstonhouse.ndo.co.uk
www.marstonhouse.ndo.co.uk
Fine art, architecture, ceramics and horticulture

Martin Dunitz
(see T&F Informa)

McGraw-Hill Education
Shoppenhangers Road, Maidenhead,
Berkshire SL6 2QL
01628 502500
www.mcgraw-hill.co.uk
Business, economics, computing and engineering

Higher Education
University textbooks on business, economics, accounting, finance, marketing, computing science, decision sciences. Imprints: McGraw-Hill Education, McGraw-Hill Irwin

Open University Press
Higher education, education, health and social welfare, cultural and media studies, psychology, criminology, sociology, counselling, study guides

Professional
Professional, business and general reference books covering computing, science, technical and medical, languages, architecture, careers, politics, management, finance, parenting, health,

sports & fitness. Imprints: McGraw-Hill Professional, McGraw-Hill Trade, McGraw-Hill Osborne, McGraw-Hill Medical Publishing, McGraw-Hill Contemporary, Harvard Business School Press, Amacom, Berrett-Koehler, CMP

Schools
Early childhood, primary and secondary school books. Imprints: Kingscourt, Glencoe and SRA, Macmillan, The Learning Group

Mercat Press
10 Coates Crescent,
Edinburgh EH3 7AL
0131 225 5324
enquiries@mercatpress.com
www.mercatpress.com
Fiction and non-fiction of Scottish interest

Merlin Press
96, Monnow Street,
Monmouth NP25 3EQ
01600 775663
info@merlinpress.co.uk
www.merlinpress.co.uk
Economics, history, leftwing politics. Imprints: Green Print, Merlin Press

Merrell Publishers
81 Southwark Street,
London SE1 0HX
020 7928 8880
mail@merrellpublishers.com
www.merrellpublishers.com
Art, architecture, design and photography

Methodist Publishing House
4 John Wesley Road,
Werrington, Peterborough,
Cambridgeshire PE4 6ZP
01733 325002
sales@mph.org.uk
www.mph.org.uk
Owned by the Methodist Church Christian books. Imprint: Epworth Press

Methuen Publishing
11/12 Buckingham Gate,
London SW1E 6LB
020 7798 1600
sales@methuen.co.uk
www.methuen.co.uk
General fiction and non-fiction. Imprint: Politicos (politics)

Michael Joseph
(see Penguin Books)

Michael O'Mara Books
9 Lion Yard, Tremadoc Road,
London SW4 7NQ
020 7720 8643
enquiries@michaelomarabooks.com
www.mombooks.com
Biography, popular history, humour, children's and pre-school

Michelin Travel Publications
Hannay House, 39 Clarendon Road,
Watford, Hertfordshire WD17 1JA
01923 205240
www.viamichelin.com
Travel books and maps

Microsoft Press
Thames Valley Park, Reading,
Berkshire RG6 1WG
0870 601 0100
mspinfo@microsoft.com
www.microsoft.com/mspress/uk
*Computing manuals to accompany
Microsoft products; also system
administration, business solutions
and security*

Miles Kelly Publishing
Unit 17 & 18, The Bardfield Centre,
Great Bardfield, Essex CM7 4SL
01371 811309
info@mileskelly.net
www.mileskelly.net
Children's titles

Milet Publishing
6 North End Parade, London W14 0SJ
020 7603 5477
info@milet.com
www.milet.com
Children's books

Millivres Prowler Group
Unit M, Spectrum House,
32/34 Gordon House Road,
London NW5 1LP
020 7424 7400
www.millivres.co.uk
*Zipper Books, Gay Men's Press, Gay Times
Books, Diva Books and Red Hot Diva Books*

Mills & Boon
(see Harlequin Mills & Boon)

MIT Press
(see Harvard University Press/
MIT Press)

Motor Racing Publications
PO Box 1318, Croydon,
Surrey CR9 5YP
020 8654 2711
mrp.books@virgin.net
www.mrpbooks.co.uk
*Motor racing, road cars, performance
and classic cars*

MQ Publications
12 The Ivories,
6-8 Northampton Street,
London N1 2HY
020 7359 2244
kim@mqpublications.com
www.mqpublications.com
Illustrated cookbooks

Murdoch Books UK
Erico House, 6th Floor,
93-99 Upper Richmond Road,
Putney, London SW15 2TG
020 8785 5995
jpickett@murdochbooks.co.uk
*Food and drink, craft, gardening, fiction
and non-fiction*

National Trust Publications
Heelis, Kemble Drive, Swindon,
Wiltshire SN2 2NA
01793 817400
enquiries@thenationaltrust.org.uk
www.nationaltrust.org.uk/bookshop
Publishing arm of The National Trust

Nautical Data
The Book Barn, Westbourne,
Emsworth, Hampshire PO10 8RS
01243 389352
info@nauticaldata.com
www.nauticaldata.com

NCVO Publications
Regent's Wharf, 8 All Saints Street,
London N1 9RL
020 7713 6161
ncvo@ncvo-vol.org.uk
www.ncvo-vol.org.uk
*Publishing imprint of the National Council
for Voluntary Organisations. Directories,
public policy and governance; trusteeship
and HR in the voluntary sector*

Neil Wilson Publishing
Suite 303, The Pentagon Centre,
36 Washington Street,
Glasgow G3 8AZ
0141 221 1117
info@nwp.co.uk
www.nwp.co.uk
*Scottish and Irish interest: food and
drink, outdoor pursuits, history, humour
and biography*

Nelson Thornes
Delta Place, 27 Bath Road,
Cheltenham,
Gloucestershire GL53 7TH
01242 267100
info@nelsonthornes.com
www.nelsonthornes.com
*Part of the Wolters Kluwer Group.
Educational*

New Beacon Books
76 Stroud Green Road,
London N4 3EN
020 7272 4889
newbeaconbooks@btconnect.com
*Black-oriented fiction, history, politics,
poetry and language*

New Holland Publishers (UK)
Garfield House,
86-88 Edgware Road,
London W2 2EA
020 7724 7773
info@nhpub.co.uk
www.newhollandpublishers.com
Non-fiction, lifestyle and self-improvement

New Riders
(see Pearson Education)

nferNelson
(see Granada Learning Group)

Nicholas Brealey Publishing
3-5 Spafield Street,
London EC1R 4QB
020 7239 0360
publicity@nbrealey-books.com
www.nbrealey-books.com
*Includes Intercultural Press. Cultural
business, self-help and travel. US imprint:
Intercultural Press*

Nick Hern Books
The Glasshouse,
49a Goldhawk Road,
London W12 8QP
020 8749 4953
info@nickhernbooks.demon.co.uk
www.nickhernbooks.co.uk
Theatre and film

Nielsen BookData
3rd Floor, Midas House,
62 Goldsworth Road, Woking,
Surrey GU21 6LQ
0870 7778710
sales@nielsenbookdata.co.uk
www.nielsenbookdata.com
*The Directory of UK and Irish Book
Publishers*

NMS Enterprises
National Museums of Scotland,
Chambers Street, Edinburgh EH1 1JF
0131 247 4026
publishing@nms.ac.uk
www.nms.ac.uk
*History, art, archaeology, natural history,
popular Scottish history, culture,
biography and geology*

Nottingham University Press
Manor Farm, Church Lane,
Thrumpton, Nottingham NG11 0AX
0115 983 1011
editor@nup.com
www.nup.com
Scientific textbooks

Oberon Books
521 Caledonian Road, London N7 9RH
020 7607 3637
info@oberonbooks.com
www.oberonbooks.com
Play texts

Octagon Press
78 York Street, London W1H 1DP
020 7168 5308
admin@octagonpress.com
www.octagonpress.com
*Philosophy, psychology, travel and
Eastern religion*

Octopus Publishing Group
2-4 Heron Quays, London E14 4JP
020 7531 8400
info@octopus-publishing.co.uk
www.octopus-publishing.co.uk
www.conran-octopus.co.uk
www.hamlyn.co.uk
www.mitchell-beazley.co.uk
www.philips-maps.co.uk
*Owned by Hachette. Illustrated adult
reference books*

Oldcastle Books
PO Box 394, Harpenden,
Hertfordshire AL5 1XJ
01582 761264
info@noexit.co.uk
info@pocketessentials.com
www.noexit.co.uk
www.pocketessentials.com
*Imprints: No Exit Press and Crime Time
(crime/noir fiction); Pocketessentials
(compact reference books on film, tv,
literature, ideas and history); High Stakes
(gambling)*

Omnibus Press
14–15 Berners Street, London W1T 3LJ
020 7434 0066
music@musicsales.co.uk
www.omnibuspress.com
Imprints: Omnibus Press (music-related biography); Vision On (upmarket music-related photo books). US imprint: Schirmer Books (self-help books, music industry)

Oneworld
(see Thomson Learning)

Onlywomen Press
40 St Lawrence Terrace, London W10 5ST
020 8354 0796
onlywomenpress@aol.com
www.onlywomenpress.com
Lesbian and feminist fiction, non-fiction theory and poetry

Open University Press
(see McGraw-Hill Education)

Orbit Press
(see Time Warner Books)

Orion Publishing Group
Orion House, 5 Upper Saint Martin's Lane, London WC2H 9EA
020 7240 3444
info@orionbooks.co.uk
www.orionbooks.co.uk
• Gollancz - *Sci-fi and fantasy*
• Orion Children's Books
• Weidenfeld & Nicolson - *History, reference, non-fiction, illustrated and literary fiction, military*
• Cassell Military - *Illustrated and paperback*
• Cassell Reference
• Everyman *Classics in paperback*
• Phoenix - *Contemporary fiction*

Osprey Publishing
Midland House, West Way, Oxford OX2 0PH
01865 727022
info@ospreypublishing.com
www.ospreypublishing.com
Military history, aviation

Oxford University
Ashmolean Museum Publications, Ashmolean Museum, Beaumont Street, Oxford OX1 2PH
01865 278010
publications@ashmus.ox.ac.uk
www.ashmolean.org
Art and archaeology

Griffith Institute
Sackler Library, 1 St John's Street, Oxford OX1 2LG
01865 278099
griffith.institute@orinst.ox.ac.uk
www.ashmolean.museum/griffith.html
Egyptology

Oxford University Press
Great Clarendon Street, Oxford OX2 6DP
01865 556767
enquiry@oup.com
www.oup.com
A department of Oxford University. Academic. Imprint: Oxford Children's Books

Palgrave Macmillan
(see Macmillan Publishers)

Pan/Pan Macmillan
(see Macmillan Publishers)

Papermac
(see Macmillan Publishers)

Paper Tiger
(see Anova Books)

Pavilion
(see Anova Books)

Peachpit Press
(see Pearson Education)

Pearson Education
Edinburgh Gate, Harlow, Essex CM20 2JE
01279 623623
enquiries@pearson.com
www.pearsoned.co.uk
• Addison-Wesley - *Computer programming*
• Allyn & Bacon - *Education, humanities and social sciences*
• Benjamin Cummings - *Science*
• Cisco Press - *Cisco systems materials*
• FT Prentice Hall - *Global business*
• Longman - *Educational materials for schools, English language teaching (ELT) materials, higher education textbooks (law, humanities, social sciences)*
• New Riders - *Graphics and design*
• Peachpit Press - *Web development*
• Penguin Books - *(see separate entry under Penguin Books)*
• Penguin Longman - *ELT books*
• Penguin English (for teachers) - www.penguinenglish.com
• Penguin Readers (for students) - www.penguinreaders.com
• Prentice Hall - *Academic and reference textbooks: business, computer science, engineering and IT*
• Prentice Hall Business - *Practical and personal development*
• QUE Publishing - *Computing*
• SAMS Publishing - *Reference books for programmers and developers, web developers, designers, networking and system administrators*
• York Notes - *Literature guides for students*

Pegasus Elliot & Mackenzie Publishers
Sheraton House, Castle Park, Cambridge CB3 0AX
01223 370012
editors@pegasuspublishers.com
www.pegasuspublishers.com
Fiction and non-fiction, crime and erotica. Imprints: Vanguard Press, Nightingale Books, Chimera

Pen & Sword Books
47 Church Street, Barnsley, South Yorkshire S70 2AS
01226 734222
enquiries@pen-and-sword.co.uk
www.pen-and-sword.co.uk
Military, naval and aviation history. Imprints: Leo Cooper, Wharncliffe Publishing

Penguin Books
80 Strand, London WC2R 0RL
020 7010 3000
penguin@penguin.co.uk
www.penguin.co.uk
Owned by Pearson
• Dorling Kindersley - *Information books and resources for children and adults*
• ePenguin - *ebooks*
• Penguin Audiobooks
• Penguin General Books - *Imprints: Penguin Paperbacks; Hamish Hamilton; Michael Joseph; Viking*
• Penguin Press - *Imprints: Allen Lane (reference inc. Roget's Thesaurus and Pears Cyclopaedia); Penguin Classics; Penguin Modern Classics*
• Puffin - *Children's*
• Rough Guides - roughguide@penguin.co.uk *Travel guides, phrase books, music guides and reference*
• Warne - *Children's, inc. Beatrix Potter, Spot, Ladybird*

Penguin Ireland
25 St Stephen's Green, Dublin 2
00 353 1 661 7695
info@penguin.ie
www.penguin.ie

Persephone Books
59 Lamb's Conduit Street, London WC1N 3NB
020 7242 9292
info@persephonebooks.co.uk
www.persephonebooks.co.uk
Reprint fiction and non-fiction, focus on women

Perseus Books Group
69-70 Temple Chambers, 3-7 Temple Avenue, London EC4Y 0HP
020 7353 7771
enquiries@perseusbooks.co.uk
www.perseusbooksgroup.com
UK office of US Perseus Books Group. Non-fiction. Imprints: PublicAffairs (current affairs); Da Capo Press (music, history, film and biography); Basic Books (current affairs, history, popular science); Counterpoint (literature and fiction); Basic Civitas Books (African American studies); Westview Press (social sciences, humanities, science)

Peter Haddock Publishing
Pinfold Lane, Bridlington, East Yorkshire YO16 6BT
01262 678121
sales@phpublishing.co.uk
www.phpublishing.co.uk
Children's books

Peter Owen Publishers
73 Kenway Road, London SW5 0RE
020 7373 5628
admin@peterowen.com
www.peterowen.com
Biography, non-fiction, literary fiction, literary criticism, history and the arts

Phaidon Press
18 Regent's Wharf, All Saints Street,
London N1 9PA
020 7843 1000
enquiries@phaidon.com
www.phaidon.com
Arts

Pharmaceutical Press
1 Lambeth High Street,
London SE1 7JN
020 7735 9141
enquiries@rpsgb.org
www.rpsgb.org
The publications division of the Royal Pharmaceutical Society of Great Britain. Medicine

Philip Berrill International
60 Leyland Road, Southport,
Merseyside PR9 9JA
01704 534725
philipberrill@hotmail.com
Art and mind, body and spirit guides

Philip Wilson Publishers
109 Drysdale Street,
The Timber Yard, London N1 6ND
020 7033 9900
pwilson@philip-wilson.co.uk
www.philip-wilson.co.uk
Art, museums and exhibition catalogues

Phillimore & Co
Shopwyke Manor Barn, Chichester,
West Sussex PO20 2BG
01243 787636
bookshop@phillimore.co.uk
www.phillimore.co.uk
Local and family history

Phoenix
(see Orion Publishing Group)

Piatkus Books
5 Windmill Street, London W1T 2JA
020 7631 0710
info@piatkus.co.uk
www.piatkus.co.uk
Fiction, biography, history, health, business and personal development

Picador
(see Macmillan Publishers)

Piccadilly Press
5 Castle Road, London NW1 8PR
020 7267 4492
books@piccadillypress.co.uk
www.piccadillypress.co.uk
Children's, teenage and parental books

Pimlico
(see Random House Group)

Pinwheel
Winchester House,
259–269 Old Marylebone Road,
London NW1 5XJ
020 7616 7200
www.pinwheel.co.uk
Imprints: Gullane (children's picture); Pinwheel (novelty); Andromeda (education)

Pluto Press
(see Thomson Learning)

Pocket Books
(see Simon & Schuster UK)

The Policy Press
University of Bristol, Fourth Floor,
Beacon House, Queen's Road,
Bristol BS8 1QU
0117 331 4054
tpp-info@bristol.ac.uk
www.policypress.org.uk
Social sciences

Politico's Publishing
(see Methuen Publishing)

Polity Press
65 Bridge Street, Cambridge CB2 1UR
01223 324315
info@polity.co.uk
www.polity.co.uk
General academic

Portland Press
3rd Floor, Eagle House,
16 Proctor Street, London WC1V 6NX
020 7280 4100
editorial@portlandpress.com
www.portlandpress.com
Biochemistry and medicine

Prentice Hall/Prentice Hall Business
(see Pearson Education)

Prestel Publishing
4 Bloomsbury Place,
London WC1A 2QA
020 7323 5004
sales@prestel-uk.co.uk
www.prestel.com
Art, architecture, photography, design and fashion

Priddy Books
(see Macmillan Publishers)

Profile Books
3A Exmouth House, Pine Street,
Exmouth Market, London EC1R 0JH
020 7841 6300
info@profilebooks.com
www.profilebooks.com
Non-fiction. Imprint: Economist Books

Profile Sports Media
5th Floor, Mermaid House,
2 Puddledock, London EC4V 3DS
020 7332 2000
info@profilesportsmedia.com
www.profilesportsmedia.com
Sporting annuals and publications

Proquest Information and Learning
The Quorum, Barnwell Road,
Cambridge CB5 8SW
01223 215512
marketing@proquest.co.uk
www.proquest.co.uk
Educational

Psychology Press
(see T&F Informa)

Publishing House
Trinity Place, Barnstaple,
Devon EX32 9HG
01271 328892
publishinghouse@
 vernoncoleman.com
www.vernoncoleman.com
Fiction, health, humour, animals and politics

Puffin
(see Penguin Books)

Pushkin Press
12 Chester Terrace, London NW1 4ND
01362 861089
info@pushkinpress.com
www.pushkinpress.com
Translated classic and contemporary European literature

Quadrille Publishing
Alhambra House,
27–31 Charing Cross Road,
London WC2H 0LS
020 7839 7117
enquiries@quadrille.co.uk
www.quadrille.co.uk
Lifestyle

Quartet Books
27 Goodge Street, London W1T 2LD
020 7636 3992
quartetbooks@easynet.co.uk
Part of the Namara Group. Contemporary literary fiction

Quarto Publishing
6 Blundell Street, London N7 9BH
020 77006700
info@quarto.com
www.quarto.com
Highly illustrated non-fiction

QUE Publishing
(see Pearson Education)

Radcliffe Publishing
18 Marcham Road, Abingdon,
Oxfordshire OX14 1AA
01235 528820
contact.us@radcliffemed.com
www.radcliffe-oxford.com

Random House Group
Random House, 20 Vauxhall Bridge
Road, London SW1V 2SA
020 7840 8400
enquiries@randomhouse.co.uk
www.randomhouse.co.uk

Random House Division
• **Arrow** – *Mass-market paperback fiction and non-fiction*
• **Century** – *General fiction and non-fiction including commercial fiction, autobiography, biography, history and self-help*
• **Chatto & Windus** – *Memoirs, current affairs, essays, literary fiction, history, poetry, politics, philosophy and translations*
• **Harvill Secker** – *Literary fiction, literature in translation, English literature, quality thrillers, some non-fiction*
• **Hutchinson** – *General fiction and non-fiction including belles-lettres, current affairs, politics, travel and history*
• **Jonathan Cape** – *Biography and memoirs, current affairs, fiction, history, photography, poetry, politics and travel*
• **Pimlico** – *Quality non-fiction paperbacks specialising in history, biography, popular culture and the arts*
• **Random House Business Books**
• **Vintage** – *Quality paperback fiction and non-fiction*
• **William Heinemann** – *General fiction and non-fiction especially history,*

literary fiction, crime, science, thrillers and women's fiction
- **Yellow Jersey Press** - *Narrative sports books*

Ebury Press Division
- **Ebury Press** - *Autobiography, biography, popular history, cookery, popular science, humour, diet and health*
- **Fodor's** - *Travel guides*
- **Rider** - *Mind, body and spirit*
- **Vermilion** - *Popular reference, lifestyle, crafts, interior design*

Random House Children's Books
Transworld Publishers, 61-63
Uxbridge Road, London W5 5SA
020 8231 6800
Imprints: Hutchinson, Jonathan Cape, The Bodley Head, Doubleday Picture Books, David Fickling Books, Corgi, Red Fox

Transworld Publishers
61-63 Uxbridge Road,
London W5 5SA
020 8579 2652
info@transworld-publishers.co.uk
www.booksattransworld.co.uk
Imprints: Bantam, Bantam Press, Corgi & Black Swan, Doubleday, Eden, Expert Books, Channel 4 Books

Ransom Publishing
Rose Cottage, Howe Hill,
Watlington, Oxfordshire OX49 5HB
01491 613711
ransom@ransom.co.uk
www.ransom.co.uk
Education and children's fiction

Reader's Digest Association
11 Westferry Circus, Canary Wharf,
London E14 4HE
020 7715 8000
gbeditorial@readersdigest.co.uk
www.readersdigest.co.uk
Cookery, history, reference, gardening and DIY

Reaktion Books
33 Great Sutton Street,
London EC1V 0DX
020 7253 1071
info@reaktionbooks.co.uk
www.reaktionbooks.co.uk
Architecture, asian and cultural studies, film, art and photography, history and geography, biography

Reardon Publishing
PO Box 919, Cheltenham,
Gloucestershire GL50 9AN
01242 231800
reardon@bigfoot.com
www.reardon.co.uk
Member of the Outdoor Writers Guild. Cotswold area local interest

Red Bird Publishing
Kiln Farm, East End Green,
Brightlingsea, Colchester,
Essex CO7 0SX
01206 303525
info@red-bird.co.uk
www.red-bird.co.uk
Special-effects books for children

Red Fox
(see Random House Group)

Redhat Press
(see John Wiley & Sons)

Reed Elsevier
1-3 Strand, London WC2N 5JR
020 7930 7077
www.reedelsevier.com
Press: 020 7166 5657/5670

Business Division
Reed Business Information,
Quadrant House, The Quadrant,
Sutton, Surrey SM2 5AS
020 8652 3500
www.reedbusiness.co.uk
Business directories, magazines, e-newsletters, websites and cd-roms
Press: 020 8652 3296

Education Division
Harcourt Education, Halley Court,
Jordan Hill, Oxford OX2 8EJ
01865 311366
uk.schools@
   harcourteducation.co.uk
www.harcourteducation.co.uk
*Textbooks and educational resources.
Imprints: Ginn; Heinemann (Primary, Secondary, FE and Vocational); Rigby UK*

Legal Division
LexisNexis Butterworths Tolley,
Halsbury House, 35 Chancery Lane,
London WC2A 1EL
020 7400 2500
competitive.intelligence@
   lexis-nexis.com
www.lexisnexis.co.uk
Legal and business materials in print and online, including The Advertiser Red Books. Butterworths Services provide access to a library of UK law
Press: 020 7400 2753

Science and Medical Division
32 Jamestown Road, Camden Town,
London NW1 7BY
020 7424 4200
eurobkinfo@clsevier.com
www.elsevier-international.com
Press: pressoffice@elsevier.com
- **Elsevier Science and Technology** -
Imprints: Academic Press (physical, applied and life sciences); Morgan Kaufmann (databases, computer networking, human computer interaction, computer graphics, multimedia information and systems, artificial intelligence, and software engineering); Syngress Media (computing reference works for IT professionals)
- **Elsevier Health Sciences** - *Imprints: Saunders (medical); Mosby (medicine, nursing, allied health and veterinary medicine); Churchill Livingstone (medical); Butterworth-Heinemann (technology, medicine and management); Hanley & Belfus (medical); Bailliere Tindall (nursing and midwifery); BC Decker (medicine, health sciences, and dentistry); GW Medical Publishing (abuse, maltreatment, sexually transmitted diseases, and domestic violence)*

Regency House Publishing
Nial House, 24-26 Boulton Road,
Stevenage, Hertfordshire SG1 4QX
01438 314488
regency-house@btconnect.com
Art and transport

Richmond House Publishing Company
70-76 Bell Street, Marylebone,
London NW1 6SP
020 7224 9666
sales@rhpco.co.uk
www.rhpco.co.uk
Theatre and entertainment directories

Rider
(see Random House Group)

Robert Hale
Clerkenwell House,
45-47 Clerkenwell Green,
London EC1R 0HT
020 7251 2661
enquire@halebooks.com
www.halebooks.com

Robson Books
(see Anova Books)

Rodale Books
7-10 Chandos Street,
London W1G 9AD
020 7291 6000
www.rodale.co.uk
Lifestyle

Roget's Thesaurus
(see Penguin Books)

RotoVision
Sheridan House,
112/116A Western Road, Hove,
East Sussex BN3 1DD
01273 727268
sales@rotovision.com
www.rotovision.com
Graphic arts and design

Rough Guides
(see Penguin Books)

Roundhouse Publishing
Millstone, Limers Lane, Northam,
North Devon EX39 2RG
01237 474474
roundhouse.group@ukgateway.net
www.roundhouse.net
Cinema and media

Routledge
(see T&F Informa)

Ryland, Peters & Small
20-21 Jockey's Fields,
London WC1R 4BW
020 7025 2200
info@rps.co.uk
www.rylandpeters.com
Illustrated lifestyle

SAF Publishing
149 Wakeman Road,
London NW10 5BH
020 8969 6099
info@safpublishing.com
www.safpublishing.com
*Experimental rock and jazz music.
Co-imprint with Helter Skelter
Publishing: Firefly Publishing
(mainstream rock and pop)*

Sage Publications

1 Olivers Yard, 55 City Road,
London EC1Y 1SP
020 7324 8500
market@sagepub.co.uk
www.sagepub.co.uk
Social sciences and humanities. Imprint: Paul Chapman (education and training)

Saint Andrew Press

Church of Scotland,
121 George Street,
Edinburgh EH2 4YN
0131 225 5722
standrewpress@cofscotland.org.uk
www.churchofscotland.org.uk
/standrewpress
Owned by the Church of Scotland. Christian, moral and ethical

Samuel French

52 Fitzroy Street, London W1T 5JR
020 7387 9373
theatre@
samuelfrench-london.co.uk
www.samuelfrench-london.co.uk
Plays

SAMS Publishing

(see Pearson Education)

Sangam Books

57 London Fruit Exchange,
Brushfield Street, London E1 6EP
020 7377 6399
sangambks@aol.com
Educational textbooks

SB Publications

14 Bishopstone Road, Seaford,
East Sussex BN25 2UB
01323 893498
sbpublications@tiscali.co.uk
www.sbpublications.co.uk
Local history, travel, guides

Scholastic

Villiers House, Clarendon Avenue,
Leamington Spa,
Warwickshire CV32 5PR
01926 887799
enquiries@scholastic.co.uk
www.scholastic.co.uk
Education

Scholastic Children's Books

Euston House, 24 Eversholt Street,
London NW1 1DB
020 7756 7756
scbenquiries@scholastic.co.uk
www.scholastic.co.uk
Fiction. Imprints: Hippo, Point

SCM Canterbury Press

9–17 St Albans Place,
London N1 0NX
020 7359 8033
admin@scm-canterburypress.co.uk
www.scm-canterburypress.co.uk
Theology and hymn books

Scala Publishers

Northburgh House,
10 Northburgh Street,
London EC1V 0AT
020 7490 9900
info@scalapublishers.com
www.scalapublishers.com
Art

Scottish Cultural Press/ Scottish Children's Press

Unit 6, Newbattle Abbey Business
Park, Newbattle Road,
Dalkeith EH22 3LJ
Cultural: 0131 660 6366
Children's: 0131 660 4757
info@scottishbooks.com
www.scottishbooks.com
Scottish-interest books for adult, tourist and academic readers

Search Press

Wellwood, North Farm Road,
Tunbridge Wells, Kent TN2 3DR
01892 510850
searchpress@searchpress.com
www.searchpress.com
Art and crafts

SEMERC

(see Granada Learning Group)

Seren

57 Nolton Street, Bridgend CF31 3AE
01656 663018
general@seren-books.com
www.seren-books.com
Wales and Welsh authors

Serpent's Tail

4 Blackstock Mews, London N4 2BT
020 7354 1949
info@serpentstail.com
www.serpentstail.com
Contemporary and gay fiction and non-fiction

Severn House Publishers

9–15 High Street, Sutton,
Surrey SM1 1DF
020 8770 3930
info@severnhouse.com
www.severnhouse.com
Hardback fiction for the library market: romance, science fiction, horror, fantasy and crime

Shepheard-Walwyn (Publishers)

Suite 604, The Chandlery,
50 Westminster Bridge Road,
London SE1 7QY
020 7721 7666
books@shepheard-walwyn.co.uk
www.shepheard-walwyn.co.uk
Ethical economics, perennial philosophy, biography, gift books, books of Scottish interest

Shetland Times

Gremsta, Lerwick, Shetland ZE1 0PX
01595 693622
adverts@shetland-times.co.uk
www.shetlandtoday.co.uk
Shetland interest

Shire Publications

Cromwell House, Church Street,
Princes Risborough,
Buckinghamshire HP27 9AA
01844 344301
shire@shirebooks.co.uk
www.shirebooks.co.uk
Original non-fiction paperbacks

Short Books

3a Exmouth House, Pine Street,
Exmouth Market, London EC1R 0JH
020 7833 9429
emily@shortbooks.biz
www.shortbooks.co.uk
Non-fiction for adults and children

Sidgwick and Jackson

(see Macmillan Publishers)

Sigma Press

5 Alton Road, Wilmslow,
Cheshire SK9 5DY
01625 531035
info@sigmapress.co.uk
www.sigmapress.co.uk
Outdoor, heritage, myth, biography

Simon & Schuster UK

Africa House, 64–78 Kingsway,
London WC2B 6AH
020 7316 1900
enquiries@simonandschuster.co.uk
www.simonsays.co.uk
General fiction and non-fiction. Imprints: Simon & Schuster, Pocket, Simon & Schuster Childrens Books, Free Press, Scribner, Simon & Schuster Audio, A CBS Company

Soundings

(see Ulverscroft Group)

Souvenir Press

43 Great Russell Street,
London WC1B 3PD
020 7580 9307
souvenirpress@ukonline.co.uk
Academic. Imprints include: Condor, Human Horizons, Independent Voices, Pictorial Presentations, Pop Universal, The Story-Tellers

Spon Press

(see T&F Informa)

Springer Science & Business Media

100 Borough High Street,
London SE1 1LB
020 7863 3000
www.springer-sbm.com
Owned by Candover & Cinven. Scientific, technical and medical textbooks. Imprints: Consultants Bureau

Springer-Verlag London

Ashbourne House, The Guildway,
Old Portsmouth Road, Guildford,
Surrey GU3 1LP
01483 734433
jean.lovell-butt@springer.com
www.springer.com
Computer science, medical, engineering, astronomy, maths

Stainer & Bell

PO Box 110, 23 Gruneisen Road,
London N3 1DZ
020 8343 3303
post@stainer.co.uk
www.stainer.co.uk
Music and hymns

Stanley Gibbons Publications
7 Parkside, Christchurch Road,
Ringwood, Hampshire BH24 3SH
01425 472363
rpurkis@stanleygibbons.co.uk
www.stanleygibbons.co.uk
*Philatelic reference catalogues and
handbooks*

TSO (The Stationery Office)
St Crispins, Duke Street, Norwich,
Norfolk NR3 1PD
01603 622211
customer.services@tso.co.uk
www.thestationeryoffice.com

Summersdale Publishers
46 West Street, Chichester,
West Sussex PO19 1RP
01243 771110
enquiries@summersdale.com
www.summersdale.com
*Travel, martial arts, self-help, cookery,
humour and gift books*

Summertown Publishing
29 Grove Street, Summertown,
Oxford OX2 7JT
01865 454130
louis@summertown.co.uk
www.summertown.co.uk
English-language teaching

Sutton Publishing
Phoenix Mill, Thrupp, Stroud,
Gloucestershire GL5 2BU
01453 731114
sales@sutton-publishing.co.uk
www.suttonpublishing.co.uk
*Owned by Haynes Publishing. Biography,
countryside, history, transport, military
and aviation*

Sweet & Maxwell Group
100 Avenue Road, London NW3 3PF
020 7393 7000
marketinginformation@
    sweetandmaxwell.co.uk
www.sweetandmaxwell.co.uk
*Part of the Thomson Corporation.
Legal and professional. Imprints:
W Green (Scotland); Round Hall*

T&F Informa
Mortimer House, 37–41 Mortimer
Street, London W1T 3JH
020 7017 5000
professional.enquiries@informa.com
www.irtfinforma.com
• **BIOS Scientific Publishers** - *Biology and
medicine*
• **Brunner-Routledge** - *psychology and
counselling*
• **Carfax** - *Social science and humanities*
• **CRC** - *Science and medical*
• **Curzon Press** - *Asian and Middle
Eastern studies*
• **Europa Publications** - *International
affairs, politics and economics*
• **Frank Cass** - *Military and strategic
studies. Also Jewish interest imprints:
Vallentine Mitchell, Jewish Chronicle
Publications*
• **Garland Science** - *Biology*
• **Martin Dunitz** - *Medical*
• **Psychology Press** - *Psychology*

• **Routledge** - *Humanities & social
sciences textbooks/ general non-fiction*
• **Routledge Curzon** - *Politics and Middle
Eastern studies*
• **Routledge Falmer** - *Education*
• **Spon Press** - *Architecture and planning*
• **Taylor & Francis** - *Science and reference
esp. ergonomics, geographical
information systems, biotechnology and
engineering*

Taschen UK
1 Heathcock Court, 5th Floor,
415 Strand, London WC2R 0NS
020 7845 8585
contact@taschen.com
www.taschen.com
*Architecture, art, atlases, Collectors'
editions, film, lifestyle, photography and
pop culture*

Taylor & Francis
(see T&F Informa)

Telegram
26 Westbourne Grove,
London W2 5RH
020 7229 2911
editorial@telegrambooks.com
www.telegrambooks.com
*International literary fiction. Imprint:
Saqi fiction*

Templar Publishing
Pippbrook Mill, London Road,
Dorking, Surrey RH4 1JE
01306 876361
alex.fieldus@templarco.co.uk
www.templarco.co.uk
Illustrated and novelty books for children

Tempus Publishing
The Mill, Brimscombe Port, Stroud,
Gloucestershire GL5 2QG
01453 883300
info@tempus-publishing.com
www.spellmount.com
History and military history

Terence Dalton
Water Street, Lavenham, Sudbury,
Suffolk CO10 9RN
01787 249290
terence@lavenhamgroup.co.uk
www.terencedalton.com
*Part of the Lavenham Group. Non-fiction:
aeronautical, aviation, maritime and
local interest*

Thalamus Publishing
4 Attorney's Walk, Bull Ring,
Ludlow, Shropshire SY8 1AA
01584 874977
roger@thalamus-books.com
www.thalamus-books.com
Family reference

Thames & Hudson
181A High Holborn,
London WC1V 7QX
020 7845 5000
mail@thameshudson.co.uk
www.thamesandhudson.com
Cultural non-fiction

Third Millennium Publishing
2-5 Benjamin Street,
London EC1M 5QL
020 7336 0144
db@tmiltd.com
www.tmiltd.com

Thomas Cook Publishing
PO Box 227,
Unit 15/16 Coningsby Road,
Peterborough PE3 8SB
01733 416477
publishing-sales@thomascook.com
www.thomascookpublishing.com
Guide books and timetables

Thomson Learning
50-51 Bedford Row,
London WC1R 4LR
020 7067 2500
communications@
    thomsonlearning.com
www.thomsonlearning.co.uk
*Part of the Thomson Corporation.
Educational. Imprints: Scientific Press,
Cherry Tree Books (children's), Business
Press, Arden Shakespeare, Computer
Press, Course Technology, Premier Press,
Texere, Wadsworth*

*Continuum International Publishing
Group*
Tower Building, 11 York Road,
London SE1 7NX
020 7922 0880
info@continuumbooks.com
www.continuumbooks.com
*Academic and religious. Imprints:
Athlone, Pinter, Sheffield Academic Press,
Geoffrey Chapman, Mowbray, TandT
Clark, Burns and Oates, Morehouse,
Claridge Press*

Evans Publishing Group
2A Portman Mansions,
Chiltern Street, London W1U 6NR
020 7487 0920
sales@evansbrothers.co.uk
www.evansbooks.co.uk
*Children's and educational. Imprints:
Cherrytree Books, Evans Brothers,
Zero to Ten*

IB Tauris
6 Salem Road, London W2 4BU
020 7243 1225
enquiries@ibtauris.com
www.ibtauris.com
*Culture, history and politics. Imprint:
New Press*

Oneworld
185 Banbury Road, Oxford OX2 7AR
01865 310597
info@oneworld-publications.com
www.oneworld-publications.com
*Religion, history, philosophy, popular
science and psychology*

Pluto Press
345 Archway Road, Highgate,
London N6 5AA
020 8348 2724
pluto@plutobooks.com
www.plutobooks.com
Academic and political non-fiction

Thorsons
(see HarperCollins Publishers)

Time Out Group
Universal House,
251 Tottenham Court Road,
London W1T 7AB
020 7813 3000
www.timeout.com
Guide and travel books

Time Warner Books (UK)
Brettenham House, Lancaster Place,
London WC2E 7EN
020 7911 8000
email.uk@twbg.co.uk
www.timewarnerbooks.co.uk
Imprints: Little, Brown (non-fiction);
Abacus (fiction, travel); Time Warner
(paperback fiction); Virago Press (women
authors only: fiction, non-fiction and
poetry); Atom (teen sci-fi); Orbit Press
(sci-fi and fantasy)

Titan Publishing
144 Southwark Street,
London SE1 0UP
020 7620 0200
editorial@titanmail.com
www.forbiddenplanet.com
Comic books, graphic novels, spin-offs

Tolkien
(see HarperCollins Publishers)

Top That Publishing
Marine House, Tide Mill Way,
Woodbridge, Suffolk IP12 1AP
01394 386651
info@topthatpublishing.com
www.topthatpublishing.com
Children's imprints: Top that!, Kids and
Tide Mill Press: Adult imprint: Kudos

Transworld Publishers
(see Random House Group)

Travel Publishing
7A Apollo House, Calleva Park,
Aldermaston, Berkshire RG7 8TN
0118 981 7777
info@travelpublishing.co.uk
www.travelpublishing.co.uk
Imprints: Hidden Places, Hidden Inns,
Golfers Guides, Country Living Rural
Guides, Off the Motorway

Trentham Books
Westview House,
734 London Road, Stoke-on-Trent,
Staffordshire ST4 5NP
01782 745567
tb@trentham-books.co.uk
www.trentham-books.co.uk
Education, culture and law for
professional readers

Trident Press
Empire House, 175 Piccadilly,
London W1J 9TB
020 7491 8770
admin@tridentpress.com
www.tridentpress.com
TV tie-ins, history, travel, geography,
culture

Trotman & Co
2 The Green, Richmond,
Surrey TW9 1PL
020 8486 1200
mail@trotman.co.uk
www.trotman.co.uk
Careers and education

Tucann Books
19 High Street, Heighington,
Lincoln LN4 1RG
01522 790009
sales@tucann.co.uk
www.tucann.co.uk
Self-publishing

Ulverscroft Group
The Green, Bradgate Road,
Anstey, Leicester LE7 7FU
0116 236 4325
sales@ulverscroft.co.uk
www.ulverscroft.com

FA Thorpe Publishing
Fiction and non-fiction large print books.
Imprints and divisions include: Linford
Romance, Linford Mystery, Linford
Western, Charnwood and Ulverscroft

Isis Publishing
7 Centremead, Osney Mead,
Oxford OX2 0ES
01865 250333
sales@isis-publishing.co.uk
www.isis-publishing.co.uk
Large-print books and audio books

Magna Large Print Books
Magna House,
Long Preston, Nr. Skipton,
North Yorkshire BD23 4ND
01729 840225
Large-print books; audio fiction and
non-fiction

Soundings
Isis House, Kings Drive, Whitley Bay,
Tyne and Wear NE26 2JT
0191 253 4155
mail@gillian2004.plus.com
Audio books

Ulverscroft Large Print Books
The Green, Bradgate Road, Anstey,
Leics LE7 7SU
0116 236 4325
Large-print books and audio books

University of Hertfordshire Press
Hatfield Campus, Learning Resource
Centre, College Lane, Hatfield,
Hertfordshire AL10 9AB
01707 284681
uhpress@herts.ac.uk
www.herts.ac.uk/UHPress/
Literary criticism and theatre studies,
Romani studies, regional and local
history, parapsychology. Imprints:
Hertfordshire Publications

University of Wales Press
10 Columbus Walk, Brigantine Place,
Cardiff CF10 4UP
029 2049 6899
press@press.wales.ac.uk
www.uwp.co.uk
Imprints: GPC Books, Gwasg Prifysgol
Cymru

University Presses of California,
Columbia & Princeton
1 Oldlands Way, Bognor Regis,
West Sussex PO22 9SA
01243 843291
lois@upccp.demon.co.uk
www.ucpress.com
www.columbia.edu/cu/cup
www.pup.princeton.edu

Unofficial Guides
(see John Wiley & Sons)

Usborne Publishing
83–85 Saffron Hill,
London EC1N 8RT
020 7430 2800
mail@usborne.co.uk
www.usborne.com
Non-fiction books for children, including
computer guides, puzzlebooks, pre-school
and books on music

Vallentine Mitchell/
Jewish Chronicle Publications
(see Frank Cass, T&F Informa)

Vermilion
(see Random House Group)

Viking
(see Penguin Books)

Vintage
(see Random House Group)

Virago Press
(see Time Warner Books)

Virgin Books
Units 5 & 6, Thames Wharf Studios,
Rainville Road, London W6 9HA
020 7386 3300
info@virgin-books.co.uk
www.virginbooks.com
TV, film, music, sport and pop culture.
Imprints: Black Lace and Nexus (erotic
fiction)

Visual
(see John Wiley & Sons)

Voyager
(see HarperCollins Publishers)

W Foulsham & Co
The Publishing House,
Bennetts Close, Slough,
Berkshire SL1 5AP
01753 526769
info@foulsham.com
www.foulsham.com
Lifestyle

Walker Books
87 Vauxhall Walk, London SE11 5HJ
020 7793 0909
enquiry@walker.co.uk
www.walkerbooks.co.uk
Children's big books, book charts,
game books. Series: Giggle Club

Wallflower Press
6A Middleton Place,
Langham Street, London W1W 7TE
020 7436 9494
info@wallflowerpress.co.uk
www.wallflowerpress.co.uk
Film, media and cultural studies

Warne
(see Penguin Books)

Watts Publishing Group
338, Euston Road, London NW1 3BH
020 7873 6000
ad@hachettechildrens.co.uk
www.hachettechildrens.co.uk
*Part of Groupe Lagardere. Children's
non-fiction, reference, fiction, picture
and novelty. Imprints: Franklin Watts,
Orchard Books, Cats Whiskers,
Aladdin/Watts*

Weidenfeld & Nicolson
(see Orion Publishing Group)

Wharncliffe Publishing
(see Pen & Sword Books)

Which?
2 Marylebone Road, London NW1 4DF
020 7770 7000
which@which.co.uk
www.which.co.uk
*Publishing arm of the Consumers'
Association*

Whittet Books
Hill Farm, Stonham Road, Cotton,
Stowmarket, Suffolk IP14 4RQ
01449 781877
annabel@whittet.dircon.co.uk
www.whittetbooks.com
*Natural history, pets and rural interest,
livestock and horticulture*

Wild Goose Publications
Iona Community,
4th Floor, The Savoy House,
140 Sauchiehall Street,
Glasgow G2 3DH
0141 332 6292
admin@ionabooks.com
www.iona.books.com
*Publishing house of the Iona Community.
Religion, spiritualism and human rights*

Wiley
(see John Wiley & Sons)

William Heinemann
(see Random House Group)

Wimbledon Publishing Company
75–76 Blackfriars Road,
London SE1 8HA
020 7401 4200
info@wpcpress.com
www.anthempress.com
*Textbooks for languages, maths, biology
and accountancy. Imprint: Anthem Press*

Windhorse Publications
11 Park Road, Moseley,
Birmingham B13 8AB
0121 449 9191
info@windhorsepublications.com
www.windhorsepublications.com
Meditation and Buddhism

WIT Press
Ashurst Lodge, Ashurst,
Southampton, Hampshire SO40 7AA
023 8029 3223
marketing@witpress.com
www.witpress.com
Scientific and technical

Wolters Kluwer (UK)
145 London Road,
Kingston-on-Thames, Surrey KT2 6SR
020 8247 1694
sales@kluwerlaw.com
www.kluwerlaw.com
*Part of Aspen Publishers, a Wolters
Kluwer company*

Women's Press
27 Goodge Street, London W1T 2LD
020 7636 3992
sales@the-womens-press.com
www.the-womens-press.com
Part of the Namara Group

Woodhead Publishing
Abington Hall, Abington,
Cambridge CB1 6AH
01223 891358
wp@woodhead-publishing.com
www.woodheadpublishing.com
*Formerly Abington Publishing.
Engineering, textiles, finance and
investment, food technology and
environmental science*

Wordsworth Editions
8b East Street, Ware,
Hertfordshire SG12 9HJ
01920 465167
enquiries@
    wordsworth-editions.com
www.wordsworth-editions.com
*Literary classics, reference, poetry,
children's classics, mystery and the
supernatural*

Working White
Chancery Court,
Lincolns Inn, Lincoln Road,
High Wycombe HP12 3RE
01494 429318
info@workingwhite.co.uk
www.workingwhite.co.uk
*Children's big books, book charts,
game books. Series: Giggle Club*

Wrox
(see John Wiley & Sons)

WW Norton & Company
Castle House, 75–76 Wells Street,
London W1T 3QT
020 7323 1579
office@wwnorton.co.uk
Academic and professional non-fiction

X Press
PO Box 25694, London N17 6FP
020 8801 2100
vibes@xpress.co.uk
www.xpress.co.uk
Black interest. Imprints: Nia, 20/20

Y Lolfa Cyf
Talybont, Ceredigion SY24 5AP
01970 832304
ylolfa@ylolfa.com
www.ylolfa.com
*Welsh and Celtic interest. Imprints and
divisions include: Dinas*

Yale University Press (London)
47 Bedford Square,
London WC1B 3DP
020 7079 4900
sales@yaleup.co.uk
www.yalebooks.co.uk

Yellow Jersey Press
(see Random House Group)

York Notes
(see Pearson Education)

Young Picador
(see Macmillan Publishers)

Zambezi Publishing
PO Box 221, Plymouth,
Devon PL2 2YJ
01752 350453
info@zampub.com
www.zampub.com
New-age and self-help

Zed Books
7 Cynthia Street, London N1 9JF
020 7837 4014
www.zedbooks.co.uk
*International and third-world affairs and
development studies*

Literary agents

Abner Stein*
10 Roland Gardens, London SW7 3PH
020 7373 0456
abner@abnerstein.co.uk
US agents and authors, some full-length fiction and general non-fiction

The Agency (London)*
24 Pottery Lane, Holland Park,
London W11 4LZ
020 7727 1346
info@theagency.co.uk
www.theagency.co.uk
Theatre, film, TV, radio and children's writers and illustrators; also film and TV rights in novels and non-fiction

Alan Brodie Representation
6th Floor, Fairgate House,
78 New Oxford Street,
London WC1A 1HB
020 7079 7990
info@alanbrodie.com
www.alanbrodie.com
Theatre, film, TV and radio scripts

Alexandra Nye
Craigower, 6 Kinnoull Avenue,
Dunblane, Perthshire FK15 9JG
01786 825114
Fiction and topical non-fiction, esp literary fiction and history

AM Heath & Co*
6 Warwick Court, London WC1R 5DJ
020 7242 2811
www.amheath.com
Fiction, general non-fiction and children's

Andrew Mann*
1 Old Compton Street,
London W1D 5JA
020 7734 4751
manscript@onetel.com
Fiction; general non-fiction; film, TV, theatre and radio scripts

Andrew Nurnberg Associates*
Clerkenwell House,
45-47 Clerkenwell Green,
London EC1R 0QX
020 7417 8800
all@nurnberg.co.uk
Foreign rights

Annette Green Authors' Agency*
1 East Cliff Road, Tunbridge Wells,
Kent TN4 9AD
01892 514275
annettekgreen@aol.com
www.annettegreenagency.co.uk
Literary and general fiction, non-fiction, fiction for teenagers, upmarket popular culture

Artellus
30 Dorset House, Gloucester Place,
London NW1 5AD
020 7935 6972
artellus@artellusltd.co.uk
General fiction and non-fiction

Andrew Lownie Literary Agency*
17 Sutherland Street,
London SW1V 4JU
020 7828 1274
lownie@globalnet.co.uk
www.andrewlownie.co.uk
Non-fiction

AP Watt*
20 John Street, London WC1N 2DR
020 7405 6774
apw@apwatt.co.uk
www.apwatt.co.uk
Full-length typescripts, including children's books, screenplays for film and TV

Barbara Levy Literary Agency*
64 Greenhill,
Hampstead High Street,
London NW3 5TZ
020 7435 9046
General fiction, non-fiction, TV presenters, film and TV rights

Bill McLean Personal Management
23B Deodar Road, London SW15 2NP
020 8789 8191
Scripts for all media

Blake Friedmann*
122 Arlington Road,
London NW1 7HP
020 7284 0408
carole@blakefriedmann.co.uk
isobel@blakefriedmann.co.uk

BookBlast
PO Box 20184, London W10 5AU
020 8968 3089
gen@bookblast.com
www.bookblast.com
Selective fiction and non-fiction

Brie Burkeman*
14 Neville Court, Abbey Road,
London NW8 9DD
0709 223 9113
brie.burkeman@mail.com
Commercial and literary fiction and non-fiction, scripts. Independent film and television consultant to literary agents

Bell Lomax Agency
James House, 1 Babmaes Street,
London SW1Y 6HF
020 7930 4447
agency@bell-lomax.co.uk
Fiction and non-fiction, biography, children's, business and sport

Campbell Thomson & McLaughlin*
1 King's Mews, London WC1N 2JA
020 7242 0958
Fiction and general non-fiction

Capel & Land*
29 Wardour Street, London W1D 6PS
020 7734 2414
yvonne@capelland.co.uk
www.capelland.com
Fiction and non-fiction; film, TV, radio presenters

Caroline Davidson Literary Agency
5 Queen Anne's Gardens,
London W4 1TU
020 8995 5768
High quality fiction of originality and non-fiction

Caroline Sheldon Literary Agency*
Thorley Manor Farm, Thorley,
Yarmouth PO41 0SJ
01983 760205
Fiction, commercial and literary novels, especially women's and children's fiction

Casarotto Ramsay and Associates
National House, 60-66 Wardour
Street, London W1V 4ND
020 7287 4450
agents@casarotto.uk.com
www.casarotto.uk.com
Scripts for TV, theatre, film and radio

Cecily Ware Literary Agents
19C John Spencer Square,
London N1 2LZ
020 7359 3787
info@cecilyware.com
Scripts for TV and film in all areas

Chapman & Vincent*
The Mount, Sun Hill, Royston,
Herts SG8 9AT
01763 245005
info@chapmanvincent.co.uk
Non-fiction

Christine Green Authors' Agent*
6 Whitehorse Mews,
Westminster Bridge Road,
London SE1 7QD
020 7401 8844
info@christinegreen.co.uk
www.christinegreen.co.uk
Literary and general fiction and non-fiction

Conville & Walsh*
2 Ganton Street, Soho,
London W1F 7QL
020 7287 3030
sue@convilleandwalsh.com
Literary and commercial fiction; serious and narrative non-fiction; childrens books

Crawford and Pearlstine Associates
31 Ashley Gardens,
Ambrosden Avenue,
London SW1P 1QE
020 7828 4212
agents@capaltd.co.uk
General non-fiction and fiction, history, current affairs, biography, health and politics

Curtis Brown Group*
5th Floor, Haymarket House,
28/29 Haymarket, London SW1Y 4SP
020 7393 4400
cb@curtisbrown.co.uk
www.curtisbrown.co.uk
Writers, directors, designers, presenters and actors

The Christopher Little Literary Agency*
10 Eel Brook Studios,
125 Moore Park Road,
London SW6 4PS
020 7736 4455
info@christopherlittle.net
www.christopherlittle.net
Commercial and literary full-length fiction and non-fiction; film scripts for established clients

Darley Anderson Literary, TV & Film Agency*
Estelle House, 11 Eustace Road,
London SW6 1JB
020 7385 6652
enquiries@darleyanderson.com
www.darleyanderson.com
Fiction: young male, American, Irish, women's, crime/mystery and humour; non-fiction; children's fiction; selected scripts for film and TV

David Godwin Associates
55 Monmouth Street,
London WC2H 9DG
020 7240 9992
assistant@
   davidgodwinassociates.co.uk
Literary and general fiction, non-fiction, biography

David Grossman Literary Agency
118b Holland Park Avenue,
London W11 4UA
020 7221 2770
Full-length fiction and general non-fiction, esp controversial

David Higham Associates*
5-8 Lower John Street,
Golden Square, London W1F 9HA
020 7434 5900
dha@davidhigham.co.uk
www.davidhigham.co.uk
Fiction; general non-fiction: biography, history, current affairs; children's; scripts

David O'Leary Literary Agents
10 Lansdowne Court,
Lansdowne Rise, London W11 2NR
020 7229 1623
d.oleary@virgin.net
Fiction (popular and literary) and non-fiction, esp thrillers, history, popular science, Russia and Ireland (history and fiction)

Deborah Owen*
78 Narrow Street, Limehouse,
London E14 8BP
020 7987 51191
do@deborahowen.co.uk

Dench Arnold Agency
10 Newburgh Street,
London W1F 7RN
020 7437 4551
www.dencharnold.com
Scripts for TV and film

Dorian Literary Agency*
Upper Thornehill, 27 Church Road,
St Marychurch, Torquay,
Devon TQ1 4QY
01803 312095
General fiction especially popular; children's (over 10 years)

Dorie Simmonds Agency*
67 Upper Berkeley Street,
London W1H 7QX
020 7569 8686
dhsimmonds@aol.com
General fiction, including commercial women's fiction, historical fiction, thrillers; commercial non-fiction, including historical and contemporary biographies, self-help, cookery; children's books and associated rights throughout the world

Duncan McAra
28 Beresford Gardens,
Edinburgh EH5 3ES
0131 552 1558
duncanmcara@hotmail.com
Literary fiction and non-fiction

Ed Victor*
6 Bayley Street, Bedford Square,
London WC1B 3HE
020 7304 4100
Mostly commercial fiction and non-fiction; children's

Edwards Fuglewicz*
49 Great Ormond Street,
London WC1N 3HZ
020 7405 6725
julia@efla.co.uk
Fiction: literary, some commercial; non-fiction: biography, history, popular culture

Elaine Steel
110 Gloucester Avenue,
London NW1 8HX
020 8348 0918
ecmsteel@aol.com
Writers and directors in film, television and publishing

Elizabeth Puttick Literary Agency*
46 Brookfield Mansions,
Highgate West Hill, London N6 6AT
020 8340 6383
agency@puttick.com
www.puttick.com
General non-fiction, esp self-help, mind, body and spirit, health and fitness, lifestyle and business

Elspeth Cochrane Personal Management
16 Old Town, London SW4 0JY
020 7819 6256
elspeth@elspethcochrane.co.uk
Fiction, non-fiction, biographies, screenplays, scripts for all media

Eric Glass
25 Ladbroke Crescent,
London W11 1PS
020 7229 9500
eglassltd@aol.com
Fiction, non-fiction and scripts

Eunice McMullen Children's Literary Agent
Low Ibbotsholme Cottage,
Off Bridge Lane, Troutbeck Bridge,
Windermere, Cumbria LA23 1HU
01539 448551
eunicemcmullen@totalise.co.uk
Children's material

Faith Evans Associates*
27 Park Avenue North,
London N8 7RU
020 8340 9920
Fiction and non-fiction

Felicity Bryan*
2A North Parade, Banbury Road,
Oxford OX2 6LX
01865 513816
agency@felicitybryan.com
Fiction and non-fiction

Felix de Wolfe
Kingsway House, 103 Kingsway,
London WC2B 6QX
020 7242 5066
info@felixdewolfe.com
Theatrical agency

Fox & Howard Literary Agency
4 Bramerton Street,
London SW3 5JX
020 7352 8691
Non-fiction: biography, history and popular culture, reference, business and lifestyle

Frances Kelly Agency*
111 Clifton Road, Kingston Upon Thames, Surrey KT2 6PL
020 8549 7830
Illustrated and academic non-fiction

Futerman, Rose & Associates*
17 Dean Hill Road, London SW14 7DQ
020 8255 7755
guy@futermanrose.co.uk
www.futermanrose.co.uk
Commercial fiction, non-fiction, biography, film and television scripts specialising in book-to-film projects

Gillon Aitken Associates*
18-21 Cavaye Place,
London SW10 9PT
020 7373 8672
reception@Gillonaitken.co.uk
Fiction and non-fiction

Greene & Heaton*
37 Goldhawk Road, London W12 8QQ
020 8749 0315
info@greeneheaton.co.uk
www.greeneheaton.co.uk
Wide range of fiction and general non-fiction (clients include Bill Bryson, Hugh Fearnley-Whittingstall, Michael Frayn, PD James and Sarah Waters)

Gregory & Co*
3 Barb Mews, London W6 7PA
020 7610 4676
info@gregoryandcompany.co.uk
www.gregoryandcompany.co.uk
Fiction: literary, commercial, crime, suspense and thrillers; general non-fiction

ICM
Oxford House, 76 Oxford Street,
London W1D 1BS
020 7636 6565
caronhurley@icmlondon.co.uk
Film, TV and theatre scripts

IMG Literary UK
McCormick House,
3 Burlington Lane, Chiswick,
London W4 2TH
020 8233 5000
www.imgworld.com
*Celebrity books, commercial fiction,
non-fiction, sports-related and how-to
business books*

Intercontinental Literary Agency*
Centric House, 390–391 Strand,
London WCTR OLT
020 7379 6611
ila@ila-agency.co.uk
Translation rights only

Jane Conway-Gordon*
1 Old Compton Street,
London W1D 5JA
020 7494 0148
Fiction and general non-fiction

Jane Judd Literary Agency*
18 Belitha Villas, London N1 1PD
020 7607 0273
*General fiction and non-fiction:
biography, investigative journalism,
health, women's interests and travel*

Janklow & Nesbit (UK)
33 Drayson Mews, London W8 4LY
020 7376 2733
queries@janklow.co.uk
*Fiction and non-fiction, commercial and
literary; US and translation rights
handled by Janklow and Nesbit
Associates in New York*

Jeffrey Simmons
15 Penn House, Mallory Street,
London NW8 8SX
020 7224 8917
jasimmons@btconnect.com
www.jeffreysimmons.com
*Biography, cinema and theatre, quality
and commercial fiction, history, law and
crime, politics and world affairs,
parapsychology and sport*

Jill Foster
9 Barb Mews, Brook Green,
London W6 7PA
020 7602 1263
Scripts for TV, film and radio

JM Thurley Management
Archery House, 33 Archery Square,
Walmer, Deal CT14 7JA
01304 371721
jmthurley@aol.com
*Full-length fiction, non-fiction, TV and
films*

Johnson & Alcock*
Clerkenwell House,
45/47 Clerkenwell Green,
London EC1R OHT
020 7251 0125
info@johnsonandalcock.co.uk
General fiction and non-fiction

**John Welch, Literary Consultant
& Agent**
Mill Cottage, Calf Lane, Chipping
Camden, Gloucestershire GL55 6JQ
01386 840237
johnwelch@cyphus.co.uk
*Military, naval and aviation history,
general history, and a little biography*

Jonathan Clowes*
10 Iron Bridge House,
Bridge Approach, London NW1 8BD
020 7722 7674
jonathanclowes@aol.com
*Fiction and non-fiction; scripts, especially
situation comedy, film and television
rights (clients include Doris Lessing,
David Nobbs, Len Deighton)*

Josef Weinberger Plays
12–14 Mortimer Street,
London W1T 3JJ
020 7580 2827
general.info@jwmail.co.uk
www.josef-weinberger.com
*Scripts for the theatre; play publisher and
licensor of stage rights; publishes plays
and acts as UK agent for US agents
including the Dramatists Play Service*

Judith Chilcote Agency*
8 Wentworth Mansions,
Keats Grove, London NW3 2RL
020 7794 3717
judybks@aol.com
*Commercial fiction, TV tie-ins, biography
and lifestyle*

Judith Murdoch Literary Agency*
19 Chalcot Square, London NW1 8YA
020 7722 4197
Full-length fiction only

Judy Daish Associates
2 St Charles Place, London W10 6EG
020 8964 8811
judy@judydaish.com
Scripts for TV, theatre, film and radio

Juri Gabriel
35 Camberwell Grove,
London SE5 8JA
020 7703 6186
Quality fiction and non-fiction

Juvenilia
Avington, near Winchester,
Hampshire SO21 1DB
01962 779656
juvenilia@clara.co.uk
*Baby to teen fiction and picture books;
non-fiction and scripts for TV and radio*

Knight Features
20 Crescent Grove,
London SW4 7AH
020 7622 1467
peter@knightfeatures.co.uk
*Motorsports, cartoon books, puzzles,
business, history, factual and
biographical material*

Laurence Fitch
Mezzanine, Quadrant House,
80–82 Regent Street,
London W1B 5AU
020 7734 9911
information@laurencefitch.com
www.laurencefitch.com
*Children's and horror books, scripts for
theatre, film, TV and radio*

Lavinia Trevor Agency*
The Glasshouse,
49A Goldhawk Road,
London W12 8QP
020 8749 8481
*General literary and commercial fiction;
non-fiction including popular science*

LAW (Lucas Alexander Whitley)*
14 Vernon Street, London W14 ORJ
020 7471 7900
*Commercial and literary fiction, non-
fiction and children's books; film and TV
scripts for established clients*

Limelight Management*
33 Newman Street, London W1T 1PY
020 7637 2529
limelight.management@virgin.net
www.limelightmanagement.com
General non-fiction

Lisa Eveleigh Literary Agency*
c/o Pollinger Limited, 9 Staple Inn,
Holborn, London WC1V 7QH
020 7399 2803
lisaeveleigh@dial.pipex.com
*Literary and commercial fiction,
non-fiction and children's fiction*

Louise Greenberg Books*
The End House, Church Crescent,
London N3 1BG
020 8349 1179
louisegreenberg@msn.com
Literary fiction and non-fiction

Lutyens and Rubinstein*
231 Westbourne Park Road,
London W11 1EB
020 7792 4855
susannah@lutyensrubinstein.co.uk
Adult fiction and non-fiction

Manuscript ReSearch
PO Box 33, Bicester,
Oxfordshire OX26 4ZZ
01869 323447
www.manuscriptresearch.co.uk
Scripts for film and TV

**Margaret Hanbury Literary
Agency***
27 Walcot Square, London SE11 4UB
020 7735 7680
maggie@mhanbury.demon.co.uk
*Quality fiction and non-fiction (clients
include JG Ballard, Simon Callow, George
Alagiah, Judith Lennox); children's
books, plays/scripts and poetry*

Marjacq Scripts
34 Devonshire Place,
London W1G 6JW
020 7935 9499
philip@marjacq.com
luke@marjacq.com
www.marjacq.com
*Fiction and non-fiction, screenplays,
radio plays and film and TV rights*

Mary Clemmey Literary Agency*
6 Dunollie Road, London NW5 2XP
020 7267 1290
*Fiction and non-fiction, high quality for
an international market*

MBA Literary Agents*
62 Grafton Way, London W1T 5DW
020 7387 2076
agent@mbalit.co.uk
*Fiction and non-fiction books, TV, film,
theatre and radio scripts*

Mic Cheetham Literary Agency
11-12 Dover Street, London W1S 4LJ
020 7495 2002
www.miccheetham.com
*General and literary fiction, fantasy and
science fiction, crime and some specific
non-fiction*

Micheline Steinberg Associates
Fourth Floor,
104 Great Portland Street,
London W1W 6PE
020 7631 1310
micheline@steinplays.com
Drama for stage, TV, radio and film

Michelle Kass Associates*
85 Charing Cross Road,
London WC2H 0AA
020 7439 1624
Literary fiction and film

Maggie Noach Literary Agency*
22 Dorville Crescent,
London W6 0HJ
020 8748 2926
m-noach@dircon.co.uk
Fiction and general non fiction

Marsh Agency
11/12 Dover Street, London W1S 4LJ
020 7399 2800
enquiries@marsh-agency.co.uk
www.marsh-agency.co.uk
*International rights specialists selling
English and foreign-language writing*

Narrow Road Company
182 Brighton Road, Coulsdon,
Surrey CR5 2NF
020 8763 9895
richardireson@narrowroad.co.uk
Scripts for TV, theatre, film and radio

Paterson Marsh*
11/12 Dover Street, London W1S 4LJ
020 7399 2800
steph@patersonmarsh.co.uk
www.patersonmarsh.co.uk
*World rights, especially psychoanalysis
and psychotherapy*

Peake Associates*
14 Grafton Crescent,
London NW1 8SL
020 7267 8033
tony@tonypeake.com
www.tonypeake.com
Fiction and non-fiction

**Peters Fraser & Dunlop Group
(PFD)***
Drury House, 34–43 Russell Street,
London WC2B 5HA
020 7344 1000
postmaster@pfd.co.uk
www.pfd.co.uk
*Fiction and children's, plus scripts for
film, theatre, radio and TV*

Pollinger*
9 Staple Inn, Holborn,
London WC1V 7QH
020 7404 0342
info@pollingerltd.com
www.pollingerltd.com
*Formerly Laurence Pollinger and Pearn,
Pollinger & Higham. General trade, non-
fiction, children's fiction and non-fiction*

PVA Management
Hallow Park, Worcester WR2 6PG
01905 640663
books@pva.co.uk
Non-fiction only

Real Creatives Worldwide
14 Dean Street, London W1D 3RS
020 7437 4188
business@realcreatives.com
www.realcreatives.com
*Represents writers and creative media
professionals*

Robert Smith Literary Agency*
12 Bridge Wharf,
156 Caledonian Road,
London N1 9UU
020 7278 2444
robertsmith.literaryagency@
   virgin.net
*Non-fiction; biography, health and
nutrition, lifestyle, showbusiness and
true crime*

Roger Hancock
4 Water Lane, London NW1 8NZ
020 7267 4418
info@rogerhancock.com
*Scripts for comedy, drama and light
entertainment*

Rogers, Coleridge & White*
20 Powis Mews, London W11 1JN
020 7221 3717
Fiction, non-fiction and children's books

Rosemary Sandberg
6 Bayley Street, London WC1B 3HE
020 7304 4110
rosemary@sandberg.demon.co.uk
Children's picture books and novels

Rosica Colin
1 Clareville Grove Mews,
London SW7 5AH
020 7370 1080
*Full-length manuscripts plus theatre,
film, television and sound broadcasting*

Rupert Crew*
1A King's Mews, London WC1N 2JA
020 7242 8586
info@rupertcrew.co.uk
*Volume and subsidiary rights in fiction
and non-fiction properties*

Rupert Heath Literary Agency
177a Old Winton Road, Andover,
Hampshire SP10 2DR
020 7788 7807
rupert.heath@rupertheath.com
www.rupertheath.com
*Fiction, history, biography, science, arts
and popular culture*

Rod Hall Agency
6th Floor, Fairgate House,
78 New Oxford Street,
London WC1A 1HB
020 7079 7987
office@rodhallagency.com
www.rodhallagency.com
Drama for film, TV and theatre

Sayle Literary Agency*
8B Kings Parade, Cambridge CB2 1SJ
01223 303035
*Fiction, crime and general; general
non-fiction*

Sayle Screen
11 Jubilee Place, London SW3 3TD
020 7823 3883
info@saylescreen.com
www.saylescreen.com
*Writers and directors for film, TV, theatre
and radio*

Sharland Organisation
The Manor House,
Manor Street, Raunds,
Northamptonshire NN9 6JW
01933 626600
tsoshar@aol.com
*Scripts for film, TV, theatre and radio;
non-fiction; specialises in national and
international film, television and theatre
negotiations*

Sheil Land Associates*
52 Doughty Street, London WC1N 2LS
020 7405 9351
info@sheilland.co.uk
*Full-length general, commercial and
literary fiction and non-fiction, including
theatre, film, radio and TV scripts*

Sheila Ableman Literary Agency
3rd Floor, Lyme House Studios,
38 Georgiana Street,
London NW1 0EB
020 7485 3409
sheila@sheilaableman.co.uk
*Non-fiction including history, science and
biography*

Shelley Power Literary Agency*
13 rue du Pre Saint Gervais,
75019 Paris, France
00 33 1 42 383649
shelley.power@wanadoo.fr
*Fiction, business, true crime, film and
entertainment, architecture, self-help
and popular psychology*

Sinclair-Stevenson
3 South Terrace, London SW7 2TB
020 7581 2550
Biography, current affairs, travel, history, fiction, the arts

Susijn Agency
3rd Floor, 64 Great Titchfield Street, London W1W 7QH
020 7580 6341
info@thesusijnagency.com
www.thesusijnagency.com
Sells rights worldwide in English and non-English language literature: literary fiction and non-fiction

Tamar Karet Literary Agency
56 Priory Road, Crouch End, London N8 7EX
020 8340 6460
tamar@btinternet.com
Fiction, leisure, biography, history, social affairs and politics

Tanja Howarth Literary Agency*
19 New Row, London WC2N 4LA
020 7240 5553
tanja.howarth@btinternet.com
Fiction and non-fiction from British writers; represents German authors in Britain on behalf of German publishers

The Tennyson Agency
10 Cleveland Avenue, Wimbledon Chase, London SW20 9EW
020 8543 5939
agency@tenagy.co.uk
www.tenagy.co.uk
Theatre, film, radio and TV scripts

Teresa Chris Literary Agency
43 Musard Road, London W6 8NR
020 7386 0633
TeresaChris@
   litagency.freeserve.co.uk
Fiction: crime, general, women's, commercial and literary and non-fiction

Toby Eady Associates
3rd Floor, 9 Orme Court, London W2 4RL
020 7792 0092
toby@tobyeady.demon.co.uk
www.tobyeadyassociates.co.uk
Fiction, non-fiction, especially China, Middle East, Africa and India

Valerie Hoskins Associates
20 Charlotte Street, London W1T 2NA
020 7637 4490
vha@vhassociates.co.uk
Scripts for film, TV and radio, especially feature films, animation and TV

Vanessa Holt*
59 Crescent Road, Leigh-on-Sea, Essex SS9 2PF
01702 473787
General fiction especially crime, commercial and literary; non-fiction; non-illustrated children's

Wade & Doherty Literary Agency
33 Cormorant Lodge, Thomas More Street, London E1W 1AU
020 7488 4171
rw@rwla.com
www.rwla.com
General fiction and non-fiction including children's books

Watson, Little*
Lymehouse Studios, 38 Georgiana Street, London NW1 0EB
020 7485 5935
office@watsonlittle.com
www.watsonlittle.co.uk
Commercial and literary fiction and non-fiction for adults and children

The Wylie Agency (UK)
17 Bedford Square, London WC1B 3JA
020 7908 5900
mail@wylieagency.co.uk
Fiction and non-fiction

William Morris Agency (UK)*
52/53 Poland Street, London W1F 7LX
020 7534 6800
ldnmailroom@wma.com
www.wma.com
Fiction; general non-fiction; TV and film scripts

William Neill-Hall
Old Oak Cottage, Ropewalk, Mount Hawke, Truro, Cornwall TR4 8DW
01209 891427
wneill-hall@msn.com
General non-fiction (clients include George Carey, Philip Yancey and Eugene Peterson)

Zebra Agency
Broadland House, 1 Broadland, Shevington, Lancashire WN6 8DH
077193 75575
admin@zebraagency.co.uk
www.zebraagency.co.uk
Non-fiction and general fiction; scripts for TV, radio, film and theatre

Trade press

Annual Bibliography of English Language and Literature
Modern Humanities Research Association, Cambridge University
01223 333058
abell@bibl.org
www.mhra.org.uk/Publication
   /Journals/abell.html
Annual. Editor: Gerard Lowe; academic editor: Jennifer Fellows

Books
Publishing News
0870 870 2345
info@publishingnews.co.uk
www.publishingnews.co.uk
Weekly. Editor: Liz Thomson

Books in the Media
VNU Entertainment Media
020 7420 6006
www.thebookseller.com
Weekly. Editor: Neil Denny; news: Joel Rickett

The Bookseller
VNU Entertainment Media
020 7420 6006
joel.rickett@bookseller.co.uk
www.thebookseller.com
Weekly. Editor: Neil Denny; news: Joel Rickett

Booksellers Association Directory of Members
The Booksellers Association of the UK and Ireland
020 7802 0802
mail@booksellers.org.uk
www.booksellers.org.uk
Annual. Editor: Meryl Halls

BookWorld Magazine
Christchurch Publishers
020 7351 4995
leonard.holdsworth@
   btopenworld.com
Monthly. Editor: Leonard Holdsworth; features: James Hughes

Digital Demand – The Journal of Printing and Publishing Technology
PIRA International
01372 802080
publications@pira.co.uk
www.piranet.com
6pa. Editor: Gareth Blatchford

London Review of Books
Nicholas Spice
020 7209 1141
edit@lrb.co.uk
www.lrb.co.uk
Fortnightly. Editor: Mary-Kay Wilmers

Publishing News
Publishing News
0870 870 2345
mailbox@publishingnews.co.uk
www.publishingnews.co.uk
Weekly. Editor: Liz Thomson

Writers Forum
Writers International
01202 589828
editorial@writers-forum.com
www.writers-forum.com
*Monthly. Editor: John Jenkins; assistant
editor: Laura Fennimore*

Writers News/Writing Magazine
Warner Group Publications
0113 200 2929
derek.hudson@writersnews.co.uk
www.writersnews.co.uk
Monthly. Editor: Derek Hudson

Associations

Academi (Yr Academi Gymreig)
Mount Stuart House, Mount Stuart
Square, Cardiff CF10 5FQ
029 2047 2266
post@academi.org
www.academi.org
*Welsh national literature promotion
agency*

Alliance of Literary Societies
22 Belmont Grove, Havant,
Hampshire PO9 3PU
023 9247 5855
rosemary.culley@ntlworld.com
www.alllitsoc.org.uk

Association for Scottish Literary Studies
c/o Department of Scottish History,
9 University Gardens,
University of Glasgow,
Glasgow G12 8QH
0141 330 5309
office@asls.org.uk
www.asls.org.uk
*Charity promoting language and
literature of Scotland*

Association of Christian Writers
All Saints Vicarage,
43 All Saints Close, Edmonton,
London N9 9AT
020 8884 4348
admin@christianwriters.org.uk
www.christianwriters.org.uk
Support, training and encouragement

Association of Freelance Writers
The Writers Bureau,
Sevendale House, 7 Dale Street,
Manchester M1 1JB
0161 228 2362
studentservices@writersbureau.com
www.writersbureau.com
Correspondence college

Association of Illustrators
150 Curtain Road, London EC2A 3AR
020 7613 4328
info@theaoi.com
www.theaoi.com
Trade association

Association of Learned and Professional Society Publishers
South House, The Street, Clapham,
Worthing, West Sussex BN13 3UU
01903 871686
sally.morris@alpsp.org
www.alpsp.org
*For not-for-profit academic and
professional publishers*

Audiobook Publishers' Association
c/o 18 Green Lanes, Hatfield,
Hertfordshire AL10 9JT
07971 280788
charlotte.mccandlish@ntlworld.com
www.theapa.net
*The UK trade association of the
audiobook industry*

AuthorsOnline
19 The Cinques, Gamlingay, Sandy,
Bedfordshire SG19 3NU
0870 7500544
theeditor@authorsonline.co.uk
www.authorsonline.co.uk
*Self-publishing and authors' services
worldwide*

Authors' Club
40 Dover Street, London W1S 4NP
020 7499 8581
mem@authorsclub.co.uk
www.authorsclub.co.uk
*Anyone involved with written words;
administers Best First Novel award
and Sir Banister Fletcher award*

Authors' Licensing & Collecting Society (ALCS)
Marlborough Court, 14–18 Holborn,
London EC1N 2LE
020 7395 0600
alcs@alcs.co.uk
www.alcs.co.uk
*UK collecting society for writers and
successors*

Bibliographical Society
c/o The Institute of English Studies,
University of London, Senate House,
Malet Street, London WC1E 7HU
020 7862 8679
admin@bibsoc.org.uk
www.bibsoc.org.uk
*Aims to encourage study of bibliography
and history of publishing*

Books 4 Publishing
Lasyard House, Underhill Street,
Bridgnorth, Shropshire WV16 4BB
0870 777 3339
editor@books4publishing.com
www.books4publishing.com
Online showcase for unpublished writers

Booksellers Association of the UK & Ireland
Minster House,
272 Vauxhall Bridge Road,
London SW1V 1BA
020 7802 0802
mail@booksellers.org.uk
www.booksellers.org.uk
*Trade association. Coordinates World
Book Day with Publishers' Association;
administers Costa Book Awards*

Booktrust
Book House, 45 East Hill,
London SW18 2QZ
020 8516 2977
info@booktrust.org.uk
www.booktrust.org.uk and
www.booktrusted.com
Educational charity

British Centre for Literary Translation
University of East Anglia, Norwich,
Norfolk NR4 7TJ
01603 592134/592785
bclt@uea.ac.uk
www.literarytranslation.com
Translation centre

British Copyright Council
Copyright House,
29–33 Berners Street,
London W1T 3AB
01986 788122
secretary@britishcopyright.org
www.britishcopyright.org
Liaison committee for copyright interest

British Science Fiction Association
8a West Avenue Road,
London E17 9SE
bsfachair@gmail.com
www.bsfa.co.uk
*Also publishes Matrix, Vector and Focus
magazines*

British Society of Comedy Writers
61 Parry Road,
Ashmore Park, Wolverhampton,
West Midlands WW11 2PS
01902 722729
info@bscw.co.uk
www.bscw.co.uk
Society of comedy writers

Children's Books Ireland
First Floor,
17 North Great Georges Street,
Dublin 1, Ireland
00 353 1 872 7475
info@childrensbooksireland.com
www.childrensbooksireland.com
*Promotes children's literature and
publishes Inis magazine*

Clé, The Irish Book Publishers' Association
25 Denzille Lane, Dublin 2,
Republic of Ireland
00 353 1 639 4868
info@publishingireland.com
www.publishingireland.com
*Provides expertise and resources; access
to directory of Irish Association of
Freelance Editors, Proofreaders and
Indexers*

Combrogos
10 Heol Don, Whitchurch,
Cardiff CF14 2AU
029 2062 3359
*Arts and media research and editorial
services; books about Wales or by Welsh
authors; contact Dr Meic Stephens*

Comedy Writers' Association UK
Wisteria Cottage, Coombe Meadow,
Bovey Tracey, Newton Abbot,
Devon TQ13 9EZ
info@cwauk.co.uk
www.cwauk.co.uk
*Independent comedy writers in the UK
and around the world*

Crime Writers' Association (CWA)
media.enquiries@thecwa.co.uk
info@thecwa.co.uk
www.thecwa.co.uk
Professional group of crime authors

Critics' Circle
c/o Catherine Cooper,
69 Marylebone Lane,
London W1U 2PH
020 7224 1410
www.criticscircle.org.uk
*Critics of drama, music, cinema & dance,
art and architecture*

Directory & Database Publishers Association
Queens House, 28 Kingsway,
London WC2B 6JR
020 8846 9707; 020 7405 0836
christine@dpa.org.uk
www.dpa.org.uk
Trade association

Drama Association of Wales
The Old Library Building,
Singleton Road, Splott,
Cardiff CF24 2ET
029 2045 2200
aled.daw@virgin.net
www.amdram.co.uk/daw

English Association
University of Leicester,
University Road, Leicester LE1 7RH
0116 252 3982
engassoc@le.ac.uk
www.le.ac.uk/engassoc
*Promotes knowledge, understanding
and enjoyment of English language and
literature*

English PEN
6–8 Amwell Street, London EC1R 1UQ
020 7713 0023
enquiries@englishpen.org
www.englishpen.org
*Association of writers and literary
professionals. Fights for right to freedom
of expression*

Federation of Worker Writers and Community Publishers (FWWCP)
Burslem School of Art, Queen Street,
Stoke on Trent ST6 3EJ
01782 822327
thefwwcp@tiscali.co.uk
www.thefwwcp.org uk
*For independent writing workshops and
community publishers*

Fellowship of Authors and Artists
PO Box 158, Hertford SG13 8FA
0870 747 2514
www.author-fellowship.co.uk
*Promotes writing and art as therapy and
self-healing*

Garden Writers' Guild
c/o Institute of Horticulture,
14/15 Belgrave Square,
London SW1X 8PS
020 7245 6943
gwg@horticulture.org.uk
www.gardenwriters.co.uk
*Promotes high-quality garden writing,
photography and broadcasting*

Gaelic Books Council (Comhairle nan Leabhraichean)
22 Mansfield Street, Glasgow G11 5QP
0141 337 6211
brath@gaelicbooks.net
www.gaelicbooks.net

Horror Writers Association
244 5th Avenue, Suite 2767,
New York, NY 10001 USA
hwa@horror.org
www.horror.org
*Worldwide organisation of writers and
publishing professionals*

Independent Publishers Guild
P O Box 93, Royston,
Hertfordshire SG8 5GH
01763 247014
info@ipg.uk.com
www.ipg.uk.com

Independent Theatre Council
12 The Leathermarket,
Weston Street, London SE1 3ER
020 7403 1727
admin@itc-arts.org
www.itc-arts.org
*Offers legal advice and training
opportunities*

Institute of Linguists
Saxon House, 48 Southwark Street,
London SE1 1UN
020 7940 3100
info@iol.org.uk
www.iol.org.uk
*Professional association; accredited exam
board; commercial contracts for
government*

Institute of Translation and Interpreting (ITI)
Fortuna House,
South Fifth Street, Milton Keynes,
Buckinghamshire MK9 2EU
01908 325250
info@iti.org.uk
www.iti.org.uk

International Booksearch Service
07939 711039
sarah.fordham@btinternet.com
www.scfordham.com
Finds out-of-print books

Irish Writers Centre
19 Parnell Square, Dublin 1,
Republic of Ireland
00 353 1 872 1302
info@writerscentre.ie
www.writerscentre.ie
*Promotes Irish writers, living in Ireland,
organises readings and workshops*
Also houses:

*Irish Playwrights and Screenwriters
Guild*
moffats@indigo.ie
www.writerscentre.ie/IPSG.html

*Irish Translators' and Interpreters'
Association*
translation@eircom.net or
secretary-itia@ntlworld.ie
www.translatorsassociation.ie

Irish Writers' Union
words@neteireann.com
www.ireland-writers.com

ISBN Agency
3rd Floor, Midas House,
62 Goldsworth Road,
Woking GU21 6LQ
0870 777 8712
isbn@nielsenbookdata.co.uk
www.nielsenbookdata.co.uk
Book numbering agency

Manuscript ReSearch
PO Box 33, Bicester,
Oxfordshire OX26 4ZZ
01869 323447/322522
www.manuscriptresearch.co.uk
Services for self-publishing authors

Medical Writers' Group
The Society of Authors,
84 Drayton Gardens,
London SW10 9SB
020 7373 6642
info@societyofauthors.org
www.societyofauthors.org
Specialist group within Society of Authors

National Archives
Kew, Richmond, Surrey TW9 4DU
020 8876 3444
enquiry@nationalarchives.gov.uk
www.nationalarchives.gov.uk
*National resource for documents relating
to British history; brings together the
Public Record Office and the Historical
Manuscripts Commission*

National Association for Literature Development
PO Box 49657, London N8 7YZ
020 8348 3846
Director@nald.org
www.nald.org

National Association of Writers' Groups
The Arts Centre, Biddick Lane,
Washington, Tyne & Wear NE38 2AB
01262 609228
nawg@tesco.net
www.nawg.co.uk
*Connecting writers' groups around the
country; yearly festivals and competitions*

National Association of Writers in Education
PO Box 1, Sheriff Hutton,
York YO60 7YU
01653 618429
paul@nawe.co.uk
www.nawe.co.uk

New Writing North
2 School Lane, Whickham,
Newcastle Upon Tyne NE16 4SL
0191 488 8580
mail@newwritingnorth.com
www.newwritingnorth.com
*Literature development agency for
north-east arts region*

Nielsen BookData
3rd Floor, Midas House,
62 Goldsworth Road, Woking,
Surrey GU21 6LQ
0870 7778710
info@nielsonbookdata.co.uk
www.nielsenbookdata.com
Bibliographic data

Nielsen BookScan
3rd Floor, Midas House,
62 Goldsworth Road, Woking,
Surrey GU21 6LQ
0870 7778710
info@nielsenbookscan.co.uk
www.nielsenbookscan.co.uk
International sales data monitoring

Player-Playwrights
9 Hillfield Park, London N10 3QT
020 8883 0371
p-p@dial.pipex.com
www.playerplaywrights.co.uk
Gives opportunities to writers new to stage, radio and TV

Public Lending Right
Richard House, Sorbonne Close,
Stockton-on-Tees TS17 6DA
01642 604699
registrar@plr.uk.com
www.plr.uk.com
Distribute government funds to authors/libraries

Publishers Association
29B Montague Street,
London WC1B 5BH
020 7691 9191
mail@publishers.org.uk
www.publishers.org.uk
Trade association

Publishers Licensing Society
37–41 Gower Street,
London WC1E 6HH
020 7299 7730
pls@pls.org.uk
www.pls.org.uk
Licensing of photocopying materials in schools and universities

Publishers Publicity Circle
65 Airedale Avenue,
London W4 2NN
020 8994 1881
ppc-@lineone.net
www.publisherspublicitycircle.co.uk
Forum for book publicists and freelance PRs

Romantic Novelists' Association
jennyhaddon@dial.pipex.com
www.rna-uk.org

Royal Society of Literature
Somerset House, Strand,
London WC2R 1LA
020 7845 4676
info@rslit.org
www.rslit.org
Holds monthly lectures promoting literature and spoken word. Annual prizes

Science Fiction Foundation
37 Coventry Road, Ilford IG1 4QR
sff@sjbradshaw.cix.co.uk
www.sf-foundation.org
Writers, academics and critics with an active interest in science fiction

Scottish Book Trust
Sandeman House, Trunk's Close,
55 High Street, Edinburgh EH1 1SR
0131 524 0160
info@scottishbooktrust.com
www.scottishbooktrust.com
Arts organiser, promotes reading and writing in Scotland; holds a resource library

Scottish Print Employers Federation
48 Palmerston Place,
Edinburgh EH12 5DE
0131 220 4353
info@spef.org.uk
www.spef.org.uk
Advice, expertise, education and training

Scottish Publishers Association
Scottish Book Centre,
137 Dundee Street,
Edinburgh EH11 1BG
0131 228 6866
enquiries@scottishbooks.org
www.scottishbooks.org
Networking and information services. Lobbying organisation for book publishing issues

Scottish Youth Theatre
Old Sheriff Court,
105 Brunswick Street,
Glasgow G1 1TF
0141 552 3988
info@scottishyouththeatre.org
www.scottishyouththeatre.org
Giving young people in Scotland opportunity to explore and reach their creative potential through art

Society for Children's Book Writers & Illustrators
8271 Beverley Boulevard,
Los Angeles, CA 90048, USA
00 1 323 782 1010
scbwi@scbwi.org
www.scbwi.org

Society for Editors and Proofreaders (SfEP)
Riverbank House,
1 Putney Bridge Approach,
London SW6 3JD
020 7736 3278
administration@sfep.org.uk
www.sfep.org.uk
Non-profit body promoting high editorial standards and recognition of the professional status of its members

Society of Authors
84 Drayton Gardens,
London SW10 9SB
020 7373 6642
info@societyofauthors.org
www.societyofauthors.org
Trade union for professional authors

Society of Civil and Public Service Writers
Adrian Danson, Editor,
37 Hollingworth Road,
Petts Wood BR5 1AQ
editor@scpsw.co.uk
www.scpsw.co.uk

Society of Indexers
Woodbourn Business Centre,
10 Jessell Street, Sheffield S9 3HY
0114 244 9561
admin@indexers.org.uk
www.indexers.org.uk

Society of Young Publishers
Endeavour House,
189 Shaftesbury Avenue,
London WC2H 8TJ
info@thesyp.org.uk
www.thesyp.org.uk
Provides a forum, organises readings and meetings

Sports Writers' Association of Great Britain
244 Perry Street, Billericay,
Essex CM12 0QP
01277 657708
trevjanbond1@aol.com

Translators Association
84 Drayton Gardens,
London SW10 9SB
020 7373 6642
info@societyofauthors.org
www.societyofauthors.org

Welsh Books Council (Cyngor Llyfrau Cymru)
Castell Brychan, Aberystwyth,
Ceredigion SY23 2JB
01970 624151
castellbrychan@cllc.org.uk
www.cllc.org.uk and
www.gwales.com
For Welsh writers

West Country Writers' Association
1 Moreton Avenue, Crown Hill,
Plymouth PL6 5AZ
01752 785540
www.westcountrywriters.co.uk
Annual congress in May

Women in Publishing
info@wipub.org.uk
www.wipub.org.uk

Writernet
Cabin V, Clarendon Buildings,
25 Horsell Road, Highbury,
London N5 1XL
020 7609 7474
info@writernet.org.uk
www.writernet.org.uk
Information and guidance for playwrights and performance writers

Writers, Artists and their Copyright Holders (Watch)
David Sutton,
Director of Research Projects,
University of Reading Library,
PO Box 223, Whiteknights,
Reading RG6 6AE
0118 931 8783
D.C.Sutton@reading.ac.uk
www.watch-file.com
Database of copyright holders

Writers' Guild of Great Britain
15 Britannia Street,
London WC1X 9JN
020 7833 0777
admin@writersguild.org.uk
www.writersguild.org.uk
Trade union for professional writers

The big cinema story of the year – as far as the UK is concerned – can be summed up in three words: Bond and Borat. Ever since the announcement, back in October 2005, that Daniel Craig was the replacement for Pierce Brosnan as 007, a steady hum of – mostly adverse – comment started up.

Craig was considered by many as too blond, too rugged, and too English to step into Brosnan's shoes. The hum became a roar as the release date for Casino Royale neared; only to swiftly become an outburst of wild applause as Craig's performance was widely praised, and the film saw record takings at the UK box office. At the time of writing, it is on course to become the most successful Bond film at the US box office, set to overhaul the previous record holder Die Another Day's $160m (£82m).

Borat, or more accurately Borat: Cultural Learnings of America for Make Benefit Glorious Nation of Kazakhstan was released a week before Casino Royale in early November. (Both films had a near-simultaneous release in the US and UK, as the film industry expends more and more energy to defeat DVD piracy.) A vehicle for Sacha Baron Cohen's already-popular TV character, Borat managed to break out of the movie world and become a genuine news phenomenon, after the president of Kazakhstan complained publicly about the way it portrayed his compatriots. Propelled by such massive publicity, Borat also recorded extraordinary figures, with an opening weekend of £6m in the UK, and $28m (£14m) in the US. This from an estimated budget of $18m (£9.2m). These two year-end box-office triumphs were balanced by an artistic one earlier in the year, when the veteran British director Ken Loach was awarded the Palme d'Or at the Cannes film festival in May for The Wind That Shakes the Barley, his film about the creation of the Irish Free State. Loach belongs to the small group of British film-makers – along with Mike Leigh, Peter Greenaway and Michael Winterbottom – who are virtually guaranteed a place at any of the world's major film festivals, but Loach had not won the Palme in seven previous attempts. The Wind That Shakes the Barley became the first British film to take it since Leigh's Secrets & Lies in 1996.

British success... Artistic excellence wins the Palme d'Or for The Wind that Shakes The Barley

Joss Barett / Pathé Distribution

● Production and spend

These high-profile stories mask some underlying problems. The financial crisis in the British film industry continued through 2005: figures released by the UK Film Council in January 2006 showed that total production investment fell massively in 2005, to £560m from £812m in 2004. (This latter figure was itself described as a "collapse" in this publication last year, after a record high of £1.15bn in 2003.) Reasons for the slump were ascribed to a falling dollar, continuing uncertainty after the dramatic abolition of "sale and leaseback" funding schemes in 2004, and the slow creep of production location to cheaper studios in Eastern Europe. Figures released in September 2006, however, showed a marked revival, with a total production spend in the UK of £486m in the first half of 2006. The downturn and subsequent upturn is generally credited to industry-wide nervousness at the impact of the government's new tax relief scheme, which was announced in March 2006. When its provisions became clear – including a relaxation of what proportion of a film's budget needs to be spent in the UK for it to qualify – numbers of projects on hold were set in motion. There was also a rush to get co-productions filming before April 1 2006, when the qualifying period under the old rules ended. Twenty-three "domestic" productions were underway in the first six months of 2006, compared with 37 in the whole of 2005. Total productions with UK involvement, including all co-productions, number 70 in the first half of 2006; the total of 124 for 2005 was 9 down on the previous year.

● Hollywood

The year in Hollywood was dominated by "fall from grace" stories. Tom Cruise had his deal with Paramount terminated in August after the disappointing returns of Mission: Impossible III, though it's generally thought that a series of controversial incidents (including a much-ridiculed appearance on the Oprah Winfrey Show) were at least partly responsible. (Cruise has since become a partner in a revived United Artists production studio.) Mel Gibson aroused much hostility after a drink-driving arrest where he subjected policemen to an anti-semitic tirade. And the failure of A Good Year at the US box office is largely put down to audience disenchantment with Russell Crowe after several years of public displays of temper and aggression.

Last year's statistics made Hollywood a tad nervous. Figures released by the Motion Picture Association of America show that admissions into US theatres dropped by 8%, while the films released (a record total of 563) increased by 7%. Within that, the major studios appear to be faring well; the average take for one of their releases was $37m (£18.6m), an increase of 7% on 2004. Eight of 2005's movies grossed over $200m at the US box office – a new high for authentic blockbusters. This year, the picture is looking healthier. At the time of writing, the total box-office in the US (according to boxofficemojo.com) stands over $8.2bn, a 4% rise year-on-year. The leading film at the US box office so far this year, by some distance, is Pirates of the Caribbean 2, which at $420m is almost exactly

Top 10 UK films released in the UK and Ireland, 2005		
Rank/Title	Country of origin	Box office gross (£ m)
1 Harry Potter and the Goblet of Fire*	UK/USA	48.59
2 Charlie and the Chocolate Factory	UK/USA	37.46
3 Wallace & Gromit: The Curse of the Were-Rabbit	UK/USA	32.00
4 Nanny McPhee	UK/USA	16.49
5 Batman Begins	UK/USA	16.42
6 Pride and Prejudice	UK/USA	14.57
7 The Hitchhiker's Guide to the Galaxy	UK/USA	10.67
8 Valiant	UK/USA	8.52
9 Closer	UK/USA	8.49
10 Kingdom of Heaven	UK/USA/Spa/Ger	7.77

Box office gross = cumulative total up to 19 February 2006   * Film was still being exhibited on 19 February 2006   Source: UK Film Council, Nielsen EDI, RSU analysis

$200m ahead of the next one, the animated film Cars. (The other three are: X-Men: The Last Stand, The Da Vinci Code and Superman Returns.)

Overseas, the picture was more encouraging, with the Walt Disney Co (in the shape of Buena Vista) leading the way with $1.49bn in international box office earnings. Their platform release was Pirates of the Caribbean 2, which took over $550m internationally. Other major overseas earners for American studios included The Da Vinci Code ($500m), Ice Age: The Meltdown ($400m), and Mission: Impossible III ($260m).

The Oscars, however, turned against the big-money tickets, awarding best picture to Paul Haggis's Crash. It was seen as a nod to modestly budgeted, socially committed drama; Haggis (previously a winner for the script for Million Dollar Baby) also won the screenplay award, with two George Clooney vehicles, his anti-censorship drama Good Night, and Good Luck and his anti-big oil drama Syriana, both achieving recognition. Reese Witherspoon won the best actress award for June Carter Cash in Walk the Line, while Philip Seymour Hoffman won best actor for his impeccable lead performance in Capote. We may have got used to British success at the Oscars, but there was little around in 2006: Steve Box and Nick Park won best animated film for The Curse of the Were Rabbit, but no other major awards were recorded. Robert Altman was given an honorary Oscar for his body of work; sadly timely, as it turned out, as the great director died in November.

Hollywood's fight against piracy is being conducted with increasing aggression; the MPAA estimates the major studios lost $6.1bn to piracy in 2005. It also says its investigators seized 81 million optical discs in 2005, an 8% increase on the year before. Inside the US, its sights are firmly trained on college students, who the MPAA claims are responsible for 44% of domestic piracy losses. Worldwide, the agency has conducted over 42,000 anti-piracy raids. At the same time, studios have developed more accessible technology on the internet to undercut pirates' window of opportunity, distributing legal downloads through websites such as Lovefilm, BitTorrent and iTunes.

● Cinema attendance

In contrast to the surge in UK production in the first half of 2006, cinema attendances have dipped, with a 2.4% drop on last year's figures. As in the US, the biggest film of the year so far is Pirates of the Caribbean 2, at over £50m; its recent release on DVD confirmed its box office clout, selling 1.5 million copies in its first 10 days.

Top 10 films released in the UK and Ireland, 2005

Rank/Title	Country of origin	Box office gross (£m)
1 Harry Potter and the Goblet of Fire*	UK/USA	48.59
2 The Chronicles of Narnia: The Lion, the Witch and the Wardrobe*	USA/NZ	43.64
3 Star Wars: Episode III: Revenge of the Sith	USA	39.43
4 Charlie and the Chocolate Factory	UK/USA	37.46
5 Wallace & Gromit: The Curse of the Were-Rabbit	UK/USA	32.00
6 War of the Worlds	USA	30.65
7 King Kong*	USA/NZ	30.04
8 Meet the Fockers	USA	28.93
9 Madagascar	USA	22.65
10 Hitch	USA	17.39

Box office gross = cumulative total up to 19 February 2006   * Films were still being exhibited on 19 February 2006   Source: Nielsen EDI, RSU analysis

Cinema release patterns have, in the past few years, reoriented themselves along similar lines as the US, to reflect major studio marketing strategies. Hence the early months of the year are dominated by "mature" dramas that are aimed at the Oscars in early March: this year's crop included the acclaimed "gay western" Brokeback Mountain, and the Johnny Cash biopic Walk the Line. In April the blockbuster season begins gearing up, with each week staked out by a studio tent-pole: The Da Vinci Code, X-Men 3, Mission: Impossible III and Superman Returns backing up Pirates' stunning performance.

Foreign language and art films have to take their chances in between the cracks, and the most remarkable impact on the UK box office was by Michael Haneke's Caché (Hidden), which took £1.45m after being released in the seasonal dead zone at the end of January. However, come autumn, the prestige movies return: Volver became the highest-grossing mainstream foreign-language film of the year so far, with £2.45m. As far as UK films are concerned, The Da Vinci Code, at £30.4m, is still ahead at the time of writing of Casino Royale (£27.2m) and Borat (£20.7m).

The main efforts of the UK Film Council continue to be focused on developing the Digital Screen Network, which will equip cinemas with the facilities to project what they term "specialist" films with digital equipment — thereby saving distributors the cost of striking expensive 35mm prints. Whether this will lead to an increase in the amount of non-major studio product achieving more than minimal distribution remains to be seen.

● What the critics thought

The year began with a bang for the Guardian's Peter Bradshaw, as Georgian director Gela Babluani made "a stunning debut" with his film 13 (Tzameti). But it was Brokeback Mountain that made the first real splash of the year, uniting critics in praise of its beauty and bravery. The expensively mounted Jarhead, directed by Sam Mendes, divided critics far more: The Observer felt it was "well made and performed", while the Sunday Times considered it has "the topical firepower of a potato gun". Werner Herzog's documentary Grizzly Man was an unexpected critical hit — "full of mystery, sadness, and a kind of awed respect for its subject", said the Sunday Telegraph — and Michael Winterbottom's Road to Guantánamo secured a cinema release despite being premiered simultaneously on TV and DVD, on the strength of a top award at Berlin and strong word of mouth. At Cannes in May, the award of the Palme d'Or to Ken Loach was a surprise, though it was generally considered a weak year, with no outstanding candidates. (Sofia Coppola's Marie Antoinette, in particular, attracted much derision: described as "rip-your-own-head-off boring" by the Daily Telegraph). Arguably the critical hit of the festival was another British feature, Red Road, directed by Andrea Arnold (a "tough and superbly intelligent surveillance thriller", said the Guardian), which meant that it had a successful general release later in the year.

Another unlikely festival-fuelled hit was Tsotsi, a South African thriller that had won the audience award at Edinburgh in 2005 before winning an Oscar for best foreign film ("gutsy and heartfelt story", said the Guardian). Two films about 9/11 emerged in the summer: the conclusive winner, critically speaking, was held to be Paul Greengrass's United 93 ("fixes you to your seat", Sunday Times) over Oliver Stone's World Trade Center (a "big pile of pseudo-redemptive hooey", Daily Telegraph.)

The summer also provided us with an instructive phenomenon: Snakes on a Plane, which its distributors deemed unnecessary to screen to critics before its release. This is not unprecedented, but normally only happens to films studios don't want anyone to notice. Not so Snakes, which took over £3.5m at the UK box office. Brian De Palma's adaptation of James Ellroy's The Black Dahlia was generally considered disappointing ("a brutal and badly signposted mess", Times), while the artist Douglas Gordon's avant-garde documentary Zidane: A 21st Century Portrait aroused some strong positive reactions ("a hypnotic experience to which you must simply abandon yourself", Guardian). And so, to return to where we began: the end-year double whammy of Bond and Borat. Daniel Craig's reviews were extremely positive across the board ("effortless presence and lethal danger", the Guardian), while Sacha Baron Cohen, initially the subject of adoring praise, has suffered a major backlash. Marcel Berlins, writing in the Guardian, described his film as "reprehensible". Allison Pearson in the Daily Mail called it "cruel sport". Whether there will be a back-backlash, we will have to wait and see.

Awards

Baftas, 2006

- *Best film:* Brokeback Mountain
- *Best director:* Ang Lee for Brokeback Mountain
- *Best actor:* Philip Seymour Hoffman in Capote
- *Best actress:* Reese Witherspoon in Walk the Line
- *Best supporting actor:* Jake Gyllenhaal in Brokeback Mountain
- *Best supporting actress:* Thandie Newton in Crash
- *Outstanding British film of the year:* Wallace & Gromit: The Curse of the Were-Rabbit
- *Best original screenplay:* Paul Haggis & Bobby Moresco for Crash
- *Best adapted screenplay:* Larry McMurtry & Diana Ossana for Brokeback Mountain
- *Best foreign film:* The Beat That My Heart Skipped

Oscars, 2006

- *Best picture:* Crash
- *Best director:* Ang Lee for Brokeback Mountain
- *Best actor:* Philip Seymour Hoffman in Capote
- *Best actress:* Reese Witherspoon in Walk the Line
- *Supporting actor:* George Clooney in Syriana
- *Supporting actress:* Rachel Weisz in The Constant Gardener
- *Best original screenplay:* Paul Haggis & Bobby Moresco for Crash
- *Best adapted screenplay:* Larry McMurtry & Diana Ossana for Brokeback Mountain
- *Best foreign language film:* Tsotsi (South Africa)
- *Best animated film:* Wallace & Gromit: The Curse of the Were-Rabbit

Cannes 2006

- *Palme d'Or:* The Wind That Shakes The Barley by Ken Loach
- *Grand Prix:* Flandres by Bruno Dumont

Is fiction dead in the cinema?

Andrew Pulver

For some years now, documentary cinema has been gaining ground at the box office. Reality programmes such as Jackass have jumped successfully to the big screen. And the huge returns for Borat has shown that a film need have hardly anything in the way of props, costume, acting personnel or, indeed, script, to flourish. At a time in cinema evolution when Hollywood's obsession with special effects, comic book franchises and sequels appears to be on the point of burning out, the question asks itself: is fiction dead? Of course, narrative drama will be produced by film-makers for the foreseeable future, in considerable quantities. But the success of the documentary movement — particularly since the release of Michael Moore's Fahrenheit 9/11 — has made the telling of non-fiction stories a viable commercial proposition. The effect it has had on other areas of the film-making world has been profound.

In the past, when film-makers incorporated documentary techniques into feature films, it has essentially been a stylistic conceit. The European new waves, for example, used non-specific lighting and lightweight cameras to give their films a freshness and naturalism that more ponderous traditional methods could not. More recently, movements such as Dogme 95 sought to utilise digital video's ease-of-use to make low-budget, stripped-down films that broke cinema's reliance on celluloid. Meanwhile, straight documentaries — most recently Touching the Void — have brought the television practice of reconstruction into their work to bring otherwise unrepresentable sections to life. But the most intriguing development is the existence of new hybrid genres. This is particularly evident in the work of British director Michael Winterbottom, whose In This World is arguably the most successful combination yet of fiction and documentary.

Beginning in a refugee camp in Peshawar, In This World follows two "actors", Jamal Udin Torabi and Enayatullah — as individuals both virtually indistinguishable from the characters they play — as they cross continents in an attempt to settle in Europe. Winterbottom and crew travelled with the pair, filming them surreptitiously in real-life situations, writing dialogue as they went along. As a fusion of a created story, and documentary response to actual events, In This World works superbly.

This hybrid style has also struck a chord in the development of mainstream documentary-making techniques, seeking to break away from traditional objective perspectives. It is now common for documentaries to follow a single character on a real-life "mission" — a practice once confined to mavericks such as Nick Broomfield (The Leader, The Driver and the Driver's Wife) and, again, Michael Moore (Roger & Me).

This was a style that transferred easily to television, the habitual home of documentary. Moore developed a series called TV Nation, and was followed in Britain by apolitical provocateurs such as Louis Theroux, Paul Kaye, Dom Joly and Sacha Baron Cohen. Another strand contributing to the merging of reality and fiction has been — surprisingly — the home-made surf and skateboard film. Pioneered in the 1960s and 70s by enthusiasts keen to capture their wipe-outs on camera, these compilations of pratfalls and head-cracking evolved directly into the Jackass series on MTV, and then into the cinema. With no continuity except the ever more dangerous stunts, and the character of the participants themselves, Jackass's main contribution to cinema is to change conclusively what can be put on the big screen in the name of entertainment. Taking advantage of cinema's more liberal attitude to censorship compared to network TV, Jackass reaches areas of fecal obsession that only John Waters, in his mid-70s counter-culture heyday, could aspire to match. In this sense, Jackass resembles pornography — no matter what the furniture of narrative or set-up, it's the clear and demonstrated actuality of the act, as captured on screen, that is the function of the film. Borat, the recent hit from Baron Cohen, is a clear fusion of both these styles: the provocateur and the prankster. Baron Cohen is by no means the first film-maker to interact and hoodwink uncomprehending members of the public, but the irritation (and potential lawsuits) his film has aroused is, however, an indication of this style's advance into mainstream culture. No one dreamed of suing Ali G, or Borat while on TV, or Jackass. Baron Cohen can hardly have anticipated the impact his film has made. But he is certainly going to go down in cinema history as a man who did something new.

● Andrew Pulver is film editor at the Guardian

Hollywood studios

Buena Vista Motion Pictures Group
500 S. Buena Vista Street,
Burbank, CA 91521
00 1 818 560 1000
http://bventertainment.go.com
Owned by Disney. President: Nina Jacobson

Icon Productions
808 Wilshire Blvd, 4th Fl,
Santa Monica, CA 90401
00 1 310 434 7300
www.iconmovies.net
Partner: Mel Gibson; partner and president: Bruce Davey

MGM Pictures
10250 Constellation Blvd,
Los Angeles, CA 90067
00 1 310 449 3000
www.mgm.com
Chairman and CEO: Alex Yemenidjian

Miramax Films
375 Greenwich Street, New York,
NY 10013
00 1 212 941 3800
www.miramax.com
Owned by Disney.

Sony Pictures Entertainment
10202 W Washington Blvd,
Culver City, CA 90232
00 1 310 244 4000
www.sonypictures.com
Chairman and CEO: Michael Lynton

Touchstone Television Productions
500 S Buena Vista St, Burbank,
CA 91521
00 1 818 560 1000
http://touchstone.movies.go.com
Owned by Disney. President: Mark Pedowitz

Twentieth Century Fox Film Corporation
10201 West Pico Blvd, Los Angeles,
CA 90035
00 1 310 369 1000
www.fox.com
Co-chairmen: Jim Gianopulos, Tom Rothman

Universal Studios
100 Universal City Plaza,
Universal City, CA 91608
00 1 818 777 1000
www.universalstudios.com
President and COO: Ron Meyer

Warner Bros Entertainment
4000 Warner Blvd, Burbank,
CA 91522
00 1 818 954 6000
www.warnerbros.com
Chairman and CEO: Barry M. Meyer

Major animators and special effects studios

Aardman Animations
Gas Ferry Rd, Bristol BS1 6UN
0117 984 8485
www.aardman.com

Bolexbrothers
Unit 6, Brunel Lock Development,
Smeaton Road, Cumberland Basin,
Bristol BS1 6SE
0117 985 8000
www.bolexbrothers.co.uk

DreamWorks Animation SKG
1000 Flower St, Glendale, CA 91201
00 1 818 695 5000
www.pdi.com

Industrial Light & Magic
PO Box 2459, San Rafael, CA 94912
00 1 415 448 9000
www.ilm.com

Pixar Animation Studios
1200 Park Ave, Emeryville, CA 94608
00 1 510 752 3000
www.pixar.com

UK film companies

Amber Films
5&9 Side, Newcastle NE1 3JE
0191 232 2000
www.amber-online.com

Bard Entertainments
7 Denmark Street, London WC2H 8LZ
020 7240 7144
office@bardentertainments.co.uk
www.bardentertainments.co.uk

BBC Films
Grafton House, 379 Euston Road,
London NW1 3AU
020 7765 0251
www.bbc.co.uk/bbcfilms
Head of BBC Films: David Thompson, 020 7765 0113; head of production: Susy Liddell, 020 7765 0379

Capitol Films
Bridge House, 2nd Floor, 63-65
North Wharf Road, London W2 1LA
020 7298 6200
films@capitolfilms.com
www.capitolfilms.com

Celador Films
39 Long Acre, London WC2E 9LG
020 7845 6800
www.celador.co.uk/films.php

Company Pictures
Suffolk House, 1-8 Whitfield Place,
London W1T 5JU
020 7380 3900
enquiries@companypictures.co.uk
www.companypictures.co.uk
MDs: Charlie Pattinson, George Faber

Dan Films
32 Maple Street, London W1T 6HB
020 7916 4771
enquiries@danfilms.com
www.danfilms.com

Ecosse Films
Brigade House, 8 Parsons Green,
London SW6 4TN
020 7371 0290
info@ecossefilms.com
www.ecossefilms.com
MD: Douglas Rae

Focus Films
Focus Films, The Rotunda Studios,
r/o 116-118 Finchley Road,
London NW3 5HT
020 7435 9004
focus@focusfilms.co.uk
www.focusfilms.co.uk

Gruber Films
eOffice, 2 Sheraton Street,
London W1F 8BH
0870 366 9313
richard.holmes@gruberfilms.com
www.gruberfilms.com

In-Motion Pictures
5 Percy Street, London W1T 1DG
020 7467 6880
enquiries@in-motionpictures.com
www.in-motionpictures.com

Ipso Facto Films
1 Pink Lane,
Newcastle upon Tyne NE1 5DW
0191 230 2585
info@ipsofactofilms.com
www.ipsofactofilms.com

Merchant Ivory Productions
46 Lexington Street,
London W1F 0LP
020 7437 1200
contact@merchantivory.com

Pathé
Kent House, 14-17 Market Place,
Great Titchfield Street,
London W1N 8AR
020 7323 5151
www.pathedistribution.com

Picture Palace Productions
13 Egbert Street, London NW1 8LJ
020 7586 8763
www.picturepalace.com

Qwerty Films
42-44 Beak Street. London W1F 9RH
020 7440 5920
info@qwertyfilms.com

Ruby Films
26 Lloyd Baker Street,
London WC1X 9AW
020 7833 9990

Scion Films
18 Soho Square, London W1D 3QL
020 7025 8003
info@scionfilms.com
www.scionfilms.com

Sigma Films
Film City Glasgow,
Summertown Road, Glasgow G51 2LY
0141 445 0400
latenights@sigmafilms.com
www.sigmafilms.com

Vertigo Films
The Big Room Studios,
77 Fortress Road, London NW5 1AG
020 7428 7555
mail@vertigofilms.com
www.vertigofilms.com
Press: press@vertigofilms.com

Working Title Films
Oxford House, 76 Oxford Street,
London W1D 1BS
020 7307 3000
www.workingtitlefilms.com

UK film finance

Screen Financiers Association
9 Wimpole Street, London W1G 9SR
info@screenfinanciers.co.uk

TV & film independent production companies

» see TV, page 172

Post-production

» see TV, page 184

TV and film studios

» see TV, page 182

UK distributors

20th Century Fox
Twentieth Century House,
31-32 Soho Square, London W1D 3AP
020 7437 7766
www.fox.co.uk

Arrow Films
Orchard Villa, Porters Park Drive,
Shenley WD7 9DS
01923 858306
alex@arrowfilms.co.uk
www.arrowfilms.co.uk

Artificial Eye
14 King Street, London WC2E 8HR
020 7240 5353
info@artificial-eye.com
www.artificial-eye.com

Blue Dolphin Films
40 Langham Street, London W1W 7AS
020 7255 2494
info@bluedolphinfilms.com
www.bluedolphinfilms.com

Buena Vista International UK/ Filmfactory
3 Queen Caroline Street,
London W6 9PE
020 8222 1000
feedback@thefilmfactory.co.uk
www.bvimovies.com

CineFrance
12 Sunbury Place, Edinburgh EH4 3BY
0131 225 6191
info@cinefile.co.uk
www.cinefrance.co.uk

Columbia TriStar UK
25 Golden Square, London W1F 9LU
020 7533 1000
www.sonypictures.co.uk

Dogwoof Pictures
Second floor, 1A Neals Yard,
Covent Garden, London WC2H 9DP
020 7395 1217
info@dogwoofpictures.com
www.dogwoofpictures.com

Entertainment Film Distributors
108-110 Jermeyn Street,
London SW1Y 6HB
020 7930 7744

Eros International
customerservice2@
 erosmultimedia.net
www.erosentertainment.com

Feature Film Company
19 Heddon Street, London W1B 4BG
020 7851 6500
www.featurefilm.co.uk
www.contentfilm.com

Gala Film Distributors
26 Danbury Street, London N1 8JU
020 7226 5085

Granada International
48 Leicester Square,
London WC2H 7FB
020 7491 1441
int.info@granadamedia.com
www.carltonint.co.uk

Icon Film Distribution
Solar House, 915 High Road,
North Finchley, London N12 82J
020 8492 6300
reception@
 icon-entertainment.co.uk
www.iconmovies.co.uk

Metrodome
5th Floor, 33 Charlotte Street,
London W1T 1RR
020 7153 4421
www.metrodomegroup.com

Momentum Pictures
184-192 Drummond Street,
London NW1 3HB
020 7391 6900
info@momentumpictures.co.uk
www.momentumpictures.co.uk

Optimum Releasing
22 Newman Street, London W1T 1PH
020 7637 5403
info@optimumreleasing.com
www.optimumreleasing.com

Pathé Distribution
Kent House, 14-17 Market Place,
Great Titchfield Street,
London W1W 8AR
020 7323 5151
www.pathedistribution.com

Redbus Film Distribution
Ariel House, 74A Charlotte Street,
London W1T 4QJ
020 7299 8800
info@redbus.com
www.redbus.co.uk

Tartan Films Distribution
Royalty House, 72-74 Dean Street,
London W1D 3SG
020 7494 1400
www.tartanfilms.com

UGC Films UK
34 Bloomsbury Street,
London WC1B 3QJ
020 7631 4683

United International Pictures
UIP House, 45 Beadon Road,
Hammersmith, London W6 OEG
020 8741 9041
enquiries@uip.com
www.uip.com

Warner Bros
98 Theobalds Road,
London WC1X 8WB
020 7984 5000
www.warnerbros.com

Creative media

Film commissions

UK Film Council
10 Little Portland Street,
London W1W 7JG
020 7861 7861
info@ukfilmcouncil.org.uk
www.ukfilmcouncil.org.uk
The government-backed strategic agency working to stimulate a successful UK film industry and culture
Press: 020 7861 7508

Bath Film Office
01225 477711
bath_filmoffice@bathnes.gov.uk
www.visitbath.co.uk

Central England Screen Commission
0121 265 7120
info@screenwm.co.uk
www.screenwm.co.uk

Eastern Screen
01603 767077
productions@
  eastern-screen.demon.co.uk
www.eastern-screen.demon.co.uk

Edinburgh Film Focus
0131 622 7337
info@edinfilm.com
www.edinfilm.com

EM Media
0115 934 9090
info@em-media.org.uk
www.em-media.org.uk

European Film Commission
00 39 067 290 5757
info@
  europeanfilmcommunication.com
www.europeanfilmcommission.com

Glasgow Film Office
0141 287 0424
info@glasgowfilm.com
www.glasgowfilm.org.uk

Isle of Man Film Commission
01624 687173
iomfilm@dti.gov.im
www.gov.im/dti/iomfilm

Northern Ireland Film and Television Commission
028 9023 2444
Info@niftc.co.uk
www.niftc.co.uk

Scottish Highlands and Islands Film Commission
01463 710221
trish@scotfilm.org
www.scotfilm.org

Scottish Screen
0141 302 1700
info@scottishscreen.com
www.scottishscreen.com

Wales Screen Commission
0800 849 8848
enquiries@
  walesscreencommission.co.uk
www.walesscreencommission.co.uk

Regional agencies

East Midlands: EM Media
0115 934 9090
info@em-media.org.uk
www.em-media.org.uk

East: Screen East
01603 776920
info@screeneast.co.uk
www.screeneast.co.uk

Film London
020 7613 7676
info@filmlondon.org.uk
www.filmlondon.org.uk
Strategic agency for film and media in London, to act as catalyst for film-making in London

North-east: Northern Film and Media
0191 269 9200
www.northernmedia.org

North-west: North West Vision
0870 609 4481
info@northwestvision.co.uk
www.northwestvision.co.uk

Screen Yorkshire
0113 294 4410
info@screenyorkshire.co.uk
http://screenyorkshire.co.uk

South-east (not London): Screen South
01303 259777
info@screensouth.org
www.screensouth.org

South-west: South West Screen
0117 952 9977
info@swscreen.co.uk
www.swscreen.co.uk

West Midlands: Screen West Midlands
0121 766 1470
info@screenwm.co.uk
www.screenwm.co.uk

TV & film training and support

» see TV, page 189

Trade press

Advance Production News
020 8305 6905
www.crimsonuk.com
Monthly. Listings for production companies. Owner: Crimson Communications. Editor: Alan Williams

British Film Magazine
020 7636 7455
terence@britishfilm-magazine.com
www.britishfilm-magazine.com
Plans to go monthly. Independently owned. Editor: Terence Doyle

Broadcast Hardware International
01628 773935
cathy@hardwarecreations.tv
www.hardwarecreations.tv
10pa. Owner: Hardware Creations. Editor: Dick Hobbs

Channel 21 International magazine
020 7729 7460
press@c21media.net
www.c21media.com
10pa. Owner: C21 Media. Editor-in-chief: David Jenkinson; editor: Ed Waller

Contacts - The Spotlight Casting Directories
020 7437 7631
info@spotlight.com
www.spotlight.com
Annual. Contacts for stage, film, TV and radio. Editor: Kate Poynton

Crewfinder
028 9079 7902
mail@adleader.co.uk
www.crewfinderwales.co.uk
Annual. Wales's film, TV and video directory. Owner: Adleader Publications. Proprietor: Stan Mairs

FilmBang
0141 334 2456
info@filmbang.com
www.filmbang.com
Annual. Scotland's film and video directory. Editor: Marianne Mellin

The Hollywood Reporter
020 7420 6000
Daily. Hollywood trade paper. UK bureau chief: Stuart Kemp

IBE
01342 717459
info@bpl_business.com
www.ibeweb.com
12pa. International broadcast engineering. Owner: BPL Business Media. Editor: Neil Nixon

Kemps Film, TV, Video Handbook (UK edition)
01342 335861
kemps@reedinfo.co.uk
www.kftv.com
Annual. Guide to international production. Owner: Reed Business Information. Editorial contact: Vivien Carne

The Knowledge
01732 377591
knowledge@cmpinformation.com
www.theknowledgeonline.com
Annual. Production directory. Owner: CMP Information. Editorial contact: Michelle Hathaway

Pact Directory of Independent Producers
020 8977 7711
lbaynes@hollis-publishing.com
www.pact.co.uk
Annual

Pro Sound News Europe
020 7921 8319
david.robinson@cmpinformation.com
www.prosoundnewseurope.com
12pa. Audio industry. Owner: CMP Information. Editor: David Robinson; managing editor: Ben Rosser

The Production Guide
020 7505 8000
david.robinson@cmpi.biz
www.theproductionguide.co.uk
12pa. Pro audio industry. Owner: CMP Information. Editor: David Robinson; managing editor: Sharon Lock

Screen Digest
020 7424 2820
guy.bisson@screendigest.com
www.screendigest.com
Monthly. Editor: David Fisher; news editor: Guy Bisson; chief analyst: Ben Keen

Screen International
020 7505 8000
screeninternational@emap.com
www.screendaily.com
Weekly. News service for global film industry. Owner: Emap Media. Editor-in-chief: Colin Brown; editor: Michael Gubbins

Stage Screen and Radio
020 7346 0900
janice@stagescreenandradio.org.uk
www.bectu.org.uk
10pa. Magazine of broadcasting union Bectu. Editor: Janice Turner

VLV Bulletin
01474 352835
info@vlv.org.uk
www.vlv.org.uk
Quarterly magazine of Voice of the Listener and Viewer. Advocates citizen and consumer interests in broadcasting. Editor: Jocelyn Hay

Zerb
01795 535468
cfox@urbanfox.com
www.gtc.org.uk
2pa. For camera operators. Owner: The Deeson Group. Managing Editors: Christina Fox; Alison Chapman

》 *Consumer film and TV magazines* see page 84

Events

Bafta Awards
195 Piccadilly, London W1J 9LN
020 7734 0022
www.bafta.org
Film, TV and interactive industries

British Independent Film Awards
81 Berwick Street, London W1F 8TW
020 7287 3833
sarah.lutton@bfi.org.uk
www.bfi.org.uk

Cannes Film Festival
3, rue Amélie 75007 Paris, France
00 33 1 53 59 61 00
festival@festival-cannes.fr
www.festival-cannes.org

London Film Festival
National Film Theatre, South Bank, London SE1 8XT
020 7815 1322
www.lff.org.uk

Raindance Film Festival
81 Berwick Street, London W1F 8TW
020 7287 3833
info@raindance.co.uk
www.raindance.co.uk

TV & film associations

》 see TV, page 190

Music

The music industry's story of the year is how music was sold. In 2006, for the first time, the internet appeared to be assuming the mantle of "the future of music" that had been draped on its shoulders with monotonous regularity since the first band set up its own website. Gnarls Barkley recorded the first UK No 1 single based solely on download sales; no fewer than three acts – Arctic Monkeys, Sandi Thom and Lily Allen – had break-throughs widely attributed to their web presence; and the social networking site MySpace came to be regarded as the future of talent-scouting, even as it was welcomed into Rupert Murdoch's embrace. But despite the spread of technology, with more means of getting more music to more people than ever before, physical sales continued to fall. Though there has been a massive surge in worldwide digital sales – up 106% to £510m, or 11% of the worldwide recorded music market – the International Federation of the Phonographic Industry reported that total music sales in the first half of 2006 fell by 4% to £7.4bn. And Ged Doherty, the UK head of Sony BMG, said he expected CD sales to have fallen by 50% within three years, with digital sales not rising fast enough to compensate. So is the music business in danger? In its present form, Doherty said, yes: "We are running our businesses like it is 1982. We're running a business model that is so out of date it's not true."

● Music downloads

It didn't really seem like a lot of downloads: just 31,000. But that was enough to make Crazy by Gnarls Barkley the first download-only No 1 in April 2006. That became possible as the result of yet another change to the rules governing the singles charts. Where in 2005, digital sales could only be counted alongside physical sales, in 2006 the rules were changed to allow digital sales to be counted so long as a physical release would be forthcoming the following week. Gnarls Barkley was the first beneficiary. But 31,000 sales, while a vast improvement on the 17,694 sales that took Orson's No Tomorrow to the top spot in March (the lowest ever sales for a No 1 single), would have made Crazy a minor hit 20 years ago. The reform of the charts proved the industry was finally waking up to the importance of the download, though in a confused manner: in 2007 the rules of the singles chart are to change yet again, with downloads to be eligible for the charts even if there is no physical release of a song to follow.

The good news for the industry was that UK consumers at last appeared to be realising that they could buy music on the web, rather than just hunting out tracks on file-sharing networks. The 2006 Digital Music Survey reported that the legal download market had grown significantly over the previous year, with 50% of music buyers now using legal downloads, against 35% in 2005.

Music to the ears... Gnarls Barkley made No 1 with download single Crazy

Mark Allan

Elsewhere, the survey painted a picture of a consumer market at least as confused as the industry itself. For instance, while around a quarter of those surveyed said they now buy fewer CDs as a result of their downloading activity (both legal and illegal), a nearly identical figure said they now bought more. And despite the success of MP3 players — the telltale white headphone lead of the iPod, such a novelty just three years ago that they made users mugging targets, are ubiquitous — music consumers have not made the leap to having music on their mobile phones, whatever the public perception of hooded youths playing hip-hop out loud on the bus might lead one to believe. Although the industry is positing mobile downloading as its next big thing, the public response has been a shrug and a "Whatever ..." In fact, only 4% of music consumers currently say they are very likely to start mobile downloading, and as the survey said: "The problem is more fundamental than a lack of consumer knowledge — [it's] a lack of consumer interest."

The prevention of music piracy continued to exercise the industry. In August, the BPI estimated that around 16.5 million sales were lost to piracy in 2005, more than 10% of total album sales of 159 million. Certainly, music reviewers felt the sharp end of the record companies' efforts to stop music leaking out: when Jay-Z's comeback album was released in November, reviewers were told that owing to security concerns, a representative of the rapper would be in the UK for one day only, leaving at 5pm, and anyone wishing to review the album in time for its release date should go to the record company's offices to hear it.

Top 20 albums 2005		
1	Back To Bedlam — James Blunt	11	Forever Faithless - The Greatest Hits — Faithless
2	X&Y — Coldplay	12	Piece By Piece — Katie Melua
3	Iintensive Care — Robbie Williams	13	Hot Fuss — Killers
4	Employment — Kaiser Chiefs	14	Now That's What I Call Music 61 — Various Artists
5	Demon Days — Gorillaz	15	Don't Believe The Truth — Oasis
6	Face To Face — Westlife	16	Ancora — Il Divo
7	Now That's What I Call Music 62 — Various Artists	17	Confessions On A Dance Floor — Madonna
8	Eye To The Telescope — KT Tunstall	18	American Idiot — Green Day
9	Breakaway — Kelly Clarkson	19	Scissor Sisters — Scissor Sisters
10	Curtain Call - The Hits — Eminem	20	Hopes and Fears — Keane

Source: BPI

● Web hype

When Arctic Monkeys' debut album crashed into the charts at No 1, with first-week sales of 363,735, observers were quick to hail the band's canny use of the web to spread their music. Similarly, Sandi Thom's success in reaching No 1 was credited to a series of self-promoted webcast gigs that brought her to record company attention, and Lily Allen's status as the star of the summer was attributed to her forthright blog on MySpace.

In fact, none of these cases was quite as it appeared, suggesting the web, for all the talk about it democratising music, has become another extension of the hype machine. Far from being masters of the internet, the Arctic Monkeys denied ever having posted music on the web. It turns out their fans had shared tracks from demo CDs, a phenomenon that eager journalists then hyped up. Sandi Thom was ruthlessly promoted with a PR campaign that stressed how she had been signed to a million-pound deal after label executives had caught one of a series of gigs she played in her basement, then broadcast on the web. As soon as she popped up in the charts, however, stories started sneaking about how Thom already had a big-league publicist on board before the basement gigs, and IT experts cast doubt on whether a starving singer — as Thom claimed to be — could possibly have afforded the bandwidth required to broadcast over the web to 70,000 people a time, as she claimed to have done. And Allen was already signed to Parlophone long before her MySpace blogs and music postings started attracting the attention of press and public, though in this case it seems as though the record company was slowest out of the blocks. In fact, she told Pitchforkmedia.com, her album had not been due to come out until January 2007, and Parlophone press department was caught on the hop by journalists calling up about an act it didn't even realise it was meant to be promoting.

Allen's story is the most telling about the shape of music in 2006. MySpace became one of the most important tools in promoting artists. Not only did it enable them to get music out early and often, it helped them demonstrate a fanbase to interested labels. Record companies now say having an effective MySpace site is the most important investment a new band can make: A&R work is now done as much by trawling MySpace listening to music as by crawling round tiny clubs catching live acts. While the conversion of MySpace from private club for teenagers to extension of commerce might have dismayed its original audience, it was sufficient to lure Rupert Murdoch into buying the site.

Top 10 downloads 2005	
1	You're Beautiful — James Blunt
2	Hung Up — Madonna
3	Bad Day — Daniel Powter
4	Push The Button — Sugababes
5	Don't Cha — Pussycat Dolls (Busta Rhymes)
6	Feel Good Inc — Gorillaz
7	That's My Goal — Shayne Ward
8	Gold Digger — Kanye West (Jamie Foxx)
9	I Like The Way — Bodyrockers
10	Speed Of Sound — Coldplay

Source: BPI

Top 10 singles 2005	
1	(Is this the way to) Amarillo — Tony Christie (Peter Kay)
2	That's My Goal — Shayne Ward
3	Axel F — Crazy Frog
4	You're Beautiful — James Blunt
5	Don't Cha — Pussycat Dolls (Busta Rhymes)
6	All About You/You've Got a Friend — Mcfly
7	Lonely — Akon
8	Hung Up — Madonna
9	You Raise Me Up — Westlife
10	Push The Button — Sugababes

Source: BPI

● In the shops

The growth of digital downloads hit the high-street record shops hard, though arguably not as hard as the increasing presence of supermarkets in the marketplace. As the last century ended, virtually every CD sold was sold by a music retailer; now supermarkets control more than a quarter of the CD market. Meanwhile, the two biggest high-street chains, HMV and Virgin, saw their sales plunging: in the first two months of 2006, HMV's sales were 16.7% down on the previous year. The answer, for both chains, has been aggressive price-cutting, with HMV moving from one of the more expensive places to buy music to one of the cheapest.

The best hope of the chains, however, might be that the supermarkets will blow their own position in music retail. The major labels have become increasingly unhappy about the supermarkets' hugely aggressive pricing policy – Richard Branson accused them in November of threatening the future of young talent by concentrating on selling established acts at knockdown prices. Tesco and Warner entered into a bitter battle, with Tesco refusing to stock CDs by key Warners acts, after the record company complained about the prices its CDs were being sold at. The result has been greater goodwill towards specialist music retailers from the people who supply them with products. That, combined with a greater willingness to adapt and set their own houses in order, could see music retailers reclaiming their central position in the selling of physical music. Morgan Stanley, the merchant bank, is predicting HMV's share of both the physical and digital markets will be significantly increased by 2010: there's life in the old dog yet.

The losers will be the shops from which people of a certain age bought their first music: WH Smith and Woolworths are expected to lose half their market share in the same period.

Awards

Brit awards 2006

- *British album:* Coldplay – X&Y
- *British group:* Kaiser Chiefs
- *British male solo artist:* James Blunt
- *British female solo artist:* KT Tunstall
- *International album:* Green Day – American Idiot
- *International group:* Green Day
- *International male solo artist:* Kanye West
- *International female solo artist:* Madonna
- *Oustanding contribution to music:* Paul Weller

Nationwide Mercury music prize 2006

- Arctic Monkeys

Q awards 2006

- *Best album:* Arctic Monkeys – Whatever People Say I Am, That's What I'm Not
- *Best live act:* Muse
- *Best new act:* Corinne Bailey Rae
- *Best single:* Crazy – Gnarls Barkley
- *Best video:* The Killers – When You Were Young

MTV Europe music awards 2006

- *Best group:* Depeche Mode
- *Best album:* Red Hot Chili Peppers – Stadium Arcadium
- *Best male singer:* Justin Timberlake
- *Best female singer:* Christina Aguilera

Gramophone awards 2006

- *Best orchestral:* Berlin Philharmonic Orchestra/Claudio Abbad – Mahler, Symphony No 6
- *Best chamber:* Vadim Repin; Ilya Gringolts; Nobuko Imai; Lunn Harrell; Mikhail Pletnev – Taneyev, Chamber Music
- *Best instrumental:* Piotr Anderszewski – Szymanowski, Piano Works
- *Best solo vocal:* Christian Gerhaher; Gerold Huber – Schubert, Abendbilder
- *Best historic archive:* Bayreuth Festival/Keilberth – Wagner, Siegfried
- *Best contemporary:* Kari Kriikku; Finnish RSO/Sakari Oramo – Magnus Lindberg, Clarinet Concerto

● Festivals

With live music in Britain in ruder health than ever before, the 2006 festival season was bigger and longer than ever before. With Glastonbury taking a year off, scores of new events sprang up to fill the gap. As it happens, there was no gap. Though the biggest events – the Carling Weekend at Reading and Leeds, the V festivals in Essex and Staffordshire, T in the Park – were the expected sell-outs, a sense of festival fatigue descended this summer. The series of Hyde Park gigs under the banner of the Wireless festival failed to sell out. The Mean Fiddler organisation's attempt at a grown-up event, Latitude, held at Suffolk's London-by-the-Sea, Southwold, couldn't attract a capacity crowd, and scores of other events suffered the same fate.

That didn't stop enterprising promoters trying to put on multiple bands on multiple stages anywhere there was a free field, with the family-oriented event being a particular favourite. Guildford's Guilfest and Leicester's Summer Sundae have shown the way for festivals that combine a handful of hipster acts with some old-timers, a sprinkling of world music and some out-and-out pop, and their model was widely copied. The problem, of course, was the lack of A-list acts to go round. That's not so much a problem if, like Solfest (at Silloth in Cumbria) you are hours away from the nearest town with a thriving gig scene, but became a fatal handicap for countless mid-sized events.

But with formerly "small" events such as The Big Chill becoming established as major dates on the festival calendar, the warm glow of affection spread. One of the best-received events of 2006 was the Trick Festival in Oxfordshire, whose capacity was limited to 5,000. Its friendliness, small scale and sense of being an event put on for love rather than profit outweighed the fact that its bill consisted almost entirely of indie bands of whom few bar their immediate family had heard.

● The industry

Much of the music industry spent the year at the edge of the dancefloor, eyeing the uneasy tango between EMI and Warner, waiting to see whether the dance of the two giants would end in union. It didn't – the merger was cancelled after the European courts struck out the European Commission's approval of another melding of majors, that between Sony and BMG. Warner and EMI had been sparring with each other all year, each twice offering to buy the other, but the court ruling on Sony BMG, which stunned the industry, ended their dance as abruptly as if the house lights had come up at a club.

The future of Sony BMG remains uncertain. The two component arms of the company have had to reapply to the European Commission to get permission for their deal. The worst case would be that, in due course, the company is ordered to break itself up, though few believe there is the political will in the industry to force such a huge turnaround. The European ruling cheered independent labels, however, who saw it as a tool to prevent the creation of further supermajors with the power to exert yet more control over the industry. Following its success with the Sony BMG decision, the umbrella group of European independent companies, Impala, turned its attention to BMG's attempt to sell its publishing arm to Universal, warning that it was a threat to competition. At the time of writing, the sale was under review by the European Commission.

Success of the indie band?

Micheal Hann

Travelling through London in a cab in November 2006; the driver turns and asks what I do. I edit the Guardian's Film & Music section, I tell him. He tells me his 14-year-old daughter is just starting to go to gigs. He worries for her, but not too much. After all, she's not listening to R&B or grime, or any of that stuff that ends with people shooting each other in nightclubs. "She listens to proper music," he says. "The Kooks, the Killers. Stuff that I can relate to."

2006 was the year, it seems when what was once known as "indie" finally died, and became the new mainstream. The year an indie band was the most-hyped and fastest-selling band in the country. But Arctic Monkeys weren't even in the vanguard of the trend. Snow Patrol's Eyes Open outsold Whatever People Say I Am, That's What I'm Not; the Kooks' Inside In—Inside Out was in the same region. Neither of those bands experienced anything like the tidal wave of adulation the Monkeys received. And yet, five years ago, these records would have been minority interests, at best. So what gives?

I think the experience of the cab driver is central. The current generation of teenagers are the first to have parents who might themselves have been teenagers at the time of punk. Guitar music, with its roots in punk, is no longer remotely threatening: the Kooks, who for all their carefully nurtured gutter accents and sub-Libertines wastrel image, are self-evidently nice boys making "proper music", as the cabbie put it. Parents and kids alike can enjoy this band, as the reference points are perfectly clear to parents, too. The last time guitar music was able to cross over on this scale was with Britpop, and it's no coincidence the reference points there — the Jam, the Who, the Beatles — were equally intelligible to the parents and the teenagers.

The doors have been opened to a flood of other slightly scruffy, slightly ragged guitar groups, and don't expect the deluge to stop with the year's end. Autumn saw the Fratellis enter the album chart at No 2, a placing no music critic older than 22 could possibly have predicted or expected. They will likely be followed to mainstream success in 2007 by the View, playing similarly aggressive (but, crucially, not violent or threatening) stomping guitar rock. But the more of these bands appear, the more indistinguishable they become. There is very little truly bad new music coming through, but nor is there much in the guitar mainstream that seems in any way inspirational.

The result of the victory of "indie" is that the term has become meaningless, and the music neutered. A music writer friend of mine posits that indie has undergone what happened to metal in the late 80s: where once everything could be bracketed together as a solid mass of non-mainstream "indie" music — no matter that there were different sub-tribes — now it has fractured into "hair indie" (the chart bands), "underground indie", "indie folk" and so on. And the interesting music is being made off in these margins, and usually — as a result of a less well-developed hype machine, meaning artists aren't pushed to prominence too early — in the United States.

So is there an alternative? A music writer is probably the last person to ask. Because the experience of the past couple of years has shown that critics are rather at a loss to call out which bands have the capacity to make the leap to the big leagues. It all comes down to marketing, airplay and exposure. And that's not always (or often) contingent on the quality of the music. UK urban music has been posited as the most inventive form of homegrown music of recent years, and autumn 2006 saw a spate of dubstep albums winning critical acclaim, but few sales outside selected postal districts of east London.

There is, however, one area where the generation gap is alive and kicking, and where the sense of "outsiderdom" has been converted into record sales: emo. No one really knows what it is — in the late 1980s it meant shouty punk bands from Washington DC slowing the music down and singing about their feelings; now it seems to mean any group of pale youths with smeared mascara playing punky pop. But the Daily Mail has been terrified by it, other bands have slated it, and its prime movers, My Chemical Romance, were showered with bottles at the Reading Festival. But, oh, the records sold, and the gigs were packed, and the parents were puzzled.

The irony is that the crucial influences on My Chemical Romance — whose current album is expected to sell 10 million worldwide, and who will sell out UK arenas in the spring — are anything but threatening to the parents of the people who buy their records. Stand up, please, for Queen, whose pomposity and silliness is also at the heart of Muse, who will make the leap to filling stadiums in 2007. Whoever thought Fat-Bottomed Girls would hold such cultural resonance?

● Michael Hann is the Guardian's film and music editor

Music contacts

Record labels

679 Recordings
020 7284 5780
www.679recordings.com

Ace Records
020 8453 1311
www.acerecords.co.uk

Additive Records
020 7605 5000
www.additiverecords.com
Owner: EMI Group
Press: 020 7324 6155

All Around the World
01254 264120
info@aatw.com
www.aatw.com

Aqwa Records
020 8519 4463
www.aqwa.com

Arista Records
020 7384 7500
www.arista.com
Owner: Sony BMG

Asylum Records
020 7761 6000
www.asylumrecords.com
Owner: Warner Music Group

Atlantic Records Group
020 7938 5500
www.atlanticrecords.com
Owner: Warner Music Group
Press: 020 7938 5566

At Large
020 7605 5000
Owner: EMI Group
Press: 020 7605 5317

Audiorec
020 8204 5000
info@audiorec.co.uk
www.audiorec.co.uk

B Unique Records
Info@b-uniquerecords.com
www.b-uniquerecords.com

Bad Boy
020 7938 5500
www.badboyonline.com
Owner: Warner Music Group

Baroque Records
024 7636 1001
info@baroquerecords.co.uk
www.baroquerecords.co.uk

Beggars Group
020 8870 9912
beggars@beggars.com
www.beggars.com

Benbecula Records
2006@benbecula.com
www.benbecula.com

BMG Classics
020 7384 7500
www.bmgclassics.com
Owner: Sony BMG

Chandos Records
01206 225200
enquiries@chandos.net
www.chandos.net

Chemikal Underground
0141 550 1919
www.chemikal.co.uk

Cherry Red
020 8740 4110
infonet@cherryred.co.uk
www.cherryred.co.uk

Columbia Records
020 7384 7500
www.columbiarecords.com
Owner: Sony BMG

Cooking Vinyl
020 8600 9200
info@cookingvinyl.com
www.cookingvinyl.com

Definite Records
01362 687956
Info@definiterecords.net
www.definiterecords.net

Detour Records
01730 815422
detour@btinternet.com
www.detour-records.co.uk

Domino
020 8875 1390
enquiries@dominorecordco.com
www.dominorecordco.com

Dorado Records
020 7287 1689
contact@dorado.net
www.dorado.co.uk

Earache
020 7240 5002
talita@earache.com
www.earache.com

Echo
020 7229 1616
info@echo.co.uk
www.echo.co.uk

Elektra
020 7938 5500
www.atlanticrecords.com
Owner: Warner Music Group
Press: 020 7938 5566

EMI Records UK
020 7605 5000
www.emirecords.co.uk
Owner: EMI Group
Press: 020 7605 5317

Epic Records
020 7384 7500
www.epicrecords.com
Owner: Sony BMG

FatCat Records
01273 747433
info@fat-cat.co.uk
www.fat-cat.co.uk

Fierce Panda
ellie@fiercepanda.co.uk
www.fiercepanda.co.uk

Flying Rhino Records
020 8969 6555
info@flying-rhino.co.uk
www.flying-rhino.co.uk

Forever Heavenly
020 7494 2998
www.heavenly100.com
Press: 020 7833 9303

Geffen Records
020 7471 5400
www.geffen.com
Owner: Universal Music Group

Gorgeous Music
020 7724 2635
davix@gorgeousmusic.net
www.gorgeousmusic.net

Gut
020 7266 0777
www.gutrecords.com

Heavenly Records
020 7494 2998
www.heavenly100.com
Owner: EMI Group
Press: 020 7833 9303

Hyperion Records
020 8318 1234
info@hyperion-records.co.uk
www.hyperion-records.co.uk

Independiente
020 8747 8111
www.independiente.co.uk

Interscope Geffen A&M
020 7471 5400
www.interscope.com
Owner: Universal Music Group

Def Jam Music
020 7471 5333
www.islanddefjam.com
Owner: Universal Music Group

J Records
020 7384 7500
www.jrecords.com
Owner: Sony BMG

Jeepster
0845 126 0621
info@jeepster.co.uk
www.jeepster.co.uk

Jive Records
020 7384 7500
www.jiverecords.com
Owner: Sony BMG

LaFace Records
020 7384 7500
www.laface.com
Owner: Sony BMG

Lava Records
020 7938 5500
www.lavarecords.com
Owner: Warner Music Group
Press: 020 7938 5566

Legacy Recordings
020 7384 7500
www.legacyrecordings.com
Owner: Sony BMG

Locoz Records
01622 890611
mail@locozrecords.com
www.locozrecords.com

Lost Highway Records
020 7471 5333
www.losthighwayrecords.com
Owner: Universal Music Group

Matador Records
020 8969 5533
mike@nospam_matadorrecords.com
www.matadorrecords.com

Maverick Records
020 7761 6000
www.maverick.com
Owner: Warner Music Group

MCA
020 7471 5300
www.umgnashville.com
Owner: Universal Music Group

Mercury
020 7471 5333
www.umgnashville.com
Owner: Universal Music Group

Mi5 Recordings UK
0161 975 6226
info@mi5recordings.co.uk
www.mi5recordings.co.uk

Mighty Atom Productions
01792 367992
dave@mightyatom.co.uk
www.mightyatom.co.uk

Ministry of Sound
0870 060 0010
arnie@ministryofsound.com
www.ministryofsound.com

Motown Records
020 7471 5300
www.motown.com
Owner: Universal Music Group

Mute Records
020 8964 2001
info@mutehq.co.uk
www.mute.com
Owner: EMI Group

Nil By Mouth Records
0121 689 0370
info@nil-by-mouth.com
www.nil-by-mouth.com

Nonesuch Records
020 7761 6003
info@nonesuch.com
www.nonesuch.com
Owner: Warner Music Group

One Little Indian
020 8772 7600
info@indian.co.uk
www.indian.co.uk

Opera Rara
020 7613 2858
info@opera-rara.com
www.opera-rara.com

Parlophone
020 7605 5000
www.parlophone.co.uk
Owner: EMI Group
Press: 020 7605 5437

Polydor
020 7471 5400
www.polydor.co.uk
Owner: Universal Music Group

Positiva
020 7605 5157
www.positivarecords.com
Owner: EMI Group
Press: 020 7324 6155

Provident Music Group
01323 431574
www.providentmusic.com
Owner: Sony BMG

RCA Records
020 7384 7500
www.rcarecords.com
Owner: Sony BMG

Real World
020 7605 5000
www.realworld.on.net
Owner: EMI Group
Press: 020 7605 5895

Reprise Records
020 7761 6000
www.repriserec.com
Owner: Warner Music Group

Riverrun Records
01767 651146
riverrun@rvrcd.co.uk
www.rvrcd.co.uk

Rough Trade Records
020 8960 9888
glen@roughtraderecords.com
www.roughtraderecords.com

Rubicon Records
0181 450 5154
rubiconrecords@btopenworld.com
www.rubiconrecords.co.uk

Sanctuary Classics
020 7300 1888
info@sanctuaryclassics.com
www.sanctuaryclassics.com

Sanctuary Music Group
020 7602 6351
www.sanctuaryrecords.co.uk

Seriously Groovy
020 7439 1947
info@seriouslygroovy.com
www.seriouslygroovy.com

Sire Records
020 7761 6000
www.sirerecords.com
Owner: Warner Music Group

Skint Records
mail@skint.net
www.skint.net

So So Def Records
020 7384 7500
www.soso-def.com
Owner: Sony BMG

Solarise Records
07980 453628
info@solariserecords.com
www.solariserecords.com

Sony Classical
020 7384 7500
www.sonyclassical.com
Owner: Sony BMG

Sony Wonder
www.sonywonder.com

Thirdwave Records
info@thirdwavemusic.com
www.thirdwavemusic.com

Topic Records
020 7263 1240
tony.engle@topicrecords.co.uk
www.topicrecords.co.uk

Universal Classics
020 7471 5000
www.iclassics.com
Owner: Universal Music Group

Universal Records
020 7471 5000
www.universalrecords.com
Owner: Universal Music Group

V2
020 7471 3000
www.v2music.com

Verity Records
020 7384 7500
www.verityrecords.com
Owner: Sony BMG

Verve Music Group
020 7471 5000
publicity@vervemusicgroup.com
www.vervemusicgroup.com
Owner: Universal Music Group

Virgin Records UK
020 8964 6000
www.the-raft.com
Owner: EMI Group
Press: 020 8964 6241

Visible Noise
020 7792 9791
julie@visiblenoise.com
www.visiblenoise.com
Press: matt@bluelight.co.uk

Wall of Sound
general@wallofsound.uk.com
www.wallofsound.net

Warner Bros Records
020 7761 6000
www.wbr.com
Owner: Warner Music Group

Warner Jazz
020 7368 2500
www.warnerjazz.co.uk
Owner: Warner Music Group
Press: 020 7368 2542

Warner Music International
020 7368 2500
www.wmg.com
Owner: Warner Music Group

Zomba
020 7384 7500

Music publishers

Big Life
020 7554 2100
reception@biglifemanagement.com
www.biglifemanagement.com

BMG Music Publishing
020 7835 5200
intl.coregeneral@bmg.com
www.bmgmusicsearch.com

Bucks Music
020 7221 4275
info@bucksmusicgroup.co.uk
www.bucksmusicgroup.com

Carlin Music
020 7734 3251
www.carlinmusic.com

Chrysalis Music Publishing
020 7221 2213
info@chrysalismusic.co.uk
www.chrysalismusic.co.uk

EMI Music Publishing
020 7434 2131
www.emimusicpub.com

Independent Music Group
020 8523 9000
erich@independentmusicgroup.com
www.independentmusicgroup.com

Kobalt Music Group
020 7401 5500
info@kobaltmusic.com
www.kobaltmusic.com

Memory Lane Music Group
020 8523 8888
www.memorylanemusicgroup.com

Notting Hill
020 7243 2921
info@nottinghillmusic.com
www.nottinghillmusic.com

Sanctuary Music Publishing
020 7602 6351
info@sanctuarygroup.com
www.sanctuarygroup.com

Sony Music Publishing
020 7911 8200
www.sonymusic.co.uk

Universal Music Publishing
020 8752 2600
ukpublishing@umusic.com
www.universalmusicpublishing.com

Warner Chappell UK
020 8563 5800
www.warnerchappell.co.uk

Sheet music publishers

Associated Board of the Royal Schools of Music Publishing
020 7636 5400
publishing@abrsm.ac.uk
www.abrsmpublishing.com

Boosey & Hawkes Music Publishers
020 7054 7200
marketing.uk@boosey.com
www.boosey.com

Brass Wind Publications
01572 737409
info@brasswindpublications.co.uk
www.brasswindpublications.co.uk

Breitkopf & Härtel
01263 768732
www.breitkopf.com

Faber Music
020 7833 7900
information@fabermusic.com
www.fabermusic.com

Music Sales
020 7434 0066
music@musicsales.co.uk
www.musicsales.com

Oxford University Press
01865 353349
music.enquiry.uk@oup.com
www.oup.co.uk

Peters Edition
020 7553 4000
www.editionpeters.com

Stainer & Bell
020 8343 3303
post@stainer.co.uk
www.stainer.co.uk

United Music Publishers
01992 703110
ranger@ump.co.uk
www.ump.co.uk

Universal Edition
020 7439 6678
uelondon@universaledition.com
www.universaledition.com

Production music companies

AKM Music
01926 864068
akm@akmmusic.co.uk
www.akmmusic.co.uk

Amphonic Music
0800 525132
www.amphonic.com

Audio Network
01787 477277
office@audiolicense.net
www.audiolicense.net

Burning Petals
0870 749 1117
enquiries@burning-petals.com
www.burning-petals.co.uk

Extreme Music
020 7485 0111
www.extrememusic.com

KPM Music
020 7412 9111
kpm@kpm.co.uk
www.playkpm.com

Mediatracks
01254 691197
info@mediatracks.co.uk
www.mediatracks.co.uk

Music House
020 7412 9111
enquiries@musichouse.co.uk
www.musichouse.co.uk

Primrose Music
020 8946 7808
www.primrosemusic.com

West One Music
020 7292 0000
info@westonemusic.com
www.westonemusic.com

Digital distributors

Amazon
020 8636 9200
www.amazon.co.uk
Free downloadable tracks from high-profile artists
Press: 020 8636 9280

Artist Direct
www.artistdirect.com
Free downloadable tracks from high-profile artists

Connect
00 1 212 833 8000
service@connect-europe.com
www.connect-europe.com
Sony site, with music from all major labels and many indies
Press: 01932 816417

eMusic
00 1 212 201 9240
www.emusic.com
Subscription-based service
Press: 00 1 212 561 7454
pr@emusic.com

Epitonic
00 1 212 320 3624
www.epitonic.com

Insound
00 1 212 777 8056
www.insound.com/mp3
Free indie MP3s

Intomusic.co.uk
020 8676 4850
info@intomusic.co.uk
www.intomusic.co.uk
Independent and alternative music

iTunes UK
0800 039 1010
www.apple.com/uk/itunes
Apple's digital jukebox and music store
Press: appleuk.pr@euro.apple.com

Mperia.com
00 1 650 388 3000
www.mperia.com
Press: pr@bitpass.com

Napster
www.napster.co.uk
Subscription service
Press: media@napster.co.uk

OD2/Loudeye
0117 910 0150
info@ondemanddistribution.com
www.ondemanddistribution.com
*Handles distribution for Big Noise Music,
Freeserve Music Club, MSN UK, MTV UK.
MyCokeMusic.com and Tiscali Music Club*

Playlouder
site@playlouder.com
www.playlouder.com
UK music site
Press: media@playlouder.com

Ricall
020 7592 1710
www.ricall.com
*Music research and licencing network for
professional buyers and sellers of music*

Streets Online
0845 601 8330
digital@streetsonline.co.uk
www.streetsonline.co.uk
Owned by Woolworths

Trax2Burn
01202 315333
www.trax2burn.com
*Three house music labels: End Recordings,
Underwater and Southern Fried*

Vitaminic.com
00 1 415 781 7670
info@vitaminic.com
www.vitaminic.com
Pan-European site

Wippit
0870 737 1100
info@wippit.com
www.wippit.com
Specialises in independent label artists

Recording studios

**Association of Professional
Recording Services (APRS)**
PO Box 22, Totnes TQ9 7YZ
01803 868600
info@aprs.co.uk
www.aprs.co.uk

MEMBERS OF APRS

Abbey Road Studios
3 Abbey Road, London NW8 9AY
020 7266 7000
info@abbeyroad.com
www.abbeyroad.com
Studio manager: Colette Barber

Air Edel Studios
18 Rodmarton Street,
London W1U 8BJ
020 7486 6466
trevorbest@air-edel.co.uk
www.air-edel.co.uk
Studio manager: Trevor Best

Air Studios
Lyndhurst Hall, Lyndhurst Road,
London NW3 5NG
020 7794 0660
information@airstudios.com
www.airstudios.com
Contact: Alison Burton

British Grove Studios
20 British Grove, Chiswick,
London W4 2NL
020 8741 8941
davidstewart@
britishgrovestudios.com
www.britishgrovestudios.com
Studio manager: David Stewart

Classic Sound
5 Falcon Park, Neasden Lane,
London NW10 1RZ
020 8208 8100
classicsound@dial.pipex.com
www.classicsound.net
Director: Neil Hutchinson

The Dairy
43–45 Tunstall Road,
London SW9 8BZ
020 7738 7777
info@thedairy.co.uk
www.thedairy.co.uk
Studio manager: Emily Taylor

Eden Studios
20–24 Beaumont Road,
London W4 5AP
020 8995 5432
eden@edenstudios.com
www.edenstudios.com
Studio manager: Natalie Horton

ICC Studios
4 Regency Mews, Silverdale Road,
Eastbourne, Sussex BN20 7AB
01323 643341/2
info@iccstudios.co.uk
www.iccstudios.co.uk
Technical director: Helmut Kaufman

ICE PR
Unit 5, Acklam Workshops,
10 Acklam Road, London W10 5QZ
020 8968 2222
info@ice-pr.com
www.ice-pr.com
MD: Jason Price

Iguana Studio
Unit 1, 88a Acre Lane,
London SW2 5QN
020 7924 0496
info@iguanastudio.co.uk
www.iguanastudio.co.uk
Director: Andrea Terrano

Jacobs Studio
Ridgeway House, Dippenhall,
Nr Farnham, Surrey GU10 5EE
01252 715546
andy@jacobs-studios.co.uk
www.jacobs-studios.co.uk
MD: Andy Fernbach

Keynote Studios
Green Lane, Burghfield Bridge,
Burghfield, Reading RG30 3XN
01189 599944
keynotestudios@btconnect.co.uk
www.keynotestudios.co.uk
Owner and partner: Noel Newton

Konk Recording Studio
84–86 Tottenham Lane,
London N8 7EE
020 8340 7873
linda@konkstudios.com
Station manager: Sarah Lockwood

Lansdowne Recording Studios
Lansdowne House, Lansdowne Road,
London W11 3LP
020 7727 0041
info@cts-lansdowne.co.uk
www.cts-lansdowne.co.uk
Client liaison: Jo Buckley

Metropolis
The Powerhouse, 70 Chiswick High
Road, London W4 1SY
020 8742 1111
studios@metropolis-group.co.uk
www.metropolis-group.co.uk
Station manager: Alison Hussey

Parr Street Studios
33–45 Parr Street, Liverpool L1 4JN
0151 707 1050
info@parrstreet.co.uk
www.parrstreet.co.uk

Phoenix Sound
Pinewood Studios, Pinewood Road,
Iver Heath, Buckinghamshire SL0 0NH
01753 785495
info@phoenixsound.net
www.phoenixsound.net
Contact: Peter Fielder

RAK Recording Studios
42–48 Charlbert Street,
St John's Wood, London NW8 7BU
020 7586 2012
trisha@rakstudios.co.uk
www.rakstudios.co.uk
Station manager: Trisha Wegg

Real World Studios
Box Mill, Mill Lane, Box, Corsham,
Wiltshire SN13 8PL
01225 743188
studios@realworld.co.uk
www.realworld.on.net
Station manager: Owen Leech

Rockfield Studios
Amberley Court, Rockfield Road,
Monmouth NP25 5ST
01600 712449
lisaward@rockfieldstudios.com
www.rockfieldstudios.com
Director: Kingsley Ward

Roundhouse Recording Studios
91 Saffron Hill, London EC1N 8PT
020 7404 3333
roundhouse@stardiamond.com
www.stardiamond.com/roundhouse
Contact: Lisa Gunther

Sain
Llandwrog, Caernarfon,
Gwynedd LL54 5TG
01286 831111
eryl@sainwales.com
www.sainwales.com
Station manager: Eryl Davies

Sanctuary Studios
150 Goldhawk Road,
London W12 8HH
020 8932 3200
julie.bateman@sanctuarygroup.com
www.sanctuarygroup.com
Head of audio studios: Julie Bateman

Sawmills Studio
Golant, Fowey, Cornwall PL23 1LW
01726 833338
ruth@sawmills.co.uk
www.sawmills.co.uk
Station manager: Ruth Taylor

Soho Recording Studios
Basement, The Heals Building, 22-24
Torrington Place, London WC1E 7HJ
020 7419 2444
dominic@sohostudios.co.uk
www.sohostudios.co.uk
Manager: Dominic Sanders

Sound Recording Technology
Edison Road, St Ives,
Cambridgeshire PE27 3LF
London: 020 8446 3218
Cambridge: 01480 461880
srt@btinternet.com
www.soundrecordingtechnology.co.uk
MD: Sarah Pownall

Sphere Studios
2 Shuttleworth Road, Battersea,
London SW11 3EA
020 7326 9450
inform@spherestudios.com
www.spherestudios.com
MD: Malcolm Atkin

Strongroom Studios
120 124 Curtain Road,
London EC2A 3SQ
020 7426 5100
mix@strongroom.co.uk
www.strongroom.co.uk
MD: Richard Boote

Whites Farm Studios
Whites Farm, Wilton Lane, Kenyon
Culcheth WA3 4BA
0161 790 4830
whitesfarmstudios@aol.com
www.whitesfarmstudios.com
Manager: Gary White

Promoters

Barfly
49 Chalk Farm Road,
London NW1 8AN
020 7691 4244
london.info@barflyclub.com
www.barflyclub.com
*Clubs based in Camden London, West
End London, Birmingham, Cardiff,
Liverpool, Glasgow and York*

Club Fandango
2 St Pauls Crescent,
London NW1 9XS
everyone@clubfandango.co.uk
www.clubfandango.co.uk
*Venues in London, Brighton, Bristol,
Manchester and Glasgow. London venues
include Dublin Castle, Metro, The
Borderline (with BMI) & the Bull & Gate*

Mean Fiddler Music Group
Head office, 16 High Street,
Harlesden, London NW10 4LX
020 8961 5490
www.meanfiddler.com
*Astoria, Jazz Cafe, Borderline, The
Garage and Glastonbury festival*

» Music venues
see page 436

Events

All Tomorrow's Parties
020 7733 8009
ken@hermana.co.uk
www.atpfestival.com
*Three-day festival held over two
consecutive weekends*

Bampton Classical Opera
Holcot House, Market Square,
Bampton, Oxfordshire OX18 2JJ
mail@bamptonopera.org
http://bamptonopera.org
Lively and accessible opera productions

BBC Proms
020 7589 8212
proms@bbc.co.uk
www.bbc.co.uk/proms
Press: 020 7765 5575

Belladrum Tartan Heart
Phoineas House, Belladrum Estate,
By Beauly, Inverness-shire IV4 7BA,
Scotland
01463 741366
info@tartanheartfestival.co.uk
www.tartanheartfestival.co.uk

Benicassim
http://fiberfib.com/en/festival
/the-festival
*Indie, electronica and pop festival on the
beach*

Bestival
Get Involved Ltd, Unit B,
Park House, 206-208 Latimer Road,
London W10 6QY
020 8962 8040
clare@getinvolvedltd.com
www.bestival.net
"Boutique" 3-day festival

Big Chill
Chillfest ltd, PO Box 52707,
London EC2P 2WE
info@bigchill.net
www.bigchill.net
Dance music

Cambridge Folk Festival
The Cambridge Corn Exchange,
3 Parsons Court, Wheeler Street,
Cambridge CB2 3QE
01223 457555
folkfest@cambridge.gov.uk
www.cambridgefolkfestival.co.uk

Camden Crawl
www.thecamdencrawl.com
The London version of SXSW

Carling Weekend (Reading, Leeds)
Mean Fiddler, 16 High Street,
Harlseden, London NW10 4LX
020 8961 5490
www.meanfiddler.com

Creamfields
Cream Group, Nation, Wolstenholme
Square, 1-3 Parr Street, Dursebury,
Holton
0151 707 1309
info@cream.co.uk
www.cream.co.uk/creamfields

D:percussion
www.dpercussion.com
Manchester's free music festival

Deeply Vale
www.deeplyvale.com
*Plans for a revival of the original 1970s
festival to take place in 2007*

Dot to Dot Festival
www.dottodotfestival.co.uk
Nottingham city based festival

Download
www.downloadfestival.co.uk

Foundation
kellie@resource-pr.com
www.foundationfestival.co.uk
Varied line-up, 6 stages and circus acts

Get Loaded
020 7247 4121
stix@turnmills.co.uk
www.get-loaded.co.uk
Touring indie/dance crossover festival

Give it a Name
info@giveitaname.co.uk
www.giveitaname.co.uk

Glade
sarah@leylinepromotions.com
www.gladefestival.com
Electronic dance music

Glastonbury Festival
28 Northload Street,
Glastonbury, Somerset BA6 9JJ
01458 834 596
office@glastonburyfestivals.co.uk
www.glastonburyfestivals.co.uk

Global Gathering
www.globalgathering.co.uk
Dance music

Glyndebourne Festival
Glyndebourne Productions,
Glyndebourne, Lewes
01273 812321
info@glyndebourne.com
www.glyndebourne.com

Gosforth Gathering
0191 227 4320
info@tentrock.com
www.gosforthgathering.com
Two-day festival in Newcastle

Great Escape
www.escapegreat.com
Brighton venues

Green Man Festival
020 7733 8009
info@thegreenmanfestival.co.uk
www.thegreenmanfestival.co.uk
Folk and folktronica
Press: ken@hermana.co.uk

Guilfest
54 Haydon Place, Guildford,
Surrey GU1 4NE
info@guilfest.co.uk
www.guilfest.co.uk
Family-friendly festival

HI:FI
info@hififestival.com
www.hififestival.com
Aiming to bridge the gap between dance and rock music

Homelands Festival
Mean Fiddler, 16 High Street,
Harlseden, London NW10 4LX
020 8961 5490
www.welovehomelands.com

Hyde Park Calling
access@getlive.co.uk
www.hydeparkcalling.co.uk
Two-day festival in Hyde Park

In The City
8 Brewery Yard, Deva Centre,
Trinity Way, Salford M3 7BB
0161 839 3930
www.inthecity2006.com/2006
Manchester showcase for new talent

Isle of Wight Festival
info@isleofwightfestival.org
www.isleofwightfestival.org

Latitude
020 7792 9400
0121 224 7453
charlie@presscounsel.com
margaret@fmguk.com
www.latitudefestival.co.uk/home
Music festival with poetry, comedy, film, theatre, books
Press: Press Counsel, 5-7 Vernon Yard, off Portobello Road, London W11 2DX

Lode Star Festival
The Guildhall, Lode,
Cambridge CB5 9HB
020 7222 1173
01993 851876
info@lodestarfestival.com
http://lodestarfestival.com
Repesents emerging new talent

London Calling
020 8232 1606
andy.center@ithacamedia.co.uk
www.londoncalling2006.com
International exhibition for artists, managers, labels, service providers, brands

The London Fleadh
Mean Fiddler, 16 High Street,
Harlseden, London NW10 4LX
020 8961 5490
www.meanfiddler.com

Middlesbroughmusiclive
01642 247 755
phil@tenfeettall.co.uk
www.middlesbroughmusiclive.co.uk
City-based festival

O2 Wireless
www.wirelessfestival.co.uk
Free festival in Hyde Park

Rock-Ness
Unit 2, Broomfield Holiday Park,
West Lane, Ullapool IV26 2UT,
Scotland
01463 238660
info@rockness.co.uk
www.rockness.co.uk
Dance music festival on Lock Ness

Summer Sundae
De Montfort Hall, Granville Road,
Leicester LE1 7RU
0116 233 3113
Kate Hendry,
    dmh.office@leicester.gov.uk
www.summersundae.co.uk
Press: 020 7833 9303
    julie@9pr.co.uk

SXSW
Cill Ruan, 7 Ard na Croise, Thurles,
County Tipperary, Ireland
00353 5042 6488
una@sxsw.com
www.sxsw.com
International showcase

Tapestry Goes West
Tapestry, PO Box 45580,
London NW1 9UN
07887 924950
info@tapestrygoeswest.com
www.tapestrygoeswest.com
Indie-folk festival featuring a medieval village and jousting display

TDK Cross Central
Cross Central Events, King's Cross
Freight Depot, York Way,
London N1 0UZ
020 7833 9944
claire@crosscentral.co.uk
www.crosscentral.co.uk

Tin Pan Alley
info@tinpanalleyfestival.co.uk
www.tinpanalleyfestival.co.uk
Takes place on Denmark Street, in association with Shelter

T in the Park
www.tinthepark.com
Press: Liana Mellotte
    0141 204 7970

V Festival
www.vfestival.com
Press: vfestival@cakemedia.com

Womad
Womad Press Department, Millside,
Mill Lane, Box, Wiltshire SN13 8PN
01225 743481
info@womad.org
www.womad.org
World music

Orchestras

BBC National Orchestra of Wales
BBC Wales, Broadcasting House,
Cardiff CF5 2YQ
0800 052 1812
now@bbc.co.uk
www.bbc.co.uk/wales/now

BBC Philharmonic
New Broadcasting House,
Oxford Road, Manchester M60 1SJ
0161 244 4001
philharmonic@bbc.co.uk
www.bbc.co.uk/orchestras
    /philharmonic

BBC Scottish Symphony Orchestra
BBC Scotland, Broadcasting House,
Queen Margaret Drive,
Glasgow G12 8DG
0141 338 2606
bbcsso@bbc.co.uk
www.bbc.co.uk/scotland
    /musicscotland/bbcsso/concerts

English Symphony Orchestra
Rockliffe House, 40 Church Street,
Malvern WR14 2AZ
01386 792623
info@eso.co.uk
www.eso.co.uk

London Philharmonic Orchestra
89 Albert Embankment,
London SE1 7TP
020 7840 4200
admin@lpo.org.uk
www.lpo.co.uk

London Symphony Orchestra
Barbican Centre, Silk Street,
London EC2Y 8DS
020 7588 1116
admin@lso.co.uk
www.lso.co.uk

Royal Philharmonic Orchestra
16 Clerkenwell Green,
London EC1R 0QT
020 7608 8800
info@rpo.co.uk
www.rpo.co.uk

Royal Scottish National Orchestra
73 Claremont Street, Glasgow G3 7JB
0141 226 3868
www.rsno.org.uk

Music schools

Birmingham Conservatoire
Paradise Place, Birmingham B3 3HG
0121 331 5901/5902
conservatoire@uce.ac.uk
www.conservatoire.uce.ac.uk

Leeds College of Music
3 Quarry Hill, Leeds LS2 7PD
0113 222 3400
enquiries@lcm.ac.uk
www.lcm.ac.uk

Royal Academy of Music
Marylebone Road, London NW1 5HT
020 7873 7373
www.ram.ac.uk

Royal College of Music
Prince Consort Road,
London SW7 2BS
020 7589 3643
info@rcm.ac.uk
www.rcm.ac.uk

Royal Northern College of Music
124 Oxford Road,
Manchester M13 9RD
0161 907 5200
info@rncm.ac.uk
www.rncm.ac.uk

Royal Scottish Academy of Music and Drama
100 Renfrew Street, Glasgow G2 3DB
0141 332 4101
www.rsamd.ac.uk

Royal Welsh College of Music and Drama
Castle Grounds, Cathays Park,
Cardiff CF10 3ER
029 2034 2854
music.admissions@rwcmd.ac.uk
www.rwcmd.ac.uk
Press: Press@rwcmd.ac.uk

Trinity College of Music
King Charles Court, Old Royal Naval
College, Greenwich, London SE10 9JF
020 8305 4444
info@tcm.ac.uk
www.tcm.ac.uk

Major record companies

EMI Group
27 Wrights Lane, London W8 5SW
020 7795 7000
www.emigroup.com
Chairman: Eric Nicoli
• *Labels: Additive Records, EMI Records,
Heavenly Records, Mute Records,
Parlophone, Positiva Records, Real
World, Virgin Records UK*
Press: Amanda Conroy
   020 7795 7529

Sony BMG Music Entertainment
550 Madison Ave, New York, NY
10022-3211, USA
00 1 212 833 8000
www.sonybmg.com
CEO: Andrew Lack
• *Labels: Arista, BMG Classics, Columbia,
Epic, J Records, Jive Records, LaFace
Records, Legacy Recordings, Provident
Music Group, RCA Records, Sony
Classical, Sony Music UK, Sony Wonder,
So So Def, Verity*
Press: 00 1 212 833 5047

Sony Music Entertainment (UK)
Bedford House, 69-79 Fulham High
Street, London SW6 3JW
020 7384 7500
www.sonymusic.co.uk
Corporate Press: 020 7384 7500

Universal Music Group
2220 Colorado Avenue, Santa
Monica, CA 90404, USA
00 1 310 865 5000
http://new.umusic.com
Chairman and CEO: Jorgen Larsen
• *Labels: Geffen, Island, Lost Highway,
MCA, Mercury, Motown Records,
Polydor, Universal Classics,
Verve Music Group*

Universal Music International
8 St James's Square,
London SW1Y 4JU
020 7747 4000
Corporate Press, UK: 020 7471 5385
corporate press, international:
   020 7747 4216

Warner Music Group
75 Rockefeller Plaza, New York,
NY 10019, USA
00 1 212 275 2000
www.wmg.com
*Chairman and CEO, Warner Music
Group: Edgar Bronfman Jr; chairman
and CEO, US recorded music, Warner
Music Group: Lyor Cohen; chairman and
CEO, Warner Music International:
Patrick Vien*
• *Labels: Asylum, Atlantic, Bad Boy,
Cordless, East West, Elektra, Lava,
Maverick, Nonesuch, Perfect Game,
Reprise, Rhino, Sire, Warner Bros.
and Word*
Press: mediainquiries@wmg.com

UK office
28 Kensington Church Street,
London W8 4EP
020 7368 2500
www.warnermusic.co.uk
Press: 020 7761 6000

Music TV shows

1 Leicester Square
MTV
Hawley Crescent, London NW1 8TT
020 7284 777
www.mtv.com

The Album Chart Show
3DD Entertainment Limited
190 Camden High Street,
London NW1 8QP
020 7428 1800
http://3ddgroup.com
Executive producer: Andrew Higgie
andrew.higgie@3DDgroup.com

CD:UK
Blaze TV
43-45 Dorset Street,
London W1U 7NA
020 7664 1613
www.zenith-entertainment.co.uk

Guerilla Gig Live
Somethin' Else
Units 1-4, 1a Old Nichol Street,
London E2 7HR
020 7613 3211
info@somethinelse.com
Executive producer: Jez Nelson

Later...With Jools Holland
3DD Entertainment Limited
190 Camden High Street,
London NW1 8QP
020 7428 1800
http://3ddgroup.com
Producers: Mark Cooper, Alison Howe

Pop World
At It Productions
68-70 Salusbury Road,
London NW6 6NU
020 7644 0000
www.atitproductions.com
Producer: Iain Wimbush

Transmission with T Mobile
At It Productions, 60-70 Salusbury
Road, London NW6 6NU
020 7644 0000
www.atitproductions.com
Series producer: Rob Baker

Music websites

● Online magazines and networks

Alternate Music Press
aussie450@lycos.com
www.alternatemusicpress.com
Publication with music archive.
Editor: Ben Kettlewell

CMU music network
chris@unlimitedmedia.co.uk
caro@unlimitedmedia.co.uk
www.cmumusicnetwork.co.uk/default
*Information network linking grassroots
music and mainstream music.*

Cool Hunting
1 917 415 3937
josh@coolhunting.com
www.coolhunting.com/music.php
Music industry intelligence.
Editor-in-chief: Josh Rubin

Drownedinsound
editor@drownedinsound.com
www.drownedinsound.com
New music. Editor: Colin Roberts

fiveeight
020 7837 1347
tim@fruktmusic.com
www.fiveeight.net
*Providing coverage and strategic
insight into the music industry.*
Editor: Eamonn Forde

Fly
020 8749 3255
damian@fly.co.uk
www.fly.co.uk/fly
World music. Editor: Damian Rafferty

Pitchfork Media
ryan@pitchformedia.com
www.pitchforkmedia.com
New music. Associate editor: Ryan Schreiber

Playlouder
site@playlouder.com
www.playlouder.com
*New music. Directors: Jim Gottlieb and
Paul Hitchman*

Popjustice
020 7352 9444
contact@popjustice.com
www.popjustice.com
Internet equivalent to Smash Hits magazine. Founder: Peter Robinson

Popmatters
editor@popmatters.com
http://popmatters.com
Cultural critique. Music editor: Sarah Zupko

Stylus Magazine
todd_burns@stylusmagazine.com
http://stylusmagazine.com
New music. Editor-in-chief: Todd Burns

● Music archives

Classical Archives
1 650 330 8050
www.classicalarchives.com
Archived classical music. Website founder: Pierre Schwob

Classical Source
www.classicalsource.co
Classical music resource site (reviews, directory of links to other sources). Managing director: Chris Caspell

Dimeadozen
www.dimeadozen.org
Audio archive. Downloadable live gigs and demo tracks

Last.fm
www.last.fm
Music discovery/cataloguing project

Pandora
www.pandora.com
Music discovery/cataloguing project. Director of communications: Michelle Husak

Rock'sbackpages
020 7589 2433
www.rocksbackpages.com
Library of rock music journalism from the 1950s onwards. Contact: Tony Keys, tony@rocksbackpages.com

Youtube
http://youtube.com
Video sharing

● Blogs

Fluxblog
perpetua@gmail.com
www.fluxblog.org
Music journalism blog

The Hype Machine
http://hype.non-standard.net
Audio blog (mp3)

Largehearted Boy
http://blog.largeheartedboy.com
Music journalism blog with free downloads

Stereogum
info@stereogum.com
www.stereogum.com
Music journalism blog

Music press

Audience
020 7486 7007
info@audience.uk.com
www.audience.uk.com
Monthly. For live international contemporary music industry. Owner: Audience Media. Managing editor: Stephen Parker; sales manager: Shane Mills

Billboard
020 7420 6000
www.billboard.com
Weekly magazine and daily email. Owner: VNU. Executive Editor: Tamara Conniff; news: Jonathan Cohen; group editorial director: Scott McKenzie

Five Eight
020 7837 1347
eamonn@fiveeight.net
www.fiveeight.net
Monthly magazine and daily email. Editor: Eamonn Forde; head of production: Nick Becker

Gramophone
020 8267 5136
www.gramophone.co.uk
Monthly. Owner: Haymarket. Editor: James Inverne

Kerrang!
020 7182 8000
www.kerrang.com
Weekly. Owner: Emap. Editor: Paul Brannigan

Mojo
020 7436 1515
www.mojo4music.com
Monthly. Owner: Emap. Editor: Phil Alexander

Music Industry News Network
00 1 718 278 0662
editor@mi2n.com
www.mi2n.com
News aggregator. Editor-in-chief: Eric de Fontenay

Music Week
020 7921 8390
martin@musicweek.com
www.musicweek.com
Weekly. Owner: CMP Information. Editor: Martin Talbot; news: Paul Williams; features: Adam Webb; chief sub: Dougal Baird; online editor: Nicola Slade

MusicAlly
020 7490 5444
mail@musically.com
www.musically.com
Fortnightly plus bulletins. Owner: Digital music. Editor: Paul Brindley; features: Toby Lewis

Musician
020 7840 5531
info@musiciansunion.org.uk
www.musiciansunion.org.uk
Quarterly. Editor: Keith Ames

NME
020 7261 5564
www.nme.com
Weekly. Owner: IPC Media. Editor: Conor McNicholas

Q
020 7182 8000
www.q4music.com
Monthly. Owner: Emap. Editor: Paul Rees

Record of the Day
020 8520 2130
info@recordoftheday.com
www.recordoftheday.com
Daily newsletter. Editor: David Balfour; music editor: James Foley

» *More consumer music magazines*
see page 84

Associations

Association of British Orchestras
20 Rupert Street, London W1D 6DF
020 7287 0333
info@abo.org.uk
www.abo.org.uk

Association of Independent Music
Lamb House, Church Street, London W4 2PD
020 8994 5599
www.musicindie.org

Association of Professional Recording Services
PO Box 22, Totnes TQ9 7YZ
01803 868600
info@aprs.co.uk
www.aprs.co.uk

Association of United Recording Artists
2 Berkeley Grove, London NW1 8XY
0870 8505 200
office@aurauk.com
www.aurauk.com

British Academy of Composers and Songwriters
British Music House, 25–27 Berners Street, London W1T 3LR
020 7636 2929
info@britishacademy.com
www.britishacademy.com

British Association of Record Dealers
Colonnade House, 1st Floor, 2 Westover Road, Bournemouth, Dorset BH1 2BY
01202 292063
www.bard.org

British Music Information Centre
1st Floor, Lincoln House, 75 Westminster Bridge Road, London SE1 7HS
020 7928 1902
info@bmic.co.uk
www.bmic.co.uk

British Music Rights
British Music House, 26 Berners
Street, London W1T 3LR
020 7306 4446
britishmusic@bmr.org
www.bmr.org

British Phonographic Industry
Riverside Building, County Hall,
Westminster Bridge Road,
London SE1 7JA
020 7803 1300
research@bpi.co.uk
www.bpi.co.uk

IFPI
54 Regent Street, London W1B 5RE
020 7878 7900
info@ifpi.org
www.ifpi.org
Represents music industry worldwide

Incorporated Society of Musicians
10 Stratford Place, London W1C 1AA
020 7629 4413
membership@ism.org
www.ism.org

Independent Music Companies Association
Rue du Trône 51, 1050 Brussels,
Belgium
00 32 2289 2600
impala@kernnet.com
www.impalasite.org
European indie label association

Mechanical-Copyright Protection Society
Copyright House, 29-33 Berners
Street, London W1T 3AB
020 7580 5544
www.mcps.co.uk

Music Industries Association
Ivy Cottage Offices, Finch's Yard,
Eastwick Road, Great Bookham,
Surrey KT23 4BA
01372 750600
enquiries@mia.org.uk
www.mia.org.uk

Music Publishers Association
6th Floor, British Music House,
26 Berners Street, London W1T 3LR
020 7839 7779
info@mpaonline.org.uk
www.mpaonline.org.uk

Musicians Union
www.musiciansunion.org.uk

Regional offices

London, east and south-east England,
60-62 Clapham Rd, London SW9 0JJ
020 7840 5534
london@musiciansunion.org.uk

Midlands, Benson House, Lombard
Street, Birmingham B12 0QN
0121 622 3870
birmingham@musiciansunion.org.uk

North of England, 40 Canal Street,
Manchester M1 3WD
0161 236 1764
manchester@musiciansunion.org.uk

Scotland and Northern Ireland,
11 Sandyford Place, Glasgow G3 7NB
0141 248 3723
glasgow@musiciansunion.org.uk

Wales and south-west England,
199 Newport Road, Cardiff CF24 1AJ
029 2045 6585
cardiff@musiciansunion.org.uk

Official UK Charts Company
4th Floor, 58/59 Great Marlborough
Street, London W1F 7JY
020 7478 8500
lucy@theofficialcharts.com
www.theofficialcharts.com

Performing Rights Society
Copyright House, 29-33 Berners
Street, London W1T 3AB
020 7580 5544
www.prs.co.uk

Phonographic Performance
UK Performer Services,
PO Box 4398, London W1A 7RU
020 7534 1234
team@ukperformerservices.com
www.ppluk.com

Producers and Composers of Applied Music
01886 884204
bobfromer@onetel.com
www.pcam.co.uk

Media services

Advertising

On the surface of it, the gradual disintegration of old media and fractionalising of audiences seems like bad news for the advertising industry. But leading thinkers say the opposite. Consider the clients – the advertisers – who haven't changed, and are suddenly faced with myriad choices of advertising possibilities and a far more complicated marketing landscape, with no idea how to approach it. Once you might have chosen between a cartel of a dozen national newspapers, two television channels and a couple of radio stations blithely putting up rates every year for declining audiences. These days, the absolute bog standard ad campaign might involve niche TV channels, a portfolio of websites (both bespoke and created with existing brands), direct mail, specialist magazines, mobile advertising, outdoor advertising, oh and maybe a newspaper ad.

Naturally, the pot of money spent on advertising is not rising particularly – it's simply that the number of outlets for it is growing fast. Sectors are suffering. Worse hit is print. Those publications that rely on advertising are feeling it hard and there is no sign that the drift will stop. Projections suggest that advertising spend online will in 2007 overtake advertising spend on newspapers. Wondering why newspapers are suddenly interested in the web? Wonder no more.

As many new business ideas in the media currently seem to be developed on a model of "build it, they will come and then the advertisers will follow", the ad industry is lone among media in having both its income assured and its phones permanently busy. Inevitable, then, that the first "virtual ad agency" opened its doors in autumn 2006.

Total advertising expenditure, by medium

	2005	2004	2003	2002	2001
National newspapers	1919	1974	1902	1930	2062
Regional newspapers	2994	3132	2962	2878	2834
Consumer magazines	827	819	784	785	779
Business & professional magazines	1064	1082	1048	1088	1202
Directories	1131	1075	1029	990	959
Press production costs	653	660	634	643	669
Total press	**8589**	**8742**	**8359**	**8314**	**8504**
Television	4820	4653	4378	4341	4147
Direct mail	2371	2469	2467	2378	2228
Outdoor & transport	1043	986	914	816	788
Radio	579	606	584	547	541
Cinema	188	192	180	180	164
Internet	1366	825	465	197	166
Total	**18956**	**18472**	**17348**	**16772**	**16537**

Note: TV, direct mail, outdoor, radio and cinema data include production costs. Internet excludes production costs.　　Source: adassoc.org.uk

Bartle Bogle Hegarty's stunt, opening the agency within the virtual-reality world Second Life, came as its rival Leo Burnett announced it would create Leo Ideas Hub, a virtual creative department that will use Second Life to bring together its agency creatives around the world.

Actually, the agencies were following their clients in many ways, as Adidas had already opened a virtual store in the 3D world (even Reuters sent in a virtual media correspondent, bless them). A rash of media followed, trying to assess the value of this new economy. In September 2006, there were around 800,000 subscribers to Second Life. In one 24-hour period, the site hosted transactions totalling $347,000. Philip K Dick would be very proud.

● Forecast for the sector

To make sense of all this movement, the industry looked, as always, to Sir Martin Sorrell, the chief executive of the world's second-largest ad firm, WPP. Sir Martin cites the rise of internet advertising and the uncertainty that goes with it to the continuing sluggishness of the UK ad market overall. Growth, he implies, is being held back because of the amount of change that's underway. Internet spend in the UK is significantly higher than in other countries – good for innovation, but bad for old media. At 14%, the UK's percentage of total ad spend on the internet is twice the average of other countries. But as quoted by Sir Martin, "Google said we spend 20% of our time online, so in theory, and I stress in theory, that's where the internet market should go. It shouldn't just be 14%, it should be more than that."

Looking ahead to the global advertising scenario, Sir Martin predicted 2007 would prove similar to this year. "2005 was a good year, 2006 has been a reasonably good year, with 34% growth, 2007 will probably see the same." He admitted although it was too early to make predictions for

Predicting a stable future for advertising, Sir Martin Sorrell

Top 20 UK creative agencies 2005	
Rank/Agency	Ad spend (m)
1 Abbot Mead Vickers	384.4
2 JWT	333.3
3 McCann Erickson Advertising	293.8
4 Publicis	283.7
5 Ogilvy & Mather	266.3
6 M&C Saatchi	263.3
7 DDB London	233.5
8 Saatchi & Saatchi	211.1
9 Euro RSCG London	209.1
10 Rainey Kelly Campbell Roalfe/Y&R	208.8
11 Bartle Bogle Hegarty	208.0
12 Grey Worldwide	189.0
13 Leo Burnett	187.5
14 Lowe	184.1
15 TBWA/London	145.6
16 Clemmow	142.9
17 Mother	140.9
18 WCRS	136.6
19 Delaney Lund Knox Warren & Partners	131.9
20 VCCP	92.7

Source: Nielsen Media Research © Tables cannot be republished without prior written permission from Nielsen Media Research.

Top 20 UK media buying agencies 2005	
Rank/Agency	Ad spend (m)
1 Mediacom	862.36
2 Mindshare	761.59
3 Carat	676.93
4 Starcom UK Group	662.44
5 ZenithOptimedia	550.53
6 OMD UK	472.76
7 Initiative london	400.87
8 Universal McCann London	342.32
9 Manning Gottlieb OMD	252.09
10 PHD	226.45
11 Walker Media	207.74
12 Mediaedge:CIA	181.50
13 Vizeum UK	154.23
14 MediaVest Manchester	114.62
15 Brilliant Media	99.62
16 Media Planning Group	82.92
17 BrandConnection	66.28
18 Mediaedge:CIA Manchester	67.27
19 Booth Locket Makin	65.52
20 Feather Brooksbank	54.46

Source: Nielsen Media Research © Tables cannot be republished without prior written permission from Nielsen Media Research.

Awards

2008, he was expecting growth to be boosted further by spending on the Beijing Olympics and the US presidential elections. "We are getting Beijing spending in advance," he added. "It's not all going to be in 2008."

WPP has the scale to adapt with consumer trends – a point it proved when it announced a deal with the digital video recorder company TiVo in September 2006. TiVo, like Sky Plus, allows viewers to fast-forward through ads and has long been seen as a threat to the advertiser-funded television industry.

WPP's deal, however, allows brands to develop longer ads and video clips that will sit within the TiVo hard drive and can be accessed by consumers via their programme guide. It also has a service called TiVo Interactive Tags that allows viewers to pause their live TV show and click through to TiVo Showcase to view ads and request information, without missing any of the show they were viewing. This innovative solution will clearly require some extremely creative work from agencies. If you're going to expect viewers to actively choose to watch ads, then they'd better be bloody good.

Elsewhere, Ofcom relaxed the rules governing sponsorship, to allow brands to sponsor channels for the first time. This followed the relaxing of product placement rules at the end of 2005 and signals yet another approach to keeping the money flowing as the viewers' attention span grows ever more similar to that of a distracted gnat.

Some analysts described a "perfect storm" set of conditions hastening the drive from traditional media to the internet, with ITV's loss of form causing a crisis of faith across the industry. City analysts and media buyers do have a talent for melodrama.

● Creative performance

In all this doom and desperation where were the big ads of 2006? Well, they were on telly, same as always. Sony's Paint ad featured 70,000 litres of paint exploding on a disused council block in Glasgow. Created by the agency Fallon, the ad was a follow-up to Balls (250,000 coloured balls in the streets of San Francisco) and required 1,700 detonators, 455 mortars, 622 bottle bombs, 65 camera positions and a crew of 200 people. ("The most expensive, most hyped, but also most genuinely anticipated commercial of the year", said MediaGuardian's advertising columnist, Naresh Ramchandani.) Balls, ostensibly for the Bravia television, but really a brand ad for Sony, controversially failed to pick up the Cannes Lion, though it won the Grand Prix at the Shark Awards. Paint, presumably, will not suffer such indignities.

"It's beautiful rather than funny. It's intelligently surreal rather than brain-numbingly literal. It's gloriously depopulated rather than strewn with people you're meant to look like or identify with. And it's a proper modern media property, not just an ad: first a rumour, then a tease clip sent out on email, then an ad, a site, an online game and a downloadable documentary of the making of," enthused Ramchandani. It also cost an estimated £2m, including a hefty fee for the director, Jonathan Glazer. Want to get viewers to actively chase your ad? This is probably the way.

While advertising delights in the big spectacle, we the consumers also love a good scandal. Or, at least, the media loves a misfire: an ad that outrages and threatens the moral fibre of the nation. Whether it's nipples, language or annoying frogs that shock us, it reveals plenty (none of it good) about the state of the nation.

In 2006, perhaps the biggest outrage was an ad from Ogilvy & Mather for the male suicide charity Calm. Charity ads are frequently misbehavers. They have to be, really, because their budgets are teeny tiny and they can't afford to explode a council block or buy 70 seconds of Coronation Street ad break. Agencies generally work for free, producing "controversial" work, hoping for unconventional exposure. So it's often the case that a single poster is unveiled in central London and the campaign relies on the newspapers to reprint it for free under the headline "shocking ad shocks people".

The Calm ad, though, really hit a nerve. The poster showed the bus blown up on the July 7 London bombings and compared the four suicide bombers to the 983 other male suicide victims that year who had not made the news. The ad was, unusually, pulled before it even launched. Thereby, the cynical might suggest, saving the purchase of even one outdoor poster site.

Less cutting-edge, perhaps, the BBC kindly unveiled a new set of "circle" themed idents for BBC1, produced by Red Bee Media and costing £1.2m. The arrival of a new set of idents prompted a row over whether our national broadcaster should be wasting licence money on such trivial matters as on-screen identity. A battle that is being fought largely within the pages of the Sun and the Daily Mail. This is a much simpler controversy, though unresolvable. Either you think that in these competitive times, brand identity is of paramount importance and £1.2m is a drop in the proverbial. Or it's a load of old balls. Don't worry if you haven't formed an opinion yet, this story will be back in three years when the BBC decides on a new set.

In taste and decency news, the Advertising Standards Authority (ASA) ruled that nudity in an ad for shower gel (Cussons Original Source) was out, because the woman in question appeared to be under 16. She wasn't, but the ad was banned anyway. Appears under 16? Good lord, Joan Collins can look under 16 in a good light these days.

In the same dispatch, the ASA also criticised an ad for Bishops Finger Kentish Ale featuring a woman in medieval costume (when medieval costumes where designed by Agent Provocateur) saying, "I love a good session on the Bishops Finger". This was inoffensive to both men and women, apparently, but it did encourage excessive drinking. If only to forget.

ASA rulings

Banned

- **November 2006** Flora was told it had made misleading health claims in an advertisement that implied corn on the cob was made "healthier" when spread with its margarine which contains Omega 3 and 6 oils. The ASA instructed Unilever, the company behind Flora, not to repeat the claim, which "misleadingly implied that adding additional fat to a plain vegetable was better for health than eating the vegetable on its own".

- **July 2006** Carphone Warehouse was banned from repeating misleading advertisements claiming that the broadband provided by its TalkTalk service was "free forever". After receiving 145 objections from both consumers and competitors, the ASA said broadband was an inclusive part of the package and could not therefore be referred to as "free". In addition, the claim that it could provide a service "forever" was found to be unsubstantiated.

- **February 2006** The ASA ordered that an advert from the online gambling company thepool.com be withdrawn. The advert showed scantily clad women and the words "Why wait 'til 18? Bet at 16." Despite 16 being the legal age for pool gambling, it was deemed to be targeting children and therefore said to be "socially irresponsible".

- **January 2006** Young & Co's Brewery plc ran two advertisements, one depicting a man with a Ram's head surrounded by women in bikinis, and the other with the same character apparently entertaining a group of well-dressed men. Both sported the phrase "This is a Ram's World."
    The complainant argued that both suggested drinking Young's beer would lead to social success and sexual attractiveness. Young's pointed out that the image of the "ram" had been the symbol of the brewery for more than 150 years, and said the ads did not intend to single out men as their target audience. The complaint was upheld.

- **December 2005** A total of 28 advertisements from British Gas were found to be in breach of ASA regulations. They were adjudged to be misleading, untruthful and inaccurate. For example, the campaign to publicise a Price Protection scheme for "no more price rises until 2010" failed to make clear that it was also announcing a rise in the standard rate by 14.2% that very day. They also falsely claimed that it was cheaper than its rivals. However, the rulings had little impact since they came after the campaigns had run their course.

Allowed

- **December 2006** Channel Five's biggest marketing campaign to date for its Five US digital service triggered nearly 100 complaints including some from US citizens. The poster campaign, with its "Nothing good ever came out of America" strapline, attracted negative public reaction from day one. However the posters were part of a two-stage campaign: the second phase of the campaign — in which the posters revealed the initial statement wrong — quickly replaced the first. The ASA ruled the campaign did not breach its rules.

- **July 2006** The Gay Police Association ran an advertisement suggesting that Christians were the main perpetrators of homophobic hate crime. The advert, placed in the Independent newspaper, was headlined "In the name of the father", and was accompanied by a photograph of a Bible next to a pool of blood. Several Christian groups complained that it implied Christianity was responsible for and, worse, condoned violence against homosexuals. While the ASA appreciated that the imagery might cause concern to some, they considered that supporting text clarified the context of the picture and headline.

- **September 2005** The marketers of a ringtone, screensaver and video for mobile phones called Crazy Frog attracted a high level of complaints. The main crux of complaints related to the computer-generated frog's genitals. The ASA did not find the advert inappropriate because the commercial encouraged viewers to order the ringtone via text, which meant an ex-kids restriction (keeping it away from children's programming) was already in place. The advertisement was not found to be offensive because the ASA did not consider the frog to have any sexual nuances.

The superstar ads of 2006

Naresh Ramchandani

Back in the balmy, globally warmed autumn of 2006, I had two very different conversations with two marketing big brains about the general electability of Gordon Brown and David Cameron. One of the big brains gave Brown a chance because, like many hugely successful brands, he actually stands for something: in Brown's case, economic substance.

The other took the view that Cameron would romp it because, like many other successful brands, he's running a more exciting model of perpetual skin-shedding where what he stands for simply equals the last five things he says or does.

Both compelling theories and in a small way, reflective of a transitional year where different and sometimes contradictory approaches to communication sat side by side waiting for new communication idioms to become clearer.

In the world of television and cinema, there were some very good commercials that did what very good commercials do. XFM gave us a deft slice of an alternative music world with its delightfully silly kid roadies commercial. Müller gave us an infectious shot of mainstream vitality with its delightfully watchable and beautifully shot dancers ad.

But in a year where ITV crumbled before it made the Grade and the potency of TV advertising was questioned once again, there rose a new breed of supercommercial to fight the dwindling power. These supercommercials, such as Coca-Cola's vending machine ad and Sony's Paint commercial, were "super-produced" pieces of "super-entertainment" that aped a Hollywood blockbuster model with pre-release snippets, making-of documentary downloads and wallpaper images; that rewarded repeated downloadable viewing because of their remarkably rich content; that made standard commercials look ordinary by being commercials that people actively found rather than waited to watch.

Indeed, net-surfing time overtook telly-watching time and Google took more ad revenue than Channel 4. Advertisers were keen to harness the pull and the pound of the net but had difficulty marrying the top-down created-here nature of advertising messages with the bottom-up co-created nature of online stars such as YouTube and MySpace.

AOL's clever Discuss campaign about the nature of the net appeared to open the door to philosophical conversation but its site seemed to host sanitised discussion rather than genuine debate. SanDisk's clever anti iPod campaign for their Sansa e200 linked more genuinely to real reviews and anti-iPod bile (including a link to a fantastically cheap spoof of the epic Apple 1984 commercial where all the drones wear white-wire headphones and the hero athlete looks like he's trained on hamburgers) but like the spoof Conservatives Tosser Inside, masqueraded a little uncomfortably as a genuine piece of internet activism.

Offering more hope was a campaign that got the internet thing accidentally and gloriously right. The film Snakes on a Plane was not marketed by its studio, New Line, but by the first-year law student Brian Finkelstein. His site snakesonablog.com became a net phenomenon and a repository of amateur movie trailers and posters for a film that hadn't yet been finished. Rather than getting grumpy or litigious, New Line did a great net thing and asked the bloggers to help make the film, authorised a reshoot for extra scenes and even ran a competition to get bloggers and clickers to write a theme song for the movie.

In the land of showbiz luminaries the stars burned brighter than ever. At the beginning of the year Ben Affleck surprised us all with a genuine piece of acting in the Lynx Click commercial; Nicole Kidman again closed the year with a genuine piece of starletry in Baz Luhrmann's Chanel extravaganza. But the year's real ad superstar was Kate Moss. Having been snapped apparently taking cocaine last September, Kate was dropped by H&M and Cavalli and others who mounted a moral high horse only to find it stuffed. Kate, badder and more beautiful than ever, rode into the sunset with new contracts worth millions crammed into her saddlebags. In a compare-and-contrast tale of showbiz and sporting sinners, disgraced snorter Moss was handed brand redemption by Virgin Mobile, Calvin Klein, Agent Provocateur and others. Disgraced headbutter Zidane could have been offered comedy brand redemption by a cycle helmet manufacturer or a chest decongestant but was given nothing other than a starring part in a dour art film-doc that three people watched in a cinema in Notting Hill.

With all these different approaches shifting against each other like tectonic plates, what will successful advertising look like in 2007? I'm going down to Ladbrokes to put money on Dulux launching a brand of desirable yet sound paints whose shades are suggested by a fan base of paintheads and whose virtues are showcased in a multi-million pound supercommercial and bundle of related downloads starring none other than Kate Moss with an opportunistic cameo by Dave Cameron. You know it's a good bet.

● Naresh Ramchandani is a columnist for MediaGuardian

Global supergroups

Aegis
43–45 Portman Square,
London W1H 6LY
020 7070 7700
www.aegisplc.com

Aegis Media/Carat
Parker Tower, 43–49 Parker Street,
London WC2B 5PS
020 7430 6000
www.carat.co.uk
Carat MD: Neil Jones; head of marketing:
Nick Gracie; head of PR: Joe Rudkin

Grey Global
777 Third Avenue, New York,
NY 10017, USA
00 1 212 546 2000
www.grey.com
Bought by WPP in 2005. CEO: Ed Meyer

Grey London
215–227 Great Portland Street,
London W1W 5PN
020 7636 3399
www.grey.co.uk
Chairman: David Alberts; MD: Chris
Hirst; deputy chairman and head of
business development: Nicola Mendelsohn;
head of PR: Merida Mudie, 020 7413 2317

Havas
2 Allée de Longchamp, 92281
Suresnes Cedex, France
00 33 1 58 47 90 00
www.havas.com
Chairman and CEO: Alain de Pouzilhac;
corporate communications: Lorella
Gessa, 00 33 1 5847 9036

Interpublic
1114 Avenue of the Americas,
New York, NY 10036, USA
00 1 212 704 1200
www.interpublic.com
Chairman and CEO: Michael Roth; senior
vice-president and director of corporate
communications: Philippe Krakowsky,
pkrakowsky@interpublic.com

Omnicom
437 Madison Avenue, New York,
NY 10022, USA
00 1 212 415 3600
PublicAffairs@OmnicomGroup.com
www.omnicomgroup.com
President and CEO: John D Wren

Publicis
133 Avenue des Champs Elysées,
75008 Paris, France
00 33 1 4443 7000
contact@publicis.com
www.publicis.com

WPP
27 Farm Street, London W1J 5RJ
020 7408 2204
enquiries@wpp.com
www.wpp.com
CEO: Sir Martin Sorrell; group
communications director: Feona McEwan

Advertising agencies

1576 Advertising
0131 473 1576
www.1576.co.uk
Independent

Abbott Mead Vickers BBDO
020 7616 3500
www.amvbbdo.com
Owner: Omnicom

AGA
020 7330 8888
www.aga.co.uk
Independent

AKA
020 7836 4747
www.akauk.com
Independent

Arc Worldwide
020 7751 1662
www.arcww.co.uk
Barnsley: 01285 741100
Edinburgh: 0131 556 0115
Owner: Publicis

Archibald Ingall Stretton
020 7467 6100
www.archibaldingallstretton.com
40% owned by Havas

ARM Direct
020 7224 3040
www.arm-direct.co.uk
Independent

Artavia Advertising
01271 323333
www.artavia.co.uk
Bournemouth: 01202 293999
Bude: 01288 355646
Exeter: 01392 495529
Manchester: 0161 833 1000
Skipton: 01756 701640
Truro: 01872 223585
Owner: Accord Holdings

Attinger Jack
01225 758222
www.aja.co.uk
Independent

AWA
0161 968 6900
www.awa.uk.net
Independent

Barkers Scotland
0141 248 5030
www.barkersscotland.co.uk
Edinburgh: 0131 229 7493
Owner: Barkers

Barrington Johnson Lorains
0161 831 7141
www.bjl.co.uk
Independent

Bartle Bogle Hegarty
020 7734 1677
www.bartleboglehegarty.com
Milton Keynes: 01908 326888
Majority owned by employees, minority
stake held by Leo Burnett

BDH\TBWA
0161 908 8600
www.bdhtbwa.co.uk
Owner: Omnicom

Beechwood
020 7439 4142
www.beechwood.com
Independent

Bespoke Communications
020 7436 0266
www.bespokecommunications.com
Independent

Big Communications
0116 299 1144
www.bigcommunications.co.uk
Independent

Blac
020 7379 7799
www.blacagency.com
Independent

Black & White Advertising
0191 493 2493
www.blackandwhite.uk.net
Independent

Bray Leino
01598 760700
www.brayleino.co.uk
Independent

The Bridge
0141 552 8384
www.thebridgeuk.com
Independent

Burkitt DDB
020 7320 9300
www.burkittddb.com
Owner: Omnicom

Camp Chipperfield Hill Murray
020 7881 3200
www.cchm.co.uk
Owner: Hill Murry

Carter Gosling
01225 465415
www.cartergosling.co.uk
Independent

cdp-travissully
020 7437 4224
www.cdp-travissully.com
Owner: Dentsu

Charterhouse Advertising
& Marketing
0161 848 9050
www.charterhouse-advertising.co.uk
Independent

Cheetham Bell JWT
0161 832 8884
www.cheethambelljwt.com
Owner: WPP

Chemistry Communications
020 7736 5355
www.chemistrygroup.co.uk
Independent

Chick Smith Trott
020 7907 1200
www.cstadvertising.com
Independent

Citigate
020 7282 8000
www.citigateaf.com
Owner: Incepta

Clark McKay & Walpole
020 7927 3600
www.cmw-uk.com
Leeds: 0113 234 2022
Independent

Claydon Heeley Jones Mason
020 7924 3000
www.claydonheeley.com
Owner: Omnicom

Clayton Graham Advertising
0141 221 3700
www.claytongraham.co.uk
Independent

Clear Marketing Communications
0161 448 8008
www.clearmarketing.co.uk
Independent

Clemmow Hornby Inge
020 7462 8500
www.chiadvertising.com
Independent

Coltas
0141 204 5665
www.coltas.com
Independent

Connectpoint Advertising
0161 817 4200
www.connectpoint.co.uk
Independent

Craik Jones Watson Mitchell Voelkel
020 7734 1650
www.craikjones.co.uk
Owner: Abbott Mead Vickers

Cravens Advertising
0191 232 6683
www.cravens.co.uk
Leeds: 0113 384 6030
Independent

CWA Creative
0116 232 7400
www.cwa.co.uk
Christchurch: 01202 482288
Independent

Da Costa & Co
020 7916 3791
www.dacosta.co.uk
Independent

David Gent Creative
01706 220388
www.davidgentcreative.com
Saffron Walden: 01799 502662
Independent

DDB London
020 7262 7755
www.ddblondon.com
Owner: Omnicom

Delaney Lund Knox Warren & Partners
020 7836 3474
www.dlkw.co.uk
Independent

Dewynters
020 7321 0488
www.dewynters.com
Independent

DFGW
020 7632 5200
www.dfgw.com
Independent

Dig For Fire
0114 281 1200
www.digforfire.co.uk
Independent

DKA Creative
020 7467 7300
www.dka.uk.com
Independent

Doner Cardwell Hawkins
020 7734 0511
www.doner.co.uk
Part of Doner

Draft London
020 7589 0800
www.draftworldwide.com
Part of Draft Worldwide

Eardrum
020 7287 2211
www.eardrum.com
Independent

EHS Brann
020 7017 1000
www.ehsbrann.com
Cirencester: 01285 644744
Leeds: 0113 207 0400
Part-owned by Euro RSCG

Euro RSCG
020 7379 3991
www.eurorscg.co.uk
Owner: Havas

Factor 3
01242 254242
www.factor3.co.uk
Independent

Fallon
020 7494 9120
www.fallon.co.uk
Owner: Publicis

Farm Communications
020 7428 1300
www.creativebrief.com
Independent

FCB Group
020 7947 8000
www.london.fcb.com
Owner: Interpublic

FEREF
020 7292 6300
www.feref.com
Independent

Fox Kalomaski
020 7691 8090
www.foxkalomaski.co.uk
Independent

GCAS
028 9055 7700
www.gcasgroup.com
Independent

Genesis Advertising
028 9031 3344
www.genesis-advertising.co.uk
Independent

Gillett & Bevan
0161 228 0023
www.gillett-bevan.com
Independent

Girardot
020 7349 6376
www.girardot.co.uk
Independent

Golley Slater & Partners
029 2078 6000
www.golleyslater.com
Birmingham: 0121 454 2323
Independent

Goode International
01491 873323
www.goode.co.uk
Independent

Harrison Troughton Wunderman
020 7611 6333
www.htw.wunderman.com
Owner: WPP

HDM Agency
020 7321 2227
www.hdmagency.co.uk
Independent

Heresy
020 7349 6800
www.heresyhq.com
Owner: Chime Communications

Hooper Galton
020 7494 6300
www.hoopergalton.co.uk
Independent

Huet & Co
0161 835 3100
www.huet.co.uk
Independent

IAS Smarts
0131 555 0425
www.iassmarts.com
Belfast: 028 9039 5500
Birmingham: 0121 456 3199
London: 020 7386 3500
Manchester: 01625 434343
Owner: Incepta

ICG
01772 679383
www.icgonline.co.uk
Independent

Ideas Eurobrand
020 7738 1900
www.ideaseurobrand.com
Independent

Inferno
020 7292 7070
www.inferno-group.com
Independent

JDA
0113 290 4290
www.jda.co.uk
Warrington: 01925 638899
Independent

Joshua Agency
020 7453 7900
www.joshua-agency.co.uk
Owner: Grey Global

JWT
020 7656 7000
www.jwt.com
Owner: WPP

Kaleidoscope Advertising Design & Marketing
0151 707 2220
www.kadm.co.uk
Independent

Karmarama
020 7612 1777
www.karmarama.com
Independent

Kastner & Partners
020 7689 6989
www.kastnernetwork.co.uk
Independent

Lavery Rowe
020 7378 1780
www.laveryrowe.com
Birmingham: 0121 212 2230
Independent

Lawton Communications
023 8082 8500
www.lawton.co.uk
Independent

Leagas Delaney
020 7758 1758
www.leagasdelaney.com
Independent

Leith Agency
020 7758 1400
www.leith.co.uk
Edinburgh: 0131 561 8600
Owner: Cello

Leo Burnett
020 7751 1800
www.leoburnett.co.uk
Owner: Publicis

Levy McCallum
028 9031 9220
www.levymccallum.co.uk
Edinburgh: 0131 225 9733
Glasgow: 0141 248 7977
Independent

Lowe London
020 7584 5033
www.loweworldwide.com
Owner: Interpublic

M&C Saatchi
020 7543 4500
www.mcsaatchi.com
Independent

Maher Bird Associates
020 7309 7200
www.mba.co.uk
Owner: Omnicom

Marr Associates
01828 632800
www.marr.co.uk
Independent

Martin Talt Redheads
0191 232 1926
www.mtra.co.uk
Independent

Masius
020 7307 9170
www.masius.com
Owner: Publicis

Matters Media
020 7224 6030
Independent

McCann Erickson
020 7837 3737
www.mccann.co.uk
Birmingham: 0121 713 3500
Bristol: 0117 921 1764
Manchester: 01625 822200
Owner: Interpublic

Mediaedge:cia
020 7803 2000
www.mecglobal.com
Independent

Merle
0141 242 1800
www.merleagency.com
Independent

Miles Calcraft Briginshaw Duffy
020 7073 6900
www.mcbd.co.uk
Independent

Mortimer Whittaker O'Sullivan
020 7379 8844
www.mwo.co.uk
Independent

Mostly Media
01935 478238
www.mostlymedia.co.uk
Independent

Mother
020 7012 1999
www.motherlondon.com
Independent

Mustoes
020 7379 9999
www.mustoes.co.uk
Independent

Nexus/H UK
01892 517777
www.nexus-h.co.uk
Independent

Nitro
020 7292 5999
www.nitro-group.com
Independent

Oakbase
01244 391391
www.oakbase.co.uk
Independent

Ogilvy & Mather
020 7345 3000
www.ogilvy.com
Owner: WPP

Ogilvy Primary Contact
020 7468 6900
www.primary.co.uk
Owner: WPP

Palmer Hargreaves Wallis Tomlinson
01926 452525
www.ph-wt.com
London: 020 7713 0999
Independent

Peacock Productions
020 7580 8868
www.peacockdesign.com
Independent

Ping Communications
020 7881 3200
www.pingdirect.com
Independent

Poulter Partners
0113 285 6500
www.poulters.com
Independent

Proximity Media
020 7298 1000
www.proximitylondon.com
Owner: Omnicom

Publicis
020 7935 4426
www.publicis.co.uk
Owner: Publicis

Publicity Bureau
01302 730303
www.publicitybureau.co.uk
Independent

Purity
020 7420 7900
www.puritylondon.com
Independent

PWLC
0113 398 0120
www.pwlc.uk.com
Independent

Quiet Storm
020 7907 1140
www.quietstorm.co.uk
Independent

Radford Advertising & Marketing
0161 832 8807
www.radfordnet.com
Independent

Radioville
020 7534 5999
www.radioville.co.uk
Independent

Rainey Kelly Campbell Roalfe/Y&R
020 7404 2700
www.rkcryr.com
Owner: Young & Rubicam

Rapier
020 7369 8000
www.rapieruk.com
Independent

Raw Media
01305 259444
www.rawmedia.co.uk
Independent

Redman Jones & Partners
0161 828 2600
www.redmanjones.co.uk
Independent

Rhythmm
0117 942 9786
www.rhythmm.co.uk
Independent

Robson Brown
0191 232 2443
www.robson-brown.co.uk
Manchester: 0161 601 4900
Independent

RPM3
020 7434 4343
www.rpm3.co.uk
Independent

Saatchi & Saatchi
020 7636 5060
www.saatchi-saatchi.com
Owner: Publicis

Scholz & Friends London
020 7961 4000
www.s-f.com
Owner: S&F Holding GmbH

Sheppard Day Associates
020 7821 2222
www.sheppard-day.com
Independent

SHOP
020 7483 9800
www.shopopen.co.uk
Independent

Smarter Communications
020 7257 2600
www.smartercomms.com
Independent. Includes Senior King

Sold Out Advertising
020 7704 0409
www.soldout.co.uk
Independent

Space City Productions
020 7371 4000
www.spacecity.co.uk
Independent

SPS Advertising
01392 464545
Independent

St Luke's Communications
020 7380 8888
www.stlukes.co.uk
Cooperative

TBA
020 7380 0953
www.tbaplc.co.uk
Independent

Team Saatchi
020 7436 6636
www.teamsaatchi.co.uk
Owner: Publicis

Tequila\London
020 7440 1100
www.tequila-uk.com
Owner: Omnicom

Tequila\Manchester
0161 908 8100
www.tequilamanchester.com
Owner: Omnicom

UK Advertising & Marketing Services
01322 228899
www.ukams.co.uk
Independent

Union Advertising Agency
0131 625 6000
www.union.co.uk
Leeds: 0113 266 6050
Independent

United London
020 7915 7575
www.unitedlondon.com
Owner: WPP

Vallance Carruthers Coleman Priest
020 7592 9331
www.vccp.com
Independent

WAA
0121 321 1411
www.waa.co.uk
London: 020 7758 2871
Independent

The Walker Agency
01202 414200
www.thewalkeragency.co.uk
Independent

Ware Anthony Rust
01223 566212
www.war.uk.com
Independent

WARL
020 7400 0900
www.warl.com
Independent

WCRS
020 7806 5000
www.wcrs.com
Independent

WFCA Integrated
01892 511085
www.wfca.co.uk
Independent

Wieden & Kennedy
020 7194 7000
www.wklondon.com
Independent

Windmill Partnership
020 7371 2868
www.windmillpartnership.com
Independent

WWAV Rapp Collins
020 8735 8000
www.wwavrc.co.uk
Bristol: 0117 929 7600
Leeds: 0113 222 6300
Owner: Omnicom

Wyatt International
0121 454 8181
www.wyattinternational.com
Independent

Young & Rubicam EMEA
020 7387 9366
www.yandr.com
Owner: WPP

Young Phillips
01202 298969
Independent

ZenithOptimedia UK
020 7961 1000
www.zenithoptimedia.com
Owner: Publicis

Media agencies

All Response Media
020 7017 1450
www.allresponsemedia.com
Leeds: 0113 394 4660
Owner: Havas

AMS Media
020 7843 6900
www.amsgroup.co.uk
Independent

Attinger Jack
01225 758222
www.aja.co.uk
Independent

BJK&E Media
020 7025 3900
www.bjke.co.uk
Owner: WPP

BLM Media
020 7437 1317
www.blm.co.uk
Independent

Bray Leino
01598 760700
www.brayleino.co.uk
Independent

Brilliant Media
0113 394 0000
www.brilliantmedia.co.uk
Manchester: 0161 214 7222
Independent

Bygraves Bushell Valladares & Sheldon
020 7734 4445
www.bbvs.co.uk
Independent

Carat
020 7430 6000
www.carat.com
Owner: Aegis

Equinox Communications
020 7864 1950
www.equinoxcomm.co.uk
Owner: Zenith Optimedia

Feather Brooksbank
0131 555 2554
www.featherbrooksbank.co.uk
Glasgow: 0141 332 3382
Manchester: 0161 834 9793
Owner: Aegis

Initiative Media London
020 7663 7000
www.initiative.co.uk
Owner: Interpublic

John Ayling & Associates
020 7439 6070
Independent

Lavery Rowe Advertising
020 7378 1780
www.laveryrowe.com
Independent

Manning Gottlieb OMD
020 7470 5300
www.mgomd.com
Owner: Omnicom

Matters Media
020 7224 6030
Independent

Media Campaign Services
020 7389 0800
www.mediacampaign.co.uk
Independent

Media Planning
020 7393 9000
www.mpg.com
Owner: Havas

Mediability
0161 925 6979
www.mediability.co.uk
Independent

MediaCom
020 7874 5500
www.mediacomuk.com
Owner: WPP

MediaCom North
0161 839 6600
www.mediacomnorth.com
Owner: WPP

MediaCom Scotland
0131 555 1500
Owner: WPP

Mediaedge:cia
020 7803 2000
www.mediaedgecia.com
Manchester: 0161 930 9000
Owner: WPP

MediaVest
020 7190 8000
www.mediavest.co.uk
Manchester: 0161 211 8032
Owner: Publicis

MediaVision Manchester
0161 838 4444
www.mvmediagroup.co.uk
Edinburgh: 0131 554 0033
Owner: Publicis

Michaelides and Bednash
020 7468 1168
www.michaelidesandbednash.com
Independent

MindShare
020 7969 4040
www.mindshareworld.com
Owner: WPP

MRM Partners UK
020 7278 3856
www.mrmpworldwide.com
Owner: Interpublic

Naked
020 7336 8084
www.nakedcomms.com
Independent

OMD
020 7893 4893
www.omd.com
Owner: Omnicom

Outdoor Connection
020 7108 6094
www.outdoorconnection.co.uk
Owner: Omnicom

PHD
020 7446 0555
www.phd.co.uk
Manchester: 0161 237 7900
Owner: Omnicom

Rathbone Media
0870 830 1850
www.rathmedia.com
Independent

Robson Brown
0191 232 2443
www.robson-brown.co.uk
Manchester: 0161 877 2004
Independent

Starcom UK
020 7453 4444
www.smvgroup.com
London: 020 7190 8000
Owner: Publicis

Total Media Group
020 7937 3793
www.totalmedia.co.uk
Warwick: 01926 840011
Independent

Universal McCann
020 7833 5858
www.mccann.co.uk
Birmingham: 0121 713 3500
Manchester: 01625 822300
Owner: Interpublic

Vizeum UK
020 7379 9000
www.vizeum.co.uk
Owner: Aegis

Walker Media
020 7447 7500
www.walkermedia.com
Part-owner: M&C Saatchi

Wallace Barnaby
01481 726052
www.wallacebarnaby.com
Jersey: 01534 759807
Independent

WWAV Rapp Collins
020 8735 8000
www.wwavrc.co.uk
Bristol: 0117 929 7600
Leeds: 0113 222 6300
Owner: Omnicom

Zed Media
020 7961 3501
www.zedmedia.co.uk
Owner: Publicis

Outdoor media

Clear Channel UK
020 7478 2200
www.clearchannel.co.uk
Independent

JC Decaux
020 7298 8000
www.jcdecaux.co.uk
Birmingham: 0121 423 3777
Glasgow: 0141 891 8100
Manchester: 0161 873 6366/77
Independent

Primesight
020 7882 1200
www.primesight.co.uk
Erith: 01322 342028
Owner: SMG

Titan
020 7838 4000
www.titanoutdoor.co.uk
Birmingham: 0121 567 2970
Dublin: 00 353 1 29 5233
Glasgow: 0141 779 5250
Leeds: 0113 244 2761
Liverpool: 0151 236 5353
Independent

Viacom Outdoor
020 7482 3000
www.viacom-outdoor.co.uk
Belfast: 028 9032 2333
Birmingham: 0121 788 5250
Bristol: 0117 964 9927
Dublin: 00 353 1669 4500
Edinburgh: 0131 555 1515
Glasgow: 0141 552 5259
Leeds: 0113 242 2294
Manchester: 0161 877 7414
Owner: Viacom

» *New media agencies*
see page 239

Direct and promotional marketing

141 Worldwide
020 7706 2306
www.141ww.com
Owner: WPP

Arc Worldwide
020 7751 1662
www.arcww.co.uk
Owner: Publicis

BD-NTWK
020 7749 5500
www.bd-ntwk.com
Glasgow: 0141 567 8000
Independent

Billington Cartmell
020 7471 1900
www.bcl.co.uk
Independent

Carlson Marketing
020 8875 0875
www.carlson-europe.com
Bristol: 01454 618811
Northampton: 01604 886000
Independent

Clark McKay and Walpole
020 7487 9750
www.cmw-uk.com
Independent

Claydon Heeley Jones Mason
020 7924 3000
www.chjm.com
Owner: Omnicom

Craik Jones Watson Mitchell Voelkel
020 7734 1650
www.craikjones.co.uk
Owner: Omnicom

Dialogue Marketing
020 8783 3100
www.dialmkg.com
Owner: WPP

Dig For Fire
0114 281 1200
www.digforfire.co.uk
Independent

Draft London
020 7589 0800
www.draftworldwide.com
Part of Draft Worldwide

dunnhumby
020 8832 9222
www.dunnhumby.com
Part-owner: Tesco

Dynamo Marketing
020 7386 0699
www.dynamo.net.uk
Owner: Incepta

EHS Brann
01285 644744
www.ehsbrann.com
London: 020 7017 1000
Leeds: 0113 207 0400
Part-owner: Euro RSCG

Euro RSCG KLP
020 7478 3478
www.klp.co.uk
Owner: Euro RSCG

Euro RSCG Skybridge
020 8254 1500
www.eurorscgskybridge.com
Owner: Havas

SBG and Finex Communications
020 7326 9191
www.finexgroup.com
Owner: Incepta

Geoff Howe
020 8941 7575
www.geoffhowe.com
Independent

GHA
01903 885672
www.g-h-a.co.uk
Independent

Harrison Troughton Wunderman
020 7611 6333
www.htw.wunderman.com
Owner: WPP

Haygarth
020 8971 3300
www.haygarth.co.uk
Independent

Iris
020 7654 7900
www.irisnation.com
Manchester: 0161 830 4750
Independent

Joshua Agency
020 7453 7900
www.joshua-agency.co.uk
Owner: Grey Global

Marketing Store
020 7745 2100
www.themarketingstore.com
Birmingham: 01675 467404
Leeds: 0113 246 8266
Owner: Harvey

OgilvyOne
020 7345 3000
www.ogilvy.com
Owner: WPP

Partners Andrews Aldridge
020 7478 2100
www.andrewsaldridge.com
Independent

Red Cell Response
020 7150 3400
www.redcellresponse.com
Owner: WPP

Proximity Media
020 7298 1000
www.proximitylondon.com
Owner: Omnicom

Rapier
020 7369 8000
www.rapieruk.com
Independent

RMG Connect (formerly Black Cat)
020 7656 7310
www.rmgconnect.com
Owner: WPP

SMP
01892 548282
www.smp.uk.com
Independent

TDA
01242 633111
www.tdaltd.com
Independent

Tequila\London
020 7440 1100
www.tequila-uk.com
Owner: Omnicom

Tequila\Manchester
0161 908 8100
www.tequilamanchester.com
Owner: Omnicom

Triangle Communications
020 7071 1500
www.thetrianglegroup.co.uk
Owner: Publicis

Tullo Marshall Warren
020 7349 4000
www.tmw.co.uk
Independent

Souk Response
020 7420 8060
www.soukcommunications.com
Independent

WWAV Rapp Collins
020 8735 8000
www.wwavrc.co.uk
Bristol: 0117 929 7600
Leeds: 0113 222 6300
Owner: Omnicom

Trade press

Advertising Age
00 1 212 210 0100
editor@adage.com
www.adage.com
Weekly. Owner: Crain Communications. Publishing and editorial director: David Klein; editor: Scott Donaton

Brand Strategy
020 7970 4000
ruth.mortimer@centaur.co.uk
www.brandstrategy.co.uk
Monthly. Owner: Centaur. Editor: Ruth Mortimer

Campaign
020 8267 4683
campaign@haynet.com
www.brandrepublic.com
Weekly. Owner: Haymarket. Editor: Claire Beale; news: Francesca Newland; features: Larissa Bannister; production: Michael Porter

Cream
020 7613 9700
www.csquared.cc
Quarterly. Creative media. Editor: Alastair Ray

Creative Review
020 7970 4000
patrick.burgoyne@centaur.co.uk
www.creativereview.co.uk
Monthly. Owner: Centaur. Editor: Patrick Burgoyne; deputy editor: Paula Carson

Design Week
020 7970 4000
lyndark@centaur.co.uk
www.designweek.co.uk
Weekly. Owner: Centaur. Editor: Lynda Relph-Knight; features: John Stones

Mad.co.uk
020 7970 4000
stuart.aitken@centaur.co.uk
www.mad.co.uk
Online magazine. Owner: Centaur. Deputy editor: Stuart Aitken; news: Sarah Lelic

Marketing
020 8267 5000
marketing@haynet.com
www.brandrepublic.com
Weekly. Owner: Haymarket. Editor: Craig Smith; news: Ben Carter; features: Drew Barrand; production manager: Emma Lawton

Marketing Direct
020 8267 5000
noelle.mcelhatton@haynet.com
www.mxdirect.co.uk
Monthly. Owner: Haymarket. Editor: Noelle McElhatton; features: Melanie May

Marketing Week
020 7970 4000
mw.editorial@centaur.co.uk
www.marketing-week.co.uk
Weekly. Owner: Centaur. Editor: Stuart Smith; deputy and news: Amanda Wilkinson

Media Week
020 8267 5000
mwnewsdesk@haynet.com
www.mediaweek.co.uk
Weekly. Owner: Haymarket. Editor: Philip Smith; news: Juliette Garside; features editor: Julia Martin; production: Glenys Trevor

New Media Age
020 7970 4000
mike.nutley@centaur.co.uk
www.nma.co.uk
Weekly. Owner: Centaur. Editor: Mike Nutley; news: Justin Pearce

Shots
020 7505 8000
lyndy.stout@shots.net
www.shots.net
International advertising. 6pa. Owner: Emap Communications. Editor: Lyndy Stout; assistant editor: Danny Edwards

Advertising associations

Advertising Association
7th Floor North, Artillery House,
11-19 Artillery Row, London SW1P 1RT
020 7340 1100
aa@adassoc.org.uk
www.adassoc.org.uk
Press: jim.rothwell@adassoc.org.uk

Advertising Standards Authority
Mid City Place, 71 High Holborn,
London WC1V 6QT
020 7492 2222
enquiries@asa.org.uk
www.asa.org.uk

Chartered Institute of Marketing
Moor Hall, Cookham, Maidenhead,
Berkshire SL6 9QH
01628 427500
info@cim.co.uk
www.cim.co.uk

Committee of Advertising Practice
Mid City Place, 71 High Holborn,
London WC1V 6QT
020 7492 2222
enquiries@cap.org.uk
www.cap.org.uk
Press: press@cap.org.uk

Direct Marketing Association
DMA House, 70 Margaret Street,
London W1W 8SS
020 7291 3300
info@dma.org.uk
www.dma.org.uk

Incorporated Society of British Advertisers
Langham House, 1b Portland Place,
London W1B 1PN
020 7291 9020
Media@isba.org.uk
www.isba.org.uk

Institute of Practitioners in Advertising
44 Belgrave Square,
London SW1X 8QS
020 7235 7020
info@ipa.co.uk
www.ipa.co.uk

International Advertising Association
521 Fifth Avenue, Suite 1807,
New York, NY 10175 USA
00 1 212 557 1133
iaa@iaaglobal.org
www.iaaglobal.org

Internet Advertising Bureau
Ingram House,
13-15 John Adam Street,
London WC2N 6LU
Press: 020 7886 8282
info@iabuk.net
www.iabuk.net

Market Research Society
15 Northburgh Street,
London EC1V 0JR
020 7490 4911
info@mrs.org.uk
www.mrs.org.uk

Nielsen/NetRatings
77 St John Street, London EC1M 4AN
020 7014 0590
info@netratings.com
www.nielsen-netratings.com
Press: 020 7014 0590

Outdoor Advertising Association of Great Britain
Summit House, 27 Sale Place,
London W2 1YR
020 7973 0315
enquiries@oaa.org.uk
www.oaa.org.uk

World Federation of Advertisers
120 Avenue Louise,
1050 Brussels, Belgium
00 32 2 502 5740
info@wfanet.org
www.wfanet.org

Public relations

Communicator of the year...
David Cameron

Organic, environmentally-friendly and digital: these three themes make up the holy trinity of PR today. The website of Abel & Cole, green purveyor of environmentally-friendly organic boxes to the middle classes, must be the envy of every PR firm in London. Having a bit of a PR crisis? Well some sort of online green thing ought to fix it.

Look at BP (championing a "carbon neutral" campaign all over the internet). Or Disney (banning junk food tie-ins to its children-focused products). Or the newly inaugurated Green Awards (shortlisting M&S and ITV, who've had their troubles). And take note how the supermarket wars have shifted from "we're the cheapest", to "we're the greenest".

In fact, so trendy has green become in what is, let's face it, an industry based on trends, that the Advertising Standards Authority has taken an interest. Companies must prove their green credentials rather than merely assert them, after Scottish and Southern Energy claimed a tree-planting scheme would absorb CO_2 equal to that created by its customers. The ASA investigated and discovered that SSE couldn't quite prove its claim and warned companies that the rash of green credentials being displayed had better be backed up by hard fact. Fortunately for the PR industry, newspapers are generally easier to fool.

The fast food companies – currently the new tobacco firms in terms of rock-bottom perceptions and facing advertising bans all over the place – are increasingly turning to PR. Pizza Hut, Pepsi and Burger King all have YouTube tie-up deals, launching branded channels on the site. In Burger King's case, it has added renowned American rapper, P Diddy, to the heady mix. Diddy TV, however, struck the wrong note with users at YouTube, who submitted a barrage of complaints about the over-commercialisation of the service. More than 2,000 posts dismissed it as a sell-out.

Other attempts to be relevant have also backfired. Most notably, a gimmick gone wrong resulted in the embarrassment of one of the world's leading PR men, Richard Edelman. Edelman was forced to apologise on his eponymous company's blog after an online stunt for Wal-Mart was exposed.

As with all this viral internet stuff, the world's media seemed at first to spontaneously notice the appearance of a blog, walmartingacross america.com, documenting the journey of a couple across the US in a motorhome, stopping overnight in Wal-Mart carparks. When it emerged that the trip was being, circuitously, funded by Wal-Mart itself to promote a positive portrayal of the company, Edelman fell on his sword.

These kinds of activities are proving far more difficult to pull off than ambitious PR firms might have initially thought. Several music stunts have been burned by all sorts of wild claims for their artists' authentic downloading-from-their-bedroom success when said artist is exposed as having had a record deal all along. A faked "video diary", (LonelyGirl15), on YouTube that was all the rage for five minutes because of its extraordinary honesty was later revealed to have been the work of an actress and a professional writer. As the commentator Jeff Jarvis regularly points out, deceiving potential customers is not ultimately helpful and in the new world order, transparency is all.

● Celebrity management

In the more defensive PR world of crisis-management, phone tapping is the hot topic, following the conviction of the News of the World's royal editor and subsequent investigation into the allegedly widespread practice in tabloid newspapers. Most leading celebrity PR agencies say they have been warning their clients about such underhand methods for years, but claim online security questions (stolen or hacked-into BlackBerrys and the like) are new worries.

Phil Hall, latterly the editor of the News of the World, proved himself to be the new king of crisis PR when he landed the toughest assignment of 2006. As the spokesman and chief defender of Heather Mills McCartney, he took on most of the tabloids, but especially the Sun and his former employer. So large was the task, her law firm, Mishcon de Reya employed its own agency (The PR Office) to handle legal calls.

Stuart Bell, the 27-year-old director of the Outside Organisation, was similarly instantly elevated to one of the industry's top names overnight as Sir Paul's chief flak-deflector. In an interview with PR Week, Bell confessed that representing a national treasure in the midst of a personal crisis requires the carrying of three mobile phones as well as a BlackBerry.

Running this campaign, with its amazing string of leaks, counter-leaks, briefings and sensational splashes, must be akin to marshalling a small army of cats. You know you've got the biggest showbiz client going when Max Clifford is giving you advice…

The spin-off legal battles surrounding the McCartneys' divorce will be keeping m'learned friends in second homes for years. And that's if even only half of the threatened lawsuits (Mills v the Mail and the London Evening Standard; Mills v the News of the World; McCartney's lawyer v Associated Newspapers) come to pass. These actions — note, they are only threatened at the time of writing — appear to mark a new development in PR warfare. If your message doesn't seem to be getting through, announcing legal action will get you at least another set of headlines. By next year, someone will have calculated how much advertising revenue has been generated by the McCartneys' divorce.

● The Press Gazette

Another of the industry's most successful self-publicists, Matthew Freud, had one of the year's biggest PR disasters. Having teamed up with former Mirror editor Piers Morgan to buy the newspaper industry trade magazine Press Gazette, Freud announced in October 2006 he would be selling the title as they had lost £500k in a year. He blamed a lack of industry support from certain editors and proprietors for the British Press Awards run by the title. The awards bankroll the magazine and without them the title is unsustainable, he said.

When the editors and proprietors appeared unmoved, the team proposed a buyout of the magazine by a trust made up of all the newspaper groups to preserve its future. Unsurprisingly, a united board of warring newspaper groups seems unlikely and the title heads for administration.

Either way, months of being at war with the newspaper industry have not been kind to Freud, whose longstanding controversial reputation has taken something of a hammering. He will undoubtedly recover.

Besides, PR, traditionally the lowest of the low in media eyes, has consolidated its reputation as an industry, following its official designation as a profession. And as if to confirm that PR is everything, the winner of the communicator of the year in the 2006 PR Week awards was the leader of the Conservative Party.

David Cameron, himself a former PR agent for Carlton Communications, was feted by his former peers for dragging the Tories from 30% in the opinion polls in December 2005 to hitting 40% for the first time in a generation and nudging ahead of New Labour. How has he done this? Well, largely through embracing environmental causes, flirting with new technology and championing the organic. The holy trinity of good PR ...

PR disasters

November 2006 Real People, the real-life weekly magazine, was hit by a PR disaster after a production error in its scratchcard competition led to every reader winning a £5,000 jackpot. The magazine was forced to convert the competition into a prize draw after readers flooded it with telephone calls to claim their prize money.

June 2006 Cadbury Schweppes was hurt by a salmonella scare that forced the company to recall 1 million of its chocolate bars. The contamination, most likely caused from a leaking pipe at a Cadbury factory, infected up to 37 people. The company struggled to regain positive sales momentum in the UK and pulled some of its sponsorship idents and television ad campaigns. The scare is said to have cost the company around £30m.

June 2006 When Sven-Goran Eriksson announced he was quitting his job as England coach following the World Cup final the FA was desperate to be seen to be doing something to replace Sven. It cheerfully confirmed the reports that Luiz Felipe Scolari was on his way to manage England. But Scolari said no — precisely because of his fears about press intrusion from our intrepid tabloid hacks.

PR coups

November 2006 The board at ITV managed to prise BBC chairman Michael Grade out of the corporation without anyone suspecting. Not only did ITV overturn months of bad press with the surprise strike, it also contributed to the downturn in the BBC's licence fee negotiations. Two birds, one big pay cheque.

June 2006 A marketing coup that has exploded all over the internet. The humble Mentos sweet has been found to have spectacular properties when mixed with Diet Coke. Popping the sweet into a large bottle of Diet Coke causes a reaction that results in a 15-foot geyser shooting into the air. Mentos found about 800 videos of the soda fountains featured on the internet and estimated the free publicity to be worth $10m, a feat lauded by the Wall Street Journal, among others.

May 2006 The unknown pop singer, Sandi Thom, became an overnight sensation and headed for the top of the charts thanks to webcasts from her basement flat. The front-page publicity also did wonders for the media profile of Quite Great, the PR company behind the scam.

PR for a good cause

Julian Henry

It's funny to think that 10 years have passed since Freud Communications first launched Pepsi Max in the UK with a promise to turn the world blue for a day. They achieved this unlikely goal by painting Concorde the colour of the Pepsi can, staging a celebrity jamboree at a London airport for TV crews to beam around the world, and by persuading the Daily Mirror to turn their red logo blue as a one-off.

This was an imaginative and large-scale PR concept that is still discussed today and it helped to set the parameters for future publicity launches. And as an exercise in generating hype it succeeded because it distracted buyers from the mundane experience of buying a can of fizz, by suggesting that they were involved in something more glamorous, confident and surprising.

The only reason I mention this now, a decade later, is because a new generation of busy Freud Communications executives in London is behind the Red campaign, which, in case you missed it, was launched in 2006 as a charitable initiative with the modest objective of tackling the problem of Aids in Africa.

You have to hand it to Freud's. They have not let their spiky reputation within the industry unsettle their limitless self-belief. They like to think big, and they are not afraid to charge headfirst at the mass market with determined aggression.

I don't mind particularly if they use the same box of tricks. Like the Blue launch the Red campaign combines brand muscle, with partners like Gap, Motorola and Amex, with famous faces (Bono of course) and sponsored media to persuade us to change our shopping habits and at the same time do our bit to make the world a better place. No matter how you chose to judge the eventual outcomes of the work, the launch of Red at least proves that you don't need a new idea to appear hot in the high street.

This type of cause-related marketing has become increasingly important to brands through 2006. As a result, charities need a strong constitution if they are going to retain their purpose and not be lured into uncomfortable situations by corporations or more likely, the celebrities that they sponsor to gain column inches.

Jemima Khan's trip to Pakistan as a Unicef ambassador earlier in the year should have been a straightforward public relations exercise for the good work that the charity does for earthquake relief. But when the story appeared as a fashion spread in the London Evening Standard's ES Magazine, Sue Ryan, an honorary fellow of the charity, ended up having to write to the Observer detailing how easily good intentions become corrupted. "Unicef, so strong and brave in the field, had been wimps when faced with the force of celebrity" Ryan wrote after quickly discovering the complications that flourish around celebrities.

In 2006, the credibility offered by ethically sound groups and individuals is a premium commodity as a result of its ability to inspire people who feel increasingly cynical and worldly wise about the business of marketing.

David Cameron knows this. But despite being named Communicator of the Year at the 2006 PR Week awards, he has had a mixed year that will be remembered for his ill-advised "hug a hoodie" sound-bite as well as the crass attempt to gain brownie points from his presence at a Thom Yorke/Friends of the Earth charity concert in June. It's always embarrassing to see politicians dribbling over rock stars.

Voters today are more primed to respond to strength of character rather than naff attempts at street cred, and this is something that Gordon Brown's people seem to understand as they seek to position their man on the top of the tree.

The fact remains that an effective PR campaign has to be rooted in a core truth. And in charity or cause-related work we need to be told precisely about the detail of the benefit and the value of the action when it is announced. A crass headline blazed across a front page in bright neon makes it harder for a reader to disinter the message.

Charles Handy, the management guru, has written an instructive and topical book on "the new philanthropists" that is relevant to PR professionals who wish to ponder new ways of connecting with a mass market through cause-related marketing. In the book celebrities, business people and entrepreneurs describe how they have swapped the pursuit of self-interest for a more magnanimous and philanthropic approach to life.

Handy opens the book with the statement "generosity is fashionable again". He's right. Thanks to the work of a relatively small number of inspirational people this embryonic market in benevolent intent and action from companies and individuals is starting to thrive. And this gives the PR and marketing communities a real opportunity to grow and show that we are much more than a simple tool for self-aggrandisement.

● Julian Henry is a director of Henry's House PR consultancy

Public relations contacts

3 x 1 Public Relations
Glasgow
0141 221 0707
info@3x1.com
www.3x1.com

AD Communications
Esher, Surrey
01372 464470
rallen@adcomms.co.uk
www.adcomms.co.uk

APR Communications
London
020 7351 2227
arobson@aprcommunications.com
www.aprcommunications.com

AS Biss & Co
London
020 7340 6200
tellmemore@asbiss.com
www.asbiss.com

Ashley Communications
Rickmansworth, Hertfordshire
01923 826150
info@ashleycomms.com
www.ashleycomms.com

Attenborough Saffron
London
020 7734 4455
info@attenborough.net
www.attenborough.net

August One
London
020 8846 8300
enquiries@augustone.com
www.augustone.com

Automotive PR
London
020 7494 8050
info@automotivepr.com
www.automotivepr.com

AxiCom
London
020 8392 4050
jtanner@axicom.com
www.axicom.com

B2B Communications
Chessington, Surrey
020 8974 2404
enquiries@b2bcommunications.co.uk
www.b2bcommunications.co.uk

Band & Brown Communications
London
020 7419 7000
info@bbpr.com
www.bbpr.com

Barkers Scotland
Glasgow
0141 248 5030
ckelly@barkers-scot.com
www.barkersscotland.co.uk

Barrett Dixon Bell
Altrincham, Cheshire
0161 925 4700
info@bdb.co.uk
www.bdb.co.uk

Beattie Communications
London
020 7053 6000
info@beattiegroup.com
www.beattiegroup.com
Birmingham: 0121 698 8625
Dundee: 01382 562881
Edinburgh: 0131 220 8269
Falkirk: 01324 602550
Glasgow: 01698 787878
Leeds: 0113 213 0300
Manchester: 0161 935 8334

Bell Pottinger Public Affairs
London
020 7861 2400
pbingle@bell-pottinger.co.uk
www.bppa.co.uk

Bell Pottinger Public Relations
London
020 7861 2424
info@bell-pottinger.co.uk
www.bell-pottinger.co.uk

Berkeley PR International
Reading
0118 988 2992
enquiries@berkeleypr.co.uk
www.berkeleypr.co.uk
Bristol: 01454 203 595
Derbyshire: 01629 826942

BGB & Associates
London
020 7233 2300
pr@bgb.co.uk
www.bgb.co.uk

The Big Partnership
Glasgow
0141 333 9585
info@bigpartnership.co.uk
www.bigpartnership.co.uk
Aberdeen: 01224 224433
Edinburgh: 0131 558 3111
Kirkcaldy: 01592 643200

Biosector 2
London
020 7632 1960
www.biosector2.com

Bite Communications
London
020 8741 1123
moreUK@bitepr.com
www.bitepr.com

BMB
Luton
01582 725454
reception@bmb.uk.com
www.bmb.uk.com

Brahm PR
Leeds
0113 230 4000
www.brahm.com

Brands2Life
London
020 7592 1200
info@brands2life.com
www.brands2life.com

Brave PR
London
020 7802 8111
charlotte.a@bravepr.com
www.bravepr.com

Bray Leino
Bristol
0117 973 1173
info@brayleino.co.uk
www.brayleino.co.uk

Brazen
Manchester
0161 923 4994
nina@brazenpr.com
www.brazenpr.com

The Bright Consultancy
Solihull, West Midlands
0121 711 5000
pr@bright-consultancy.co.uk
www.bright-consultancy.co.uk

Broadgate
London
020 7726 6111
contact@bgate.co.uk
www.bgate.co.uk

Brower Lewis Pelham PR
London
020 7259 1550
www.blppr.com

Brunswick
London
020 7404 5959
info@brunswickgroup.com
www.brunswickgroup.com

Buchanan Communications
London
020 7466 5000
www.buchanan.uk.com
Leeds: 01943 883990

Buffalo Communications
London
020 7292 8680
info@buffalo.co.uk
www.buffalo.co.uk

Burson-Marsteller
London
020 7831 6262
bm-london_reception@uk.bm.com
www.bm.com

Cairns & Associates
London
020 7235 7773
ruth.barker@cairnsassociates.co.uk
www.cairnsassociates.co.uk

Camargue
London
020 7636 7366
www.camarguepr.com
Birmingham: 0121 2376063
Cheltenham: 01242 577277

Camron PR
London
020 7420 1700
genevieve@camron.co.uk
www.camron.co.uk

Capital MS&L
London
020 7307 5330
steffan.williams@capitalmsl.com
www.capitalmsl.co.uk

Capitalize
London
020 7940 1700
info@capitalize.co.uk
www.capitalize.co.uk

Carat
London
020 7430 6000
nick.gracie@carat.com
www.carat.co.uk

Carrot Communications
London
020 7386 4860
richard.houghton@
    carrotcomms.co.uk
www.carrotcomms.co.uk

Chameleon PR
London
020 7680 5500
www.chameleonpr.com

Cherton Enterprise
Belfast
028 9065 4007
robin.guthrie@cherton.co.uk
www.cherton.co.uk

CIB Communications
Leatherhead, Surrey
01372 371800
gavint@cibcommunications.co.uk
www.cibcommunications.co.uk

Citigate Communications
London
020 7282 2880
info@citigatec.co.uk
www.citigatecommunications.co.uk
Birmingham: 0845 119 9911

Citigate Dewe Rogerson
London
020 7638 9571
perri.taylor@citigatedr.co.uk
www.citigatedr.co.uk

Citigate Public Affairs
London
020 7826 2699
warwick.smith@citigatepa.co.uk
www.citigatepa.com

Citypress PR
Manchester
0161 606 0260
www.citypress.co.uk

Clareville Communications
London
020 7736 4022
mail@clareville.co.uk
www.clareville.co.uk

**Clear Communication
Consultancy & Training**
London
020 7432 2500
clear@clearco.co.uk
www.clearco.co.uk

Cohesive Communications
London
020 7470 8777
www.cohesive.uk.com
Chepstow: 01291 626200

Cohn & Wolfe
London
020 7331 5300
jonathan_shore@cohnwolfe.com
www.cohnwolfe.com

Colette Hill Associates
London
020 7622 8252
cha@chapr.co.uk
www.chapr.co.uk

College Hill
London
020 7457 2020
pr@collegehill.com
www.collegehill.com

Colman Getty PR
London
020 7631 2666
pr@colmangetty.co.uk
www.colmangetty.co.uk
Edinburgh: 0131 558 8851

The Communication Group
London
020 7630 1411
enquiries@
    thecommunicationgroup.co.uk
www.thecommunicationgroup.co.uk

Communique PR
Manchester
0161 228 6677
www.communiquepr.co.uk
London: 020 7300 6300

Companycare Communications
Reading
0118 939 5900
www.companycare.com

Consolidated Communications
London
020 7287 2087
sarahr@consol.co.uk
www.consol.co.uk

Corixa Communications
Bristol
0117 949 3394
www.corixa.co.uk

Cow Communications
London
020 7684 6969
dirk.singer@cowpr.com
www.cowpr.com

Cubitt Consulting
London
020 7367 5100
www.cubitt.com

Darwall Smith Associates
London
020 7553 3700
gill@dsapr.co.uk
www.dsapr.co.uk

Dialogue Agency
Twickenham
020 8607 0340
enquiry@dialogueagency.com
www.dialogueagency.com

DTW
London
020 7233 8903
office@dtw.co.uk
www.dtw.co.uk
Canterbury: 01227 454023
Guisborough, Cleveland:
    01287 610404

Edelman
London
020 7344 1200
london@edelman.com
www.edelman.co.uk

Edson Evers
Stafford
01785 255146
www.edsonevers.com

**EHPR (Elizabeth Hindmarch
Public Relations)**
Windsor, Berkshire
01753 842017
info@ehpr.co.uk
www.ehpr.co.uk

EML
Kingston-upon-Thames, Surrey
020 8408 8000
info@eml.com
www.eml.com

Eulogy!
London
020 7927 9999
pr@eulogy.co.uk
www.eulogy.co.uk

EuroPR Group
London
020 8971 6400
info@europrgroup.com
www.europrgroup.com

Euro RSCG Riley
London
020 7022 4000
www.eurorscg-riley.co.uk

Financial Dynamics
London
020 7831 3113
amy.hewitt@fd.com
www.fd.com

Finsbury PR
London
020 7251 3801
info@finsbury.com
www.finsbury.com

Firefly Communications
London
020 7386 1400
claire.walker@fireflycomms.com
www.fireflycomms.com

Fishburn Hedges
London
020 7839 4321
info@fishburn-hedges.com
www.fishburn-hedges.co.uk

Flagship Consulting
London
020 7886 8440
info@flagshipconsulting.co.uk
www.flagshipconsulting.co.uk

Fleishman-Hillard (UK)
London
020 7306 9000
www.fleishman.com
Dublin: 00 353 1 618 8444
Edinburgh: 0131 226 2162

Focus PR
London
020 7432 9432
vision@focuspr.co.uk
www.focuspr.co.uk

Four Communications
London
07973 893 208
info@fourcommunications.com
www.fourcommunications.com

Fox Parrack Singapour
London
020 7436 4336
tparrack@foxps.com
www.foxps.com

Freshwater Marketing Commuications
Cardiff
029 2054 5370
info@freshwater-uk.com
www.freshwater-uk.com
Birmingham: 0121 633 7775
Bristol: 0117 906 6565
Edinburgh: 0131 220 8209
Glasgow: 0141 570 0205
London: 020 7486 9445

Freud Communications
London
020 7580 2626
jackie.edgar@freud.com
www.freud.com

Galliard Healthcare Communications
London
020 7663 2250
www.galliardhealth.com

Garnett Keeler Public Relations
Surbiton, Surrey
020 8399 1184
pr@garnett-keeler.com
www.garnett-keeler.com

GCI London
London
020 7072 4000
pr@gciuk.com
www.gciuk.com

Geronimo Communications
Leeds
0113 306 0000
welcome@
    geronimocommunications.com
www.geronimocommunications.com
Bury St Edmunds: 01284 768935
London: 020 7323 7170
Nottingham: 0115 934 7340

Geronimo PR
London
020 7299 8740
welcome@
    geronimocommunications.com
www.geronimopr.co.uk

GolinHarris
London
020 7067 0600
www.golinharris.com

Golley Slater PR
London
020 7240 9920
www.golleyslater.com
Birmingham: 0121 454 2323
Bristol: 0117 921 1131
Cardiff: 029 2038 8621
Cirencester: 01285 741111
Leeds: 0113 297 9737
Manchester: 0161 832 7178
Newcastle: 0191 245 9020
Twickenham: 020 8744 2630

Good Relations
London
020 7861 3030
afossey@goodrelations.co.uk
www.goodrelations.co.uk

Gough Allen Stanley
Bromsgrove, Worcs
01527 579555
info@gough.co.uk
www.gough.co.uk

Grant Butler Coomber
London
020 8322 1922
www.gbc.co.uk

Grayling
London
020 7255 1100
info@uk.grayling.com
www.grayling.com

Great Circle Communications
Edinburgh
0131 225 4646
info@greatcircle.co.uk
www.greatcircle.co.uk

Green Issues Communications
London
020 7321 3767
www.greenissues.com
Cardiff: 029 2050 4050
Manchester: 0161 209 3850
Reading: 0118 959 1211

Hallmark Public Relations
Winchester
01962 892900
inspired@hallmarkpr.com
www.hallmarkpr.com

Halogen PR
London
020 7487 9191
www.halogenuk.com
Cheltenham: 01242 227499

Harrison Cowley
London
020 7404 6777
info@harrisoncowley.com
www.harrisoncowley.com
Birmingham: 0121 367532
Bristol: 0117 983 6400
Cardiff: 029 2034 4717
Edinburgh: 0131 226 2363
Leeds: 0113 237 0777
Manchester: 0161 839 5666
Southampton: 0208 337237

Haslimann Taylor
Birmingham
0121 355 3446
bron@haslimanntaylor.com
www.haslimanntaylor.com

Haygarth
London
020 8971 3300
stephen.m@haygarth.co.uk
www.haygarth.co.uk

Henry's House
London
020 7291 3000
www.henryshouse.com

Hill & Knowlton
London
020 7973 5926
wfick@hillandknowlton.com
www.hillandknowlton.co.uk

Hills Balfour Synergy
London
020 7922 1100
info@hillsbalfour.com
www.hillsbalfour.com

The Hoffman Agency
Egham, Surrey
01784 487 920
lhoffman@hoffman.com
www.hoffman.com

Hotwire PR
London
020 7608 2500
kristin.syltevik@hotwirepr.com
www.hotwirepr.com

Houston Associates
London
020 8778 1900
info@houston-associates.com
www.houston-associates.com

IAS Smarts
Edinburgh
0131 555 0425
www.iassmarts.com
Belfast: 028 9039 5500
Birmingham 0121 456 3199
Glasgow: 0141 222 2040
Manchester: 01625 434343

ICAS PR
Hemel Hempstead
01442 261199
pr@icas.co.uk
www.icas.co.uk
London: 020 7632 2400

The Ideas Network
London
020 7351 4719
enquiries@ideasnetwork.co.uk
www.ideasnetwork.co.uk

The Impact Agency
London
020 7580 1770
mail@impactagency.co.uk
www.theimpactagency.com

Insight Marketing & Communications
London
020 7861 3999
info@insightmkt.com
www.insightmkt.com
Heathrow: 020 8564 6397
Manchester: 01625 500800

The ITPR Group
Chertsey, Surrey
01932 578800
www.itpr.co.uk

Jackie Cooper PR
London
020 7208 7208
Info@jcpr.com
www.jcpr.com

JBP Public Relations
Bristol
0117 907 3400
www.jbp.co.uk

Johnson King
London
020 7357 7799
mikek@johnsonking.co.uk
www.johnsonking.com

Julia Hobsbawm Consulting
London
020 7272 8898
www.juliahobsbawm.com

Kaizo
London
020 7580 8852
crispin.manners@kaizo.net
www.kaizo.net

Kavanagh Communications
Guildford
01483 238840
anne@kavanaghcommunications.com
www.kavanaghcommunications.com

Keene Public Affairs Consultants
London
020 7287 0652
kpac@keenepa.co.uk
www.keenepa.co.uk

Kelso Consulting
London
020 7388 8886
pr@kelsopr.com
www.kelsopr.com

Kenyon Fraser
Liverpool
0151 706 9931
richardk@kenyons.co.uk
www.kenyons.co.uk

Kestrel WorldCom
London
020 8543 2299
kestrel@kestrelcomms.co.uk
www.kestrelworldcom.com

Ketchum
London
020 7611 3500
david.gallagher@ketchum.com
www.ketchum.com

Kinross & Render
London
020 7592 3105
sr@kinrossrender.com
www.kinrossrender.com

Kysen PR
London
020 7323 3230
www.kysenpr.co.uk

Lansons Communications
London
020 7490 8828
pr@lansons.com
www.lansons.com

Lawson Dodd
London
020 7535 1355
iam@lawsondodd.co.uk
www.lawsondodd.co.uk

Leader Communications
Warwickshire
01564 796200
ms@leader.co.uk
www.leader.co.uk

Lewis PR
London
020 7802 2626
kathp@lewispr.com
www.lewispr.com

Lexis Public Relations
London
020 7908 6488
www.lexispr.com

Lighthouse PR
London
020 7494 6590
www.lighthousepr.com

London Communications Agency
London
020 7479 2830
lca@londoncommunications.co.uk
www.londoncommunications.co.uk

M: Communications
London
020 7153 1530
info@mcomgroup.com
www.mcomgroup.com

Manning Selvage & Lee
London
020 7878 3000
results@mslpr.co.uk
www.mslpr.co.uk

Mantra Public Relations
London
020 7907 7800
dsmith@mantra-pr.com
www.mantra-pr.com

Market Engineering
Banbury, Oxon
01295 277050
www.marketengineering.co.uk

Mary Rahman PR
London
020 7749 1136
www.mr-pr.com

Mason Williams
London
020 7534 6080
info@mason-williams.com
www.mason-williams.com
Manchester: 0161 273 5923

McCann Erickson Public Relations
Solihull
0121 713 3500
brendan.callaghan@
  europe.mccann.com
www.mccann.com

McCluskey International
London
020 8237 7979
info@mccluskey.co.uk
www.mccluskeyinternational.co.uk

Media Strategy
London
020 7400 4480
clewington@mediastrategy.co.uk
www.mediastrategy.co.uk

Medicom Group
Hampton Court, Surrey
020 8481 8100
enquiries@medicomgroup.com
www.medicomgroup.com

MediTech Media
London
020 7398 0500
info@meditech.co.uk
www.meditech-media.com
Manchester: 0161 236 2367

Midas PR
London
020 7584 7474
info@midaspr.co.uk
www.midaspr.co.uk

Midnight Communications
Brighton
01273 666 200
enquiries@midnight.co.uk
www.midnight.co.uk

Mulberry Marketing Communications
London
020 7928 7676
info@mulberrymc.com
www.mulberrymc.com

Munro & Forster Communications
London
020 7815 3900
www.munroforster.com

Neesham PR
Wendover, Buckinghamshire
01296 628180
admin@neesham.co.uk
www.neesham.co.uk

Nelson Bostock Communications
London
020 7229 4400
info@nelsonbostock.com
www.nelsonbostock.com

Nexus Communications Group
London
020 7808 9808
www.nexuspr.com

NorthBank Communications
Congleton
01260 296500
info@northbankcommunications.com
www.northbankcommunications.com
London: 020 3008 7556

Northern Lights
Harrogate
01423 562400
mail@northernlightspr.com
www.northernlightspr.com

Ogilvy Public Relations
London
020 7309 1000
www.ogilvypr.com

Pagoda PR
Edinburgh
0131 447 8999
info@pagodapr.com
www.pagodapr.co.uk
Belfast: 028 9032 8291

Parkgreen Communications
London
020 7493 3713
info@parkgreenmedia.com
www.parkgreenmedia.com

Partners Group
York
01904 610077
postbox@partners-group.co.uk
www.partners-group.co.uk

Pegasus PR
Worthing, West Sussex
01903 821550
info@pegasuspr.co.uk
www.pegasuspr.co.uk

Penrose Financial
London
020 7786 4888
pr@penrose.co.uk
www.penrose.co.uk

PFPR Communications
Maidstone, Kent
01622 691361
info@pfpr.com
www.pfpr.com

Phipps Public Relations
London
020 7759 7400
askus@phippspr.co.uk
www.phippspr.com

Pinnacle Marketing Communications
Pinner, Middlesex
020 8869 9339
simon@pinnaclemarcom.com
www.pinnacle-marketing.com

Piranhakid
London
020 7973 5938
www.piranhakid.com

Pleon
London
020 7479 5656
www.pleon.com

Porter Novelli
London
020 7853 2222
www.porternovelli.com
Banbury: 01295 224400
Edinburgh: 0131 470 3400

Portfolio Communications
London
020 7240 6959
www.portfoliocomms.com

Portland PR
London
020 7404 5344
info@portlandpr.co.uk
www.portlandpr.co.uk

Positive Profile
London
020 7489 2028
henryg@positiveprofile.com
www.positiveprofile.com

PPS Group
London
020 7629 7377
www.ppsgroup.co.uk
Birmingham: 0121 200 0813
Bristol: 01454 275 630
Edinburgh: 0131 226 1951
Manchester: 0161 832 2139

Prowse & Co
Leatherhead, Surrey
01372 363386
reception@prowse.co.uk
www.prowse.co.uk

Ptarmigan Consultants
Leeds
0113 242 1155
www.ptarmiganpr.co.uk

Public Relations Consultants Association
London
020 7233 6026
pressoffice@prca.org.uk
www.prca.org.uk

Purple PR
London
020 7439 9888
enquiries@purplepr.com
www.purplepr.com

QuayWest Communications
Coggeshall, Essex
01376 563156
s.morrison@quay-west.co.uk
www.quay-west.co.uk

Radiator PR
London
020 7404 8264
www.radiatorpr.com

Rainier PR
London
020 7494 6570
rainier@rainierpr.co.uk
www.rainierpr.co.uk
Cambridge: 01359 250641

The Red Consultancy
London
020 7025 6500
red@redconsultancy.com
www.redconsultancy.com

Red Door Communications
London
020 8392 8040
info@rdcomms.com
www.rdcomms.com

Regester Larkin
London
020 7831 3839
enquiries@regesterlarkin.com
www.regesterlarkin.com

Republic
London
020 7379 5000
www.republicpr.com

Resolute Communications
London
020 7357 8187
info@resolutecommunications.com
www.resolutecommunications.com

Revolver Communications
London
020 7251 5599
enquiries@revolvercomms.com
www.revolvercomms.com
Leeds: 0113 287 0077

Richard Lewis Communications
Southampton
01962 771111
info@crossculture.com
www.crossculture.com

Ruder Finn UK
London
020 7462 8900
mail@ruderfinn.co.uk
www.ruderfinn.com

Salt
London
020 8870 6777
info@saltlondon.com
www.saltlondon.com

Seal Communications
Birmingham
0121 200 0780
www.sealcommunications.co.uk
London: 020 7336 7313

Shine Communications
London
020 7553 3333
brilliance@shinecom.com
www.shinecom.com

Shire Health Group
London
020 7108 6400
matt.degruchy@
    shirehealthlondon.com
www.shirehealthlondon.com

Six Degrees
Marlow, Buckinghamshire
01628 480280
mail@sixdegreespr.com
www.sixdegreespr.com

Spark Marketing Communications
London
020 7357 8612
info@sparkcomms.co.uk
www.sparkcomms.co.uk

Spinoza Kennedy Vesey Public Relations
Manchester
0161 236 9909
www.skvpr.co.uk

Spreckley Partners
London
020 7388 9988
info@spreckley.co.uk
www.spreckley.co.uk

Staniforth
London
020 7573 7480
urgent@staniforth.co.uk
www.staniforth.co.uk
Manchester: 0161 919 8495

Starfish Communications
London
020 7323 2121
fearfield@star-fish.net
www.star-fish.net

Storm Communications
London
020 7240 2444
info@stormcom.co.uk
www.stormcom.co.uk
Beaconsfield: 01494 670444

StrategicAlliance International
Old Amersham, Bucks
01494 434434
nicholasf@strategicpr.net
www.strategicpr.net

Target Public Relations
Cheltenham
01242 633100
www.targetgroup.co.uk

Taylor Alden
London
020 8543 3866
pr@tayloralden.co.uk
www.tayloralden.com
Newbury: 01635 521103

Taylor Herring
London
020 8206 5151
james@taylorherring.com
www.taylorherring.com

TBWA UK Group
London
020 7573 6666
www.tbwa-london.com

Text 100
London
020 8846 0700
stacey.hinds@text100.co.uk
www.text100.com

Trimedia
London
020 7025 7500
www.trimediagroup.com
Glasgow: 0141 333 6440

Twelve Consultancy
London
020 7631 0737
graham@twelvepr.co.uk
www.twelvepr.co.uk

Warman Group
Birmingham
0121 605 1111
enquiries@warmangroup.com
www.warmangroup.com

Weber Shandwick
London
020 7067 0000
enquiriesuk@webershandwick.co.uk
www.webershandwick.co.uk

Westbury Communications
London
020 7751 9170
www.westburycom.co.uk

Whiteoaks Consultancy
Farnham, Surrey
01252 727313
comms@whiteoaks.co.uk
www.whiteoaks.co.uk

Wild Card PR
London
0207 355 0655
deck@wildcardpr.co.uk
www.wildcard.co.uk

William Murray PR
London
020 8256 1360
www.williammurraypr.co.uk

Willoughby PR
Birmingham
0121 456 3004
angelah@willoughby-pr.co.uk
www.willoughby-pr.co.uk

Write Image
London
020 7959 5400
info@write-image.co.uk
www.write-image.com

Wyatt International
Birmingham
0121 454 8181
info@wyattinternational.com
www.wyattinternational.com

Yellow Door Creative Marketing
London
020 7580 0707
www.yellow-door.co.uk

PR trade press

Black Book
020 8267 5000
directories@haynet.com
www.prweek.co.uk
Annual. Press and PR contacts. Formerly known as Contact. Owner: Haymarket. Publisher of Haymarket directories: Paula Fox

Hollis UK Public Relations Annual
020 8977 7711
orders@hollis-pr.co.uk
www.hollis-pr.com
Annual. Press and PR contacts. Owner: Hollis Publishing. Editor: Sarah Hughes

PR Week
020 8267 4429
prweek@haynet.com
www.prweek.com
Weekly. Owner: Haymarket. Editor: Danny Rogers; news: Ravi Chandiramani; features: Peter Crush; sub: Chris Young

Associations

Association of Public Relations Consultants
Willow House, Willow Place,
London SW1P 1JH
020 7233 6026
info@prca.org.uk
www.prca.org.uk

British Association of Communicators in Business
GA2 Oak House,
Woodlands Business Park,
Breckland, Linford Wood West,
Milton Keynes MK14 6EY
01908 313755
enquiries@cib.uk.com
www.cib.uk.com
Professional body for internal and corporate communications staff

Chartered Institute of Public Relations
32, St James's Square,
London SW1Y 4JR
020 7766 3333
info@cipr.co.uk
www.cipr.co.uk
Press: 020 7553 3772

Media law

You would think there were no more privacy boundaries left to cross by the British press in its relentless quest to shatter every remaining societal taboo. Well, you would – predictably – be wrong. Heather Mills McCartney and Madonna are our new celebrity media law figureheads, replacing Catherine Zeta Jones and Naomi Campbell, for so long the twin pioneers of their fields. For what Catherine did for copyright (the endless legal ins and outs of her wedding photos were more than just a Hello! moment) and Naomi did for intrusion (do we have a right to know she's been to rehab?), Mills McCartney and Madonna are doing for privacy.

Madonna's adoption of a Malawian baby was a global news story that, to be fair, she did little to discourage. Though she clearly didn't enjoy much of the comment and scrutiny of her methods, she launched the adoption with full press coverage of her philanthropic efforts in Malawi and followed it with an extensive tour of credible TV interviews in the US and the UK. Hard to believe now but she was interviewed on Newsnight.

As part of the PR tour, she released several private photographs of the baby with her other children. This was controversial at best. UK privacy laws and the Data Protection Act have all but stopped images of celebrities with their children. When you see a "candid" shot of Kate Moss or Gwyneth Paltrow with baby Lila or Apple, the child's face is routinely obscured, even if they have appeared in a public place.

Added to the law, the code of conduct of the Press Complaints Commission states absolutely that children under 16 must not be photographed or have details of their lives published on the grounds of the fame, notoriety or position of its parent.

Madonna's case was slightly odd. When her staff was bringing the baby to London, he was shielded from photographers. In Malawi, however, she had been happy to pose with him. She does have the right to call a halt, however, even now and use the courts to protect him and any arguments along the lines of "you put him in the public domain" would not apply. Of course, the regulators can only protect the baby if the parents choose to have him protected ...

Heather Mills McCartney, by contrast, has endured an extraordinary six months of negative press. First revelations about her previous glamour modelling career, then allegations that she worked as a call girl. After that, details from apparently leaked court documents relating to her divorce exposed all sorts of choice details about her marriage.

She announced she would sue, but the path to court seemed far from smooth. Defamation is hard to prove in a situation where she has so repeatedly been termed a liar, fantasist or even "former hooker". She announced she would sue the Mail, the London Evening Standard and, possibly, the Sun over specific details. The latter paper has been absolutely relentless in its coverage and perhaps even more brutal after her legal threats. Its position is that she has no reputation left to defend and has declared open season. Tricky.

The McCartney divorce provoked another legal question when some newspapers decided to be circumspect in their reporting of the allegations contained within the leaked court papers. The Daily Mail led the way, breaching the Judicial Proceedings (Regulation of Reports) Act 1926, which restricts reporting of divorces and printing the allegations in full. Once the Mail had leapt feet first, most other newspapers decided to a greater or lesser extent to follow.

As the Guardian's legal columnist Marcel Berlins pointed out, the Mail did a similar thing in the same week. This time it named a woman whose false allegations of rape led an innocent man to spend three years in prison. The Mail was the only paper to name the woman and under the Sexual Offences (Amendment) Act 1976, an alleged victim of rape is automatically entitled to lifelong anonymity. The Mail, Berlins concluded, seems to have decided that because the woman was named in Hansard, the record of parliamentary debate, the paper would be covered by qualified privilege, a legal protection that allows papers to report goings-on in parliament and is supposed to protect them from being sued if an MP, say, commits libel in the House. As Berlin says, "I cannot believe the law on privilege can be used to justify the newspaper committing a clear criminal offence."

● Defamation and libel

There was better news for journalists from the law lords in 2006 when the highest court moved to protect genuine old-school investigative journalism. A judgment in favour of a "public interest" defence for important stories was generally agreed to bring English libel law closer to that of the US, where the media have long been able to write more freely about public figures, as long as it can be argued to have been responsible.

The case in question was a December 2003 ruling against the Wall Street Journal. The paper had been ordered to pay damages of £40,000 to a Saudi billionaire businessman and his companies over an article that said the Saudi Arabian authorities were monitoring the bank accounts of prominent Saudis for evidence of supporting terrorism.

Using the "Reynolds defence" (a series of questions about the methods used by the journalist, including a right of reply, reasonable time to make that reply, a proportionate level of coverage and so on), the WSJ had argued its reporting had been important and reasonable. The law lords ruled that where the topic of an investigation is of public importance, even when the allegations could not be proved true subsequently, they should not attract libel damages if they have been published responsibly.

This may seem abstruse and complex, but in terms of investigative journalism its significance is overwhelming. As mainstream media outlets become increasingly sensitive to commercial pressures, newsrooms simply can't afford to gamble the shop on difficult and often hard to prove stories. It is overstating the case to say this development protects the future of investigative journalism as there are so many other commercial pressures, but as Lady Hale, one of the law lords, said: "We need more such serious journalism in this country and defamation law should encourage rather than discourage it."

Geoffrey Robertson QC, author of the textbook Media Law, who represented the Wall Street Journal, said: "The decision provides the media in Britain with an increased freedom to publish newsworthy stories. It frees serious investigative journalism from the chilling effect of libel actions, so long as the treatment is not sensational and the editorial behaviour is responsible.

Siobhain Butterworth, the legal director for Guardian Newspapers, pointed out that it had taken a US publisher "with First Amendment sensibilities to put English law back on track and improve protections for investigative journalism".

● Press regulation

Meanwhile, in Ireland, sweeping reforms to defamation legislation and the creation of a new privacy law were announced. The Irish government proposes to create a new press council with statutory powers (unlike the PCC), despite advice from the PCC that this would stifle press freedom.

Significantly for UK newspapers, the creation of this press council, if a success, will provide another argument for those who feel the PCC does not offer sufficient protection to members of the public from newspapers. The PCC can only offer censure and uphold rulings against editors rather than impose statutory punishments for infringements of its code. Obviously, the Irish editions of UK papers will be subject to the new rules.

The Irish justice minister, Michael McDowell, introducing the proposed legislation, said that anyone who sues a newspaper for defamation will have to swear a verifiable affidavit that they know the article to be untrue. This is an attempt to make "bluff" libels more difficult, the minister said.

He said the new privacy law was necessary to bring Ireland into line with European legislation following the landmark case of Princess Caroline of Monaco, in which the European court of human rights judged that the princess's privacy had been breached by paparazzi photographs of her shopping.

● Intellectual property

Finally, moves are underway to reform the UK's copyright protection laws and intellectual property framework. With the current vogue for "the long tail" – a business theory that states that the new economy will support a near infinite number of "niche markets" stretching back through the mists of time – it was inevitable that creators would want to hang on to the rights to their creations for as long as possible.

In music terms, for example, the success of online retailers such as Amazon proves that you can sell almost anything to someone, as long as you can access it in your vast warehouse of stock, because it's no longer prohibitively expensive to do so. So musicians are at the forefront of the campaign to end the "50 year rule" of UK copyright protection, which states that after 50 years you are no longer entitled to royalties. As artists can be expected to live longer these days, all those ageing musicians of the 60s are about to see their pensions fall out of copyright and a penniless old age approach.

Andrew Gowers, the former editor of the Financial Times, is conducting the review into copyright law. Reform is by no means certain, but that some sort of movement is needed seems to be the general consensus. At least among minor 60s popstars.

Law and the media, 2005-06

December 2006

The court dismissed an appeal by author Niema Ash to overturn a high-court injunction against her unauthorised book about the private life of Canadian folk singer Loreena McKennitt. The book contained details about McKennitt's life and feelings as well as some relatively innocuous detail, such as a description of her home. The content was deemed to be part of her private life, with the appeal court deciding that someone's right to protect their private life outweighs someone else's freedom to tell their story, unless there is a "very real" public interest. The ruling marks a seismic shift in media law protecting the privacy of the famous.

August 2006

Sir Elton John failed in an attempt to prevent the Daily Mail publishing an unflattering picture of him taken in public. Paparazzi pictures in which the singer appeared to be balding were not found to be evidence of harassment, ruled the High Court in London.

July 2006

In February 2006 the News of the World reported that there had been a "homosexual orgy" involving two Premiership footballers and a "pal well known in the music industry". They and the Sun newspaper later printed more details and a pixilated photo. England footballer Ashley Cole was not named but his identity was implied.

Cole won his legal action against News International after his lawyers proved that hints at his identity were enough to implicate him. The case demonstrates that publishers can be found guilty of libel without actually naming a person. This is called "jigsaw identification".

May 2006

Red magazine succeeded in a long-running struggle against Real magazine over trademark infringement and "passing off". In 2003, Real magazine had changed its logo. In doing so, Red argued the logo had become so similar to its own that readers were mistakenly buying Real. The dispute was settled outside of court with Real magazine agreeing to pay Red's legal fees and redesign its logo.

December 2005

Robbie Williams sued the People, Star and Hot Stars over allegations that he had "engaged in casual and sordid homosexual encounters with strangers". The People ran a story that suggested his forthcoming biography, Feel, would "deceive the public" by pretending that he had sex only with women. Similar allegations were printed by the Star and Hot Star magazines. All three publications issued formal apologies and paid "substantial" libel damages plus court fees to the pop star.

Law contacts

Media law firms

A&L Goodbody
International Financial Services
Centre, North Wall Quay, Dublin 1
00 353 1 649 2000
London: 020 7382 0800
law@algoodbody.ie
www.algoodbody.ie
*Specialist media and entertainment law
group, Ireland. IP and e-commerce; film
financing; production law; contracts;
defamation*

Adlex Solicitors
76A Belsize Lane, London NW3 5BJ
020 7317 8404
adamt@adlexsolicitors.co.uk
www.adlexsolicitors.co.uk
*Internet law; co-branding; software
licensing; IT; IP; trademark registration*

Akin Gump Strauss Hauer and Feld
Citypoint, Level 32,
One Ropemaker Street,
London EC2Y 9AW
020 7012 9600
londoninfo@akingump.com
www.akingump.com
*IP; licensing; finance; media infringement
(esp digital music online); defamation;
employment inc credit disputes, contracts,
confirmation of minors' contracts*

Allen and Overy
One New Change, London EC4M 9QQ
020 7330 3000
claire.meeghan@allenovery.com
www.allenovery.com
*IP; finance; regulatory and antitrust. For
IT, publishing, film, video, radio and TV,
programming, live performance, music,
sports, ads and PR*

Arnold and Porter (UK)
Tower 42, 25 Old Broad Street,
London EC2N 1HQ
020 7786 6100
www.arnoldporter.com
*Patents, trademarks, copyright and trade
secrets*

Ashurst
Broadwalk House, 5 Appold Street,
London EC2A 2HA
020 7638 1111
enquiries@ashurst.com
www.ashurst.com
*Commercial agreements, transactions
and litigation; acquisitions, disposals,
mergers; advice on European and UK law,
licensing, regulation esp pan-European
broadcasting; regulators, governments,
broadcasters, producers, telecoms,
multiplex and satellite operators;
specialist film practice*

Astburys
210 High Street, Lewes,
East Sussex BN7 2NH
01273 403935
jastbury@astburys-law.co.uk
www.astburys-law.co.uk
*Services for broadcasting, publishing and
advertising*

Baily Gibson
30 High Street, High Wycombe,
Buckinghamshire HP11 2AG
01494 442661
Beaconsfield: 01494 672661
wycombe@bailygibson.co.uk
www.bailygibson.co.uk
E-commerce; IP

Baker and McKenzie
100 New Bridge Street,
London EC4V 6JA
020 7919 1000
info@bakernet.com
www.bakernet.com
*E-commerce; IT licensing; broadcast
media regulation inc pay-per-view
contracts, digital copyright, convergence
of media and network technologies*

Beachcroft
100 Fetter Lane, London EC4A 1BN
020 7242 1011
London Eastcheap: 020 7208 6800
Birmingham: 0121 698 5200
Bristol: 0117 918 2000
Manchester: 0161 934 3000
Leeds: 0113 251 4700
Winchester: 01962 705500
info@beachcroft.co.uk
www.beachcroft.co.uk
*Interactive commerce and new media inc
branding; data protection and privacy;
franchising; IP; IT*

Beale and Company
Garrick House, 27-32 King Street,
Covent Garden, London WC2E 8JB
020 7240 3474
Dublin: 00 353 1 799 6213
reception@beale-law.com
www.beale-law.com
*IT inc software, hardware supply and
retail; e-commerce; internet; web design;
database licensing*

Berwin Leighton Paisner
Adelaide House, London Bridge,
London EC4R 9HA
020 7760 1000
media@blplaw.com
www.blplaw.com

Bevan Brittan
Head Office, 35 Colston Avenue,
Bristol, Avon BS1 4TT
0870 194 1000
info@bevanbrittan.com
www.bevanbrittan.com
*IP; IT. Also has offices in Birmingham and
London*

Bird and Bird
90 Fetter Lane, London EC4A 1JP
020 7415 6000
london@twobirds.com
www.twobirds.com
*IP; IT; broadcasting; film finance;
advertising; sponsorship; film
production; music; publishing*

Blake Lapthorn Linnell
Holbrook House, 14 Great Queen
Street, London WC2B 5DG
020 7430 1709
Oxford: 01865 248607
Southampton: 023 8063 1823
Fareham: 01489 579990
Portsmouth: 023 9222 1122
info@bllaw.co.uk
www.bllaw.co.uk
IP; IT

BM Nyman and Co
181 Creighton Avenue,
London N2 9BN
020 8365 3060
bernie.nyman@iname.com
www.bmnyman.co.uk
*Publishing law: copyright; defamation;
contracts*

Bournemouth Media School
Talbot Campus, Fern Barrow, Poole,
Dorset BH12 5BB
01202 965360
eforbes@bournemouth.ac.uk
http://media.bournemouth.ac.uk
*Media law consultancy to press,
broadcast, film and creative industries.
See also careers and training*

Briffa
Business Design Centre, Upper
Street, Islington, London N1 0QH
020 7288 6003
info@briffa.com
www.briffa.com
*IP inc brand protection; personality rights
in sport; rights for ad industry and
designers*

Brightley Commercial
Lower Landrine, Mitchell, Newquay,
Cornwall TR8 5BB
01872 519087
robert@brightley.com
www.brightley.com
*Commercial/company law; contracts; IP;
music business agreements*

Bristows
3 Lincoln's Inn Fields,
London WC2A 3AA
020 7400 8000
info@bristows.com
www.bristows.com
*IP and media law inc publishing, ads and
marketing. Defamation; sponsorship and
merchandising; TV distribution; privacy;
competition law*

Campbell Hooper
35 Old Queen Street,
London SW1H 9JD
020 7222 9070
ch@campbellhooper.com
www.campbellhooper.com
*IP; commercial and media dispute
resolutions; defamation and media
management; theatre; merchandising
and sponsorship; advertising and
marketing law; brand and domain name
management; ICT; e-commerce; software
licensing; data protection; licensing
agreements*

Capital Law Commercial
One Caspian Point, Caspian Way,
Cardiff CF10 4DQ
0870 224 1819
www.capitallaw.co.uk
Formerly Palser Grossman. IP

Carter-Ruck
International Press Centre,
76 Shoe Lane, London EC4A 3JB
020 7353 5005
lawyers@carter-ruck.com
www.carter-ruck.com
*Defamation; human rights; IP;
employment law*

Charles Lucas and Marshall
Eastcott House, 4 High Street,
Swindon SN1 3EP
01793 511055 Newbury: 01635
521212 Wantage: 01235 771234
Hungerford: 01488 682506
www.clmsolicitors.co.uk
IT

Charles Russell
8-10 New Fetter Lane,
London EC4A 1RS
020 7203 5000
Guildford: 01483 252525
Cheltenham: 01242 221122
enquiry@cr-law.co.uk
www.charlesrussell.co.uk
*Telecoms, IT, e-commerce, competition
and regulatory law specialists. Data
protection team; internet law;
entertainment work for film, TV, literary
and music sectors inc reputation
management and IP*

Clarke Willmott
Burlington House, Botleigh Grange
Business Park, Hedge End,
Southampton SO30 2DF
023 8062 4400
Birmingham: 0121 236 0076
Bristol: 0117 941 6600
Taunton: 01823 442266
info@clarkewillmott.com
www.clarkewillmott.com

Clifford Chance
10 Upper Bank Street, Canary Wharf,
London E14 5JJ
020 7006 1000
info@cliffordchance.com
www.cliffordchance.com
*Full IP service: patents, trademarks,
copyright, design, trade secrets and
unfair competition*

Clifford Miller
Burnhill Business Centre,
50 Burnhill Road, Beckenham,
Kent BR3 3LA
020 8663 0044
generalmail@ntlworld.com
www.cliffordmiller.com
IP; competition (anti-trust); IT law

Clintons
55 Drury Lane, Covent Garden,
London WC2B 5RZ
020 7379 6080
info@clintons.co.uk
www.clintons.co.uk
*Film and TV: finance; development; IP;
production; catalogue acquisition and
disposal; distribution and exploitation;
rights clearance. Radio: contracts; digital
exploitation; IP; licence agreements;
licence applications; regulation. Talent
agencies: contracts and individual
freelance broadcast and bi-media service
agreements. Publishing: contracts, libel,
disputes, rights exploitation*

Cobbetts
Ship Canal House, King Street,
Manchester M2 4WB
0845 404 2404 (also offices in
Birmingham and Leeds)
enquiries@cobbetts.co.uk
www.cobbetts.co.uk
*Software development, outsourcing, data
protection, distance selling and ad
regulations; defamation; IP; ICT;
experience in gaming, music publishing
and events, interactive TV, new media,
film and TV*

Collins Long
24 Pepper Street, London SE1 0EB
020 7401 9800
info@collinslong.com
www.collinslong.com
*Contracts; litigation; development;
production; financing; distribution*

Collyer-Bristow
4 Bedford Row, London WC1R 4DF
020 7242 7363
cblaw@collyerbristow.com
www.collyerbristow.com
*IP; IT and e-commerce; artists and
managers, composers and publishers,
record producers and distributors,
scriptwriters, indies, film producers,
actors and performers*

Constant and Constant
Sea Containers House, 20 Upper
Ground, London SE1 9QT
020 7261 0006
twoconstants@constantlaw.com
www.constantlaw.com
*Media and e-commerce: development,
production and financing; distribution
and sales; broadcasting and publishing;
advertising; IP*

Couchman Harrington Associates
20-22 Bedford Row, London WC1R
4EB
020 7611 9660
enquiries@couchmanharrington.com
www.chass.co.uk
Sports law, IP and broadcasting

Courts and Co
15 Wimpole Street, London W1G 9SY
020 7637 1651
law@courtsandco.com
www.courtsandco.com
*IP inc electronic delivery of AV material;
UK trademarks, community trademarks
and Madrid Protocol applications;
members of International Trademark
Association; classical music contracts -
recording, film and video*

**Covington and Burling - Registered
Foreign Lawyers and Solicitors -
London**
265 Strand, London WC2R 1BH
020 7067 2000
www.cov.com
*IP and data protection; broadcasting,
telecoms, multichannel video
distribution, PCS/cellular*

Cripps Harries Hall
Wallside House,
12 Mount Ephraim Road,
Tunbridge Wells, Kent TN1 1EG
01892 515121
reception@crippslaw.com
www.crippslaw.co.uk
*IP; technology; copyright and other media
rights; defamation, libel and slander*

**Cumberland Ellis (incorporating
Barth and Partners)**
Atrium Court, 15 Jockey's Fields,
London WC1R 4QR
020 7242 0422
contact@cumberlandellis.com
www.cep-law.co.uk
*Specialist sports law team advising on
issues such as sponsorship, licensing
agreements and media rights; IP;
specialist charity law team advising on
issues including commercial activities
and contracts, donations, constitutions
and dispute resolutions*

Davenport Lyons
30 Old Burlington Street,
London W1S 3NL
020 7468 2600
dl@davenportlyons.com
www.davenportlyons.com
*Specialist areas: defamation; film
and TV; music; IP; publishing; ads;
IT, e-commerce, interactive and new
media; sport*

**David Price Solicitors and
Advocates**
21 Fleet Street, London EC4Y 1AA
020 7353 9999
enquiries@lawyers-media.com
www.lawyers-media.com
*Defamation (libel and slander), breach
of confidence and privacy, contempt and
copyright, pre-publication advice,
internet defamation*

Dean Marsh and Co
1892 Building, 54 Kingsway Place,
Sans Walk, London EC1R 0LU
020 7553 4400
info@deanmarsh.com
www.deanmarsh.com
Music and entertainment

Denton Wilde Sapte
Five Chancery Lane, Clifford's Inn,
London EC4A 1BU
020 7242 1212
info@dentonwildesapte.com
www.dentonwildesapte.com
*IP; services for ads and marketing,
broadcasting, IT, live performance,
music, publishing, sponsorship, sport and
telecoms; film and TV production, film
financing*

Dickinson Dees
St Ann's Wharf, 112 Quayside,
Newcastle Upon Tyne NE99 1SB
0191 279 9000
law@dickinson-dees.com
www.dickinson-dees.com
IT and e-commerce

DLA Piper Rudnick Gray Cary
3 Noble Street, London EC2V 7EE
0870 011 1111
(also offices in Birmingham,
Liverpool, Manchester, Leeds,
Sheffield, Edinburgh, Glasgow)
info@dlapiper.com
www.dlapiper.com
*Defamation, confidentiality and privacy,
digital media, data protection and
freedom of information, publishing,
gaming, contractual, IT. Clients include
Time Warner Book Group, ITV plc,
Thomson and IPC*

DMA Legal
4th Foor, 15-16 New Burlington
Street, London W1S 3BJ
020 7534 5850
info@dmalegal.com
www.dmalegal.com
*IP, defamation, contracts, licensing,
distribution, multimedia agreements,
royalty arrangements*

DMH Stallard
100 Queens Road, Brighton,
East Sussex BN1 3YB
01273 329833
Brighton: 01273 329833
Gatwick: 01293 605000
London: 020 7423 1000
enquiries@dmhstallard.com
www.dmhstallard.com
*Technology, media and telecoms;
charities and public sector*

Dorsey and Whitney
21 Wilson Street, London EC2M 2TD
020 7588 0800
london@dorsey.com
www.dorsey.com
IP litigation

DWF
5 Castle Street, Liverpool,
Merseyside L2 4XE
0151 907 3000
Manchester: 0161 603 5000
enquiries@dwf.co.uk
www.dwf.co.uk
IP; contracts

Dyer Burdett and Co
64 West Street, Havant,
Hampshire PO9 1PA
023 9249 2472
mail@dyerburdett.com
www.dyerburdett.com
*IP; sport; TV, radio, film and theatre
production and licensing*

Edwin Coe
2 Stone Buildings, London WC2A 3TH
020 7691 4000
law@edwincoe.com
www.edwincoe.com
IP

Eversheds
Senator House,
85 Queen Victoria Street,
London EC4V 4JL
020 7919 4500
Birmingham: 0121 232 1000
Cambridge: 01223 443666
Ipswich: 01473 284428
Leeds: 0113 243 0391
Manchester: 0161 831 8000
Cardiff: 029 2047 1147
Newcastle: 0191 241 6000
Norwich: 01603 272727
Nottingham: 0115 950 7000
www.eversheds.com
*E-commerce, IT; music, TV and related
areas; IP*

Farrer and Co
66 Lincoln's Inn Fields,
London WC2A 3LH
020 7242 2022
enquiries@farrer.co.uk
www.farrer.co.uk
IP and media law

Fennemores
200 Silbury Boulevard,
Central Milton Keynes,
Buckinghamshire MK9 1LL
01908 678241
info@fennemores.co.uk
www.fennemores.co.uk
*Data protection and contracts in
e-business and technology*

Ferdinand Kelly
21 Bennetts Hill, Birmingham,
West Midlands B2 5QP
0121 643 5228
pm@ferdinandkelly.co.uk
www.ferdinandkelly.co.uk
E-commerce, franchising, IT, IP

Field Fisher Waterhouse
35 Vine Street, London EC3N 2AA
020 7861 4000
info@ffw.com
www.ffw.com
*Services to broadcasters and publishers
esp licensing book and magazine
publishing rights in TV programmes; IP*

Finers Stephens Innocent
179 Great Portland Street,
London W1W 5LS
020 7323 4000
enquiries@fsilaw.co.uk
www.fsilaw.com
*Specialist areas: ads and sales promotion;
anti-counterfeiting; copyright; cultural
property; defamation; design rights; IT
and e-commerce; obscenity; publishing;
sports law; trademark and brand
management; visual arts; photo agencies
and libraries; TV and film*

Fladgate Fielder
25 North Row, London W1K 6DJ
020 7323 4747
fladgate@fladgate.com
www.fladgate.com
IP, IT and sports law

Foot Anstey
21 Derrys Cross, Plymouth,
Devon PL1 2SW
01752 675000 Exeter: 01392 411221
Taunton: 01823 337151
info@foot-ansteys.co.uk
www.foot-ansteys.co.uk
*Specialist media, commercial, and
employment advice to newspapers,
publishers and ISPs*

Freshfields Bruckhaus Deringer
65 Fleet Street, London EC4Y 1HS
020 7936 4000
www.freshfields.com
*IP; IT; specialist telecoms, media and
technology (TMT) group*

Gamlins
31-37 Russell Road, Rhyl,
Denbighshire LL18 3DB
01745 343500
gamlins@gamlins.co.uk
www.gamlins.co.uk
IP

George Davies
Fountain Court, 68 Fountain Street,
Manchester, Lancashire M2 2FB
0161 236 8992
mail@georgedavies.co.uk
www.georgedavies.co.uk
*IP, contracts and franchising; also sports
personalities and major sporting bodies*

Gersten and Nixon
National House, 60-66 Wardour
Street, London W1F 0TA
020 7439 3961
law@gernix.co.uk
www.gernix.co.uk
All aspects of media and entertainment law

Goodman Derrick
90 Fetter Lane, London EC4A 1PT
020 7404 0606
law@gdlaw.co.uk
www.gdlaw.co.uk
*Media law: disputes and litigation;
contracts and documentation;
programme clearance; regulatory
advice. Film: banking, securitisation;
distribution, writer and talent contracts;
mergers and acquisitions; sponsorship
and merchandising agreements; script
clearance*

Gray and Co
Habib House, 3rd Floor,
9 Stevenson Square,
Piccadilly, Greater Manchester,
Lancashire M1 1DB
0161 237 3360
grayco@grayand.co.uk
www.grayand.co.uk
*Entertainment industry in Manchester
and north-west esp. music and record
companies, film and TV contracts and
finance, sport*

Greenwoods Solicitors
Monkstone House,
City Road, Peterborough,
Cambridgeshire PE1 1JE
01733 887700
www.greenwoods.co.uk
*IP; e-commerce and IT; property and
planning issues for production companies;
corporate and commercial law*

Grundberg Mocatta Rakison
Imperial House, 15–19 Kingsway,
London WC2B 6UN
020 7632 1600
post@gmrlaw.com
www.gmrlaw.com
IP

H2O Law
40–43 Chancery Lane,
London WC2A 1JQ
020 7405 4700
enquiries@h2o-law.com
www.h2o-law.com
*Art and photography: advise artists and
photographers on IP, contracts and
licensing; Publishing: manages authors
rights, advises on contract and dispute
issues, IP and libel vetting*

Halliwells
St James's Court, Brown Street,
Manchester M2 2JF
0870 365 8000 (also offices in
Liverpool, London and Sheffield)
info@halliwells.com
www.halliwells.com
*Services to music and sports industries;
IP; financing*

Hamlins
Roxburghe House,
273–287 Regent Street,
London W1B 2AD
020 7355 6000
enquiries@hamlins.co.uk
www.hamlins.co.uk
IP and copyright

Hammonds
7 Devonshire Square,
Cutlers Gardens, London EC2M 4YH
0870 839 0000
enquiries@hammonds.com
www.hammonds.com
*ICT, e-commerce, data protection, media,
sport and entertainment*

Harbottle and Lewis
Hanover House, 14 Hanover Square,
London W1S 1HP
020 7667 5000
www.harbottle.com
*All areas inc film, TV, broadcasting, IT,
sport, music, publishing, fashion,
advertising, marketing and theatre;
IP, defamation, employment, property,
immigration, finance, tax and admin*

Haynes Phillips
113–117 Farringdon Road,
London EC1R 3BX
020 7242 2213
hello@haynesphillips.com
www.haynesphillips.com
*IP; music: contracts, rights, licensing,
management, merchandising, music
publishing, videos*

HBJ Gateley Wareing
One Eleven Edmund Street,
Birmingham B3 2HJ
0121 234 0000
Nottingham: 0115 983 8200
Leicester: 0116 285 9000
info@hbj-gw.com
www.gateleywareing.co.uk
*IP, esp in computers and software;
technology sector: trademarks, patents,
e-commerce, databases and rights*

Herbert Smith
Exchange House, Primrose Street,
London EC2A 2HS
020 7374 8000
contact@herbertsmith.com
www.herbertsmith.com
*Litigation, competition, corporate, IP,
piracy, copyright and defamation;
TV and radio, IT, books and publishing,
media, music, ads and marketing*

Hewitsons
Shakespeare House,
42 Newmarket Road, Cambridge,
Cambridgeshire CB5 8EP
01223 461155
Northampton: 01604 233233
Saffron Walden: 01799 522471
mail@hewitsons.com
www.hewitsons.com
IP; IT inc internet, e-commerce, ICT

Hextalls
28 Leman Street, London E1 8ER
020 7488 1424
info@hextalls.com
www.hextalls.com
*Telecoms, media and technology dept
serving music, entertainment, publishing
and telecoms sector*

Hill Dickinson
Pearl Assurance House,
2 Derby Square, Liverpool L2 9XL
0151 236 5400
London: 020 7695 1000
Manchester: 0161 817 7200
Chester: 01244 896600
law@hilldickinson.com
www.hilldickinson.com
*Broadcasting, theatre and film;
e-commerce; endorsement,
merchandising and sponsorship; IT; libel
and slander; publishing; sports law*

HLW
Princess House, 122 Queen Street,
Sheffield, South Yorkshire S1 2DW
0114 276 5555
info@hlwlaw.co.uk
www.hlwlaw.co.uk
IP

Holme Roberts and Owen
124 Chancery Lane,
London EC4A 1BU
020 7320 6464
www.hro.com
*IP; film, telecoms, sport and
entertainment*

Howard Kennedy
Harcourt House, 19 Cavendish
Square, London W1A 2AW
020 7636 1616
enquiries@howardkennedy.com
www.howardkennedy.com
IP; film, TV, music, theatre, sports

Howell-Jones Partnership
75 Surbiton Road,
Kingston upon Thames,
Surrey KT1 2AF
020 8549 5186
kingston@hjplaw.co.uk
www.hjplaw.co.uk
IP

Humphreys and Co
14 King Street, Bristol BS1 4EF
0117 929 2662
lawyers@humphreys.co.uk
www.humphreys.co.uk
*IP; sports contracts; IT; also advises
artists, publishers, writers, managers and
record companies in music and
entertainment industries*

Ingram Winter Green
Bedford House, 21A John Street,
London WC1N 2BL
020 7845 7400
back-chat@iwg.co.uk
www.iwg.co.uk
*E-business and IT; clients in TV, print
media, film, radio, music, printing and
ad industries; film finance, syndication,
distribution, regulation and broadcasting
complaints*

Kemp Little
Cheapside House, 138 Cheapside,
London EC2V 6BJ
020 7600 8080
amanda.millar@kemplittle.com
www.kemplittle.com
IP; IT and telecoms regulation

Kent Jones and Done
Churchill House,
Regent Road, Stoke-On-Trent,
Staffordshire ST1 3RQ
01782 202020
mail@kjd.co.uk
www.kjd.co.uk
*IT, e-commerce, technology licensing,
trademarks and copyright, entertainment*

Kimbells
Power House, Harrison Close,
Knowlhill, Milton Keynes MK5 8PA
01908 668555
www.kimbells.com
IT and IP

Kirkland and Ellis International
30 St Mary Axe, London EC3A 8AF
020 7469 2000
info@kirkland.com
www.kirkland.com
*IP inc transactions and litigation relating
to internet and e-commerce*

**Kirkpatrick and Lockhart Nicholson
Graham**
110 Cannon Street, London EC4N 6AR
020 7648 9000
mbennett@klng.com
www.klng.com
IP; IT and technologies

Kuit Steinart Levy
3 St Marys Parsonage, Manchester,
Lancashire M3 2RD
0161 832 3434
ksllaw@kuits.com
www.kuits.com
*Licensing and brand acquisitions; sports
merchandising; e-commerce*

Latham and Watkins
11th Floor, 99 Bishopsgate,
London EC2M 3XF
020 7710 1000
owen.williams@lw.com
www.lw.com
*IP and technology; acquisition, financing,
licensing and dispute resolution*

Lawdit Solicitors
No 1 Brunswick Place,
Southampton SO15 2AN
023 8023 5979
info@lawdit.co.uk
www.lawdit.co.uk
*IP inc domain names, data protection,
e-commerce, IT contracts, media law,
trademarks and websites*

Laytons
Carmelite, 50 Victoria Embankment,
Blackfriars, London EC4Y 0LS
020 7842 8000
Guildford: 01483 407000
Manchester: 0161 834 2100
london@laytons.com
www.laytons.com
*IP, IT and related UK and EU competition
law*

Leathes Prior
74 The Close, Norwich,
Norfolk NR1 4DR
01603 610911
info@leathesprior.co.uk
www.leathesprior.co.uk
*IP inc counterfeiting, domain names,
passing-off and trade libel; data
protection; employment; e-commerce
and IT*

Lee and Thompson
Greengarden House,
15-22 St Christophers Place,
London W1U 1NL
020 7935 4665
mail@leeandthompson.com
www.leeandthompson.com
*All aspects of media work covered
(contracts, business structures, IP,
litigation etc) esp in the fields of music,
film and television (finance and
production), sport and celebrity
representation*

Lennox Bywater
9 Limes Avenue, London NW7 3NY
020 8906 1206
lennox.bywater@virgin.net
www.lennoxbywater.com
Sports law

Leonard Lowy and Co
500 Chiswick High Road,
London W4 5RG
020 8956 2785
leonard@leonardlowy.co.uk
www.leonardlowy.co.uk
Music industry

Lester Aldridge
Russell House, Oxford Road,
Bournemouth, Dorset BH8 8EX
01202 786161
info@LA-law.com
www.lesteraldridge.com
IP

Lewis Silkin
5 Chancery Lane, Clifford's Inn,
London EC4A 1BL
020 7074 8000
info@lewissilkin.com
www.lewissilkin.com
Media brands and technology

Linklaters
One Silk Street, London EC2Y 8HQ
020 7456 2000
rupert.winlaw@linklaters.com
www.linklaters.com
*IP; IT and comms law - inc telecoms and
satellites; broadcasting; e-commerce and
internet; outsourcing; data protection*

Lovells
Atlantic House, Holborn Viaduct,
London EC1A 2FG
020 7296 2000
information@lovells.com
www.lovells.com
IP; technology, media and telecoms

Macfarlanes
10 Norwich Street, London EC4A 1BD
020 7831 9222
penny.rutterford@macfarlanes.com
www.macfarlanes.com
*IP: IT; e-commerce; advertising and
marketing*

Maclay Murray and Spens
151 St Vincent Street,
Glasgow G2 5NJ
0141 248 5011
London: 020 7002 8500
Edinburgh: 0131 226 5196
Aberdeen: 01224 356130
magnus.swanson@mms.co.uk
www.mms.co.uk
*IP; technology (software, electronics and
engineering), film and media, internet
and e-commerce*

Magrath and Co
52-54 Maddox Street,
London W1S 1PA
020 7495 3003
admin@magrath.co.uk
www.magrath.co.uk
*IP; agreements for recording artists and
recording companies, actors, sports
people, TV and filmmakers*

Manches
Aldwych House, 81 Aldwych,
London WC2B 4RP
020 7404 4433
manches@manches.com
www.manches.com
*IT, IP, internet, publishing and media inc
sponsorship, merchandising, financing,
litigation, defamation, data protection,
ad and sales promotion laws*

Mann and Partners
New Court Chambers,
23-25 Bucks Road, Douglas,
Isle Of Man IM99 2EN
01624 695800
law@mannandpartners.com
www.mannandpartners.com
*Contracts, disputes and general work for
the film industry*

**Marks and Clerk Patent and
Trademark Attorneys**
90 Long Acre, London WC2E 9RA
020 7420 0000
london@marks-clerk.com
www.marks-clerk.com
*Patents; trademarks; copyright; design;
domain names; licensing*

Marks and Clerk solicitors
90 Long Acre, London WC2E 9RA
020 7420 0250
solicitors@marks-clerk.com
www.marks-clerk.com
IP; IT; publishing

Marriott Harrison
12 Great James Street,
London WC1N 3DR
020 7209 2000
www.marriottharrison.co.uk
*Corporate finance; media/
entertainment; commercial/IT*

Martineau Johnson
1 Colmore Square,
Birmingham B4 6AA
0870 763 2000
lawyers@martjohn.com
www.martineau-johnson.co.uk
*IP; IT inc hardware acquisition, software
licensing, internet and e-commerce*

McClure Naismith
Equitable House,
47 King William Street,
London EC4R 9AF
020 7929 3770
Edinburgh: 0131 228 4994
Glasgow: 0141 204 2700
london@mcclurenaismith.com
www.mcclurenaismith.com
IP; IT; dispute resolution and litigation

McCormicks
Britannia Chambers, 4 Oxford Place,
Leeds, West Yorkshire LS1 3AX
0113 246 0622
Harrogate: 01423 530630
p.mccormick@
    mccormicks-solicitors.com
www.mccormicks-solicitors.com
*IP; defamation and media law;
sponsorship; sports law; rights
management and exploitation;
charity law; general commercial and
corporate law*

McGrigors
5 Old Bailey, London EC4M 7BA
020 7054 2500
enquiries@mcgrigors.com
www.mcgrigors.com
IP

Memery Crystal Solicitors
44 Southampton Buildings,
London WC2A 1AP
020 7242 5905
info@memerycrystal.com
www.memerycrystal.com
*Digital technology inc branding, software
development, licensing agreements, IP,
data protection, rights protection,
litigation, domain name disputes and
internet libel*

MLM
Pendragon House, Fitzalan Court,
Newport Road, Cardiff,
South Glamorgan CF24 0BA
029 2046 2562
enquiries@mlmsolicitors.com
www.mlmsolicitors.com
*IP; IT, technology companies,
TV companies and broadcasters*

Moorcrofts
Mere House, Mere Park,
Dedmere Road, Marlow,
Buckinghamshire SL7 1PB
01628 470000
info@moorcrofts.com
www.moorcrofts.com
*Corporate, IP and regulation. Clients
include RDF, Video Arts and TV Network*

Morgan Cole
Buxton Court, 3 West Way, Oxford,
Oxfordshire OX2 0SZ
01865 262600
Cardiff: 029 2038 5385
Reading: 0118 955 3000
London: 020 8774 6700
oxford@morgan-cole.com
www.morgan-cole.com
IP

Morrison and Foerster MNP
CityPoint, 1 Ropemaker Street,
London EC2Y 9AW
020 7920 4000
london@mofo.com
www.mofo.com
*IP; new media and technology; telecoms
and other regulation; all aspects of
project and corporate finance*

Myers Fletcher and Gordon
15 Cambridge Court,
210 Shepherds Bush Road,
Hammersmith, London W6 7NJ
020 7610 4433
mfg@mfglon.co.uk
www.mfg-law.com
*Entertainment law, internet, copyright,
appropriation of personality, IP, dispute
litigation*

Nabarro Nathanson
Lacon House, Theobalds Road,
London WC1X 8RW
020 7524 6000
info@nabarro.com
www.nabarro.com
E-commerce, telecoms, IT

Network Law
Anvil Court, Denmark Street,
Wokingham, Berkshire RG40 2BB
0118 989 7110
info@networklaw.org
www.networklaw.org
*National IT IP firm. Clients include
Microsoft and Dell*

New Media Law
102 Dean Street, London W1D 3TQ
020 7734 9777
ian.penman@newmedialaw.biz
www.newmedialaw.biz
*Specialise in media/entertainment law,
including copyright (film, music and TV)
and new media*

Nexus Solicitors
Carlton House, 16-18 Albert Square,
Manchester, Lancashire M2 5PE
0161 819 4900
help@nexussolicitors.co.uk
www.nexussolicitors.co.uk
*Sports and media inc sponsorship,
endorsement agreements, merchandising
and licensing, football transfers, event
regulation, publishing*

Norton Rose
Kempson House,
35-37 Camomile Street,
London EC3A 7AN
020 7283 6000
www.nortonrose.com
All aspects of media law

Olswang
90 High Holborn, London WC1V 6XX
020 7067 3000
london@olswang.com
www.olswang.com
*Media communications, technology and
property*

Orchard Brayton Graham
24 Britton Street, London EC1M 5UA
0870 874 7477
info@orchardlaw.com
www.obglaw.com
*Film, marketing, music, publishing, TV
and radio, IT, internet*

Osborne Clarke
One London Wall, London EC2Y 5EB
020 7105 7000
www.osborneclarke.com
*IP; IT and telecoms; advertising and
marketing*

Peachey and Co
95 Aldwych, London WC2B 4JF
020 7316 5200
email@peachey.co.uk
www.peachey.co.uk
*Broadcasting; creative media (ads and
marketing); new media; software and IT
services; sport; telecoms*

Penningtons
Bucklersbury House, 83 Cannon
Street, London EC4N 8PE
020 7457 3000
information@penningtons.co.uk
www.penningtons.co.uk
E-business and IP

Pictons
28 Dunstable Road, Luton,
Beds LU1 1DY
01582 870870
marketing@pictons.co.uk
www.pictons.co.uk
Technology IP

Pinsent Masons
Dashwood House,
69 Old Broad Street,
London EC2M 1NR
020 7418 7000
Birmingham: 0121 200 1050
Bristol: 0117 924 5678
Edinburgh: 0131 225 0000
Glasgow: 0141 248 4858
Leeds: 0113 244 5000
Manchester: 0161 250 0100
enquiries@pinsentmasons.com
www.pinsentmasons.com
*IP; IT inc resolution of IT and telecoms
disputes*

Putsman Solicitors
Britannia House,
50 Great Charles Street,
Birmingham, West Midlands B3 2LT
0121 237 3000
www.pwlc.co.uk
*IP etc for TV production, band and media
managers, celeb agents, publishers,
media personalities, signed bands and
artists, casting agents, venues*

Rawlison Butler
Griffin House, 135 High Street,
Crawley, West Sussex RH10 1DQ
01293 527744
info@rawlisonbutler.com
www.rawlisonbutler.com
*IP and brand protection; IT and
e-commerce; data protection; EU and
UK competition law; contracts*

Reed Smith
Minerva House, 5 Montague Close,
London SE1 9BB
020 7403 2900
mrutherford@reedsmith.com
www.reedsmith.com
*Pre-publication and pre-broadcast inc
libel, invasion of privacy etc; non-
litigation such as protecting IP, general
corporate, negotiation of industry-related
agreements, labour and employment,
comms regulatory, and ad branding;
media management*

Reid Minty
Moss House, 15-16 Brooks Mews,
London W1K 4DS
020 7318 4444
lawyers@reidminty.co.uk
www.reidminty.co.uk
*Defamation: libel, slander and malicious
falsehood; employment and litigation*

Reynolds Porter Chamberlain
Tower Bridge House,
St Katharine's Way, London E1W 1AA
020 3060 6000
enquiries@rpc.co.uk
www.rpc.co.uk
*Content-related issues for press,
publishers, TV*

Richard Howard and Co
45-51 Whitfield Street,
London W1T 4HB
020 7831 4511
richard.howard@richardhoward.co.uk
www.richardhoward.tv
*TV, paper and electronic publishing,
multimedia and telecoms; IP*

Richards Butler International
Beaufort House, 15 St Botolph Street,
London EC3A 7EE
020 7247 6555
rjp@richardsbutler.com
www.richardsbutler.com
*IP; telecoms; IT, data protection and
e-business*

Ricksons
6 Winckley Square, Preston PR1 3JJ
01772 556677
Leeds: 0113 243 1555
Manchester: 0161 833 3355
info@ricksons.co.uk
www.ricksons.co.uk
*E-commerce and computer contracts; IP;
confidentiality agreements and data
protection*

Robert Muckle
Norham House,
12 New Bridge Street West,
Newcastle upon Tyne NE1 8AS
0191 232 4402
enquiries@robertmuckle.co.uk
www.robertmuckle.co.uk
IP; IT; dispute resolution

Roiter Zucker
Regent House,
5-7 Broadhurst Gardens,
Swiss Cottage, London NW6 3RZ
020 7328 9111
mail@roiterzucker.co.uk
www.roiterzucker.co.uk
IP and disputes

Rollits
Wilberforce Court, High Street, Hull,
North Humberside HU1 1YJ
01482 323239
info@rollits.com
www.rollits.com
*IP and telecoms; media and
entertainment law; IT/ technology*

Rooks Rider
Challoner House, 19 Clerkenwell
Close, London EC1R ORR
020 7689 7000
lawyers@rooksrider.co.uk
www.rooksrider.co.uk
IP

Rosenblatt
9-13 St Andrew Street,
London EC4A 3AF
020 7955 0880
info@rosenblatt-law.co.uk
www.rosenblatt-law.co.uk
Defamation and IP

Ross and Craig
12a Upper Berkeley Street,
London W1H 7QE
020 7262 3077
reception@rosscraig.com
www.rosscraig.com
*Co-production arrangements; IP and
copyright; film and TV funding; rights
acquisition; production and artistes'
contracts; defamation; IT and e-commerce*

Rowberry Morris
17 Castle Street, Reading,
Berkshire RG1 7SB
0118 958 5611
admin@rowberrymorris.co.uk
www.rowberrymorris.co.uk
*All aspects of media law. Specialist unit
advises new bands and writers*

RT Coopers Solicitors
Telfords Yard, 6/8 The Highway,
London E1W 2BS
020 7488 2985
enquiries@rtcoopers.com
www.rtcoopers.com
*Film, TV, music, IP, copyright, branding,
licensing, publishing etc*

Salans
Millennium Bridge House,
2 Lambeth Hill, London EC4V 4AJ
020 7429 6000
london@salans.com
www.salans.com
IP; IT and communications law

Schillings
Royalty House, 72-74 Dean Street,
London W1D 3TL
020 7453 2500
legal@schillings.co.uk
www.schillings.co.uk
IP and media management

Seddons
5 Portman Square, London W1H 6NT
020 7725 8000
enquiries@seddons.co.uk
www.seddons.co.uk
Entertainment and music industry

Shepherd And Wedderburn
12 Arthur Street, London EC4R 9AB
020 7763 3200
www.shepwedd.co.uk
*IP and trademark litigation, copyright,
sport law*

Sheridans
Whittington House, Alfred Place,
London WC1E 7EA
020 7079 0100
info@sheridans.co.uk
www.sheridans.co.uk
*Agreements; music, book and magazine
publishing; distribution; licensing;
merchandising; sponsorship; trademarks
and domain names*

Simmons and Simmons
Citypoint, 1 Ropemaker Street,
London EC2Y 9SS
020 7628 2020
enquiries@simmons-simmons.com
www.simmons-simmons.com
*IT litigation; technology, media and
telecommunications*

Simons Muirhead and Burton
50 Broadwick Street, Soho,
London W1F 7AG
020 7734 4499
mail@smab.co.uk
www.smab.co.uk
*Film and TV regulatory and production
law; dispute resolution, copyright and
libel advice*

SJ Berwin
10, Queens Street Place,
London EC4R 1BE
020 7111 2222
info@sjberwin.com
www.sjberwin.com
*IP; film, TV and radio work (content
and carriage), music, telecoms, sport,
animation, digital media, e-commerce
and online*

Slaughter and May
One Bunhill Row, London EC1Y 8YY
020 7600 1200
www.slaughterandmay.com
IP; IT; technology, media and telecoms

Spearing Waite
41 Friar Lane, Leicester,
Leicestershire LE1 5RB
0116 262 4225
info@spearingwaite.co.uk
www.spearingwaite.co.uk
Franchising, agency and licensing; IP

Spring Law
40 Craven Street, London WC2N 5NG
020 7930 4158
tim.perry@springlaw.co.uk
www.Springlaw.co.uk
*IP, franchise arrangements, sponsorship,
rights exploitation, distribution,
merchandising, licensing, marketing, ads
and promotions*

Squire Sanders and Dempsey
1st Floor, 60 Cannon Street,
London EC4N 6NP
020 7189 8000
ssdinfo@ssd.com
www.ssd.com
*Communications law inc IP, internet,
licensing, regulatory restructuring,
satellite communications, broadcasting
and cable*

Steeles
Bedford House, 21A John Street,
London WC1N 2BF
020 7421 1720
media@steeleslaw.co.uk
www.steeleslaw.co.uk
*For record labels, agents, managers,
event organisers, artists, publishers,
writers, broadcasters, unions and
professional bodies*

Stringer Saul
17 Hanover Square, London W1S 1HU
020 7917 8500
info@stringersaul.co.uk
www.stringersaul.co.uk
IP; IT and internet; publishing

Tarlo Lyons
Watchmaker Court,
33 St John's Lane, London EC1M 4DB
020 7405 2000
simon.stokes@tarlolyons.com
www.tarlolyons.com
*IP; digital media; IT; data protection;
ads; website development and
e-commerce; information security
and fraud; telecoms*

Taylor Wessing
Carmelite, 50 Victoria Embankment,
London EC4Y 0DX
020 7300 7000
london@taylorwessing.com
www.taylorwessing.com
Patents, copyright and other IP

Teacher Stern Selby
37–41 Bedford Row, London WC1R 4JH
020 7242 3191
g.shear@tsslaw.com
www.tsslaw.com
*Defamation and reputation management;
IT; IP; internet and e-commerce; data
protection; telecoms and risk management*

Thompsons
Congress House,
23–28 Great Russell Street,
London WC1B 3LW
020 7290 0000
info@thompsons.law.co.uk
www.thompsons.law.co.uk
*Represents media unions and their
members including NUJ, Bectu and Amicus*

Thomson Snell and Passmore
3 Lonsdale Gardens,
Tunbridge Wells, Kent TN1 1NX
01892 510000
info@ts-p.co.uk
www.ts-p.co.uk
E-commerce and IP law

TLT Solicitors
Sea Containers House,
20 Upper Ground, Blackfriars Bridge,
London SE1 9LH
020 7620 1311
www.tltsolicitors.com
IT inc internet and e-commerce; sports law

Travers Smith
10 Snow Hill, London EC1A 2AL
020 7295 3000
travers.smith@traverssmith.com
www.TraversSmith.com
*IT and e-commerce; media and IP;
contracts*

Truman and Co Solicitors, Truelegal
76 Fore Street, Topsham,
Exeter, Devon EX3 0HQ
01392 879414
info@truelegal.co.uk
www.truelegal.co.uk
*Commercial, media and e-law for
advertising, marketing, PR, web, new
media companies in London and South
West. Anglo German specialist.*

Turner Parkinson
Hollins Chambers,
64a Bridge Street, Manchester,
Lancashire M3 3BA
0161 833 1212
tp@tp.co.uk
www.tp.co.uk
IP; computer contracts and e-commerce

Veale Wasbrough
Orchard Court, Orchard Lane,
Bristol BS1 5WS
0117 925 2020
central@vwl.co.uk
www.vwl.co.uk
*IP esp tech, computer systems and
e-commerce*

Vizards Tweedie
42 Bedford Row, London WC1R 4JL
020 7405 1234
www.vizardstweedie.co.uk
Media and IT law

Wake Smith
68 Clarkehouse Road, Sheffield,
South Yorkshire S10 2LJ
0114 266 6660
legal@wake-smith.com
www.wake-smith.co.uk
*Media and entertainment law; global tech
licensing contracts; agency, distribution
and marketing agreements*

Watson Farley and Williams
15 Appold Street, London EC2A 2HB
020 7814 8000
info@wfw.com
www.wfw.com
*Telecoms, media and tech: for operators,
regulators, equipment and maintenance
providers, internet services, content
providers, e-commerce users and
developers*

Wiggin
95 Promenade, Cheltenham,
Gloucestershire GL50 1WG
01242 224114
law@wiggin.co.uk
www.wiggin.co.uk
*Broadcast media, telecoms, e-commerce,
advertising, publishing, gaming, music,
IP, content and regulation*

**Willoughby and Partners
(Rouse and Co International)**
The Isis Building, Thames Quay,
193 Marsh Wall, London E14 9SG
020 7345 8888
Harrogate: 01423 850800
Oxford: 01865 318400
rouse@iprights.com
www.iprights.com
*IP services worldwide in TV, film,
entertainment and publishing sectors inc
agreements, rights, licensing and defence
of infringement*

**Wilmer Cutler Pickering Hale
and Dorr**
Alder Castle House, 10 Noble Street,
London EC2V 7QJ
020 7645 2400
www.wilmerhale.com
*IP; services for telecoms, internet,
e-commerce and software industries*

Wollastons
Brierly Place, New London Road,
Chelmsford, Esssex CM2 0AP
01245 211211
enquiries@wollastons.co.uk
www.wollastons.co.uk
*IP inc agreements, licensing, trademark
registration, infringement of copyright,
passing off, breach of confidence,
warranties and liability, internet trade
and portal development*

Wragge and Co
55 Colmore Row,
Birmingham B3 2AS
0870 903 1000
mail@wragge.com
www.wragge.com
*Media business services from content
creation and exploitation to financing
and corporate development. Offices in
London and Brussels*

Wright Hassall Solicitors
9 Clarendon Place, Leamington Spa,
Warwickshire CV32 5QP
01926 886688
email@wrighthassall.co.uk
www.wrighthassall.co.uk
*IP and transactional support to
technology, new media and advertising
clients. Emphasis on branding, design,
merchandising, sponsorship, sales
promotion and all copyright issues.*

Wright, Johnston and Mackenzie
302 St Vincent Street,
Glasgow G2 5RZ
0141 248 3434
Edinburgh: 0131 221 5560
enquiries@wjm.co.uk
www.wjm.co.uk
IP and dispute resolution

Media law journals

International Journal of Communications Law and Policy
00 49 251 833 8640
IJCLP@digital-law.net
www.digital-law.net/IJCLP
2pa: Jan and July

IP Law and Business
ALM
Editor: 001 212 313 9130
efriedlander@amlaw.com
www.ipww.com
Monthly, plus annual digest issue.
Editor: Emily Friedlander
Press: 001 401 848 5494

Media Law and Policy
New York Law School
00 1 212 431 2160
www.nyls.edu/pages/1572.asp

PA Media Lawyer
01932 700 907
Medialawyer@pa.press.net
www.medialawyer.press.net
Bi-monthly. Editor: Mike Dodd

Copyright associations

Authors' Licensing and Collecting Society (ALCS)
Marlborough Court, 14–18 Holborn,
London EC1N 2LE
020 7395 0600
alcs@alcs.co.uk
www.alcs.co.uk
UK collecting society for writers and their successors

British Copyright Council
Copyright House,
29–33 Berners Street,
London W1T 3AB
01986 788122
secretary@britishcopyright.org
Copyright watchdog

Copyright Licensing Agency
Saffron House, 6–10 Kirby Street,
London EC1N 8TS
020 7400 3100
cla@cla.co.uk
www.cla.co.uk
Administers copyrights

Design and Artists Copyright Society (DACS)
33 Great Sutton Street,
London EC1V 0DX
020 7336 8811
info@dacs.org.uk
www.dacs.org.uk
Copyright and collecting society for visual artists

Federation Against Copyright Theft (FACT)
Unit 7, Victory Business Centre,
Worton Road, Isleworth, Middlesex
TW7 6DB
020 8568 6646
contact@fact-uk.org.uk
www.fact-uk.org.uk
UK film anti-piracy body

Irish Copyright Licensing Agency
25 Denzille Lane, Dublin 2
00 353 1 662 4211
info@icla.ie
www.icla.ie
Ireland's reproduction rights organisation

Mechanical-Copyright Protection Society
29–33 Berners Street,
London W1T 3AB
020 7580 5544
www.mcps.co.uk
Collects and distributes music royalties: record companies, broadcasters, novelties, online

Patent Office
Concept House, Cardiff Road,
Newport NP10 8QQ
0845 950 0505
enquiries@patent.gov.uk
www.patent.gov.uk
Patents, trademarks, design and copyright

Performing Rights Society
29–33 Berners Street,
London W1T 3AB
020 7580 5544
www.prs.co.uk
Collects and distributes music royalties: pubs, clubs, broadcasters, online

Public Lending Right
Richard House, Sorbonne Close,
Stockton-on-Tees TS17 6DA
01642 604699
registrar@plr.uk.com
www.plr.uk.com
Library payment scheme for authors

Publishers Licensing Society
37–41 Gower Street,
London WC1E 6HH
020 7299 7730
pls@pls.org.uk
www.pls.org.uk
Supports Copyright Licensing Agency

UK Copyright Bureau
110 Trafalgar Road, Portslade,
East Sussex BN41 1GS
info@copyrightbureau.co.uk
www.copyrightbureau.co.uk
Copyright service for authors, playwrights, scriptwriters, poets, musicians and associated literary crafts

Writers, Artists and their Copyright Holders (Watch)
David Sutton, Director of Research
Projects, University of Reading
Library, PO Box 223, Whiteknights,
Reading RG6 6AE
0118 931 8783
UK: d.c.sutton@reading.ac.uk
US: rworkman@mail.utexas.edu
www.watch-file.com
Database primarily containing names and addresses of copyright holders and contacts for authors and artists whose archives are housed in libraries in North America and UK

Associations

International Bar Association – Media Law Committee
10th Floor, 1 Stephen Street,
London W1T 1AT
020 7691 6868
member@int-bar.org
www.ibanet.org

Stanhope Centre for Communications Policy Research
Stanhope House, Stanhope Place,
London W2 2HH
020 7479 5900
www.stanhopecentre.org/
Media law and policy forum

Libraries and research

Specialist libraries and archives

Bank of England Information Centre
Threadneedle Street,
London EC2R 8AH
020 7601 4715
informationcentre@
  bankofengland.co.uk
www.bankofengland.co.uk
Central banking and finance

Barbican Library
Silk Street, London EC2Y 8DS
020 7638 0569
barbicanlib@corpoflondon.gov.uk
www.cityoflondon.gov.uk
Lending library with strong arts and music sections

BBC Written Archives Centre
Peppard Road, Caversham Park,
Reading, Berkshire RG4 8TZ
0118 948 6281
wac.enquiries@bbc.co.uk
www.bbc.co.uk/heritage

BFI
21 Stephen Street, London W1T 1LN
020 7255 1444
library@bfi.org.uk
www.bfi.org.uk/nationallibrary
  /index.html
World's largest collection of documentation on film and television

British Architectural Library
Royal Institute of British Architects,
66 Portland Place, London W1B 1AD
020 7580 5533
bal@inst.riba.org
www.architecture.com

British Library
96 Euston Road, London NW1 2DB
0870 444 1500
reader-admissions@bl.uk
www.bl.uk

British Newspaper Library
Colindale Avenue, London NW9 5HE
020 7412 7353
newspaper@bl.uk
www.bl.uk/catalogues
  /newspapers.html

CAA Library and Information Centre
Aviation House, Gatwick Airport,
West Sussex RH6 0YR
01293 573725
infoservices@caa.co.uk
www.caa.co.uk

Catholic Central Library
St Michael's Abbey, Farnborough
Road, Farnborough GU14 7NQ
020 7732 8379
librarian@catholic-library.org.uk
www.catholic-library.org.uk

City Business Library
1 Brewers' Hall Garden,
London EC2V 5BX
020 7332 1812
cbl@cityoflondon.gov.uk
www.cityoflondon.gov.uk
  /citybusinesslibrary

City of Westminster Archives Centre
10 St Ann's Street, London SW1P 2DE
020 7641 5180
archives@westminster.gov.uk
www.westminster.gov.uk/archives

DigiReels Media Monitoring
45 Foubert's Place, London W1F 7QH
020 7437 7743
info@digireels.co.uk
www.digireels.co.uk
Online ad database

Foreign and Commonwealth Office
Library E213, King Charles Street,
London SW1A 2AH
020 7270 3925
library.enquiries@fco.gov.uk
www.fco.gov.uk

Forestry Commission Library
Forest Research Station, Alice Holt
Lodge, Wrecclesham, Farnham,
Surrey GU10 4LH
01420 222555
library@forestry.gsi.gov.uk
www.forestry.gov.uk/forest_research

French Institute Library
Institut francais, 17 Queensberry
Place, London SW7 2DT
020 7073 1350
library@ambafrance.org.uk
www.institut.ambafrance.org.uk

Goethe-Institut Library
50 Princes Gate, Exhibition Road,
London SW7 2PH
020 7596 4000
mail@london.goethe.org
www.goethe.de/london
German literature and reference

Harry Price Library of Magical Literature
University of London Library,
Senate House, Malet Street,
London WC1E 7HU
020 7862 8470
historic@ull.ac.uk
www.ull.ac.uk/historic
  /collections.shtml
Magic literature

Institute of Education Library (London)
20 Bedford Way, London WC1H 0AL
020 7612 6080
lib.enquiries@ioe.ac.uk
www.ioe.ac.uk
Over 300,000 volumes including special sections on educational studies. 2,000 periodicals

Instituto Cervantes
102 Eaton Square,
London SW1W 9AN
020 7201 0757
biblon@cervantes.es
www.cervantes.es
Spain

International Booksearch Service
020 7639 8900
admin@scfordham.com
www.scfordham.com
Finds out-of-print books

Italian Cultural Institute
39 Belgrave Square,
London SW1X 8NX
020 7396 4425
icilondon@esteri.it
www.icilondon.esteri.it

Linen Hall Library
17 Donegall Square North,
Belfast BT1 5GB
028 9032 1707
info@linenhall.com
www.linenhall.com
Ireland and politics

Llyfrgell Genedlaethol Cymru/ National Library of Wales
Aberystwyth, Ceredigion SY23 3BU
01970 632800
holi@llgc.org.uk
www.llgc.org.uk

London Metropolitan Archives (LMA)
40 Northampton Road, Clerkenwell, London EC1R 0HB
020 7332 3820
ask.lma@cityoflondon.gov.uk
www.cityoflondon.gov.uk/lma
Largest local authority archive in the UK

Murder Files
Dommett Hill Farm,
Hare Lane, Buckland St Mary,
Somerset TA20 3JS
01460 234065
enquiry@murderfiles.com
www.murderfiles.com
UK murders since 1400

National Archives
Kew, Richmond, Surrey TW9 4DU
020 8392 5300
www.nationalarchives.gov.uk
11th-20th-century national records

National Film and TV Archive
Kingshill Way, Berkhamsted,
Herts HP4 3TP
01442 876301
darren.long@bfi.org.uk
www.bfi.org.uk
Contains more than 275,000 films and 200,000 TV programmes, dating from 1895 to the present

National Library for the Blind
Far Cromwell Road, Bredbury,
Stockport SK6 2SG
0161 355 2000
enquiries@nlbuk.org
www.nlb-online.org

National Library of Scotland
George IV Bridge, Edinburgh EH1 1EW
0131 226 4531
enquiries@nls.uk
www.nls.uk

National Meteorological Archive
The Scott Building, Sterling Centre,
Eastern Road, Bracknell,
Berkshire RG12 2PW
01344 861629
metarc@metoffice.com
www.metoffice.com

National Museum of Scotland
NMS Enterprises, Chambers Street,
Edinburgh EH1 1JF
0131 247 4026
nmsphoto@nms.ac.uk
www.nms.ac.uk

Natural History Museum Library
Cromwell Road, London SW7 5BD
020 7942 5460
library@nhm.ac.uk
www.nhm.ac.uk/library/index.html

Office for National Statistics
1 Drummond Gate, London SW1V 2QQ
0845 601 3034
info@statistics.gov.uk
www.statistics.gov.uk

Polish Library
238–246 King Street, London W6 0RF
020 8741 0474
bibliotekapolska@
   posklibrary.fsnet.co.uk
www.posk.library.fs.net

Royal Geographical Society Library (with the Institute of British Geographers)
1 Kensington Gore, London SW7 2AR
020 7591 3000
press@rgs.org
www.rgs.org

Royal Society Library
6-9 Carlton House Terrace,
London SW1Y 5AG
020 7451 2606
library@royalsoc.ac.uk
www.royalsoc.ac.uk
Science

Royal Society of Medicine Library
1 Wimpole Street, London W1G 0AE
020 7290 2940
library@rsm.ac.uk
www.rsm.ac.uk

Science Fiction Foundation Research Library
Liverpool University Library,
PO Box 123, Liverpool L69 3DA
0151 794 3142
asawyer@liverpool.ac.uk
www.liv.ac.uk/~asawyer
   /sffchome.html

Science Museum Library
Imperial College Road,
London SW7 5NH
020 7942 4242
smlinfo@nmsi.ac.uk
www.sciencemuseum.org.uk

Theatre Museum Library and Archive
1e Tavistock Street, London WC2E 7PR
020 7943 4700
tmenquiries@vam.ac.uk
www.theatremuseum.org

Westminster Music Library
Victoria Library, 160 Buckingham
Palace Road, London SW1W 9UD
020 7641 4292
musiclibrary@westminster.gov.uk
www.westminster.gov.uk/libraries
   /special/music

Wiener Library
4 Devonshire Street, London W1W 5BH
020 7636 7247
info@wienerlibrary.co.uk
www.wienerlibrary.co.uk
Modern Jewish history, the Holocaust and German 20th-century history

Women's Library
25 Old Castle Street, London E1 7NT
020 7320 2222
moreinfo@thewomenslibrary.ac.uk
www.thewomenslibrary.ac.uk

Zoological Society Library
Regent's Park, London NW1 4RY
020 7449 6293
library@zsl.org
www.zsl.org

Research data

AC Nielsen
ACNielsen House, London Road,
Headington, Oxford OX3 9RX
01865 742742
www.acneilson.com
Marketing research worldwide

Audit Bureau of Circulations (ABC)
Saxon House, 211 High Street,
Berkhamsted, Hertfordshire HP4 1AD
01442 870800
marketing@abc.org.uk
www.abc.org.uk
Circulation figures for newspapers and magazines

Broadcasters' Audience Research Board (Barb)
2nd Floor, 18 Dering Street,
London W15 1AQ
020 7529 5531
enquiries@barb.co.uk
www.barb.co.uk
TV audience data

Communications Research Group
Anvic House, 84 Vyse Street,
Jewellery Quarter,
Birmingham B18 6HA
0121 523 9595
research@crghq.com
www.crghq.com
Market and audience research

LemonAd United Kingdom
Nielsen/NetRatings UK, 2nd Floor,
4 Elder Street, London E1 6BT
020 7420 9268
barney@netcrawling.com
www.lemonad.com
Advertising monitoring in Europe

National Readership Survey (NRS)
40 Parker Street, London WC2B 5PQ
020 7242 8111
stevemillington@nrs.co.uk
www.nrs.co.uk
Newspaper and magazine readership estimates

Nielsen BookScan
3rd Floor Midas House,
62 Goldsworth Road, Woking,
Surrey GU21 6LQ
01483 712222
info@nielsenbookscan.co.uk
www.nielsenbookscan.co.uk
International sales data monitoring and analysis service for the English-language book industry worldwide

Rajar
Paramount House,
162-170 Wardour Street,
London W1F 8XZ
020 7292 9040
info@rajar.co.uk
www.rajar.co.uk
Measures and profiles the audiences of UK radio stations

Media Monitoring

Precise Media Group
The Registry, Royal Mint Court,
London EC3N 4QN
020 7264 4700
sales.admin@precise-media.co.uk
www.precise-media.co.uk
*Media monitoring across print, web and
broadcast*

Library associations

**Association of Independent
Libraries**
Leeds Library, 18 Commercial Street,
Leeds, West Yorkshire LS1 6AL
0113 245 3071
admin@hlsi.demon.co.uk
www.independentlibraries.co.uk

Association of UK Media Libraries
Editorial Information Services,
Financial Times, One Southwark
Bridge, London SE1 9HL
020 7873 3920
www.aukml.org.uk
Represents librarians in media industry

**Chartered Institute of Library
and Information Professionals**
7 Ridgmount Street, London WC1E 7AE
020 7255 0500
info@cilip.org.uk
www.cilip.org.uk

**Chartered Institute of Library
and Information Professionals
in Scotland**
1st Floor, Building C, Brandon Gate,
Leechlee Road, Hamilton ML3 6AU
01698 458888
cilips@slainte.org.uk
www.slainte.org.uk

Focal International
Pentax House, South Hill Avenue,
South Harrow HA2 0DU
020 8423 5853
info@focalint.org
www.focalint.org
*Represents commercial film/audiovisual,
stills and sound libraries, plus facility
houses, film researchers and producers*

Museum Libraries & Archives Council
16 Queen Anne's Gate,
London SW1H 9AA
020 7273 1444
www.mla.gov.uk
*Development agency for museums,
libraries and archives*

A career in media

Careers and training

Ask any student if they would like a career in "the media", and they would probably say yes. Ask anyone in the media industry if they would rather still be a student, and they would most likely give the same answer. While a "creative" career might sound glamorous, everyone else thinks so too; and many employers, recognising this, get away with paying low or mediocre salaries for long hours, and even then offer little formal training to help employees develop. To get your foot in the door, most people will probably at some stage have to work for free; to develop professionally, many end up having to train at their own expense. Some give it up and go off to become an accountant instead.

That said, if accountancy is not for you, there are many different kinds of media roles to choose from. In press and publishing, to name but a few roles, you could be a news reporter, a writer of features or specialist articles, a subeditor, a production editor, a commissioning editor, or a writer for the web; in broadcasting, you could be a journalist, a presenter, a researcher, a camera operator, a director or producer. You could be a creative in advertising, a PR agent, or a media buyer whose job it is to know the industry inside out (tip: read this book). And most, if not all these areas, need their designers, graphic artists, production gurus, marketers, sales managers, distributors and managers who – in theory at least – make the whole enterprise tick. Which is better than spending all day sitting in front of a spreadsheet.

● Entry-level: courses and work experience

There are two ways of getting into any media career: first, go off and train yourself to do the job; second, do the job. You don't always have to do the first. You always have to do the second.

More and more entrants into the media are well qualified, with good degrees in media studies or other subjects; having such a degree will not necessarily make you stand out from the crowd. Indeed, rightly or wrongly – and partly as a result of articles written by wizened hacks who worked their way up through the regional press – "media studies" still has a poor reputation among employers as a soft option. What can make the difference is a practical qualification which suggests you have the commitment and ability to do the job.

Many parts of the media have accrediting bodies for postgraduate and training courses. In journalism, this is the National Council for the Training of Journalists (NCTJ); the courses it accredits are run either through a training contract at a regional or local paper – the traditional route, with much to recommend it – or, popularly but competitively, at a university. Courses try to be as practical as possible: those in newspaper journalism, for example, will include all the knowledge you need plus

Journalism and Media: shape your future

If you're considering a degree in journalism or media, the School of Arts and Humanities at Nottingham Trent University has some fantastic opportunities on offer.

Nottingham is an excellent place to study journalism and media. It is a vibrant city with its own award-winning newspaper, four local radio stations and a wealth of other media opportunities. NTU benefits from the support of these media partners.

Graduates from our popular **BA (Hons) Broadcast Journalism** course have won many awards and are enjoying considerable career success. Our new **BA (Hons) Print Journalism** course will provide similar opportunities for students in this area of journalism. Both courses are offered through the Centre for Broadcasting and Journalism which provides extensive facilities with industry-standard equipment. This enables you to develop the knowledge and skills essential for your future career and to receive specialist training in a variety of fields. Work placements provide you with experience and insight into the media industry.

The Centre for Broadcasting and Journalism also offers an **MA/PgDip,** in **Newspaper, Online, Radio** or **Television Journalism,** which will provide you with the necessary skills, knowledge and experience to start your chosen career.

These courses are highly regarded within the media industry, indicated by the fact that our **MA/PgDip** in **Newspaper Journalism** is currently considered the best performing course in the country by the NCTJ (National Council for the Training of Journalists).

BA (Hons) Media is designed to offer you maximum flexibility, allowing you to design your own degree according to your interests. You can choose to do a general Media degree or to specialise in one of the following named pathways: Communications, Creative Industries, Film and TV, Journalism Studies, Media Practices or Popular Culture.

Media Joint Honours degrees offer the opportunity to study media with another subject to degree level.

The new and exciting **MA Media and Globalisation** course is designed to deliver a highly advanced and sophisticated level of understanding of the many facets of today's communications media.

For further information please contact:
Tel: **0115 848 5806 (Journalism)**
0115 848 3111 (Media)
Visit: **www.ntu.ac.uk/gmg**

We offer both undergraduate and postgraduate courses which will provide you with opportunities to develop the knowledge and skills needed for a successful career. Opportunities for work experience will provide insight into the media industry.

Undergraduate

BA (Hons) Broadcast Journalism

BA (Hons) Print Journalism

BA (Hons) Media (with pathways)

Media Joint Honours degrees combine Media with another subject from our Joint Honours Programme

Postgraduate

MA/PgDip Newspaper Journalism

MA/PgDip Online Journalism

MA/PgDip Radio Journalism

MA/PgDip Television Journalism

MA/PgDip Media and Globalisation

Our postgraduate journalism courses also offer an international option which develops English language skills

"Studying at Nottingham Trent helped me learn the ropes and develop a news discipline which I never had before. The lecturers were happy to talk things through in a supportive way and they always had time for me. The highlight for me was winning the Student Journalist of the Year award from The Guardian.*"*

Olav Bjortomt, MA Newpaper Journalism, currently working for *The Times* in London

NOTTINGHAM
TRENT UNIVERSITY

4529/11/06

100wpm of shorthand; while journalism students at Preston are issued with a stylebook as if working in a newsroom. Courses will also include work experience, although students usually need work experience to get on the course in the first place.

In broadcasting, journalism courses are accredited by the Broadcast Journalism Training Council (BJTC). There are also a few highly competitive broadcast training schemes, often funded by Skillset – the skills council for the broadcast industry in general. In most parts of TV and radio, many people start as a "runner" or in a similar junior training position and gain experience and qualifications as they progress, often from BBC Training.

In PR, the Chartered Institute of Public Relations approves training courses. Many successful journalism schools now also run PR courses alongside their journalism courses, a trend that started in the US.

The real key to getting any job in the media, though, is work experience. The best way to get work experience is to target an individual in the organisation closest to where you want to work; send them your CV and follow it up a day or two later with a phone call. Be persistent but polite; if they are busy (and they will always say they are), ask when would be the best time to call, or – as a last resort – if there is someone else they think might be able to help you. When doing work experience, dress fairly smartly, put on your most plausible manner, and try to be as helpful as you can. If in doubt, make tea.

● The job market

Jobs in the media are advertised in the Guardian on a Monday, on Guardian Unlimited Jobs (jobs.guardian.co.uk) and in other newspapers and the trade press. Most jobs that are advertised nationally attract large numbers of applications, so spend time targeting your CV and covering letter by thinking hard about how your skills and experience best relate to the job description. Keep the CV down to one page (two at most); use a simple font such as Times New Roman (Arial if you love sans serif); and get someone who knows how to spell to read it through (not just Bill Gates).

Remember, most jobs aren't advertised: with the happy exception of the inclusive BBC, many media organisations simply recruit internally or give a job to a freelancer who's been around a while. So if you're looking for a job, the best place to be is working: carry on working for free, or if you are experienced enough, charge freelance rates. So don't apply for jobs simply because they're advertised in the Guardian; better to target the right job for you, or you'll end up back where you started in a few months.

One other problem to bear in mind when looking for a job: the vast majority of media jobs – perhaps up to 80% – are based in London and the south-east. National newspapers, TV production and advertising are based almost exclusively in London; most magazines are in London, with small concentrations elsewhere; only radio, some TV, and (of course) the regional press are truly nationwide.

A career in media

Journalism at Preston is cutting edge and professional. Our courses cater for all - from the experienced journalist (MA Journalism Leadership) to the next generation of storytellers (BA Hons Digital Journalism Production). With great facilities, outstanding tutors and more than 40 years' experience of teaching journalism, we've earned a national reputation for quality. But don't take our word for it. Ask our alumni. You'll find them in newsrooms across the UK.

Learn it. Do it. Live it.

Undergraduate

BA(Hons) Journalism

BA(Hons) Sports Journalism

BA(Hons) Digital
Journalism Production

BA(Hons) International
Journalism

BA(Hons) Journalism
and English Literature

Combined Honours Journalism

Postgraduate

MA Journalism Leadership

MA Newspaper Journalism

PgDip Newspaper Journalism

MA Broadcast Journalism

PgDip Broadcast Journalism

MA Online Journalism

MA Magazine Journalism

MA International Journalism

MA International
Documentary Production

uclan

For information about our courses and how to apply go to
www.ukjournalism.org or telephone **01772 894730.**
Department of Journalism, University of Central Lancashire, Preston PR1 2HE

FACULTY OF THE ARTS

Media Courses

We can prepare you for a variety of exciting careers in the media and cultural industries. Many of our graduates have achieved rewarding and highly successful career opportunities and are employed in organisations such as the BBC, Channel 4, Harper Collins, Transworld Publishing and Saatchi & Saatchi.

BA (Hons) Advertising

BA (Hons)/DipHE Broadcasting

BA (Hons) Creative Advertising

BA (Hons)/DipHE Film: Video Production with Film Studies

BA (Hons)/DipHE Media and Event Management

BA (Hons) Media Studies

BA (Hons) New Media Journalism

BA (Hons) New Media Journalism and Radio Broadcasting

BA (Hons) Photography and Digital Imaging

BA (Hons) Public Relations

MA Creative Screenwriting

MA Film and the Moving Image

MA Media

MA Photography

MA Video Production with Film Studies

For further information on all our Media courses, please contact us.

0800 036 8888

learning.advice@tvu.ac.uk
www.tvu.ac.uk
apply online at: www.tvu.ac.uk/apply

Thames Valley University
London Reading Slough

● Freelancing

Many people who work in the media are freelancers; that is, they are self-employed workers who are paid by the day or by the job. Many experienced journalists and producers become freelancers out of choice, for the relative freedom it offers; there are others who are freelance by necessity because they are looking for a job. In broadcasting, according to the annual Skillset survey, a quarter of the workforce was freelance; though this under-represented the actual freelance population, as many will not have been working on the day of the survey. Many newspaper and magazine journalists also work on a freelance basis, either writing from home or coming into the office to do reporting or subediting shifts.

There are a few major advantages to freelancing: you get to be your own boss, no one tells you what time you have to get up in the morning, and above all you have the freedom to move your career in whatever direction you choose. That's about the size of it. On the other hand, there are many major disadvantages: you never know where the next pay cheque is coming from; you have little power against companies who pay too little, too late, or attempt to appropriate the rights for your work; and you have to fill in a tax return. Remember, you should be entitled to statutory holiday pay in addition to the pay you receive, but many companies will not pay up unless you ask for it.

In broadcasting, you will work a lot of short-term contracts; so ask to see a contract up front, check their rates of pay with broadcasters' union Bectu, and watch out for terms covering intellectual property and statutory holiday pay (companies often try to include holiday pay in the headline figure). In journalism, the biggest issue is rates of pay: publishers are paying reporters and subeditors less and less in real terms each year for a shift, usually by setting arbitrarily low "ceilings" for a day rate. It is up to freelancers and the NUJ to work together to get the pay they deserve.

● Further training

Training and professional development, or the lack of it, is a serious problem for the media. In the broadcast industry, Skillset subsidises 60% of the cost a range of short courses for freelances; but freelancers will often have to pay the rest themselves. The BBC also subsidises training, and the industry body Pact can organise training for its members, but regular freelancers will often have less formal training than if they worked for a big in-house team such as the BBC.

10 ways to get that media job
Chris Alden

1. Research

It's the number one media skill, so apply it to your job search. Watch plenty of TV; listen to the radio; get digital; read newspapers; surf the web. Read MediaGuardian and MediaGuardian.co.uk, plus the trade press, particularly Broadcast, Televisual and Press Gazette.

2. Build contacts

Media is all about contacts. So if you know a friend of a friend who's in the media, call or email, mentioning the person you know in common. Without being pushy or needy, ask them if they can make time for a quick chat — and ask them questions about their work. Don't, however, ask them to find you a job.

3. Get work experience

Nothing prepares you better for working in the media than doing the job. So work experience is a useful way in; and in TV, working as a "runner" is the traditional first rung.

4. Show off your work

In journalism and artistic jobs, build a portfolio; in TV or radio, create a showreel or a demo tape to show off what you can do. Work for whatever media outfits you can — newsletters, websites, hospital radio, whoever will use you — to make that portfolio bigger and better.

5. Consider a course

A course with a strong practical element can help you increase your technical knowledge; and in journalism, it may give you skills such as shorthand, law and knowledge of public life. Ultimately, though, it helps you make contacts, get experience, and build that portfolio.

6. Consider a niche

Genuine expertise is always bankable. So if you have an interest in and knowledge about a subject — be it arts, travel, health or a region of the country — consider making it your niche.

7. Get the tech skills

If you're going for a technical job, you should get some basic experience of the skills involved; if you're not technically minded, you should know how technical concerns affect others. Media is about teamwork: the more knowledge you have, the better the team works, and the more employable you are.

8. Target your CV

The traditional CV is not always required to get a job in media, as jobs are often won informally by word of mouth. But if you are using one, then the secret is to prepare a different CV for each job for which you are applying. Use simple, clear design in a well-known font, at a readable point size.

9. Prepare for the interview

Interviews are about the stories you tell, and how you tell them. So remind yourself what you said your skills were; then take time to remember something that happened that backs them up. Other than that, dress smartly, speak slowly, make eye contact and project your voice; come up with intelligent questions — and expect the unexpected.

10. Consider freelancing

You do not need a permanent job to have a successful career in media. You could be freelance — that is, paid only for the work you do, or on a short-term contract. Freelancing can be highly stressful and isolating; but once you have been doing it for a while, it can seem like the only way to live.

● Chris Alden is a freelance journalist. His own online portfolio is at www.chrisalden.co.uk

The largest centre of professional education for the media industries in the UK.

Designated as a Centre for Excellence in Media Practice by Higher Education Funding Council for England, and also an accredited Skillset Screen Academy, the endorsements firmly establish the School as a major training and higher education centre.

Students at all levels work with industry-standard equipment and have won major awards for excellence in all disciplines. Our industry and professional links mean we offer placement and graduate employment opportunities and a range of industry accreditations.

- Broadcast Journalism Training Council

- Chartered Institute of Marketing

- Chartered Institute of Public Relations

- Periodicals Training Council

- Skillset

- National Council for Training of Journalists

The School's international reputation is built on strong theoretical foundations supported by applied research into the dynamics of communication and the creative industries together with professional expertise.

If you would like to know more about Bournemouth Media School, contact us on 01202 965360 or email: media@bournemouth.ac.uk

Head of School: Stephen Jukes, MA (Oxon).

Universities and training providers

General media See also PR, marketing and advertising
Press, journalism and writing See also publishing and broadcasting
TV, radio and film See also press and multimedia
PR, marketing and advertising
Publishing See also press and multimedia
Multimedia Includes new media, photography, animation, special effects, art and design
Music See also broadcasting

	general media	press, journalism & writing	TV, radio & film	PR, marketing & advertising	publishing	multimedia	music
Aberdeen, University of			•				•
Abertay, Dundee, University of	•			•		•	
Adam Smith College, Fife		•		•		•	
Anglia Polytechnic University			•	•	•	•	•
Arts Institute at Bournemouth			•			•	
Aston University				•		•	
University Centre Barnsley		•				•	•
Basingstoke College of Technology	•					•	
Bath Spa University College	•	•				•	•
Bath, University of			•			•	
Bell College		•	•	•			
Birkbeck, University of London	•	•	•	•		•	•
Birmingham College of Food, Tourism and Creative Studies				•			
Birmingham Conservatoire							•
Birmingham, University of	•	•	•	•		•	•
Blackburn College			•		•	•	•
Bolton, University of	•	•	•	•		•	
Bournemouth University	•	•	•	•		•	•
Bradford College			•	•		•	•
Bradford, University of	•	•	•	•		•	•
Brighton, University of	•	•	•	•		•	•
Bristol, University of		•	•			•	•
Brunel University	•	•	•	•		•	•
Buckingham, University of	•	•		•		•	
Bucks Chilterns University College	•	•	•	•		•	•
Camberwell College of Arts					•	•	
Cambridge, University of							•
Canterbury Christ Church University College	•	•	•	•		•	•
Canterbury College	•	•	•	•		•	•
Cardiff University	•	•	•	•		•	•
Cardonald College	•	•	•				
Central England in Birmingham, University of	•	•	•	•		•	•
Central Lancashire, University of	•	•	•	•		•	•
Central Saint Martins College of Art and Design	•	•	•			•	
Central School of Speech and Drama		•	•			•	•
Central Sussex College	•		•				
Chelsea College of Art and Design				•		•	
University College Chester	•	•	•	•		•	•
Chichester College	•		•				
University College Chichester		•	•			•	•
City College Brighton and Hove		•	•			•	•
City Lit		•	•	•	•	•	•
City Of Wolverhampton College	•	•					•

	general media	press, journalism & writing	TV, radio & film	PR, marketing & advertising	publishing	multimedia	music
City University, London	●	●	●		●	●	●
Cleveland College of Art & Design			●			●	
Coleg Gwent		●	●			●	●
Coleg Menai						●	
Coleg Sir Gar (Carmarthenshire College)			●			●	●
Conservatoire for Dance and Drama			●				
Cornwall College		●	●			●	
Coventry University	●	●	●	●		●	●
Cumbria Institute of the Arts		●	●			●	
Darlington College Of Technology	●	●	●	●		●	●
De Montfort University	●	●	●	●		●	●
Derby, University of	●	●	●	●		●	●
Doncaster College			●	●		●	●
Dublin Institute of Technology	●	●		●		●	●
Dundee, University of						●	
Durham University							●
Ealing, Hammersmith and West London College	●					●	●
East Anglia, University of	●	●	●	●			●
East London, University of	●	●	●	●	●	●	●
East Surrey College	●		●			●	●
Edge Hill College of Higher Education	●	●	●	●		●	
Edinburgh College of Art				●			
Edinburgh, University of		●	●			●	●
Editorial Centre		●	●			●	
Editorial Training Consultants	●	●	●	●	●	●	
Essex, University of		●	●			●	●
Exeter, University of	●	●	●				
University College Falmouth	●	●	●	●	●	●	
Glamorgan, University of	●	●	●	●		●	●
Glasgow Caledonian University		●		●			●
Glasgow Metropolitan College		●	●	●	●	●	
Glasgow School of Art						●	
Glasgow, University of	●		●			●	●
Gloucestershire, University of		●	●	●	●	●	
Goldsmiths College	●	●	●			●	●
Greenwich, University of	●	●	●	●		●	●
Grimsby Institute of Further & Higher Education	●	●	●	●		●	●
Guildford College	●		●	●		●	
Harlow College		●				●	●
Harrow College	●	●	●			●	●
Henley College Coventry	●		●			●	
Hertfordshire, University of			●	●		●	●
Highbury College, Portsmouth	●	●	●		●	●	●
Huddersfield, University of	●	●	●	●		●	●
Hull, University of	●	●	●	●		●	●
Journalism Training Centre		●					
Keele, University of	●						●
Kensington and Chelsea College						●	●
Kent Institute of Art and Design			●	●	●	●	
Kent, University of		●	●	●		●	●
King's College London	●		●			●	●
Kingston University	●	●	●	●		●	●

	general media	press journalism & writing	TV, radio & film	PR, marketing & advertising	publishing	multimedia	music
Lambeth College	●	●	●			●	
Lancaster University	●	●	●	●		●	●
Leeds College of Art and Design				●		●	
Leeds College of Music			●				●
Leeds Metropolitan University	●		●	●			●
Leeds Trinity & All Saints	●	●	●	●			
Leeds, University of		●	●	●		●	
Leicester, University of			●				
Lincoln, University of	●	●	●	●		●	●
Liverpool Community College	●	●	●			●	●
Liverpool Hope University College	●		●	●			●
Liverpool John Moores University	●	●	●	●	●	●	●
Liverpool, University of	●		●	●		●	●
London Business School				●			
London College of Communication	●	●	●	●	●	●	●
London College of Fashion		●		●		●	
London College of Music & Media							
London Film School			●				
London Metropolitan University	●	●	●	●		●	●
London School of Economics and Political Science	●			●		●	
London School of Journalism		●					
London South Bank University	●	●	●	●		●	●
University College London			●		●		
Luton, University of	●	●	●	●		●	●
Manchester Metropolitan University	●	●	●	●		●	
Manchester, University of	●	●	●				●
Marjon, College of St Mark & St John	●	●	●	●			
Mid-Cheshire College						●	●
Middlesex University	●	●	●	●	●	●	
Mid-Kent College	●		●		●		●
Napier University	●	●	●	●	●	●	
National Broadcasting School			●				
National Film and Television School			●			●	●
Neath Port Talbot College			●			●	●
New College Nottingham	●		●			●	●
Newcastle College			●			●	
Newcastle Upon Tyne, University of	●	●	●	●		●	
North East Surrey College of Technology (NESCOT)	●		●			●	●
North East Wales Institute of Higher Education	●	●		●		●	●
North East Worcestershire College	●		●			●	●
North West Kent College	●	●				●	●
Northbrook College Sussex		●		●		●	●
University College Northampton	●	●	●	●			
Northumbria University	●	●	●	●		●	●
Norwich School of Art and Design		●			●	●	
noSweat Journalism Training		●					
Nottingham Trent University	●	●	●	●		●	
Nottingham, University of			●				●
Open University	●						
Oxford Brookes University			●	●	●	●	●
Oxford, University of		●					●
Paisley University	●		●	●		●	●

373

	general media	press, journalism & writing	TV, radio & film	PR, marketing & advertising	publishing	multimedia	music
Peterborough Regional College	●	●	●				●
Plymouth College of Art and Design			●		●	●	●
Plymouth, University of	●	●	●	●	●	●	●
PMA Training	●	●	●	●		●	
Portsmouth, University of	●	●	●	●		●	●
Queen Margaret University College, Edinburgh	●		●	●			
Queen Mary, University of London			●			●	●
Queen's University Belfast			●				●
Radio and TV School			●				
Ravensbourne College of Design and Communication			●			●	●
Robert Gordon University		●		●	●	●	
Roehampton University	●	●	●	●	●	●	●
Royal Academy of Music							●
Royal College of Music							●
Royal Holloway, University of London		●	●			●	●
Royal Northern College of Music							●
Royal Scottish Academy of Music and Drama							●
Royal Welsh College of Music and Drama			●	●			●
St Helens College, Merseyside			●			●	●
St Martin's College, Lancaster		●					
St Mary's College, Twickenham		●	●			●	
Salford, University of	●	●	●	●		●	●
Salisbury College			●			●	●
School of Oriental and African Studies	●		●				●
Sheffield College, The	●		●			●	●
Sheffield Hallam University	●	●	●	●		●	
Sheffield, University of		●	●				●
Solihull College	●			●			
South Birmingham College			●	●		●	●
South Devon College	●		●				●
South East Essex College	●	●	●		●	●	●
South Kent College	●		●	●			●
South Nottingham College			●			●	
South Thames College	●		●			●	●
Southampton Institute	●	●	●	●		●	●
Southampton, University of			●			●	●
Staffordshire University	●	●	●			●	●
Stevenson College Edinburgh			●	●			●
Stirling, University of	●	●	●	●	●		
Stockport College of Further and Higher Education	●		●				
Strathclyde, University of		●		●		●	●
Sunderland, University of	●	●	●	●	●	●	●
Surrey Institute of Art and Design	●	●	●	●		●	
Surrey, University of			●				●
Sussex, University of	●	●	●			●	●
Sutton Coldfield College	●	●					
Swansea Institute of Higher Education		●	●	●		●	●
Swansea University	●	●	●	●			
Tameside College			●			●	
Teesside, University of	●	●	●	●		●	●
Thames Valley University	●	●	●	●		●	●
Trinity College, Carmarthen	●	●	●	●		●	

	general media	press, journalism & writing	TV, radio & film	PR, marketing & advertising	publishing	multimedia	music
Trinity College of Music							●
Tyne Metropolitan College			●			●	
UHI Millennium Institute	●		●	●		●	●
Ulster, University of	●	●	●	●		●	●
Wakefield College	●					●	●
University of Wales, Aberystwyth	●		●	●			
University of Wales, Bangor	●	●	●	●		●	●
University of Wales Institute, Cardiff		●	●			●	●
University of Wales, Lampeter	●	●	●				
University of Wales, Newport	●	●	●	●		●	●
Warwick, University of	●	●	●	●			
Warwickshire College		●		●		●	
West Herts College			●	●			
West Kent College	●	●	●				
West of England, University of the	●		●	●		●	●
Westminster, University of		●	●	●		●	●
University College Winchester (formerly King Alfred's College)	●	●	●				
Wirral Metropolitan College	●		●				●
Wolverhampton, University of	●	●	●	●		●	●
University College Worcester	●		●			●	
York St John College	●	●				●	●
York, University of			●			●	●
Yorkshire Coast College of Further Education						●	

Aberdeen, University of
King's College, Aberdeen AB24 3FX
01224 272000
communications@abdn.ac.uk
www.abdn.ac.uk
• *MA (ug) film* • *BMus music*

Abertay, Dundee, University of
40 Bell Street, Dundee DD1 1HG
01382 308000
enquiries@abertay.ac.uk
www.abertay.ac.uk
• *BA (Hons) media, culture and society* • *BA (Hons) marketing and business* • *BSc (Hons) web design and development. BA (Hons) computer arts. BSc multimedia development (no year 4)*

Adam Smith College, Fife
St Brycedale Avenue, Kirkcaldy, Fife, Scotland KY1 1EX
0800 413280
enquiries@fife.ac.uk
www.fife.ac.uk
Formerly Fife College of Further and Higher Education and Glenrothes College
• *HNC/HND practical journalism* • *HNC/HND communication with media; events management* • *HNC/HND interactive multimedia. AdvDip interactive graphic design. BSc multimedia development*

Anglia Polytechnic University
East Road, Cambridge CB1 1PT
Bishop Hall Lane, Chelmsford, Essex CM1 1SQ
0845 271 3333
answers@apu.ac.uk
www.apu.ac.uk
• *BA (Hons) film, film with art history* • *BA (Hons) marketing* • *BA (Hons) illustration and animation; graphic design; graphic and web design* • *Fdg/BA (Hons) pop. (Hons) music with drama, English, psychosocial studies. MA music*

Arts Institute at Bournemouth
Wallisdown, Poole, Dorset BH12 5HH
01202 533011
general@aib.ac.uk
www.aib.ac.uk
• *BA (Hons) acting for theatre, film and TV; film production* • *Fdg commercial photography; interactive media. BA (Hons) graphic design; photography; photography; animation production*

Aston University
Aston Triangle, Birmingham B4 7ET
0121 204 3000
www.aston.ac.uk
• *BSc marketing* • *BSc multimedia tech; multimedia digital systems*

Barnsley, University Centre
PO Box 266, Church Street, Barnsley S70 2YW
01226 216267
admissions@barnsley.ac.uk
www.barnsley.ac.uk
• *Fdg journalism and media production* • *FdSc multimedia. BSc creative multimedia tech (top-up)* • *BA (Hons) creative music tech and sound recording; pop*

Basingstoke College of Technology
Worting Road, Basingstoke RG21 8TN
01256 354141
info@bcot.ac.uk
www.bcot.ac.uk
• *BTec FirstDip/NatDip media* • *BTec NatDip/NatCert graphic design; multimedia. OCN level 3 photography. Short courses: intro to using a digital camera; web page design with Dreamweaver*

Bath Spa University College
Newton Park, Newton St Low, Bath BA2 9BN
01225 875875
enquiries@bathspa.ac.uk
www.bathspa.ac.uk
• *BA/BSc (Hons) media communication (joint)* • *MA creative writing; writing for young people* • *Fdg design for digital tech. PgCert/PgDip/MA interactive multimedia* • *Fdg commercial music. PgCert/PgDip/ BA(Hons)/MA creative music tech. BA (Hons) music*

Bath, University of
Claverton Down, Bath BA2 7AY
01225 388388
admissions@bath.ac.uk
www.bath.ac.uk
• *Fdg digital media arts (moving image production) (Wiltshire College, Chippenham 01249 464644)* • *Fdg digital media arts (multimedia) (Wiltshire College, Trowbridge 01225 766241)*

Bell College
Almada Street, Hamilton, Lanarkshire ML3 0JB
01698 283100
enquiries@bell.ac.uk
www.bell.ac.uk
• *BA journalism*; Prelim journalism (NCTJ). NatCert journalism (NCTJ). Block-release newspaper journalism. Short courses in subediting, shorthand, law, freelancing, features* • *PgDip broadcast journalism. Short courses: freelance broadcasting, moviemaking without budget, radio journalism (reporting and interviewing; news and scriptwriting; production using Cool Edit Pro)* • *DipHE/CertHE communication. Short course in marketing*

Birkbeck, University of London
Malet Street, Bloomsbury, London WC1E 7HX
020 7631 6000
info@bbk.ac.uk
www.bbk.ac.uk
• *Fdg media and business application. Cert/Dip media practice. BA media and humanities* • *Cert/MA creative writing. Short courses in journalism* • *Cert/Dip/BA film and media. PhD/MPhil film; TV; media. MA/MRes history of film and visual media. Short courses: film; history of cinema and screenwriting; radio, docs and video* • *Dip science communication. Short courses in PR* • *Dip multimedia and web authoring; new media management; web design and development* • *Cert/Dip musical techniques and composition; opera studies. Fcourse/ Dip/AdvDip performance studies: concert singing, opera, dance. Short courses in music*

Birmingham College of Food, Tourism and Creative Studies
Summer Row, Birmingham B3 1JB
0121 604 1000
marketing@bcftcs.ac.uk
www.bcftcs.ac.uk
• *Fdg/BA(Hons) marketing management; marketing with events/ hospitality management. FdA marketing and PR*

Birmingham Conservatoire
Paradise Place, Birmingham B3 3HG
0121 331 5901/2
conservatoire@uce.ac.uk
www.conservatoire.uce.ac.uk
• *HND music performance. BMus (Hons) jazz; music. BSc (Hons) music tech*

* subject to validation

Birmingham, University of
Edgbaston, Birmingham B15 2TT
0121 414 3344
postmaster@bham.ac.uk
www.bham.ac.uk
• BA culture, society and communication (Europe); media, culture and society (single and joint) • BA (Hons) creative writing • MPhil American film and literature; film; history, film and TV • MSc marketing • BEng/MEng computer interactive systems (business management option). BSc/MSc multimedia computer systems. MEng computer interactive systems with international study. MSc/PgDip/PgCert comms engineering; multimedia computer systems • BMus/ BA (joint)/MPhil/MLitt/MMus/PhD music

Blackburn College
Feilden Street, Blackburn BB2 1LH
01254 55144
studentservices@blackburn.ac.uk
www.blackburn.ac.uk
• BTec NatDip media (moving image). Pre-entry media production. Short courses: makin' music breakin' news; DJ skills Cert/Dip/PgDip marketing professional • BTec NatDip multimedia; photography. HND photography. Fdg multimedia (Lancaster University) • NOCN IntDip/ AdvDip contemporary and pop

Bolton, University of
Deane Road, Bolton BL3 5AB
01204 900600
enquiries@bolton.ac.uk
www.bolton.ac.uk
• BA (Hons) fashion media* • BA (Hons) media, writing and production; creative writing. MA creative writing • BA (Hons) writing for stage, screen and radio • BA (Hons) marketing; creative advertising. MSc e-marketing • BA (Hons) animation and illustration. HND/BSc (Hons) multimedia and website development. Short courses in internet site design, web site promotion

Bournemouth University
Bournemouth Media School, Weymouth House,
Fern Barrow, Poole, Dorset BH12 5BB
01202 524111
bms@bournemouth.ac.uk
www.bournemouth.ac.uk
• BA (Hons) communication and media (University Centre Yeovil) • MA magazine journalism; • Fdg video production (Weymouth College). BA (Hons) scriptwriting for film and TV; TV production; media production (top up Bournemouth and Poole College/ Weymouth College/University Centre Yeovil); radio production (Bournemouth and Poole College). MA TV production; radio production; screenwriting; broadcast and film management • Fdg marketing (Bournemouth and Poole College). BA (Hons) PR; ad and marketing comms; marketing; international marketing; international leisure marketing (top-up); international retail marketing (top-up); marketing comms. MA corporate/political comms; PR practice; consumer marketing • Fdg multimedia (Bournemouth and Poole College); CAD - 3D computer modelling and animation (Bournemouth and Poole College/Salisbury College); CAD - engineering modelling and animation* (Bournemouth and Poole College/Cornwall College); CAD - design engineering (Cornwall College)/ CAD - graphics and packaging (University Centre Yeovil). BA (Hons) multimedia journalism; interactive media production; computer visualisation and animation; photomedia (top-up at Salisbury College). BSc (Hons) CAD - 3D computer/engineering modelling and animation (both top-up at Bournemouth and Poole College). MA multimedia journalism; post-production - sound design/editing; interactive media; 3D computer animation; digital effects. MSc computer animation • Fdg music (at Weymouth College); music tech (at Weymouth College); pop (at Bournemouth and Poole College). BA (Hons) music design (top-up). MA post-production: composing

Bradford College
Great Horton Road, Bradford BD7 1AY
01274 433333
admissions@bradfordcollege.ac.uk
www.bradfordcollege.ac.uk
• PgDip/MA politics of visual representation; representation in film • BTec HNC advertising and marketing comms. HND marketing comms and advertising. BA (Hons) advertising and marketing comms; marketing comms. MA marketing practice. PgDip/Cert/Dip marketing CIM. NatCert business and marketing. PgDip/MA marketing practice. HE courses in law and marketing • BTec HND computing (software development). BTec NatDip multimedia design. Dip digital applications. HND media and special effects (beauty therapy). BA (Hons) graphic media communication; interactive multimedia. Short courses in multimedia design (photography, web page design, animation, CD-Rom design, digital moving image) and Autodesk Inventor • NatDip music performance; music tech

Bradford, University of
Richmond Road, Bradford BD7 1DP
01274 232323
course-enquiries@bradford.ac.uk
www.brad.ac.uk
• BA/BSc media (with options). BSc media tech and production. EurMA media, communication and cultural studies • BA creative writing and identity; creative writing (with options) • BA cinematics (joint); TV (joint). PgDip/MSc entertainment tech; radio frequency comms engineering • BSc marketing (options) • BSc animatronics; computer animation and special effects; e-commerce tech; creative media and tech; internet, law and society; multimedia computing. BA digital media; digital tech (joint). BEng electronic, telecomms and internet engineering. PgDip/MSc personal, mobile and satellite comms; creative media and tech (options). EurMA computer animation and special effects • BA music tech (joint)

Brighton, University of
Mithras House, Lewes Road, Brighton BN2 4AT
01273 600900
admissions@brighton.ac.uk
www.brighton.ac.uk
• BA (Hons) English and sociology (NCTJ) • BA (Hons) sport journalism • Fcert eSystems design and tech. BSc (Hons) digital media development • BA (Hons) communication and media; communication and digital media • FCert graphics communication. FCert/BA (Hons) multimedia. BA (Hons) graphic design • FCert music production. BA (Hons) digital music; music and visual art; music composition for professional media music performance; music production

Bristol, University of
Senate House, Tyndall Avenue, Bristol BS8 1TH
0117 928 9000
Press: public-relations@bristol.ac.uk
www.bristol.ac.uk
• BA drama: theatre, film and TV. MA cinema; film and TV production; TV • MSc advanced computing (character animation; global computing and multimedia; internet tech; machine learning and data mining) • BA music. MA music: advanced musical studies; composition of music for film and television

Brunel University
Uxbridge, Middlesex UB8 3PH
01895 274000
admissions@brunel.ac.uk
www.brunel.ac.uk
• MSc health, risk and the media; risk, insecurity and the media
• BA English with creative writing. MA creative and transactional writing • BA film and TV; English, drama, music options. MA documentary practice • BSc social anthropology and communication; sociology and communication; communication and media. MSc marketing, business and management; public affairs and lobbying. MA public policy; media and comms
• BSc multimedia tech and design. MSc multimedia computing for e-commerce; digital broadcast systems; globalisation and new media; multimedia computing • BA music (also with drama, English, film, TV); creative music tech. MA creative music

Buckingham, University of
Hunter Street, Buckingham MK18 1EG
01280 814080
admissions@buckingham.ac.uk
www.buckingham.ac.uk
• BA (Hons) English with multimedia journalism, media comms and other options • BSc economics with business journalism
• BSc (Hons) marketing with media comms (and other options). MSc international marketing management • BA (Hons) English literature with multimedia journalism

Bucks Chilterns University College
Queen Alexander Road, High Wycombe, Bucks HP11 2JZ
01494 522141
marketing@bcuc.ac.uk
www.bcuc.ac.uk
• BA (Hons) media (joint and with options) • BA (Hons) creative writing (joint and with options); journalism (joint) • HNC/HND live TV production. BA applied performing arts (top-up); applied TV production (top-up). BA (Hons) video production; drama production; film or film studies (all joint and with options)
• BA (Hons) ad and promotions management; business and ad management; business and marketing management; business management with marketing; business management with marketing comms; marketing (joint and with options); PR management. PgDip marketing (CIM) • HND internet and multimedia computing; BA applied graphic studies (top-up); applied photography and digital imaging (top-up). BA (Hons) design for digital media; graphic design and advertising. BSc (Hons) multimedia tech (options). Short course: dynamic web page design • BSc (Hons) audio and music tech. BA (Hons) international music management; music entertainment and arts management; music industry management

Camberwell College of Arts
Peckham Road, London SE5 8UF
020 7514 6302
enquiries@camberwell.arts.ac.uk
www.camberwell.arts.ac.uk
• BA/MA conservation; illustration. MA book arts
• BA photography. BA/MA graphic design. MA digital arts; digital arts online

Cambridge, University of
The Old Schools, Trinity Lane, Cambridge CB2 1TN
01223 333308
admissions@cam.ac.uk
www.cam.ac.uk
• BA (Hons) music

Canterbury Christ Church University College
Department of Media, North Holmes Road, Canterbury, Kent CT1 1QU
01227 767700
admissions@cant.ac.uk
www.cant.ac.uk
• BA (Hons) media and cultural studies (also joint and with options). MA popular culture and the media • PgDip/MA journalism; MA creative writing • BA (Hons) film, radio and TV (joint and with options). PgDip/MA broadcast journalism. MA media production • BA (Hons) business studies with advertising*; marketing with advertising*; marketing (joint and with options)
• DipHE/ BA (Hons) digital media. BA (Hons) digital culture, arts and media (joint and with options) • Cert/Dip music. BA (Hons) music (also joint and with options); commercial music. MMus music

Canterbury College
New Dover Road, Canterbury, Kent CT1 3AJ
01227 811111
courseenquiries@cant-col.ac.uk
www.cant-col.ac.uk
• BTec NatDip media • HND media production. OCN intro to scriptwriting • HND graphic design and advertising. BA (Hons) visual art and communication* • HNC/HND CAD and 3D animation. OCN basic multimedia modelmaking techniques; stop motion animation for beginners • BTec FirstDip/NatDip music tech. BTec NatDip music. HND music production. BA (Hons) creative music production. OCN intro to DJ tech; creative DJ tech; intro to music tech for beginners; intro to digital audio; intro to multi-track recording

Cardiff University
Student Recruitment Office, Cardiff University, 46 Park Place, Cardiff CF10 3XQ
029 2087 4000
prospectus@cardiff.ac.uk
www.cardiff.ac.uk
• BA language and communication. MA teaching and practice of creative writing • BA journalism film and media. PgDip/MA journalism studies. MA international journalism. Short courses: writing, exploring media • BA journalism film and media
• PgDip public and media relations. MA international PR; political communication. MSc strategic marketing • Short courses in photography, creative website design, creative digital video production • BMus/BA (Hons - single and joint) music. MA musicology; music, culture and politics; performance studies; composition. Short courses in music

Cardiff, University of Wales Institute
PO Box 377, Western Avenue, Cardiff CF5 2SG
029 2041 6070
uwicinfo@uwic.ac.uk
www.uwic.ac.uk
• BA (Hons) art and creative writing • BA (Hons) broadcast media with popular culture • HND business information tech. BA (Hons) graphic communication; design for interactive media. BSc (Hons) business information systems • HND/BSc (Hons) music and audio electronic systems

Cardonald College
690 Moss Park Drive, Glasgow G52 3AY
0141 272 3333
enquiries@cardonald.ac.uk
www.cardonald.ac.uk
• HNC/HND media and comms • Prelim Cert journalism (NCTJ). HNC/ HND practical journalism • HNC/HND TV operations and production

Central England in Birmingham, University of
Perry Barr, Birmingham B42 2SU
0121 331 5000
info@ucechoices.com
www.uce.ac.uk
• BA (Hons) media and communication • BA (Hons) media and communication (journalism) • BA (Hons) media and communication (radio production; TV and video); TV tech and production • BA (Hons) advertising (joint only); marketing (options); marketing, advertising and PR; media and communication (PR); PR. CIM Dip marketing • HND digital media tech; multimedia; multimedia and networks tech. BA (Hons) media and communication (media photography, multimedia); multimedia tech; sound and multimedia • BSc (Hons) music tech; sound and multimedia; sound engineering and audio production

Central Lancashire, University of
Preston, Lancashire PR1 2HE
01772 201201
cenquiries@uclan.ac.uk
www.uclan.ac.uk
• BA (Hons) creative writing (joint course) • BA (Hons) digital journalism production; international journalism; journalism; journalism and English lang or lit; sports journalism. MA/PgDip broadcast/newspaper/ online journalism. MA international journalism; magazine journalism • BA (Hons) film, media and American studies; film, media and visual culture; film and media; TV (minor). BSc (Hons) media production and tech (AV media, journalism options); TV production. MA experimental film • BA (Hons) advertising (options); communication studies; digital comms; management and PR; marketing (options); press comms; PR (also with management/marketing). BSc (Hons) marketing. MA/PGDip/PGCert strategic communication. MA marketing. MSc international applied communication; fundraising and sponsorship; marketing management • BSc (Hons) interactive digital media; web and multimedia (also with business information systems) • BA(Hons) multimedia and sonic arts; music practice; music theatre

Central Saint Martins College of Art and Design
12–42 Southampton Row, London WC1B 4AP
020 7514 7022
info@csm.arts.ac.uk
www.csm.arts.ac.uk
• MA creative practice for narrative environments • BA criticism, communication and curation for arts and design; fashion communication with promotion. MA fashion journalism • BA acting; directing. MA European classical acting; performance (pathways in screen acting, directing, scriptwriting, movement direction); scenography • BA graphic design. PgCert professional studies: photography. PgDip character animation. MA communication design

Central School of Speech and Drama
Embassy Theatre, Eton Avenue, London NW3 3HY
020 7722 8183
enquiries@cssd.ac.uk
www.cssd.ac.uk
• MA writing for stage and broadcast media • MA theatre (inc theatre journalism). MA acting for screen. Short course: intro to acting for screen • MA advanced theatre practice (visual media for performance) • BA theatre practice (theatre sound); acting (music theatre). MA acting musical theatre; advanced theatre practice (sound design and music for performance). Short course in singing

Central Sussex College
College Road, Crawley, West Sussex RH10 1NR
01293 442200
information@crawley-college.ac.uk
www.crawley-college.ac.uk
• BTec Dip media • BTec NatDip media production

Chelsea College of Art and Design
16 John Islip Street, London SW1P 4JP
020 7514 7751
enquiries@chelsea.arts.ac.uk
www.chelsea.arts.ac.uk
• BA design communication • BA fine art: new media

University of Chester
Parkgate Road, Chester CH1 4BJ
01244 511000
enquiries@chester.ac.uk
www.chester.ac.uk
• BA (Hons) media; cultural studies. MA media and cultural studies • BA (Hons) journalism • BA (Hons) film; media (TV/radio production). MA TV production • BA (Hons) communication studies; advertising; marketing • BA (Hons) graphic design; internet tech; multimedia tech; photography. BSc/BA (Hons) internet tech; multimedia tech; fine art: new media • BA (Hons) media (commercial music production); pop

Chichester College
Westgate Fields, Chichester, West Sussex PO19 1SB
01243 786321
info@chichester.ac.uk
www.chichester.ac.uk
• BTec FirstDip/NatDip media • BTec HND media (radio production)

Chichester, University College
Bishop Otter Campus, College Lane, Chichester,
West Sussex PO19 6PE
01243 816000
admissions@ucc.ac.uk
www.ucc.ac.uk
• BA (Hons) English and creative writing; MA creative writing • BA (Hons) media production and media • BA (Hons) IT and media; media • Fdg instrumental and vocal teaching; music tech. BA (Hons) music. MA music

City College Brighton and Hove
Pelham Street, Brighton, East Sussex BN1 4FA
01273 667788
info@ccb.ac.uk
www.ccb.ac.uk
• Cert magazine journalism (NCTJ); newspaper journalism (NCTJ). OCN level 3 print journalism • OCN level 3 video production • Short courses: 3D Studio Max, animation, digital imaging for managers, digital photography, Quark, Flash animation, intro to digital imaging, multimedia, web design, PhotoShop for photographers, • Short courses: intro to music tech; Cubase SX for PC; Logic Audio for Apple Mac

City Lit
Keeley Street, London WC2B 4BA
020 7492 2600
infoline@citylit.ac.uk
www.citylit.ac.uk
• Short courses in creative writing, freelance journalism, travel journalism, computer skills for journalists, etc • Short courses in broadcast journalism, writing comedy, scriptwriting, screenwriting • Short course in how to write a press release • Short course in how to get published • Short courses: HTML, web design and hosting, Dreamweaver and Fireworks, Javascript, using Apple computers, sound and video editing, desktop video and digital editing, Premiere, Final Cut, After Effects, producing animated titles, PhotoShop, digital techniques for printmakers, animation, Maya and 3D animation, digital imaging, digital photography, colour management • Short courses: Cubase sequencing, Pro-tools, Logic Pro, digital music production techniques, Loop-based music using Ableton Live, Reason, Sibelius, Mixing and mastering techniques, drum-and-bass masterclass with Davide Carbone

City of Wolverhampton College
Wulfrun Campus, Paget Road, Wolverhampton WV6 0DU
01902 836000
mail@wolverhamptoncollege.ac.uk
www.wolverhamptoncollege.ac.uk; www.mediacove.com
• Dip/NatDip media • Pre-entry journalism (NCTJ). OCN level 3 art of writing • NatCert music tech

subject to validation

City University, London
Department of Journalism, Northampton Square,
London EC1V 0HB
020 7040 5060; journalism: 020 7040 8221
ugadmissions@city.ac.uk; journalism@city.ac.uk
www.city.ac.uk
• *MSc media research and analysis. MA transnational media and society* • *BA journalism with social science or contemporary history. PGDip newspaper journalism; magazine journalism (PTC). PgDip/MA international journalism. MA creative writing (novels/plays and scripts)* • *PGDip broadcast journalism (BJTC)/ TV current affairs journalism* • *PgDip/MA publishing studies; electronic publishing.* • *BSc computer science with games tech; music informatics. BEng media communication systems. BSc/BEng multimedia and internet systems* • *BMus/BSc music. MA musicology; music performance studies. PgDip/ MSc music IT*

Cleveland College of Art & Design
Green Lane, Linthorpe, Middlesbrough TS5 7RJ
01642 288000
StudentRecruitment@ccad.ac.uk
www.ccad.ac.uk
• *BTec Dip media (moving image). Fdg TV and film production* • *BTec Dip multimedia*

Coleg Gwent
The Rhadyr, Usk NP15 2FD
01495 333333
info@coleggwent.ac.uk
www.coleggwent.ac.uk
• *OCN writing for the media* • *BTec NatDip media (moving image). OCN video and editing production* • *BTec Dip multimedia and animation. BTec NatDip/HNC/HND graphic design. BTec NatDip photography and digital imaging; multimedia. HND photography and digital imaging. Fdg multimedia. C&G 9231/6922/6923/OCN photography. OCN web design; animation; cartooning and comic strip; CEL animation (traditional); computer graphics and animation; electronic imaging* • *BTec Dip performing arts (music/rock and pop). BTec NatDip music practice (performing, performance); music tech. OCN music tech; percussion and guitar; level 1 guitar*

Coleg Menai
Ffriddoedd Road, Bangor, Gwynedd, North Wales LL57 2TP
01248 370125
student.services@menai.ac.uk
www.menai.ac.uk
• *Dip/NatDip e-media*

Coleg Sir Gar (Carmarthenshire College)
Graig Campus, Sandy Road, Llanelli,
Carmarthenshire SA15 4DN
01554 748000
admissions@colegsirgar.ac.uk
www.colegsirgar.ac.uk
• *NatDip media (moving image). EdexcelCert film & TV acting* • *OCN web page design* • *Dip performing arts - music. NatDip music tech. Short course in music composition portfolio development*

Conservatoire for Dance and Drama
1-7 Woburn Walk, London WC1H 0JJ
020 7387 5101
info@cdd.ac.uk
www.cdd.ac.uk
• *MA dance for the screen (London Contemporary Dance School). DipHE costume for theatre, film and TV (Bristol Old Vic Theatre School)*

Cornwall College
Trevenson Road, Pool, Redruth, Cornwall TR15 3RD
01209 611611
enquiries@cornwall.ac.uk
www.cornwall.ac.uk
• *HNC media (writing). Fdg newspaper and magazine journalism. PGDip journalism (NCTJ). Short course in creative writing* • *NatDip media (moving image).* • *BTec NatDip media (e-media). HNC creative photography in commerical practice. HND multimedia. Fdg animation; multimedia design; graphic and communication design*

Coventry University
Priory Street, Coventry CV1 5FB
024 7688 7688
rao.cor@coventry.ac.uk
www.coventry.ac.uk
• *BA (Hons) communication, culture and media; media. MA communication, culture and media* • *BA (Hons) journalism and English; journalism and media. MA automotive journalism; international media journalism* • *BA (Hons) media production* • *BA business and marketing. BA (Hons) advertising and business/media; creative industries management; marketing (joint and options); marketing management. MA marketing. MSc communication management* • *BA (Hons) creative computing; digital entertainment tech; English; graphic design; media; multimedia computing. BSc/BEng (Hons) internet and broadband comms tech. MA design and digital media; media arts* • *BA (Hons) music composition and professional practice. BEng (Hons) music tech. BA (Hons) music and professional practice*

Cumbria Institute of the Arts
Brampton Road, Carlisle, Cumbria CA3 9AY
01228 400300; enquiries: 0845 607 6563
info@cumbria.ac.uk
www.cumbria.ac.uk
• *BA (Hons) journalism (NCTJ, BJTC); creative writing and contemporary culture; creative writing and film* • *BA (Hons) media production; film and creative writing; film and contemporary culture* • *MA graphic design; digital media; media futures.* • *BA (Hons) photography; graphic design; multimedia design and digital animation*

Darlington College of Technology
Cleveland Avenue, Darlington, County Durham DL3 7BB
01325 503050
enquire@darlington.ac.uk
www.darlington.ac.uk
• *Dip media* • *Pre-entry journalism (NCTJ)* • *NatDip media production (moving image)* • *ProfDip marketing (CIM)* • *NatDip multimedia. Level4 Cert digital photo journalism (NCTJ*)* • *NatCert audio production*

De Montfort University
The Gateway, Leicester LE1 9BH
0116 255 1551
enquiry@dmu.ac.uk
www.dmu.ac.uk
• *BA (Hons) media* • *BA (Hons) journalism. PgDip journalism (NCTJ)* • *BSc (Hons) media production; media tech, broadcast tech. BA (Hons) film. MA TV scriptwriting* • *BA (Hons) arts management; marketing; advertising and marketing comms; design management and innovation* • *BA (Hons) graphic/ interactive/animation/game art design; internet computing; photography and video. BSc (Hons) multimedia computing; tech. MA/PgDip photography. MSc/PgDip/PGCert multimedia comms engineering* • *HND music tech. BA/BSc (Hons) music, tech and innovation (BA for creative musicians working with technology). BSc (Hons) audio and recording tech; radio production*

Derby, University of
School of Arts, Design & Technology, Kedleston Road,
Derby DE22 1GB
01332 590500
admissions@derby.ac.uk
www.derby.ac.uk
• BA media; popular culture and media (with options) • BA media
writing (with options) • Fdg/BA (top-up) video and photography;
video production. BA broadcast media (options); film and TV
(single and with options); film and video; film • BA/PgCert/
PgDip/MA marketing management. Cert/Dip/ PgDip marketing
(CIM) • BSc computer games programming; design tech;
multimedia tech • BA design for digital media (top-up);
illustration for animation • BSc multimedia tech and music
production; music tech and audio system design; sound, light and
live event tech. BA pop with music tech. PgDip acoustics and noise
control. MSc applied acoustics

Doncaster College
Waterdale, Doncaster DN1 3EX
01302 553553
infocentre@don.ac.uk
www.don.ac.uk
• BA (Hons) scriptwriting • Cert/Dip/PgDip marketing (CIM).
MA marketing management • HNC multimedia. Fdg animation
and games art. BA (Hons) theatre or dance practice with digital
performance. MA digital performance • NCFE InterCert music
tech (mix DJ skills); BA (Hons) music tech (top-up); music
(top-up); applied new music; creative music tech

Dublin Institute of Technology
Fitzwilliam House, 30 Upper Pembroke Street, Dublin 2
00 353 1 402 3000
school of media: 00 353 1 402 3098
www.dit.ie
• BA media arts • BA (Hons) journalism with a language.
MA journalism • MA PR • BA (Hons) photography. MA digital
media tech • FCert music. BMus (Hons). MMus performance

Dundee, University of
Nethergate, Dundee DD1 4HN
01382 344000
srs@dundee.ac.uk
www.dundee.ac.uk and www.imaging.dundee.ac.uk
• BA (Hons) animation and electronic media; time-based art;
illustration. MSc animation and visualisation; electronic imaging

Durham University
University Office, Old Elvet, Durham DH1 3HP
0191 334 2000
admissions@durham.ac.uk
www.dur.ac.uk
• BA (Hons) music; education studies with music

Ealing, Hammersmith and West London College
Gliddon Road, Barons Court, London W14 9BL
0800 980 2175
Marketing@wlc.ac.uk
www.wlc.ac.uk
• BTec FirstDip/NatDip media • BTec NatDip/HND interactive
media. BTec Dip design. BTec NatDip graphic design; multimedia;
graphics. Fdg digital animation. Short courses in web page
creation and design • BTec NatAward/NatDip music tech. BTec Dip
performing arts (music). BTec NatDip music practice

East Anglia, University of
Norwich, Norfolk NR4 7TJ
01603 456161
admissions@uea.ac.uk
www.uea.ac.uk
• BA politics with media; society, culture and media. MA economics
and the mass media • BA English literature with creative writing.
MA creative writing • BA film with American studies, English
studies, TV. MA film; film with archiving; studies in fiction • MA
culture and communication • BA music; music with computing;
music with mathematics. MMus music performance studies

East London, University of
Docklands Campus, University Way, London E16 2RD
020 8223 3000
admiss@uel.ac.uk
www.uel.ac.uk
• BA (Hons) media and creative industries; media. MA media;
global media • BA (Hons) creative writing; journalism
• BA (Hons) film and video: theory and practice/ film history.
• BA (Hons) media and advertising; communication studies
• BA (Hons) photographic and print media. MA consumer and
promotional culture • HND multimedia tech. BA (Hons) digital
arts; interactive media. BSc (Hons) multimedia; multimedia tech.
MA interactive media practice; cybernetic culture • BA (Hons)
music culture: theory and production. MA sonic culture

East Surrey College
Reigate School of Art Design and Media, Gatton Point,
Claremont Road, Redhill, Surrey RH1 2JX
01737 772611
studentservices@esc.ac.uk
www.esc.ac.uk
• FDip art, design and media • HNC/HND 3D media crafts and
sculpture; moving image production. InterDip media: audio, video
and photography. NatDip media (moving image) • InterDip
multimedia. NatDip photography. HNC/Dip digital photography
• NatDip media (audio)

Edge Hill College of Higher Education
St Helen's Road, Ormskirk, Lancashire L39 4QP
01695 575171
enquiries@edgehill.ac.uk
www.edgehill.ac.uk
• BA (Hons) media • BA (Hons) journalism (NCTJ). BSc (Hons)
creative writing. PgDip print journalism • BA (Hons) media (film
and TV); film; film with film and TV production. PgDip broadcast
journalism • BA (Hons) media (advertising); PR • BA (Hons)
media (digital media design); animation

Edinburgh College of Art
Lauriston Place, Edinburgh EH3 9DF
0131 221 6000
registry@eca.ac.uk
www.eca.ac.uk
• BA (Hons)/MDes/Dip visual communication - animation;
film and TV, graphic design; illustration; photography

Edinburgh, University of
57 George Square, Edinburgh EH8 9JU
0131 650 1000
sra.enquiries@ed.ac.uk
www.ed.ac.uk
• MSc English literature: creative writing; nation, writing,
culture; writing and cultural politics • MSc film • MSc sound
design; design and digital media • MA (Hons) (undergrad) music;
music tech. MSc (postgrad) research music. Dip music therapy
(Nordoff-Robbins). MMus composition; keyboard performance
studies; musicology; organology

Editorial Centre
Hanover House, Marine Court, St Leonards-on-Sea,
East Sussex TN38 0DX
01424 435991
enquiries@editorial-centre.co.uk
www.editorial-centre.co.uk
• NatDip journalism (15-week pre-entry newspaper journalism,
Newspaper Qualifications Council). Dip journalism (overseas);
subediting; press photography. Short courses inc reporting,
writing, features, subediting, desk editing, editing, design, law,
government, FoI, photography, pictures, publishing business,
marketing, Quark, InDesign, PhotoShop, etc • Short courses in
video camera and editing, presenting for TV and multimedia,
reporting for TV and multimedia, editing for TV and multimedia,
radio • Short course in multimedia basics, designing for the web,
editorial staff and the web

Editorial Training Consultants
13 Petworth Road, Haslemere, Surrey GU27 2JB
01428 644123
info@etc-online.co.uk
www.etc-online.co.uk
• Short tailored courses for businesses. Law: IP inc copyright, defamation update, IP update. Journalism: interviewing, style, styles of writing, subbing, research, etc. Broadcast media training; faster, funnier comic writing. PR: presentation, creative thinking, writing, media training etc. Publishing: editorial management and craft skills. • New media: online writing and research; improving site traffic

Essex, University of
Wivenhoe Park, Colchester CO4 3SQ
01206 873333
admit@essex.ac.uk
www.essex.ac.uk
• BA journalism (South East Essex College) • BA film and literature/ history of art; history with film; American studies with film; TV production and screen theory* (at South East Essex College). MACert film; film and literature • BSc multimedia production and internet tech (taught in conjunction with South East Essex College) • BA music production (South East Essex College)

Exeter, University of
The Queen's Drive, Exeter, Devon EX4 4QJ
01392 661000
www.ex.ac.uk
• BA English, also with film. • MA/PhD creative writing • BA film (cinema and practice)/ film with a modern language; MA film; PhD film by practice

Falmouth, University College
Woodlane Campus, Falmouth, Cornwall TR11 4RH
01326 211077
admissions@falmouth.ac.uk
www.falmouth.ac.uk
• BA (Hons) English with media • BA (Hons) English with creative writing; journalism. PgDip/MA professional writing. MA international journalism* • BA (Hons) film; broadcasting. PgDip/MA broadcast journalism (BJTC) (MA options in arts, media, travel/investigative/science/sports journalism; TV production • PgDip creative advertising • MA illustration: authorial practice • BA (Hons) graphic design. BA (Hons)/MA photography. MA interactive art and design

Glamorgan, University of
Pontypridd, Wales CF37 1DL
0800 716925
enquiries@glam.ac.uk
www.glam.ac.uk
• BA (Hons) English, also with media; drama (theatre and media); media and communication studies; media, with options
• BA (Hons) creative and professional writing; journalism. MPhil writing • BSc (Hons) digital media and broadcasting tech; lighting tech; live event tech. BA (Hons) film and TV set design; film (Joint); film, radio and TV; media production (with options); media production (radio). MPhil/PhD film practice. MSc film producing and business management • BA (Hons)/Fdg/MSc/PgD/ PgC/CIM Dip marketing. BSC (Hons) media production with marketing • FCert media and information tech. HND/Fdg media tech. BSc (Hons) interactive new media tech; media tech (also as BSc); multimedia; multimedia tech. BA (Hons) media production (photography) • HND/Fdg/BSc/BSc (Hons) music tech; sound tech. BA (Hons) pop. MSc advanced music production; music engineering and production

Glasgow Caledonian University
70 Cowcaddens Road, Glasgow G4 0BA
0141 331 3000
enquiries@gcal.ac.uk
www.gcal.ac.uk
• BA/BA (Hons) journalism (NCTJ). PGDip journalism studies (NCTJ) • BA (Hons) marketing • Dip multimedia visualisation with product design. BSc multimedia tech. MA digital media design • BSc/BSc (Hons) audio tech with electronics; multimedia

Glasgow Metropolitan College
60 North Hanover Street, Glasgow G1 2BP
0141 566 6226
enquiries@glasgowmet.ac.uk
www.glasgowmet.ac.uk
• HNC/HND journalism: broadcast and print • HNC/HND TV operations and production • HNC/HND event management
• HNC/HND digital media for publishing and print; publishing.
• HNC/HND interactive multimedia creation; graphic design; visual information: design and illustration. HND professional photography and digital imaging. AdvDip illustrative photography

Glasgow School of Art
167 Renfrew Street, Glasgow G3 6RQ
0141 353 4500
registry@gsa.ac.uk
www.gsa.ac.uk
• MPhil 2D/3D motion graphics

Glasgow, University of
Glasgow G12 8QQ
0141 330 2000
admissions@gla.ac.uk
www.gla.ac.uk
• MA (Hons) creative and cultural studies (undergraduate)
• MA (Hons) theatre; film and TV (undergrad). MLitt theatre; film and TV • MA (Hons) arts and media informatics (undergrad)
• BMus/MA (Hons) music

Gloucestershire, University of
The Park, Cheltenham GL50 2RH
0870 721 0210
admissions@glos.ac.uk
www.glos.ac.uk
• BA (Hons) journalism and professional writing; creative writing
• BA (Hons) broadcast journalism; film; media comms • BA (Hons) advertising; PR; multimedia marketing • BA (Hons) publishing
• BA (Hons) multimedia; design for interactive media

Goldsmiths College
Dept of Media and Communications,
University of London, New Cross, London SE14 6NW
020 7919 7171
media-comms@gold.ac.uk
www.goldsmiths.ac.uk
• BA media and anthropology/sociology/modern literature/comms; international media; transnational comms and global media. MPhil/PhD/MRes/FCert/BA media and comms. Practice courses in journalism, radio, TV, film, photography
• MA journalism (accredited by PTC and recognised by NUJ)
• MA feature film; filmmaking; TV journalism; radio (BJTC); screen documentary; scriptwriting • MA digital media: tech and cultural form; image and communication (photography or electronic graphics); interactive media: critical theory and practice
• BMus music; music (extension degree); pop studies. PgCert music. MMus composition; contemporary music studies; ethnomusicology; historical musicology; music theory and analysis; performance and related studies; Russian music studies. MPhil/PhD music. Dip jazz and pop. PgDip music teaching to adults. Cert music studies; music workshop skills. FCert integrated degree in music

Greenwich, University of
Old Royal Naval College, Park Row, Greenwich,
London SE10 9LS
020 8331 8000
courseinfo@greenwich.ac.uk
www.gre.ac.uk
• BA (Hons) creative industries; media, culture and comms;
media and comms • HND professional writing. BA creative writing
(options). BA (Hons) media writing (options) • HND TV
production tech. BA film (with options) • BA(Hons) international
marketing; marketing (options); marketing comms. MA
professional services marketing*; sports marketing*; strategic
marketing (also executive track); strategic marketing comms
• HNC/HND/BA (Hons) graphic and digital design. HND
photography. Fdg creative industries (multimedia; image-based
media)*. BA (Hons) photography*; 3D digital design and
animation. BSc (Hons) multimedia and internet tech; multimedia
tech (options); entertainment tech; interactive multimedia games
development. BEng (Hons) games and entertainment systems.
MA critical studies, new media and practising arts; website
architecture. MSc games and entertainment systems software
engineering; multimedia and internet tech • Fdg creative
industries (music production)

Grimsby Institute of Further & Higher Education
Nuns Corner, Grimsby DN34 5BQ
01472 311222
infocent@grimsby.ac.uk
www.grimsby.ac.uk
• Dip media; bespoke media law training • NatDip media
(journalism and publishing). OCN novel/short story writing. BA
(Hons) professional writing; digital media production - journalism
(both with Lancaster University) • HND media production; media
(TV, film and video). NatDip media (moving image). Fdg digital
media (broadcast). BA (Hons) digital media production - TV, film,
video (with Lancaster University). OCN intro to script writing.
ProfCert video journalism; digital video editing • Fdg media and
marketing • BTec NatDip e-media; games media development.
HNC photography and digital imaging. HNC/HND interactive
media. HND multimedia. BA (Hons) digital media production -
photography; multimedia (with Lancaster University)
• ProfCert digital audio editing. HND music production.
Dip performing arts (music). NatDip music tech. BA (Hons)
creative music* (University of Hull)

Guildford College
Stoke Park, Guildford, Surrey GU1 1EZ
01483 448500
info@guildford.ac.uk
www.guildford.ac.uk
• NatCert media • NatDip media (moving image). HND/ BA (Hons)
media production. • IntroCert/ ProfCert/Dip/PgDip marketing
(CIM) • SROCN level 2 and 3/NatDip photography. Short courses
in PhotoShop and Quark Xpress on the Mac

Harlow College
Velizy Avenue, Town Centre, Harlow, Essex CM20 3LH
01279 868000
full-time@harlow-college.ac.uk
www.harlow-college.ac.uk
• One-year journalism: newspapers (NCTJ). BA (Hons) journalism
(Middlesex University). Pg journalism: newspapers (NCTJ);
magazines (NCTJ, PTC) • NatDip graphic design. Short courses:
Apple Mac workshop, webpage design, digital photography,
advanced digital photography • NatDip pop. Short course in music
tech

Harrow College
Brookshill, Harrow Weald, Middlesex HA3 6RR
020 8909 6000
enquiries@harrow.ac.uk
www.harrow.ac.uk
• BTec NatCert/NatDip media • Short courses: creative writing
• Short courses speaking with confidence • Short courses in
using digital photography (PhotoShop), web design using
Dreamweaver/ Front Page • Short courses in music theory
beginner to grade 5, piano keyboard, singing and vocal workout

Henley College Coventry
Henley Road, Bell Green, Coventry CV2 1ED
024 7662 6300
info@henley-cov.ac.uk
www.henley-cov.ac.uk
• BTec Dip media • BTec NatDip media - moving image
• BTec NatDip e-media

Hertfordshire, University of
College Lane, Hatfield AL10 9AB
01707 284000
admissions@herts.ac.uk
www.herts.ac.uk
• BSc (Hons) media tech and digital broadcast • BA (Hons)
marketing. BA (Hons) digital animation; lens media; model design
and special effects. BA/BSc (Hons) software systems for the arts
and media. BSc (Hons) digital tech; internet tech and e-commerce
• BSc (Hons) music composition and tech; music; commercial
composition and tech; music tech; sound design tech

Highbury College, Portsmouth
Dept of Media and Journalism, Dovercourt Road,
Portsmouth, Hampshire PO6 2SA
023 9238 3131
info@highbury.ac.uk
www.highbury.ac.uk
• BTec Dip art, design and media; media • Pre-entry newspaper
journalism (NCTJ); magazine journalism (PTC). HND media
(journalism). Short course introduction to newspaper and
magazine journalism • Pre-entry broadcast journalism (BJTC).
BTec NatDip media production (moving image). HND media
(moving image). Short course intro to digital video editing • BTec
NatDip media production (publishing) • BTec NatDip multimedia;
media production (games design). • BTec NatDip music tech

Huddersfield, University of
Queensgate, Huddersfield HD1 3DH
01484 422288
admissions@hud.ac.uk
www.hud.ac.uk
• BA (Hons) English (with media, creative writing, journalism);
media and sports journalism; drama and media • BA (Hons) media
and print journalism • BA (Hons) media and TV production • BA
(Hons) advertising with media and design management; creative
imaging (advertising); marketing with innovation; PR with media;
PR with media and design management • HNC/HND multimedia.
BA/BSc (Hons) virtual reality design; interaction design for media
tech; multimedia design. BA (Hons) creative imaging (graphic
design/illustration/media and animation); interactive
multimedia; multimedia with installation art; multimedia
(options); video, 3D and popular music; video and 3D for popular
music; virtual reality design with animation. BSc (Hons)/BSc
multimedia computing. BSc (Hons) multimedia computing/tech.
MA creative imaging. MSc electronic and computer based systems
design. MA/MSc innovation for the digital future; interactive
multimedia production. PgCert/PgDip/MSc multimedia and
e-learning • BMus (Hons) music; creative music tech. BA (Hons)
drama with music; music tech; music tech and pop; music with a
modern language; music with English; pop production; media and
radio journalism. BSc (Hons) music tech software development;
music tech and audio systems; pop production. PgDip/ MA music
(single and joint); music (composition; electro-acoustic
composition; performance; performance; contemporary music
studies; historical musicology). MA music (musicology)

Hull, University of
Cottingham Road, Hull HU6 7RX
01482 346311
admissions@hull.ac.uk
www.hull.ac.uk
• BA culture, media and society • BA creative writing (options). Cert creative writing • BA film (with options). MA contemporary literature and film • BA marketing (options) • BA creative music tech with digital arts; design for digital media; digital arts. BSc creative media computing. BSc internal computing with creative media; creative music tech. BSc computer science with games development. • BA music; creative music tech (single or with digital arts); drama and music; English and music; music and modern languages. BSc music tech and computing. BMus music. MMus music (musicology, composition, performance). MRes creative music tech. MPhil/PhD music; creative music tech

Journalism Training Centre
29 Harley Street, London W1G 9QR
020 7798 5618
info@jtc.co.uk
www.jtc.co.uk
• Dip periodicals journalism (NUJ). Short courses: subediting, feature writing, media law

Keele, University of
Keele, Staffordshire ST5 5BG
01782 621111
www.keele.ac.uk
• BA/BSc media, comms and culture • BA/BSc music (options); music tech (options)

Kensington and Chelsea College
Hortensia Road, London SW10 0QS
020 7573 5333
enquiries@kcc.ac.uk
www.kcc.ac.uk
• BTec NatCert/HNC multimedia; graphic design. BTec animation for video and DVD production (Level 2); LOCN web page design Flash, Dreamweaver, Fireworks; e-commerce and business websites with Dreamweaver, PHP and Apache • BTec FirstDip performing musician* (in partnership with Access to Music). LOCN music tech. Music tech with Deep Recording Studios. LOCN studio programming level 1, 2 and 3.

Kent Institute of Art and Design
Oakwood Park, Maidstone, Kent ME16 8AG
01622 620000
info@kiad.ac.uk
www.kiad.ac.uk
• BA (Hons) video media arts; video and photography. MA artists' film, video and photography • BA (Hons) design, branding and marketing; fashion promotion. • BA (Hons) illustration • BTec NatDip multimedia. Fdg graphic communication. BA (Hons) animation; digital 3D design; graphic design; photography; photography and media arts. PgCert contemporary photographic practice; graphic design. MA graphic design; photography

Kent, University of
The Registry, Canterbury, Kent CT2 7NZ
01227 764000
recruitment@kent.ac.uk
www.kent.ac.uk
• MA English and American literature and creative writing • BA (Hons) American studies (art and film); European studies (film); film; film and contemporary arts; visual and performed arts. MA/MPhil/PhD film • BA (Hons) marketing; business administration (marketing) • BA (Hons) multimedia tech and design. MRes/MPhil/PhD cartoons and caricature. MSc computer animation • BA (Hons) music tech

King's College London
School of Humanities, Strand, London WC2R 2LS
020 7836 5454
ceu@kcl.ac.uk
www.kcl.ac.uk
• MA cultural and creative industries • BA English with film; film and American studies; other BA honours programmes with film. MA contemporary cinema cultures • MA digital culture and tech. MSc information tech and internet law • BMus music; BA German and music. MMus music.

Kingston University
River House, 53-57 High Street, Kingston-upon-Thames, Surrey KT1 1LQ
020 8547 2000
admissions-info@kingston.ac.uk
www.kingston.ac.uk
• BA (Hons) visual and material culture; media and cultural studies. BSc (Hons) media tech. • BA (Hons) creative writing (joint); journalism. MA creative writing • BA (Hons) history of art, design and film/TV; TV design and production; film. MA production design/screen design for film and TV • Fdg graphic comms. MA communication design; marketing; strategic marketing management; political communication • BA (Hons) graphic design. BA (Hons)/MA illustration and animation • BA (Hons) live arts. BMus (Hons) music. MA composing for film and TV; music; music composition; music education; musicology; music performance; pop

Lambeth College
45 Clapham Common South Side, London SW4 9BL
020 7501 5100
courses@lambethcollege.ac.uk
www.lambethcollege.ac.uk
• BTec FirstDip media • Fdg journalism (London Metropolitan University). Pre-entry newspaper journalism (NCTJ)
• BTec NatDip media (moving image). BTec NatAward radio. C&G Cert video production techniques. • LOCN video, photography and digital publishing; web design and animation. C&G Dip/AdvDip web design. BTec FirstDip multimedia and photography. BTec NatDip web design and animation (e-media)

Lampeter, University of Wales
Ceredigion SA48 7ED
01570 422351, dept of film and media: 01570 424790
admissions@lamp.ac.uk
www.lamp.ac.uk
• BA media. MA/PgDip Welsh media • BA English with creative writing. MA/PgDip creative writing • BA film; film and media. BA/MA/PgDip media production. MA/PgDip screenwriting (bilingual); screen studies

Lancaster University
Bailrigg, Lancaster LA1 4YW
01524 65201
ugadmissions@lancaster.ac.uk
www.lancs.ac.uk
• BA (Hons) creative arts; English language and the media; media and cultural studies. MA globalisation and the information age; visual culture • BA (Hons) English language or literature with creative writing. MA creative writing; women's writing
• BA (Hons) film and cultural studies; film and philosophy; sociology. PgDip/MSc media production and distribution
• BA (Hons) advertising and marketing. BSc (Hons) marketing; marketing management. MSc advanced marketing management
• BSc (Hons) computer science with multimedia systems. BSc (Hons)/MSc communication and computer systems. PgDip/MA/MRes IT, management and organisational change. MSc mobile and ubiquitous computing; multimedia networking. PgDip/MSc mobile game design and m-commerce systems*; multimedia courseware engineering • BA (Hons)/BSc (Hons) computer science and music. BA (Hons) music tech; musicology. BA (Hons)/BMus (Hons) music. MMus music; music theory

Leeds College of Art and Design
Blenheim Walk, Leeds, West Yorkshire LS2 9AQ
0113 202 8000
info@leeds-art.ac.uk
www.leeds-art.ac.uk
• Fdg advertising. BA (Hons) visual comms • Fdg photography; digital media

Leeds College of Music
3 Quarry Hill, Leeds LS2 7PD
0113 222 3400
enquiries@lcm.ac.uk
www.lcm.ac.uk
• Fdg music production for film and television • BA (Hons) jazz studies; music studies; pop studies; music production. MMus jazz studies; music studies. PgCert advanced piano performance

Leeds Metropolitan University
Civic Quarter, Leeds LS1 3HE
0113 283 2600
course-enquiries@leedsmet.ac.uk
www.leedsmet.ac.uk
• BA (Hons) media and popular culture • CertHE/Fdg film and TV production. BA (Hons) film and moving image production (level 3 top-up) • HND business and PR; consumer marketing. BA (Hons) PR; PR with a European language; consumer marketing; marketing. BA/BA (Hons) managing cultural and major events. BSc (Hons) marketing media and systems. MA PR management; PR. MSc marketing • Fdg creative tech. HND/BSc (Hons) games design; multimedia tech. BSc (Hons) animation tech and special effects. BA (Hons) web media management. BA/BSc (Hons) education and new media. MSc creative tech; digital imaging tech; web engineering • BSc (Hons) creative music and sound tech; design tech for music; music tech; music and new media tech. MSc music tech

Leeds Trinity & All Saints
Brownberrie Lane, Horsforth, Leeds LS18 5HD
0113 283 7100
admissions@tasc.ac.uk
www.tasc.ac.uk
• BA English, also with film, media and other options. BA media; media and marketing. Cert media education • BA sports journalism. PgDip/MA bi-media (radio and TV); radio or print journalism (NCTJ) • BA film • PgDip/MA public communication. BA marketing (options)

Leeds, University of
Leeds LS2 9JT
0113 243 1751
enquiry@leeds.ac.uk
www.leeds.ac.uk
• BA creative writing. MA international journalism: production and consumption. PgDip/MA creative writing • BA broadcasting; broadcast journalism; cinema, photography and TV. MA scriptwriting for TV • BA comms. MA comms studies; international comms; media management; political communication • BA new media • BA/BMus music. BA/BSc music, multimedia and electronics. BA popular and world music; music - philosophy; music - theology and religious studies. MMus music (composition; musicology; performance; tech and computer music). PgCert/PgDip/MA music and liturgy

Leicester, University of
University Road, Leicester LE1 7RH
0116 252 2522
admissions@le.ac.uk
www.le.ac.uk
• BA film and the visual arts. MA humanities and film
• BSc comms, media and society. MA/PGDip mass comms; globalisation and comms; media and communication research

Lincoln, University of
Brayford Pool, Lincoln LN6 7TS
01522 882000
enquiries@lincoln.ac.uk
www.lincoln.ac.uk
Some courses held at Hull School of Art & Design • BA (Hons) media, culture and comms. MA/MRes/MPhil/PhD media and cultural studies • BA/PgDip/MA journalism • BA (Hons) contemporary lens media; digital and interactive TV; TV and film. BA (Hons)/MA media production. MA documentary and factual programme production • BA (Hons) advertising and art direction; marketing. MSc international marketing strategy. MBA strategic marketing • BA (Hons) animation; games design; interactive and screen-based graphics; interactive multimedia; web design. BSc (Hons) media tech; multimedia tech. BSc (Hons)/MSc games computing • BSc audio tech

Liverpool Community College
Broad Green Road, Old Swan, Liverpool L13 5SQ
0151 252 1515
www.liv-coll.ac.uk
• BTec FirstDip/HND/Fdg media • Pre-entry journalism (NCTJ). Dip print/periodical journalism (fast-track, NCTJ) • BTec NatDip media (moving image) • BTec NatDip multimedia; photography • BTec FirstDip/NatAward/NatDip music tech. ProfDip creative music tech.

Liverpool Hope University College
Hope Park, Liverpool L16 9JD
0151 291 3000
admission@hope.ac.uk
www.hope.ac.uk
• BA creative and performing arts; media (single and joint)
• BA film (joint) • BA marketing (joint) • BA music (joint); music, pop, music tech. MA music

Liverpool John Moores University
Roscoe Court, 4 Rodney Street, Liverpool L1 2TZ
0151 231 5090
recruitment@ljmu.ac.uk
www.ljmu.ac.uk
• BA (Hons) media and cultural studies; media, cultural studies and marketing • BA (Hons) journalism (NCTJ); international journalism (NCTJ); imaginative writing. MA journalism; international journalism; writing • BA (Hons) media professional studies; screen studies. MA screen writing • BA (Hons) business and PR; marketing; business and information. BSc (Hons) e-business communication • PgDip/MA information and library management • BA (Hons) English literature and electronic creative tech • BA (Hons) pop studies

Liverpool, University of
Liverpool L69 3BX
0151 794 2000
uksro@liv.ac.uk
www.liv.ac.uk
• BA (Hons) English and communication studies (joint)
• BA (Hons) film (European) and a modern language
• BA (Hons) communication and business studies (joint); politics and communication studies; marketing. MA politics and the mass media • BSc (Hons) computer and multimedia systems. BEng (Hons)/ MEng (Hons) wireless comms and 3G tech. MSc internet computing • BA (Hons) communication, media and pop (joint). BA (Hons) music/ pop. MA pop studies. MMus music

London Business School
Regent's Park, London NW1 4SA
020 7000 7000
www.london.edu
• MBA marketing strategy (full-time executive MBA)

subject to validation

London College of Communication
Elephant & Castle, London SE1 6SB
020 7514 6569
info@lcc.arts.ac.uk
www.lcc.arts.ac.uk
• Fdg media practice. BA media and cultural studies
• Fdg/BA/PgDip/MA journalism. GradCert periodical journalism
• BA film and video. MA screenwriting; documentary research.
PgDip broadcast journalism and documentary photography
• Fdg/BA marketing and advertising. BA/MA PR. MA marketing
and comms • Dip print production. BA print media, marketing and
advertising. GradCert bookbinding and restoration/publishing.
Postgraduate programme in publishing/publishing production
• Dip animation; pro photography practice; 3D modelling and
animation; new media publishing. NatDip/BA graphic and media
design. Fdg digital media production; interactive games
production; photojournalism; design for graphic; display design.
GradCert photography practice; design for visual communication.
BA digital media production; photography. MA/PgDip interactive
media. MSc digital colour imaging. MA digital media and print;
photography; graphic design. Short courses: digital orientation/
media • Dip sound design and music tech. BA sound arts and
design. GradCert sonic arts; music publishing

London College of Fashion
20 John Prince's Street, London W1G 0BJ
020 7514 7344
enquiries@fashion.arts.ac.uk
www.fashion.arts.ac.uk
• PgCert fashion and lifestyle journalism. MA fashion journalism
• Fdg fashion marketing and promotion (also online); fashion
design and marketing. GradCert fashion marketing. BA fashion
promotion. MA fashion photography; digital fashion

London College of Music & Media
see Thames Valley University

London Film School
24 Shelton Street, London WC2H 9UB
020 7836 9642
info@lfs.org.uk
www.lfs.org.uk
• MA filmmaking; screenwriting

London Metropolitan University
31 Jewry Street, London EC3N 2EY
020 7423 0000
admissions@londonmet.ac.uk
www.londonmet.ac.uk
• BA (Hons) media* • BA (Hons) creative writing. Fdg/BA (Hons)
journalism. MA professional writing • Fdg audio production for
broadcast media. BA (Hons) film; film and broadcast production.
PgCert/PgDip/MA screenwriting. MA AV production; filmmaking
• BA (Hons) ad and marketing communication*; arts management
(joint); comms and visual culture; events management and music
and media management; marketing; PR. HND/BA (Hons) events
management. BSc mass comms. MA international marketing
comms; marketing; mass comms; sport management • Fdg/ BSc
(Hons) multimedia. BSc (Hons) digital media; computer
animation; computer visualisation and games; digital media and
mass comms/multimedia tech and apps; multimedia tech and
apps. MA digital information management/media/media
management/ moving image. MSc multimedia systems
• Fdg musical instruments. /BA (Hons) music and media
management. BSc (Hons) music tech (audio systems). BA (Hons)
music education; sound and media. Cert sound recording tech

London School of Economics and Political Science
Houghton Street, London WC2A 2AE
020 7405 7686
stu.rec@lse.ac.uk
www.lse.ac.uk
• MSc gender and the media • MSc global media and comms;
media and comms; media and comms regulation and policy;
politics and communication; social and public communication
• MSc new media, information and society

London School of Journalism
126 Shirland Road, Maida Vale, London W9 2BT
020 7289 7777
info@lsjournalism.com
www.lsj.org
• PgDip journalism (also online) (NUJ). Short and distance courses
inc news/feature/internet/freelance journalism, subediting,
novel/short story writing, writing for children, law etc

London South Bank University
90 London Road, London SE1 6EN
020 7815 7815
enquiries@lsbu.ac.uk
www.lsbu.ac.uk
• BA (Hons) English/ media; BSc (Hons) media and society;
MA creative media arts (cultural and media; digital film
production; media education; media writing; new media)
• BA (Hons) creative writing and English • BA (Hons) film (joint)
• BA (Hons) arts management; marketing. MSc/PgDip international
marketing. E-marketing award (CIM) • BA (Hons) digital
photography/media arts; game cultures. MSc/PgDip/PgCert
internet and multimedia information systems/engineering
• BA (Hons) sonic media

London, University College
Gower Street, London WC1E 6BT
020 7679 2000
www.ucl.ac.uk
• MA film studies • MA library and information studies.
PgCert/PgDip/MA electronic communication and publishing

Luton, University of
Park Square, Luton, Beds LU1 3JU
01582 734111
enquiries@luton.ac.uk
www.luton.ac.uk
• MA media, culture and tech. MRes media arts • Fdg creative
writing. BA (Hons) creative writing; journalism; journalism and
public relations. MRes creative writing • Fdg media production
(Barnfield/Bedford/ Dunstable/Milton Keynes). BA (Hons) media
performance; TV production. MA international cinema; media
production (documentary) • Fdg ad and marketing comms. BA
(Hons) ad and marketing comms; marketing; marketing and
media practices; PR; media advertising; media practices (mass
comms). MSc marketing and business management; marketing
comms. MA media arts (mass comms) • Fdg creative and editorial
photography (Dunstable College); digital imaging and design for
media (Milton Keynes College); media art and design. BA (Hons)
digital photography and video art; animation. BSc (Hons)
computer games development. MA art design and internet tech;
new media and internet tech. MSc computer animation
• Fdg music tech (Bedford). BA (Hons) music tech

Manchester, University of
Oxford Road, Manchester M13 9PL
0161 306 6000
www.manchester.ac.uk
• BA (Hons) media, culture and society • MA/PhD creative writing
• BA (Hons) film with options • BMus (Hons) music. BA (Hons)
music and drama. MMus musicology; composition,
electroacoustic music composition. MPhil/PhD musicology;
composition

Manchester Metropolitan University
All Saints Building, All Saints, Manchester M15 6BH
0161 247 2000
enquiries@mmu.ac.uk
www.mmu.ac.uk
• MA media arts; representation in cinema and media; design and
art direction • BA (Hons) English and creative writing • BA (Hons)
English and film; contemporary film and video; film and media
• BA (Hons) ad and brand management; communication;
corporate communication; communication in culture and media;
human communication • Fdg new media design. BSc (Hons)
multimedia tech; media tech; multimedia computing. BA (Hons)
photography; interactive arts.

---

* subject to validation

387

Marjon, College of St Mark & St John
Derriford Road, Plymouth, Devon PL6 8BH
01752 636700
admissions@marjon.ac.uk
www.marjon.ac.uk
• BA (Hons) media • BA (Hons) writing for the media; creative writing • BA (Hons) creative media practice • BA (Hons) PR

Mid-Cheshire College
Hartford Campus, Chester Road, Northwich, Cheshire CW8 1LJ
01606 74444
info@midchesh.ac.uk
www.midchesh.ac.uk
• BTec NatDip multimedia; photography. Fdg new and interactive media. • BTec NatDip music practice; music tech

Middlesex University
Admissions Enquiries, North London Business Park, London N11 1QS
020 8411 5555
admissions@mdx.ac.uk
www.mdx.ac.uk
• BA (Hons) media and cultural studies • BA (Hons) creative and media writing; journalism and communication studies; journalism. MA writing (prose fiction, poetry or scriptwriting) • BA film arts/ filmmaking. BA (Hons) film studies; film video interactive arts; TV production • MA media and comms management. BA marketing • BA (Hons) publishing and media • HND/HNC graphic design. DipHE visual communication design - graphic design. Fdg graphic design. BA (Hons) graphic/games design; illustration; photography. MA/MSc design for interactive media. MA electronic arts; graphic design • BA (Hons) music; music and arts management. BA/BSc (Hons)/MA sonic arts. MA music

Mid-Kent College
Horsted Centre, Maidstone Road, Chatham, Kent ME5 9UQ
01634 402020
www.midkent.ac.uk
• BTec IntroDip art, design and media • BTec NatDip media (moving image) • BTec NatDip media (publishing) • BTec NatDip music tech. BTec NatAward music tech

Napier University
Craiglockhart Campus, Edinburgh EH14 1DJ
08452 60 60 40
info@napier.ac.uk
www.napier.ac.uk
• BA/BA (Hons) culture, media and society • BA/BA (Hons) journalism. MSc/PgDip journalism • MA screen project development; screenwriting • BA (Hons) communication; marketing management. MSc/PgDip creative advertising; international communication; marketing • BA/BA (Hons) publishing media. MSc/ PgDip publishing • BA/BA (Hons) design futures; photography, film and imaging. BEng / BEng (Hons) internet computing; multimedia systems; software engineering. MDes interdisciplinary design • BMus/ BMus (Hons) music. BA/BA (Hons) pop

National Broadcasting School
The Innovation Centre, University of Sussex, Brighton BN1 9SB
01273 704510
www.nationalbroadcastingschool.com
• PgDip NBS radio presentation and production; radio journalism

National Film and Television School
Beaconsfield Studios, Station Road, Beaconsfield, Bucks HP9 1LG
01494 731425/13
info@nftsfilm-tv.ac.uk
www.nftsfilm-tv.ac.uk
• Dip script development; sound recording for film and TV; fundamentals of fiction direction. MA producing; production design; screenwriting; sound post-production; cinematography; doc/fiction direction; editing; producing for TV entertainment. Doc summer school. Feature development workshop. Short courses in art and design; camera and lighting; directing; editing; production; sound; writing • Dip digital post production; visual and special effects producing. MA animation direction • MA composing for film and TV

Neath Port Talbot College
Dwr-y-Felin Road, Neath SA10 7RF
01639 648000
enquiries@nptc.ac.uk
www.nptc.ac.uk
• HNC/HNDmedia production • HNC/ HND computing (multimedia) • HND music performance (pop). BA (Hons) music performance and production

New College Nottingham
City Campus, Adams Building, Stoney Street, Lace Market, Nottingham NG1 1NG
0115 910 0100
enquiries@ncn.ac.uk
www.ncn.ac.uk
• BTec FirstDip/NatDip/HND media • C&G TV and video production. BTec ProfCert digital video editing • BTec NatDip e-media production. Fdg multimedia. Short courses: 3D Studio Max 6 beginner, intermediate, advanced - character modelling and animation • HND music performance; music production. FirstDip/NatDip music practice (pop); music tech. Short course music production

Newcastle College
Rye Hill Campus, Scotswood Road, Newcastle NE4 5BR
0191 200 4000
enquiries@ncl-coll.ac.uk
www.newcastlecollege.co.uk
• Fdg TV and media practice • HNC interactive media/graphic design. Fdg multimedia design; illustration and animation; graphic design; graphics design for news media

Newcastle Upon Tyne, University of
Newcastle NE1 7RU
0191 222 6000
enquiries@ncl.ac.uk
www.ncl.ac.uk
• BA (Hons) media, communication and cultural studies
• PgCert/MA creative writing. MA literary studies: writing, memory, culture • MA modern and contemporary studies
• BA (Hons) marketing and management. BSc (Hons) marketing
• MSc e-business and information systems; system design for internet apps

Newport, University of Wales
Caerleon Campus, PO Box 179, Newport, South Wales NP18 3YG
01633 432432
uic@newport.ac.uk
www.newport.ac.uk
• MA sports media • BA (Hons) creative writing
• BA(Hons) documentary film and TV; film and video; cinema and scriptwriting. MA film • BA (Hons) advertising. BSc marketing
• BA (Hons) animation; computer games design. BSc (Hons) games development and artificial intelligence. MA animation
• BA (Hons) creative sound and music

North East Surrey College of Technology (NESCOT)
Reigate Road, Ewell, Epsom, Surrey KT17 3DS
020 8394 3038
info@nescot.ac.uk
www.nescot.ac.uk
• FirstDip media • NatDip media production • NatDip multimedia.
Fdg media and multimedia (OUVS); photography and digital
imaging (OUVS). BA (Hons) photography and imaging • NatDip
music tech

North East Wales Institute of Higher Education
Plas Coch, Mold Road, Wrexham LL11 2AW
01978 290666
enquiries@newi.ac.uk
www.newi.ac.uk
• BA (Hons) media • BA (Hons) writing • BA (Hons) media comms;
marketing. ProfCert/ProfDip/ PgDip marketing (CIM) • HND
internet and multimedia computing; graphic design. Fdg (Hons)
internet and multimedia computing. Fdg digital media. BA (Hons)
animation; graphic/multimedia. BSc (Hons) internet and
multimedia computing. MA animation • Fdg sound/studio tech.
BSc (Hons) studio recording and performance tech

North East Worcestershire College
Peakman Street, Redditch, Worcestershire B98 8DW
01527 570020
info@ne-worcs.ac.uk
www.ne-worcs.ac.uk
• BTec FirstDip/NatDip media • HNC/HND media (moving image)
• HNC/HND multimedia development • BTec FirstDip performing
arts, media and music tech. NatDip music tech

North West Kent College
Oakfield Lane, Dartford, Kent DA1 2JT
0800 074 1447
course.enquiries@nwkcollege.ac.uk
www.nwkcollege.ac.uk
• BTec IntroDip art, design and media; BTec Dip media; BTec
NatDip media • HND professional writing • BTec NatDip graphic
design; multimedia. Short courses: interactive web design,
advanced interactive web design • InterDip music tech;
performance. Dip advanced music tech; advanced acting and music

Northbrook College Sussex
Little Hampton Road, Worthing, West Sussex BN12 6NU
01903 606060   0800 183 6060
enquiries@nbcol.ac.uk
www.northbrook.ac.uk
• HND media, the moving image • BA (Hons) communication
design • ABC Dip/ BA (Hons) media arts • BTec NatDip music tech.
HND music performance (pop). Fdg music production.
BA (Hons) music composition; performance; production (top-up).
BA (Hons) music composition for professional media

Northampton, University College
Park Campus, Boughton Green Road,
Northampton NN2 7AL
0800 358 2232
study@northampton.ac.uk
www.northampton.ac.uk
• BA (Hons) media • HND/BA (Hons) journalism. BA (Hons)
creative writing • HND media production. BA (Hons) contemporary
media practice; film and TV; film, TV and popular culture
• BA (Hons) marketing

Northumbria University
Ellison Place, Newcastle Upon Tyne NE1 8ST
0191 232 6002
er.admissions@northumbria.ac.uk
www.northumbria.ac.uk
• BA (Hons) media, culture and society. BA/MA visual culture
• MA creative writing • BA (Hons) English and film; film and TV*;
media production; history of modern art, design for industry
• BSc (Hons) communication. BA (Hons) politics and media
• BA (Hons) contemporary photographic practice/multimedia
design. BSc (Hons) multimedia and digital entertainment
computing; multimedia computing. MA art practices (media)
• BA (Hons) performance. MA music management and promotion

Norwich School of Art and Design
Francis House, 3-7 Redwell Street, Norwich,
Norfolk NR2 4SN
01603 610561
info@nsad.ac.uk
www.nsad.ac.uk
• BA (Hons) creative writing. MA writing the visual • BA (Hons)
graphic design (design for publishing) • Fdg games art and design;
graphic design. BA (Hons) graphic design (graphic design,
photography, animation). MA animation and sound design; digital
practices

noSweat Journalism Training
16/17 Clarkenwell Close, London EC1R 0AN
020 7490 2006
info@nosweatjt.co.uk
www.nosweatjt.co.uk
• Prelim Cert newspaper journalism (NCTJ). Dip magazine journalism

Nottingham Trent University
Burton Street, Nottingham NG1 4BU
0115 941 8418
advice.shop@ntu.ac.uk
www.ntu.ac.uk
• BA (Hons) media (with pathways in communications, creative
industries, film and TV, journalism studies, media practices and
popular culture). PgDip/MA media and globalisation • BA (Hons)
English with creative writing. PGDip/MA newspaper journalism;
television journalism; radio journalism; online journalism (all also
international). PgCert/ PgDip/MA creative writing • BA (Hons)
broadcast journalism. BA (Hons) print journalism. • BA(Hons)/MA
fashion marketing and communication. ProfDip/ PgDip marketing
(CIM) • BA (Hons) photography; photography in Europe. BA/BSc
(Hons) multimedia. BSc (Hons) computer science (games tech;
imaging and display tech). PGDip/MA online journalism (also
international). PgDip/MSc computer games systems; multimedia
engineering/games engineering

Nottingham, University of
University Park, Nottingham NG7 2RD
0115 951 5151
undergraduate-enquiries@nottingham.ac.uk
postgraduate-enquiries@nottingham.ac.uk
www.nottingham.ac.uk
• BA film and American studies/sociology/theology.
BA (Hons) film and TV. MA/PgDip film. Research opportunities:
institute welcomes applications from students interested in
analysis of film and TV production and consumption • BA music;
music and philosophy

Open University
Walton Hall, Milton Keynes MK7 6AA
01908 274066
general-enquiries@open.ac.uk
www.open.ac.uk
• MA cultural and media

Oxford Brookes University
Headington Campus, Oxford OX3 0BP
01865 484848
query@brookes.ac.uk
www.brookes.ac.uk
• BA/BSc (Hons) film (joint) • Fdg communication at work.
BA/BSc (Hons) arts management and administration (joint);
communication, media and culture (single or joint) • BA/BSc
(Hons) publishing (single or joint). MA education/educational
studies with publishing; international publishing; publishing;
publishing and language. MBA (specialism in publishing)
• Fdg art and design. BA/ BSc (Hons) fine art (single or joint);
multimedia systems (joint). BSc (Hons) media tech (joint);
multimedia production (joint). MA interactive media publishing.
MSc digital media production; e-commerce computing; web tech
• BA/BSc (Hons) music (single or joint). BSc (Hons) sound tech
and digital music. MA composition and sonic art; contemporary
arts and music

Oxford, University of
St Aldate's, Oxford OX1 1DB
01865 276125
www.music.ox.ac.uk
• Dip/Mstud creative writing • BA (Hons) music

Paisley University
High Street, Paisley, Scotland PA1 2BE
0141 848 3000
info@paisley.ac.uk
www.paisley.ac.uk
• BA (Hons) media • BA (Hons) cinema; screen practice
• BA (Hons) marketing; international marketing. MSc
international marketing • BSc (Hons) multimedia tech; media
tech; multimedia with interactive entertainment tech*; computer
games tech; computer animation; digital art • BA (Hons)
commercial music; music tech

Peterborough Regional College
Park Crescent, Peterborough PE1 4DZ
01733 767366
info@peterborough.ac.uk
www.peterborough.ac.uk
• BTec FirstDip/HNC/HND media • C&G 7790 journalism (media
techniques). HNC/HND journalism • BTec NatDip media (moving
image, video) • BTec NatDip media (audio/radio); music practice

Plymouth College of Art and Design
Tavistock Place, Plymouth PL4 8AT
01752 203434
enquiries@pcad.ac.uk
www.pcad.ac.uk
• NatDip moving image. Fdg media production and the
environment* • NatDip media publishing • NatDip interactive
media; graphic design; photography. BA (Hons) photomedia and
design communication. Fdg film and animation; photography and
electronic imaging; graphic design and production • NatAward
music tech (music for media). Fdg music and sound for media*

Plymouth, University of
Drake Circus, Plymouth, Devon PL4 8AA
01752 600600
prospectus@plymouth.ac.uk
www.plymouth.ac.uk
• BA (Hons) media arts (with options); media practice and society.
BSc (Hons) science and the media • PgDip/MA creative writing
• MA contemporary film practice • BA (Hons) marketing
• PgDip/MA publishing • BA (Hons) design: illustration;
photography. BA/BSc (Hons) digital art and tech. BSc (Hons)
media lab arts; multimedia production and tech. MA/MSc/MRes
digital art and tech. MA/MSc digital futures • BA (Hons) music.
MA music education

PMA Training
PMA Group, PMA House, Free Church Passage,
St Ives, Cambs PE27 5AY
020 7278 0606
training@pma-group.com
www.pma-group.com
• One- to three-day short courses. Journalism: news, features,
style, subediting and proofing, writing for different mediums,
production, investigation, launching a publication etc; also two-
day journalism school for school and college leavers; nine-week
postgrad course in magazine journalism (PTC). Broadcasting:
writing, interviewing and public speaking PR: law, writing,
strategy, event management, pitching, internal comms etc.
Software: Quark XPress, Adobe Illustrator/ Photoshop/ Acrobat,
PowerPoint, HTML, Macromedia Flash/ Dreamweaver, DVD Studio
Pro, Adobe Premiere, Final Cut Pro. Also media law; marketing;
blogging; public speaking, interviewing and presentation skills

Portsmouth, University of
University House, Winston Churchill Avenue,
Portsmouth PO1 2UP
023 9284 8484
info.centre@port.ac.uk
www.port.ac.uk
• BA (Hons) English with media, creative writing and film as
options • BA (Hons) creative writing and drama; English lang/lit
and journalism; languages and creative writing. MA creative
writing • BA (Hons) film with options including entertainment
tech, creative writing, drama, languages. BA (Hons) media (single
or with creative writing, drama, entertainment tech) • BA (Hons) ;
marketing. MA communication and language skills; technical
communication. MPA masters in public administration
• BA (Hons) animation; communication design; design for
interactive media; 3D design; video production. BSc (Hons)
computer animation; computer games tech; creative computing
tech; digital media; digital video tech; enterprise in computer
games tech/entertainment tech; entertainment tech; multimedia
programming. MA art, design and media; design for digital media;
real-time media comms. MSc computer animation; digital media;
scientific and technical comms • BSc (Hons) music and sound
tech. MSc creative and computational sound

Queen Margaret University College, Edinburgh
Corstophine Campus, Clerwood Terrace,
Edinburgh EH12 8TS
0131 317 3000
marketing@qmuc.ac.uk
www.qmuc.ac.uk
• BA/BA (Hons) media; media and culture; psychology and
media • BA/BA (Hons) film and media; performance production
and management. MFA/MA/PgDip advanced screen practice
• BA/BA (Hons) marketing (options); retail business;
PR and media/ marketing/psychology; event management.
CIPR diploma. MSc PR

Queen Mary, University of London
Mile End Road, London E1 4NS
020 7882 5555
admissions@qmul.ac.uk
www.qmul.ac.uk
• MA/BA film (with options) • BEng/MEng multimedia systems
tech • MSc digital music processing

Queen's University Belfast
University Road, Belfast BT7 1NN
028 9024 5133
admissions@qub.ac.uk
www.qub.ac.uk
• BA (Hons)/MA/MPhil film • BSc (Hons) music tech.
BA (Hons)/BMus music

Radio and TV School
High Street, Staplehurst, Kent TN12 0AX
01580 895256
mail@radioschool.co.uk
www.radioschool.co.uk
• One-to-one radio courses, covering presentation styles,
techniques and production values. Core 1 for beginners with
no technical or radio experience; Core 2 for hospital/uni/RSL
presenters and nightclub DJs; Core 3 for pro and semi-pro
broadcasters working on-air now. One-to-one TV presenter
mini-courses for demos and showreels

Ravensbourne College of Design and Communication
Walden Road, Chislehurst, Kent BR7 5SN
020 8289 4900
info@rave.ac.uk
www.ravensbourne.ac.uk
Fdg broadcast post-production; broadcast operations and
production; broadcast media tech. BA (Hons) content creation for
broadcasting and new media. BSc (Hons) broadcast tech (top-up)
• Fdg computer visualisation and animation. BA (Hons) animation
(top-up)/ moving image design. MA interactive digital media;
networked media environments • Fdg creative sound design

* subject to validation

Robert Gordon University
School Hill, Aberdeen AB10 1FR
01224 262000
admissions@rgu.ac.uk
www.rgu.ac.uk
• BA/BA (Hons) publishing with journalism • BA/BA (Hons) corporate communication • BA/BA (Hons) publishing; publishing with journalism • BA (Hons) photographic and electronic media. BSc (Hons) graphics design. BSc/BSc (Hons) computing for internet and multimedia. BDes (Hons) design for digital media

Roehampton University
Erasmus House, Roehampton Lane, London SW15 5PU
020 8392 3000
enquiries@roehampton.ac.uk
www.roehampton.ac.uk
• BA media and culture. PgDip/MA media and cultural studies
• BA/BSc creative writing; journalism and new media. PgDip/MA translation (AV); creative and professional writing; women, gender and writing • BA film and screen practice. BA/BSc film
• BSc marketing; business information management
• PgCert/PgDip/MA children's literature • BA/BSc internet and multimedia computing; computing • BMus/BA/BSc music. PgDip/MA choral education and music education; music and culture

Royal Academy of Music
Marylebone Road, London NW1 5HT
020 7873 7373
go@ram.ac.uk
www.ram.ac.uk
• BMus (4yr) composition; performance. PgDip performance (options in musical theatre and opera). MMus/MPhil/PhD composition; performance

Royal College of Music
Prince Consort Road, London SW7 2BS
020 7589 3643
info@rcm.ac.uk
www.rcm.ac.uk
• BMus (Hons) music. PGDip/MMus integrated masters programme in performance

Royal Holloway, University of London
Egham, Surrey TW20 0EX
01784 434455
admissions@rhul.ac.uk
www.rhul.ac.uk
• MA creative writing • MA doc by practice; feature film screenwriting (MAFFS); producing film and TV; screen studies; screenwriting for TV and film (retreat programme) • BA media arts • BMus music. MMus composition; performance studies (joint with Royal College of Music); advanced musical studies (composition; ethnomusicology; historical musicology; opera studies; performance; performance studies; theory and analysis)

Royal Northern College of Music
124 Oxford Road, Manchester M13 9RD
0161 907 5200
info@rncm.ac.uk
www.rncm.ac.uk
• BMus(Hons). PGDip performance; composition; repetiteur studies. MMus/MPhil performance; composition

Royal Scottish Academy of Music and Drama
100 Renfrew Street, Glasgow G2 3DB
0141 332 4101
registry@rsamd.ac.uk
www.rsamd.ac.uk
• BA (Hons) music; Scottish music; Scottish music - piping. MMus performance; opera. Master of opera. MMus composition; conducting. PgDip music. Master of performance in musical theatre

Royal Welsh College of Music and Drama
Castle Grounds, Cathays Park, Cardiff CF10 3ER
029 2034 2854
info@rwcmd.ac.uk
www.rwcmd.ac.uk
• BA (Hons)/PgDip acting; stage management; theatre design
• PgDip/MA arts management • BMus (Hons) music. PgDip/MA music therapy

St Helens College
Brook Street, St Helens, Merseyside WA10 1PZ
01744 733766
enquire@sthelens.ac.uk
www.sthelens.ac.uk
• BA (Hons) TV and video production (Liverpool John Moores University). • HNC multimedia (design route). BTec NatCert multimedia. Fdg interactive multimedia arts and animation (Liverpool John Moores University). BA (Hons) digital arts (LJM Uni) • FirstDip performing arts (music). NatCert music tech. Fdg music tech and sound design* (Huddersfield University)

St Martin's College
Bowerham Road, Lancaster LA1 3JD
01524 384384
www.ucsm.ac.uk
• PgCert/PgDip/MA creative writing

St Mary's College
Waldegrave Road, Twickenham TW1 4SX
020 8240 4000
recruit@smuc.ac.uk
www.smuc.ac.uk
• BA (Hons) professional and creative writing (single or with options) • BA Hons film and TV (joint) • BA (Hons) media arts (joint)

Salford, University of
Salford, Greater Manchester M5 4WT
0161 295 5000
course-enquiries@salford.ac.uk
www.salford.ac.uk
• BA (Hons) media, language and business • BA (Hons) journalism (options); English and creative writing • HND media production; media performance; audio and video broadcast technology. BSc (Hons) media tech. BA (Hons) media and performance; TV and radio; journalism and broadcasting • BA (Hons) advertising design
• BA (Hons) digital 3D design; visual arts; animation. BSc (Hons) computer and video games; multimedia and internet tech
• BA (Hons) pop and recording; music. BSc (Hons) audio tech

Salisbury College
Southampton Road, Salisbury, Wiltshire SP1 2LW
01722 344344
enquiries@salisbury.ac.uk
www.salisbury.ac.uk
• BTec NatAward/Dip/NatDip performing arts. BTec NatDip media (moving image) • BTec Dip design; art. BTec FDip/NatDip art and design. HNC/ HND fine art • BTec Dip/NatDip pop. BTec NatDip music tech.

School of Oriental and African Studies
Thornaugh Street, Russell Square, London WC1H 0XG
020 7637 2388
study@soas.ac.uk
www.soas.ac.uk
• MA critical media and cultural studies; anthropology of media; global media and postnational communication • MA cinemas of Asia and Africa • BA music. MMus ethnomusicology; performance

Sheffield College, The
The Norton Centre, Dyche Lane, Sheffield S8 8BR
0114 260 3603
course-enquiries@sheffcol.ac.uk
www.sheffcol.ac.uk
• BTec media • Short courses: journalism reporter (NCTJ), journalism/photography (NCTJ), press photography
• BTec NatDip multimedia • BTec Dip/NatDip music practice

Sheffield Hallam University
City Campus, Howard Street, Sheffield S1 1WB
0114 225 5555
admissions@shu.ac.uk
www.shu.ac.uk
• BA (Hons)/MA/PgDip/PgCert media • MA/PgDip/PgCert
broadcast journalism; international broadcast journalism; writing
• BA (Hons) film and literature; film and media production; film
and history; film. MA/PgDip/PgCert film and media production
• BA (Hons) communication studies. MA/PgDip/ PgCert
communication studies; corporate/professional/tech
communication • BA (Hons) photographic practice; multimedia
and communication design; interactive product design. BSc (Hon)
software development (games). MSc/PgDip/PgCert multimedia
and internet; entertainment software development

Sheffield, University of
Western Bank, Sheffield S10 2TN
0114 222 2000
www.shef.ac.uk
• BA (Hons)/MA journalism (options). PGDip/MA print journalism.
• MA web journalism • PGDip/MA broadcast journalism (BJTC)
• MA musicology; music theatre studies

Solihull College
Blossomfield Road, Solihull B91 1SB
0121 678 7000
enquiries@solihull.ac.uk
www.solihull.ac.uk
• BTec Dip/NatDip media • Cert sales and marketing (Level 2
and3) (ISMM). FCert marketing (CIM). Cert marketing (Stage 1)
(CIM). ProfDip marketing (Stage 2) (CIM). ProfPgDip marketing
(Stage 3) (CIM)

South Birmingham College
High Street Deritend, Digbeth, Birmingham B5 5SU
0121 694 5000
info@sbc.ac.uk
www.sbc.ac.uk
• BTec NatDip media (moving image) • HND media and
communication • BTec national media (e-media). HND multimedia
• BTec national media (audio). HND media production – audio
pathway

South Devon College
Vantage Point, Long Road, Paignton TQ4 7EJ
01803 540540
enquiries@southdevon.ac.uk
www.southdevon.ac.uk
• FirstDip media • BTec NatDip media (moving image)
• FirstDip music production. NatDip music tech (audio engineering;
studio production)

South East Essex College
Luker Road, Southend-on-Sea, Essex SS1 1ND
01702 220400
learning@southend.ac.uk
www.southend.ac.uk
• BTec FirstDip media • BA (Hons) journalism. Short courses:
writing your first novel, creative writing • BTec NatDip moving
image. BA (Hons) TV production and screen media; short course
TV presenting skills • BTec NatDip publishing • BTec NatDip
digital animation; multimedia. Short course: basic 3D animation
• HND performing arts (music production). BTec FirstDip/NatDip
contemporary music; music tech. BTec FirstDip/NatDip radio. BA (Hons)
music production

South Kent College
Folkestone Campus, Shorncliffe Road, Folkestone,
Kent CT20 2TZ
01303 858200
www.southkent.ac.uk
• Dip media • FirstDip/NatCert/NatDip performing arts. NatDip
media (moving image) production • IntroCert/ProfCert/ProfDip/
PgDip marketing (CIM) • InterCert/NatCert/NatDip music tech.
NatAward music tech - DJ skills

South Nottingham College
Greythorn Drive, West Bridgford, Nottingham NG2 7GA
0115 914 6400
enquiries@snc.ac.uk
www.snc.ac.uk
• HNC/HND media production • HNC/HND multimedia;
photography and digital imaging; print, media and digital design

South Thames College
Wandsworth High Street, London SW18 2PP
020 8918 7777
studentservices@south-thames.ac.uk
www.south-thames.ac.uk
• BTec Dip/NatDip media • ProfDev Cert 16mm film making; film
and TV. BTec NatDip media (moving image). HNC 16mm film
making; TV production; media production • Dip design. NatCert
multimedia (graphics and photography). ProfDev Cert graphic
design. HNC graphic design; photography; art and design (graphic
design) • Entry-level course music, TV and video production.
C&G/BTec Dip/NatCert/NatDip music tech. BTec NatAward music
production - music for media. BTec NatAward/NatDip music
practice. NatAward/HNC music production

Southampton Institute
East Park Terrace, Southampton, Hampshire SO14 0YN
023 8031 9000
enquiries@solent.ac.uk
www.solent.ac.uk
• BA (Hons) media with cultural studies.MA media. • BA (Hons)
journalism (NCTJ, PTC, BJTC); media writing; writing fashion and
culture; writing popular fiction* • BSc (Hons) film and video tech
(BKSTS); media tech. BA (Hons) film and TV; film; screenwriting;
TV and video production*. MA film and filmmaking
• HND advertising and media comms. Dip marketing (CIM). BA
(Hons) marketing with media and design; PR and communication.
• BA (Hons) animation; digital media; multimedia design;
photography • BSc (Hons) audio tech (BKSTS); music studio tech
(BKSTS). BA (Hons) pop and record production; multimedia sound*

Southampton, University of
University Road, Highfield, Southampton SO17 1BJ
023 8059 5000
www.soton.ac.uk
• BA film (with options) • BA fine art theory and practice
(new media); textiles, fashion and fibre (new media). BSc/MEng
computer science with image and multimedia systems
• BA music (options). BEng/MEng acoustical engineering

Staffordshire University
Stoke-on-Trent, Staffordshire ST4 2DE
01782 294000
study@staffs.ac.uk
www.staffs.ac.uk
• BA media • BA (Hons) English and journalism (NCTJ)
• BA (Hons)/MA broadcast journalism (BJTC). BA film; film, TV
and radio studies; music technology; TV and radio studies; media
production • BA multimedia graphics; graphics; animation; design
innovation. MA media futures; interactive multimedia
• BA music broadcasting

Stevenson College Edinburgh
Bankhead Avenue, Edinburgh EH11 4DE
0131 535 4600; course enquiries: 0131 535 4700
info@stevenson.ac.uk
www.stevenson.ac.uk
• HNC/HND AV tech. HND TV operations. Fdg film and TV
• HNC advertising and PR • Fdg classical music. HND/Fdg pop

subject to validation

Stirling, University of
Stirling FK9 4LA
01786 473171
admissions@stir.ac.uk
www.stir.ac.uk
• MSc/PGDip media management (available online); media research • BA (Hons) journalism studies • BA (Hons) film and media; European film and media • BA (Hons)/PGDip/MSc marketing. PGDip/MSc PR (online learning available) • MLitt publishing studies

Stockport College of Further and Higher Education
Wellington Road South, Stockport, Cheshire SK1 3UQ
0161 958 3100
enquiries@stockport.ac.uk
www.stockport.ac.uk
• Dip media. IntroDip art, design and media • HND media (moving image - broadcasting). NatDip media broadcasting. NatCert/NatDip performing arts: media make-up.

Strathclyde, University of
16 Richmond Street, Glasgow G1 1XQ
0141 552 4400
www.strath.ac.uk
• BA (Hons) journalism and creative writing (joint). MLitt/PgDip in journalism studies (Scottish Centre for Journalism with Glasgow Caledonian - 0141 950 3281) • BA/Mres/MSc/PgDip marketing. MSc/PgDip marketing, international. MSc marketing, international (online) • BEng/MEng design computing; digital multimedia systems. BSc internet computing; software engineering. MSc/PgDip computer and internet tech. MSc/PgDip/PgCert digital multimedia and communication systems • BA applied music

Sunderland, University of
Edinburgh Building, Chester Road, Sunderland SR1 3SD
0191 515 3000
student-helpline@sunderland.ac.uk
www.sunderland.ac.uk
• BA (Hons) media, culture and communication. MA/PgDip/PgCert media and cultural studies • BA (Hons)/MA journalism (NCTJ) • BA (Hons) English and film; broadcast journalism*; film and media; media production (TV and radio). MA/PgDip/PgCert film and cultural studies; media production (TV and video) • BA (Hons) marketing; PR (CIPR); ads and design • Fdg media design (publishing) • BA (Hons) photography, video and digital imaging; media production (video and new media); animation and design; design: multimedia and graphics; illustration and design; 3D design innovation; graphic communication; graphic design (top-up). BSc (Hons) product design. MA/PgDip/PgCert design: multimedia and graphics; illustration and design. 3D design innovation; design studies; photography • BA (Hons) music (top-up). MA/PgDip/PgCert radio (production and management)

Surrey Institute of Art and Design
Falkner Road, Farnham, Surrey GU9 7DS
01252 722441
registry@surrart.ac.uk
www.surrart.ac.uk
• BA (Hons) arts and media • BA (Hons) journalism (PTC, BJTC, recognised by NUJ); fashion journalism • BA (Hons) film and video (BKSTS). MA film and video • BA (Hons) ad and brand management • BA (Hons) animation; digital screen arts; photography. MA animation; photography; digital games design; graphic communication (branding, printed and interactive media); graphic design and new media

Surrey, University of
Guildford, Surrey GU2 7XH
01483 300800
information@surrey.ac.uk
www.surrey.ac.uk
• MA radio. All at Farnborough College of Technology • BMus (Hons) music (also with professional placement year, or with computer sound design) MMus/PgDip/MRes/MPhil/PhD music

Sussex, University of
Falmer, Brighton BN1 9RH
01273 606755
information@sussex.ac.uk
www.sussex.ac.uk
• BA media; media practice and theory. PgDip/MA/MPhil/DPhil media and cultural studies. MA gender and media. MSc social research methods (media and cultural studies) • MPhil/DPhil creative and critical writing. MA English literature: creative and critical writing; dramatic writing • BA film (with options). MA film • MA digital media • BA music; music and cultural studies; music and film; music with languages. BA/BSc music informatics. MA music

Sutton Coldfield College
Lichfield Road, Sutton Coldfield, West Midlands B74 2NW
0121 355 5671
infoc@sutcol.ac.uk
www.sutcol.ac.uk
• HND media and communication. • Pre-entry Cert newspaper journalism (NCTJ). C&G desktop publishing; 7790 Cert in media techniques: journalism and radio competences

Swansea Institute of Higher Education
Mount Pleasant, Swansea SA1 6ED
01792 481000
enquiry@sihe.ac.uk
www.sihe.ac.uk
• BA (Hons) photojournalism • BA (Hons) English studies, video • BA (Hons) design for advertising; marketing. PgDip marketing (CIM) • HND/BA/BSc (Hons) 3D computer animation; multimedia. BSc (Hons) computer games development. BA (Hons) creative computer games design; photojournalism (contemporary practice). MA photography; visual arts enterprise; visual communication. MA 3D computer animation. MSc multimedia • BSc (Hons) music tech

Swansea University
Singleton Park, Swansea SA2 8PP
01792 205678
admissions@swansea.ac.uk
www.swansea.ac.uk
• BA (Hons) media (with options). MA media talk • MA comparative journalism; creative and media writing • BA (Hons) screen studies (options) • BA (Hons) public and media relations

Tameside College
Beaufort Road, Ashton-under-Lyne, Greater Manchester OL6 6NX
0161 908 6600
info@tameside.ac.uk
www.tameside.ac.uk
• NatDip media (moving image) • NatDip multimedia. HNC/NatDip photography.

Teesside, University of

Middlesbrough, Tees Valley TS1 3BA
01642 218121
registry@tees.ac.uk
www.tees.ac.uk
• BA (Hons) English with media; media; media with history
• Fdg journalism • Fdg TV and film production; performance and event production. BA (Hons) media production professional practice; TV production professional practice • BA (Hons) marketing; marketing and retail management/ad management; PR; creative advertising and promotions. PgCert professional development: marketing. PgDip marketing (CIM). MSc marketing management • HND web design/development. Fdg digital media. BA (Hons) computer animation; creative digital media/visualisation; computer games art/design; digital character animation; web design. BSc (Hons) computer games programming/ science; computer graphics science; web development. MA computer animation; computer games art; web design; creative digital media. MSc visual and web apps; computer games programming; CGI; web enterprise; web services development • HND music tech. BSc (Hons) media and music tech; digital music. BA (Hons) digital music creation

Thames Valley University

St Mary's Road, Ealing, London W5 5RF
020 8579 5000
learning.advice@tvu.ac.uk
www.tvu.ac.uk
• BA (Hons) media arts; MA/PgDip/MPhil/PhD media • BA (Hons) new media journalism (options). MPhil/PhD journalism
• BA (Hons) digital broadcast media. BA (Hons)/DipHE/MA film: video production with film. MA film and the moving image
• BA (Hons) advertising (options); creative advertising (options). PR (options); event management (combinations)
• HND multimedia; media tech; photography and digital imaging. Fdg digital animation; BA (Hons) design for interactive media (options); digital animation (options); media, creative tech and event management (combinations); photography and digital imaging; professional photographic imaging (final year). BA (Hons)/DipHE design for interactive media. creative computing; media tech; multimedia computing (options); new media journalism (joint). BA (Hons)/MPhil/PhD digital arts (options). MA photography; computer arts • Fdg music and multimedia tech; music performance; musical theatre; pop studies. HND music production (music tech); music performance; performing arts (theatre). BA (Hons)/DipHE music tech. BMus (Hons)/DipHE pop performance. BA (Hons) music and event management; music and media; combinations of the above; music: performance/composition (options); music tech (options). BSc (Hons) performance tech. BMus (Hons) music (performance, composition). MA audio tech. MMus composing concert music; composing for film and television; composing for musical theatre. MPhil/PhD music; music tech

Trinity College Carmarthen

Wales SA31 3EP
01267 676767
registry@trinity-cm.ac.uk
www.trinity-cm.ac.uk
• BA media • BA/MA creative writing • BA film • BA advertising. MBA arts management • BA web systems

Trinity College of Music

King Charles Court, Old Royal Naval College, Greenwich, London SE10 9JF
020 8305 4444
admissions@tcm.ac.uk
www.tcm.ac.uk
• BMus (Hons) - intensive performance-centred training. BMus (Hons) Early Music, Jazz, Western Classical Music or Indian Classical Music (in assoc with Bharatiya Vidya Bhavan Institute of Indian Art and Culture*) - see www.bhavan.net. PgDip/masters – areas of specialisation in creative performance

Tyne Metropolitan College

Embleton Avenue, Wallsend, Tyne and Wear NE28 9NJ
0191 229 5000
enquiries@tynemet.ac.uk
www.tynemet.ac.uk
• HND TV and video • HNC graphic design

UHI Millennium Institute

Executive Office, Ness Walk, Inverness IV3 5SQ
01463 279000
eo@uhi.ac.uk
www.uhi.ac.uk
• BA (Hons) Gaelic and media • HND TV and multimedia
• HNC/HND advertising and PR • HNC/HND interactive multimedia creation • HNC/HND music. BA (Hons) pop performance

Ulster, University of

Cromore Road, Co Londonderry, Northern Ireland BT52 1SA
0870 040 0700
online@ulster.ac.uk
www.ulster.ac.uk
• BA media; media arts. BSc (Hons) business with media. BA (Hons) English with media; media (with options). PgDip/MA international media • BSc/BA (Hons) journalism and publishing studies (options). MA journalism studies. • BA Hons film (options)
• BSc (Hons) PR; government/politics with PR; communication (options); communication, advertising and marketing; marketing; government with communication; leisure events and cultural management. BDes design and communication. MSc future communication. PgDip/MDes design and communication
• BSc (Hons) interactive multimedia design; multimedia computer games. BDes design for visual communication. BA (Hons) tech and design • BMus (Hons). BA Hons music (options). MMus music

Wakefield College

Margaret Street, Wakefield, West Yorks WF1 2DH
01924 789789
info@wakcoll.ac.uk
www.wakcoll.ac.uk
• HND interactive use of media • HND photography • FirstDip pop

University of Wales, Aberystwyth

Old College, King Street, Aberystwyth, Ceredigion SY23 2AX
01970 623111
ug-admissions@aber.ac.uk
www.aber.ac.uk
• BA/MA/MPhil/PhD media and communication studies
• BA/MA/MPhil/ PhD tv; film; scriptwiting • BSc marketing

University of Wales, Bangor

Gwynedd LL57 2DG
01248 351151
admissions@bangor.ac.uk
www.bangor.ac.uk
• BA (Hons) creative studies; theatre and media. MA creative studies • BA (Hons) history with journalism; creative writing; journalism and media. • BA Hons English with film; English language with film; history with film • BA (Hons) Communication and media (Welsh) • BA (Hons) (part time) internet, learning and organisations • BA (Hons)/BMus (Hons) music. MA music

Warwick, University of

Coventry CV4 7AL
024 7652 3523
www.warwick.ac.uk
• BA English literature and creative writing. MA ancient visual and material culture; creative and media enterprises
• MA writing • BA film and literature; film with TV. MA film and TV
• MSc marketing and strategy

Warwickshire College
Leamington Centre, Warwick New Road, Leamington
Spa, Warwickshire CV32 5JE
0800 783 6767
enquiries@warkscol.ac.uk
www.warkscol.ac.uk
• Pre-entry journalism (NCTJ) • BTec Multimedia (Visual
Communications) • BTec art & design

West Herts College
Watford Campus, Hempstead Road, Watford,
Herts WD17 3EZ
01923 812345
admissions@westherts.ac.uk
www.westherts.ac.uk
• Fdg/BA (Hons) media production • Fdg business (with
advertising, PR, marketing). BA (Hons) advertising and marketing
comms

West Kent College
Brook Street, Tonbridge, Kent TN9 2PW
01732 358101
enquiries@wkc.ac.uk
www.wkc.ac.uk
• BA (Hons) media and communication • Pre-entry newspaper
journalism (NCTJ) • HND TV production tech

West of England, University of the
Frenchay Campus, Coldharbour Lane, Bristol BS16 1QY
0117 965 6261
enquiries@uwe.ac.uk
www.uwe.ac.uk
• BA (Hons)/MA cultural and media. PhD media practice: theory
• BA (Hons) film. • BA/BSc marketing (options). MA marketing
• BA (Hons) drawing and applied arts with animation; graphic
design (animation option); illustration with animation; media
practice (animation option). BSc (Hons) internet computing;
internet systems (joint); internet tech (joint); multimedia
computing. MA media (animation/interactive media/ research);
multimedia (research) • BSc (Hons) creative music tech; music
systems engineering.

Westminster, University of
309 Regent Street, London W1B 2UW
020 7911 5000
www.wmin.ac.uk
• BA (Hons) media. PgDip journalism (NCTJ). MA journalism
studies (part-time); journalism for international students. All with
print and online journalism options • BA (Hons) media (TV/radio
production pathways); film and TV production; contemporary
media practice. PgDip journalism (broadcast pathway). MA
journalism (part-time; broadcast pathway); journalism for
international students (broadcast pathway); screenwriting and
producing for film and TV; film: culture and industry • BA (Hons)
media (PR pathway). MA communication; communication policy
• BA (Hons) animation • BA (Hons) commercial music. MA audio
production; music business management

**University College Winchester
(formerly King Alfred's College)**
Hampshire SO22 4NR
01962 841515
admissions@winchester.ac.uk
www.winchester.ac.uk
• Fdg creative industries. BA media; drama • BA journalism;
creative writing (joint). MA creative and critical writing; writing
for children • BA film and American culture; film; media
production

Wirral Metropolitan College
Conway Park Campus, Europa Boulevard, Conway Park,
Birkenhead, Wirral CH41 4NT
0151 551 7777
enquiries@wmc.ac.uk
www.wmc.ac.uk
• BA media • Short courses: writing film scripts, writing scripts
for film and TV • BTec FirstDip performing arts (music). BTec
NatCert music tech. BTec NatDip music practice

Wolverhampton, University of
Wulfruna Street, Wolverhampton WV1 1SB
01902 321000
enquiries@wlv.ac.uk
www.wlv.ac.uk
• BA (Hons) media and cultural studies • BA (Hons) creative and
professional writing; journalism and editorial design • Fdg (arts)
broadcast journalism. BA (Hons) film studies; literary, film and
theatre studies • BA (Hons) media and comms studies; marketing;
PR; public services • HNC/HND/ BA (Hons) photography. BA
(Hons) animation; computer games design; design; design for
multimedia; digital + arts media; graphic comms; interactive
multimedia; video. BSc (Hons) computer science (games
development, software engineering); computing (multimedia);
design tech; multimedia apps development; mobile computing;
virtual reality design; web computing • BA (Hons) music; music
tech and music; music tech and pop; pop; pop (top-up from HND)

University College Worcester
Henwick Grove, Worcester WR2 6AJ
01905 855000
study@worc.ac.uk
www.worc.ac.uk
• HND media. BA (Hons) media and cultural studies • HND
filmmaking. BA (Hons) drama and performance; performance
costume and make-up (top-up) • BA (Hons) visual arts; creative
digital media; interactive digital media; time-based digital media

York St John College
Lord Mayor's Walk, York YO31 7EX
01904 624624
admissions@yorksj.ac.uk
www.yorksj.ac.uk
• BA (Hons) media • PgDip/MA literature studies and creative
writing • Fdg creative industries and tech • BA (Hons)
performance: music

York, University of
Heslington, York YO10 5DD
01904 430000
admissions@york.ac.uk
www.york.ac.uk
• BA/MA writing and performance (drama, film, TV). • BEng/MEng
media tech • BA music. BEng/MEng music tech systems. MA
music; community music. Dip/MPhil/PhD/MA/MSc music tech

Yorkshire Coast College of Further Education
Lady Edith's Drive, Scarborough, North Yorks YO12 5RN
01723 372105
admissions@ycoastco.ac.uk
www.yorkshirecoastcollege.ac.uk
• Fdg applied digital media (design)

* subject to validation

In-house training courses

Archant
Prospect House, Rouen Road,
Norwich, Norfolk NR1 1RE
paul.durrant@archant.co.uk
www.archant.co.uk
EDP assistant editor: Paul Durrant. Takes applicants within, or with strong link to, circulation area. Ask in July for info on following year's recruitment. One month induction, followed by fast-track training course

BBC Training and development: Broadcast Training
35 Marylebone High Street,
London W1U 4PX
0870 122 0216
training@bbc.co.uk
www.bbctraining.com
Development executive: Andrew Carmichael. All strands of broadcast training

Johnston Training Centre
Upper Mounts,
Northampton NN1 3HR
01604 477755
www.johnstonpress.co.uk
Usually only takes trainees who have preliminary NCTJ certificate

Midland News Association
MNA Training Centre,
Rock House, Old Hill, Tettenhall,
Wolverhampton WV6 8QB
01902 742126
c.clark@expressandstar.co.uk
www.expressandstar.com
Training coordinator: Crispin Clark. Recruits non-company editorial trainees, usually eight per year

Newsquest Media Group
58 Church Street,
Weybridge KT13 8DP
01932 821212
www.newsquest.co.uk
Each region operates its own training system

The Press Association
292 Vauxhall Bridge Road,
London SW1V 1AE
0870 120 3200
tony.johnston@
    pressassociation.co.uk
www.pa.press.net
Head of PA editorial training: Tony Johnston. In-house trainee journalist programmes in multimedia, sport and production

Trinity Mirror Training Centre
Thomson House, Groat Market,
Newcastle-upon-Tyne NE1 1ED
0191 201 6043
paul.jones@ncjmedia.co.uk
www.trinitymirror.com
Foundation course leader: Paul Jones 0191 201 6039. 16-week preliminary course, primarily in-house but external places available

Media recruitment companies

Career Moves
London: 020 7292 2900
www.cmoves.co.uk

Davis Company
London: 020 7025 4424
www.daviscompany.co.uk

Hudson Media
London: 020 7187 6000
Aberdeen: 01224 620 262
Birmingham: 0121 633 0010
Dublin: 00 353 01676 5000
Edinburgh: 0131 555 4321
Glasgow: 0141 221 8182
Guildford: 01483 303 300
Leeds: 0113 297 9500
Manchester: 0161 832 7728
Milton Keynes: 01908 547 995
Reading: 0118 939 1003
St Albans: 01727 840 660
http://uk.hudson.com

Leed Recruitment
Ipswich: 01473 402627
www.leedrecruitment.com

Marketing Stars
Isleworth: 020 8892 1848
www.marketingstars.co.uk

Media Contacts
London: 020 7359 8244
www.media-contacts.co.uk

The Media Exchange
London: 020 7636 6777
www.themediaexchange.com

The Media Network
London: 020 7637 9227
www.tmn.co.uk

MediaCentrix
London: 020 7812 7180
www.mediacentrix.com

Michael Page Marketing
Birmingham: 0121 634 6920
Bristol: 0117 927 6509
Glasgow: 0141 331 7900
Leeds: 0113 246 9155
London: 020 7831 2000
Manchester: 0161 819 5500
St Albans: 01727 730 111
Weybridge: 01932 264 000
www.michaelpage.co.uk

Moriati Media
London: 020 7307 1280
www.moriati.co.uk

Network Recruitment
London: 020 7580 5151
www.networkdesign.cc

Online Content UK
Harpenden: 0845 123 5717
www.onlinecontentuk.org

Pathfinders
London: 020 7434 3511
www.pathfindersrecruitment.com

Phee Farrer Jones
London, Manchester:
    0870 048 9100
www.pheefarrerjones.co.uk

Price Jamieson
London: 020 7580 7702
www.pricejam.com

Profiles Creative
London, Leeds, Reading:
    0870 414 6288
www.profilescreative.com

Real Recruitment
London: 020 7499 5955
www.real-recruitment.com/

Recruit Media
London: 020 7758 4550
www.recruitmedia.co.uk

Reilly People
London: 020 7240 8080
www.reillypeople.co.uk

Swindale Parks Recruitment
Halesowen: 0121 585 6079
www.swindaleparks.co.uk

Workstation
London: 020 7371 7161
www.workstation.co.uk

Media training associations

BKSTS – The Moving Image Society
Pinewood Studios, Iver Heath,
Bucks SL0 0NH
01753 656656
Info@bksts.com
www.bksts.com
Film foundation, TV and digital tech, foundation sound for film and video, broadcasting engineering

British Universities Film & Video Council
77 Wells Street, London W1T 3QJ
020 7393 1500
ask@bufvc.ac.uk
www.bufvc.ac.uk
To promote the use of media within higher education

Broadcast Journalism Training Council
The Secretary, 18 Miller's Close,
Rippingale, Lincolnshire PE10 0TH
01778 440025
Sec@bjtc.org.uk
www.bjtc.org.uk
Accredits courses

City & Guilds
1 Giltspur Street, London EC1A 9DD
020 7294 2800
enquiry@city-and-guilds.co.uk
www.city-and-guilds.co.uk
Vocational qualifications

FT2 – Film and Television Freelance Training
Fourth Floor, Warwick House,
9 Warwick Street, London W1B 5LY
020 7734 5141
info@ft2.org.uk
www.ft2.org.uk
Training for new broadcast freelancers

Film Education
21-22 Poland Street,
London W1F 8QQ
020 7851 9450
postbox@filmeducation.org
www.filmeducation.org

First Film Foundation
info@firstfilm.co.uk
www.firstfilm.co.uk
*Training for new film writers, producers
and directors*

**National Council for the
Training of Journalists**
The New Granary, Station Road,
Newport, Saffron Walden,
Essex CB11 3PL
01799 544014
info@NCTJ.com
www.nctj.com
*Runs schemes for print journalists.
Accredits courses*

Periodicals Training Council
Queens House, 28 Kingsway,
London WC2B 6JR
020 7400 7523
www.ppa.co.uk
Training arm of PPA

**Skillset:
The Sector Skills Council
for the Audio Visual Industries**
Prospect House,
80-110 New Oxford Street,
London WC1A 1HB
020 7520 5757
info@skillset.org
www.skillset.org
*Owned by broadcast industry; accredits
courses, publishes handbooks and runs
Skillsformedia (www.skillsformedia.com)*

yourcreativefuture.org
education@designcouncil.org.uk
www.yourcreativefuture.org
*Guide to a creative career; sponsored by
government, Design Council and Arts
Council*

Agents

The more creative your role in the media, the greater the chance that there is an agent to represent you. The best authors, scriptwriters, actors, directors and presenters will always be in demand, but the number of wannabes far exceeds the number of talents. So the agent's role is to be the middle man: to find the talent, sell it, and make themselves a profit into the bargain.

There are more than 200 literary agents in the UK, of which about 75 are members of the association of authors' agents; the agents' association has more than 400 entertainment agencies among its members. Agencies can range from large multinational organisations such as PFD or ICM to tiny operations managed by just one overworked soul. The best agents will have an eye for a talent, a wide range of industry contacts, and above all a hard head for a business deal.

● Talent agents

Talent agencies have a reputation – cemented in films such as Little Voice and Some Like It Hot – as a hard-headed, wheeler-dealing bunch. In the real world they come in a vast variety of forms: specialisms include television presenters, voice-overs for radio ads, directors of short films, actors, singers, make-up artists, cruise ship entertainers, lookalikes and of course models; many agencies will handle some but not all of these, even though they work under the broad umbrella of "entertainment". Agents employed by artists charge about 15% commission, rising to 20% for musicians and models in particular; or they may act as talent-brokers, earning their commission as a mark-up charged to the event hirer. There are few hard and fast rules – but the agents' association does have a code of conduct; artists should never, for example, pay a fee to join an agency's books. Other bodies include the personal managers' association, which represents actors' agents; and the association of voice-over agents.

● Literary agents

It is increasingly difficult to acquire the services of a good literary agent; but then, it is harder still to sell a novel or a script without one. A good agent will not only advise an author in an editorial capacity, at least in order to make a script more saleable; they will also be able to sell writing for much more than the writer could on their own. In particular, agents aim to separate out rights for different media (such as paperback, film, television, multimedia and novelisation in the case of a script), for different markets (such as potentially lucrative US rights) and even, in this post-Potter world, for merchandising. Thus they hope to earn more for the writer than if all the rights were sold at once. In return, they charge a commission that normally ranges from 10% to 15%.

Agents complain that they are so busy trying to sell their existing authors that they have little time to find new talent. The result is that many agents, at one point or another, are either not accepting new writers or only accepting writers recommended to them by people they know and trust. Those that do receive unsolicited manuscripts are deluged: some agents receive up to 50 a day, which will usually mean the agent is looking for a reason to reject them.

The advice to an author seeking any agent, then, is to make life as easy as possible for them. Don't send work to an agent who doesn't accept unsolicited manuscripts, or who doesn't handle the genre you write in; you'll only be wasting your time and theirs. Check the agent's website to find the authors they already handle: this will help you target to agents who you know will like the kind of work you write. Spend a few moments finding out in what form the agent prefers to see a manuscript: whether complete, or in the form of a few chapters plus synopsis, and how they like the type to be set (normally use a simple font such as Times New Roman, on decent-quality white paper, double-spaced to allow room for notes; don't forget to enclose a stamped addressed envelope). Asked when they like to see a manuscript, many agents will helpfully reply that the best time is when you've improved it as best you can: make of that what you will. Finally, if an agent offers to represent you, trust your instinct: an agent who likes you and your writing will be your best advocate. To put it another way, the better your relationship with your agent, the more likely you are to sell your work.

Finally, don't lose hope: one day it could be your script that is being sold by a top agent such as Jonny Geller for a seven-figure sum at the Frankfurt book fair. It won't be, but it could.

Agents contacts

Alexander Personal Management
PO Box 834, Hemel Hempstead,
Hertfordshire HP3 9ZP
01442 252907
apm@apmassociates.net
www.apmassociates.net
Actors, voiceovers

Amanda Howard Associates
21 Berwick Street, London W1F 0PZ
020 7287 9277
mail@amandahowardassociates.co.uk
www.amandahowardassociates.co.uk
*Actors, directors, designers, composers,
voiceovers and writers*

Andrew Manson
288 Munster Road, London SW6 6BQ
020 7386 9158
post@andrewmanson.com
www.talentroom.com
Actors, voiceovers (for US)

Another Tongue Voices
10-11 D'Arblay Street,
London W1F 8DS
020 7494 0300
Info@anothertongue.com
www.anothertongue.com
Voiceovers

Arlington Enterprises
1-3 Charlotte Street,
London W1T 1RD
020 7580 0702
info@arlington-enterprises.co.uk
www.arlingtonenterprises.co.uk
TV presenters

Billy Marsh Associates
76A Grove End Road,
St John's Wood, London NW8 9ND
020 7449 6930
talent@billymarsh.co.uk
TV presenters and personalities

Blackburn Sachs Associates
2-4 Noel Street, London W1F 8GB
020 7292 7555
presenters@
   blackburnsachsassociates.com
www.blackburnsachsassociates.com
TV and radio presenters and personalities

Bryan Drew
Mezzanine, Quadrant House,
80-82 Regent Street,
London W1B 5AU
020 7437 2293
bryan@bryandrewltd.com
Actors, writers, voiceovers

Calypso Voices
25-26 Poland Street,
London W1F 8QN
020 7734 6415
calypso@calypsovoices.com
www.calypsovoices.com
Actors for voiceover work

Castaway
Suite 3, 15 Broad Court,
London WC2B 5QN
020 7240 2345
sheila@castaway.org.uk
www.castaway.org.uk
Voiceovers

Celebrity Management
12 Nottingham Place,
London W1M 3FA
020 7224 5050
info@celebrity.co.uk
www.celebrity.co.uk
Celebrity booking

Chase Personal Management
Model Plan 4th Floor,
4 Golden Square, London W1F 9HT
020 7287 8444
michelle@modelplanlondon.co.uk
www.modelplan.co.uk
Presenters and celebrities

Complete Talent Agency
200 London Road, Hadleigh,
Benfleet, Essex SS7 2PD
01702 427100
gary@entertainers.co.uk
www.entertainers.co.uk
*AV, celebrity guests, comedians, lights,
productions and speakers*
*Also at: The Old Forge, Kingfield Road,
Woking, Surrey GU22 9EG*

Conway Van Gelder
3rd Floor, 18-21 Jermyn Street,
London SW1Y 6HP
020 7287 1070
kate@conwayvg.co.uk
www.conwayvangelder.com
Actors, commercials, voiceovers, directors

Crawfords
PO Box 44394, London SW20 0YP
020 8947 9999
info@crawfordsagency.com
www.crawfords.tv
Actors and models for TV commercials

Curtis Brown Group
Haymarket House,
28-29 Haymarket, London SW1Y 4SP
020 7393 4400
info@curtisbrown.co.uk
www.curtisbrown.co.uk
*Writers, directors, actors, playwrights
and celebrities*

David Anthony Promotions
PO Box 286, Warrington,
Cheshire WA2 8GA
01925 632496
dave@davewarwick.co.uk
www.davewarwick.co.uk
TV presenters

Downes Presenters Agency
96 Broadway, Bexleyheath,
Kent DA6 7DE
020 8304 0541
info@presentersagency.com
www.presentersagency.com
TV presenters

Dynamic FX
Regent House, 291 Kirkdale,
London SE26 4QD
020 8659 8130
mail@dynamicfx.co.uk
www.dynamicfx.co.uk
Magical entertainment

Eric Glass
25 Ladbroke Crescent, Notting Hill,
London W11 1PS
020 7229 9500
eglassltd@aol.com
Actors, writers

Evans O'Brien
115 Humber Road, London SE3 7LW
020 8293 7077
info@evansobrien.co.uk
www.evansobrien.co.uk
Voiceovers

Excellent Talent Company
19-21 Tavistock Street,
London WC2E 7PA
020 7520 5656
liz@excellentvoice.co.uk
www.excellentvoice.co.uk
Voiceovers and TV presenters

Extras Unlimited
9 Hansard Mews, London W14 8BJ
020 7603 9995
info@extrasunlimited.com
www.extrasunlimited.com
Extras

FBI Agency
PO Box 250, Leeds LS1 2AZ
07050 222747
casting@fbi-agency.ltd.uk
www.fbi-agency.ltd.uk
*Models, dancers, walk-ons, presenters,
actors, stand-ins*

Foreign Legion
1 Kendal Road London NW10 1JH
020 8450 4451
getem@foreignlegion.co.uk
www.foreignlegion.co.uk
*Foreign-language voiceovers and
translations*

Foreign Versions
60 Blandford Street,
London W1U 7JD
020 7935 0993
info@foreignversions.co.uk
www.foreignversions.com
*Translators and voiceovers in foreign
languages*

Fox Artist Management
Concorde House,
101 Shepherds Bush Road,
London W6 7LP
020 7602 8822
fox.artist@btinternet.com
www.foxartistmanagement.tv
TV presenters

Gordon & French
12–13 Poland Street, London W1F 8QB
020 7734 4818
mail@gordonandfrench.net
Actors and voiceovers

Hobson's Voices
62 Chiswick High Road,
London W4 1SY
020 8995 3628
voices@hobson-international.com
www.hobsons-international.com
Actors, voiceovers, children, singers

ICM Artists (London)
4–6 Soho Square, London W1D 3PZ
020 7432 0800
infouk@icmtalent.com
www.icmtalent.com
Conductors and musicians

Icon Actors Management
Tanzaro House, Ardwick Green North,
Manchester M12 6FZ
0161 273 3344
info@iconactors.net
www.iconactors.net
Actors

International Artists
4th Floor, Holborn Hall,
193–197 High Holborn,
London WC1V 7BD
020 7025 0600
reception@intart.co.uk
www.intart.co.uk
Presenters, actors and comedians

J Gurnett Personal Management
12 Newburgh Street,
London W1F 7RP
020 7440 1850
info@jgpm.co.uk
www.jgpm.co.uk
TV and radio presenters

Jacque Evans Management
Suite 1, 14 Holmesley Road,
London SE23 1PJ
020 8699 1202
jacque@jacqueevans.com
www.jacqueevans.com
*Presenters, journalists, broadcasters and
experts*

James Grant Management
94 Strand on the Green,
London W4 3NN
020 8742 4950
www.jamesgrant.co.uk
TV presenters

Jane Morgan Management
Thames Wharf Studios,
Rainville Road, London W6 9HA
020 7386 5345
enquiries@janemorganmgt.com
www.janemorganmgt.com

Jeremy Hicks Associates
114–115 Tottenham Court Road,
London W1T 5AH
020 7383 2000
info@jeremyhicks.com
www.jeremyhicks.com
Presenters, writers, comedians and chefs

JLA (Jeremy Lee Associates)
4 Stratford Place, London W1C 1AT
020 7907 2800
talk@jla.co.uk
www.jla.co.uk
Presenters, speakers, entertainers

John Miles Organisation
Cadbury Camp Lane,
Clapton-in-Gordano,
Bristol BS20 7SB
01275 854675
john@johnmiles.org.uk
www.johnmiles.org.uk
Presenters

John Noel Management
2nd Floor, 10A Belmont Street,
London NW1 8HH
020 7428 8400
john@johnnoel.com
www.johnnoel.com
TV presenters and radio DJs

Julie Ivelaw-Chapman
The Chase, Chaseside Close,
Cheddington, Beds LU7 0SA
01296 662441
jivelawchapman@gmail.com
Broadcasters

KBJ Management
7 Soho Street, London W1D 3DQ
020 7434 6767
general@kbjmgt.co.uk
www.kbjmgt.co.uk
Presenters and comics

Knight Ayton Management
114 St Martin's Lane,
London WC2N 4BE
020 7836 5333
info@knightayton.co.uk
www.knightayton.co.uk
TV presenters and news people

Lip Service
60–66 Wardour Street,
London W1F 0TA
020 7734 3393
bookings@lipservice.co.uk
www.lipservice.co.uk
Voiceovers

Liz Hobbs Group
1st Floor, 65 London Road, Newark,
Notts NG24 1RZ
0870 070 2702
info@lizhobbsgroup.com
www.lizhobbsgroup.com
Musical theatre, actors and presenters

**Mark Summer Management
& Agency**
137 Freston Road, London W10 6TH
020 7243 1984
info@marksummers.com
www.marksummers.com
*Choreographers and actors, adults and
children*

**Markham & Froggatt Personal
Management**
4 Windmill Street, London W1T 2HZ
020 7636 4412
admin@markhamfroggatt.co.uk
www.markhamfroggatt.com
Actors, voiceovers and radio

McLean-Williams Management
212 Piccadilly, London W1J 9HG
020 7917 2806
alex@mclean-williams.com
Actors

MPC Entertainment
MPC House, 15–16 Maple Mews,
London NW6 5UZ
020 7624 1184
info@mpce.com
www.mpce.com
Radio, TV and sports personalities

NCI Management
51 Queen Anne Street,
London W1G 9HS
020 7224 3960
nicola@nci-management.com
www.nci-management.com
TV presenters

Noel Gay Artists
19 Denmark Street,
London WC2H 8NA
020 7836 3941
mail@noelgay.com
www.noelgay.com
*TV presenters, voiceovers, writers,
directors*

Off The Kerb Productions
3rd Floor, Hammer House,
113–117 Wardour Street,
London W1F 0UN
020 7437 0607
info@offthekerb.co.uk
www.offthekerb.co.uk
Comedians
Also at:
22 Thornhill Crescent, London N1 1BJ
020 7700 4477

PFD
Drury House, 34–43 Russell Street,
London WC2B 5HA
020 7344 1000
postmaster@pfd.co.uk
www.pfd.co.uk
*Writers, directors, producers, actors,
technicians, composers, sportsmen and
women, public speakers and illustrators*

PHA Casting
Tanzaro House, Ardwick Green North,
Manchester M12 6FZ
0161 273 4444
info@pha-agency.co.uk
www.pha-agency.co.uk
Models, extras, actors

Princess Talent Management
Princess Studios, Whiteleys Centre,
151 Queensway, London W2 4SB
020 7985 1985
talent@princesstv.com
www.princesstv.com
TV and radio presenters

PVA Management
Hallow Park, Hallow,
Worcester WR2 6PG
01905 640663
pvamanltd@aol.com
www.pva.co.uk
*TV and radio presenters and classical
musicians*

Qvoice
4th Floor, Holborn Hall,
193-197 High Holborn,
London WC1V 7BD
020 7025 0660
info@qvoice.co.uk
www.qvoice.co.uk
Voiceovers

Rabbit Vocal Management
2nd Floor, 18 Broadwick Street,
London W1F 8HS
020 7287 6466
info@rabbit.uk.net
www.rabbit.uk.net
Voiceovers

Rhubarb
1st Floor, 1a Devonshire Road,
Chiswick, London W4 2EU
020 8742 8683
enquiries@rhubarb.co.uk
www.rhubarb.co.uk
Voiceovers

Richard Stone Partnership
2 Henrietta Street, London WC2E 8PS
020 7497 0849
all@richstonepart.co.uk
Actors, presenters, voiceovers, comedians

RK Commercials
205 Chudleigh Road, London SE4 1EG
020 8690 6542
enquiries@rkcommercials.com
www.rkcommercials.com
*Actors for commercials and presenting
work*

Roseman Organisation
51 Queen Anne Street,
London W1G 9HS
020 7486 4500
info@theromanorganisation.co.uk
www.theromanorganisation.co.uk
News and TV presenters

Roxane Vacca Management
73 Beak Street, London W1F 9SR
020 7734 8085
roxane@roxanevacca.co.uk
www.roxanevaccavoices.com
Actors and voiceovers

Sally Hope Associates
108 Leonard Street,
London EC2A 4XS
020 7613 5353
casting@sallyhope.biz
www.sallyhope.biz
*Actors, voiceovers, directors, designers,
lighting, hair and make-up*

Shining Management
12 D'Arblay Street, London W1F 8DU
020 7734 1981
info@shiningvoices.com
www.shiningvoices.com
Voiceovers

Speak
59 Lionel Road North, Brentford,
Middlesex TW8 9QZ
020 8758 0666
info@speak.ltd.uk
www.speak.ltd.uk
Voiceovers

Speak-Easy
1 Dairy Yard, High Street, Market
Harborough, Leicestershire LE16 7NL
0870 013 5126
enquiries@speak-easy.co.uk
www.speak-easy.co.uk
TV presenters and voiceovers

Storm
1st Floor, 5 Jubilee Place,
London SW3 3TD
020 7368 9967
info@stormmodels.com
www.stormmodels.com
Model and celebrity management

Susi Earnshaw Management
68 High Street, Barnet,
Herts EN5 5SJ
020 8441 5010
casting@susiearnshaw.co.uk
www.susiearnshaw.co.uk
Actors and musical theatre performers

Susy Wootton Voices
75 Shelley Street, Kingsley,
Northampton NN2 7HZ
0870 765 9660
suzy@suzywoottonvoices.com
www.suzywoottonvoices.com
Voiceovers

Take Three Management
110 Gloucester Avenue,
Primrose Hill, London NW1 8HX
020 7209 3777
info@take3management.com
www.take3management.co.uk
TV presenters, after-dinner speakers

Talking Heads
2/4 Noel Street, London W1F 8GB
020 7292 7575
voices@talkingheadsvoices.com
www.talkingheadsvoices.com
Voiceovers

Tongue & Groove
3 Stevenson Square,
Manchester M1 1DN
0161 228 2469
info@tongueandgroove.co.uk
www.tongueandgroove.co.uk
Voiceovers

Unique Management Group
Power Road Studios, 114 Power Road,
Chiswick, London W4 5PY
020 8987 6406
celebrities@uniquegroup.co.uk
www.unique-management.co.uk
TV presenters, radio hosts

Upfront Celebrity Services
39-41 New Oxford Street,
London WC1A 1BN
020 7836 7702/3
info@upfronttv.com
www.celebritiesworldwide.com
Celebrity bookings

Vincent Shaw Associates
186 Shaftesbury Avenue,
London WC24 8JB
020 8509 2211
info@vincentshaw.com
www.vincentshaw.com
Actors

Vocal Point
25 Denmark Street,
London WC2H 8NJ
020 7419 0700
enquiries@vocalpoint.net
www.vocalpoint.net
Voiceovers

Voice & Script International
Aradco House, 132 Cleveland St,
London W1T 6AB
020 7692 7700
info@vsi.tv
www.vsi.tv
*Translators and voiceovers in foreign
languages*

Voice Shop
1st Floor, 1a Devonshire Road,
London W4 2EU
020 8742 7077
info@voice-shop.co.uk
www.voice-shop.co.uk
Voiceovers

Voice Squad
1 Kendal Road, London NW10 1JH
020 8450 4451
bookem@voicesquad.com
www.voicesquad.com
Voiceovers

**Voicebank, The Irish Voice-Over
Agency**
The Barracks, 76 Irishtown Road,
Dublin 4
00 353 1 668 7234
voicebank@voicebank.ie
www.voicebank.ie
Voiceovers

Voicecall
67A Gondar Gardens, Fortune Green,
London NW6 1EP
020 7209 1064
voicecall@blueyonder.co.uk
www.voicecall-online.co.uk
Voiceovers

The Voiceover Gallery
PO Box 213, Chorlton,
Manchester M21 9ED
0161 881 8844
info@thevoiceovergallery.co.uk
www.thevoiceovergallery.co.uk
Voiceovers

Whatever Artists Management
F24 Argo House, Kilburn Road,
London NW6 5LF
020 7372 4777
info@wamshow.biz
www.wamshow.biz
Artists in light entertainment

Yakety Yak
8 Bloomsbury Square,
London WC1A 2NE
020 7430 2600
info@yaketyyak.co.uk
www.yaketyyak.co.uk
Voiceovers

Literary agents

» see Books page 280

Associations

Agents Association
54 Keyes House, Dolphin Square,
London SW1V 3NA
020 7834 0515
association@agents-uk.com
www.agents-uk.com
Trade association of entertainment agents

Association of Authors' Agents
A P Watt, 20 John Street, London
WC1N 2DR
020 7405 6774
aaa@apwatt.co.uk
www.agentsassoc.co.uk

Personal Managers' Association
1 Summer Road, East Molesey,
Surrey KT8 9LX
020 8398 9796
aadler@thepma.com
www.thepma.com

A career in media

Media awards

Press

Amnesty International Media Awards
020 7033 1500
www.amnesty.org.uk
Human rights journalism

AOP Online Publishing Awards
020 7400 7532
www.ukaop.org.uk/events
/annual-awards

BAPLA Picture Editor's Award
020 7713 1780
www.pbf.org.uk
For nationals that show best practice in crediting images

British Garden Writers' Guild
020 7245 6943
www.gardenwriters.co.uk/awards
/2006/awards2k.html

British Press Awards
020 8565 4392
www.britishpressawards.com
Organised by Press Gazette

British Society of Magazine Editors
020 8906 4664
www.bsme.com

Emmas (Ethnic Multicultural Media Academy awards)
020 7636 1233
www.emma.tv
Multicultural media

Foreign Press Association Annual Media Awards
020 7930 0445
www.foreign-press.org.uk
International journalism by British media

Glenfiddich Food & Drink awards
020 7355 0655
http://events.glenfiddich-whisky.co.
uk/food-and-drink-awards

Guardian Student Media Awards
01727 898 141
Student journalists, designers and photographers
Press: 020 7713 4087

The Herald Scottish Student Press Awards 2003
0141 302 7000
www.theherald.co.uk
Open to full-time students in Scotland

ICIJ Award for Outstanding International Investigative Reporting
00 1 202 466 1300
www.icij.org

Local Reporting Awards
020 7632 7400
www.newspapersoc.org.uk
Under-30s

Medical Journalism Awards
023 8037 2414
www.norwichunion.co.uk
/medical_journalism_awards

NetMedia European Online Journalism Awards
020 7637 7097
www.net-media.co.uk

Newspaper Awards
01869 340788
www.newspaperawards
.newstech.co.uk
Technical innovation in newspaper and new media production

Observer Hodge Award
01727 799987
www.observer.co.uk/hodgeaward
Young photographers

Picture Editors' Awards
administrator@pictureawards.net
www.pictureawards.net
Photographic journalism

Plain English Media Awards
01663 744409
www.plainenglish.co.uk/mediaawards
Campaign against gobbledygook

PPA Awards
020 7404 4166
www.ppa.co.uk
Periodicals

Press Gazette Student Journalism Awards
020 7936 6420
www.studentjournalismawards.co.uk
Open to students enrolled on a journalism course

Race in the Media Awards
020 7939 0000
www.cre.gov.uk
Organised by Commission for Racial Equality

Regional Press Awards
020 7693 0439
www.regionalpressawards.co.uk
Organised by Press Gazette

What the Papers Say Awards
020 7620 1620
www.granadamedia.com
National newspaper journalists

TV and film

Academy Awards (US)
00 1 310 247 3000
www.oscars.org
Film

Bafta Awards
020 7734 0022
www.bafta.org
Film, TV and interactive industries

British Comedy Awards
020 8987 6400
www.britishcomedyawards.com

British Independent Film Awards
020 7287 3833
www.bifa.org.uk

Broadcast Awards
020 7505 8115
www.broadcastnow.co.uk
Programme ideas and execution

Emmy Awards (US)
00 1 818 754 2800
www.emmys.com
TV
Press: 00 1 323 965 1990

Evening Standard British Film Awards
020 7938 6247
www.thisislondon.co.uk

First Light Film Awards
0121 753 4866
www.firstlightmovies.com
Short films made by 5- to 18-year-olds

Golden Globes (US)
00 1 310 657 1731
www.hfpa.org
TV and film, worldwide

Indie Awards (Pact)
020 7067 4367
www.pact.co.uk
Film, TV, animation and new media producers

National TV Awards
020 7486 4443
Winners picked by viewers

Royal Television Society Awards
020 7822 2810
www.rts.org.uk

Radio

NTL Commercial Radio Awards
020 7306 2603
www.crca.co.uk

Sony Radio Academy Awards
020 7255 2010
www.radioacademy.org/awards

Student Radio Awards
events@studentradio.org.uk
www.studentradio.org.uk

Music

Brits
020 7803 1301
www.brits.co.uk
Press: 020 7439 7222

Broadband from BT Digital Music Awards
sam@dma05.com
www.dma04.com

Classical Brit Awards
020 7803 1301
www.classicalbrits.co.uk

Dancestar
00 1 305 371 2450
www.dancestar.com
Dance music

Grammys (US)
00 1 310 392 3777
www.grammy.com

Gramophone Awards
020 8267 5136
www.gramophone.co.uk
Classical music

Ivor Novello Awards
www.britishacademy.com/awards
/ivorsmenu/ivorshome.html
British songwriters, composers and music publishers
Press: 020 8621 2345
TV and radio: 020 7299 7979

Kerrang Awards
020 7436 1515
www.kerrangawards.com
Rock

Mobo Awards
www.mobo.net
Music of black origin
Press: 020 7419 8055
press@mobo.com

MTV Europe Awards
www.mtve.com

Music Week Awards
020 7921 8308
www.musicweekawards.com

NME Awards
020 7261 5564
www.nmeawards.com
Voted for by NME readers

Nationwide Mercury Prize
020 8964 9964
www.nationwidemercurys.com
Best album in UK and Ireland

Q Awards
020 7312 8182
www.qawards.co.uk

Radio 3 Awards for World Music
020 7765 5887
www.bbc.co.uk/radio3/awards2006

Books

British Book Design and Production Awards
020 7915 8334
www.britishbookawards2006.com

Costa Book Awards
01582 844 346
Dionne.Parker@Whitbread.com
www.costabookawards.com
Contemporary British writing
Press: 01582 844 346

Guardian First Book Award
020 7278 2332
www.guardian.co.uk/firstbook
First-time writers of fiction, poetry, biography, memoirs, history, politics, science and current affairs
Press: 020 7713 4087

Orange Prize for Fiction
www.orangeprize.co.uk
Women's fiction
Press: 020 7544 3894

The Man Booker Prize
www.themanbookerprize.com
Best novel in English by citizen of Commonwealth, Ireland, Pakistan or South Africa
Press: 020 7631 2666

Advertising and PR

Advertising, Marketing & Digital Media Awards
020 7693 0428
www.newspapersoc.org.uk

British Television Advertising Awards
020 7734 6962
www.btaa.co.uk

Campaign Direct/Media/Poster Advertising Awards
020 8267 4090
www.brandrepublic.com
/magazines/campaign

Cannes Lions International Advertising Festival Awards
020 7239 3400
www.canneslions.com

Communicators in Business Awards
01908 313755
www.cib.uk.com

Creative Juice Awards
020 7632 7400
www.newspapersoc.org.uk
Young creative teams with maximum of three years' experience

Institute of Public Relations Excellence Awards
020 7766 3333
www.ipr.org.uk

London International Advertising Awards
020 8426 1670
www.liaawards.com

Marketing Week Effectiveness Awards
020 7970 4772
www.marketingweek.co.uk

Media Week Awards
020 8267 4344
www.mediaweekawards.co.uk

PR Week Awards
020 8267 4017
www.prweek.com

The Pride Awards
01158 419699
www.ipr.org.uk/prideawards

TUC/Bank of Scotland Press and PR Awards
020 7467 1242
www.tuc.org.uk
Journalism about Scottish issues and in Scottish publications

New media

AOP Online Publishing Awards
020 7400 7532
www.ukaop.org.uk/Events
/Annual-Awards

Bafta Games Awards
020 7734 0022
www.bafta.org
Video games

Bloggies
2006.bloggies.com

New Media Age Awards
020 7970 4848
www.nma.co.uk

New Statesman New Media Awards
020 7730 3444
www.newstatesman.co.uk/nma

Revolution Awards
020 8267 4947
www.revolutionmagazine.com
/awards
Digital marketing and business

Webby Awards
00 1 212 675 3555
www.webbyawards.com
Press: 00 1 212 627 8098

A career in media

406

Glossary

Press

ABC: The Audit Bureau of Circulation, the company that monitors and verifies magazines and newspaper sales. "ABCs" is the popular term for the circulation figures it publishes: see explainer

average issue readership: The number of people who, when surveyed, say they have read a newspaper or magazine within the lifespan of the issue. Also known as AIR

Brad: British Rate and Data, a company that records every periodical that carries advertising in the UK

broadsheet: Larger size of paper, used by the news sections of most quality UK papers; usually 580mm × 380mm

bulks: Copies of newspapers distributed free to targeted places such as hotels and airlines. *See explainer on ABCs*

byline: A journalist's name next to an article. Reporters live for bylines like salesmen live for bonuses

circulation: The number of copies a newspaper or magazines sells or distributes in a defined period (usually a month). Not the same as average issue readership

compact: A less downmarket term for tabloid

copy: Words for publication

DPS: Double-page spread

freesheet: A newspaper or magazine distributed free of charge, and usually paid for by advertising

journalist: Someone who works on the editorial side of a newspaper or magazine

leader: Editorial opinion column expressing the views of the newspaper (or its owner)

masthead: The bit with the title of the newspaper or magazine at the top of the front page

news agency: Company that sells news stories to a newspaper or magazine, usually delivered electronically to each journalist's desktop over the wires. The biggest are Reuters, the UK-based Press Association (PA) and the US-based Associated Press (AP)

Newspaper Society: Body representing the UK's regional press

PPA: The Periodical Publishers Association. Represents magazine publishers in the UK

reporter: Someone who writes news stories. Just one of many kinds of journalist

scoop: The act of printing a news story (or, these days, a celebrity interview) before a rival. The "scoop culture" of the UK press has been criticised for getting in the way of balanced news reporting

standfirst: The short paragraph at the top of a feature article, below the headline, that summarises it for the reader. Usually written by a subeditor

subeditor: Someone who lays out and edits the copy in a newspaper or magazine. Will also write the headline, standfirst and other page furniture such as picture captions

tabloid: Smaller size of paper, until recently used by more downmarket titles and the features sections of some quality papers; usually half the size of broadsheet. Also known as a compact

wires: Electronic delivery of news and pictures, sent by agencies to a journalist's desktop

TV and film

analogue television: Television transmitted in "radio waves"; in other words, not digitally. Most terrestrial TV in the UK is still transmitted in analogue

Barb: The Broadcasters Audience Research Board, which measures television audiences

BBC: The British Broadcasting Corporation. Britain's public service broadcaster

best boy: The second-in-command of a lighting team

BSkyB: Britain's only satellite broadcaster, owned by Rupert Murdoch's News Corporation

cable television: Television delivered through a cable under the ground into the home. Largely concentrated in urban areas. Can be digital or analogue

digital television: Television transmitted in binary format; can be delivered by cable, by satellite or terrestrially. Allows greater choice of channels, better quality and interactive services

EPG: the electronic programme guide

encryption: The encoding of television signals for security purposes, usually so they can only be watched by paying subscribers

free-to-air: A television service that can be received without decoding or paying a fee

Freeview: A commercial free-to-air digital terrestrial service; a partnership between BBC, BSkyB and transmission firm Crown Castle

grip: Someone who handles the equipment that enables a camera to move

HD: High-definition

ITV network: The 15 regional franchises that together make up the ITV1 channel

ITV plc: Company, formed from the merger of Carlton and Granada, that controls 11 of the 15 ITV network franchises, including all those in England and Wales

licence fee: How the BBC generates most of its revenue. A colour licence cost £126.50 in 2005

multichannel television: TV that includes more than just the five analogue terrestrial channels. If you receive cable, satellite or digital terrestrial, you are defined as being in a "multichannel home"

multiplex: A single digital terrestrial transmission comprising several channels. There are six television multiplexes in all

Ofcom: Broadcasting super-regulator

Pact: Producers' alliance for cinema and television. Represents independent television production companies

pay-per-view: An individual programme that the viewer has to pay to see

pay-TV: A general term for subscription services that the viewer has to pay to see

radio spectrum: The total capacity of radio frequencies that can be received. A small part of the electromagnetic spectrum, which is made up of a range of phenomena including gamma rays, X-rays, ultraviolet radiation and visible light

satellite television: Television received through a satellite dish, controlled in Britain by BSkyB. BSkyB has switched all its television services to digital

Section 42, Section 48: British tax breaks for the film industry. Until reform of the tax system, film producers wasted no time in claiming both of them, a practice known as "double-dipping"

terrestrial television: Television beamed from a ground transmitter directly to the home; can be analogue or digital

UK Film Council: Lottery-funded body charged with attracting investment to the British film industry

watershed: Before 9pm, nothing may shown on television that is considered unsuitable for children; after 9pm, nothing may shown that is considered unsuitable for adults. 9pm is therefore the "watershed"

Radio

access radio: The old name for community radio

analogue radio: Radio transmitted in waves; in other words, not digitally. Most terrestrial radio in the UK is still transmitted in analogue

audience share: In Rajar figures, the percentage of all radio listening hours that a station accounts for within its transmission area

BBC: The British Broadcasting Corporation. Britain's public service broadcaster

community radio: Not-for-profit, community-based radio. Formerly access radio

DAB digital radio: Digital terrestrial radio

digital radio: Shorthand for digital terrestrial radio. More accurately, refers to any radio transmitted in binary format - either through DAB digital radio, or via a television or the internet

multiplex: A single digital terrestrial transmission, comprising several channels. There are two national and almost 50 local multiplexes

Ofcom: Broadcasting super-regulator

podcasting: A way of publishing audio to the internet; users download podcasts to a PC or portable audio player

Rajar: Radio Joint Audience Research, the company that calculates radio audience figures

radio spectrum: The total capacity of radio signals that can be received

reach: In Rajar figures, the number of people aged 15 or over who tune to a radio station within at least a quarter-hour period over the course of a week, and have listened to the station for at least five minutes within that quarter-hour

Digital media

3G: Third-generation mobile phones, capable of video messaging, location mapping and other technical wizardry

ADSL: Broadband over a BT phone line (but not necessarily bought from BT)

blog: Diary-style web page in which new entries are added at the top and old ones drift to the bottom; popular among those who want a web page but don't necessarily know much about the internet. Short for "weblog"

broadband: High-speed internet access, usually 512kbps (kilobytes per second) as opposed to the 52kbps of a standard modem

browser: Software usually used to surf, or "browse", the internet. Internet Explorer and Netscape Communicator are the most popular

coverage: The percentage of the country or the population that can be reached by a mobile phone network

search engine: Service allowing you to find a word or image anywhere on the world wide web

short message service (SMS): Text messaging

Wi-Fi: Wireless internet access

Books

A-format, B-format: The two main "sizes" in which paperbacks are published. A-format are smaller (110mm × 178mm) and usually more downmarket; B-format are larger (130mm × 198mm) and usually further upmarket

acquisition editor: Someone in a publishing house who identifies and negotiates to acquire new titles for publication

advance: Initial payment to authors against which any royalties are offset

commissioning editor: Someone in a publishing house who looks for authors to write particular books for publication; sometimes also an acquiring editor

imprint: The name of the publisher; usually a brand operating under the auspices of a large publishing house

literary agent: Person who finds marketable authors and tries to sell rights in their work to publishers, taking a commission in the process

Nielsen Bookscan: Company that produces bestseller lists and other analysis of the UK book industry

royalties: Payment received by the author as a percentage of sales. Usually set off against the advance

rights: The main commodity in the books business. Rights can be separated out to include film, television, multimedia, merchandising and rights to publish abroad

Music

A&R: "Artist and repertoire"; the department of a record label that manages musicians

British Phonographic Industry: Association representing the music industry in the UK

indie: Independent record label

iPod: The most popular digital music (usually MP3) player, manufactured by Apple

label: Organisation that produces music; could be an indie, or a brand operating under the auspices of a large record company

MP3: Most popular digital music format

Advertising & PR

Advertising Association: Body representing the advertising and promotional marketing industries

Advertising Standards Authority: Regulator for advertising below the line: Marketing services such as PR, direct marketing, market research and sales promotion are said to be "below the line"; advertising directly in media is "above the line"

creatives: In advertising, art directors and copywriters, who often work in pairs on an ad

Chartered Institute of Public Relations: PR professional organisation

display: Advertising in the main body of a publication (as opposed to classified)

demographic data: Information defining a population according to factors such as age, sex and income; used to target an ad or marketing campaign

media agency: Agency that controls the purchase of advertising space, and often the strategic direction of a campaign

pitch: The lifeblood of the advertising industry is the pitch for an account

press release: Information sent by PR agencies and other publicists to journalists

Public Relations Consultants Association: PR trade body

solus: In publishing, the only advert on a page

Media law

contempt of court: A crime that carries imprisonment or a fine. Journalists could be in contempt of a court by publishing information about a defendant or other person granted privacy under a court order or injunction; or by speculating about the guilt or innocence of a defendant; or by publishing a photograph of a defendant when identity is an issue

culture select committee: Influential cross-party parliamentary committee that examines issues in culture, media and sport

European convention on human rights: European Union legislation, incorporated in British law through the Human Rights Act 1998. Includes articles protecting right to freedom of expression, but also the right to privacy

European court of human rights: Highest European court dealing with human rights law

law commission: Senior lawyers who meet to recommend changes in legislation

libel: A civil "tort", for which a complainant may sue for damages. Generally speaking, a journalist commits libel by publishing or broadcasting something that is defamatory, even by implication, to a person or a small enough group of people; *unless* the journalist can prove that what they wrote or published was true, or it was fair comment based firmly in fact, or it was an accurate, contemporaneous report of something said in parliament or court. But that isn't the half of it: see the latest edition of *McNae's Essential Law for Journalists*

Careers and training

Bectu: Broadcasting, entertainment, cinematograph and theatre union. Represents workers in broadcasting, film, theatre, entertainment, leisure and interactive media

BJTC: Broadcast journalism training council. Accredits broadcast journalism courses

FT2: Freelance Training for Film and Television, a respected training body

NCTJ: National council for the training of journalists. Accredits newspaper and magazine journalism courses

NUJ: National union of journalists. Represents journalists

Pact: Producers' alliance for cinema and television. Represents independent television production companies

Skillset: National training organisation for broadcast, film, video and interactive media

Glossary

Contacts book

Government: **UK government**

Downing Street

Prime Minister's Office
10 Downing Street,
London SW1A 2AA
020 7270 3000
www.number-10.gov.uk
Prime minister: Tony Blair*
Parliamentary private secretary:
Keith Hill
Press: 020 7930 4433

Government departments

Cabinet Office
70 Whitehall, London SW1A 2AS
020 7276 3000
www.cabinet-office.gov.uk
Cabinet Office minister: Hilary Armstrong*
Parliamentary secretaries: Pat McFadden,
Ed Miliband
Press: 020 7276 1191

Deputy Prime Minister
26 Whitehall, London SW1A 2WH
020 7944 4400
www.communities.gov.uk
Deputy prime minister: John Prescott*
Press: 020 7944 4297

**Communities and
Local Government**
Eland House, Bressenden Place,
London SW1E 5DU
020 7944 4400
www.communities.gov.uk
Communities and local government
secretary: Ruth Kelly*
Minister of state: Phil Woolas; minister
of state: Yvette Cooper; parliamentary
under-secretaries: Angela E Smith,
Meg Munn, Baroness Andrews

Constitutional Affairs
54 Victoria Street, London SW1E 6QW
020 7210 8614
www.dca.gov.uk
Constitutional affairs secretary and Lord
Chancellor: Lord Falconer of Thoroton*
Minister of state: Harriet Harman;
parliamentary under secretaries:
Baroness Ashton of Upholland; Bridget
Prentice, Vera Baird
Press: 020 7210 8512

Culture, Media and Sport
2–4 Cockspur Street,
London SW1Y 5DH
020 7211 6200
www.culture.gov.uk
Culture secretary: Tessa Jowell*
Minister of state: Richard Caborn;
parliamentary under-secretaries: David
Lammy, Shaun Woodward
Press: 020 7211 6145

Defence
Horseguards Avenue,
London SW1A 2HB
020 7218 9000
www.mod.uk
Defence secretary: Des Browne*
Minister of state: Adam Ingram;
parliamentary under-secretaries:
Lord Drayson, Tom Watson
Press: 020 7218 7907

Education and Skills
Great Smith Street,
London SW1P 3BT
0870 000 2288
www.dfes.gov.uk
Education secretary: Alan Johnson*
Minister of state for schools: Jim Knight;
minister of state for children and
families: Beverley Hughes; minister of
state for higher education and lifelong
learning: Bill Rammell; parliamentary
under-secretary for schools: Lord Andrew
Adonis; under-secretary for skills: Phil
Hope; under-secretary for children,
young people and families: Parmjit
Dhanda
Press: 020 7925 6789

**Environment, Food and
Rural Affairs**
17 Smith Square, London SW1P 3JR
020 7238 6000
www.defra.gov.uk
Environment secretary: David Miliband*
Minister of state: Ian Pearson; minister
of state (Lords): Lord Rooker;
parliamentary under-secretaries:
Ben Bradshaw, Barry Gardiner
Press -
animal welfare: 020 7238 6044
environment: 020 7238 6054
rural affairs: 020 7238 5608
sustainable farming and food:
   020 7238 6146

Foreign Office
Whitehall, London SW1A 2AH
020 7270 1500
www.fco.gov.uk
Foreign secretary: Margaret Beckett*
Minister of state for Europe: Geoff
Hoon*; minister of state for trade: Ian
McCartney*; minister of state: Dr Kim
Howells; parliamentary under-secretary:
Lord Triesman
Press: 020 7008 3100

Health
79 Whitehall, London SW1A 2NS
020 7210 4850
www.dh.gov.uk
Health secretary: Patricia Hewitt*
Minister of state for reform: Lord Warner;
minister of state: Rosie Winterton;
minister of state for public health:
Caroline Flint; minister of state for
delivery and quality: Andy Burnham;
parliamentary under-secretary of state
for care services: Ivan Lewis
Press: 020 7210 5221

Home Office
Direct Communications Unit,
2 Marsham Street,
London SW1P 4DF
020 7035 3535
www.homeoffice.gov.uk
Home secretary: John Reid*;
Minister for police and security:
Tony McNulty; under-secretary for police
and security: Vernon Coaker; minister
for justice: Baroness Scotland;
under-secretary for justice: Gerry
Sutcliffe; minister for immigration:
Liam Byrne; under-secretary for
immigration: Joan Ryan
Press: 020 7035 4381

International Development
1 Palace Street, London SW1E 5HE
020 7023 0000
www.dfid.gov.uk
International development secretary
of state: Hilary Benn*
Parliamentary under-secretary:
Gareth Thomas
Press: 020 7023 0600

Law Officers' Department
9 Buckingham Gate,
London SW1E 6JP
020 7271 2400
www.lslo.gov.uk
Attorney general: Lord Goldsmith*
Solicitor general: Mike O'Brien
Press: 020 7271 2440

Northern Ireland Office
11 Millbank, London SW1P 4PN
028 9052 0700
www.nio.gov.uk
Northern Ireland secretary of state:
Peter Hain*
Minister of state: David Hanson;
parliamentary under-secretaries: Paul
Goggins, Maria Eagle, David Cairns:
Speaking for the Lords: Lord Rooker
Press: 020 7210 0260/0213

Privy Council
2 Carlton Gardens, London SW1Y 5AA
020 7210 1033
www.privy-council.org.uk
Leader of the Lords and Lord President
of the Council: Baroness Amos*
Leader of the Commons and Lord
Privy Seal: Jack Straw*; deputy leader:
Nigel Griffiths
Press: 020 7210 1092

Scotland Office
Whitehall, London SW1A 2AU
020 7270 6754
www.scotlandoffice.gov.uk
Secretary of state: Douglas Alexander*
Parliamentary under-secretary:
David Cairns
Press: 0131 244 9053

* cabinet minister

413

Trade and Industry
1 Victoria Street, London SW1H OET
020 7215 5000
www.dti.gov.uk
Trade and industry secretary:
Alistair Darling*
Minister of state for trade: Ian McCartney*;
Minister of state: Margaret Hodge;
minister of state for energy: Malcolm
Wicks; under-secretary for science and
innovation: Lord Sainsbury of Turville;
under-secretary: Jim Fitzpatrick
Press: 020 7215 5961/5967/6405

Transport
76 Marsham Street,
London SW1P 4DR
020 7944 8300
www.dft.gov.uk
Transport secretary: Douglas Alexander*
Minister of state: Dr Stephen Ladyman;
parliamentary under-secretaries:
Derek Twigg, Gillian Merron
Press -
rail: 020 7944 3108
roads: 020 7944 3066
sea and air: 020 7944 3108

Treasury
1 Horse Guards Road,
London SW1A 2HQ
020 7270 4558
www.hm-treasury.gov.uk
Chancellor of the Exchequer:
Gordon Brown*
Chief secretary: Stephen Timms*;
paymaster general: Dawn Primarolo;
financial secretary: John Healey;
economic secretary: Ed Balls
Press: 020 7270 5238

Wales Office
Whitehall, London SW1A 2ER
020 7270 0534
www.walesoffice.gov.uk
Wales secretary: Peter Hain*
Parliamentary under-secretary:
Nick Ainger
Press: 020 7270 0566

Work and Pensions
79 Whitehall, London SW1A 2NS
020 7238 0800
www.dwp.gov.uk
Work and pensions secretary: John Hutton*
Minister of state for employment and
welfare reform: Jim Murphy; minister of
state for pensions reform: James Purnell;
parliamentary under-secretaries: Lord
Hunt of Kings Heath (Lords), Anne
McGuire (disabled people), James Plaskitt
(Commons)
Press: 020 7238 0866

Minister without portfolio
Hazel Blears*
Lords chief whip
Lord Grocott of Telford*
Chief Whip
Jacqui Smith*

● Wales
National Assembly for Wales
Cardiff Bay, Cardiff CF99 1NA
029 2082 5111
www.wales.gov.uk
First minister: Rhodri Morgan
Ministers: business: Jane Hutt; culture,
Welsh language and sport: Alun Pugh;
enterprise, innovation and networks:
Andrew Davies; education and lifelong
learning: Jane Davidson; environment,
planning and countryside: Carwyn Jones;
finance, local government and public
services: Sue Essex; health and social
services: Brian Gibbons; social justice and
regeneration: Edwina Hart
Press: 029 2089 8099

● Scotland
Scottish Executive
St Andrews House,
Edinburgh EH1 3DG
0131 556 8400
www.scotland.gov.uk
First minister: Jack McConnell
Ministers - deputy first minister and
enterprise and lifelong learning: Nicol
Stephen; communities: Malcolm
Chisholm; health and community care:
Andy Kerr; education and young people:
Peter Peacock; environment and rural
development: Ross Finnie; finance and
public service reform: Tom McCabe;
justice: Cathy Jamieson; parliamentary
business: Margaret Curran; tourism,
culture and sport: Patricia Ferguson;
transport and telecommunications:
Tavish Scott
Press: 0131 244 2664

● Northern Ireland
Northern Ireland Assembly
(suspended October 2002)
www.niassembly.gov.uk
Northern Ireland Executive
(suspended October 2002)
www.northernireland.gov.uk

Local and regional government

Local Government Association
020 7664 3131
www.lga.gov.uk
Press: 020 7664 3333
County Councils Network
020 7664 3011
www.lga.gov.uk/ccn
Audit Commission for Local Authorities
020 7828 1212
www.audit-commission.gov.uk
Press: 020 7166 2128
 020 7166 2111
Convention of Scottish Local Authorities
0131 474 9200
www.cosla.gov.uk
Press: 0131 474 9205
Improvement and Development Agency
020 7296 6600
www.idea-knowledge.gov.uk
Press: 020 7296 6529
Local government ombudsman
020 7217 4900
www.lgo.org.uk
Scotland
0800 377 7330
www.scottishombudsman.org.uk
Wales
01656 641150
www.ombudsman-wales.org

Professional bodies

Association of Council Secretaries and Solicitors
www.acses.org.uk
Association of Electoral Administrators
0151 281 8246
www.aea-elections.co.uk
Association of Local Authority Chief Executives
www.alace.org.uk

England

● London

Greater London Authority
020 7983 4000
www.london.gov.uk
Press: 020 7983 6553

Association of London Government
020 7934 9999
www.alg.gov.uk
Press -
daytime: 020 7934 9620/9755
evening: 07717 435184/
07917 227216

City of London
020 7606 3030
www.cityoflondon.gov.uk
Press: 020 7332 1906

● London boroughs

Barking and Dagenham
020 8592 4500
www.barking-dagenham.gov.uk
Press: 020 8227 2107

Barnet
020 8359 2000
www.barnet.gov.uk
Press: 020 8359 7796

Bexley
020 8303 7777
www.bexley.gov.uk
Press: 020 8294 6222

Brent
020 8937 1234
www.brent.gov.uk
Press: 020 8937 1066

Bromley
020 8464 3333
www.bromley.gov.uk
Press: 020 8313 4415

Camden
020 7278 4444
www.camden.gov.uk
Press: 020 7974 5717

Croydon
020 8686 4433
www.croydon.gov.uk
Press: 020 8760 5644

Ealing
020 8825 5000
www.ealing.gov.uk
Press: 020 8825 8686

Enfield
020 8379 1000
www.enfield.gov.uk
Press: 020 8379 4470

Greenwich
020 8854 8888
www.greenwich.gov.uk
Press: 020 8921 5040

Hackney
020 8356 5000
www.hackney.gov.uk
Press: 020 8356 3736

Hammersmith and Fulham
020 8748 3020
www.lbhf.gov.uk
Press: 020 8753 2164

Haringey
020 8489 0000
www.haringey.gov.uk
Press: 020 8489 2997

Harrow
020 8863 5611
www.harrow.gov.uk
Press: 020 8424 1295

Havering
01708 434343
www.havering.gov.uk
Press: 01708 432012

Hillingdon
01895 250111
www.hillingdon.gov.uk
Press: 01895 250534

Hounslow
020 8583 2000
www.hounslow.gov.uk
Press: 020 8583 2180

Islington
020 7527 2000
www.islington.gov.uk
Press: 020 7527 3376

Kensington and Chelsea
020 7937 5464
www.rbkc.gov.uk
Press: 020 7361 2826

Kingston upon Thames
020 8547 5757
www.kingston.gov.uk
Press: 020 8547 4710

Lambeth
020 7926 1000
www.lambeth.gov.uk
Press: 020 7926 2841

Lewisham
020 8314 6000
www.lewisham.gov.uk
Press: 020 8314 7337

Merton
020 8274 4901
www.merton.gov.uk
Press: 020 8274 4901

Newham
020 8430 2000
www.newham.gov.uk
Press: 020 8430 6892

Redbridge
020 8554 5000
www.redbridge.gov.uk
Press: 020 8708 2151

Richmond upon Thames
020 8891 1411
www.richmond.gov.uk
Press: 020 8891 7766

Southwark
020 7525 5000
www.southwark.gov.uk
Press: 020 7525 7306

Sutton
020 8770 5000
www.sutton.gov.uk
Press: 020 8770 5145

Tower Hamlets
020 7364 5000
www.towerhamlets.gov.uk
Press: 020 7364 4969

Waltham Forest
020 8496 3000
www.lbwf.gov.uk
Press: 020 8496 4855

Wandsworth
020 8871 6000
www.wandsworth.gov.uk
Press: 020 8871 6031

Westminster
020 7641 6000
www.westminster.gov.uk
Press: 020 7641 2259

● County councils

Bedfordshire
01234 363222
www.bedfordshire.gov.uk
Press: 01234 228888

Buckinghamshire
01296 395000
www.buckscc.gov.uk
Press: 01296 382055

Cambridgeshire
01223 717111
www.cambridgeshire.gov.uk
Press: 01223 717612

Cheshire
01244 602424
www.cheshire.gov.uk
Press: 01244 602216

Cornwall
01872 322000
www.cornwall.gov.uk
Press: 01872 322186

Cumbria
01228 606060
www.cumbria.gov.uk
Press: 01228 606334

Derbyshire
0845 605 8058
www.derbyshire.gov.uk
Press: 01629 585035

Devon
01392 382000
www.devon.gov.uk
Press: 01392 383290

Dorset
01305 251000
www.dorsetcc.gov.uk
Press: 01305 224725

Durham
0191 383 3000
www.durham.gov.uk
Press: 0191 383 3373

East Sussex
01273 481000
www.eastsussex.gov.uk
Press: 01273 481552

Essex
01245 492211
www.essexcc.gov.uk
Press: 01245 434979

Gloucestershire
01452 425000
www.gloucestershire.gov.uk
Press: 01452 425226

Hampshire
01962 870500
www.hants.gov.uk
Press: 01962 847666

Herefordshire
01432 260000
www.herefordshire.gov.uk/
Press: 01432 260224

Hertfordshire
01438 737555
www.hertsdirect.org
Press: 01992 555539

Kent
0845 824 7247
www.kent.gov.uk
Press: 01622 694177

Lancashire
0845 053 0000
www.lancashire.gov.uk
Press: 01772 530726

Leicestershire
0116 232 3232
www.leics.gov.uk
Press: 0116 265 6274

Lincolnshire
01522 552222
www.lincolnshire.gov.uk
Press: 01522 552301

Norfolk
0844 800 8020
www.norfolk.gov.uk
Press: 01603 222716

North Yorkshire
01609 780780
www.northyorks.gov.uk
Press: 01609 532206

Northamptonshire
01604 236236
www.northamptonshire.gov.uk
Press: 01604 237322

Northumberland
01670 533000
www.northumberland.gov.uk
Press: 01670 534850

Nottinghamshire
0115 982 3823
www.nottinghamshire.gov.uk
Press: 0115 977 3791

Oxfordshire
01865 792422
www.oxfordshire.gov.uk
Press: 01865 810256

Rutland
01572 722577
www.rutland.gov.uk
Press: 01572 758328

Shropshire
0845 678 9000
www.shropshireonline.gov.uk
Press: 01743 252813

Somerset
0845 345 9166
www.somerset.gov.uk
Press: 01823 355020

Staffordshire
01785 223121
www.staffordshire.gov.uk
Press: 01785 276829

Suffolk
01473 583000
www.suffolkcc.gov.uk
Press: 01473 264397

Surrey
0845 600 9009
www.surreycc.gov.uk
Press: 020 8541 9548

Warwickshire
0845 090 7000
www.warwickshire.gov.uk
Press: 01926 412758

West Sussex
01243 777100
www.westsussex.gov.uk
Press: 01243 777408

Wiltshire
01225 713000
www.wiltshire.gov.uk
Press: 01225 713114

Worcestershire
01905 763763
www.worcestershire.gov.uk
Press: 01905 766642

Isle of Wight
01983 821000
www.iwight.com
Press: 01983 823693

City and district councils

AVON

» see Somerset & Avon

BEDFORDSHIRE

Bedford
01234 267422
www.bedford.gov.uk
Press: 01234 221622

Luton
01582 546000
www.lutonline.gov.uk

Mid Bedfordshire
01525 402051
www.midbeds.gov.uk

South Bedfordshire
01582 472222
www.southbeds.gov.uk

BERKSHIRE

Reading
0118 939 0900
www.reading.gov.uk
Press: 0118 939 0301

Bracknell Forest
01344 352000
www.bracknell-forest.gov.uk

Slough
01753 552288
www.slough.gov.uk

West Berkshire
01635 42400
www.westberks.gov.uk

Windsor and Maidenhead
01628 798888
www.rbwm.gov.uk

Wokingham
0118 974 6000
www.wokingham.gov.uk

BUCKINGHAMSHIRE

Milton Keynes
01908 691691
www.mkweb.co.uk
Press: 01908 252009

Aylesbury Vale
01296 585858
www.aylesburyvaledc.gov.uk

Chiltern
01494 729000
www.chiltern.gov.uk

South Bucks
01895 837200
www.southbucks.gov.uk

Wycombe
01494 461000
www.wycombe.gov.uk

CAMBRIDGESHIRE

Cambridge
01223 457000
www.cambridge.gov.uk

Peterborough
01733 747474
www.peterborough.gov.uk

East Cambridgeshire
01353 665555
www.eastcambs.gov.uk

Fenland
01354 654321
www.fenland.gov.uk

Huntingdonshire
01480 388388
www.huntsdc.gov.uk

South Cambridgeshire
0845 045 0500
www.scambs.gov.uk

CHANNEL ISLANDS

Isles of Scilly
01720 422537
www.scilly.gov.uk
Press: 01720 424043

States of Jersey
01534 445500
www.gov.je
Press: 01534 603430

States of Guernsey
01481 717000
www.gov.gg
Press: 01481 717131

CHESHIRE

Chester
01244 324324
www.chester.gov.uk
Press: 01244 402362

Congleton
01270 763231
www.congleton.gov.uk

Crewe and Nantwich
01270 537777
www.crewe-nantwich.gov.uk

Ellesmere Port and Neston
0151 356 6789
www.ellesmereport-neston.gov.uk

Halton
0151 424 2061
www.halton.gov.uk

Macclesfield
01625 500500
www.macclesfield.gov.uk

Vale Royal
01606 862862
www.valeroyal.gov.uk

Warrington
01925 444400
www.warrington.gov.uk

CLEVELAND

Hartlepool
01429 266522
www.hartlepool.gov.uk
Press: 01429 523510

Middlesbrough
01642 245432
www.middlesbrough.gov.uk
Press: 01642 729502

Redcar and Cleveland
0845 612 6126
www.redcar-cleveland.gov.uk

CORNWALL

Caradon
01579 341000
www.caradon.gov.uk
Carrick
01872 224400
www.carrick.gov.uk
Kerrier
01209 614000
www.kerrier.gov.uk
North Cornwall
01208 893333
www.ncdc.gov.uk
Penwith
01736 362341
www.penwith.gov.uk
Restormel
01726 223300
www.restormel.gov.uk

COUNTY DURHAM

Durham
0191 383 3000
www.durham.gov.uk
Press: 0191 383 3373
Chester-le-Street
0191 387 1919
www.chester-le-street.gov.uk
Darlington
01325 380651
www.darlington.gov.uk
Derwentside
01207 693693
www.derwentside.gov.uk
Easington
0191 527 0501
www.easington.gov.uk
Sedgefield
01388 816166
www.sedgefield.gov.uk
Teesdale
01833 690000
www.teesdale.gov.uk
Wear Valley
01388 765555
www.wearvalley.gov.uk

CUMBRIA

Carlisle
01228 817000
www.carlisle.gov.uk
Press: 01228 817150
Allerdale
01900 326333
www.allerdale.gov.uk
Barrow-in-Furness
01229 894900
www.barrowbc.gov.uk
Copeland
01946 852585
www.copelandbc.gov.uk
South Lakeland
01539 733333
www.southlakeland.gov.uk

DERBYSHIRE

Derby
01332 293111
www.derby.gov.uk
Press: 01332 256207

Amber Valley
01773 570222
www.ambervalley.gov.uk
Bolsover
01246 240000
www.bolsover.gov.uk
Chesterfield
01246 345345
www.chesterfield.gov.uk
Derbyshire Dales
01629 761100
www.derbyshiredales.gov.uk
Erewash
0115 907 2244
www.erewash.gov.uk
High Peak
0845 129 7777
www.highpeak.gov.uk
North East Derbyshire
01246 231111
www.ne-derbyshire.gov.uk
South Derbyshire
01283 221000
www.south-derbys.gov.uk

DEVON

Exeter
01392 277888
www.exeter.gov.uk
Press: 01392 265103
Plymouth
01752 668000
www.plymouth.gov.uk
Press: 01752 304913
East Devon
01395 516551
www.eastdevon.gov.uk
Mid Devon
01884 255255
www.middevon.gov.uk
North Devon
01271 327711
www.northdevon.gov.uk
South Hams
01803 861234
www.southhams.gov.uk
Teignbridge
01626 361101
www.teignbridge.gov.uk
Torbay
01803 201201
www.torbay.gov.uk
Torridge
01237 428700
www.torridge.gov.uk
West Devon
01822 813600
www.westdevon.gov.uk

DORSET

Bournemouth
01202 451451
www.bournemouth.gov.uk
Press: 01202 454668
Christchurch
01202 495000
www.dorsetforyou.com
East Dorset
01202 886201
www.dorsetforyou.com
North Dorset
01258 454111
www.north-dorset.gov.uk

Poole
01202 633633
www.boroughofpoole.com
Purbeck
01929 556561
www.purbeck.gov.uk
West Dorset
01305 251010
www.dorsetforyou.com
Weymouth and Portland
01305 838000
www.weymouth.gov.uk

EAST SUSSEX

Brighton and Hove
01273 290000
www.brighton-hove.gov.uk
Press: 01273 291040
Eastbourne
01323 410000
www.eastbourne.gov.uk
Hastings
01424 781066
www.hastings.gov.uk
Lewes
01273 471600
www.lewes.gov.uk
Press: 01273 484141
Rother
01424 787878
www.rother.gov.uk
Wealden
01892 653311
www.wealden.gov.uk

ESSEX

Southend-on-Sea
01702 215000
www.southend.gov.uk
Press: 01702 215020
Basildon
01268 533333
www.basildon.gov.uk
Braintree
01376 552525
www.braintree.gov.uk
Brentwood
01277 312500
www.brentwood.gov.uk
Castle Point
01268 882200
www.castlepoint.gov.uk
Chelmsford
01245 606606
www.chelmsford.gov.uk
Colchester
01206 282222
www.colchester.gov.uk
Epping Forest
01992 564000
www.eppingforestdc.gov.uk
Harlow
01279 446655
www.harlow.gov.uk
Maldon
01621 854477
www.maldon.gov.uk
Rochford
01702 546366
www.rochford.gov.uk
Tendring
01255 686868
www.tendringdc.gov.uk

Thurrock
01375 652652
www.thurrock.gov.uk
Uttlesford
01799 510510
www.uttlesford.gov.uk

GLOUCESTERSHIRE

Gloucester
01452 522232
www.gloucester.gov.uk
Press: 01452 396133
Cheltenham
01242 262626
www.cheltenham.gov.uk
Press: 01242 775050
Cotswolds
01285 623000
www.cotswold.gov.uk
Press: 01285 623120
Forest of Dean
01594 810000
www.fdean.gov.uk
South Gloucestershire
01454 868686
www.southglos.gov.uk
Stroud
01453 766321
www.stroud.gov.uk
Tewkesbury
01684 295010
www.tewkesbury.gov.uk

GREATER MANCHESTER

Manchester
0161 234 5000
www.manchester.gov.uk
Press: 0161 234 3534
Bolton
01204 333333
www.bolton.gov.uk
Bury
0161 253 5000
www.bury.gov.uk
Oldham
0161 911 3000
www.oldham.gov.uk
Rochdale
01706 647474
www.rochdale.gov.uk
Salford
0161 794 4711
www.salford.gov.uk
Stockport
0161 480 4949
www.stockport.gov.uk
Tameside
0161 342 8355
www.tameside.gov.uk
Trafford
0161 912 2000
www.trafford.gov.uk
Wigan
01942 244991
www.wiganmbc.gov.uk

HAMPSHIRE

Portsmouth
023 9283 4092
www.portsmouth.gov.uk
Press: 023 9283 4043
Southampton
023 8022 3855
www.southampton.gov.uk
Press: 023 8083 2000
Basingstoke and Deane
01256 844844
www.basingstoke.gov.uk
East Hampshire
01730 266551
www.easthants.gov.uk
Eastleigh
023 8068 8068
www.eastleigh.gov.uk
Fareham
01329 236100
www.fareham.gov.uk
Gosport
023 9258 4242
www.gosport.gov.uk
Hart
01252 622122
www.hart.gov.uk
Havant
023 9247 4174
www.havant.gov.uk
New Forest
023 8028 5000
www.newforest.gov.uk
Rushmoor
01252 398398
www.rushmoor.gov.uk
Test Valley
01264 368000
www.testvalley.gov.uk
Winchester
01962 840222
www.winchester.gov.uk

HERTFORDSHIRE

St Albans
01727 866100
www.stalbans.gov.uk
Press: 01727 819316
Broxbourne
01992 785555
www.broxbourne.gov.uk
Dacorum
01442 228000
www.dacorum.gov.uk
East Hertfordshire
01279 655261
www.eastherts.gov.uk
Hertsmere
020 8207 2277
www.hertsmere.gov.uk
North Hertfordshire
01462 474000
www.north-herts.gov.uk
Stevenage
01438 242242
www.stevenage.gov.uk
Watford
01923 226400
www.watford.gov.uk
Welwyn Hatfield
01707 357000
www.welhat.gov.uk

KENT

Canterbury
01227 862000
www.canterbury.gov.uk
Press: 01227 862050
Ashford
01233 331111
www.ashford.gov.uk
Dartford
01322 343434
www.dartford.gov.uk
Dover
01304 821199
www.dover.gov.uk
Gravesham
01474 337000
www.gravesham.gov.uk
Maidstone
01622 602000
www.digitalmaidstone.co.uk
Medway
01634 306000
www.medway.gov.uk
Sevenoaks
01732 227000
www.sevenoaks.gov.uk
Shepway
01303 850388
www.shepway.gov.uk
Swale
01795 424341
www.swale.gov.uk
Thanet
01843 577000
www.thanet.gov.uk
Tonbridge and Malling
01732 844522
www.tmbc.gov.uk
Tunbridge Wells
01892 526121
www.tunbridgewells.gov.uk

LANCASHIRE

Lancaster
01524 582000
www.lancaster.gov.uk
Press: 01524 582041
Preston
01772 906900
www.preston.gov.uk
Press: 01772 906464
Blackburn with Darwen
01254 585585
www.blackburn.gov.uk
Blackpool
01253 477477
www.blackpool.gov.uk
Burnley
01282 425011
www.burnley.gov.uk
Chorley
01257 515151
www.chorley.gov.uk
Fylde
01253 658658
www.fylde.gov.uk
Hyndburn
01254 388111
www.hyndburnbc.gov.uk
Pendle
01282 661661
www.pendle.gov.uk

Ribble Valley
01200 425111
www.ribblevalley.gov.uk
Rossendale
01706 217777
www.rossendale.gov.uk
South Ribble
01772 421491
www.south-ribblebc.gov.uk
West Lancashire
01695 577177
www.westlancsdc.gov.uk
Wyre
01253 891000
www.wyrebc.gov.uk

LEICESTERSHIRE

Leicester
0116 252 7000
www.leicester.gov.uk
Press: 0116 252 6081
Blaby
0116 275 0555
www.blaby.gov.uk
Charnwood
01509 263151
www.charnwood.gov.uk
Harborough
01858 828282
www.harborough.gov.uk
Hinckley and Bosworth
01455 238141
www.hinckleyandbosworthonline
.org.uk
Melton
01664 502502
www.meltononline.co.uk
North West Leicestershire
01530 454545
www.nwleics.gov.uk
Oadby and Wigston
0116 288 8961
www.oadby-wigston.gov.uk

LINCOLNSHIRE

Lincoln
01522 881188
www.lincoln.gov.uk
Press: 01522 873384
Boston
01205 314200
www.boston.gov.uk
East Lindsey
01507 601111
www.e-lindsey.gov.uk
North East Lincolnshire
01472 313131
www.nelincs.gov.uk
North Kesteven
01529 414155
www.n-kesteven.gov.uk
North Lincolnshire
01724 296296
www.northlincs.gov.uk
South Holland
01775 761161
www.sholland.gov.uk
South Kesteven
01476 406080
www.southkesteven.gov.uk
West Lindsey
01427 676676
www.west-lindsey.gov.uk

MERSEYSIDE

Liverpool
0151 233 3000
www.liverpool.gov.uk
Press: 0151 225 5509
Knowsley
0151 489 6000
www.knowsley.gov.uk
Sefton
0151 922 4040
www.sefton.gov.uk
St Helens
01744 456789
www.sthelens.gov.uk
Wirral
0151 606 2000
www.wirral.gov.uk

NORFOLK

Norwich
01603 212212
www.norwich.gov.uk
Press: 01603 212167/212991
Breckland
01362 695333
www.breckland.gov.uk
Broadland
01603 431133
www.broadland.gov.uk
Great Yarmouth
01493 856100
www.great-yarmouth.gov.uk
King's Lynn and West Norfolk
01553 616200
www.west-norfolk.gov.uk
North Norfolk
01263 513811
www.north-norfolk.gov.uk
South Norfolk
01508 533633
www.south-norfolk.gov.uk

NORTH AND EAST YORKSHIRE

York
01904 613161
www.york.gov.uk
Press: 01904 552005
Craven
01756 700600
www.cravendc.gov.uk
East Riding of Yorkshire
01482 393939
www.eastriding.gov.uk
Hambleton
0845 121 1555
www.hambleton.gov.uk
Harrogate
01423 500600
www.harrogate.gov.uk
Kingston upon Hull
01482 300300
www.hullcc.gov.uk
Richmondshire
01748 829100
www.richmondshire.gov.uk
Ryedale
01653 600666
www.ryedale.gov.uk
Scarborough
01723 232323
www.scarborough.gov.uk

Selby
01757 705101
www.selby.gov.uk
Stockton-on-Tees
01642 393939
www.stockton-bc.gov.uk

NORTHAMPTONSHIRE

Northampton
01604 837837
www.northampton.gov.uk
Corby
01536 464000
www.corby.gov.uk
Daventry
01327 871100
www.daventrydc.gov.uk
East Northamptonshire
01832 742000
www.east-northamptonshire.gov.uk
Kettering
01536 410333
www.kettering.gov.uk
South Northamptonshire
0845 230 0226
www.southnorthants.gov.uk
Wellingborough
01933 229777
www.wellingborough.gov.uk

NORTHUMBERLAND

Alnwick
01665 510505
www.alnwick.gov.uk
Berwick-upon-Tweed
01289 330044
www.berwick-upon-tweed.gov.uk
Blyth Valley
01670 542000
www.blythvalley.gov.uk
Castle Morpeth
01670 535000
www.castlemorpeth.gov.uk
Tynedale
01434 652200
www.tynedale.gov.uk
Wansbeck
01670 532200
www.wansbeck.gov.uk

NOTTINGHAMSHIRE

Nottingham
0115 915 5555
www.nottinghamcity.gov.uk
Press: 0115 915 4686
Ashfield
01623 450000
www.ashfield-dc.gov.uk
Bassetlaw
01909 533533
www.bassetlaw.gov.uk
Broxtowe
0115 917 7777
www.broxtowe.gov.uk
Gedling
0115 901 3901
www.gedling.gov.uk
Mansfield
01623 463463
www.mansfield.gov.uk

Newark and Sherwood
01636 650000
www.newark-sherwooddc.gov.uk
Rushcliffe
0115 981 9911
www.rushcliffe.gov.uk

OXFORDSHIRE

Oxford
01865 249811
www.oxford.gov.uk
Press: 01865 252096
Cherwell
01295 252535
www.cherwell-dc.gov.uk
South Oxfordshire
01491 823000
www.southoxon.gov.uk
Vale of White Horse
01235 520202
www.whitehorsedc.gov.uk
West Oxfordshire
01993 861000
www.westoxon.gov.uk

SHROPSHIRE

Bridgnorth
01746 713100
www.bridgnorth-dc.gov.uk
North Shropshire
01939 232771
www.northshropshiredc.gov.uk
Oswestry
01691 671111
www.oswestrybc.gov.uk
Shrewsbury and Atcham
01743 281000
www.shrewsbury.gov.uk
South Shropshire
01584 813000
www.southshropshire.gov.uk
Telford & Wrekin
01952 202100
www.telford.gov.uk

SOMERSET AND AVON

Bath and North-east Somerset
01225 477000
www.bathnes.gov.uk
Bristol
0117 922 2000
www.bristol-city.gov.uk
Press: 0117 922 2650
Mendip
01749 648999
www.mendip.gov.uk
North Somerset
01934 888888
www.n-somerset.gov.uk
Sedgemoor
0845 408 2540
www.sedgemoor.gov.uk
South Somerset
01935 462462
www.southsomerset.gov.uk
Taunton Deane
01823 356356
www.tauntondeane.gov.uk
West Somerset
01643 703704
www.westsomersetonline.gov.uk

SOUTH YORKSHIRE

Doncaster
01302 734444
www.doncaster.gov.uk
Rotherham
01709 382121
www.rotherham.gov.uk
Sheffield
0114 272 6444
www.sheffield.gov.uk
Press: 0114 203 9082

STAFFORDSHIRE

Stoke-on-Trent
01782 234567
www.stoke.gov.uk
Press: 01782 232900
Cannock Chase
01543 462621
www.cannockchasedc.gov.uk
East Staffordshire
01283 508000
www.eaststaffsbc.gov.uk
Lichfield
01543 250011
www.lichfield.gov.uk
Newcastle-under-Lyme
01782 717717
www.newcastle-staffs.gov.uk
South Staffordshire
01902 696000
www.sstaffs.gov.uk
Stafford
01785 619000
www.staffordbc.gov.uk
Staffordshire Moorlands
01538 483483
www.staffsmoorlands.gov.uk
Tamworth
01827 709709
www.tamworth.gov.uk

SUFFOLK

Ipswich
01473 432000
www.ipswich.gov.uk
Press: 01473 432031
Babergh
01473 822801
www.babergh.gov.uk
Forest Heath
01638 719000
www.forest-heath.gov.uk
Mid Suffolk
01449 720711
www.midsuffolk.gov.uk
St Edmundsbury
01284 763233
www.stedmundsbury.gov.uk
Suffolk Coastal
01394 383789
www.suffolkcoastal.gov.uk
Waveney
01502 562111
www.waveney.gov.uk

SURREY

Elmbridge
01372 474474
www.elmbridge.gov.uk
Epsom and Ewell
01372 732000
www.epsom-ewell.gov.uk
Guildford
01483 505050
www.guildford.gov.uk
Mole Valley
01306 885001
www.molevalley.gov.uk
Reigate and Banstead
01737 276000
www.reigate-banstead.gov.uk
Runnymede
01932 838383
www.runnymede.gov.uk
Surrey Heath
01276 707100
www.surreyheath.gov.uk
Tandridge
01883 722000
www.tandridgedc.gov.uk
Waverley
01483 523333
www.waverley.gov.uk
Woking
01483 755855
www.woking.gov.uk

TYNE AND WEAR

Newcastle upon Tyne
0191 232 8520
www.newcastle.gov.uk
Press: 0191 211 5057
Gateshead
0191 433 3000
www.gateshead.gov.uk
North Tyneside
0191 200 5000
www.northtyneside.gov.uk
South Tyneside
0191 427 1717
www.southtyneside.gov.uk
Sunderland
0191 553 1000
www.sunderland.gov.uk

WARWICKSHIRE

Warwick
01926 450000
www.warwickdc.gov.uk
North Warwickshire
01827 715341
www.northwarks.gov.uk
Nuneaton and Bedworth
024 7637 6376
www.nuneatonandbedworth.gov.uk
Rugby
01788 533533
www.rugby.gov.uk
Stratford-on-Avon
01789 267575
www.stratford.gov.uk

WEST MIDLANDS

Birmingham
0121 303 9944
www.birmingham.gov.uk
Press: 0121 303 3287
Coventry
024 7683 3333
www.coventry.gov.uk
Press: 024 7683 4848
Dudley
01384 818181
www.dudley.gov.uk
Sandwell
0121 569 2200
www.sandwell.gov.uk
Solihull
0121 704 6000
www.solihull.gov.uk
Walsall
01922 650000
www.walsall.gov.uk
Wolverhampton
01902 556556
www.wolverhampton.gov.uk
Press: 01902 554077

WEST SUSSEX

Adur
01273 263000
www.adur.gov.uk
Arun
01903 737500
www.arun.gov.uk
Mid Sussex
01444 458166
www.midsussex.gov.uk
Chichester
01243 785166
www.chichester.gov.uk
Crawley
01293 438000
www.crawley.gov.uk
Horsham
01403 215100
www.horsham.gov.uk
Worthing
01903 239999
www.worthing.gov.uk

WEST YORKSHIRE

Leeds
0113 234 8080
www.leeds.gov.uk
Press: 0113 247 4328
Bradford
01274 431000
www.bradford.gov.uk
Calderdale
01422 357257
www.calderdale.gov.uk
Kirklees
01484 221000
www.kirklees.gov.uk
Wakefield
01924 306090
www.wakefield.gov.uk

WILTSHIRE

Kennet
01380 724911
www.kennet.gov.uk
North Wiltshire
01249 706111
www.northwilts.gov.uk
Salisbury
01722 336272
www.salisbury.gov.uk
Press: 01722 434561
Swindon
01793 463000
www.swindon.gov.uk
Press: 01793 463105
West Wiltshire
01225 776655
www.westwiltshire.gov.uk

WORCESTERSHIRE

Worcester
01905 723471
www.cityofworcester.gov.uk
Press: 01905 722230
Bromsgrove
01527 873232
www.bromsgrove.gov.uk
Malvern Hills
01684 862151
www.malvernhills.gov.uk
Redditch
01527 64252
www.redditchbc.gov.uk
Wychavon
01386 565000
www.wychavon.gov.uk
Wyre Forest
01562 732928
www.wyreforestdc.gov.uk

Government offices for the regions

East of England
01223 372500
www.go-east.gov.uk
East Midlands
0115 971 9971
www.goem.gov.uk
London
020 7217 3328
www.go-london.gov.uk
North-east
0191 201 3300
www.go-ne.gov.uk
North-west
0161 952 4000
www.gonw.gov.uk
South-east
01483 882255
www.gose.gov.uk
South-west
0117 900 1700
www.gosw.gov.uk
West Midlands
0121 352 5050
www.go-wm.gov.uk
Yorkshire and the Humber
0113 280 0600
www.goyh.gov.uk

Government News Network offices

www.gnn.gov.uk
East
01223 372780
East Midlands
0115 971 2780
London
020 7261 8325
North-east
0191 202 3600
North-west
0161 952 4513
South-east
01483 88228/8
South-west
0117 900 3551
West Midlands
0121 352 5500
Yorkshire and the Humber
0113 283 6599
Scotland
0131 244 9060/1
Wales
0844 800 6823

Regional development agencies

East of England
01223 713900
www.eeda.org.uk
Press: 01223 484624
East Midlands
0115 988 8300
www.emda.org.uk
Press: 0115 988 8375
London
020 7680 2000
www.lda.gov.uk
Press: 020 7954 4100
North-east
0191 229 6200
www.onenortheast.co.uk
Press: 0191 229 6311
North-west
01925 400100
www.nwda.co.uk
Press: 01925 400232
South-east
01483 484200
www.seeda.co.uk
Press: 01483 484216
South-west
01392 214747
www.southwestrda.org.uk
Press: 01392 229567
West Midlands
0121 380 3500
www.advantagewm.co.uk
Press: 0121 503 3228
Yorkshire
0113 394 9600
www.yorkshire-forward.com
Press: 0113 394 9923

UK government : Government

421

Wales

National Assembly for Wales
» see page 414
Cardiff
029 2087 2000
www.cardiff.gov.uk
Press: 029 2087 2964
Swansea
01792 636000
www.swansea.gov.uk
Press: 01792 636092

Carmarthenshire
01267 234567
www.carmarthenshire.gov.uk
Ceredigion
01970 617911
www.ceredigion.gov.uk
Denbighshire
01824 706000
www.denbighshire.gov.uk
Flintshire
01352 752121
www.flintshire.gov.uk
Gwynedd
01286 672255
www.gwynedd.gov.uk
Isle of Anglesey
01248 750057
www.ynysmon.gov.uk
Monmouthshire
01633 644644
www.monmouthshire.gov.uk
Newport
01633 656656
www.newport.gov.uk
Pembrokeshire
01437 764551
www.pembrokeshire.gov.uk
Powys
01597 826000
www.powys.gov.uk

● County borough councils

Blaenau Gwent
01495 350555
www.blaenau-gwent.gov.uk
Bridgend
01656 643643
www.bridgend.gov.uk
Caerphilly
01443 815588
www.caerphilly.gov.uk
Conwy
01492 574000
www.conwy.gov.uk
Merthyr Tydfil
01685 725000
www.merthyr.gov.uk
Neath Port Talbot
01639 763333
www.npt.gov.uk
Rhondda Cynon Taff
01443 424000
www.rhondda-cynon-taff.gov.uk
Torfaen
01495 762200
www.torfaen.gov.uk

Vale of Glamorgan
01446 700111
www.valeofglamorgan.gov.uk
Wrexham
01978 292000
www.wrexham.gov.uk

Scotland

Scottish Executive
» see page 414
Aberdeen
01224 523406
www.aberdeencity.gov.uk
Press: 01224 522821
Dundee
01382 434000
www.dundeecity.gov.uk
Press: 01382 434500
Edinburgh
0131 200 2000
www.edinburgh.gov.uk
Press: 0131 529 4044
Glasgow
0141 287 2000
www.glasgow.gov.uk
Press: 0141 287 0906

Aberdeenshire
01467 620981
www.aberdeenshire.gov.uk
Angus
0845 277 7778
www.angus.gov.uk
Argyll and Bute
0141 578 8000
www.eastdunbarton.gov.uk
Clackmannanshire
01259 450000
www.clacksweb.org.uk
Dumfries and Galloway
01387 260000
www.dumgal.gov.uk
East Ayrshire
01563 576000
www.east-ayrshire.gov.uk
East Dunbartonshire
0141 578 8000
www.eastdunbarton.gov.uk
East Lothian
01620 827827
www.eastlothian.gov.uk
East Renfrewshire
0141 577 3001
www.eastrenfrewshire.gov.uk
Falkirk
01324 506070
www.falkirk.gov.uk
Fife
01592 414141
www.fifedirect.org.uk
Highland
01463 702000
www.highland.gov.uk
Inverclyde
01475 717171
www.inverclyde.gov.uk
Midlothian
0131 270 7500
www.midlothian.gov.uk

Moray
01343 543451
www.moray.gov.uk
North Ayrshire
0845 603 0590
www.north-ayrshire.gov.uk
North Lanarkshire
01698 332000
www.northlan.gov.uk
Orkney Islands
01856 873535
www.orkney.gov.uk
Perth and Kinross
01738 475000
www.pkc.gov.uk
Renfrewshire
0141 842 5000
www.renfrewshire.gov.uk
Scottish Borders
01835 824000
www.scottishborders.gov.uk
Shetland Islands
01595 693535
www.shetland.gov.uk
South Ayrshire
01292 612000
www.south-ayrshire.gov.uk
South Lanarkshire
01698 454444
www.southlanarkshire.gov.uk
Stirling
0845 277 7000
www.stirling.gov.uk
West Dunbartonshire
01389 737000
www.west-dunbarton.gov.uk
West Lothian
01506 775000
www.westlothian.gov.uk
Western Isles
01851 703773
www.w-isles.gov.uk

Northern Ireland

Belfast
028 9032 0202
www.belfastcity.gov.uk
Press: 028 9027 0221
Lisburn
028 9250 9250
www.lisburncity.gov.uk

ANTRIM

Antrim
028 9446 3113
www.antrim.gov.uk
Ballymena
08456 581 581
www.ballymena.gov.uk
Ballymoney
028 2766 0200
www.ballymoney.gov.uk
Carrickfergus
028 9335 8000
www.carrickfergus.org
Larne
028 2827 2313
www.larne.gov.uk
Moyle
028 2076 2225
www.moyle-council.org

Newtownabbey
028 9034 0000
www.newtownabbey.gov.uk

ARMAGH

Armagh
028 3752 9600
www.armagh.gov.uk
Craigavon
028 3831 2400
www.craigavon.gov.uk

COUNTY DERRY

Coleraine
028 7034 7034
www.colerainebc.gov.uk
Derry
028 7136 5151
www.derrycity.gov.uk
Press: 028 7137 6504
Limavady
028 7772 2226
www.limavady.gov.uk
Magherafelt
028 7939 7979
www.magherafelt.gov.uk

DOWN

Ards
028 9182 4000
www.ards-council.gov.uk
Banbridge
028 4066 0600
www.banbridge.com
Castlereagh
028 9049 4500
www.castlereagh.gov.uk
Down
028 4461 0800
www.downdc.gov.uk
Newry and Mourne
028 3031 3031
www.newryandmourne.gov.uk
North Down
028 9127 0371
www.northdown.gov.uk

FERMANAGH

Fermanagh
028 6632 5050
www.fermanagh.gov.uk

TYRONE

Cookstown
028 8676 2205
www.cookstown.gov.uk
Dungannon and South Tyrone
028 8772 0300
www.dungannon.gov.uk
Omagh
028 8224 5321
www.omagh.gov.uk
Strabane
028 7138 2204
www.strabanedc.com

Government: **parliament and politics**

Parliaments and assemblies

Parliament
020 7219 3000
www.parliament.uk
Commons information office:
020 7219 4272
Commons press: 020 7219 0898
Lords information office:
020 7219 3107
National Assembly for Wales
029 2082 5111
www.wales.gov.uk
Press: 029 2089 8099
Scottish Parliament
0131 348 5000
www.scottish.parliament.uk
Press: 0131 348 5000

Main political parties

Labour party
0870 590 0200
www.labour.org.uk
Conservative party
020 7222 9000
www.conservatives.com
Press: 020 7984 8121
Liberal Democrat party
020 7222 7999
www.libdems.org.uk
Press: 020 7340 4949

Regional parties

● Wales

Plaid Cymru
029 2064 6000
www.plaidcymru.org
Press: 01824 709890
Welsh Labour party
029 2087 7700
www.welshlabour.org.uk
Press: 029 2087 7707
Welsh Conservative party
029 2061 6031
www.welshconservatives.com
Press: 029 2089 8395
Welsh Liberal Democrats
029 2031 3400
www.welshlibdems.org.uk
Press: 029 2089 8426

● Scotland

Scottish Conservative party
0131 247 6890
www.scottishconservatives.com
Press: 0131 348 5620
Scottish Green party
0870 077 2207
www.scottishgreens.org.uk
Press: 0131 348 6360

Scottish Labour party
0141 572 6900
www.scottishlabour.org.uk
Press: 0141 572 6905
Scottish Liberal Democrats
0131 337 2314
www.scotlibdems.org.uk
Press: 0131 348 5810
Scottish National party
0131 525 8900
www.snp.org
Scottish Socialist party
0141 429 8200
www.scottishsocialistparty.org

● Northern Ireland

Alliance party
028 9032 4274
www.allianceparty.org
Democratic Unionist party
028 9047 1155
www.dup.org.uk
Press: 028 9065 4479
Progressive Unionist party
028 9022 5040
www.pup-ni.org.uk
Sinn Féin
00 353 1 872 6100
www.sinnfein.ie
Social Democratic and Labour party
028 9024 7700
www.sdlp.ie
Press: 028 9052 1364
UK Unionist party
028 9147 9860
www.ukup.org
Ulster Unionist party
028 9076 5500
www.uup.org
Press: 028 9076 5521

Minor parties

British National party
0870 757 6267
www.bnp.org.uk
Press: 07074 530267
Communist League party
mail@communistleague.org.uk
www.communistleague.org.uk
Communist party of Britain
office@communist-party.org.uk
www.communist-party.org.uk
Cooperative party
020 7367 4150
www.co-op-party.org.uk
Press: 020 7367 4160
English Independence party
020 7278 5221
www.englishindependenceparty.com
Green party
020 7272 4474
www.greenparty.org.uk
Press: 020 7561 0282

Liberal party
0151 259 5935
www.liberal.org.uk
Separate from the Liberal Democrats
National Front
0121 246 6838
www.natfront.com
Official Monster Raving Loonies
01484 665226
www.omrlp.com
Press: 01484 665226
Socialist party
020 8988 8777
www.socialistparty.org.uk
Press: 020 8988 8778
Socialist Party of Great Britain
www.worldsocialism.org
UK Independence party
0121 333 7737
www.ukip.org
Press: 020 7222 9365
Workers Revolutionary party
020 7232 1101
www.wrp.org.uk

Parliamentary and electoral bodies

Electoral Commission
020 7271 0500
www.electoralcommission.gov.uk
Press: 020 7271 0529
Electoral Reform Society
020 7928 1622
www.electoral-reform.org.uk
Press: 07984 644138
Hansard Society
020 7438 1222
www.hansardsociety.org.uk
Press: 020 7438 1225
Parliamentary Counsel
020 7210 6644
www.parliamentary-counsel.gov.uk
Cabinet Office press office:
020 7276 0317

Thinktanks

Adam Smith Institute
020 7222 4995
www.adamsmith.org
Free market economics
Bow Group
020 7431 6400
www.bowgroup.org
Centre-right
Centre for Economic Policy Research
020 7878 2900
www.cepr.org
European network of research fellows
Centre for Global Energy Studies
020 7235 4334
www.cges.co.uk

Centre for Policy Studies
020 7222 4488
www.cps.org.uk
*Established 1974 by Margaret Thatcher
and Keith Joseph*

Centre for the Study of Financial Innovation
020 7493 0173
www.csfi.org.uk

Centre Forum
020 7340 1160
www.centreforum.org
Independent liberal

Chatham House
020 7957 5700
www.chathamhouse.org.uk

Civitas
020 7799 6677
www.civitas.org.uk
Civil society

Demos
0845 458 5949
www.demos.co.uk
Everyday democracy

Fabian Society
020 7227 4900
www.fabian-society.org.uk
Centre-left

Federal Trust
020 7735 4000
www.fedtrust.co.uk

Foreign Policy Centre
020 7388 6662
www.fpc.org.uk
Established 1998 by Labour government

International Institute for Environment and Development
020 7388 2117
www.iied.org

Institute for European Environmental Policy
020 7799 2244
www.ieep.org.uk

Institute for Global Ethics
020 7486 1954
www.globalethics.org

HLSP Limited. (formerly Institute for Health Sector Development)
020 7253 5064
www.hlspinstitute.org

Institute for Jewish Policy Research
020 7935 8266
www.jpr.org.uk

Institute for Public Policy Research
020 7470 6100
www.ippr.org.uk
Centre-left

International Institute for Strategic Studies
020 7379 7676
www.iiss.org

Institute of Economic Affairs
020 7799 8900
www.iea.org.uk
UK's original free market thinktank

Institute of Fiscal Studies
020 7291 4800
www.ifs.org.uk

Institute of Ideas
020 7269 9220
www.instituteofideas.com

New Economics Foundation
020 7820 6300
www.neweconomics.org

New Policy Institute
020 7721 8421
www.npi.org.uk
Progressive thinktank

New Politics Network
020 7278 4443
www.new-politics.com
Democracy and participation in politics

Overseas Development Institute
020 7922 0300
www.odi.org.uk

Policy Studies Institute
020 7911 7500
www.psi.org.uk

Politeia
020 7240 5070
www.politeia.co.uk
Role of the state

Scottish Council Foundation
0131 225 4709
www.scottishcouncilfoundation.org

Smith Institute
020 7823 4240
www.smith-institute.org.uk
Social values and economic imperatives

Social Affairs Unit
020 7637 4356
www.socialaffairsunit.org.uk

Social Market Foundation
020 7222 7060
www.smf.co.uk

Alternative and protest

Anarchist Federation
info@ afed.org.uk

Anti-Nazi League
020 7924 0333
www.anl.org.uk

Big Green Gathering
01458 834629
www.big-green-gathering.com

British Democracy Campaign
www.britishdemocracycampaign.com

Campaign Against Racism and Facism (CARF)
020 7837 1450
www.carf.demon.co.uk

Charter 88
0845 450 7210
www.charter88.org.uk

Creative Exchange
020 7065 0980
www.creativexchange.org

Democracy Movement
020 8570 5681
www.democracymovement.org.uk

Freedom Association
01746 861267
www.tfa.net

Globalise Resistance
020 7053 2071
www.resist.org.uk

Green Events
020 7424 9100
www.greenevents.co.uk

GreenNet
0845 055 4011
www.gn.apc.org

Indymedia
www.indymedia.org.uk
Network of independent media activists

Love Music Hate Racism
020 7924 0333
www.lmhr.org.uk

OneWorld
020 7239 1400
www.oneworld.net
Anti-globalisation

Peoples' Global Action
www.agp.org

Protest Net
rabble-rouser@protest.net
www.protest.net

Red Star Research
07960 865601
www.red-star-research.org.uk

Revolutionary Communist Group
020 7837 1688
www.revolutionarycommunist.com

Rising Tide
07708 794665
www.risingtide.org.uk

Squall
squall@squall.co.uk
www.squall.co.uk

The Land is Ours
01460 249 204
www.tlio.org.uk
Press: 0117 944 6219

Undercurrents News Network (UNN)
01792 455900
www.undercurrents.org
Alternative news videos

Unite Against Fascism
020 7833 4916
020 7837 4522
www.uaf.org.uk

Urban 75
www.urban75.com

Wombles
wombles@hushmail.com
www.wombles.org.uk
Anarchist and libertarian

Freemasons

Freemasons
grandsecretary@grandlodge.org.uk
www.grandlodge.org.uk

Government: **global politics**

Government departments

Foreign Office
020 7270 1500
www.fco.gov.uk
Press: 020 7008 3100
International Development
020 7023 0000
www.dfid.gov.uk
Press: 020 7023 0600

International

United Nations
00 1 212 963 1234
www.un.org
Press -
spokesman of the secretary general:
00 1 212 963 7160
media accreditation:
00 1 212 963 6937/34
Regional United Nations Information Centre
00 32 2788 8484
www.unric.org
UN Commission on International Trade Law (UNCITRAL)
00 43 1 26 060 4061
www.uncitral.org
Press: 00 43 1 26 060 3325
UN Conference on Trade & Development (UNCTAD)
00 41 22 917 0042
www.unctad.org
UN Educational, Scientific & Cultural Organisation (Unesco)
00 33 1 4568 1000
www.unesco.org
Press: 00 33 1 4568 1743
UN High Commissioner for Human Rights (UNHCHR)
00 41 22 917 9000
www.ohcr.org
Press: 00 41 22 917 9602
UN High Commissioner for Refugees (UNHCR)
020 7759 8090
00 41 22 739 8502
www.unhcr.org.uk
Press: gbrloea@unhcr.org
UN Relief & Works Agency for Palestinian Refugees (UNRWA)
00 972 8 677 7333
www.un.org/unrwa
Press: 00 972 8 677 7526
UN World Food Programme
00 39 06 65131
www.wfp.org
Press: 00 39 06 65131
Unicef
020 7405 5592
www.unicef.org.uk
Press: 020 7430 0162

International Labour Organisation (ILO)
00 41 22 799 6111
www.ilo.org
Press: 00 41 22 799 7912
International Maritime Organisation (IMO)
020 7735 7611
www.imo.org
Press: 020 7587 3153
International Monetary Fund (IMF)
00 1 202 623 7000
www.imf.org
Press: 00 1 202 623 7100
International Whaling Commission
01223 233971
www.iwcoffice.org
Nato
0032 2 707 72 11
www.nato.int
Press: 00 32 2 707 5041
OneWorld
020 7239 1400
www.oneworld.net
Press: 020 7239 1424
World Bank
00 1 202 473 1000
www.worldbank.org
UK Press: 020 7930 8511
World Health Organisation (WHO)
00 41 22 791 2111
www.who.int
Press: 00 41 22 791 2222
World Trade Organisation (WTO)
00 41 22 739 5111
www.wto.org
Press: 00 41 22 739 50 07

EU Institutions

European Parliament
London: 020 7227 4300
Edinburgh: 0131 557 7866
www.europarl.europa.eu
Press: 020 7227 4300
European Commission
00 800 6789 1011
www.europa.eu.int/comm/
Press: 00 32 2 296 5745
Committee of the Regions of the European Union
00 32 2 282 2211
www.cor.europa.eu
Press: 00 32 2 282 2155
Council of the European Union
00 32 2 281 6111
http://ue.eu.int
Press: 00 32 2 281 6319
Court of Justice of the European Communities
00 352 43031
www.curia.europa.eu
Press: 00 49 69 1344 7455
European Central Bank
00 49 69 1 3440
www.ecb.int
Press: 00 49 69 1344 7454/5

European Court of Auditors
00 352 43 984 5410
www.eca.eu.int
Press: 00 352 43 984 5410
European Economic and Social Committee
00 32 2 546 9011
www.esc.eu.int
Press: 00 32 2 546 9011
European Environment Agency
00 45 33 367000
http://org.eea.europa.eu
Press: 00 45 33 367 269
European Investment Bank
00 352 4379 3122
www.eib.org
Press: 00 352 4379 2159
The European Ombudsman
00 33 3 8817 2313
www.euro-ombudsman.eu.int
European Police Office
00 31 70 302 5000
www.europol.eu.int
Office for Official Publications of the European Communities
00 352 29291
http://publications.europa.eu
Translation Centre for the Bodies of the European Union
00 352 42 17111
www.cdt.europa.eu
Western European Union
www.weu.int

Other European contacts

Council of Europe
00 33 3 8841 2033
www.coe.int
Press: 00 33 3 8841 2560
Council of European Municipalities and Regions
00 32 2 511 7477
00 33 1 4450 5959
www.ccre.org
Press: 00 32 2 500 0534
European Court of Human Rights
00 33 3 8841 2018
www.echr.coe.int
Press: 00 33 3 8841 2560
European Space Agency
00 33 1 5369 7654
www.esa.int
Press: 00 33 1 5369 7155
European University Institute, Florence
00 39 055 46851
www.iue.it
Press: 00 39 055 468 5313
European Youth Parliament
00 49 30 9700 5095
www.eypuk.org
Organisation for Economic Cooperation and Development
00 33 1 4524 8200
www.oecd.org
Press: 00 33 1 4524 9700

Organisation for Security and Cooperation in Europe
00 43 1 514360
www.osce.org
Press: 00 43 1 514360
Eurocorps
00 33 388 43 20 03
www.eurocorps.net
Press: 00 33 388 43 20 06

Political parties

Confederal Group of the European United Left/Nordic Green Left
00 32 2 284 2683/2686
www.guengl.org
Press: 00 32 475 646628
European Liberal Democrats
00 32 2 237 01 40
www.eldr.org
Greens-European Free Alliance
00 32 2 284 3045
00 33 3 8817 5879
www.greens-efa.org
Press: 00 32 2 284 4683
00 33 3 8817 4760
Independence/Democracy Group in the European Parliament
ind-dem@europarl.europa.eu
http://indemgroup.org
Group of European People's Party (Christian Democrats) and European Democrats
00 32 2 284 2234
00 33 3 8817 4144
www.epp-ed.org
Press: 00 32 2284 2228
Parliamentary Group of the Party of European Socialists
00 32 2 284 2111
00 33 3 88 1 74873
www.socialistgroup.org
Press: 00 32 2 28 43099
Union for Europe of the Nations Group
00 32 2 284 2971
www.uengroup.org
Press: 00 32 2 28 42249

Pro-Europe and anti-Europe lobbies

Bruges Group
020 7287 4414
www.brugesgroup.com
Eurosceptic thinktank
European Movement
020 7820 9965
www.euromove.org.uk
Pro-European
Federation of Small Businesses
01253 336000
www.fsb.org.uk
Powerful anti-euro lobby
Press: 020 7592 8128
The No Campaign
info@no-euro.com
www.nocampaign.com
Pro-Europe, anti-euro
Press: 020 7222 9100

Commonwealth and British international

British Council
020 7389 4268
www.britcoun.org
Press: 020 7389 4939
Commonwealth Institute
020 7024 9822
www.commonwealth.org.uk
Press: 020 7861 8574
Commonwealth Secretariat
020 7747 6500
www.thecommonwealth.org
Press: 020 7747 6385

British overseas territories

Anguilla
Governor: 00 1 264 497 2621/2
Small east Caribbean island
Bermuda
Governor, Hamilton:
00 1 441 292 3600
100 small islands, 20 inhabited, 600 miles off North Carolina, USA
British Antarctic Territory
Commissioner, London:
020 7008 2614
Uninhabited part of Antarctica, including South Orkney and South Shetland islands
British Indian Ocean Territory
Commissioner, London:
020 7008 2890
Group of Chagos Archipelago islands in central Indian Ocean, south of India
British Virgin Islands
Governor, Tortola:
00 1 284 494 2345/2370
Eastern Caribbean group of 46 islands, 11 inhabited, near Anguilla
Cayman Islands
Governor, Georgetown:
00 1 345 244 2434
Three tax-free, wealthy islands south of Cuba
Falkland Islands
Governor, Stanley: 00 500 27433
Largest islands in the south Atlantic
Gibraltar
Governor: 00 350 45440
Promontory of southernmost Spain
Montserrat
Governor, Olveston:
00 1 664 491 2688/9
East Caribbean volcanic island
Pitcairn Islands
Governor, Auckland:
00 09 64 366 0186
Eastern group in Pacific, between north New Zealand and Peru. Home of mutineers from HMS Bounty, 1790
St Helena
Governor, Jamestown: 00 290 2555
Island in south Atlantic, 1,100 miles off Angola. Two dependencies
Ascension Island
Administrator: 00 247 7000
700 miles north-west of St Helena

Tristan da Cunha
Administrator: 00 870 764 341 816
Island group 1,850 miles west of Cape Town
South Georgia & Sandwich Islands
Governor, Stanley: 00 500 27433
Scattered islands east and south-east of Cape Horn. South Georgia is military, South Sandwich uninhabited and volcanic
Turks & Caicos Islands
Governor, Grand Turk:
00 1 649 946 2309
30 Caribbean islands, north of Haiti

International aid

ActionAid
020 7561 7561
www.actionaid.org.uk
Press: 020 7561 7614
Baby Milk Action
01223 464420
www.babymilkaction.org
Book Aid International
020 7733 3577
www.bookaid.org
British Leprosy Relief Association
01206 216700
0845 121 2121
www.lepra.org.uk
British Overseas NGOs for Development (Bond)
020 7837 8344
www.bond.org.uk
British Red Cross
0870 170 7000
www.redcross.org.uk
Press: 020 7877 7046/7039
Care International
020 7934 9334
www.careinternational.org.uk
Press: 020 7934 9315
Casa Alianza
00 502 2433 9600
www.casa-alianza.org
Catholic Agency for Overseas Development
020 7733 7900
www.cafod.org.uk
Press: 020 7326 5557
Christian Aid
020 7620 4444
www.christian-aid.org.uk
Press: 020 7523 2421
Christian Vision
0121 522 6087
www.christianvision.com
Church Mission Society
020 7928 8681
www.cms-uk.org
Disasters Emergency Committee
020 7387 0200
www.dec.org.uk
International Care and Relief
01892 519 619
www.icrcharity.com
International Committee of Red Cross
00 41 22 734 6001
www.icrc.org
Press: 00 41 22 730 2282

International HIV/Aids Alliance
01273 718900
www.aidsalliance.org

International Rescue Committee
00 1 212 551 3000
www.theirc.org
Press: 020 7692 2741

Islamic Relief
020 8531 6752
www.islamic-relief.org.uk
Press: 0121 622 0649

Médecins sans Frontières (UK)
020 7404 6600
www.uk.msf.org

Methodist Relief and Development Fund
020 7467 5132
www.mrdf.org.uk

Muslim Aid
020 7377 4200
www.muslimaid.org.uk

Oxfam
0870 333 2700
01865 473727
www.oxfam.org.uk
Press: 01865 472498

Plan UK
020 7482 9777
www.plan-uk.org

Sightsavers
01444 446600
www.sightsavers.org.uk
Press: 01444 446671

Tear Fund
0845 355 8355
www.tearfund.org
Press: 020 8943 7779

Voluntary Services Overseas
020 8780 7200
www.vso.org.uk
Press: 020 8780 7365

WaterAid
020 7793 4500
www.wateraid.org
Press: 020 7793 4793

World Development Movement
020 7820 4900
www.wdm.org.uk
Press 07711 875345

World Emergency Relief
0870 429 2129
www.wer-uk.org

World Vision UK
01908 841000
www.worldvision.org.uk
Press: 01908 244418

Human rights

ActionAid
020 7561 7561
www.actionaid.org.uk
Press: 020 7561 7614

Amnesty International
020 7033 1500
www.amnesty.org.uk
Press: 020 7033 1548

Anti-Slavery
020 7501 8920
www.antislavery.org
Press: 020 7501 8934

Asian Human Rights Commission
00 852 2698 6339
www.ahrchk.net

Association for Civil Rights in Israel
00 9722 652 1218
www.acri.org.il

British Institute of Human Rights
020 7848 1818
www.bihr.org

British Refugee Council
020 7346 6700
www.refugeecouncil.org.uk
Press: 020 7346 1213

Burma Campaign
020 7324 4710
www.burmacampaign.org.uk
Press: 020 7324 4713

Campaign Against Criminalising Communities
020 7586 5892
www.cacc.org.uk

Campaign Against Sanctions on Iraq
info@casi.org.uk
www.casi.org.uk

Campaign Against the Arms Trade
020 7281 0297
www.caat.org.uk

Centre for Research on Globalisation
00 1 514 425 3814
http://globalresearch.ca

Citizens for Global Solutions
00 1 202 546 3950
www.globalsolutions.org
Press: 00 1 202 546 3950

Coalition for the International Criminal Court
00 1 212 687 2863
00 31 70 363 4484
www.iccnow.org

Concern Worldwide
0800 032 4000
www.concern.net
Press: 00 353 1 417 7700

Derechos Human Rights
00 31 71 798634
www.derechos.org

Eliminate Child Labour in Tobacco
00 41 22 306 1444
www.eclt.org

European Roma Rights Centre
00 36 1 413 2200
http://errc.org

Free Tibet Campaign
020 7324 4605
www.freetibet.org

Gendercide Watch
office@gendercide.org
www.gendercide.org

Global Action to Prevent War
00 1 212 818 1815
www.globalactionpw.org

Global Fund for Women
00 1 415 202 7640
www.globalfundforwomen.org
Press: 001 415 202 7640 x338

Human Rights Watch
020 7713 1995
www.hrw.org

International Fellowship of Reconciliation
00 31 72 512 3014
www.ifor.org

International Physicians for the Prevention of Nuclear War
00 1 617 868 5050
www.ippnw.org

Kurdish Human Rights Project
020 7405 3835
www.khrp.org

Labour Behind the Label
01603 666160
www.labourbehindthelabel.org

One World Action
020 7833 4075
www.oneworldaction.org

Safer World
020 7324 4646
www.saferworld.co.uk
Press: 020 7324 4671

Stop the War Coalition
020 7278 6694
www.stopwar.org.uk
Press: 07939 242229

Transcend
00 40 742 079 716
www.transcend.org

Unrepresented Nations and Peoples Organisation
00 31 70 364 6504
www.unpo.org

War Resistors International
info@wri-irg.org
www.wri-irg.org

Womankind Worldwide
020 7549 0360
www.womankind.org.uk

World Commission for Peace and Human Rights Council
00 92 51 411704
www.worphco.cjb.net

World Organization For Human Rights USA
00 1 202 296 5702
www.humanrightsusa.org

Government: **overseas embassies in the UK**

Afghanistan
020 7589 8891
www.afghanembassy.co.uk
Albania
020 7828 8897
Algeria
020 7221 7800
Andorra
020 8874 4806
Angola
020 7299 9850
www.angola.org.uk
Antigua and Barbuda
020 7258 0070
www.antigua-barbuda.com
Argentina
020 7318 1300
www.argentine-embassy-uk.org
Armenia
020 7938 5435
Australia
020 7379 4334
www.australia.org.uk
Austria
020 7235 3731
www.austria.org.uk
Azerbaijan
020 7938 3412
www.president.az
Bahamas
020 7408 4488
Bahrain
020 7201 9170
Bangladesh
020 7584 0081
www.bangladeshhighcommission
.org.uk
Barbados
020 7631 4975
Belarus
020 7937 3288
http://belembassy.org/uk
Belgium
020 7470 3700
www.diplobel.org/uk
Belize
020 7723 3603
www.bzhc-lon.co.uk
Bolivia
020 7235 4248
www.embassyofbolivia.co.uk
Bosnia and Herzegovina
020 7373 0867
Botswana
020 7499 0031
Brazil
020 7499 0877
www.brazil.org.uk
Brunei
020 7581 0521
Bulgaria
020 7584 9400
www.bulgarianembassy.org.uk
Burma
020 7499 4340
www.myanmar.com
Burundi
00 32 2 230 45 35
Nearest embassy is in Belgium

Cameroon
020 7727 0771
Canada
020 7258 6600
www.dfait-maeci.gc.ca/canada
europa/united_kingdom
Chile
020 7580 6392
China
020 7299 4049
www.chinese-embassy.org.uk
Colombia
020 7589 9177
www.colombianembassy.co.uk
Congo
020 7922 0695
Congo, Democratic Republic of
020 7278 9825
Costa Rica
020 7706 8844
http://costarica.embassyhomepage
.com
Croatia
020 7387 2022
Cuba
020 7240 2488
Cyprus
020 7499 8272
Czech Republic
020 7243 1115
www.mzv.cz/london
Denmark
020 7333 0200
www.denmark.org.uk
Dominica, Commonwealth of
020 7370 5194/5
www.dominica.co.uk
Dominican Republic
020 7727 6285
www.serex.gov.do
Ecuador
020 7584 2648
Egypt
020 7499 3304
El Salvador
020 7436 8282
Eritrea
020 7713 0096
Estonia
020 7589 3428
www.estonia.gov.uk
Ethiopia
020 7589 7212-5
www.ethioembassy.org.uk
Fiji
020 7584 3661
Finland
020 7838 6200
www.finemb.org.uk
France
020 7073 1000
www.ambafrance-uk.org
Gabon
020 7823 9986
Gambia, The Republic of
020 7937 6316

Georgia
020 7603 7799
www.embassyofgeorgia.org.uk
Germany
020 7824 1300
www.german-embassy.org.uk
Ghana
020 7235 4142
www.ghana-com.co.uk
Greece
020 7229 3850
www.greekembassy.org.uk
Grenada
020 7631 4277
Guatemala
020 7351 3042
Guinea
020 7078 6087
Guyana
020 7229 7684
Holy See
020 8944 7189
Honduras
020 7486 4880
Hungary
020 7201 3440
www.huemblon.org.uk
Iceland
020 7259 3999
www.iceland.org.uk
India
020 7836 8484
www.hcilondon.org
Indonesia
020 7499 7661
www.indonesianembassy.org.uk
Iraq
020 7581 2264
Iran
020 7225 3000
www.iran-embassy.org.uk
Ireland
020 7235 2171
Israel
020 7957 9500
http://london.mfa.gov.il/
Italy
020 7312 2200
www.amblondra.esteri.it
Ivory Coast
020 7201 9601
Jamaica
020 7823 9911
www.jhcuk.com
Japan
020 7465 6500
www.uk.emb-japan.go.jp
Jordan
020 7937 3685
www.jordanembassyuk.org
Kazakhstan
020 7581 4646
www.kazakhstanembassy.org.uk
Kenya
020 7636 2371/5
Korea, DPR (North Korea)
020 8992 4965
www.koreanembassy.org.uk

Korea, Republic of (South Korea)
020 7227 5500
http://korea.embassyhomepage.com
Kuwait
020 7590 3400
www.kuwaitinfo.org.uk
Kyrgyzstan
020 7935 1462
www.kyrgyz-embassy.org.uk
Latvia
020 7312 0040
www.london.am.gov.lv/en
Lebanon
020 7229 7265
Lesotho
020 7235 5686
www.lesotholondon.org.uk
Liberia
020 7388 5489
Libya
020 7201 8280
Lithuania
020 7486 6401
http://amb.urm.lt/jk
Luxembourg
020 7235 6961
Macedonia
020 7976 0535
www.macedonianembassy.org.uk
Madagascar
020 3008 4550
Malawi
020 7491 4172
Malaysia
020 7235 8033
Maldives
020 7224 2135
www.maldiveshighcommission.org
Malta
020 7292 4800
Mauritania
020 7478 9323
Mauritius
020 7581 0294-8
Mexico
020 7499 8586
www.embamex.co.uk
Moldova
020 8995 6818
Mongolia
020 7937 0150
www.embassyofmongolia.co.uk
Morocco
020 7581 5001
Mozambique
020 7383 3800
Namibia
020 7636 6244
Nepal
020 7229 1594
www.nepembassy.org.uk
Netherlands
020 7590 3200
www.netherlands-embassy.org.uk
New Zealand
020 7930 8422
www.nzembassy.com
Nicaragua
020 7938 2373
http://freespace.virgin.net/
emb.ofnicaragua
Nigeria
020 7839 1244
www.nigeriahc.org.uk

Norway
020 7591 5500
www.norway.org.uk
Oman
020 7225 0001
Pakistan
020 7664 9200
www.pakmission-uk.gov.pk
Panama
020 7493 4646
Papua New Guinea
020 7930 0922
Paraguay
020 7610 4180
www.paraguayembassy.co.uk
Peru
020 7838 9223
www.peruembassy-uk.com
Philippines
020 7937 1600
www.philemb.org.uk
Poland
0870 774 2700
www.polishembassy.org.uk
Portugal
020 7235 5331
www.portembassy.gla.ac.uk
Qatar
020 7493 2200
Romania
020 7937 9666
www.roemb.co.uk
Russia
020 7229 2666
Rwanda
020 7224 9832
www.ambarwanda.org.uk
**Saint Christopher and Nevis
(St Kitts and Nevis)**
020 7937 9718
St Lucia
020 7370 7123
St Vincent and the Grenadines
020 7565 2874
San Marino
020 7823 4762
Saudi Arabia
020 7917 3000
www.saudiembassy.org.uk
Senegal
020 7937 7237
www.senegalembassy.co.uk
Serbia and Montenegro
020 7235 9049
www.yugoslavembassy.org.uk
Sierra Leone
020 7404 0140
www.slhc-uk.org.uk
Singapore
020 7235 8315
www.mfa.gov.sg/london
Slovakia
020 7243 0803
www.slovakembassy.co.uk
Slovenia
020 7222 5400
www.gov.si/mzz/dkp/vlo/eng
Solomon Islands
00 32 2 732 7085
Nearest embassy is in Belgium
South Africa
020 7451 7299
www.southafricahouse.com

Spain
020 7235 5555
Sri Lanka
020 7262 1841
www.slhclondon.org
Sudan
020 7839 8080
www.sudan-embassy.co.uk
Swaziland
020 7630 6611
Sweden
020 7917 6400
www.swedish-embassy.org.uk
Switzerland
020 7616 6000
www.swissembassy.org.uk
Syria
020 7245 9012
www.syrianembassy.co.uk
Tanzania
020 7569 1470
www.tanzania-online.gov.uk
Thailand
020 7225 5512
Togo
00 33 1 4380 1213
Nearest embassy is in Paris
Tonga
020 7724 5828
Trinidad and Tobago
020 7245 9351
Tunisia
020 7584 8117
Turkey
020 7393 0202
www.turkconsulate-london.com
Turkmenistan
020 7255 1071
Uganda
020 7839 5783
Ukraine
020 7727 6312
www.ukremb.org.uk
United Arab Emirates
020 7581 1281
United States
020 7499 9000
www.usembassy.org.uk
Uruguay
020 7589 8835
Uzbekistan
020 7229 7679
www.uzbekembassy.org
Venezuela
020 7584 4206
www.venezlon.co.uk
Vietnam
020 7937 1912
www.vietnamembassy.org.uk
Yemen
020 7584 6607
www.yemenembassy.org.uk
Zambia
020 7589 6655
www.zhcl.org.uk
Zimbabwe
020 7836 7755
http://zimbabwe.embassy
homepage.com

Government: **overseas diplomatic contacts**

Key
E   Embassy
HC   High Commission
DHC   Deputy High Commission
CG   Consulate-General
C   Consulate
HonC   Honorary Consulate
VC   Honorary Vice-consulate   *Source: Foreign Office*

Afghanistan
E: Kabul 00 93 70 102: 000
     www.britishembassy.gov.uk/afghanistan

Albania
E: Tirana 00 355 42 34973/4/5
     www.britishembassy.gov.uk/albania

Algeria
E: Algiers 00 213 2123 0068
     www.britishembassy.gov.uk/algeria

Andorra
C: Andorra La Vella 00 376 839 840 *www.ukinspain.com*

Angola
E: Luanda 00 244 2 334582/3, 392991, 387681
     www.britishembassy.gov.uk/angola

Antigua and Barbuda
HC: St John's 00 1 268 462 0008/9, 463 0010

Argentina
E: Buenos Aires 00 54 11 4808 2200 *www.britain.org.ar*

Armenia
E: Yerevan 00 3741 264301 *www.britishembassy.am*

Australia
HC: Canberra 00 61 2 6270 6666 *www.britaus.net*
CG: Brisbane 00 61 7 3223 3200
CG: Melbourne 00 61 3 9652 1600
CG: Perth 00 61 8 9224 4700
CG: Sydney 00 61 2 9247 7521
C: Adelaide 00 61 8 8212 7280

Austria
E: Vienna 00 43 1 716 130 *www.britishembassy.at*
C: Bregenz 00 43 5574 78586
C: Graz 00 43 316 8216 1621
C: Innsbruck 00 43 512 588320
C: Salzburg 00 43 662 848133

Azerbaijan
E: Baku 00 99 412 497 5188/89/90
     www.britishembassy.gov.uk/azerbaijan

Bahrain
E: 00 973 574100 *www.ukembassy.gov.bh*

Bangladesh
HC: Dhaka 00 880 2 882 2705
     www.britishhighcommission.gov.uk/bangladesh

Barbados
HC: Bridgetown 00 1 246 430 7800
     www.britishhighcommission.gov.uk/barbados

Belarus
E: Minsk 00 375 172 105920
     www.britishembassy.gov.uk/belarus

Belgium
E: Brussels 00 32 2 287 6211
     www.britishembassy.gov.uk/belgium

Belize
HC: Belmopan 00 501 822 2146 *www.britishhighbze.com*

Bolivia
E: La Paz 00 591 2 243 3424
     www.britishembassy.gov.uk/bolivia

Bosnia and Herzegovina
E: Sarajevo 00 387 3328 2200 *www.britishembassy.ba*

Botswana
HC: Gaborone 00 267 395 2841
     www.britishhighcommission.gov.uk/botswana

Brazil
E: Brasilia 00 55 61 329 2300 *www.uk.org.br*
CG: Rio de Janeiro 00 55 21 2555 9600
CG: São Paulo 00 55 11 3094 2700
     www.gra-bretanha.org.br
C: Belém 00 55 91 222 5074, 223 0990
C: Belo Horizonte 00 31 3261 2072
C: Curitiba 00 55 41 322 1202
C: Fortaleza 00 55 85 466 8580/2
C: Manáus 00 55 92 613 1819
C: Porto Alegre 00 55 51 3232 1414
C: Rio Grande 00 55 53 233 7700
C: Salvador 00 55 71 243 7399
C: Santos 00 55 13 3211 2300

Brunei
HC: Bandar Seri Begawan 00 673 2 222231/223121
     www.britishhighcommission.gov.uk/brunei

Bulgaria
E: Sofia 00 359 2 933 9222 *www.british-embassy.bg*
C: Varna 00 359 52 665 5555

Burma
E: Rangoon 00 95 1 370863

Burundi
E-liaison: Bujumbura 00 257 827602

Cambodia
E: Phnom Penh 00 855 23 427124, 428295
     www.britishembassy.gov.uk/cambodia

Cameroon
HC: Yaoundé 00 237 222 0545/0796 *www.britcam.org*

Canada
HC: Ottawa 00 1 613 237 1530
CG: Montreal 00 1 514 866 5863
CG: Toronto 00 1 416 593 1290
CG: Vancouver 00 1 604 683 4421
C: Halifax/Dartmouth 00 1 902 461 1381
C: St John's 00 1 709 579 2002
C: Winnipeg 00 1 204 896 1380
C: Quebec City 00 1 418 521 3000

Chad
E: Ndjamena 00 237 222 05 45, 07 96

Chile
E: Santiago 00 56 2 370 4100
     www.britishembassy.gov.uk/chile
C: Valparaíso 00 56 32 213063
C: Punta Arenas 00 56 61 211535

China
E: Beijing 00 86 10 5192 4000
     www.britishembassy.org.cn
CG: Shanghai 00 86 21 6279 7650 *www.uk.cn*
CG: Guangzhou 00 86 20 8314 3000 *www.uk.cn/gz*
CG: Chongqing 00 023 6369 1500
     www.britishcouncil.org.cn
CG: Hong Kong 00 852 2901 3000
     www.britishconsulate.org.hk
CG: Macao 00 853 685 0886

Colombia
E: Bogotá 00 57 1 326 8300 *www.britain.gov.co*
C: Cali 00 57 2 653 6089
C: Medellin 00 57 4 377 9966

Congo, Democratic Republic of
E: Kinshasa 00 243 8171 50761

Costa Rica
E: San José 00 506 258 2025 *www.britishembassycr.com*

Croatia
E: Zagreb 00 385 1 600 9100
   www.britishembassy.gov.uk/croatia
C: Split 00 385 21 341 464
C: Dubrovnik 00 385 20 324597

Cuba
E: Havana 00 53 7 204 1771
   www.britishembassy.gov.uk/cuba

Cyprus
HC: Nicosia 00 357 22 861100 *www.britain.org.cy*

Czech Republic
E: Prague 00 420 2 5740 2111 *www.britain.cz*

Denmark
E: Copenhagen 00 45 3544 5200
   www.britishembassy.dk
C: Aabenraa 00 45 7462 3500
C: Aalborg 00 45 9811 3499
C: Aarhus 00 45 8627 3338
C: Esbjerg 00 45 7518 1476
C: Fredericia 00 45 7592 2000
C: Herning 00 45 9627 7300
C: Odense 00 45 6614 4714
C: Torshavn, Faroe Islands 00 45 2 9835 0077

Djibouti
C: Djibouti 00 253 38 5007

Dominica, Commonwealth of
HC: Roseau 00 1 246 430 7800
HONC: Roseau 00 1 767 448 7655

Dominican Republic
E: Santo Domingo 00 1 809 472 7111
C: Puerto Plata 00 1 809 586 4244/8464

East Timor
E: Dili 00 670 332 2838

Ecuador
E: Quito 00 593 2 2970 800/1 *www.britembquito.org.ec*
C: Guayaquil 00 593 4 256 0400 x318
C: Galápagos 00 593 5 526157/9

Egypt
E: Cairo 00 20 2 794 0850/2/8
   www.britishembassy.gov.uk/egypt
CG: Alexandria 00 20 3 546 7001/2, 522 3717, 522 0507
C: Suez 00 20 62 313872

El Salvador
C: San Salvador 00 503 281 5555
E: Guatemala City 00 502 2367 5425,6,7,8,9

Eritrea
E: Asmara 00 291 1 120145

Estonia
E: Tallinn 00 372 667 4700 *www.britishembassy.ee*

Ethiopia
E: Addis Ababa 00 251 11 661 2354
   www.britishembassy.gov.uk/ethiopia

Fiji
HC: Suva 00 679 322 9100
   www.britishhighcommission.gov.uk/fiji

Finland
E: Helsinki 00 358 9 2286 5100 *www.britishembassy.fi*
C: Jyväskylä 00 358 14 446 9211
C: Kotka 00 358 5 234 4281
C: Kuopio 00 358 17 368 1800
C: Åland Islands 00 358 18 13591, 47720
C: Oulu 00 358 83 310 7117
C: Rovaniemi 00 358 16 317831
C: Tampere 00 358 3 256 5701
C: Turku 00 358 2 274 3410
C: Vaasa 00 358 6 282 2000

France
E: Paris 00 33 1 4451 3100 *www.amb-grandebretagne.fr*
CG: Bordeaux 00 33 5 5722 2110
CG: Lille 00 33 3 2012 8272
CG: Lyon 00 33 4 7277 8170
CG: Marseille 00 33 4 9115 7210
C: Amiens 00 33 3 2272 0848
C: Boulogne-sur-Mer 00 33 3 2187 1680
C: Calais 00 33 3 2196 3376
C: Cayenne, French Guiana 00 594 311034
C: Cherbourg 00 33 2 3378 0183
C: Dunkirk 00 33 3 2866 1198
C: Fort de France, Martinique 00 596 618892
C: Guadeloupe 00 590 825757
C: La Réunion 00 33 2 6234 7576
C: Le Havre 00 33 2 3519 7888
C: Lorient 00 33 6 1732 6310
C: Montpellier 00 33 4 6715 5207
C: Nantes 00 33 2 5172 7260
C: New Caledonia 00 687 273627/282153
C: Papeete, French Polynesia 00 689 706382
C: Saumur 00 33 2 4152 9054
C: St Malo-Dinard 00 33 2 2318 3030
C: Toulouse 00 33 5 6130 3791
C: Tours 00 33 2 4743 5058

Gabon
C: Libreville 00 241 762200/742041

Gambia, The Republic of
HC: Banjul 00 220 449 5133/4
   www.britishhighcommission.gov.uk/thegambia

Georgia
E: Tbilisi 00 995 32 274747
   www.britishembassy.gov.uk/georgia

Germany
E: Berlin 00 49 30 204570 *www.britischebotschaft.de*
CG: Düsseldorf 00 49 211 94480
   www.british-consulate-general.de
CG: Hamburg 00 49 40 448 0320
CG: Munich 00 49 89 211090
CG: Stuttgart 00 49 711 162690
C: Bremen 00 49 421 59090
C: Hanover 00 49 511 388 3808
C: Kiel 00 49 431 331971
C: Nuremburg 00 49 911 2404 303

Ghana
HC: Accra 00 233 21 701 0650/ 00 233 21 221665
   www.britishhighcommission.gov.uk/ghana

Greece
E: Athens 00 30 210 727 2600 *www.british-embassy.gr*
C: Heraklion (Crete) 00 30 2810 224012
C: Rhodes 00 30 22410 22005
C: Thessaloniki 00 30 2310 278006
VC: Corfu 00 30 26610 30055
VC: Kos 00 30 22420 21549
VC: Patras 00 30 2610 277329
VC: Syros 00 30 22810 82232/88922
VC: Zakynthos 00 30 26950 22906/48030

Grenada
HC: St George's 001 473 440 3536/3222

Guatemala
E: Guatemala City 00 502 2367 5425-9

Guinea
CG: Conakry 00 224 45 5807

Guyana
HC: Georgetown 00 592 22 65881,2,3,4
   www.britishhighcommission.gov.uk/guyana

Haiti
C: Port-au-Prince 00 509 257 3969

Holy See
E: Rome 00 39 06 422 04000
   www.britishembassy.gov.uk/holysee

Honduras
C: San Pedro Sula 00 504 550 2337
C: Tegucigalpa 00 504 237 6577/0645/0324
E: Guatemala City 00 502 2367 5425,6,7,8,9

Hungary
E: Budapest 00 36 1 266 2888 *www.britishembassy.hu*

Iceland
E: Reykjavik 00 354 550 5100
VC: Akureyri 00 354 463 0102

India
HC: New Delhi 00 91 11 2687 2161
www.britishhighcommission.gov.uk/india
DHC: Chennai 00 91 44 5219 2151
DHC: Kolkata 00 91 33 2288 5172
DHC: Mumbai 00 91 22 2283 0517/2330/3602

Indonesia
E: Jakarta 00 62 21 315 6264
www.britain-in-indonesia.or.id
C: Medan 00 62 061 661 3476

Iran
E: Tehran 00 98 21 66705011/7
www.britishembassy.gov.uk/iran

Iraq
E: Basra 00 964 0 7901 926 280
www.britishembassy.gov.uk/iraq

Ireland
E: Dublin 00 353 1 205 3700 *www.britishembassy.ie*

Israel
E: Tel Aviv 00 972 3 725 1222 *www.britemb.org.il*
C: Eilat 00 972 8 634 0810
CG: Tel Aviv 00 972 3 5100166

Italy
E: Rome 00 39 06 4220 0001 *www.britain.it*
CG: Milan 00 39 02 723001
C: Bari 00 39 080 554 3668
C: Cagliari 00 39 070 828628
C: Catania 00 39 095 715 1864
C: Genoa 00 39 010 5740071
C: Florence 00 39 055 284133
C: Naples 00 39 081 423 8911
C: Palermo 00 39 091 582 533
C: Trieste 00 39 040 347 8303
C: Venice 00 39 041 505 5990

Ivory Coast
E: Abidjan 00 225 2030 0800 *www.britaincdi.com*

Jamaica
HC: Kingston 00 1 876 510 0700
www.britishhighcommission.gov.uk/jamaica
C: Montego Bay 00 1 876 999 9693

Japan
E: Tokyo 00 81 3 5211 1100 *www.uknow.or.jp*
HonC: Fukuoka 00 81 92 476 2155
CG: Osaka 00 81 6 6120 5600
C: Nagoya 00 81 52 223 5031

Jerusalem
CG: 00 972 2 541 4100
CG: West Jerusalem 00 972 2 671 7724

Jordan
E: Amman 00 962 6 590 9200 *www.britain.org.jo*

Kazakhstan
E: Almaty 00 75731 502200
www.britishembassy.gov.uk/kazakhstan

Kenya
HC: Nairobi 00 254 20 284 4000
www.britishhighcommission.gov.uk/kenya
C: Mombasa 00 254 41 313609/220023

Kiribati
HC: Tarawa 00 679 3229100
www.britishhighcommission.gov.uk/fiji

Korea (North)
E: Pyongyang 00 850 2 381 7980

Korea (South)
E: Seoul 00 82 2 3210 5500 *www.uk.or.kr*
C: Pusan 00 82 5 1463 4630

Kuwait
E: 00 965 240 3335 *www.britishembassy-kuwait.org*

Kyrgystan
HC: Bishkek 00 996 312 584245

Laos
E: Vientiane 00 856 21 413606

Latvia
E: Riga 00 371 777 4700 *www.britain.lv*

Lebanon
E: Beirut 00 961 1 990400
www.britishembassy.gov.uk/lebanon
C: Mount Lebanon 00 961 4 723502
C: Tripoli 00 961 4 431320

Lesotho
HC: Pretoria 00 27 12 421 7500 *www.britain.org.za*
C: Maseru 00 266 223 13929

Liberia
HonC: Freetown 00 231 226056

Libya
E: Tripoli 00 218 21 340 3644/5
www.britishembassy.gov.uk/libya

Lithuania
E: Vilnius 00 370 5 246 2900 *www.britain.lt*

Luxembourg
E: 00 352 229864 *www.britain.lu*

Macedonia
E: Skopje 00 389 2 3299 299
www.britishembassy.gov.uk/macedonia
C: Toamasina 00 261 20 533 2548/69

Malawi
HC: Lilongwe 00 265 1 772400
www.britishhighcommission.gov.uk/malawi

Malaysia
HC: Kuala Lumpur 00 60 3 2170 2200 *www.britain.org.my*

Malta
HC: Valletta 00 356 2323 0000
www.britishhighcommission.gov.uk/malta

Mauritania
HC: Nouakchott 00 222 525 8331

Mauritius
HC: Port Louis 00 230 202 9400
C: Rodrigues 00 230 832 0120

Mexico
E: Mexico City 00 52 55 5 242 8500
www.britishembassy.gov.uk/mexico
L: Monterrey 00 52 818 315 2049
C: Veracruz 00 52 229 931 1285 / 931 0955

Moldova
E: Chisinau 00 3732 2225902
www.britishembassy.gov.uk/moldova

Monaco
C: 00 377 9350 9954

Mongolia
E: Ulaanbaatar 00 976 11 458133
www.britishembassy.gov.uk/mongolia

Morocco
E: Rabat 00 212 37 633333 *www.britain.org.ma*
CG: Casablanca 00 212 22 85 74 00
C: Agadir 00 212 48 823401/2
C: Marrakech 00 212 44 435095
C: Tangier 00 212 39 936939/40

Mozambique
HC: Maputo 00 258 21 356 000
www.britishhighcommission.gov.uk/mozambique
C: Beira 00 258 23 325 997

Namibia
HC: Windhoek 00 264 61 274800
www.britishhighcommission.gov.uk/namibia

Nepal
E: Kathmandu 00 977 1 441 0583/1281/1590/4588
www.britishembassy.gov.uk/nepal

Netherlands
E: The Hague 00 31 70 427 0427   *www.britain.nl*
CG: Amsterdam 00 31 20 676 4343
C: Willemstad (Curacao) 00 599 9 747 3322

New Zealand
HC: Wellington 00 64 4 924 2888   *www.britain.org.nz*
CG: Auckland 00 64 9 303 2973
C: Christchurch 00 64 3 337 9933

Nigeria
HC: Abuja 00 234 9 413 2010/2011/3885-7
www.ukinnigeria.com
DHC: Lagos 00 234 1 261 9531/9537/9541/9543

Norway
E: Oslo 00 47 2313 2700   *www.britain.no*
C: Alesund 00 47 7011 7500
C: Bergen 00 47 5536 7810
C: Bodo 00 47 7556 5800
C: Kristiansand 00 47 3812 2070
C: Stavanger 00 47 5152 9713
C: Tromso 00 47 7762 4500
C: Trondheim 00 47 7360 0200

Oman
E: Muscat 00 968 609000
www.britishembassy.gov.uk/oman

Pakistan
HC: Islamabad 00 92 51 201 2000
www.britishhighcommission.gov.uk/pakistan
DHC: Karachi 00 92 21 582 7000
C: Lahore 00 92 04263 16589/90

Panama
E: Panama City 00 507 269 0866
www.britishembassy.gov.uk/panama

Papua New Guinea
HC: Port Moresby 00 675 325 1677
www.britishhighcommission.gov.uk/papuanewguinea

Paraguay
HONC: Asunción 00 595 21 210 405
E: Buenos Aires 00 54 11 4808 2200   *www.britain.org.ar*

Peru
E: Lima 00 51 1 617 3000   *www.britemb.org.pe*
C: Arequipa 00 51 54 241 340
C: Cusco 00 51 84 226671/239974
C: Trujillo 00 51 44 245935

Philippines
E: Manila 00 63 2 816 7116
www.britishembassy.gov.uk/philippines
C: Angeles City 00 63 45 323 4187
C: Cebu 00 63 32 346 0525
C: Olongapo 00 63 47 252 2222

Poland
E: Warsaw 00 48 22 311 0000   *www.britishembassy.pl*
C: Gdansk 00 48 58 341 4365
C: Katowice 00 48 32 206 9801
C: Krakow 00 48 12 421 7030
C: Lodz 00 48 42 631 18 18
C: Lublin 00 48 81 742 0101
C: Poznan 00 48 61 665 8850
C: Szczecin 00 48 91 487 0302
C: Wroclaw 00 48 71 344 8961

Portugal
E: Lisbon 00 351 21 392 4000   *www.uk-embassy.pt*
C: Oporto 00 351 22 618 4789
C: Portimao 00 351 282 490 750
HONC: Azores 00 351 296 628 175

Qatar
E: Doha 00 974 442 1991
www.britishembassy.gov.uk/qatar

Romania
E: Bucharest 00 40 21 201 7200
www.britishembassy.gov.uk/romania

Russia
E: Moscow 00 7 095 956 7200   *www.britaininrussia.ru*
CG: St Petersburg 00 7 812 320 3200   *www.britain.spb.ru*

Rwanda
E: Kigali 00 250 584098, 585771, 585773
www.britishembassykigali.org.rw

St Kitts and Nevis
HC: Basseterre 001 268 462 0008/9

St Lucia
HC: Castries 001 758 45 22484/5

St Vincent
HC: Kingstown 001 784 457 1701

Samoa
HC: Apia 00 64 4 924 2888

San Marino
CG: Florence 00 39 055 284133

São Tomé and Principe
C: São Tomé 00 239 12 21026/7

Saudi Arabia
E: Riyadh 00 966 1 488 0077
www.britishembassy.gov.uk/saudiarabia
CG: Jeddah 00 966 2 622 5550

Senegal
E: Dakar 00 221 823 7392/9971
www.britishembassy.gov.uk/senegal

Serbia and Montenegro
E: Belgrade 00 381 11 3060 900
www.britishembassy.gov.uk

Seychelles
HC: Victoria 00 248 283666   *www.bhcvictoria.sc*

Sierra Leone
HC: Freetown 00 232 22 232 961/362/563-5
www.britishhighcommission.gov.uk/sierraleone

Singapore
HC: 00 65 6424 4200   *www.britain.org.sg*
C: Singapore 00 65 6473 1111

Slovakia
E: Bratislava 00 421 2 5998 2000
www.britishembassy.sk

Slovenia
E: Ljubljana 00 386 1 200 3910   *www.british-embassy.si*

Solomon Islands
HC: Honiara 00 677 21705/6

Somalia
E: Mogadishu 00 252 1 20288/9

South Africa
HC: Pretoria 00 27 12 421 7500   *www.britain.org.za*
CG: Cape Town 00 27 21 405 2400
C: Durban 00 27 31 202 6823
C: Port Elizabeth 00 27 41 363 8841

Spain
E: Madrid 00 34 91 700 8200   *www.ukinspain.com*
CG: Barcelona 00 34 93 366 6200
C: Bilbao 00 34 94 415 7600/7711/7722
C: Alicante 00 34 96 521 6022
C: Las Palmas, Canary Islands 00 34 928 262 508
C: Málaga 00 34 95 235 23 00
C: Palma 00 34 971 712445, 712085, 716048, 718501, 712696

c: Santa Cruz de Tenerife, Canary Islands
00 34 922 28 6863/6653
c: Santander 00 34 942 220000
c: Vigo 00 34 986 437133
vc: Ibiza 00 34 971 30 1818
vc: Menorca 00 34 971 367818

Sri Lanka
HC: Colombo 00 94 11 2 437336/43
www.britishhighcommission.gov.uk/srilanka

Sudan
E: Khartoum 00 249 11 777105
www.britishembassy.gov.uk/sudan

Suriname
c: Paramaribo 00 597 402 558/870

Sweden
E: Stockholm 00 46 8 671 3000 *www.britishembassy.se*
CG: Gothenburg 00 46 31 339 3300
c: Sundsvall 00 46 60 164000

Switzerland
E: Berne 00 41 31 359 7700 *www.britishembassy.ch*
CG: Geneva 00 41 22 918 2400
vc: Basel 00 41 61 483 0977
vc: Lugano 00 41 91 950 0606
vc: Montreux/Vevey 00 41 21 943 3263
vc: Valais 00 41 27 480 3210
vc: Zurich 00 41 1 383 6560

Syria
E: Damascus 00 963 11 373 9241-3/7
c: Aleppo 00 963 21 267 2200

Tajikistan
E: Dushanbe 00 992 372 24 22 21/24 14 77
www.britishembassy.gov.uk/tajikistan

Tanzania
HC: Dar es Salaam 00 255 22 211 0101
www.britishhighcommission gov.uk/tanzania

Thailand
c: Aleppo 00 963 21 267 2200

Togo
E: Dushanbe 00 992 372 24 22 21/24 14 77
www.britishembassy.gov.uk/tajikistan

Trinidad and Tobago
HC: Port of Spain 001 868 6 222748/81234/81068
www.britishhighcommission.gov.uk

Tunisia
E: Tunis 00 216 7110 8700
www.britishembassy.gov.uk/tunisia
Honc: Fax 00 216 7422 3971

Turkey
F: Ankara 00 90 312 455 3344 *www.britishembassy.org.tr*
vc: Antalya 00 90 242 244 5313
cg· Istanbul 00 90 212 334 6400
c: Bodrum 00 90 252 319 0093/4
c: Izmir 00 90 232 463 5151
c: Marmaris 00 90 252 412 6486

Turkmenistan
E: Ashgabat 00 993 12 363462-4
www.britishembassy.gov.uk/turkmenistan

Uganda
HC: Kampala 00 256 31 312000 *www.britain.or.ug*

Ukraine
E: Kiev 00 380 44 490 3660 *www.britemb-ukraine.net*

United Arab Emirates
E: Abu Dhabi 00 971 2 610 1100
www.britishembassy.gov.uk/uae
E: Dubai 00 971 4 309 4444

United States
E: Washington 00 1 202 588 6500 *www.britainusa.com*
CG: Atlanta 00 1 404 954 7700
CG: Boston 00 1 617 245 4500
CG: Chicago 00 1 312 970 3800
CG: Houston 00 1 713 659 6270
CG: Los Angeles 00 1 310 481 0031
CG: New York 00 1 212 745 0200
CG: San Francisco 00 1 415 617 1300
c: Anchorage 00 1 907 786 4848
c: Charlotte 00 1 704 383 4359
c: Denver 00 1 303 592 5200
c: Kansas City 00 1 913 469 9786
c: Miami 00 1 305 374 1522
c: Nashville 00 1 615 743 3061
c: New Orleans 00 1 504 524 4180
c: Philadelphia 00 1 215 557 7665
c: Pittsburgh 00 1 412 624 4200
c: Portland 00 1 503 227 5669
c: Puerto Rico 00 1 787 758 9828
c: Salt Lake City 00 1 801 297 6922
c: San Diego 00 1 619 459 8231
c: Seattle 00 1 206 622 9255
c: Orlando 00 1 407 581 1540

Uruguay
E: Montevideo 00 598 2 622 3630/50
www.britishembassy.org.uy

Uzbekistan
E: Tashkent 00 99871 120 6451/6288/7852-4
www.britain.uz

Vanuatu
HC: Suva 00 679 3229100
www.britishhighcommission.gov.uk/fiji

Venezuela
E: Caracas 00 58 212 263 8411 *www.britain.org.ve*
c: Maracaibo 00 58 2 61 797 7003
c: Margarita 00 0295 257 05 18
c: Mérida 00 0274 417 37 46
c: San Cristobal 00 58 276 356 67 32

Vietnam
E: Hanoi 00 84 4 936 0500 *www.uk-vietnam.org*
CG: Ho Chi Minh City 00 84 8 829 8433

Yemen
E: Sana'a 00 967 1 264081-4
www.britishembassy.gov.uk/yemen
c: Hodeidah 00 967 3 238130/1

Zambia
HC: Lusaka 00 260 1 251133
www.britishhighcommission.gov.uk/zambia

Zimbabwe
E: Harare 00 263 4 772990
www.britishembassy.gov.uk/zimbabwe

》WEBSITES
Where a website is not listed, visit
www.britishembassy.gov.uk for a country list

435

Arts

Government departments

Culture, Media and Sport
020 7211 6200
www.culture.gov.uk
Press: 020 7211 6145

Arts councils

Arts Council England
0845 300 6200
www.artscouncil.org.uk
Press: 020 7973 6459

Arts Council for Northern Ireland
028 9038 5200
www.artscouncil-ni.org
Press: 028 9038 5210

Arts Council of Wales
029 2037 6500
www.artswales.org.uk
Press: 029 2037 6506

British Council
0161 957 7755
www.britishcouncil.org
Press: 020 7389 4939

Design Council
020 7420 5200
www.design-council.org.uk
Press: 020 7420 5248

Scottish Arts Council
0131 226 6051
www.scottisharts.org.uk
Press: 0131 240 2404

UK Film Council
020 7861 7861
www.ukfilmcouncil.org.uk
Press: 020 7861 7508

Galleries and museums

24 Hour Museum
01273 820044
www.24hourmuseum.org.uk

Ashmolean Museum, Oxford
01865 278000
www.ashmolean.org
Press: 01865 288298

Association of Independent Museums
023 9258 7751
www.museums.org.uk/aim

British Library
0870 444 1500
www.bl.uk
Press: 020 7412 7110

British Museum
020 7323 8000
www.thebritishmuseum.ac.uk
Press: 020 7323 8583

Gallery of Modern Art, Glasgow
0141 229 1996
www.glasgowmuseums.com

Geffrye Museum
020 7739 9893
www.geffrye-museum.org.uk

Imperial War Museum
020 7416 5320
www.iwm.org.uk
Press: 020 7416 5311

Institute of Contemporary Arts
020 7930 3647
www.ica.org.uk
Press: 020 7766 1406

Lowry, Salford
0870 787 5780
www.thelowry.com
Press: 0161 876 2044

Modern Art Oxford
01865 722733
www.modernartoxford.org.uk
Press: 01865 813813

Museum of London
0870 444 3852
www.museumoflondon.org.uk
Press: 020 7814 5503

Museums Association
020 7426 6970
www.museumsassociation.org

National Art Collections Fund
020 7225 4800
www.artfund.org
Press: 020 7225 4822

National Galleries of Scotland
0131 624 6200
www.nationalgalleries.org,
www.natgalscot.ac.uk

National Gallery
020 7747 2885
www.nationalgallery.org.uk
Press: 020 7747 2865

National Maritime Museum
020 8858 4422
www.nmm.ac.uk
Press: 020 8312 6790

National Museum and Gallery of Wales
029 2039 7951
www.nmgw.ac.uk

National Museum of Science and Industry
0870 870 4771
www.nmsi.ac.uk
Press: 020 7942 4357

National Museums Liverpool
0151 207 0001
www.liverpoolmuseums.org.uk
Press: 0151 478 4612

National Museums of Scotland
0131 247 4422
www.nms.ac.uk

National Portrait Gallery
020 7306 0055
www.npg.org.uk
Press: 020 7312 2452

Natural History Museum
020 7942 5000
www.nhm.ac.uk
Press: 020 7942 5654

Royal Academy of Arts
020 7300 8000
www.royalacademy.org.uk
Press: 020 7300 5615

Royal College of Art
020 7590 4444
www.rca.ac.uk
Press: 020 7590 4114

Royal Marines Museum
023 9281 9385
www.royalmarinesmuseum.co.uk

Tate
020 7887 8000
www.tate.org.uk
Press: 020 7887 8730

Victoria and Albert Museum
020 7942 2000
www.vam.ac.uk
Press: 020 7942 2502

Performing arts

Almeida Theatre Company
020 7288 4900
www.almeida.co.uk
Press: 020 7292 8330

Barbican Centre
020 7638 4141
www.barbican.org.uk

BBC Proms
proms@bbc.co.uk
www.bbc.co.uk/proms
Press: 020 7765 5575

British Film Institute
020 7255 1444
www.bfi.org.uk
Press: 020 7957 8919

Carling Apollo, Manchester
0161 273 6921
www.getlive.co.uk

Earls Court
020 7385 1200
www.eco.co.uk

Edinburgh Festival Fringe
0131 226 0026
www.edfringe.com
Press: 0131 240 1919

English National Ballet
020 7581 1245
www.ballet.org.uk

English National Opera
020 7836 0111
www.eno.org
Press: 020 7845 9378

Glastonbury Festival
01458 834596
www.glastonburyfestivals.co.uk

Glyndebourne Festival
01273 812321
www.glyndebourne.com
Press: 01273 812321

London Astoria
020 7434 9592
www.meanfiddler.co.uk

Millennium Centre, Cardiff
029 2063 6400
www.wmc.org.uk

NEC, Birmingham
0121 780 4141
www.necgroup.co.uk
Press: 0121 780 2828

Ronnie Scott's
020 7439 0747
www.ronniescotts.co.uk
Royal Academy of Dance
020 7326 8000
www.rad.org.uk
Press: 020 7326 8003/8044
Royal Albert Hall
020 7589 3203
www.royalalberthall.com
Royal Ballet School
020 7836 8899
www.royal-ballet-school.org.uk
Press: 020 7845 7073
Royal College of Music
020 7589 3643
www.rcm.ac.uk
Press: 020 7591 4372
Royal Concert Hall, Glasgow
0141 353 8080
www.grch.com
Press: 0141 353 8016
Royal National Theatre
020 7452 3333
www.nt-online.org
Press: 020 7452 3235
Royal Opera House, Covent Garden
020 7240 1200
www.royaloperahouse.org
Royal Shakespeare Company
01789 296655
www.rsc.org.uk
Sage, Gateshead
0191 443 4666
www.thesagegateshead.org
Press: 0191 443 4613
South Bank Centre
020 7921 0600
www.rfh.org.uk
Theatres Trust
020 7836 8591
www.theatrestrust.org.uk
Wembley Arena
020 8902 8833
www.livenation.co.uk/wembley
Press: 020 8585 3536

History and heritage

Alexandra Palace and Park
020 8365 2121
www.alexandrapalace.com
Press: 020 8365 4328
Ancient Monuments Society
office@
ancientmonumentssociety.org.uk
www.ancientmonumentssociety
.org.uk
Architectural Heritage Fund
020 7925 0199
www.ahfund.org.uk
British Archaeological Association
www.britarch.ac.uk/baa
Civic Trust
020 7539 7900
www.civictrust.org.uk
Council for British Archaeology
01904 671417
www.britarch.ac.uk

English Heritage
0870 333 1181
www.english-heritage.org.uk
Press: 020 7973 3250
Garden History Society
020 7608 2409
www.gardenhistorysociety.org
Historic Royal Palaces
020 8781 9750
www.hrp.org.uk
Press: 020 3166 6166
Banqueting House
0870 751 5178
Hampton Court Palace
0870 752 7777
Kensington Palace State Apartments
0870 751 5170
Kew Palace and Queen Charlotte's Cottage
0870 751 5179
Tower of London
0870 756 6060
Historical Diving Society
enquiries@thehds.com
www.thehds.com
Historical Metallurgy Society
01792 233223
http://hist-met.org
Institute of Historic Building Conservation
01747 873133
www.ihbc.org.uk
International Council on Monuments & Sites in UK
020 7566 0031
www.icomos.org/uk
Jewish Historical Society of Britain
020 7723 5852
www.jhse.org
Keltek Trust
bells@keltek.org
www.keltek.org
Church bell preservation society
Landmark Trust
01628 825920
www.landmarktrust.org.uk
National Archives
020 8876 3444
www.nationalarchives.gov.uk
Press: 020 8392 5277
National Association of Decorative & Fine Arts Associations
020 7430 0730
www.nadfas.org.uk
National Trust
0870 458 4000
www.nationaltrust.org.uk
Press: 0870 600 2127
National Trust for Scotland
0131 243 9300
www.nts.org.uk
Press: 0131 243 9349
Royal Commission on the Ancient & Historic Monuments of Wales
01970 621200
www.rcahmw.org.uk
Save Britain's Heritage
020 7253 3500
www.savebritainsheritage.org
Scottish Railway Preservation Society
01506 825855
www.srps.org.uk

Society for the Protection of Ancient Buildings
020 7377 1644
www.spab.org.uk
Press: 020 7456 0905
Ulster Architectural Heritage Society
028 9055 0213
www.uahs.co.uk
United Kingdom Institute for Conservation of Historic & Artistic Works
020 7785 3805
www.icon.org.uk
Vivat Trust
0845 090 0194
www.vivat.org.uk

Business

Government departments

Treasury
020 7270 4558
www.hm-treasury.gov.uk
Press: 020 7270 5238
Trade and Industry
020 7215 5000
www.dti.gov.uk
Press: 020 7215 5961/5967/6405
Work and Pensions
020 7238 0800
www.dwp.gov.uk
Press: 020 7238 0866

Central banks

Bank of England
020 7601 4444
www.bankofengland.co.uk
Press: 020 7601 4411
European Central Bank
00 49 69 13440
www.ecb.int

Businesses

● Business associations

Trade Association Forum
020 7395 8283
www.taforum.org
Confederation of British Industry
020 7379 7400
www.cbi.org.uk
Press: 020 7395 8239
Ethnic Minority Business Forum
embf@sbs.gsi.gov.uk
www.ethnicbusiness.org
Federation of Small Businesses
01253 336000
www.fsb.org.uk
Press: 020 75928128

● FTSE 100 companies

3i Group
020 7928 3131
www.3i.com
Press: 020 7975 3573
Alliance & Leicester
0116 201 1000
www.alliance-leicester-group.co.uk
Press: 0116 200 3355
Alliance Boots
01932 870550
www.alliance-unichem.com
Press: 01932 870 550
Amvescap
020 7638 0731
www.amvescap.com
Press: 00 1 404 479 2886
Anglo American
020 7968 8888
www.angloamerican.co.uk
Press: 020 7698 8555

Antofagasta
020 7808 0988
www.antofagasta.co.uk
Associated British Foods
020 7399 6500
www.abf.co.uk
AstraZeneca
01582 836000
www.astrazeneca.co.uk
Aviva
020 7283 2000
www.aviva.com
Press: 020 7662 8221
BAE Systems
01252 373232
www.baesystems.com
Press: 01252 384605
Barclays
020 7699 5000
www.barclays.co.uk
Press: 020 7116 64755
BG Group
0118 935 3222
www.bg-group.com
Press: 0118 929 3717
BHP Billiton
020 7802 4000
www.bhpbilliton.com
Press: 020 7802 4177
BOC Group
01276 477222
www.boc.com
Press: 01276 807594
BP
020 7496 4000
www.bp.com
Press: 020 7496 4076
Brambles
020 7659 6000
www.brambles.com
British Airways
0870 850 9850
www.britishairways.com
Press: 020 8738 5100
British American Tobacco
020 7845 1000
www.bat.com
Press: 020 7845 2888
British Energy Group
01452 652222
www.british-energy.com
Press: 01452 652233
British Land
020 7486 4466
www.britishland.com
Press: 020 7467 2899
BSkyB
0870 240 3000
www.sky.com
Press: 0870 240 3000
BT Group
020 7356 5000
www.btplc.com
Press - national: 020 7356 5369
Cadbury Schweppes
020 7409 1313
www.cadburyschweppes.com
Press:020 7830 5011

Cairn Energy
0131 475 3000
www.cairn-energy.plc.uk
Capita Group
020 7799 1525
www.capita.co.uk
Press: 0870 240 0488
Carnival
00 1 305 599 2600
www.carnivalcorp.com
Centrica
01753 494000
www.centrica.co.uk
Press: 01753 494085
Compass Group
01932 573000
www.compass-group.com
Press: 01932 573116
Corus Group
020 7717 4444
www.corusgroup.com
Press: 020 7717 4597
Diageo
020 7927 5200
www.diageo.com
Drax Group Plc
01757 618 381
www.draxgroup.plc.uk
DSGI PLC
0870 850 3333
www.dsgiplc.com
Enterprise Inns
0121 733 7700
www.enterpriseinns.com
Friends Provident
0870 6071352
www.friendsprovident.co.uk
City and corporate press:
020 7760 3133
Gallaher Group
01932 859777
www.gallaher-group.com
Press: 01932 832531
Glaxo SmithKline
020 8047 5000
www.gsk.com
Press: 020 8047 5502
Gus
020 7495 0070
www.gus.co.uk
Press: 020 7251 3801
Hammerson
020 7887 1000
www.hammerson.com
Press: 020 7887 1881
Hanson
020 7245 1245
www.hansonplc.com
Press: 01454 316000
HBOS
0870 600 5000
www.hbosplc.com
Press - general:
pressoffice@HBOSplc.com
Bank of Scotland:
0131 243 7195, 0845 606 6696
Bank of Scotland corporate:
0845 606 6696
Halifax: 01422 333253

HSBC
020 7991 8888
www.hsbc.com
Press: 020 7992 1573
ICAP
020 7000 5000
www.icap.com
ICI
020 7009 5000
www.ici.com
Press: 020 7009 5000
Imperial Tobacco
0117 963 6636
www.imperial-tobacco.com
Press: 0117 933 7241
Intercontinental Hotel Group
01753 410100
www.intercontinental.com
International Power
020 7320 8600
www.ipplc.com
ITV
020 7843 8000
www.itv.com
Press: 020 7620 1620
J Sainsbury
020 7695 6000
www.j-sainsbury.co.uk
Press: 020 7695 7295
Johnson Matthey
020 7269 8400
www.matthey.com
Press: 020 7269 8410
Kazakhmys
0845 080 2369
www.kazakhmys.com
Kelda Group
01274 600 111
www.keldagroup.com
Press: 01274 692954
Kingfisher
020 7372 8008
www.kingfisher.co.uk
Press: 020 7644 1030
Land Securities Group
020 7413 9000
www.landsecurities.co.uk
Press: 020 7024 5462
Legal & General Group
020 7528 6200
www.legalandgeneral.com
Press: 01737 375353/375351
Liberty International
020 7960 1200
www.liberty-international.co.uk
Press: 020 7887 7029
Lloyds TSB
020 7626 1500
www.lloydstsb.com
Press: 020 7356 2493
Lonmin
020 7201 6000
www.lonmin.com
Press: 020 7201 6060
Man Group
020 7144 1000
www.mangroupplc.com
Press: 020 7653 6620
Marks & Spencer
020 7935 4422
www.marksandspencer.com
Press: 020 7268 1919
Morrison Supermarkets
01274 356000
www.morereasons.co.uk
Press: 01274 356807

National Grid Transco
01926 653000
www.nationalgrid.com/uk
Press: 01926 656536
Next
0845 600 7333
www.next.co.uk
Press: 0116 284 2503
Northern Rock
0845 600 8401
www.northernrock.co.uk
Press: 0191 279 4676
Old Mutual
020 7002 7000
www.oldmutual.com
Press: 020 7002 7133
PartyGaming
00 350 78700
www.partygaming.com
Press: 020 7337 0100
Pearson
020 7010 2000
www.pearson.com
Press - general: 020 7825 8076
corporate: 020 7010 2314/07
FT Group: 020 7873 4447
Pearson Education: 00 1 212 782 3482
Penguin UK: 020 7010 3000
Persimmon
01904 642199
www.persimmon.plc.uk
Prudential
020 7220 7588
www.prudential.co.uk
Press - general: 020 7548 3719
Egg: 020 7526 2600
M&G: 020 7548 3222
UK insurance: 020 7150 2203
Reckitt Benckiser
01753 217800
www.reckitt.com
Reed Elsevier
020 7930 7077
www.r-e.com
Press - general: 020 7166 5657/46
business publishing: 020 8652 3296
educational: 00 1 407 345 3987
legal: 00 1 937 865 8838
science and medical:
00 31 20 485 2736
Rentokil Initial
01342 833022
www.rentokil-initial.co.uk
Press: 01342 830274
Reuters Group
020 7250 1122
www.reuters.com
Press: 020 7542 8404
Rexam
020 7227 4100
www.rexam.com
Press: 020 7227 4141
Rio Tinto
020 7930 2399
www.riotinto.com
Press: 020 7753 2305
Rolls Royce
020 7222 9020
www.rolls-royce.com
Royal & Sun Alliance
01403 232323
www.royalsunalliance.com
Press - UK: 020 7337 5146
world: 020 7111 7047

Royal Bank of Scotland
020 7250 1122
www.rbs.co.uk
Press - general: 0131 523 4414
corporate banking and financial
markets: 0131 523 4414
Coutts: 020 7957 2427
Direct Line: 0141 308 4100
Lombard: 020 7672 1921
NatWest: 020 7672 1932/31/27
One Account: 01603 707154
RBS: 020 7672 1928
RBS cards: 020 7672 5086
RBS insurance: 0845 878 2367
Ulster Bank: 00 353 1 608 4573
Royal Dutch Shell
020 7934 1234
www.shell.com
Press: 020 7934 3505
SABMiller
020 7659 0100
www.sab.co.za
Press: 01483 264156
Sage Group
0191 294 3000
www.sage.co.uk
Press: 0191 294 3036
Schroders
020 7658 6000
www.schroders.com
Press: 020 7658 6000
Scottish & Newcastle
0131 528 2000
www.scottish-newcastle.com
Press: 0131 528 2131
Scottish & Southern Energy
0845 143 4005
www.scottish-southern.co.uk
Scottish Power
0845 272 7111
www.scottishpower.plc.uk
Press: 0141 636 4515
Severn Trent
0121 722 4000
www.stwater.co.uk
Press - general: 0121 722 4273
Biffa: 01494 521 221
Severn Trent Water: 0121 722 4121
**Slough Estates Shire
Pharmaceuticals**
01256 894 000
www.shiregroup.com
Press: 01256 894280
Smith & Nephew
020 7401 7646
www.smith-nephew.com
Press: 020 7831 3113
Smiths Group
020 8458 3232
www.smiths-group.com
Press: 020 8457 8403
Standard Chartered
020 7280 7500
www.standardchartered.com
Press: 020 7280 7708
Tate & Lyle
020 7626 6525
www.tateandlyle.com
Press: 020 7977 6143
Tesco
01992 632222
www.tesco.com
Press: 01992 644 645

Unilever
020 7822 5252
www.unilever.co.uk
Press: 020 7822 5252

United Utilities
01925 237 000
www.unitedutilities.com
Press: 01925 537 366

Vedanta Resources
020 7499 5900
www.vedantaresources.com

Vodafone
01635 33251
www.vodafone.co.uk
Press - group: 01635 674268
UK: 07000 500100

Wolseley
0118 929 8700
www.wolseley.com

WPP Group
020 7408 2204
www.wpp.com
Press: 020 7408 2204

Xstrata
020 7968 2800
www.xstrata.com
Press: 020 7968 2812

Yell Group
0118 959 2111
www.yellgroup.com
Press: 0118 950 6999

Watchdogs

● Regulators and government agencies

Advertising Standards Authority
020 7492 2222
www.asa.org.uk
Press: 020 7492 2123
      020 7492 2222

British and Irish Ombudsman Association
020 8894 9272
www.bioa.org.uk

British Board of Film Classification
020 7440 1570
www.bbfc.co.uk
Press: 020 7440 3285

British Standards Institution
020 8996 9000
www.bsi-global.com
Press: 020 8996 6330

Competition Commission
020 7271 0100
www.competition-commission.org.uk
Press: 020 7271 0242

Council of Mortgage Lenders
020 7437 0075
www.cml.org.uk

Financial Ombudsman Service
020 7964 1000
www.financial-ombudsman.org.uk

Financial Services Authority
020 7066 1000
www.fsa.gov.uk

Food Standards Agency
020 7276 8000
www.foodstandards.gov.uk

Health and Safety Executive
0845 345 0055
www.hse.gov.uk

Health and Safety Executive for Northern Ireland
0800 0320 121
028 9024 3249
www.hseni.gov.uk

Independent Committee for the Supervision of Telephone Information Services
020 7940 7474
www.icstis.org.uk
Press: 020 7940 7408

Information Commissioner
01625 545 745
www.ico.gov.uk
Press: 020 7025 7580

National Lottery Commission
020 7016 3400
www.natlotcomm.gov.uk
Press: 020 7016 3430

Ofcom
020 7981 3000
www.ofcom.org.uk
Press: 020 7981 3033

Office of Fair Trading
08457 224499
www.oft.gov.uk

Office of the Rail Regulator
020 7282 2000
www.rail-reg.gov.uk
Press: 020 7282 2007

Ofgem
020 7901 7000
www.ofgas.gov.uk/ofgem
Press: 020 7901 7158

Ofwat
0121 625 1300/1373
www.ofwat.gov.uk
Press: 0121 625 1442

Ombudsman for Estate Agents
01722 333306
www.oea.co.uk

Pensions Ombudsman
020 7834 9144
www.pensions-ombudsman.org.uk

Serious Fraud Office
020 7239 7272
www.sfo.gov.uk

Small Business Service
020 7215 5000
www.sbs.gov.uk

Trading Standards Institute
0870 872 9000
www.tsi.org.uk
Press: 0870 872 9030

● Consumer bodies

Which?
020 7770 7000
0845 307 4000
www.which.net/corporate
Press: 020 7770 7062/7373

General Consumer Council for Northern Ireland
028 9067 2488
www.gccni.org.uk

National Association of Citizens Advice Bureaux
020 7833 7000
www.adviceguide.org.uk

National Consumer Council
020 7730 3469
www.ncc.org.uk

Scottish Consumer Council
0141 226 5261
www.scotconsumer.org.uk

Welsh Consumer Council
029 2025 5454
www.wales-consumer.org.uk

Employment

● Employment bodies

Employment Tribunals
Enquiry line: 0845 795 9775
www.employmenttribunals.gov.uk

Equal Opportunities Commission (EOC)
020 7222 0004
www.eoc.org.uk

Equality Commission for Northern Ireland
028 9050 0600
www.equalityni.org

Investors in People UK
020 7467 1900
www.iipuk.co.uk

Labour Relations Agency
028 9032 1442
www.lra.org.uk

Low Pay Commission
020 7467 7207
www.lowpay.gov.uk
Press: 020 7467 7279

Pay & Employment Rights Service
01924 439587
www.pers.org.uk

● Unions

Trades Union Congress
020 7636 4030
www.tuc.org.uk

Abbey National Group Union
01442 891122
www.angu.org.uk

Accord
0118 934 1808
www.accord-myunion.org
HBDS Group employees

Alliance and Leicester Group Union of Staff
0116 285 6585
www.algus.org.uk

Amicus
020 8462 7755
www.amicustheunion.org
Manufacturing, technical and skilled workers

Aslef
020 7317 8600
www.aslef.org.uk
Associated Society of Locomotive Engineers and Firemen
Press: 020 7317 8607

Aspect
01226 383420
www.aspect.org.uk

Association for College Management
01858 461 110
www.acm.uk.com

Association of Educational Psychologists
0191 384 9512
www.aep.org.uk

Association of Flight Attendants
001 202 434 1300
www.afanet.org

Association of Magisterial Officers
020 7403 2244
www.amo-online.org.uk

Association of Teachers and Lecturers
020 7930 6441
www.askatl.org.uk
Press: 020 7782 1589

Association of University Teachers
020 7670 9700
www.aut.org.uk

Bakers, Food and Allied Workers Union
01707 260150
www.bfawu.org

Britannia Staff Union
01538 399627
www.britanniasu.org.uk

British Air Line Pilots Association
020 8476 4000
www.balpa.org.uk
Press: 020 7924 7555

British and Irish Orthoptic Society
020 7387 7992
www.orthoptics.org.uk

British Association of Colliery Management – Technical, Energy and Administrative Management
01302 815551
www.bacmteam.org.uk

British Dietetic Association
0121 200 8080
www.bda.uk.com
Press: 01626 362473

Broadcasting, Entertainment, Cinematograph and Theatre Union
020 7346 0900
www.bectu.org.uk

Card Setting Machine Tenters Society
01924 400206

Ceramic and Allied Trades Union
01782 272755
www.catu.org.uk

Chartered Society of Physiotherapy
020 7306 6666
www.csp.org.uk
Press: 020 7306 6163

Communication Workers Union
020 8971 7200
www.cwu.org

Community and District Nursing Association
020 8231 0180
www.cdna.tvu.ac.uk

Community and Youth Workers' Union
0121 244 3344
www.cywu.org.uk

Connect
020 8971 6000
www.connectuk.org
Communications professionals
Press: 020 8971 6027

Diageo Staff Association
020 8978 6069
Staff grades at Diageo, including Guinness, in the UK

Educational Institute of Scotland
0131 225 6244
www.eis.org.uk

Equity
020 7379 6000
www.equity.org.uk
Performers and artists
Press: 020 7670 0259

FDA
020 7343 1111
www.fda.org.uk
Senior managers and professionals in public service
Press: 020 7343 1121

Fire Brigades Union
020 8541 1765
www.fbu.org.uk

General Union of Loom Overlookers
01254 51760

GMB
020 8947 3131
www.gmb.org.uk
General union
Press: 020 8971 4224

Hospital Consultants and Specialists Association
01256 771777
www.hcsa.com

ISTC
020 7239 1200
www.istc-tu.org
Steel and metal industry and communities

Musicians' Union
020 7840 5504
www.musiciansunion.org.uk

NASUWT
0121 453 6150
www.nasuwt.org.uk
National Association of Schoolmasters Union of Women Teachers

NATFHE
020 7837 3636
www.natfhe.org.uk
University and college lecturers

National Association of Colliery Overmen, Deputies and Shotfirers
01226 203743
www.nacods.co.uk

National Association of Cooperative Officials
0161 351 7900

National Association of Probation Officers
020 7223 4887
www.napo.org.uk

National Union of Domestic Appliances and General Operatives
020 7387 2578
www.gftu.org.uk

National Union of Journalists
020 7278 7916
www.nuj.org.uk

National Union of Knitwear, Footwear and Apparel Trades
020 7239 1200
www.kfat.org.uk
Manufacturing, retail and logistics

National Union of Lock and Metal Workers
01902 366651

National Union of Marine, Aviation and Shipping Transport Officers
020 8989 6677
www.numast.org

National Union of Mineworkers
01226 215555
www.num.org.uk

National Union of Teachers
020 7388 6191
www.teachers.org.uk

Nationwide Group Staff Union
01295 710767
www.ngsu.org.uk

Prison Officers Association
020 8803 0255
www.poauk.org.uk

Professional Footballers' Association
0161 236 0575
www.givemefootball.com

Prospect
020 7902 6600
www.prospect.org.uk
Engineers, scientists, managers and specialists

Public and Commercial Services Union
020 7924 2727
www.pcs.org.uk
Press: 020 7801 2820

RMT
020 7387 4771
www.rmt.org.uk
Rail, maritime and transport workers
Press: 020 7529 8803

Society of Chiropodists and Podiatrists
0845 450 3720
www.feetforlife.org

Society of Radiographers
020 7740 7200
www.sor.org

Transport and General Workers' Union
020 7611 2500
www.tgwu.org.uk
Press: 020 7611 2555

Transport Salaried Staffs' Association
020 7387 2101
www.tssa.org.uk

UBAC
01653 697634
Staff at Bradford and Bingley Group and Alltel Mortgage Solutions

UCAC National Union of Welsh Teachers
01970 639950
www.athrawon.com

Union of Construction, Allied Trades and Technicians
020 7622 2442
www.ucatt.org.uk
Press: 020 7622 2422

Union of Shop, Distributive and Allied Workers
0161 224 2804/249 2400
www.usdaw.org.uk

Unison
0845 355 0845
www.unison.org.uk
Public service union

Writers' Guild of Great Britain
020 7833 0777
www.writersguild.org.uk

Yorkshire Independent Staff Association
01274 472453
www.ybs.co.uk

Diversity

Media diversity associations

Age Concern
Astral House, 1268 London Road,
London SW16 4ER
020 8765 7200
ace@ace.org.uk
www.ageconcern.co.uk

Age Positive
Department for Work and Pensions,
Room W8d, Moorfoot,
Sheffield S1 4PQ
Press: 020 7299 8757
agepositive@dwp.gsi.gov.uk
www.agepositive.gov.uk/
Age diversity in employment

Bird's Eye View
Unit 310A, Aberdeen Centre,
22–24 Highbury Grove,
London N5 2EA
020 7288 7444
rosiestrang@birds-eye-view.co.uk
www.birds-eye-view.co.uk
Platform for emerging female film-makers

Employers' Forum on Disability
Broadcaster and Creative Industries
Disability Network, Nutmeg House,
60 Gainsford Street,
London SE1 2NY
020 7403 3020
jenny.stevens@
    employers-forum.co.uk
www.employers-forum.co.uk
Employers' organisation

Commission for Racial Equality (CRE)
St Dunstan's House,
201–211 Borough High Street,
London SE1 1GZ
020 7939 0000
info@cre.gov.uk
www.cre.gov.uk

The Creative Collective
The Business Design Centre,
Suite Forum P, 52 Upper Street,
Islington, London N1 0QH
020 7359 3535
info@thecreativecollective.com
www.thecreativecollective.com
Aims to develop social policy on diversity and to empower community groups to harness media

Cultural Diversity Network (CDN)
c/o ITV, London Television Centre,
Upper Ground, London SE1 9LT
020 7261 3006
cdnetwork@itv.com
www.itv.com
Online directory of black, Asian and other ethnic minority TV freelancers and staff

Digital Media Access Group
Applied Computing,
University of Dundee,
Dundee DD1 4HN
01382 345050
dmag@computing.dundee.ac.uk
www.dmag.org.uk
Promotes new media accessibility

Disability Rights Commission
Freepost MID02164,
Stratford upon Avon CV37 9BR
0845 762 2633
enquiry@drc-gb.org
www.drc-gb.org

Emma Awards
67–69 Whitfield Street,
London W1T 4HF
020 7636 1233
mail@emma.tv
www.emma.tv
Multicultural media awards and online humanitarian information portal

Equal Opportunities Commission
Arndale House, Arndale Centre,
Manchester M4 3EQ
0845 601 5901
info@eoc.org.uk
www.eoc.org.uk

International Association of Women in Radio and Television
nik@netactive.co.za
www.iawrt.org

International Women's Media Foundation
1625K Street NW, Suite 1275,
Washington, DC 20006, USA
00 1 202 496 1992
info@iwmf.org
www.iwmf.org

Ligali
PO Box 1257, London E5 0UD
020 8986 1984
mail@ligali.org
www.ligali.org
African British equality organisation

MediaWise Trust
38 Easton Business Centre,
Felix Road, Bristol BS5 0HE
0117 941 5889
pw@mediawise.org.uk
www.mediawise.org.uk
Independent media ethics charity

Society of Women Writers & Journalists
Calvers Farm, Thelveton,
Diss IP21 4NG
01379 740 550
zoe@zoeking.com
www.swwj.co.uk

Women and Equality Unit
1 Victoria Street, London SW1H 0ET
0207 215 5000
info-womenandequalityunit@
    dti.gsi.gov.uk
www.womenandequalityunit.gov.uk

Women in Film and Television
6 Langley Street, London WC2H 9JA
020 7240 4875
angela@wftv.org.uk
www.wftv.org.uk

Women in Publishing
c/o Multilingual Matters,
Channel View Publications,
Frankfurt Lodge, Clevedon Hall,
Victoria Road, Clevedon BS21 7HH
info@wipub.org.uk
www.wipub.org.uk

Women's Radio Group
27 Bath Road, London W4 1LJ
020 8995 5442
wrg@zelo.demon.co.uk
www.womeninradio.org.uk
Training, info and production facilities

Education

Government department

Education and Skills
0870 000 2288
www.dfes.gov.uk
Press: 020 7925 6789

Government agencies

Adult Learning Inspectorate
024 7671 6600
www.ali.gov.uk
Press: 020 7618 9189
Arts and Humanities Research Board
0117 987 6500
www.ahrb.ac.uk
Council for Science and Technology
020 7215 6518
www.cst.gov.uk
Education and Learning Wales
08456 088 066
www.elwa.ac.uk
Higher Education Funding Council for England (HEFCE)
0117 931 7317
www.hefce.ac.uk
Press: 0117 931 7363/7431
Learning and Skills Council
0870 900 6800
www.lsc.gov.uk
Learning and Skills Development Agency
020 7297 9000
www.lsda.org.uk
Learning and Teaching Scotland
0870 0100 297
www.ltscotland.com
National Grid for Learning
www.ngfl.gov.uk
Ofsted
0845 6404 045
www.ofsted.gov.uk
Press: 020 7421 6617
Qualifications and Curriculum Authority
020 7509 5555
www.qca.org.uk
Press: 020 7509 6789
Quality Assurance Agency for Higher Education
01452 557000
www.qaa.ac.uk
Press: 01452 557074
Scottish Qualifications Authority
0845 279 1000
www.sqa.org.uk
Sector Skills Development Agency
01709 765444
www.ssda.org.uk
Student Loans Company
0800 405010
www.slc.co.uk
Press: 0141 306 2120

Teacher Training Agency (TTA)
0845 600 0991
www.canteach.gov.uk
Ucas
01242 222444
www.ucas.com

Professional bodies

Association of Teachers and Lecturers
020 7930 6441
www.askatl.org.uk
Press: 020 7782 1541
Association of University Administrators
0161 275 2063
www.aua.ac.uk
Association of University Teachers
020 7670 9700
www.aut.org.uk
Press: 020 7782 1589
British Educational Research Association
01625 504062
www.bera.ac.uk
National Association of School-masters Union of Women Teachers
0121 453 6150
www.teachersunion.org.uk
National Union of Students
England: 020 7561 6577
Wales: 029 2068 0070
Scotland: 0131 556 6598
Ireland: 028 9024 4641
www.nus.org.uk
National Union of Teachers
020 7388 6191
www.teachers.org.uk

Associations of schools and universities

1994 Group
01273 678208
www.1994group.ac.uk
16 small and medium-sized universities
Boarding Schools' Association
020 7798 1580
www.boarding.org.uk
Girls' Schools Association
0116 254 1619
www.gsa.uk.com
Independent Schools Association
01799 523619
www.isaschools.org.uk
National Association of Independent Schools and Non-Maintained Special Schools
01904 621243
www.nasschools.org.uk
National Grammar Schools Association
01543 251517
www.ngsa.org.uk

Russell Group
0151 794 2010
www.russellgroup.ac.uk
19 major research-intensive universities, including Oxford and Cambridge
State Boarding Schools' Association
020 7798 1580
www.sbsa.org.uk
Universities UK
020 7419 4111
www.universitiesuk.ac.uk

Voluntary bodies

Afasic
020 7490 9410
www.afasic.org.uk
Speech, language and communication charity
Campaign for Learning
020 7930 1111
www.campaign-for-learning.org.uk
ContinYou
024 7658 8440
www.continyou.org.uk
Learning Through Action
0870 770 7985
www.learning-through-action.org.uk
Life Education Centres
020 7831 9311
www.lifeeducation.org.uk
National Literacy Trust
020 7828 2435
www.literacytrust.org.uk
Press: 020 7828 2435
UFI/Learn Direct
0114 291 5000
www.ufi.com

Universities

Aberdeen, University of
01224 272000
www.abdn.ac.uk
Press: 01224 272014
Abertay Dundee, University of
01382 308080
www.abertay.ac.uk
Aberystwyth - University of Wales
01970 623 111
www.aber.ac.uk
Anglia Polytechnic University
0845 271 3333
www.apu.ac.uk
Aston University, Birmingham
0121 204 3000
www.aston.ac.uk
Bangor - University of Wales
01248 351151
www.bangor.ac.uk
Press: 01248 383 298
Bath Spa University College
01225 875875
www.bathspa.ac.uk

Bath, University of
01225 388388
www.bath.ac.uk
Bell College
01698 283100
www.bell.ac.uk
Birmingham, University of
0121 414 3344
www.bham.ac.uk
Press: 0121 414 6680
Bishop Grossteste College
01522 527347
www.bgc.ac.uk
Bolton, University of
01204 900600
www.bolton.ac.uk
Bournemouth University
01202 524111
www.bournemouth.ac.uk
Bournemouth, Arts Institute at
01202 533011
www.aib.ac.uk
Bradford, University of
01274 232323
www.bradford.ac.uk
Press: 1274 233084
Brighton, University of
01273 600900
www.brighton.ac.uk
Press:
   communications@brighton.ac.uk
Bristol, University of
0117 928 9000
www.bris.ac.uk
Brunel University
01895 274000
www.brunel.ac.uk
Press: 01895 265585
Buckingham Chilterns University College
01494 522141
www.bcuc.ac.uk
Buckingham, University of
01280 814080
www.buckingham.ac.uk
Press: 01280 820338
Cambridge, University of
01223 337733
www.cam.ac.uk
Press: 01223 332300
Christ's College
01223 334900
www.christs.cam.ac.uk
Churchill College
01223 336000
www.chu.cam.ac.uk
Clare College
01223 333200
www.clare.cam.ac.uk
Corpus Christi College
01223 338000
www.corpus.cam.ac.uk
Downing College
01223 334800
www.dow.cam.ac.uk
Emmanuel College
01223 334200
www.emma.cam.ac.uk
Fitzwilliam College
01223 332000
www.fitz.cam.ac.uk

Girton College
01223 338999
www.girton.cam.ac.uk
Gonville & Caius College
01223 332447
www.cai.cam.ac.uk
Homerton College
01223 507111
www.homerton.cam.ac.uk
Hughes Hall
01223 334898
www.hughes.cam.ac.uk
Jesus College
01223 339339
www.jesus.cam.ac.uk
Kings College
01223 331100
www.kings.cam.ac.uk
Lucy Cavendish College
01223 332190
www.lucy-cav.cam.ac.uk
Magdalene College
01223 332100
www.magd.cam.ac.uk
New Hall
01223 762100
www.newhall.cam.ac.uk
Newnham College
01223 335700
www.newn.cam.ac.uk
Pembroke College
01223 338100
www.pem.cam.ac.uk
Peterhouse College
01223 338200
www.pet.cam.ac.uk
Queen's College
01223 335511
www.quns.cam.ac.uk
Robinson College
01223 339100
www.robinson.cam.ac.uk
St Catharine's College
01223 338300
www.caths.cam.ac.uk
St Edmund's College
01223 336250
www.st-edmunds.cam.ac.uk
St John's College
01223 338703
www.joh.cam.ac.uk
Selwyn College
01223 335846
www.sel.cam.ac.uk
Sidney Sussex College
01223 338800
www.sid.cam.ac.uk
Canterbury Christ Church University College
01227 767700
www.cant.ac.uk
Cardiff – University of Wales Institute
029 2041 6070
www.uwic.ac.uk
Cardiff University
029 2087 4000
www.cardiff.ac.uk

Central England in Birmingham, University of
0121 331 5595
www.uce.ac.uk
Press: 0121 331 6738
Central Lancashire, University of
01772 201201
www.uclan.ac.uk
Central School of Speech and Drama
020 7722 8183
www.cssd.ac.uk
City University
020 7040 5060
www.city.ac.uk
Press: 020 7040 8783
Conservatoire for Dance & Drama
020 7387 5101
www.cdd.ac.uk
Coventry University
024 7688 7688
www.coventry.ac.uk
Cumbria Institute of the Arts
01228 400300
www.cumbria.ac.uk
Dartington College of Arts
01803 862224
www.dartington.ac.uk
De Montfort University
0116 255 1551
www.dmu.ac.uk
Derby, University of
01332 590500
www.derby.ac.uk
Dundee, University of
01382 344000
www.dundee.ac.uk
Durham, University of
0191 374 2000
www.dur.ac.uk
East Anglia, University of
01603 456161
www.uea.ac.uk
Press: 01603 592203
East London, University of
020 8223 3000
www.uel.ac.uk
Edge Hill College
01695 575171
www.edgehill.ac.uk
Edinburgh College of Art
0131 221 6000
www.eca.ac.uk
Edinburgh, University of
0131 650 1000
www.ed.ac.uk
Essex, University of
01206 873333
www.essex.ac.uk
Exeter, University of
01392 661000
www.ex.ac.uk
Falmouth, University College
01326 211077
www.falmouth.ac.uk
Glamorgan, University of
0800 716 925
www.glam.ac.uk
Glasgow Caledonian
0141 331 3000
www.caledonian.ac.uk

Glasgow School of Art
0141 353 4500
www.gas.ac.uk
Glasgow, University of
0141 330 2000
www.gla.ac.uk
Gloucestershire, University of
0870 721 0210
www.glos.ac.uk
Goldsmiths College, University of London
020 7919 7171
www.goldsmiths.ac.uk
Greenwich, University of
020 8331 8000
www.gre.ac.uk
Harper Adams University College
01952 820820
www.harper-adams.ac.uk
Heriot-Watt University
0131 449 5111
www.hw.ac.uk
Hertfordshire, University of
01707 284000
www.herts.ac.uk
Press: 01707 286331
Huddersfield, University of
01484 422288
www.hud.ac.uk
Hull, University of
01482 346311
www.hull.ac.uk
Imperial College, London
020 7589 5111
www.ic.ac.uk
Press: 07803 886248
Keele University
01782 621111
www.keele.ac.uk
Kent, University of
01227 764000
www.ukc.ac.uk
Kent Institute of Art & Design
01622 620000
www.kiad.ac.uk
Press: 01622 620164
King's College London
020 7836 5454
www.kcl.ac.uk
Kingston University
020 8457 2000
www.kingston.ac.uk
Press: 020 8517 7952
Lampeter – University of Wales
01570 422351
www.lamp.ac.uk
Lancaster University
01524 65201
www.lancs.ac.uk
Leeds Metropolitan University
0113 283 2600
www.lmu.ac.uk
Leeds, University of
0113 243 1751
www.leeds.ac.uk
Press: 0113 343 4030
Leicester, University of
0116 252 2522
www.le.ac.uk
Lincoln, University of
01522 882000
www.lincoln.ac.uk

Liverpool Hope University College
0151 291 3000
www.hope.ac.uk
Liverpool John Moores University
0151 231 2121
www.livjm.ac.uk
Liverpool, University of
0151 794 2000
www.liv.ac.uk
Press: 0151 794 2247
London Metropolitan University
020 7423 0000
www.londonmet.ac.uk
London School of Economics and Political Science (LSE)
020 7405 7686
www.lse.ac.uk
London – University of the Arts
Camberwell College of Arts
020 7514 6302
www.camberwell.arts.ac.uk
Central St Martin's College of Art & Design
020 7514 7000
www.csm.arts.ac.uk
Chelsea College of Art & Design
020 7514 7751
www.chelsea.arts.ac.uk
London College of Communication
020 7514 6500
www.lcc.arts.ac.uk
London College of Fashion
020 7514 7500
www.fashion.arts.ac.uk
Loughborough University
01509 263171
www.lboro.ac.uk
Luton, University of
01582 734111
www.luton.ac.uk
Manchester Metropolitan University
0161 247 2000
www.mmu.ac.uk
Manchester, University of
0161 306 6000
www.man.ac.uk
Middlesex University
020 8411 5000
www.mdx.ac.uk
Napier University
08452 60 60 40
www.napier.ac.uk
Press: 0131 455 6301
Newcastle upon Tyne, University of
0191 222 6000
www.ncl.ac.uk
Newman College
0121 476 1181
www.newman.ac.uk
Press: 0121 476 1181
Newport – University of Wales
01633 432432
www.newport.ac.uk
North East Wales Institute of Higher Education
01978 290666
www.newi.ac.uk
Press: 01978 293121

Northern School of Contemporary Dance
0113 219 3000
www.nscd.ac.uk
Northumbria, University of
0191 232 6002
www.unn.ac.uk
Press: 0191 227 3477
Norwich School of Art & Design
01603 610561
www.nsad.ac.uk
Nottingham Trent University
0115 941 8418
www.ntu.ac.uk
Nottingham, University of
0115 951 5151
www.nottingham.ac.uk
Press: 0115 951 5765
Oxford Brookes University
01865 741111
www.brookes.ac.uk
Oxford, University of
01865 270000
www.ox.ac.uk
Admissions
01865 288000
www.admissions.ox.ac.uk
Balliol College
01865 277777
www.balliol.ox.ac.uk
Brasenose College
01865 277510
www.bnc.ox.ac.uk
Christ Church
01865 276150
www.chch.ox.ac.uk
Corpus Christi College
01865 276700
www.ccc.ox.ac.uk
Exeter College
01865 279600
www.exeter.ox.ac.uk
Harris Manchester College
01865 271006
www.hmc.ox.ac.uk
Hertford College
01865 279400
www.hertford.ox.ac.uk
Jesus College
01865 279700
www.jesus.ox.ac.uk
Keble College
01865 272727
www.keble.ox.ac.uk
Lady Margaret Hall
01865 274300
www.lmh.ox.ac.uk
Lincoln College
01865 279800
www.lincoln.ox.ac.uk
Magdalen College
01865 276000
www.magd.ox.ac.u
Mansfield College
01865 270999
www.mansfield.ox.ac.uk
Merton College
01865 276310
www.merton.ox.ac.uk
New College
01865 279555
www.new.oc.ac.uk

Oriel College
01865 276555
www.oriel.ox.ac.uk
Pembroke College
01865 276444
www.pmb.ox.ac.uk
The Queen's College
01865 279120
www.queens.ox.ac.uk
Regent's Park College
01865 288120
www.rpc.ox.ac.uk
St Anne's College
01865 274800
www.stannes.ox.ac.uk
St Catherine's College
01865 271 701
www.stcatz.ox.ac.uk
St Edmund Hall
01865 279008
www.she.ox.ac.uk
St Hilda's College
01865 276884
www.sthildas.ox.ac.uk
St Hugh's College
01865 274900
www.st-hughs.ox.ac.uk
St John's College
01865 277318
www.sjc.ox.ac.uk
St Peter's College
01865 278900
www.spc.ox.ac.uk
Somerville College
01865 270600
www.some.ox.ac.uk
Trinity College
01865 279900
www.trinity.ox.ac.uk
University College
01865 276602
www.univ.ox.ac.uk
Wadham College
01865 277900
www.wadham.ox.ac.uk
Worcester College
01865 278300
www.worcester.ox.ac.uk
Paisley, University of
0141 848 3000
www.paisley.ac.uk
Plymouth, University of
01752 600600
www.plymouth.ac.uk
Portsmouth, University of
023 9284 8484
www.port.ac.uk
Queen Margaret University College
0131 317 3000
www.qmuc.ac.uk
Queen Mary, University of London
020 7882 5555
www.qmul.ac.uk
Queen's University Belfast
02890 245133
www.qub.ac.uk
Press: 028 9097 3091
Ravensbourne College of Design & Communication
020 8289 4900
www.rave.ac.uk

Reading, University of
0118 987 5123
www.reading.ac.uk
Press: 0118 378 7388
Robert Gordon University, Aberdeen
01224 262000
www.rgu.ac.uk
Roehampton – University of Surrey
020 8392 3000
www.roehampton.ac.uk
Rose Bruford College
020 8308 2600
www.bruford.ac.uk
Royal Academy of Music
020 7873 7373
www.ram.ac.uk
Royal Agricultural College
01285 652531
www.royagcol.ac.uk
Royal College of Music
020 7589 3643
www.rcm.ac.uk
Royal Holloway, University of London
01784 434455
www.rhul.ac.uk
Royal Northern College of Music
0161 907 5200
www.rncm.ac.uk
Royal Scottish Academy of Music & Drama
0141 332 4101
www.rsamd.ac.uk
Royal Veterinary College
020 74685000
www.rvc.ac.uk
Royal Welsh College of Music & Drama
029 2034 2854
www.rwcmd.ac.uk
St Andrews, University of
01334 476161
www.st-andrews.ac.uk
St George's Hospital Medical School
020 8672 9944
www.sghms.ac.uk
St Mark & St John College
01752 636 700
www.marjon.ac.uk
St Martin's College
01524 384384
www.ucsm.ac.uk
St Mary's College
020 8240 4000
www.smuc.ac.uk
Salford, University of
0161 295 5000
www.salford.ac.uk
School of Oriental and African Studies (SOAS)
020 7637 2388
www.soas.ac.uk
School of Pharmacy, University of London
020 7753 5800
www.ulsop.ac.uk
Scottish Agricultural College
0131 535 4000
www.sac.ac.uk/education

Sheffield Hallam University
0114 225 5555
www.shu.ac.uk
Sheffield, University of
0114 222 2000
www.sheffield.ac.uk
South Bank University
020 7928 8989
www.sbu.ac.uk
Southampton Institute
023 8031 9000
www.solent.ac.uk
Southampton, University of
023 8059 5000
www.soton.ac.uk
Press: 023 8059 3212
Staffordshire University
01782 294000
www.staffs.ac.uk
Stirling, University of
01786 473171
www.stir.ac.uk
Stranmillis University College
028 9038 1271
www.stran-ni.ac.uk
Strathclyde, University of
0141 552 4400
www.strath.ac.uk
Sunderland, University of
0191 515 2000
www.sunderland.ac.uk
Surrey Institute of Art & Design, University College
01252 722441
www.surrart.ac.uk
Surrey, University of
01483 300800
www.surrey.ac.uk
Sussex, University of
01273 606755
www.sussex.ac.uk
Swansea – University of Wales
01792 205678
www.swan.ac.uk
Swansea Institute of Higher Education
01792 481000
www.sihe.ac.uk
Teesside, University of
01642 218121
www.tees.ac.uk
Thames Valley University
020 8579 5000
www.tvu.ac.uk
Trinity & All Saints College
0113 283 7100
www.tasc.ac.uk
Trinity College, Carmarthen
01267 676767
www.trinity-cm.ac.uk
Trinity College of Music
020 8305 4444
www.tcm.ac.uk
UHI Millennium Institute
01643 27900
www.uhi.ac.uk
Ulster, University of
0870 0400 700
www.ulster.ac.uk
University College Chester
01244 511000
www.chester.ac.uk

University College Chichester
01243 816000
www.ucc.ac.uk
University College London
020 7679 2000
www.ucl.ac.uk
Press: 020 7679 9728
University College Northampton
01604 735500
www.northampton.ac.uk
University College Winchester
01962 841515
www.winchester.ac.uk
University College Worcester
01905 855000
www.worc.ac.uk
Warwick, University of
024 7652 3523
www.warwick.ac.uk
West of England, University of the
0117 965 6261
www.uwe.ac.uk
Westminster, University of
020 7911 5000
www.westminster.ac.uk
Wimbledon School of Art
020 8408 5000
www.wimbledon.ac.uk
Wolverhampton, University of
01902 321000
www.wlv.ac.uk
Press: 01902 322736
Writtle College
01245 424200
www.writtle.ac.uk
York St John College
01904 624624
www.yorksj.ac.uk
York, University of
01904 430000
www.york.ac.uk

Environment

Government and agencies

Department for the Environment, Food and Rural Affairs
020 7238 6000
www.defra.gov.uk
Press -
animal welfare: 020 7238 6044
environment: 020 7238 6054
rural affairs: 020 7238 5608
sustainable farming and food:
 020 7238 6146
British Waterways Board
01923 201120
www.britishwaterways.co.uk
Press: 01923 201329
Countryside Agency
01242 521381
www.countryside.gov.uk
Press: 01242 533306
Environment Agency
08708 506 506
www.environment-agency.gov.uk
Press: 020 7863 8710
Food Standards Agency
020 7276 8000
www.foodstandards.gov.uk
Press: 020 7276 8888
Forestry Commission
0131 334 0303
www.forestry.gov.uk
Press: 0131 314 6500
Meat and Livestock Commission
01908 677577
www.mlc.org.uk
Press: 01908 844106
The Pesticides Safety Directorate
01904 640500
www.pesticides.gov.uk
Press: 020 7238 6698
United Kingdom Atomic Energy Authority
01235 820220
www.ukaea.org.uk
Press: 01235 436900

Rural and environmental bodies

Country Land and Business Association
020 7235 0511
www.cla.org.uk
Press: 020 7460 7936
English Heritage
0870 333 1181
www.english-heritage.org.uk
Press: 020 7973 3250
English Nature
01733 455000
www.english-nature.org.uk
Press: 01733 455190

Friends of the Earth
020 7490 1555
www.foe.co.uk
England, Wales and Northern Ireland
Press: 020 7566 1649
Friends of the Earth Scotland
0131 554 9977
www.foe-scotland.org.uk
Game Conservancy Trust
01425 652381
www.gct.org.uk
Press: 01425 651000
Greenpeace
020 7865 8100
www.greenpeace.org.uk
Press: 020 7865 8255
National Farmers Union
024 7685 8500
www.nfu.org.uk
Press: 024 7685 8686
National Trust
0870 242 6620
www.nationaltrust.org.uk
National Trust for Scotland
0131 243 9300
www.nts.org.uk
Press: 0131 243 9349
Ramblers Association
020 7339 8500
www.ramblers.org.uk
Press: 020 7339 8531/2
Worldwide Fund for Nature UK
01483 426444
www.wwf-uk.org

National parks

Brecon
01874 624437
www.breconbeacons.org
Dartmoor
01626 832093
www.dartmoor-npa.gov.uk
Exmoor
01398 323665
www.exmoor-nationalpark.gov.uk
Lake District
01539 724555
www.lake-district.gov.uk
Norfolk & Suffolk Broads
01603 610734
www.broads-authority.gov.uk
Northumberland
01434 605555
www.northumberland-national-park.org.uk
North Yorkshire Moors
01439 770657
www.moors.uk.net
Peak District
01629 816200
www.peakdistrict.org
Pembrokeshire Coast
0845 345 7275
www.pembrokeshirecoast.org.uk

Snowdonia
0845 130 6229
www.ccw.gov.uk
Yorkshire Dales
0870 1 666333
www.yorkshiredales.org.uk

Voluntary sector

● Animal welfare

Animal Aid
01732 364546
www.animalaid.org.uk
Animal Defenders
020 8846 9777
www.animaldefenders.org.uk
Animal Health Trust
0870 050 2424
www.aht.org.uk
Bat Conservation Trust
020 7627 2629
www.bats.org.uk
Battersea Dogs Home
020 7622 3626
www.dogshome.org
Press: 020 7627 9294
Blue Cross
01993 822651
www.bluecross.org.uk
Pet welfare charity
British Deer Society
01425 655434
www.bds.org.uk
British Hedgehog Protection Trust
01584 890801
www.britishhedgehogs.org.uk
British Union for Abolition of Vivisection
020 7700 4888
www.buav.org
Brooke Hospital for Animals
020 7930 0210
www.brooke-hospital.org.uk
Working animals in developing world
Butterfly Conservation Trust
0870 774 4309
www.butterfly-conservation.org
Canine Lifeline UK
0870 758 1401
www.caninelifeline.fsnet.co.uk
Cat Action Trust
01555 660784
www.catactiontrust.co.uk
Cats Protection
0870 209 9099
www.cats.org.uk
Celia Hammond Animal Trust
01892 783367
www.celiahammond.org
Dog Trust
020 7837 0006
www.dogstrust.org.uk
Donkey Sanctuary
01395 578222
www.thedonkeysanctuary.org.uk

Farm Animal Welfare Council
020 7904 6534
www.fawc.org.uk
Fauna & Flora International
01223 571000
www.fauna-flora.org
Federation of Zoos
www.zoofederation.org.uk
Feline Advisory Board
0870 742 2278
www.fabcats.org
Humane Slaughter Society
01582 831919
www.hsa.org.uk
Hunt Saboteurs Organisation
0845 450 0727
www.huntsabs.org.uk
International Dolphin Watch
01482 632650
www.idw.org
International Fund for Animal Welfare
020 7587 6700
www.ifaw.org
International League for the Protection of Horses
0870 870 1927
www.ilph.org
League Against Cruel Sports
0845 330 8486
www.league.uk.com
London Wildlife Trust
020 7261 0447
www.wildlondon.org.uk
Mammal Society
020 7350 2200
www.abdn.ac.uk/mammal
Mare & Foal Sanctuary
01626 355969
www.mareandfoal.org.uk
Marine Conservation Society
www.mcsuk.org
National Federation of Badger Groups
020 7228 6444
www.nfbg.org.uk
Otter Trust
01986 893470
www.ottertrust.org.uk
People and Dogs Society
01924 897732
01977 678593
www.padsonline.org
People for the Ethical Treatment of Animals (PETA)
020 7357 9229
www.peta.org.uk
People's Dispensary for Sick Animals (PDSA)
01952 290999
www.pdsa.org.uk
Rare Breeds Survival Trust
024 7669 6551
www.rare-breeds.com
Redwings Horse Sanctuary
01508 481000
www.redwings.co.uk
Royal Society for the Prevention of Cruelty to Animals
0870 555 5999
www.rspca.org.uk
Press: 0870 754 0288/44

Royal Society for the Protection of Birds
01767 680551
www.rspb.org.uk
Press: 01767 681577
Save the Rhino
020 7357 7474
www.savetherhino.org
Scottish Society for the Prevention of Cruelty to Animals
0131 339 0222
www.scottishspca.org
Scottish Wildlife Trust
0131 312 7765
www.swt.org.uk
Society for the Protection of Animals Abroad
020 7831 3999
www.spana.org
TRAFFIC
01223 277427
www.traffic.org
Combats damaging trade in plants & animals
Ulster Wildlife Trust
028 4483 0282
www.ulsterwildlifetrust.org
Uncaged
0114 272 2220
www.uncaged.co.uk
Anti-vivisection campaigner
Veteran Horse Society
01239 881300
www.veteran-horse-society.co.uk
Whale & Dolphin Conservation Society
0870 870 0027
www.wdcs.org.uk
Wildfowl & Wetlands Trust
01453 891900
www.wwt.org.uk
The Wildlife Trusts
0870 036 7711
www.wildlifetrusts.org
Wood Green Animal Shelters
08701 904090
www.woodgreen.org.uk
World Society for the Protection of Animals
020 7587 5000
www.wspa-international.org
www.wspa.org.uk
WWF UK
01483 426444
www.wwf.org.uk

● Conservation

Black Environment Network
01286 870715
www.ben-network.co.uk
British Association for Shooting and Conservation
01244 573000
www.basc.org.uk
Press: 01244 573031
British Trust for Conservation Volunteers
01302 572244
www.btcv.org

Campaign for Real Events
www.c-realevents.demon.co.uk
Provides renewable energy and 'alt tech' support for events
Campaign to Protect Rural England
020 7981 2800
www.cpre.org.uk
Carbon Neutral Company
020 7833 6000
www.carbonneutral.com
Centre for Alternative Technology
01654 705950
www.cat.org.uk
Community Composting Network
0114 258 0483
0114 255 3720
www.communitycompost.org
Community Service Volunteers – Environment
020 7278 6601
www.csv.org.uk
Conservation Foundation
020 7591 3111
www.conservationfoundation.co.uk
Council for Environmental Education
0118 950 2550
www.cee.org.uk
Council for National Parks
020 7924 4077
www.cnp.org.uk
Earth First! In Britain
www.earthfirst.org.uk
Earth Rights
01279 870391
www.earthrights.org.uk
Environmental public interest law firm
Earthwatch Institute
01865 318838
www.uk.earthwatch.org
Conservation of natural environments and cultural heritage
Eco-Village Network
0117 373 0346
www.evnuk.org.uk
Energywatch
0845 906 0708
www.energywatch.org.uk
Environmental Campaigns
01942 612621
www.encams.org
European Rivers Network
00 33 47 102 0814
www.rivernet.org
Based in southern France
Forest Action Network
00 1 250 799 5800
www.fanweb.org
Forum for the Future
020 7324 3630
www.forumforthefuture.org.uk
Gaia Energy Centre
01840 213321
www.gaiaenergy.co.uk
Promotes renewable energy
Game Conservancy Trust
01425 652381
www.gct.org.uk
People and Planet
01865 245678
www.peopleandplanet.org
UK student action on human rights, poverty and the environment

Rising Tide
07708 794665
www.risingtide.org.uk
Action against climate change

Royal Society for Nature Conservation
0870 036 1000
www.wildlifetrusts.org

Solar Energy Society
07760 163559
www.thesolarline.com

Surfers Against Sewage
0845 458 3001
www.sas.org.uk

UNEP World Conservation Monitoring Centre
01223 277314
www.unep-wcmc.org

Woodland Trust
01476 581135
www.woodland-trust.org.uk

● Farming and food

Farm
020 7713 9250
www.farm.org.uk
Campaigners for the future of independent and family farms

Farm Animal Welfare Council
020 7904 6534
www.fawc.org.uk

Farming & Wildlife Advisory Group
024 7669 6699
www.fwag.org.uk

Biodynamic Agricultural Association
01453 759501
www.biodynamic.org.uk

Campaign for Real Ale
01727 798443
www.camra.org.uk

Compassion in World Farming
01730 264208
www.ciwf.org.uk

Dig It Up!
www.dig-it-up.uk.net
Action against planting of GM rape crops

Eat the View
01242 533222
www.countryside.gov.uk/lar
    /landscape/etv/index.asp

FARMA
0845 458 8420
www.farma.org.uk

Food from Britain
020 7233 5111
www.foodfrombritain.com
Promoting sustainable local products

Five Year Freeze Campaign
020 7837 0642
www.fiveyearfreeze.org
Anti-GM activists group

Food & Drink Federation
020 7836 2460
www.fdf.org.uk

Food Dudes
01248 38 3973
www.fooddudes.co.uk
Teaching children about healthy eating

Foundation for Local Food Initiatives
0845 458 9525
www.localfood.org.uk

Free Range Activism Website
www.fraw.org.uk

Future Harvest
00 1 703 548 4540
www.futureharvest.org
Promoting environmentally sound agricultural methods

Henry Doubleday Research Society
024 7630 3517
www.hdra.org.uk
Researches and promotes organic methods and produce

Herb Society
01295 768899
www.herbsociety.co.uk
Herbs for health

National Federation of City Farms
0117 923 1800
www.farmgarden.org.uk

Permaculture Society
0845 458 1805
www.permaculture.org.uk

Pesticide Action Network
020 7065 0905
www.pan-uk.org

Soil Association
0117 314 5000
www.soilassociation.org

Sustain
020 7837 1228
www.sustainweb.org
Alliance for better food and farming

UK Food Group
020 7523 2369
www.ukfg.org.uk
Network for NGOs working on global food and agriculture issues

Veggies Catering Campaign
0845 458 9595
www.veggies.org.uk

Willing Workers on Organic Farms
01273 476286
www.wwoof.org/wwoof_uk

● Gardening

Royal Horticultural Society
020 7834 4333
www.rhs.org.uk

Health

Government departments

Department of Health
020 7210 4850
www.dh.gov.uk
Press: 020 7210 5221
Scottish Executive DoH
0131 556 8400
www.scotland.gov.uk
Press: 0131 244 2797
Northern Ireland DoH
028 9052 0500
www.dhsspsni.gov.uk
Press: 028 9052 0636

Government agencies

Centre for Emergency Preparedness and Response
01980 612100
Centre for Infections
020 8200 4400
Centre for Radiation, Chemical and Environmental Hazards
01235 831600
Health and Safety Executive
0845 345 0055
www.hse.gov.uk
Press: 020 7717 6700
out of hours: 020 7928 8382
Health Care Commission
020 7448 9200
www.healthcarecommission.org.uk
Press: 020 7448 9210
Health Professions Council
020 7582 0866
www.hpc-uk.org
Health Protection Agency
020 7759 2700/1
www.hpa.org.uk
Health Service Ombudsman
0845 015 4033
www.ombudsman.org.uk
Human Fertilisation and Embryology Authority
020 7291 8200
www.hfea.gov.uk
Human Genetics Commission
020 7972 4351
www.hgc.gov.uk
Press: 020 8675 1066
Medical Research Council
020 7636 5422
www.mrc.ac.uk
Medicines and Healthcare products Regulatory Agency
020 7084 2000
www.mhra.gov.uk
Press: 020 7084 2657
National Blood Service
0845 7711 711
www.blood.co.uk
National Institute for Health and Clinical Excellence (NICE)
020 7067 5800
www.nice.org.uk

National Patient Safety Agency
020 7927 9500
www.npsa.nhs.uk
NHS Executive
0113 254 5000
www.nhs.uk
Press: 020 7210 5221
NHS Health Scotland
0131 536 5500
www.healthscotland.com
NHS Quality Improvement, Scotland
0131 623 4300
www.nhshealthquality.org
NHS State Hospitals Board for Scotland
01555 840293
www.show.scot.nhs.uk/tsh

Professional bodies

Royal College of Anaesthetists
020 7092 1500
www.rcoa.ac.uk
Royal College of General Practitioners
020 7581 3232
www.rcgp.org.uk
Press: 020 7344 3135/29/37
Royal College of Nursing
020 7409 3333
www.rcn.org.uk
Press: 020 7647 3633
Royal College of Obstetricians & Gynaecologists
020 7772 6200
www.rcog.org.uk
Press: 020 7772 6357
Royal College of Ophthalmologists
020 7935 0702
www.rcophth.ac.uk
Royal College of Paediatrics and Child Health
020 7307 5600
www.rcpch.ac.uk
Royal College of Pathologists
020 7451 6700
www.rcpath.org
Press: 020 7451 6752
Royal College of Physicians of Edinburgh
0131 225 7324
www.rcpe.ac.uk
Press: 0131 247 3693
Royal College of Physicians of Ireland
00 353 1 661 6677
www.rcpi.ie
Royal College of Physicians of London
020 7935 1174
www.rcplondon.ac.uk
Press: x254, x468
Faculty of Public Health Medicine
020 7935 0243
www.fphm.org.uk
Press: 020 7487 1185

Royal College of Physicians & Surgeons of Glasgow
0141 221 6072
www.rcpsglasg.ac.uk
Royal College of Psychiatrists
020 7235 2351
www.rcpsych.ac.uk
Press: x154, x127
Royal College of Radiologists
020 7636 4432
www.rcr.ac.uk
Press: x1138
Royal College of Surgeons of Edinburgh
0131 527 1600
www.rcsed.ac.uk
Royal College of Surgeons of England
020 7405 3474
www.rcseng.ac.uk
Press: 020 7869 6045
Royal College of Surgeons in Ireland
00 353 1 402 2100
www.rcsi.ie
Press: 00 353 1 402 8610

Patient groups

Patients Association
020 8423 9111
www.patients-association.com

Voluntary sector

● General health

Action Medical Research
01403 210406
www.action.org.uk
Press: 01403 327404
Alzheimer's Society
020 7306 0606
www.alzheimers.org.uk
Press: 020 7306 0813/39
Arthritis Care
020 7380 6500
www.arthritiscare.org.uk
Press: 020 7380 6551
Arthritis Research Campaign
0870 850 5000
www.arc.org.uk
Press: 01246 541107
Association for International Cancer Research
01334 477910
www.aicr.org.uk
Bliss
020 7378 1122
www.bliss.org.uk
National charity for premature or sick babies
Breakthrough Breast Cancer
020 7025 2400
www.breakthrough.org.uk
Press: 020 7025 2432/2460

Breast Cancer Campaign
020 7749 3700
www.bcc-uk.org
Breast Cancer Care
020 7384 2984
www.breastcancercare.org.uk
Press: 020 7384 4696
British Dietetic Association
0121 200 8080
www.bda.uk.com
British Heart Foundation
020 7935 0185
www.bhf.org.uk
Press: 020 7487 7172 (24 Hour)
British Pregnancy Advisory Service
0870 365 5050
www.bpas.org
Press: 020 7612 0206 07788 725185
CLIC Sargent
0845 301 0031
www.clicsargent.org.uk
Children's cancer charity
Press: 0117 314 8621
Cancer Research UK
020 7121 6699
www.cancerresearchuk.org
Press: 020 7061 8300
Consensus Action on Salt and Health
020 8725 2409
www.actiononsalt.org.uk
Press: 07711 698984
        020 8853 1349
Cystic Fibrosis Trust
020 8464 7211
www.cftrust.org.uk
Press: 020 7940 3800
Diabetes UK
020 7424 1000
www.diabetes.org.uk
Press: 020 7424 1165
Eating Disorders Association
0870 770 3256
www.edauk.com
Press: 0870 770 3221
Epilepsy Action
0113 210 8800
www.epilepsy.org.uk
Great Ormond St Children's Charity
020 7916 5678
www.gosh.org
Guy's & St Thomas' Charity
020 7188 7700
www.gsttcharity.org.uk
Press: 020 7188 1218
HIT
0870 990 9702
www.hit.org.uk
Campaigning and providing helplines
Institute of Cancer Research
020 7352 8133
www.icr.ac.uk
Press: x5312, x5359
International HIV/AIDS Alliance
01273 718900
www.aidsalliance.org
International Obesity Taskforce
020 7691 1900
www.iotf.org
Leukaemia Research Fund
020 7405 0101
www.lrf.org.uk
Press: 020 7269 9019

Macmillan Cancer Support
020 7840 7840
www.macmillan.org.uk
Press: 020 7840 7821
Marie Curie Cancer Care
020 7599 7777
www.mariecurie.org.uk
Press: 020 7599 7700
Marie Stopes International
020 7574 7400
www.mariestopes.org.uk
Reproductive healthcare worldwide
Press: 020 7574 7353
Meningitis Trust
01453 768000
www.meningitis-trust.org
Mind
020 8519 2122
www.mind.org.uk
National Association for Mental Health
Press: 020 8522 1743
Motor Neurone Disease Association
01604 250505
www.mndassociation.org
Press: 01604 611840
Multiple Sclerosis Society
020 8438 0700
www.mssociety.org.uk
Press: 020 7082 0820
Muscular Dystrophy Campaign
020 7720 8055
www.muscular-dystrophy.org
National Asthma Campaign
020 7786 4900
www.asthma.org.uk
Press: 020 7786 4949
National Heart Forum
020 7383 7638
www.heartforum.org.uk
National Kidney Research Fund
0845 070 7601
www.kidneyresearchuk.org
Parkinson's Disease Society of the UK
020 7931 8080
www.parkinsons.org.uk
St John Ambulance
08700 104950
www.sja.org.uk
Press: 020 7324 4210
Stroke Association
020 7566 0300
www.stroke.org.uk
Press: 020 7566 1500
Terrence Higgins Trust
0845 1221 200
www.tht.org.uk
HIV/Aids
Press: 020 7812 1600
The Wellcome Trust
020 7611 8888
www.wellcome.ac.uk
Health research charity
Press: 020 7611 8866
World Cancer Research Fund UK
020 7343 4200
www.wcrf-uk.org
Yorkshire Cancer Research
01423 501269
www.ycr.org.uk

● **Drugs, alcohol and addiction**

Addaction
020 7251 5860
www.addaction.org.uk
Adfam
020 7928 8898
www.adfam.org.uk
Families, drugs and alcohol
Alchemy Project
0845 165 1197
www.alchemyproject.co.uk
Alcohol Concern
020 7928 7377
www.alcoholconcern.org.uk
Alcohol Focus Scotland
0141 572 6700
www.alcohol-focus-scotland.org.uk
Alcoholics Anonymous
01904 644026
www.alcoholics-anonymous.org.uk
Arrest Referral Forum
01484 550604
www.drugreferral.org
Support for workers on drugs referral projects
ASH: Action on Smoking and Health
020 7739 5902
www.ash.org.uk
Association of Nurses in Substance Abuse
0870 241 3503
www.ansa.uk.net
Clouds
01747 830733
www.clouds.org.uk
Treatment for addiction
Crew 2000
0131 220 3404
www.crew2000.co.uk
Drug advice service
Drugscope
020 7928 1211
www.drugscope.org.uk
Information resource
European Association for the Treatment of Addiction
020 7922 8753
www.eata.org.uk
Legalise Cannabis Alliance
07984 255015
www.lca-uk.org
Life or Meth
www.lifeormeth.com
Methamphetamine awareness campaign
Narcotics Anonymous
020 7251 4007
www.ukna.org
National Treatment Agency
020 7972 2214
www.nta.nhs.uk
No Smoking Day – March 8
0870 770 7909
www.nosmokingday.org.uk
Parents Against Drug Abuse
0845 702 3867
www.btinternet.com/-padahelp
Promis Recovery Centre
01304 841700
www.promis.co.uk
Multi-addiction awareness and treatment

Release
020 7729 5255
www.release.org.uk
Provides for health, welfare and legal needs of drug users
Re-Solv
01785 817885
www.re-solv.org
Society for prevention of solvent abuse
Ride Foundation
01372 467708
www.ridefoundation.org.uk
Drug awareness programmes for schools
Scottish Drugs Forum
0141 221 1175
www.sdf.org.uk
Substance Misuse Management in General Practice
www.smmgp.org.uk
Transform
0117 941 5810
www.tdpf.org.uk
Anti-prohibition campaign
UK Harm Reduction Alliance
www.ukhra.org
Campaigning for health and ethical treatment of drug users

Health helplines

NHS Direct
0845 4647
Alcoholics Anonymous
08457 697555
Alzheimers Helpline
08453 000336
Arthritis Care Helpline
0808 800 4050
Asthma UK Advice Line
08457 010203
British Allergy Foundation Helpline
01322 619898
Carers Line
0808 808 7777
Diabetes UK Careline
0845 120 2960
Doctors' Supportline
0870 765 0001
Drinkline
0800 917 8282
Eating Disorders Association Helpline
0845 634 1414
Eating Disorders Association Youth Helpline
0845 634 7650
Epilepsy Action Helpline
0808 800 5050
Frank (National Drugs Helpline)
0800 776600
Miscarriage Association Helpline
01924 200799
NHS Asian Tobacco Helpline
0800 169 0881 (Urdu)
0800 169 0882 (Punjabi)
0800 169 0883 (Hindi)
0800 169 0884 (Gujerati)
0800 169 0885 (Bengali)
NHS Pregnancy Smoking Helpline
0800 169 9169
NHS Smoking Helpline
0800 169 0169
Organ Donor Line
0845 606 0400
Parents Against Drug Abuse
0845 702 3867
Re-Solv
0808 800 2345
RNID Tinnitus Helpline
0808 808 6666
Sexual Health Direct
08453 101334
Sexual Health Information Line
0800 567123
Smokers Quitline
0800 002200
Still Births and Neonatal Deaths Helpline
020 7436 5881
Women's Health Concern Helpline
0845 123 2319
Women's Health Enquiry Line
0845 125 5254

The NHS

● Strategic health authorities, England

East Midlands Strategic Health Authority
0115 968 4444
www.eastmidlands.nhs.uk
East of England Strategic Health Authority
01223 597500
www.eoe.nhs.uk
London Strategic Health Authority
020 7016 8872
www.london.nhs.uk
North East Strategic Health Authority
0191 210 6400
www.northeast.nhs.uk
North West Strategic Health Authority
0161 237 2397
www.northwest.nhs.uk
South Central Strategic Health Authority
01865 337000
www.southcentral.nhs.uk
South East Coast Strategic Health Authority
01293 778899
www.southeastcoast.nhs.uk
South West Strategic Health Authority
01935 384000
www.southwest.nhs.uk
West Midlands Strategic Health Authority
0121 695 2222
www.westmidlands.nhs.uk
Yorkshire and The Humber Strategic Health Authority
0113 295 2000
www.yorksandhumber.nhs.uk

● Local health boards, Wales

Anglesey
01248 751229
www.wales.nhs.uk
Blaenau Gwent
01495 325400
www.wales.nhs.uk
Bridgend
01656 754400
www.wales.nhs.uk
Caerphilly
01443 862056
www.wales.nhs.uk
Cardiff
029 2055 2212
www.wales.nhs.uk
Carmarthenshire
01554 744400
www.wales.nhs.uk
Ceredigion
01570 424100
www.wales.nhs.uk
Conwy
01492 536586
www.wales.nhs.uk

Denbighshire
01745 589601
www.wales.nhs.uk
Flintshire
01352 803434
www.wales.nhs.uk
Gwynedd
01286 672451
www.gwyneddhealth.org
Merthyr Tydfil
01685 358500
www.wales.nhs.uk
Monmouthshire
01600 710000
www.wales.nhs.uk
Neath/Port Talbot
01639 890916
www.wales.nhs.uk
Newport
01633 261430
www.wales.nhs.uk
Pembrokeshire
01437 771220
www.wales.nhs.uk
Powys
01874 711661
www.wales.nhs.uk
Rhondda Cynon Taff
01443 824400
www.wales.nhs.uk
Swansea
01792 784800
www.wales.nhs.uk
Torfaen
01495 332200
www.wales.nhs.uk
Vale of Glamorgan
029 2035 0600
www.wales.nhs.uk
Wexham
01978 346500
www.wales.nhs.uk

● NHS boards, Scotland
Argyll and Clyde
0141 842 7200
www.nhsac.scot.nhs.uk
Ayrshire and Arran
01563 577037
www.nhsayrshireandarran.com
Borders
01896 825500
www.nhsborders.org.uk
Dumfries and Galloway
01387 246246
www.nhsdg.scot.nhs.uk
Fife
01592 643355
www.nhsfife.scot.nhs.uk
Forth Valley
01786 463031
www.nhsforthvalley.com
Grampian
0845 456 6000
www.nhsgrampian.org
Greater Glasgow and Clyde
0141 201 4444
www.nhsggc.org.uk
Press: 0141 201 4429
Highland
01463 717123
www.nhshighland.scot.nhs.uk

Lanarkshire
01698 281313
www.nhslanarkshire.co.uk
Lothian
0131 536 9000
www.nhslothian.scot.nhs.uk
Orkney
01856 888000
www.show.scot.nhs.uk/ohb
Shetland
01595 743060
www.show.scot.nhs.uk/shb
Tayside
01382 818479
www.nhstayside.scot.nhs.uk
Western Isles
01851 702997
www.wihb.scot.nhs.uk
Scottish Ambulance Service
0131 446 7000
www.scottishambulance.com

● Health & social services boards, Northern Ireland
Eastern
028 9032 1313
www.ehssb.n-i.nhs.uk
Northern
028 2531 1000
www.nhssb.n-i.nhs.uk
Southern
028 3741 0041
www.shssb.n-l.nhs.uk
Western
028 7186 0086
www.whssb.n-l.nhs.uk

● NHS foundation trusts
Monitor
020 7340 2400
www.monitor-nhsft.gov.uk
Monitor and independent regulator of
NHS foundation trusts
Press: 020 7340 2440
Barnsley Hospital NHS Foundation Trust
01226 730000
Basildon and Thurrock Hospitals NHSFT
01268 533911
Bradford Teaching Hospitals NHSFT
01274 542200
Cambridge University Hospitals NHSFT
01223 245151
Chesterfield Royal Hospital NHSFT
01246 277271
City Hospitals Sunderland NHSFT
0191 565 6256
Countess of Chester Hospital NHSFT
01244 365000
Derby Hospitals NHSFT
01332 347141
Doncaster and Bassetlaw Hospitals NHSFT
01302 366666
Frimley Park Hospital NHSFT
01276 604604

Gateshead Health NHSFT
0191 482 0000
Gloucestershire Hospitals NHSFT
08454 222222
Guy's and St Thomas's NHSFT
020 7188 7188
Harrogate and District NHSFT
01423 885959
Heart of England NHSFT
0121 424 2000
Homerton University Hospital NHSFT
020 8510 5555
Lancashire Teaching Hospitals NHSFT
01772 716565
Liverpool Women's NHSFT
0151 708 9988
Moorfields Eye Hospital NHSFT
020 7253 3411
Papworth Hospital NHSFT
01480 830541
Peterborough and Stamford Hospitals NHSFT
01733 874000
Queen Victoria Hospital NHSFT
01342 414000
The Rotherham NHSFT
01709 820000
The Royal Bournemouth & Christchurch Hospitals NHSFT
01202 303626
Royal Devon & Exeter NHSFT
01392 411611
The Royal Marsden NHSFT
020 7352 8171
The Royal National Hospital for Rheumatic Diseases NHSFT
01225 465941
Sheffield Teaching Hospitals NHSFT
0114 271 1100
South Tyneside NHSFT
0191 454 8888
Stockport NHSFT
0161 483 1010
University College London Hospitals NHSFT
0845 155 5000
University Hospital Birmingham NHSFT
0121 432 3232

NHS hospitals: England

A

Abingdon Community Hospital, Abingdon
01235 205700

Accrington Victoria Community Hospital, Accrington
01254 687342

Addenbrooke's Hospital, Cambridge
01223 245151

Airedale General Hospital, Keighley
01535 652511

Alcester Hospital, Alcester
01789 762470

Alder Hey Children's Hospital, Liverpool
0151 228 4811

Alderney Hospital, Poole
01202 735537

Alexandra Hospital, Chatham
01634 687166

Alexandra Hospital, Redditch
01527 503030

Alfred Bean Hospital, Driffield
01377 241124

Alnwick Infirmary
01665 626 700

Altrincham General Hospital, Altrincham
0161 928 6111

Amberstone Hospital, Hailsham
01323 440022

Amersham Hospital, Amersham
01494 526161

Arrowe Park Hospital, Wirral
0151 678 5111

Ashburton & Buckfastleigh Hospital
01364 652203

Ashfield Community Hospital, Kirkby in Ashfield
01636 681681

Ashford Hospital
01784 884488

Ashton House Hospital, Merseyside
0151 653 9660

Ashworth Hospital, Liverpool
0151 473 0303

Axminster Hospital, Axminster
01297 630400

B

Babington Hospital, Belper
01773 824171

Barking Hospital, Essex
020 8983 8000

Barnet Hospital, London
0845 111 4000

Barnsley District General Hospital
01226 730000

Basildon Hospital, Essex
01268 533911

Bassetlaw Hospital, Worksop
01909 500990

Beacon Day Hospital, Wigan
01695 626034

Beccles & District Hospital
01502 719800

Beckenham Hospital
01689 863000

Bedford Hospital, Bedford
01234 355122

Beighton Community Hospital, Sheffield
0114 271 6500

Bensham Hospital, Gateshead
0191 482 0000

Berkeley Hospital, Berkley
01453 562000

Berwick Infirmary, Berwick-on-Tweed
01289 356600

Beverley Westwood Hospital
01482 886600

Bexhill Hospital, Bexhill-on-Sea
01424 755255

Bicester Hospital
01869 604000

Bickley Day Hospital, Norfolk
01953 457342

Bingley Hospital
01274 563438

Birch Hill Hospital, Rochdale
01706 377777

Birmingham Children's Hospital
0121 333 9999

Birmingham Dental Hospital
0121 236 8611

Birmingham Heartlands Hospital
0121 424 2000

Birmingham Women's Hospital
0121 472 1377

Bishop Auckland General Hospital
01388 455000

Bishops Castle Community Hospital
01588 638220

Blackberry Hill Hospital, Bristol
0117 965 6061

Blackburn Royal Infirmary, Blackburn
01254 263555

Blackpool Victoria Hospital
01253 300000

Blandford Community Hospital
01258 456541

Blyth Community Hospital
01670 396400

Bodmin Hospital
01208 251301

Bolingbroke Hospital, London
020 7223 7411

Booth Hall Children's Hospital, Manchester
0161 795 7000

Bovey Tracey Hospital, Bovey Tracey
01626 832279

Bradford Royal Infirmary
01274 542200

Bradford-on-Avon Community Hospital
01225 862975

Bradwell Hospital, Newcastle
01782 425400

Brampton War Memorial Community Hospital, Brampton
01697 72534

Bridgnorth Hospital
01746 762641

Bridgwater Community Hospital
01278 451501

Bridlington & District Hospital
01262 606666

Bridport Community Hospital
01308 422371

Brighton General Hospital
01273 696011

Bristol Eye Hospital
0117 928 4771

Bristol General Hospital
0117 928 6223

Bristol Homoeopathic Hospital
0117 973 1231

Bristol Royal Hospital for Children
0117 927 6998

Bristol Royal Infirmary
0117 923 0000

Brixham Hospital
01803 882153

Broadgreen Hospital, Liverpool
0151 282 6000

Broadmoor Hospital
01344 773111

Bromyard Community Hospital
01885 485700

Broomfield Hospital, Chelmsford
01245 440761

Buckland Hospital, Dover
01304 201624

Bucknall Hospital, Stoke-on-Trent
01782 273510

Budleigh Salterton Hospital
01395 442020

Burnham-on-Sea War Memorial Hospital
01278 773118

Burnley General Hospital
01282 425071

Bushey Fields Hospital, Dudley
01384 457373

Buxton Hospital
01246 277271

C

Calderdale Royal Hospital, Halifax
01422 357171

Calderstones Hospital, Clitheroe
01254 822121

Camborne/Redruth Community Hospital, Redruth
01209 881688

Cannock Chase Hospital, Cannock
01543 572757

Carlton Court, Lowestoft
01502 527900

Carshalton War Memorial Hospital
020 8770 8000

Cassell Hospital, Richmond
020 8940 8181

Castle Hill Hospital, Cottingham
01482 875875

Castleberg Hospital, Settle
01729 823515

Castleford & Normanton District Hospital
01924 327000

Caterham Dene Hospital
01883 837500

Central Middlesex Hospital, London
020 8965 5733

Chantry House Day Hospital, Frome
01373 455817

Chapel Allerton Hospital, Leeds
0113 262 3404

Chard & District Hospital
01460 238220

Charing Cross Hospital, London
020 8846 1234

Charles Clifford Dental Hospital,
Sheffield
0114 271 7800

Chase Farm Hospital, Enfield
0845 111 4000

Chase Hospital, Bordon
01420 488801

Cheadle Hospital, Stoke-on-Trent
01538 487500

Chelsea and Westminster Hospital,
London
020 8746 8000

Cheltenham General Hospital
08454 222222

Cherry Knowle Hospital,
Sunderland
0191 565 6256

Cherry Tree Hospital, Stockport
0161 483 1010

Chester le Street Hospital
0191 333 6262

Chesterfield Royal Hospital
01246 277271

Chingford Hospital
020 8529 7141

Chippenham Community Hospital
01249 447100

Chipping Norton Community
Hospital
01608 648450

Chorley & South Ribble District
General Hospital, Chorley
01257 261222

Christchurch Hospital
01202 486361

Christie Hospital, Manchester
0161 446 3000

Churchill Hospital, Headington
01865 741841

Cirencester Hospital
01285 655711

City General Hospital,
Stoke-on-Trent
01782 715444

City Hospital, Birmingham
0121 554 3801

Clacton Hospital
01255 201717

Clatterbridge Hospital, Wirral
0151 334 4000

Clayton Hospital, Wakefield
01924 201688

Clifton Hospital, Lytham St Annes
01253 306204

Clitheroe Hospital
01200 427311

Cobham Cottage Hospital
020 8296 2000

Cockermouth Cottage Hospital,
Cockermouth
01900 822226

Colchester General Hospital
01206 747474

Colman Hospital, Norwich
01603 286286

Congleton & District War Memorial
Hospital, Congleton
01260 294800

Conquest Hospital,
St Leonards on Sea
01424 755255

Cookridge Hospital, Leeds
0113 267 3411

Coppetts Wood Hospital, London
020 7794 0500

Coquetdale Cottage Hospital,
Morpeth
01669 620555

Corbett House, Stourbridge
01384 456111

Corby Community Hospital
01536 400070

Coronation Hospital, Ilkley
01943 609666

Cossham Hospital, Bristol
0117 967 1661

Countess of Chester Hospital
01244 365000

County Hospital, Durham
0191 333 6262

Coventry and Warwickshire
Hospital, Coventry
024 7622 4055

Crawley Hospital
01293 600300

Crediton Hospital
01363 775588

Crewkerne Hospital
01460 72491

Cromer Hospital
01263 513571

Crowborough War Memorial
Hospital
01892 652284

Cumberland Infirmary, Carlisle
01228 523444

D

Danesbury Hospital, Welwyn
01438 714447

Danetre Hospital, Daventry
01327 705610

Darent Valley Hospital, Dartford
01322 428100

Darlington Memorial Hospital
01325 380100

Dartmouth & Kingswear Hospital,
Dartmouth
01803 832255

Dawlish Hospital, Dawlish
01626 868500

Delancey Hospital, Cheltenham
01242 222222

Derby City General Hospital
01332 340131

Derby Royal Infirmary
01332 347141

Derbyshire Children's Hospital,
Derby
01332 340131

Dereham Hospital
01362 692391

Derriford Hospital, Plymouth
01752 777111

Devizes Community Hospital
01380 723511

Devonshire Road Hospital,
Blackpool
01253 303364

Dewsbury and District Hospital
01924 512000

Diana, Princess of Wales Hospital,
Grimsby
01472 874111

Didcot Hospital
01235 205860

Dilke Memorial Hospital,
Gloucester
01594 598100

Doncaster Gate Hospital,
Rotherham
01709 304802

Doncaster Royal Infirmary
01302 366666

Dorking Hospital
01306 887150

Dorset County Hospital, Dorchester
01305 251150

Dunston Hill Hospital, Gateshead
0191 445 6414

E

Ealing Hospital, Southall
020 8967 5000

Earls House Hospital, Durham
0191 333 6262

East Surrey Hospital, Redhill
01737 768511

Eastbourne District General
Hospital, Eastbourne
01323 417400

Eastman Dental Hospital, London
020 7915 1000

Edenbridge & District War Memorial
Hospital, Edenbridge
01732 862137

Edgware Community Hospital
020 8952 2381

Edward Hain Hospital, St Ives
01736 576100

Ellen Badger Hospital,
Shipston-on-Stour
01608 661410

Ellesmere Port Hospital
01244 365000

Elmwood Day Hospital, Chester
01244 364122

Epsom General Hospital
01372 735735

Erith & District Hospital
020 8308 3131

Essex County Hospital, Colchester
01206 747474

Evesham Community Hospital
01386 502345

Exmouth Hospital
01395 282000

F

Fairfield General Hospital, Bury
0161 764 6081

Fairford Hospital
01285 712212

Faversham Cottage Hospital
01795 562066

Feilding Palmer Hospital,
Lutterworth
01455 552150

Felixstowe General Hospital
01394 458848

Fenwick Hospital, Lyndhurst
023 8028 2782

Fieldhead Hospital, Wakefield
01924 327000

Finchley Memorial Hospital,
London
020 8349 6300

Fleetwood Hospital
01253 306000

Fordingbridge Hospital
01425 652255
Fowey Hospital
01726 832241
Freeman Hospital,
Newcastle-upon-Tyne
0191 233 6161
Frenchay Hospital, Bristol
0117 970 1212
Friarage Hospital, Northallerton
01609 779911
Frimley Park Hospital, Frimley
01276 604604
Frome Victoria Hospital
01373 463591
Furness General Hospital,
Barrow-in-Furness
01229 870870

G

George Eliot Hospital, Nuneaton
024 7635 1351
Glenfield Hospital, Leicester
0116 287 1471
Gloucestershire Royal Hospital,
Gloucester
01452 528555
Goldie Leigh Hospital, London
020 8319 7100
Good Hope Hospital, Sutton
Coldfield
0121 378 2211
Goole & District Hospital
01405 720720
Gordon Hospital, London
020 8746 5505
Gorse Hill Hospital, Leicester
0116 225 5400
Goscote Hospital, Walsall
01922 721172
Gosport War Memorial Hospital
023 9252 4611
Grantham & District Hospital
01476 565232
Gravesend & North Kent Hospital
01474 360500
Great Ormond Street Hospital for
Children, London
020 7405 9200
Great Western Hospital, Swindon
01793 604020
Green Lane Hospital, Devizes
01380 731200
Greenfields Hospital, Birmingham
0121 465 8750
Guest Hospital, Dudley
01384 456111
Guisborough General Hospital
01287 284000
Guy's Hospital, London
020 7188 7188

H

Halstead Hospital
01787 291022
Halton Hospital, Runcorn
01928 714567
Haltwhistle War Memorial Hospital
01434 320225
Hammersmith Hospital, London
020 8383 1000
Hammerwich Hospital, Burntwood
01543 686224

Harefield Hospital
01895 823737
Harold Wood Hospital, Romford
01708 345533
Harpenden Memorial Hospital
01582 760196
Harplands Hospital, Stoke-on-Trent
01782 441600
Harrogate District Hospital
01423 885959
Harry Watton House, Birmingham
0121 685 6001
Harwich Hospital
01255 201200
Havant War Memorial Hospital
023 9248 4256
Hawkhurst Cottage Hospital,
Hawkhurst
01580 753345
Haywood Hospital, Stoke-on-Trent
01782 715444
Heanor Memorial Hospital
01773 710711
Heartlands Hospital, Birmingham
0121 424 2000
Heath Lane Hospital, West
Bromwich
0845 146 1800
Heatherwood Hospital, Ascot
01344 623333
Heavitree Hospital, Exeter
01392 411611
Hellesdon Hospital, Norwich
01603 421421
Helston Hospital
01326 435800
Hemel Hempstead General Hospital
01442 213141
Herbert Hospital, Bournemouth
01202 584300
Hereford County Hospital
01432 355444
Hertford County Hospital
01438 314333
Herts & Essex Hospital,
Bishop's Stortford
01279 444455
Hexham General Hospital
0844 811 8118
Highbury Hospital, Nottingham
0115 977 0000
Highfield Day Hospital,
Chester le Street
0191 333 6262
Highfield Hospital, Widnes
0151 495 5079
Hill Crest Mental Health Unit,
Redditch
01527 500575
Hillingdon Hospital, Uxbridge
01895 238282
Hinchingbrooke Hospital,
Huntingdon
01480 416416
Holbeach Hospital, Spalding
01406 422283
Holme Valley Memorial Hospital,
Holmfirth
01484 681711
Homeopathic Hospital, Tunbridge
Wells
01892 522598

Homerton University Hospital,
London
020 8510 5555
Honiton Hospital
01404 540540
Hope Hospital, Salford
0161 206 4840
Hornsea Cottage Hospital
01964 533146
Horsham Hospital
01403 227000
Horton Hospital, Banbury
01295 275500
Hospital for Tropical Diseases,
London
0845 155 5000
Hospital of St Cross, Rugby
01788 572831
Huddersfield Royal Infirmary
01484 342000
Hull Royal Infirmary
01482 328541
Hundens Lane Day Hospital,
Darlington
01325 380100
Hunters Moor Hospital,
Newcastle-upon-Tyne
01670 512121
Hurstwood Park Neurosciences
Centre, Haywards Heath
01444 441881
Hyde Hospital, Cheshire
0161 366 8833
Hythe Hospital, Southampton
023 8084 5955

I

Ilkeston Community Hospital
0115 930 5522
Ipswich Hospital
01473 712233

J

James Cook University Hospital,
Middlesbrough
01642 850850
James Paget Hospital, Great
Yarmouth
01493 452452
John Coupland Hospital,
Gainsborough
01427 816500
John Radcliffe Hospital, Oxford
01865 741166
Johnson Hospital, Spalding
01476 565232
Julian Hospital, Norwich
01603 421800

K

Kendray Hospital, Barnsley
01226 777811
Kent & Canterbury Hospital,
Canterbury
01227 766877
Kent and Sussex Hospital,
Tunbridge Wells
01892 526111
Kettering General Hospital
01536 492000
Keynsham Hospital, Bristol
0117 986 2356

Kidderminster Hospital
01562 823424
King Edward VII Hospital, Windsor
01753 860441
King George Hospital, Ilford
020 8983 8000
King's College Hospital, London
020 7737 4000
King's Mill Hospital, Sutton in
Ashfield
01623 622515
Kings Park Hospital, Bournemouth
01202 303757
Kingston Hospital,
Kingston-upon-Thames
020 8546 7711
Knutsford and District Community
Hospital
01565 757220

L

Lady Eden Hospital, Bishop
Auckland
01388 455060
Launceston General Hospital
01566 765650
Leatherhead Hospital
01372 384384
Leeds Dental Hospital
0113 244 0111
Leeds General Infirmary
0113 243 2799
Leek Moorlands Hospital
01538 487100
Leicester General Hospital,
Leicester
0116 249 0490
Leicester Royal Infirmary, Leicester
0116 254 1414
Leigh Infirmary, Leigh
01942 672333
Leighton Hospital, Crewe
01270 255141
Leominster Community Hospital,
Leominster
01568 614211
Lewes Victoria Hospital
01273 474153
Lincoln County Hospital
01522 512512
Lings Bar Hospital, Nottingham
0115 945 5577
Liskeard Community Hospital
01579 335600
Lister Hospital, Stevenage
01438 314333
Little Brook Hospital, Dartford
01322 622222
Little Court Day Hospital,
Burnham-on-Sea
01278 786876
Liverpool Women's Hospital,
Liverpool
0151 708 9988
Livingstone Hospital, Dartford
01322 622222
London Chest Hospital
020 7377 7000
Longton Cottage Hospital,
Stoke-on-Trent
01782 425600
Louth County Hospital
01507 600100

Lowestoft Hospital
01502 587311
Lucy Baldwyn Hospital,
Stourport-on-Severn
01299 827327
Ludlow Hospital
01584 872201
Luton & Dunstable Hospital
0845 127 0127
Lydney and District Hospital
01594 598220
Lymington Hospital
01590 677011
Lynfield Mount Hospital, Bradford
01274 494194
Lytham Hospital, Lytham St Annes
01253 303953

M

Macclesfield District General
Hospital, Macclesfield
01625 421000
Maidstone Hospital, Maidstone
01622 729000
Malmesbury Community Hospital
01666 823358
Malton and Norton Hospital
01653 693041
Malvern Community Hospital,
Malvern
01684 612600
Manchester Royal Eye Hospital
0161 276 1234
Manchester Royal Infirmary
0161 276 1234
Manor Hospital, Walsall
01922 721172
Mansfield Community Hospital
01623 785050
Market Harborough & District
Hospital, Market Harborough
01858 410500
Mary Hewetson Community
Hospital, Keswick
01768 767000
Maudsley Hospital, London
020 7703 6333
Mayday University Hospital,
Croydon
020 8401 3000
Medway Maritime Hospital,
Gillingham
01634 830000
Melksham Community Hospital
01225 701000
Melton War Memorial Hospital,
Melton Mowbray
01664 854800
Memorial Hospital, London
020 8836 8500
Mile End Hospital, London
020 7377 7000
Milford-on-Sea Hospital
01590 648110
Mill View Hospital, Hove
01273 696011
Millom Hospital, Cumbria
01229 772631
Milton Keynes General Hospital
01908 660033
Minehead Hospital
01643 707251

Montagu Hospital, Mexborough
01709 585171
Moore Hospital, Cheltenham
01451 820228
Moorgreen Hospital, Southampton
023 8047 2258
Moreton-in-Marsh Hospital
01608 650456
Moretonhampstead Hospital,
Newton Abbot
01647 440217
Morpeth Cottage Hospital
01670 395600
Moseley Hall Hospital, Birmingham
0121 442 4321
Mount Gould Hospital, Plymouth
01752 268011
Mount Vernon Hospital, Barnsley
01226 777835
Mount Vernon Hospital, Northwood
01923 826111
Musgrove Park Hospital, Taunton
01823 333444

N

National Hospital for Neurology
& Neurosurgery, London
020 7837 3611
Nelson Hospital, London
020 8296 2000
Nevill Hospital, Hove
01273 821680
New Cross Hospital,
Wolverhampton
01902 307999
New Epsom and Ewell Cottage
Hospital
01372 734834
Newark Hospital
01636 681681
Newcastle Dental Hospital,
Newcastle upon Tyne
0191 233 6161
Newcastle General Hospital,
Newcastle upon Tyne
0191 233 6161
Newham General Hospital, London
020 7476 4000
Newport Hospital, Shropshire
01952 820893
Newquay and District Hospital
01637 893600
Newton Abbot Hospital
01626 354321
Newton Community Hospital,
Newton-le-Willows
01925 222731
Newtown Hospital, Worcester
01905 763333
Norfolk & Norwich University
Hospital
01603 286286
North Devon District Hospital,
Barnstaple
01271 322577
North Hampshire Hospital,
Basingstoke
01256 473202
North Manchester General Hospital
0161 795 4567
North Middlesex University
Hospital, London
020 8887 2000

North Tyneside General Hospital, North Shields
0191 259 6660
Northampton General Hospital
01604 634700
Northern General Hospital, Sheffield
0114 243 4343
Northgate Hospital, Great Yarmouth
01493 337652
Northgate Hospital, Morpeth
01670 394000
Northwick Park Hospital, Harrow
020 8864 3232
Northwood & Pinner Hospital, Northwood
01923 824782
Norwich Community Hospital
01603 776776
Nottingham City Hospital
0115 969 1169

O

Okehampton Community Hospital
01837 658000
Oldchurch Hospital, Romford
01708 345533
Ongar War Memorial Hospital
01277 362629
Orchard Hill Hospital
020 8770 8000
Ormskirk and District General Hospital, Ormskirk
01695 577111
Orpington Hospital
01689 863000
Orsett Hospital
01268 533911
Ottery St Mary Hospital
01404 816000
Oxford Community Hospital
01865 225505

P

Paignton Hospital
01803 557425
Palmer Community Hospital, Jarrow
0191 451 6000
Papworth Hospital, Cambridge
01480 830541
Patrick Stead Hospital, Halesworth
01986 872124
Paulton Memorial Hospital, Bristol
01761 412315
Peasley Cross Hospital, St Helens
01744 458459
Pembury Hospital, Tunbridge Wells
01892 823535
Pendle Community Hospital, Nelson
01282 425071
Penrith Hospital
01768 245300
Pershore Cottage Hospital, Worcestershire
01386 502070
Peterborough District Hospital
01733 874000
Peterlee Community Hospital
0191 586 3474

Petersfield Hospital
01730 263221
Pilgrim Hospital, Boston
01205 364801
Pinderfields General Hospital, Wakefield
01924 201688
Plympton Hospital, Plymouth
01752 314500
Poltair Hospital, Penzance
01736 575570
Pontefract General Infirmary
01977 600600
Poole Hospital
01202 665511
Portland Hospital, Dorset
01305 820341
Potters Bar Community Hospital
01707 653286
Preston Hall Hospital, Aylesford
01622 710161
Primrose Hill Hospital, Jarrow
0191 451 6375
Princess Alexandra Hospital, Harlow
01279 444455
Princess Anne Hospital, Southampton
023 8077 7222
Princess Louise Hospital, London
020 8969 0133
Princess Marina Hospital, Northampton
01604 752323
Princess of Wales Community Hospital, Bromsgrove
01527 488000
Princess of Wales Hospital, Ely
01353 652000
Princess Royal Hospital, Haywards Heath
01444 441881
Princess Royal Hospital, Hull
01482 701151
Princess Royal Hospital, Telford
01952 641222
Princess Royal University Hospital, Orpington
01689 863000
Prospect Park Hospital, Reading
0118 960 5000
Prudhoe Hospital
01670 394000
Purley War Memorial Hospital
020 8401 3000

Q

Queen Alexandra Hospital, Portsmouth
023 9228 6000
Queen Charlotte's Hospital
020 8383 1111
Queen Elizabeth Hospital, Gateshead
0191 482 0000
Queen Elizabeth Hospital, King's Lynn
01553 613613
Queen Elizabeth Hospital, London
020 8836 6000
Queen Elizabeth II Hospital, Welwyn Garden City
01707 328111

Queen Elizabeth Medical Centre, Birmingham
0121 472 1311
Queen Elizabeth The Queen Mother Hospital, Margate
01843 225544
Queen Mary's Hospital, Roehampton, London
020 8487 6000
Queen Mary's Hospital, Sidcup
020 8302 2678
Queen Victoria Hospital, East Grinstead
01342 414000
Queen Victoria Hospital, Morecambe
01524 405700
Queen Victoria Memorial Hospital, Herne Bay
01227 594700
Queen's Hospital, Burton-upon-Trent
01283 566333
Queens Medical Centre, Nottingham
0115 924 9924
Queens Park Hospital, Blackburn
01254 263555

R

Radcliffe Infirmary, Oxford
01865 311188
Ramsbottom Cottage Hospital, Bury
01706 823123
Ravenscourt Park Hospital, London
020 8846 7777
Redcliffe Day Hospital, Wellingborough
01933 440181
Retford Hospital
01777 274400
Ribbleton Hospital, Preston
01772 401600
Richardson Hospital, Barnard Castle
01833 696500
Ridge Lea Hospital, Lancaster
01524 586200
Ridley Day Hospital, Wincanton
01963 34708
Ripley Hospital, Derbyshire
01773 743456
Ripon Community Hospital, Ripon
01765 602546
Robert Jones and Agnes Hunt Orthopaedic Hospital, Oswestry
01691 404000
Roborough Day Hospital, Eastbourne
01323 638972
Rochdale Infirmary
01706 377777
Romsey Hospital, Romsey
01794 834700
Ross Community Hospital, Ross-on-Wye
01989 562100
Rossall Hospital, Fleetwood
01253 655104
Rossendale Hospital
01706 215151

Rotherham District General Hospital
01709 820000

Rowan House EMI Facility and Day Hospital, Malvern
01684 612763

Rowley Regis Hospital
0121 607 3465

Roxbourne Hospital, Harrow
020 8237 2000

Royal Albert Edward Infirmary, Wigan
01942 244000

Royal Alexandra Hospital for Sick Children, Brighton
01273 328145

Royal Berkshire Hospital, Reading
0118 322 5111

Royal Bolton Hospital
01204 390390

Royal Bournemouth General Hospital
01202 303626

Royal Brompton Hospital, London
020 7352 8121

Royal Cornwall Hospital, Truro
01872 250000

Royal Devon and Exeter Hospital
01392 411611

Royal Eye Infirmary, Plymouth
01752 315123

Royal Free Hospital, London
020 7794 0500

Royal Hallamshire Hospital, Sheffield
0114 271 1900

Royal Hampshire County Hospital, Winchester
01962 863535

Royal Lancaster Infirmary, Lancaster
01524 65944

Royal Leamington Spa Rehabilitation Hospital, Warwick
01926 317700

Royal Liverpool Children's Hospital, Alder Hey
0151 228 4811

Royal Liverpool University Dental Hospital
0151 706 2000

Royal Liverpool University Hospital
0151 706 2051

Royal London Homeopathic Hospital
020 7391 8833

Royal London Hospital
020 7377 7000

Royal Manchester Children's Hospital
0161 794 4696

Royal Marsden Hospital, London
020 7352 8171

Royal Marsden Hospital, Sutton
020 8642 6011

Royal National Hospital for Rheumatic Diseases, Bath
01225 465941

Royal National Orthopaedic Hospital, London
020 8954 2300

Royal National Throat, Nose and Ear Hospital, London
020 7915 1300

Royal Oldham Hospital
0161 624 0420

Royal Orthopaedic Hospital, Birmingham
0121 685 4000

Royal Preston Hospital
01772 716565

Royal Shrewsbury Hospital
01743 261000

Royal South Hants Hospital, Southampton
023 8063 4288

Royal Surrey County Hospital, Guildford
01483 571122

Royal Sussex County Hospital, Brighton
01273 696955

Royal United Hospital, Bath
01225 428331

Royal Victoria Hospital, Folkestone
01303 850202

Royal Victoria Infirmary, Newcastle-upon-Tyne
0191 233 6161

Royston Hospital
01763 242134

Rushden Hospital
01933 440666

Russells Hall Hospital, Dudley,
01384 456111

Ruth Lancaster James Hospital, Alston
01434 381218

Rutland Memorial Hospital, Oakham
01572 722552

Ryhope General Hospital, Sunderland
0191 565 6256

S

Saffron Walden Community Hospital
01799 562900

St Albans City Hospital
01727 866122

St Andrew's Hospital, London
020 7476 4000

St Ann's Hospital, Poole
01202 708881

St Anne's Hospital, Altrincham
0161 928 5851

St Anne's Orchard Psychiatric Day Hospital, Malvern
01684 561659

St Austell Community Hospital
01726 291199

St Barnabas Hospital, Saltash
01752 857400

St Bartholomew's Day Hospital, Liverpool
0151 489 6241

St Bartholomew's Hospital, London
020 7377 7000

St Barholomew's Hospital, Rochester
01634 810900

St Catherine's Hospital, Birkenhead
0151 678 7272

St Charles Hospital, London
020 8969 2488

St Christopher's Hospital, Fareham
01329 286321

St Clement's Hospital, Ipswich
01473 329000

St Clement's Hospital, London
020 8880 6296

St George's Hospital, Lincoln
01522 512 512

St George's Hospital, London
020 8672 1255

St George's Hospital, Morpeth
01670 512121

St George's Hospital, Stafford
01785 257888

St Helens Hospital
0151 426 1600

St Helier Hospital, Carshalton
020 8296 2000

St James' Hospital, Portsmouth
023 9282 2444

St James's University Hospital, Leeds
0113 243 3144

St John's Hospital, Chelmsford
01245 440761

St Leonard's Community Hospital, Ringwood
01202 584200

St Luke's Hospital, Bradford
01274 734744

St Luke's Hospital, Market Harborough
01858 410300

St Luke's Hospital, Middlesbrough
01642 516147

St Margaret's Hospital, Epping
01992 902010

St Mark's Hospital, Maidenhead
01628 632012

St Mark's Hospital, Harrow
020 8235 4000

St Martin's Hospital, Bath
01225 831500

St Martin's Hospital, Canterbury
01227 459584

St Mary's Hospital, Isle of Wight
01983 524081

St Mary's Hospital, Isles of Scilly
01720 422392

St Marys Hospital, Kettering
01536 410141

St Mary's Hospital, London
020 7886 6666

St Mary's Hospital, Manchester
0161 276 1234

St Mary's Hospital, Melton Mowbray
01664 854800

St Mary's Hospital, Portsmouth
023 9228 6000

St Michael's Hospital, Braintree
01245 440761

St Michael's Hospital, Bristol
0117 921 5411

St Michael's Hospital, Hayle
01736 753234

St Michael's Hospital, Warwick
01926 406789

St Monica's Hospital, York
01347 821214

St Nicholas Hospital, Newcastle-upon-Tyne
0191 213 0151

St Pancras Hospital, London
020 7530 3500
St Peter's Hospital, Chertsey
01932 872000
St Peter's Hospital, Maldon
01621 725323
St Richard's Hospital, Chichester
01243 788122
St Thomas' Hospital, London
020 7188 7188
Salisbury District Hospital,
Salisbury
01722 336262
Sandwell General Hospital,
West Bromwich
0121 553 1831
Savernake Hospital, Marlborough
01672 517200
Scarborough General Hospital
01723 368111
Scott Hospital, Plymouth
01752 314343
Scunthorpe General Hospital
01724 282282
Seacroft Hospital, Leeds
0113 264 8164
Seasons Day Hospital, Clevedon
01275 870316
Seaton Hospital
01297 23901
Sedgefield Community Hospital,
Stockton-on-Tees
01740 626600
Selby War Memorial Hospital
01757 702664
Selly Oak Hospital, Birmingham
0121 627 1627
Sevenoaks Hospital
01732 470200
Severalls Hospital, Colchester
01206 228630
Sheffield Children's Hospital
0114 271 7000
Shelton Hospital, Shrewsbury
01743 261000
Sheppey Community Hospital,
Isle of Sheppey
01795 879100
Shepton Mallet Community
Hospital
01749 342931
Shipley Hospital
01274 773390
Shotley Bridge Hospital, Consett
0191 333 2333
Sir Alfred Jones Memorial Hospital,
Liverpool
0151 494 3198
Sir GB Hunter Memorial Hospital,
Wallsend
0191 220 5953
Sir Robert Peel Hospital, Tamworth
01827 263800
Sittingbourne Memorial Hospital
01795 418300
Skegness & District General
Hospital
01754 762401
Skipton General Hospital
01756 792233
Solihull Hospital
0121 424 2000
South Hams Hospital, Kingsbridge
01548 852349

South Moor Hospital, Stanley
0191 333 6262
South Petherton Hospital
01460 240333
South Shore Hospital, Blackpool
01253 306106
South Tyneside District General
Hospital, South Shields
0844 811 3030
Southampton General Hospital
023 8077 7222
Southend Hospital,
Westcliff-on-Sea
01702 435555
Southlands Hospital,
Shoreham-by-Sea
01273 455622
Southmead Hospital, Bristol
0117 950 5050
Southport & Formby District
General Hospital, Southport
01704 547471
Southport General Infirmary
01704 547471
Southwold Hospital, Suffolk
01502 723333
Springfield University Hospital,
London
020 8672 9911
Staffordshire General Hospital,
Stafford
01785 257731
Stamford and Rutland Hospital
01780 764151
Stead Memorial Hospital, Redcar
01642 282282
Stepping Hill Hospital, Stockport
0161 483 1010
Stewart Day Hospital, St Helens
01744 458393
Stoke Mandeville Hospital,
Aylesbury
01296 315000
Stone House Hospital, Dartford
01322 622222
Stratford Hospital,
Stratford-upon-Avon
01789 205831
Stratton Hospital, Bude
01288 287700
Stretford Memorial Hospital,
Manchester
0161 881 5353
Stroud General Hospital
01453 562200
Stroud Maternity Hospital
01453 562140
Sunderland Eye Infirmary
0191 565 6256
Sunderland Royal Hospital
0191 565 6256
Surbiton Hospital
020 8399 7111
Sussex Eye Hospital, Brighton
01273 606126
Sutton Hospital, Surrey
020 8296 2000
Swanage Hospital, Swanage
01929 422282

T

Tameside General Hospital,
Ashton-under-Lyne
0161 331 6000
Tavistock Hospital
01822 612233
Teddington Memorial Hospital
020 8714 4000
Teignmouth Hospital
01626 772161
Tenbury and District General
Hospital, Tenbury Wells
01584 810643
Tewkesbury Hospital
01684 293303
Thornbury Hospital, Bristol
01454 412636
Tickhill Road Hospital, Doncaster
01302 796000
Tiddington Fields,
Stratford-upon-Avon
01789 261455
Tiverton & District Hospital
01884 235400
Tolworth Hospital, Surrey
020 8390 0102
Tonbridge Cottage Hospital
01732 353653
Torbay District General Hospital,
Torquay
01803 614567
Totnes Hospital
01803 862622
Trafford General Hospital,
Manchester
0161 748 4022
Trengweath Hospital, Redruth
01209 881900
Trowbridge Community Hospital
01225 752558

U

Uckfield Hospital
01825 769999
Ulverston Hospital
01229 484045
University College Hospital,
London
0845 155 5000
University Dental Hospital,
Manchester
0161 275 6666
University Hospital Aintree,
Liverpool
0151 525 5980
University Hospital Lewisham,
London
020 8333 3000
University Hospital of Hartlepool
01429 266654
University Hospital of North
Durham
0191 333 2333
University Hospital of North Tees,
Stockton-on-Tees
01429 266654
University of Bristol Dental Hospital
0117 928 4383
Upton Hospital, Slough
01753 821441

V

Verrington Hospital, Wincanton
01963 32006

Victoria Central Hospital, Merseyside
0151 678 7272

Victoria Cottage Hospital, Havant
01243 376041

Victoria Cottage Hospital, Maryport
01900 812634

Victoria Hospital, Deal
01304 865400

Victoria Hospital, Lichfield
01543 442000

Victoria Hospital, Sidmouth
01395 512482

Victoria Infirmary, Northwich
01606 564000

W

Walkergate Hospital, Newcastle upon Tyne
0191 233 6161

Wallingford Community Hospital
01491 208500

Walsgrave Hospital, Coventry
024 7660 2020

Walton Hospital, Chesterfield
01246 515151

Walton Hospital, Liverpool
0151 525 3611

Wansbeck General Hospital, Ashington
01670 521 212

Wantage Hospital
01235 205801

Wareham Community Hospital
01929 552433

Warminster Community Hospital
01985 212076

Warrington Hospital
01925 635911

Warwick Hospital
01926 495321

Waterside Mental Health Day Hospital
01386 502510

Watford General Hospital
01923 244366

Wathwood Hospital, Rotherham
01709 870800

Weardale Hospital, Stanhope
01388 528233

Welland Hospital, Spalding
01476 565232

Wellington & District Cottage Hospital
01823 662663

West Cornwall Edward Bolitho House Hospital
01736 575555

Wembley Community Hospital, London
020 8903 1323

Wesham Hospital Rehabilitation Unit, Preston
01253 655404

West Berkshire Community Hospital, Thatcham
01635 273300

West Cornwall Hospital, Penzance
01736 874000

West Cumberland Hospital, Whitehaven
01946 693181

West Heath Hospital, Birmingham
0121 627 1627

West Mendip Community Hospital
01458 836450

West Middlesex University Hospital, Isleworth
020 8560 2121

West Park Hospital, Wolverhampton
01902 444000

West Suffolk Hospital, Bury St Edmunds
01284 713000

West View Hospital, Tenterden
01580 261500

Westbourne Green Hospital, Bradford
01274 227599

Westbury Community Hospital
01373 823616

Western Community Hospital, Southampton
023 8047 5401

Western Eye Hospital, London
020 7886 6666

Westhaven Hospital, Weymouth
01305 786116

Westminster Memorial Hospital, Shaftesbury
01747 851535

Westmorland General Hospital, Kendal
01539 732288

Weston General Hospital, Weston-super-Mare
01934 636363

Weston Park Hospital, Sheffield
0114 226 5000

Westwood Hospital, Beverley
01482 886600

Wexham Park Hospital, Slough
01753 633000

Weymouth Community Hospital
01305 760022

Wharfedale Hospital, Otley
01943 465522

Whelley Hospital, Wigan
01942 244000

Whipps Cross University Hospital, London
020 8539 5522

Whiston Hospital, Prescot
0151 426 1600

Whitby Community Hospital
01947 604851

Whitchurch Hospital
01948 666292

Whitstable & Tankerton Hospital
01227 594400

Whittington Hospital, London
020 7272 3070

Whitworth Hospital, Matlock
01246 277271

Wigton Hospital, Cumbria
01697 366600

Willesden Hospital, London
0208 438 7000

William Harvey Hospital, Ashford
01233 633331

William Julien Courtauld Hospital, Braintree
01245 440761

Williton Hospital
01984 635600

Wimborne Hospital
01202 858200

Winchcombe Hospital, Cheltenham
01242 602341

Windsor Day Hospital, Shepton Mallet
01749 343911

Withernsea Community Hospital
01964 614666

Withington Hospital, Manchester
0161 434 5555

Witney Community Hospital
01993 209400

Woking Community Hospital
01483 715911

Wokingham Hospital
0118 949 5000

Wolverhampton and Midland Eye Infirmary
01902 307999

Woodlands Hospital, St Leonards on Sea
01424 755470

Woods Hospital, Glossop
01457 860783

Worcestershire Royal Hospital, Worcester
01905 763333

Workington Infirmary
01946 693181

Worthing Hospital
01903 205111

Wotton Lawn, Gloucester
01452 891500

Wrightington Hospital, Wigan
01942 244000

Wycombe Hospital, High Wycombe
01494 526161

Wythenshawe Hospital, Manchester
0161 998 7070

Y

Yeatman Hospital, Sherborne
01935 813991

Yeovil District Hospital
01935 475122

York Hospital
01904 631313

NHS England hospitals © NHS Connecting for Health

NHS hospitals: Wales

Aberbargoed Hospital
01443 828728

Aberdare General Hospital
01685 883811

Abergele Hospital
01745 832295

Abertillery & District Hospital
01495 214123

Amman Valley Hospital, Ammanford
01269 822226

Barry Hospital
01446 704000

Blaenavon Hospital
01495 790236

Blaina & District Hospital, Nantyglo
01495 293250

Bodnant EMI Unit, Llandudno
01492 862347

Brecon War Memorial Hospital, Brecon
01874 622443

Bro Cerwyn Day Hospital, Haverfordwest
01437 773157

Bro Ddyfi Community Hospital, Powys
01654 702266

Bron y Garth Hospital, Gwynedd
01766 770310

Bronglais General Hospital, Aberystwyth
01970 623131

Bronllys Hospital, Brecon
01874 711255

Bryn Beryl Hospital, Pwllheli
01758 701122

Bryn y Neuadd Hospital, Conwy
01248 682682

Brynmair Day Hospital, Llanelli
01554 772768

Bryntirion Hospital, Llanelli
01554 756567

Builth Wells Hospital
01982 552221

Caerphilly and District Miners' Hospital
029 2085 1811

Cardiff Royal Infirmary
029 2049 2233

Cardigan and District Memorial Hospital
01239 612214

Cefn Coed Hospital, Swansea
01792 561155

Cefni Hospital, Anglesey
01248 750117

Chepstow Community Hospital, Chepstow
01291 636636

Chirk Community Hospital
01691 772430

Cimla Hospital, Neath
01639 862000

Colwyn Bay Community Hospital
01492 515218

Conwy Hospital
01492 564300

County Hospital, Torfeen
01495 768768

Dan-y-Bryn Unit, Ebbw Vale
01495 353700

Deeside Community Hospital, Deeside
01244 830461

Denbigh Infirmary
01745 812624

Dewi Sant Hospital, Pontypridd
01443 486222

Dolgellau Hospital
01341 422479

Eryri Hospital, Caernarfon
01286 672481

Fairwood Hospital, Swansea
01792 203192

Ffestiniog Memorial Hospital
01766 831281

Flint Community Hospital
01352 732215

Garngoch Hospital, Swansea
01792 892921

Gellinudd Hospital, Swansea
01792 862221

Glan Clwyd District General Hospital, Rhyl
01745 583910

Glanrhyd Hospital, Bridgend
01656 752752

Glantraeth Day Hospital, Rhyl
01745 443270

Gorseinon Hospital, Swansea
01792 702222

Gorwelion Day Hospital, Aberystwyth
01970 615448

Groeswen Hospital, Port Talbot
01639 862000

Hill House Hospital, Swansea
01792 203551

HM Stanley Hospital, St Asaph
01745 583275

Holywell Community Hospital
01352 713003

Knighton Hospital
01547 528633

Llandough Hospital, Penarth
029 2071 1711

Llandovery Hospital
01550 722200

Llandrindod Wells Hospital
01597 822951

Llandudno General Hospital
01492 860066

Llanfrechfa Grange Hospital, Cwmbran
01633 623623

Llangollen Community Hospital
01978 860226

Llanidloes War Memorial Hospital
01686 412121

Lluesty Hospital, Holywell
01352 710581

Llwynypia Hospital, Rhondda
01443 440440

Maesteg Community Hospital
01656 752752

Maindiff Court Hospital, Abergavenny
01873 735500

Minffordd Hospital, Bangor
01248 352308

Mold Community Hospital
01352 758744

Monmouth Hospital
01600 713522

Montgomery County Infirmary, Newtown
01686 617200

Morriston Hospital, Swansea
01792 702222

Mountain Ash General Hospital
01685 872411

Mynydd Mawr Hospital, Llanelli
01269 841343

Neath Port Talbot Hospital, Port Talbot
01639 862000

Oakdale Hospital, Blackwood
01495 225207

Pontypridd & District Cottage Hospital
01443 486144

Prestatyn Community Hospital
01745 853487

Prince Charles Hospital, Merthyr Tydfil
01685 721721

Prince Phillip Hospital, Llanelli
01554 756567

Princess of Wales Hospital, Bridgend
01656 752752

Redwood Memorial Hospital, Rhymney
01685 840314

Rookwood Hospital, Cardiff
029 2041 5415

Royal Alexandra Hospital, Rhyl
01745 443000

Royal Glamorgan Hospital, Llantrisant
01443 443443

Royal Gwent Hospital, Newport
01633 234234

Ruthin Hospital
01824 702692

St Brynach's Day Hospital, Haverfordwest
01437 773157

St Cadoc's Hospital, Newport
01633 436700

St David's Hospital, Cardiff
029 2053 6666

St David's Hospital, Carmarthen
01267 237481

St Tydfil's Hospital, Merthyr Tydfil
01685 723244

St Woolos Hospital, Newport
01633 234234

Singleton Hospital, Swansea
01792 205666

South Pembrokeshire Hospital, Pembroke Dock
01646 682114

Swn-y-Gwynt Day Hospital, Ammanford
01269 595473

Tenby Cottage Hospital
01834 842040

Tonna Hospital, Neath
01639 862000

Tredegar General Hospital
01495 722271

Tregaron Hospital
01974 298203

Trevalyn Hospital
01244 570446
Ty Sirhowy Health Centre,
Blackwood
01495 229010
Tywyn & District War Memorial
Hospital, Tywyn
01654 710411
University Dental Hospital, Cardiff
029 2074 7747
University Hospital of Wales,
Cardiff
029 2074 7747
Victoria Memorial Hospital,
Welshpool
01938 553133
Whitchurch Hospital, Cardiff
029 2069 3191
Withybush General Hospital,
Haverfordwest
01437 764545
Wrexham Maelor Hospital,
Wrexham
01978 291100
Ysbyty George Thomas, Treorchy
01443 440440
Ysbyty Gwynedd, Bangor
01248 384384
Ysbyty Penrhos Stanley, Anglesey
01407 766000
Ysbyty'r Tri Chwm, Blaenau Gwent
01495 353200
Ystrad Mynach Hospital, Hangoed
01443 811411
Ystradgynlais Community Hospital,
Swansea
01639 844777

NHS hospitals: Scotland

Abbotsford Park Hospital,
Edinburgh
0131 447 2674
Aberdeen Maternity Hospital,
Aberdeen
0845 456 6000
Aberdeen Royal Infirmary
01224 681818
Aberfeldy Community Hospital
01887 820314
Aboyne Community Hospital
01339 886433
Adamson Hospital, Fife
01334 652901
Ailsa Hospital, Ayr
01292 610556
Annan Hospital
01461 203425
Arbroath Infirmary
01241 872584
Argyll & Bute Hospital, Argyll
01546 602323
Arran War Memorial Hospital,
Lamlash
01770 600777
Ashludie Hospital, Angus
01382 423000
Astley Ainslie Hospital, Edinburgh
0131 537 9000
Ayr Hospital
01292 610555
Ayrshire Central Hospital
01294 274191
Balfour Hospital, Kirkwall
01856 888000
Bannockburn Hospital
01786 813016
Belford Hospital, Fort William
01397 702481
Belhaven Hospital, Dunbar
01368 862246
Benbecula Hospital
01870 603603
Biggart Hospital
01292 470611
Birch Avenue Day Hospital, Perth
01738 553920
Blairgowrie Community Hospital
01250 874466
Blawarthill Hospital
0141 211 9030
Bo'ness Hospital
01506 829580
Bonnybridge Hospital
01324 814685
Borders General Hospital, Melrose
01896 826000
Brechin Infirmary
01356 622291
Brooksby Day Hospital
01475 676318
Caithness General Hospital, Wick
01955 605050
Cameron Hospital, Fife
01592 712472
Campbell Hospital, Banff
01261 842202
Campbell House, Gartnavel Royal
Hospital, Glasgow
0141 211 3600

Campbeltown Hospital, Argyll
01586 552224
Castle Douglas Hospital
01556 502333
Chalmers Hospital, Banff
01261 812567
Chalmers Hospital, Edinburgh
0131 536 1000
City Hospital, Edinburgh
0131 536 6000
Clackmannan County Hospital,
Alloa
01259 727374
Coathill Hospital, Coatbridge
01236 707769
Coldstream Cottage Hospital
01890 882417
Corstorphine Hospital, Edinburgh
0131 537 5000
County Community Hospital,
Invergordon
01349 852496
Crieff Community Hospital
01764 653173
Crosshouse Hospital, Kilmarnock
01563 521133
Dalrymple Hospital, Stranraer
01776 706900
Davidson Cottage Hospital, Girvan
01465 712571
Dr Gray's Hospital, Elgin
01343 543131
Dr Mackinnon Memorial Hospital,
Isle of Skye
01471 822491
Drumchapel Hospital, Glasgow
0141 211 6000
Dumbarton Joint Hospital
01389 812036
Dumfries and Galloway Royal
Infirmary, Dumfries
01387 246246
Dunaros Hospital, Isle of Mull
01680 300392
Dunbar Hospital, Thurso
01847 893263
Dundee Dental Hospital
01382 660111
Dunoon General Hospital
01369 704341
Dunrowan Day Hospital, Falkirk
01324 639009
Dykebar Hospital, Paisley
0141 884 5122
East Ayrshire Community Hospital
01290 429429
Eastern General Hospital,
Edinburgh
0131 536 7000
Edenhall Hospital, Musselburgh
0131 536 8000
Edinburgh Dental Hospital,
Edinburgh
0131 536 4900
Edinburgh Orthopaedic Trauma Unit
0131 536 1000
Edington Cottage Hospital, North
Berwick
01620 897040
Eyemouth Day Hospital
01890 751101

Falkirk & District Royal Infirmary,
Falkirk
01324 624000
Fleming Hospital, Aberlour
01340 871464
Forfar Infirmary, Angus
01307 464551
Forth Park Hospital, Kirkcaldy
01592 643355
Fraserburgh Hospital
01346 513151
Garrick Hospital, Stranraer
01776 702323
Gartnavel General Hospital,
Glasgow
0141 211 3000
Gilbert Bain Hospital, Lerwick
01595 743000
Glasgow Dental Hospital
0141 211 9600
Glasgow Homoeopathic Hospital
0141 211 1600
Glasgow Royal Infirmary
0141 211 4000
Glaxo Day Hospital, Monifieth
01382 527831
Glen O'Dee Hospital, Banchory
01330 822233
Glencoe Hospital, Glencoe
01855 811254
Glenrothes Hospital
01592 743505
Hairmyres Hospital, East Kilbride
01355 585000
Hartwood Hill Hospital, Shotts
01501 824575
Hawick Cottage Hospital
01450 372162
Hawick Day Hospital
01450 364300
Hawkhill Day Hospital, Dundee
01382 668300
Hay Lodge Hospital, Peebles
01721 722080
Herdmanflat Hospital, Haddington
0131 536 8300
Holmhead Hospital, Cumnock
01290 422220
Ian Charles Hospital,
Grantown-on-Spey
01479 872528
Insch Hospital
01464 820213
Inverclyde Royal Hospital,
Greenock
01475 633777
Inverurie Hospital
01467 620454
Irvine Memorial Hospital, Pitlochry
01796 472052
Islay Hospital, Isle of Islay
01496 301000
Johnstone Hospital, Johnstone
01505 331471
Kello Hospital, Biggar
01899 220077
Kelso Community Hospital
01573 223441
Kildean Hospital, Stirling
01786 446615
Kilsyth Victoria Memorial Hospital
01236 822172
Kirkcudbright Hospital
01557 330549

Kirklands Hospital, Bothwell
01698 245000
Knoll Hospital, Duns
01361 883373
Lady Home Hospital, Lanark
01555 851210
Lady Margaret Hospital, Isle of
Cumbrae
01475 530307
Lawson Memorial Hospital, Golspie
01408 633157
Leanchoil Hospital, Forres
01309 672284
Lightburn Hospital, Glasgow
0141 211 1500
Little Cairnie Hospital, Arbroath
01241 872584
Loanhead Hospital, Edinburgh
0131 440 0174
Lochmaben Hospital
01387 810255
Lorn and Islands District General
Hospital, Oban
01631 567500
Lynebank Hospital, Fife
01383 623623
Mackinnon Memorial Hospital,
Isle of Skye
01471 822491
Macmillan House, Perth
01738 639303
Maud Hospital
01771 613236
Merchiston Hospital, Johnstone
01505 328261
Mid Argyll Hospital, Argyll
01546 602449
Migdale Hospital, Bonar Bridge
01863 766211
Moffat Hospital
01683 220031
Monklands Hospital, Airdrie
01236 748748
Montrose Royal Infirmary
01674 830361
Murray Royal Hospital, Perth
01738 621151
Netherlea Hospital,
Newport-on-Tay
01382 543223
Newton Stewart Hospital
01671 402015
Ninewells Hospital, Dundee
01382 660111
Orchard House Day Hospital,
Stirling
01786 849717
Orleans Day Hospital, Dundee
01382 667322
Parkhead Hospital, Glasgow
0141 211 8300
Perth Royal Infirmary, Perth
01738 623311
Peterhead Community Hospital
01779 478234
Portree Hospital, Skye
01478 613200
Princes Street Day Hospital, Stirling
01786 474161
Princess Alexandra Eye Pavilion,
Edinburgh
0131 536 1000

Princess Royal Maternity Hospital,
Glasgow
0141 211 5400
Queen Margaret Hospital,
Dunfermline
01383 623623
Queen Mother's Hospital, Glasgow
0141 201 0550
Raigmore Hospital, Inverness
01463 704000
Randolph Wemyss Memorial
Hospital, Buckhaven
01592 712427
Ravenscraig Hospital, Greenock
01475 633777
Roadmeetings Hospital, Carluke
01555 772271
Roodlands Hospital, Haddington
0131 536 8300
Ross Memorial Hospital, Dingwall
01349 863313
Rosslynlee Hospital, Midlothian
0131 536 7600
Roxburghe House, Aberdeen
0845 456 6000
Royal Aberdeen Children's Hospital
0845 456 6000
Royal Alexandra Hospital, Paisley
0141 887 9111
Royal Cornhill Hospital, Aberdeen
0845 456 6000
Royal Dundee Liff Hospital
01382 423000
Royal Edinburgh Hospital
0131 537 6000
Royal Hospital for Sick Children,
Edinburgh
0131 536 0000
Royal Hospital for Sick Children,
Glasgow
0141 201 0000
Royal Infirmary of Edinburgh
0131 536 1000
Royal Northern, Inverness
01463 704000
Royal Scottish National Hospital,
Larbert
01324 570700
Royal Victoria Hospital, Dundee
01382 423000
Royal Victoria Hospital, Edinburgh
0131 537 5000
St Andrews Memorial Hospital, Fife
01334 472327
St Brendan's Hospital, Isle of Barra
01871 810465
St John's Hospital at Howden,
Livingston
01506 419666
St Margaret's Hospital,
Auchterarder
01764 662246
St Michael's Hospital, Linlithgow
01506 842053
St Vincent's Hospital, Kingussie
01540 661219
Sauchie Hospital, Alloa
01259 722060
Seafield Hospital, Buckie
01542 832081
Sister Margaret Hospital, Jedburgh
01835 863212

Southern General Hospital,
Glasgow
0141 201 1100
Spynie Hospital, Elgin
01343 567835
Stephen Hospital, Dufftown
01340 820215
Stirling Royal Infirmary, Stirling
01786 434000
Stobhill Hospital, Glasgow
0141 201 3000
Stracathro Hospital, Brechin
01356 647291
Strathclyde Hospital, Motherwell
01698 245000
Stratheden Hospital, Fife
01334 652611
Strathmartine Hospital, Dundee
01382 423000
Sunnyside Royal Hospital, Montrose
01674 830361
Thomas Hope Hospital, Langholm
01387 380417
Thornhill Hospital
01848 330205
Threshold Day Hospital, Dundee
01382 322026
Tippethill House, West Lothian
01501 745917
Town & County Hospital, Caithness
01955 604025
Town & County Hospital, Nairn
01667 452101
Turner Memorial Hospital, Keith
01542 882526
Turriff Hospital
01888 563293
Udston Hospital, Hamilton
01698 723200
Ugie Hospital, Peterhead
01779 472011
Uist and Barra Hospital
01870 603603
Vale of Leven District General
Hospital, Alexandria
01389 754121
Victoria Hospital, Isle of Bute
01700 503938
Victoria Infirmary, Glasgow
0141 201 6000
Victoria Infirmary, Helensburgh
01436 672158
Westbank Day Hospital, Falkirk
01324 624111
Wester Moffat Hospital, Airdrie
01236 763377
Western General Hospital,
Edinburgh
0131 537 1000
Western Infirmary, Glasgow
0141 211 2000
Western Isles Hospital, Stornoway
01851 704704
Weston Day Hospital, Fife
01334 652163
Whitehills Hospital, Angus
01307 475222
Whytemans Brae Hospital, Fife
01592 643355
Wishaw General Hospital
01698 361100
Woodend Hospital, Aberdeen
0845 456 6000

NHS hospitals: Northern Ireland

Alexandra Gardens Day Hospital,
Belfast
028 9080 2150
Altnagelvin Area Hospital,
Londonderry
028 7134 5171
Antrim Hospital
028 9442 4000
Ards Hospital, Newtownards
028 9181 2661
Armagh Community Hospital
028 3752 2281
Bangor Community Hospital
028 9147 5100
Belvoir Park Hospital, Belfast
028 9032 9241
Belfast City Hospital
028 9032 9241
Braid Valley Hospital, Ballymena
028 2563 5200
Causeway Hospital, Coleraine
028 7032 7032
Craigavon Area Hospital
028 3833 4444
Daisy Hill Hospital, Newry
028 3083 5000
Dalriada Hospital, Ballycastle
028 2766 6600
Downe Hospital, Downpatrick
028 4461 3311
Erne Hospital, Enniskillen
028 6638 2000
Forster Green Hospital, Belfast
028 9094 4444
Gransha Hospital, Londonderry
028 7186 0261
Holywell Hospital, Antrim
028 9441 3620
Knockbracken Mental Health
Services, Belfast
028 9056 5656
Lagan Valley Hospital, Lisburn
028 9266 5141
Longstone Hospital, Armagh
028 3752 2381
Lurgan Hospital
028 3832 9483
Mater Hospital, Belfast
028 9074 1211
Mid-Ulster Hospital, Magherafelt
028 7963 1031
Mourne Hospital, Co Down
028 4176 2235
Moyle Hospital, Larne
028 2827 5431
Muckamore Abbey Hospital,
Muckamore
028 9446 3333
Mullinure Hospital, Armagh
028 3752 2381
Musgrave Park Hospital, Belfast
028 9090 2000
Royal Belfast Hospital for Sick
Children, Belfast
028 9024 0503
Royal Maternity Hospital, Belfast
028 9024 0503
Royal Victoria Hospital, Belfast
028 9024 0503

St Luke's Hospital, Armagh
028 3752 2381
Shaftesbury Square Hospital,
Belfast
028 9032 9808
South Tyrone Hospital, Dungannon
028 8772 2821
Tyrone and Fermanagh Hospital,
Omagh
028 8283 3100
Tyrone County Hospital, Omagh
028 8283 3100
Ulster Hospital, Dundonald
028 9048 4511
Whiteabbey Hospital,
Newtownabbey
028 9086 5181

Private healthcare

● Main private
healthcare providers

Abbey Hospitals
020 7563 6550
www.abbeyhospitals.co.uk
BMI Healthcare
020 7009 4500
www.bmihealthcare.co.uk
British Pregnancy Advisory Sevice
0870 365 5050
www.bpas.org
Press: 020 7612 0206
BUPA Hospitals
020 7656 2000
www.bupahospitals.co.uk
Capio Healthcare
01234 273473
www.capio.co.uk
Four Seasons Health Care
01625 417800
www.fshc.co.uk
HCA International
020 7616 4848
www.hcainternational.com
Nuffield Hospitals
020 8390 1200
www.nuffieldhospitals.org.uk
Partnerships in Care
01763 255600
www.partnershipsincare.co.uk
Priory Healthcare
01372 860400
www.prioryhealthcare.co.uk

Law

Government

Home Office
0870 000 1585
www.homeoffice.gov.uk
Press: 020 7035 4381
Attorney General's Office
020 7271 2400
Press: 020 7271 2405/65
Department for Constitutional Affairs
020 7210 8614
www.lcd.gov.uk
Press: 020 7210 8512
Scottish Executive
0131 556 8400
www.scotland.gov.uk
Press office, justice desk:
0131 244 1111

● Government agencies

Law Commission
020 7453 1220
www.lawcom.gov.uk
Legal Services Commission
020 7759 0000
www.legalservices.gov.uk

The legal system

● Ombudsmen

Legal Services Ombudsman
0845 601 0794
www.olso.org
Scottish Legal Services Ombudsman
0131 556 9123
www.slso.org.uk

● Law associations

Administrative Law Bar Association
020 7583 1770
www.adminlaw.org.uk
Association of Personal Injury Lawyers
0870 609 1958
www.apil.com
Bar Council
020 7242 0082
www.barcouncil.org.uk
Press: 020 7222 2525
Chancery Bar Association
020 8883 1700
www.chba.org.uk
Commercial Bar Association
020 7404 2022
www.combar.com
Family Law Bar Association
020 7242 1289
www.flba.co.uk
Institute of Barristers' Clerks
020 7831 7144
www.barristersclerks.com

Institute of Legal Executives
01234 841000
www.ilex.org.uk
Press: 01234 845713
Justices' Clerks' Society
0151 255 0790
www.jc-society.co.uk
Law Society
020 7242 1222
www.lawsoc.org.uk
Press: 020 7320 5764
Legal Aid Practitioners' Group
020 7960 6068
www.lapg.co.uk
Magistrates' Association
020 7387 2353
www.magistrates-association.org.uk
Solicitors' Criminal Law Association
01273 676725
www.clsa.co.uk
Solicitors' Family Law Association
01689 850227
www.sfla.org.uk
Press: 020 7357 9215

The judiciary

● Justice agencies

Appeals Service
020 7712 2600
www.appeals-service.gov.uk
Children and Family Court Advisory and Support Service (Cafcass)
020 7510 7000
www.cafcass.gov.uk
See website for details of regional offices
Civil Justice Council
020 7947 6670
www.civiljusticecouncil.gov.uk
Court Service, Northern Ireland
028 9032 8594
www.courtsni.gov.uk
Press: 028 9041 2345
Courts Service
020 7189 2000
www.hmcourts-service.gov.uk
Press: 020 7210 8512
Criminal Cases Review Commission
0121 633 1800
www.ccrc.gov.uk
Criminal Records Bureau
0870 909 0811
www.crb.gov.uk
Crown Office and Procurator Fiscal Service, Scotland
0131 226 2626
www.crownoffice.gov.uk
Crown Prosecution Service
020 7796 8000
www.cps.gov.uk
Press: 020 7796 8442

HM Revenue & Customs
0845 010 9000
www.hmrc.gov.uk
Press -
business: 020 7147 2328/0798
personal: 020 7147 2318/319/333
law enforcement:
020 7147 0052/2314/2331
social: 020 7147 0452/2337/0051
Inspectorate of Court Administration
020 7217 4355
www.hmica.gov.uk
Scottish Courts Administration
0131 229 9200
www.scotcourts.gov.uk
Press: 0131 556 8400
Youth Justice Boards for England and Wales
020 7271 3033
www.youth-justice-board.gov.uk
Press: 020 7271 3014/2988

● Appeal courts

Court of Appeal
Civil cases: 020 7947 6409
Criminal: 020 7947 6014
Press -
individual cases: 020 7947 6000
policy: 020 7210 8512
High Court
020 7947 6000
Judicial Committee of the Privy Council
020 7276 0483/5/7
Supreme Courts, Scotland
0131 225 2595
High Court (criminal) and Court of Session (civil)
High Court of Justiciary, Scotland
0131 240 2906
Press: 0131 244 2642/2656/2939/3073
Supreme Court of Northern Ireland
028 9072 4661
Press: 028 9041 2385

● Crown courts

Central Criminal Court - Old Bailey
020 7248 3277
Aylesbury
01296 434401
Barnstaple
01271 373286
Basildon Combined Court
01268 458000
Birmingham
0121 681 3300
Blackfriars
020 7922 5800
Bolton Combined Court Centre
01204 392881
Bournemouth
01202 502800

Bradford Combined Court Centre
01274 840274
Bristol
0117 976 3030
Burnley Combined Court Centre
01282 416899
Bury St Edmunds
01473 228585
Caernarfon
01286 675753
Cambridge
01223 488321
Canterbury Combined Court Centre
01227 819200
Cardiff
029 2041 4400
Carlisle Combined Court Centre
01228 520619
Carmarthen
01792 637000
Chelmsford
01245 603000
Chester
01244 317606
Chichester Combined Court Centre
01243 520700
Coventry Combined Court Centre
024 7653 6166
Croydon
020 8410 4700
Derby Combined Court Centre
01332 622600
Dolgellau
01341 423081
Doncaster
01302 322211
Dorchester
01305 752510
Durham
0191 386 6714
Exeter Combined Court Centre
01392 415300
Gloucester
01452 420100
Great Grimsby Combined Court Centre
01472 265250
Guildford
01483 468500
Harrow
020 8424 2294
Hereford
01432 276118
Hove Trial Centre
01273 229200
Inner London
020 7234 3100
Ipswich
01473 228 585
Isleworth
020 8380 4500
King's Lynn
01553 760847
Kingston-upon-Hull Combined Court Centre
01482 586161
Kingston-upon-Thames
020 8240 2500
Knutsford
01565 624020
Lancaster Crown Court
01772 844700

Leeds Combined Court Centre
0113 306 2800
Leicester Crown Court
0116 222 5800
Lewes Combined Court Centre
01273 480400
Lincoln
01522 525222
Liverpool
0151 473 7373
Luton
01582 522000
Maidstone
01622 202000
Manchester (Crown Square)
0161 954 1800
Manchester at Minshull St
0161 954 7500
Merthyr Tydfil Combined Court Centre
01685 358222
Middlesex Guildhall
020 7202 0370
Mold
01352 707340
Newcastle upon Tyne Combined Court Centre
0191 201 2000
Newport (South Wales)
01633 266211
Newport, I.O.W.
01983 535100
Northampton Combined Court
01604 470400
Norwich Combined Court Centre
01603 728200
Nottingham
0115 910 3551
Oxford Combined Court Centre
01865 264200
Peterborough Combined Court Centre
01733 349161
Plymouth Combined Court
01752 677400
Portsmouth Combined Court Centre
023 9289 3000
Preston Combined Court Centre
01772 844700
Reading
0118 967 4400
Salisbury Combined Court Centre
01722 325444
Sheffield Combined Court Centre
0114 281 2400
Shrewsbury
01743 260820
Snaresbrook
020 8530 0000
Southampton Combined Court Centre
023 8021 3200
Southend
01268 458000
Southwark
020 7522 7200
St. Albans
01727 753220
Stafford Combined Court Centre
01785 610730
Stoke-on-Trent Combined Court
01782 854000

Swansea
01792 637000
Swindon Combined Court
01793 690500
Taunton
01823 281100
Teesside Combined Court Centre
01642 340000
Truro
01872 222328
Warrington Combined Court Centre
01925 256700
Warwick Combined Court Centre
01926 495428
Welshpool
01938 553144
Weymouth and Dorchester Combined Court Centre
01305 752510
Winchester Combined Court Centre
01962 814100
Wolverhampton Combined Court Centre
01902 48100
Wood Green
020 8826 4100
Woolwich
020 8312 7000
Worcester Combined Court Centre
01905 730800
York
01904 645121

● County courts

Aberdare
01685 888575
Aberystwyth
01970 636370
Accrington
01254 237490
Aldershot & Farnham
01252 796800
Altrincham
0161 975 4760
Ashford
01233 632464
Aylesbury
01296 393498
Banbury
01295 452090
Barnet
020 8343 4272
Barnsley
01226 777550
Barnstaple
01271 372252
Barrow-In-Furness
01229 840370
Basildon Combined Court
01268 458000
Basingstoke
01256 318200
Bath
01225 310282
Bedford
01234 760400
Birkenhead
0151 666 5800
Birmingham Civil Justice Centre
0121 681 4441
Bishop Auckland
01388 660251
Blackburn
01254 680640
Blackpool
01253 754020
Blackwood
01495 223197
Bodmin
01208 74224/73735
Bolton Combined Court
01204 392881
Boston
01205 366080
Bournemouth
01202 502800
Bow
020 8536 5200
Bradford Combined Court Centre
01274 840274
Brecknock
01685 358222
Brentford
020 8231 8940
Bridgend
01656 673 833
Brighton
01273 674421
Brighton County Court Family Centre
01273 811333
Bristol
0117 910 6700
Bromley
020 8290 9620

Burton Upon Trent County Court
01283 568241
Burnley Combined Court
01282 416899
Bury
0161 447 8699
Bury St Edmunds
01284 753254
Buxton
01298 23734
Caernarfon
01286 684600
Cambridge
01223 224500
Canterbury Combined Court
01227 819200
Cardiff Civil Justice Centre
029 2037 6400
Carlisle Combined Court Centre
01228 520619
Carmarthen
01267 228010
Central London
020 7917 5000
Cheltenham
01452 834900
Chelmsford
01245 264670
Chester Civil Justice Centre
01244 404200
Chesterfield
01246 501200
Chichester
01243 520700
Chorley
01257 262778
Clerkenwell
020 7250 7200
Colchester
01206 717200
Consett
01207 502854
Conwy & Colwyn
01492 530807
Coventry Combined Court Centre
024 7653 6166
Crewe
01270 539300
Croydon Combined Court
020 8410 4797
Darlington
01325 463224
Dartford
01322 629820
Derby Combined Court
01332 622600
Dewsbury
01924 466135
Doncaster
01302 381730
Dudley
01384 480799
Durham
0191 3865941
Eastbourne
01323 735195
Edmonton
020 8884 6500
Epsom
01372 721801
Evesham
01386 442287

Exeter Combined Court
01392 415300
Gateshead
0191 477 2445
Gloucester
01452 834900
Grantham
01476 539030
Gravesend
01474 321771
Great Grimsby Combined Court
01472 265200
Guildford
01483 595200
Halifax
01422 344700
Harlow
01279 443291
Harrogate
01423 503921
Hartlepool
01429 268198
Hastings
01424 435128
Haverfordwest
01437 772060
Haywards Heath
01444 447970
Hertford
01992 503954
Hereford
01432 357233
High Wycombe
01494 436374
Hitchin
01462 443750
Horsham
01403 252474
Huddersfield
01484 421043
Huntingdon
01480 450932
Ilford
020 8478 1132
Ipswich
01473 214256
Keighley
01535 602803
Kendal
01539 721218
Kettering
01536 512471
Kidderminster
01562 822480
King's Lynn
01553 772067
Kingston upon Hull
01482 586161
Kingston-upon-Thames
020 8546 8843
Lambeth
020 7091 4410/20
Lancaster
01524 68112
Leeds
0113 306 2800
Leicester
0116 222 5700
Leigh
01942 673639
Lewes Combined Court
01273 480400

Lincoln Combined Court
01522 883000
Liverpool Combined Court
0151 296 2200
Llanelli
01554 757171
Llangefni
01248 750225
Lowestoft
01502 501060
Ludlow
01584 872091
Luton
01582 506700
Macclesfield
01625 412800
Maidstone Combined Court
01622 202000
Manchester
0161 954 1800
Mansfield
01623 656406
Mayor's & City Of London Court
020 7796 5400
Medway
01634 810720
Melton Mowbray
01664 485100
Merthyr Tydfil Combined Court
01685 358200
Middlesborough County Court at
Teesside Combined Court
01642 340000
Milton Keynes
01908 302800
Mold
01352 707330
Morpeth & Berwick
01670 512221
Neath and Port Talbot
01639 642267
Nelson
01282 601177
Newark
01636 703607
Newbury County Court
01635 642210
Newcastle Combined Court
0191 201 2000
Newport (Gwent) County Court
01633 227150
Newport (Isle Of Wight)
01983 526821
North Shields
0191 2982339
Northampton Combined Court
01604 470400
Northwich
01606 42554
Norwich Combined Court
01603 728200
Nottingham
0115 910 3500
Nuneaton
024 7648 2970
Oldham
0161 290 4200
Oswestry
01691 652127
Oxford Combined Court Centre
01865 264200
Penrith
01768 862535

Penzance
01736 362987
Peterborough Combined Court
01733 349161
Plymouth Combined Court
01752 677400
Pontefract
01977 702357
Pontypool
01495 762248
Pontypridd
01443 490800
Poole
01202 741150
Portsmouth Combined Court
023 9289 3000
Preston Combined Court
01772 844700
Rawtenstall
01706 214614
Reading
0118 987 0500
Redditch
01527 67822
Reigate
01737 763637
Rhyl
01772 844700
Romford
01708 775353
Rotherham
01709 364786
Rugby
01788 542543
Runcorn
01928 716533
St Albans
01727 856925
St Helens
01744 27544
Salford
0161 745 7511
Salisbury
01722 325444
Scarborough
01723 366361
Scunthorpe
01724 289111
Sheffield Combined Court
0114 281 2400
Shrewsbury
01743 289069
Skegness
01205 366080
Skipton
01756 692650
Slough
01753 690300
South Shields
0191 456 3343
Southampton Combined Court
023 8021 3200
Southend
01702 601991
Southport
01704 531541
Stafford
01785 610730
Staines
01784 459175
Stockport
01614 747707

Stoke On Trent Combined Court
01782 854000
Stourbridge
01384 394232
Stratford upon Avon
01789 293056
Sunderland
0191 568 0750
Swansea Civil Justice Centre
01792 510350
Swindon Combined Court
01793 690500
Tameside
0161 331 5614
Tamworth
01827 62664
Taunton
01823 281110
Teesside Combined Court
01642 340000
Telford
01952 238280
Thanet
01843 221722
Torquay & Newton Abbot
01803 616791
Trowbridge
01225 752101
Truro Combined Court
01872 222340
Tunbridge Wells
01892 515515
Uxbridge
020 8561 8562
Wakefield
01924 370268
Walsall
01922 728855
Wandsworth
020 8333 4351
Warrington Combined Court
01925 256700
Warwick Combined Court Centre
01926 492276
Watford
01923 699400/1
Wellingborough
01933 226168/222393
Welshpool And Newtown
01938 552004
West London
020 8600 6868
Weston Super Mare
01934 626967
Weymouth & Dorchester
01305 752510
Whitehaven
01946 67788
Wigan
01942 246481
Winchester Combined Court
01962 814100
Willesden
020 8963 8200
Wolverhampton Combined Court
01902 481000
Woolwich
020 8854 2127
Worcester Combined Court
01905 730800
Worksop
01909 472358

Worthing
01903 221920
Wrexham
01978 296140
Yeovil
01935 382150
York
01904 629935

● Sheriff courts, Scotland

Aberdeen
01224 657200
Airdrie
01236 751121
Alloa
01259 722734
Arbroath
01241 876600
Ayr
01292 268474
Banff
01261 812140
Campbeltown
01586 552503
Cupar
01334 652121
Dingwall
01349 863153
Dornoch
01862 810224
Dumbarton
01389 763266
Dumfries
01387 262334
Dundee
01382 229961
Dunfermline
01383 724666
Dunoon
01369 704166
Duns
01835 863231
Edinburgh
0131 225 2525
Elgin
01343 542505
Falkirk
01324 620822
Forfar
01307 462186
Fort William
01397 702087
Glasgow
0141 429 8888
Greenock
01475 787073
Haddington
01620 822936
Hamilton
01698 282957
Inverness
01463 230782
Jedburgh
01835 863231
Kilmarnock
01563 550024
Kirkcaldy
01592 260171
Kirkcudbright
01557 330574
Kirkwall
01856 872110

Lanark
01555 661531
Lerwick
01595 693914
Linlithgow
01506 842922
Livingston
01506 462118
Lochmaddy
01876 500340
Oban
01631 562414
Paisley
0141 887 5291
Peebles
01721 720204
Perth
01738 620546
Peterhead
01779 476676
Portree
01478 612191
Rothesay
01700 502982
Selkirk
01750 21269
Stirling
01786 462191
Stonehaven
01569 762758
Stornoway
01851 702231
Stranraer
01776 702138
Tain
01862 892518
Wick
01955 602846

● Northern Ireland courts

Antrim
028 9446 2661
Armagh
028 3572 2816
Ballymena
028 2564 9416
Banbridge
028 4062 3622
Bangor
028 9147 2626
Belfast
028 9032 8594
Coleraine
028 7034 3437
Craigavon
028 3834 1324
Derry
028 7136 3448
Downpatrick
028 4461 4621
Dungannon
028 8772 2992
Enniskillen
028 6632 2356
Larne
028 2827 2927
Limavady
028 7772 2688
Lisburn
028 9267 5336
Londonderry
028 7136 3448

Magherafelt
028 7963 2121
Newry
028 3025 2040
Newtownards
028 9181 4343
Omagh
028 8224 2056
Strabane
028 7138 2544

Law centres

Law Centres Federation
020 7387 8570
www.lawcentres.org.uk
Avon & Bristol
0117 924 8662
Barnet
020 8203 4141
Battersea
020 7585 0716
Bradford
01274 306617
Brent Community
020 8451 1122
Bury
0161 272 0666
Cambridge House Law Centre
020 7703 3051
Camden Community
020 7284 6510
Cardiff
029 2049 8117
Carlisle
01228 515129
Central London
020 7839 2998
Chesterfield
01246 550674
Coventry
024 7622 3053
Croydon & Sutton Law Centre (SWLLC)
020 8667 9226
Derby
01332 344557
Devon
01752 519794
Enfield Law Centre
020 8807 8888
Gateshead
0191 440 8585
Gloucester
01452 423492
Greenwich Community
020 8305 3350
Hackney Community
020 8985 8364
Hammersmith & Fulham
020 8741 4021
Harehills & Chapeltown
0113 249 1100
Haringey
020 8808 5354
Hillingdon
020 8561 9400
Hounslow
020 8570 9505
Isle of Wight Law Centre
01983 524715
Islington
020 7607 2461

Kingston & Richmond Law Centre (SWLLC)
020 8547 2882
Lambeth
020 7737 9780
Leicester
0116 242 1160
Lewisham
020 8692 5355
Liverpool
0151 709 7222
Luton
01582 481000
Newcastle
0191 230 4777
North Kensington
020 8969 7473
North Manchester
0161 205 5040
Nottingham
0115 978 7813
Oldham
0161 627 0925
Paddington
020 8960 3155
Plumstead Community
020 8855 9817
Rochdale
01706 657766
Rotherham
01709 838988
Saltley & Nechells
0121 328 2307
Sheffield
0114 273 1888
South Manchester
0161 225 5111
Southwark
020 7732 2008
Springfield
020 8767 6884
Stockport
0161 476 6336
Streetwise Community
020 8778 5854
Surrey
01483 215 000
Thamesmead
020 8311 0555
Tottenham
020 8800 5354
Tower Hamlets
020 7247 8998
Trafford Law Centre
0161 872 3669
Vauxhall Law and Information Centre
0151 482 2001
Wandsworth & Merton
020 8767 2777
Warrington Community
01925 651104
Wiltshire
01793 486926
Wythenshawe
0161 498 0905/6
Northern Ireland: Belfast
028 9024 4401
Northern Ireland: western area
028 7126 2433

Prisons

● Prison services

National Offender Management Service
0870 000 1585
www.noms.homeoffice.gov.uk
Press: 020 7035 4381
Victim helpline: 0845 758 5112
Her Majesty's Inspectorate of Prisons for England and Wales (HMIP)
020 7035 2136
www.homeoffice.gov.uk
Northern Ireland Prison Service
028 9052 5065
www.niprisonservice.gov.uk
Parole Board for England and Wales
0870 420 3505
www.paroleboard.gov.uk
Prisons Ombudsman for England and Wales
020 7035 2876
www.ppo.gov.uk
Scottish Parole Board
0131 244 8373
www.scottishparoleboard.gov.uk
Scottish Prison Service
0131 244 8745
www.sps.gov.uk
Scottish Prisons Inspectorate
0131 244 8481

● Professional bodies

Prison Governors Association
020 7217 8591
www.prisongovernors.org.uk
Prison Officers Association
020 8803 0255
www.poauk.org.uk
National Association of Official Prison Visitors
01234 359763
www.brittain.plus.com/naopv
National Association of Probation Officers (Napo)
020 7223 4887
www.napo.org.uk
Trade union and professional association for family court and probation staff

● Campaign groups

Action for Prisoners' Families
020 8812 3600
www.prisonersfamilies.org.uk
Apex Trust
020 7638 5931
www.apextrust.com
Campaign for Freedom of Information
020 7831 7477
www.cfoi.org.uk
Committee on the Administration of Justice (Northern Ireland)
028 9096 1122
www.caj.org.uk

Howard League for Penal Reform
020 7249 7373
www.howardleague.org
Inquest
020 7263 1111
www.inquest.org.uk
Justice
020 7329 5100
www.justice.org.uk
Liberty
020 7403 3888
www.liberty-human-rights.org.uk
Minority Rights Group
020 7422 4200
www.minorityrights.org
National Association for the Care and Resettlement of Offenders
020 7582 6500
www.nacro.org.uk
Prison Reform Trust
020 7251 5070
www.prisonreformtrust.org.uk
Prisoners Advice Service
020 7253 3323
www.prisonersadviceservice.org.uk
Prisoners Family and Friends
020 7403 4091/9359
www.prisonersfamiliesandfriends.org.uk
Unit for the Arts and Offenders
01227 470 629
www.apcentre.org.uk
Unlock
01634 247350
www.unlockprison.org.uk
National association of ex-offenders
Women in Prison
020 7226 5879
www.womeninprison.org.uk

● Prisons for men

Acklington
01670 762300
Albany
01983 556300
Altcourse*
0151 522 2000
Ashfield*
0117 303 8000
Ashwell
01572 884100
Aylesbury
01296 444000
Bedford
01234 373000
Belmarsh
020 8331 4400
Birmingham
0121 345 2500
Blakenhurst
01527 400500
Blantyre House
01580 213200
Blundeston
01502 734500
Brinsford
01902 532450
Bristol
0117 372 3100
Brixton
020 8588 6000
Brockhill
01527 552650
Bullingdon
01869 353100
Camp Hill
01983 554600
Canterbury
01227 862800
Cardiff
02920 923100
Castington
01670 382100
Channings Wood
01803 814600
Chelmsford
01245 272000
Coldingley
01483 804300
Dartmoor
01822 892000
Deerbolt
01833 633200
Doncaster*
01302 760870
Dorchester
01305 214500
Dovegate*
01283 829400
Downview
020 8929 3300
Durham
0191 332 3400
Edmunds Hill
01440 743500
Elmley
01795 882000
Erlestoke
01380 814250
Everthorpe
01430 426500

Featherstone
01902 703000
Feltham
020 8844 5000
Ford
01903 663000
Forest Bank*
0161 925 7000
Foston Hall
01283 584300
Frankland
0191 332 3000
Full Sutton
01759 475100
Garth
01772 443300
Gartree
01858 436600
Glen Parva
0116 228 4100
Gloucester
01452 453000
Grendon
01296 443000
Guys Marsh
01747 856400
Haverigg
01229 713000
Hewell Grange
01527 552000
High Down
020 8722 6300
Highpoint
01440 743100
Hindley
01942 855000
Hollesley Bay
01394 412400
Holme House
01642 744000
Hull
01482 282200
Huntercombe
01491 643100
Kingston
023 9295 3100
Kirkham
01772 675400
Kirklevington Grange
01642 792600
Lancaster Castle
01524 565 100
Lancaster Farms
01524 563450
Latchmere House
020 8500 6650
Leeds
0113 203 2600
Leicester
0116 228 3000
Lewes
01273 785100
Leyhill
01454 264000
Lincoln
01522 663000
Lindholme
01302 524700
Littlehey
01480 333000
Liverpool
0151 530 4000
Long Lartin
01386 835100

Lowdham Grange*
0115 966 9200
Maidstone
01622 775300
Manchester
0161 817 5600
Moorland
01302 523000
The Mount
01442 836300
Northallerton
01609 785100
North Sea Camp
01205 769300
Norwich
01603 708600
Nottingham
0115 872 3000
Onley
01788 523400
Parc*
01656 300200
Parkhurst
01983 554000
Pentonville
020 7023 7000
Peterborough*
01733 217500
Portland
01305 825600
Prescoed
01291 675000
Preston
01772 444550
Ranby
01777 862000
Reading
0118 908 5000
Risley
01925 733000
Rochester
01634 803100
Rye Hill*
01788 523300
Send
01483 471000
Shepton Mallett
01749 823300
Shrewsbury
01743 273000
Spring Hill
01296 443000
Stafford
01785 773000
Standford Hill
01795 884500
Stocken
01780 795100
Stoke Heath
01630 636000
Sudbury
01283 584000
Swaleside
01795 804100
Swansea
01792 485300
Swinfen Hall
01543 484000
Thorn Cross
01925 805100
Usk
01291 671600
The Verne
01305 825000

Wakefield
01924 246000
Wandsworth
020 8588 4000
Warren Hill
01394 412400
Wayland
01953 804100
Wealstun
01937 848500
The Weare
01305 825400
Wellingborough
01933 232700
Werrington
01782 463300
Wetherby
01937 544200
Whatton
01949 859200
Whitemoor
01354 602350
Winchester
01962 723000
Wolds*
01430 428000
Woodhill
01908 722000
Wormwood Scrubs
020 8588 3200
Wymott
01772 444000

● Prisons for women

Askham Grange
01904 772000
Bronzefield*
01784 425690
Buckley Hall
01706 514300
Bullwood Hall
01702 562800
Cookham Wood
01634 202500
Drake Hall
01785 774100
East Sutton Park
01622 845000
Eastwood Park
01454 382100
Exeter
01392 415650
Holloway
020 7979 4400
Low Newton
0191 376 4000
Morton Hall
01522 666700
New Hall
01924 844200
Peterborough*
01733 217500
Styal
01625 553000

Law

● Prisons in Scotland

Aberdeen
01224 238300
Barlinnie
0141 7702000
Castle Huntly
01382 319333
Cornton Vale
01786 832591
Dumfries
01387 261218
Edinburgh
0131 444 3000
Glenochil
01259 760471
Greenock
01475 787801
Inverness
01463 229000
Kilmarnock*
01563 548800
Low Moss
0141 7624848
Noranside
01382 319333
Perth
01738 622293
Peterhead
01779 479101
Polmont
01324 711558
Shotts
01501 824000

● Prisons in Northern Ireland

Hydebank Wood
028 9025 3666
Maghaberry
028 9261 1888
Magilligan
028 7776 3311

● Immigration removal centres

Dover
01304 246400
Haslar
023 9260 4000

Legal advice

Activists Legal Project
01865 243772
www.activistslegalproject.org.uk
Legal information for activists
Asylum Aid
020 7377 5123
www.asylumaid.org.uk
Advice line: 020 7247 8741
CHAS Central London
020 7723 5928
www.chascl.org.uk
Housing and debt advice
Children's Legal Centre
01206 872466
www.childrenslegalcentre.com
Community Legal Service
0845 345 4345
www.clsdirect.org.uk
Counsel & Care
020 7241 8555
www.counselandcare.org.uk
Advice line: 0845 300 7585
Disability Law Service
020 7791 9800
Environmental Law Foundation
020 7404 1030
www.elflaw.org
Housing Justice
020 7723 7273
www.housingjustice.org.uk
Joint Council for the Welfare of Immigrants
020 7251 8708
www.jcwi.org.uk
Legal Action Group
020 7833 2931
www.lag.org.uk
Legal Services Research Centre
www.lsrc.org.uk
Liberty (the National Council for Civil Liberties)
www.yourrights.org.uk
Advice line: 0845 123 2307
National Youth Advocacy Service
0151 649 8700
www.nyas.net
Young people helpline:
0800 616101
Prisoners Advice Service
020 7253 3323
www.prisonersadviceservice.org.uk
Advice line: 0800 018 2156
Prisoners' Families Helpline
0808 808 2003
www.prisonersfamilieshelpline.org.uk
Public Law Project
020 7697 2190
www.publiclawproject.org.uk
Refugee Legal Centre
020 7780 3200
www.refugee-legal-centre.org.uk
Advice line: 020 7780 3220
UK Legal
0845 2801976
www.uklegal.com

Religion

Inter Faith Network for the UK
020 7931 7766
ifnet@interfaith.org.uk
www.interfaith.co.uk

Anglicanism

Anglican Communion
020 7313 3900
www.anglicancommunion.org
Archbishop of Canterbury
020 7898 1200
www.archbishopofcanterbury.org
Archbishop of York
01904 707021
www.bishopthorpepalace.co.uk/arch
bishop.html
Church in Wales
029 2034 8200
suebrookman@churchinwales.org.uk
www.churchinwales.org.uk
Church of England
020 7898 1000
www.cofe.anglican.org
Church of Ireland
00 353 1 497 8422
enquiries@ireland.anglican.org
www.ireland.anglican.org
Record Centre
020 7898 1400
www.lambethpalacelibrary.org
Scottish Episcopal Church
0131 225 6357
office@scotland.anglican.org
www.scotland.anglican.org

Catholicism

Catholic Church
020 7630 8220
www.catholic-ew.org.uk
Media Office
020 7901 4800
Provinces/ Archbishops
Armagh 028 3752 2045
Birmingham 0121 236 5535
Edinburgh 0131 452 8244
Glasgow 0141 226 5898
Cardiff 029 2022 0411
Liverpool 0151 522 1000
Southwark 020 7928 5592
Westminster 020 7798 9055
Catholic Enquiry Office
020 8458 3316
www.life4seekers.co.uk

Other Christian

Baptist Union
01235 517700
www.baptist.org.uk
Church of Christ, Scientist
00 1 617 450 2000
www.themotherchurch.org
Church of Jesus Christ of Latter Day Saints (Mormons)
0121 712 1207
www.lds.org
Church of Scotland
0131 225 5722
www.churchofscotland.org.uk
Churches Together in Britain & Ireland
020 7654 7254
www.ctbi.org.uk
Churches Together in England
020 7529 8141
www.churches-together.org.uk
Congregational Federation
0115 911 1460
www.congregational.org.uk
Association of Interchurch Families
020 7654 7254
www.interchurchfamilies.org
Eastern Orthodox Churches
Greek: 020 7723 4787
Russian: 020 7584 0096
Free Church of England
admin@fce-ec.org.uk
www.fce-ec.org.uk
Free Presbyterian Church of Scotland
daross@
    donaldalexander.freeserve.co.uk
www.fpchurch.org.uk
Independent Methodist Churches
emoore@fimc.org.uk
www.fimc.org.uk
International Churches of Christ
info@icoc.org.uk
www.icoc.org.uk
Jehovah's Witnesses
020 8906 2211
www.watchtower.org
Jesus Army
0845 123 5550
www.jesusarmy.org.uk
Lutheran Council of GB
020 7554 2900
www.lutheran.org.uk
Methodist Church
020 7467 5221
www.methodist.org.uk
Moravian Church
020 8883 3409
www.moravian.org.uk
New Testament Church of God
01604 643311
www.ntcg.org.uk
Pentecostal Assemblies of God
0115 921 7272
www.aog.org.uk

Presbyterian Church in Ireland
028 9032 2284
www.presbyterianireland.org
Presbyterian Church of Wales
029 2062 7465
www.ebcpcw.org.uk
Quakers
020 7663 1000
www.quaker.org.uk
Salvation Army
020 7332 0101
www.salvationarmy.org
Seventh Day Adventist Church
01923 672251
www.adventist.org.uk
Unitarian Churches
020 7240 2384
www.unitarian.org.uk
United Free Church of Scotland
0141 332 3435
www.ufcos.org.uk
United Reform Church
020 7916 2020
www.urc.org.uk
World Council of Churches
00 41 22 791 6111
www.wcc-coe.org

Buddhism

BuddhaNet
bdea@buddhanet.net
www.buddhanet.net
London Buddhist Centre (LBC)
0845 458 4716
www.lbc.org.uk
London Buddhist Vihara
020 8995 9493
www.londonbuddhistvihara.org
The Buddhist Society
020 7834 5858
www.thebuddhistsociety.org
Cardiff Buddhist Centre
029 2046 2492
www.cardiffbuddhistcentre.com
Edinburgh Buddhist Centre
0131 662 6699
www.edinburghbuddhistcentre
    .org.uk
Friends of the Western Buddhist Order
0845 458 4716
www.fwbo.org
Network of Buddhist Organisations
0845 345 8978
www.nbo.org.uk
Potala Buddhist Centre, Belfast
028 9023 8090
www.potalacentre.org.uk
Society Krishna Consciousness
01923 857244
www.iskcon.org.uk

Islam

Islamic Centre of England
020 7604 5500
www.ic-el.org
Islamic Cultural Centre
020 7724 3363
www.iccuk.org
Islamic Digest
00 255 744 078830
www.islamicdigest.net
Muslim Council of Britain
020 8432 0585/6
www.mcb.org.uk
Muslim Directory
020 8799 4455
www.muslimdirectory.co.uk

Hinduism

Hindu Centre, London
020 7485 8200
Hindunet
hsc@hindunet.org
www.hindunet.org
Hindu Links
www.hindulinks.org

Judaism

Board of Deputies of British Jews
020 7543 5400
www.bod.org.uk
The Jewish Leadership Council
020 7242 9734
www.jlc.gb.com
Jewish Network
07976 220273
www.jewish.co.uk
United Synagogue
020 8343 8989
www.unitedsynagogue.org.uk

Sikhism

Sikh Missionary Society
020 8574 1902
www.sikhs.org
Sikhnet
00 505 753 3117
www.sikhnet.com
Sikh Women's Network
info@sikhwomen.com
www.Sikhwomen.com

Spiritualism and paganism

Aetherius Society
020 7736 4187
www.aetherius.org
British Druid Order
sparrowhawk@
    britishdruidorder.co.uk
www.druidorder.demon.co.uk
Order of Bards, Ovates & Druids
01273 470 888
www.druidry.org
Pagan Federation
020 8470 8643
www.paganfed.org
Satanism
HPNadramia@churchofsatan.com
www.churchofsatan.com
Spiritualist Association of Great Britain
info@spiritualuk.com
www.spiritualuk.com
Spiritualists' National Union
0845 4580 768
www.snu.org.uk
Theosophical Society
020 7935 9261
info@thesociety.org
www.theosophical-society.org.uk
Transcendental Meditation
08705 143733
www.transcendental-meditation
    .org.uk.

Other religions

Baha'i Community of UK
020 7584 2566
www.bahai.org.uk
Church of Scientology
01342 318229
www.scientology.org
Jainism
vinod@jainworld.com
www.jainworld.com
World Zoroastrian Organisation
President@w-z-o.org
www.w-z-o.org

Humanism and atheism

Association of Irish Humanists
00 353 1286 9870
www.irish-humanists.org
British Humanist Assoc
020 7079 3580
www.humanism.org.uk
Gay and Lesbian Humanist Association
01926 858 450
www.galha.freeserve.co.uk/
    galha.htm
International Humanist and Ethical Union
www.iheu.org
National Secular Society
020 7404 3126
www.secularism.org.uk
Rationalist Press Association
020 7436 1151
www.rationalist.org.uk
South Place Ethical Society
library@ethicalsoc.org.uk
www.ethicalsoc.org.uk

Society

Government

Department for Communities and Local Government
020 7944 4400
www.communities.gov.uk
Press: 020 7944 4297

Health
020 7210 4850
www.dh.gov.uk
Press: 020 7210 5221

Home Office
0870 000 1585
www.homeoffice.gov.uk
Press: 020 7035 4381

Work and Pensions
020 7238 0800
www.dwp.gov.uk
Press: 020 7238 0866

Government agencies

Charity Commission
0845 3000218
www.charity-commission.gov.uk
Press: 020 7674 2323/32/33

Children and Family Court Advisory Service
020 7510 7000
www.cafcass.gov.uk
Press: 020 7510 7036

Child Support Agency
08457 133133
www.csa.gov.uk
Press: 020 7238 0866

Commission for Racial Equality (CRE)
020 7939 0000
www.cre.gov.uk

Connexions
0808 001 3219
www.connexions.gov.uk
Advice and support for 13-19-year-olds

Housing Corporation
0845 230 7000
www.housingcorp.gov.uk
Funding and regulation of housing associations

Immigration and Nationality Directorate
0870 606 7766
www.ind.homeoffice.gov.uk

Office of the Immigration Services Commissioner
020 7211 1500
www.oisc.gov.uk

Charity association

Institute of Fundraising
020 7840 1000
www.institute-of-fundraising.org.uk

Media Trust
020 7874 7600
www.mediatrust.org
Helping charities communicate

Major charities

Action for Blind People
020 7635 4800
www.afbp.org
Press: 020 7635 4898

ActionAid
020 7561 7561
www.actionaid.org.uk
Press: 020 7561 7614

Age Concern England
020 8765 7200
www.ageconcern.org.uk
Press: 020 8765 7200

Alzheimer's Society
020 7306 0606
www.alzheimers.org.uk
Press: 020 7306 0813/39

ARC Addington Fund
024 7669 0587
www.arc-addingtonfund.org.uk

Arthritis Research Campaign
0870 850 5000
www.arc.org.uk
Press: 01246 541107

Association for International Cancer Research
01334 477910
www.aicr.org.uk

Asthma UK
020 7786 4900
www.asthma.org.uk
Press: 020 7786 4949

Barnardo's
020 8550 8822
www.barnardos.org.uk
Press: 020 8498 7555

Battersea Dogs' & Cats' Home
020 7622 3626
www.dogshome.org
Press: 020 7627 9294

BBC Children in Need Appeal
020 8576 7788
www.bbc.co.uk/pudsey

Benenden Hospital Trust
01580 240333
www.benendenhospital.org.uk
Press: 01580 242472

Birmingham Diocesan Trust
0121 236 5535
www.birminghamdiocese.org.uk
Press: 0121 427 2780

Blue Cross
01993 822651
www.bluecross.org.uk
Press: 020 7932 4060

British and Foreign Bible Society
01793 418100
www.biblesociety.org.uk
Press: 01793 418241

British Heart Foundation
020 7935 0185
www.bhf.org.uk
Press: 020 7487 7172
out of hours: 07764 290381

British Red Cross
0870 170 7000
www.redcross.org.uk
Press: 020 7877 7046

British Tennis Foundation
020 7381 7000
www.lta.org.uk
Press: 020 7381 7009

Cambridge Foundation
01223 332288
www.foundation.cam.ac.uk
Press: 01223 332300

Cancer Research UK
020 7121 6699
www.cancerresearchuk.org
Press: 020 7061 8300

Catholic Agency for Overseas Development
020 7733 7900
www.cafod.org.uk
Press: 020 7326 5557

Cats Protection
0870 209 9099
www.cats.org.uk
Press: 08707 708 612

ChildLine
020 7650 3200
www.childline.org.uk
Press: 020 7825 2516

Children with Leukaemia Foundation
020 7404 0808
www.leukaemia.org
Press: 023 8045 4570

Children's Society
0845 300 1128
www.childrenssociety.org.uk
Press: 020 7841 4422

Choice Support
020 7261 4100
www.choicesupport.org.uk

Christian Aid
020 7620 4444
www.christian-aid.org.uk
Press: 020 7523 2421

Christian Vision
0121 522 6087
www.christianvision.com

Christie Hospital Charitable Fund
0161 446 3988
www.christies.org
Press: 0161 446 3613

Church of Jesus Christ of Latter Day Saints Great Britain
0121 712 1207
www.lds.org.uk

Church of Scotland Unincorporated Boards and Committees
0131 225 5722
www.churchofscotland.org.uk
Press: 0131 240 2243

Comic Relief
020 7820 5555
www.comicrelief.com

Community Integrated Care
0151 420 3637
www.c-i-c.co.uk
Press: 0151 422 5352

Concern Worldwide
0800 032 4000
www.concern.net
Press: 020 7906 4629

Diabetes UK
020 7424 1000
www.diabetes.org.uk
Press: 020 7424 1165

Disasters Emergency Committee
020 7387 0200
www.dec.org.uk

Dogs Trust
020 7837 0006
www.dogstrust.org.uk
Press: 020 7837 0006

Donkey Sanctuary
01395 578222
www.thedonkeysanctuary.org.uk
Press: 01395 573097

Fremantle Trust
01296 393055
www.fremantletrust.org

Great Ormond St Children's Charity
020 7916 5678
www.gosh.org

Guide Dogs for the Blind Association
0118 983 5555
www.guidedogs.org.uk
Press: 0118 983 8380

Help the Aged
020 7278 1114
www.helptheaged.org.uk
Press: 020 7239 1942

International Planned Parenthood Federation
020 7939 8200
www.ippf.org
Press: 020 7939 8233

Islamic Relief
0121 605 5555
www.islamic-relief.com/uk
Press: 0121 605 0663

Jewish Care
020 8922 2000
www.jewishcare.org
Press: 020 8922 2812

Leonard Cheshire
020 7802 8200
www.leonard-cheshire.org
Provider of support to disabled people

Leukaemia Research Fund
020 7405 0101
www.lrf.org.uk
Press: 020 7269 9019

Liverpool Roman Catholic Archdiocesan Trust
0151 522 1000
www.archdiocese-of-liverpool.co.uk
Press: 0151 522 1007

Macmillan Cancer Relief
020 7840 7840
www.macmillan.org.uk
Press: 020 7840 7821

Marie Curie Cancer Care
020 7599 7777
www.mariecurie.org.uk
Press: 020 7599 7700

Mencap
020 7454 0454
www.mencap.org.uk
Press: 020 7696 5524

Mind
020 8519 2122
www.mind.org.uk
National Association for Mental Health
Press: 020 8522 1743

Motability
01279 635999
www.motability.co.uk
Press: 01279 632024

Multiple Sclerosis Society
020 8438 0700
www.mssociety.org.uk
Press: 020 7082 0820

National Council of YMCAs
020 8520 5599
www.ymca.org.uk
Press: 020 7421 3008

National Galleries of Scotland
0131 624 6200
www.nationalgalleries.org
www.natgalscot.ac.uk

National Missing Persons Helpline
020 8392 4545
www.missingpersons.org
Press: 020 8392 4510-3

National Museum of Science and Industry
0870 870 4771
www.nmsi.ac.uk
Press: 020 7942 4357

National Society for the Prevention of Cruelty to Children (NSPCC)
020 7825 2500
www.nspcc.org.uk
Press: 020 7825 2514/1373

National Trust
0870 458 4000
www.nationaltrust.org.uk
Press: 0870 600 2127

National Trust for Scotland
0131 243 9300
www.nts.org.uk
Press: 0131 243 9349

NCH
020 7704 7000
www.nch.org.uk
Press: 020 7704 7111

Oxfam
0870 333 2700
01865 311311
www.oxfam.org.uk
Press: 01865 472498

Parkinson's Disease Society of the UK
020 7931 8080
www.parkinsons.org.uk

PDSA
0800 917 2509
www.pdsa.org.uk
Press: 01952 290999

Plan UK
020 7482 9777
www.plan-uk.org

Portsmouth Roman Catholic Diocesan Trustees Registered (PRCDTR)
01329 835583
www.portsmouth-dio.org.uk
Press: 07770 538693

Prince's Trust
020 7543 1234
www.princes-trust.org.uk
Press: 020 7543 1318

Royal National Institute of the Blind (RNIB)
020 7388 1266
www.rnib.org.uk
Press: 020 7391 2223

Royal National Institute for Deaf People (RNID)
020 7296 8000
www.rnid.org.uk
Press: 020 7296 8137

Roman Catholic Diocese of Hexham & Newcastle
0191 243 3300
www.rcdhn.org.uk
Press: 0191 228 0003

Roman Catholic Diocese of Southwark
020 7928 2495
www.rcsouthwark.co.uk

Royal British Legion
020 7973 7200
www.britishlegion.org.uk
www.poppy.org.uk
Press: 020 7973 7296

Royal Horticultural Society
020 7834 4333
www.rhs.org.uk
Press: 020 7821 3043

Royal Marsden Hospital Charity
020 7352 8171
www.royalmarsden.org
Press: 020 7808 2605

Royal National Lifeboat Institution (RNLI)
0845 122 6999
www.rnli.org.uk
Press: 01202 662218
/663184/663127

Royal Society for the Prevention of Cruelty to Animals (RSPCA)
Helpline: 0870 555 5999
enquiries: 0870 333 5999
www.rspca.org.uk
Press: 0870 754 0244

Royal Society for the Protection of Birds (RSPB)
01767 680551
www.rspb.org.uk

Salford Diocesan Trust
0161 736 1421
www.salforddiocese.org.uk
Press: 0161 330 2777

Salvation Army
020 7367 4500
www.salvationarmy.org.uk
Press: 020 7367 4700

Samaritan's Purse International
020 8559 2044
www.samaritanspurse.org.uk
Press: 0131 624 1155

Save the Children (UK)
020 7012 6400
www.savethechildren.org.uk
Press: 020 7012 6841

Scope
020 7619 7100
www.scope.org.uk
Press: 020 7619 7200

Sense
020 7272 7774
www.sense.org.uk
Press: 020 7561 3405

Sheffield City Trust
0114 243 5355
www.sivltd.com
Press: 0114 221 0380

Shelter
0845 458 4590
www.shelter.org.uk
Press: 020 7505 2162

Sightsavers
01444 446600
www.sightsavers.org.uk
Press: 01444 446655

St John Ambulance
08700 10 49 50
www.sja.org.uk
Press: 020 7324 4210

Stewardship
08452 26 26 27
www.stewardship.org.uk

Stroke Association
020 7566 0300
www.stroke.org.uk
Press: 020 7566 1500

Tate
020 7887 8000
www.tate.org.uk
Press: 020 7887 8730

Tear Fund
0845 355 8355
www.tearfund.org
Press: 020 8943 7779

Unicef
020 7405 5592
www.unicef.org.uk
Press: 020 7430 0162

United Jewish Israel Appeal
020 8369 5000
www.ujia.org
Press: 020 8369 5028

Victoria and Albert Museum
020 7942 2000
www.vam.ac.uk
Press: 020 7942 2502

**Watch Tower Bible and Tract
Society of Britain**
020 8906 2211
www.watchtower.org

WaterAid
020 7793 4500
www.wateraid.org.uk
Press: 020 7793 4793

**Westminster Roman Catholic
Diocesan Trust**
020 7798 9036
www.rcdow.org.uk
Press: 020 7798 9031

World Emergency Relief
0870 429 2129
www.wer-uk.org

World Vision UK
01908 841000
www.worldvision.org.uk
Press: 01908 841020

WWF UK
01483 426444
www.wwf.org.uk
Press: 01483 412383

Other charities and campaign groups

● Children

4Children
020 7512 2112
www.4children.org.uk

Acorns Children's Hospice Trust
0845 128 4444
www.acorns.org.uk

**Adoption and Fostering
Information Line**
0800 783 4086
www.adoption.org.uk

Anna Freud Centre
020 7794 2313
www.annafreudcentre.org
Psychoanalysis for children

Barnardo's
020 8550 8822
www.barnardos.org.uk

BBC Children in Need
020 8576 7788
www.bbc.co.uk/pudsey

Bliss
020 7378 1122
www.bliss.org.uk
National charity for premature or sick babies

Care and Relief For The Young
01489 788300
www.cry.org.uk

Child Concern
0161 832 8113
www.childconcern.org.uk

ChildHope
020 7065 0950
www.childhopeuk.org
Defending street children worldwide

ChildLine
020 7650 3200
www.childline.org.uk

Children and Armed Conflict Unit
01206 873483
www.essex.ac.uk/armedcon

**Children with Leukaemia
Foundation**
020 7404 0808
www.leukaemia.org

Children's Society
0845 300 1128
www.childrenssociety.org.uk

CLIC Sargent
0845 301 0031
www.clicsargent.org.uk
Children's cancer charity

Coram Family
020 7520 0300
www.coram.org.uk
Working with vulnerable children

End Child Poverty
020 7278 6541
www.ecpc.org.uk

EveryChild
020 7749 2468
www.everychild.org.uk

Foyle Foundation
020 7430 9119
www.foylefoundation.org.uk
Distributes grants to arts, health and learning charities

Girlguiding UK
020 7834 6242
www.girlguiding.org.uk

Great Ormond St Children's Charity
020 7916 5678
www.gosh.org

Hope
01442 234561
www.hope-for-children.org
International charity for handicapped, orphaned, poor and exploited children

Hope and Homes for Children
01722 790111
www.hopeandhomes.org

**Hyperactive Children's Support
Group**
01243 551313
www.hacsg.org.uk

**International Planned Parenthood
Federation**
020 7939 8200
www.ippf.org

National Children's Bureau
020 7843 6000
www.ncb.org.uk

National Youth Agency
0116 242 7350
www.nya.org.uk

NCH
020 7704 7000
www.nch.org.uk
Support for vulnerable children

NSPCC
020 7825 2500
www.nspcc.org.uk

Plan UK
020 7482 9777
www.plan-uk.org
Children in developing countries

Prince's Trust
020 7543 1234
www.princes-trust.org.uk

Relate
0845 1 304016
www.relate.org.uk
Relationship guidance
Press: 0845 456 1210

Ride Foundation
01372 467708
www.ridefoundation.org.uk
Drug awareness, life skills and citizenship programmes for schools

Save the Children (UK)
020 7012 6400
www.savethechildren.org.uk

Second Chance
023 9287 2790
www.second-chance.org.uk
Camping and fishing for disadvantaged children

The Site
020 7226 8008
www.thesite.org.uk
Advice and help for young people
Press: 020 7288 7309

Task Brasil Trust
020 7735 5545
www.taskbrasil.org.uk
UK charity for street children in Brazil

Trident Trust
020 7014 1400
www.thetridenttrust.org.uk

Unicef
020 7405 5592
www.unicef.org.uk

Society

United Kingdom Missing Children
www.missingkids.co.uk

Variety Club Children's Charity
020 7428 8100
www.varietyclub.org.uk

War Child UK
020 7916 9276
www.warchild.org.uk

Whizz Kidz
020 7233 6600
www.whizz-kidz.org.uk
Children with disabilities

World Villages for Children
020 7629 3050
www.worldvillages.org

Young Enterprise
01865 776845
www.young-enterprise.org.uk

● Citizenship

Association for Citizenship Teaching
020 7566 4133
www.teachingcitizenship.org.uk
Information and direct action across a number of areas

Citizenship Foundation
020 7566 4141
www.citizenshipfoundation.org.uk

● Community

Anchor Trust
020 7759 9100
www.anchor.org.uk
Press: 020 7759 9104

Army Benevolent Fund
020 7591 2000
www.armybenfund.org

Business in the Community
0870 600 2482
www.bitc.org.uk

Changemakers
020 7702 1511
www.changemakers.org.uk

Citizens Advice Bureaux
020 7833 2181
www.citizensadvice.org.uk

Civil Service Benevolent Fund
020 8240 2400
www.csbf.org.uk

Coalfields Regeneration Trust
0800 064 8560
www.coalfields-regen.org.uk

Common Purpose
020 7608 8100
www.commonpurpose.org.uk

Communities that Care
020 7619 0123
www.communitiesthatcare.org.uk

Community Development Foundation
020 7833 1772
www.cdf.org.uk

Community Foundation
0191 222 0945
www.communityfoundation.org.uk
Serving Tyne & Wear and Northumberland

Community Integrated Care
0151 420 3637
www.c-i-c.co.uk

Community Service Volunteers
020 7278 6601
www.csv.org.uk

Directory of Social Change
0845 077 7707
www.dsc.org.uk

Duke of Edinburgh's Award
01753 727400
www.theaward.org

Erskine Home
0141 812 1100
www.erskine.org.uk
For ex-servicemen

Groundwork
0121 236 8565
www.groundwork.org.uk
Community improvement schemes in rundown areas

Gurkha Welfare Trust
020 7251 5234
www.gwt.org.uk

Nacro
020 7582 6500
www.nacro.org.uk
Crime reduction charity

National Federation of Community Organisations
020 7837 7887
www.communitymatters.org.uk

Neighbourhood Initiatives Foundation
0870 7700339
www.nif.co.uk

Neighbourhood Renewal Unit
08450 828383
www.neighbourhood.gov.uk

Norwood Ravenswood Foundation
020 8954 4555
www.norwood.org.uk

Outward Bound Trust
020 7928 1991
www.outwardbound-uk.org

Police Rehabilitation Centre
01491 874499
www.flinthouse.co.uk

Prince's Trust
020 7543 1234
www.princes-trust.org.uk

Princess Royal Trust for Carers
020 7480 7788
www.carers.org

Raleigh International Trust
020 7371 8585
www.raleighinternational.org

Rathbone
0161 236 5358
www.rathbonetraining.co.uk
Learning and training support for the disadvantaged

Royal Air Force Benevolent Fund
020 7580 8343
www.rafbf.org.uk

Royal Air Forces Association
020 8286 6667
www.rafa.org.uk

Royal British Legion
08457 725725
www.britishlegion.org.uk
www.poppy.org.uk

Royal Commonwealth Ex-Services League
020 7973 7263
www.bcel.org.uk

Samaritans
020 8394 8300
www.samaritans.org

Scottish Community Foundation
0131 524 0300
www.scottishcommunityfoundation.com

Soldiers, Sailors, Airmen and Families Association – Forces Help
020 7403 8783
www.ssafa.org.uk

Sue Ryder Care
020 7400 0440
www.sueyrdercare.org
National volunteering campaign for community welfare

Time Bank
0845 456 1668
www.timebank.org.uk

Victim Support
020 7735 9166
www.victimsupport.org
Helps victims of crime

Voluntary Service Overseas
020 8780 7200
www.vso.org.uk

● Disability

Disability Rights Commission
0845 762 2633
www.drc-gb.org
Independent body established by statute

Action for Blind People
020 7635 4800
www.afbp.org
Press: 020 7635 4898

Afasic
020 7490 9410
www.afasic.org.uk
For children and young adults with communication impairments

Christian Blind Mission
01223 484700
www.cbmuk.org.uk

Council for Disabled Children
020 7843 6000
www.ncb.org.uk

Dogs For the Disabled
08700 776600
www.dogsforthedisabled.org

Elizabeth Foundation for Pre-School Deaf Children
023 9237 2735
www.elizabeth-foundation.org

Employment Opportunities for People with Disabilities
020 7448 5420
www.opportunities.org.uk

Guide Dogs for the Blind
0118 983 5555
www.guidedogs.org.uk

Leonard Cheshire
020 7802 8200
www.leonard-cheshire.org
Creating opportunities with disabled people

Mencap
020 7454 0454
www.mencap.org.uk

Motability
01279 635999
www.motability.co.uk

National Autistic Society
020 7833 2299
www.nas.org.uk
National Deaf Children's Society
020 7490 8656
www.ndcs.org.uk
National Library for the Blind
0161 355 2000
www.nlb-online.org
**Northern Counties School
for the Deaf**
0191 281 5821
www.northern-counties-school
.co.uk
**Physically Handicapped and
Able Bodied Children**
020 8667 9443
www.phabengland.org.uk
Riding for the Disabled
0845 658 1082
www.riding-for-disabled.org.uk
**Royal National Institute of the
Blind (RNIB)**
020 7388 1266
www.rnib.org.uk
**Royal National Institute for Deaf
People (RNID)**
020 7296 8000
www.rnid.org.uk
Royal Hospital for Neuro-disability
020 8780 4500
www.rhn.org.uk
Royal London Society for the Blind
01732 592500
www.rlsb.org.uk
Royal Star and Garter Home
020 8439 8000
www.starandgarter.org
St Dunstan's
020 7723 5021
www.st-dunstans.org.uk
Scope
020 7619 7100
www.scope.org.uk
**Sense - National Deafblind and
Rubella Association**
020 7272 7774
www.sense.org.uk
Sightsavers
01444 446600
www.sightsavers.org.uk
The Shaw Trust
01225 716300
www.shaw-trust.org.uk
Provides training and work opportunities
United Response
020 8246 5200
www.unitedresponse.org.uk
*Support for those with learning
difficulties and mental health problems*
**West Midlands Special Needs
Transport**
0121 333 3107
www.ringandride.org.uk
**Westminster Society for Mentally
Handicapped Children and Adults**
020 8968 7376
www.wspld.org.uk
WheelPower
01296 395995
www.wheelpower.org.uk
World Vision UK
01908 841000
www.worldvision.org.uk

● **Diversity**

Equal Opportunities Commission
0845 601 5901
www.eoc.org.uk

AGE

Age Concern England
020 8765 7200
www.ageconcern.org.uk
Age Positive
www.agepositive.gov.uk
Age diversity in employment
Press: 020 7299 8757
Help the Aged
020 7278 1114
www.helptheaged.org.uk

RACE

1990 Trust
020 7582 1990
www.blink.org.uk
Black community organisation
Black Enterprise
Helper@colourfulnetwork.net
www.blackenterprise.co.uk
Ethnic Minority Foundation
020 8432 0307
www.emf-cemvo.co.uk

SEXUALITY

**Armed Forces Lesbian and Gay
Association**
0870 740 7755
www.aflaga.org.uk
**Gay and Lesbian Association of
Doctors and Dentists**
0870 765 5606
www.gladd.org.uk
**Lesbian and Gay Christian
Movement**
020 7739 1249
www.lgcm.org.uk
Lesbian and Gay Foundation
0161 235 8035
www.lgf.org.uk
Metro Centre
020 8265 3311
www.metrocentreonline.org
*Services for people questioning their
sexuality*
Outrage
020 8240 0222
outrage@blueyonder.co.uk
Direct action for gay rights
Queerspace
info@queerspace.org.uk
www.queerspace.org.uk
Northern Ireland
Stonewall
020 7881 9440
www.stonewall.org.uk
The Gay Vote
webmaster@thegayvote.co.uk
www.thegayvote.co.uk
**UK Lesbian and Gay Immigration
Group**
020 7620 6010
www.uklgig.org.uk

» *Diversity in the media*
see page 442

● Housing

Broadway
020 7089 9500
www.broadwaylondon.org
Working to house the homeless
Centrepoint
0845 466 3400
www.centrepoint.org.uk
Agency for young homeless
Chartered Institute of Housing
024 7685 1700
www.cih.org
*Promoting high standards in housing
provision*
Connection at St Martin's
020 7766 5544
www.connection-at-stmartins
.org.uk
Facilities for London's homeless
Crash
020 8742 0717
www.crash.org.uk
*Construction and property industry
homeless charity*
Crisis
0870 011 3335
www.crisis.org.uk
Homeless charity
Defend Council Housing
020 7987 9989
www.defendcouncilhousing.org.uk
Empty Homes Agency
020 7828 6288
www.emptyhomes.com
FEANTSA
00 32 2 538 6669
www.feantsa.org
*European federation of homeless
organisations*
Foyer Federation
020 7430 2212
www.foyer.net
*Accommodation and opportunities for
the young*
Groundswell
020 7737 5500
www.groundswell.org.uk
Support projects for the homeless
Homeless Link
020 7960 3010
www.homeless.org.uk
*UK membership network for homeless
agencies*
Homes for Homeless People
01582 481426/481484
www.homeline.dircon.co.uk
Housing Quality Network
01723 350099
www.hqnetwork.org.uk
*Aims to improve quality of housing
services*
Joseph Rowntree Foundation
01904 629241
www.jrf.org.uk
*Policy research and action on housing
and social care*
National Housing Federation
020 7067 1010
www.housing.org.uk
*Representing the independent social
housing sector*
**Paddington Churches Housing
Association**
020 8150 4200
www.pcha.org.uk
London housing association founded 1965

Society

Peabody Trust
020 7021 4000
www.peabody.org.uk
London housing association
ROOMatRTPI
01789 763006
www.room.org.uk
Forum for debate on housing and regeneration issues
Rural Housing Trust
020 7793 8114
www.ruralhousing.org.uk
Affordable housing in English villages
Shelter
0845 458 4590
www.shelter.org.uk
Thames Reach Bondway
020 7702 4260
www.thamesreachbondway.com
London homeless charity
Press: 020 7702 5646
UK Co-Housing Network
johnston@garradhassan.com
www.cohousing.org.uk
Network of resident-developed neighbourhoods

● Immigration and refugees
Asylum Aid
020 7377 5123
www.asylumaid.org.uk
COSLA Refugee&Asylum Seekers Consortium
0141 248 2396
www.asylumscotland.org.uk
Immigration Advisory Service
020 7967 1200
www.iasuk.org
Immigration Law Practitioners' Association
020 7251 8383
www.ilpa.org.uk
Information Centre about Asylum & Refugees
020 7040 4596
www.icar.org.uk
Joint Council for the Welfare of Immigrants
020 7251 8708
www.jcwi.org.uk
Human rights for immigrants and asylum seekers in UK
Migration Research Unit
020 7679 7569
www.geog.ucl.ac.uk/mru
Refugee Action
020 7654 7700
www.refugee-action.org.uk
Refugee Council
020 7346 6700
www.refugeecouncil.org.uk
Scottish Refugee Council
0141 248 9799
www.scottishrefugeecouncil.org.uk

● Women
Abortion Rights
020 7923 9792
www.abortionrights.org.uk
Breast Cancer Campaign
020 7749 3700
www.bcc-uk.org

Breast Cancer Care
020 7384 2984
www.breastcancercare.org.uk
British Association of Women Entrepreneurs
01786 446044
www.bawe-uk.org
Campaign Against Domestic Violence
020 8520 5881
www.cadv.org.uk
Child and Woman Abuse Studies Unit
020 7133 5014
www.cwasu.org
Emily's List
contact@emilyslist.org.uk
www.emilyslist.org.uk
Campaign for Labour women MPs
European Women's Lobby
00 32 2 217 9020
www.womenlobby.org
Everywoman
0870 746 1800
www.everywoman.co.uk
The Fawcett Society
020 7253 2598
www.fawcettsociety.org.uk
Equality campaign
Justice for Women
0113 262 5101
www.jfw.org.uk
League of Jewish Women
020 7242 8300
www.theljw.org
Marie Stopes International
020 7574 7400
www.mariestopes.org.uk
Reproductive healthcare worldwide
Meet A Mum Association
0845 120 3746
www.mama.co.uk
National Association for Premenstrual Syndrome
0870 777 2178
www.pms.org.uk
National Council of Women
01325 367375
www.ncwgb.org
National Federation of Women's Institutes
020 7371 9300
www.womens-institute.co.uk
Older Feminist Network
020 8346 1900
www.ofn.org.uk
Rights of Women
020 7251 6575
www.row.org.uk
Scottish Women's Aid
0131 226 6606
www.scottishwomensaid.co.uk
Single Parent Action Network
0117 951 4231
www.spanuk.org.uk
Suzy Lamplugh Trust
020 7091 0014
www.suzylamplugh.org
Personal safety
Womankind Worldwide
020 7549 0360
www.womankind.org.uk
Women and Manual Trades
020 7251 9192
www.wamt.org

Women's Aid
0117 944 4411
www.womensaid.org.uk
Women's Aid, Ireland
028 2563 2136
www.womens-aid.org.uk
The Women's Library
020 7320 2222
www.thewomenslibrary.ac.uk
Women's Link
020 7248 1200
www.womenslink.org.uk
Women's National Commission
020 7215 6933
www.thewnc.org.uk
YWCA (London)
01865 304200
www.ywca-gb.org.uk

Useful helplines

Afasic
0845 355 5577
Benefit Enquiry Line
0800 882200
Childline
0800 1111
Churches Child Protection Advisory Service
0845 120 4550
Deafblind UK
0800 132 320
Disability Living Allowance
0845 712 3456
Elder Abuse Response line
0808 808 8141
Gamblers Anonymous
0870 050 8880
Gingerbread Advice Line
0800 018 4318
Healthy Start
0845 607 6823
Kidscape
0845 120 5204
Learning Disability Helpline
0808 808 1111
National Missing Persons Helpline
0500 700700
NSPCC National Child Protection Helpline
0808 800 5000
Parent Line
0808 800 2222
Refugee Helpline
0800 413 848
Relate
0845 130 4016
Runaway Helpline
0808 800 7070
Samaritans
08457 90 90 90
Saneline
0845 767 8000
Shelter London Line
0808 800 4444
Supportline for Survivors of Professional Abuse
0845 4 500 300
Victim Supportline
0845 303 0900
Winter Warmth Advice Line
0800 085 7000
Women's Aid National Domestic Violence Helpline
0808 2000 247

Sport

Government department

Department for Culture, Media and Sport
020 7211 6200
www.culture.gov.uk
Press: 020 7211 6145

Official bodies

UK Sport
020 7211 5100
www.uksport.gov.uk
Press: 020 7211 5106
Sport England
0845 850 8508
London: 020 8778 8600
East: 01234 345222
East Midlands: 0115 982 1887
North: 0191 384 9595
North-west: 0161 834 0338
South-east: 0118 948 3311
South-west: 01460 73491
West Midlands: 0121 456 3444
Yorkshire: 0113 243 6443
www.sportengland.org
Press: 020 7273 1590
Sport Scotland
0131 317 7200
Glenmore Lodge: 01479 861256
Cumbrae: 01475 530757
Inverclyde: 01475 674666
www.sportscotland.org.uk
Press: 0131 472 3309
Sports Council for Northern Ireland
028 9038 1222
www.sportni.net
Sports Council for Wales
0845 045 0904
www.sports-council-wales.co.uk
Press: 029 2030 0597

Olympics and Paralympics

London 2012
020 3201 2000
www.london2012.org
Press: 020 3201 2700
British Olympic Association
020 8871 2677
www.olympics.org.uk
Press: 020 8871 2677 x233
British Paralympic Association
020 7211 5222
www.paralympics.org.uk
Press: 01225 323518
International Olympic Committee
00 41 21 621 6111
www.olympic.org
International Paralympic Committee
00 49 228 209 7200
www.paralympic.org

Football

● Governing bodies

Fifa
00 41 222 7777
www.fifa.com
Deutsche Fussball-Bund (German FA)
00 49 69 67880
www.dfb.de
UEFA
00 41 0848 00 2727
www.uefa.com
Press: 00 41 0848 04 2727
Euro 2008, Austria and Switzerland
00 41 848 002008
Press: 00 41 22 707 2002
FA
020 7745 4545
www.the-fa.org
Press: 020 7745 4720
Women's Football
www.thefa.com/womens
FA Premier League
020 7864 9000
www.premierleague.com
Press: 020 7864 9190
Football League
020 7864 9000
www.football-league.co.uk
Press: 020 7864 9190
Nationwide Conference
conference@fastwebmedia.co.uk
www.footballconference.co.uk
Press: pressoffice@
footballconference.co.uk
Irish Football Association
028 9066 9458
www.irishfa.com
Scottish Football Association
0141 616 6000
www.scottishfa.co.uk
Football Association of Wales
029 2043 5830
www.faw.org.uk

● National stadiums

Millennium Stadium, Cardiff
0870 5582 582
www.millenniumstadium.com
Wembley Stadium
020 8902 8833
www.wembleystadium.com

● Premiership 2006-07

Arsenal FC
020 7704 4000
www.arsenal.com
Press: 020 7704 4010
Aston Villa FC
0121 327 2299
www.avfc.co.uk
Press: 0121 326 1561

Blackburn Rovers FC
0870 111 3232
www.rovers.co.uk
Press: 01254 296171
Bolton Wanderers FC
01204 673673
www.bwfc.co.uk
Press: 01204 673675
Charlton AFC
020 8333 4000
www.cafc.co.uk
Press: 020 8333 4000
Chelsea FC
0870 300 1212
www.chelseafc.co.uk
Press: 020 7957 8285
Everton FC
0151 330 2200
www.evertonfc.com
Press: 0151 330 2278
Fulham FC
0870 442 1222
www.fulham-fc.co.uk
Press: 020 8336 7510
Liverpool FC
0151 263 2361
www.liverpoolfc.net
Press: 0151 230 5721
Manchester City FC
0161 231 3200
www.mcfc.co.uk
Press: 0161 438 7631
Manchester United FC
0161 868 8000
www.manutd.com
Press: 0161 868 8720
Middlesbrough FC
0870 421 1986
www.mfc.co.uk
Press: 01325 729916
Newcastle United FC
0191 201 8400
www.nufc.co.uk
Press: 0191 201 8420
Portsmouth FC
023 9273 1204
www.pompeyfc.co.uk
Reading FC
0118 968 1100
www.readingfc.co.uk
Sheffield United FC
0870 787 1960
www.sufc.co.uk
Tottenham Hotspur FC
0870 420 5000
www.spurs.co.uk
Press: 020 8506 9043
Watford FC
01923 496000
www.watfordfc.com
West Ham United FC
020 8548 2748
www.whufc.co.uk
Wigan Athletic FC
01942 774000
www.wiganathletic.tv
Press: 01942 770411

483

● Coca-Cola Football League Championship

Barnsley FC
01226 211211
www.barnsleyfc.co.uk
Birmingham FC
0871 226 1875
www.blues.premiumtv.co.uk
Press: 0121 244 1501
Burnley FC
0870 443 1882
www.burnleyfootballclub.com
Cardiff City FC
029 20 221001
www.cardiffcityfc.co.uk
Colchester United FC
01206 508800
www.cu-fc.com
Coventry City FC
0870 421 1987
www.ccfc.co.uk
Crystal Palace FC
020 8768 6000
www.cpfc.co.uk
Derby County FC
0870 444 1884
www.dcfc.co.uk
Hull City FC
0870 837 0003
www.hullcityafc.net
Ipswich Town FC
01473 400500
www.itfc.co.uk
Leeds United FC
0113 367 6000
www.lufc.co.uk
Leicester City FC
0870 040 6000
www.lcfc.co.uk
Luton Town FC
01582 411622
www.lutontown.co.uk
Norwich City FC
01603 760 760
www.canaries.co.uk
Plymouth Argyle FC
01752 562561
www.pafc.co.uk
Preston North End FC
0870 442 1964
www.pnefc.net
Queens Park Rangers FC
020 8743 0262
www.qpr.co.uk
Sheffield Wednesday FC
0870 999 1867
www.swfc.co.uk
Southampton FC
0870 220 0000
www.saintsfc.co.uk
Southend United FC
01702 304050
www.southendunited.co.uk
Stoke City FC
01782 592 222
www.stokecityfc.com
Sunderland FC
0191 551 5000
www.safc.com
Press: 0191 551 5060
West Bromwich Albion FC
0870 066 8888
www.wba.co.uk
Press: 0870 066 2860 x4010
Wolverhampton Wanderers FC
0870 442 0123
www.wolves.co.uk

● Coca-Cola League One

AFC Bournemouth
01202 726300
www.afcb.co.uk
Blackpool FC
0870 443 1953
www.blackpoolfc.co.uk
Bradford City FC
01274 773355
www.bradfordcityfc.co.uk
Brentford FC
08453 456 442
www.brentfordfc.co.uk
Brighton and Hove Albion FC
01273 695 400
www.seagulls.co.uk
Bristol City FC
0117 963 0630
www.bcfc.co.uk
Carlisle United FC
01228 526 237
www.carlisleunited.premiumtv.co.uk
Cheltenham Town FC
01242 573558
www.ctfc.com
Chesterfield FC
01246 209765
www.chesterfield-fc.co.uk
Crewe Alexandra FC
01270 213 014
www.crewealex.net
Doncaster Rovers FC
01302 539441
www.doncasterroversfc.co.uk
Gillingham FC
01634 300000
www.gillinghamfootballclub.com
Huddersfield Town FC
0870 4444677
www.htafc.com
Leyton Orient FC
020 8926 1111
www.leytonorient.net
Millwall FC
020 723 21222
www.millwallfc.co.uk
Northampton Town FC
01604 757773
www.ntfc.co.uk
Nottingham Forest FC
0115 982 4444
www.nottinghamforest.co.uk
Oldham Athletic FC
08712 262 235
www.oldhamathletic.co.uk
Port Vale FC
01782 655800
www.port-vale.co.uk
Rotherham FC
01709 512 434
www.themillers.co.uk
Scunthorpe United FC
01724 848077
www.scunthorpe-united.co.uk
Swansea City FC
01792 616600
www.swanseacity.net
Tranmere Rovers FC
0151 609 3333
www.tranmererovers.co.uk
Yeovil Town FC
01935 423662
www.ytfc.net

● Coca-Cola League Two

Accrington Stanley FC
01254 356950
www.accringtonstanley.co.uk
Barnet FC
020 8441 6932
www.barnetfc.premiumtv.co.uk
Boston United FC
01205 364406
www.bostonunited.co.uk
Bristol Rovers FC
0117 909 6648
www.bristolrovers.co.uk
Bury FC
0161 764 4881
www.buryfc.co.uk
Chester City FC
01244 371376
www.chestercityfc.net
Darlington FC
01325 387000
www.darlington-fc.net
Grimsby Town FC
01472 605050
www.gtfc.co.uk
Hartlepool United FC
01429 272584
www.hartlepoolunited.co.uk
Hereford United FC
01432 276666
www.herefordunited.co.uk
Lincoln City FC
01522 880011
www.redimps.com
Macclesfield Town FC
01625 264686
www.mtfc.co.uk
Mansfield Town FC
0870 756 3160
www.mansfieldtown.net
Milton Keynes Dons FC
01908 607090
www.mkdons.com
Notts County FC
0115 952 9000
www.nottscountyfc.co.uk
Peterborough United FC
01733 563947
www.theposh.com
Rochdale FC
01706 644648
www.rochdaleafc.co.uk
Shrewsbury Town FC
01743 360111
www.shrewsburytown.co.uk
Stockport County FC
0161 286 8888
www.stockportcounty.com
Swindon Town FC
0870 443 1969
www.swindontownfc.co.uk
Torquay United FC
01803 328666
www.torquayunited.com
Walsall FC
0870 442 0442
www.saddlers.co.uk
Wrexham AFC
01978 262129
www.wrexhamafc.co.uk
Wycombe Wanderers FC
01494 472100
www.wycombewanderers.co.uk

● Scottish premier league

Aberdeen FC
01224 650400
www.afc.co.uk
Press: 01224 650406
Celtic FC
0845 671 1888
www.celticfc.co.uk
Press: 0141 551 4276
Dundee United FC
01382 833166
www.dundeeunitedfc.co.uk
Dunfermline Athletic FC
01383 724295
www.dafc.co.uk
Falkirk FC
01324 624121
www.falkirkfc.co.uk
Heart of Midlothian FC
0131 200 7200
www.heartsfc.co.uk
Hibernian FC
0131 661 2159
www.hibernianfc.co.uk
Inverness Caledonian Thistle FC
01463 222880
www.caleythistleonline.com
Kilmarnoch FC
01563 545300
www.kilmarnockfc.co.uk
Motherwell FC
01698 333333
www.motherwellfc.co.uk
Rangers FC
0870 600 1972
www.rangers.co.uk
St MIrren FC
0141 889 2558
www.saintmirren.net

● Football: other bodies

Professional Footballers' Association
0161 236 0575
www.givemefootball.com
Referees Association
024 7660 1701
www.footballreferee.org
Football Supporters' Federation
01634 319461
www.fsf.org.uk
Kick It Out
020 7684 4884
www.kickitout.org
Football's anti-racism campaign
Show Racism the Red Card
0191 291 0160
www.srtrc.org
Supporters Direct
0870 160 0123
www.supporters-direct.org

Other sports

AMERICAN FOOTBALL

British American Football Association
01661 843179
www.bafa.org.uk

ANGLING

National Federation of Anglers
0115 9813535
www.nfadirect.com
National Federation of Sea Anglers
01364 644643
www.nfsa.org.uk
Salmon and Trout Association
020 7283 5838
www.salmon-trout.org

ARCHERY

The Grand National Archery Society
01952 677888
www.gnas.org

ATHLETICS

British Athletics
0161 406 6320
www.britishathletics.info
International Association of Athletics Federations
00 377 9310 8888
www.iaaf.org

BADMINTON

Badminton Association of England
01908 268100
www.baofe.co.uk
Welsh Badminton Union
029 2049 7225
www.welshbadminton.net
Scottish Badminton Union
0141 445 1218
www.scotbadminton.demon.co.uk
Badminton Union of Ireland
00 353 1 839 3028
www.badmintonireland.com

BALLOONING

British Balloon & Airship Club
0117 953 1231
www.bbac.org

BASEBALL

British Baseball Federation
020 7453 7055
www.baseballsoftballuk.com

BASKETBALL

English Basketball Association
0870 7744225
www.englandbasketball.co.uk
Basketball Association of Wales
01443 771576
www.basketballwales.com
Basketball Scotland
0131 317 7260
www.basketball-scotland.com

BIATHLON

British Biathlon Union
01874 730562
www.britishbiathlon.com

BOBSLEIGH

British Bobsleigh Association
01225 386802
www.british-bobsleigh.com

BOWLING

English Bowling Association
01903 820222
www.bowlsengland.com
Welsh Bowling Association
01446 733745
Scottish Bowling Association
01292 294623
www.scottish-bowling.co.uk
Irish Bowling Association
028 2827 0008
www.bowlsireland.com

BOXING

Amateur Boxing Association of England
020 8778 0251
www.abae.co.uk
Amateur Boxing Scotland
07900 003206
www.garnockboxing.com
British Boxing Board of Control
029 2036 7000
www.bbbofc.com
International Boxing Federation
00 1 973 414 0300
www.ibf-usba-boxing.com
Irish Amateur Boxing Association
00 353 1 453 3371
www.iaba.ie
World Boxing Association (Venezuela)
00 58 244 663 1584
www.wbaonline.com
World Boxing Organisation
00 1 787 765 4444
www.wbo-int.com

CANOEING

British Canoe Union
0115 982 1100
www.bcu.org.uk

CAVING

British Caving Association
www.british-caving.org.uk

CRICKET

England and Wales Cricket Board
020 7432 1200
www.ecb.co.uk
Cricket Scotland
0131 313 7420
www.scottishcricket.org
Marylebone Cricket Club (Lord's)
020 7616 8500
www.lords.org.uk

CROQUET

Croquet Association
01242 242318
www.croquet.org.uk

CURLING

British Curling Association
01234 315174
www.britishcurlingassociation.org.uk
Royal Caledonian Curling Club
0131 333 3003
www.royalcaledoniancurlingclub.org

CYCLING

British Cycling Federation
0870 871200
www.bcf.uk.com

EQUESTRIANISM

British Equestrian Federation
024 7669 8871
www.bef.co.uk
British Show Jumping Association
024 7669 8800
www.bsja.co.uk

FENCING

British Fencing Association
020 8742 3032
www.britishfencing.com

GOLF

English Golf Union
01526 354500
www.englishgolfunion.org
Welsh Golfing Union
01633 430830
www.welshgolf.org
Scottish Golf Union
01382 549500
www.scottishgolfunion.org
Golfing Union of Ireland, Ulster branch
00 353 1 505 4000
www.gui.ie
Ladies Golf Union
01334 475811
www.lgu.org
R&A, St Andrews
01334 460000
www.randa.org
Open Championship
www.opengolf.com
St Andrews Links
01334 466666
www.standrews.org.uk

GYMNASTICS

British Gymnastics
01952 820330
www.baga.co.uk

HANDBALL

England Handball
01706 229354
www.englandhandball.com

HOCKEY

English Hockey Association
01908 544644
www.englandhockey.co.uk
Welsh Hockey Union
029 2057 3940
www.welsh-hockey.co.uk
Scottish Hockey Union
0131 453 9070
www.scottish-hockey.org.uk
Irish Hockey Assoc
00 353 1 260 0028
www.hockey.ie

HORSE RACING

The Horse Racing Association
020 7189 3800
www.thehra.org
Ascot
0870 727 4321
www.ascot.co.uk
Aintree (Grand National)
0151 523 2600
www.aintree.co.uk
Epsom (Derby)
01372 726311
www.epsomderby.co.uk

ICE HOCKEY

Ice Hockey UK
020 8732 4505
www.icehockeyuk.co.uk

ICE SKATING

National Ice Skating Association of UK
0115 988 8060
www.iceskating.org.uk

MARTIAL ARTS

British Aikido Board
020 8304 8430
www.aikido-baa.org.uk
British Ju-Jitsu Association
01254 396806
www.bjjagb.com
British Judo Association
01509 631670
www.britishjudo.org.uk
British Kendo Association
john.howell@kendo.org.uk
www.kendo.org.uk
English Karate Governing Body
01628 487555
www.ekgb.org.uk
Tae Kwon-Do Association of Great Britain
0800 052 5960
www.tagb.biz

KORFBALL

British Korfball Association
chairman@korfball.co.uk
www.korfball.co.uk

LACROSSE

English Lacrosse Association
0161 834 4582
www.englishlacrosse.co.uk

LUGE

Great Britain Luge Association
01684 576604
www.gbla.org.uk

MODERN PENTATHLON

Modern Pentathlon Association of Great Britain
01225 386808
www.mpagb.org.uk

MOTOR SPORTS

Auto-Cycle Union
01788 566400
www.acu.org.uk
Federation Internationale de L'Automobile (FIA)
00 33 1 4312 4455
www.fia.com
Royal Automobile Club Motor Sports Association
01753 765 000
www.msauk.org

MOUNTAINEERING

British Mountaineering Council
0870 010 4878
www.thebmc.co.uk

NETBALL

All England Netball Association
01462 442344
www.england-netball.co.uk
Welsh Netball Association
029 2023 7048
www.welshnetball.co.uk
Netball Scotland
0141 572 0114
www.netballscotland.com

ORIENTEERING

British Orienteering Federation
01629 734042
www.britishorienteering.org.uk

PARACHUTING

British Parachute Association
0116 278 5271
www.bpa.org.uk

PETANQUE

British Petanque Association
01360 660723
www.britishpetanque.org.uk

POLO

Hurlingham Polo Association
01367 242828
www.hpa-polo.co.uk

POOL

English Pool Association
01706 642770
www.epa.org.uk

ROUNDERS

National Rounders Association
0114 248 0357
www.nra-rounders.co.uk

ROWING

Amateur Rowing Association
0870 060 7100
www.ara-rowing.org

RUGBY

The Rugby Football League
0113 232 9111
www.rfl.uk.com
British Amateur Rugby League Association
01484 544131
www.barla.org.uk
Rugby Football Union
020 8892 2000
www.rfu.com
Welsh Rugby Union
0870 013 8600
www.wru.co.uk
Scottish Rugby Union
0131 346 5000
www.sru.org.uk
Irish Rugby Union
00 353 1 647 3800
www.irishrugby.ie
Rugby Football Union for Women
020 8831 7996
www.rfu-women.co.uk

SAILING

Royal Yachting Association
08453 450400
www.rya.org.uk

SCUBA DIVING

British Sub-Aqua Club
0151 350 6200
www.bsac.com

SHOOTING

Great Britain Target Shooting Federation
01483 486948
www.gbtsf-worldclass.co.uk

SKIING AND SNOWBOARDING

British Ski & Snowboard Federation
0131 445 7676
www.snowsportgb.com
Snowsport Scotland
0131 445 4151
www.snowsportscotland.org

SOFTBALL

British Softball Federation
020 7453 7055
www.baseballsoftballuk.com

SQUASH

England Squash
0161 231 4499
www.englandsquash.com
Scottish Squash
0131 317 7343
www.scottishsquash.org
Squash Wales
01633 682108
www.squashwales.co.uk

Ulster Squash
028 9038 1222
www.ulstersquash.com

SURFING

British Surfing Association
01673 876474
www.britsurf.co.uk

SWIMMING

Amateur Swimming Federation of Great Britain
01509 618700
www.britishswimming.org

TABLE TENNIS

English Table Tennis Association
01424 722525
www.englishtabletennis.org.uk

TENNIS

Lawn Tennis Association
020 7381 7000
www.lta.org.uk
Tennis and Rackets Association
020 8333 4267
www.irtpa.com

TENPIN BOWLING

British Tenpin Bowling Association
020 8478 1745
www.btba.org.uk

TRIATHLON

British Triathlon Association
01509 226161
www.britishtriathlon.org

VOLLEYBALL

English Volleyball Association
01509 631699
www.volleyballengland.org

WATER SKIING

British Water Ski Federation
01932 575364
www.britishwaterski.co.uk

WEIGHTLIFTING

British Weight Lifting Association
01952 604201
www.bawla.com

WRESTLING

British Amateur Wrestling Association
01246 236443
www.britishwrestling.org

YOGA

British Wheel of Yoga
01529 306851
www.bwy.org.uk

Institutes of sport

English Institute of Sport
0870 759 0400
www.eis2win.co.uk
Press: 07866495872
Scottish Institute of Sport
01786 460100
www.sisport.com
Press: 01786 460119

National sports centres

Bisham Abbey, Bucks
01628 476911
www.bishamabbeynsc.co.uk
Crystal Palace, south London
020 8778 0131
www.crystalpalacensc.co.uk
Cumbrae, Ayrshire
0131 317 7200
www.nationalcentrecumbrae.org.uk
Glenmore Lodge, Aviemore
01479 861256
www.glenmorelodge.org.uk
Inverclyde, Largs
01475 674666
www.nationalcentreinverclyde.org.uk
Lilleshall, Shropshire
01952 603003
www.lilleshallnsc.co.uk
National Water Sports Centre – Holme Pierrepont, Nottinghamshire
0115 982 1212
www.nationalsportscentres.co.uk
Plas Menai, Gwynedd
01248 673943
www.plasmenai.co.uk
Plas y Brenin, Conwy
01690 720214
www.pyb.co.uk
Tollymore, County Down
028 4372 2158
www.tollymore.com
Welsh Institute, Cardiff
029 2030 0500
www.welsh-institute-sport.co.uk

Sport and disability

British Amputee and Les Autres Sports Association
0120 449 4308
www.balasa.org
British Blind Sport
08700 789000
www.britishblindsport.org.uk
British Deaf Sports Council
Fax: 01268 510621
www.britishdeafsportscouncil.org.uk
Wheelpower British Wheelchair Sports
01296 395995
www.wheelpower.org.uk

Sport

Sport and education

British Universities Sports Association
  020 7633 5080
  www.busa.org.uk

Central Council of Physical Recreation
  020 7854 8500
  www.ccpr.org.uk

National Council for School Sport
  0115 923 1229
  www.ncss.org.uk

Physical Education Association of UK
  0118 931 6240
  www.pea.uk.com

Youth Sport Trust
  01509 226600
  www.youthsporttrust.org

Other bodies

The Big Lottery Fund
  0845 410 2030
  www.biglotteryfund.org.uk

Sports Aid Foundation
  020 7273 1975
  www.sportsaid.org.uk

Sports Coach UK
  0113 274 4802
  www.sportscoachuk.org

Women's Sports Foundation
  020 7273 1740
  www.wsf.org.uk

Travel

Department for Transport
020 7944 8300
www.dft.gov.uk
Press -
roads: 020 7944 3066
marine, aviation: 020 7944 3232
railways: 020 7944 3248
Commission for Integrated Transport
cfit@dft.gsi.gov.uk
www.cfit.gov.uk

Urban transport

● London

Transport for London
020 7222 5600
www.tfl.gov.uk/tfl
Press: 0845 600 4141
Congestion charging
0845 900 1234
www.cclondon.com
London Buses
0845 300 7000
www.tfl.gov.uk/buses
London River Services
020 7941 2400
www.tfl.gov.uk/river
London Underground
020 7222 5600
www.tube.tfl.gov.uk
Docklands Light Rail
020 7363 9700
www.tfl.gov.uk/dlr
London Cycling Campaign
020 7234 9310
www.lcc.org.uk
London Travel Watch
020 7505 9000
www.londontravelwatch.org.uk
Press: 020 7726 9953

● The regions

Centro
0121 200 2787
www.centro.org.uk
West Midlands
Press: 0121 214 7073
GMPTE
0161 242 6000
www.gmpte.gov.uk
Greater Manchester
Press: 0161 242 6245
Merseytravel
0151 227 5181
www.merseytravel.gov.uk
Merseyside
Press: 0151 330 1151
Metro
0113 251 7272
www.wymetro.com
West Yorkshire
Press: 0113 251 7213

Nexus
0191 203 3333
www.nexus.org.uk
Tyne & Wear
Press: 0191 203 3112
South Yorkshire
0114 276 7575
www.sypte.co.uk
Press: 0114 221 1335
Strathclyde
0141 332 6811
www.spt.co.uk
Press: 0141 333 3282
Passenger Transport Executive Group
0113 251 7204
www.pteg.net
Association of all seven passenger transport executives
Press: 0113 251 7445

Rail

● Rail companies

Network Rail
020 7557 8000
www.networkrail.co.uk
Infrastructure operator
National press: 020 7557 8292/3
London and south-east:
   020 7557 8107
Midlands: 0121 345 3100
North-east: 01904 522825
North-west: 0161 228 8582
Scotland: 0141 555 4109
South and south-west:
   020 7922 4747
West Country and Wales:
   01793 515267
Arriva Trains Wales
0845 6061 660
www.arrivatrainswales.co.uk
Press: 029 2072 0522
C2C
0845 601 4873
www.c2c-online.co.uk
Press: 020 7713 2168
Central Trains
0121 634 2040
www.centraltrains.co.uk
Press: 0121 654 1278
Chiltern Railways
0845 600 5165
www.chilternrailways.co.uk
Press: 020 7282 2930
English Welsh & Scottish Railways
01302 766801
www.ews-railway.co.uk
Press: 0870 060 0260
First Capital Connect
0845 026 4700
www.firstcapitalconnect.co.uk
Press: 020 7620 5253
First Great Western Link
0845 600 5604
www.firstgreatwesternlink.co.uk
Press: 01793 499499

First Scotrail
0845 601 5929
www.firstgroup.com
Press: 0141 335 4788
Freightliner
020 7200 3974
www.freightliner.co.uk
Press: 020 7200 3900/2
Gatwick Express
0845 850 15 30
www.gatwickexpress.co.uk
Press: 020 8750 6622
GNER
0845 722 5333
www.gner.co.uk
Press: 01904 523072
Heathrow Express
0845 600 1515
www.heathrowexpress.co.uk
Press: 020 8750 6680
Hull Trains
0845 071 0222
www.hulltrains.co.uk
Press: 01482 867867
Island Line
01983 812591
www.island-line.co.uk
London Eastern Railway
0845 600 7245
www.onerailway.com
Press: 01206 363947/8/9
Midland Mainline
0845 722 1125
www.midlandmainline.com
Press: 01332 262010
Northern Rail
0845 600 1159
www.northernrail.org
Press: 0161 228 4501
Silverlink
0845 601 4867/8
www.silverlink-trains.com
Press: 020 7713 2168
Southern
08451 27 29 20
www.southcentraltrains.co.uk
Press: 020 8929 8673
South West Trains
0845 600 0650
www.swtrains.co.uk
Press: 020 7620 5229
Translink
028 9066 6630
www.translink.co.uk
Press: 028 9089 9455
Virgin Trains
0870 789 1234
www.virgintrains.co.uk
Press: 0870 789 1111
West Anglia Great Northern Railway (WAGN)
0845 781 8919
www.wagn.co.uk
Press: 020 7713 2168
Wessex Trains
0845 600 0880
www.wessextrains.co.uk

● Overseas rail travel

EuRail
www.eurail.com
Press: 00 31 30 750 83 92
Eurostar
01777 77 78 79
www.eurostar.com
Press: 020 7922 6030/4494
Rail Europe
0870 584 8848
www.raileurope.co.uk
Main distributor of continental rail travel in the UK; including Eurostar, Inter-Rail, Snow Trains, French Motorail and TGV
Press: 01732 526729/14

● Rail associations

Association of Train Operating Companies
020 7841 8000
www.atoc.org
Trade association
Press: 020 7841 8020
National Rail Enquiries
08457 484950
www.nationalrail.co.uk
Passenger Focus
08453 022022
www.railpassengers.org.uk
General Consumer Council Northern Ireland
028 9067 2488
www.gccni.org.uk

● Government and agencies

Strategic Rail Authority
020 7654 6000
www.sra.gov.uk
Health and Safety Executive: railways
020 7717 6533
www.hse.gov.uk/railways
Office of the Rail Regulator
020 7282 2000
www.rail-reg.gov.uk
Press: 020 7282 2007
library: 020 7282 2001
Rail Safety and Standards Board
020 7904 7777
www.railwaysafety.org.uk

Air travel

● Airports

BAA
020 7834 9449
www.baa.co.uk
Operates UK's biggest airports
Press: 020 7932 6654
London City
020 7646 0088
www.londoncityairport.com
Press: 020 7646 0054
London Gatwick
0870 000 2468
www.baa.co.uk/main/airports/gatwick
Press: 01293 505000
London Heathrow
0870 000 0123
www.baa.com/main/airports/heathrow
Press: 020 8745 7224
London Heliport (Battersea)
020 7228 0181/2
www.weston-aviation.com
London Luton
01582 405100
www.london-luton.co.uk
Press: 01582 395119
London Stansted
0870 000 0303
www.baa.com/main/airports/stansted
Press: 01279 680534

Aberdeen
0870 040 0006
www.aberdeenairport.com
Press: 0131 272 2111
Alderney
01481 822624
www.alderney.gov.gg/index.php/pid/40
Barrra
01871 890212
www.hial.co.uk/barra-airport.html
Belfast International Airport (Aldergrove)
028 9448 4848
www.belfastairport.com
Press: 07766 475453
Benbecula
01870 602051
www.hial.co.uk/benbecula-airport.html
Biggin Hill
01959 578500
www.bigginhillairport.com
Birmingham
0870 733 5511
www.bhx.co.uk
Press: 0121 767 7094
Blackpool
08700 273777
www.blackpoolairport.com
Bournemouth
01202 364000
www.flybournemouth.com
Press: 01202 364106
Bristol
0870 1212747
www.bristolairport.co.uk
RAF Brize Norton
01993 842551
www.raf.mod.uk/rafbrizenorton

Cambridge City Airport
01223 373765
www.cambridgecityairport.com
Campbeltown
01586 553797
www.hial.co.uk/campbeltown-airport.html
Cardiff International Airport
01446 711111
www.cial.co.uk
Carlisle
01228 573641
www.carlisleairport.co.uk
Coventry
02476 308600
www.coventryairport.co.uk
RNAS Culdrose
01326 574121
www.royal-navy.mod.uk
Doncaster Sheffield Robin Hood Airport
08708 33 22 10
www.robinhoodairport.com
Dundee
01382 662200
www.dundeecity.gov.uk/airport
East Midlands
0871 919 9000
www.eastmidlandsairport.com
Press: 0845 108 8542
Edinburgh
0870 040 0007
www.edinburghairport.com
Press: 0131 272 2111
Exeter
01392 367433
www.exeter-airport.co.uk
Press: 01392 354945
George Best Belfast (City)
028 9093 9093
www.belfastcityairport.com
Press: 028 9448 4035
Glasgow
0870 040 0008
www.glasgowairport.com
Press: 0131 272 2111
Gloucester
01452 857700
www.gloucestershireairport.co.uk
Guernsey
01481 237766
www.guernsey-airport.gov.gg
Inverness
01667 464000
www.hial.co.uk/inverness-airport.html
Islay
01496 302361
www.hial.co.uk/islay-airport.html
Isle of Man (Ronaldsway)
01624 821600
www.iom-airport.com
Jersey
01534 492000
www.jersey-airport.com
Kent International, Manston
01843 823600
www.kia-m.com
Lands End
01736 788771
Leeds Bradford International Airport
0113 250 9696
www.lbia.co.uk
Press: 0113 391 3333

Liverpool John Lennon Airport
0870 750 8484
www.liverpooljohnlennonairport
.com
Press: 0151 907 1622
Lydd
01797 322411
www.lydd-airport.co.uk
Manchester
0161 489 3000
www.manairport.co.uk
Press: 0161 489 2700
Newcastle
0870 122 1488
www.newcastleairport.com
Press: 0191 214 3568
Newquay Cornwall Airport
01637 860600
www.newquayairport.com
Norwich
01603 411923
www.norwichairport.co.uk
Orkney (Kirkwall)
01856 872421
www.hial.co.uk/kirkwall-
airport.html
Penzance Heliport
01736 363871
Plymouth City Airport
01752 204090
www.plymouthairport.com
Press: 01872 276276
Prestwick
0871 223 0700
www.gpia.co.uk
St Mary's, Isles of Scilly
01720 422677
Sheffield City Airport
0114 201 1998
www.sheffieldcityairport.com
Shetland
01950 460654
Shoreham (Brighton City)
01273 296900
www.shorehamairport.co.uk
Southampton
0870 040 0009
www.southamptonairport.com
Press: 023 8062 7141
Southend
01702 608100
www.southendairport.net
Stornoway
01851 707400
www.hial.co.uk/stornoway
-airport.html
Sumburgh
01950 461000
www.hial.co.uk/sumburgh
-airport.html
Teesside
01325 332811
www.teessideairport.com
Tiree
01879 220456
www.hial.co.uk/tiree-airport.html
Tresco Heliport
01720 422970
www.tresco.co.uk
Wick
01955 602215
www.hial.co.uk/wick-airport.html

● Airlines

Aer Lingus
00 353 818 365 044
www.aerlingus.ie
Press: 00 353 1 886 3420
Aeroflot
00 1 212 944 2300
www.aeroflot.com
Air Berlin
0870 738 8880
www.airberlin.com
Press: 00 49 30 3434 1510
Air Canada
0871 220 1111
www.aircanada.ca
Air France
0870 142 4343
www.airfrance.com
Press: mail.mediarelations.gbi@
airfrance.fr
Air India
020 7495 7950
www.airindia.com
Air Malta
00 356 2169 0890
www.airmalta.com
Air New Zealand
0800 028 4149
www.airnewzealand.com
Air Scotland
0141 222 2363
www.air-scotland.com
Air Seychelles
01293 596656
www.airseychelles.net
Ajet
00 357 24 815 735
www.ajet.com
Alitalia
020 8814 7700
www.alitalia.com
Alaska Airlines
01992 441517
www.alaskaair.com
America West Airlines
00 1 480 693 0800
www.americawest.com
Press: 00 1 480 693 5729
American Airlines
0845 778 9789
www.aa.com
Press: 020 8577 4804
ANA Europe
0870 837 8866
www.anaskyweb.com
Press: 020 7808 1356
ATA
00 1 800 435 9282
www.ata.com
Austrian Airlines
020 7766 0300
www.aua.com
Avianca (Colombia)
0870 576 7747
www.avianca.com
British Airways
0870 850 9850
www.british-airways.com
Press: 020 8738 5100

BMI (British Midland)
01332 854000
www.britishmidland.com
Press: 01332 854687
Cathay Pacific
020 8834 8888
www.cathaypacific.com
Press: 020 8834 8800
China Airlines
020 7436 9001
www.china-airlines.com
Continental Airlines
01293 776464
www.continental.com
Cyprus Airways
020 8359 1333
www.cyprusair.com
Press: 020 8359 1366
Delta Express
001 404 715 2600
www.delta.com
Press: 020 7932 8376
EasyJet
0871 244 2366
www.easyjet.com
Press: 01582 525252
El Al Israel Airlines
020 7121 1450
www.elal.com
Press: 020 7121 1455
Emirates
0870 243 2222
www.emirates.com
Press: 020 7861 2424
Finnair
0870 241 4411
www.finnair.com
Flybe
01392 366669
www.flybe.com
Press: 0845 675 0681
Flyglobespan
0870 556 1522
www.flyglobespan.com
GB Airways
01293 664239
www.gbairways.com
Press: 01293 664000
Germanwings
0870 252 1250
www.germanwings.com
Press: presse@germanwings.com
Gulf Air
0870 777 1717
www.gulfairco.com
HLX (Hapag-Lloyd Express)
0870 606 0519
www.hlx.com
Iberia
0870 609 0500
www.iberia.com
Icelandair
0870 787 4020
www.icelandair.net
Press: 020 78741007
Japan Airlines
0845 774 7700
www.jal.com
JAT - Yugoslav Airlines
020 7629 2007
www.jat.com

Jet 2
0871 226 1737
www.jet2.com

Kenya Airways
01784 888222
www.kenya-airways.com

KLM Royal Dutch
0870 243 0541
www.klm.com

Kuwait Airways
020 7412 0006
www.kuwait-airways.com

LanChile
0800 917 0572
www.lanchile.com

LOT – Polish Airlines
0870 414 0088
www.lot.com

Lufthansa
0870 837 7747
www.lufthansa.com
Press: 020 8750 3415

Malaysia Airlines
020 7341 2000
www.malaysia-airlines.com

Monarch
01582 400000
www.monarch-airlines.com
Press: 01582 398146

Olympic Airways
0870 606 0460
www.olympic-airways.gr
Press: 00 30 210 926 7251

Portugalia Airlines
0161 250 0385
www.pga.pt

Qantas Airways
0845 774 7767
www.qantas.com.au
Press: 020 8846 0501

Royal Air Maroc
020 7307 5800
www.royalairmaroc.com

Royal Jordanian Airlines
020 7878 6300
www.rja.com.jo
Press: 020 7878 6337

RyanAir
0871 246 0000
www.ryanair.co.uk
Press: 00 353 181 21212

SAS Scandinavian Airlines
00 46 8 797 0000
www.scandinavian.net
Press: 00 46 70 997 4893

Saudi Arabian Airlines
020 7798 9898
www.saudiairlines.com

Singapore Airlines
0844 800 2380
www.singaporeair.com
Press: 020 8563 6788/41

Sky Europe
0905 7222 747
www.skyeurope.com

South African Airways
020 8897 3645
www.flysaa.com

Spanair
0870 1266710
www.spanair.com

Sri Lankan Airlines
020 8538 2001
www.srilankan.aero

Swiss
0845 758 1333
www.swiss.com

TAP Air Portugal
0870 607 2024
www.tap.pt
Press: 00 351 21 841 5000

Thai Airways
020 7491 7953
www.thaiairways.com
Press: 020 7907 9524

Transavia
020 7365 4997
www.transavia.com

United Airlines
0845 844 4777
www.ual.com
Press: 020 8276 6800

Varig – Brazilian Airlines
0870 120 3020
www.varig.co.uk

Virgin Atlantic
01293 562345
www.virgin-atlantic.com
Press: 01293 747 373

Virgin Express
0870 730 1134
www.virgin-express.com

Volare
00 380 44 537 52 96
www.volare.kiev.ua

Wizz Air
00 48 22 351 9499
www.wizzair.com

Yemen Airways
020 8759 0385
www.yemenairways.co.uk

● Air associations
   and authorities

Air Accidents Investigation Branch
01252 510300
24-hour accident reporting line:
   01252 512299
www.aaib.dft.gov.uk

Air Transport Users Council
020 7240 6061
www.auc.org.uk

Airport Operators Association
020 7222 2249
www.aoa.org.uk

British Airline Pilots Association
020 8476 4000
www.balpa.org
Press: 020 7924 7555

Civil Aviation Authority
020 7379 7311
www.caa.co.uk
Regulator

International Air Transport Association
020 8607 6200
www.iata.org

National Air Traffic Services
020 7309 8666
www.nats.co.uk
Press: 01489 615945

Water travel

● Ports

Aberdeen
01224 597000
www.aberdeen-harbour.co.uk

Ayr
01292 281687
www.abports.co.uk

Barrow
01229 822911
www.abports.co.uk

Barry
0870 609 6699
www.abports.co.uk

Belfast
028 9055 4422
www.belfast-harbour.co.uk

Boston
01205 365571
www.portofboston.co.uk

Brightlingsea
01206 302200?
www.brightlingseaharbour.org

Bristol
0117 982 0000
www.bristolport.co.uk

Brixham
01803 853321

Cardiff
0870 609 6699
www.abports.co.uk

Cowes
01983 293952
www.cowes.co.uk

Dartmouth
01803 832337
www.dartharbour.org.uk

Dover
01304 240400
www.doverport.co.uk
Press: x4806

Dundee
01382 224121
www.forthports.co.uk

**Ellesmore Port
(Manchester Ship Canal)**
01928 508550
www.shipcanal.co.uk

Eyemouth
01890 750223

Falmouth
01326 312285
www.falmouthport.co.uk

Felixstowe
01394 604500
www.portoffelixstowe.co.uk

Fife
0131 554 2703
www.forthports.co.uk

Fleetwood
01253 872323
www.abports.co.uk

Folkestone
01303 254597
www.folkestoneharbour.com

Garston
0151 427 5971
www.abports.co.uk

Goole
01482 327171
www.abports.co.uk

Grangemouth
01324 482591
www.forthports.co.uk
Great Yarmouth
01493 335500
www.gypa.co.uk
Grimsby
01472 359181
www.abports.co.uk
Harwich
01255 243030
www.hha.co.uk
Heysham
01524 852373
Hull
01482 327171
www.abports.co.uk
Immingham
01472 359181
www.abports.co.uk
Inverness Harbour Trust
01463 715715
www.invernessharbour.co.uk
Ipswich
01473 231010
www.abports.co.uk
Isle of Man
01624 686628
King's Lynn
01553 691555
www.abports.co.uk
Larne
028 2887 2100
www.portoflarne.co.uk
Leith
0131 555 8750
www.forthports.co.uk
Lerwick
01595 692991
www.lerwick-harbour.co.uk
Liverpool
0151 949 6000
www.merseydocks.co.uk
Port of London
020 7743 7900
www.portoflondon.co.uk
Londonderry
028 7186 0555
www.londonderryport.com
Lowestoft
01553 691 555
www.abports.co.uk
Medway Ports
01795 596596
www.medwayports.com
Milford Haven
01646 696100
www.mhpa.co.uk
Montrose Port Authority
01674 672302
www.montroseport.co.uk
Mostyn Docks, Holywell
01745 560335
Newport
0870 609 6699
www.abports.co.uk
Peterhead
01779 474020
www.peterhead-bay.co.uk
Plymouth
01752 662191
www.abports.co.uk

Poole
01202 440200
www.phc.co.uk
Portsmouth
023 9229 7395
www.portsmouthand.co.uk
Port Talbot
0870 609 6699
www.abports.co.uk
Ramsgate
01843 587661
www.ramsgatenewport.co.uk
Rosyth
01383 413366
www.forthports.co.uk
Saundersfoot
01834 812094
Scarborough
01947 602354
Seaham
0191 516 1700
www.victoriagroup.co.uk
Shoreham
01273 598100
www.portshoreham.co.uk
Silloth
016973 31358
www.abports.co.uk
Southampton
023 8048 8800
www.abports.co.uk
Stonehaven
01569 762 741
Stornoway
01851 702688
www.stornoway-portauthority.com
Sunderland
0191 553 2100
www.portofsunderland.org.uk
Swansea
0870 609 6699
www.abports.co.uk
Tees & Hartlepool
01642 877000
www.thpal.co.uk
Teignmouth
01626 774044
www.abports.co.uk
Tilbury
01375 852200
www.forthports.co.uk
Troon
01292 281687
www.abports.co.uk
Tyne, Port of
0191 455 2671
www.portoftyne.com
Weymouth
01305 838000
www.weymouth.gov.uk
Whitby, Port of
01947 602354
www.portofwhitby.co.uk

● Ferries and cruises
Brittany Ferries
08703 665333
www.brittany-ferries.com
Caledonian MacBrayne
01475 650100
www.calmac.co.uk

Condor Ferries
01202 207207
www.condorferries.co.uk
Cunard Cruise Line
0845 071 0300
www.cunard.com
DFDS Seaways
08702 520524
www.dfdsseaways.co.uk
EasyCruise
0906 292 9000
www.easycruise.com
Fjord Line
0870 143 9669
www.fjordline.com
Hoverspeed
0870 240 8070
www.hoverspeed.com
Press: 020 7805 5845
Hovertravel
01983 811000
www.hovertravel.co.uk
Irish Ferries
08705 171717
www.irishferries.com
Isle of Man Steam Packet Company
01624 645645
www.steam-packet.com
Norfolk Line
00 31 7035 27400
www.norfolkline.com
Orkney Ferries
01856 872044
www.orkneyferries.co.uk
P&O Cruises
0845 678 00 14
www.pocruises.com
P&O Ferries
0870 520 2020
www.poferries.com
Press: 01304 863833
Red Funnel Ferries
0870 444 8898
www.redfunnel.co.uk
Sea Containers Irish Sea Operations
020 7805 5000
www.seacontainers.com
SeaFrance
01304 828300
www.seafrance.com
Press: 020 7233 2300
Stena Line
08705 70 70 70
www.stenaline.com
Superfast Ferries Scotland
0870 234 0870
www.superfast.com
Swansea Cork Ferries
01792 456116
www.swansea-cork.ie
Thomson Cruises
0870 607 1642
www.thomson-cruises.co.uk
Wightlink
0870 240 4323
www.wightlink.co.uk
Woolwich Ferry
020 8921 5978

Travel

● Water travel associations and authorities

Associated British Ports
020 7430 1177
www.abports.co.uk
Press: 020 7430 6820/60

Association of Inland Navigation Authorities
0113 243 3125
www.aina.org.uk

British Marine Federation
01784 223634
www.britishmarine.co.uk

British Ports Association
020 7242 1200
www.britishports.org.uk

British Waterways
01923 201120
www.britishwaterways.co.uk
Press: 01923 201350

Hydrographic Office
01823 723366
www.hydro.gov.uk

Inland Waterways Association
01923 711114
www.waterways.org.uk

International Maritime Organisation
020 7735 7611
www.imo.org

Lloyd's Register – Fairplay
01737 379000
www.fairplay.co.uk

Lloyd's Register
020 7709 9166
www.lr.org

Lloyd's List
0220 7017 5531
www.lloydslist.com

Maritime & Coastguard Agency
023 8032 9100
www.mcga.gov.uk

Royal Institute of Navigation
020 7591 3130
www.rin.org.uk

Royal Yachting Association
0845 345 0400
www.rya.org.uk

Road travel

● Motoring bodies

AA
0870 600 0371
www.theaa.co.uk
Press: 01256 492927

British Motorcyclists Federation
0116 284 5380
www.bmf.co.uk

British Parking Association
01444 447 300
www.britishparking.co.uk

Coach Operators Federation
01934 832074
http://users.tinyworld.co.uk
/somerbus/index.htm

Confederation of Passenger Transport
020 7240 3131
www.carlton-group.co.uk
/passtransport.html

DVLA (Drivers & Vehicles Licensing Authority)
01792 782341
www.dvla.gov.uk
Press: 01792 782318

Greenflag
0845 246 1557
www.greenflag.com
Press: 0113 399 1427

Institute of Logistics & Transport
01536 740104
www.iolt.org.uk

Institute of the Motor Industry
01992 511 521
www.motor.org.uk

International Road Transport Union
www.iru.org

Licensed Taxi Drivers Association
020 7286 1046
www.ltda.co.uk

Motor Industry Research Association
01268 290100
www.mira.co.uk

National Federation of Bus Users
023 9281 4493
www.nfbu.org

RAC
020 8917 2500
www.rac.co.uk
Press: 020 8917 2742

Road Haulage Association
01932 841515
www.rha.net

Road Operators Safety Council
01865 775552
www.rosco.org.uk

Society of Motor Manufacturers
020 7235 7000
www.smmt.co.uk

Transport & General Workers Union
020 7611 2500
www.tgwu.org.uk

World Road Association (PIARC)
00 33 1 47 96 81 21
www.piarc.org

● Pedestrians, cyclists and campaign groups

Brake
01484 559909
www.brake.org.uk
Road safety charity

British Cycling Federation
0870 871 2000
www.bcf.uk.com
pressoffice@britishcycling.org.uk

Campaign Against Drinking & Driving
0845 123 5541
www.cadd.org.uk

Cycle Campaign Network
ccn@cyclenetwork.org.uk
www.cyclenetwork.org.uk

Cyclists Touring Club
0870 873 0060
www.ctc.org.uk
Press: 0870 873 0063

Environmental Transport Association
0800 212810
www.eta.co.uk
Environmental campaigner and provider of roadside recovery service

European Federation of Road Victims
fevr@worldcom.ch
www.fevr.org

Lift Share
08700 780225
www.liftshare.com
Online car-sharing scheme

Living Streets
020 7820 1010
www.livingstreets.org.uk
Fighting for cleaner, safer streets

London Cycling Campaign
020 7928 7220
www.lcc.org.uk

Motorcycle Action Group
0870 444 8448
www.mag-uk.org

National Cycle Network
0845 113 0065
www.sustrans.org.uk
Press: 0117 927 7555

Nationwide Cycle Registration
0117 964 2187
www.cycleregistration.com

Ramblers Association
020 7339 8500
www.ramblers.org.uk
Press: 020 7339 8531/8532

Reclaim the Streets
rts@gn.apc.org
http://rts.gn.apc.org

RoadPeace
020 8838 5102
www.roadpeace.org

Slower Speeds Initiative
0845 345 8459
www.slower-speeds.org.uk

Sustrans
0845 113 0065
www.sustrans.org.uk
Sustainable transport charity
Press: 0117 927 7555

● Buses

Arriva
0191 520 4000
www.arriva.co.uk
Press: 0191 520 4106

Firstgroup
020 7291 0505
www.firstgroup.com
Press: 0161 627 7218

The Go-ahead Group
0191 232 3123
www.go-ahead.com

London United Busways
020 8400 6665
www.lonutd.co.uk

Lothian Buses
0131 554 4494
www.lothianbuses.co.uk
Press: 0131 555 6363

Metroline
020 8218 8888
www.metroline.co.uk

National Express
08705 808080
www.nationalexpress.com
Press: 0121 625 1122

Scottish Citylink
0141 332 9644
www.citylink.co.uk
Press: 0141 333 9585

Stagecoach
01738 442111
www.stagecoachplc.com

Translink
028 9066 6630
www.translink.co.uk

Tourism

● Major tour operators

First Choice
0870 750 0001
www.firstchoice.co.uk
Press: 01293 588762

MyTravel
01706 742000
www.mytravel.com
Press: 0161 232 6464

Thomas Cook
01733 417100
www.thomascook.com
Press: 01733 417272

Thomson
024 7628 2828
www.thomson.co.uk
Press: 01582 645363

● Tourism associations

Air Travel Organisers' Licensing (ATOL)
020 7453 6424
www.caa.co.uk/cpg/atol
Press: 020 7453 6030

Association of British Travel Agents
020 7637 2444
www.abtanet.com
Press: 020 7307 1900

British Tourist Authority
020 8846 9000
www.visitbritain.com
Press: 020 8563 3220

Tourism Concern
020 7133 3330
www.tourismconcern.org.uk

Visit London
020 8234 5000
www.visitlondon.com

Youth Hostels Association
01629 592600
www.yha.org.uk
Press: 01629 592575

Travel

Utilities

Energy

● Energy companies

BNFL
01925 832000
www.bnfl.com
British Nuclear Fuels
Press: 01925 832000

British Gas
0845 600 0560
www.house.co.uk
Gas and electricity supplier. Owned by Centrica
Press: 01784 874433

British Energy
01452 652222
www.british-energy.com
Electricity producer
Press: 01506 408801

Ecotricity
01453 756111
www.ecotricity.co.uk
Electricity supplier
Press: 01453 769317

EDF Energy
020 7242 9050
www.edfenergy.com
Gas and electricity supplier. Owns SWEB, Seeboard and London Energy
Press: 020 7752 2266

Green Energy UK
0845 456 9550
www.greenenergy.uk.com

Good Energy
0845 456 1640
www.good-energy.co.uk
Renewable electricity supplier. Owned by Monkton Group

National Grid Transco
020 7004 3000
www.ngtgroup.com
Energy distribution
Press: 020 7004 3147

Powergen 024 7642 4000
www.powergen.co.uk
Gas and electricity supplier. Owned by E.ON UK
Press: 02476 425741

RWE npower
01793 877777
www.rwenpower.com
Gas and electricity supplier
Press: 0845 070 2807

Scottish and Southern
01738 456000
www.scottish-southern.co.uk
Gas and electricity supplier
Press: 0870 900 0410

Scottish Power
0141 248 8200
www.scottishpower.com
Gas and electricity supplier
Press: 0141 636 4515

● Energy bodies and associations

British Hydropower Association
01202 886622
www.british-hydro.org
Trade association

British Nuclear Energy Society
020 7222 7722
www.bnes.com

British Wind Energy Association
020 7689 1960
www.bwea.com
Trade association

Centre for Sustainable Energy
0117 929 9950
www.cse.org.uk
Charity

Energy Retail Association
020 7930 9175
www.energy-retail.org.uk

Energywatch
0845 906 0708
www.energywatch.org.uk
Independent watchdog
Press: 08459 060708

National Energy Foundation
01908 665555
www.natenergy.org.uk
Charity

Nuclear Industry Association
020 7766 6640
www.niauk.org
Trade association
Press: 020 7766 6640

Solar Trade Association
01908 442290
www.greenenergy.org.uk/sta
Trade association

● Government and regulation

Defra
08459 335577
www.defra.gov.uk

DTI Energy Group
020 7215 5000
www.dti.gov.uk/energy
Press: 020 7215 6407

Nuclear Decommissioning Authority
01925 802001
www.nda.gov.uk
Press: 01925 80 2075

Ofgem
020 7901 7000
www.ofgem.gov.uk
Official regulator
Press: 020 7901 7006

Water

● Water companies

Anglian Water
08457 919155
www.anglianwater.co.uk
Press: 0870 600 5600

Dwr Cymru Welsh Water
01443 452300
www.dwrcymru.co.uk
Press: 029 2055 6140

Northumbrian Water
0870 608 4820
www.nwl.co.uk

Scottish Water
0845 601 8855
www.scottishwater.co.uk
Press: 01383 848445

Severn Trent Water
0800 783 4444
www.stwater.co.uk
Press: 0121 722 4121

South West Water
01392 446688
www.southwestwater.co.uk
Press: 01392 443020

Southern Water
01903 264444
www.southernwater.co.uk

Thames Water
0118 373 8936
www.thames-water.com

United Utilities
01925 234000
www.unitedutilities.com
Press: 01925 537366

Wessex Water
01225 526000
www.wessexwater.co.uk
Press: 01225 526323/9

Yorkshire Water
01274 691111
www.yorkshirewater.com

● Water associations

British Water
020 7957 4554
www.britishwater.co.uk
Trade association

Water UK
020 7344 1844
www.water.org.uk
Trade association

● Government and regulation

Defra
08459 335577
www.defra.gov.uk

Drinking Water Inspectorate
020 7082 8024
www.dwi.gov.uk
Watchdog

Ofwat
0121 625 1300/73
www.ofwat.gov.uk
Regulator
Press: 0121 625 1416/96/42
Water Industry Commissioner for Scotland
01786 430200
www.watercommissioner.co.uk

Post

Royal Mail
08457 740740
www.royalmail.com

● Regulator

Postcomm (Postal Services Commission)
020 7593 2100
www.postcomm.gov.uk
Press: 020 7593 2114

Telecoms

British Telecom
020 7356 5000
www.bt.com
Press: 020 7356 5369
Cable and Wireless
01908 845000
www.cableandwireless.co.uk
Press: 01344 818888
Colt
0207 390 3900
www.colt.co.uk
Press: 07017 100100
Hutchinson 3G
08707 330333
www.three.co.uk
Press: 01628 765000
Kingston Communications
01482 602100
www.kcltd.co.uk
Press: 01482 602711
mmO2
0113 272 2000
www.mmo2.com
Press: 01753 628402
NTL
01256 752000
www.ntl.com
Press: 01256 752669
Orange
01454 624600
www.orange.co.uk
Press: 020 7984 2001
Telewest
01483 750900
www.telewest.co.uk
Press: 020 7299 5115
Thus
0800 0275 8487
www.thus.co.uk
Press: 0141 567 1234
T-Mobile
01707 315000
www.t-mobile.co.uk
Press: 07017 150150

Verizon
0118 905 5000
www.verizon.com
Virgin Mobile
01225 895555
www.virginmobile.com
Press: 0845 600 6272
Vodafone
01635 33251
www.vodafone.co.uk
Press: 07000 500100

● Regulator

Ofcom
020 7981 3040
www.ofcom.org.uk
Press: 020 7981 3033

Emergency and services

Police

● Government and agencies

Home Office
0870 000 1585
www.homeoffice.gov.uk
Press: 020 7035 4381

Forensic Science Service
0121 329 5200
www.forensic.gov.uk
Press: 0121 329 5295

HM Inspectors of Constabulary
01527 882000
www.inspectorates.homeoffice
.gov.uk

Independent Police Complaints Commission (IPCC)
0845 300 2002
www.ipcc.gov.uk
Press: 020 7166 3214

》 Police forces
see pages 500–2

● Police services

Police Service
www.police.uk

Centrex
01256 602100
www.centrex.police.uk
National police training
Press: 01256 602949

Civil Nuclear Constabulary (CNC)
www.cnc.police.uk

Interpol
00 33 4 7244 7000
www.interpol.int

Northern Ireland Police Service
028 9065 0222
www.psni.police.uk
Press: 028 9070 0084

Northern Ireland Policing Board
028 9040 8500
www.nipolicingboard.org.uk
Press: 028 9040 8539/8542

Police Forces in Scotland
www.scottish.police.uk

Police IT Organisation
020 8358 5555
www.pito.org.uk
National computer

Scottish Drug Enforcement Agency
01224 783289
www.sdea.police.uk

Scottish Police Information Strategy
0141 582 1000
www.spis.police.uk

Serious Organised Crime Agency (SOCA)
020 7238 8000
www.soca.gov.uk
Press: 0870 268 8100

● Professional bodies

Association of Chief Police Officers
020 7227 3434
www.acpo.police.uk
Press: 020 7227 3425

Association of Chief Police Officers in Scotland
0141 532 2052
www.scottish.police.uk
Press: 0141 532 2658

Association of Police Authorities
020 7664 3185
www.apa.police.uk

British Association for Women in Policing
0870 766 4056
www.bawp.org

Institute of Traffic Accident Investigators
01332 292447
www.itai.org

Police Federation
020 8335 1000
www.polfed.org

Police Federation for Northern Ireland
028 9076 4200
www.policefed-ni.org.uk

Police Superintendents' Association
0118 984 4005
www.policesupers.com

Fire

Office of the Deputy Prime Minister
020 7944 4400
www.communities.gov.uk
Press: 020 7944 4297

FRS Development Division
020 7944 6923
www.frsonline.fire.gov.uk

HM Fire Service Inspectorate
020 7944 5569

》 Fire and rescue authorities
see pages 500–2

● Professional bodies

Fire Brigades Union
020 8541 1765
www.fbu.org.uk
Press: 07736 818 100

Chief Fire Officers' Association (CFOA)
01827 302300
www.cfoa.org.uk

Fire Protection Association
01608 812 500
www.thefpa.co.uk

Ambulance

Department of Health
020 7210 4850
www.dh.gov.uk
Press: 020 7210 5221

》 Ambulance services
see pages 500–2

● Ambulance associations

Ambulance Service Association
020 7928 9620
www.asa.uk.net

Association of Professional Ambulance Personnel
0870 167 0999
www.apap.org.uk

Search and rescue

Maritime and Coastguard Agency
0870 600 6505
www.mcga.gov.uk

Mountain Rescue Council of England and Wales
08702 404024
www.mountain.rescue.org.uk
Network of voluntary rescue teams

RAF Mountain Rescue Association
www.rafmountainrescue.com

Search and Rescue Dog Association
chairman@nsarda.org.uk
www.nsarda.org.uk

Military

Ministry of Defence
020 7218 9000
www.mod.uk
Press: 020 7218 7907

British Army
www.army.mod.uk
Press: 020 7218 7907

Royal Air Force
www.raf.mod.uk
Press: 020 7218 7907

Royal Navy
www.royal-navy.mod.uk
Press: 020 7218 7907

Army Training and Recruitment Agency
01980 615041
www.army.mod.uk/atra

Central Data Management Authority
01793 555391
www.cdma.mod.uk

Computer Emergency Response Team
020 7218 2640
www.cert.mod.uk

Defence Analytical Services Agency
020 7807 8792
www.dasa.mod.uk
UK defence statistics

Defence Procurement Agency
0117 913 0000
www.mod.uk/defenceinternet
/microsite/dpa
Press: 0117 913 0257
Defence Scientific Advisory Council
020 7218 9000
www.dsac.mod.uk
Provides independent advice to the
defence secretary
GCHQ (Government Communications
Headquarters
01242 221491
www.gchq.gov.uk
Press: 01242 221491 x33847
International Visits Control Office
ivco@dpa.mod.uk
www.mod.uk/ivco
Provides security clearance and advice
for visitors to and from the UK defence
industry
Ministry of Defence Police
01371 854000
www.mdp.mod.uk
Press: 01371 854416
Sabre
0800 389 5459
www.sabre.mod.uk
Supports Britain's reservists
and employers
Territorial Army
0845 603 8000
www.ta.mod.uk
Reserve force
Veterans Agency
0800 169 2277, 01253 866043
www.veteransagency.mod.uk
MoD contact for veterans and dependants
MI5
www.mi5.gov.uk
UK's defensive security intelligence agency
Press: 020 7035 3535 (Home Office)
MI6
www.fco.gov.uk
Secret intelligence service
Press: 020 7008 3100
(Foreign Office)

● **Military associations**
Army Base Repair Organisation
01264 383295
www.abro.mod.uk
Commonwealth War Graves
Commission
01628 634221
www.cwgc.org
Press: 01628 507163
Military Heraldry Society
01952 270221
Military Historical Society
020 7730 0717
Orders and Medals Research
Society
01295 690009
www.omrs.org.uk
Reserve Forces' and Cadets'
Associations' in Scotland
Lowland: 0141 945 4951
Highland: 01382 668283
www.rfca.org.uk

Royal British Legion
020 7973 7200
www.britishlegion.org.uk
www.poppy.org.uk
Press: 020 7973 7296
SSAFA Forces Help
020 7403 8783
www.ssafa.org.uk
National charity helping serving and ex-
service men, women and their families

Emergency planning

● Government
Air Accidents Investigation Branch
01252 510300
24-hour accident reporting line:
01252 512299
www.aaib.dft.gov.uk
Press: 020 7944 3387
Civil Contingencies Secretariat
020 7276 3267
www.cabinetoffice.gov.uk
Formerly the Emergency Planning
Division
Press: 020 7276 1191
Emergency Planning College,
Easingwold
01347 821406
www.ukresilience.info/college
Government training college
London Fire and Emergency
Planning Authority
020 7587 2000
www.london-fire.gov.uk
London Prepared
enquiries-lrt@gol.gsi.gov.uk
www.londonprepared.gov.uk
National Infrastructure Security
Co-ordination Centre (NISCC)
020 7821 1330
www.niscc.gov.uk
Health Protection Agency, Centre
for Radiation, Chemical and
Environmental Hazards, Radiation
Protection Division
01235 831600
www.hpa.org.uk/radiation
Scottish Executive Justice
Department
0131 556 8400
www.scotland.gov.uk
Anti-Terrorist Hotline
0800 789321

● Professional body
Emergency Planning Society
0845 600 9587
www.the-eps.org

Voluntary services

Basics
0870 165 4999
www.basics.org.uk
Medical help at disasters
British Red Cross
0870 170 7000
www.redcross.org.uk
Casualties Union
08700 780590
www.casualtiesunion.org.uk
Simulated injuries for emergency
exercises
Crimestoppers
020 8254 3200
Hotline: 0800 555 111
www.crimestoppers-uk.org
Royal Life Saving Society
01789 773 994
www.lifesavers.org.uk
Royal National Lifeboat Institution
0845 122 6999
www.rnli.org.uk
St Andrews Ambulance Association
Aberdeen: 01224 877271
Dundee: 01382 322389
Fife: 01592 631758
Edinburgh: 0131 229 5419
Glasgow: 0141 332 4031
www.firstaid.org.uk
St John Ambulance
08700 104950
www.sja.org.uk
Victim Support
020 7735 9166
Victim support line: 0845 3030 900
www.victimsupport.org
Supports victims of crime
Press: 020 7896 3809

Fire, police and ambulance

England

Avon
FIRE: 0117 926 2061
PRESS: x216
POLICE: 0845 456 7000
PRESS: 01275 816350
AMBULANCE: 0117 927 7046
PRESS: 0117 928 0265/0870 241 0857

Bedfordshire
FIRE: 01234 351081
PRESS: 01234 326198
POLICE: 01234 841212
PRESS: 01234 842390
AMBULANCE: 01234 408999
PRESS: 01234 408999

Berkshire
FIRE: 0118 945 2888
PRESS: 0118 932 2214/83
POLICE: 0845 850 5505
PRESS: 01865 846699
AMBULANCE: 0118 936 5500
PRESS: 0118 936 5500

Buckinghamshire
FIRE: 01296 424666
PRESS: 01296 424666
POLICE: 0845 850 5505
PRESS: 01865 846699
AMBULANCE: 01908 262422
PRESS: 01908 264945

Cambridgeshire
FIRE: 01480 444500
PRESS: 01480 444558
POLICE: 0845 456 4564
PRESS: 01480 422393
AMBULANCE: 01603 424255
PRESS: 01603 422729

Cheshire
FIRE: 01606 868700
PRESS: 01606
868657/868422/868786
POLICE: 01244 350000
PRESS: 01244 612030
AMBULANCE: 0151 260 5220
PRESS: 0151 261 2585

Cleveland
FIRE: 01429 872311
POLICE: 01642 326326
PRESS: 01642 301245/54
AMBULANCE: 01904 666000
PRESS: 01904 666041

Cornwall
FIRE: 01872 273117
PRESS: 01872 322785
POLICE: 0845 277 7444
PRESS: 01392 452151/200
AMBULANCE: 01392 261500
PRESS: 01392 261506

Cumbria
FIRE: 01900 822503
PRESS: 01900 822503
POLICE: 01768 891999
PRESS: 01768 217009
AMBULANCE: 01228 596909
PRESS: 01228 403006

Derbyshire
FIRE: 01332 771221
PRESS: 01332 771221
POLICE: 0845 123 3333
PRESS: 01773 572033/034/979
AMBULANCE: 0115 929 6151
PRESS: 0115 929 6151

Devon
FIRE: 01392 872200
PRESS: 01392 872318
POLICE: 0845 277 7444
PRESS: 01392 452151/200
AMBULANCE: 01392 261500
PRESS: 01392 261506

Dorset
FIRE: 01305 251133
PRESS: 01305 252084
POLICE: 01202 222222
PRESS: 01202 223893
AMBULANCE: 01202 851640
PRESS: 01202 851640

Durham
FIRE: 0191 384 3381
PRESS: 0191 384 3381
POLICE: 0845 606 0365
PRESS: 0191 375 2157
AMBULANCE: 0191 273 1212
PRESS: 0191 273 1212

East Sussex
FIRE: 0845 130 8855
PRESS: 01323 462388
POLICE: 0845 607 0999
PRESS: 01273 404173
AMBULANCE: 01273 489444
PRESS: 01273 897859

Essex
FIRE: 01277 222531
PRESS: 01277 222531
POLICE: 01245 491491
PRESS: 01245 452450
AMBULANCE: 01245 443344
PRESS: 01245 444444

Gloucestershire
FIRE: 01452 753333
PRESS: 01452 753333
POLICE: 0845 090 1234
PRESS: 01242 276070
AMBULANCE: 01452 753030
PRESS: 01452 753030

Greater Manchester
FIRE: 0161 736 5866
PRESS: 0161 608 4090
POLICE: 0161 872 5050
PRESS: 0161 856 2220
AMBULANCE: 0161 796 7222
PRESS: 0161 834 9836

Hampshire
FIRE: 023 8064 4000
PRESS: 023 8062 6812
POLICE: 0845 045 4545
PRESS: 01962 871619
AMBULANCE: 01962 863511
PRESS: 01962 843165

Hereford & Worcester
FIRE: 01905 24454
PRESS: 01905 725060
POLICE: 0845 744 4888
PRESS: 01432 347340
AMBULANCE: 01886 834200
PRESS: 01886 834200

Hertfordshire
FIRE: 01992 507507
PRESS: 01992 507546
POLICE: 0845 330 0222
PRESS: 01707 354588
AMBULANCE: 01234 408999
PRESS: 01234 408999

Humberside
FIRE: 01482 565333
PRESS: 01482 567466
POLICE: 0845 606 0222
PRESS: 01482 578372
AMBULANCE: 01904 666000
PRESS: 01904 666041

Isle of Wight
FIRE: 01983 823194
PRESS: 01983 823107
POLICE: 0845 045 4545
PRESS: 01962 871619
AMBULANCE: 01983 534111
PRESS: 01983 534184

Kent
FIRE: 01622 692121
PRESS: 01622 692121
POLICE: 01622 690690
PRESS: 01622 652231-3
Port of Dover POLICE: 01304 240400
AMBULANCE: 01622 747010
PRESS: 01622 740331

Lancashire
FIRE: 01772 862545
PRESS: 01772 866939, 07769
907887
POLICE: 01772 614444
PRESS: 01772 412658/444
AMBULANCE: 01772 862666
PRESS: 01772 773005

Leicestershire
FIRE: 0116 287 2241
PRESS: 0116 229 2194
POLICE: 0116 222 2222
PRESS: x2798
AMBULANCE: 0115 929 6151
PRESS: 0115 929 6151

Lincolnshire
FIRE: 01522 582222
PRESS: 01522 552302
POLICE: 01522 532222
PRESS: 01522 558026
AMBULANCE: 0845 045 0422
PRESS: 01522 832638

London
FIRE: 020 7587 2000
PRESS: 020 7587 6100
METROPOLITAN POLICE: 020 7230 1212
PRESS: 020 7230 2171
CITY OF LONDON POLICE:
020 7601 2222
PRESS: 020 7601 2220
AMBULANCE: 020 7921 5100
PRESS: 020 7921 5113

Merseyside
FIRE: 0151 296 4000
PRESS: 0151 296 4419
POLICE: 0151 709 6010
PRESS: 0151 777 8566
AMBULANCE: 0151 260 5220
PRESS: 0151 261 2585

Norfolk
FIRE: 01603 810351
PRESS: 01603 819759
POLICE: 0845 456 4567
PRESS: 01953 423666/07626 952342
AMBULANCE: 01603 424255
PRESS: 01603 422729

North Yorkshire
FIRE: 01609 780150
PRESS: 01609 788595
POLICE: 0845 606 0247
PRESS: 01609 789959
AMBULANCE: 01904 666000
PRESS: 01904 666041

Northamptonshire
FIRE: 01604 797000
PRESS: 01536 516400
POLICE: 01604 700700
PRESS: 01604 703197
AMBULANCE: 01908 262422
PRESS: 01908 262422

Northumberland
FIRE: 01670 533000
PRESS: 01670 533208
POLICE: 01661 872555
PRESS: 01661 868888
AMBULANCE: 0191 273 1212
PRESS: 0191 273 1212

Nottinghamshire
FIRE: 0115 967 0880
PRESS: 0115 977 4918
POLICE: 0115 967 0999
PRESS: 0115 967 2080
AMBULANCE: 0115 929 6151
PRESS: 0115 929 6151

Oxfordshire
FIRE: 01865 842999
PRESS: 01865 842999
POLICE: 0845 850 5505
PRESS: 01865 846699
AMBULANCE: 01865 740100
PRESS: 01865 740117

Rutland
FIRE: 0116 287 2241
PRESS: 0116 229 2194
POLICE: 0116 222 2222
PRESS: x2798
AMBULANCE: 0115 929 6151
PRESS: 0115 929 6151

Shropshire
FIRE: 01743 260200
PRESS: 01743 260286
POLICE: 0845 744 4888
PRESS: 01743 237491
AMBULANCE: 01384 215555
PRESS: 01384 246395

Somerset
FIRE: 01823 364500
PRESS: 01823 364582
POLICE: 0845 456 7000
PRESS: 01275 816350
AMBULANCE: 01392 261500
PRESS: 01392 261506

South Yorkshire
FIRE: 0114 272 7202
PRESS: 0114 253 2353
POLICE: 0114 220 2020
PRESS: 0114 252 3848
AMBULANCE: 01709 820520
PRESS: 01709 302026

Staffordshire
FIRE: 08451 22 11 55
PRESS: 01785 898581
POLICE: 0845 330 2010
PRESS: 01785 234864
AMBULANCE: 01785 253521
PRESS: 01785 273309

Suffolk
FIRE: 01473 588888
PRESS: 01473 264392
POLICE: 01473 613500
PRESS: 01473 613996/7
AMBULANCE: 01603 424255
PRESS: 01603 422729

Surrey
FIRE: 01737 242444
PRESS: 01737 224027
POLICE: 0845 125 2222
PRESS: 01483 482322
AMBULANCE: 01737 353333
PRESS: 01737 363815

Tyne and Wear
FIRE: 0191 444 1500
PRESS: 0191 444 1542
POLICE: 01661 872555
PRESS: 01661 868888
AMBULANCE: 0191 273 1212
PRESS: 0191 273 1212

Warwickshire
FIRE: 01926 423231
PRESS: 01926 423231
POLICE: 01926 415000
PRESS: North: x3366; South: x4266
AMBULANCE: 01926 881331
PRESS: 01926 881331

West Midlands
FIRE: 0121 359 5161
PRESS: 0121 380 6101
POLICE: 0845 113 5000
PRESS: 0121 626 5858
AMBULANCE: 01384 215555
PRESS: 01384 246395

West Sussex
FIRE: 01243 786211
PRESS: 01243 752448
POLICE: 0845 607 0999
PRESS: 01273 404173
AMBULANCE: 01273 489444
PRESS: 01273 897859

West Yorkshire
FIRE: 01274 682311
PRESS: 01274 655717
POLICE: 0845 606 0606
PRESS: 01924 292045
AMBULANCE: 01924 582000
PRESS: 01924 582204

Wiltshire
FIRE: 01380 723601
PRESS: 01380 723601
POLICE: 0845 408 7000
PRESS: 01380 734126
AMBULANCE: 01249 443939
PRESS: 01249 443939

Worcestershire
» see Hereford & Worcester

Wales

Mid Wales
FIRE: 0870 606 0699
PRESS: 01267 226866
POLICE: 01267 222020
PRESS: 01267 222274
AMBULANCE: 01745 532900
PRESS: 02920 344888

West Wales
FIRE: 0870 606 0699
PRESS: 01267 226866
POLICE: 0845 330 2000
PRESS: 01267 222274
AMBULANCE: 01745 532900
PRESS: 02920 344888

North Wales
FIRE: 01745 343431
PRESS: 01745 535283
POLICE: 01492 517171
PRESS: 01492 511157-9
AMBULANCE: 01745 532900
PRESS: 02920 344888

South Wales
FIRE: 01443 232000
PRESS: 01443 232164
POLICE: 01656 655555
PRESS: 01656 869291
AMBULANCE: 01745 532900
PRESS: 02920 344888

Scotland

Central Scotland
FIRE: 01324 716996
PRESS: 01324 716990
POLICE: 01786 456000
PRESS: 01786 456370
AMBULANCE: 0131 446 7000
PRESS: 07974 017937

Dumfries and Galloway
FIRE: 01387 252222
PRESS: 01387 252222
POLICE: 01387 252112
PRESS: 01387 260576
AMBULANCE: 0131 446 7000
PRESS: 07974 017937

Fife
FIRE: 01592 774451
PRESS: x2082 (voicebank), x2069
POLICE: 01592 418888
PRESS: 01592 418813
AMBULANCE: 0131 446 7000
PRESS: 07974 017937

Grampian
FIRE: 01224 696666
PRESS: 01224 696666
POLICE: 0845 600 5700
PRESS: 01224 386431
AMBULANCE: 0131 446 7000
PRESS: 07974 017937

Highland and Islands
FIRE: 01463 227000
PRESS: 01463 227009
POLICE: 01463 715555
PRESS: 01463 720396
AMBULANCE: 0131 446 7000
PRESS: 07974 017937

Lothian and Borders
FIRE: 0131 228 2401
PRESS: 0131 228 2401
POLICE: 0131 311 3131
PRESS: 0131 311 3423
AMBULANCE: 0131 446 7000
PRESS: 07974 017937

Strathclyde
FIRE: 01698 300999
POLICE: 0141 532 2000
PRESS: 0141 532 2658
AMBULANCE: 0131 446 7000
PRESS: 07974 017937

Tayside
FIRE: 01382 322222
PRESS: 01382 322222
POLICE: 01382 223200
PRESS: 01382 596730
AMBULANCE: 0131 446 7000
PRESS: 07974 017937

Northern Ireland

HQ, Lisburn
FIRE: 028 9266 4221
PRESS: 028 9266 4221
POLICE: 028 9065 0222
PRESS: 028 9070 0084
AMBULANCE: 028 9040 0999
PRESS: 028 9040 0999

British Transport Police

020 7830 8800

PRESS

London and south-east
Breaking news:
020 7957 1527
Follow-ups:
London Underground:
020 7918 3547
South London and south-east:
020 7023 6973
North London through East Anglia:
020 7830 8854

Midlands, Wales and west
Breaking news: 0121 654 2244
Follow-ups: 0121 654 2052

North-east
Breaking news: 0113 245 9149
Follow-ups: 0113 247 9149

North-west
Breaking news: 0161 228 5685
Follow-ups: 0161 228 42398

Scotland
Breaking news: 0141 335 3198
Follow-ups: 0141 335 2814

National and policy enquiries
020 7830 8854

Index

E

I

J

M

O

T